T0181100

Lecture Notes in Computer Science 10882

Commenced Publication in 1973
Founding and Former Series Editors:
Gerhard Goos, Juris Hartmanis, and Jan van Leeuwen

Aurélio Campilho · Fakhri Karray
Bart ter Haar Romeny (Eds.)

Image Analysis
and Recognition

15th International Conference, ICIAR 2018
Póvoa de Varzim, Portugal, June 27–29, 2018
Proceedings

 Springer

Editors
Aurélio Campilho (iD)
University of Porto
Porto
Portugal

Fakhri Karray (iD)
University of Waterloo
Waterloo, ON
Canada

Bart ter Haar Romeny (iD)
Biomedical Engineering
Eindhoven University of Technology
Eindhoven
The Netherlands

ISSN 0302-9743   ISSN 1611-3349 (electronic)
Lecture Notes in Computer Science
ISBN 978-3-319-92999-6   ISBN 978-3-319-93000-8 (eBook)
https://doi.org/10.1007/978-3-319-93000-8

Library of Congress Control Number: 2018944436

LNCS Sublibrary: SL6 – Image Processing, Computer Vision, Pattern Recognition, and Graphics

Printed on acid-free paper

This Springer imprint is published by the registered company Springer International Publishing AG
part of Springer Nature
The registered company address is: Gewerbestrasse 11, 6330 Cham, Switzerland

Preface

ICIAR 2018 was the 15th edition of the series of annual conferences on image analysis and recognition, offering a forum to the participants to interact and present their latest research contributions in theory, methodology and applications of image analysis and recognition. ICIAR 2018, the International Conference on Image Analysis and Recognition, was held in Póvoa de Varzim, Portugal, June 27–29, 2018. ICIAR is organized by AIMI, the Association for Image and Machine Intelligence, a not-for-profit organization registered in Ontario, Canada.

We received a total of 179 papers from 44 countries. Before the review process, all the papers were checked for similarity using a comparison database of scholarly work. The review process was carried out by members of the Program Committee and other reviewers. Each paper was reviewed by at least two reviewers, and checked by the conference chairs. A total of 106 papers were finally accepted and appear in these proceedings. We would like to sincerely thank the authors for responding to our call, and to thank the reviewers for the careful evaluation and feedback provided to the authors. It is this collective effort that resulted in the strong conference program and high-quality proceedings.

We were very pleased to include three outstanding keynote talks: "Deep Learning for Imaging Diagnostics" by Bram van Ginneken, Radboud University, The Netherlands; "Learning to Understand Human Behavior: In Multimedia, Surveillance, and Automotive" by Rita Cucchiara, Università di Modena e Reggio Emilia, Italy; and "Eyes Are the Windows of the Body: The Analysis of Corneal and Retinal Images" by Alfredo Ruggeri, University of Padua, Italy. We would like to express our gratitude to the keynote speakers for accepting our invitation to share their vision and recent advances in their areas of expertise.

Two successful parallel events took place: the special session on "Novel Imaging Methods for Diagnosis and Screening of Ophthalmic Diseases" co-chaired by Koen Vermeer, Rotterdam Eye Hospital, The Netherlands and by Ana Maria Mendonça, University of Porto, Portugal; and the "Grand Challenge on Breast Cancer Histology Images," organized by Teresa Araújo and Guilherme Aresta (INESC TEC, Institute for Systems and Computer Engineering, Technology and Science, Portugal), Catarina Eloy, António Polónia and Paulo Aguiar (I3S – Instituto de Investigação e Inovação em Saúde, Portugal). Awards were distributed among the four teams with best performance in the challenge. We were also very pleased to announce that a Springer prize was awarded to the three best papers of the conference.

We would like to thank Dr. Khaled Hammouda, the webmaster of the conference, for maintaining the website, managing the registrations and reviews logistics, interacting with the authors, and preparing the proceedings. We are also grateful to Springer's editorial staff, for supporting this publication in the LNCS series. Furthermore, we would like to acknowledge the members of the local Organizing Committee and Abreu Events for supporting the organization of the conference.

The event took place in the wonderful setting of the Axis Vermar Conference and Beach Hotel, Póvoa de Varzim, Portugal, which guaranteed many scientific and social interactions.

Finally, we were very pleased to welcome all the participants to ICIAR 2018. For those who were not able to attend, we hope this publication provides a good overview of the research presented at the conference, and we look forward to meeting you at the next ICIAR conference.

June 2018   Aurélio Campilho
                                                                                                        Fakhri Karray
                                                                                          Bart ter Haar Romeny

Organization

General Chairs

Aurélio Campilho   University of Porto, Portugal
                        campilho@fe.up.pt
Fakhri Karray   University of Waterloo, Canada
                        karray@uwaterloo.ca
Bart ter Haar Romeny   Eindhoven University of Technology,
                          The Netherlands
                        B.M.terHaarRomeny@tue.nl

Local Organizing Committee

Adrián Galdrán   INESC TEC, Portugal
Catarina Carvalho   INESC TEC, Portugal
Hélder Oliveira   INESC TEC, Portugal

Conference Secretariat

Abreu Events
Porto, Portugal
www.abreuevents.com

Webmaster

Khaled Hammouda   Waterloo, Canada
                        khaledh@aimiconf.org

Supported by

AIMI – Association for Image and Machine Intelligence

Center for Biomedical Engineering Research
INESC TEC – Institute for Systems and Computer Engineering, Technology
and Science
Portugal

U. PORTO

FEUP **FACULDADE DE ENGENHARIA**
UNIVERSIDADE DO PORTO
Department of Electrical and Computer Engineering
Faculty of Engineering
University of Porto
Portugal

C P A M I
INTELLIGENT RESEARCH EXCELLENCE
CPAMI – Centre for Pattern Analysis and Machine Intelligence
University of Waterloo
Canada

Program Committee

A. Abate	University of Salerno, Italy
P. Aguiar	INEB - Inst Nac Eng Biomédica, Portugal
J. Alba-Castro	University of Vigo, Spain
E. Alegre	University of Leon, Spain
L. Alexandre	University of Beira Interior, Portugal
H. Araújo	University of Coimbra, Portugal
G. Azzopardi	University of Groningen, The Netherlands
J. Barron	University of Western Ontario, Canada
J. Batista	University of Coimbra, Portugal
E. Bekkers	Eindhoven University of Technology, The Netherlands
R. Bernardes	University of Coimbra, Portugal
I. Bloch	Telecom ParisTech - CNRS LTCI, France
H. Bogunovic	Medical University Vienna, Austria
J. Boisvert	CNRC, Canada
V. Bolon Canedo	Universidade da Coruña, Spain
F. Camastra	University of Naples Parthenope, Italy
B. Cancela	INESC TEC, Portugal
J. Cardoso	INESC TEC, Portugal
F. Ciompi	Radboud University Medical Center, The Netherlands
M. Correia	University of Porto, Portugal
J. Debayle	Ecole Nationale Supérieure des Mines de Saint-Etienne (ENSM-SE), France
M. Dimiccoli	Universitat de Barcelona, Spain
L. Duong	Ecole de Technologie Superieure, Canada
A. El Khatib	University of Waterloo, Canada
P. Fallavollita	University of Ottawa, Canada
A. Farahat	Hitachi America, Ltd. R&D, USA

J. Fernandez	CNB-CSIC, Spain
R. Fisher	University of Edinburgh, UK
I. Fondon	University of Seville, Spain
D. Frejlichowski	West Pomeranian University of Technology, Poland
V. Gonzalez-Castro	University of Leon, Spain
G. Grossi	University of Milan, Italy
L. Igual	Universitat de Barcelona, Spain
A. Janowczyk	Case Western Reserve University, USA
M. Kampel	Vienna University of Technology, Austria
Y. Kita	National Institute AIST, Japan
R. Kolar	Brno University of Technology, Czech Republic
M. Koskela	CSC - IT Center for Science Ltd., Finland
A. Kuijper	TU Darmstadt and Fraunhofer IGD, Germany
G. Litjens	Eindhoven University of Technology, The Netherlands
J. Lorenzo-Ginori	Universidad Central Marta Abreu de Las Villas, Cuba
J. Marques	Instituto Superior Técnico, Portugal
M. Melkemi	Univerisité de Haute Alsace, France
A. Mendonça	University of Porto, Portugal
P. Morrow	University of Ulster, UK
M. Nappi	University of Salerno, Italy
H. Ogul	Baskent University, Turkey
C. Ou	University of Waterloo, Canada
C. Ouali	University of waterloo, Canada
E. Ovreiu	University Politehnica of Bucharest, Romania
X. Pardo	CiTIUS, Universidade de Santiago de Compostela, Spain
M. Penedo	University of Coruna, Spain
P. Pina	Instituto Superior Técnico, University of Lisbon, Portugal
A. Pinho	University of Aveiro, Portugal
J. Pinto	Instituto Superior Técnico, Portugal
J. Pluim	Eindhoven University of Technology, The Netherlands
L. Prevost	ESIEA, France
S. Rahnamayan	UOIT, Canada
B. Remeseiro	Universidad de Oviedo, Spain
H. Ren	Samsung Research USA, USA
D. Riccio	University of Naples Federico II, Italy
J. Rodrigues	University of the Algarve, Portugal
N. Rodriguez	University of A Coruña, Spain
P. Roth	Graz University of Technology, Austria
J. Rouco	University of A Coruña, Spain
K. Roy	North Carolina A&T State University, USA
A. Ruggeri	University of Padua, Italy
R. Sablatnig	TU Wien, Austria
A. Sappa	ESPOL Polytechnic University, Ecuador; and Computer Vision Center, Spain

G. Schaefer	Loughborough University, UK
P. Scheunders	University of Antwerp, Belgium
J. Silva	University of Porto, Portugal
N. Strisciuglio	University of Groningen, The Netherlands
S. Sural	Indian Institute of Technology, India
A. Taboada-Crispi	Universidad Central Marta Abreu de Las Villas, Cuba
X. Tan	Nanjing University of Aeronautics and Astronautics, China
J. Tavares	Universidade do Porto, Portugal
A. Torsello	Università Ca' Foscari Venezia, Italy
F. Tortorella	Universitá degli Studi di Cassino e del Lazio Meridionale, Italy
J. Traver	Universitat Jaume I, Spain
A. Uhl	University of Salzburg, Austria
M. Vento	Università di Salerno, Italy
K. Vermeer	Rotterdam Ophthalmic Institute, Rotterdam Eye Hospital, The Netherlands
E. Vrscay	University of Waterloo, Canada
Z. Wang	University of Waterloo, Canada
M. Wirth	University of Guelph, Canada
A. Wong	University of Waterloo, Canada
J. Xue	University College London, UK
P. Yan	Rensselaer Polytechnic Institute, USA
P. Zemcik	Brno University of Technology, Czech Republic
H. Zhou	Queen's University Belfast, UK
R. Zwiggelaar	Aberystwyth University, UK

Additional Reviewers

T. Araújo	INESC Technology and Science, Portugal
G. Aresta	INESC Technology and Science, Portugal
A. Barkah	University of Waterloo, Canada
C. Caridade	ISEC, Portugal
C. Carvalho	INESC TEC, Portugal
P. Carvalho	INESC TEC, Portugal
A. Cunha	INESC TEC, Portugal
B. Dashtbozorg	Eindhoven University of Technology, The Netherlands
A. Galdran	INESC TEC Porto, Portugal
A. Gerós	i3S - Instituto de Investigação e Inovação em Saúde, Portugal
U. Markowska-Kaczmar	Wroclaw University of Science and Technology, Polska
F. Monteiro	IPB, Portugal
J. Novo	University of A Coruña, Spain
H. Oliveira	INESC TEC, Portugal

A. Pinto   INESC TEC, Portugal
M. Sánchez Brea   University of A Coruña, España
F. Sattar   Nanyang Technological University, Singapore
E. Talavera   Universidade de Barcelona, Spain

Contents

Detection, Classification and Recognition

Indexing and Retrieval

Biomedical Image Analysis

Diagnosis and Screening of Ophthalmic Diseases

Challenge on Breast Cancer Histology Images

Enhancement, Restoration and Reconstruction

Projection Selection for Binary Tomographic Reconstruction Using Global Uncertainty

Gábor Lékó$^{(\boxtimes)}$, Péter Balázs, and László G. Varga

Department of Image Processing and Computer Graphics,
University of Szeged, Árpád tér 2, Szeged 6720, Hungary
{leko,pbalazs,vargalg}@inf.u-szeged.hu

Abstract. Binary tomography focuses on the problem of reconstructing homogeneous objects from a small number of their projections. In many applications, incomplete projection data holds insufficient information for the correct reconstruction of the original object. In this paper, we provide an optimization based method to select the "most informative" projection set, using information of global uncertainty. Beside the projection data we assume no further knowledge of the image to be reconstructed. Still, we achieve approximately as accurate reconstruction results, as it is possible to gain with a former method that uses blueprint images to find the optimal set of projections. We give experimental results for validating our approach on artificial images of various structures.

Keywords: Binary tomography · Reconstruction · Uncertainty
Projection selection · Optimization

1 Introduction

The goal of tomographic reconstruction is to discover the inner structure of objects using their projections, in a slice-by-slice manner. Most often, the projections are produced by X-rays. Measuring the attenuation of the beams passing through the object can give information of the density of the materials along the paths of the beams. Collecting such projection data from many angles one can produce an image showing the inner structure of the object [5,6].

Ideally, in the noiseless case, the exact reconstruction needs at least $\frac{m\Pi}{2}$ projections, when the number of detectors is m. Taking so many projections, however, is not always possible or can cause unwanted effects. For example, in medical CT diagnosis it would mean a high radiation dosage and could cause harm to the patient. Furthermore, in non-destructive testing of objects we often

This research was supported by the NKFIH OTKA [grant number K112998] and by the project "Integrated program for training new generation of scientists in the fields of computer science", no EFOP-3.6.3-VEKOP-16-2017-0002. The project has been supported by the European Union and co-funded by the European Social Fund.

© Springer International Publishing AG, part of Springer Nature 2018
A. Campilho et al. (Eds.): ICIAR 2018, LNCS 10882, pp. 3–10, 2018.
https://doi.org/10.1007/978-3-319-93000-8_1

cannot take more than a few (say, up to 18) projections, due to physical and/or time considerations. This brings new approaches of reconstruction alive ensuring accurate results from fewer projections. For example, in binary tomography we use the prior information that the object consists of a single material and air in between. In some cases, this constraint can lead to an accurate result, even from just 4–8 projections.

In their paper [7], Nagy et al. noted that when using a low number of projections, the accuracy of a binary reconstruction can depend on the projection angles. Further investigated in [9], this phenomenon was found to depend on the structure of the object of study, and in [10] the authors proposed different projection selection algorithms when a blueprint of the object is available. Without a blueprint, the authors of [2] gave a heuristic approach for in-situ projection angle selection that chooses the next projection direction based on metrics calculated for a previous projection set [1]. For the general case, on the other hand, Haque et al. [4] proposed an adaptive heuristic projection selection method, that fine tunes the stepping angle between consecutive projections by trying to approximate the information content of single projections. Although, the above methods give solutions capable of improving the reconstruction, they are either of heuristic nature, or rely strongly on the blueprint of the object.

Recently, two research groups independently discovered the concept of pixel uncertainty in reconstructions and gave different ways for measuring it [3,11]. The idea is that the projections determine the pixels of reconstructions to different degrees. Some pixels are exactly determined, while others are ambiguous by the projections, therefore reconstruction methods have a chance to produce erroneous pixel values. These results also imply that by minimizing the uncertainty of pixels one can gain better reconstructions.

In this paper, we provide a projection selection method for binary reconstruction based on the summed pixel uncertainty. Our method selects the projection angles solely using the projection data and does not use any blueprint. The structure of the paper is the following. In Sect. 2, we summarize previous works, the theoretical background of our algorithm and the state-of-art. In Sect. 3, we give a detailed description of the proposed method. Then, in Sect. 4, we present experimental results. Finally, Sect. 5 is for the conclusion.

2   Preliminaries

We use the algebraic formulation of the reconstruction problem. Our aim is to recover a 2-dimensional binary image (describing a cross section of a 3D object) from its parallel-beam projections. Without the loss of generality we can assume, that the image is of size $n \times n$. In this way, the reconstruction problem can be formulated as a system of equations

$$\mathbf{A}\mathbf{x} = \mathbf{b}, \quad \mathbf{x} \in \{0,1\}^{n^2}, \tag{1}$$

where $\mathbf{x}$ is the vector of all n^2 unknown image pixels; $\mathbf{b}$ is the vector of all m projection values; and $\mathbf{A}$ is a projection coefficient matrix of size $m \times n^2$ that describes the projection geometry by all a_{ij} elements representing the intersection of the i-th projection line and the j-th pixel. The formulation is illustrated in Fig. 1. Solving (1) yields also a solution of the reconstruction problem. In binary tomography, an approximate solution of (1) is often found by a thresholded version of the Simulated Iterative Reconstruction Technique (SIRT) [5].

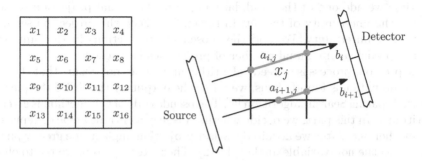

Fig. 1. Equation system-based representation of the parallel-beam projection geometry on a discrete image.

Given the reconstruction task, we can also formulate the uncertainty of a projection set, by using the results of [11] for calculating the uncertainty of reconstructions. Due to the incomplete information in the projection data, there can be several solutions of (1) in which the pixel values may vary. Knowing all the reconstructions we could calculate the probability of $x_i (i = 1, \ldots, n)$ taking the value $x_i = 1$, by

$$p_i = \frac{\mathcal{N}_b^A (x_i = 1)}{\mathcal{N}_b^A}, \tag{2}$$

where $\mathcal{N}_b^A$ denotes the number of solutions of (1), and $\mathcal{N}_b^A (x_i = 1)$ stands for the number of binary solutions with $x_i = 1$. The probabilities given, we can determine the uncertainty of pixel x_i as

$$\mathcal{H}(x_i) = -(p_i \log_2(p_i) + (\bar{p}_i) \log_2(\bar{p}_i)), \tag{3}$$

where $\bar{p}_i = 1 - p_i$. Furthermore, we can also calculate the global uncertainty of the whole reconstruction by summing the pixel uncertainties as

$$\mathcal{U}(\mathbf{x}) = \frac{\sum_{i=1}^{n} \mathcal{H}(x_i)}{\frac{1}{p} \sum_{j=1}^{m} b_j}, \tag{4}$$

where p is the number of projections. This global uncertainty measure also describes the uncertainty of the projection set.

Calculating (4) needs in practice an unreasonable amount of processing time, since all the reconstructions satisfying the projection set have to be generated. Fortunately, in [11], the authors gave two ways of measuring the uncertainty: a stochastic one by sampling the possible reconstructions, and a deterministic approximation of the values. In this paper, we will use the latter one.

3   Proposed Method

We propose an optimization algorithm aiming to minimize the global uncertainty. At the beginning two initial integer angles are randomly chosen. Using these angles we acquire the projections from the unknown object. To select the next projection angle we examine all integer angles between 0 and 179°, one by one. Each time we add one of the candidate angles to the actual projection set and compute the uncertainty of the set. In the end, we keep the projection set with the smallest uncertainty. We add the subsequent projections in the same way until the predefined maximal number of projections is reached.

The previous process is a greedy algorithm and it does not ensure that the best angle combination is found. Thus, we refine the output by the SFFS (Sequential Forward Floating Search) algorithm [8]. The pseudo code of this method is given in Algorithm 1. In this part, we decide whether we keep a current angle or replace it with another one. After we acquired the last projection angle in the greedy phase, we fix it, as the non-variable angle (Line 2). Then, step by step, we try to eliminate one of the non-fixed projections and compute the uncertainty. We keep the projection angle combination belonging to the smallest uncertainty (Line 8). In the second part of the algorithm, we take again all the integer angles between 0 and 179 and compute the uncertainty value by adding each of them to the current set of projections (Line 9–12). We insert the angle with the smallest uncertainty value into the projection set (Line 13) and fix it (Line 14). Lines 4–14 are repeated until the stopping criteria is met. In our implementation we stop the process when uncertainty cannot be decreased any more.

The final result depends on the initially chosen two angles. If these are not properly chosen, the algorithm can easily stick in a local minimum. To reduce the probability of such an unwanted event to occur, we start the algorithm from 18 different random initial angle pairs. Thereby, 18 projection sets are generated. They may all be different, but same sets may also occur. In the end, we choose the one with the smallest uncertainty value.

4   Experimental Results

4.1   Test Frameset

We conducted experiments on binary software phantoms to show empirically that even without a blueprint we can select nearly as informative projection sets as it is possible with the aid of the ground truth. Our image database consisted of 22 phantoms of different structural complexity, with the same size of 256 by 256 pixels. Some of them can be seen in Fig. 2. All the images have been reconstructed from a set of 4 projection angles determined by the algorithm described in Sect. 3 in two different ways. First, in the algorithm, uncertainty is calculated by approximating (4) in a deterministic way as was given in [11]. Then, we reconstructed the image from its projection set by a binarized and

Algorithm 1. Angle selection with SFFS algorithm

```
1: function SFFS(A)                                    ▷ A - set of the actual angles
2:     fixΘ ← the last element inserted into A
3:     repeat
4:         for each angle θ ∈ A \ {fixΘ} do
5:             calculate uncertainty(A \ {θ})
6:             θ_min ← angle corresponding to the smallest uncertainty value
7:         end for
8:         A ← A \ {θ_min}
9:         for θ ← 0 to 179 do
10:            calculate uncertainty(A ∪ {θ})
11:            θ_min ← angle corresponding to the smallest uncertainty value
12:        end for
13:        A ← A ∪ {θ_min}
14:        fixΘ ← θ_min
15:    until stopping criteria is met
16: end function
```

bounded version of the SIRT algorithm [5]. The quality of the reconstruction was measured by the Relative Mean Error (RME) defined as

$$RME(\mathbf{x}^*, \mathbf{y}) = \frac{\sum_i |x_i^* - y_i|}{\sum_i x_i^*}, \tag{5}$$

where $\mathbf{x}^*$ denotes the vector of the pixel values of the original phantom and $\mathbf{y}$ is the reconstructed image. We refer to this algorithm as Alg-UNC.

In the second approach (referred to as Alg-RME) we assumed that the original image is known in advance. We followed the same strategy as in Sect. 3. However, each time the calculation of uncertainty was replaced with an RME calculation. We reconstructed a grayscale image by a bounded SIRT algorithm [5] from the current projection set, binarized the result, calculated the RME value (by comparing the result to the blueprint) and used that value for the optimization to choose the proper angles.

4.2 Results

Using the RME values we compared the reconstructions provided by Alg-UNC and Alg-RME. The results are summarized in Table 1. In the sixth column one can see the difference of the RME values given in the second and fourth column. If the value is negative Alg-UNC performed better, otherwise Alg-RME did. Anyway, the differences are rather small, and in Fig. 3 it can be also visually followed that the RME values of the two mentioned algorithms highly correlate.

Table 2 shows the RME values achieved by Alg-UNC, for higher number of projections, in case of the phantoms of Fig. 2. The same is visualized in Fig. 4. Indeed, there are easier and more complicated phantoms, but our proposed method works well on both of them. Clearly, the more projections we can use, the better the reconstruction is. The price we pay is that the projection selection algorithm will need more time to find optimal projection sets of bigger sizes.

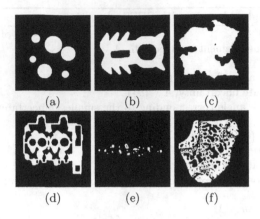

(a)   (b)   (c)

(d)   (e)   (f)

Fig. 2. Some of the software phantoms used for testing. A general image with 6 randomly placed disks (a), an object with complex structure (b), a shape with a small hole (c), a cross section of an engine phantom (d), a set of small shapes (e), and a cross section of a mouse femur (f). Figures from (a) to (f) are in Table 1 Phantom 1, 8, 13, 14, 15 and 16, respectively.

Table 1. Best uncertainty and RME results provided by Alg-UNC and Alg-RME

	Alg-UNC		Alg-RME		Difference
	Uncertainty	RME	Uncertainty	RME	RME
Phantom 1	0.498686	0.054054	0.525388	0.052858	0.001196
Phantom 2	0.614922	0.053567	0.552586	0.067159	−0.013592
Phantom 3	0.293671	0.029400	0.293773	0.035786	−0.006386
Phantom 4	0.607451	0.069475	0.659946	0.060987	0.008488
Phantom 5	0.687311	0.088321	0.692301	0.089693	−0.001372
Phantom 6	0.527275	0.061344	0.509842	0.064690	−0.003346
Phantom 7	0.582135	0.089337	0.597854	0.067330	0.022007
Phantom 8	0.578104	0.116264	0.596882	0.119123	−0.002859
Phantom 9	0.310081	0.044787	0.326152	0.042202	0.002585
Phantom 10	0.350083	0.037991	0.324438	0.030669	0.007322
Phantom 11	0.526202	0.074057	0.535776	0.089109	−0.015052
Phantom 12	0.135703	0.011891	0.136618	0.007658	0.004233
Phantom 13	0.311714	0.049153	0.314140	0.054103	−0.004950
Phantom 14	1.324257	0.416702	1.337183	0.404755	0.011947
Phantom 15	2.337384	0.425000	2.481358	0.350000	0.075000
Phantom 16	1.405617	0.472347	1.430437	0.481177	−0.008830
Phantom 17	2.156736	0.873173	2.218493	0.866745	0.006428
Phantom 18	1.428904	0.413737	1.479656	0.408491	0.005246
Phantom 19	0.278831	0.052162	0.318267	0.051140	0.001022
Phantom 20	0.295304	0.037180	0.295760	0.035964	0.001216
Phantom 21	0.612189	0.127827	0.615520	0.133426	−0.005599
Phantom 22	1.598097	0.436369	1.724271	0.430816	0.005553
Average	0.793666	0.183370	0.816666	0.179267	0.004103

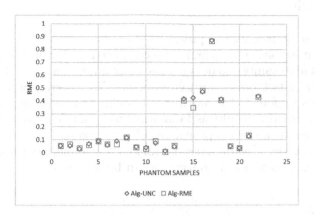

Fig. 3. RME values belonging to Alg-UNC and Alg-RME

Table 2. RME values of sample images for different number of projections

#Projs.	Fig. 2a	Fig. 2b	Fig. 2c	Fig. 2d	Fig. 2e	Fig. 2f
4	0.054054	0.116264	0.049153	0.416702	0.425000	0.472347
6	0.028103	0.039972	0.019268	0.264441	0.205208	0.404389
9	0.011839	0.013183	0.006876	0.120124	0.082291	0.333075
12	0.005142	0.007253	0.002984	0.065348	0.031250	0.273380
15	0.002989	0.003600	0.001209	0.033092	0.016666	0.218539
18	0.000956	0.001747	0.000604	0.018875	0.009375	0.185128

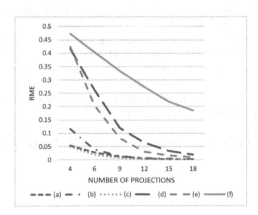

Fig. 4. RME values achieved by Alg-UNC on the phantoms of Fig. 2, for different number of projections

5   Conclusion

We proposed an optimization approach to select projection sets with high information content for binary tomographic reconstruction. The method is based on the concept of uncertainty and does not need any prior information (or blueprint) of the image to select proper projection angles. By experimental test on software phantoms we found that our method is able to provide approximately as accurate reconstruction results as former methods can do, which, however, use blueprint images to find the optimal set of projections. The results presented here can be primarily used in industrial tomography of homogeneous objects, of which only a small number of projections can be gathered.

References

1. Batenburg, K.J., Fortes, W., Hajdu, L., Tijdeman, R.: Bounds on the difference between reconstructions in binary tomography. In: Debled-Rennesson, I., Domenjoud, E., Kerautret, B., Even, P. (eds.) DGCI 2011. LNCS, vol. 6607, pp. 369–380. Springer, Heidelberg (2011). https://doi.org/10.1007/978-3-642-19867-0_31
2. Batenburg, K.J., Palenstijn, W.J., Balázs, P., Sijbers, J.: Dynamic angle selection in binary tomography. Comput. Vis. Image Underst. **117**(4), 306–318 (2013)
3. Frost, A., Renners, E., Hotter, M., Ostermann, J.: Probabilistic evaluation of three-dimensional reconstructions from X-Ray images spanning a limited angle. SENSORS **13**(1), 137–151 (2013)
4. Haque, M.A., Ahmad, M.O., Swamy, M.N.S., Hasan, M.K., Lee, S.Y.: Adaptive projection selection for computed tomography. IEEE Trans. Image Process. **22**(12), 5085–5095 (2013)
5. Herman, G.T.: Image Reconstruction from Projections, Fundamentals of Computerized Tomography, 2nd edn. Springer, London (2009)
6. Kak, A.C., Slaney, M.: Principles of Computerized Tomographic Imaging. IEEE Press, New York (1999)
7. Nagy, A., Kuba, A.: Reconstruction of binary matrices from fan-beam projections. Acta Cybern. **17**(2), 359–385 (2005)
8. Pudil, P., Novovicová, J., Kittler, J.: Floating search methods in feature selection. Pattern Recogn. Lett. **15**(11), 1119–1125 (1994)
9. Varga, L., Balázs, P., Nagy, A.: Direction-dependency of binary tomographic reconstruction algorithms. Graph. Models **73**(6), 365–375 (2011)
10. Varga, L., Balázs, P., Nagy, A.: Projection selection dependency in binary tomography. Acta Cybern. **20**, 167–187 (2011)
11. Varga, L.G., Nyúl, L.G., Nagy, A., Balázs, P.: Local and global uncertainty in binary tomographic reconstruction. Comput. Vis. Image Underst. **129**, 52–62 (2014)

Reconstruction of Binary Images with Fixed Number of Strips

Péter Balázs and Judit Szűcs[(✉)]

Department of Image Processing and Computer Graphics,
University of Szeged, Árpád tér 2, Szeged 6720, Hungary
{pbalazs,jszucs}@inf.u-szeged.hu

Abstract. We consider the problem of reconstructing a binary matrix from its row and column sums with the additional constraint that for each row and column the number of strips (consecutive 1 s of maximal length) is given. The problem is connected both to binary tomography and to nonogram puzzles, and is in general NP-hard. Here, we propose an integer programming framework and an approximation algorithm based on simulated annealing to solve this issue. The effectiveness of the two methods are compared on randomly generated binary matrices.

Keywords: Binary tomography · Reconstruction · Nonogram
Linear programming · Simulated annealing

1 Introduction

The goal of *Binary tomography* [8] is to reconstruct binary images from their projections. In the most common applications of this field, e.g., electron tomography [1] and non-destructive testing [5], projections can be gathered from just a few directions, since the acquisition process can be expensive or damage the object. Owing to the insufficient amount of available data the binary reconstruction can be extremely ambiguous. A common way to reduce the number of solutions of the reconstruction problem is to exploit prior information (e.g., convexity, connectedness, smoothness, similarity to a model image, etc.) of the image to be reconstructed. In the reconstruction process the prior knowledge is often incorporated into an energy function, thus the reconstruction issue is equivalent to a function minimization problem. There are various methods to solve that kind of problems, which can be deterministic [11,14,16] as well as stochastic ones [2,7,10]. Motivated by nonogram puzzles, in this paper we introduce a novel prior to describe the expected texture of the reconstructed image:

This research was supported by the NKFIH OTKA [grant number K112998] and by the project "Integrated program for training new generation of scientists in the fields of computer science", no EFOP-3.6.3-VEKOP-16-2017-0002. The project has been supported by the European Union and co-funded by the European Social Fund.

the number of strips in each row and column. We first reformulate the reconstruction as a Constraint Satisfaction Problem (CSP) that is solved by a system of linear equations. Although this method gives an exact solution it is hardly applicable in practice, as the problem turns out to be NP-complete. As an alternative approach we present also a method based on simulated annealing that gives generally just an approximate solution, but works much faster than the CSP-based approach. The effectiveness of the two methods are compared on an artificial dataset.

The paper is structured as follows. In Sect. 2 we introduce the binary reconstruction problem, the nonogram puzzles, and define the intermediate problem of reconstructing binary matrices with fixed number of strips, from their row and column sums. In Sect. 3 we provide two approaches to solve the above problem. In Sect. 4 we present experimental results and provide an explanation of them. Finally, we summarize our work in Sect. 5.

2 Binary Tomography, Nonograms, and the Intermediate Problem

First, we consider the basic problem of binary tomography where the aim is to reconstruct a two-dimensional binary image from two projections. The image can be represented by a binary matrix, where 1 stands for the object (black) and 0 for the background (white) pixels, respectively. Furthermore, the *horizontal and vertical projection* of the image can be defined as the vector of the row and column sums, respectively, of the image matrix. Thus, formally the following problem is investigated.

Problem. BINARY TOMOGRAPHY (BT)
Input: Two non-negative integer vectors $H \in \mathbb{Z}^m$ and $V \in \mathbb{Z}^n$.
Output: A binary matrix of size $m \times n$, if it exists, with row sum vector H and column sum vector V.

This problem is known to be solvable in polynomial time, although usually not in a unique way [13]. A *switching component* in a binary matrix $A \in \{0,1\}^{m \times n}$ is a set of four positions $(i,j), (i',j), (i,j'), (i',j')$ ($1 \leq i, i' \leq m$, $1 \leq j, j' \leq n$) such that $a_{ij} = a_{i'j'}$ and $a_{i'j} = a_{ij'} = 1 - a_{ij}$. In [13] it is also proven that the presence of switching components ensures non-uniqueness of the solution. The above problem has a natural connection to the logic puzzles called nonograms. To formally describe this problem, we introduce the notion of *strips* which are non-extendible (i.e. maximal) segments of black pixels of a row or column.

Definition 1. *Given a binary matrix A of size $m \times n$, a sequence of consecutive positions $(i, j_s), (i, j_{s+1}), \ldots, (i, j_{s+l-1})$ (where l is a positive integer, and $1 \leq j_s \leq n$) in the i-th row ($1 \leq i \leq m$) form a strip if $a_{i,j_s} = 1, a_{i,j_{s+1}} = 1, \ldots, a_{i,j_{s+l-1}} = 1$, and $a_{i,j_s-1} = 0$ and $a_{i,j_s+l} = 0$ (if the latter two positions* *exist). The length of the strip is given by l. Strips of columns can be defined in an analogous way.*

The length of each strip in the rows of the matrix A can be encoded by an integer matrix LH of size $m \times n$, where lh_{ij} is the length of the j-th strip from the left, in the i-th row. Entries not used to indicate strips are set to 0. Similarly, a matrix LV of size $n \times m$ can describe the length of each strip in the columns of A. Now, the problem is given as follows.

Problem. NONOGRAM
Input: Two non-negative integer matrices LH of size $m \times n$ and LV of size $n \times m$.
Output: A binary matrix of size $m \times n$, if it exists, in each row and column having strips of length prescribed by LH and LV, respectively.

In contrast to BINARY TOMOGRAPHY, NONOGRAM is in general an NP-complete problem (see, e.g., [4]). We define the following intermediate problem.

Problem. STRIP CONSTRAINED BINARY TOMOGRAPHY (SCBT)
Input: Four non-negative integer vectors $H \in \mathbb{Z}^m$, $V \in \mathbb{Z}^n$, $SH \in \mathbb{Z}^m$, and $SV \in \mathbb{Z}^n$.
Output: A binary matrix of size $m \times n$, if it exists, with row sum vector H, column sum vector V, and in each row and column having the number of strips prescribed by SH and SV, respectively.

The motivation of studying this problem comes from the fact that the SH and SV vectors carry information about the texture of the image, and such descriptors can reduce the ambiguity of the reconstruction [15].

If the two vectors SH and SV contain exclusively 1 values, then SCBT reduces to the problem of reconstructing so-called hv-convex images (where the black pixels in each row and column must be consecutive). This latter problem is also NP-complete in general [17], thus so is SCBT. The three problems and their connections are presented in Fig. 1.

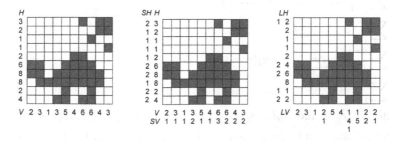

Fig. 1. Instances of the BT (left), SCBT (middle), and NONOGRAM (right) problems. Padding zero elements of the matrices LH and LV are not indicated

Proposition 1. *The solution of the* SCBT *problem is not always uniquely determined.*

Proposition 2. *For an arbitrary solution of a fixed instance of the* SCBT *problem it holds that the number of pairs of adjacent 1s in the i-th row* $(i = 1, \ldots, m)$ *is equal to* $h_i - sh_i$ *and the number of pairs of adjacent 1s in the j-th column* $(j = 1, \ldots, n)$ *is equal to* $v_j - sv_j$.

For an example of Proposition 1 see Fig. 2. If there is only a single strip in the row (column), Proposition 2 naturally holds, while 'cutting' a strip into two parts decreases the number of adjacent 1s by 1, and increases the number of strips by 1.

Fig. 2. Example of the non-uniqueness of the SCBT problem

3   Proposed Methods

3.1   Constraint Satisfaction

Now, consider the input instance $H \in \mathbb{Z}^m$, $SH \in \mathbb{Z}^m$, $V \in \mathbb{Z}^n$, and $SV \in \mathbb{Z}^n$ of the SCBT problem. Our goal is to construct a binary matrix X of size $m \times n$ according to the given vectors. Following the idea of [6] we formulate SCBT as a Constraint Satisfaction Problem.

Let $YH^{m \times (n-1)}$ and $YV^{(m-1) \times n}$ two unknown binary matrices to indicate the locations of adjacent 1s in the solution, i.e., the $\begin{bmatrix} 1 & 1 \end{bmatrix}$ and $\begin{bmatrix} 1 \\ 1 \end{bmatrix}$ components of the solution image, respectively. The conditions of the model are as follows:

$$\sum_{j=1}^{n} x_{ij} = h_i (i = 1, \ldots, m) \tag{1}$$

$$\sum_{i=1}^{m} x_{ij} = v_j \ (j = 1, \ldots, n) \tag{2}$$

$$\sum_{j=1}^{n-1} yh_{ij} = h_i - sh_i (i = 1, \ldots, m) \tag{3}$$

$$\sum_{i=1}^{m-1} yv_{ij} = v_j - sv_j (j = 1, \ldots, n) \tag{4}$$

$$yh_{ij} \leq x_{ij} \quad \text{and} \quad yh_{ij} \leq x_{i(j+1)} (i = 1, \ldots, m; j = 1, \ldots, (n-1)) \tag{5}$$

$$yv_{ij} \leq x_{ij} \quad \text{and} \quad yv_{ij} \leq x_{(i+1)j} (i = 1, \ldots, (m-1); j = 1, \ldots, n) \tag{6}$$

Equations (1) and (2) ensure that the reconstructed image has the given row and column sums, respectively, whereas the conditions (3) and (4) are to satisfy Proposition 2. Finally, (5) builds the connection between the solution image and its components formed by the adjacent 1 s in rows. If $(x_{ij}, x_{i,j+1}) \in \{(0,0), (0,1), (1,0)\}$ then $yh_{ij} = 0$ must hold, indicating that the pair of positions (i, j) and $(i, j + 1)$ do not form a component of consecutive ones. However, $yh_{ij} = 1$ can hold if both x_{ij} and $x_{i,j+1}$ are equal to 1. In fact, together with the constraints (1), (2), (3), and (4), $yh_{ij} = 1$ is always true, whenever $x_{ij} = 1$ and $x_{i,j+1} = 1$ (thus the condition is necessary and sufficient). The same relation is ensured for the consecutive ones in columns, by condition (6).

To implement the constraint satisfaction model we used the `intlinprog` MATLAB built-in function, which is a mixed-integer linear programming solver, setting a constant 1 objective function.

3.2 Simulated Annealing

Although the mixed integer programming based method gives always an exact solution, it is hardly applicable in practice, as the SCBT problem is NP-complete. As an alternative approach we present also a method based on simulated annealing (SA) [9] that gives generally just an approximate solution. The pseudocode of the algorithm is given in Algorithm 1.

Algorithm 1. Simulated Annealing

1: $s \leftarrow$ initial state;
2: $T_1 \leftarrow$ initial temperature;
3: $k \leftarrow 1$;
4: $\alpha \in (0.5, 1)$
5: $\beta \in (0, 1)$
6: **while** $stoppingCriteria == FALSE$ **do**
7:     $tempStay := 0$
8:     **while** $(tempStay < \beta \cdot f(s))$ **do**
9:         $actual := neighbor(s)$
10:        **if** $(f(actual) < f(s))$ **then**
11:           $s := actual$
12:        **else if** $(e^{\frac{f(s)-f(actual)}{T_k}} > rand(0,1))$ **then**
13:           $s := actual$
14:        **end if**
15:        $tempStay := tempStay + 1$
16:     **end while**
17:     $T_{k+1} := T_k \cdot \alpha$
18:     $k := k + 1$
19: **end while**

The function we want to minimize is

$$f(x) = ||H - H'||^2 + ||V - V'||^2 + ||SH - SH'||^2 + ||SV - SV'||^2,$$

where vectors H, V, SH, SV are given as input and H', V', SH', SV' are the corresponding vectors belonging to the current solution. The method starts each time from a random binary image. Choosing a neighbor means randomly choosing and inverting a pixel. The parameters of the SA algorithm were set manually in an empirical way. The stopping criteria of the algorithm is to reach 300 000 iterations or to perform 3 000 iterations without improving the solution. The initial temperature is set to $T_1 = 350$ and the cooling schedule is controlled by $\alpha = 0.99$. The SA algorithm may stay in identical temperature for some iteration, in our case this is defined by $\beta = 0.035$.

4   Experimental Results

We evaluated the methods on 50–50 binary images of sizes $3 \times 3, 4 \times 4, \ldots, 256 \times 256$, containing $0\%, 10\%, \ldots, 100\%$ randomly chosen object pixels (Fig. 3). Thus, the test set contained a total of $50 \cdot 254 \cdot 11 = 139\ 700$ images.

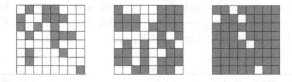

Fig. 3. Images with 30%, 60%, and 90% randomly chosen object pixels (from left to right, respectively)

Figure 4 shows the pixel error of the two methods for the different image classes calculated by

$$E(O, R) = \frac{\sum_{ij} |o_{ij} - r_{ij}|}{mn},$$

where O and R is the original and the reconstructed image, respectively, and $m \times n$ is the size of the image. In the figure (and also later in Fig. 5), for the SA method only the graphs of matrices with 0–50% object pixels are plotted. For 60–100% object pixel density we achieve very similar curves. We can deduce that the closer the image is to the uniform random the higher is the pixel error. This is relatively high even when the exact method (`intlinprog`) is applied. The reason is that a structure close to the uniform random one gives more freedom to switching components to occur (see also Fig. 2), and the solution can be highly ambiguous. If a big portion of the pixels are fixed to belong to the foreground/background, this less often happens.

Regarding the average running time, in Fig. 5 we can observe that `intlinprog` needs an unreasonable amount of time to produce the solution, even for small matrices (that is why we present only statistics for small matrices). It is not surprising, as the problem is NP-complete. SA facilitates the problem by searching for an image which may just partially satisfy the conditions. Thus, it works for bigger images, too. Since SA starts from a uniform random matrix, the running time excessively increases as the relative number of object pixels

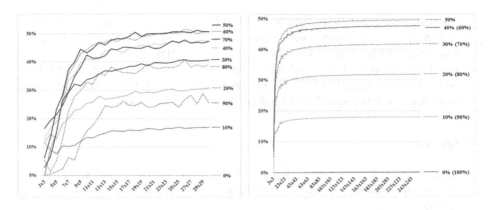

Fig. 4. Average pixel error (vertical axis) of the `intlingprog` (left) and the SA (right) methods for different sized images (horizontal axis)

gets far from 50%. The explanation is that in these cases more invertations are needed to reach a matrix with the proper density.

Beside these, the fact that SA seeks just an approximate solution makes it more preferable in practical applications where the projections are noisy and the structure of the image is also just approximately known in advance.

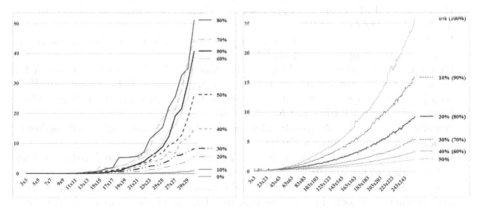

Fig. 5. Average running time in seconds (vertical axis) of the `intlingprog` (left) and the SA (right) methods for different sized images (horizontal axis)

5 Conclusions and Further Work

We defined the problem of reconstructing binary images from their horizontal and vertical projections and the number of strips per row and column. We proposed an exact deterministic and an approximate stochastic method to solve the problem. We evaluated tests on simulated datasets and found that the exact method is hardly applicable in practice, whereas the stochastic approach is much more suitable for practical purposes. The results obtained here can provide a better understanding of binary tomographic reconstruction with structural priors.

Since SA is rather sensitive to the choice of the initial state, in a further work, we aim to develop sophisticated strategies for choosing a starting image, e.g., by using Ryser's algorithm [13]. Beside that, we will investigate how switching components affect the speed and quality of the reconstruction.

References

1. Aert, S.V., Batenburg, K.J., Rossell, M.D., Erni, R., Tendeloo, G.V.: Three-dimensional atomic imaging of crystalline nanoparticles. Nature **470**, 374–377 (2011)
2. Balázs, P., Gara, M.: An evolutionary approach for object-based image reconstruction using learnt priors. In: Salberg, A.-B., Hardeberg, J.Y., Jenssen, R. (eds.) SCIA 2009. LNCS, vol. 5575, pp. 520–529. Springer, Heidelberg (2009). https://doi.org/10.1007/978-3-642-02230-2_53
3. Batenburg, K.J., Bals, S., Sijbers, J., Kuebel, C., Midgley, P.A., Hernandez, J.C., Kaiser, U., Encina, E.R., Coronado, E.A., Tendeloo, G.V.: 3D imaging of nanomaterials by discrete tomography. Ultramicroscopy **109**(6), 730–740 (2009)
4. Batenburg, K.J., Kosters, W.A.: Solving Nonograms by combining relaxations. Pattern Recogn. **42**(8), 1672–1683 (2009)
5. Baumann, J., Kiss, Z., Krimmel, S., Kuba, A., Nagy, A., Rodek, L., Schillinger, B., Stephan, J.: Discrete tomography methods for nondestructive testing. In: [8], pp. 303–331 (2007)
6. Dahl, G., Flatberg, T.: Optimization and reconstruction of hv-convex $(0,1)$-matrices. Disc. Appl. Math. **151**, 93–105 (2005)
7. Di Gesù, V., Lo Bosco, G., Millonzi, F., Valenti, C.: A memetic algorithm for binary image reconstruction. In: Brimkov, V.E., Barneva, R.P., Hauptman, H.A. (eds.) IWCIA 2008. LNCS, vol. 4958, pp. 384–395. Springer, Heidelberg (2008). https://doi.org/10.1007/978-3-540-78275-9_34
8. Herman, G.T., Kuba, A. (eds.): Advances in Discrete Tomography and its Applications. Birkhäuser, Boston (2007)
9. Kirkpatrick, S., Gelatt, C.D., Vecchi, M.P.: Optimization by simulated annealing. Science **220**, 671–680 (1983)
10. Kiss, Z., Rodek, L., Nagy, A., Kuba, A., Balaskó, M.: Reconstruction of pixel-based and geometric objects by discrete tomography. Simulation and physical experiments. Electron. Notes Discret. Math. **20**, 475–491 (2005)
11. Lukic, T., Lukity, A.: A spectral projected gradient optimization for binary tomography. In: Rudas, I.J., Fodor, J., Kacprzyk, J. (eds.) Computational Intelligence in Engineering. SCI, vol. 313, pp. 263–272. Springer, Heidelberg (2010). https://doi.org/10.1007/978-3-642-15220-7_21
12. Russell, S., Norvig, P.: Artificial Intelligence, A Modern Approach, 2nd edn. Prentice-Hall, Englewood Cliffs (2003)
13. Ryser, H.J.: Combinatorial properties of matrices of zeros and ones. Canad. J. Math. **9**, 371–377 (1957)
14. Schüle, T., Schnörr, C., Weber, S., Hornegger, J.: Discrete tomography by convex concave regularization and DC programming. Disc. Appl. Math. **151**(1), 229–243 (2005)

15. Szűcs, J., Balázs, P.: Binary image reconstruction using local binary pattern priors. Int. J. Circuits Syst. Sig. Process. **11**, 296–299 (2017)
16. Varga, L., Balázs, P., Nagy, A.: Discrete tomographic reconstruction via adaptive weighting of gradient descents. Comput. Methods Biomech. Biomed. Eng. Imaging Vis. **3**(2), 100–109 (2015)
17. Woeginger, G.W.: The reconstruction of polyominoes from their orthogonal projections. Inform. Process. Lett. **77**, 225–229 (2001)

Alternate Direction Method of Multipliers for Unconstrained Structural Similarity-Based Optimization

Daniel Otero[1], Davide La Torre[2,3], Oleg V. Michailovich[4],
and Edward R. Vrscay[5(✉)]

[1] Department of Electronic Engineering,
Faculty of Engineering, Pontificia Universidad Javeriana, Bogotá, Colombia
`oterod@javeriana.edu.co`
[2] Dubai Business School, University of Dubai, Dubai, UAE
`dlatorre@ud.ac.ae`
[3] Department of Economics, Management, and Quantitative Methods,
University of Milan, Milan, Italy
`davide.latorre@unimi.it`
[4] Department of Electrical and Computer Engineering, Faculty of Engineering,
University of Waterloo, Waterloo, ON N2L 3G1, Canada
`olegm@uwaterloo.ca`
[5] Department of Applied Mathematics, Faculty of Engineering,
University of Waterloo, Waterloo, ON N2L 3G1, Canada
`ervrscay@uwaterloo.ca`

Abstract. Recent studies have demonstrated that the Structural Similarity Index Measure (SSIM) is the top choice for quantifying both visual quality and image similarity. Although the SSIM is not convex, it has been successfully employed in a wide range of imaging tasks over the last years. In this paper, the authors propose a new method based on the Alternate Direction Method of Multipliers (ADMM) for solving an unconstrained SSIM-based optimization problem. We focus our analysis on the case in which the regularizing term is convex. The paper also includes numerical examples and experiments that showcase the effectiveness of the proposed method.

1 Introduction

As is well known, it is customary to employ Euclidean-based metrics in a wide variety of image processing tasks. These metrics are quite convenient to use since they are mathematically tractable and easily computed. For instance, the squared Euclidean distance is convex and differentiable, which makes it well suited as, say, the objective function of an optimization problem. As such, it is usually included as the fidelity term in imaging tasks that can be carried out by optimizing a cost function. In general, such functions have the following form:

$$\min_x \frac{1}{2}\|A(x) - y\|_2^2 + \lambda h(x), \tag{1}$$

© Springer International Publishing AG, part of Springer Nature 2018
A. Campilho et al. (Eds.): ICIAR 2018, LNCS 10882, pp. 20–29, 2018.
https://doi.org/10.1007/978-3-319-93000-8_3

where $A(\cdot)$ is generally a linear operator (e.g., blurring kernel, subsampling operator, etc.), y is a given observation, $h(x)$ is a regularizing term, and the constant λ is a regularization parameter.

The role of the fidelity term $\|A(x) - y\|_2^2$ is to maintain the solution to (1) close to the observed data y. As for the regularization term $h(x)$, this has two main purposes: (i) It prevents over-fitting and (ii) ensures the solution will have certain expected features which are based on prior information or assumptions. For example, if the optimal solution is assumed to have bounded variation, a typical regularization term is $h(x) = \|x\|_{TV}$, where $\|\cdot\|_{TV}$ is the Total Variation (TV) seminorm [6–8].

Despite the advantages that Euclidean-based metrics offer, it has been shown that they are not appropriate for measuring similarity between images [19,20]. Given this, many measures of visual quality have been proposed in an attempt to model the Human Visual System (HVS). In particular, the Structural Similarity Index Measure (SSIM), originally proposed by Wang et al. [20], has become the top choice for quantifying both visual quality and image similarity.

Although the SSIM is not convex and not as mathematically tractable as the Euclidean-based metrics, it has been successfully employed in a wide range of imaging tasks over the last years. For instance, in [3] the authors find the best approximation coefficients in the SSIM sense when an orthogonal transformation is used (e.g., Discrete Cosine Transform (DCT), Fourier, etc.). Very briefly, a contrast-enhanced version of the best ℓ_2-based approximation is obtained. Based on this result, Rehman et al. [15] address the SSIM version of the image restoration problem proposed by Elad et al. in [10], where the denoising of images is performed using sparse and redundant representations over learned dictionaries. Furthermore, in [15], the authors also introduce a super-resolution algorithm—also based on the SSIM—to recover from a given low resolution image its high resolution version.

Another interesting application for reconstruction and denoising was proposed in [9]. Here, the authors define the statistical SSIM index (statSSIM), an extension of the SSIM for wide-sense stationary random processes. By optimizing the statSSIM, an optimal filter in the SSIM sense is found. The non-convex nature of the statSSIM is overcome by reformulating its maximization as a quasi-convex optimization problem, which is solved using the bisection method [1,9]. Nevertheless, it is not mentioned that the SSIM—under certain conditions—is a quasi-convex function (see [4]). As a result, it can be minimized using quasi-convex programming techniques, which permits the consideration of a much broader spectrum of SSIM-based optimization problems. Such techniques have already been introduced in [11,13].

More recently, Brunet et al. proposed a systematic framework for the design of SSIM-based restoration algorithms [5]. Applications such as optimal SSIM image denoising and soft-thresholding are introduced in this work. Other imaging techniques based on the SSIM can also be found in [16,18]. In these works, optimization of rate distortion, video coding and image classification are explored using the SSIM as a measure of performance.

Also, in [12], the authors introduced a general framework for carrying out *unconstrained SSIM-based optimization*. In particular, two algorithms are proposed for solving optimization problems of the form

$$\min_x T(\Phi(x), y) + \lambda h(x), \tag{2}$$

where Φ is usually a linear transformation, λ is a regularization parameter, $h(x)$ is a convex regularizing term, and $T(\cdot, \cdot)$ is a dissimilarity measure, which is given by

$$T(x, y) = 1 - \text{SSIM}(x, y). \tag{3}$$

In this paper, we propose a new method based on the Alternate Direction Method of Multipliers (ADMM) for solving problem (2). In particular, we focus our attention on the case in which the regularizing term $h(x)$ is convex. Experiments that showcase the effectiveness of the proposed method are also included.

2 The Structural Similarity Index Measure (SSIM)

Structural similarity (SSIM) [20] provides a measure of visual closeness of two images (or local image patches) by quantifying similarities in three fundamental characteristics: luminance, contrast and structure. Luminances are compared in terms of a relative change in means. Contrasts are compared in terms of relative variance. Finally, structures are compared in terms of the correlation coefficient between the two images. The SSIM value is computed by simply taking the product of these changes.

In what follows, we let $x, y \in \mathbb{R}^n$ denote two n-dimensional signal/image blocks. The SSIM between x and y is defined as [20],

$$\text{SSIM}(x, y) = \left(\frac{2\mu_x \mu_y + C_1}{\mu_x^2 + \mu_y^2 + C_1} \right) \left(\frac{2\sigma_x \sigma_y + C_2}{\sigma_x^2 + \sigma_y^2 + C_2} \right) \left(\frac{\sigma_{xy} + C_3}{\sigma_x \sigma_y + C_3} \right). \tag{4}$$

Here, μ_x and μ_y denote the mean values of x and y, respectively, and σ_{xy} denotes the cross correlation between x and y, from which all other definitions follow. The small positive constants, C_1, C_2, C_3 provide numerical stability and can be adjusted to accommodate the HVS. Note that $-1 \leq \text{SSIM}(x, y) \leq 1$. Furthermore, $\text{SSIM}(x, y) = 1$ if and only if $x = y$. As such, x and y are considered to be more similar the closer $\text{SSIM}(x, y)$ is to 1.

Setting $C_3 = C_2/2$ leads to the following definition of the SSIM index found in [20] and used in [3] and elsewhere,

$$\text{SSIM}(x, y) = \left(\frac{2\mu_x \mu_y + C_1}{\mu_x^2 + \mu_y^2 + C_1} \right) \left(\frac{2\sigma_{xy} + C_2}{\sigma_x^2 + \sigma_y^2 + C_2} \right). \tag{5}$$

Since the statistics of images vary greatly spatially, the $\text{SSIM}(x, y)$ is computed using a sliding window of 8×8 pixels. The final result, i.e., the so-called *SSIM index*, is basically an average of the individual SSIM measures.

A further simplification results when x and y have zero mean, i.e., $\mu_x = \mu_y = 0$. In this special case, we obtain the following expression

$$\mathrm{SSIM}(x,y) = \frac{2x^T y + C}{\|x\|_2^2 + \|y\|_2^2 + C},\tag{6}$$

where $C = (n-1)C_2$ (see [11,12] for more details). For the remainder of this paper, unless otherwise stated, we shall be working with zero mean vectors, so that Eq. (6) will be employed in all computations of the SSIM.

The corresponding distance/dissimilarity function $T(x,y)$ in Eq. (3) becomes

$$T(x,y) = 1 - \mathrm{SSIM}(x,y) = \frac{\|x - y\|_2^2}{\|x\|_2^2 + \|y\|_2^2 + C}.\tag{7}$$

Note that $0 \leq T(x,y) \leq 2$. Furthermore, $T(x,y) = 0$ if and only if $x = y$. As mentioned earlier, since $\mathrm{SSIM}(x,y)$ is a measure of similarity, $T(x,y)$ can be considered as a measure of dissimilarity between x and y.

3   Unconstrained SSIM-Based Optimization

We shall focus on unconstrained SSIM-based optimization problems of the form,

$$\min_x T(\Phi x, y) + \lambda h(x),\tag{8}$$

where $\lambda > 0$ is a regularization parameter and $h : \mathbb{R}^n \to \mathbb{R}$ is a regularization functional, which is often defined to be convex. Notice that the first term in (8) is not convex, thus the entire cost function is not convex either. This implies that the existence of a unique global minimizer of (8) cannot be generally guaranteed. Despite this, it is still possible to devise efficient numerical methods capable of converging to either a locally or a globally optimal solution, as will be shown in the following Section of the paper.

3.1   ADMM-Based Approach

In order to solve problem in (8) we follow an approach based on the Augmented Lagrangian Method of Multipliers (ADMM). This methodology is convenient since it allows us to solve a wide variety of unconstrained SSIM-based optimization problems by splitting the cost function to be minimized into simpler optimization problems that are easier to solve.

The problem in (8) can be solved efficiently by taking advantage of the fact that the objective function is separable. Let us write Problem (8) in its equivalent constrained form:

$$\min_{x,z} T(\Phi x, y) + \lambda h(z),$$

$$\text{subject to } x - z = 0,\tag{9}$$

where $z \in \mathbb{R}^n$ [2]. Clearly, (9) is equivalent to problem (8), thus by solving it, we automatically obtain a minimizer of the original optimization problem in (8).

As is customary in the ADMM methodology, let us first form the corresponding augmented Lagrangian of (9),

$$L_\rho(x, z, u) = T(\Phi x, y) + \lambda h(z) + \frac{\rho}{2}\|x - z + u\|_2^2, \tag{10}$$

where $u = v/\rho$ is a scaled dual variable [2]. As expected, the iterations of the proposed algorithm for solving (9) will be the minimization of Eq. (10) with respect to variables x and z in an alternate fashion, and the update of the dual variable u, which accounts for the maximization of the dual function $g(u)$:

$$g(u) := \inf_{x,y} L_\rho(x, z, u). \tag{11}$$

Thus, we define the following iteration for minimizing the cost function of the equivalent counterpart of problem (8):

$$x^{k+1} := \operatorname*{argmin}_x \left(T(\Phi x, y) + \frac{\rho}{2}\|x - z^k + u^k\|_2^2 \right), \tag{12}$$

$$z^{k+1} := \operatorname*{argmin}_z \left(h(z) + \frac{\rho}{2\lambda}\|x^{k+1} - z + u^k\|_2^2 \right), \tag{13}$$

$$u^{k+1} := u^k + x^{k+1} - z^{k+1}. \tag{14}$$

Observe that the x-update can be computed using the algorithm introduced in [12] for differentiable regularizing terms. Furthermore, when h is convex, the z-update is equal to the *proximal operator* of $(\lambda/\rho)h$ [14]. Recall that for a convex function $f : \mathbb{R}^n \to \mathbb{R}$ its proximal operator $\mathbf{prox}_f : \mathbb{R}^n \to \mathbb{R}^n$ is defined as

$$\mathbf{prox}_f(v) := \operatorname*{argmin}_x \left(f(x) + \frac{1}{2}\|x - v\|_2^2 \right). \tag{15}$$

It then follows that

$$z^{k+1} := \mathbf{prox}_{\frac{\lambda}{\rho}h}(x^{k+1} + u^k). \tag{16}$$

Given the latter, we introduce the following algorithm for solving Problem (8).

Algorithm I: ADMM-BASED METHOD FOR UNCONSTRAINED
SSIM-BASED OPTIMIZATION

initialize $x = z = x_0$, $u = \mathbf{0}$;
data preprocessing $y = y - \frac{1}{n}\mathbf{1}^T y$;
repeat
    $x := \operatorname*{argmin}_x \left(T(\Phi x, y) + \frac{\rho}{2}\|x - z + u\|_2^2 \right)$;
    $z := \operatorname*{argmin}_z \left(h(z) + \frac{\rho}{2\lambda}\|x - z + u\|_2^2 \right)$;
    $u := u + x - z$;
until stopping criterion is satisfied.
return x.

---

4   Applications

As anticipated, by choosing different types regularization terms and linear operators, a wide variety of SSIM-based imaging tasks can be performed. In this section, due to space limitations, we review just one application that has been barely studied, namely, SSIM-TV denoising. For the interested reader, more applications and experimental results can be found in [11–13].

4.1   SSIM-TV Denoising

Until now we have worked with vectors, nevertheless, the proposed algorithm can be easily adapted for dealing with matrices, which are the digital counterparts of images. In the particular case of denoising, images can be denoised in the following fashion. Let $Y \in \mathbb{R}^{m \times n}$ be a noisy image. Also, let $V : \mathbb{R}^{m \times n} \to \mathbb{R}^{mn \times 1}$ be a linear transformation that converts matrices into column vectors, that is,

$$V(A) = \text{vec}(A) = [a_{11}, a_{21}, \ldots, a_{(m-1)n}, a_{mn}]^T, \tag{17}$$

where $A \in \mathbb{R}^{m \times n}$.

As mentioned before, it is more convenient to employ an average of local SSIMs as a fidelity term. Let $\{Y_i\}_{i=1}^N$ be a partition of the given image Y such that $\cup_{i=1}^N Y_i = Y$. Further, let $\{X_i, Z_i\}_{i=1}^N$ also be partitions of the variables X and Z such that $\cup_{i=1}^N X_i = X$ and $\cup_{i=1}^N Z_i = Z$. Also, let $MT : \mathbb{R}^{m \times n} \times \mathbb{R}^{m \times n} \to \mathbb{R}$ be given by

$$MT(X, Y) = \frac{1}{N} \sum_{i=1}^N T(V(X_i), V(Y_i)). \tag{18}$$

Then, the optimization problem that is to be solved is

$$\min_X MT(X, Y) + \lambda \|X\|_{TV}, \tag{19}$$

where the regularizing term is a discretization of the isotropic TV seminorm for real-valued images [6].

If $\{Y_i, X_i Z_i\}_{i=1}^N$ are partitions of non-overlapping blocks, the problem in (19) can be solved by carrying out the following iterations,

$$X_i^{k+1} := \underset{X_i}{\text{argmin}} \left(T(V(X_i), V(Y_i)) + \frac{N\rho}{2} \|X_i - Z_i^k + U_i^k\|_F^2 \right), \tag{20}$$

$$Z^{k+1} := \underset{Z}{\text{argmin}} \left(\|Z\|_{TV} + \frac{\rho}{2\lambda} \|Z - X^{k+1} - U^k\|_F^2 \right), \tag{21}$$

$$U^{k+1} := U^k + X^{k+1} - Z^{k+1}, \tag{22}$$

where $\|\cdot\|_F$ is the Frobenius norm and U_i is an element of the partition of the dual variable U. As expected, $\cup_{i=1}^N U_i = U$, and $U_i \cap U_j = \varnothing$ for all $i \neq j$. Notice that the Z-update may be computed efficiently by using the algorithm introduced by Chambolle in [6]. The extension of this algorithm when a weighted average of local SSIMs is used as a measure of similarity between images is straightforward.

We close this section by mentioning that to the best of our knowledge, the contributions reported in [11, 13, 17] along with the applications presented above are the only approaches in the literature that combine TV and the SSIM.

5   Experiments

In the following experiments, the denoising of some images corrupted with Additive White Gaussian Noise (AWGN) was performed. Although from a maximum a posteriori (MAP) perspective the ADMM-SSIM approach is not optimal, it is worthwhile to see how denoising is carried out when the SSIM-based metric is employed as a fidelity term.

It is important to mention that in order to reduce blockiness in the reconstructions the mean of each non-overlapping pixel block is not subtracted prior to processing. This implies that the fidelity term defined in (18) is not equivalent, but is based on the dissimilarity measure introduced in Sect. 2. Despite this, the experiments presented below suggest that this fidelity measure may be used as a substitute of the SSIM.

In all experiments, we employed non-overlapping pixel blocks. Performance of the ℓ_2- and SSIM-based approaches is assessed by computing the MSSIM of the original images and their corresponding reconstructions. Here, the MSSIM is simply the average of the SSIM values of all non-overlapping blocks.

As expected, the noiseless approximation is obtained by solving Problem (19). To evaluate the performance of the proposed ADMM-SSIM method, we compare it with its ℓ_2 counterpart, namely,

$$\min_X \|X - Y\|_2^2 + \lambda \|X\|_{TV}. \tag{23}$$

Naturally, Chambolle's algorithm can be employed for solving this optimization problem [6]. In order to compare the effectiveness of the proposed approach and Chambolle's method (TV), regularization was carried out in such a way that the TV seminorms of the reconstructions yielded by both methods are the same.

In Fig. 1, some visual results are shown. We employed the test image *Lena*. The noisy image, as well as the SSIM map, can be observed in the first row. The reconstructed and original images are presented in the second row. The TV seminorm of the reconstruction is 2500 for *Lena*. The Peak Signal-to-Noise Ratio (PSNR) prior to denoising was 18.067 dB in all experiments.

It is evident that the proposed method performs significantly better than its ℓ_2 counterpart. Notice that some features of the original *Lena* are better reconstructed (e.g., the eyes in *Lena*), whereas in the ℓ_2 reconstruction these features are considerably blurred. This is mainly due to the fact that the noise does not completely hide some of the more important attributes of the original image. Since the fidelity term enforces the minimizer of problem (19) to be visually as similar as possible as the given noisy observation, while denoising is still accomplished, the reconstruction yielded by the ADMM-SSIM approach is visually more similar to the noiseless image. As for MSSIM values, these are 0.4386 and 0.6468 for the ℓ_2 and ADMM-SSIM reconstructions, respectively.

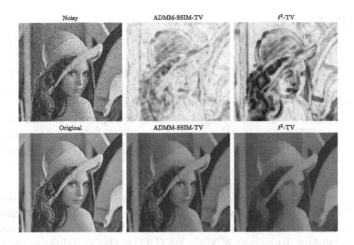

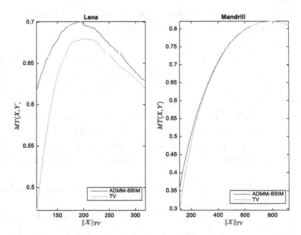

Fig. 1. Some visual results for the denoising of the test image *Lena*. The TV seminorm of both reconstructed images is 2500. **Top row:** Noisy image along with SSIM maps between each reconstructed image and the original. **Bottom row:** Original and ADMM-SSIM- and ℓ^2-based denoised images, with MSSIM values 0.6468 and 0.4386, respectively.

Fig. 2. The behaviour of the average SSIM of reconstructed images obtained from the proposed SSIM-based method and the classical ℓ_2 method as a function of the TV seminorm of the reconstruction. **Left:** The *Lena* image. **Right:** The *Mandrill* image. In the case of the *Lena* image, the SSIM-based approach clearly outperforms the classical ℓ_2 method. For the *Mandrill* image, however, the performance of both methods is, in general, very similar.

In order to have a general idea of the effectiveness of the SSIM-based methodology when regularization varies, in Fig. 2, we show the behaviour of the MSSIM as a function of the TV seminorm of the reconstructions obtained by both the ADMM-SSIM and the ℓ_2 approaches. The plot on the left shows the behaviour of the MSSIM for a noisy image patch of *Lena* whereas the plot on the right shows the results for a corrupted image patch of *Mandrill*. As expected, the plot on the right hand side shows that for images with low regularity—such as *Mandrill*—the ADMM-SSIM and ℓ_2 methods exhibit similar effectiveness over a wide range of regularization values. On the other hand, for the image *Lena*, one observes a significant difference between the performances of the two methods. This suggests that when strong regularization is required, it is more advantageous to employ SSIM-based techniques over ℓ_2 methods if certain visual features need to be recovered, provided that the reconstruction possesses some degree of regularity.

Acknowledgements. This work has been supported in part by Discovery Grants (ERV and OM) from the Natural Sciences and Engineering Research Council of Canada (NSERC). Financial support from the Faculty of Mathematics and the Department of Applied Mathematics, University of Waterloo (DO) is also gratefully acknowledged.

References

1. Boyd, S., Vandenberghe, L.: Convex Optimization. Cambridge University Press, Cambridge (2004)
2. Boyd, S., Parikh, N., Chu, E., Peleato, B., Eckstein, J.: Distributed optimization and statistical learning via the alternating direction method of multipliers. Found. Trends Mach. Learn. **3**, 1–122 (2010)
3. Brunet, D., Vrscay, E.R., Wang, Z.: Structural similarity-based approximation of signals and images using orthogonal bases. In: Campilho, A., Kamel, M. (eds.) ICIAR 2010. LNCS, vol. 6111, pp. 11–22. Springer, Heidelberg (2010). https://doi.org/10.1007/978-3-642-13772-3_2
4. Brunet, D., Vrscay, E.R., Wang, Z.: On the mathematical properties of the structural similarity index. IEEE Trans. Image Process. **21**, 1488–1499 (2012)
5. Brunet, D., Channappayya, S., Wang, Z., Vrscay, E.R., Bovik, A.: Optimizing image quality. In: Handbook of Convex Optimization Methods in Imaging Science, pp. 15–41 (2017)
6. Chambolle, A.: An algorithm for total variation minimization and applications. J. Math. Imaging Vis. **20**, 89–97 (2004)
7. Chambolle, A., Caselles, V., Cremers, D., Novaga, M., Pock, T.: An introduction to total variation for image analysis. Theor. Found. Numer. Methods Sparse Recover. **9**, 263–340 (2010)
8. Chambolle, A., Pock, T.: A first-order primal-dual algorithm for convex problems with applications to imaging. J. Math. Imaging Vis. **40**, 120–145 (2011)
9. Channappayya, S., Bovik, A.C., Caramanis, C., Heath Jr., R.W.: Design of linear equalizers optimized for the structural similarity index. IEEE Trans. Image Process. **17**, 857–872 (2008)
10. Elad, M., Aharon, M.: Image denoising via sparse and redundant representations over learned dictionaries. IEEE Trans. Image Process. **15**, 3736–3745 (2006)
11. Otero, D.: Function-valued mappings and SSIM-based optimization in imaging, Ph.D. thesis, University of Waterloo, Waterloo, ON, Canada (2015)
12. Otero, D., Vrscay, E.R.: Unconstrained structural similarity-based optimization. In: Campilho, A., Kamel, M. (eds.) ICIAR 2014. LNCS, vol. 8814, pp. 167–176. Springer, Cham (2014). https://doi.org/10.1007/978-3-319-11758-4_19

13. Otero, D., Vrscay, E.R.: Solving optimization problems that employ structural similarity as the fidelity measure. In: Proceedings of the International on Image Processing, Computer Vision and Pattern Recognition, pp. 474–479. CSREA Press (2014)
14. Parikh, N., Boyd, S.: Proximal algorithms. Found. Trends Optim. **1**, 123–231 (2013)
15. Rehman, A., Rostami, M., Wang, Z., Brunet, D., Vrscay, E.R.: SSIM-inspired image restoration using sparse representation. EURASIP J. Adv. Signal Process. **2012**, 1–12 (2012)
16. Rehman, A., Gao, Y., Wang, J., Wang, Z.: Image classification based on complex wavelet structural similarity. Signal Process. Image Commun. **28**, 984–992 (2013)
17. Shao, Y., Sun, F., Li, H., Liu, Y.: Structural similarity-optimal total variation algorithm for image denoising. In: Sun, F., Hu, D., Liu, H. (eds.) Foundations and Practical Applications of Cognitive Systems and Information Processing. AISC, vol. 215, pp. 833–843. Springer, Heidelberg (2014). https://doi.org/10.1007/978-3-642-37835-5_72
18. Wang, S., Rehman, A., Wang, Z., Ma, S., Gao, W.: SSIM-motivated rate-distortion optimization for video coding. IEEE Trans. Circuits Syst. Video Techn. **22**, 516–529 (2012)
19. Wang, Z., Bovik, A.C.: A universal image quality index. IEEE Signal Process. Lett. **9**, 81–84 (2002)
20. Wang, Z., Bovik, A.C., Sheikh, H.R., Simoncelli, E.P.: Image quality assessment: from error visibility to structural similarity. IEEE Trans. Image Process. **13**, 600–612 (2004)

A Flexible Statistical Model
for Image Denoising

Ines Channoufi[1,2], Sami Bourouis[1,3(✉)], Nizar Bouguila[4],
and Kamel Hamrouni[1]

[1] Lab: LR-SITI Signal Image et Technologies de l'Information,
Université de Tunis El Manar, ENIT, 1002 Tunis, Tunisie
`kamel.hamrouni@enit.rnu.tn`
[2] ESPRIT School of Engineering, Tunis, Tunisia
`ines.channoufi@esprit.tn`
[3] Taif University, Taif, Saudi Arabia
`s.bourouis@tu.edu.sa`
[4] The Concordia Institute for Information Systems Engineering (CIISE),
Concordia University, Montreal, QC H3G 1T7, Canada
`nizar.bouguila@concordia.ca`

Abstract. In this paper, we examine an important problem in the context of image processing which is image denoising. Although conventional Gaussian distributions have been widely used, they fail to fit the shape of heavy-tailed data produced by the presence of noise. In this paper, we propose an unsupervised algorithm based on finite mixtures of bounded generalized Gaussian distributions (BGGMD) to achieve smooth denoising results. The proposed framework has the flexibility to fit different shapes of observed data and bounded support data in the case of noisy images. Experimental results demonstrate that the proposed method has superior performance than some conventional approaches.

Keywords: Image denoising · Mixture models
Bounded generalized Gaussian distribution · Expectation maximization

1 Introduction

Image denoising still remains a fundamental problem in the area of image processing, since the quality of an image is degraded by noise which will negatively influence the accuracy of many computer vision operations such as image segmentation, object tracking and recognition, etc. Thus, a preprocessing denoising step is required before exploiting images in challenging applications. In the literature, various denoising techniques have been developed to enhance the quality of images. It is possible to divide these techniques into two categories [17]: spatial-based filtering and transform-based filtering. Spatial-based filtering deal with spatial pixels to enhance the entire image, while transform-based filtering uses a linear combination of few basis elements to estimate the true signal. Moreover, it

© Springer International Publishing AG, part of Springer Nature 2018
A. Campilho et al. (Eds.): ICIAR 2018, LNCS 10882, pp. 30–38, 2018.
https://doi.org/10.1007/978-3-319-93000-8_4

is possible to solve the problem of denoising through a statistical multiresolution criterion [8,18] in which a smoothing parameter was applied for regularization purpose. On the other hand, finite mixture models are employed with success in this area of research. In particular, an interesting work was developed in [1] that investigates the generalized Gaussian mixture model with edge information for modelling and denoising noisy medical images. Several other works based on the so called -Gaussian scale mixture model (GSM)- are developed in the literature to deal with the problem of noise removal [7,16,20,21]. For instance, GSM was applied in wavelet domain [16] as a local denoising solution which has been generalized later to a discrete mixture of linear projected Gaussian scale mixtures [7]. GSM was also used as a prior model in a Bayesian wavelet framework for multi-component images denoising [20]. Another extension of GSM [21] is proposed as a bilateral filtering in the shiftable complex directional pyramid domain. Gaussian mixture models (GMM) have also been used in image denoising such as the method based on a Gaussian mixture Markov random field (GM-MRF) which is proposed for image denoising and reconstruction [22]. Despite the advantages of GMMs such as their flexibility in data modeling, they are sensitive to noise. Indeed, in real world, data has different shapes that cannot be modelled with simple Gaussian distributions. To solve this problem, a generalized Gaussian model (GGM) has been proposed in [3,5,12,13], which provides a flexibility to fit the shape of the data. GGM was also applied to denoise medical MRI images [4]. Although GGMs are applied with success for image denoising, their distri butions are unbounded with a support range of $(-\infty, +\infty)$. In practice, many sources have a bounded support which can be exploited to select the appropriate model shape. It is also noteworthy to mention that the bounded Gaussian mixture model (BGMM) and the bounded Generalized Gaussian mixture model (BGGMM) have more promising results than the GMM and the GGMM for the case of speech modeling [9] and image segmentation [14]. These models have never been adopted before for such application. In fact, we want to exploit their flexibility to fit different shapes and their ability to model the observed data with various bounded support regions. The remainder of this paper is organized as follows. A BGGMM model for image denoising is presented in Sect. 2. Then, in Sect. 3, obtained results and a comparative study are presented. Finally, we end with conclusions in Sect. 4.

2   Proposed Denoising Model

2.1   Bounded Generalized Gaussian Mixture Model

Let $\mathcal{Y}$ be an observed noisy image characterized by N pixels $\mathcal{Y} = \{Y_1, ..., Y_N\}$. In general, noisy images are modeled as follow:

$$\mathcal{Y} = \mathcal{X} + \mathcal{N} \tag{1}$$

where $\mathcal{X} = \{X_1, ..., X_N\}$ is the noise-free image, and $\mathcal{N}$ is the Gaussian white noise with zero mean and standard deviation σ_N. Since an image is composed of several regions, so it could be described using a mixture model with K components:

$$p(X_i|\Theta) = \sum_{j=1}^{K} \pi_j f(X_i|\theta_j) \tag{2}$$

where $\pi_j \geq 0$ and $\sum_{j=1}^{K} \pi_j = 1$, $f(X_i|\theta_j)$ is the probability density function associated with the region j, θ_j represents the set of parameters defining jth component, π_j are the mixing proportions and $\Theta = \{\theta_1, ..., \theta_K, \pi_1, ..., \pi_K\}$ is a complete set of parameters of the mixture model. The likelihood of data $\mathcal{X}$ with N independent and identically distributed data points can be expressed as:

$$p(\mathcal{X}|\Theta) = \prod_{i=1}^{N} \sum_{j=1}^{K} \pi_j f(X_i|\theta_j) \tag{3}$$

The density function of the BGGMM is defined as follows:

$$f(X_i|\theta_j) = \frac{f_{ggd}(X_i|\theta_j)H(X_i|\Omega_j)}{\int_{\partial_j} f_{ggd}(u|\theta_j)du} \tag{4}$$

where $H(X_i|\Omega_j) = \begin{cases} 1 & \text{if } X_i \in \partial_j \\ 0 & \text{Otherwise} \end{cases}$ is the indicator function which defines ∂_j to be the bounded support region in $\Re$ for each component Ω_j and f_{ggd} represents the generalized Gaussian distribution:

$$f_{ggd}(X_i|\theta_j) = \frac{\lambda_j \sqrt{\frac{\Gamma(3/\lambda_j)}{\Gamma(1/\lambda_j)}}}{2\partial_j \Gamma(1/\lambda_j)} \exp\left(-\left[\frac{\Gamma(3/\lambda_j)}{\Gamma(1/\lambda_j)}\right]^{\lambda_j/2} \left|\frac{X_i - \mu_j}{\sigma_j}\right|^{\lambda_j}\right) \tag{5}$$

where $\Gamma(.)$ represents gamma function and the parameter λ controls the tail of this distribution which is peaked with a lower value of λ and becomes flat for higher values. According to Eqs. (2) and (3), the complete data likelihood function for BGGMM can be described as follows:

$$p(\mathcal{X}|\Theta) = \prod_{i=1}^{N} \sum_{j=1}^{K} Z_{ij} \pi_j \left\{ \frac{f_{ggd}(X_i|\theta_j)H(X_i|\Omega_j)}{\int_{\partial_j} f_{ggd}(u|\theta_j)du} \right\} \tag{6}$$

where Z_{ij} is the membership indicator (i.e., $Z_{ij} = 1$ is X_i belongs to component j, and 0 otherwise).

2.2   BGGMM-Based Image Denoising

According to previous Eqs. 1 and 2, we have:

$$p(\mathcal{Y}) = \int p(\mathcal{Y}|\mathcal{X})p(\mathcal{X})d\mathcal{X} = \int f(\mathcal{Y}|\mathcal{X},\sigma_N^2) \prod_{i=1}^{N} \sum_{j=1}^{K} Z_{ij}\pi_j^X f(X_i|\lambda_j^X,\mu_j^X,\sigma_j^X)d\mathcal{X}$$

$$= \int \prod_{i=1}^{N} \sum_{j=1}^{K} Z_{ij}\pi_j^X f(Y_i|X_i,\sigma_N^2) f(X_i|\lambda_j^X,\mu_j^X,\sigma_j^X)d\mathcal{X}$$

$$= \prod_{i=1}^{N} \sum_{j=1}^{K} Z_{ij}\pi_j^X f(Y_i|\lambda_j^X,\mu_j^X,\sigma_j^X + \sigma_N^2) = \prod_{i=1}^{N} \sum_{j=1}^{K} Z_{ij}\pi_j^Y f(Y_i|\lambda_j^Y,\mu_j^Y,\sigma_j^Y)$$

$$(7)$$

The distribution parameters of each component of the noise-free image can be deduced from those of the noisy image as follows:

$$\pi_j^X = \pi_j^Y \qquad \lambda_j^X = \lambda_j^Y \qquad \mu_j^X = \mu_j^Y \qquad \sigma_j^X = \sigma_j^Y - \sigma_N^2 \qquad (8)$$

Then we apply the minimum mean square error estimator (MMSE), we can obtained the filtered image data $\hat{X}$ which is estimated from $\mathcal{Y}$ as:

$$\hat{X} = \arg\min_X \int p(\mathcal{X}|\mathcal{Y})(X - \mathcal{X})^2 d\mathcal{X} = \arg\min_X \frac{\int p(\mathcal{X}\mathcal{Y})(X-\mathcal{X})^2 d\mathcal{X}}{p(\mathcal{Y})} = \arg\min_X Q(X) \quad (9)$$

Setting $\frac{\partial Q(X)}{dX} = 0$, we obtain the estimator of $\mathcal{X}$ as: $\hat{X} = \frac{\int \mathcal{X}p(\mathcal{X}\mathcal{Y})d\mathcal{X}}{p(\mathcal{Y})}$ Finally $\hat{X}$ can be expressed as :

$$\hat{X} = \frac{\prod\limits_{i=1}^{N} \sum\limits_{j=1}^{K} Z_{ij}\pi_j^Y f(Y_i|\lambda_j^Y,\mu_j^Y,\sigma_j^Y) \left(\sum_j^Y\right)^{-1} (\sigma_N^2 \mu_j^X + \sigma_j^X Y_i)}{\prod\limits_{i=1}^{N} \sum\limits_{j=1}^{K} Z_{ij}\pi_j^Y f(Y_i|\lambda_j^Y,\mu_j^Y,\sigma_j^Y)} \quad (10)$$

To evaluate the previous equation for $\hat{X}$, we opt for the well known "maximum likelihood" technique [11,15]. In practice, we use the expectation maximization (EM) algorithm to estimate the model's parameters of the noisy and the noise-free images. The developed algorithm is summarized as follow:

1. Initialize the model parameters of the noisy image $\mathcal{Y}$ as: $\Theta = \{\pi_j, \mu_j, \sigma_j, \lambda_j\}$: choose an initial value for K as the number of regions in the image.
2. Update the mixture parameters Θ by altering the following two steps:
   - E-Step: Compute the posterior probability.
   - M-Step: Update the mixture parameters $\{\pi_j, \mu_j, \sigma_j, \lambda_j\}$. probability.
3. Repeat 2 until convergence.
4. According to Eq.(8), compute the $\pi_j^X, \lambda_j^X, \mu_j^X, \sigma_j^X (1 \le j \le K)$;
5. According to Eq.(10), determine the filtered region $\hat{X}_i$.
6. Finally, the filtered image is determined as $\hat{X} = \left\{\hat{X}_1, \hat{X}_2, ..., \hat{X}_M\right\}$.

3   Experiments and Results

3.1   Experiment 1

In this section we evaluate our proposed method using some well known images such as Lena, Fingerprint, Boat, etc. These images are contaminated with an additive Gaussian white noise with 6 different levels. In order to quantify the obtained performances, we use three different measures which are: The Peak Signal-to-Noise Ratio (PSNR), the Structural Similarity Index (SSIM) [10] and the Sattar's index [19]. The best performances are delivered with higher PSNR, SSIM and Sattar's indices. From Fig. 1, we notice that almost all models are able to provide acceptable qualitative results. This is can be also observed from Tables 1 and 2. Moreover, we can notice that the BGGMM-based method provides the most smoothed denoising results (under PSNR metric). In addition, the SSIM and Sattar values for BGGMM (depicted in Table 2) outperform the other method's values.

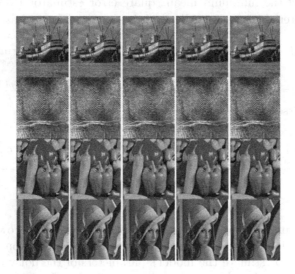

Fig. 1. Denoising results: 1st column: Original noisy images: Boat image with $\sigma_N = 25\%$; Fingerprint with $\sigma_N = 30\%$; Peppers with $\sigma_N = 20\%$; and Lena image with $\sigma_N = 30\%$; 2nd column: GMM; 3rd column: BGMM; 4th column: GGMM; 5th column: BGGMM.

3.2   Experiment 2: Medical Image Denoising

Image denoising is also a crucial step for medical applications. In particular, removing noise from magnetic resonance imaging (MRI) images is often desired for routine clinical tasks as a preprocessing step. In this work, we compare the denoising performance among the tested methods based on GMM, BGMM, GGMM and BGGMM using the public available benchmark dataset BrainWeb.

Table 1. Average PSNR values for different 2D images.

$\sigma_N(\%)$	GMM	BGMM	GGMM	BGGMM
5	27,3453	30,1158	29,5683	31,9996
10	26,4127	29,2212	28,1523	31,3348
15	25,7641	28,9034	27,7503	30,0984
20	26,1014	26,9523	27,2290	28,8847
25	25,8112	26,158	26,5960	27,9549
30	25,4827	25,9454	25,9698	27,1305

Table 2. Average SSIM and Sattar values for different 2D images.

SSIM					Sattar				
$\sigma_N(\%)$	GMM	BGMM	GGMM	BGGMM	$\sigma_N(\%)$	GMM	BGMM	GGMM	BGGMM
5	0,8747	0,9376	0,9082	0,9636	5	0,9940	0,9997	0,9939	0,9939
10	0,8401	0,9007	0,8650	0,9212	10	0,9847	0,9998	0,9867	0,9867
15	0,8023	0,8364	0,8395	0,8701	15	0,9775	0,9998	0,9778	0,9781
20	0,7907	0,8081	0,8043	0,8338	20	0,9934	0,9911	0,9935	0,9933
25	0,7595	0,7537	0,7529	0,8093	25	0,9893	0,9989	0,9897	0,9901
30	0,7076	0,7338	0,7361	0,7708	30	0,9922	0,9961	0,9924	0,9934

Table 3. Average PSNR values found for all 2D MRI images in the simulated BrainWeb Database.

$\sigma_N(\%)$	GMM	BGMM	GGMM	BGGMM
3	11,9525	15.1843	15,2263	22,8901
5	15,3693	18.5834	18,2454	23,2359
7	18,4162	20.2974	21,1743	22,6392
9	18,9034	19.1653	19,6888	21,1314

The MRI data are provided with different levels of Rician noise (3%, 5%, 7%, 9%, and more). We noticed again that obtained denoising results for BGGMM-based method are promising as illustrated in Fig. 2. The average metrics depicted in Tables 3 and 4 show that BGGMM-based method can achieve very competitive denoising performance and outperforms the rest of methods w.r.t different used metrics, in particular, for the case of $\sigma_N = 9\%$ (PSNR metric). Therefore, according to these results, we can state that image denoising has been improved with the BGGMM model.

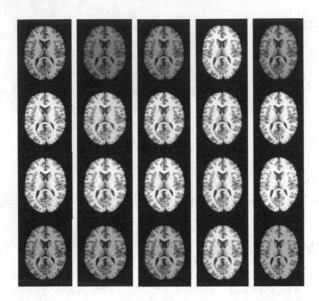

Fig. 2. Denoising results for the MRI Slice No 85: 1st row: $\sigma_N = 3\%$, 2nd row: $\sigma_N = 5\%$, 3rd row: $\sigma_N = 7\%$, 4th row: $\sigma_N = 9\%$; 1st column: Original images; 2nd column: GMM; 3rd column: GGMM; 4th column: BGMM; 5th column: BGGMM.

Table 4. Average SSIM and Sattar values found for all 2D MRI images in the simulated BrainWeb Database.

SSIM					Sattar				
$\sigma_N(\%)$	GMM	BGMM	GGMM	BGGMM	$\sigma_N(\%)$	GMM	BGMM	GGMM	BGGMM
3	0,8095	0.8013	0,8021	0,9034	3	0,9886	0.9886	0,9888	0,9893
5	0,7910	0.8173	0,7909	0,8707	5	0,9769	0.9769	0,9770	0,9773
7	0,7958	0.7945	0,7945	0,8175	7	0,9809	0.9810	0,9810	0,9809
9	0,7646	0.7386	0,7280	0,7705	9	0,9693	0.9691	0,9691	0,9693

4   Conclusion

In this paper, we have presented a new approach for image denoising based on the bounded generalized Gaussian distributions (BGGMD) which is more flexible to fit different shapes with bounded support than classic Gaussian-based models. We evaluated the performance of the proposed method for denoising some natural images and for simulated MRI brain images. According to this study, it's obvious that BGGMM can improve the visual quality of noisy images and can achieve very competitive denoising performances than conventional models. In our future works we plan to improve again results by taking into account the contextual information and feature selection process like in [2,6].

References

1. Cao, Y., Luo, Y., Yang, S.: Image denoising with gaussian mixture model. In: Image and Signal Processing, 2008, CISP 2008, Congress on, vol. 3, pp. 339–343 (2008)
2. Channoufi, I., Bourouis, S., Bouguila, N., Hamrouni, K.: Color image segmentation with bounded generalized gaussian mixture model and feature selection. In: 4th International Conference on Advanced Technologies for Signal and Image Processing (ATSIP'2018) (2018)
3. Cho, D., Bui, T.D.: Multivariate statistical approach for image denoising. In: IEEE International Conference on Acoustics, Speech, and Signal Processing, 2005. Proceedings, (ICASSP 2005), vol. 4, p. iv-589 (2005)
4. Cong-Hua, X., Jin-Yi, C., Wen-Bin, X.: Medical image denoising by generalised gaussian mixture modelling with edge information. IET Image Process. $8(8)$, 464–476 (2014)
5. Elguebaly, T., Bouguila, N.: Bayesian learning of generalized gaussian mixture models on biomedical images. In: Schwenker, F., El Gayar, N. (eds.) ANNPR 2010. LNCS (LNAI), vol. 5998, pp. 207–218. Springer, Heidelberg (2010). https://doi.org/10.1007/978-3-642-12159-3_19
6. Fan, W., Sallay, H., Bouguila, N., Bourouis, S.: A hierarchical dirichlet process mixture of generalized dirichlet distributions for feature selection. Comput. Electr. Eng. 43, 48–65 (2015)
7. Goossens, B., Pizurica, A., Philips, W.: Image denoising using mixtures of projected gaussian scale mixtures. IEEE Trans. Image Process. $8(8)$, 1689–1702 (2009)
8. Hotz, T., Marnitz, P., Stichtenoth, R., Davies, L., Kabluchko, Z., Munk, A.: Locally adaptive image denoising by a statistical multiresolution criterion. Comput. Stat. Data Anal. $56(3)$, 543–558 (2012)
9. Lindblom, J., Samuelsson, J.: Bounded support gaussian mixture modeling of speech spectra. IEEE Trans. Speech Audio Process. $11(1)$, 88–99 (2003)
10. López-Rubio, E., Florentín-Núñez, M.N.: Kernel regression based feature extraction for 3D MR image denoising. Med. Image Anal. $15(4)$, 498–513 (2011)
11. Meignen, S., Meignen, H.: On the modeling of small sample distributions with generalized gaussian density in a maximum likelihood framework. IEEE Trans. Image Process. $15(6)$, 1647–1652 (2006)
12. Najar, F., Bourouis, S., Bouguila, N., Belghith, S.: A fixed-point estimation algorithm for learning the multivariate GGMM: application to human action recognition. In: 31st IEEE Canadian Conference on Electrical and Computer Engineering (CCECE 2018) (2018)
13. Najar, F., Bourouis, S., Bouguila, N., Belguith, S.: A comparison between different gaussian-based mixture models. In: 14th IEEE International Conference on Computer Systems and Applications, Tunisia. IEEE (2017)
14. Nguyen, T.M., Wu, Q.J., Zhang, H.: Bounded generalized gaussian mixture model. Pattern Recogn. $47(9)$, 3132–3142 (2014)
15. Pi, M.: Improve maximum likelihood estimation for subband GGD parameters. Pattern Recogn. Lett. $27(14)$, 1710–1713 (2006)
16. Portilla, J., Strela, V., Wainwright, M.J., Simoncelli, E.P.: Image denoising using scale mixtures of gaussians in the wavelet domain. IEEE Trans. on Image process. $12(11)$, 1338–1351 (2003)
17. Rajni, R., Anutam, A.: Image denoising techniques-an overview. Int. J. Comput. Appl. $86(16)$, 13–17 (2014)

18. Rajpoot, N., Butt, I.: A multiresolution framework for local similarity based image denoising. Pattern Recogn. **45**(8), 2938–2951 (2012)
19. Sattar, F., Floreby, L., Salomonsson, G., Lovstrom, B.: Image enhancement based on a nonlinear multiscale method. IEEE Trans. Image Process. **6**(6), 888–895 (1997)
20. Scheunders, P., De Backer, S.: Wavelet denoising of multicomponent images using gaussian scale mixture models and a noise-free image as priors. IEEE Trans. on Image Process. **16**(7), 1865–1872 (2007)
21. Yang, H.Y., Wang, X.Y., Qu, T.X., Fu, Z.K.: Image denoising using bilateral filter and gaussian scale mixtures in shiftable complex directional pyramid domain. Comput. Electr. Eng. **37**(5), 656–668 (2011)
22. Zhang, R., Bouman, C.A., Thibault, J.B., Sauer, K.D.: Gaussian mixture markov random field for image denoising and reconstruction. In: Global Conference on Signal and Information Processing (GlobalSIP), 2013 IEEE, pp. 1089–1092 (2013)

Towards Automatic Calibration of Dotblot Images

André R. S. Marcal[1(✉)] (iD), Joana Martins[2], Elena Selaru[2], and Fernando Tavares[2,3] (iD)

[1] Departamento de Matemática Faculdade de Ciências, Universidade do Porto, Porto, Portugal
andre.marcal@fc.up.pt
[2] Faculdade de Ciências, Universidade do Porto, Porto, Portugal
[3] CIBIO - Centro de Investigação em Biodiversidade e Recursos Genéticos, Vairão, Portugal

Abstract. This paper addresses the issue of calibration (or normalization) of macroarray (dotblot) images. It proposes 3 parameters for the evaluation of the impact on the recorded markers of under- and over-exposure during the experimental acquisition of dotblot images – volume (V), saturation (S) and apparent radius (R). These parameters were evaluated using 101 dotblot images obtained from 16 different experiments, with 404 control markers in total. A procedure to simulate the changes on markers by increasing and decreasing exposure times is also presented. This can be the basis of a normalization procedure for dot blot images, which would be an important improvement in the current laboratory image acquisition protocol, reducing the subjectivity both at the acquisition level and at the subsequent image analysis stage.

Keywords: Macroarrays · Dot blot images · Calibration · Normalization

1 Introduction

A rapid and faithful detection of microorganisms from environmental samples is extremely important in diagnostic microbiology [1]. Unlike PCR (Polymerase Chain Reaction), where only one or a very limited number of markers can be detected in a single assay, the hybridization techniques, such as microarrays and macroarrays (Fig. 1) allow the simultaneous analysis of several molecular markers, increasing the robustness of detection. Currently, macroarrays allows for a higher cost-benefit in routine analysis than the much more expensive and elaborate microarray platform [2]. One of the main difficulties in the implementation of protocols for detecting microorganisms based on macroarrays is to unify the images' analysis to avoid bias in the results interpretation by an operator. Some efforts have been done recently in order to automate the image analysis of macroarray/dotblot images [2, 3], but surprisingly there are no papers available from other research groups on this innovative topic. Despite the progresses reported in [2, 3], there are still open some issues regarding image consistency, for example related to the time of film exposure to chemiluminescence.

It should be noted that in macroarrays by dot blot an ideal positive dot will be a dark mark in a light grey background, whereas a negative dot will ideally be undistinguishable from the background. However, the different affinities of hybridization between probes

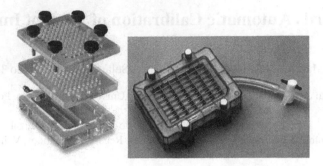

Fig. 1. Hybridization using macroarray with Bio-Dot apparatus [2].

and targets, as well as heterogeneity of the background noise, results in a grayscale image from which it is not always easy to distinguish a positive from a negative signal [2].

The dot blot images used in this work were acquired with a ChemiDoc System (Bio-Rad) [4], producing grayscale images with roughly 850 by 1300 pixels. Each dot blot had a pre-defined grid of evenly spaced dots, in this case, 96 dots arranged in 8 rows and 12 columns. Figure 2 presents 6 dotblot images, acquired with various exposure times. On the top row, there is an under-exposed image (left), a correct acquisition (centre) and a slightly over-exposed image (right). The bottom row presents 3 over-exposed images. In particular, the extreme over-exposure (right) clearly shows a number of markers which could potentially be false positive identifications.

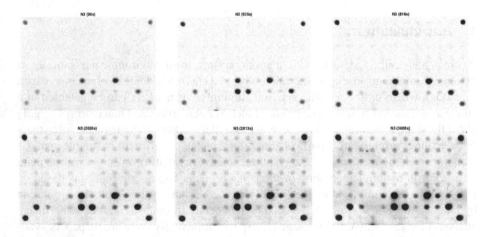

Fig. 2. Example of dotblot images acquired with different exposure times (experiment N3).

The purpose of this paper is to present 3 parameters for the evaluation of the impact of under- and over-exposure during the experimental acquisition of dotblot images on the recorded marker's signal, as well as to present a method for the simulation of changes on markers by increasing and decreasing exposure times, towards the development of an automatic calibration (or normalisation) method for dotblot images.

2   Materials and Methods

The procedures developed are general, for a N by M grid of evenly spaced dots. However, for this particular work, all the images used have the same grid size (N = 8, M = 12). The mark radius is also fixed at 0.15 mm, and the distances between the control marks located in the grid corners are 6.3 mm and 9.9 mm (short and long distance in the rectangular grid). An initial estimate for the mark radius (R_0) is 16 pixels.

2.1   Detection of the Control Marks

A sub-image size is established, by computing the number of lines (L_{sub}) and columns (C_{sub}) from the number pixels of lines (L) and columns (C) in the dotblot image, using (1) and (2). Four sub-images with this size are extracted from the dotblot image, from each image corner.

$$L_{sub} = \left\{ round\left(\frac{1.2\,L}{N} \right) \right\} \qquad (1)$$

$$C_{sub} = \left\{ round\left(\frac{1.2\,C}{M} \right) \right\} \qquad (2)$$

A local threshold value is computed for each sub-image, using the Otsu algorithm [5]. The four binary sub-images are then placed over a fully ON binary image (all pixels 1), of the same size as the original dotblot image. The morphological operation closing and opening are subsequently applied, both with a circular structuring element of radius R_0 [6]. Further operations are applied (labelling separate objects, extraction of the largest objects), to obtain a final binary image with a single object on each sub-region.

The image scale (pixels/mm) is computed as the average of 6 estimates, using all pairs of control marks. For each pair, the measured distance in pixels between the centres of the two marks is divided by the expected distance in mm. The scale is used to compute the regular (expected) marker radius in pixels (R_r).

2.2   Marker Evaluation Parameters

Three parameters are used to evaluate each control marker – volume, saturation and apparent radius – in order to characterise the image exposure. The exposure of a dotblot image is considered correct when saturation of a reference marker starts to occur.

For each control marker, a reference background intensity (I_b) is computed as the median intensity value of a margin (area between the external and internal rectangles centred on the marker). The internal rectangle size is 0.9 the average distance between markers, and the external rectangle has an additional 20 pixels in each length (margin of 10 pixels around the internal rectangle). Figure 3 shows a dot blot image (left) and a detail view of the control markers (right) with the corresponding internal (green) and external (red) rectangles overlaid.

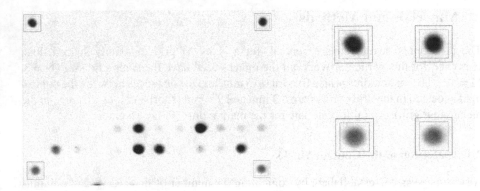

Fig. 3. Dotblot image with correct exposure (left) and a detail of the control marks rectangular regions (right), used to extract the reference background intensity for each mark.

The volume of a control marker (V) is computed using (3), with j corresponding to each pixel in the internal rectangle centered on the mark, with intensity I_j.

$$V = \sum_j max\{0, I_b - I_j\} \tag{3}$$

A pixel j is considered to be saturated when its intensity is 0 or nearly 0 – when its value is $I_j < 0.02I_b$. The saturation (S) is computed as the number of saturated pixels for the internal rectangle centered on the control marker.

A local thresholding is applied to the internal rectangle sub-image, using the Otsu algorithm [5]. The resulting binary image, with values 1 for background and 0 for foreground (mark), is used to compute the area of the marker A (in pixels^2) and the apparent radius R (in pixels), computed by (4).

$$R = \sqrt{A/\pi} \tag{4}$$

2.3   Simulation of Exposure

The goal of the simulation process is to transform a marker with volume V_{in} in a new version with volume V_{out}, to simulate the effect of increasing and decreasing the exposure time at the image acquisition stage. Initially, the marker centre coordinates (x,y) and the regular (expected) radius (R_r) are used to create a bitmap (mask), with ON values in the circular region corresponding to the marker. A maximum volume (V_{max}) is then computed, which corresponds to the case where all ON pixels are saturated.

The gamma (γ) transformation function (5) can be used to change the intensity levels of a greyscale image [7], where I_{in} and I_{out} are the pixel levels before and after the transformation, and K is a normalization factor (K = 1 for images in the [0,1] range).

$$I_{out} = K I_{in}^{\gamma} \tag{5}$$

Two different approaches are considered in order to achieve the target volume (V_{out}) for the marker. If $V_{out} < V_{max}$ the volume of the marker is changed by applying a gamma transformation function (5), with the values of γ set by increments of 0.01 (positive or negative) in succession until the volume reaches V_{out}.

If $V_{out} > V_{max}$, a similar process is initially performed, until the volume of the marker reaches V_{max}. After this level, the mark is further changed by applying the morphologic operation erosion, with a circular structuring element of increasing size, until the target volume V_{out} is reached.

2.4   Test Dataset

A total of 101 dotblot images were used, acquired with various exposure times from 16 experimental setups. Table 1 presents a summary of the image characteristics. For each experiment, there is a correct exposure and a number of under-exposures or/and over-exposures. Figure 2 presents 6 of the 8 dotblot images of experiment N3, with exposure times of 90 s (under-exposure), 635 s (correct), and 816, 2026, 2813, 3600 s (over-exposures).

Table 1.   Summary of the dotblot images used for testing.

	No images (regarding exposure)				Exposure time [s] (range)		
Experiment	Under	Correct	Over	Total	Under	Correct	Over
A1	1	1	6	8	151	211	1845
E1	0	1	5	6	–	211	1724
E2	1	1	4	6	332	695	2208
F1	2	1	3	6	574	937	1179
F2	0	1	6	7	–	332	1300
F3	0	1	8	9	–	151	1845
N1	2	1	3	6	574	1058	2026
N2	1	1	2	4	90	151	1119
N3	1	1	6	8	90	635	3600
R1	2	1	2	5	574	1300	2510
R2	2	1	2	5	151	453	1663
S1	4	1	1	6	90	1058	1119
S2	5	1	2	8	90	2813	3600
V1	0	1	4	5	–	211	1724
V2	0	1	6	7	–	332	2208
V3	0	1	4	5	–	574	2026
TOTAL	21	16	64	101	–	–	–

The range of exposure times varies considerably between experiments. The correct exposure time for these experiments is between 151 and 2813 s, which corresponds to a ratio of nearly 20 (longest/shortest time). These values clearly show the difficulty in establishing laboratory protocols for dotblot image acquisition that are independent from operator interpretation.

3 Results

3.1 Exposure Evaluation Parameters

The impact of the exposure on the parameters volume (V), saturation (S) and apparent radius (R) was evaluated for all 16 experiments. Figure 4 shows how these parameters vary with the exposure time, for experiment A1, where the correct exposure was achieved at the 2nd image (exposure time 211 s). The volume increases nearly linearly with the exposure time for all control markers, in the time range tested in A1. The saturation starts to decrease for extreme exposure times, due to a contamination of the backgroud, which is used as reference. The relations between the marker's characterisation parameters – V, S and R – are presented in Fig. 5, for all 404 markers tested. The figure shows scatterplots of the parameters V and S versus R.

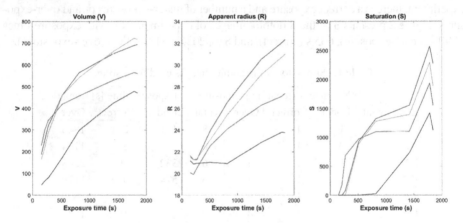

Fig. 4. Volume (left), apparent radius (centre) and saturation (right) for experiment A1.

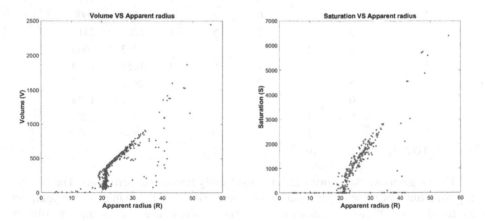

Fig. 5. Scatterplots of the volume (left) and saturation (right), both versus the apparent radius.

3.2 Simulation of Exposure

The simulation of exposure is illustrated with experiment F1 (6 images). The saturation of a control mark first occurred at the 3rd image (exposure time of 937 s), due to the saturation of 106 pixels on mark 2 (bottom left corner), thus resulting in 2 under-exposed and 3 over-exposed images. For this experiment, only two marks saturated – mark 2 and mark 4 (on the 5th image).

The volumes computed for the various marks/images were used to simulate under- and over-exposures, from the control marks of the reference image (correct exposure). Figure 6 shows the simulated (top rows) and real (bottom rows) control marks for the 6 images of experiment F1, for the 4 control marks. It is worth noting that the non-saturated simulated marks only use the regular (expected) marker radius, with the background set to white. The simulated marks closely resemble the original recorded marks, although some differences can be observed, particularly for saturated marks.

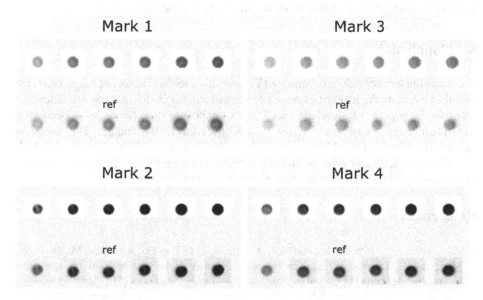

Fig. 6. Simulation of under- and over-exposure on the 4 control marks of experiment F1.

4 Discussion

The control markers of a dotblot image are expected to be all clearly ON, thus providing a solid reference to evaluate the remaining markers. However, as the experimental results presented here show, the actual recorded signal for a marker (the intensity levels of the corresponding image pixels) vary considerably with the exposure time. Furthermore, the signal of the 4 control markers is not the same for any given exposure.

The correct exposure time was found to be very diverse for the 16 experiments carried out (from 151 to 2813 s), which clearly shows how difficult it is to establish a robust independent laboratory protocol for dotblot image acquisition (not based on the subjective interpretation of an operator). It is therefore almost inevitable that the analysis of dotblot images is performed on under-exposed or over-exposed images.

A normalisation procedure can be implemented, by simulating the increase or decrease of exposure time. The goal is to obtain an image similar to what would result from an image acquisition with the perfect exposure time (just when the signal of a control marker starts to saturate). The simulation procedures proposed in this paper can be applied to the control marker to establish the ideal modification, and then applied to all image markers. There is still some validation work that needs to be done in order to confirm the worth of the simulated markers, both for automatic and human analysis.

A further open issue is whether or not the normalisation procedure should be equal for all markers. As the 4 control markers usually start to saturate at different exposure times, there could be potentially 4 reference exposure times to be used to simulate the final normalised image. The actual correction on an observed marker would then be a linear interpolation between the 4 reference markers. However, this approach still requires considerable validation work in order to be considered.

5   Conclusions

The 3 parameters considered – volume (V), saturation (S) and apparent radius (R) – are useful to evaluate the level of exposure of control marker in dot blot images. They can assist in the process of simulating a change of exposure time (increase or decrease), which can be the basis of a normalization procedure for dot blot images. This would be an important improvement in the current laboratory image acquisition protocol, which is still very much dependent on subjective human interpretation, and further increase the reliability of microorganisms detection based on macroarrays.

References

1. Albuquerque, P., Ribeiro, N., Almeida, A., Panschin, I., Porfirio, A., Vales, M., Diniz, F., Madeira, H., Tavares, F.: Application of a Dot Blot Hybridization Platform to Assess Streptococcus uberis Population Structure in Dairy Herds, Frontiers in Microbiology 8 (2017)
2. Caridade, C.M.R., Marcal, A.R.S., Albuquerque, P., Mendes, M.V., Tavares, F.: Automatic analysis of dot blot images. Intell. Autom. Soft Comput. **21**(4), 607–622 (2015)
3. Caridade, C.M.R., Marcal, A.R.S., Mendonça, T., Albuquerque, P., Mendes, M.V., Tavares, F.: Automatic analysis of macroarrays' images, In: Proceedings of the 32nd IEEE EMBS - EMBC 2010 Conference, pp. 6122–6125 (2010)
4. Bio-Rad.   http://www.bio-rad.com/en-pl/product/chemidoc-imaging-systems/chemidoc-xrs-system. Accessed 31 Jan 2018
5. Otsu, N.: A threshold selection method from gray-level histograms. IEEE Trans. Syst. Man Cybern. **9**(1), 62–69 (2002)
6. MATLAB and Image Processing Toolbox Release 2017a, The MathWorks, Inc., Natick, Massachusetts, United States (2017)
7. Gonzalez, R.C., Woods, R.E.: Digital Image Processing, 3rd edn. Prentice Hall, Upper Saddle River (2008)

Improving Picture Quality
with Photo-Realistic Style Transfer

Ilya Makarov$^{(\boxtimes)}$ (iD), Diana Polonskaya, and Anastasia Feygina

National Research University Higher School of Economics, Moscow, Russia
iamakarov@hse.ru, polonskaya.d@mail.ru, a.g.feygina@gmail.com
http://www.hse.ru/en/staff/iamakarov

Abstract. In this paper, we study style transfer applications for the
photo-realistic image processing tasks. First, we present the results on
image quality improvement based with photo style transfer. Second, we
describe the problems of learning style transfer under geometrical constraints for processing portrait images and multi-style transfer. Finally,
we give a short glimpse on application of image-to-image translation
methods for updating realistic graphics for video games.

Keywords: Style transfer · Photo-realistic image correction
Digital art · Generative Adversarial Networks
Image-to-image translation

1 Introduction

Creating digital art objects is now available not only for professionals but also
computer scientists and common people via different applications. One of such
an examples is the problem of transferring artistic or photo-realistic style from
one object onto another. It could be seen as copying style of famous paining
artist while not having skills to create original art.

Recently, style transfer became very popular method among computer
vision and machine learning applications to image processing. One of the first
approaches was artistic style transfer [1] based on pretrained convolutional neural
network VGG-19 [2] designed for deep image recognition. The authors suggested
using inner layers of VGG deep neural network for extracting content feature
maps as they preserve the information about the general content of the scenery
and semantic information. In [3], the authors demonstrated model based on
convolutional neural network with trained feature space for generating textures
from a given pattern. However, both models were slow and memory-consuming
in terms of optimization.

In [4], the authors described a model that works faster and with better quality
in comparison with [1]. The main idea of their approach was to combine all the
computational work with learning stage. Such an approach was used for style
transfer and texture generating from an image, however, random pasted textures

© Springer International Publishing AG, part of Springer Nature 2018
A. Campilho et al. (Eds.): ICIAR 2018, LNCS 10882, pp. 47–55, 2018.
https://doi.org/10.1007/978-3-319-93000-8_6

from style may sometimes be pasted to content image. To reduce this effect, more region-based style transfer was represented in [5], where researchers are jointly training all of the styles in a single model.

In standard style transfer and texture synthesis models, there are some restrictions connected with inability to control the process of training. The histogram-based methods and local losses could partially improve the quality control, as was shown in [6]. The problem arises whenever basic algorithms of style transfer switch colours of the content image to colours of style image, sometimes causing undesirable interference in output image. This problem was solved in [7] suggesting the following two techniques. The first idea was matching color histograms of the style image with the colors of the content image. The second approach consists of luminance-only transfer.

Another way to produce the texture or scale the existing one is using Generative Adversarial Networks, which produce images by sampling from uniform noise distribution. Recent trends in this field consist of two main ideas: using spacial tensor instead of single vector to extend the distribution of input noise [8] and consistently generating structure of image using Structure-GAN and then, producing the image with Style-GAN, which takes surface normal map as an input [9]. An interesting approach was represented in [10], where authors have combined Generative Adversarial Networks operating on Markov random fields, and deep CNNs. Compared with separate using of MFR-based and CNN based approaches, this combined technology increase visual plausibility of graphic content. It allows to maintain considerable variability while matching local features. Moreover, the idea of using only Markov random field instead of CNN in texture synthesis was put forward by Kwatra in [11]. This approach is based on idea of minimizing energy function under EM-like optimization algorithm, however, the idea was not widely spread due to the progress and popularity of neural networks applications. However, in [12], the authors has represented the extended version of Kwatra's algorithm by adding complicated segmentation and reaching the quality comparable with CNN-based approaches.

2   Related Work

Style transfer to an existing photo is complicated, but interesting task which can be completed using several approaches. Some of them are using luminance mechanism of colour preservation like described in [7] suit style transfer to photo. The generation of perceptual-appealing styles using decomposition of style to perceptual factors was presented in [13]. In [14], the idea of using oRGB colour theory and simple statistical analysis was described as the core feature while global luminance histogram was used to achieve better image quality. The key feature of this approach is compatibility with CUDA and highly parallel computations. A multimodal CNN-based approach was discussed in [15], where authors are struggling with quality reduction in small, complicated and exquisite textures. The proper quality has been obtained using hierarchical stylization with multiple losses of increasing scales.

In [16], the authors showed that using CNNs for transferring style between photos may reveal some kind of unnecessary distortions. A way to reduce unnecessary distortions was presented in [17]. The authors suggested the two main ideas: the maximization of photo-realism and semantic segmentation of the inputs to avoid the content-mismatch problem. They added regularization to prevent colors undergo non-affine transformations and the masks as additional channels of input image processing. The way to improve quality and speed in the mentioned approach was presented in [18].

Perceptual loss based on features of network can be used instead of using per-pixel loss giving no semantic information about the input image. The evolution of this approach was described in [19], where researchers from NVIDIA and MIT Media Lab have modified the loss function by adding perceptually-motivated losses and adding differentiable error function. This research has shown that it is possible to reach significantly better results even by just improving the loss function, when the network architecture remains unchanged. Another problem of transferring style to photo is discussed in [20], where a robust tool for stylization photos, which is based on Superpixel-based Bipartite Graph, was introduced. The main idea of this approach consists of two steps: extracting hierarchical features in order to construct a bipartite graph to produce superpixels and rematching superpixels by bipartite matching to form a new bipartite graph. The results have shown success in transferring style even on night photos.

3   Our Method

3.1   Network Architecture

We use convolutional neural network (CNN) for photo style transfer. In particular, CNN called VGG-16 was used in our experiments. VGG-style networks have roughly the same architecture consisting of repeated convolution, ReLu, and MaxPool layers. It allows to use deep image representation as tensor factorization upon the layers of neural network.

3.2   Loss Function

Mixed image should contain both texture and content of input images. Thus, it is important to take into consideration the measure of significant difference between input images and output picture during the learning process.

In this paper, we want to improve the existing model of using feature activations $F^l(x)$ and Gram matrix $G^l(x)$ at layer l, by adding a term to the that will measure the quality of output picture, so that an overall loss can be written as weighted sum of style and content loss, and penalty for bad image quality:

$$L = \alpha \sum_l ||F^l(t) - F^l(x)||_2^2 + \beta \sum_l ||G^l(t) - G^l(x)||_2^2 + \gamma L_{quality},$$

where $L_{quality}$ is L_1 norm of the picture gradient.

4 Experiments

4.1 Paintings

First group of experiments was related to photo style transfer to paintings. The goal was to make a state of art look for the famous art paintings like they are a real photo. Input image and painting should satisfy similarity criterion: style and content picture should be semantically similar.

Fig. 1. Photo Style Transfer

As it can be seen from Fig. 1, different implementations of the learning with image quality metric in loss function showed good results in style transfer to paintings task.

4.2 Portraits

Another experiment was about transferring style from portrait to portrait. This task is more difficult due to significant image distortions. It is important to preserve some geometrical proportions when transferring portrait style without compromising quality by arbitrary occurrences of content misplacement.

Figure 2 represents the output from two CNNs. As it can be seen from illustrations, results are very different. In the first row, Fig. 2a was style for grey-scale of itself. In second and third row, to the grey-scale Fig. 2a styles of N. Campbell and E. Fanning Style were applied, respectively. It can be clearly seen that Neural art was good for skin color transfers as for hair color compared to JcJohnson. However, on Fig. 2e skin color of output image was transferred from grey t-shirt of input style photo. Results with gradient sparseness were better then with non-modified loss.

4.3 Multi-style Transfer

In this experiment, we consider transfer of style from two different paintings to one photo. Our approach was based on consistent application of style to picture and then to output from first CNN.

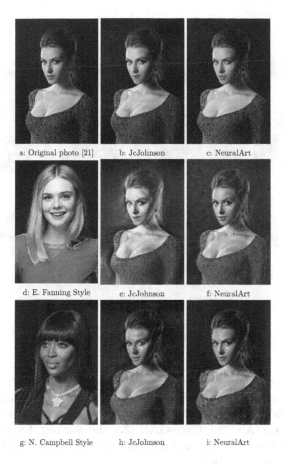

Fig. 2. Portrait Style Transfer

The first column is the result of application Fig. 3j and k. The second column represents the reverse order. It is noticeable that both, straight and reverse order gives approximately the same result and quality while slightly preferring color scheme of the latter one. For future work we consider to make possible simultaneous once by splitting loss function between two style images.

4.4 Image-to-Image Translation

The problem of choosing single "style" for all the segments of realistic image arise in real-world application. The idea of image-to-image translation inferring texture model from training mapping two image datasets was suggested in [22]. We used a post-processing algorithm rendering high-quality graphics training image-to-image translation on two datasets of images from GTA: San Andreas [23] (old graphics) and new version of video game GTA: V [24] (modern graphics) while both game locations have the same original city. The example of images

a   b   c

d: Photo 2   e   f   j: Style 1

k: Style 2

g   h   i

Fig. 3. Multi-style Transfer

from both datasets could be seen at Fig. 4. We adjust the graphics to a new virtual world rendering using unpaired image-to-image translation improving basic graphics and texture quality. We use several GAN architectures, such as CoGAN [25], DiscoGAN [26], CycleGAN [27] and our own CycleWGAN [under review] obtaining stable quality and real-time post-processing of rendered virtual scene, which is shown at Fig. 5.

Fig. 4. Image translation from left to right domains

Fig. 5. At the bottom you can see the original GTA San Andreas images, then starting from the top left of the first row the results of CoGAN and DiscoGAN, the second row with CycleGAN (left) and new CycleGAN with WGAN implementation (right)

5   Discussion

We have presented a style transfer algorithm with the quality loss function, which can be applied to photo-based style transfer. In photo style transfer, input images were selected according to their similarity making the experiments not scalable. It is important to enlarge test sample space without deterioration in quality. One of the possible improvements can be done using GAN-based method introduced in [28]. We also aim to include semantic segmentation of the portrait images in order to present a photo-style transfer that could be of great interest for fashion industry and compare it with image-to-image translation based on pix-to-pix methods [29, 30].

Acknowledgments. The article was supported within the framework of a subsidy by the Russian Academic Excellence Project '5–100'.

References

1. Gatys, L.A., Alexander, S., Ecker, M.B.: A neural algorithm of artistic style. arXiv preprint arXiv:1508.06576 (2015)
2. Simonyan, K., Zisserman, A.: Very deep convolutional networks for large-scale image recognition. CoRR abs/1409.1556 (2014)
3. Gatys, L.A., Ecker, A.S., Bethge, M.: Texture synthesis using convolutional neural networks. In: Cortes, C., Lawrence, N.D., Lee, D.D., Sugiyama, M., Garnett, R. (eds.) Advances in Neural Information Processing Systems 28: Annual Conference on NIPS 2015, 7–12 December 2015, Montreal, Quebec, Canada, pp. 262–270 (2015)
4. Ulyanov, D., Lebedev, V., Vedaldi, A., Lempitsky, V.S.: Texture networks: feed-forward synthesis of textures and stylized images. In: Balcan, M., Weinberger, K.Q. (eds) Proceedings of the 33nd International Conference on Machine Learning, ICML 2016, 19–24 June 2016, New York City, NY, USA, JMLR Workshop and Conference Proceedings, JMLR.org, vol. 48, pp. 1349–1357 (2016)
5. Chen, D., Yuan, L., Liao, J., Yu, N., Hua, G.: Stylebank: An explicit representation for neural image style transfer. CoRR abs/1703.09210 (2017)
6. Wilmot, P., Risser, E., Barnes, C.: Stable and controllable neural texture synthesis and style transfer using histogram losses. CoRR abs/1701.08893 (2017)
7. Gatys, L.A., Bethge, M., Hertzmann, A., Shechtman, E.: Preserving color in neural artistic style transfer. CoRR abs/1606.05897 (2016)
8. Jetchev, N., Bergmann, U., Vollgraf, R.: Texture synthesis with spatial generative adversarial networks. CoRR abs/1611.08207 (2016)
9. Wang, X., Gupta, A.: Generative image modeling using style and structure adversarial networks. CoRR abs/1603.05631 (2016)
10. Li, C., Wand, M.: Combining markov random fields and convolutional neural networks for image synthesis. CoRR abs/1601.04589 (2016)
11. Kwatra, V., Essa, I.A., Bobick, A.F., Kwatra, N.: Texture optimization for example-based synthesis. ACM Trans. Graph. **24**(3), 795–802 (2005)
12. Elad, M., Milanfar, P.: Style-transfer via texture-synthesis. CoRR abs/1609.03057 (2016)
13. Gatys, L.A., Ecker, A.S., Bethge, M., Hertzmann, A., Shechtman, E.: Controlling perceptual factors in neural style transfer. CoRR abs/1611.07865 (2016)
14. Zhao, H., Jin, X., Shen, J., Wei, F.: Real-time photo style transfer. In: 11th International Conference on Computer-Aided Design and Computer Graphics, CAD/Graphics 2009, 19–21 August 2009, Huangshan, China, pp. 140–145. IEEE (2009)
15. Wang, X., Oxholm, G., Zhang, D., Wang, Y.: Multimodal transfer: A hierarchical deep convolutional neural network for fast artistic style transfer. CoRR abs/1612.01895 (2016)
16. Gatys, L.A., Ecker, A.S., Bethge, M.: Image style transfer using convolutional neural networks. In: 2016 IEEE Conference on Computer Vision and Pattern Recognition, CVPR 2016, 27–30 June 2016, Las Vegas, NV, USA, pp. 2414–2423. IEEE Computer Society (2016)
17. Luan, F., Paris, S., Shechtman, E., Bala, K.: Deep photo style transfer. arXiv preprint arXiv:1703.07511 (2017)
18. Johnson, J., Alahi, A., Fei-Fei, L.: Perceptual losses for real-time style transfer and super-resolution. In: Leibe, B., Matas, J., Sebe, N., Welling, M. (eds.) ECCV 2016. LNCS, Part II, vol. 9906, pp. 694–711. Springer, Cham (2016). https://doi.org/10.1007/978-3-319-46475-6_43

19. Zhao, H., Gallo, O., Frosio, I., Kautz, J.: Loss functions for neural networks for image processing. CoRR abs/1511.08861 (2015)
20. Liu, J., Yang, W., Sun, X., Zeng, W.: Photo stylistic brush: Robust style transfer via superpixel-based bipartite graph. CoRR abs/1606.03871 (2016)
21. Kartashov, E.: Lesson # 19 shooting portraits on a black background (2017). https://photoshop-master.org/disc92/
22. Isola, P., Zhu, J.Y., Zhou, T., Efros, A.A.: Image-to-image translation with conditional adversarial networks. arXiv preprint arXiv:1611.07004 (2016)
23. Rockstar North, W.D.S.: Grand theft auto: San andreas (2004). http://www.rockstargames.com/sanandreas/. Accessed 26 Oct 2004
24. Rockstar Games, R.N.: Grand theft auto: V (2013). http://www.rockstargames.com/V/. Accessed 17 Sept 2013
25. Liu, M.Y., Tuzel, O.: Coupled generative adversarial networks. In: Advances in Neural Information Processing Systems, NIPS, pp. 469–477 (2016)
26. Kim, T., Cha, M., Kim, H., Lee, J., Kim, J.: Learning to discover cross-domain relations with generative adversarial networks. arXiv preprint arXiv:1703.05192 (2017)
27. Zhu, J.Y., Park, T., Isola, P., Efros, A.A.: Unpaired image-to-image translation using cycle-consistent adversarial networks. arXiv preprint arXiv:1703.10593 (2017)
28. Ulyanov, D., Vedaldi, A., Lempitsky, V.S.: Improved texture networks: Maximizing quality and diversity in feed-forward stylization and texture synthesis. CoRR abs/1701.02096 (2017)
29. Chen, Q., Koltun, V.: Photographic image synthesis with cascaded refinement networks. In: International Conference on Computer Vision (ICCV), vol. 1. IEEE (2017)
30. Wang, T.C., Liu, M.Y., Zhu, J.Y., Tao, A., Kautz, J., Catanzaro, B.: High-resolution image synthesis and semantic manipulation with conditional gans. arXiv preprint arXiv:1711.11585 (2017)

K-Means Color Image Quantization with Deterministic Initialization: New Image Quality Metrics

Mariusz Frackiewicz[(✉)] and Henryk Palus

Silesian University of Technology, ul. Akademicka 16, 44-100 Gliwice, Poland
{Mariusz.Frackiewicz,Henryk.Palus}@polsl.pl

Abstract. Color image quantization is used in several tasks of color image processing as an image segmentation, image compression, image watermarking, etc. In this paper we consider four traditional (MSE, PSNR, DE76 and DM) and four new perceptual metrics (DSCSI, HPSI, MDSIs and MDSIm) as useful tools for evaluating quantized images. The values of these metrics confirm that Wu's algorithm can be used as effective deterministic initialization of K-Means method. No empty clusters are produced by this method of quantization. The experiments were realized using 24 benchmark color images for different numbers of quantization levels. The same quantization with additional Floyd-Steinberg dithering generates the images with even better values of tested perceptual metrics.

Keywords: Color image quantization · Image quality assessment
K-Means · Initialization · Dithering

1 Introduction

Color image quantization is a process of reduction of the number of colors in true color images. Obtaining a small quantization error needs a color palette designed for the particular image. The quantization error depends on the number of colors in the palette (e.g. 8, 16, 32, 64, 128, 256 colors), the method of building a color palette and the pixel classifying technique. The color quantization is still applied to different tasks of computer vision and computer graphics. Among the color quantization methods the splitting techniques, e.g. median-cut (MC) [5], Wu's algorithm [13] and clustering techniques, e.g. most popular K-Means (KM) technique [8] can be distinguished. The splitting techniques are faster than the clustering techniques, but they give larger quantization errors. KM clustering results depend on the method of initialization, i.e. determining the initial cluster centers. The classic version of KM uses a random choice of initial centers, but in this case we will not have repeated results. Therefore, it makes sense to search for a deterministic initialization, which allows to get a small quantization error. An important issue remains a way to assess this error.

© Springer International Publishing AG, part of Springer Nature 2018
A. Campilho et al. (Eds.): ICIAR 2018, LNCS 10882, pp. 56–61, 2018.
https://doi.org/10.1007/978-3-319-93000-8_7

Previous searches for deterministic initializations of KM method were based on the use of heuristic approaches (KMDC, KMSD; see below) or the use of splitting quantization (MC, WU) as KM initialization (KMMC, KMWU). An example of such work is in the article [10]. In it was shown for five benchmark images and using traditional quality metrics (MSE, DE76, DM), that KMWU technique offers a better performance than KM technique with other initializations. In our paper we would like to get an answer to the question: How the four new perceptual metrics assess the investigated initializations of the KM method used for color image quantization?

This paper is organized in four sections. In Sect. 2 we present the traditional and new image quality metrics, which are used for the quality assessment of color quantization. In Sect. 3 we describe the use of four perceptual metrics to evaluate selected splitting and combined KM quantization methods. Finally, the Sect. 4 concludes the paper.

2   Color Quantization Quality Assessment

The most popular and widely used in image processing metric is the MSE, that version for color images is defined as:

$$MSE = \frac{1}{3MN} \sum_{i=1}^{M} \sum_{j=1}^{N} [(R_{ij} - R_{ij}^*)^2 + (G_{ij} - G_{ij}^*)^2 + (B_{ij} - B_{ij}^*)^2] \quad (1)$$

where MN represents the resolution of the image, R_{ij}, G_{ij}, B_{ij} are the color value components of the pixel (i,j) in the original image and R_{ij}^*, G_{ij}^*, B_{ij}^* are the color value components in the same pixel of the quantized image. Another metric applied to color quantization, well correlated with MSE value and usually expressed in decibels is PSNR:

$$PSNR = 10 \log_{10} \frac{255^2}{MSE} \quad (2)$$

The quantization error can be treated as a color error calculated on the whole image. From the point of view of the color science, such color error should be determined in a perceptually uniform color space, i.e. CIELAB space. An average color error calculated in the CIELAB color space can be expressed as:

$$DE76 = \frac{1}{MN} \sum_{i=1}^{M} \sum_{j=1}^{N} \sqrt{(L_{ij} - L_{ij}^*)^2 + (a_{ij} - a_{ij}^*)^2 + (b_{ij} - b_{ij}^*)^2} \quad (3)$$

where L_{ij}, a_{ij}, b_{ij} are the color value components of the pixel (i,j) in the original image and L_{ij}^*, a_{ij}^* and b_{ij}^* are the CIELAB color value components in the same pixel of the quantized image.

The loss of image colorfulness [4] can be used as an additional measure of quantization error:

$$DM = |M_{orig} - M_{quant}| \quad (4)$$

where M_{orig} and M_{quant} are respectively the colorfulness of the original and quantized images. The formula for computing of image colorfulness is simple and good correlate with perceptual colorfulness of the image:

$$M = \sqrt{\sigma_{rg}^2 + \sigma_{yb}^2} + 0.3\sqrt{\mu_{rg}^2 + \mu_{yb}^2} \qquad (5)$$

where σ_{rg}, σ_{yb}, μ_{rg}, μ_{yb} are respectively standard deviations and means of opponent color components calculated on the whole image. The opponent color components are approximated by following simplified equations: $rg = R - G$, $yb = 0.5(R + G) - B$, where rg represents the red-green opponency and yb represents the yellow-blue opponency.

In the last few years many new perceptual image quality assessment (IQA) metrics have been developed. A good example of such metrics is the DSCSI [7], which consists of three steps. The first step is the image transformation from the RGB into the S-CIELAB color space. In a second step, the local features for color similarity are calculated to three color components: hue, chroma and lightness. In this way we obtain the following six features: the hue mean similarity, the hue dispersion similarity, the chroma mean similarity, the chroma contrast similarity, the lightness contrast similarity and the lightness structural similarity. In the third step, these six features are combined into two scores: the chromatic similarity S_C and achromatic similarity S_A, which are directly used in the final DSCSI formula:

$$Q(I, I^*) = S_A \cdot (S_C)^\lambda \qquad (6)$$

where I - original image, I^* - distorted image and λ is a weighting factor. The smaller the difference between the original and distorted images, the value of DSCSI metric is closer to 1. In papers [2, 11] the usefulness of the DSCSI metric for assessment of color quantization is shown.

Other new perceptual metric is called HPSI (Haar wavelet-based Perceptually Similarity Index) [12]. This metric is based on the coefficients of three stages of a discrete Haar wavelet transform. These coefficients assess the local similarities between two compared images. The six simple 2D Haar wavelet filters to detect horizontal and vertical edges are used. It is built in both local similarity maps (horizontal and vertical) and both weight functions. In addition, a non-linear mapping in the form of the logistic function is introduced in the HPSI computation process. HPSI metric can be considered as a simplified version of the FSIM metric. Also, here the YIQ color space for the generalization to color is used. Discussion on the similarities and differences between HPSI and FSIM can be found in [12].

The last considered metric is named MDSI (Mean Deviation Similarity Index) [9]. Firstly are redefined both gradient and chromaticity similarities. Gradient similarity (GS) represents the local structural distortions and chromaticity similarity (CS) represents the color distortions. These both image features in the form of maps are further pooling by novel deviation technique into a single quality index. Two similarity maps are combined by summation (MDSIs version) or multiplication (MDSIm version). Further details can be found in [9].

Table 1. Average values of quality metrics of quantized Kodak images ($k = 8$)

Method	MSE	PSNR	DE76	DM	DSCSI	HPSI	MDSIs	MDSIm
MC	234.24	24.83	8.65	10.44	0.5572	0.6608	0.3759	0.3013
WU	158.77	26.58	7.78	6.22	0.5976	0.7014	0.3548	0.2848
KMDC	149.39	26.76	7.75	6.62	0.6032	0.7111	0.3501	0.2795
KMSD	**146.66**	26.86	**7.37**	6.43	0.6099	0.7126	0.3500	0.2799
KMMC	149.60	26.78	7.45	6.65	0.6025	0.7072	0.3529	0.2817
KMWU	146.70	**26.87**	7.64	6.23	0.6060	0.7093	0.3493	0.2792
KMWU+FS	205.37	25.49	8.17	**5.57**	**0.6697**	**0.7750**	**0.3179**	**0.2512**

Table 2. Average values of quality metrics of quantized Kodak images ($k = 64$)

Method	MSE	PSNR	DE76	DM	DSCSI	HPSI	MDSIs	MDSIm
MC	36.71	32.95	3.71	2.65	0.8442	0.9105	0.2374	0.1818
WU	21.49	35.30	3.32	1.07	0.9070	0.9462	0.2011	0.1519
KMDC	23.40	34.86	3.44	1.16	0.8930	0.9409	0.2112	0.1602
KMSD	23.14	34.86	3.23	1.03	0.8913	0.9355	0.2126	0.1620
KMMC	22.29	35.08	3.15	1.04	0.9003	0.9421	0.2054	0.1564
KMWU	**19.43**	**35.72**	**3.14**	0.93	0.9142	0.9506	0.1943	0.1464
KMWU+FS	27.60	34.26	3.50	**0.68**	**0.9403**	**0.9661**	**0.1738**	**0.1300**

In a new paper [2] we considered an application of four above-mentioned perceptual quality metrics for assessment of quantized images. All these perceptual metrics achieved the highest correlation coefficients with Mean Opinion Scores (MOS) after tests on many images, what encourages to choose these metrics for assessment. Statistical analysis of these correlation coefficients showed that the differences between the four perceptual metrics are not statistically significant.

3   The Experiment and Its Results

The experiment was done on 24 Kodak images [6] for the whole range of typical palette sizes $k = 8, 16, .., 256$. Six quantization methods were tested: MC, WU, KMDC, KMSD, KMMC and KMWU. The results of quantization with dithering by Floyd-Steinberg method [1] were also included as KMWU+FS. More on the properties of FS dithering can be found in the paper [11]. The values of individual metrics (averages for 24 images) are given in Tables 1, 2 and 3. The best result for each metric is bolded. Due to limited space of this paper we do not present results for $k = 16, 32, 128$. These results were very similar to the presented here results.

The results in Tables 1, 2 and 3 show that adding dithering to KMWU color quantization improves the values of four perceptual quality metrics and achieves

Table 3. Average values of quality metrics of quantized Kodak images ($k = 256$)

Method	MSE	PSNR	DE76	DM	DSCSI	HPSI	MDSIs	MDSIm
MC	12.29	37.69	2.25	0.86	0.9368	0.9709	0.1710	0.1286
WU	7.56	39.78	2.16	0.32	0.9685	0.9831	0.1440	0.1077
KMDC	10.56	38.15	2.20	0.48	0.9435	0.9705	0.1711	0.1293
KMSD	10.56	38.15	2.20	0.48	0.9435	0.9705	0.1711	0.1293
KMMC	7.99	39.50	**2.01**	0.40	0.9628	0.9806	0.1487	0.1108
KMWU	**6.82**	**40.25**	2.02	0.35	0.9717	0.9841	0.1393	0.1037
KMWU+FS	9.40	38.86	2.27	**0.12**	**0.9800**	**0.9893**	**0.1265**	**0.0941**

the best results. The DM metric behaves similarly to perceptual metrics. By the contrast, the values of three classic metrics (MSE, PSNR, DE76) then get worse. If you do not use dithering, then the KMWU continues to quantize images with results evaluated as the best by all eight metrics. Exceptions are the results for $k = 8$ where KMWU is indicated by the half of metrics.

Table 4. Average computation time for quality metrics

Metric	MSE	PSNR	DE76	DM	DSCSI	HPSI	MDSIs	MDSIm
Time [s]	0.005	0.005	0.038	0.011	0.499	0.038	0.019	0.022

In addition, it was verified that the best initialization method does not generate the empty clusters, i.e., the number of colors obtained after quantization is always equal to k. This is not the case for KMDC and KMSD initializations. Finally, the calculation times for eight quality metrics were compared (Table 4). Calculations were performed a hundred times for each metrics using following setup: Intel i7 920, 8.0 GB RAM, Windows 7 Professional and Matlab R2016b. For the high quality of DSCSI metric, we pay a calculation time that is much higher than the times for other metrics. In work [3] we showed that there are no statistically significant differences (Friedman test with post-hoc procedures) between these new metrics, therefore we can use any of them. The best choice from the point of view of the calculation time is the MDSIs metric.

4   Conclusions

In this paper we looked for the effective deterministic initialization of the K-Means method used for color quantization. Of the few tested initializations, the best results give the initialization based on the palette from the Wu's algorithm (KMWU). Eight image quality metrics were used for assessment of 24 quantized images. Additional inclusion of Floyd-Steinberg dithering procedure improves the quantization results (KMWU+FS) judged by newly created perceptual metrics. This represents a significant advantage of these metrics.

Acknowledgments. This work was supported by the Polish Ministry for Science and Education under internal grant BK-204/RAU1/2017/t-4 for the Institute of Automatic Control, Silesian University of Technology, Gliwice, Poland.

References

1. Floyd, R.W.: An adaptive algorithm for spatial gray-scale. Proc. Soc. Inf. Disp. **17**, 75–77 (1976)
2. Frackiewicz, M., Palus, H.: New image quality metric used for the assessment of color quantization algorithms. In: Ninth International Conference on Machine Vision, pp. 103411G–103411G. SPIE (2017)
3. Frackiewicz, M., Palus, H.: Toward a perceptual image quality assessment of color quantized images. In: Tenth International Conference on Machine Vision, Vienna, Austria. SPIE (in press)
4. Hasler, D., Suesstrunk, S.: Measuring colourfulness for natural images. In: Electronic Imaging 2003: Human Vision and Electronic Imaging VIII, Proceedings of SPIE, vol. 5007, pp. 87–95 (2003)
5. Heckbert, P.: Color image quantization for frame buffer display. ACM SIGGRAPH Comput. Graph. **16**(3), 297–307 (1982)
6. Kodak: Kodak images. http://r0k.us/graphics/kodak/. Accessed Mar 2018
7. Lee, D., Plataniotis, K.N.: Towards a full-reference quality assessment for color images using directional statistics. IEEE Trans. Image Process. **24**(11), 3950–3965 (2015)
8. MacQueen, J.: Some methods for classification and analysis of multivariate observations. In: Proceedings of the 5th Berkeley Symposium on Mathematics, Statistics, and Probabilities, Berkeley, USA, pp. 281–297 (1967)
9. Nafchi, H.Z., Shahkolaei, A., Hedjam, R., Cheriet, M.: Mean deviation similarity index: efficient and reliable full-reference image quality evaluator. IEEE Access **4**, 5579–5590 (2016)
10. Palus, H., Frackiewicz, M.: New approach for initialization of K-means technique applied to color quantization. In: 2nd IC on Information Technology (ICIT), Gdansk, Poland, pp. 205–209 (2010)
11. Palus, H., Frackiewicz, M.: Further applications of the DSCSI metric for evaluating color quantization. In: Ninth International Conference on Machine Vision, pp. 103411H–103411H. SPIE (2017)
12. Reisenhofer, R., Bosse, S., Kutyniok, G., Wiegand, T.: A Haar wavelet-based perceptual similarity index for image quality assessment. arXiv preprint arXiv:1607.06140 (2016)
13. Wu, X.: Color quantization by dynamic programming and principal analysis. ACM Trans. Graph. (TOG) **11**(4), 348–372 (1992)

Singular Value Decomposition in Image Compression and Blurred Image Restoration

Katerina Fronckova, Pavel Prazak, and Antonin Slaby[✉]

University of Hradec Kralove, Hradec Kralove, Czech Republic
{Katerina.Fronckova,Pavel.Prazak,Antonin.Slaby}@uhk.cz

Abstract. The singular value decomposition (SVD) is an important and very versatile tool for matrix computations with a variety of uses. The contribution briefly introduces the concept of the SVD and basic facts about it and then describes two classes of its applications in image processing - image compression and blurred image restoration. Calculations are implemented in MATLAB software. Our experiences and the results are presented in the text.

Keywords: Singular value decomposition · Matrix computations
Image processing · Image compression · Image deblurring

1 Introduction

The SVD is one of the most important and most versatile matrix computations tools. Its application can be found both in mathematical theory and in various practical areas. The SVD is related to many other concepts of linear algebra [3]. It is possible to use it for example to determine matrix rank, the Frobenius norm or spectral norm of a matrix, the condition number of a matrix, an orthonormal basis for the null space and the column space of a matrix, the approximation of a matrix by a matrix of lower rank. Further large application domain is in statistics in the context of principal component analysis and correspondence analysis. Another major application of the SVD is the area of signal processing including compression or data filtering [6], also it is used for data registration [1], recognition [7], steganography watermarking [5], latent semantic indexing and analysis [2] etc.

2 Basic Theoretical Facts About SVD

The following theorem states the existence of the SVD for any real matrix.

Theorem 1. *Let $A \in \mathbb{R}^{m \times n}$ and $p = \min\{m, n\}$. Then there exist orthogonal matrices $U \in \mathbb{R}^{m \times m}$, $V \in \mathbb{R}^{n \times n}$ and a diagonal matrix $\Sigma \in \mathbb{R}^{m \times n}$ with diagonal elements $\sigma_1 \geq \sigma_2 \geq \cdots \geq \sigma_p \geq 0$ so that it holds*

$$A = U\Sigma V^T. \tag{1}$$

© Springer International Publishing AG, part of Springer Nature 2018
A. Campilho et al. (Eds.): ICIAR 2018, LNCS 10882, pp. 62–67, 2018.
https://doi.org/10.1007/978-3-319-93000-8_8

Diagonal elements $\sigma_{jj} = \sigma_j, j = 1, \ldots, p$, of the matrix $\boldsymbol{\Sigma}$ are called the singular values of the matrix $\boldsymbol{A}$. Let $\boldsymbol{u}_j$ resp. $\boldsymbol{v}_j$ denote the jth column of the matrix $\boldsymbol{U}$ respectively matrix $\boldsymbol{V}$. Vectors $\boldsymbol{u}_j, j = 1, \ldots, m$, are called the left singular vectors and vectors $\boldsymbol{v}_j, j = 1, \ldots, n$, are called the right singular vectors of the matrix $\boldsymbol{A}$.

The singular values are uniquely determined, and if we in addition to it suppose that they are written in sorted order $(\sigma_1 \geq \sigma_2 \geq \cdots \geq \sigma_p \geq 0)$ then the matrix $\boldsymbol{\Sigma}$ is uniquely determined too. On the other hand, the left singular vectors and the right singular vectors and consequently the matrices $\boldsymbol{U}$ and $\boldsymbol{V}$ are not uniquely determined.

The rank r of a matrix $\boldsymbol{A}$ is equal to the number of non-zero (positive) singular values

$$\sigma_1 \geq \sigma_2 \geq \cdots \geq \sigma_r > 0, \ \sigma_{r+1} = \sigma_{r+2} = \ldots = \sigma_p = 0, \ \ p = \min\{m, n\}.$$

However, the above-mentioned fact is correct only if we assume the SVD calculated in the exact arithmetic. When we apply numerical calculations on computer, it can be assumed that numbers $\sigma_{r+1}, \ldots, \sigma_p$ will not be exact zeros. In this case it is not clear which of the singular values are really zero and which are just almost zero. The concept of the numerical rank of a matrix is introduced from this reason. A matrix has the numerical rank of k if k singular values are greater than the chosen tolerance $\delta > 0$, the other singular values are considered to be zero.

3   Low-Rank Matrix Approximation and Data Compression

The task of finding for a matrix $\boldsymbol{A} \in \mathbb{R}^{m \times n}$ of rank $\mathrm{rank}(\boldsymbol{A}) = r$ another matrix $\boldsymbol{A}_k \in \mathbb{R}^{m \times n}$ having rank $\mathrm{rank}(\boldsymbol{A}_k) = k < r$ which is in some sense its best approximation is useful in many applications. Here, the best approximation will be considered in the sense of minimizing the spectral norm of error $\boldsymbol{A} - \boldsymbol{A}_k$, i.e.

$$\|\boldsymbol{A} - \boldsymbol{A}_k\|_2 = \min_{\substack{\boldsymbol{X} \in \mathbb{R}^{m \times n} \\ \mathrm{rank}(\boldsymbol{X}) = k}} \|\boldsymbol{A} - \boldsymbol{X}\|_2. \tag{2}$$

The following Theorem 2 indicates the way of using the SVD to solve this problem. It is used the following form of the so-called economy-size SVD

$$\boldsymbol{A} = \boldsymbol{U}_r \boldsymbol{\Sigma}_r \boldsymbol{V}_r^T = \sum_{j=1}^{r} \sigma_j \boldsymbol{u}_j \boldsymbol{v}_j^T, \tag{3}$$

where $\boldsymbol{U}_r = \boldsymbol{U}_{\bullet,1:r}$, $\boldsymbol{\Sigma}_r = \boldsymbol{\Sigma}_{1:r,1:r}$ and $\boldsymbol{V}_r = \boldsymbol{V}_{\bullet,1:r}$.

Theorem 2 (Eckart, Young, Mirsky). *Let us have a matrix $\boldsymbol{A} \in \mathbb{R}^{m \times n}$ of rank r and let k be a natural number, $k < r$. Let us consider the SVD of the* *matrix $\boldsymbol{A}$ given by (3). Then the matrix*

$$\boldsymbol{A}_k = \sum_{j=1}^{k} \sigma_j \boldsymbol{u}_j \boldsymbol{v}_j^T$$

is the best rank k approximation of the matrix $\boldsymbol{A}$ in terms of (2).

A grayscale digital image can be represented by a matrix of type $m \times n$ whose element at position ij corresponds to the intensity of the ijth pixel of the image. Grayscale images will be taken for simplicity. The case of color image compression could be solved analogously by applying the further described procedure to each of the RGB color channels separately.

A photograph of the Large Square in the city of Hradec Kralove (Czech Republic) is used as a demonstration (see the leftmost image in Fig. 1). The image can be represented by the matrix $\boldsymbol{A}$ of size 706×670. In accordance with the Theorem 2 the matrices $\boldsymbol{A}_{200}$ and $\boldsymbol{A}_{20}$ are constructed. Only the elements of $\boldsymbol{u}_j$, $\boldsymbol{v}_j$ and the numbers σ_j, $j = 1, \ldots, k$, are stored in the memory for each of these matrices when using the economy-size SVD, which represents the total amount of $(m + n + 1)k$ values. The amount of $(m + n + 1)r$ values must be stored for the initial matrix $\boldsymbol{A}$ of rank r. Thus, the compression ratio is given by fraction $\frac{r}{k}$.

Memory savings are 70.15 % for the approximation $\boldsymbol{A}_{200}$ and 97.01 % for $\boldsymbol{A}_{20}$ compared to the original image. However, the quality of approximation is getting worse with decreasing k. Figure 1 shows the obtained results.

Fig. 1. Initial image and compression of the image corresponding to the approximation matrices for $k = 200, 20$

4 Ill-Posed Problems and Regularization

The further described application of the SVD will concern blurred image restoration. A grayscale image represented by a matrix $\boldsymbol{X} \in \mathbb{R}^{m \times n}$ will be assumed. This matrix will represent the ideal sharp image and consequently at the same time the solution to be sought as the result of reconstruction (Fig. 2a). But in practice, we only have at our disposal an image given by a matrix $B \in \mathbb{R}^{m \times n}$ that is degraded by blurring, for example due to the motion or poorly focused optical system of the camera (Fig. 2b). If the blurring is linear and the blurring of the columns in the image is independent of the blurring of the rows, the blurring process can be represented by the following matrix equation

$$A_C X A_R^T = B. \tag{4}$$

The matrix $A_C \in \mathbb{R}^{m \times m}$ represents the blurring of the columns and $A_R \in \mathbb{R}^{n \times n}$ the blurring of the rows.

Equation (4) can be rewritten to common form of a system of linear algebraic equations

$$A x = b, \tag{5}$$

where $A = A_R \otimes A_C \in \mathbb{R}^{mn \times mn}$ is a Kronecker product of the matrices A_R and A_C. The vectors x and b represent vectorization of the matrices X and B, i.e. $x = \text{vec}(X) = (X_{\bullet 1}^T, \ldots, X_{\bullet n}^T)^T \in \mathbb{R}^{mn}$ and $b = \text{vec}(B) = (B_{\bullet 1}^T, \ldots, B_{\bullet n}^T)^T \in \mathbb{R}^{mn}$.

When working with real data, it often happens that the vector b contains noise (measurement inaccuracies, rounding errors, discretization errors, etc.). So it holds

$$b = b_{\text{EXACT}} + b_{\text{NOISE}},$$

where b_{EXACT} is the exact right hand side of the system of equations and b_{NOISE} is the noise vector. It will be assumed that $\|b_{\text{EXACT}}\|_2 \gg \|b_{\text{NOISE}}\|_2$.

If $\text{rank}(A_C) = m$ and $\text{rank}(A_R) = n$ then the matrix A is nonsingular and the solution of the system of equations (5), usually referred to as naive, can simply be written as $x_{\text{NAIVE}} = A^{-1} b$. This solution would correspond to the desired solution $x_{\text{EXACT}} = A^{-1} b_{\text{EXACT}}$ if the vector b did not contain noise. In case the vector b contains noise, for x_{NAIVE} holds

$$x_{\text{NAIVE}} = A^{-1} b = x_{\text{EXACT}} + A^{-1} b_{\text{NOISE}}. \tag{6}$$

Reconstruction of a blurred image is a typical example of ill-posed problems. Figure 2c shows that the naive solution (6) is dominated by the inverse noise $A^{-1} b_{\text{NOISE}}$, and this noise completely overlaps the solution x_{EXACT}. The solution x_{NAIVE} can be written using the SVD of the matrix A as

$$x_{\text{NAIVE}} = \sum_{j=1}^{mn} \frac{u_j^T b_{\text{EXACT}}}{\sigma_j} v_j + \sum_{j=1}^{mn} \frac{u_j^T b_{\text{NOISE}}}{\sigma_j} v_j. \tag{7}$$

Furthermore, it is assumed that the vector b_{EXACT} meets the discrete Picard condition. This condition can be formulated like this: Magnitude of the $u_j^T b_{\text{EXACT}}$ components is with increasing j dropping to zero on average faster than the absolute value of the corresponding singular values σ_j. The noise vector b_{NOISE} does not have to meet this condition. Values $u_j^T b_{\text{NOISE}}$ do not usually decrease to zero, and their influence will increase as a result of division by small

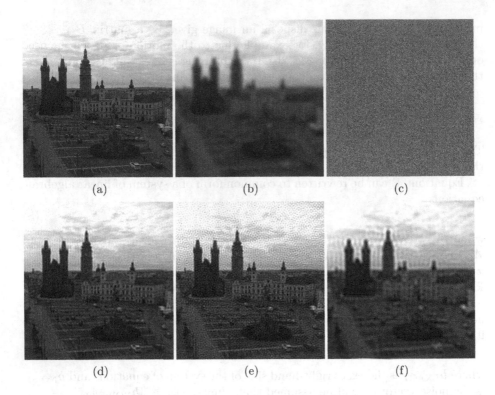

(a)   (b)   (c)

(d)   (e)   (f)

Fig. 2. Blurred image restoration: (a) initial sharp image (exact solution), (b) blurred image with additive noise, (c) naive solution, (d) solution for the appropriate choice of the truncation parameter ($k = 12693$), (e) undersmoothed solution with influence from high-frequency components of noise ($k = 15351$), (f) oversmoothed solution missing high-frequency information (noise, but also image details) ($k = 3602$)

singular values. The second sum dominates in the naive solution (7), which explains the result in Fig. 2c.

The way in which ill-posed problems can be solved is regularization. The goal is to find an approximation of the exact solution x_{EXACT} in order to suppress the impact of noise. One of the classic regularization methods is Truncated SVD (TSVD). TSVD regularization is based on the replacement of the matrix $\boldsymbol{A}$ by its best approximation of lower rank according to the Theorem 2

$$\boldsymbol{A}_k = \sum_{j=1}^{k} \sigma_j \boldsymbol{u}_j \boldsymbol{v}_j^T, \qquad k < mn.$$

The corresponding solution of the problem (5) (in the least squares sense) has the form

$$\boldsymbol{x}_{\text{REG}(k)} = \boldsymbol{A}_k^\dagger \boldsymbol{b} = \sum_{j=1}^{k} \frac{\boldsymbol{u}_j^T \boldsymbol{b}}{\sigma_j} \boldsymbol{v}_j.$$

The components mostly dominated by noise, corresponding to division by small singular values $\sigma_j, j = k + 1, \ldots, mn$, are simply removed.

Figure 2d – f shows solutions corresponding to various values of the truncation parameter k, for more details see [4].

5 Conclusion

The SVD has a variety of uses, some have been known for many years and have been developed by various authors over the course of time, while other applications are related to relatively new domains associated with the development of computing. The article briefly presents our experience with the SVD in the field of image compression and blurred image restoration. Additional outputs could not be included due to the limited scope of the text.

Acknowledgments. This work and the contribution were supported by a project of Students Grant Agency – FIM, University of Hradec Kralove, Czech Republic. Katerina Fronckova is a student member of the research team.

References

1. Arun, K.S., Huang, T.S., Blostein, S.D.: Least-squares fitting of two 3-D point sets. IEEE Trans. Pattern Anal. Mach. Intell. **9**(5), 698–700 (1987). https://doi.org/10.1109/TPAMI.1987.4767965
2. Deerwester, S., Dumais, S.T., Furnas, G.W., Landauer, T.K., Harshman, R.: Indexing by latent semantic analysis. J. Am. Soc. Inf. Sci. **41**(6), 391–407 (1990). https://doi.org/10.1002/(SICI)1097-4571(199009)41:6⟨391::AID-ASI1⟩3.0.CO;2-9
3. Golub, G.H., Van Loan, C.F.: Matrix Computations, 4th edn. Johns Hopkins University Press, Baltimore (2013)
4. Hansen, P.C., Nagy, J., O'Leary, D.P.: Deblurring images: Matrices, Spectra, and Filtering, 1st edn. Society for Industrial and Applied Mathematics, Philadelphia (2006)
5. Liu, R., Tan, T.: An SVD-based watermarking scheme for protecting rightful ownership. IEEE Trans. Multimed. **4**(1), 121–128 (2002). https://doi.org/10.1109/6046.985560
6. Sadek, R.A.: SVD based image processing applications: state of the art, contributions and research challenges. Int. J. Adv. Comput. Sci. Appl. **3**(7), 26–34 (2012). arXiv:1211.7102
7. Turk, M.A., Pentland, A.P.: Eigenfaces for recognition. J. Cognit. Neurosci. **3**(1), 71–86 (1991). https://doi.org/10.1162/jocn.1991.3.1.71

Image Segmentation

Fully Convolutional Neural Network for Lungs Segmentation from Chest X-Rays

Rabia Rashid$^{(\boxtimes)}$, Muhammad Usman Akram$^{(\boxtimes)}$, and Taimur Hassan$^{(\boxtimes)}$

College of Electrical and Mechanical Engineering,
National University of Sciences and Technology, Islamabad, Pakistan
rabiar27@hotmail.com, usmakram@gmail.com,
engr.taimoorhassan@gmail.com

Abstract. Deep neural networks have entirely dominated the machine vision space in the past few years due to their astonishing human comparable performance. This paper applies power of such network to segment out lungs from chest x-rays, which is a crucial step in any computer aided diagnostic (CAD) system design. A fully convolutional network was used to extract lungs region from the x-rays. Post processing was done to fill holes, separate left and right lung from each other and remove unwanted objects that appeared in few cases. The process was repeated ten times, with random split of data into a 60:40 ratio as training and testing sets respectively, to calculate the average accuracy. The methodology was tested on three datasets: Japanese Society of Radiological Technology (JSRT), Montgomery County (MC), and a local dataset that achieved average accuracy of 97.1%, 97.7% & 94.2% respectively. The results proved that the proposed methodology is efficient enough and can be generalized for other such segmentation problems in medical imaging domain.

Keywords: Chest radiography · Computer aided diagnostic system
Deep neural networks · Fully convolutional network · Lungs segmentation

1 Introduction

Technology is revolutionizing the world and aims at automating processes, reducing manual work as much as possible and thus aiding the mankind in every field. In the past decades, it tries to automate things by enabling systems to follow a set of commands and act according to the programmed instructions. Lately a concept of artificial intelligence is waved, in this process of automation, which tries to mimic the learning capability of human brain. To create intelligent systems that can adapt, learn and potentially act autonomously rather than simply executing predefined instructions is primary battleground for technology vendors through at least 2020 [1]. One of such systems is an intelligent computer-aided diagnosis (CAD) system that tries to mimic the brain of a radiologist by learning how to differentiate between normal and diseased radiographs. CAD systems offer more objective evidence, increase the diagnostic confidence of radiologists, shorten the detection time, and are used as a "second opinion" in assisting radiologist's image interpretations.

© Springer International Publishing AG, part of Springer Nature 2018
A. Campilho et al. (Eds.): ICIAR 2018, LNCS 10882, pp. 71–80, 2018.
https://doi.org/10.1007/978-3-319-93000-8_9

Pulmonary diseases are life threatening, contagious and are immensely spread worldwide, therefore, early and accurate diagnosis is a critical priority for containing their spread. One common epidemic among them is Tuberculosis, which was among top 10 causes of death worldwide in 2015 according to World Health Organization (WHO) global TB report 2016 [2]. This leads to a crying need of a CAD system that can facilitate timely detection of such diseases and hence, can save many lives.

Chest x-rays (CXRs) are ubiquitous in clinical practice for the diagnosis of pulmonary abnormalities and more reliable as compared to other imaging techniques especially for mass screening purpose. One of the major milestones in the CAD system design is to correctly segment out the lungs region from the CXR. Low contrast of the images and hidden region of interest due to overlapping ribcage and other superimposed anatomical structures makes the segmentation a challenging task. Even experienced and skilled radiologists have trouble differentiating infiltrates from the normal pattern of branching blood vessels in the lungs, or identifying subtle nodules that suggests lung cancer. Several endeavors have been done by researchers for tackling this problem in the past five years. Chondroa et al. [3] used low order adaptive region growing technique, Arbabshirani et al. [4], Kalinovskya and Kovalev [5] used different deep network architectures and Li et al. [6] proposed statistical shape and appearance models. Ngo and Carneiro [7] used combination of level sets and deep-structured learning and inference, Saad et al. [8] suggested edge detection and morphology approach and Candemir [9] used non-rigid registration method. Among all these techniques, deep neural networks are the latest and most influential. Hence, this research presents a deep convolutional neural network (CNN) architecture for solving the segmentation problem. A U-Net [10] model, which is a fully convolutional network, was used with little modifications. It was trained and then tested on three datasets: Japanese Society of Radiological Technology (JSRT), Montgomery County (MC) and a local dataset. The segmentation output generated by the model was post-processed and the final results obtained, were quite accurate.

The rest of the paper is organized as follows. Section 2 consists of the proposed methodology in detail. The experimental results are discussed in detail with all desired figures and tables in Sect. 3. Section 4 concludes the research and reveals its future scope.

2   Methodology

The segmentation is done to extract the region of interest from the image. Here, in the chest x-rays, our region of interest is left and right lung. A Fully Convolutional Network (FCN) was used for the lungs segmentation. It basically classifies each pixel as a foreground or background pixel. The dataset was randomly split into a 60:40 ratio as training and testing set respectively. Then, the FCN model was trained using the training images and their corresponding manual masks (or ground truth). The testing data was then inputted to the trained model, which accurately segmented them. Very few resultant images contained some minor holes in the lung region and/or small unnecessary objects/ dots and/or fused left and right lung. Post processing was done to cater this. In postprocessing, holes were filled using flood-fill algorithm, small objects were removed by choosing top two foreground objects (i.e. left and right lung region) in terms of area, and the left and right lung was separated from each other using morphological opening iteratively. This way, the final segmentation was achieved that is depicted in Fig. 1. The whole process was repeated ten times and the average accuracy was declared as the final accuracy.

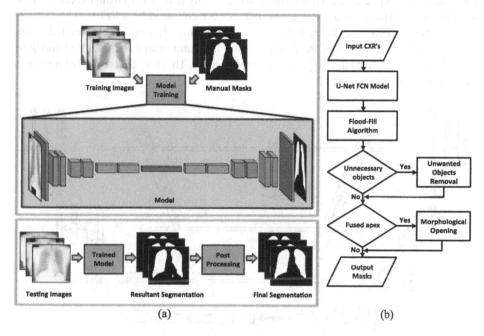

Fig. 1. Segmentation methodology (a) Block diagram (b) Flow chart diagram

2.1 Fully Convolutional Networks

In fully convolutional networks, all the learnable layers are convolutional, or in other words, it doesn't have any fully connected layer. They are used for image segmentation. In segmentation, we just not only need to classify whether a pixel belongs to foreground or background but also its location (i.e. spatial info) needs to be preserved. Typical example of FCN is an Encoder-Decoder network. Encoder gradually decreases the spatial dimension (or resolution) using pooling layers while decoder gradually recovers the spatial dimension and object details. Encoder aggregates image information from fine minute details to global concept while decoder recovers image details at different levels, with the initial layers encoding overall image information and final layers capturing fine details. Usually, there are shortcut connections from encoder to decoder that helps decoder to recover the object details better.

U-Net [10] is a popular architecture from this class and it was used with slight modifications (Fig. 2). The CXR's were resized to 224 × 240 resolution and inputted to the U-Net model without any pre-processing. The model consists of a contraction module (encoder) followed by an expansion module (decoder). The contraction module takes each image, performs two padded 3 × 3 convolutions, each followed by a ReLU and downsamples the image into half using max pooling of 2 × 2. The number of convolutional filters is doubled after each pooling. The process is iterated many times and after each iteration, the depth of resultant feature maps becomes double and their spatial dimensions (length and width) becomes half. The expansion module upsamples the feature map, concatenates it with the corresponding feature map from the contraction module, and performs two 3 × 3 convolutions each followed by a ReLU. The number of convolutional filters is halved after each upsampling. The process is iterated many times and after each iteration, the depth of resultant feature maps becomes half and their spatial dimensions (length and width) becomes double. This way the original dimensions of the image are preserved.

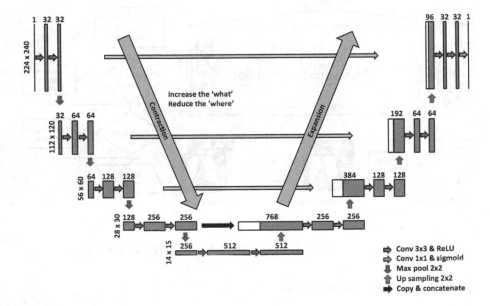

Fig. 2. Model architecture

2.2 Flood Fill Algorithm for Holes Filling

The flood-fill is a recursive algorithm used for filling connected, similar colored region to a new desired target color. It takes three parameters as input: starting node, target color and the replacement color. Starting node is the pixel from where we start filling. Target color is the old color we want to change or replace. Replacement color is the desired resultant color. The algorithm starts with the starting node and checks for two conditions and move to the next pixel without any change if one of the following conditions is true:

- If the color of node is not equal to target-color i.e. the pixel belongs to some other object or any boundary and we don't aim to change that color.
- If target-color is equal to replacement-color i.e. there is no need to replace the color as the desired color is already there.

If both conditions are false that means the pixel color needs to be changed, so the starting node color is changed to the replacement color. Then it moves to the next pixel using 4 or 8 connectivity and repeats the same procedure recursively.

Few cases in the lung segmentation results had holes in the lungs due to the presence of acquisition equipment in the original x-ray. For removing these artifacts, flood-fill algorithm was used. The top left corner pixel (0, 0) was set as the starting node. The target color was the same as of starting node i.e. black (0), and white (1) was the replacement color. After flood filling, the resultant image was inverted and added to the original image that produced the desired results without holes, as illustrated in Fig. 3.

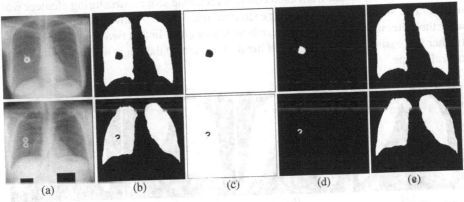

(a)   (b)   (c)   (d)   (e)

Fig. 3. Holes filing (a) Original image (b) Model segmentation result (c) Flood-fill algorithm result (d) Inverted flood-fill algorithm result (e) Inverted image added to the model result

2.3 Unwanted Objects Removal

Few segmentation results had unwanted tiny objects that were eliminated by choosing top two foreground objects in terms of area and removing the remaining objects. As tiny objects have very small area as compared to the lungs area, they were easily eradicated as shown in Fig. 4.

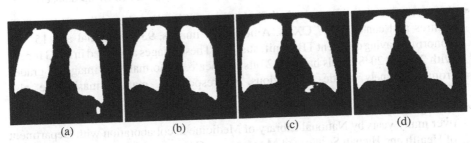

(a)   (b)   (c)   (d)

Fig. 4. Small unwanted objects removal (a), (c) Model segmentation results (b), (d) Corresponding results after unnecessary objects removal

2.4 Morphological Opening

Opening is a morphological operation defined as erosion followed by dilation. It uses the same structuring element for both operations. Consider A as an input image and SE as a structuring element then opening can be represented as:

$$A \circ SE = (A \ominus SE) \oplus S$$

(1)

For lungs segmentation, opening was used as post-processing in some cases where left and right lungs were fused or merged at the apex. Opening was performed iteratively until both were separated from each other. A rectangle shaped structuring element was used and its size was increased after each iteration. Figure 5 shows the opening results after three iterations. We can see there is no major effect in first two iterations, but after further increasing the SE size, fourth iteration separated the lungs without distortion in overall shape.

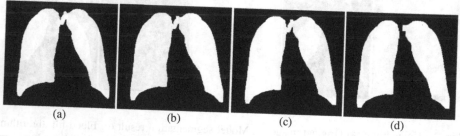

(a)	(b)	(c)	(d)

Fig. 5. Morphological opening three iterations (a) Model segmentation result (b) Opening iteration 1 (c) Iteration 2 (d) Iteration 3

3 Experimental Results

3.1 Datasets

Performance of the proposed methodology is evaluated on the following datasets:

- Japanese Society of Radiological Technology: JSRT is gathered from 14 medical centres and contains 247 CXRs. Among 247 images, 93 are normal and 154 are abnormal having different TB manifestations. These images are stored in PNG format with 2048 × 2048 pixels having 12 bits grayscale. Abnormality of images is graded from extremely subtle to obvious. Corresponding manual masks are also provided [11].
- Montgomery County: MC dataset is a subset of a larger CXRs repository gathered over many years by National Library of Medicine in collaboration with Department of Health and Human Services of Montgomery Country (MC), Maryland. It contains 138 x-rays, among which 80 are normal and 58 are abnormal. The images are stored in PNG format with pixel resolution of 4020 × 4892 or 4892 × 4020 with 12 bits grayscale. Corresponding manual lung masks are also available which were generated under the supervision of radiologists [12].

- Local Dataset: The local dataset was collected from the Peoples University of Medical and Health Sciences (PUMHS) Nawabshah, Sindh, Pakistan. It consists of 37 CXR's among which few have resolution of 1760 × 1760 pixels and remaining have 1760 × 2140 pixels resolution. The corresponding manual masks were generated using Adobe Illustrator by tracing the lung boundaries.

3.2 Performance Measures

The common parameters for evaluation of the results are dice similarity coefficient (DSC), sensitivity (SEN), specificity (SPE), and accuracy (ACC). DSC, SEN and SPE are sometimes also referred as overlap index, True Positive Rate (TPR) and True Negative Rate (TNR) respectively. The parameters are defined in terms of true positive (TP), false positive (FP), true negative (TN) and false negative (FN) values. Where, in segmentation, TP is the no. of foreground pixels correctly classified as foreground. FP is the no. of background pixels wrongly classified as foreground. TN is the no. of background pixels correctly classified as background and FN is the no. of foreground pixels wrongly classified as background pixels.

3.3 Results

The segmentation methodology was evaluated on JSRT, MC and local dataset. The JSRT and MC datasets achieved average accuracy of 97.1% and 97.7% respectively. The local dataset, in spite of having too less images, still achieved average accuracy of 94.2%. The value of other performance evaluation parameters is shown in Table 1.

Table 1. Segmentation results statistics

Database	Total images	Training (60%)	Testing (40%)	DSC (%)	SEN (%)	SPE (%)	ACC (%)
JSRT	247	147	100	95.1%	95.1%	98.0%	97.1%
MC	138	82	56	95.4%	95.4%	98.5%	97.7%
Local	37	22	15	88.0%	86.2%	97.0%	94.2%

The training and testing accuracy trend of some random iteration is plotted in Fig. 6. The no. of epochs were set to 120 to see the trend, but it can be clearly seen that the maximum accuracy was attained at 20–40 epochs and after that, it remains almost constant. The trend of JSRT and MC is quite smooth while that of local dataset is little bumpy and that can be completely justified by the scarcity of x-rays in local dataset.

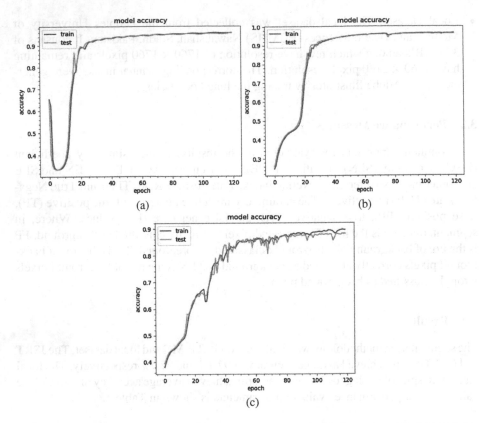

Fig. 6. Training and testing accuracy trend with respect to no. of epochs of (a) JSRT (b) MC (c) Local dataset

Figure 7 visually compares the final segmentation results with the original manual masks or ground truth of JSRT, MC and local dataset respectively. The results show that no matter how elongated, small, wide or thin the shape is, the model is generalized enough to segment all the cases accurately with very few FP and FN pixels.

The comparison of different segmentation techniques from the past five years is shown in Table 2. The proposed algorithm has achieved highest accuracy as compared to other convolutional networks proposed by Arbabshirani et al., Kalinvosky and kovalev. The achieved accuracy of MC is highest till date and that of JSRT (97.1%) is also very close to the highest accuracy achieved by Li et al. i.e. 97.7%.

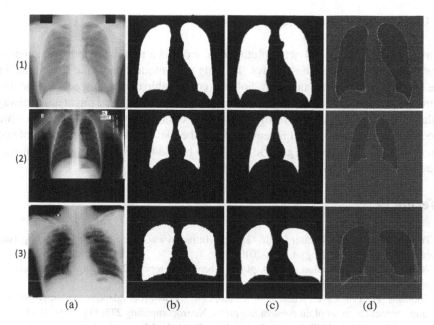

Fig. 7. Segmentation results (1) JSRT, (2) MC, (3) Local dataset, (a) Original image (b) Segmented mask (c) Ground truth (d) Superimposition of segmented mask on ground truth where green represents TP, magenta represents TN, red represents FP, cyan represents FN (Color figure online)

Table 2. Comparison of segmentation methodologies

Year	Author	Technique	Database	ACC (%)	DSC/IOU/OVL (%)
2018	Our	FCN (U-Net)	JSRT	97.1%	DSC=95.1%
			MC	97.7%	DSC=95.4%
			Local	94.2%	DSC=88.0%
2017	Chondro et al [3]	Low order adaptive region growing	JSRT	96.3%	
			MC	96.6%	
2017	Arbabshirani et al [4]	Deep CNN	Geisinger		IOU=96%
2016	Kalinovsky and Kovalev [5]	Encoder-Decoder CNN (ED-CNN)	Belarus + JSRT	96.2%	Min DSC=92.6% Max DSC=97.4%
2016	Li et al [6]	Statistical Shape and Appearance Models	JSRT	97.7%	OVL=93.1%
2015	Ngo and Carneiro [7]	Distance Regularized Level Set (DRLS) & Deep-Structured Learning & Inference	JSRT	94.8% to 98.5%.	
2014	Saad et al [8]	Edge Detection & Morphology	JSRT	82.9%	
2014	Candemir et al [9]	Anatomical Atlases with Nonrigid Registration	JSRT	95.4%	
			MC	94.1%	
			India	91.7%	

4 Conclusions and Future Work

The results show that a fully convolutional network is a promising tool for automatic lungs segmentation from chest x-rays. Training such models may take some time, but once a model is trained it can give radiologist comparable results in seconds. One limitation is that we need manually segmented masks for its training, that might not be always available, but this problem can resolved to some extent using transfer learning in which a model trained on one dataset is reused for another dataset. One major benefit of such deep network is that they are generic enough to be used for variety of similar medical image segmentation problems with little modifications.

References

1. Technology Trends-Smarter with Gartner. https://www.gartner.com/smarterwithgartner/gartners-top-10-technology-trends-2017/
2. World Health Organization (WHO), global tuberculosis report (2016). http://www.who.int/tb/publications/global_report/en/
3. Chondro, P., Yao, C.-Y., Ruan, S.-J., Chien, L.-C.: Low order adaptive region growing for lung segmentation on plain chest radiographs. Neurocomputing **275**(31), 1002–1011 (2018)
4. Arbabshirani, M.R., Dallal, A.H., Agarwal, C., Patel, A., Moore, G.: Accurate segmentation of lung fields on chest radiographs using deep convolutional networks. In: Proceedings of Medical Imaging, vol. 10133 (2017)
5. Kalinovsky, A., Kovalev, V.: Lung image segmentation using deep learning methods and convolutional neural networks. In: XIII International Conference on Pattern Recognition and Information Processing, 3–5 October, pp. 21–24. Belarus State University, Minsk (2016)
6. Li, X., et al.: Automatic lung field segmentation in X-ray radiographs using statistical shape and appearance models. J. Med. Imaging Health Inform. **6**, 338–348 (2016)
7. Ngo, T.A., Carneiro, G.: Lung segmentation in chest radiographs using distance regularized level set and deep-structured learning and inference. In: 2015 IEEE International Conference on Image Processing (ICIP) (2015)
8. Saad, M.N., Muda, Z., Ashaari, N.S., Hamid, H.A.: Image segmentation for lung region in chest x-ray images using edge detection and morphology. In: 2014 IEEE International Conference on Control System, Computing and Engineering, 28–30 November 2014, Penang, Malaysia (2014)
9. Candemir, S., et al.: Lung segmentation in chest radiographs using anatomical atlases with nonrigid registration. IEEE Trans. Med. Imaging **33**(2), February 2014
10. Ronneberger, O., Fischer, P., Brox, T.: U-Net: convolutional networks for biomedical image segmentation. In: Navab, N., Hornegger, J., Wells, W.M., Frangi, A.F. (eds.) MICCAI 2015. LNCS, vol. 9351, pp. 234–241. Springer, Cham (2015). https://doi.org/10.1007/978-3-319-24574-4_28
11. Japanese Society of Radiological Technology Database. http://db.jsrt.or.jp/eng.php
12. National Library of Medicine, National Institutes of Health, Bethesda, MD, USA. https://ceb.nlm.nih.gov/repositories/tuberculosis-chest-x-ray-image-data-sets/

DTI Segmentation Using Anisotropy Preserving Quaternion Based Distance Measure

Sumit Kaushik$^{(\boxtimes)}$ and Jan Slovak

Department of Mathematics and Statistics, Faculty of Science, Masaryk University,
Kotlářská 2, 611 37 Brno, Czech Republic
sumitkaushik24@gmail.com, slovak@muni.cz,
http://www.math.muni.cz

Abstract. In brain research, the second order tensor model of the diffusion tensor imaging (DTI) encodes diffusion of water molecules in microstructures of tissues. These tensors are real matrices lying in a nonlinear space enjoying the Riemannian symmetric space structure. Thus, there are natural intrinsic metrics there, together with their extrinsic approximations. The effective implementations are based on the extrinsic ones employing their vector space structure. In processing DTI, the Log-Euclidean (LogE) metric is most popular, though very far from optimal. The spectral decomposition approach yields the distance measures which respect the anisotropy much better. In the present work, we propose to use the spherical linear interpolation (slerp-SQ) which performs much better than the LogE one and provides better interpolation of geodesics than the spectral-quaternion one. We have implemented the localized active contour segmentation method for these metrics, providing much better handling of the inhomogeneity of the data than global counterpart.

Keywords: Diffusion tensor imaging · Anisotropy
Riemannian symmetric spaces

1 Introduction

The non-invasive DW-MRI method can quantify the degree of diffusion of water molecules in the brain. The second order diffusion model was introduced in [13]. In this model, the tensors encoding diffusion are 3×3 symmetric positive definite matrices with six degrees of freedom, lying in the $\mathbb{S}^+(3)$ space. The anisotropic tensors in DTI represent white matter micro-structures which allow more diffusion oriented along axons. The segmentation of white matter structures has

Sumit Kaushik has been supported by the grant MUNI/A/1138/2017 of Masaryk University, Jan Slovak gratefully acknowledges support from the Grant Agency of the Czech Republic, grant Nr. GA17-01171S.

© Springer International Publishing AG, part of Springer Nature 2018
A. Campilho et al. (Eds.): ICIAR 2018, LNCS 10882, pp. 81–89, 2018.
https://doi.org/10.1007/978-3-319-93000-8_10

relevance in diagnosis and clinical studies of patients with multiple sclerosis, stroke, and brain-connectivity issues. For segmentation, the deformable models were long been used for intensity images in earlier works, called snakes, cf. [9]. These contours are guided by an energy function which deals with topological changes while evolving. For example, [14,15] used edge based function but had disadvantage because of inability to deal with noise and it required initial curve to be placed near to the boundary of the object of interest. The level sets (geometrically known as implicit curves in hypersurface) were exploited in [2] to deal with topological changes of the evolving curve. In their remarkable paper [3], Chan-Vese incorporated region based energy model based on Mumford-Shah formulation [1]. The method was based on minimization of global energy which was formulated as a variational problem. This resolved the problem with edge based methods, but such global methods fail to segment the objects whose parts have non-homogenous statistics. To resolve this issue, localized curve model was introduced by Lankton et al. in [11] and subsequently was used by them in [12] for fibre bundle segmentation. Further, they advocated that the efficiency of the method relies upon the choice of distance measure or metric. This is one of the motivation for current work.

The space of tensors in DTI is well studied and known as a non-Euclidean Riemannian symmetric space. The work [16] provided a Riemann framework for computing. Affine invariant metrics on the homogenous space $\mathbb{S}^+$ are well known in differential geometry texts [17], while in statistics, they are known as Fisher information metrics [18]. The use of the latter technique for DTI was advocated in [20].

In the current work, we implement the localized segmentation method for DTI based on the so called slerp-SQ metric and we have chosen the widely used Log-Euclidean metric, introduced in [21], for comparison. This spherical linear interpolation of quaternion slerp-SQ distance measure is an extension of the spectral-quaternion (SQ) measure for curve evolution. We provide arguments why is this metric better in providing smooth interpolation of geodesics. We achieved very fast and effective segmentation of white matter structure as compared to the Log Euclidean metric for 2D cross section. It works very well for structures with quickly varying curvatures (e.g. corpus collasum). At the same time, it enables the segmentation curve to deal with the heterogeneity of the tensors in the underlying image, which is due to variation in the orientation and eigen-values. Results on both synthetic images and on real human brain images are shown.

2   Localization of Global Energy Formulation

In early works for scalar images, deformable models were called snakes. Kass et al. [9] introduced an energy function to evolve the curve which was fast but had difficulty in handling topological changes. The evolution of curves is guided by the curvature motion and edge function: $g(|\nabla u_0|) = (1 + |\nabla(G_\sigma \star u_0)|)^{-1}$. Here, u_0 is image, G_σ is the Gaussian function and $\star$ is the convolution operation.

In [14,15] g acts as evolving and a stopping term for the curve as its value is zero near the boundaries of object. The disadvantage of these edge based methods is their inability to deal with noise because in the process of smoothing noise, Gaussian also smoothes the boundaries. Another shortcoming is that the initial curve needs to be placed near the boundary of object of interest. Osher and Sethian in [10] used level-sets to deal the topological changes during curve evolution, the evolving curve is embedded in high dimensional surface. Further, based on Mumford Shah model [1], as a special case, Chan-Vese [3] model evolved the curve without requiring edges as stopping condition, they used energy formulation based on first moments of energy distribution in the interior and exterior regions of the curve. Minimization of the energy converges the evolving curve to boundary of the object. It enables to segment the objects with or without discontinuous boundaries, and it is robust to noise. Let ϕ be the surface embedding the curve, i.e. $\partial\phi/\partial t = F|\nabla\phi|$. Various choices of the function F exist in literature. Region based techniques works well for the objects with uniform features but fails where sub-region of the object has non-uniformity i.e. the statistics of the object's (local) region has variation. Authors in [5] incorporated local statistics into variational framework to deal heterogeneity. [6–8,11] are some works in this direction.

In the current work, we are using [11] energy functional which they used in followed up paper [12] for fibre bundle segmentation for 3D DTI. They used Log-Euclidean metric and advocated the improvement under a better similarity measures/metric. A bounding ball mask $\mathcal{B}(x,y)$ is selected with a fixed radius r across the length of contour, with value 1 inside and zero outside. The reader is referred to [11] for details on the variational setup. The iterative optimization of the energy is implemented with the help of the Euler-Lagrange equation

$$\frac{\partial\phi}{\partial t}(x) = \delta\phi(x)\int_{\Omega_y}\mathcal{B}(x,y)\cdot\nabla_{\phi(y)}F(I(y),\phi(y))\,dy + \lambda\delta\phi(x)\operatorname{div}\frac{\nabla\phi(x)}{|\nabla\phi(x)|}.$$

3   Distance Measures for Second Order Tensors

These tensors can be considered to lie either in a Euclidean space (extrinsically) or the embedded space (intrinsically). With Euclidean space approach, the advantage is that it is a vector space and all statistics are easily performed but at the cost of accuracy and closure property. Embedded space has inherent non-scalar curvature. However, advantage is that it reduces the dimension of the problem and under proper metric promises accurate results. Computational speed is an issue in this case when it involves enormous data (e.g. DTI). The symmetric positive definite (SPD) matrices forms a manifold called Riemann symmetric space. Geometrically, these matrices forms a cone (because of positive definite constraint) in $\mathbb{R}^n$. Euclidean space approach in [24] gives a unique mean but smoothing operations may result in negative or null eigenvalues, which are non-physical for diffusion process. Further, it gives rise to problems like the swelling effect.

3.1   State of the Art

Notice, the matrix exponential is a diffeomorphism from the embedding space $\mathbb{R}^6$ of the symmetric 3 by 3 matrices to the tensor space $\mathbb{S}^+$ (the manifold of the positive definite ones).

Log-Euclidean Metric: The latter mathematical observation was exploited by the authors in [21] and gave a Lie group structure to the tensor space. With this structure computations become easy in three steps: Take log of the tensor space, process the vector data (symmetric matrices), use exp to map the data back to the manifold. This is a popular metric for DTI processing. The composition operation is not the usual matrix multiplication (under which it is not a Lie group). It is given by:

$$p_1 \bullet p_2 = \exp(\log(p_1) + \log(p_2)) \tag{1}$$

$$\text{dist}^2(p_1, p_2) = \text{trace}((\log(p_1) - \log(p_2))^2 \tag{2}$$

and the interpolation curve between two tensors p_1 and p_2 is

$$p(t) = \exp(1 - t)\log(p_1) + t\log(p_2). \tag{3}$$

This extrinsic metric is an approximation of intrinsic affine invariant metric. They are very close to each other near to the identity. It is invariant with respect to the similarity transformations (rotation or scaling). Log Euclidean interpolation curve provides a closed-form mean for two or more tensors.

Spectral Metric: For the first time, [19] used spectral treatment for regularization of noisy diffusion tensors. The key idea is to treat eigenvalues and eigenvectors separately. An interpolation curve between any two tensors u_1 and u_2 is given by:

$$p(t) = u(t)\Lambda(t)u^T(t) \tag{4}$$

$$u(t) = u_1 \exp(t\log(u_1^T u_2)) \tag{5}$$

$$\Lambda(t) = \exp(1 - t)\log(\Lambda_1) + t\log(\Lambda_2) \tag{6}$$

where $u_1, u_2 \in \mathbb{SO}(3)$ (the rotational group) and Λ_1 and Λ_2 are diagonal matrices with eigen values entries. This interpolation curve is a geodesic in the product of Lie groups $\mathbb{SO}(3) \times \mathbb{D}^+(3)$, where $\mathbb{D}^+(3)$ is the group of diagonal matrices with positive elements. This Lie group is a four-fold covering of $\mathbb{S}^+(3)$. The tensor has four distinct orientations, determined by rotations of principle axes by π, and one due to identity. Let G be one such four-tuple of u_2. Then distance between the any two rotations u_1 and u_2:

$$\text{dist}(u_1, u_2) = \arg \min_{u \in G} \text{dist}(u_1, u) = \arg \min\|\log(u_1 u_2^T)\|_2 \tag{7}$$

The calculations here require four matrix exp and log operations. To reduce the number of computations, rotation is performed in the quaternion space in [22]. We have extended the spectral quaternion metric which is based on Lerp (linear interpolation) and we use inner-product based metric for the rotation space.

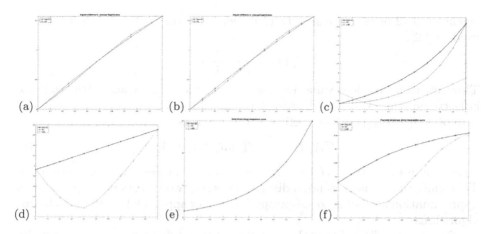

Fig. 1. Comparison of smoothness of the interpolation curves depicted by angular difference in principle eigenvectors. Blue curve is for slerp-SQ and red for SQ in (a) with $n = 4$ tensors, (b) $n = 10$. Green is for LogE in (c). Mean diffusivity (MD) evolves monotonically better in slerp-SQ than SQ but not with LogE metric. In (d) the Hilbert anisotropy evolves similar in both slerpSQ and SQ, in comparison to LogE. In (e), the determinant evolves similar in all three cases. In (f), the fractional anisotropy evolves similar in both slerpSQ and SQ, in comparison to LogE. (Color figure online)

3.2   Slerp-SQ

We propose to use the spherical version of the linear interpolation spectral quaternion distance measure. The Hopf-Rinow-De Rham theorem indicates that among all possible geodesics between any two points on a complete manifold there exists at least one geodesic with minimum length which can be considered as distance between two points. We exploit spherical linear interpolation (Slerp) of quaternions. Slerp produces smoother curves in quaternion space and resulting geodesic is thus closer to the geodesic distance in the Lie group $\mathbb{SO}(3) \times \mathbb{D}^+(3)$.

The slerp interpolation between two quaternions q_1 and q_2 is

$$q_m(q_1, q_2, t) = \frac{sin[(1-t)\theta]}{sin\theta} q_1 + \frac{sin[t\theta]}{sin\theta} q_2 \qquad (8)$$

where $\theta = \arccos(|q_1.q_2|)$. Notice, θ is a metric and we shall denote it $d_{slerpSQ}$.
This seems to be a better choice than the metric

$$d_{SQ} = 1 - \cos(d_{slerpSQ})$$

used in [22]. Notice, d_{SQ} metric is an chordal distance approximation in S^3 quaternion space. Further, it converges to 0 at a slower rate and not bounded equivalent to other metrics [23] for rotation space.

Anisotropy carries useful information and requires to be preserved during processing of DTI tensors. The Eq. 4 for the interpolation curve between tensors is valid for those with distinct eigenvalues. To account for the tensors with same eigenvalues (2 or more), a smooth transition function $f(x)$ (keeping $\beta = 0.6$) is used in [22],

$$f(x) = \frac{(\beta x)^4}{1 + (\beta x)^4} \tag{9}$$

This function gets low value in case of isotropic tensors and high value for anisotropic ones. The true distance between two tensor is given by a weighted sum of $d_\lambda + \alpha d_{slerpSQ}$. The coefficient α is given as

$$\alpha(HA_1, HA_2) = f(\min(HA_1, HA_2)), \tag{10}$$

where Hilbert anisotropy $HA = \log \frac{\lambda_{max}}{\lambda_{min}}$ with λ_i being eigenvalues of the tensors. This similarity measure is not a distance between two tensors but it provides an approximation according to anisotropy. The latter approach lead to the following algorithms.

The Fig. 1 indicates that the evolution of scalar anisotropies, i.e., mean diffusitivity and fractional anisotropy, is much closer to linear in SQ and Slerp-SQ than in LogE cases. Moreover, Slerp-SQ behaves better than SQ. As the number of tensors increases, Slerp-SQ converges to SQ (Fig. 2).

3.3   The Algorithms

We present the computation of the means and distance measures now.

Algorithm 1. Weighted mean.
Input: Tensors p_i with $i = 1$ to N with weights w_i, such that $\sum w_i = 1$.
Output: p_μ the mean tensor.

1. Spectral decomposition of N tensors.
2. Evaluate weighted mean $\lambda_{\mu,k} = \exp\left(\sum_{i=1}^{N} w_i \log(\lambda_{i,k})\right)$, $k = 1, 2, 3$.
3. Select the reference tensor which maximizes $w_i HA_i$ i.e. q^{ref}
4. With respect to q^{ref}, the realigned quaternion is given by
   $q_i^a = \arg\min_{q_i \in Q_i} \arccos(|q^{ref}.q_i|)$
5. The weighted mean q_μ is given by: 8 and $q_\mu = \frac{q_m}{|q_m|}$
6. Compute rotation matrix u_μ from q_μ
7. Finally, $P_\mu = u_\mu \Lambda u_\mu^T$

Algorithm 2. The distance approximation.
Input: Tensors p_1 and p_2.
Output: The distance $\text{dist}(p_1, p_2)$

1. Spectral decomposition of the tensors and get quaternions from the rotation matrix.
2. The distance between eigenvalues is given by: $d_\lambda = \sum |\log \frac{\lambda_i(p_1)}{\lambda_i(p_2)}|$
3. The weighting factor is given by: $\alpha(p_1, p_2) = f(x)$ by equation 9, where $x = \min(HA_1, HA_2)$
4. With q_1 as the reference quaternion, realigned quaternion is calculated as $q_2^a = \arg\min_{q_2 \in Q} \arccos(|q_1.q_2|)$, and $d_{slerpSQ} = \arccos(|q_1.q_2^a|)$.
5. $\text{dist}(p_1, p_2) = \alpha(p_1, p_2)d_q + d_\lambda$.

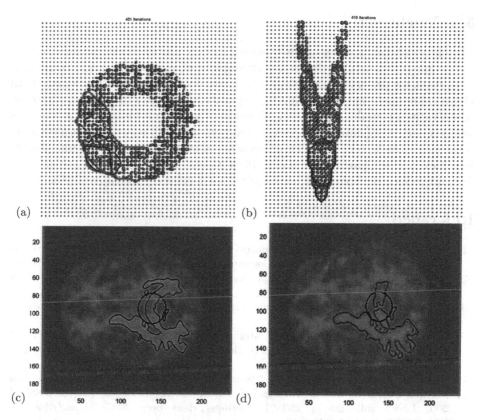

Fig. 2. In (a), slerp-SQ is faster (both curves shown at 521 iterative step, both are able to segment the object). In (b), LogE fails to evolve after 50th iteration, whereas slerp-SQ continued segmenting the whole object. Segmentation inside region of interest (roi) shown with ellipse, localization radius = 20, z-slice = 86, data size = $191 \times 236 \times 171$. In (c), LogE fails to deal with heterogeneity present in roi, while in (d), slerp-SQ is able to discern the heterogeneous data present within roi.

4   Results

We used two 2D structures, parabola and circle, having high and constant curvature respectively. Background is kept uniform and various degree of heterogeneity in structures is obtained by inducing randomness in eigenvalues and eigenvectors. Curve with slerp-SQ distance measure is shown in green and that of LogE in black color in the figures. A slice of the human brain image is chosen[1] and algorithm is run to segment an arbitrary region, where heterogeneity is visible. LogE fails to discern the non-homogenous region (encircled). Results are overlapped on image with darker region showing the white matter presence.

---

[1] Brain Image Source: http://brainimaging.waisman.wisc.edu/~chung/DTI.

5   Conclusion

The choice of distance measure in localized curve evolution is crucial in extracting white matter structure effectively. Decoupling of eigenvalues and rotations is important for preserving anisotropy and representation of Rotational space with Quaternion space not only reduces computations but also maintains anisotropy preservation. Introducing spherical linear interpolation for quaternions produces smooth curves in quaternion space and in turn in tensor space. It guarantees the geodesic distance to be closer approximation of metric with correct segmentation is achieved. Next part of our work will be to extract white matter structure in 3D and reduce the computations required for localized contour evolution.

References

1. Mumford, D., Shah, J.: Optimal approximation by piecewise smooth functions and associated variational problems. Commun. Pure Appl. Math. **42**, 577–685 (1989)
2. Sethian, J.: Level Set Methods and Fast Marching Methods. Springer, New York (1999)
3. Chan, T., Vese, L.: Active contours without edges. IEEE Trans. Image Process. **10**(2), 266–277 (2001)
4. Yezzi, A., Tsai, A., Willsky, A.: A statistical approach to snakes for bimodal and trimodal imagery. In: Proceedings of the International Conference on Computer Vision, vol. 2, pp. 898–903 (1999)
5. Brox, T., Cremers, D.: On the statistical interpretation of the piecewise smooth Mumford-Shah functional. In: Sgallari, F., Murli, A., Paragios, N. (eds.) SSVM 2007. LNCS, vol. 4485, pp. 203–213. Springer, Heidelberg (2007). https://doi.org/10.1007/978-3-540-72823-8_18
6. Li, C., Kao, C.-Y., Gore, J.C., Ding, Z.: Implicit active contours driven by local binary fitting energy. Presented at the computer vision and pattern recognition, June 2007
7. Piovano, J., Rousson, M., Papadopoulo, T.: Efficient segmentation of piecewise smooth images. In: Sgallari, F., Murli, A., Paragios, N. (eds.) SSVM 2007. LNCS, vol. 4485, pp. 709–720. Springer, Heidelberg (2007). https://doi.org/10.1007/978-3-540-72823-8_61
8. An, J., Rousson, M., Xu, C.: Γ-convergence approximation to piecewise smooth medical image segmentation. In: Ayache, N., Ourselin, S., Maeder, A. (eds.) MICCAI 2007. LNCS, vol. 4792, pp. 495–502. Springer, Heidelberg (2007). https://doi.org/10.1007/978-3-540-75759-7_60
9. Kass, M., Witkin, A., Terzopoulos, D.: Snakes: active contour models. Int. J. Comput. Vis. **1**, 321–331 (1987)
10. Osher, S., Sethian, J.: Fronts propagating with curvature-dependent speed: algorithms based on Hamilton-Jacobi formulations. J. Comput. Phys. **79**, 12–49 (1988)
11. Lankton, S., Tannenbaum, A.: Localizing region-based active contours. IEEE Trans. Image Process. **17**(11), 2029–2039 (2008)
12. Lankton, S., Melonakos, J., Malcolm, J., Dambreville, S., Tannenbaum, A.: Localized statistics for DW-MRI fiber bundle segmentation. In: Proceedings of 21st CVPR Workshops, pp. 1–8 (2008)
13. Basser, P.J., Mattiello, J., LeBihan, D.: Estimation of the effective self-diffusion tensor from the NMR spin-echo. J. Magn. Reson., Ser. B **103**(3), 247–254 (1994)

14. Caselles, V., Kimmel, R., Sapiro, G.: Geodesic active contours Int. J. Comput. Vision **22**(1), 61–79 (1997)
15. Malladi, R., Sethian, J.A., Vemuri, B.C.: Shape modeling with front propagation: a level set approach. IEEE Trans. Pattern Anal. Mach. Intell. **17**(2), 158–175 (1995)
16. Pennec, X., Fillard, P., Ayache, N.: A Riemann framework for tensor computing. Int. J. Comput. Vis. **66**(1), 41–66 (2006)
17. Bhatia, R.: On the exponential metric increasing property. Linear Algebra Appl. **375**, 211–220 (2003)
18. Skovgaard, L.: A Riemann geometry of the multivariate normal model. Scand. J. Stat. **11**, 211–223 (1984)
19. Tschumperle, D., Deriche, R.: Diffusion tensor regularization with constraints preservation. In: Proceedings of the 2001 IEEE Computer Society Conference on Computer Vision and Pattern Recognition, CVPR 2001, vol. 1, pp. 948–953 (2001)
20. Lenglet, C., Rousson, M., Deriche, R., Faugeras, O., Lehericy, S., Ugurbil, K.: A Riemannian approach to diffusion tensor images segmentation. In: Christensen, G.E., Sonka, M. (eds.) IPMI 2005. LNCS, vol. 3565, pp. 591–602. Springer, Heidelberg (2005). https://doi.org/10.1007/11505730_49
21. Arsigny, V., Commowick, O., Pennec, X., Ayache, N.: A Log-Euclidean framework for statistics on diffeomorphisms. In: Larsen, R., Nielsen, M., Sporring, J. (eds.) MICCAI 2006. LNCS, vol. 4190, pp. 924–931. Springer, Heidelberg (2006). https://doi.org/10.1007/11866565_113
22. Collard, A., Bonnabel, S., Phillips, C., Sepulchre, R.: An anisotropy preserving metric for DTI processing. Int. J. Comput. Vis. Arch. **107**(1), 58–74 (2014)
23. Huynh, D.Q.: Metrics for 3D rotations: comparison and analysis. J. Math Imaging Vis. **35**(2), 155–104 (2009)
24. Fletcher, P.T., Joshi, S.: Principal geodesic analysis on symmetric spaces: statistics of diffusion tensors. In: Sonka, M., Kakadiaris, I.A., Kybic, J. (eds.) CVAMIA/MMBIA -2004. LNCS, vol. 3117, pp. 87–98. Springer, Heidelberg (2004). https://doi.org/10.1007/978-3-540-27816-0_8

Affinely Registered Multi-object Atlases as Shape Prior for Grid Cut Segmentation of Lumbar Vertebrae from CT Images

Weimin Yu[1], Wenyong Liu[2], Liwen Tan[3], Shaoxiang Zhang[3], and Guoyan Zheng[1(✉)]

[1] Institute for Surgical Technology and Biomechanics,
University of Bern, Bern, Switzerland
guoyan.zheng@istb.unibe.ch

[2] School of Biological Science and Medical Engineering, Beijing Advanced Innovation Centre for Biomedical Engineering, Beihang University, Beijing, China

[3] The Institute of Digital Medicine, The Third Military Medical University, Chongqing, China

Abstract. In this paper, we present a method for automatic segmentation of lumbar vertebrae from a given lumbar spinal CT image. More specifically, our automatic lumbar vertebrae segmentation method consists of two steps: affine atlas-target registration-based label fusion and bone-sheetness assisted multi-label grid cut which has the inherent advantage of automatic separation of the five lumbar vertebrae from each other. We evaluate our method on 21 clinical lumbar spinal CT images with the associated manual segmentation and conduct a leave-one-out study. Our method achieved an average Dice coefficient of $93.9 \pm 1.0\%$ and an average symmetric surface distance of $0.41 \pm 0.08\,\mathrm{mm}$.

Keywords: Lumbar vertebrae · CT · Segmentation
Multi-object atlas · Grid cut

1 Introduction

Vertebra segmentation is challenging because the overall morphology of the vertebral column has a basic similarity, with the exception of the first two cervical vertebrae and the sacrum. Although the shape of the individual vertebrae changes significantly along the spine, most neighboring vertebrae look very similar and are difficult to distinguish. In recently years, a number of spine segmentation algorithms for CT images have been proposed. The proposed methods range from unsupervised image processing approaches, such as level set [1] and graph cut methods [1], to geometrical model-based methods such as statistical anatomical models or probabilistic atlas-based methods [1], to more recently machine learning and deep learning based methods [2,3].

W. YU and W. Liu mdash Contributed equally to this paper.

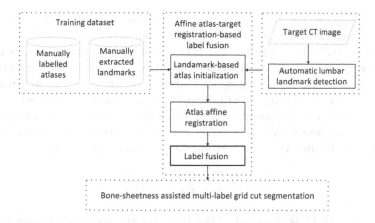

Fig. 1. The flowchart of our proposed segmentation method. See text for details.

In this paper, we proposed a two-stage method consists of the localization stage and the segmentation stage. The localization stage aims to identify each lumbar vertebra, while the segmentation stage handles the problem of labeling each lumbar vertebra from a given 3D image. Previously, we have developed a method to fully automatically localize landmarks for each lumbar vertebra in CT images with context features and reported a mean localization error of 3.2 mm [4]. In this paper, we focus on the segmentation stage where the detected landmarks in the localization stage are used to initialize our segmentation method. To this end, we propose to use an affinely registered multi-object atlases as shape prior for grid cut segmentation of lumbar vertebrae from a given target CT image. More specifically, our segmentation method consists of two steps: affine atlas-target registration-based label fusion and bone-sheetness assisted multi-label grid cut. The initial segmentation obtained from the first step will be used as the shape prior for the second step.

2 Method

Figure 1 presents a schematic overview of the complete work-flow of our proposed approach. Without loss of generality, we assume that for the lth ($l \in \{1, 2, 3, 4, 5\}$) lumbar vertebra, there exists a set of N_l atlases with manually labeled segmentation and manually extracted landmarks. In the following, details of each step will be presented.

2.1 Affine Atlas-Target Registration-Based Label Fusion

Given the unseen lumbar spinal CT image, we assume that a set of landmarks have been already detected for each lumbar vertebra. The following steps are conducted separately for each lumbar vertebra.

Using the detected anatomical landmarks, paired-point scaled rigid registration are performed to align all N_l atlases of the lth lumbar vertebra to the target image space. We then select $N_{l,s} \ll N_l$ atlases with the least paired-point registration errors for the atlas affine registration step as described below.

Each selected atlas consists of a CT volume and a manual segmentation of the corresponding lumbar vertebra. For every selected atlas, we perform a pair-wise atlas-target affine registration using the intensity-based registration toolbox "Elastix" [5]. Using the obtained 3D affine transformation, we can align the associated manual segmentation of the selected atlas to the target image space. Then the probability of labeling a voxel x in the target image space as part of the lth lumbar vertebra is computed with average voting:

$$p_{l,x} = \frac{1}{N_{l,s}} \sum_{i=1}^{N_{l,s}} A_i(x) \tag{1}$$

where $A_i(x) \in \{0,1\}$ is the label of the ith atlas at voxel x after aligned to the target image space.

A simple thresholding is then conduct to get an initial binary segmentation of the lth lumbar vertebra.

$$L_l(x) = \begin{cases} 0; \ p_{l,x} < T \\ 1; \ p_{l,x} \geqslant T \end{cases} \tag{2}$$

where T is the threshold and is empirically selected as 0.35.

Above steps are conducted for all five lumbar vertebrae.

2.2 Bone-Sheetness Assisted Grid Cut

The initial segmentation obtained in the last step is usually not accurate enough as only affine atlas-target registrations are used. To further improve the segmentation accuracy, we proposed to use bone-sheetness assisted multi-label grid cut taking the initial segmentation as the shape prior.

Grid cut is a fast multi-core max-flow/min-cut solver optimized for grid-like graphs [6]. The task of multi-label grid cut is to assign an appropriate label $L(x)$ to every voxel x in the image space Ω of the target image I. In our case, labels $L(x) \in \{0,1,2,3,4,5\}$ are employed for the purpose of labeling the target image into six different regions including background region (BK, $L(x) = 0$), and the five lumbar vertebral regions (for the lth lumbar vertebra L_l, $L(x) = l$). After segmentation, the target image will be partitioned into 6 sub-image regions, i.e., $\Omega = \{\Omega_{BK} \cup \Omega_{l_1} \cup \Omega_{l_2} \cup \Omega_{l_3} \cup \Omega_{l_4} \cup \Omega_{l_5}\}$.

Grid cut, similar to graph cut, is an energy minimization segmentation framework based on combinatorial graph theory. The energy function of a multi-label grid cut $E(L)$ is defined as

$$E(L) = \sum_{x \in \Omega} R_x(L(x)) + \lambda \sum_{(x,y) \in \mathcal{N}} B_{x,y}(L(x), L(y)) \tag{3}$$

where $R_x(L(x))$ is the pixel-wised term which gives the cost of assigning label $L(x) \in \{0,1,2,3,4,5\}$ to voxel x, $B_{x,y}(L(x), L(y))$ is the pair-wised term which gives the cost of assigning labels to voxel x and y in a user-defined neighborhood system $\mathcal{N}$, and λ adjusts the balance between the pixel-wised term and pair-wised term.

In general, grid cut methods define the energy based on intensity information. However, weak bone boundaries, narrow inter-bone space, and low intensities in the trabecular bone make image intensity alone a relatively poor feature to discriminate adjacent joint structures. This can be addressed by applying image enhancement using sheetness filter to generate a new feature image (sheetness score map) [7]. For each voxel in the target image space Ω, a sheetness score BS is computed from the eigenvalues $|\lambda_1| \leq |\lambda_2| \leq |\lambda_3|$ of local Hessian matrix with scale σ as

$$BS_x(\sigma) = (\exp(\frac{-R_{sheet}^2}{2\alpha^2}))(1 - \exp(\frac{-R_{blob}^2}{2\gamma^2}))(1 - \exp(\frac{-R_{noise}^2}{2\xi^2})) \qquad (4)$$

where α, γ, ξ are the parameters [7]. $R_{sheet} = \frac{|\lambda_2|}{|\lambda_3|}$, $R_{blob} = \frac{|2\lambda_3 - \lambda_2 - \lambda_1|}{|\lambda_3|}$, $R_{noise} = \sqrt{\lambda_1^2 + \lambda_2^2 + \lambda_3^2}$.

For every pixel x, we have the computed sheetness score $BS_x \in [0, 1]$, where larger score associates with higher possibility that this pixel belongs to a bone region. With the computed sheetness score map and the initial segmentation, we define each term of the energy function as described below:

Pixel-Wised Term. Based on the initial segmentation obtained in the last step, the target image space Ω can be separated into 6 sub-image regions, i.e., $\Omega = \{\Omega'_{BK} \cup \Omega'_{l_1} \cup \Omega'_{l_2} \cup \Omega'_{l_3} \cup \Omega'_{l_4} \cup \Omega'_{l_5}\}$, where each sub-image region is obtained from the corresponding initial segmentation. By further employing the computed sheetness score map and the Hounsfield units (HU) of different tissues, the exclusion regions for each structure can be defined as

$$\begin{cases} E_{\neg L_1} = \{v \notin \Omega'_{L_1} \text{ and } \mathcal{I}(x) \leq -50\text{HU}\} \\ E_{\neg L_2} = \{v \notin \Omega'_{L_2} \text{ and } \mathcal{I}(x) \leq -50\text{HU}\} \\ E_{\neg L_3} = \{v \notin \Omega'_{L_3} \text{ and } \mathcal{I}(x) \leq -50\text{HU}\} \\ E_{\neg L_4} = \{v \notin \Omega'_{L_4} \text{ and } \mathcal{I}(x) \leq -50\text{HU}\} \\ E_{\neg L_5} = \{v \notin \Omega'_{L_5} \text{ and } \mathcal{I}(x) \leq -50\text{HU}\} \\ E_{\neg BK} = \{v \notin \Omega'_{BK} \text{ and } \mathcal{I}(x) \geq 200\text{HU} \ \wedge \ BS_v > 0\} \end{cases} \qquad (5)$$

where -50HU and 200HU are empirically selected. The $R_x(L(x))$ is then defined as

$$R_x(L(x)) = \begin{cases} 1 & \text{if } L(x) = 0 \text{ and } x \in E_{\neg BK} \\ 1 & \text{if } L(x) = 1 \text{ and } v \in E_{\neg L_1} \\ 1 & \text{if } L(x) = 2 \text{ and } v \in E_{\neg L_2} \\ 1 & \text{if } L(x) = 3 \text{ and } v \in E_{\neg L_3} \\ 1 & \text{if } L(x) = 4 \text{ and } v \in E_{\neg L_4} \\ 1 & \text{if } L(x) = 5 \text{ and } v \in E_{\neg L_5} \\ 0 & \text{otherwise} \end{cases} \qquad (6)$$

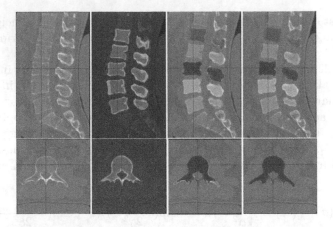

Fig. 2. A lumbar vertebrae segmentation example. Top row: saggital view. Bottow row: axial view. For both rows, from left to right: the input image, the probability map, the initial segmentation obtained from the label fusion step, and the final results.

Pair-Wised Term. As the sheetness filter enhances the bone boundaries, we employ the computed sheetness score map to define the pair-wised term:

$$B_{x,y}(L(x), L(y)) \propto \exp\{-\frac{|BS_x - BS_y|}{\sigma_s}\} \cdot \delta(L(x), L(y)) \qquad (7)$$

where σ_s is a constant scaling parameter and

$$\delta(L(x), L(y)) = \begin{cases} 1 & \text{if } L(x) \neq L(y) \\ 0 & \text{otherwise} \end{cases} \qquad (8)$$

3   Experimental Results

We evaluated our method on 21 clinical lumbar spinal CT data with the associated manual segmentation. In this paper, we conducted a standard leave-one-out (LOO) cross-validation study to evaluate the performance of the present method. In each time, the segmented results of the test data were compared with the associated ground truth manual segmentation. For each vertebra in a test CT data, we evaluate the Average Symmetric Surface Distance (ASSD), the Dice Coefficient (DC), precision and recall.

Table 1 presents the segmentation results of the cross validation study, where the results on each individual vertebra as well as on the entire lumbar region are presented. Our approach achieves a mean DC of $93.9 \pm 1.0\%$ and a mean ASSD of 0.41 ± 0.08 mm on the entire lumbar region. In each fold, it took about 12 min to finish segmentation of all five lumbar vertebrae of one test image. Figure 2 shows a segmentation example.

Table 1. Segmentation results of the leave-one-out cross validation on 21 clinical spinal CT data.

	DC (%)	ASSD (mm)	Precision (%)	Recall (%)
L1	94.2 ± 0.8	0.39 ± 0.06	91.9 ± 1.7	96.7 ± 1.6
L2	94.1 ± 0.8	0.39 ± 0.05	91.6 ± 1.9	96.7 ± 1.6
L3	93.8 ± 1.0	0.42 ± 0.07	91.0 ± 2.3	96.8 ± 1.7
L4	94.0 ± 0.9	0.40 ± 0.06	91.4 ± 2.0	96.9 ± 1.6
L5	93.7 ± 1.1	0.45 ± 0.11	91.2 ± 2.6	96.3 ± 2.1
Lumbar	93.9 ± 1.0	0.41 ± 0.08	91.4 ± 2.1	96.7 ± 1.8

4 Discussions and Conclusions

In conclusion, we proposed a method for automatic segmentation of lumbar vertebrae from clinical CT images. The results obtained from the LOO experiment demonstrated the efficacy of the proposed approach.

Acknowledgments. The work is supported by the Swiss National Science Foundation (Grant no. 205321_157207) and Beijing Natural Science Foundation (Grant no. Z170001).

References

1. Yao, J., Burns, J., Forsberg, D., et al.: A multi-center milestone study of clinical vertebral CT segmentation. Comput. Med. Imaging Graph. **49**, 16–28 (2016)
2. Chu, C., Belavy, D., et al.: Fully automatic localization and segmentation of 3d vertebral bodies from CT/MR images via a learning-based method. PLoS One **10**(11), e0143327 (2015)
3. Sekuboyina, A., Kukacka, J., Kirschke, J., Menze, B., Valentinitsch, A.: Attention-driven deep learning for pathological spine segmentation. In: Proceedings of the 2017 MICCAI-MSKI Workshop, pp. 104–115 (2017)
4. Damopoulos, D., Glocker, B., Zheng, G.: Automatic localization of the lumbar vertebral landmarks in CT images with context features. In: Proceedings of the 2017 MICCAI-MSKI Workshop, pp. 56–68 (2017)
5. Klein, S., Staring, M., Murphy, K., Viergever, M., Pluim, J.: Elastix: a toolbox for intensity-based medical image registration. IEEE Trans. Med. Imaging **29**(1), 196–205 (2010)
6. Jamriška, O., Sýkora, D., Hornung, A.: Cache-efficient graph cuts on structured grids. In: Proceedings of the CVPR 2012, pp. 3673–3680 (2012)
7. Descoteaux, M., Audette, M., Chinzei, K., Siddiqi, K.: Bone enhancement filtering: application to sinus bone segmentation and simulation of pituitary surgery. In: Proceedings of the MICCAI 2005, pp. 9–16 (2005)

Pixel-Based Leaf Segmentation from Natural Vineyard Images Using Color Model and Threshold Techniques

Carlos S. Pereira[1], R. Morais[2], and M. J. C. S. Reis[3(✉)]

[1] Instituto Politécnico do Porto, Escola Superior de Tecnologia e Gestão, Rua do Curral,
Casa do Curral–Margaride, 4610-156 Felgueiras, Portugal
cmp@estg.ipp.pt
[2] INESC TEC/UTAD, Quinta de Prados, 5001-801 Vila Real, Portugal
rmorais@utad.pt
[3] IEETA/UTAD, Quinta de Prados, 5001-801 Vila Real, Portugal
mcabral@utad.pt

Abstract. The presence in natural vineyard images of savage foliage, weed, multiple leaves with overlapping, occlusion, and obstruction by objects due to the shadows, dust, insects and other adverse climatic conditions that occur in natural environment at the moment of image capturing, turns leaf segmentation a challenging task. In this paper, we propose a segmentation algorithm based on region growing using color model and threshold techniques for classification of the pixels belonging to vine leaves from vineyard color images captured in real field environment. To assess the accuracy of the proposed vine leaf segmentation algorithm, a supervised evaluation method was employed, in which a segmented image is compared against a manually-segmented one. Concerning boundary-based measures of quality, an average accuracy of 94.8% over a 140 image dataset was achieved. It proves that the proposed method gives suitable results for an ongoing research work for automatic identification and characterization of different endogenous grape varieties of the Portuguese Douro Demarcated Region.

Keywords: Leaf segmentation · Natural vineyard images · Color model
Threshold techniques

1 Introduction and Related Work

Most of the proposed automatic detection and classification systems for agricultural products are primarily developed for robotic/automated harvesting purposes. An automated harvesting process is crucial to improve efficiency, productivity and cost reduction in the agricultural labor. Subsequently, a set of the daily farming tasks as grading, sorting, and fruit counting, plant disease early detection, varieties identification, crop yield prediction, pest damage, and spraying system optimization are likely developed by researchers with the main purpose of reducing the farmer's manual monitoring and visual decision-making procedures. Segmentation is one of the most important image

© Springer International Publishing AG, part of Springer Nature 2018
A. Campilho et al. (Eds.): ICIAR 2018, LNCS 10882, pp. 96–106, 2018.
https://doi.org/10.1007/978-3-319-93000-8_12

processing techniques, which divides an entire image into several parts which turns out to be more meaningful and easier for subsequent processing.

Visually, the plants are easily identified based on flowers and fruits (Harish et al. 2013). Gwo and Wei (2013) add that "plants may be recognized through the leaves, flowers, roots, and fruits, which reflect the diversity of plant shapes available within an organism. In particular, the shape of leaves is especially important with the leaves considered an especially useful characteristic for variety identification". Leaves carry a lot of information about the plant species, such as color, texture, vein structure and shape (Harish et al. 2013). Ideally, to extract these features it will be necessary to get an image of a unique and perfect leaf.

Scharr et al. (2015) highlight the problem of leaf segmentation versus leaf identification, and isolated leaf segmentation to be not similar. An accurate segmentation of each leaf in an image showing a whole plant is exceptionally complex, due to the lack of clearly discernible boundaries among overlapping leaves with typical imaging conditions. On the other hand, the leaf segmentation that uses several image datasets showing leaves isolated from plants, or showing leaves on the plant with a leaf appearing in an image with a large field of view, tends to decrease segmentation complexity and increase accuracy.

Whalley and Shanmuganathan (2013) focus on the challenging of applying image processing techniques over in-field and on-the-vine digital images. Given that grape berries occur in clusters, many of the berries can be occluded by other berries and by the leaves. One last reason pointed out by these researchers is the fact that vineyard management practices, such as vine training systems (firstly, aiming at controlling the volume of the foliage; secondly, to facilitate the mechanization process of many vineyards tasks) and pruning systems (to cut and remove selected parts of a grape vine) can also affect the quality of the images captured on natural vineyards. Yet, according to the authors, "the harvest can significantly vary from year to year and also within the vineyard due to soil conditions, disease, pests, climate and variation in vineyard management practices".

Reis et al. (2012) have developed a system for the detection and location of bunches of grapes in natural color images captured from the vineyards of the Portuguese Douro Demarcated Region. The proposed grape recognition system distinguishes the type of grape (red or white) and detect bunches represented by black areas. Based on the pixel distribution and density around the center of each detected black area, the bunch stem location is computed. From a dataset of 190 images containing bunches of white grapes, and 35 images of red grapes, the proposed visual inspection system is able to automatically distinguish between red and white grapes, and has achieved 97% and 91% of correct classifications, respectively.

Yanne et al. (2011) have proposed a grape variety identification method via leaf image processing. The identification method select a set of features based on the size and circumference of blade and Hu's 7 moment invariants, and build a software classifier based on the features extracted from digital images of the sample leaves. The classification algorithm was tested to classify 354 leaf images belonging to 20 varieties. A correct classification rate of 87% was obtained.

A classification system to automatically identify the existence of foliar diseases from digital images of cotton crops was developed by Bernardes et al. (2013). Feature vectors that represents five distinct classes (diagnostics) based on the energy of the Discrete Wavelet Transform from each sub-band obtained from the three-level decomposition of the original image was extracted. These feature vectors were used for training a Support Vector Machine classifier, reaching an overall average of correct guesses around 89.5%.

Vibhute and Bagalkote (2014) have developed an algorithm that gives the user the ability to identify the variety of grape plant species based on images of the plant's leaf taken by a camera. The proposed system acquires statistical features of the leaves, and then classifies the species based on a novel combination of the computed texture and color analysis, namely, four measures from the gray-level co-occurrence matrices: contrast, correlation, energy and homogeneity. Classification accuracy up to 87% is reached.

The leaf segmentation algorithm proposed here is part of an ongoing computer vision application, which started with a work of Pereira et al. (2017) that reviewed and categorized the newest literature on computer analysis of fruit images in agricultural operations gathered from natural environments. It involves five basic processes: image acquisition, pre-processing, segmentation, object detection and classification.

The proposed segmentation algorithm was developed using: (1) The pixel-based technique (categorized as similarity-based), in which pixels that are related to the bunches of grapes and the background are removed from the image, (2) The color model technique to classify pixels belonging to the bunches of grapes and the background of the image, and (3) The threshold technique to bound with pixel-based and color model techniques turning the detected leaf area a closed one and, therefore, the boundaries to be identified for segmentation.

The remaining of this paper is organized as follows. Section 2 describes the vineyard image dataset. Section 3 deals with the vine leaf segmentation algorithm on its different development phases. The assessment of the segmentation results against the manually segmented images is reported in Sect. 4. Finally, conclusions and ongoing work are presented in Sect. 5.

2 Image Dataset

The main Portuguese local grape varieties from *Vitis vinifera L.* growing in the Douro Demarcated Region (DDR) include red grapes *Touriga Nacional, Tinta Roriz, Touriga Franca, Tinto Cão* and *Tinta Barroca* as the prime dark-skinned grape varieties. *Tinta Amarela* has come later to be included among the varieties of the DDR. A sample for each grape variety used in this work is shown in Fig. 1.

Fig. 1. A sample of the six red grape varieties at the Douro Demarcated Region: (a) Touriga Nacional; (b)Tinta Roriz; (c) Touriga Franca; (d), Tinto Cão; (e) Tinta Barroca and (f) Tinta Amarela.

The DDR typical vineyards are characterized by having more than one caste per parcel and even per bard. As such, it would be very relevant the possibility to automatically identify the type of the grape variety (type of caste), for example, during the operation of an autonomous harvesting system.

The collection of images used in this work, which we called Douro Red Grape Varieties (DRGV), as stated above, was captured in the 2016 harvest season, August, during a full sunny day time with a CANON EOS 600D camera, with a resolution of 5184 × 3456 pixels and image aspect ratio of 3:2.

A set of 140 images was acquired in two vineyards at the DDR (Quinta da Pacheca and Quinta do Vale Abraão) subdivided into the six most significant castes, with an average of nearly 23 images per caste, as shown in Table 1.

Table 1. Distribution of the images per caste.

Caste	Number of images	Vineyard
Tinta Amarela	24	*Quinta da Pacheca*
Tinto Cão	25	
Tinta Barroca	23	*Quinta do Vale Abraão*
Touriga Franca	23	
Touriga Nacional	22	
Tinta Roriz	23	

3   Vine Leaf Segmentation System

The algorithm presented in this paper is intended to be used as the initial phase for classification of the most significant castes produced at the vineyards of the DDR in Portugal. The code was implemented in MatLab[TM] 9.3 (R2017b) platform.

Basically, the segmentation system comprises three distinct phases: pre-processing, segmentation and post-processing. The output of the algorithm comprises an image of the vine leaf region only, and it is crucial for the discriminative feature extraction process from the leaf texture, because vine leaves is one of the most important visual inspecting elements present on the vineyard and that best help the agriculturist to distinguish different castes. The three phases of the algorithm are detailed in the following subsections.

3.1   Pre-processing Phase

In the first step of the pre-processing phase, the image was resized to 640×960 pixels to significantly reduce the processing time of the algorithm and run with the low memory capacity of the computer available. To run our segmentation algorithm with these reduced resolution images on the computer installed with Windows 10 Home, Intel Core^{TM} processor i7-7500U at 2.70 GHz and 8 GB DDR4, it takes an average of 1.13 s per image, whereas using the original images with resolution of 3456×5184 pixels, it spends an average of 2.03 min per image, over the 140 images of the DRGV dataset.

In the second step of the pre-processing phase, the range of the histogram intensity values in each one of the three RGB channels of the previously resized image is automatically adjusted to increase the contrast of the image. At the end of this phase, the RGB to HSI color model conversion was processed for the original and their enhanced images, while the RGB to L*a*b* color model conversion was performed for the original image only. Figure 2 shows an original vineyard image and its enhanced image, the HSI and L*a*b* components from these two images and the original image, respectively.

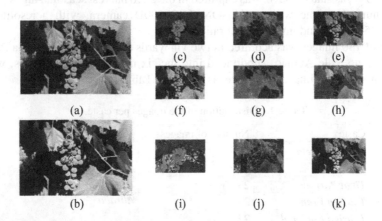

Fig. 2. Pre-processing phase: (a)–(b) Original vineyard image and its enhanced image; (c)–(e) H, S and I components from (a); (f)–(h) L*, a* and b* components from (a); (i)–(k) H, S and I components from (b).

3.2   Segmentation Phase

We begin the detection of shadowed regions in the RGB image using the luminance component (L*) of the CIELAB color model, as described in Murali and Govindan

(2013). A binary image is produced, setting to 0 (black) the pixels classified as shadow pixels, which have a luminance component value less or equal than the difference between the mean and one third of the standard deviation, computed over the luminance component of the image (Fig. 3b). The corresponding original image (Fig. 3a) over the shadowed region is shown in Fig. 3c.

(a)   (b)   (c)

Fig. 3. Shadow region detection: (a) Original image (b) Binary image of the detected shadow region (black pixels) (c) The non-shaded part of the color image.

The detected non-shadow and shadow regions are processed by our algorithm sequentially in the following order. Over the non-shadow region of the image, bunches of grapes are removed from the image. For that, a pixel is classified as grape, and set to 0 (black), if the blue channel value of the RGB image is greater than the summation of the red and green channel component values of that pixel. Next, a morphological opening is applied to the resulting binary image to remove all 8-connected components that have less than 30 pixels and a dilation operation with a square structuring element whose width is 5 × 5 pixels followed by a morphological reconstruction using a MatLab™ function "imfill" to fill in the holes on the resulting binary image (Fig. 4b). Next, all the remaining background of the image of the non-shadow region is removed. Here, the HSI color space applied to the original and enhanced RGB images is used to classify the pixel as a background pixel (or not). So, the threshold range values between 0.1402 and 0.6 obtained experimentally implying that a given pixel at the non-shadow region will be classified as a background pixel when its hue component value is outside the referred range of values. In this case, this pixel is set to 0 (black). Next, the sequence of morphological operations previously described for the detected bunches of grapes area on the non-shadow region was also applied to the detected background area, only replacing the number of pixels to 295 and the width of the square structuring element to 3 × 3 pixels for the opening and dilation operations, respectively (see Fig. 4c). An example of the output image is shown in Fig. 4d.

(a)   (b)   (c)   (d)

Fig. 4. Non-shadow region processing: (a) Original image; (b) Binary image with bunches of grapes; (c) Binary image with the background; (d) Resulting image, with non-shadow region.

In the next step, the shadow region is processed to remove bunches of grapes and the remaining background on this region. To remove bunches of grapes in the shadow region, the HSI color model conversion over the original and enhanced RGB images is computed. A pixel is set to black if the hue component value is between 0.45 and 0.85 in the enhanced HSI image, or the same range of values is applied to the hue component value in the original image, and simultaneously the a* component value is greater than 74 and the b* component value is less than 86 occurring in the CIELAB color model. An example of the output binary image is presented in Fig. 5b.

(a)   (b)   (c)   (d)

Fig. 5. Shadow region processing: (a) Original image; (b) Binary image with bunches of grapes; (c) Binary image with the background; (d) Resulting image, with shadow region.

In the next step, all the remaining background of the image in the shadow region is removed. As it was done with the non-shadow region, the HSI color model is applied to the original and enhanced RGB image to classify the pixel (set it to black) as a background pixel. The difference is in the boundaries over the hue component value. In this case, the lower and upper bounds, determined experimentally, are 0.145 and 0.575, respectively (see Fig. 5c). Yet, other morphological operations were also applied, namely, removing small objects using the MatLab^{TM} function "bwareaopen" and dilating the binary image using a square structuring element of 3×3 pixels, which result is depicted in the output image shown in Fig. 5d.

3.3 Post-processing Phase

In this phase, we are attempting to fill small holes that were not detected, and that typically are due to the presence of diseases, pests, sun burnings, insects, and dust on leaves, that generally displaying coloring reddish-brown blurs inside the leaves which resemble to the background of the image.

To try ensuring the segmentation of the entire leaf, every small hole, until a maximum area of 4,850 pixels, was selected. This value is related to the size of the image patches (64×64 pixels) that will be extracted automatically from the leaf segmented images and will be inputted in a future grape varieties classification. So, for each selected hole, a morphological dilation operation with a structuring element of shape "square" and two different sizes, 9 (3×3) and 100 (10×10) were used. To each structuring element, the mean of the hue intensity values from the enhanced HSI image inside the hole and the ring around it (computed as the difference between two regions: the output of the dilation operation and the hole itself) are computed. The hole is selected to be filled if the difference of the mean values of the two regions is nearly zero (we considered ± 0.067). An example of the detection of small holes inside one leaf is shown in Fig. 6a. The corresponding resulting image (with filling the detected small holes) is presented in Fig. 6b.

(a)   (b)

Fig. 6. Detection of the coloring reddish-brown of blurs inside the segmented leaves: (a) Detection of small holes inside a leaf; (b) Filling of the detected small holes.

4   Results and Discussion

The proposed segmentation algorithm was tested using every image in the DRGV dataset as an input image. Figure 7 shows a set of images of the six castes with the correspondent binary boundary segmented image produced by the algorithm.

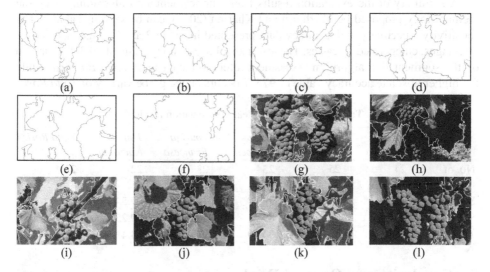

(a)   (b)   (c)   (d)

(e)   (f)   (g)   (h)

(i)   (j)   (k)   (l)

Fig. 7. Segmented images: (a)–(f) Boundary lines of the leaves; (g)–(l) Vine leaf segmented images from (a)–(f), respectively.

The testing/evaluation procedure of our segmentation algorithm is more adequate using the pixel-based measures, given its output scheme: final classification of the pixel as a leaf or not.

In order to easily collect manual segmentation from every image in the dataset, we have developed a simple MatLab™ application that allows the processing of free-hand drawing line segments on the images. The segmentation produced by this program comprises a set of continuous black pixels that divide an image into segments.

We have created a ground-truth image dataset for segmentation evaluation containing 140 binary segmented images grouped in six classes. An example of two binary ground-truth (Fig. 8c–d) and machine-segmented (Fig. 8e–f) images of the leaves from the segmented images (Fig. 8a–b) is presented in Fig. 8.

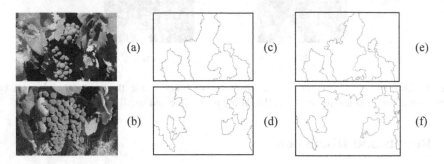

Fig. 8. Ground-truth versus machine-segmented images for algorithm assessment: (a)–(b) Original images; (c)–(d) Ground-truth images; (e)–(f) Machine-segmented images.

A summary of the evaluation results from our segmentation algorithm, using the methodology proposed be Mazhurin and Kharma (2013), can be seen in Table 2. The sensitivity, specificity and accuracy data presented in Table 2 are average values over all images, categorized by castes. The lower absolute accuracy value of 89.35% obtained on the segmentation algorithm assessment refers to the caste of *Tinta Barroca*, while the higher absolute accuracy value of 97.9% occurs on the grape variety of *Tinta Roriz*.

Table 2. Summary of leaf segmentation results.

	Tinta Amarela	*Tinto Cão*	*Tinta Barroca*	*Touriga Francesa*	*Touriga Nacional*	*Tinta Roriz*
No. of images	24	25	23	23	22	23
Sensitivity	99.55	99.51	99.57	99.53	99.54	99.67
Specificity	90.68	89.91	89.21	88.6	89.25	92.07
Accuracy	95.12	94.71	94.39	94.06	94.4	95.87

5   Conclusion and Ongoing Work

In this paper we propose an algorithm based on color and threshold techniques for vine leaf segmentation from real vineyard environment images. A high-resolution camera was used to take pictures of six different species of grapes. The images were pre-processed and after detecting and processing separately the non-shadow/shadow regions on the images, vine leaf homogeneous regions were extracted based on color and threshold techniques. At the post-processing phase, small holes inside the segmented leaf regions that were not detected due to the presence of diseases on leaves were filled.

A set of manually-segmented images was created to evaluate the quality of the proposed algorithm. An average accuracy of 94.8% over our 140 image dataset using pixel-based measures was obtained.

The main difficulty in our work was taking all the images in vineyards during daylight, subject to any kind of adverse climatic conditions that occur in natural environment. In opposition, the majority of the research works uses images of a unique and perfect leaf as the basis for the automatic classification of plant leaf into its belonging class using image processing techniques.

The proposed leaf segmentation algorithm is intended for an ongoing research work for automatic identification and characterization of six different grape varieties originated from the Portuguese Douro Demarcated Region. The classification stage will be applied on the previously segmented vine leaves. We expect that the good performance of the proposed segmentation algorithm will give suitable results for an efficient recognition of castes during the harvesting season at the Douro Region.

Acknowledgment. The Institute of Electronics and Informatics Engineering of Aveiro (IEETA) research unit is funded by National Funds through the FCT – Foundation for Science and Technology, in the context of the project UID/CEC/00127/2013.

References

Bernardes, A.A., Rogeri, J.G., Oliveira, R.B., Marranghello, N., Pereira, A.S., Araujo, A.F., Tavares, J.M.R.S.: Identification of foliar diseases in cotton crop. In: Tavares, J., Natal Jorge, R. (eds.) Topics in Medical Image Processing and Computational Vision. Lecture Notes in Computational Vision and Biomechanics, vol. 8, pp. 67–85. Springer, Dordrecht (2013). https://doi.org/10.1007/978-94-007-0726-9_4

Gwo, C., Wei, C.: Plant identification through images: using feature extraction of key points on leaf contours. Appl. Plant Sci. **1**, 11 (2013)

Harish, B., Hedge, A., Venkatesh, O., Spoorthy, D., Sushma, D.: Classification of plant leaves using morphological features and Zernike moments. In: IEEE International Conference on Advances in Computing, Communications and Informatics, pp. 827–1831 (2013)

Murali, S., Govindan, V.K.: Shadow detection and removal from a single image using LAB color space. Cybernet. Inf. Technol. **13**(1), 95–103 (2013)

Mazhurin, A., Kharma, N.: An image segmentation assessment tool ISAT 1.0. In: Proceedings of the International Conference on Computer Vision Theory and Applications, vol. 1, pp. 436–443 (2013)

Pereira, C.S., Morais, R., Reis, M.J.C.S.: Recent advances in image processing techniques for automated harvesting purposes: a review. In: Proceedings of the Intelligent Systems Conference 2017, pp. 566–575 (2017)

Reis, M.J.C.S., Morais, R., Peres, E., Pereira, C., Contente, O., Soares, S., Valente, A., Baptista, J., Ferreira, P.J.S.G., Bulas-Cruz, J.: Automatic detection of bunches of grapes in environment from color images. J. Appl. Logic **10**(4), 285–290 (2012)

Scharr, H., Minervini, M., French, A., Klukas, C., Kramer, D., Liu, X., Luengo, I., Pape, J., Polder, G., Vukadinovic, D., Yin, X., Tsaftaris, S.: Leaf segmentation in plant phenotyping: a collation study. Mach. Vis. Appl., 1–22 (2015)

Vibhute, A., Bagalkote, I.: Identification of grape variety plant species using image processing. Avishkar – Solapur Univ. Res. J. **3**, 45–51 (2014)

Whalley, J., Shanmuganathan, S.: Applications of image processing in viticulture: a review. In: 20th International Congress on Modelling and Simulation, pp. 531–537 (2013)

Yanne, P., Zhang, J., Li, H.: Automatic grape varieties identification by computer. Bulletin de l'Organisation Internationale de la Vigne et du Vin **84**, 5–14 (2011)

Handling Specularity in Intrinsic Image Decomposition

Siraj Muhammad[1](✉), Matthew N. Dailey[1], Imari Sato[2](✉),
and Muhammad F. Majeed[3](✉)

[1] Asian Institute of Technology (AIT), Khlong Luang, Thailand
{Siraj.Muhammad,mdailey}@ait.asia
[2] National Institute of Informatics (NII), Tokyo, Japan
imarik@nii.ac.jp
[3] Shaheed Benazir Bhutto University, Sheringal (SBBU Sheringal),
Sheringal, Pakistan
m.faran.majeed@ieee.org

Abstract. Intrinsic image decomposition (IID), the process of separating an image into reflectance and shading components, is one of the fundamental problems in computer vision. Various approaches for IID have been proposed, but most assume Lambertian surfaces. In this paper, we propose a method that handles specularity while decomposing an input image into reflectance and shading components. The method first removes specularities from the image, and then it decomposes the image into reflectance and shading components. We propose a new algorithm for reconstruction of an image's diffuse component and demonstrate the effectiveness of the method under specularity based on the extracted reflectance and shading images. Future work will focus on a more extensive empirical evaluation against ground truth and handling of shadows.

Keywords: Di-chromatic reflection model · Specularity · Reflectance
Shading · Intrinsic image decomposition

1 Introduction

In many computer vision applications, steps such as segmentation, object detection or recognition, three-dimensional modeling, and albedo and shading analysis are adversely affected by lighting conditions. In particular, specularity can disrupt a variety of different visual processing steps.

Intrinsic image decomposition (IID) is one such step that aims to decompose an image into reflectance, shading, and illumination components, simplifying the robustness of downstream processes. We find that, like other vision processes, IID algorithms are disrupted by the kinds of specularities seen in practical applications such as video surveillance. If IID is to be useful across a wide spectrum of practical applications, then we require methods that are robust to specularities. Therefore, in this paper, we develop a method for handling specularity prior to decomposing an image into reflectance and shading with IID.

© Springer International Publishing AG, part of Springer Nature 2018
A. Campilho et al. (Eds.): ICIAR 2018, LNCS 10882, pp. 107–115, 2018.
https://doi.org/10.1007/978-3-319-93000-8_13

Many algorithms for IID have been proposed. Land and McCann's classic retinex method [1] was among the first to decompose images into illumination and reflectance components and is used as a basic approach in many of today's methods. Rother et al. [2] address the problem of decoupling material-dependent properties (reflectance, albedo, and diffuse reflectance) and light-dependent properties (specular reflectance, shading, and inter-object reflection) from a single image using a prior on the reflectance component. Similarly, Barron et al. [3] decompose images into albedo and illumination components. Barron and Malik [4] recover shape, surface color, and illumination color from a single image. Laffont et al. [5] propose a method that decomposes an input image into intrinsic images from multiple view angles of a scene, without a priori knowledge of scene geometry. The method uses multi-view stereo to reconstruct a 3D point cloud. Although the cloud is sparse and incomplete, it provides the necessary information about illumination at each point. The authors optimize the point cloud and estimate sun visibility, i.e., decomposing illumination into sun, sky, and indirect illumination layers. Shi et al. [6] present an approach that decomposes input RGBD images into reflectance and shading images. The method assumes piecewise constant reflectance, allowing superpixel clustering of the reflectance image. Pixels lying in the same superpixel are assumed to have identical reflectance; any color variation is assumed to arise from shading. Kang et al. [7] perform IID on hyper-spectral images and extract features from the image set thus obtained. They use a method by Shen et al. [8] for the IID step.

Despite the richness of this literature, most IID methods assume Lambertian surfaces and diffuse lighting and are thus not robust under more adverse conditions, especially specular reflections common in practical applications with less-than-ideal illumination, such as video surveillance.

Therefore, in this paper, we propose to handle specularities while decomposing an image into reflectance and shading components. Our method comprises two steps. In the first step, we decompose the image into a specular component and a diffuse component with a new method that improves upon the state of the art. In the second step, the resulting image is decomposed into its specularity free reflectance and shading components. In the future we will add shadow handling and compare our pipeline with that of Fan et al [9]. We evaluate our method qualitatively by conducting experiments on synthetic and real images. The results show that our approach is successful at producing specularity-free reflectance and shading components. Our method may help computer vision applications such as object detection, segmentation, and tracking under adverse lighting conditions.

In the next section, we present the method in detail. In Sect. 3, we discuss our experimental setup and results, and in Sect. 4, we conclude and discuss future work.

2   Proposed Model

A schematic of our method is shown in Fig. 1. It consists of two components: specularity removal and IID. We describe each component separately in Sects. 2.1 and 2.2.

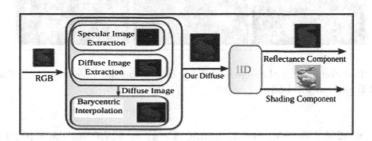

Fig. 1. Proposed model for specularity-aware intrinsic image decomposition (IID).

2.1   Specularity Removal

In the specularity removal component, we begin with the well-known dichromatic reflection model for image formation [10]. This model has been used in many researchers' work [11–14]. According to the dichromatic reflection model, the RGB color $V(p)$ of observed pixel with index p is the combination of diffuse and specular reflection

$$V(p) = \alpha(p)V_d(p) + \beta(p)V_s(p), \tag{1}$$

where $V_d(p)$ is the (unknown) underlying diffuse color value of pixel p, $V_s(p)$ is the (unknown) underlying specular color value of pixel p, and $\alpha(p)$ and $\beta(p)$ represent the (unknown) contributions of diffuse and specular reflection to the observed pixel p, respectively. We use row vectors to denote RGB intensities for a pixel.

Clearly, the problem of finding $\alpha(p)$, $V_d(p)$, $\beta(p)$, and $V_s(p)$ consistent with $V(p)$ is underconstrained. Our method extends that of H.L. Shen et al. [14]. First, following H.L. Shen et al., we categorize each pixel p as either diffuse or specular based on whether all three color components are above (specular) a threshold or not (diffuse). Next, let p be the diffuse pixel with the highest value of R, G, or B. Set $V_d(p) = V(p)$ and $V_s(p) = [0, 0, 0]$. After that, for each diffuse pixel q whose chromaticity (normalized RGB vector) is within a threshold distance of that of p, the method calculates $\alpha(q)$ and $\beta(q)$ as

$$\begin{bmatrix} \alpha(q) \\ \beta(q) \end{bmatrix} = \begin{bmatrix} V_d(p)^T & L^T \end{bmatrix}^+ V(q)^T, \tag{2}$$

Original	Diffuse [14]	Our Approach

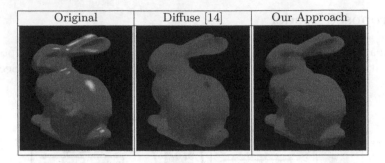

Fig. 2. Diffuse component of image with large bright specularities using H.L. Shen et al. method [14] and our method.

where $L = \begin{bmatrix} 255\ 255\ 255 \end{bmatrix}$. By assuming $V_d(q) = V_d(p)$ for each pixel q similar to p, we are left with two simple linear equations with one unknown each, allowing direct solution for $V_s(q)$. The process is repeated with another p not yet considered until every diffuse pixel is resolved.

In H.L. Shen et al.'s method, after each diffuse pixel q has been assigned values for $V_d(q)$ and $V_s(q)$, a similar procedure is applied to the specular pixels, assuming that the diffuse component for each specular pixel q is the same as the diffuse pixel p with the most similar chromaticity.

This method works well in some cases, but it does not work well in the case of large, bright specularities, which are common in real world situations. Bright specularity dominates the diffuse component of the light to the point that the original diffuse chromaticity cannot be recovered, and the assumption that the specular pixel's diffuse component should be same as that of the diffuse pixel with the most similar chromaticity introduces artifacts in the estimated diffuse image. An example is shown in Fig. 2.

To handle this issue and provide more accurate reconstruction of the diffuse component of the image under such conditions, we propose a simple interpolation method able to accurately reconstruct the diffuse component of bright specular regions. Our method uses barycentric interpolation of the RGB components of the diffuse image based on the boundary of the specular region, as determined in the first step. An example is shown in Fig. 2. Diffuse pixel value $V_d(q)$ for pixel q within a specular region is reconstructed as

$$V_d(q) = \sum_{j \in B(q)} [\omega_{jq} V_d(j)], \tag{3}$$

where $B(q)$ represents the set of pixels on the boundary of the specular region containing pixel q, $V_d(j)$ represents the RGB diffuse component of boundary pixel j, and ω_{jq} is a barycentric weight calculated as

$$\omega_{jq} = \frac{\exp\left(-\gamma \|j - q\|\right)}{\sum_{j \in B(q)} \exp\left(-\gamma \|j - q\|\right)}. \tag{4}$$

Here $||j - q||$ represents the spatial Euclidean distance between specular pixel q and boundary pixel j. $\gamma > 0$ is a normalization constant. Large values of γ give high relative weights to the closest boundary points, and lower values of γ give more uniform weights over boundary points. It would be possible to make γ adaptive to the size of the specular region in question, but we find that $\gamma = 0.25$ gives good weight distributions for most specular region size. We pass the diffuse component of the input image to the next step, intrinsic image decomposition.

2.2 Intrinsic Image Decomposition (IID)

After removing specularities, the next step is to decompose the image into reflectance and shading components. We use the well-known intrinsic image decomposition model of Rother et al. [2], which has been used by many other researchers [5,8,15,16]. We adopt their basic approach following Shen et al. [8], assuming that after specularity removal,

$$V_d(p) = L(p)R(p), \tag{5}$$

where $V_d(p)$ represents an input diffuse image pixel, $L(p)$ represents the diffuse illumination, and $R(p)$ represents the diffuse reflectance of pixel p. J. Shen et al. [8] assume that neighbor pixels having similar intensity will have similar reflectance, leading them to minimize the energy function

$$E(R, L) = \sum_p \left(R(p) - \sum_{q \in \mathcal{N}(p)} w_{pq} R(q) \right)^2 + \sum_p (V_d(p)/L(p) - R(p))^2, \tag{6}$$

where R is the reflectance image, L is the shading image, $\mathcal{N}(p)$ is a local neighborhood around pixel p (for example a 3×3 window), and w_{pq} is a weight indicating the similarity of pixels p and q:

$$w_{pq} = e^{-[\langle \widetilde{V}_d(p), \widetilde{V}_d(q) \rangle^2 / \rho_{pT}^2 + (Y(p) - Y(q))^2 / \rho_{pY}^2]}, \tag{7}$$

where $\langle \widetilde{V_d}(p), \widetilde{V_d}(q) \rangle$ is the cosine of the angle between normalized RGB vectors $\widetilde{V_d}(p)$ and $\widetilde{V_d}(q)$, and $Y(p)$ denotes the intensity or luminosity of pixel p in V. ρ_{pT}^2 and ρ_{pY}^2 represent the variance of the angles and intensities, respectively, around pixel p.

3 Empirical Evaluation

To evaluate the method described in the previous section, we use two datasets. First, we generated a new dataset in which well-known 3D models (monkey, bunny, and teapot) are rendered with specularity using the Blender software package. For purposes of quantitative analysis using Local Mean Squared Error (LMSE) [17], we also rendered corresponding ground-truth reflectance and shading images without specularity. Second, we use a dataset of images provided by H.L. Shen et al. [14]. No ground truth is available for these images, so the results can only be evaluated qualitatively. We performed two sets of experiments. In Experiment I, we ran dataset 1 through the pipeline of Fig. 1, and in Experiment II, we ran dataset 2 through the pipeline of Fig. 1. We report local mean square error and show qualitative results for the case (dataset 1) where we have ground truth, and we show qualitative results for dataset 2, where we have no ground truth.

3.1   Experiment I: Images with Specularity

As dataset 1 (consisting of synthetic images rendered by Blender) has ground truth, we compare the results of specularity removal and IID with the ground truth reflectance and shading components obtained from Blender. A quantitative comparison is shown in Fig. 3. The evaluation shows that our proposed framework produces better results than those of J. Shen et al. [8].

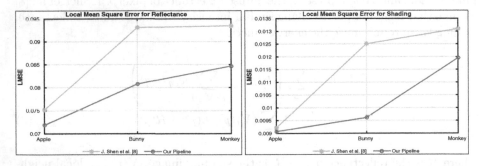

Fig. 3. Quantitative analysis of proposed framework using local mean squared error (LMSE)

Qualitative results are shown in Fig. 4. It can be seen that our proposed framework produces better specular-free reflectance and shading images than those provided by Shen et al. [8].

3.2   Experiment II: Specularity from [14]

This experiment uses images provided by Shen et al. [14]. Qualitative experimental results are shown in Fig. 4. By visual inspection, it is clear that our proposed model produces better specularity-free reflectance and shading images than produced by the method of Shen et al. [8].

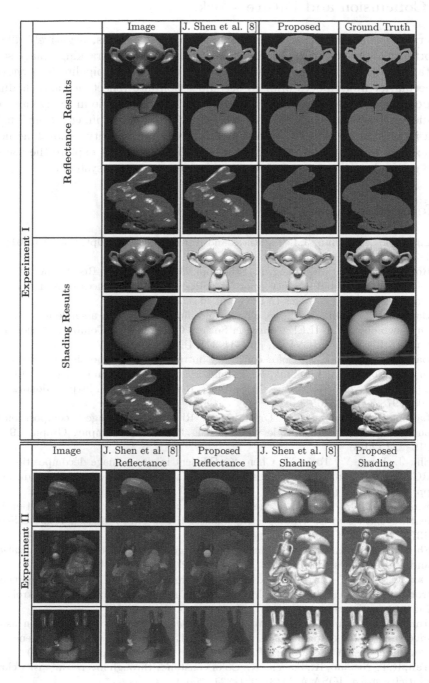

Fig. 4. Experiment I & II results. Proposed method produces reflectance images closer to the ground truth than the original J. Shen et al. method.

4   Conclusion and Future Work

Adverse lighting conditions, particularly specular reflections, negatively affect important computer vision tasks such as feature detection, tracking, image segmentation, and object detection. In this paper, we propose a pipeline for removal of specularity from images prior to decomposition into reflectance and shading components. We find that the proposed framework is capable in many cases of producing accurate specularity-free reflectance and shading images from single input images. In future work, we plan to improve the specularity removal method and extend our pipeline to handle shadows. Finally, we will explore the use of these methods in the context of real-world video processing systems.

References

1. Land, E.H., McCann, J.J.: Lightness and retinex theory. J. Opt. Soc. Am. **61**(1), 1–11 (1971)
2. Rother, C., Kiefel, M., Zhang, L., Schölkopf, B., Gehler, P.V.: Recovering intrinsic images with a global sparsity prior on reflectance. In: Advances in Neural Information Processing Systems (NIPS), pp. 765–773 (2011)
3. Barron, J.T., Malik, J.: Shape, albedo, and illumination from a single image of an unknown object. In: IEEE Computer Society Conference on Computer Vision and Pattern Recognition (CVPR), pp. 334–341. IEEE (2012)
4. Barron, J.T., Malik, J.: Color constancy, intrinsic images, and shape estimation. In: Fitzgibbon, A., Lazebnik, S., Perona, P., Sato, Y., Schmid, C. (eds.) ECCV 2012. LNCS, vol. 7575, pp. 57–70. Springer, Heidelberg (2012). https://doi.org/10.1007/978-3-642-33765-9_5
5. Laffont, P.Y., Bousseau, A., Drettakis, G.: Rich intrinsic image decomposition of outdoor scenes from multiple views. IEEE Trans. Vis. Comput. Graph. **19**(2), 210–224 (2013)
6. Shi, J., Dong, Y., Tong, X., Chen, Y.: Efficient intrinsic image decomposition for RGBD images. In: ACM Symposium on Virtual Reality Software and Technology, pp. 17–25. ACM (2015)
7. Kang, X., Li, S., Fang, L., Benediktsson, J.A.: Intrinsic image decomposition for feature extraction of hyperspectral images. IEEE Trans. Geosci. Remote Sens. **53**(4), 2241–2253 (2015)
8. Shen, J., Yang, X., Li, X., Jia, Y.: Intrinsic image decomposition using optimization and user scribbles. IEEE Trans. Cybern. **43**(2), 425–436 (2013)
9. Fan, C., Zhu, H., Lin, G., Cao, L.: Deriving reflectance and shading components from a single image. In: Fourth International Conference on Intelligent Control and Information Processing (ICICIP), pp. 139–143. IEEE (2013)
10. Tan, R.T., Nishino, K., Ikeuchi, K.: Illumination chromaticity estimation using inverse-intensity chromaticity space. In: IEEE Computer Society Conference on Computer Vision and Pattern Recognition (CVPR), vol. 1, p. I-673 (2003)
11. Tan, R.T., Nishino, K., Ikeuchi, K.: Color constancy through inverse-intensity chromaticity space. JOSA A **21**(3), 321–334 (2004)
12. Tan, R.T., Ikeuchi, K.: Separating reflection components of textured surfaces using a single image. IEEE Trans. Pattern Anal. Mach. Intell. **27**(2), 178–193 (2005)

13. Mallick, S.P., Zickler, T., Belhumeur, P., Kriegman, D.: Dichromatic separation: specularity removal and editing. In: ACM SIGGRAPH 2006 Sketches, p. 166. ACM (2006)
14. Shen, H.L., Zhang, H.G., Shao, S.J., Xin, J.H.: Chromaticity-based separation of reflection components in a single image. Pattern Recognit. **41**(8), 2461–2469 (2008)
15. Carroll, R., Ramamoorthi, R., Agrawala, M.: Illumination decomposition for material recoloring with consistent interreflections. ACM Trans. Graph. **30**(4), 43 (2011)
16. Chen, Q., Koltun, V.: A simple model for intrinsic image decomposition with depth cues. In: Proceedings of the IEEE International Conference on Computer Vision, pp. 241–248 (2013)
17. Grosse, R., Johnson, M.K., Adelson, E.H., Freeman, W.T.: Ground truth dataset and baseline evaluations for intrinsic image algorithms. In: IEEE International Conference on Computer Vision (ICCV), pp. 2335–2342. IEEE (2009)

An Improvement on GrabCut with CLAHE for the Segmentation of the Objects with Ambiguous Boundaries

Murat Aykut$^{(\boxtimes)}$ ⓘ and Saffet Murat Akturk

Karadeniz Technical University, 61080 Trabzon, Turkey
murat_aykut@ktu.edu.tr

Abstract. Interactive image segmentation scheme provides an opportunity to select/mark initial region(s) of the target object(s) with user interactions. In this way, the foreground objects are segmented easily and successfully from the scenes which have cluttered backgrounds and multiple objects. GrabCut technique that utilize graph theory, Gaussian Mixture Model and iterative energy minimization can be considered in this context. This study concentrate on the weakness that occur on the low-contrast images. Using a contrast enhancement technique as a preprocessing step in GrabCut is proposed to improve the segmentation performance. CLAHE, which is a successful adaptive contrast enhancement method is used with RGB color channels in this work. Experimental results show that the proposed approach gives much better results (4% accuracy improvement) than the original GrabCut method on the images sampled from the Caltech 256 image dataset.

Keywords: GrabCut · Interactive image segmentation · Low-contrast images
CLAHE

1 Introduction

Interactive image segmentation, which uses prior knowledge by interacting with the users, is preferred in many applications due to its superior performance [1]. In this approach the users mark some regions belong to foreground and background and initialize the method with them. The most used interactive segmentation methods are GraphCut [2] and its variants (especially GrabCut).

The GraphCut method considers the image as a graph and utilize the mathematical operations and algorithms developed for graph theory. It equalizes the boundary and region features on all segments [2]. Many studies have been focused on the GraphCut and new methods have been developed. For example: Adding some other information to the energy functions [3, 4]; using region and boundary information together [5]. Among these methods the most interested one is the GrabCut method [1].

GrabCut method has improved the optimization of the GraphCut method, converted it to an iterative procedure and used the "border matting" to enhance the boundary

© Springer International Publishing AG, part of Springer Nature 2018
A. Campilho et al. (Eds.): ICIAR 2018, LNCS 10882, pp. 116–122, 2018.
https://doi.org/10.1007/978-3-319-93000-8_14

segmentation performance. It also ask for users to select a rectangular region only, as an initial interaction.

In recent years some works have been implemented to improve the performance of the original GrabCut segmentation method. In [6], the depth information is also used on the energy function. Similarly, in [7] the texture information is used additionally. Khattab et al. [8] enhance the method to give the ability to find more than two objects and reduce the user interaction. In [9], the authors proposed to use the saliency map.

GrabCut is a segmentation method based on iterative energy minimization that use the probability model for color distributions of pixels. Hence, unexpected results may occur when the boundaries between the foreground and background have low contrast. To resolve this problem, the energy function of the method is reformulated in [10].

In this work we propose to use contrast enhancement methods as a preprocessing step for the GrabCut method. Thus, we aim to improve the original GrabCut method's segmentation performance. From the contrast enhancement methods, Contrast Limited Adaptive Histogram Equalization (CLAHE) method [11] has been chosen and used for this study, because it operates on local regions and it is robust to noisy images. In the literature there are two works in which CLAHE and GrabCut methods have been used [12, 13]. On the other hand these works are application-specific and there are some other steps between CLAHE and GrabCut (in [12] CLAHE + brightness preserving dynamic fuzzy histogram + CLAHE + morphological operations + Gabor wavelets + GrabCut; in [13] preprocessing + CLAHE + thresholding and morphological operations + GrabCut have been proposed). Furthermore, they did not applied the CLAHE on all of the RGB channels (e.g. in [13] on the grey-level of the image only).

2   Methodology

2.1   GrabCut Method

GrabCut [1] is one of the best known GraphCut-based methods in the literature. Rother et al. proposed to use color information with GMM; minimize the energy function iteratively; and use incomplete trimaps, additionally. Basic steps of the method are:

Step 1. Initialize the trimap T which consists of known background T_B, unknown T_U and foreground T_F regions, by drawing a rectangle on the image. Outside of the rectangle is determined as T_B and the complement of it as T_U. The initial T_F is empty.
Step 2. Perform initial segmentation $\alpha = (\alpha_1, ..., \alpha_i, ..., \alpha_N)$:

$$\alpha_i = 0, \, for \, i \in T_B; \, \alpha_i = 1, \, for \, i \in T_U \tag{1}$$

Step 3. Initialize two Gaussian Mixture Model (GMM), (one for background and other for foreground) with the previously obtained α segmentation.
Step 4. For each pixel in the unknown trimap T_U, find the most appropriate Gaussian components from the background and foreground GMMs, separately.

$$k_i = arg \, min \, k_i D_i(\alpha_i, \, k_i, \, \theta, \, z_i) \tag{2}$$

where $k_i \in \{1,...,K\}$ is an additional parameter assigned to each pixel to define the most likely GMM component of a pixel, K is the number of GMM components, and D_i is the data term of the Gibbs energy function. The D_i can be calculated by:

$$D\left(\alpha_i, k_i, \theta, z_i\right) = - \log \pi\left(\alpha_i, k_i\right) + 0.5 \log \det \Sigma\left(\alpha_i, k_i\right)$$
$$+ 0.5\left[z_i - \mu\left(\alpha_i, k_i\right)\right]^T \Sigma\left(\alpha_i, k_i\right) \left[z_i - \mu\left(\alpha_i, k_i\right)\right] \tag{3}$$

where $\pi(.)$ is the mixture weighting coefficient, μ is the mean vector, Σ is the covariance matrix and z_i is the intensity value of a pixel.

Step 5. Update the GMM parameters from the data previously clustered.

$$\theta = \arg\min_\theta \Sigma_i\left[D\left(\alpha_i, k_i, \theta, z_i\right)\right] \tag{4}$$

Step 6. To find the new clustering of the pixels perform the min cut algorithm as [1].

$$\min_{\{\alpha i : i \epsilon Tu\}} \min_k E(\alpha, k, \theta, z) \tag{5}$$

where Gibbs Energy function can be derived by the formula:

$$E(\alpha, k, \theta, z) = \Sigma_i\left[D\left(\alpha_i, k_i, \theta, z_i\right)\right] + V(\alpha, z) \tag{6}$$

$$V(\alpha, z) = \gamma \sum_{(i,j) \epsilon C} [\alpha_i \neq \alpha_j] \exp\left(-\beta\left\|z_i - z_j\right\|^2\right) \tag{7}$$

where V is the smoothness term of the energy function, C is a set of neighboring pixels, γ is the smoothness coefficient, β is a constant.

Step 7. Repeat steps 4–6 until the energy function converges to the predefined value.

In this work, we only use the hard segmentation process described above. The number of the Gaussian components, β constant, and the smoothness coefficient γ are determined empirically as 5, 5 and 50, respectively.

2.2   The Proposed Method

The original GrabCut method gives poor results for some images (especially for the images with low contrast object boundaries). To get rid of this weakness, Khattab et al. [10] proposed to reformulate the energy function of the method. On the contrary, we have not changed the original method, and proposed to use a contrast enhancement method before the original method as a preprocessing step.

In this work the Contrast Limited Adaptive Histogram Equalization (CLAHE) method is preferred for the contrast enhancement task due to these reasons: (1) it enhance the contrast of the local regions, which provides more information; (2) it is not greatly affected by the image noise because of the contrast limitation.

CLAHE Method

The CLAHE method is proposed by Pizer et al. in [11]. Main steps of the CLAHE can be summarized as follows:

Step 1. Divide the image into non-overlapping local regions (grids). Minimum size of the grid should be 32 × 32. And calculate the histogram for all grids, separately.

Step 2. Clip the histogram to avoid being affected by the noise. If the number of pixels for any intensity value is greater than a predetermined threshold value, it should be fixed to that threshold. In this case, to equalize the total number of pixels, the clipped number of pixels are distributed to the histogram uniformly.

Step 3. Perform the histogram equalization on the histograms obtained in step 2. Combine the neighboring grids and use the bilinear interpolation to eliminate the boundary artifacts. For the pixels in the center of the grids use interpolation of the four neighboring pixels. Although, the original method is developed for the gray level images, it has been used for color images with different schemes. In this work we use the "CLAHE on RGB model" described in [14].

3 Experiments and Results

3.1 Data Set

To evaluate the performance of the proposed approach we began with constituting a data set. The images are selected from the Caltech 256 images dataset [15] according to the following criteria: (1) do not select the images that have uniform backgrounds; (2) maximally select one image per object category; (3) select images which have cluttered backgrounds and complex shaped objects. Although most of the studies performed the experiments on 25 images, 40 images are chosen for this work.

3.2 Experimental Results

The performance of the proposed method has been evaluated visually and quantitatively with the segmentation results of the images on the constituted data set. Six well known performance metrics were used in the experiments for quantitative evaluation: Accuracy, Dice Coefficient, Jaccard Index, Precision, Sensitivity, and Specificity. In the experiments the region that is marked as known background is not taken into account, because there is no possibility to segment erroneously. Table 1. shows the average values of the quality metrics, for the proposed method compared to original method.

It is clear from Table 1. that the proposed method achieved better results than the original GrabCut method for all the metrics. There is approximately 4% improvement with the proposed method.

To interpret the results much better, all the segmentation results of the images for both methods were analyzed visually. Figure 1 shows some images from the data set and their segmentation results in a comparative manner.

Table 1. Quantitative results of the proposed and original GrabCut methods on the image set.

Performance metric	Segmentation method	
	GrabCut	Proposed
Accuracy	0.9208	**0.9580**
Dice coefficient	0.9012	**0.9557**
Jaccard Index	0.8422	**0.9117**
Precision	0.8849	**0.9564**
Sensitivity	0.9149	**0.9511**
Specificity	0.9292	**0.9698**

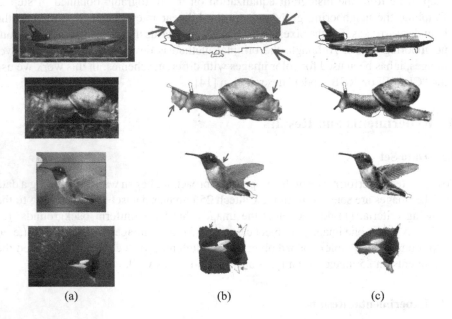

(a)   (b)   (c)

Fig. 1. Sample images and segmentation results for various scenarios. (a) Original image and initial bounding box; b, (c) Segmentation results of the GrabCut and the proposed method.

In the first two lines sample images which have low contrast are given. For these images, the proposed method gives better results noticeably. In the first image, although a part of the sky is included in the foreground; the bottom casing of the airplane and the logo of the airline company are not included in the foreground with the GrabCut method. In the second image, the snail is not successfully separated from the background with the original method. Third image contains a humming bird which flaps its wings at high frequency that results with some uncertainties on the boundaries. The proposed method also overcome this problem by enhancing the contrast in a local manner. Another scene is underexposed images taken under the sea. These images have low contrast and high noise as shown in the last line. Although the original GrabCut method gives weak performance, the proposed method provides sufficiently good results.

For the other schemes which are not visually shown above, both methods give very similar segmentation results.

4   Discussion

In this paper, an improvement to the GrabCut method is proposed to deal with the segmentation difficulties occurred when the images have low-contrast regions. The improvement has been done by using a contrast enhancement method (CLAHE on RGB colour bands) before the GrabCut method as a preprocessing step. The performance tests have been achieved on a data set consists of 40 images. According to the obtained results it is evident that the proposed method is superior to the original GrabCut method, especially for the low-contrast images. It has no drawbacks for the other images.

For the future work, the effect of the other contrast enhancement and image preprocessing techniques to the original GrabCut method might be studied.

References

1. Rother, C., Kolmogorov, V., Blake, A.: "GrabCut": interactive foreground extraction using iterated graph cuts. ACM Trans. Graph. **23**, 309–314 (2004)
2. Boykov, Y., Jolly, M.P.: Interactive graph cuts for optimal boundary and region segmentation of objects in N-D images. In: International Conference on Computer Vision, pp. 105–112. IEEE Press, Vancouver (2001)
3. Shan, J., Tu, J., Lu, X., Yao, J., Li, L.: Optimal seamline detection for multiple image mosaicking via graph cuts. ISPRS J. Photogramm. Remote Sens. **113**, 1–16 (2016)
4. Najjar, A., Gamra, S.B., Zagrouba, E.: Model-based graph-cut method for automatic flower segmentation with spatial constraints. Image Vis. Comput. **32**, 1007–1020 (2014)
5. Han, S., Chen, Q., Sun, Q., Ji, Z., Wang, T.: Image segmentation based on weighting boundary information via graph cut. J. Vis. Commun. Image Represent. **33**, 10–19 (2015)
6. Vaiapury, K., Aksay, A., Izquierdo, E.: GrabcutD: improved GrabCut using depth information. In: ACM International Conference on Multimedia, pp. 57–62. ACM Press, Firenze (2010)
7. Han, S., Tao, W., Wang, D., Tai, X.C., Wu, X.: Image segmentation based on GrabCut framework integrating multiscale nonlinear structure tensor. IEEE Trans. Image Process. **18**, 2289–2302 (2009)
8. Khattab, D., Ebied, H.M., Hussein, A.S., Tolba, M.F.: Multi-label automatic GrabCut for image segmentation. In: 14th International Conference on Hybrid Intelligent Systems, pp. 152–157. IEEE Press, Kuwait (2014)
9. Kim, K.S., Yoon, Y.J., Kang, M.C., Sun, J.Y., Ko, S.J.: An improved GrabCut using a saliency map. In: 3rd Global Conference on Consumer Electronics, pp. 317–318. IEEE, Tokyo (2014)
10. Khattab, D., Theobalt, C., Hussein, S.A., Tolba, F.M.: Modified GrabCut for human face segmentation. Ain Shams Eng. J. **5**, 1083–1091 (2014)
11. Pizer, S.M., Amburn, E.P., Austin, J.D., Cromartie, R., Geselowitz, A., Greer, T., Romeny, B.H., Zimmerman, J.B., Zuiderveld, K.: Adaptive histogram equalization and its variations. Comput. Vis. Graph. Image Process. **39**, 335–368 (1987)

12. Gutierrez, J.E., Barrena, J.T., Aroca, P.R., Valls, A., Puig, D.: Interactive optic disk segmentation via discrete convexity shape knowledge using high-order functionals. In: International Conference of the Catalan Association for Artificial Intelligence, pp. 39–44. UPC, Barcelona (2016)
13. Okuboyejo, DA., Olugbara, OO., Odunaike, SA.: CLAHE inspired segmentation of dermoscopic images using mixture of methods. In: World Congress on Engineering and Computer Science (WCECS), pp. 355–365. IAENG Press, San Francisco (2013)
14. Hitam, M.S., Awalludin, E.A., Yussof, W.N., Bachok, Z.: Mixture contrast limited adaptive histogram equalization for underwater image enhancement. In: International Conference on Computer Applications Technology (ICCAT), pp. 1–5. IEEE Press, Sousse (2013)
15. Griffin, G., Holub, A., Perona, P.: The Caltech-256 Object Category Dataset. Technical report, Caltech (2017)

Detection, Classification and Recognition

A Computational Model of Multi-scale Spatiotemporal Attention in Video Data

Roman Palenichka[1(✉)], Rafael Falcon[1,2], Rami Abielmona[1,2],
and Emil Petriu[1]

[1] University of Ottawa, Ottawa, Canada
rpalenyc@uottawa.ca
[2] Larus Technologies, Ottawa, Canada

Abstract. This paper describes a spatiotemporal saliency-based attention model in applications for the rapid and robust detection of objects of interest in video data. It is based on the analysis of feature-point areas, which correspond to the object-relevant focus-of-attention (FoA) points extracted by the proposed multi-scale spatiotemporal operator. The operator design is inspired by three cognitive properties of the human visual system: detection of spatial saliency, perceptual feature grouping, and motion detection. The model includes attentive learning mechanisms for object representation in the form of feature-point descriptor sets. The preliminary test results of attention focusing for the detection of feature-point areas have confirmed the advantage of the proposed computational model in terms of its robustness and localization accuracy over similar existing detectors.

Keywords: Spatiotemporal attention · Video data · Attention operator
Local scale · Object detection · Spatial saliency · Property coherence
Temporal change

1 Introduction

The study of biologically-inspired vision systems can be considered as a two-way street. On the one hand, biological systems can provide a source of inspiration for new computationally-efficient and robust models while, on the other hand, computer vision approaches reveal new insights for understanding biological sensing systems such as the Human Visual System (HVS) [1]. This paper is dedicated to a saliency-based multi-scale spatiotemporal attention in video data mostly for computer vision objectives. We consider applications for object detection in video data of dynamic scenes, which usually proceeds by initially extracting some object-relevant spatiotemporal features [2]. Their extraction is based on the detection of spatiotemporal attention points. The bio-inspired approach has certain advantages over the conventional methods using the object-background segmentation, because video segmentation of dynamic scenes is a computationally complex and error-prone process [3, 4].

Most of the existing computational attention models deal with still images [5–8] and few actually tackle video data. One of such spatiotemporal detector models was proposed in [9] as a generalization of the spatial saliency-based attention [6]. This method was

© Springer International Publishing AG, part of Springer Nature 2018
A. Campilho et al. (Eds.): ICIAR 2018, LNCS 10882, pp. 125–135, 2018.
https://doi.org/10.1007/978-3-319-93000-8_15

further extended to detect objects in dynamic scenes by capitalizing on coherent motion characteristics in video frames [10]. Another general spatiotemporal attention model was described in [11]. A spatiotemporal isotropic attention (STIA) operator was proposed to detect attention points, which explicitly combines spatial saliency and temporal change [12]. It is a multi-scale area-based operator, in which the spatial saliency is defined as the area isotropic spatial contrast relative to the homogeneity of an image area.

An entire class of attention models is represented by detectors of spatiotemporal feature (interest) points in video data. Detection of feature points is based on various local image properties such as area saliency, temporal change, motion, shape, local area homogeneity, etc. [13]. The feature point extraction is a computationally simpler and more reliable procedure than the spatiotemporal image segmentation. The first spatiotemporal feature-point detector, called the Harris 3D detector, was proposed in [14] as a space-time extension of the Harris detector [15]. It is based on the computation of a spatiotemporal second-moment matrix at each video point using scale selection, Gaussian smoothing functions, and space-time gradients. Another detector of feature points is the generalization of the Laplacian-of-Gaussian (LoG) operator to the space-time domain with the selection of spatial and temporal scales [16]. The Hessian detector was proposed in [17] as a spatiotemporal version of the Hessian saliency measure used in [18] for blob detection in images. The Cuboid detector of feature points is mostly based on the spatiotemporal Gabor filters [19].

The main drawback of the abovementioned detectors is that simple extensions of spatial detectors to the temporal domain, through the introduction of the time variable, will result in poor detection of still and moving objects at the same time. Another weakness of the existing models is their inability to computationally represent the perceptional grouping of local low-level features to avoid getting distracted by irrelevant low-level features. This is an important element of the so-called *gestalt* model for the HVS's attention focusing [20]. Neural networks and the Deep Learning models are biologically inspired approaches too that can be utilized for feature extraction and object detection [21, 22]. They are not considered in our current study as they do not provide attention focusing mechanisms.

The computational model of visual attention proposed in this paper is primarily aimed at eliminating or diminishing shortcomings of the existing models in computer vision applications. It is achieved through the introduction of a new spatiotemporal attention operator, which combines basic cognitive hypothesises of the HVS such as the multi-scale attention through spatial saliency, temporal change detection and perceptual feature grouping. Another contribution is the tuneable attention operator via machine learning algorithms to make it relevant to the objects of interest. In the literature, except for the deep learning approach, no attention focusing models related to learning processes are considered.

The rest of this paper is concentrated on the extraction of spatiotemporal attention points based on the proposed computational model. Section 2 gives an overview of the adopted approach in the context of object detection tasks. The cornerstone of the model is our proposed spatiotemporal attention operator (Sect. 3). The model's application capability for object detection is shortly discussed in Sect. 4 since the detailed handling is out of scope of the current paper. The experimental results (Sect. 5) and the algorithm's advantageous characteristics (Sect. 6) for the attention-point detection confirm the viability of this approach.

2 Spatiotemporal Visual Attention

The computational model of spatiotemporal visual attention consists in attention-guided image sequence analysis by first extracting multi-scale spatiotemporal attention regions called feature-point areas (FPAs) and sequentially analyzing in detail the neighborhoods of the FPAs for object detection and classification. The attention-point area, which is currently analyzed in detail, is called the focus-of-attention (FoA) area. The FoA points are determined by the local maxima locations of the proposed multi-scale spatiotemporal attention operator. It considers three spatiotemporal image area characteristics for the determination of FPAs: spatial saliency, area properties' coherence (e.g., area homogeneity by an image local property) and temporal change (e.g., motion).

The flowchart of the proposed computational model is shown in Fig. 1. In the latter, all the attention points are first determined at a single spatiotemporal resolution of the video data. Initially, some simple image properties are time-efficiently extracted in a dense mode, i.e., pixel-by-pixel. The current FoA point is determined as the new local maximum of the attention operator excluding previously analyzed FoA-point areas. Object detection, tracking and classification is based on spatiotemporal descriptor sets estimated in the corresponding FPAs. No image pre-segmentation into object and background regions is required. Figure 1 describes a single-stage spatiotemporal attention model for multi-scale image analysis; however, a multi-stage hierarchical computational model is a straightforward generalization [2]. During the first stage, attention focusing at a single largest scale or narrow scale range is performed, while in subsequent stages, the FoA areas are analyzed at lower scale ranges (or higher image resolutions) by the same computational model in Fig. 1.

The proposed model is a multi-scale approach to image sequence analysis, which involves the concept of local spatial scale [12]. It is the diameter of a circular area, which is homogeneous according to one or more image properties. A local temporal scale can also be introduced in the video data analysis similarly to the definition proposed in [23]. It characterizes how fast the temporal change or motion occurs at a given location and for the determined local spatial scale. The model in Fig. 1 includes a machine learning stage powered by the attentive learning mechanisms. The goal is to effectively store objects' spatiotemporal descriptors in the form of reference sets of video descriptors to perform matching of descriptor sets. Another objective of the attentive learning is to automatically tune the parameter values of the computational attention model such as the saliency coefficients in the attention operator (Sect. 3). The attentive machine learning uses FPA extraction to obtain reference sets of FPA descriptors from the training samples of short-duration videos as the centers of descriptor-set clusters [24].

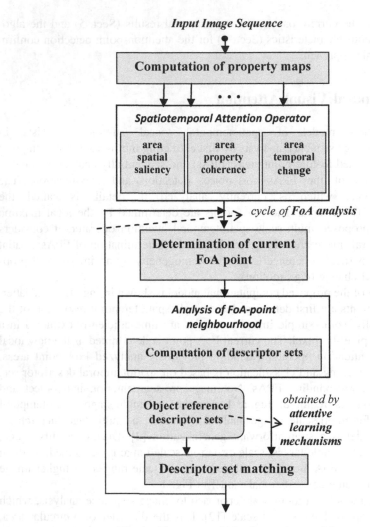

Fig. 1. The proposed visual attention model.

3 Multicomponent Spatiotemporal Attention Operator

The cornerstone of the proposed model is the multi-scale spatiotemporal attention operator designed to fulfil the extraction of attention points in *spatiotemporally salient* (i.e., detectable), *locally unique* (i.e., unambiguous), and *object-relevant* (i.e., object-positioning) locations of video data. To achieve that, the operator is applied to multiple components of the input video data and contains three response factors for each component: spatial saliency, temporal change, and area homogeneity as a measure of coherence. The proposed multi-scale spatiotemporal attention operator $F[\{g(i, j,t)\}, \rho]$ as applied to the intensity image sequence $\{g(i,j,t)\}$ is composed of three terms, which are aggregated into a single attention function of pixel coordinates (i,j), time t, and scale ρ,

$$F[i,j,t,\rho] = c(i,j,t,\rho) + \alpha \cdot e(i,j,t,\rho) - \gamma \cdot h(i,j,t,\rho), \tag{1}$$

where $c(i,j,t,\rho)$ is the area spatial saliency, $e(i,j,t,\rho)$ is the area temporal change, $h(i,j,t,\rho)$ is the area inhomogeneity measure, and $\alpha > 0$ and $\gamma > 0$ are the change and coherence coefficients, respectively. The values of α and γ can be determined by the maximum likelihood rule using a representative training sample of FoA areas to determine the conditional distribution parameters, which provide the coefficients' optimal values. It is based on the probabilistic formulation of the attention-focusing mechanisms and derivation of the attention function in Eq. (1) by the maximum likelihood rule [25]. The spatial saliency $c(i,j,t,\rho)$ is defined as an area isotropic contrast [12], which is the mean value of squared intensity deviations in the background ring $Q_\rho(i,j)$ with respect to the mean intensity in the disk $S_\rho(i,j)$ for the feature area $W_\rho = S_\rho \cup Q_\rho$ (Fig. 2). The area inhomogeneity $h(i,j,t,\rho)$ is the intensity mean deviation inside the disk $S_\rho(i,j)$ [12]. The computational scheme for the temporal change $e(i,j,t,\rho)$ in Eq. (1) consists of the accumulated temporal differentiation using consecutive video frames and the isotropic contrast computation over the accumulated differentiation result.

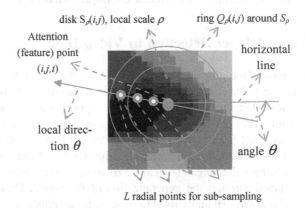

Fig. 2. Attention point detection and estimation of area direction: example of a corner area.

The operator in Eq. (1) is generalized as acting on multiple video (image) property maps. The property maps include sensors' raw components such as the three-color components, infrared and multispectral components if available. Additionally, computationally simple property maps such as the spatial and temporal derivatives of different orders, smoothing filters as well as other local object-relevant functions can be included as the property maps. The multi-component spatiotemporal isotropic attention (MSIA) function $F[i,j,t,\rho]$ becomes:

$$F[i,j,t,\rho] = \sum_{n=1}^{N} \beta_n \cdot s_n(i,j,t,\rho), \tag{2}$$

where $s_n(i, j, t, \rho)$ is the nth spatiotemporal saliency component corresponding to nth property map and β_n is the nth saliency coefficient. The derivation of the optimized values for $\{\beta_n\}$ in the MSIA operator is based on the Fisher's Linear Discriminant Analysis (LDA) method [25]. The LDA-based transformation of N saliency components onto a single axis of $F[i, j, t, \rho]$ values is aimed at maximizing the difference between the $F[i, j, t, \rho]$ values for object and background points respectively while minimizing differences between $F[i, j, t, \rho]$ values corresponding to the object points only.

The sequential detection and analysis of the FoA points $\{(u, v, \tau)_k\}$ and their associated local scale values $\{r_k\}$ as the FPAs' diameters proceeds as follows:

$$(u, v, \tau, r)_k = \underset{(i,j,t) \in A, \rho \in \Omega}{\arg \max} \{F[i, j, t, \rho], (i, j, t) \in Z_{k-1}\}, \qquad (3)$$

where Z_{k-1} is the set of previously detected FoA points, Ω is the scale range of the attention operator, and A is a subset of video data under current analysis. A *fast-recursive implementation* of the MSIA operator alike the recursive STIA algorithm described in [12] makes the computation independent of the window size and becomes $O(N)$ per pixel and per scale value, where N is the total number of property maps (Eq. 2). It is based on the recursive implementation of 2D filters with the square window shape, which approximate the circular (isotropic) window $W_\rho = S_\rho \cup Q_\rho$.

4   Application to Object Detection in Video Data

One of the applications of the proposed attention model is the fast and robust detection of objects of interest in video data. Multiple-object detection proceeds by sequentially detecting object-relevant subsets of FPAs in the input image sequence. This is implemented through the clustering of feature-point areas around the current FoA-point. A descriptor set is extracted for each subset of FPAs. Three different types of descriptors are extracted to form a single descriptor set: (1) area pose; (2) local appearance; and (3) temporal change. To achieve rotation invariance, local appearance descriptors are extracted through the generalization of the Radial Descriptor Pattern (RDP) algorithm, which was originally used to rotation-invariantly extract planar shape descriptors [26]. The RDP algorithm consists of two basic steps: (a) determination of a dominant direction; and (b) estimation of angular-radial descriptor components (Fig. 2). The dominant direction is the *local direction* angle θ included in the pose descriptors [26]. The second step is the angular-radial sub-sampling of image intensity within the window $W_\rho = S_\rho \cup Q_\rho$, for M angle values and L radial points per angular position (Fig. 2). The values of L and M are determined by considering a tradeoff between the accuracy of description and computational costs. To detect and classify objects of interest, the computational model in Fig. 1 proceeds by matching the observed FPA descriptors with the reference ones obtained during the machine learning stage. The Euclidian distance between descriptor sets can be used as the dissimilarity measure of matching.

5 Experimental Results

We conducted numerous experiments to investigate several basic performance characteristics of the proposed attention model. The latter was tested on the operator adequate response (detection capability) to high-contrast areas, high property-coherence areas, and areas with object rigid motion. Another type of experiments was the accuracy of the FoA point localization and spatial scale determination. We used the Singapore maritime datasets (https://sites.google.com/site/dilipprasad/home/singapore-maritime-dataset). The application is vessel detection in maritime scenes.

The testing was comparative with respect to existing computational models. We compared the model's performance with the following algorithms: attention model-based STIA algorithm [12] and feature-point detector in the HSIP method (Harris' Spatiotemporal Interest Points) [14]. Figure 3 illustrates the computation of the MSIA operator and the process of attention-point extraction for the color maritime videos. The MSIA operator uses 8 spatial scales and 5 spatiotemporal saliency components in Eq. (2): three normalized RGB components, mean intensity component, and temporal change. Coefficients $\{\beta_1 = 0.15, \beta_2 = 0.08, \beta_3 = 0.05, \beta_4 = 0.19, \beta_5 = 0.35\}$ in Eq. (2) were learned by the LDA approach (Sect. 3).

The performance of attention focusing in terms of correct response to such video stimuli as spatial saliency, coherence and motion presence is reported in Table 1 as the F-measure, which combines the standard precision and recall rates [24]. Table 1 provides the comparative performance of attention-point detection in general. The MSIA operator provides adequate detection of FoA points due to the effective combination of saliency components in Eq. (2) and the introduction of a new temporal change filter. Many false attention points were detected by the HSIP method in water ripples, specular reflections and ship wakes. A drawback of the HSIP detector as well as other feature-point detectors is the instability of feature point extraction due to their sensitivity to irrelevant spatiotemporal changes (Fig. 3f). The MSIA operator locates the FPAs with the priority to be inscribed into object regions (Fig. 3e). Estimated errors for the FoA-point localization and local scale estimation are given in Table 2. The normalized root mean-squares error (RMSE) was used to characterize the localization accuracy.

The normalized run-time for the proposed MSIA operator is summarized in Table 3. The normalization consists in dividing the current run-time by that of the minimal window size (3×3 pixels) to get rid of a particular CPU speed figure. For comparison purposes, we estimated the run-time of direct (non-recursive) implementation for the MSIA-based attention focusing as well as the HSIP-based attention model using the fast (iterative) Gaussian smoothing algorithm.

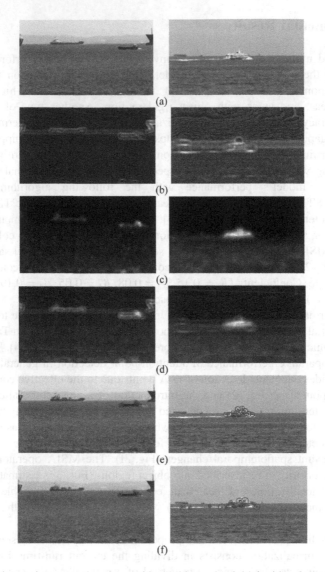

Fig. 3. Attention point extraction in maritime videos: (a) initial video images; (b) spatial saliency map; (c) temporal change map; (d) MSIA operator map; (e) MSIA points; (f) HSIP points;

Table 1. *F*-measure of attention focusing models by the stimuli response.

Response of attention focusing to	HSIP detector	Attention operator STIA	Attention operator MSIA
Area saliency	0.81	0.80	**0.86**
Area coherence	0.71	0.78	**0.92**
Area motion	0.75	0.79	**0.91**
Attention point	0.72	0.77	**0.87**

Table 2. RMSE-based accuracy of FoA-point localization and local scale estimation.

Algorithm	FoA localization		Local scale	
	Low scale range	High scale range	Low scale range	High scale range
MSIA operator	0.03	0.18	0.11	0.09
HSIP detector	0.31	0.34	0.3	0.18
STIA operator	0.23	0.2	0.05	0.13

Table 3. Normalized run-time per pixel of the attention-focusing process.

Window (scale) size:	HSIP-based attention	Direct computation MSIA	Fast recursive computation MSIA
3 x 3	1	1	**1**
5 x 5	1.7	2.6	**1.2**
7 x 7	2.6	3.8	**1.6**
15 x 15	4.8	9.1	**1.6**
31 x 31	9.2	24.5	**1.6**

6 Conclusions

A computational model for spatiotemporal attention-guided analysis of videos is put forth. Our technique is based on the sequential detection of FoA points, identification of FPAs and matching of the FPA's descriptor sets with the reference ones. The proposed approach showed the following advantageous characteristics confirmed by the preliminary experiments reported herein: (1) localization of FoAs points inside object-relevant and homogeneous areas by selected properties; (2) local uniqueness of feature-point areas achieved through the isotropic definition of the multi-scale local contrast; (3) enhanced sensitivity in motion detection due to the temporal change determination using the area-time accumulated differentiation.

Acknowledgement. We gratefully acknowledge the financial support of the Ontario Centers of Excellence (OCE) and the National Sciences and Engineering Research Council of Canada (NSERC) towards the project "Big Data Analytics for the Maritime Internet of Things".

References

1. Cristóbal, G., Perrinet, L., Keil, M.S. (eds.): Biologically Inspired Computer Vision: Fundamentals and Applications, 458 p. (2015)
2. Frintrop, S., et al.: Computational visual attention systems and their cognitive foundation: a survey. ACM Trans. Appl. Percept. **7**(1), 1–46 (2010)
3. Feichtenhofer, C., Pinz, A., Wildes, R.: Dynamic scene recognition with complementary spatiotemporal features. IEEE Trans. PAMI **38**(12), 2389–2401 (2016)
4. Bregonzio, M., Gong, S., Xiang, T.: Recognizing action as clouds of space-time interest points. In: Proceedings of the CVPR, pp. 1948–1955 (2009)
5. Felzenszwalb, P.F., et al.: Object detection with discriminatively trained part-based models. IEEE Trans. PAMI **32**(9), 1627–1645 (2010)
6. Itti, L., Koch, C., Niebur, E.: A model of saliency-based visual attention for rapid scene analysis. IEEE Trans. PAMI **20**(11), 1254–1259 (1998)
7. Kadir, T., Brady, M.: Saliency, scale and image description. Int. J. Comput. Vis. **45**(2), 83–105 (2001)
8. Bruce, N.B., Tsotsos, J.K.: Saliency, attention, and visual search: an information theoretic approach. J. Vis. **9**(3), 1–24 (2009)
9. Itti, L., Baldi, P.: A principled approach to detecting surprising events in video. In: IEEE Conference Computer Vision and Pattern Recognition, pp. 631–637 (2005)
10. Mahadevan, V., Vasconcelos, N.: Spatiotemporal saliency in highly dynamic scenes. IEEE Trans. PAMI **32**(1), 171–177 (2010)
11. Adelson, E.H., Bergen, J.R.: Spatiotemporal energy models for the perception of motion. Opt. Soc. Am. **2**, 284–299 (1985)
12. Palenichka, R., et al.: A spatiotemporal attention operator using isotropic contrast and regional homogeneity. J. Electron. Imaging **20**(2), 1–15 (2011)
13. Shabani, A., Clausi, D., Zelek, J.S.: Evaluation of local spatiotemporal salient feature detectors for human action recognition. In: Proceedings of the CRV 2012, pp. 468–475 (2012)
14. Laptev, I.: On space-time interest points. Int. J. Comp. Vis. **64**(2/3), 107–123 (2005)
15. Harris, C., Stephens, M.J.: A combined corner and edge detector. In: Alvey Vision Conference, pp. 147–151 (1988)
16. Lindeberg, T.: Generalized Gaussian scale-space axiomatics comprising linear scale-space, affine scale-space and spatiotemporal scale-space. J. Math. Imaging Vis. **40**(1), 36–81 (2011)
17. Willems, G., Tuytelaars, T., Van Gool, L.: An efficient dense and scale-invariant spatio-temporal interest point detector. In: Forsyth, D., Torr, P., Zisserman, A. (eds.) ECCV 2008. LNCS, vol. 5303, pp. 650–663. Springer, Heidelberg (2008). https://doi.org/10.1007/978-3-540-88688-4_48
18. Lindeberg, T.: Feature detection with automatic scale selection. IJCV **30**(2), 79–116 (1998)
19. Dollar, P., Rabaud, V., Cottrell, G., Belongie, S.: Behavior recognition via sparse spatiotemporal features. In: Proceedings of the VS-PETS, pp. 65–72 (2005)
20. Treisman, A., Gelade, G.: A feature integration theory of attention. Cogn. Psychol. **12**, 97–136 (1980)
21. Erhan, D., et al.: Scalable object detection using deep neural networks. In: Proceedings of the CVPR, pp. 2147–2154 (2014)
22. Curtis, P., Harb, M., Abielmona, R., Petriu, E.: Feature selection and neural network architecture evaluation for real-time video object classification. In: IEEE CEC, pp. 1038–1045 (2016)

23. Lindeberg, T.: Spatio-temporal scale selection in video data. J. Math. Imaging Vis., 1–38 (2017)
24. Jain, A.K., Dubes, R.C.: Algorithms for Clustering Data. Prentice-Hall, Englewood Cliffs (1988)
25. McLachlan, G.J.: Discriminant Analysis and Statistical Pattern Recognition. Wiley Interscience, Hoboken (2004)
26. Palenichka, R., et al.: Model-based extraction of image area descriptors using a multi-scale attention operator. In: ICPR, Tokyo, pp. 853–856 (2012)

Feature Selection for Big Visual Data: Overview and Challenges

Verónica Bolón-Canedo[1], Beatriz Remeseiro[2(✉)], and Brais Cancela[1]

[1] Department of Computer Science, Universidade da Coruña, A Coruña, Spain
{vbolon,brais.cancela}@udc.es
[2] Department of Computer Science, Universidad de Oviedo, Gijón, Spain
bremeseiro@uniovi.es

Abstract. The unprecedented amount of visual data that is available nowadays has created new research opportunities and challenges in the areas of computer vision and machine learning. When dealing with large scale datasets, with a huge number of samples and features, the use of feature selection plays an important role for dimensionality reduction whilst allowing model interpretation, data understanding and knowledge extraction. This manuscript is focused on feature selection as applied to big visual data, including both traditional and deep approaches, and tries to give an overview of the cutting-edge techniques to deal with large-scale vision problems and identify technical challenges in the field.

Keywords: Feature selection · Visual information · Big Data
Deep learning

1 Introduction

The amount of visual data is exponentially growing day by day, mainly because the increasing availability of cameras of all types [10]. On the one hand, people daily acquire, transmit and share both images and videos through the Internet and different social networks. On the other hand, huge amounts of visual information is being stored and processed by different agents in the industrial world with different purposes, such as automatic inspection in manufacturing applications [25] or detecting events in visual surveillance systems [14].

This huge amount of visual data has led to new problems that pose a challenge for machine learning and computer vision researchers. Image datasets have grown not only in the number of examples, but also in the number of features that describe them. In this situation, it might be reasonable to think that having more features would give us more information and thus better results. However, this is not happening because of the *curse of dimensionality*, a colorful term coined by Richard Bellman back in 1957 to describe the difficulty of optimization by exhaustive enumeration on product spaces [1]. It refers to the different phenomena that appear when analyzing high-dimensional datasets (with hundreds or thousands of features) that do not occur in low-dimensional settings.

© Springer International Publishing AG, part of Springer Nature 2018
A. Campilho et al. (Eds.): ICIAR 2018, LNCS 10882, pp. 136–143, 2018.
https://doi.org/10.1007/978-3-319-93000-8_16

A possible solution to this situation is the use of dimensionality reduction techniques, aiming at reducing the number of input features for a given problem. In particular, this manuscript is focused on the use of feature selection methods in the area of big visual data. Note that traditional approaches of computer vision can be seen as two-step methods in which a set of image properties is first computed to obtain a descriptor, i.e. a feature vector that then feed machine learning algorithms that may include feature selection methods and/or learning models. But when dealing with big visual data, it is quite common to use deep learning algorithms due to their computational power and generalization ability [19]. As opposed to traditional methods, deep learning techniques can be seen as models that perform feature computation and inductive learning as part of the same process. This paper addresses both approaches, traditional and deep, and presents an overview of different techniques as well as the main challenges that need to be faced in the near future.

The rest of this manuscript is structured as follows: Sect. 2 includes an overview of feature selection applied to large-scale computer vision problems, Sect. 3 deals with deep learning approaches for feature selection, Sect. 4 includes some technical challenges, and Sect. 5 closes with the conclusions.

2   Feature Selection

As stated in the introduction, dimensionality reduction techniques are used to reduce the number of input features. These dimensionality reduction techniques usually come in two flavors: *feature selection* and *feature extraction*. On the one hand, feature extraction techniques achieve dimensionality reduction by *combining* the original features (i.e. the features extracted from the images that are fed as input to the FS algorithms). In this manner, they are able to generate a set of *new* features, which is usually more compact and of stronger discriminating power. It is the typical choice in applications such as image analysis, signal processing, or information retrieval. On the other hand, feature selection achieves dimensionality reduction by *removing* the irrelevant and redundant features. Due to the fact that feature selection maintains the *original* features, it is especially useful for applications where the original features are important for model interpreting and knowledge extraction.

As mentioned above, feature extraction is the preferred approach when dealing with image analysis, and therefore there are plenty of works analyzing the application of these methods to this field [11,16,24,33]. However, although not so common, feature selection has also been applied to image analysis, and it is expected to be more important in the future, now that the interpretability of the results is gaining importance. Therefore, the remaining of this paper will be focused on feature selection (FS).

FS methods are typically divided into three major approaches according to the relationship between a FS algorithm and the inductive learning method used to infer a model [12]: filters, which are independent of the induction model; and wrappers and embedded methods, which involve a learning algorithm to determine the useful features. When dealing with Big Data, the preferred approach is to use filters, since they are advantageous in terms of computational cost. For more details, refer to the specialized books [3,12].

DNA microarray images are a typical application of classical feature selection [5]. This type of data consists in measuring the simultaneous expression of thousands of genes, which then can be used as inputs to large-scale data analysis. Typically, these datasets have thousands of features and very small samples (often less than 100), so feature selection plays an extremely important role and there are thousands of works in the literature acknowledging its effectiveness in this domain. The interested reader may find some works that review the FS methods used most for microarray data. Saeys et al. [28] provided a basic taxonomy of classical FS techniques and discuss their use in a number of bioinformatics applications. Lazar et al. [18] presented a survey focusing on filter methods in a unified framework. During the last decade, in addition to the application of state-of-the-art methods, an important number of new filter approaches have been proposed and applied to microarray data, which are reviewed by Bolón-Canedo et al. [5].

Many other works can be found in the literature that apply feature selection to different computer vision problems with high-dimensional datasets. Jia et al. [15] analyzed the effect of receptive field designs on image classification accuracy, and proposed a learning algorithm based on incremental feature selection that outperforms the state-of-art on the CIFAR-10 dataset. Tan et al. [31] proposed a novel adaptive scaling scheme for high-dimensional FS on Big Data, and demonstrated the effectiveness of the method by performing experimentation on different synthetic and real-world large-scale datasets, including image datasets such as MNIST. Zhao et al. [34] presented a new framework to select relevant features in multi-modal, often high-dimensional datasets by applying deep neural networks and FS with LASSO, and carried out an experimental study on three image classification datasets. Cao et al. [7] proposed a measure to evaluate the relevance of feature groups in image classification by employing the well-known feature selection filter *minimum Redundancy Maximum Relevance* (mRMR), and demonstrated the importance of using well-designed features after applying this measure to different image datasets and several image descriptors.

3   Deep Feature Selection

Deep learning algorithms are normally used to *extract* relevant features. By removing the last layer, one can take the final layer as a feature vector (these are the so-called *deep features*). As it is mentioned, this is a feature extraction procedure which is not the focus of this manuscript. However, as previously explained, feature selection methods maintain the original features, so they can be used for model interpretability and knowledge extraction. Assuming this idea, there are some deep learning techniques that can be included as *hybrid* feature selection methods, since they take advantage of feature extraction properties to infer which image pixels are relevant to the task. Note that these methods are not as fast as classic feature selection approaches (see Sect. 2), since an intermediate step is required to obtain the relevant information.

All these algorithms try to obtain the *saliency* features, and deep learning techniques were proven to be a powerful tool to detect them. By definition, *saliency* is the characteristic that stands out compared with its neighborhood. In our study field, it means the detection of relevant features within an image, discarding those that are not necessary (e.g. foreground vs. background). This approach is somehow different from classic feature selection since here the idea is to detect those features that help the model to trigger any given output, rather than just taking a fixed subset. Although no dimensionality reduction can be performed if spatial information is used (for instance, in Convolutional Neural Networks), feature selection can be used by putting irrelevant features to zero, and thus helping the model to avoid overfitting.

Training algorithms can be classified in two different approaches: weakly-supervised and fully-supervised. In weakly-supervised algorithms, the classification task indicates what kind of information appears in the image, but not where it is located. Thus, only by visualizing the neural network node activation we can infer where the object of interest is located. On the contrary, fully-supervised algorithms requires a segmentation image to compare against it.

Simonyan et al. [30] use a two-step algorithm to obtain a saliency map. First, a deep Convolutional Neural Network (CNN) for class classification is trained. Then, for every image, it recognizes the pixels that are contributing the most to select the winner class. Two different approaches were created to deal with this information, either to select a smaller ROI within the image or to perform an object segmentation, discarding the information that is considered as background. It is very interesting because there is no information provided to the CNN about where the object is placed within the scene, and yet the network highest activations are usually correctly placed [27]. However, this effect can also be used to break the system, as it was demonstrated that incoherent images can be created to completely fool a CNN [26].

This idea of evaluating the activation weights was also used in [20], but introducing a pool of different CNNs. Wei et al. [32] extended a similar version, introducing both deep CNN and semantic segmentation. Zhou et al. [36] introduce the concept of *class activation maps*, a weight-based heat map associated to each image. Different final layer possibilities were tested in [22], selecting Global Average Pooling as the most suitable one. Li and Yu [21] used a Conditional Random Field (CRF) as final step in order to improve the spatial coherence. Similar idea was addressed in [35], but combining a paired-CNN (two different CNNs with shared weights in some layers) to introduce both global and local context information, respectively. Pre-trained CNNs were also proven to be valid architectures to provide saliency information [13].

Despite the detection of salient regions, there is also a field of study that addresses the issue of detecting objects in the scene. It is often referred as *salient object detection*. We are not interested in the segmentation part, since it is a classification problem, far from the feature selection methods we are addressing in this paper. However, some remarkable salient techniques were created, and we want to mention them. A comprehensive analysis and study of existing works was reported in [6], where both a review and a benchmark study were conducted. Cheng et al. [9] used the saliency map to successfully detect the foreground objects within an image. Li et al. [23] uses a fully-supervised regularized nonlinear regression model, developing a multi-task learning scheme for inferring the correlations between saliency detection and semantic image segmentation.

4 Challenges

Ongoing advances in computer-based technologies have enabled researchers to collect data at an increasingly fast pace. It is more frequent than ever to have to deal with high-dimensional data, so feature selection becomes an imperative preprocessing step [4]. However, this advent of Big Data has brought an important number of challenges, both in traditional and deep learning approaches, and some of them are discussed in the following.

- **Real-time processing.** Data is being collected at an unprecedented fast pace and, correspondingly, needs to be processed rapidly. Social media networks and portable devices dominate our day-to-day, and they require sophisticated methods capable of dealing with vast amounts of data in real time, e.g. for video/image retrieval. Although online learning is a quite popular field among researchers, online feature selection has not received the same amount of attention. In this new Big Data scenario, online feature selection methods should be capable of (i) modifying the selected subset of features as new training samples arrive, and (ii) being executed in a dynamic feature space that would initially be empty but would add features as new information arrived. Online deep learning should be also a focus of attention for researchers, due to its limited progress in recent years. In this sense, the strategy of stochastic gradient descent and the update of parameters on a mini-batch basis used for training deep learning algorithms may be adapted for online learning [8].
- **Feature cost.** Typically, feature selection methods only focus on detecting the relevant features, but there are some situations in which these features have an associated cost which should not be ignored. For example, the cost for computing different image features may be not homogeneous [2], so the fact that the computational cost of extracting each feature varies implies different computational times. Time complexity is crucial with the advent of Big Data, especially in real-time processing. Although the issue of reducing costs in feature selection has received some attention in the last few years, we still definitely need new feature selection methods that can match the accuracy of state-of-the-art algorithms while reducing computational cost.
- **Interpretability.** As mentioned before, feature extraction is the preferred approach to reduce image dimensionality. However, these techniques have the limitation that the features being selected are transformations of the original ones. Thus, when model interpretability is important, FS is necessary to discover the good features of a model. And not only to deal with images, but also on other types of big databases it is necessary to develop user-friendly

visualization tools to enhance interpretability. There is an important necessity of more interactive model visualizations where (i) users can change input parameters to better interact with the model and visualize future scenarios, and (ii) users can iterate through different feature subsets rather than be tied to a specific subset chosen by an algorithm.

- **Acceptability.** In the context of interpretability previously mentioned, deep learning models are often seen as *black-boxes* difficult to interpret, which implies a problem of user acceptance in critical sectors such as health or robotics. Saliency maps (see Sect. 3) may be useful to understand output models by providing information about the pixels that contribute to generate this output. Other techniques have been presented to generate visual explanations from deep learning models [29], although their full deployment has not taken place yet. Thus, the benefits of using visual analytics tools need to be communicated to the potential users in order to overcome any possible barrier [17].

5   Conclusions

The growing size of visual datasets, composed by not only a great amount of samples (images and/or videos) but also a huge number of features, makes indispensable the use of dimensionality reduction techniques. These methods can be useful to reduce the number of input features and alleviate the computational burden with no degradation in performance. As opposed to feature extraction, feature selection is also helpful in model interpretation and knowledge extraction.

Traditional approaches of feature selection have been successfully applied to different problems, including DNA microarray analysis and image classification. When dealing with Big Data, particularly in computer vision problems, the use of deep learning seems to be inevitable due to its computational power. However, using deep models involves sacrificing interpretation to gain abstraction and integration [29]. In this context, saliency features can be computed by deep learning techniques to detect the relevant regions within an image.

In conclusion, both traditional and deep feature selection approaches have demonstrated to be useful in different large-scale problems of computer vision. However, some technical challenges need to be addressed to increase model interpretability and user acceptability, and to allow real-time processing.

Acknowledgments. This research has been partially funded by the Spanish Ministerio de Economía y Competitividad and FEDER funds of the European Union (projects TIN2015-65069-C2-1-R and TIN2015-65069-C2-2-R); and by the Consellería de Industria of the Xunta de Galicia (project GRC2014/035). Brais Cancela acknowledges the support of the Xunta de Galicia under its postdoctoral program.

References

1. Bellman, R.: Dynamic Programming. Princeton University Press, Princeton (1957)
2. Bolón-Canedo, V., Remeseiro, B., Sánchez-Maroño, N., Alonso-Betanzos, A.: mC-ReliefF: an extension of ReliefF for cost-based feature selection. In: International Conference on Agents and Artificial Intelligence, vol. 1, pp. 42–51 (2014)
3. Bolón-Canedo, V., Sánchez-Maroño, N., Alonso-Betanzos, A.: Feature Selection for High-Dimensional Data. AIFTA. Springer, Cham (2015). https://doi.org/10.1007/978-3-319-21858-8
4. Bolón-Canedo, V., Sánchez-Maroño, N., Alonso-Betanzos, A.: Recent advances and emerging challenges of feature selection in the context of big data. Knowl. Based Syst. **86**, 33–45 (2015)
5. Bolón-Canedo, V., Sánchez-Maroño, N., Alonso-Betanzos, A., Benítez, J.M., Herrera, F.: A review of microarray datasets and applied feature selection methods. Inf. Sci. **282**, 111–135 (2014)
6. Borji, A., Cheng, M.M., Jiang, H., Li, J.: Salient object detection: a benchmark. IEEE Trans. Image Process. **24**(12), 5706–5722 (2015)
7. Cao, Z., Principe, J.C., Ouyang, B.: Group feature selection in image classification with multiple kernel learning. In: International Joint Conference on Neural Networks, pp. 1–5 (2015)
8. Chen, X.W., Lin, X.: Big data deep learning: challenges and perspectives. IEEE Access **2**, 514–525 (2014)
9. Cheng, M.M., Mitra, N.J., Huang, X., Torr, P.H., Hu, S.M.: Global contrast based salient region detection. IEEE Trans. Pattern Anal. Mach. Intell. **37**(3), 569–582 (2015)
10. Fang, Z., Hwang, J.N., Huo, X., Lee, H.J., Denzler, J.: Emergent Techniques and Applications for Big Visual Data. Int. J. Digit. Multimed. Broadcast. **2017**, 2 (2017). Article ID 6468502
11. Guo, G., Fu, Y., Dyer, C.R., Huang, T.S.: Image-based human age estimation by manifold learning and locally adjusted robust regression. IEEE Trans. Image Process. **17**(7), 1178–1188 (2008)
12. Guyon, I.: Feature Extraction: Foundations and Applications, vol. 207. Springer, Heidelberg (2006)
13. Hong, S., You, T., Kwak, S., Han, B.: Online tracking by learning discriminative saliency map with convolutional neural network. In: International Conference on Machine Learning, pp. 597–606 (2015)
14. Hu, W., Tan, T., Wang, L., Maybank, S.: A survey on visual surveillance of object motion and behaviors. IEEE Trans. Syst. Man Cybern. Part C (Appl. Rev.) **34**(3), 334–352 (2004)
15. Jia, Y., Huang, C., Darrell, T.: Beyond spatial pyramids: receptive field learning for pooled image features. In: IEEE Conference on Computer Vision and Pattern Recognition, pp. 3370–3377 (2012)
16. Juan, L., Gwun, O.: A comparison of SIFT, PCA-SIFT and SURF. Int. J. Image Process. **3**(4), 143–152 (2009)
17. Keim, D.A., Mansmann, F., Schneidewind, J., Ziegler, H.: Challenges in visual data analysis. In: International Conference on Information Visualization, pp. 9–16 (2006)
18. Lazar, C., Taminau, J., Meganck, S., Steenhoff, D., Coletta, A., Molter, C., de Schaetzen, V., Duque, R., Bersini, H., Nowe, A.: A survey on filter techniques for feature selection in gene expression microarray analysis. IEEE/ACM Trans. Comput. Biol. Bioinf. **9**(4), 1106–1119 (2012)

19. LeCun, Y., Bengio, Y., Hinton, G.: Deep learning. Nature **521**(7553), 436–444 (2015)
20. Li, G., Yu, Y.: Visual saliency based on multiscale deep features. In: IEEE Conference on Computer Vision and Pattern Recognition, pp. 5455–5463 (2015)
21. Li, G., Yu, Y.: Deep contrast learning for salient object detection. In: IEEE Conference on Computer Vision and Pattern Recognition, pp. 478–487 (2016)
22. Li, G., Yu, Y.: Visual saliency detection based on multiscale deep CNN features. IEEE Trans. Image Process. **25**(11), 5012–5024 (2016)
23. Li, X., Zhao, L., Wei, L., Yang, M.H., Wu, F., Zhuang, Y., Ling, H., Wang, J.: DeepSaliency: Multi-task deep neural network model for salient object detection. IEEE Trans. Image Process. **25**(8), 3919–3930 (2016)
24. Maaten, L., Hinton, G.: Visualizing data using t-SNE. J. Mach. Learn. Res. **9**, 2579–2605 (2008)
25. Malamas, E.N., Petrakis, E.G., Zervakis, M., Petit, L., Legat, J.D.: A survey on industrial vision systems, applications and tools. Image Vis. Comput. **21**(2), 171–188 (2003)
26. Nguyen, A., Yosinski, J., Clune, J.: Deep neural networks are easily fooled: High confidence predictions for unrecognizable images. In: IEEE Conference on Computer Vision and Pattern Recognition, pp. 427–436 (2015)
27. Oquab, M., Bottou, L., Laptev, I., Sivic, J.: Is object localization for free?-weakly-supervised learning with convolutional neural networks. In: IEEE Conference on Computer Vision and Pattern Recognition, pp. 685–694 (2015)
28. Saeys, Y., Inza, I., Larrañaga, P.: A review of feature selection techniques in bioinformatics. Bioinformatics **23**(19), 2507–2517 (2007)
29. Selvaraju, R.R., Cogswell, M., Das, A., Vedantam, R., Parikh, D., Batra, D.: Grad-CAM: visual explanations from deep networks via gradient-based localization. In: IEEE Conference on Computer Vision and Pattern Recognition, pp. 618–626 (2017)
30. Simonyan, K., Vedaldi, A., Zisserman, A.: Deep inside convolutional networks: Visualising image classification models and saliency maps. arXiv preprint arXiv:1312.6034 (2013)
31. Tan, M., Tsang, I.W., Wang, L.: Towards ultrahigh dimensional feature selection for big data. J. Mach. Learn. Res. **15**, 1371–1429 (2014)
32. Wei, Y., Liang, X., Chen, Y., Shen, X., Cheng, M.M., Feng, J., Zhao, Y., Yan, S.: STC: A simple to complex framework for weakly-supervised semantic segmentation. IEEE Trans. Pattern Anal. Mach. Intell. **39**(11), 2314–2320 (2017)
33. Weinberger, K.Q., Saul, L.K.: Unsupervised learning of image manifolds by semidefinite programming. Int. J. Comput. Vis. **70**(1), 77–90 (2006)
34. Zhao, L., Hu, Q., Wang, W.: Heterogeneous feature selection with multi-modal deep neural networks and sparse group LASSO. IEEE Trans. Multimed. **17**(11), 1936–1948 (2015)
35. Zhao, R., Ouyang, W., Li, H., Wang, X.: Saliency detection by multi-context deep learning. In: IEEE Conference on Computer Vision and Pattern Recognition, pp. 1265–1274 (2015)
36. Zhou, B., Khosla, A., Lapedriza, A., Oliva, A., Torralba, A.: Learning deep features for discriminative localization. In: IEEE Conference on Computer Vision and Pattern Recognition, pp. 2921–2929 (2016)

Model Compression for Faster Structural Separation of Macromolecules Captured by Cellular Electron Cryo-Tomography

Jialiang Guo[1], Bo Zhou[2], Xiangrui Zeng[2], Zachary Freyberg[3], and Min Xu[2(✉)]

[1] Xi'an Jiaotong University, Xi'an, China
[2] School of Computer Science, Carnegie Mellon University, Pittsburgh, USA
mxu1@cs.cmu.edu
[3] Departments of Psychiatry and Cell Biology, University of Pittsburgh, Pittsburgh, USA

Abstract. Electron Cryo-Tomography (ECT) enables 3D visualization of macromolecule structure inside single cells. Macromolecule classification approaches based on convolutional neural networks (CNN) were developed to separate millions of macromolecules captured from ECT systematically. However, given the fast accumulation of ECT data, it will soon become necessary to use CNN models to efficiently and accurately separate substantially more macromolecules at the prediction stage, which requires additional computational costs. To speed up the prediction, we compress classification models into compact neural networks with little in accuracy for deployment. Specifically, we propose to perform model compression through knowledge distillation. Firstly, a complex teacher network is trained to generate soft labels with better classification feasibility followed by training of customized student networks with simple architectures using the soft label to compress model complexity. Our tests demonstrate that our compressed models significantly reduce the number of parameters and time cost while maintaining similar classification accuracy.

Keywords: Model compression · Knowledge distillation · Cellular Electron Cryo-Tomography · Macromolecule classification

1 Introduction and Related Work

Maintenance of cellular homeostasis is largely based upon the coordinated activities of an array of intracellular macromolecular complexes. The structural and functional roles of many of these complexes, to date, have been inferred from in vitro studies, often from purified samples. While such studies are extremely useful, the ability to study macromolecular complexes within their native cellular contexts may be even more informative. At present, live cell imaging does

---

J. Guo, B. Zhou—Contributed equally.

A. Campilho et al. (Eds.): ICIAR 2018, LNCS 10882, pp. 144–152, 2018.
https://doi.org/10.1007/978-3-319-93000-8_17

not have sufficient resolution to visualize the structure or distribution of individual macromolecular complexes within cells. Cellular Electron Cryo-Tomography (CECT), on the other hand, has the resolution to potentially visualize individual macromolecular complexes in three dimensions within cells preserved in a near-native state [6]. However, the systematic structural identification and recovery of the macromolecules captured by CECT is difficult due to the structural complexity and imaging limits in CECT tomograms. First, a key contributor of this complexity is the makeup of these large macromolecular structures which are composed of numerous components with highly dynamic conformations and interactions, thus limiting the overall complex resolution. Secondly, imaging limits of CECT such as low signal-to-noise ratio (SNR) and missing data effects (i.e. missing wedge) have further complicated systematic macromolecular structural recovery [8]. Therefore, it is critical to develop effective computational approaches to separate and average huge numbers (at least millions) of highly structurally diverse macromolecules represented by subtomograms (a *subtomogram* is a cubic sub-image that is likely to contain only one macromolecule). Recently, we have developed deep learning-based macromolecular structure classification approaches [2,8] with high discriminative ability and scalability to automatically process subtomograms. According to this methodology, convolutional neural networks (CNN) equipped with 3D filters were used to extract features from subtomograms and separate them into structurally homogeneous subgroups.

In order to achieve a significantly increased particle separation accuracy, it is necessary to search for a CNN model that has more layers and larger capacities. This is especially relevant given the rapid advances in the automation of CECT data acquisition, where efficient and accurate separation of tens of millions of macromolecules captured by CECT will soon become a new computational bottleneck towards achieving significantly improved systematic macromolecular structural identification and recovery. However, implementation of such a model would incur substantially increased computational and (GPU memory) storage costs compared with previously proven models. Indeed, in testing CNN models on subtomograms with a size of 40^3 voxels and a voxel spacing of 0.92 nm [8], on a computer with a single GPU, the training of previous CNN models using one million of these subtomograms for 20 epochs took more than 19 h, and the separation of one million subtomograms could take up to 2 h. It is desirable to reduce the computation and storage costs. Therefore, it is critical to compress the CNN models into smaller ones with fewer parameters while maintaining the same accuracy, once highly accurate CNN models are obtained.

Use of compressed models has many notable advantages compared to the above models, including less prediction time, better deployment to other datasets, and often higher generalization ability [5]. Much previous work has been done to develop methods for model compression [1,4,7]. However, these methods were only tested on 2D images. To our knowledge, to date, little is known about the performance of model compression on CNN models designed for 3D image classification. In this paper, we will focus on reducing the complexity of deep neural networks by knowledge distillation. Among the preexisting models [2], we chose the DSRF3D-v2 (Deep Small Receptive Field) model for compression on the basis of considerations for processing time and performance. Corresponding student models are simpler versions of the original model. Knowledge in the teacher networks is compressed by generating soft labels which contain more information than the original labeled data. The student networks are trained with the soft labels. Our experiments show that with acceptable loss in classification accuracy, the size of distilled models can be significantly reduced. The reduction in the number of layers, and the simplification of structure significantly reduces the number of total parameters and processing time. Among the three student models we proposed, DSRF3D-v2-s1 achieved the best performance, which only requires approximately 1/20 of the original parameters, half of the original prediction time, but only loses 3% of accuracy as compared to the complex teacher model.

2   Method

In our previous work [8], a deep learning approach was proposed to subdivide structurally highly heterogeneous subtomograms into structurally more homogeneous smaller subsets through supervised feature extraction using CNN. Subtomograms are 3D grayscale sub-images representing particles within a cell, denoted as a function $f : \mathbb{R}^3 \rightarrow \mathbb{R}$. Each input f of our CNN model is attached with a class label $\mathbf{y} := (y_1, \cdots, y_L)$, where $y_i \in \{0,1\}, \sum_i y_i = 1$, and L is the number of possible classes. The CNN outputs a probability vector $\mathbf{p} := (p_1, \cdots, p_L)$, where $p_i \in [0,1]$ and predict the inputs f to be in class $\arg\max_i p_i$. To achieve higher accuracy, we may still need to complicate the structure of our models. On the other hand, our testing data can contain millions of subtomograms and the image size can significantly increase under a higher resolution. Thus, it is necessary to find models with simpler structure for deployment.

2.1   Knowledge Distillation

Based on features extracted by prior convolutional and pooling layers, the last hidden layer in a convolutional neural network outputs logits z_i, which indicate the likelihood for each class and are converted into probabilities p_i by the softmax function using Eq. 1.

$$p_i = \frac{\exp\{z_i/T\}}{\sum_j \exp\{z_j/T\}} \tag{1}$$

The function compares each logit with others and uses the temperature T to control the relative sizes of the output probabilities. The knowledge distillation technique [5] asserts that with more information than the original hard labels, the class probabilities produced by large neural networks can be used to guide small models to generalize information from the training data in the same way as large models. However, the probability vector tends to include many values near zero and only one value very close to 1; according to [5], the information that resides in the ratios of very small probabilities has very little influence on the cross-entropy cost function when training small models because the probabilities are too small. To recover the information learned by large models, [1] directly used logits may be employed as soft labels to transfer knowledge. The more generalized method knowledge distillation generates a soft target distribution as the soft label for each training case by using a high temperature in the softmax layer.

Figure 1 illustrates the procedure of knowledge distillation for Deep Neural Networks that separates subtomograms extracted from CECT data. Phase 1 is regular supervised DNN training with labeled 3D images on the teacher network. The rather complex network structure is capable of finding a proper way to generalize information through training, with the knowledge of the learned function mostly stored in the logit layer. In Phase 2, we remove the softmax layer of the trained teacher network and obtain a DNN that outputs logits of the input subtomograms. Notably, since we do not need hard labels to generate logits, we can extend the training set with unlabeled images, if available [5]. The yielded logits are converted into soft labels in Phase 3 by the softmax function with a proper high temperature. The softened probabilities are then attached to the corresponding image to train the student network, typically a simplified version of the teacher network. [5] has explained that since the soft labels have high entropy, they provide much more information per training case than hard labels. Additionally, they possess much less variance in the gradient between training cases, so the small model can often be trained on much less data than the original, more cumbersome model. Furthermore, the compact student network uses a much higher learning rate but retain accuracy. In the deployment stage, the compact student network predicts the input subtomogram to be in the category corresponding to the max value in the output soft label.

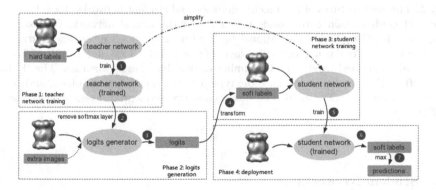

Fig. 1. Knowledge distillation flowchart for the deep-learning based subtomogram classification. The algorithm takes labeled tomographic data and a complex structure for the teacher network as inputs, and outputs a trained compact subtomogram classifier

2.2   Teacher Network

The previous models in [2] have achieved a high accuracy of over 90% at separation of macromolecules extracted from CECT images. However, these models
are relatively big in terms of the total number of parameters. Though the three
models, DSRF3D-v2, RB3D and CB3D, are appropriate to serve as the pro-
totypes of the teacher network, considering that the training process of CB3D
takes too long and the performance of RB3D is relatively poor, we have opted
to use DSRF3D-v2 as the teacher network in our compression.

As shown in Fig. 2, connected to the input layer are three sequential sets of
stacked layers, each set consisting of two $3 \times 3 \times 3$ 3D convolutional layers and
one $2 \times 2 \times 2$ 3D max pooling layer. Then it is followed by two fully connected
layers with 70% dropout. All hidden layers are activated by ReLU. The final
fully connected output layer has the same number of neurons as the number of
possible structure class and uses softmax activation for outputs.

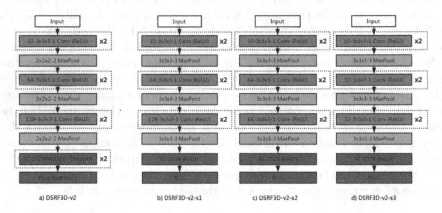

Fig. 2. The architectures of the teacher network and student networks. Each box with
type and configuration corresponds to a layer in the neural network. For example,
'32-3 $\times$ 3 $\times$ 3-1 Conv' is a convolutional layer with 32 3 $\times$ 3 $\times$ 3 filters and a stride of
1.'3 $\times$ 3x3-3 MaxPool' is a max pooling layer of a size of $3 \times 3 \times 3$ and a stride of 3. 'FC-
L' is a full connected layer with L (number of possible classes) neurons. The 'ReLU'
and 'Softmax' in the bracket denote the type of activation function (Linear activation
if not mentioned). "x2" outside the box means two sequential layers with the same
configuration.

2.3   Student Networks

The student network is a simpler version of the teacher network. To simplify
the teacher model, we chose to reduce the number of layers. However, directly
connecting the first convolutional layer and pooling layer to the full connected
layer brings more parameters due to the overwhelming number of local features

in the first convolution operation. Therefore, the compression is implemented by simplifying the convolutional layers, pooling layers and eliminating one of the two fully connected layers. Essentially, the training samples with soft labels brings easier knowledge for the CNN to learn. The student network with 'weaker' layers has sufficient capability for the classification task, as the information in the soft labels distill the knowledge about how the teacher network learned from the dataset. To weaken convolutional layers, the simplest way is to reduce the number of filters. Increasing the pooling size of pooling layers makes the pooling operation performed on a greater region and ignores some local features.

We demonstrate three different student network configurations in Fig. 2, which we believe have best maintained the accuracy while efficiently compressing the model. The student networks share similar structure with the teacher network, except that the dropout layers and one fully connected layer with 1024 neurons were dismissed. Based on that, details of the additional student networks' modifications are listed as follows: (a) In DSRF3D-v2-s1, the pooling size and stride of all the three max pooling layers are increased from $2 \times 2 \times 2$ to $3 \times 3 \times 3$. (b) In DSRF3D-v2-s2, besides performing modification in (a), the last two convolutional layers drop half of original 128 filters. (c) In DSRF3D-v2-s3, besides performing modification in a), the number of filters in the six convolutional layers change from (32, 32, 64, 64, 128, 128) to (16, 16, 32, 32, 32, 32).

These modifications lead to a significant drop in the total number of parameters. Removal of one FC-1024 at the end of the network reduces approximately 1 million parameters. Increasing the stride of the pooling layer from $2 \times 2 \times 2$ to $3 \times 3 \times 3$ has decreased the overall number of parameters by nearly 70%. Applying the modification to all three pooling layers has resulted in a decrease of 97%. Halving the number of filters in a convolutional layer halves the overall number of parameter of this layer.

3   Implementation Details

The input of our models is labeled subtomogram, which is the volumetric image data extracted from CECT data. In [2], 12 datasets of simulated subtomograms were generated with different levels of SNR and tilt angle ranges. In this work, we chose simulated subtomograms with a tilt angle range of $\pm 60°$ and a SNR level equal to 0.05 as our training data, which is further split into 14720 training samples, 3680 validation samples and 4600 test samples.

4   Experimental Results

In this paper, we are using three student models to distill knowledge and compare them with the original uncompressed model. Our student networks are trained with the same configuration as in our previous work [2]. We use a stochastic gradient descent (SGD) optimizer and minimize the categorical cross-entropy cost function by adding Nesterov momentum of 0.9. The initial learning rate is set at 0.005 with a decay factor of 1e−7. The training processes are performed

Table 1. Comparison between teacher and students

Model	#Parameter	Accuracy[1]	Accuracy[2]	Test time (s)
DSRF3D-v2	18,316,599	95.89%	/	15.91
DSRF3D-v2-s1	1,014,071	85.65%	93.82%	9.41
DSRF3D-v2-s2	506,039	84.26%	91.17%	8.95
DSRF3D-v2-s3	161,639	72.17%	89.83%	5.58

[1] test accuracy when the model is trained with hard labels
[2] test accuracy when the model is trained with soft labels

with a batch size of 64 for 20 epochs and will stop early if the classification performance shows no improvement over 5 consecutive epochs based on the loss function. The temperature in the softmax function is set to 5 heuristically by experience.

As shown in Table 1, the teacher network is significantly compressed with a remarkable decrease in the total number of parameters. In assaying test time, our results indicates a significant reduction in test duration, demonstrating a great potential for deployment. On the other hand, the classification accuracy of three student network suffers little loss. The DSRF3D-v2-s1 maintains almost the same accuracy, with the next two models at an accuracy of approximately 90%. An important fact we should note is that if we use the original hard labels to train our student networks, the test accuracy is relatively unsatisfactory and significantly lower than the accuracy when the model is trained with soft labels, which contain information from the more capable teacher network. This improvement in accuracy, to some degree, provides proof that the student networks themselves are not strong enough in structure to extract sufficient information from the training data and that the knowledge distilled from the teacher network accounts for the high accuracy of the student networks.

Table 2. Evaluation of different student networks

Model	Compression rate[1]	Accuracy rate[2]	Speedup[3]
DSRF3D-v2	1	1	1
DSRF3D-v2-s1	18.1	0.978	1.69
DSRF3D-v2-s2	36.2	0.951	1.78
DSRF3D-v2-s3	113.3	0.937	2.85

[1] the ratio of number of parameters
[2] the ratio of test accuracy
[3] the ratio of test time (all ratios are of the teacher network to model of interest)

Table 2 gives three evaluation metrics [3] of the student networks. Naturally, as the compression rate and the speedup increase, the accuracy preserved in the student model gradually decreases. Therefore, when simplifying the teacher network, we must prevent the layers from being oversimplified so that the obtained student network has enough capability of imitating the teacher network. In practice, we must consider the trade-off between loss of accuracy and parameter compression. Like the student networks demonstrated above, choosing proper student network architectures that have fewer parameters but that remain within the range of acceptable accuracy loss is critical.

5 Conclusion

In this paper, we have proposed a model compression approach for CECT data based on knowledge distillation to compress previously proposed high-accuracy deep neural network models for subtomogram classification. To our knowledge, this is the first time the model compression applied to 3D CECT classification. With DSRF3D-v2 as the teacher network, we have correspondingly designed relatively compact models serving as student networks, among which DSRF3D-v2-s1 achieves the best classification accuracy. Typically, a higher compression rate will result in a greater loss of accuracy. In contrast, our distilled models significantly reduce the number of parameters and processing time cost, while keeping almost the same classification accuracy. Therefore, computation cost and storage cost are effectively reduced, making it possible to deploy our neural networks in practice to classify massive datasets of CECT images, especially those with a large image size. The high-performance deep learning inference optimizer technique, like TensorRT, can optimize the student network and will be included in our future work.

Acknowledgements. This work was supported in part by U.S. National Institutes of Health (NIH) grant P41 GM103712. M.X acknowledges support of Samuel and Emma Winters Foundation.

References

1. Caruana, R., Niculescu-Mizil, A.: Model compression. In: ACM SIGKDD International Conference on Knowledge Discovery and Data Mining, pp. 535–541 (2006)
2. Che, C., Lin, R., Zeng, X., Elmaaroufi, K., Galeotti, J., Xu, M.: Improved deep learning based macromolecules structure classification from electron cryo tomograms. arXiv preprint arXiv:1707.04885 (2017)
3. Cheng, Y., Wang, D., Zhou, P., Zhang, T.: A survey of model compression and acceleration for deep neural networks (2017)
4. Han, S., Mao, H., Dally, W.J.: Deep compression: Compressing deep neural network with pruning, trained quantization and huffman coding (2015)
5. Hinton, G., Vinyals, O., Dean, J.: Distilling the knowledge in a neural network. Comput. Sci. **14**(7), 38–39 (2015)
6. McIntosh, R., Nicastro, D., Mastronarde, D.: New views of cells in 3D: an introduction to electron tomography. Trends Cell Biol. **15**(1), 43–51 (2005)

7. Meng, W., Gu, Z., Zhang, M., Wu, Z.: Two-bit networks for deep learning on resource-constrained embedded devices (2017)
8. Xu, M., Chai, X., Muthakana, H., Liang, X., Yang, G., Zeevbenmordehai, T., Xing, E.P.: Deep learning-based subdivision approach for large scale macromolecules structure recovery from electron cryo tomograms. Bioinformatics **33**(14), i13 (2017)

Video-Based Person Re-identification by 3D Convolutional Neural Networks and Improved Parameter Learning

Naoki Kato[1(✉)], Kohei Hakozaki[1], Masamoto Tanabiki[2], Junko Furuyama[2], Yuji Sato[2], and Yoshimitsu Aoki[1]

[1] Keio University, Tokyo, Japan
nkato@aoki-medialab.jp
[2] Panasonic Corporation, Osaka, Japan

Abstract. In this paper we propose a novel approach for video-based person re-identification that exploits convolutional neural networks to learn the similarity of persons observed from video camera. We take 3-dimensional convolutional neural networks (3D CNN) to extract fine-grained spatiotemporal features from the video sequence of a person. Unlike recurrent neural networks, 3D CNN preserves the spatial patterns of the input, which works well on re-identification problem. The network maps each video sequence of a person to a Euclidean space where distances between feature embeddings directly correspond to measures of person similarity. By our improved parameter learning method called entire triplet loss, all possible triplets in the mini-batch are taken into account to update network parameters. This parameter updating method significantly improves training, enabling the embeddings to be more discriminative. Experimental results show that our model achieves new state of the art identification rate on iLIDS-VID dataset and PRID-2011 dataset with 82.0%, 83.3% at rank 1, respectively.

1 Introduction

Person re-identification is a problem of matching the same individuals observed from non-overlapping cameras or single camera that does not share time. It is a fundamental task in video surveillance, applicable to wide-area human tracking system, human retrieval from videos, and so on. Matching persons captured from different cameras is challenging due to large varying viewpoints, human poses, illuminations, background clutters, and occlutions. The classification problem must only discriminate interclass objects; re-identification needs to distinguish different identities among intraclass. Therefore, re-identification must detect the finer differences among individuals, which are not included in the training data.

Most of the existing re-identification algorithms [1,3,14,18,28,30] are based on still images. In contrast, we tackle the multi-shot scenario, so-called video-based person re-identification problem. It is natural idea to use video data for re-identification because a person's images are normally obtained by video cameras

© Springer International Publishing AG, part of Springer Nature 2018
A. Campilho et al. (Eds.): ICIAR 2018, LNCS 10882, pp. 153–163, 2018.
https://doi.org/10.1007/978-3-319-93000-8_18

in a surveillance system. Video data should contribute to more accurate re-identification than single-shot images for several reasons. First, video data simply have a lot of information than single image, contraining various human body direction, camera viewpoint, and walking phase. Second, video data provide not only appearance information but also the temporal patterns of the frame transformation, including the gait features (e.g., the way of posture changing and the walking cycle), the temporal transformations of background objects, and occlusions. Appropriately extracting and modeling appearance cues and motion cues must improve re-identification accuracy.

Recently, convolutional neural networks (CNNs) have achieved significant success in visual recognition problems, such as classification [8,13], object detection [21], and semantic segmentation [2,16]. CNNs have also been applied to similarity learning tasks [10,20,25], which include person re-identification. However, despite the many person re-identification studies based on CNNs [1,3,14,18], video re-identification has been largely neglected. To our knowledge, only [19,27,31] applied deep learning approaches to video re-identification. Mclaughlin et al. extracted temporal features from a sequence using simple recurrent neural networks (RNNs) and reported superior results [19]. However, as RNN requires a sequential order of the input images, it consumes a long computational time. Moreover, the network parameters are learned by contrastive loss [7], which is prone to overfit.

In this paper, we introduce a method that learns a mapping function from a person sequence to a Euclidean space, in which the distances between embeddings directly correspond to measures of person similarity. Our algorithm extracts the temporal features from the input sequence using 3D convolution [11,24] and employs an effective parameter-learning method. In video re-identification, 3D CNN has several advantages over RNNs including long short-term memory (LSTM) [9] and gated recurrent unit (GRU) [4]. Unlike RNN, 3D CNN process all temporal locations at the same time. Such parallelization notably reduces the computational time. Moreover, RNN based on fully-connected layers inevitably shuffles the spatial pattern of the input image; convolution represents a receptive field with sparse connections among the input and output neurons, which preserves the spatial pattern of the input image. Our method trains the network by simple expansion of triplet loss: it calculates the gradients based on all possible set of triplets at each parameter update. Thus, each parameter update considers significant number of combinations of triplets, which lead to better convergence. Evaluations show that proposed method significantly improves the re-identification accuracy.

2   Approach

2.1   Overall System

We propose video-based person re-identification method which exploits CNN to learn similarity of persons observed by a video camera. The network input is a video sequence of a person, denoted as $X = [x_1, ..., x_T]$, where x_t represents the

Table 1. Network architecture of proposed 3D CNN. The input and output sizes are denoted as *height × width × temporal length × channels*. The kernel and the stride sizes are described by *height × width × temporal length*.

Layer	Size-in	Size-out	Kernel	Stride
conv1	$112 \times 48 \times T \times 3$	$112 \times 48 \times T \times 24$	$3 \times 3 \times 1$	$1 \times 1 \times 1$
maxpool1	$112 \times 48 \times T \times 24$	$56 \times 24 \times T \times 24$	$2 \times 2 \times 1$	$2 \times 2 \times 1$
3dconv2	$56 \times 24 \times T \times 24$	$56 \times 24 \times (T-2) \times 24$	$3 \times 3 \times 3$	$1 \times 1 \times 1$
maxpool2	$56 \times 24 \times (T-2) \times 24$	$28 \times 12 \times (T-2) \times 24$	$2 \times 2 \times 1$	$2 \times 2 \times 1$
3dconv3	$28 \times 12 \times (T-2) \times 24$	$28 \times 12 \times (T-4) \times 24$	$3 \times 3 \times 3$	$1 \times 1 \times 1$
avepool3	$28 \times 12 \times (T-4) \times 24$	$14 \times 6 \times 1 \times 24$	$2 \times 2 \times (T-4)$	$2 \times 2 \times 1$
fc4	$1 \times 1 \times 1 \times 2016$	$1 \times 1 \times 1 \times 128$		
L2	$1 \times 1 \times 1 \times 128$	$1 \times 1 \times 1 \times 128$		

person image in frame t. Each frame of the sequence is processed by a 3D CNN (as described in Sect. 2.2), and its spatiotemporal features are extracted. The extracted feature embedding $f(X)$ contains semantic information of the person sequence. This process can be regarded as an application of a nonlinear function $f(.)$ that maps a sequence into a feature space. We define the feature space as a Euclidean space, as in [19]. The similarity between a pair of sequences X_i, X_j, is defined according to the squared Euclidean distance between their embeddings:

$$D_{i,j} = \|f(X_i) - f(X_j)\|_2^2 \qquad (1)$$

The larger the distance $D_{i,j}$ is, the more dissimilar are the two sequences. Our purpose is to learn the mapping function $f(.)$ so that embeddings from the same individual mapped close, different individuals mapped apart discriminatively. Once the proper feature embeddings have been obtained, the classification problem can be replaced by the nearest neighbor problem in Euclidean space. A major advantage of embedding learning is that it allows to solve classification problems for classes not included in training data. Although several loss functions for embedding learning already exist, we derive a new loss function called entire triplet loss, which is a variant of triplet loss (as described in Sect. 2.3).

2.2 Feature Extraction

In this section we explain the feature extraction procedure of our method. RNN is among the most popular approaches for extracting features from sequential data. RNN learns the long-term dependencies of the input sequences by maintaining the previous information, which is beneficial in natural language processing tasks [4,23] and video recognition tasks, such as action recognition [5]. However, in video re-identification, RNN is problematic for several reasons. First, RNN units, including LSTM and GRU, based on fully-connected layer, inevitably shuffle the spatial patterns of the input image to compute the hidden state, so it cannot handle small spatial variations between consecutive frames.

Second, although RNN is able to capture the dependencies of sequential data, standard application of RNN tends to bias the embeddings of person sequences toward later time steps. Thus, obtained embeddings keep little information of former frames which may be important. Third, RNN variants such as LSTM have a lot of parameters (e.g., LSTM has 8 weight matrices), which typically requires large-scale training data. In contrast, we extract the spatiotemporal features by convolution in the time direction. In sequential images, feature extraction is performed by 3D convolution, which computes each hidden layer as feature maps. This approach extracts the features of the fine motion patterns of the target person and backgrounds, preserving the spatial patterns of the person images that are important for re-identification. Compared with LSTM and GRU, 3D convolution requires fewer parameters so it has low overfitting risk.

Table 1 describes the architecture of our network. Each frame of the input sequence X is processed by the conv1 layer. The 3dconv layer then computes the feature maps considering the temporal patterns of the inputs. The conv1 and 3dconv2 layers are followed by a rectified linear unit as the activation function. The avepool3 layer outputs the average of the input feature maps over all time steps, enabling the network to cope with variable length inputs. In observations, avepool3 outperformed the average-embeddings approach. The output of avepool3 is processed by fc4 and then normalized by L2 to obtain the feature embedding of the sequence.

2.3 Parameter Learning

Review of the Embedding Methods. As a preliminary remark, we review two major methods for learning discriminative embeddings using CNNs: contrastive loss and triplet loss. These methods learn the distance metric of static-image pairs, but for convenience, are here regarded as applicable to video sequences.

Contrastive loss [7] take the sequence pairs of a person (X_i, X_j, y_{ij}). A label $y_{ij} \in \{0,1\}$ returns 1 if the sequence pair is from the same person, and 0 otherwise. This loss function forces the squared Euclidean distance of embeddings from the same identity to 0 and separates different identities by some margin. In each iteration of mini-batch training, the loss function is given by

$$L = \frac{1}{2N} \sum_{(i,j)}^{N} y_{ij} D_{i,j} + (1 - y_{ij}) max(\alpha - D_{i,j}, 0) \tag{2}$$

where N is the mini-batch size and α is a margin enforced on negative pairs. This loss function penalizes embeddings from the same identity at single points in the embedding space, regardless of the image appearance (e.g., the person's ambient environment and the camera angle). Such embeddings prone to overfit to training data.

Triplet loss [22,25] requires a triplet sample (X_a, X_p, X_n), where X_p is a sequence from the same person as X_a and X_n is from the different person, respectively. This loss function penalize so that the squared Euclidean distance of negative pair in the triplet exceed that of positive pair by some margin. The loss function is defined as follows:

$$L = \frac{1}{N} \sum_{(a,p,n)}^{N} max(D_{a,p} - D_{a,n} + \beta, 0) \tag{3}$$

where N is the mini-batch size, and β is a margin parameter. Because this loss function penalizes the relative distance between the positive and negative pair, embeddings can reside at various points in the feature space provided that they are discriminative. Feature embeddings of the same person mapped to different points, depending on the person's appearance and background environment.

Improved Parameter Learning. The objective function of our method is fundamentally equivalent to triplet loss, but alters the parameter updating method. While normal triplet loss use N triplets for calculating the loss, where N is the mini-batch size, the proposed method defines the mini-batch size as the number of identities required to calculate the loss. The loss function per mini-batch is defined as triplet loss averaged over all possible triplets in the mini-batch:

$$L = \frac{1}{|T|} \sum_{(a,p,n) \in T}^{|T|} max(D_{a,p} - D_{a,n} + \beta, 0) \tag{4}$$

where T is the set of all possible triplets in the mini-batch. We call Eq. 4 the entire triplet loss. This loss function markedly increases the number of triplets in each parameter update. Given the number of cameras that observe persons K and the number of identity used for composing mini-batch N, the number of triplets used for each parameter updating is $_KP_2KN(N-1)$ with entire triplet loss. Although the number of triplets to be considered increases in the order of N^2, the number of samples requiring feature extraction by CNN, which is relatively large in calculation cost, is KN, which has linear relationship with the number of cameras and mini-batch size. We use $K = 2$ in the experiments for reducing computational cost. On the other hand, triplet loss considers N triplets in each parameter update, and $3N$ samples need feature extraction. With entire triplet loss, since the loss calculation is performed on the low-dimensional embedding vectors after feature extraction, even if the number of combinations increases, both computational cost and memory consumption do not become very large. Because the number of combinations of triplets in a dataset is typically very large, normal triplet loss requires a lot of iterations to cover all triplets. In contrast, our entire triplet loss computes the loss considering a large number of triplets, so it enables faster convergence. Entire triplet loss not only speeds training faster but also has better convergence than triplet loss because large number of triplets provide proper gradients for generalization. This parameter learning method enables effective model training without hard sample mining.

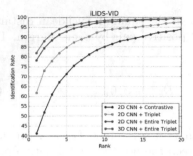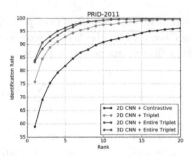

Fig. 1. CMC curves of our models evaluated on each dataset. (Color figure online)

3   Experiments

Datasets: Experiments were conducted on two public datasets of video-based person re-identification, iLIDS-VID and PRID-2011. The iLIDS-VID dataset includes 300 different pedestrians observed by two disjoint cameras in public space. Each image sequence ranges from 23 to 192 frames, with an average of 73 frames. This dataset is challenging as it includes occlusions and background clutters. The PRID-2011 dataset contains 400 image sequences of 200 people observed from the viewpoints of two adjacent cameras. The sequences vary from 5 to 675 frames, with an average number of 100.

Evaluation Protocol: In these experiments, we randomly split each dataset into 50% of persons for training and 50% of persons for testing. The results were quantitatively evaluated by the Cumulative Matching Characteristics (CMC) curves which is widely used in evaluations of person re-identification. In each dataset, the sequences from cameras A and B were used as the query and gallery sequences, respectively. The gallery set comprised one sequence per person. For each sequence in the query set, we first computed the L2 distance between the query sequence and all gallery sequences using the feature embeddings produced by the trained network, then returned the top n nearest sequences in the gallery set. If a sequence in the returned list and the query sequence featured the same person at the k-th position, the query was considered a success of rank k. We conducted 10 trials in each experiment and report the averaged results.

Implementation Details: The hyper-parameters were set as follows: mini-batch size $N = 64$, embedding size $d = 128$, margin parameters $\alpha = 2.0$, and $\beta = 0.2$. To reduce overfitting, data augmentation is applied in the form of cropping and mirroring. The same augmentation was applied to all the frames in a sequence. The network inputs were normalized to have zero mean and unit variance. For regularization, dropout with $p = 0.5$ is arranged before fully-connected layer. During training, each embedding was computed from a sub-sequence of $T = 5$ consecutive frames, randomly selecting a different subset from the full sequence at each epoch. For optimization we used Adam [12] with a learning rate of 0.001. All models were trained for a maximum of 100,000 iterations.

3.1   Effect of 3D Convolution

We compare 3D CNN described in Sect. 2.2 with 2D CNN, in which the 3D convolution is replaced with 2D convolution. The CMC curves of 2D CNN and 3D CNN trained with entire triplet loss are plotted as the blue and red lines in Fig. 1, respectively. 3D CNN outperformed 2D CNN on the iLIDS-VID dataset, but delivered slightly low performance on the PRID-2011 dataset. This deterioration occurs because the PRID-2011 dataset contains fewer occlusions and clearer backgrounds than the iLIDS-VID dataset; therefore, the temporal information is less important. The performance enhancement on iLIDS-VID can be explained that 3D CNN captures the between-frame transitions of persons and backgrounds as well as simply containing multi-frame appearances of persons.

3.2   Embedding Method

We conducted a experiment comparing different embedding learning methods with 2D CNN described in Sect. 3.1. We compared performance of contrastive loss, triplet loss, and entire triplet loss. The results are shown in Fig. 1. On both datasets, the identification rate improved in the order of contrastive loss, triplet loss, and proposed entire triplet loss. The results show the choice of embedding learning method greatly influences the model performance. Comparing the triplet and entire triplet losses, which are based on the same loss function, we confirm that improving the manner of updating the network parameters significantly enhances convergence. Additionally, the rank 1 re-identification rate improves as the training on the iLIDS-VID dataset proceeds (see Fig. 2). The entire triplet loss function improves both the convergence speed and the final re-identification rate, indicating that it is better choice for embedding learning.

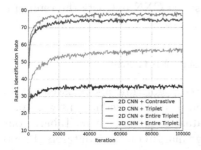
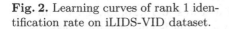
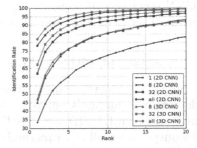

Fig. 2. Learning curves of rank 1 identification rate on iLIDS-VID dataset.

Fig. 3. CMC curves of each model as a function of sequence length.

3.3   Sequence Lengths

We next investigate the effect of sequence length on the re-identification rate. In this evaluation, 2D and 3D CNNs were trained on the iLIDS-VID dataset.

Table 2. Comparison of our method with the state of the art methods.

Dataset	iLIDS-VID				PRID-2011			
CMC rank	1	5	10	20	1	5	10	20
DVR [26]	39.5	61.1	71.7	81.0	40.0	71.7	84.5	92.2
STFV3D + KISSME [15]	44.3	71.7	83.7	91.7	64.1	87.3	89.9	92.0
TDL [29]	56.3	87.6	95.6	98.2	56.7	80.0	87.6	93.6
AvgTAPR [6]	55.0	87.5	93.8	97.2	68.6	94.6	97.4	98.9
Deep RCN + KISSME [27]	46.1	76.8	89.7	95.6	69.0	88.4	93.2	96.4
CNN + XQDA [31]	53.0	81.4	-	95.1	77.3	93.5	-	99.3
RNN + Contrastive [19]	58.0	84.0	91.0	96.0	70.0	90.0	95.0	97.0
3D CNN + Entire Triplet	**82.0**	**95.5**	**98.3**	**99.3**	**83.3**	**95.3**	**99.2**	**99.8**

Test sequences of the desired lengths were taken from the start frames of the sequences. If the sequence length was below the desired length, the maximum number of available frames was taken as the test sequence. Intuitively, longer sequences should improve the performance. Figure 3 confirms this expectation. In 2D CNN, the re-identification rate of rank 1 was greatly improved from 33.5% with a sequence length of 1 (a single still image) to 78.2% with all frames in the sequence (averaging 73 frames), indicating the advantage of the video-based approach in re-identification. 2D CNN embeds the sequence by inputting the final feature map (averaged over the feature maps computed by the network over the whole time series) into the fully-connected layer. Simple averaging over the time series was successful because the embeddings produced by averaging over the feature maps incorporated the multi-frame information and decreased the noise component in the whole. However, 2D CNN was outperformed by 3D CNN regardless of sequence length because 3D CNN extracts the temporal features rather than a simple ensemble.

3.4 Comparison with the State of the Art Methods

We compare the performances of our proposed algorithm and existing video re-identification methods published in the literature. The evaluations were performed on the iLID-VID and PRID-2011 datasets. As shown in Table 2, our model outperforms all other methods by a large margin on both datasets. Previous methods based on deep convolutional networks [19,27,31] report relatively better results over methods using low-level features [6,15,26,29]. This confirms that data-driven feature extraction by deep learning is effective for video-based person re-identification. The superiority of our model can be explained by its refined manner of training the embedding function.

Fig. 4. t-SNE [17] visualization of our embedding on the test split of the iLIDS-VID dataset. Numbers and colors represent the identity of an individual and the camera that captured the individual's sequence, respectively. (Color figure online)

3.5 Visualization of the Embeddings

We visualized our embeddings of person sequences using t-SNE [17]. For this purpose, we plotted 100 person embeddings in the test split constructed from the iLIDS-VID dataset. Figure 4 shows the visualization result. The numbers in this figure represent the person identities, and their colors denote the cameras that captured the person sequence. Embeddings of the same person were closely mapped, whereas those of different persons were mapped apart. This visualization confirms the high discriminative ability of the embeddings in the proposed feature extraction method with improved parameter learning.

4 Conclusion

This paper described a novel method based on convolutional neural networks for video-based person re-identification. The proposed method makes two important contributions: the use of 3D convolution and improved parameter learning for the video-based person re-identification problem. The 3D CNN extracts the spatiotemporal features from a sequence of a person while saving parameter increase. The feature maps obtained by 3D CNN preserve the spatial patterns of human body parts, improving the discriminative representation of human features. The parameter update is based on the gradients calculated from all possible triplets in the mini-batch, which increases the efficiency of distance-metric learning and ensures good convergence. In experiments with the public datasets, our approach outperformed existing methods by a large margin.

References

1. Ahmed, E., Jones, M., Marks, T.K.: An improved deep learning architecture for person re-identification. In: CVPR (2015)
2. Badrinarayanan, V., Kendall, A., Cipolla, R.: Segnet: A deep convolutional encoder-decoder architecture for image segmentation. arXiv preprint arXiv:1511.00561 (2015)

3. Cheng, D., Gong, Y., Zhou, S., Wang, J., Zheng, N.: Person re-identification by multi-channel parts-based CNN with improved triplet loss function. In: CVPR (2016)
4. Cho, K., Van Merriënboer, B., Gulcehre, C., Bahdanau, D., Bougares, F., Schwenk, H., Bengio, Y.: Learning phrase representations using rnn encoder-decoder for statistical machine translation. arXiv preprint arXiv:1406.1078 (2014)
5. Donahue, J., Anne Hendricks, L., Guadarrama, S., Rohrbach, M., Venugopalan, S., Saenko, K., Darrell, T.: Long-term recurrent convolutional networks for visual recognition and description. In: CVPR (2015)
6. Gao, C., Wang, J., Liu, L., Yu, J.G., Sang, N.: Temporally aligned pooling representation for video-based person re-identification. In: ICIP (2016)
7. Hadsell, R., Chopra, S., LeCun, Y.: Dimensionality reduction by learning an invariant mapping. In: CVPR (2006)
8. He, K., Zhang, X., Ren, S., Sun, J.: Deep residual learning for image recognition. In: CVPR (2016)
9. Hochreiter, S., Schmidhuber, J.: Long short-term memory. Neural Comput. 9(8), 1735–1780 (1997)
10. Huang, C., Loy, C.C., Tang, X.: Local similarity-aware deep feature embedding. In: NIPS (2016)
11. Ji, S., Xu, W., Yang, M., Yu, K.: 3d convolutional neural networks for human action recognition. IEEE Trans. Pattern Anal. Mach. Intell. 35(1), 221–231 (2013)
12. Kingma, D., Ba, J.: Adam: A method for stochastic optimization. arXiv preprint arXiv:1412.6980 (2014)
13. Krizhevsky, A., Sutskever, I., Hinton, G.E.: Imagenet classification with deep convolutional neural networks. In: NIPS (2012)
14. Li, W., Zhao, R., Xiao, T., Wang, X.: Deepreid: Deep filter pairing neural network for person re-identification. In: CVPR (2014)
15. Liu, K., Ma, B., Zhang, W., Huang, R.: A spatio-temporal appearance representation for viceo-based pedestrian re-identification. In: ICCV (2015)
16. Long, J., Shelhamer, E., Darrell, T.: Fully convolutional networks for semantic segmentation. In: CVPR (2015)
17. Maaten, L., Hinton, G.: Visualizing data using t-SNE. J. Mach. Learn. Res. 9(Nov), 2579–2605 (2008)
18. McLaughlin, N., Del Rincon, J.M., Miller, P.: Data-augmentation for reducing dataset bias in person re-identification. In: AVSS (2015)
19. McLaughlin, N., Martinez del Rincon, J., Miller, P.: Recurrent convolutional network for video-based person re-identification. In: CVPR (2016)
20. Oh Song, H., Xiang, Y., Jegelka, S., Savarese, S.: Deep metric learning via lifted structured feature embedding. In: CVPR (2016)
21. Ren, S., He, K., Girshick, R., Sun, J.: Faster R-CNN: Towards real-time object detection with region proposal networks. In: NIPS (2015)
22. Schroff, F., Kalenichenko, D., Philbin, J.: Facenet: A unified embedding for face recognition and clustering. In: CVPR (2015)
23. Sutskever, I., Vinyals, O., Le, Q.V.: Sequence to sequence learning with neural networks. In: NIPS (2014)
24. Tran, D., Bourdev, L., Fergus, R., Torresani, L., Paluri, M.: Learning spatiotemporal features with 3D convolutional networks. In: ICCV (2015)
25. Wang, J., Song, Y., Leung, T., Rosenberg, C., Wang, J., Philbin, J., Chen, B., Wu, Y.: Learning fine-grained image similarity with deep ranking. In: CVPR (2014)
26. Wang, T., Gong, S., Zhu, X., Wang, S.: Person re-identification by discriminative selection in video ranking. In: PAMI (2016)

27. Wu, L., Shen, C., Hengel, A.v.d.: Deep recurrent convolutional networks for video-based person re-identification: An end-to-end approach. arXiv preprint arXiv:1606.01609 (2016)

28. Xiao, T., Li, H., Ouyang, W., Wang, X.: Learning deep feature representations with domain guided dropout for person re-identification. In: CVPR (2016)

29. You, J., Wu, A., Li, X., Zheng, W.S.: Top-push video-based person re-identification. In: CVPR (2016)

30. Zhao, R., Ouyang, W., Wang, X.: Person re-identification by salience matching. In: ICCV (2013)

31. Zheng, L., Bie, Z., Sun, Y., Wang, J., Su, C., Wang, S., Tian, Q.: Mars: a video benchmark for large-scale person re-identification. In: ECCV (2016)

Emotional Faces in the Wild: Feature Descriptors for Emotion Classification

Huthaifa Abuhammad$^{(\boxtimes)}$ and Richard Everson$^{(\boxtimes)}$

Department of Computer Science, University of Exeter, Exeter, UK
{hzaa201,R.M.Everson}@exeter.ac.uk

Abstract. We present an automated new approach for facial expression recognition of seven emotions. Three types of texture features (HOG, D-SURF and LBP) from static images are combined, and the resulting features are classified using random forests. We achieve better than state-of-the-art accuracies using multiple texture feature descriptors. The use of random forests allows identification of the most important feature types and locations for emotion classification. Regions around the eyes, forehead, sides of the nose and mouth are found to be most significant.

We introduce the "Emotional Faces in the Wild" dataset (eLFW), a citizen-labelling of 1310 faces from the Labelled Faces in the Wild data. Like people, machine classification of these and the Karolinska Directed Emotional Faces data obtained from actors; poorest results are obtained in distinguishing the sad, angry and fearful emotions. We describe a new weighted voting algorithm, in which the weighted predictions of classifiers trained on pairs of classes are combined with the weights learned using an evolutionary algorithm. This method yields superior results, particularly for the hard-to-distinguish emotions.

1 Introduction

Facial expression recognition a rapidly growing research topics due to an increased interest in applications of human-computer interaction. In 1978 Suwa et al. presented an early automatic facial the expressions system by tracking 20 identified spots on an image sequence [1]. After that, many research has been made to build computer systems to help us to understand human face. Recently Some research concentrating on geometric features, Oztel et al. [2] used SVM classifier on frontal-facial points to achieve a testing accuracy of 75.52% on RaFD dataset after training KDEF database. Diego et al. [3] tracked a set of 68 facial landmarks and obtained an overall recognition rate of 85% on the KDEF.

Appearance-based methods have become more prominent recently [4] such as Histograms of Gradients (HOG) [5], Dense Speeded Up Robust Features (D-SURF) [6,7] and Local Binary Patterns (LBP) [8]. A recent work by Ali et al. [9], where the used PCA, LBP and HOG to represent facial image feature vector, then the extracted feature vector was processed for dimensionality reduction using further principal component analysis. Rao et al. [10] used SURF

© Springer International Publishing AG, part of Springer Nature 2018
A. Campilho et al. (Eds.): ICIAR 2018, LNCS 10882, pp. 164–174, 2018.
https://doi.org/10.1007/978-3-319-93000-8_19

features with One-against-All logistic regression model we trained as weak classifier during boosting; then the weak classifier is selected to combine a final multi-pose classifier, their experiments achieved a rate of 90.64% on the RaFD database and 74.05% on the KDEF database.

In this paper we investigate the use of the combination three feature descriptors, HOG, LBP and D-SURF for more accurate classification. We show that the combination gives a strong image descriptor. Classification with random forests, which embody natural feature selection, further allows us to find the location of the most important image descriptors.

Obtaining labelled data for training emotion classification algorithms costly and researchers are usually forced to resort to using emotions displayed by actors, such as the famous Karolinska Directed Emotional Faces (KDEF) database [11]. To obtain more realistic data we have used citizen volunteers to label a subset of the Labelled Faces in the Wild [12] database with the emotion being displayed. We describe the collection of this emotional Labelled Faces in the Wild (eLFW) dataset and illustrate the performance of the texture-based classifiers on it.

Following the description of the eLFW dataset in Sect. 2, we describe the feature extraction and classification in Sect. 3, followed by the results obtained with proposed method (Sect. 4). The difficulties encountered by people and machines in distinguishing expressions displaying fear, anger and sadness lead us to consider alternative classifiers. So in Sect. 5 we describe a pairwise random forest classifier in which the pairwise classifiers have a weighted vote to determine the overall class. We show how to optimise the weights using an evolutionary algorithm and present results showing the efficacy of the method. Finally, conclusions are drawn in Sect. 6.

2   Emotional Faces in the Wild

Seven elementary categories are typically used for emotion classification: happy, fear, anger, sad, disgust, surprise and neutral. Researchers developing emotion classification algorithms have often used databases of images of professional actors portraying these emotions. Preeminent among these is the Karolinska Directed Emotional Faces (KDEF) database collected by Lundqvist et al. [11], which contains images of 70 individuals, each displaying the seven elementary emotional expressions, each expression being photographed (twice) from five different angles. In our experiments with KDEF, we used only frontal faces making a total of 490 images. Figure 1 shows some sample images from the KDEF data.

2.1   Emotional Labelled Faces in the Wild (eLFW)

In order to develop and test algorithms on images of people displaying emotions in natural settings, without the subject being required to pose a particular emotion, we turned to the Labelled Faces in the Wild (LFW) dataset. This dataset comprises 13,233 images automatically collected from the web and aligned [12].

| Fearful | Angry | Disgusted | Happy | Neutral | Sad | Surprise |

Fig. 1. Example faces from the KDEF database.

Table 1. Summary statistics for the eLFW database.

	KDEF	LFW
Number of accepted images	278	1310
Mean number of votes for accepted images	4.989	7.203
Average entropy for accepted images (bits)	0.668	0.905

Each image is labelled with the name of the person shown and 1680 of the people pictured have two or more distinct photos in the data set.

We obtained labels for the emotions displayed in the LFW data by inviting members of the public to assign an emotional label on our web page, http://www.emotional-faces.ex.ac.uk. The 135 citizens who participated were allowed to label as many or as few images as they wished. Figure 2 shows some example images and their labels from the 1310 images in the eLWF data.

Since the labels assigned differ between annotators, images were retained in a pool of images to be labelled until they had been assigned labels by at least 4. Citizens and the consensus emotion, that is the modal classification, was sufficiently unequivocal. Ambiguous classifications were avoided by calculating the entropy of the empirical distribution of classifications. Let p_n be the proportion of citizens' votes for the nth class ($n = 1, \ldots, 8$), then the entropy, $H = -\sum_n p_n \log_2 p_n$, measures the agreement between the annotators. The entropy is maximised when all classes are assigned in equal proportion and is minimised when images are assigned to only a single class. We therefore kept an image in the pool of images to be labelled until the entropy of the citizens' assignments was less than 1 bit. Images that did not receive an unambiguous classification after 15 votes and images for which the consensus was "don't know" were rejected.

In addition to the LFW images, approximately one in ten images presented to the citizens was a KDEF posed image. This allowed us to check the veracity of individual annotators and, as discussed below, investigate human performance on the KDEF data. As Table 1 shows, the KDEF images were, unsurprisingly, easier than the LFW data for citizens to classify, requiring fewer votes to reduce the entropy below the acceptance threshold. After labelling by citizens, the eLFW database comprises 190 fear images, 120 anger, 160 disgust, 330 happy, 240 neutral, 200 sad and 70 surprise images.

Fearful	Angry	Disgusted	Happy	Neutral	Sad	Surprise

Fig. 2. Example images from the eLWF database together with their citizen consensus emotion labels.

Table 2. Confusion matrices for the citizens' performance on KDEF images. True classes are shown by rows, with assigned classes in columns. FE: fear; AN: anger; DI: disgust; HA: happiness; NE: neutral; SA: sadness; SU: surprise.

	FE	AN	DI	HA	NE	SA	SU
FE	**0.429**	0.020	0.347	0.000	0.000	0.061	0.143
AN	0.057	**0.800**	0.086	0.000	0.000	0.029	0.029
DI	0.000	0.024	**0.786**	0.000	0.000	0.048	0.143
HA	0.000	0.000	0.000	**1.000**	0.000	0.000	0.000
NE	0.000	0.000	0.000	0.000	**1.000**	0.000	0.000
SA	0.059	0.000	0.059	0.000	0.000	**0.853**	0.029
SU	0.139	0.056	0.000	0.000	0.000	0.028	**0.778**

2.2 Citizens' Classification of KDEF Faces

The citizens classified the 278 KDEF photos as shown in Table 2, which were distributed as: 49 fear, 35 anger, 42 disgust, 47 happy, 35 neutral, 34 sad and 36 surprised. The overall agreement of citizens with the KDEF labelling was 80.6%. As the confusion matrix in Table 2 shows, there was complete agreement with the KDEF labelling for happy and neutral faces expressions, but only 42.9% for fear (confused principally with disgust and surprise); 77.8% for surprise (confused principally with fear and anger); and 78.6% for disgust (confused principally with sadness and surprise). Figure 3 shows examples of faces for which the citizen consensus differed from the KDEF labelling.

Fear	Anger	Sad

Surprised	Disgusted	Fear

Fig. 3. Examples of faces for which citizens' votes differ from the KDEF labelling. KDEF labels are shown above each image with the citizens' consensus below.

Fig. 4. Texture feature importances. *Left:* Colours indicate the most important feature in each patch: Red HOG; Green LBP; Blue D-SURF. Image masks identifying the most informative regions for emotion classification: *Middle:* KDEF; *Right* eLWF. (Color figure online)

3   Emotion Classification with Texture Features

In our proposed system, there are four main steps to extract and classify facial features: face detection, face alignment, texture feature extraction (LBP, HOG and D-SURF) and classification. Faces and, within them, eyes and mouth were detected using a Viola-Jones detector [13], after which faces were aligned with an affine transformation to the mean shape found via Procrustes analysis [14]. Texture features were extracted from points on a 25×25 grid of patches covering the images rescaled to 400×400 pixels. Each image patch was characterised by three image descriptors: Local Binary Patterns (LBP), Histogram of Oriented Gradients (HOG) and Dense Speeded Up Robust Features (D-SURF). For each of LBP, HOG and D-SURF, the extracted feature vectors at each grid location were concatenated to characterise the image regarding that texture descriptor.

A random forest classifier [15,16] with 5000 trees was used to classify the displayed emotion into one of the seven classes. Random forests have proved to be accurate and robust classifiers, but also they can be used to gauge the importance of individual features by calculating how much the prediction error increases or decreases when out-of-bag data for a variable is permuted while all others are passed on unaltered. 10-fold cross-validation was used in all the experiments reported here.

4   Combined Texture-Feature Classification

We initially tested each of the texture feature descriptors individually. Using the 490 images in the KDEF database the overall accuracies for the three methods were: LBP 79.9%, HOG 73.0%, D-SURF 70.3%.

In addition, the three texture descriptors by concatenating the feature vectors from LBP, HOG and D-SURF to form a combined feature vector of length 96250. Overall classification accuracy using the combined features was 82.2%, showing that each of the image descriptors provides additional information. The regions in which the separate image descriptors are most informative can be visualised by mapping the most important image descriptor (as measured by the change in prediction error) back to the image patch that generated it. Figure 4 presents the result of this procedure, showing that HOG and LBP features are predominant.

Feature selection also allows the most informative regions of the face for emotion detection to be discovered. To achieve this we summed the feature importance values for each patch to indicate the overall importance of that patch. These were then thresholded, using a threshold chosen by Otsu's method [17], to convert the importance values to a binary mask, which was then rescaled to the original image size. As Fig. 4 shows, this procedure identifies the eyes, mouth, creases at the side of the nose and the forehead as most informative. We point out that this is an empirically determined mask rather than one chosen *a priori* and we obtain slightly different masks for the acted and wild faces.

Table 3. Confusion matrices for random forest classification of the KDEF and eLFW databases. True classes are shown by rows, with assigned classes in columns.

KDEF

	FE	AN	DI	HA	NE	SA	SU
FE	**0.671**	0.143	0.043	0.000	0.000	0.143	0.000
AN	0.000	**0.857**	0.071	0.000	0.000	0.071	0.000
DI	0.000	0.043	**0.929**	0.000	0.000	0.029	0.000
HA	0.000	0.000	0.000	**0.986**	0.014	0.000	0.000
NE	0.000	0.000	0.000	0.014	**0.986**	0.000	0.000
SA	0.043	0.029	0.043	0.000	0.000	**0.886**	0.000
SU	0.014	0.000	0.014	0.000	0.000	0.000	**0.971**

eLFW

	FE	AN	DI	HA	NE	SA	SU
FE	**0.263**	0.153	0.200	0.016	0.042	0.168	0.158
AN	0.083	**0.725**	0.042	0.000	0.000	0.042	0.108
DI	0.063	0.031	**0.775**	0.038	0.031	0.031	0.031
HA	0.000	0.006	0.009	**0.973**	0.012	0.000	0.000
NE	0.004	0.004	0.017	0.054	**0.908**	0.008	0.004
SA	0.150	0.130	0.065	0.010	0.010	**0.535**	0.100
SU	0.157	0.129	0.157	0.029	0.000	0.086	**0.443**

Table 3 shows confusion matrices for random forest classification of the KDEF and eLFW data using the feature importance mask. Overall accuracy for the KDEF data was 89.8% and 71.6% for the eLFW data, which is more difficult to classify due to the unposed nature of the images. The happy and neutral expressions are most easily classified in both datasets and fear is most often misclassified, particularly in the eLFW data, where it is confused with all the other classes except happy and neutral. We point out the similarity of citizens' "misclassifications" of the KDEF data: they achieved a lower overall accuracy of 80.6% and also most frequently confused fear, surprise and disgust (see Sect. 2.2). Further evidence of the similarity between machine and human classification is provided by the entropy of the citizens' classification. Table 4 shows the average entropy of the distributions of citizens' votes for images that were correctly and incorrectly classified. For each of the emotion classes, the average entropy for the misclassified images is greater than or equal to the average entropy of the correctly classified images displaying the same emotion. This indicates that there was more disagreement between the citizens about the emotion displayed there was about correctly classified images. Overall accuracies of other methods on the eLFW data are not available. However, as Table 5 demonstrates, when evaluated on the KDEF data our proposed method using random forest classifiers

Table 4. Average entropy of citizens' voting distributions for correctly and incorrectly classified eLWF images.

Emotion	Entropy (bits)	
	Correct	Misclassified
Fear	0.962	0.981
Anger	0.956	0.982
Disgust	0.983	0.983
Happy	0.777	0.902
Neutral	0.869	0.943
Sad	0.956	0.963
Surprised	0.937	0.976
Overall	0.920	0.961

Table 5. Comparison of classification accuracy of random forest classification using masked LBP, HOG and D-SURF texture features with other recent techniques. Evaluation on the KDEF data.

Method	Accuracy
Rao et al. (2015) [10]	74.05%
Santra et al. (2016) [18]	83.51%
Santra et al. (2016) [19]	84.07%
Yuqian et al. (2017) [4]	88.7%
Random forests with masked texture features	89.8%
Pairwise weighted random forests with masked texture features (Sect. 5)	95.1%

and masked LBP, HOG and D-SURF features compares favourably with another state of the art techniques.

The most informative features for the KDEF database yield an overall accuracy of 89.8% compared with 82.2% obtained using all the features. Likewise, accuracy on the eLFW data rose from 67.3% to 71.6% by using the importance mask.

We also examined the accuracy of support vector machines (SVMs) for this task. On the KDEF data, a one-versus-all SVM with an RBF kernel obtained a classification rate of 72.4%, which rose to 80.8% by restricting the features to those chosen above. Similarly, on the eLWF data, the classification rate using the importance mask was 65.2%, 4.2% greater than using all the features (61%). As Table 6 shows, masking unimportant features improved the classification accuracy of all emotions. The pattern of misclassifications is similar to that found with random forests, with anger, fear, disgust and sadness most often confused. We emphasise that these are the emotions for which citizens' opinions most often contradicted the nominal acted emotions. Similar results were obtained on the eLFW database.

Table 6. Confusion matrices for SVM classification of the KDEF database with and without the importance mask shown in Fig. 4.

Without mask

	FE	AN	DI	HA	NE	SA	SU
FE	**0.643**	0.014	0.057	0.100	0.029	0.071	0.086
AN	0.043	**0.671**	0.071	0.000	0.043	0.086	0.086
DI	0.086	0.057	**0.714**	0.000	0.000	0.071	0.071
HA	0.000	0.000	0.000	**0.900**	0.057	0.014	0.029
NE	0.000	0.000	0.014	0.071	**0.843**	0.057	0.014
SA	0.068	0.043	0.071	0.000	0.029	**0.657**	0.114
SU	0.157	0.057	0.043	0.014	0.014	0.071	**0.643**

Masked

	FE	AN	DI	HA	NE	SA	SU
FE	**0.714**	0.057	0.043	0.000	0.000	0.100	0.086
AN	0.043	**0.686**	0.071	0.000	0.029	0.086	0.086
DI	0.043	0.057	**0.786**	0.000	0.000	0.057	0.057
HA	0.000	0.000	0.000	**0.957**	0.029	0.000	0.014
NE	0.000	0.000	0.000	0.057	**0.900**	0.029	0.014
SA	0.057	0.057	0.043	0.000	0.000	**0.771**	0.071
SU	0.071	0.029	0.014	0.014	0.000	0.029	**0.843**

5 Weighted Pairwise Classification

Random forest classifiers combine decision trees which are naturally capable of multi-class classification, as opposed to dichotomous classifiers, such as SVMs, for which strategies such as one-versus-all or pairwise voting must be employed. In an effort to reduce the misclassifications of fear, anger, disgust and surprise, we also investigated the use of pairwise classifiers for classifying emotions. In this framework a single classifier is trained to discriminate between a pair of classes. The item is then assigned to the class which receives the majority of votes from the pairwise classifiers. In most pairwise architectures each of the constituent classifiers has an equal vote. Here we weight the votes from each classifier and learn appropriate weights by optimising the classification accuracy on a validation set. More specifically, suppose $y_{ij}(\mathbf{x}_n) \in [0, 1]$ is the output of the classifier discriminating between classes i and j for image features $\mathbf{x}_n$. Here we use random forests for each dichotomous classifier, so that $y_{ij}(\mathbf{x}_n)$ is the proportion of decision trees in the (i, j)-th forest that voted for class i. Then the overall score for class i is

$$Y_i(\mathbf{x}_n) = \sum_{j \neq i} \lambda_{ij} y_{ij}(\mathbf{x}_n) \tag{1}$$

where the weights are λ_{ij}, and the image is assigned to the class with the largest overall score: $\operatorname{argmax}_i Y_i(\mathbf{x}_n)$. The weights are constrained to be non-negative, $\lambda_{ij} \geq 0$ for all i and j, and we demand that $\sum_j \lambda_{ij} = 1$ for all i.

Training takes place in two phases. First, the constituent classifiers are independently trained on the pairs of classes. Secondly, the accuracy of the overall classifier on a second training data set is maximised by optimising the voting weights using an evolutionary optimiser. Here we used CMA-ES [20], a popular and effective evolutionary optimiser. Constraints were enforced by working in terms of variables θ_{ij} with

$$\lambda_{ij} = \frac{\theta_{ij}}{\sum_k \theta_{ik}}. \tag{2}$$

Table 7. Confusion matrices weighted pairwise classification of the KDEF and eLFW databases.

KDEF

	FE	AN	DI	HA	NE	SA	SU
FE	**0.914**	0.029	0.000	0.000	0.000	0.000	0.057
AN	0.000	**0.943**	0.014	0.000	0.000	0.043	0.000
DI	0.000	0.014	**0.971**	0.000	0.000	0.014	0.000
HA	0.000	0.000	0.000	**0.986**	0.014	0.000	0.000
NE	0.000	0.000	0.000	0.014	**0.986**	0.000	0.000
SA	0.043	0.029	0.043	0.000	0.000	**0.886**	0.000
SU	0.014	0.000	0.014	0.000	0.000	0.000	**0.971**

eLFW

	FE	AN	DI	HA	NE	SA	SU
FE	**0.495**	0.089	0.142	0.011	0.042	0.074	0.147
AN	0.025	**0.792**	0.050	0.000	0.000	0.083	0.050
DI	0.056	0.019	**0.788**	0.044	0.031	0.025	0.038
HA	0.003	0.012	0.003	**0.970**	0.009	0.003	0.000
NE	0.004	0.013	0.000	0.017	**0.938**	0.029	0.000
SA	0.150	0.130	0.065	0.010	0.010	**0.535**	0.100
SU	0.086	0.086	0.071	0.014	0.129	0.086	**0.529**

We note that the procedure is efficient because once the pairwise classifiers have been trained, classification scores $y_{ij}(\mathbf{x}_n)$ need only be calculated once before optimisation of the weights. Table 7 shows the confusion matrices obtained with the optimised pairwise classification using 10-fold cross-validation testing. The accuracies for the data sets have increased to 95.1% for KDEF and 76.6% for eLFW. As can be seen from the confusion matrices, classification accuracies of fear, anger, surprise and disgust have increased substantially, although for the eLFW data there is still considerable misclassification of fear (confused with disgust and surprise), sadness (confused with fear and anger) and surprise (confused with neutral, fear, anger and disgust). We remark that these emotions are all often expressed through a grimacing expression which may account for the difficulty in distinguishing them. Furthermore, these are the emotions about which the citizens showed the most disagreement.

6 Conclusion

Work on machine recognition of emotional expressions has been hampered by the lack of unposed labelled data. In this paper we have described the new emotional Labelled Faces in the Wild (eLFW) database, a citizen labelling of LFW faces. The eLFW database is available for research use at http://www.emotional-faces. ex.ac.uk.

Rather than using a single type of texture descriptor for appearance-based classification of emotions, we showed that a combination of LBP, HOG and D-SURF significantly increases classification accuracy. Furthermore, the random forest's feature selection was used to empirically identify the important regions of the faces for classifying emotion. As might be expected these are mainly around the eyes, mouth, creases on either side of the nose and the forehead. Use of our empirically defined importance mask enhances classification accuracy.

Further improvements to classification accuracy were obtained by pairwise weighted voting between dichotomous classifiers, and we showed how to learn optimal weights using an evolutionary algorithm. The resulting accuracies are significantly better than current published state of the art results on the posed KDEF data. Nonetheless, particularly for unposed data, classification of fear, anger, disgust, sadness and surprise remains imperfect and we obtain classification accuracies of about 77%. We observe that these are the emotions that humans find more difficult to classify from static images in the eLFW data. Current work is to build upon these methods to take advantage of the additional information in dynamic expressions using video data.

References

1. SOWN, M.: A preliminary note on pattern recognition of facial emotional expression. In: The 4th International Joint Conferences on Pattern Recognition (1978)
2. Oztel, I., Yolcu, G., Oz, C., Kazan, S., Bunyak, F.: iFER: facial expression recognition using automatically selected geometric eye and eyebrow features. J. Electron. Imaging **27**(2), 023003 (2018)
3. Faria, D.R., Vieira, M., Faria, F.C., Premebida, C.: Affective facial expressions recognition for human-robot interaction. In: IEEE RO-MAN17: IEEE International Symposium on Robot and Human Interactive Communication, Lisbon, Portugal (2017)
4. Yuqian, Z., Bertram, E.: Action unit selective feature maps in deep networks for facial expression recognition. In: The 2017 International Joint Conference on Neural Networks (IJCNN 2017) (2017)
5. Dalal, N., Triggs, B.: Histograms of oriented gradients for human detection. In: 2005 IEEE Computer Society Conference on Computer Vision and Pattern Recognition (CVPR 2005), vol. 1, pp. 886–893. IEEE (2005)
6. Lowe, D.G.: Distinctive image features from scale-invariant keypoints. Int. J. Comput. Vis. **60**(2), 91–110 (2004)
7. Bay, H., Ess, A., Tuytelaars, T., Van Gool, L.: Speeded-up robust features (SURF). Comput. Vis. Image Underst. **110**(3), 346–359 (2008)
8. Ojala, T., Pietikäinen, M., Harwood, D.: A comparative study of texture measures with classification based on featured distributions. Pattern Recogn. **29**(1), 51–59 (1996)
9. Ali, G., Iqbal, M.A., Choi, T.S.: Boosted NNE collections for multicultural facial expression recognition. Pattern Recogn. **55**, 14–27 (2016)
10. Rao, Q., Qu, X., Mao, Q., Zhan, Y.: Multi-pose facial expression recognition based on surf boosting. In: 2015 International Conference on Affective Computing and Intelligent Interaction (ACII), pp. 630–635. IEEE (2015)
11. Lundqvist, D., Flykt, A., Öhman, A.: The Karolinska directed emotional faces (KDEF) (1998)
12. Huang, G., Mattar, M., Lee, H., Learned-Miller, E.G.: Learning to align from scratch. In: Advances in Neural Information Processing Systems, pp. 764–772 (2012)
13. Viola, P., Jones, M.J.: Robust real-time face detection. Int. J. Comput. Vis. **57**(2), 137–154 (2004)
14. Kendall, D.G.: A survey of the statistical theory of shape. Stat. Sci. **4**, 87–99 (1989)
15. Breiman, L.: Bagging predictors. Mach. Learn. **24**(2), 123–140 (1996)
16. Breiman, L.: Random forests. Mach. Learn. **45**(1), 5–32 (2001)
17. Otsu, N.: A threshold selection method from gray-level histograms. Automatica **11**(285–296), 23–27 (1975)

18. Santra, B., Mukherjee, D.P.: Local dominant binary patterns for recognition of multi-view facial expressions. In: Proceedings of the Tenth Indian Conference on Computer Vision, Graphics and Image Processing, p. 25. ACM (2016)
19. Santra, B., Mukherjee, D.P.: Local saliency-inspired binary patterns for automatic recognition of multi-view facial expression. In: IEEE International Conference on Image Processing (ICIP), pp. 624–628. IEEE (2016)
20. Hansen, N.: The CMA evolution strategy: a comparing review. In: Lozano, J., Larranaga, P., Inza, I., Bengoetxea, E. (eds.) Towards a New Evolutionary Computation. STUDFUZZ, vol. 192, pp. 75–102. Springer, Heidelberg (2006). https://doi.org/10.1007/3-540-32494-1_4

From Windows to Logos: Analyzing Outdoor Images to Aid Flyer Classification

Payam Pourashraf[1]([⊠]), Noriko Tomuro[1],
and Saeed Bagheri Shouraki[2]

[1] DePaul University, 243 S. Wabash Ave, Chicago, IL, USA
ppourash@depaul.edu, tomuro@cs.depaul.edu
[2] Department of Electrical Engineering,
Sharif University of Technology, Tehran, Iran
bagheri-s@sharif.ir

Abstract. The goal of this paper was to create a new method for analyzing the online real estate flyers based on their property types. We created an algorithm which identifies the buildings and windows from the buildings in order to extract some useful features for classifying the flyers. Our novel approach for building recognition has two main steps: 1- Building Detector 2- Region Growing. Our novel window detection algorithm uses vanishing point to identify nearly the best angle for applying window detection. It transforms the 2D image into 3D and rotates the 3D image around the z-axis and picks the appropriate angle based on the vanishing points. Using these two novel techniques we were be able to extract a new feature vector which is used to build our final model. This final model is able to classify Retail spaces very well based on the Window and logo features.

Keywords: Flyer · Window detection · Building recognition · Object detection

1 Introduction

Online flyers are a common information media for many commercial industries. Although several large centralized product data repositories/databases have been developed lately for some industries such as residential real estate[1], they may be proprietary. Also for industries that do not have a centralized database or established repository, local dealers, brokers and agents still rely on traditional media such as flyers to accumulate and dissimilate information. They typically create flyers (usually in pdf) of the products they want to sell (or lease) and place them on their websites. The commercial real estate industry in the US is one such industry.[2] Brokers collect local commercial property data using information from flyers, contacting brokers, or visiting physical sites.

---

[1] The US Multiple Listing Services (MLS) represents the US residential real estate.
[2] LoopNet (http://www.loopnet.com/) is the most heavily trafficked online commercial real estate marketplace that also covers the largest geographical area in the US, but only has 800,000 listings (as of May 14, 2017).

© Springer International Publishing AG, part of Springer Nature 2018
A. Campilho et al. (Eds.): ICIAR 2018, LNCS 10882, pp. 175–184, 2018.
https://doi.org/10.1007/978-3-319-93000-8_20

The current real-estate databases are manual based which is tiresome, time consuming and error prone; therefore, automatic building and indexing these databases has advantages and practical applications for brokers. A real-estate flyer typically contains textual descriptions, and some images such as pictures and logos. An example of a real estate flyer is shown in Fig. 1. In one of our previous works, we categorized the images embedded in the flyers into five genres: indoor-building, outdoor-building, map, aerial, and drawing [1]. However, a major problem in flyer classification is the problem of the semantic gap between the low-level visual and textual features and the high-level labels of property type (e.g. retail, industrial, office; labels commonly used in the real estate industry). The problem is that property types are essentially based on the usage of the property, rather than the attributes or objects that are described in the text or captured in the images. Furthermore, since a flyer might include several images, the determination of the final property type by an automatic system is non-trivial. These factors together are making the relation between the two levels extremely complex and the semantic gap much more pronounced in the domain of real estate flyers. The properties are already indicated on property listing forums they have been done by humans and manually.

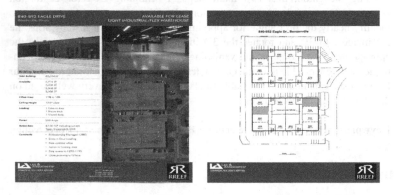

Fig. 1. A commercial real estate flyer of an industrial property (© Lee & Associates)

The work we present in this paper is an attempt to reduce the semantic gap and improve the flyers classification, by focusing on images of Outdoor-buildings. Outdoor images by capturing the external features such as window properties could correlate with the usage of the property. Thus focusing on the outdoor image genre has been chosen as a current step in the classification of the flyers, based on the image genres. The results of this work can improve the classification of flyers which has a practical import for the brokers. Another important benefit of this work is to reduce the semantic gap which has been an obstacle for modeling of this system.

The hypothesis of the current work is that focusing on the outdoor-building genre and extracting physical features from the images, such as window and logo features, could help in the classification of flyers and help to reduce the semantic gap.

2 Related Works

Previous independent work has been done on text and image within the flyers [1–3]. In one of the previous works for the text side various techniques in IE and Text Categorization has been used. The combinations of textual (e.g. token and token kind) and visual features (e.g. font color, size, position in the flyer) were used to accurately extract various information about the property. The results showed that overall visual features improved performance significantly [2].

In a study that has been completed about the flyer images, we described our exploratory work on supplementing our dataset of images extracted from real estate flyers with images from a large general image repository to enhance the breadth of the samples and create a classification model which would perform well for totally unseen, new instances. We selected some images from the Scene UNderstanding (SUN) database which are annotated with the scene categories that seem to match with our flyer images, and added them to our flyer dataset. We ran a series of experiments with various configurations of flyer vs. SUN data mix. The results showed that the classification models trained with a mixture of SUN and flyer images produced comparable accuracies as the models trained solely with flyer images [3].

Some approaches have been proposed for learning from multimodal data. In [4] they showed that utilizing tags with image features (such as Spatial Color Mode, MPEG-7 Edge Histogram, MPEG-7 Edge Histogram) could boost the classification performance of SVM model. In [5], an approach has presented that on different object recognition tasks, by adding the text modality the accuracy of SVM classifier can be boosted. In [6], in order to learn a model with multiple input modalities, a Deep Boltzmann Machine has been proposed.

As mentioned above, the independent previous works on the text side have obtained fairly good promising results but to problem of semantic gap the current work has been designed to improve the classification models. However, in going forward, the current system has been designed to improve the accuracy of classification of the flyers just based on the image side.

3 Methodology and Experimental Design

3.1 Image Dataset

We utilized the real estate flyer dataset used in [2]. 144 flyers that included outdoor images have been selected from the original dataset. We focused on outdoor images in this work, because we thought outdoor images by capturing the external features such as properties of the windows could help us to find the property type, especially the retail rather than other kinds of property types. Thus focusing on the outdoor image genre has been chosen as a current step in the classification of the flyers, based on the image genres. Then in order to extract the images inside the flyers, we wrote our own code and utilized software tools to filter 'noisy' non-content images (such as image fragments, color borders and company logos).

Table 1. Distribution of the number of flyers and their proportion in the dataset

	I	I-O	I-L	I-M	L	L-O	L-R	O	O-R	R	M
Aerial	107	25	3		115	2	2	60	23	110	3
Map	135	36	3		337	2	2	160	63	266	57
Inside	130	20			2			287	36	193	21
Outside	265	50		2	45		8	253	85	398	68

We put together an analysis that categorized flyers by their property types. The flyers could have single label (Industrial, Office, ...) or multi-label (Industrial-Office, Industrial-Land). Below you can see what the results were (Table 1):

As can be seen there are considerable amounts of images which belongs to Office-Retail and Industrial-Office categories. This makes it difficult for the algorithms to differentiate between the Retail, Office and Industrial categories. To solve this, our hypothesis is that window size can be used by the algorithm to differentiate between retail, industrial and office. This is because retail buildings typically have large windows and office buildings have smaller frequent windows and industrial has smaller but less frequent windows. For example, in the Fig. 2 we can tell its retail because the windows size is large compared to the building size and also there are few windows. In Fig. 3 it is clear that this is an industrial building because the windows are small and infrequent. Finally, the Fig. 4 is an Office since the windows are medium size and frequent.

Fig. 2. An example of retail property

Fig. 3. An example of industrial property

Fig. 4. An example of office property

Our initial analysis included those multi-label flyers however for our final analysis we decided to analyze based on just single label flyers. The reason for this is because we felt that analyzing multi-label and single-label flyers together was too broad.

Finally, we selected 844 outdoor images out of the original flyers which have better resolutions. The distribution of the number of flyers and their proportion in the dataset are shown in Table 2.

Table 2. Distribution of different property types with their number of images and their proportion in the dataset

Property type	Industrial	Multi-family	Office	Retail	Land	Total
Number of images	216	65	182	338	43	844
Proportion of images	26%	8%	21%	40%	5%	100%

3.2 The Framework

The framework that we have developed will look for objects like Logos, Features from Windows and General features from the buildings. We start with outside building images and we then from the outside image we recognize the building by our recognition algorithm (see Sect. 3.3) From that we extrapolate the Windows (see Sect. 3.4) Logos (see Sect. 3.5) and General features from the building. Finally, we extract 38 features from detected building, logo, and windows. The framework of our approach can be seen in Fig. 5.

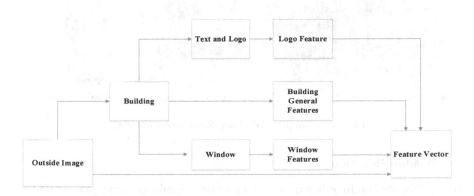

Fig. 5. The framework of our work

3.3 Building Recognition

We thought that there are some useful features inside the building that can be helpful for the task of classifying flyers based on their property types. For instance, after identifying buildings the task of identifying windows would become easier and more accurate. Our approach for building recognition has two main steps: 1- Building Detector 2- Region Growing. Reference Figs. 6a and b for the visual representation of both steps.

1- Building Detector: For building recognition we first apply the object detector by Viola and Jones which uses Haar-like features and trained by 6000 building images from SUN database [7, 8]. The training set included both occluded and non-occluded samples. However, with this algorithm we are not able to find the area of the entire building. We made approximations of the regions that buildings could exist. In order to solve this issue, we applied the Region Growing algorithm.

2- Region Growing: This algorithm has been used multiple times for image segmentation [9, 10]. In this algorithm, finding the initial seed is very vital. If the
selected seed is inside a door or wall, then we will be unable to find the whole area.
Because the doors and windows are negative spaces, the algorithm will only find
the area of that space, unable to spread past the confines of the door or window.
However, If the seed would be selected inside the wall then we are hopeful to
capture the whole building area. We determined that the pixels with highest color
frequency are more likely to be the wall because it is the largest part of the
building. So out of the set of pixels with highest color frequency, we select the one
which is closest to the center of the building and apply the region growing algorithm to the seed.

(a) Shows the outcome of the step 1   (b) The result of applying region growing algorithm

Fig. 6. A sample of Building Recognition process.

3.4   Window Detection

After finding the building dimensions by using the formula, the next goal would be to
identify the window dimensions. In order to detect the windows, we proposed an
alternative approach that functions based on the changing vanishing points. This
alternative algorithm identifies the largest vanishing points of a rectangular shape.
Specifically, we are analyzing windows and finding the best angle to apply window
detection. The reason why we are performing this approach is because our window
detector program performs optimally when looking at the object straight on. If the
shape has an angle, the program is unable to detect the object because our window
detector is trained to recognize only rectangular shapes.

In order to begin, we first transform the 2D image into 3D by using Make3D [11].
Then we rotate the 3D objects around their z-axis and for each angle we compute the
vanishing points. We use the vanishing points because as you rotate the object the
angle changes from a fixed perspective. As the vanishing point decreases, the angle of
the window is sharper. But as the vanishing point becomes larger the object moves to a
more head on view. So when we find the angle with the largest vanishing point we will
transform the 3D object back into its original 2D dimension. After that we will apply
the window detection on the newly rotated object. Similar to building and car detection,
we used Viola and Jones object detector which uses Haar-like features and trained by

15000 window images from SUN database [7, 8]. The training set included both occluded and non-occluded samples. Other studies that have used window detection never rotate the original object because they simplified the problem by using the straight on images. However, our method is unique because we don't necessarily need the straight forward image for the task of object recognition. As a result, this method is unique and applicable to other object detection tasks. This process eliminates the need for huge training datasets which are hard to access in certain tasks. It also simplifies the method used for object detection.

3.5 Logo Detection

For logos, the algorithm will simply detect the text from the building area (referenced in Sect. 3.3) whether there is a logo or not. We used the Tesseract Optical Character Recognizer (OCR) API for recognizing characters in the building image [12, 13]. If there is a logo, this might tell us that it is a retail building, if not that flyer might be hinting at other property types. To indicate a logo, we are looking for texts that are bigger than a certain threshold (within 1/10th of the building size or greater), and we want the logo dimensions to be proportional to the building size. We may filter out all smaller texts and numbers since they are not necessary in detecting logos and they could refer to building addresses. As it shows below in Fig. 7 this would be an example of a building address which we are not interested in. Figure 8 is showing the logo that we are interested in.

Fig. 7. Building with no interested embedded text

Fig. 8. Building with interested embedded text found through logo detection system

4 Flyer Categorization

The flyer categorization task involves labeling all flyers with appropriate transaction property types, such as; Retail, Industrial, Multi family, Office, and Land. This is a multi-label classification task as in all cases a flyer can have more than one label; however, some can have more than one but we decided to focus on single label flyers. We applied a supervised Machine Learning approach to the task utilizing Support Vector Machines (SVM) using the LibSVM library [17].

To see the effect of different features we ran 3 different test scenarios, because we were interested to reduce the number of features without sacrificing the classification accuracy. In the first scenario we used just GIST features and we consider this as the baseline scenario. In the second scenario, we included the GIST, Window, and Logo features and the third scenario we just included the Window and Logo Features. Table 3 illustrates the results for these scenarios.

Table 3. Results from applying SVM on the task of identifying flyer property type (retail, office, industrial, land, multi-family).

Property type		GIST	GIST-Window-Logo	Window-Logo
	Accuracy	0.405	0.478	0.486
	(p-value)	(–)	(0.005)	(0.003)

Table 4. Accuracy per class for scenario 3

	Retail	Office	Multi-family	Industrial	Land
Correctly classified	72%	29%	19%	45%	23%

As Table 3 shows, the accuracy level increases by adding Window and Logo features to the GIST features. We compared the first scenario with the other two scenarios. There is an observable difference between the accuracy levels depending on the number of features. The difference between accuracies was statistically significant with the p-value < 0.01 by a 1-sided t-test, where the null hypothesis is there is no significant difference between the baseline scenario and the other two scenarios with new approaches on extracting features. The alternative hypothesis is that scenarios 2 and 3 produced higher accuracies compared to the baseline.

In the third scenario, by excluding GIST features we got a better accuracy. GIST gets the global configuration of the scene and doesn't portray any interior details that could help inform the system about the classification of the flier based on their property types. Therefore, the other features (Window and Logo) that try to get more detail information from the buildings are more helpful to this task.

As can be seen in Table 4, the retail properties are correctly predicted 72%. So the model predicted the retail properties effectively and this is considered as one of the significant parts of this work. Even Though we could not classify all of the categories very well, but this approach is good for identifying images of retail. Based on the relatively effective prediction of the retail property type, we can conclude that we can lessen the semantic gap between the low-level visual features and the high-level labels of property type.

5   Conclusions and Future Work

In conclusion, in this work we presented our work on classifying the outdoor images embedded in the real estate flyers by the property type. We were trying to find a new algorithm in order to categorize the online flyers based on their property types. We decided to use new feature vector which includes windows, logos, and general building features and run them in to the algorithm. We also proposed new ideas for Building identification and Window recognition. As a results of this study we concluded that windows and logos were features that differentiated retail properties very well and our model showed the relatively effective prediction of the retail property type. Although the other features did not provide the same distinct differentiation, our results still can be useful for the flyer categorization.

For future work, we plan to bridge the problem of semantic gap by building a multimodal system using both texts and images. Other future studies with a focus on the other image genres besides outdoor-building (map, schematic drawing, aerial photo and indoor-building) would also be helpful for improvement of flyers classification.

References

1. Pourashraf, P., Tomuro, N., Apostolova, E.: Genre-based image classification using ensemble learning for online flyers. International Conference on Image Processing (ICDIP) (2015)
2. Apostolova, E., Tomuro, N.: Combining visual and textual features for information extraction from online flyers. In: Empirical Methods in Natural Language Processing (EMNLP) (2014)
3. Pourashraf, P., Tomuro, N.: Use of a large image repository to enhance domain dataset for flyer classification. In: ISVC (2015)
4. Huiskes, M.J., Thomee, B., Lew, M.S.: New trends and ideas in visual concept detection: the MIR flickr retrieval evaluation initiative. In: Proceedings of the International Conference on Multimedia Information Retrieval, pp. 527–536. ACM, March 2010
5. Guillaumin, M., Verbeek, J., Schmid, C.: Multimodal semi-supervised learning for image classification. In: 2010 IEEE Conference on Computer Vision and Pattern Recognition (CVPR), pp. 902–909. IEEE, June 2010
6. Srivastava, N., Salakhutdinov, R.R.: Multimodal learning with deep boltzmann machines. In: Advances in Neural Information Processing Systems (2012)
7. Viola, P., Jones, M.: Rapid object detection using a boosted cascade of simple features. In: Proceedings of the 2001 IEEE Computer Society Conference on Computer Vision and Pattern Recognition, CVPR 2001, vol. 1, p. I. IEEE (2001)
8. Xiao, J., Hays, J., Ehinger, K. A., Oliva, A., Torralba, A.: Sun database: Large-scale scene recognition from abbey to zoo. In: 2010 IEEE Conference on Computer Vision and Pattern Recognition (CVPR), pp. 3485–3492. IEEE, June 2010
9. Mohammed, M.A., et al.: Automatic segmentation and automatic seed point selection of nasopharyngeal carcinoma from microscopy images using region growing based approach. J. Comput. Sci. **20**, 61–69 (2017)
10. Duan, H.H., Gong, J., Nie, S.D.: Two-pass region growing combined morphology algorithm for segmenting airway tree from CT chest scans. In: 2016 UKACC 11th International Conference on Control (CONTROL), pp. 1–6. IEEE, August 2016
11. Saxena, A., Sun, M., Ng, A.Y.: Make3D: learning 3-D scene structure from a single still image. IEEE Trans. Pattern Anal. Mach. Intell. (PAMI) (2008)
12. Google. "tesseract-ocr". https://code.google.com/tesseract-ocr/. Accessed 2008-07-12
13. Kay, Anthony: Tesseract: an open-source optical character recognition engine. Linux J. **2007** (159), 2 (2007)

14. Irving, B.: Aspects and extensions of a theory of human image understanding. In: Computational Processes in Human Vision: An Interdisciplinary Perspective, pp. 370–428 (1998)
15. Khosla, A., K., Das Sarma, A., Hamid, R.: What makes an image popular? In Proceedings of the 23rd International Conference on World Wide Web, pp. 867–876 (2014)
16. Oliva, A., Torralba, A.: Modeling the shape of the scene: a holistic representation of the spatial envelope. Int. J. Comput. Vis. **42**(3), 145–175 (2001)
17. Chang, C.C., Lin, C.J.: LIBSVM: a library for support vector machines. ACM Trans. Intell. Syst. Technol. (TIST) **2**(3), 27 (2011)

Deep Convolutional-Shepard Interpolation Neural Networks for Image Classification Tasks

Kaleb E. Smith[1(✉)], Phillip Williams[2], Tatsanee Chaiya[1], and Max Ble[1]

[1] Florida Institute of Technology, Melbourne, FL 32901, USA
ksmith012007@my.fit.edu
[2] University of Ottawa, Ottawa, Canada

Abstract. With the power of deep learning taking over image classification and computer vision problems, it is no wonder that many algorithms look to their architecture to leverage better results. With Shepard Interpolation Neural Networks (SINN), there is no need for this deep architecture, but rather a shallow and wide approach is taken. SINNs fall short in the ability to take raw input information and extract meaningful features from them. This task is excelled however by deep learning approaches, more specifically, a deep convolutional neural network (CNN) which naturally learns important features from the raw input data for better discrimination. For this paper, we look to collide the power of deep learning features with the speed and efficiency of the shallow learning framework into one cohesive architecture that produces competitive results with a tenth of the computational cost. We start by using different CNNs to extract features from three popular image classification data sets (MNIST, CIFAR-10, and CIFAR-100), and then use those features to efficiently and effectively train a shallow SINN to classify the images accordingly. This method has the ability to not only produce competitive results to the state-of-the-art in image classification, but also blow their computational cost of running an efficient network out of the water by nearly ten times the speed.

1 Introduction

Although deep learning has changed many of the benchmark data sets' "state-of-the-art" accuracy, the overall concept of image classification hasn't changed. That is, to classify well on any data set you need a crucial component - features. However, not just any feature will suffice. For instance, the pixel colors in the RGB color space are indeed features, but with just those three numbers in a feature vector the task ability is limited. This is where deep learning actually shines, in its ability to naturally extract meaningful and useful features from any image and then have those features be unique to certain aspects of the image class it's describing [5,6]. It is here where we look to utilize deep learning for its ability to extract better features for image classification.

© Springer International Publishing AG, part of Springer Nature 2018
A. Campilho et al. (Eds.): ICIAR 2018, LNCS 10882, pp. 185–192, 2018.
https://doi.org/10.1007/978-3-319-93000-8_21

The reason for not using stacked convolutional neural networks for the image classification task is shown in the computational complexity. Though these algorithms excel in classification tasks the computational costs are extremely high and complex [4]. This leads to current state-of-the-art models having an extreme training time due to the billions of tunable parameters. The network is then limited to only being trained on large massive computer servers or clusters in order to get a network that can perform a classification task. Our proposed algorithm looks to advance this computational complexity to a feasible amount that can be achieved on a local CPU or laptop. Shepard Interpolation neural networks (SINN) map the input feature vectors to a set of hypersurfaces which approximates the functions in the feature space to a certain amount of precision. SINN make an impact in image classification tasks in the fact that they can compete in accuracy, but at a huge reduction in the memory footprint and computational cost of the network to be trained (to an order of ten). For images, the input vector is the flattened RGB data of the image, and from there the information is encoded in the relative position of the pixels [7]. This flattening does not help the SINN because it fails to extract meaningful features from these RGB input vectors. This is where CNNs come into play, using their feature extracting ability, meaning features can be utilized in the SINN architecture and achieve high accuracy with efficient speeds [6].

In this paper, the issue of obtaining great performance results (both accuracy and computational) on image classification is addressed. We obtain features from several small CNN architectures and then extract features from three popular image classification data sets: MNIST, CIFAR-10, and CIFAR-100. Then these features are utilized in the SINN framework to classify the images into the appropriate categories. Experiments show that at a tenth of the cost of large bulky CNNs, our approach achieves competitive results in accuracy across all data sets. The rest of the paper first looks at previous related works of Shepard interpolation methods in machine learning and image classification. Second, the CNN features are briefly explained while looking more into how a SINN is formed. Next, experimental results are presented from the three data sets mentioned above. Finally, a brief conclusion looking back on the work done and future outlook for our approach.

2   Related Works

The Shepard Interpolation Neural Network architecture is new, having just being published within the last year. As a result, there are little to no advancements made on this architecture or improvements to the classification results [3]. SINN use a Shepard and metric node inside the hidden layer, which can be thought of as one node essentially since the Shepard node can not activate without a metric node's output. By utilizing the interpolation technique of Shepard [9], this network can design hyper-parameters which require very little tuning, resulting in a decrease of the computational complexity of the network. As mentioned, this network design is still fresh in the community, therefore looking deeply into

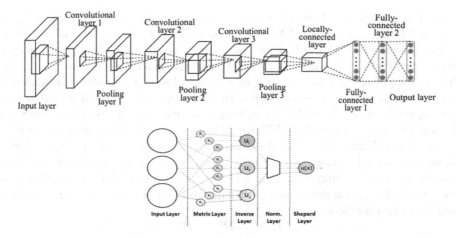

Fig. 1. Illustration of a CNN (top) and SINN (bottom) Architecture.

SINN for literature is difficult; however, this method of Shepard interpolation has been used for tasks outside of image classification.

Park and Sandberg [2] describe a Radial Basis Function Network that functions in much the same manner as the Shepard Interpolation in that they are both based off of exact interpolation and function using a single hidden layer. The Shepard Interpolation Neural Network architecture departs from Radial Basis Function Networks through implementation as well as a few characteristics of the activation functions used. For example, Radial Basis Function Networks require that the activation function be radially symmetric [2], while Shepard Interpolation Neural Networks do not place such a constraint on the metric and Shepard activation functions [3].

Ren et al. [8] outline the application of Shepard Interpolation to convolutional neural networks. The proposed method is the addition of a Shepard Interpolation layer as an augmentation on architectures used for low-level image processing tasks such as inpainting and super resolution. This showed promise in the work, but was never advanced from looking at more literature reviews.

We all know of the vast amount of literature relating to deep learning and convolutional neural networks [1]. To summarize, the concept was brought to light by Lecun in the 1990's for a new way of classifying images [13]. It didn't gain extreme popularity until ImageNet was won by Krizhevsky in 2012 using a deep CNN, blowing all other algorithms away in accuracy [16]. Since then, his paper has been cited over eighteen thousand times and deep learning took off.

3   Deep Feature Based Shepard Interpolation Neural Networks

For any image classification task, the SINN transforms a feature vector to a space of classification vectors. If the Shepard Interpolation Neural Network is treated as a transform from the feature space to the output classification space, a second transform is needed from the image space to the feature space. Prior to the introduction of the feature-based input layers to the Shepard Interpolation architecture, the mapping from the image space to the feature space is simply flattening the image matrix to a vector; the key innovation proposed is to replace the image flattening step with more sophisticated feature extraction techniques from the deep CNN, resulting in a much better overall accuracy for the model. An overview of a CNN architecture and a SINN architecture can be seen in Fig. 1. Notice, the SINN shows an independent Metric and Shepard layer. These activation functions work in unison and can be visualized as just one layer in a higher level architecture. This leads to the idea of a shallow learning process, which is much quicker, more efficient, and competitive in accuracy versus standard deep methods.

$$R^{i \times j} \to R^m \to R^n \tag{1}$$

where $R^{i \times j}, R^m, R^n$ are the image space, feature space and classification space respectively.

3.1   Network Compression

In the Shepard Interpolation Neural Network architecture [3], the metric nodes contain the vast majority of learnable parameters. Furthermore, it is possible to reduce the total memory footprint of the metric layer by a third after training while maintaining exactly the same behavior. The metric activation function is as follows:

$$\Phi(x) = |\alpha(wx + b)| \tag{2}$$

By allowing all three free parameters (α, w and b) to be updated during training, the network converges much more quickly and achieves superior validation accuracy once the training is completed. However, the activation can be written under a slightly different form:

$$\Phi(x) = |\alpha wx + \alpha b| \tag{3}$$

This shows two input digits from MNIST before and after training. You can see the difference in what the Metric node and Shepard node learns depending on their input. In comparison, the features learned from a CNN can also be seen in the same figure.

3.2   K-means Initialization

The performance of the model is directly related to the coverage of the nodes across the areas of interest in the feature space. This concept leads to interesting possibilities for the initiation of the metric nodes. Therefore, to achieve better efficiency in training, the k-means clustering algorithm is used on the feature vectors in the feature space to initialize the metric nodes for the approximation needed to cover the complete feature space surface [10].

4   Experiments

In order to validate that the our deep feature approaches show significant improvements over existing methods, we explore our method on three popular data sets: MNIST data set [13] of 28×28 grayscale images of handwritten numbers and the CIFAR-10 and CIFAR-100 [14] data sets of 32×32 RGB images of various objects.

We pull features from three smaller CNNs to feed into our SINN of only 50 nodes in the hidden layer. These CNN networks are of the following sizes: CNN-1: $32\times(3 \times 3)$, $32\times(5 \times 5)$, $32\times(3 \times 3)$ CNN-2: $32\times(5 \times 5)$, $64\times(3 \times 3)$, $32\times(5 \times 5)$ and CNN-3: $64\times(3 \times 3)$, $64\times(3 \times 3)$, $64\times(3 \times 3)$, these names denote the architecture in the results tables. Each CNN is trained using a ReLU activation function and having a dropout of 0.3 between the convolutional layers; the output is a fully connected layer going to a softmax activation function. These networks were trained over 200 epochs and the middle convolutional layer features were used in the SINN. The middle layer was used from comparison of the three layers, showing a small increase in accuracy while using the middle layer. The training parameters shown in the results below take into account the parameters needed to train the CNN used for pulling features. This is to compare the parameters needed for feature extraction and testing that a regular deep learning approach takes. You can see a reduction in parameters from the original SINN using the raw images to the SINN using deep features; the differences are larger in the CIFAR data because of the third dimension of color given in the original data.

4.1   MNIST

For the MNIST data set, we see an average of 2% increase in performance using the deep CNN features. This is good, considering our later model shows results almost rivaling that of the state-of-the-art Deep Multi Column (DMC) network which has roughly four times the amount of trainable parameters in the network [11]. DMC tries to better mimic the complex human brain and have several smaller deep neural networks that are trained on different preprocessed data. These networks then combined in a multi column approach making the recognition of the DMC boosted compared to the individual networks. This is similar to our approach since we use a smaller deep neural network for features, however, this is done once and several features from multiple trained networks are

Table 1. Classification accuracy on MNIST data set using various variants of feature extraction architectures

Architecture	SINN	SINN-1	SINN-2	SINN-3	DMC [11]
Accuracy	96.50%	97.92%	98.45%	99.71%	99.77%
Parameters	189,065	123,811	216,210	242,180	839,650
Features	None	CNN-1	CNN-2	CNN-3	Deep

not combined into one. Further results for each network can be seen in Table 1. To note, the best result obtained was a testing accuracy of 99.79%, while most models attained a performance of 99.6% to 99.7%. It is also clear looking at the results for MNIST that using a deep CNN to pull features is an improvement over the original SINN with no feature extraction used.

4.2   CIFAR-10 and CIFAR-100

Deep features are then learned and fed into the SINN for training on the CIFAR data sets. The resulting accuracy of CIFAR-10 can be seen in Table 2 while the accuracy of CIFAR-100 can be seen in Table 3. As seen in Tables 2 and 3, the deep features are a drastic improvement from the original image being flattened and trained in the SINN. Even with such a small CNN to extract features, these improvements are almost two times that of the original in both data set cases. This solidifies our approach of the SINN being better at separating the feature space to become a more efficient classifier than a feature extractor. Though it did not reach state-of-the-art accuracy on either data set, it is good to note the size difference in trainable parameters having a decrease of a large order of magnitudes. The state-of-the-art method for CIFAR-10, Aggregated Residual Transformation for Deep Neural Networks (ART), looks to improve the residual network design by being able to have multiple transformation in a block but having the same complexity as the original ResNet [12]. This network contains parameters in the millions which they needed 8 GPUs with only 300 epochs to perform their training. While SINN contains significantly less parameters to achieve decent accuracy, the network can be trained to several thousand epochs with only a single GPU in epoch times less than one second per. Wide Residual Networks (WRN) hold the leading accuracy for the CIFAR-100 data set and once again look to better the implementation architecture of residual networks [15]. This method looks to widen each block of the residual network for better accuracy instead of cascading multitudes of layers on top of one another. Even with this improvement on stacked layers in large deep residual networks, WRN boasts nearly fifty-six million parameters for training. They also are restricted to convolutions of size (3×3) due to the computational performance of large convolutions. These issues do not occur in our SINN architecture, due to its widening of the hidden layer (similar to ART and WRN) we are able to use meaningful features from any convolution size in the CNN to be extracted to the SINN with limited computation loss. It is also interesting to note the size changes of our model depending on the data set. In CIFAR-10, the SINN is a smaller model since there are only ten classes; this means each Shepard node only contains ten metric nodes. This causes the overall width of the network to stay the same, but the internal node difference to be rather easy to tune. Since CIFAR-100 is just ten times the amount of classes per metric node, it fits that the parameters are of an order ten higher than CIFAR-10. Now to mention again, the total number of parameters in the SINN models do include those which were needed to find the features in the CNN. This is the only fair way to assess the feature extraction to classification that these deep models do in

Table 2. Classification accuracy on CIFAR-10 data set using various variants of feature extraction architectures

Architecture	SINN	SINN-1	SINN-2	SINN-3	ART [12]
Accuracy	48.50%	84.84%	89.35%	90.50%	96.44%
Parameters	729,541	254,103	285,230	295,852	68,000,000
Features	None	CNN-1	CNN-2	CNN-3	Deep

comparison to our shallow model. These parameter reductions show a promise in application, having an efficient algorithm which holds high classification accuracy while maintaining low computational cost. It achieves near top performance and translates to training speed having some of our experiments training and testing in under an hour.

Table 3. Classification accuracy on CIFAR-100 data set using various variants of feature extraction architectures

Architecture	SINN	SINN-1	SINN-2	SINN-3	WRN[15]
Accuracy	36.50%	68.52%	70.25%	72.86%	81.7%
Parameters	7,436,967	2,652,052	2,978,502	3,143,025	56,000,000
Features	None	CNN-1	CNN-2	CNN-3	Deep

5   Conclusion

In this paper, we look at utilizing and harnessing the power of deep learning for feature extraction using a CNN. These features were then used in our SINN architecture to show high accuracy on the data sets tested. Though the SINN is still rather new, the results show promising accuracy in image classification against the state-of-the-art. What shows even more promise of SINN is that of lowering the computational cost for this caliber of accuracy, by thirty - three hundred times less than that of the leading deep learning frameworks. This shows it is not always necessary to scale a deep framework to immense extents when smaller frameworks with a SINN work in comparison. Possible future work could be to expand the architecture of the SINN to see if accuracy performance can increase (while of course decreasing computational performance) with more nodes. There could be some use to see SINN in other machine learning tasks, such as natural language processing, time series analysis and forecasting, or medical image analysis. Since the approach is still new, there are many open areas for research interest. Also to note, a stacked method could be possible, however, this would neglect our rebuttal that deep isn't always the best way, and our shallow approach is fast and efficient.

References

1. Masci, J., Meier, U., Cireşan, D., Schmidhuber, J.: Stacked convolutional auto-encoders for hierarchical feature extraction. In: Honkela, T., Duch, W., Girolami, M., Kaski, S. (eds.) ICANN 2011. LNCS, vol. 6791, pp. 52–59. Springer, Heidelberg (2011). https://doi.org/10.1007/978-3-642-21735-7_7
2. Park, J., Sandberg, I.W.: Universal approximation using radial-basis-function networks. Neural Comput. **3**(2), 246–257 (1991)
3. Williams, P.: SINN: Shepard Interpolation Neural Networks. In: Bebis, G., et al. (eds.) ISVC 2016. LNCS, vol. 10073, pp. 349–358. Springer, Cham (2016). https://doi.org/10.1007/978-3-319-50832-0_34
4. Le, Q.V.: Building high-level features using large scale unsupervised learning. In: 2013 IEEE International Conference on Acoustics, Speech and Signal Processing (ICASSP), pp. 8595–8598. IEEE, May 2013
5. Clevert, D.A., Unterthiner, T., Hochreiter, S.: Fast and accurate deep network learning by exponential linear units (ELUS). arXiv preprint arXiv:1511.07289 (2015)
6. Wan, L., Zeiler, M., Zhang, S., Cun, Y.L., Fergus, R.: Regularization of neural networks using dropconnect. In: Proceedings of the 30th International Conference on Machine Learning (ICML 2013), pp. 1058–1066 (2013)
7. Petrov, Y., Zhaoping, L.: Local correlations, information redundancy, and sufficient pixel depth in natural images. JOSA A **20**(1), 56–66 (2003)
8. Ren, J.S., Xu, L., Yan, Q., Sun, W.: Shepard convolutional neural networks. In: Advances in Neural Information Processing Systems, pp. 901–909 (2015)
9. Donald, S.: A two-dimensional interpolation function for irregularly-spaced data. In: Proceedings of the 1968 23rd ACM National Conference. ACM (1968)
10. Arthur, D., Vassilvitskii, S.: k-means++: the advantages of careful seeding. In: Proceedings of the Eighteenth Annual ACM-SIAM Symposium on Discrete Algorithms, pp. 1027–1035. Society for Industrial and Applied Mathematics, January 2007
11. Ciregan, D., Meier, U., Schmidhuber, J.: Multi-column deep neural networks for image classification. In: 2012 IEEE Conference on Computer Vision and Pattern Recognition (CVPR), pp. 3642–3649. IEEE, June 2012
12. Xie, S., et al.: Aggregated residual transformations for deep neural networks. In: 2017 IEEE Conference on Computer Vision and Pattern Recognition (CVPR). IEEE (2017)
13. LeCun, Y., Bengio, Y.: Convolutional networks for images, speech, and time series. In: The Handbook of Brain Theory and Neural Networks, vol. 3361, no. 10 (1995)
14. Krizhevsky, A., Hinton, G.: Learning multiple layers of features from tiny images. Technical report, University of Toronto (2009)
15. Zagoruyko, S., Komodakis, N.: Wide residual networks. arXiv preprint arXiv:1605.07146 (2016)
16. Krizhevsky, A., Sutskever, I., Hinton, G.E.: ImageNet classification with deep convolutional neural networks. In: Advances in Neural Information Processing Systems (2012)

Emotion Assessment Using Adaptive Learning-Based Relevance Analysis

C. Torres-Valencia(✉), A. Alvarez-Meza, and A. Orozco-Gutierrez

Automatics Research Group, Universidad Tecnológica de Pereira,
Pereira - Risaralda, Colombia
{cristian.torres,andres.alvarez1,aaog}@utp.edu.co

Abstract. The study of brain electrical activity (BEA) allows to describe and analyze the different cognitive and physiological process that occurs inside the human body. The Electroncephalogram (EEG) is often chosen over other neuroimaging techniques, but the non-stationarity nature of the EEG data and the variability between subjects have to be sorted to design reliable methodologies for neural activity identification. In this work, we propose the use of adaptive filtering for the relevance analysis of EEG segments in emotion assessment experiments. First, a windowing stage of the EEG data is performed, from which brain connectivity measures are extracted as BEA descriptors. The correlation and the time-series generalized measure of association (TGMA) are selected at this stage. Then, the connectivity data is used for galvanic skin response (GSR) and Blood Volume pressure (BVP) estimation employing the quantized kernel mean least squares (QKLMS) strategy. Finally, from the QKLMS algorithm, a set of relevant centroids in the estimation of physiological responses are used in the classification of the specific emotional state. The results obtained validate the proposed methodology and give clear evidence that a selection of segments from BEA improve further stages of classification for emotion assessment tasks.

Keywords: Emotion assessment · Brain connectivity
Relevance analysis · Adaptive filtering

1 Introduction

Human brain controls, reflects, and regulates all the processes that occur in the biological systems that compose the human body. So, the analysis of the brain electrical activity (BEA) can improve our understanding of several physiological processes as reflects of our body functioning [9]. The BEA is analyzed following different neuroimaging techniques, such as: Electroencephalography (EEG), Magnetoencephalography, Magnetic Resonance Imaging, functional MRI, among others. The EEG presents some advantages in comparison with other technologies; such as: low cost, less invasive scheme of acquisition, and higher temporal

© Springer International Publishing AG, part of Springer Nature 2018
A. Campilho et al. (Eds.): ICIAR 2018, LNCS 10882, pp. 193–200, 2018.
https://doi.org/10.1007/978-3-319-93000-8_22

resolution. Following this advantages, EEG is preferred for BEA; nevertheless, there are some challenges associated with the processing of EEG signals, indeed, the non-stationarity nature of the recordings, the low spatial resolution, and the variability that exists between studies of different subjects with similar conditions, make the EEG processing task a very challenging one [14].

Some strategies for BEA processing has been proposed to deal with the aforementioned challenges. Most of them are based on data transformations, namely, temporal, spectral, and, time-frequency are employed to deal with the EEG non-stationarity behaviors [9]. However, classical spectral and time-frequency approaches provide redundant information that derives in suboptimal classification results [7]. On the other hand, the analysis of brain connectivity has emerged as a way to characterize and understand brain functions [2]. In this case, segregated regions of the brain are integrated to perform a specialized information processing and the resulting interactions between different areas are quantized. These measures of interdependences among channels can be understood as a spatio-temporal representation, which is used in further stages of BEA discrimination, i.e., emotion classification or motor tasks recognition [12].

In this work, we propose the development of an adaptive learning-based relevance analysis (ALRA) for BEA data in an emotion recognition context. We use brain connectivity measures to characterize the spatio-temporal dependencies of EEG channels. In particular, two functions of connectivity quantification are used: the correlation and the time-series generalized measure of association (TGMA) [4]. Besides, we carried out a segmentation stage of the BEA towards a sliding window. In addition, we use a physiological response (galvanic skin response (GSR) and the blood volume pressure (BVP)) to select relevant EEG time windows holding relevant connectivity patterns. So, an adaptive filter algorithm, termed the quantized Kernel mean least squares (QKLMS), is used for the physiological response estimation. The data of each window is used for the adjustment of the filter parameters using an online learning strategy, and a classifier is trained over the filter codebooks. Achieved results show an improvement using relevant spatio-temporal EEG dependencies for emotion classification in comparison to state-of-the-art approaches.

The remainder of this paper includes a theoretical background in Sect. 2, followed by a description of the experimental setup in Sect. 3. Finally, a description of the obtained results is presented in Sect. 4 and some remarks are included also in Sect. 5.

2   Relevance Analysis Based on Kernel Adaptive Filtering for Emotion Assessment

BEA Data Processing. For a particular subject, let $\chi = \{X_n \in \mathbb{R}^{C \times T}; y_n \in \mathbb{R}^T; l_n \in [l_{min}, l_{max}]\}_{n=1}^N$ be and EEG set data with C channels at T time instants, where X_n holds the n–th EEG trial with emotional level l_n and physiological response y_n. Then, a windowing function is applied to segment the data into W windows holding t time samples per window, yielding

$\mathcal{Z}_n = \{\bar{\boldsymbol{X}}_{n,k} \in \mathbb{R}^{C \times t}; \bar{\boldsymbol{y}}_{n,k} \in \mathbb{R}^t\}$, with $n = \{1, \ldots, N\}$ and $k = \{1, \cdots, W\}$. Now, a feature extraction stage is performed over $\mathcal{Z}_n$ based on a given connectivity measure to obtain the representation set $\mathcal{U}_n = \{\boldsymbol{U}_{n,k} \in \mathbb{R}^{C \times C}; \boldsymbol{d}_{n,k} \in \mathbb{R}\}$. In particular, $\boldsymbol{U}_{n,k} = \phi_e(\bar{\boldsymbol{X}}_{n,k}) \in \mathbb{R}^{C \times C}$ codes the connectivity quantification and $\boldsymbol{d}_{n,k} = \phi_p(\bar{\boldsymbol{y}}_{n,k}) \in \mathbb{R}^W$ characterizes the physiological response, both within the k-th window. Here, we employ the correlation index and the time generalized measure of association (TGMA) as connectivity measures to capture the channel dependencies [10]. A detailed explanation of the correlation index and the TGMA could be found in [2] and [4], respectively. For simplicity and taking into account the symmetric property of the correlation and the TGMA measures, the feature space is rearranged via vector concatenation to build the set $\Omega_n = \{\boldsymbol{U}_{n,k} \in \mathbb{R}^{(C*(C-1)/2)}; \boldsymbol{d}_{n,k} \in \mathbb{R}\}$.

Physiological Responses Estimation and BEA Data Selection. With the aim of estimating $\boldsymbol{d}_{n,k}$ from Ω_n, a kernel induced mapping $\kappa(\cdot, \cdot)$ is employed to transform $\boldsymbol{U}_{n,k}$ into a higher dimensional feature space $\mathbb{F}$ through the nonlinear mapping function $\boldsymbol{\psi} : \mathbb{R}^{C*(C-1)/2} \to \mathbb{F}$. Then, an adaptive learning approach is applied, termed the kernel least mean squares (KLMS), which minimizes the following cost function [6]:

$$\min_{\boldsymbol{w}} \sum_{k=1}^{W} (\boldsymbol{d}_{n,k} - \boldsymbol{\omega}(k-1)^\top \boldsymbol{\psi}(\boldsymbol{U}_{n,k}))^2, \tag{1}$$

where an updating scheme can be inferred as $\boldsymbol{\omega}(k) = \eta \sum_{j=1}^{i} e(j)\boldsymbol{\psi}(j)$, allowing to efficiently estimate the desired output as $\eta \sum_{j=1}^{k} e(j)\kappa(\boldsymbol{U}_{n,j}, \boldsymbol{u}')$, being $\eta \in [0, 1]$ a learning rate parameter and $e(j) = \boldsymbol{d}_{n,j} - \boldsymbol{\omega}(j-1)^\top \boldsymbol{\psi}(\boldsymbol{U}_{n,j})$. Now, to extract relevant BEA patterns, the quantized-KLMS (QKLMS) algorithm is used via the following novelty criterion:

$$D_k = \min_{\boldsymbol{c}(j) \in C_k} \|\boldsymbol{U}_{n,k+1} - \boldsymbol{c}(j).\|_2 \tag{2}$$

where $\boldsymbol{c}(j) \in \mathbb{R}^{(C*(C-1)/2)}$ is the j-th codeword in the codebook C_k. If $D_k < \delta$, ($\delta \in \mathbb{R}^+$) then the new input $\boldsymbol{U}_{n,k+1}$ will be not added into the dictionary, otherwise, $\boldsymbol{U}_{n,k+1}$ is added as a new codeword of C_k. So, not only the estimation of the physiological response is performed but also the most relevant centroids will be stored. Then, at this stage only the selected centroids as well as the QKLMS coefficients correspond to relevant BEA data.

3   Experimental Setup

Database. EEG signals are obtained from a publicly available dataset for affective computing. The database for emotion recognition using physiological data "DEAP" contains a set of recordings of physiological signals under a set of 40 emotion elicitation experiments applied to 32 subjects. Physiological responses such as EEG (32 channels), Galvanic skin response (GSR), temperature, blood volume pressure (BVP), and the respiratory pattern were acquired and then down-sampled to 128 Hz. For each emotion elicitation experiment, the ratings of arousal and valence are stored, following a scale between 1 to 9 [5].

Implementation Details. For the initial step of BEA data processing, a partition of the time series into 2 s segments is performed, resulting in $W = 19$ possible windows [10]. A second step corresponds to the brain connectivity computation, using the correlation and TGMA measures that are applied to the EEG data. Then, the physiological estimation from the adaptive filtering is performed using two different signals, the GSR, and the BVP as the desired outputs. The data is divided in two classes from the l labels by splitting the data into high and low ratings in each dimension (arousal and valence), with $1 - 3$ for the low class and $7 - 9$ for the high-class [13]. In this stage, the subjects with non-balanced classes are discarded for classification consistency. Now, for the relevance analysis using QKLMS, a validation procedure is employed by using the 80% of the data for training and the left 20% for testing purposes, a mean square error is computed in the testing set at each condition. Some parameters needed in the ALRA and the classification methodologies are settled, the Kernel bandwidth $\sigma = 10$, the novelty criterion $\delta_1 = \sqrt{\frac{1}{2}\sigma}$ [6] and the learning rate $\eta = 0.9$ are fixed for the QKLMS algorithm. Likewise, in the classification stage, a strategy of cross-validation with 80% for training and 20% for testing within 10 fold repetitions is performed. The value of σ_{svm} is selected by heuristic search into a grid of predefined values within the cross-validation scheme. For further reference, the $\kappa(\cdot, \cdot)$ Kernel function used in the QKLMS algorithm implementation and for classification purposes is the Gaussian Kernel.

BEA Classification. From the connectivity measures and the application of the QKLMS strategy, discrimination of the BEA patterns of each condition could be developed. Under a supervised learning scheme, the l_n labels for all the conditions are used to partition the data into biclass problems, but only for those subjects with balanced classes. As a matching criterion, both datasets, $\mathcal{Z}$ containing the connectivity data and Ω holding the relevant data, are employed in the following experiments.

- Classification of emotional states by using relevant data. The number of Nc selected centroids varies at each condition, and the data is ordered by weighting each selected window by the corresponding QKLMS expansion coefficients.
- Classification using connectivity data. The mean and variance for each $\mathcal{Z}_n$ along the whole time windows is stored in the matrices $\Delta \in \mathbb{R}^{C \times C}$ and $\Omega \in \mathbb{R}^{C \times C}$. Next, the feature vector coding the variability of the connectivity measures is built after vector concatenation of Δ and Ω resulting in the set $\{\boldsymbol{X}_C \in \mathbb{R}^{N \times P}; \boldsymbol{l}^{\top} \in \mathbb{R}^N\}$.

4   Results and Discussion

Examples of the physiological estimation results obtained by the QKLMS algorithm using BEA are discussed first. Estimation of the GSR by the correlation measure for subject 12 under a particular condition with valence rating of 7 is presented in Fig. 1. Likewise, an estimation of the BVP using the TGMA measure for subject 2 with an arousal rating of 2 is presented in Fig. 2. The top row on both figures presents the filter output against the reference value at each one of the 19 windows. At this point, the mean square error is computed for the complete test set of realizations for each subject. For the valence dimension, the error obtained is around 9.34 ± 2.11 and 4.30 ± 1.82 for GSR and BVP respectively when the correlation measure is used; and approximately 5.22 ± 1.85 and 7.15 ± 2.15 for GSR and BVP respectively when TGMA is used instead. On the other hand, for the Arousal dimension, the mean error is around 10.00 ± 2.44 for GSR and 8.74 ± 2.32 for BVP whit the correlation index and finally a mean error of 6.45 ± 1.87 for GSR and 8.85 ± 2.23 for BVP with the TGMA measure.

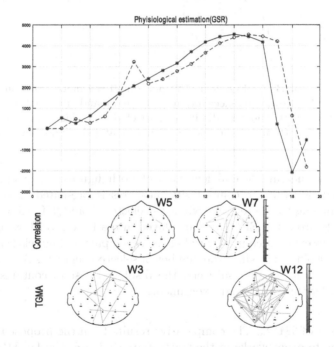

Fig. 1. Estimation of GSR physiological response and relevance selection of connectivity patterns. Top row, reference output (solid line) and filter output estimation (dashed line) for the 19 windows. Middle row, selected centroids at $\{5, 7\}$ windows for correlation and bottom row the selected centroids at $\{3, 12\}$ windows for TGMA.

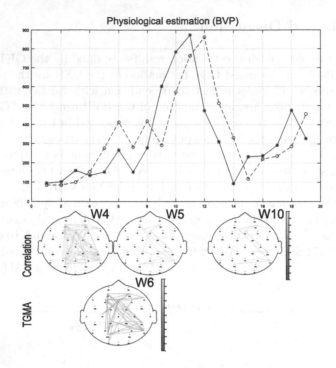

Fig. 2. Estimation of BVP physiological response and relevance selection of connectivity patterns. Top row, reference output (solid line) and filter output estimation (dashed line) for the 19 windows. Middle row, selected centroids at $\{4, 5, 10\}$ windows for correlation and bottom row the selected centroids at $\{6\}$ window for TGMA

Likewise, at the middle and low rows of both figures, an example of the relevance analysis from the connectivity measures is presented. The displayed data corresponding to the relevant windows selected from QKLMS on a scheme of 32 electrodes from the EEG array displayed into a head model, with the lines representing the existent connectivity between each pair of channels that satisfies a defined threshold. Also, since the number of selected centroids $\mathcal{X}$ varies across the different conditions and subjects, the displayed results contains only the selected data for that particular experiment.

Classification of BEA. The comparative results from the proposed approach in comparison to other works in the state-of-art that uses the DEAP database, are presented in Table 1. As can be seen in Table 1, there is an improvement on the classification results when the proposed ALRA approach is employed. The number of selected subjects in each dimension that satisfies the balanced class experiments are 10 subjects for the valence dimension and 9 subjects for the arousal dimension. The highest results were obtained by the ALRA approach when employing the GSR signal with $76.62\% \pm 5.81$ for the arousal dimension, and by the ALRA when employing the BVP response with 76.21% ± 4.06 for the valence dimension.

Table 1. Mean emotion classification results [%] for selected DEAP subjects, only mean value for comparison consistency against reported works in [8]

Reference	Approach	Arousal	Valence
Koelstra et al. [5]	Linear features, power spectral - SVM	62.00	57.50
Soleymani et al. [11]	Power spectral - SVM	50.00	62.00
Gupta et al. [3]	Power spectral - HJORT - SVM	60.00	60.00
Castellanos et al. [8]	MSP - ROI signal - SVM	58.6	55.76
Daimi et al. [1]	Wavelet Packet - SVM	67.00	65.00
Torres et al. [12]	RFCV - KNN	66.00	65.73
This work	SVM - correlation	65.31	69.63
This work	SVM - TGMA	65.31	69.99
This work	**ALRA - GSR**	**76.62**	74.38
This work	**ALRA - BVP**	75.19	**76.21**

5   Conclusions

To the best of our knowledge, the estimation of physiological responses by emotional stimulus from BEA data was not developed before, although the emotion recognition was performed by using descriptors of this data. The use of adaptive filtering learning seems adequate for BEA data analysis since this data is particular for each subject and the methodologies of processing must be adapted to these particularities. The QKLMS algorithm allows the estimation of the physiological value from the connectivity measures. The amounts of the estimation error enable to conclude that this framework can be used with a high degree of confidence as evidenced in the results. Also, an additional essential outcome is the implicit selection of some centroids via the novelty criterion, which allows extracting the connectivity data holding relevant information for classification purposes on the absence of labeling in most of the BEA. An improvement in the classification accuracy is observed when using the relevant selected data in comparison to the case when the whole connectivity data is used. Also, higher values of classification accuracy were obtained in comparison with the state-of-art works as detailed in Table 1. As future work, a scheme of automatic tagging of BEA could be derived from this strategy as a remarkable outcome of the proposed methodology. Finally, the adjustment of the parameters in each stage could be improved since the heuristic search may result in non-optimal parameter selection.

Acknowledgments. Under grants supported by the project: "Sistema de visualización de conectividad cerebral efectiva utilizando representaciones kernel orientado a tareas de memoria de trabajo"–(6-18-1), and C. Torres is partially funded by and "Análisis discriminante de señales de electroencefalografía utilizando representaciones en espacios de Hilbert de Kernel Reproductivo"–(E6-18-1), funded by Vicerrectoria de investigaciones, Innovación, y Extensión of the Universidad Tecnológica de Pereira.

References

1. Daimi, S.N., Saha, G.: Classification of emotions induced by music videos and correlation with participants' rating. Expert Syst. Appl. **41**(13), 6057–6065 (2014)
2. Friston, K.J.: Functional and effective connectivity: a review. Brain Connectivity **1**(1), 13–36 (2011)
3. Gupta, R., Laghari, K.U.R., Falk, T.H.: Relevance vector classifier decision fusion and EEG graph-theoretic features for automatic affective state characterization. Neurocomputing **174**(PB), 875–884 (2016)
4. Fadlallah, B.H., Brockmeier, A., Seth, S., Li, L., Keil, A., Principe, J.: An association framework to analyze dependence structure in time series, pp. 6176–6179 (2012)
5. Koelstra, S., Muhl, C., Soleymani, M., Lee, J.-S., Yazdani, A., Ebrahimi, T., Pun, T., Nijholt, A., Patras, I.: DEAP: a database for emotion analysis; using physiological signals. IEEE Trans. Affect. Comput. **3**(1), 18–31 (2012)
6. Liu, W., Principe, J.C., Haykin, S.: Kernel Adaptive Filtering: A Comprehensive Introduction, 1st edn. Wiley Publishing, New York (2010)
7. Motamedi-Fakhr, S., Moshrefi-Torbati, M., Hill, M., Hill, C.M., White, P.R.: Signal processing techniques applied to human sleep EEG signals-a review. Biomed. Sign. Process. Control **10**(Supplement C), 21–33 (2014)
8. Padilla-Buritica, J.I., Martinez-Vargas, J.D., Castellanos-Dominguez, G.: Emotion discrimination using spatially compact regions of interest extracted from imaging EEG activity. Front. Comput. Neurosci. **10**, 55 (2016)
9. Sanei, S.: Adaptive Processing of Brain Signals. Wiley, London (2013)
10. Silva, C.S., Hazrati, M.K., Keil, A., Principe, J.C.: Quantification of neural functional connectivity during an active avoidance task. In: 38th International Conference of the IEEE Engineering in Medicine and Biology Society (EMBC), pp. 708–711, August 2016
11. Soleymani, M., Pantic, M., Pun, T.: Multimodal emotion recognition in response to videos. IEEE Trans. Affect. Comput. **3**(2), 211–223 (2012)
12. Torres-Valencia, C., Alvarez-Meza, A., Orozco-Gutierrez, A.: Emotion assessment based on functional connectivity variability and relevance analysis. In: Ferrández Vicente, J.M., Álvarez-Sánchez, J.R., de la Paz López, F., Toledo Moreo, J., Adeli, H. (eds.) IWINAC 2017. LNCS, vol. 10337, pp. 353–362. Springer, Cham (2017). https://doi.org/10.1007/978-3-319-59740-9_35
13. Torres-Valencia, C., Álvarez-López, M., Orozco-Gutiérrez, Á.: SVM-based feature selection methods for emotion recognition from multimodal data. J. Multimodal User Interfaces **11**(1), 9–23 (2016)
14. Wang, R., Wang, J., Yu, H., Wei, X., Yang, C., Deng, B.: Power spectral density and coherence analysis of Alzheimer's EEG. Cogn. Neurodyn. **9**(3), 291–304 (2015)

Improved Edge Detection Algorithms Based on a Riesz Fractional Derivative

Carmina Georgescu[✉]

Department of Mathematical Methods and Models,
University Politehnica of Bucharest, Bucharest, Romania
carmina.georgescu@upb.ro

Abstract. In this paper we generalize some classical edge detectors using the second-order Riesz fractional derivative. Taking advantages of fractional differential method we improve the shortcomings of conventional operators like Roberts, Prewitt and Sobel. Consequently, three improved edge detection algorithms are gained. The experimental results show that the proposed models enhance edge information effectively and reveal more detailed information than traditional operators.

1 Introduction

Edge detection is the process of localizing pixel intensity transitions in images, being an important component of digital image processing and computer vision applications. There are many ways to perform edge detection. The most common method used for detecting sharp intensity variations employs first and second order differential operators that include Roberts, Sobel, Prewitt, Canny, Scharr and Laplacian techniques. All of these are integer-order differential algorithms and have several shortcomings. While first order operators produce wide edges, the second order ones are very sensitive to noise and generate double responses in the grey scale variations. Therefore, extracting edges while reducing noise is a key challenge in edge detection.

It is well known that the Sobel operator is more sensitive to the diagonal edges than to the horizontal and vertical edges, while the Prewitt operator is more sensitive to horizontal and vertical edges. The performance of the Roberts-cross operator is slightly superior to these operators but inferior to other operators. The Canny operator is by far one of the best edge operators as it can provide localisation at minimal response. However, it suffers some drawbacks due to the use of the Gaussian filter as smoothing technique.

Recently, fractional differential operators were used in image quality enhancement, image texture enhancement, image denoising and image edge analysis, with very promising results. In contrast to integer-order operators, the fractional derivative preserves high frequency edge features in the grey prominent variations and also high frequency texture features in the grey small variations. There are several alternatives for generalizing the concept of an integer-order

© Springer International Publishing AG, part of Springer Nature 2018
A. Campilho et al. (Eds.): ICIAR 2018, LNCS 10882, pp. 201–209, 2018.
https://doi.org/10.1007/978-3-319-93000-8_23

derivative: Grünwald-Letnikov, Riemann-Liouville, Caputo, Weil-Riesz operators. It seems like a reasonable thing to combine fractional differential methods with traditional edge detectors, this procedure leading to higher signal to noise, high accuracy, more details and fine distinction.

There is no edge detection method which works perfectly for all the applications. Referring the traditional Sobel and Prewitt edge detectors and based on the Grünwald-Letnikov fractional derivative, Yang et al. [7] have proposed the Tiansi fractional differential gradient operator and the experiments revealed that the model can not only extract the image edge features, but also have a good noise inhibition. It can also detect more image texture details, which is better than the commonly used integer order differential edge detection algorithm.

Chiwueze et al. [3] developed an algorithm based on the Caputo fractional derivative, which generalizes the classical Prewitt gradient operator. Jiang et al. [4] combined the fractional-order differential with the Laplacian operator, proposed a new image edge detection model and compared with the existing integer-order edge detection methods. Yu et al. [8] proposed a new texture enhancement method based on the second order Riesz fractional differential operator, using a Lagrange 3-point interpolation formula, to get the gray value of non-integer step pixel. The method was then applied for both grey scale and colour image enhancement. In [1], Yirenkyi et al. presented a new fractional-based convolution edge detector using Gaussian and cubic spline based smoothing technique. Using the Riemann-Liouville fractional derivative, in paper [2] the authors constructed another fractional derivative mask and compared the proposed fractional edge detector with Canny detector [5] and Tiansi detector [7].

In this paper we propose three new fractional-order gradient edge detectors, based on the Riesz fractional differential operator. The experimental results show that our new models provide significantly better performance in enhancing the edge information and superior image quality over existing methods. Moreover, the proposed algorithms not only can preserve the edge information of the processed images adequately, but they also effectively suppress the noise in the smooth area. The paper is organized as follows. In Sect. 2, we provide brief review of classical edge detectors and second-order Riesz fractional derivative. Section 3 describes the construction of three fractional edge detection algorithms. In Sect. 4 we discuss how numerical experiments are setup and compare the results with previous edge detectors used in medical imaging applications.

2   First Order Differential Edge Operators

Many edge-detecting operators are based in some way on measuring the intensity gradient at a point in the image. If $f(x, y)$ represents the image value at coordinates (x, y), its gradient is defined as the two-dimensional vector $\nabla f(x, y) = (f'_x, f'_y)^T$. The gradient magnitude represents the strength of the edge and gives the amount of the difference between pixels in the neighborhood. It is common practice, however, to approximate the gradient magnitude by absolute values: $|\nabla f(x, y)| = \sqrt{(f'_x)^2 + (f'_y)^2} \simeq |f'_x| + |f'_y|$ or $|\nabla f(x, y)| = max\{|f'_x|, |f'_y|\}$.

The Roberts cross operator uses the differences between two diagonally adjacent pixels. Every point in an image should use the following two kernels to do convolution:

$$\begin{pmatrix} 1 & 0 \\ 0 & -1 \end{pmatrix} \quad \begin{pmatrix} 0 & 1 \\ -1 & 0 \end{pmatrix}.$$

Put $f'_x = f(x, y) - f(x + 1, y + 1)$ for the convolution with the first kernel and $f'_y = f(x + 1, y) - f(x, y + 1)$ for the convolution with the second one. Even if f'_x and f'_y are not specifically derivatives with respect to x and y, they are derivatives with respect to the two diagonal directions. The Roberts operator approximates the gradient magnitude in the following way

$$g(x, y) = \left\{ [f(x, y) - f(x + 1, y + 1)]^2 + [f(x + 1, y) - f(x, y + 1)]^2 \right\}^{\frac{1}{2}} \quad (1)$$

The Roberts kernels are in practice too small to reliably find edges in the presence of noise.

The Prewitt operator is based on the approximation of the first-order derivative by the central difference. The convolution is performed by using the following two kernels:

$$\begin{pmatrix} -1 & 0 & 1 \\ -1 & 0 & 1 \\ -1 & 0 & 1 \end{pmatrix} \quad \begin{pmatrix} -1 & -1 & -1 \\ 0 & 0 & 0 \\ 1 & 1 & 1 \end{pmatrix}.$$

Putting $g_x = f(x + 1, y - 1) - f(x - 1, y - 1) + f(x + 1, y) - f(x - 1, y) + f(x + 1, y + 1) - f(x - 1, y + 1)$ and $g_y = f(x - 1, y + 1) - f(x - 1, y - 1) + f(x, y + 1) - f(x, y - 1) + f(x + 1, y + 1) - f(x + 1, y - 1)$ and using backward difference, the two components can be rewritten under the following differential form:

$$g_x = 2 \left[f'_x(x + 1, y - 1) + f'_x(x + 1, y) + f'_x(x + 1, y + 1) \right] \quad (2)$$

$$g_y = 2 \left[f'_y(x - 1, y + 1) + f'_y(x, y + 1) + f'_y(x + 1, y + 1) \right] \quad (3)$$

The Sobel operator also relies on central differences. Unlike the Prewitt operator, this operator places an emphasis on pixels that are closer to the center of the mask. The two convolution kernels are:

$$\begin{pmatrix} -1 & 0 & 1 \\ -2 & 0 & 2 \\ -1 & 0 & 1 \end{pmatrix} \quad \begin{pmatrix} -1 & -2 & -1 \\ 0 & 0 & 0 \\ 1 & 2 & 1 \end{pmatrix}.$$

The Sobel operator can provide more accurate edge direction information but it will also detect many false edges with coarse edge width. While the Prewitt operator is more sensitive to horizontal and vertical edges, the Sobel operator is more sensitive to the diagonal edges than to the horizontal and vertical edges. Convoluting the image with the above masks we get:

$$g_x = f(x+1, y-1) - f(x-1, y-1) + 2f(x+1, y) - 2f(x-1, y) + f(x+1, y+1) - f(x-1, y+1)$$

$$g_y = f(x-1, y+1) - f(x-1, y-1) + 2f(x, y+1) - 2f(x, y-1) + f(x+1, y+1) - f(x+1, y-1)$$

and using the differential form related to the backward difference formula:

$$g_x = 2\left[f'_x(x+1, y-1) + 2f'_x(x+1, y) + f'_x(x+1, y+1)\right] \qquad (4)$$

$$g_y = 2\left[f'_y(x-1, y+1) + 2f'_y(x, y+1) + f'_y(x+1, y+1)\right] \qquad (5)$$

Fractional order derivative has been used in various scientific fields, including image processing. In the sequel, we adopt the Riesz fractional derivative. Let $u(t)$ be an analytic function on $\mathbb{R}$ and $\nu > 0$, but not an integer. In order to better approximate the Riesz fractional derivative, Ortigueira [6] proposed a second order scheme based on the fractional centered difference method with step h:

$$\frac{\partial^\nu u(t)}{\partial |t|^\nu} \simeq -\frac{1}{2\cos(\pi\nu/2)h^\nu}\left[\sum_{k=0}^{\infty} \omega_k u(t-kh) + \sum_{k=-\infty}^{0} \omega_k u(t-kh)\right],$$

where the coefficients are defined by

$$\omega_0 = -\frac{\Gamma(1-\nu/2)}{\nu\Gamma(1+\nu/2)\Gamma(-\nu)}, \; \omega_k = \frac{(-1)^{k+1}\Gamma(\nu/2)\Gamma(1-\nu/2)}{\Gamma(\nu/2-k+1)\Gamma(\nu/2+k+1)\Gamma(-\nu)}, \; k \in \mathbb{Z}^*.$$

Generally, we assume that $h = 1$. In the context of a two dimensional digital image, $f(x, y)$, we divide the duration of the signal into n equal frames within the interval $[0, x]$ and based on the values of $n+1$ causal pixels, $f(0, y)$, $f(x/n, y)$,..., $f(x, y)$, we approximate the fractional partial differential on the positive x-axis

$$\frac{\partial^\nu f(x, y)}{\partial x^\nu} \simeq -\frac{1}{2\cos(\pi\nu/2)}\sum_{k=0}^{n} \omega_k f(x-k, y), \; n \in \mathbb{N}^*. \qquad (6)$$

A similar expression holds for the positive y-axis. It can be proven that the distinct difference between fractional based processing and an integral based one is the fact that the summation of the nonzero coefficients is not zero.

3   Design of the Improved Riesz Fractional Differential Based Masks

In this section we combine the fractional order differentiation with classical edge detector operators to propose three new and improved edge detection masks. In order to construct our new models, the fractional gradient magnitude of the filtered image will be achieved by using the following formula:

$$|\nabla^\nu g(x, y)| = \sqrt{\left(\frac{\partial^\nu g}{\partial x^\nu}\right)^2 + \left(\frac{\partial^\nu g}{\partial y^\nu}\right)^2} \simeq \left|\frac{\partial^\nu g}{\partial x^\nu}\right| + \left|\frac{\partial^\nu g}{\partial y^\nu}\right|. \qquad (7)$$

Combination of Roberts Operator and Riesz Fractional Order Derivative. We convolve first, the classical Roberts operator with the image and consider that $g(x, y)$ is the processed image. If fractional order differential operator is combined with the Robert operator it enhances the image texture and recognizes the edges of small and prominent. Replacing the initial image values $f(x, y)$ by $g(x, y)$ in (6), we obtain the following combination formula on the positive x-coordinate:

$$\frac{\partial^\nu g(x, y)}{\partial x^\nu} \simeq -\frac{1}{2\cos(\pi\nu/2)} \sum_{k=0}^{n} \omega_k g(x-k, y) = -\frac{1}{2\cos(\pi\nu/2)}$$

$$\times \sum_{k=0}^{n} \omega_k \left\{ [f(x-k, y) - f(x-k+1, y+1)]^2 + [f(x-k+1, y) - f(x-k, y+1)]^2 \right\}^{\frac{1}{2}}$$

In order to achieve a better edge detection, we take the former three items of the fractional differential expression.

Combination of Prewitt Operator and Riesz Fractional Order Derivative. Replacing the integer-order derivatives in (2)–(3) by the fractional-order ones described in (6), we get the improved gradient:

$$\frac{\partial^\nu g}{\partial x^\nu}(x, y) = 2\left[\frac{\partial^\nu f}{\partial x^\nu}(x+1, y-1) + \frac{\partial^\nu f}{\partial x^\nu}(x+1, y) + \frac{\partial^\nu f}{\partial x^\nu}(x+1, y+1)\right]$$

$$\frac{\partial^\nu g}{\partial y^\nu}(x, y) = 2\left[\frac{\partial^\nu f}{\partial y^\nu}(x-1, y+1) + \frac{\partial^\nu f}{\partial y^\nu}(x, y+1) + \frac{\partial^\nu f}{\partial y^\nu}(x+1, y+1)\right]$$

Put $c_i = -\dfrac{\omega_i}{\cos(\pi\nu/2)}$, $i \in \mathbb{N}$. Taking into account the first three terms in the fractional differential expression (6), we obtain the following improved fractional Prewitt operator, along x direction:

$$\frac{\partial^\nu g}{\partial x^\nu}(x, y) = c_0\Big(f(x+1, y-1) + f(x+1, y) + f(x+1, y+1)\Big)$$

$$+ c_1\Big(f(x, y-1) + f(x, y) + f(x, y+1)\Big)$$

$$+ c_2\Big(f(x-1, y-1) + f(x-1, y) + f(x-1, y+1)\Big).$$

A similar formula holds for the fractional order y component. The fractional-order kernels for the improved Prewitt detector are as follows:

$$\begin{pmatrix} c_2 & c_1 & c_0 \\ c_2 & c_1 & c_0 \\ c_2 & c_1 & c_0 \end{pmatrix} \qquad \begin{pmatrix} c_2 & c_2 & c_2 \\ c_1 & c_1 & c_1 \\ c_0 & c_0 & c_0 \end{pmatrix}.$$

Combination of Sobel and Riesz Fractional Order Differential Mask. Replacing the integer-order derivatives in (4)–(5) by the fractional-order ones and following the same algorithm as for the fractional order Prewitt detector, we get the following fractional-order kernels:

$$\begin{pmatrix} c_2 & 2c_1 & c_0 \\ c_2 & 2c_1 & c_0 \\ c_2 & 2c_1 & c_0 \end{pmatrix} \qquad \begin{pmatrix} c_2 & c_2 & c_2 \\ 2c_1 & 2c_1 & 2c_1 \\ c_0 & c_0 & c_0 \end{pmatrix}.$$

4   Numerical Simulation and Analysis

Our algorithms are build upon the following technique for edge enhancing the input: we perform first a convolution filter with the two gradient components of each edge detector designed in the previous section; we compute then the gradient magnitude in (7); edge detection is then accomplished by utilizing a thresholding scheme to binarize the output. To test our proposed algorithms we selected an abdominal CT scan showing sigmoid diverticulitis (arrow) and free air (star). The experiments were carried out in MATLAB 7.

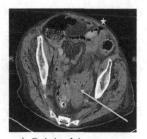   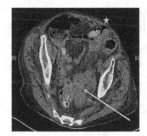

a) Original image;   b) Noisy image with $\sigma = 0.02$

Fig. 1. An abdominal CT scan.

Experimental Analysis of Noise-Free and Noisy Images. During image acquisition, the resulting image could be affected by various artifact regarded as noise. The simulation results are conducted on a noise-free abdominal CT image (Fig. 1(a)) and on a noisy abdominal image distorted with Gaussian white noise (noise is 0.02) (Fig. 1(b)). It could be found that the enhancement degree of image edges with fractional differential (Fig. 2(d)–(f)) is better than the first order one, this fact illustrating the capability of fractional order operators to extract more image structure feature details. The results in Fig. 3(d)–(f) show better noise immunity in edge detection. The threshold value T was selected,

$$T = \frac{\tau}{mn} \cdot \sum_{\substack{i=\overline{1,m} \\ j=\overline{i,n}}} (\nabla^\nu g)_{i,j}, \text{ where } \tau \geq 1 \text{ is a predetermined parameter and } m \text{ and}$$

n represent the height and width of the image. Of the three new edge detectors, the fractional Sobel operator seems to be better than the fractional Roberts and fractional Prewitt operators in handling noisy images. It not only performs reasonably well in the presence of noise but also provides good edges.

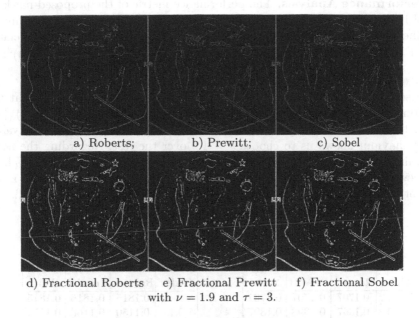

a) Roberts;   b) Prewitt;   c) Sobel

d) Fractional Roberts   e) Fractional Prewitt   f) Fractional Sobel
with $\nu = 1.9$ and $\tau = 3$.

Fig. 2. Results of the detected image in Fig. 1(a), with different filters.

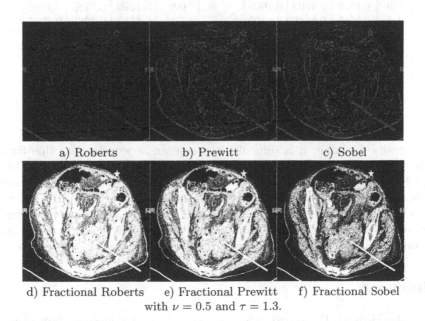

a) Roberts   b) Prewitt   c) Sobel

d) Fractional Roberts   e) Fractional Prewitt   f) Fractional Sobel
with $\nu = 0.5$ and $\tau = 1.3$.

Fig. 3. Results of the detected noisy image in Fig. 1(b), with different filters.

Performance Analysis. The performance metric of the proposed masks is tested by measuring the mean squared error (MSE) between the original image and the filtered one. If I_A and I_B are two $m \times n$ given images, the associated error based on quality is defined by MSE $= \frac{1}{mn} \sum\limits_{\substack{i=\overline{1,m} \\ j=\overline{1,n}}} (I_A(i,j) - I_B(i,j))^2$. In the case of the noise-free abdominal CT image, Table 1(a) indicates that the fractional masks have a linear behaviour along the ν values. For $\nu \in (0,2)\backslash\{1\}$, it can be seen that the higher the fractional order, the higher the MSE value. This behaviour allows us to choose $\nu = 1.9$ over the rest. Regarding the noisy abdominal CT image, Table 1(b) shows that the proposed fractional masks have a piecewise linear relationship with the fractional order. Selecting $\nu = 0.5$, one can notice the presence of diverticulitis (arrows) and free air (star) as well.

Table 1. MSE values for the filtered images:

$\sigma = 0$ Order	MSE Roberts	MSE Prewitt	MSE Sobel	$\sigma=0.02$ Order	MSE Roberts	MSE Prewitt	MSE Sobel
	0.1707	0.1707	0.1707		0.1815	0.1815	0.1815
0.1	0.1397	0.1398	0.1397	0.1	0.1150	0.1166	0.1174
0.3	0.1400	0.1402	0.1400	0.3	0.1270	0.1287	0.1316
0.5	0.1411	0.1412	0.1412	0.5	**0.1415**	**0.1433**	**0.1498**
0.7	0.1440	0.1442	0.1444	0.7	0.1598	0.1610	0.1691
0.9	0.1598	0.1603	0.1606	0.9	0.1690	0.1788	0.1886
1.1	0.1645	0.1648	0.1650	1.1	0.1887	0.1990	0.2087
1.3	0.1685	0.1693	0.1694	1.3	0.2100	0.2161	0.2238
1.5	0.1758	0.1761	0.1762	1.5	0.2189	0.2219	0.2252
1.7	0.1785	0.1788	0.1788	1.7	0.2171	0.2207	0.2221
1.9	**0.1795**	**0.1795**	**0.1795**	1.9	0.2150	0.2181	0.2179
a) in Fig. 2 d)-f)				b) in Fig.3 d)-f).			

Generally speaking, it is difficult to choose an appropriate ν value for the designed masks. A smaller value of the average gradient is needed to enhance image textures, while a larger fractional order is required to enhance textural details. When processing with image restoration and compression, the lower the MSE value, the better the edge information extracted. However, in terms of image edge detection, the MSE value might be higher to ensure it found more edge points on the image and also was capable to detect weak edge points.

References

1. Amoako-Yirenkyi, P., Appati, J.K., Dontwi, I.K.: Performance analysis of image smoothing techniques on a new fractional convolution mask for image edge detection. Open J. Appl. Sci. **6**, 478–488 (2016)

2. Amoako-Yirenkyi, P., Appati, J.K., Dontwi, I.K.: A new construction of a fractional derivative mask for image edge analysys based on Riemann-Liouville fractional derivative. Adv. Differ. Equ. **238**, 1–23 (2016)
3. Chiwueze, O.I., Cloot, A.: Possible application of fractional order derivative to image edges detection. Life Sci. J. **10**(4), 171–176 (2013)
4. Jiang, W., Ding, Z.-Q., Liu, Y.-E.: New image edge detection model based on fractional-order partial differentiation. J. Comput. Appl. **10**, 2848–2858 (2012)
5. Ma, X., Li, B., Zhang, Y., Yan, M.: The Canny edge detection and its improvement. In: Lei, J., Wang, F.L., Deng, H., Miao, D. (eds.) AICI 2012. LNCS (LNAI), vol. 7530, pp. 50–58. Springer, Heidelberg (2012). https://doi.org/10.1007/978-3-642-33478-8_7
6. Ortigueira, M.D.: Riesz potential operators and inverses via fractional centred derivatives. Int. J. Math. Math. Sci. **2006**, 1–12 (2006). https://doi.org/10.1155/IJMMS/2006/48391. Article ID 48391
7. Yang, Z., Lang, F., Yu, X., Zhang, Y.: The construction of fractional differential gradient operator. J. Comput. Inf. Syst. **7**(12), 4328–4342 (2011)
8. Yu, Q., Vegh, V., Liu, F., Turner, I.: A variable order fractional differential-based texture enhancement algorithm with application in medical imaging. PLoS One **10**(7), e0132952 (2015)

Facial Expression Based Emotion Recognition Using Neural Networks

Ekin Yağış and Mustafa Unel[✉]

Faculty of Engineering and Natural Sciences, Sabanci University,
34956 Tuzla, Istanbul, Turkey
{ekinyagis,munel}@sabanciuniv.edu

Abstract. Facial emotion recognition has been extensively studied over the last decade due to its various applications in the fields such as human-computer interaction and data analytics. In this paper, we develop a facial emotion recognition approach to classify seven emotional states (joy, sadness, surprise, anger, fear, disgust and neutral). Seventeen action units tracked by Kinect v2 sensor have been used as features. Classification of emotions was performed by artificial neural networks (ANNs). Six subjects took part in the experiment. We have achieved average accuracy of 95.8% for the case in which we tested our approach with the same volunteers took part in our data generation process. We also evaluated the performance of the network with additional volunteers who were not part of the training data and achieved 67.03% classification accuracy.

Keywords: Facial expression · Emotion recognition
Action Units (AU) · Kinect · Artificial Neural Networks (ANN)

1 Introduction

Facial expressions are the integral part of human communication. Along with intonation and accentuation, facial expressions complement the communication by shaping the intended meaning. Facial expressions are the most basic and primitive reflections of human emotions, which are at the same time the most effective and inevitable part of any communication.

In human to human interaction, non-verbal part of the communication such as tone and facial expressions are analyzed internally. These supporters allow a human to comprehend the emotional state of a person and intended meaning of a communication. In 1968, Mehrabian pointed out that 55% of message conveying information about feelings and attitudes is transmitted through facial expressions [1]. Thus, facial expression recognition has been widely studied for measuring the emotional state of human beings.

Being the pioneers of ERFE field (Emotion Recognition via Facial Expressions), Ekman and Friesen proposed a discrete categorization for basic facial emotions under six groups: anger, disgust, fear, happiness, sadness and surprise; and the seventh subset can be identified as neutral state of expression [2]. In the

© Springer International Publishing AG, part of Springer Nature 2018
A. Campilho et al. (Eds.): ICIAR 2018, LNCS 10882, pp. 210–217, 2018.
https://doi.org/10.1007/978-3-319-93000-8_24

research, they have developed the FACS system (Facial Action Coding System) in which changes in facial expressions deriving from specific muscle activity have been described as special coefficients - Action Units (AUs). For instance, Orbicularis oculi and pars orbitalis muscles are active in the movement of cheeks. Upper movement of checks is defined by coefficient "Action Unit 6" which has been called "cheek raiser". Using the earlier version of Kinect sensor only 6 action units could be detected, whereas 17 action units (AUs) can be tracked with the new Kinect v2 and the high definition face tracking API. Enumeration of action units tracked with Kinect v1 and Kinect v2 sensors is shown in Fig. 1.

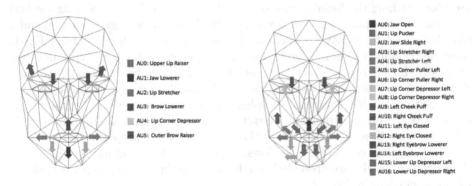

Fig. 1. Visualization of action units (AUs) extracted from Kinect v1 and v2, respectively. Color-coded labels of AUs indicate the position of that specific muscle. The arrow signs are used to illustrate the muscle movement. (Color figure online)

Over the past few decades facial and emotion recognition have attracted a great deal of research interest. Existing research efforts can be classified as image-based, video-based, and 3D surface-based methods [3]. While 3D facial recognition techniques were investigated in the literature to some extent, most of the studies have focused on two-dimensional (2D) algorithms which are computationally expensive [4–8].

Mao et al. [9] proposed a real-time EFRE method, in which, six action units (AUs) and 45 feature point positions (FPP) are used as features. Using these two features respectively, the classification of emotions has been done using support vector machine (SVM) classifiers and the recognition results of 30 consecutive frames are fused by the fusion algorithm based on improved emotional profiles (IEPs). In 2013, Youssef et al. [10] constructed a dataset containing 3D data for 14 different persons performing the 6 basic facial expressions. SVM and k-NN are used to classify emotions. They have achieved 38.8% (SVM) and 34.0% (k-NN) accuracy for individuals who did not participate in training of the classifiers, whereas observed 78.6% (SVM) and 81.8% (k-NN) accuracy levels considering individuals who did participate in training. Zhang et al. [11] collected the 3D facial points recorded by Kinect from 52 subjects (34 female and 18 male). The best accuracy reached was 80% for three emotions in only female data with decision tree classification. Lastly, in 2017, Tarnowski et al. [12] performed emotion classification using 6 action units tracked by Kinect v1 sensor as features to neural network. They have constructed the dataset with six men performing 7 emotional states, total of 256 facial expressions.

In this paper, we propose a facial emotion recognition approach based on several action units (AUs) tracked by a Kinect v2 sensor to recognize six basic emotions (i.e., anger, disgust, fear, happiness, sadness, and surprise) and neutral. Classification is performed through artificial neural networks (ANNs) where inputs of the network are features obtained from a 3D depth camera. Microsoft Kinect for Windows sensor v2 and high definition face tracking SDK have been used for tracking the facial action units (AUs) [13]. Unlike the existing method [12] where 6 features were employed for classification, we use 17 action units (AUs) derived from FACS system as features. As it can be seen from Fig. 1, these newly added 11 action units are mainly located in the lower face and thus provide a better representation for emotions that involve movement of muscles around mouth area. It should be noted that the new set of features plays a distinctive role in classifying complex human emotions. Several experiments are conducted on a homemade dataset which consists of 3 male and 3 female subjects. Classification results show the potential of our proposed method.

This paper is organized as follows: Sect. 2 describes our method in detail. Classification results are presented and discussed in Sect. 3. The paper is finalized with a conclusion in Sect. 4.

2   Method

2.1   Dataset and Experimental Setup

Six volunteers (3 women and 3 men) took part in data generation process. The participants were seated at a distance of two meters away from the Kinect sensor. Two sessions were held in which subjects mimicked all seven emotional states: neutral, joy, surprise, anger, sadness, fear and disgust. Each participant took 10 second breaks between emotional states and performed each emotion for a minute. Sample images from our dataset is shown in Fig. 2. For each session, 5 peak frames have been chosen per participant per emotion. As a result, 70 frames (5 peak frames × 2 sessions × 7 emotions) were collected for each subject. Overall dataset consisted of 420 (70 frames × 6 participants) facial expressions.

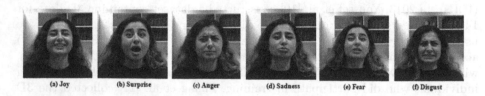

(a) Joy   (b) Surprise   (c) Anger   (d) Sadness   (e) Fear   (f) Disgust

Fig. 2. Example of facial expressions of one subject from dataset.

The high definition face tracking API developed by Microsoft, was employed to extract seventeen action units (AUs). 14 out of 17 AUs are expressed as a numeric weight varying between 0 and 1 whereas the remaining 3, Jaw Slide Right, Right Eyebrow Lowerer, and Left Eyebrow Lowerer, vary between -1 and $+1$, representing the displacement from a neutral AU expression. The action unit features coming from each frame can be written in the vector form:

$$a = (AU_0, AU_1, AU_2...AU_{16}) \tag{1}$$

Then, these action units were used as features in the classification process. Table 1 illustrates the exemplary values of action units for different emotional states (neutral, joy, surprise, anger, sadness, fear and disgust) of one participant.

Table 1. Numerical values of action units corresponding to various facial expressions.

	neutral	joy	surprise	anger	sadness	fear	disgust
AU0	0.045	0.160	0.337	0.088	0.091	0.229	0.197
AU1	0.231	0.000	0.347	0.216	0.392	0.246	0.289
AU2	0.057	-0.019	0.018	-0.055	0.001	-0.067	-0.037
AU3	0.133	0.204	0.010	0.101	0.052	0.015	0.022
AU4	0.115	0.161	0.032	0.101	0.151	0.188	0.030
AU5	0.000	0.820	0.023	0.020	0.010	0.024	0.084
AU6	0.015	0.903	0.023	0.025	0.014	0.002	0.013
AU7	0.040	0.056	0.174	0.118	0.421	0.241	0.116
AU8	0.044	0.080	0.134	0.036	0.437	0.277	0.193
AU9	0.034	0.022	0.019	0.026	0.035	0.020	0.022
AU10	0.031	0.010	0.016	0.018	0.025	0.021	0.024
AU11	0.201	0.179	0.047	0.132	0.055	0.083	0.304
AU12	0.216	0.127	0.033	0.044	0.046	0.034	0.366
AU13	0.340	-0.049	-0.246	0.156	-0.118	-0.201	0.117
AU14	0.371	0.063	-0.221	0.376	-0.025	-0.085	0.258
AU15	0.000	0.550	0.036	0.045	0.017	0.001	0.137
AU16	0.000	0.482	0.026	0.044	0.018	0.005	0.114

2.2   Classification

Having extracted the action units from Kinect sensor, we provided this features to our classifier as input. The flowchart of our proposed method can be seen in Fig. 3.

We have used a neural network classifier with one hidden layer to classify emotional states. 10 neurons and sigmoid action function have been used in hidden layer. Input layer consisted of seventeen action units (AUs). The output was one of the seven emotional states. We trained the neural network using scaled conjugate gradient backpropagation algorithm. The structure of the neural network can be seen in Fig. 4.

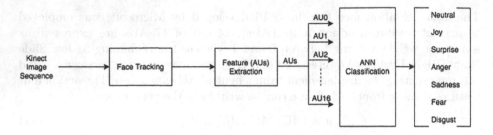

Fig. 3. Schematic representation of the methodology.

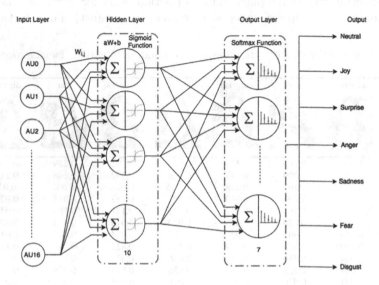

Fig. 4. The neural network classifier.

3   Experimental Results

We first tested our method for subject dependent case in which all the data were randomly divided into training, testing and the validation parts. Training part consisted of 70% of our overall data (294 samples) whereas testing and validation parts were 15% each (63 samples). The validation data is used to measure model generalization, and to terminate training when generalization stops improving. Testing samples which have no effect on training is used to measure network performance. In subject dependent case, we have tested our approach for the same volunteers took part in our data generation process. The network was trained 50 times using scaled conjugate gradient backpropagation. The average classifier accuracy was 95.8% for testing set and 96.2% for validation set (Table 2).

Afterwards, we evaluated our approach through training our network with samples collected from 5 volunteers and testing it with 6th volunteer who was

Table 2. Classification performances.

Training data	Validation data	Test data	Test accuracy (%)
70% of dataset	15% of dataset	15% of dataset	95.80

Table 3. Classification performances.

Test subject	Classification accuracy (%)
1	74.3
2	57.1
3	80.6
4	52.8
5	66.2
6	71.2
Average	67.03

	Training Data	Test Data	Accuracy (%)
Data	Male dataset	Female dataset	56.20
Number of Samples	210	210	

Fig. 5. The neural network classifier.

not part of the training data. This experiment is repeated for each subject. The network's average performance was 67.03% for classifying images which were not part of its training dataset (Table 3).

It has been known that skin color, facial hair and gender play a significant role in the quality of emotion recognition system. To examine the effect of gender in our classification approach, we performed an additional test. We divided our dataset into half and used the samples collected from men as training data. We then tested the network with remaining samples coming from our three female volunteers. For this gender-based test, we obtained 56% classification accuracy. Samples from both training and test set are shown in the Fig. 5, along with the classification accuracy.

				Target Class			
Emotions	neutral	joy	surprise	anger	sadness	fear	disgust
neutral	10	0	0	0	0	0	1
joy	0	8	0	0	0	0	0
surprise	0	0	13	0	0	0	0
anger	0	0	0	7	0	0	0
sadness	0	0	0	0	8	0	0
fear	0	0	0	0	0	8	1
disgust	0	0	0	0	0	0	7

Fig. 6. Test confusion matrix.

Confusion matrices are shown in Fig. 6 to determine easiest and most difficult emotions in term of classification. Distribution of 63 test samples into the classes neutral, joy, surprise, anger, sadness, fear and disgust can be seen from Fig. 6. According to the confusion matrix, disgust, neutral and fear are most likely to be misclassified. Lighting of the environment, head orientation of subject, distance from the sensor, and distinctive characteristics of human expressions are the main challenges for which Kinect could identify the feature points.

4   Conclusion

In this paper, we have presented our facial emotion recognition approach to classify seven different emotional states. We have created our own dataset of 420 samples collected from six volunteers with different gender and ethnicity. Each sample is labeled as neutral, joy, sadness, anger, surprise, fear or disgust. We have achieved average accuracy of 95.8% for subject dependent case and 67.03% accuracy for images of a different subject which did not take part in training. Moreover, we have examined the impact of gender by training the network with samples collected from male volunteers and testing it with female subjects. In this case, we have obtained 56% classification accuracy which is significantly lower compared to previous cases. In the future work, to eliminate the effect of gender, we plan to work on a fusion algorithm based on action units (AUs) and feature point positions (FPPs) and use principal component analysis (PCA) for feature selection process. Furthermore, we will expand our dataset by adding people with different ages.

References

1. Mehrabian, A.: Communication without words. In: Mortensen, C.D. (ed.) Communication Theory, pp. 193–200. Transaction Publishers, New Brunswick (2008)
2. Ekman, P., Friesen, W.: Facial Action Coding System. Consulting Psychologists Press, Stanford University, Palo Alto (1977)
3. Wang, P., Barrett, F., Martin, E., Milonova, M., Gur, R.E., Gur, R.C., Kohler, C., Verma, R.: Automated video-based facial expression analysis of neuropsychiatric disorders. J. Neurosci. Methods **168**(1), 224–238 (2008)
4. Tong, Y., Chen, R., Cheng, Y.: Facial expression recognition algorithm using LGC based on horizontal and diagonal prior principle. Optik-Int. J. Light Electron. Optics **125**, 4186–4189 (2014)
5. Jabid, T., Kabir, M.H., Chae, O.: Facial expression recognition using local directional pattern (IDP). In: 17th IEEE International Conference on Image Processing (ICIP). IEEE (2010)
6. Guo, Y., Tian, Y., Gao, X., Zhang, X.: Micro-expression recognition based on local binary patterns from three orthogonal planes and nearest neighbor method. In: International Joint Conference on Neural Networks (IJCNN). IEEE (2014)
7. Gizatdinova, Y., Surakka, V., Zhao, G., Makinen, E., Raisamo, R.: Facial expression classification based on local spatiotemporal edge and texture descriptors. In: Proceedings of the 7th International Conference on Methods and Techniques in Behavioral Research. ACM (2010)
8. Kabir, M.H., Jabid, T., Chae, O.: Local directional pattern variance (IDPV): a robust feature descriptor for facial expression recognition. Int. Arab. J. Inf. Technol. **9**(4), 382–391 (2012)
9. Mao, Q., Pan, X., Zhan, Y., Shen, X.: Using Kinect for real-time emotion recognition via facial expressions. Front. Inf. Technol. Electron. Eng. **16**(4), 272–282 (2015)
10. Youssef, A.E., Aly, S.F., Ibrahim, A.S., Abbott, A.L.: Auto-optimized multimodal expression recognition framework using 3D kinect data for ASD therapeutic aid. Int. J. Model. Optim. **3**(2), 112–115 (2013)
11. Zhang, Z., Cui, L., Liu, X., Zhu, T.: Emotion detection using Kinect 3D facial points. In: International Conference on Web Intelligence (2016)
12. Tarnowski, P., Kolodziej, M., Majkowkski, A., Rak, R.: Emotion recognition using facial expressions. In: International Conference on Computer Science, ICCS (2017)
13. Microsoft SDK for Face Tracking. http://msdn.microsoft.com/enus/library/jj130970.aspx

Robust Detection of Water Sensitive Papers

André R. S. Marcal$^{(\boxtimes)}$ (iD)

Departamento de Matemática, Faculdade de Ciências, Universidade do Porto, Porto, Portugal
andre.marcal@fc.up.pt

Abstract. The automatic analysis of water-sensitive papers (WSP) is of great relevance in agriculture. SprayImageMobile is a software tool developed for mobile devices (iOS) that provides full processing of WSP, from image acquisition to the final reporting. One of the initial processing tasks on SprayImage-Mobile is the detection (or segmentation) of the WSP on the image acquired by the device. This paper presents the method developed for the detection of the WSP that was implemented in SprayImageMobile. The method is based on the identification of reference points along the WSP margins, and the modeling of a quadrilateral that takes into account possible false positive and negative identifications. The method was tested on a set of 360 images, failing to detect the WSP in only 1 case (detection accuracy of 99.7%). The segmentation accuracy was evaluated using references obtained by a semi-automatic method. The average values obtained for the 359 images tested were: 0.9980 (precision), 0.9940 (recall) and 0.9921 (Hammoude metric).

Keywords: Water sensitive paper · Detection · Segmentation

1 Introduction

Spraying is the most common process of applying pesticides to crops because it is a fast and low cost method. It is however generally accepted that crop-pesticide application by spraying is an inefficient process [1], as the quantity of the chemicals that reaches the target is significantly less than that released from sprayer, which have negative economic and environmental impacts. There is therefore a need to compute agricultural spray parameters, with water-sensitive papers (WSP) being the most popular artificial targets for this evaluation [2]. WSP are coated papers with a yellow surface which turns dark blue by impinging aqueous droplets [2]. This color change in the WSP is due to the reaction of the water with the bromophenol-blue which changes the pH from 2.8 to 4.6 [3]. Since water in the spray stains the WSP, the spot size on the paper can be observed and measured [2]. The most commonly used WSP format is 26×76 mm, with other standard formats available, such as 52×76 mm, 26×500 mm.

There are generally two different approaches used in WSP image analysis tools. The first is a conventional one, with the WSP digitised with a scanner and the resulting image processed in a computer at the office. Examples of such systems are Gotas [4], Stain-Master [5], Image tool [6], Stain Analysis [7], Agro Scan [8], Droplet Scan [9] and Spr@y_Image [10]. A review of the performance of these software is presented in [2].

© Springer International Publishing AG, part of Springer Nature 2018
A. Campilho et al. (Eds.): ICIAR 2018, LNCS 10882, pp. 218–226, 2018.
https://doi.org/10.1007/978-3-319-93000-8_25

An obvious disadvantage of all these tools is that no immediate processing can be performed in the field, as the WSP needs to be digitized. An alternative approach is now possible using smartphone technology. A mobile device (smartphone or tablet) has the acquisition and processing capabilities to acquire a WSP image and process it on-site. Examples of such systems are SnapCard [11] and SprayImageMobile, developed by the University of Porto (Faculdade de Ciências) for Syngenta Crop Protection AG.

The SprayImageMobile image acquisition protocol requires that the WSP is placed over a red or pink homogeneous background, preferably centred and aligned with the image frame, but without touching the image edges. As an illustration of the typical WSP images that need to be analysed, Fig. 1 shows some examples of WSP images acquired for SprayImageMobile. The WSP in these images are all 26 × 76 mm format except for those on the 2 rightmost columns, which are 52 × 76 mm format. Images 01, 02 and 05 are nearly prefect acquisition, although the WSP is slightly off-centre in images 02 and 05. The remaining images presented in Fig. 1 illustrate some of the challenges that need to be addressed: rotated WSP (images 03, 04); small size of the imaged WSP (04, 11); specular reflectance (06, 07, 08); low contrast (04, 11); heterogeneous background due to the presence of shadows (07, 12); deformed WSP and resulting shadows (09, 10).

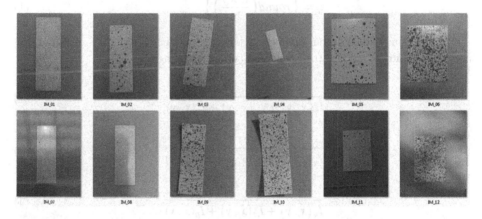

Fig. 1. Examples of WSP images acquired for SprayImageMobile processing. (Color figure online)

The purpose of this paper is to present a method developed for the detection of a WSP, which was implemented in SprayImageMobile, and to test it with a set of WSP images acquired under various conditions.

2   Materials and Methods

2.1   WSP Identification Strategy

The general goal is to identify a quadrilateral in the image that best matches the WSP. The process has to be robust and computationally light, as the subsequent analysis of

WSP on SprayImageMobile, based on mathematical morphology [10], requires considerable computational effort and time.

The processing is carried out in 5 stages: (1) identification of candidate points on the
long edges (left and right); (2) adjustment of left and right lines; (3) identification of
points on the top and bottom edges; (4) adjustment of top and bottom lines; (5) computation of corner co-ordinates of the quadrilateral.

A final validation of the detection process is done by computing the average ratio
between the short and long edges of the quadrilateral. If valid, SprayImageMobile uses
its corner coordinates to apply an affine transformation, mapping it to a rectangle.

2.2 WSP Identification Method

Let $I(x, y)$ be the input image, which has three color components: red – $I_R(x, y)$, green –
$I_G(x, y)$ and blue – $I_B(x, y)$. The image size is L (no lines) by C (no columns) pixels. A
margin of M pixels, with $M = round(C/30)$, is considered on both the right and left parts
of the image. A total of 15 image lines are selected, sampled uniformly from $I(x, y)$ using
(1), with $i = \{1, 2, \ldots, 15\}$.

$$x_i = \left\{ round\left(\frac{L \times i}{16}\right) \right\}$$ (1)

For each line i, the 3 colour components are normalized using (2–4), resulting in 3
sequences of number in the [0, 1] range – $r_i(y)$, $g_i(y)$ and $b_i(y)$.

$$r_i(y) = \frac{I_R(x_i, y)}{I_R(x_i, y) + I_G(x_i, y) + I_B(x_i, y)}$$ (2)

$$g_i(y) = \frac{I_G(x_i, y)}{I_R(x_i, y) + I_G(x_i, y) + I_B(x_i, y)}$$ (3)

$$b_i(y) = \frac{I_B(x_i, y)}{I_R(x_i, y) + I_G(x_i, y) + I_B(x_i, y)}$$ (4)

Reference values are computed by averaging the pixel values on both the left and
right margins for each color sequence, resulting in r_i^M, g_i^M and b_i^M. A new sequence of
numbers is computed from the normalized color sequences and reference values, using
(5). A reference value (n_i^M) is also computed from $n_i(y)$, by averaging the pixel values
on the left and right margin.

$$n_i(y) = r_i^M - r_i(y) + |g_i(y) - g_i^M| + |b_i(y) - b_i^M|$$ (5)

A final binary sequence $d_i(y)$ is computed from $n_i(y)$ and n_i^M. The value of $d_i(y)$ is 1
if $n_i(y) - n_i^M > 0.12$ else $d_i(y)$ is 0. The detection process is finished by searching for
the first 5 consecutive values of 1 in $d_i(y)$. If available, the first detection corresponds
to a point in the left edge of the WSP and the last one (or first one detected on the swapped

sequence) correspond to a point in the right edge of the WSP. An image (IM_12, bottom right corner of Fig. 1) was selected to illustrate the process. Figure 2 shows plots of $n_i(y)$ (top row) and $d_i(y)$ (bottom row), for 5 values of i (2, 5, 8, 11, 14). For this image, the detection of edge points is successful for values of i between 6 and 12.

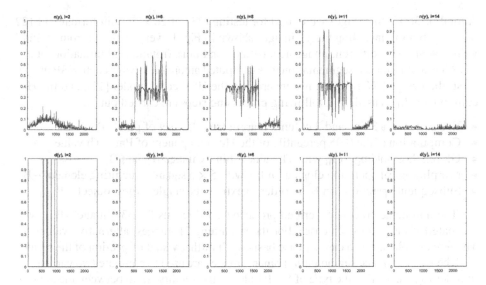

Fig. 2. Illustration of the detection process on a test image (IM_12) – plots of $n_i(y)$ (top row) and $d_i(y)$ (bottom row), for 5 values of i (2, 5, 8, 11, 14).

As the WSP are usually not perfectly aligned with the image grid, there is a possibility that the first and last points detected can belong to the top or bottom edge of the WSP. For this reason, they are disregarded for further processing. The remaining points detected are used to adjust lines that establish the left and right edges of the WSP. This is achieved by least square fitting to determine the polar coordinates ρ and θ of a line (6). The polar coordinates system was chosen as the left and right lines that model the WSP can be vertical, which would cause difficulties using affine coordinates.

$$\rho = x\cos\theta + y\sin\theta \qquad (6)$$

An average slope (θ_a) is computed using the slopes of the left (θ_l) and right (θ_r) lines. It is used to extract 5 sequences of numbers from the image, using parallel lines equally spaced between the left and right edges of the WSP. A similar processing to the one described to detect edge points is performed to detect up to 5 points in the top and bottom edges of the WSP. These points are used to determine lines that model the top and bottom edges of the WSP. Finally the lines are intersected to compute the x, y (or line, column) coordinates of the 4 points that define a quadrilateral that best matches the WSP in the image.

The final step is to validate the WSP detection, by using the computed average ratio of the short edges (top and bottom) and the long edges (left and right), assuming that the quadrilateral is in fact a distorted representation of a rectangle. If this value is different by more than 10% than the ratio expected for standard format WSP (0.342 for 26 × 76 mm and 0.684 for 52 × 76 mm), the detection is considered to have failed.

2.3 Test Dataset

A total of 360 WSP images were used for testing (238 of 26 × 76 mm format and 122 of 52 × 76 mm), including the 12 images shown in Fig. 1, were obtained from 19 individual WSP using different image acquisition conditions (rotation, illumination, etc.).

An initial reference segmentation was computed automatically for each WSP image. First, the original RGB image is converted to the HSV color model [12], and the Hue component (I_H) is used. The following processing steps are carried out [13]:

- Extraction of a 3 line and 3 column margin from I_H – set of pixels Pm.
- Computation of the 0.05 percentile of the Hue component of Pm – Th value.
- Global thresholding of I_H with Th value – binary image B_0, and $B_1 = 1-B_0$.
- Morphological operation closing on B_1, with 5 × 5 square structuring element – B_2.
- Subsequent operations on B_2 in order to extract the single largest object – B_{final}.

The automatic process described produced good results for 339 images (B_{final} was evaluated visually for each case). For the remaining 21 images, alternative values for Th were established on a case by case basis, with further visual inspection of the results.

The final reference segmentation binary images are used to compute two parameters in order to characterize the type of WSP image – the solidity (ratio between the areas of the binary object and its convex hull) and the orientation (absolute value of the angle between the binary object major axis and the vertical) [13].

As the output of the WSP detection method is simply the x, y (line, column) coordinates of the quadrilateral's 4 corners, a function to create a corresponding binary image was implemented in order to allow for a comparison with the reference segmentation.

2.4 Segmentation Evaluation

Three area based metrics were used to quantify the differences between the segmentation results: precision (P), recall (R) and Hammoude metric (H) [14]. To define these metrics let S_c and S_r be the computed and reference segmentations. The values computed for the metrics P (7), R (8) and H (9) all range from 0 to 1, with 1 corresponding to a perfect segmentation result (when the computed and reference segmentations are equal). P and R penalize over-segmentation (P) and under-segmentation (R) only, whereas H penalizes both over- and under-segmentation.

$$P = \frac{S_c \cap S_r}{S_c} \tag{7}$$

$$R = \frac{S_c \cap S_r}{S_r} \tag{8}$$

$$H = \frac{S_c \cap S_r}{S_c \cup S_r} \qquad (9)$$

3   Results

3.1   Results for a Sample Image

A sample image was selected from those presented in Fig. 1 for more detailed analysis. The image selected was IM_10, which has as the main challenges the deformation of the WSP and the resulting shadow over the background. The use of color space values from the image pixels is presented in Fig. 3 for 4 common color models – RGB, HSV, YcbCr and L*a*b* [12]. As can be seen in Fig. 3, all color models provide a reasonable but not perfect separation between the two main regions of the image (WSP and background). The automatic reference segmentation was successful in this case.

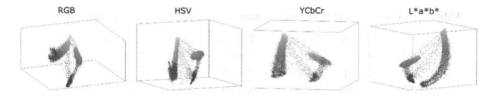

Fig. 3. Use of color space values in 4 color models: RGB, HSV, YcbCr and L*a*b* (IM_10). (Color figure online)

The results of the WSP detection for the test image (IM_10) are presented in Fig. 4. The left image shows the edge points and resulting lines adjusted to those points, and the image on the center shows the final quadrilateral obtained for the WSP, both

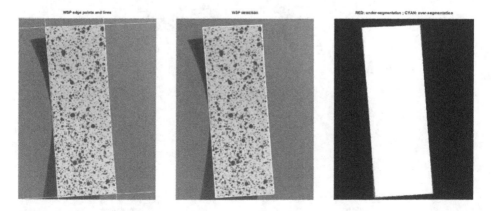

Fig. 4. Example of WSP detection for sample image. Detection of edge points and lines (left), resulting quadrilateral for the WSP detection (center) and segmentation result overlaid (right). (Color figure online)

presented in white over the original RGB image. The image on the right shows the segmentation results overlaid - red for under-segmentation and cyan for over-segmentation (white pixels are positive in both methods, and black negative in both).

This image has a solidity of 0.96611 and an orientation angle of 4.4°, both values computed from the reference segmentation. The segmentation results for this image are P = 0.99706, R = 0.98423 and H = 0.98139.

3.2   Results for the Test Dataset

The detection method failed to detect the WSP in 1 image, out of the 360 images tested (detection accuracy of 99.7%). The image was rejected due to a failed detection of the bottom edge, which resulted in an invalid ratio between the short and long edges.

For the remaining 359 images, a summary of the WSP image parameters and segmentation evaluation results is presented in Table 1. The average values obtained for the 3 metrics were: 0.9980 (precision), 0.9940 (recall) and 0.9921 (Hammoude metric).

Table 1. Summary of the WSP image parameters and segmentation evaluation results.

	Solidity	Orientation	Precision	Recall	Hammoude
Min.	0.954	0.01°	0.9853	0.9637	0.9637
Mean	0.991	3.73°	0.9980	0.9940	0.9921
Max.	0.998	18.55°	1.0000	0.9999	0.9974

The results from the 3 metrics used to evaluate the segmentation are generally similar. However, as the Hammoude metric (H) is the most demanding, penalizing both over-segmentation (false positives) and under-segmentation (false negatives), it will be further used. An evaluation of the relation between the Hammoude metric and the WSP

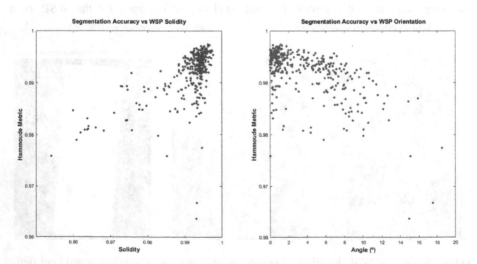

Fig. 5. Scatterplots of the Hammoude segmentation evaluation metric (H) versus WSP solidity (left) and orientation (right).

solidity and orientation is presented in Fig. 5. As expected, there is a clear relation between H and both solidity and orientation, with the best results obtained for low values of the orientation angle (WSP well aligned with the image grid) and high values of the solidity parameter (less deformed WSP).

4 Conclusions

The method developed is robust and efficient for the detection of a water sensitive paper (WSP) over red or pink homogeneous background, such as the image acquisition requirements of the SprayImageMobile software tool. The computational time was found to be less than 1 s (between 0.7 and 0.9 s). The method was tested with 360 images of 26 × 76 and 52 × 76 mm standard formats, failing to detect the WSP in only 1 case (detection accuracy of 99.7%). The test images include a number of challenges, such as rotated, small sized and deformed WSP, specular reflectance, low contrast and heterogeneous background (shadows). The average segmentation accuracy was 0.9980 (precision), 0.9940 (recall) and 0.9921 (Hammoude metric). A clear relation between the segmentation accuracy and the image acquisition conditions was found, with the best results obtained for less deformed WSP well aligned with the image grid.

References

1. Salyani, M., Farooq, M., Sweeb, R.D.: Spray deposition and mass balance in citrus orchard applications. Trans. ASABE 50(6), 1963–1969 (2007)
2. Cunha, M., Carvalho, C., Marcal, A.R.S.: Assessing the ability of image processing software to analyse spray quality on water-sensitive papers used as artificial targets. Biosys. Eng. 111(1), 11–23 (2012)
3. Turner, C.R., Huntington, K.A.: The use of water sensitive dye for the detection and assessment of small spray droplets. J. Agric. Eng. Res. 15, 385–387 (1970)
4. Chaim, A., Pessoa, M., Neto, J.C., Hermes, L.C.: Comparison of microscopic method and computational program for pesticide deposition evaluation of spraying. Pesqui. Agropecu. Bras. 37, 493–496 (2002)
5. StainMaster. http://www.stainmaster.com.ar
6. UTHSCSA: UTHSCSA Image Tool IT Version 2.0. San Antonio, Texas (USA): University of Texas Health Science Center at San Antonio (1997)
7. REMSpC: Stainalysis Manual. Ayr, ON Canada: REMSpC Spray Consulting (2002)
8. Araujo, E., Araujo, R.: Análise de gotas em pulverizações agrícolas utilizando digitalização de imagem ("AgroScan"). Agrotec Tecnologia Agrícola e Industrial, LTDA, Pelotas, RS, Brasil (2001)
9. Whitney, R.W., Gardisser, D.R.: WRK DropletScanTm Version 2.2 Software Manual, 4th edn. WRK, Inc. (2003)
10. Marcal, A.R.S., Cunha, M.: Image processing of artificial targets for automatic evaluation of spray quality. Trans. ASABE 51, 811–821 (2008)
11. Nansen, C., Ferguson, J.C., Moore, J., Groves, L., Emery, R., Garel, N., Hewitt, A.: Optimizing pesticide spray coverage using a novel web and smartphone tool. SnapCard, Agron. Sustain. Dev. 35(3), 1075–1085 (2015)

226   A. R. S. Marcal

12. Gonzalez, R.C., Woods, R.E., Eddins, S.L.: Digital Image Processing Using MATLAB, 2nd edn. Gatesmark Publishing, USA (2009)
13. MATLAB and Image Processing Toolbox Release 2017a, The MathWorks, Inc., Natick, Massachusetts, United States (2017)
14. Hammoude, A.: Computer-assisted endocardial border identification from a sequence of two-dimensional echocardiographic images. Ph.D. dissertation, University Washington, Seattle, WA (1988)

Classification of Icon Type and Cooldown State in Video Game Replays

Jeremias Eichelbaum, Ronny Hänsch$^{(\boxtimes)}$, and Olaf Hellwich

Computer Vision and Remote Sensing, Technische Universität Berlin,
Straße des 17 Juni. 135, 10623 Berlin, Germany
eichelbaum@campus.tu-berlin.de, r.haensch@tu-berlin.de

Abstract. The potential to positively influence research developments in seemingly unrelated areas leads to an increasing interest in the analysis of video games. As game publishers rarely provide an open interface to gain access to in-game information, the proposed system relies on the availability of video game recordings and broadcasts and operates completely in the visual domain. The classification of video game icons and associated metadata serves as an example task to assess the potential of several image recognition methods, including Random Forests (RFs), Support Vector Machines (SVMs), and Convolutional Networks (ConvNets). The experiments show that all machine learning approaches are able to successfully classify game icons in their original state, but performance is significantly decreased for icons in a cooldown state. SVMs fail to estimate the correct cooldown state, while RFs are outperformed by ConvNets.

Keywords: eSports · Image classification · Convolutional networks

1 Introduction

Playing video games competitively, also known as *eSports*, has become one of the most rapidly growing forms of new media. While in 2013, 70 million people watched eSports broadcasts [1], this number increased to 258 million people only four years later. Another indication for the growing popularity of competitive gaming is that the total revenue generated by eSports valued at \$1.5B in 2017 alone [2]. Companies and academia focus on two areas related to competitive gaming: Performance analysis and the development of artificial intelligence. Both disciplines need access to in-game information, such as the status and availability of items often visualized by icons and a corresponding cooldown state. In reality this often requires either reverse engineering - to which publishers usually do not agree - or an individual Application Programming Interface (API) for each game - which is seldom provided by the publishers. A more general and unrestrictive approach (illustrated in Fig. 1) is to analyze games in the visual domain, i.e. extracting in-game information from the user interface and other visual components.

© Springer International Publishing AG, part of Springer Nature 2018
A. Campilho et al. (Eds.): ICIAR 2018, LNCS 10882, pp. 227–234, 2018.
https://doi.org/10.1007/978-3-319-93000-8_26

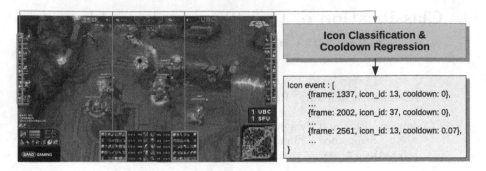

Fig. 1. Screenshot of a League of Legends World Championship replay. We extract the icons in the highlighted rectangles, classify their type as well as cooldown state, and thus extract parts of the game state. (Color figure online)

Tracking performance via the visual domain has been practiced for a long time for prominent sports like soccer or baseball. Similar to those examples, analysing a eSports player's performance can highlight what he excels or lacks in and provides valuable indicators to coaches and scouts. Furthermore, information about a player's performance is crucial to increase the success of both, the individual and the team [7]. However, the sophisticated tracking approaches of the mainstream sports can not directly be applied to eSports performance tracking, as the interactions in video games do not fit into an established sports category [7]. Motivated by the immense amount of players that want to receive personal training, several companies have automated analysis to provide players with individual feedback on their performance. Another example is the use of in-game information to predict the outcome of the eSports matches (e.g. in [9]), which is of high interest for fans, commentators, sponsors, and the media [8].

We aim to support research efforts in performance tracking and analysis by providing a general method to extract information associated with icons in video games. While there are multiple visual approaches to communicate in-game information, we focus on icons, due to their broad usage in game interfaces (see Fig. 1). They can communicate complex information fast, as they rely on the human ability to quickly perceive form and shape [3]. Icons from League of Legends (LoL) replays are a good example as it is one of the biggest and most successful video games in eSports history. These icons communicate two pieces of information: Item-/ability-type and its cooldown state. The former is visualized by shape and color of the icon, the latter by a certain amount of occlusion.

As eSports are a relatively young phenomena, very little research has been conducted on this emerging market. Only recently researchers started to study eSports in particular with respect to its potential of positively influencing research developments in other areas [1]. Most eSports research is focused on match outcome prediction [11]. In [9] information from the game state are used as features to predict the outcome of the match - with a surprisingly high accuracy of 71.49%. Such an approach requires real time access to a detailed game state. Most eSports titles do not provide a sufficient API and if they do, it is often limited to the parties involved in the match. This limits the applicability of outcome prediction to very few eSports titles and motivates our approach which rather depends on highly available data such as videos and broadcasts. One of the very few examples of automatic information extraction from eSports videos is the work in [5], which aims at detecting highlight moments in eSport videos.

While work on icon classification for the analysis of video games is relatively rare, there are many examples in other computer vision areas which aim to classify a set of small images. One of the earliest and probably best known datasets is MNIST, i.e. 28 × 28 px large images of handwritten digits [6]. Another example is CIFAR-100 [4] with 32 × 32 px large images with objects of 100 different classes. The dataset of LoL icons compiled for our work (see Sect. 2) consists of 20 × 20 large images of 103 different icon classes and is thus comparable in image size and class number to CIFAR. In [17] a simple k-Nearest-Neighbor classifier achieves an accuracy of 98.24% on the MNIST dataset. The work of [14] applies a Random Forest (RF) for image classification and achieves high classification rates despite the simplicity of the underlying model. This indicates that a RF is able to learn complex pattern [16]. Other approaches first encode the image before handing it over to the classifier, as for example in [15] which applies a Support Vector Machine (SVM) to a Histogram of oriented Gradients (HoG, [13]) descriptor and achieves 97.25% accuracy on the MNIST dataset. Deep Convolutional Networks (ConvNets) exhibit state of the art classification accuracy on complex image recognition tasks and successfully classify MNIST [10] as well as CIFAR-100 [12] with near human accuracy. Yahoo eSports uses ConvNets to detect highlights in eSport videos [5] by learning visual cues that signal the start or end of a video period.

Those classifiers require a sufficiently large training set, i.e. example images with known icon type and cooldown state. Such a dataset is (to the best of our knowledge) not available for any eSports title. Section 2 provides details about the dataset compiled for the experiments in Sect. 3, which evaluate the performance of kNN, SVMs, RFs, and ConvNets on the two tasks of classifying the icon type and the corresponding cooldown state.

2   Dataset

Professional players change strategies more often than casual players, which leads to a more diverse range of displayed icons in replays of professional matches. That is why we use replays from the League of Legends World Championship, in particular six hand annotated videos, as basis of our dataset. Figure 1 shows a typical scene from such an eSports replay. We are only interested in scenes that show the game itself and thus manually removed unrelated scenes. Icons in video games often appear at the same position, e.g. those marked by rectangles in Fig. 1. Using this information together with a pixel mask allows for easy extraction. In case of a 1280 × 720 pixel LoL replay, the size of each icon is 20 × 20 pixels. These icons are rendered as partially transparent overlay to the game and

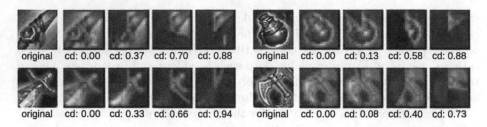

Fig. 2. Four example classes of icons extracted from video game replays. Each example group consists of the original icon and samples in various cooldown (cd) states.

Table 1. Sample distribution for our collected datasets.

	Classes	Samples	Samples cd = 0	Samples cd > 0
Train	103	10117	8678	1439
Validation	103	3072	2525	547
Test	103	5114	4202	912

thus contain some background scenery, which introduces noise and a varying brightness to the extracted icons. If an item is on cooldown, it is additionally occluded where the occlusion ranges from 0 to 100%. Figure 2 shows several examples of icons that appear in LoL replays (and are part of our dataset).

Because icons in LoL replays change infrequently, icons occurring in consecutive frames are near equals. That is why we only process one frame per second and only use a sample if all other samples of the same class are at least three seconds apart. Some icons appear more often than others as they are either more frequently provided by the game or preferred by the players. From the approximately 180 icon classes of LoL, only 133 classes appear within the six annotated videos. After limiting the number of maximum samples per icon class to avoid an unbalanced dataset and removing underrepresented icon classes, a total of 103 classes remains. Only a third of all icon classes can be on cooldown. For those classes, 50% of the samples show the icon in various states of cooldown. Icon type as well as the amount of cooldown are manually labelled for all samples in the dataset. The complete dataset is divided into three subsets, subsequently used for training, validation, and testing, which contain roughly 100, 30, 50 samples per icon class, respectively (see Table 1). Each of these datasets includes samples from two unique videos to avoid learning recording or encoding artifacts.

3   Methodology and Experiments

The following two subsections evaluate the performance of several machine learning approaches for two distinctive tasks, namely the classification of the icon type (Sect. 3.1) and the regression of the cooldown state (Sect. 3.2). Both sets of experiments are based on the same dataset as described in Sect. 2.

Table 2. Results for all four icon identification methods.

	No Cooldown	<50%	50 – 75%	>75%	Total
kNN	0.798	0.215	0.010	0.078	0.675
RF	0.990	**0.935**	0.927	0.807	0.971
SVM	0.993	0.894	**0.947**	0.885	0.976
ConvNet	**1.000**	0.910	0.932	**0.908**	**0.985**

3.1 Icon Classification

As a baseline we investigate the performance of a kNN classifier that is not based on a big training dataset but instead uses only a few reference images. We create this reference set directly from game assets (often found in the game directory) by using downsized version of the original icon. Using a kdTree with leaf size of 20, the euclidean distance, and $k = 1$ results in 79.8% accuracy on unoccluded icons, but is highly unreliable for partially or fully occluded icons.

Despite the mediocre performance, this method is sufficiently accurate to suggest multiple annotations during the manual video annotation process. For an unoccluded query icon the correct label is in 95% of the cases under the top five suggestions ($k = 5$).

The remaining classifiers, namely SVM, RF, and ConvNet, are trained on the training set, while the validation set is exploited to fix hyperparameters, and the test set is used only to estimate the final classification accuracies which are shown in Table 2.

The RF and SVM are based on the HoG descriptor of an icon, i.e. the concatenated gradient histograms of 4×4 cells of size 5×5 pixel. The RF consists of 100 trees with a maximum height of 20 and achieves an accuracy of 97.1%. It seems that the RF assigns less importance to the upper part of the icon, which allows it to achieve high performance for icons with 0–50% occlusion. Icons that are more than 75% occluded are slightly underrepresented in our dataset. This causes a slight overfitting of the RF to less occluded samples and a drastic decrease in classification accuracy on icons that are more than 75% occluded. The SVM uses a linear kernel. It only marginally outperforms the RF by 0.4% with the main difference that it better classifies strong occluded icons.

The ConvNet is applied directly to the image data without the computation of a predefined descriptor. It consists of two convolution layers, two max pooling layers, one fully connected layer, and one output layer. The convolution layers have a receptive field of 5×5 pixel, a stride of one, no zero-padding, and use a ReLU activation function. The first convolution layer applies 32, the second 64 filters, respectively. The pooling layers apply a 2×2 max-pooling with a stride of two. The fully connected layer consists of 1024 units, which connect to the output layer with 103 units. The learning step uses stochastic gradient descent in combination with a softmax loss function. The drop out rate is set to 40%. After only five epochs, the overall classification accuracy is 98.5%, with the lowest

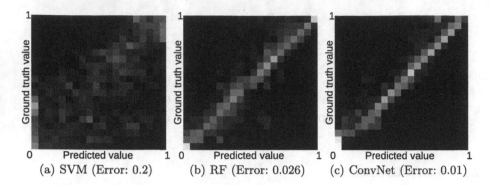

(a) SVM (Error: 0.2)   (b) RF (Error: 0.026)   (c) ConvNet (Error: 0.01)

Fig. 3. Confusion matrices and mean error for cooldown regression.

accuracy of 90.8% on icons that are more than 75% occluded. It outperforms the other models at the cost of a relatively long training time.

3.2   Cooldown Regression

All methods use the same hyperparameters as during the task of icon type classification. However, there are two important changes: First, SVM as well as RF are now used as regressors and estimate a value between 0 and 1 that corresponds to the amount of occlusion. Second, instead of using the HoG descriptor as input (as during icon type classification, see Sect. 3.1), the icon images are used directly since experiments showed a superior performance. The cooldown state of an icon is visualized by occluding/darkening a specific amount of the pixel (see Fig. 2 for examples). While gradient orientations describe the shape of the icon well and are thus useful for icon type classification, they cannot sufficiently capture the amount of dark pixels which leads to a loss in performance.

The RF achives a mean error of 0.026 and thus provides reliable estimates of the cooldown state. The confusion matrix in Fig. 3(b) shows that the RF provides reliable, yet not completely accurate estimates of the cooldown state. There are no major misassignments but adjacent cooldown states are partially mixed leading to the overall small error. The SVM performs poorly with a mean error of 0.2 and is basically unable to distinguish different cooldown states as the confusion matrix in Fig. 3(a) shows. Small to medium cooldown states are assigned to the no-cooldown class, while larger cooldown states are confused with other high cooldown classes. ConvNets are usually not well suited for regression tasks which is why we cast it as a classification problem by dividing the range of cooldown states into 20 intervals and treat them as individual class labels. The final estimate of the cooldown state is computed as weighted average over the activation of the output neurons. The ConvNet achieves a nearly perfect accuracy with a mean error of only 0.01 and thus outperforms the already good results of the RF. A certain cooldown state causes the appearance of an oriented edge within the image. The orientation of this edge is a good indicator of the cooldown state. Another strong cue is the number of dark pixels inside of the image. Both image characteristics are usually well detected by a ConvNet which explains its outstanding performance that is further illustrated in Fig. 3(c).

4 Conclusion

This paper presents first results in the relatively young research area of performance tracking in eSports. Icons are heavily used in video games to convey important information and thus allow to gain insights into the performance of the player as well as the current game state. We focused on the task of classifying the type of an icon, i.e. the correct icon class has to be estimated independent from whether it is shown completely or nearly completely occluded due to a low cooldown state. The second task is given by the regression problem to estimate the correct cooldown state of a given icon. Both tasks are challenging, as the icon images are small (i.e. 20×20 px), as transparent overlays partially corrupted with the background image, and - if in a cooldown state - blurred, occluded, and of low contrast.

Based on the success of machine learning methods on image databases with similar properties such as number of classes and size of images, we investigated three different machine learning approaches namely SVMs, RFs, and ConvNets. While all methods produce reliable icon type predictions for the classification task, in particular close to perfect results for unoccluded icons, the ConvNet achieves the highest accuracy on average. SVMs are not able to estimate the cooldown state of an icon, while RFs and ConvNets achieve low error rates in this case, too. For both tasks ConvNets are the winning approach and lead to the best overall performance at the cost of a significantly higher amount of computation time.

The occlusion caused by a given cooldown state is the major reason for a decreased performance during icon type classification. Interestingly, the cooldown filter does not fully occlude the icon but still retains some information. A first preliminary inspection of the remaining signal indicates the possibility to restore the occluded parts by deblurring and contrast enhancement. This would lead to a reconstructed icon which should be easier to be correctly classified then its occluded version. Future work will investigate this line of thought. However, different games apply different strategies to visualize the cooldown states so that a solution for one game might not be completely transferable to another game.

Icons are only one way to communicate information in video games to the player. While the game state of simple games can be fully accessed by analyzing icons, more complex games visualize the game state in multiple ways. Accessing the whole game state of complex games through visual recognition requires more sophisticated methods as well as larger datasets. In the future we aim to provide a categorization of visual recognition challenges related to game state extraction across games. Given the recent success of neural networks it seems plausible that most of the recognition tasks related to video games can be solved by adapting successful approaches of similar real world challenges to the video game domain.

We further plan to track the performance of eSports athletes and teams using information from video replays. A future goal is to find behavioral patterns that put players at an advantage or disadvantage. This information can be translated into identifying aspiring talent, augmenting coaches with additional insights, and allow for a reliable match outcome prediction.

References

1. Wagner, M.G.: On the scientific relevance of eSports. In: International Conference on Internet Computing, pp. 437–442 (2006)
2. Esports Market Report: Courtside-Playmakers of 2017. https://www.superdataresearch.com/market-data/esports-market-report/
3. Blattner, M., Sumikawa, D., Greenberg, R.: Earcons and icons: their structure and common design principles. Hum. Comput. Interact. **4**, 11–44 (1989)
4. Krizhevsky, A.: Learning multiple layers of features from tiny images. Technical Report, Department of Computer Science, University of Toronto, (2009)
5. Song, Y.: Real-Time Video Highlights for Yahoo Esports (2016). arXiv preprint: arXiv:1611.08780
6. LeCun, Y., Bottou, L., Bengio, Y., Haffner, P.: Gradient-based learning applied to document recognition. Proc. IEEE **86**, 2278–2324 (1998)
7. Hughes, M., Bartlett, R.: The use of performance indicators in performance analysis. J. Sports Sci. **20**, 739–754 (2002)
8. Spann, M., Skiera, B.: Sports forecasting: a comparison of the forecast accuracy of prediction markets, betting odds and tipsters. J. Forecast. **28**, 55–72 (2009)
9. Yang, Y., Qin, T., Lei, Y.H.: Real-time eSports Match Result Prediction (2016). arXiv preprint: arXiv:1701.03162
10. Cireşan, D., Meier, U., Masci, J., Schmidhuber, J.: Multi-column deep neural network for traffic sign classification. Neural Netw. **32**, 333–338 (2012)
11. Semenov, A., Romov, P., Korolev, S., Yashkov, D., Neklyudov, K.: Performance of machine learning algorithms in predicting game outcome from drafts in Dota 2. In: International Conference on Analysis of Images, Social Networks and Texts, pp. 26–37 (2016)
12. Srivastava, N., Hinton, G.E., Krizhevsky, A., Sutskever, I., Salakhutdinov, R.: Dropout: a simple way to prevent neural networks from overfitting. J. Mach. Learn. Res. **15**, 1929–1958 (2014)
13. Lowe, D.G.: Distinctive image features from scale-invariant keypoints. Int. J. Comput. Vis. **60**(2), 91–110 (2004)
14. Bosch, A., Zisserman, A., Munoz, X.: Image classification using random forests and ferns. In: IEEE 11th International Conference on Computer Vision, pp. 1–8 (2007)
15. Ebrahimzadeh, R., Jampour, M.: Efficient handwritten digit recognition based on histogram of oriented gradients and SVM. Int. J. Comput. Appl. **104**, 10–13 (2014)
16. Kleinberg, E.M.: An overtraining-resistant stochastic modeling method for pattern recognition. Ann. Stat. **24**(6), 2319–2349 (1996)
17. Zhang, B., Srihari, S.: Fast k-nearest neighbor classification using cluster-based trees. IEEE Trans. Pattern Anal. Mach. Intell. **26**, 525–528 (2004)

Multimodal Deep Learning for Robust Recognizing Maritime Imagery in the Visible and Infrared Spectrums

Kheireddine Aziz[(✉)] and Frédéric Bouchara[(✉)]

SIIM Team, Laboratoire LIS, UMR CNRS 7296, Université du Sud Toulon-Var,
B.P. 20132, 83957 La Garde, France
{Kheir-Eddine.Aziz,Frederic.bouchara}@univ-tln.fr

Abstract. The robust recognition of objects is an essential element of many maritime video surveillance systems. This paper builds on recent advances in convolutional neural networks (CNN) and proposes a new visible-infrared spectrum architecture for ship recognition. Our architecture is composed of two separate CNN processing streams, which will be consecutively combined with a merge network. This merge allows the classification to be performed and provide a rich semantic information such as appearance. It also allows to remedy some problems related to the quality of the visible images due to the weather conditions (rain, fog, etc.) and very complex maritime environment (foam, etc.). Using this architecture, we are able to achieve an average recognition accuracy of 87%.

Keywords: Data fusion · CNN · Classification
Maritime video surveillance

1 Introduction

Maritime video-surveillance is an important application which finds several both civilian and military applications such as the protection of the marine environment, the safety of people and merchandise. However, with the rapid development of image processing, there is a growing interest in automated solutions for sea surface control which ensure a visual ship recognition with few human intervention. In the other hand, beyond the complexity of the environment caused by the dynamic sea background, the typical recognition challenges stay making recognition with different angle of view, a large variation in lighting conditions and scale. In this context, most target recognition systems are completely separate tasks: collecting and processing of data. In fact, if data are found to be noisy or ambiguous during processing and there are not available supplementary data to reduce those deficiencies, the accuracy and robustness of the recognition process may be insufficient. For example, the visual spectrum cameras cannot be used in the dark and their seeing distance drops very quickly in the unfavorable weather conditions such as fog or heavy rain. In this condition, the better

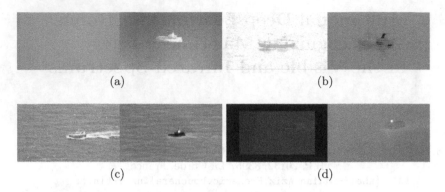

(a)   (b)

(c)   (d)

Fig. 1. Daylight scene captured with a normal camera and an infrared camera. (a) fog, (b) sun glitter, (c) foam, (d) low illumination.

performance can be obtained with camera operating in the infrared range as can be seen in Fig. 1.

In the state-of-the-art, some active multimodal sensor systems based on visual spectrum or long-wave IR sensor have been proposed (Withagen99 [1], Teutsch10 [2], Kumlu13 [3], Broek14 [4], Pan15 [5], Bloisi15 [6], Makedonas15 [7], Bousetouane16 [8], Guo17 [9], Huang17 [10]).

Paul et al. [1] made classification of ships from infrared images. 32 features were calculated (size, location of the hot spot and moment invariant functions). Classification has been performed using a k-Nearest Neighbor (k-NN), a linear, and a quadratic classifier. Teutsch et al. [2] focused their research on variations of boat appearance, image quality and environmental condition. A support vector machines (SVMs) classification are used to distinguish between three object classes: clutter, irrelevant objects and suspicious boats. Kumlu et al. [3] proposed to use a synthetic images for learning and a real images for validation. For classification, they used as features the oriented histogram of the binary edge and SVM (support vector machine). Ødegaard et al. [11] proposed also to use the simulated data for SAR images and a convolutional neural network for classification. Broek et al. [4] suggested to make ship recognition from electro-optical imagery. It consists in analysis the effect of the combination of the key-points SIFT and compact representation of this descriptor. Pan et al. [5] proposed an approach based on active learning and trained a composite kernel SVM for ship recognition. Two SVM kernel matrix are calculated by the two types of features (shape and texture), and the final composite kernel is obtained by the weighted sum. Bloisi et al. [6] made fusion of 11 features extracted from the vessel image and then, several classifiers such as k-NN and clustering have been tested for ship recognition. Makedonas et al. [7] used a hierarchical vessel classification approach based on features such as scale, shape and texture. These features allows to represent the structure, material and orientation of civilian vessels into three distinct types: cargo, small ship, and tanker. Bousetouane et al. [8] proposed an adapted R-CNN [12] surveillance pipeline for vessel localization and classification.

It consists a fine-grained classification using CNN features and a SVM classifier for object verification. Guo et al. [9] proposed a ship recognition method based on variational inference. They used features based on local spatial gray information and obtained from the aerial view image. Huang et al. [10] proposed to learn a multiple features for ship classification in optical remote sensing imagery. The overall classification framework consists of multiple texture features.

In summary, the large majority of these literature above used directly the data collected from the sensor and applied mature algorithms such as SVMs to improve different task of target recognition. It did not consider the interaction with the sensors for supplementing the information such as shape. This combination present a robust way to improve the recognition accuracy.

In our study, the multimodal sensor system is composed of two synchronized streams: visible and long-wave IR. We combine images from these sensors and demonstrate that the sensor-wise combination may improve the classification accuracy. Our architecture as depicted in Fig. 2, consists on a pipeline of two convolutional networks that operate on synchronized visible and IR streams respectively. The network learns and combines finally the features obtained from each stream. We initialize both visible and IR stream network with weights from a Caffe network [13] pre-trained on our large-scale ship database. We devise the ship recognition architecture accordingly into two pathways as shown in Fig. 2. Each pathway is implemented using a deep CaffeNet, softmax scores of which are combined by the fusion of twice fully connected layers. Both pathways of the model joins in one the fully connected and a softmax classifier layer.

2   Multimodal Architecture for Visible-IR Ship Recognition

The pipeline that we propose consists on fusion of two CaffeNet networks as shown in Fig. 2.

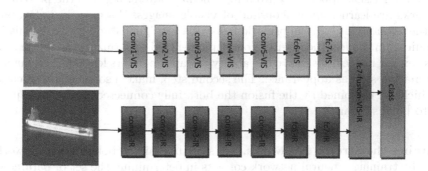

Fig. 2. Multimodal convolutional neural network for visible and IR stream. The top branch operates on visible images and the bottom branch operates on IR images.

Each pathway of the pipeline consists of a CaffeNet [13] network that has been pre-trained on our large-scale ship database. This database is composed of visible images captured with an airborne camera and fused with the other vessel database. Our database consists of 25 classes that contain each of them over thousands of images. For a robust training, we make a data augmentation on the whole of database such as flipping, cropping, rotation, smoothing, contrast/brightness adjustment and jpeg compression. Training of our multimodal CNN is performed in two stages. In the first stage, we fine-tune the parameters of each individual stream network and proceed with the training task for ship classification. In the second stage, we jointly train the parameters of the fusion network. The different stage will be described in the following sections.

2.1   Paired Visible and Infrared Ship Image Processing

We start training using CaffeNet definition. The input images should be formatted to 256×256 color jpeg. On the other hand, we have updated the CaffeNet implementation because our system should be able to take two input images (Visible, IR) and a label of the class for the joint images. For that, we used the HDF5 layer DATA of the library HDF5[1]. We note that HDF5 is a key value store, where each key is a string, and each value is a multidimensional array. To use the HDF5 DATA layer, we add a new key for each top we want to use and set the value of that key to store the image we could use.

2.2   Network Training

The training task will train on one set of images and test its accuracy on the other set of images. The training of the model consists on a two-step strategy. In the first step, we train both stream networks (Visible, IR) individually. We take our pre-trained CaffeNet network and fine-tune the parameters on new custom data (VAIS[2]). The advantage of this approach is the capture the semantics of the general visual appearance from intermediate layers, because the pre-trained networks are learned on a thousand of visible images. However, in unfavorable weather conditions, this information may be ambiguous and create a missing classification. Hence, the interest to complement this information with the other ones (ex: IR images) resides in the ability to capture others less noised semantics information such as appearance. The second step, make a softmax classification of which are combined by the fusion the both fully connected layers corresponding to both streams.

Training the Stream Networks. We start by training both stream networks. Usually, training a neural network consists in determining the set of parameters $\theta = \{\mathbf{W}, \mathbf{b}\}$ that minimize the overall errors made by the network. The error

---

[1] https://support.hdfgroup.org/HDF5/.
[2] http://vcipl-okstate.org/pbvs/bench/.

function is the sum of the squared difference between the desired output t_k and the network output a_k. This problem is solved using gradient descent, which requires determining $\frac{\partial E}{\partial \theta}$ for all θ in the model. This task is applied on the visible and IR data separately.

After all convolution, pooling and fully-connected layers, a softmax classifier layer is used to calculate the class probability of each instance of each pathway of multimodal CNN. The softmax function is a generalization of the multinomial logistic function that generates a K-dimensional vector of real values in the range $(0,1)$ which represents a categorical probability distribution. Equation 1 shows how softmax function predicts the probability for the $j-th$ class given a sample vector X. After training, the resulting networks can be used to perform separate classification of each stream as shown in Figs. 3 and 4.

$$P(y = j|X; W, b) = \frac{exp^{X^T w_j}}{\sum_{k=1}^{K} exp^{X^T W_k}} \tag{1}$$

Sloop	0.94	Cargo	0.94	Fishing ship	0.68
Ketch	0.06	Container ship	0.03	Trawler	0.31
Pleasure craft	0.03	Bulk carrier	0.05	Tug boat	0.00
Sail boat	0.00	Sail boat	0.01	Sail boat	0.00
Yawl	0.00	Offshor boat	0.00	Offshor boat	0.00

Fig. 3. First five predictions accuracy for three visible images.

Training the Fusion Network. Once the both individual stream networks are trained, we discard their softmax weights, concatenate their last layer responses $\theta_{Vis} = \{\mathbf{W_{Vis}}, \mathbf{b_{Vis}}\}$ and $\theta_{IR} = \{\mathbf{W_{IR}}, \mathbf{b_{IR}}\}$ and feed them through an additional fusion stream. Let $\theta_{joint} = \{\mathbf{W_{joint}}, \mathbf{b_{joint}}\}$ be the representation extracted from the concatenation of both last fully connected layer ($fc7_{Vis}$ and $fc7_{IR}$) of the CaffeNet of each stream (gray layer fc1-fus in Fig. 2). The fused network can therefore be trained by jointly optimizing all parameters to minimize the loss function. Then, the updated softmax classifier layer is obtained using the following equation:

$$P(y = j|X_{Vis}, X_{IR}; W_{joint}, b_{joint}) = \frac{exp^{X_{Vis,IR}^T W^{joint}_j}}{\sum_{k=1}^{K} exp^{X_{Vis,IR}^T W_k^{joint}}} \tag{2}$$

After training, the resulting networks can be used to perform classification of joint stream as shown in Fig. 5.

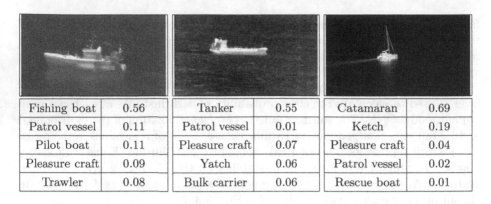

Fishing boat	0.56	Tanker	0.55	Catamaran	0.69
Patrol vessel	0.11	Patrol vessel	0.01	Ketch	0.19
Pilot boat	0.11	Pleasure craft	0.07	Pleasure craft	0.04
Pleasure craft	0.09	Yatch	0.06	Patrol vessel	0.02
Trawler	0.08	Bulk carrier	0.06	Rescue boat	0.01

Fig. 4. First five predictions accuracy for three IR images.

3 Experiments

3.1 Experimental Dataset

To validate our multimodal CNN for ship classification, we use the public VAIS [14] database. For now, it is the only existing database of paired visible and infrared ship imagery. The dataset contains 2865 images (1623 visible and 1242 IR), of which 1088 "Visible-IR" pairs. The database includes 6 categories: merchant ships, sailing ships, medium passenger ships, medium "other" ships, tugboats and small boats. The paired visible-IR image set is partitioned into train and validation data. In our experiment, we have used 544 image pairs for training and 360 image pairs for validation of which we applied data augmentation for increasing the number of image pairs.

For testing our model on images captured in the unfavorable weather condition, we construct another set contains 107 image pairs acquired from airborne video camera. We distinguished 66 image pairs in ideal weather conditions and 41 others in the unfavorable weather conditions (fog, sun glitter, foam, low illumination).

3.2 Results and Analysis

Our approach is compared mainly with existed state-of-the-art methods such as the work of Zhang et al. [14].

The comparison result for the VAIS datasets are shown respectively in Table 1. We notice that for various ship image classes, the visible and IR images are complementary and improve significantly the classification accuracy (86.67%). We notice also that combining two stream could assist the classification process in some confused conditions such as fog, low illumination as shown in Fig. 5. This is explained by the fact that some information that is absent in the visible image could be supplemented by other information coming from

Couple of visible and IR image

Bulk Carrier	0.53
Cargo	0.35
Offshor boat	0.09
Container ship	0.02
Patrol vessel	0.02

(a) Visible

Bulk carrier	0.85
Cargo	0.08
Tanker	0.02
Patrol vessel	0.01
Pilot boat	0.01

(b) IR

Bulk carrier	0.91
Tanker	0.02
Cargo	0.01
Patrol vessel	0.01
Pilot boat	0.01

(c) Visible+IR

Couple of visible and IR image.

Cargo	0.37
Petrolier	0.17
Vraqiuer	0.02
Tugboat	0.089
Offshore boat	0.045

(a) Visible

Bulk carrier	0.25
Offshore boat	0.16
Cargo	0.15
Cruiser ship	0.11
Yatch	0.07

(b) IR

Cargo	0.76
Bulk carrier	0.19
Tanker	0.04
Patrol vessel	0.00
Rescue boat	0.00

(c) Visible+IR

Fig. 5. Example of classification accuracy for one target in ideal and bad weather conditions. Three tables shows the first five predictions accuracy using: (a) Visible pathway. (b) IR pathway. (c) Combining both pathways.

the IR image. Table 2 summarize the classification accuracy obtained from the second set of validations.

The proposed method achieves superior classification performance (Table 1) compared to the existed methods, which demonstrates the effectiveness for classification problem. Especially, for IR images, the CNN obtains higher overall accuracy than deep learning method [14] and the visible Images obtains nearly the same overall accuracy for VAIS dataset. Therefore, the proposed approach, which combine multiple streams, have the overall accuracy most important than deep learning method [14].

Table 1. Comparison of classification accuracy (%) with existed state-of-the-art methods for the VAIS database.

	IR	Visible	IR + Visible
Gnostic field [14]	58.7%	82.4%	82.4%
CNN [14]	54%	81.9%	82.1%
Gnostic field + CNN [14]	56.8%	81%	87.4%
Our multimodal CNN	63.47%	80.17%	86.67%

Table 2. Classification accuracy using our multimodal CNN for two weather conditions classes.

	IR	Visible	Visible + IR
Ideal weather conditions	66.35%	81.41%	87.01%
Unfavorable weather conditions (fog, low illumination...)	51.29%	70.68%	79.2%

In addition, to demonstrate the enhanced power of stream fusion for ship classification, we calculated the accuracy classification of the proposed multimodal CNN approach on each ship class and compare them with the performance of the method that use each individual stream. The accuracy per class is reported in Fig. 6. It is apparent that the proposed approach outperforms all the individual streams approaches.

Class	IR	Visible	IR + Visible
Cargo	76,67%	85,00%	93,33%
Medium other	63,33%	78,33%	85,00%
Pessenger	61,67%	81,67%	83,33%
Sailing	61,67%	76,67%	90,00%
Small	58,33%	71,67%	80,00%
Tug	51,67%	85,00%	88,33%

Fig. 6. Classification accuracy (%) per class for the VAIS database.

Confusion matrix of the multimodal CNN for the VAIS database is listed in Fig. 7. Using only IR images, as shown in Fig. 7a, there is 40% the confusion between different classes. The major confusion occurs between class 4 (i.e., sailing) and class 5 (i.e., small), because some sailing images are like the small images. In the other hand, using only visible images decrease significantly this confusion (Fig. 7b) and even more when we merge features of both pathway corresponding to each stream as shown in Fig. 7c.

Figure 7c shown the confusion matrix of streams fusion. It is observed that the small number of confusion occurs always within class 4 and class 5, class 5 and class 6. Some sailing ships are similar to passenger ships. Visually, some small ships have high similarity to medium passenger ships. Hence, the necessity to complete the classification by other semantic information such as dimension.

Class	Cargo	Medium other	Pessenger	Sailing	Small	Tug	Recall
Cargo	46	2	9	1	2	0	0,77
Medium other	2	38	7	3	5	5	0,63
Pessenger	1	15	37	1	5	1	0,62
Sailing	0	7	3	37	11	2	0,62
Small	2	3	6	9	35	5	0,58
Tug	5	6	7	4	7	31	0,52
Precision	0,82	0,54	0,54	0,67	0,54	0,70	

IR

Class	Cargo	Medium other	Pessenger	Sailing	Small	Tug	Recall
Cargo	51	2	5	0	2	0	0,85
Medium other	0	47	2	2	0	9	0,78
Pessenger	0	8	49	0	3	0	0,82
Sailing	0	0	3	46	11	0	0,77
Small	0	1	2	8	43	6	0,72
Tug	2	2	4	0	1	51	0,85
Precision	0,96	0,78	0,75	0,82	0,72	0,77	

Visible

Class	Cargo	Medium other	Pessenger	Sailing	Small	Tug	Recall
Cargo	56	0	3	0	1	0	0,93
Medium other	0	51	0	0	2	7	0,85
Pessenger	0	5	50	0	2	3	0,83
Sailing	0	0	2	54	4	0	0,90
Small	0	1	1	6	48	4	0,80
Tug	0	6	0	0	1	53	0,88
Precision	1	0,81	0,89	0,90	0,83	0,79	

Visible+IR

Fig. 7. Confusion matrix for VAIS database

4 Conclusion

In this paper, we presented a method for ship classification using joint visible and IR stream based on CaffeNet architecture. This method consists in combining semantics information from two streams. These two stream are complementary to each other and the combination of them is a powerful and comprehensive representation of ship images. We notice that the multimodal CNN became more discriminative than using only an individual stream. Experimental results over visible-IR database ensured that the proposed model consistently achieves a superior classification performance.

The scarcity of public image databases make the task of evaluation very difficult. We plan to build a Visible-IR image/videos database of boats making the evaluation of the algorithms of the scientific community more objective and allowing to compare the different existing approaches.

References

1. Withagen, P., Schutte, K., Vossepoel, A., Breuers, M.: Automatic classification of ships from infrared (FLIR) images (1999)
2. Teutsch, M., Krager, W.: Classification of small boats in infrared images for maritime surveillance. In: 2010 International WaterSide Security Conference, pp. 1–7, November 2010
3. Kumlu, D., Jenkins, B.K.: Autonomous ship classification using synthetic and real color images (2013)
4. van den Broek, S.P., Bouma, H., den Hollander, R.J.M., Veerman, H.E.T., Benoist, K.W., Schwering, P.B.W.: Ship recognition for improved persistent tracking with descriptor localization and compact representations (2014)
5. Pan, B., Jiang, Z., Wu, J., Zhang, H., Luo, P.: Ship recognition based on active learning and composite kernel SVM. In: Tan, T., Ruan, Q., Wang, S., Ma, H., Di, K. (eds.) IGTA 2015. CCIS, vol. 525, pp. 198–207. Springer, Heidelberg (2015). https://doi.org/10.1007/978-3-662-47791-5_23
6. Bloisi, D.D., Iocchi, L., Pennisi, A., Tombolini, L.: ARGOS-Venice boat classification. In: 2015 12th IEEE International Conference on Advanced Video and Signal Based Surveillance (AVSS), pp. 1–6 (2015)
7. Makedonas, A., Theoharatos, C., Tsagaris, V., Anastasopoulos, V., Costicoglou, S.: Vessel classification in COSMO-SkyMed SAR data using hierarchical feature selection. In: ISPRS - International Archives of the Photogrammetry, Remote Sensing and Spatial Information Sciences, vol. XL-7/W3, pp. 975–982 (2015)
8. Bousetouane, F., Morris, B.: Fast CNN surveillance pipeline for fine-grained vessel classification and detection in maritime scenarios. In: 2016 13th IEEE International Conference on Advanced Video and Signal Based Surveillance (AVSS), pp. 242–248, August 2016
9. Guo, W., Xia, X.: A ship recognition method of variational inference-based probability generative model using optical remote sensing image. Optik Int. J. Light Electron. Opt. 145(Suppl. C), 365–376 (2017)
10. Huang, L., Li, W., Chen, C., Zhang, F., Lang, H.: Multiple features learning for ship classification in optical imagery. In: Multimedia Tools and Applications, July 2017
11. Ødegaard, N., Knapskog, A.O., Cochin, C., Louvigne, J.C.: Classification of ships using real and simulated data in a convolutional neural network. In: 2016 IEEE Radar Conference (RadarConf), pp. 1–6, May 2016
12. Girshick, R.: Fast R-CNN. In: Proceedings of the International Conference on Computer Vision (ICCV) (2015)
13. Jia, Y., Shelhamer, E., Donahue, J., Karayev, S., Long, J., Girshick, R., Guadarrama, S., Darrell, T.: Caffe: convolutional architecture for fast feature embedding. In: Proceedings of the 22nd ACM International Conference on Multimedia, MM 2014, pp. 675–678. ACM, New York (2014)
14. Zhang, M.M., Choi, J., Daniilidis, K., Wolf, M.T., Kanan, C.: VAIS: a dataset for recognizing maritime imagery in the visible and infrared spectrums. In: 2015 IEEE Conference on Computer Vision and Pattern Recognition Workshops (CVPRW), pp. 10–16, June 2015

Shape Classification Using Hilbert Space Embeddings and Kernel Adaptive Filtering

J. S. Blandon[1](✉), C. K. Valencia[1](✉), A. Alvarez[1], J. Echeverry[1], M. A. Alvarez[2], and A. Orozco[1]

[1] Automatics Research Group, Universidad Tecnológica de Pereira, Pereira, Colombia
{jsblandon,ckvalencia}@utp.edu.co
[2] Department of Computer Science, University of Sheffield, Sheffield, UK

Abstract. Shape classification is employed for realizing image object identification and classification tasks. Most of the state-of-the-art approaches use sequential features extracted from contours to classify shapes, either directly, i.e., k-nearest neighbors (KNN), or through stochastic models, i.e., hidden Markov models (HMMs). Here, inspired by probability based metrics using Hilbert space embedding (HSE), we introduce a novel scheme for efficient shape classification. To this end, we highlight relevant curvature patterns from binary images towards a Kernel Adaptive Filtering (KAF)-based enhancement of the maximum mean discrepancy metric. Namely, we test the performance of our approach on the well-known *MPEG-7* and *99-Shapes* databases. Results show that our strategy can code relevant shape properties from binary images achieving competitive classification results.

Keywords: Shape classification · Binary images · HSE · KAF

1 Introduction

Nowadays, shape classification (SC) from binary images is a widely studied field, which mainly favors object recognition tasks through contour-based features; for instance, to support hand recognition [3], object tracking [7], image sensing [5], among others. Commonly, curvature coefficients are computed from input binary images, which locally describe shape variations. However, coding relevant patterns from curvature features is a challenging task due to the contour length changes and because of the presence of complex shape dynamics. Regarding this, authors in [1,6] proposed stochastic-based models to capture shape variations from curvature coefficients. Likewise, in [6] a contour-based feature estimation stage is coupled with an HMM classifier. Nonetheless, such approaches require an exhaustive parameter tuning. On the other hand, authors in [5] employ a manifold-based representation to discriminate among shapes using the well-known Maximum Mean Discrepancy (MMD) metric. However, the conventional

© Springer International Publishing AG, part of Springer Nature 2018
A. Campilho et al. (Eds.): ICIAR 2018, LNCS 10882, pp. 245–251, 2018.
https://doi.org/10.1007/978-3-319-93000-8_28

MMD does not code the relevance of each sample [8], i.e., a curvature coefficient within a shape, yielding to biased results.

Here, we introduce a shape classification approach based on a curvature-based representation and a weighted extension of the MMD metric. Namely, a kernel adapting filtering (KAF) strategy is carried out to learn salient patterns from curvature-based features [4]. In turn, such patterns are used to compute the probability density of each object shape from a HES-based perspective. Lastly, a k-nearest neighbors classifier is trained using the enhanced MMD metric to discriminate shapes from binary images. Our proposal is tested on the well-known *MPEG-7* and *99-Shapes* databases [6]. As a benchmark, we employ the stochastic model hinge on likelihood maximization presented in [6], and a straightforward MMD algorithm [5]. Overall, our methodology reaches competitive results concerning the average classification accuracy. The remainder of this paper is organized as follows: Sect. 2 describes the mathematical background, Sect. 3 presents the experimental set-up, Sect. 4 describes the results obtained, and Sect. 5 the conclusions.

2   Kernel Adaptive Filtering-Based MMD Enhancement for Shape Classification

Preprocessing and Curvature Estimation from Binary Images [1]. Given a binary image $M \in \mathbb{R}^{W \times H}$ holding $W \times H$ pixels, a Canny filter is applied as edge detector to reveal the object shape. Then, some morphological operations are carried out to prevent non-closed trajectories and a set of curvature coefficients $\{x_n \in \mathbb{R}\}_{n=1}^{N}$ is extracted based on first order changes. In fact, the trajectories are extracted from farthest horizontal point to the right, getting each curvature point from this first coordinate in a counter-clockwise manner.

Shape Classification. To compare two different objects from their curvature sets $\{x_n\}_{n=1}^{N}$ and $\{y_m\}_{m=1}^{M}$, we introduce a Reproducing Kernel Hilbert Space Embedding-based distance as follows: let $\mathcal{P}$ be the space of all probability distributions and let $X, Y \subset \mathcal{X}$ be two random variables that follow the distribution functions $\mathbb{P}$ and $\mathbb{Q}$, respectively; then $\mathbb{P}, \mathbb{Q} \in \mathcal{P}$, $x_n \in X$, and $y_m \in Y$. Let $\mu\{\cdot\}$ be a marginal embedding operator mapping a given sample $x \in X$ from a probability distribution $\mathbb{P}$ to a Reproducing Kernel Hilbert Space (RKHS) $\mathcal{H}$, as follows: $\mu(\mathbb{P}) = \mathbb{E}_X[\phi(x)] = \int_{\mathcal{X}} \phi(x) d\mathbb{P}(x)$, where $\phi : \mathcal{X} \to \mathcal{H}$. This embedding of probability distributions into RKHS allows us to compute distances between them. According to [8], the RKHS-based distance over the probability measures $\mathbb{P}$ and $\mathbb{Q}$, yields: $d_\kappa^2(\mathbb{P}, \mathbb{Q}) = \|\mu(\mathbb{P}) - \mu(\mathbb{Q})\|_{\mathcal{H}}^2$, which can be rewritten as: $d_\kappa^2(\mathbb{P}, \mathbb{Q}) = \left\| \int_{\mathcal{X}} \phi(x) d\mathbb{P}(x) - \int_{\mathcal{X}} \phi(y) d\mathbb{Q}(y) \right\|_{\mathcal{H}}^2$.

Afterward, we define a function $\kappa(x, x') = \langle \phi(x), \phi(x') \rangle_{\mathcal{H}}$, $\forall x, x' \in \mathcal{X}$ as a reproducing characteristic kernel on $\mathcal{H}$. If the probability distributions $\mathbb{P}(x)$ and $\mathbb{Q}(y)$ admit density functions $p(x)$ and $q(y)$, respectively, we have $d\mathbb{P}(x) = p(x)dx$ and $d\mathbb{Q}(y) = q(y)dy$. Also, the density functions $p(x)$ and $q(y)$ can be computed as a dot product between a function $f \in \mathcal{F}$ and the mapping φ into the RKHS $\mathcal{F}$, e.g, $p(x) = \langle f, \varphi(x) \rangle_{\mathcal{F}} = \int_{\mathcal{X}} \alpha_{x'} \varphi(x) dx'$, where $\varphi : \mathcal{X} \rightarrow \mathcal{F}$ and $\alpha_{x'} \in [0,1]$. Next, we rewrite $d_\kappa^2(\mathbb{P}, \mathbb{Q})$ in terms of the α parameters as follows [9]:

$$d_\kappa^2(\mathbb{P}, \mathbb{Q} | \alpha_x, \alpha_y) = \int_{\mathcal{X}} \int_{\mathcal{X}} \alpha_x \alpha_{x'} \kappa(x, x') \zeta(x, x') dx dx' + \int_{\mathcal{X}} \int_{\mathcal{X}} \alpha_y \alpha_{y'} \kappa(y, y') \zeta(y, y') dy dy'$$

$$- 2 \int_{\mathcal{X}} \int_{\mathcal{X}} \alpha_x \alpha_y \kappa(x, y) \zeta(x, y) dx dy, \tag{1}$$

where $\zeta(x, x') = \langle \varphi(x), \varphi(x') \rangle_{\mathcal{F}}$. The expression in (1) can be seen as a weighted enhancement of the well-known maximum mean discrepancy distance (WMMD) with regard to the mapping function φ in the $p(x)$ and $p(y)$ estimation. In this sense, to code relevant curvature patterns, we propose to learn the weights in WMMD towards a kernel adaptive filtering (KAF) technique. Namely, the quantized kernel least mean square (QKLMS) algorithm is selected as a straightforward solution [2]. So, the densities are computed from an input-output pair of samples $\{x_{n+1}, x_n\}_{n=1}^{N-1}$ and QKLMS predictions: $\hat{x}_{n+1} = \sum_{x' \in \Omega_n} \beta_{x'} \zeta(x_{n+1}, x')$, being Ω_n the filter codebook at the n-th iteration and $\beta_{x'} \in \mathbb{R}$. Therefore, QKLMS estimates the curvature sequence into a RKHS following a Markovian constraint to preserve the spatial dependencies of the object. Besides, the QKLMS includes a novelty criterion (NC) based on the euclidean distance $d_E(x_n, \Omega_{n-1})$, with $i \in \{1, 2, \ldots, N\}$. Later, given two curvature sequences from X and Y, that is, $\{x_n\}_{n=1}^{N} \sim \mathbb{P}$ and $\{y_n\}_{m=1}^{M} \sim \mathbb{Q}$, the densities are computed as: $\hat{p}(x) = \sum_{x' \in \Omega_{N-1}^x} \hat{\alpha}_{x'} \zeta(x, x')$ and $\hat{p}(y) = \sum_{y' \in \Omega_{N-1}^y} \hat{\alpha}_{y'} \zeta(y, y')$. Furthermore, to preserve the metric properties in WMMD, the weights are normalized as: $\hat{\alpha}_{x'} = |\beta_{x'}| / \sum_{\beta_{x'} \in \Omega_{N-1}^x} |\beta_{x'}|$ and $\hat{\alpha}_{y'} = |\beta_{y'}| / \sum_{\beta_{y'} \in \Omega_{M-1}^y} |\beta_{y'}|$. Finally, using a Gaussian kernel $\kappa_G(\cdot, \cdot) \in \mathbb{R}^+$ to infer the RKHSs, the WMMD is written as:

$$\tilde{d}_\kappa^2(\mathbb{P}, \mathbb{Q} | \alpha_x, \alpha_y) = \sum_{x, x' \in \Omega_{N-1}^x} \alpha_x \alpha_{x'} \kappa_G(x, x' | \sigma + 2\sigma_x) + \sum_{y, y' \in \Omega_{M-1}^y} \alpha_y \alpha_{y'} \kappa_G(y, y' | \sigma + 2\sigma_y)$$

$$- 2 \sum_{x \in \Omega_{N-1}^x, y \in \Omega_{M-1}^y} \alpha_x \alpha_y \kappa_G(x, y | \sigma + \sigma_x + \sigma_y), \tag{2}$$

where $\sigma, \sigma_x, \sigma_y \in \mathbb{R}^+$ are the bandwidth values for the characteristic and the QKLMS kernels, respectively.

3   Experimental Set-up

To assess the WMMD we used two databases (DB): the *99-Shape Database*[1], and the *MPEG-7_CE-Shape-1 Part B*[2], holding 9 and 13 classes, respectively. Both datasets comprise binary images with different resolutions and perturbations, e.g., occlusion and rotation. To get the shape curvatures we replicate the feature

---

[1] http://vision.lems.brown.edu/content/.
[2] http://www.dabi.temple.edu/~shape/MPEG7/dataset.html.

estimation methodology presented by authors in [1], tuning experimentally the length parameter to compute the curvature at each spatial point. We implement a 1-NN classifier from the WMMD-based distances among shapes. For concrete testing, a training-testing validation is carried out fixing the training set as the 80% and 50% of the input images for *99-Shape Database MPEG-7_CE-Shape-1 Part B*, respectively. With respect to the QKLMS parameters, a grid of 100 values is build, varying ϵ_U from 1 to 10, while e_t is computed based on the input data standard deviation. The kernel bandwidth σ_x is fixed according to a Parzen-based density estimation of each curvature sequence. Further, the characteristic kernel bandwidth σ is tuned in terms of the classification accuracy, building a grid of 5 points from 0.003 to 0.3 in *99-Shape Database*, and from 0.001 to 0.03 in *MPEG-7_CE-Shape-1 Part B*. The QKLMS learning rate is set as 0.9 for both experiments [4]. As baseline, we test two state-of-the art techniques: a HMM classifier based on highest likelihood as discussed in [6], and a 1-NN classifier from a MMD representation [5].

4   Results and Discussion

Figure 1(Left bottom) shows a data sample contour plot from *99-Shapes* DB. As seen, points holding high curvature coefficient values (see color intensities) are related to extremities, whose has greater morphological changes concerning the rest of the shape. Besides, from marker sizes, the QKLMS-based relevance analysis is able to code the main shape variations. Now, Fig. 1(Right bottom) shows the filter prediction against the target curvature sequence. Curvature beginning is labeled by x_0, and as was exposed in Sect. 2, following counter-clockwise it is found the midpoint of the sequence, labeled as x_{40}. In general, it is clear that the KAF-based adjustment is low concerning the curvature predictions. Since our goal is to classify shapes towards a relevant curvature representation, the code-book and the filter weights are more appropriate for further discrimination task, e.g., the 1-NN-based classification, than for the curvature value prediction. So, the training stage requires a trade-off between classification and filtering fitting.

In addition, Table 1 shows the results of classification for the *99-Shapes* DB. Overall, the accuracy obtained in this experiment was 77.8%, which is lower than the HMM and MMD approaches. However, in Quadrupeds, Humans, Hands, Rays, Rabbits, and Wrenches classes, our proposal achieves the highest performances. Moreover, for the Airplanes class, our methodology fails; this is ought to sharp changes along its contour and low curvature sequences in comparison to the other classes, which induces biased prediction results in the QKLMS filter. Further, Table 2 presents the classification results for the *MPEG-7_CE-Shape-1* DB. This experiment was successful since our methodology overcomes MMD and HMM schemes. However, for Shoe and Bone classes, their outcomes could be due to their class heterogeneity. For Bottle, Children, Flatfish, and Fountain classes, WMMD allows discriminating each of them properly.

In general, WMMD is competitive with other state-of-the-art methodologies. Previous results allow us to say that our WMMD-based methodology performs

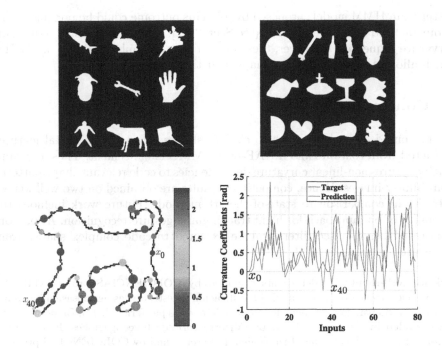

Fig. 1. Left top: 99-Shapes DB which has 11 samples per class. Right top: MPEG-7 DB which has 20 samples per class. Left bottom: $\{x_n\}_{n=1}^N$ for image 63 in the 99-Shape, where color indicates a x_n value and marker size code the QKLMS-based relevance. Right bottom: QKLMS curvature prediction.

Table 1. *99-Shapes* classification results.

Class	Proposal TP(%)	HMM TP(%)	MMD TP(%)
Quadrupeds	100.0	100.0	50.0
Humans	100.0	100.0	100.0
Airplanes	0.0	81.8	50.0
Grebes	50.0	100.0	50.0
Fish	50.0	72.7	100.0
Hands	100.0	90.9	100.0
Rays	100.0	90.9	100.0
Rabbits	100.0	81.8	100.0
Wrenches	100.0	72.7	100.0
Accuracy(%)	**77.8**	87.9	83.3

Table 2. *MPEG-7* classification results.

Class	Proposal TP(%)	HMM TP(%)	MMD TP(%)
Bone	60.0	100.0	60.0
Glas	100.0	100.0	100.0
HCircle	90.0	80.0	80.0
Heart	90.0	90.0	70.0
Misk	100.0	80.0	100.0
Apple	70.0	80.0	60.0
Bottle	100.0	70.0	90.0
Children	100.0	90.0	90.0
Face	100.0	90.0	90.0
Flatfish	100.0	80.0	90.0
Fountain	100.0	80.0	90.0
Shoe	50.0	60.0	90.0
Teddy	80.0	90.0	100.0
Accuracy(%)	**87.7**	83.8	85.4

better than HMM models proposed by [6]. This outcome could be possible ought to our method introduces the NC (see Sect. 2) [2], which avoids using redundant curvature sequences. Moreover, these input filters are embedded into an RKHS, which allows to maps nonlinear shape structures.

5   Conclusions

We presented a novel approach to classify shapes based on sequential features extracted from contours and a KAF-based MMD enhancement. Thus, our approach captures non-linear curvature dependencies to code relevant shape patterns from binary images. Hence, competitive results are obtained on two well-known datasets in comparison to state-of-the-art methods. Future work includes the extension of our approach for hand tracking and gesture recognition. Also, more elaborated kernel-based filters will be explored·to code complex shapes from curvature features.

Acknowledgments. Under grants provided by COLCIENCIAS project 1110-744-55958: "Desarrollo de un sistema de identificación de estructuras nerviosas en imágenes de ultrasonido para la asistencia de bloqueo de nervios periféricos". J.S. Blandon is partially funded by the project E6-18-09 (Vicerrectoria de Investigaciones, Innovación y Extensión) from Universidad Tecnológica de Pereira, and by COLCIENCIAS program 775: "Jóvenes Investigadores e Innovadores por la Paz 2017".

References

1. Bicego, M., Murino, V.: Investigating Hidden Markov models' capabilities in 2D shape classification. IEEE Trans. Pattern Anal. Mach. Intell. **26**(2), 281–286 (2004)
2. Chen, B., Zhao, S., Zhu, P., Principe, J.C.: Quantized Kernel least mean square algorithm. IEEE Trans. Neural Netw. Learn. Syst. **23**(1), 22–32 (2012)
3. Keskin, C., Kıraç, F., Kara, Y.E., Akarun, L.: Hand pose estimation and hand shape classification using multi-layered randomized decision forests. In: Fitzgibbon, A., Lazebnik, S., Perona, P., Sato, Y., Schmid, C. (eds.) ECCV 2012, Part VI. LNCS, vol. 7577, pp. 852–863. Springer, Heidelberg (2012). https://doi.org/10.1007/978-3-642-33783-3_61
4. Liu, W., Principe, J.C., Haykin, S.: Kernel Adaptive Filtering: A Comprehensive Introduction, vol. 57. John Wiley & Sons, New York (2011)
5. Luo, C., Ma, L.: Manifold regularized distribution adaptation for classification of remote sensing images. IEEE Access (2018)
6. Pun, C.M., Lin, C.: Geometric invariant shape classification using hidden markov model. In: 2010 International Conference on DICTA, pp. 406–410. IEEE (2010)
7. Rathi, Y., Vaswani, N., Tannenbaum, A., Yezzi, A.: Tracking deforming objects using particle filtering for geometric active contours. IEEE Trans. Pattern Anal. Mach. Intell. **29**(8), 1470–1475 (2007)

8. Sriperumbudur, B.K., Gretton, A., Fukumizu, K., Schölkopf, B., Lanckriet, G.R.: Hilbert space embeddings and metrics on probability measures. J. Mach. Learn. Res. **11**, 1517–1561 (2010)
9. Zuluaga, C.D., Valencia, E.A., Álvarez, M.A., Orozco, Á.A.: A parzen-based distance between probability measures as an alternative of summary statistics in approximate bayesian computation. In: Murino, V., Puppo, E. (eds.) ICIAP 2015. LNCS, vol. 9279, pp. 50–61. Springer, Cham (2015). https://doi.org/10.1007/978-3-319-23231-7_5

Interactive Photo Liveness
for Presentation Attacks Detection

Galina Lavrentyeva[1]([✉]), Oleg Kudashev[2], Aleksandr Melnikov[1],
Maria De Marsico[3], and Yuri Matveev[1]

[1] ITMO University, St. Petersburg, Russia
{lavrentyeva,melnikov-a}@speechpro.com,
matveev@mail.ifmo.ru
[2] STC-innovations Ltd., St. Petersburg, Russia
kudashev@speechpro.com
[3] Sapienza University of Rome, Rome, Italy
demarsico@di.unroma1.it
www.ifmo.ru, www.speechpro.com,
http://en.uniroma1.it/

Abstract. This paper presents an interactive liveness detection approach against presentation attacks. It aims to minimize the impact on the
user, who is only asked to produce single head movements. The described
approach combines two methods: (1) single-photo liveness estimation
based on CNN implementation, and (2) interactive liveness estimation
based on head movements detected from two video frames extracted
before and during the movement. The resulting system is designed to
work on smartphones and by web-cameras. An appropriate database was
collected for experiments. These achieved EER of less than 5% for paper
spoofing attacks, less than 4% for monitor and 0.6% for tablet, while the
Failure to Capture (FTC) was less than 3% for the most user-friendly
scenario.

Keywords: Spoofing · Anti-spoofing · Liveness detection

1 Introduction and Related Work

Biometric face recognition technologies became more commonplace in our every-
day life, however they can be cheated by spoofing attacks (attempts to steal the
identity of a genuine user). Face spoofing techniques usually include placing a
users photograph on a paper or screen (presentation attacks) or playing a video
recording (replay attacks) in front of the verification system. Here only presentation attacks are considered as they are more likely to be used by the impostor,
since, nowadays, a photograph can be easily found in social networks or taken
at a distance. However, these attacks cannot reproduce the face 3D structure
or characteristics, or effectively respond to interactive challenges. This can be
used by anti-spoofing approaches [1]. Most devices also leave specific artifacts

or produce effects on the photo or video, that can be detected automatically: blurry images of a digital screen caused by slow autofocus, or reduced sharpness due to the built-in filters.

Anti-spoofing techniques can be classified in 4 categories [2]: texture-based, analyzing image quality and texture artifacts; liveness-based, searching for any evidence of liveness on the face; motion-based; and spoofing detection in the presence of additional devices (i.e. infra-red camera).

Methods of the first category usually rely on the differences in reflectance properties between real and spoofed faces [3]. Popular examples of effective texture operators for face antispoofing are Local Binary Pattern (LBP) [4] and Weber Local Descriptor (WLD) [5] with related methods.

Liveness detection methods of the second type focus on spontaneous user behavior, e.g., on detecting eye-blinking or mouth movements. A number of papers use optical flow for motion estimation of the live faces as 3D objects [6]. In [7] an eye-blink-based liveness detection approach using *eye closity* is proposed.

The described methods are not robust enough for spoofing attacks using high quality video of a valid user, who can be recorded without knowing. Interactive liveness detection can solve this problem. The method presented in [8] requires the user to rotate his head by looking in a certain direction, according to randomly generated instructions. In [9] the user is asked to utter a specific sequence of digits, that is randomly defined by the system. Our previous work [10] introduced a text-dependent anti-spoofing system based on estimation of synchrony between audio stream and lip movements. However, after the detailed analysis of its applicability it was deemed too intrusive for some applications, e.g., people refused to use it in a public place and it has limitations in noisy conditions.

In this research we tried to reduce the impact on the user during the process of liveness detection by excluding the voice modality. The proposed interactive photo liveness system asks the user to perform a single specific head movement. It captures 2 frames before and during the user answer and estimates whether the requested movement was done by the real human. The proposed approach combines a photo-liveness method, that analyzes each of two captured images separately, and an interaction-based method where the movements of the head are determined through the characteristic landmarks of the face in these 2 photos. Different movements were compared in order to select the most appropriate in terms of the compromise between user friendliness and accuracy.

2   System Description

This research considers the combination of single-photo liveness and interactive liveness techniques. The main idea is to minimize the interaction with the user, considering a single simple movement, that will not require too much user effort. The proposed system is expected to be mainly used in applications that use smart-phones and web-cameras. Due to specific set-up there were no available databases with samples of real accesses and spoofing attacks, so that an appropriate one was collected.

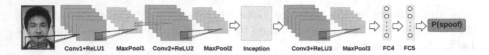

Conv1+ReLU1 MaxPool1 Conv2+ReLU2 MaxPool2 Inception Conv3+ReLU3 MaxPool3 FC4 FC5

Fig. 1. CNN architecture for single-photo liveness detection

Single-Photo Liveness Module Description. Convolutional neural networks are successful in many tasks, e.g., face recognition. We implemented a CNN to distinguish real from fake faces by a single image. Convolution layers can learn distinctive features from the images, and help extract informative features for face liveness detection [11].

Our CNN contains two convolutional layers before the inception module and one after, which is followed by two fully-connected layers (Fig. 1) and a dropout layer, in order to avoid over-fitting. The softmax activation function is used as a classifier. The network was trained with Nesterov accelerated gradient method and advanced learning rate. Input images are resized to 110×110 pixels and normalized by subtracting the mean image computed from the training set.

Training of the single-photo liveness module relied on the combination of the public databases CASIA Face Anti-Spoofing database [12], and NUAA Photo Impostor database [3], and of the Face database collected for this research. CASIA database consists of 600 videos of 50 users captured by Sony NEX-5-HD (1280×720), USB camera and Webcam (640×480 both); 150 videos represent attacks via paper prints and iPad. NUAA was collected by a Webcam (640×480) from 15 users. For impostors sessions high definition color photos were used, printed on photographic paper and A4 paper. Our Face database contains 5094 spoofing attacks collected by taking pictures of the faces from the Google images and displayed on the monitor (1920×1080). The training and testing subsets of these databases were separately combined (train = 25742, test = 1920 images).

Interactive Liveness Module Description. The most evident difference between real face video and 2D spoofing attacks is the effect produced by specific movements during the video record due to the 3D nature of the real head. The proposed system asks the user to produce a single movement from the following: left-right rotations, head tilt up or down, or movements towards the camera.

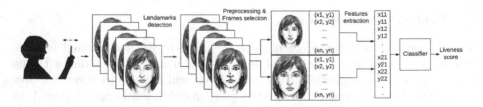

Fig. 2. Interactive liveness detection

Table 1. Conditions for primary and analyzed frames selection

Movement	Primary frame	Analyzed frame
Head is turned left	(1) $-0.1 < x1 < 0.1$	(1) $0.2 < x1 < 0.4$ (2) $min(x1 - 0.3)$
Head is turned right	(2) $min(x1)$	(1) $-0.4 < x1 < -0.2$ (2) $min(x1 + 0.3)$
Head is tilted up	(1) $0 < x2 < 0.5$	(1) $0.5 < x2 < 0.75$ (2) $min(x2 - 0.75)$
Head is tilted down	(2) $min(x2 - 0.25)$	(1) $-0.5 < x2 < -0.1$ (2) $min(x2 + 0.2)$
Head is moved towards	(1) $1 < x3 < 1.15$ (2) $min(x3 - 1)$	(1) $1.5 < x3 < 3$ (2) $min(x3 - 1.75)$

According to the described scenario the analysis of head movements is a key issue and the success of liveness detection system mainly depends on the accuracy of landmarks detection. During the last decade head pose tracking algorithms based on face points distribution model (PDM) were actively investigated. Constrained Local Model (CLM) framework proposed in [13] has proven to be a powerful and robust method for frontal and near frontal facial movements tracking. In our system it was used on the first step of the algorithm (Fig. 2), by applying it to the recorded input video frame by frame. For each of them, the output included 68 landmarks and likelihood of the derived face presence in the frame. Only those with a face likelihood above a given threshold were further processed. This threshold was defined equal to -0.1 after analyzing the results from experiments on the training dataset. In order to generalize the input data we applied rotation and scaling: the remaining frames were rotated in such a way that the localized eyes lie on a horizontal line and the center of the frame matches the center between the eyes; frames were then scaled along the x-axis so that the distance between the eyes was equal to 1 and along y-axis so that the distance between the eye-line and mouth center was equal to 1. Using the updated landmarks the primary (before movement) and analyzed (during movement) frames were selected. The selection of such frames was done by the analysis of parameters according to the conditions presented in Table 1: $x'_1 = \frac{x_1}{D}; x'_2 = \frac{x_2}{L}; x'_3 = \frac{D}{D_{min}}$, where D is the distance between the eyes, L is the distance between the eye-line and mouth center, x_1 is distance from the center between the eyes to tip of nose along the x-axis and x_2 is the same distance along the y-axis. D_{min} is estimated on the whole database. These parameters should be estimated before the scaling described above. The conditions were movement-dependent and were formulated during our experiments on the training data. A frame was selected if it satisfied the first condition and got the minimum value in the second one.

The final feature vector for each trial was built from the landmarks positions in the selected frames (Fig. 2). In order to achieve decorrelation, the vector was transformed with respect to a eigenvector basis computed over the training database. The transformed feature vectors were submitted to a Support Vector Machine (SVM) with linear kernel, to get a real access/spoofing response.

To test the interactive liveness approach we collected video recordings using 3 different mobile phones: LG Nexus 5, HTC One Mini and Samsung Galaxy S4.

60 different users (30 male and 30 female) were recorded by each device to collect a real access database. The spoofing database contains presentation attacks using paper prints, tablet (LG Nexus 7) and computer monitor (DELL P2213). For each movement the same amount of real and spoofing sessions was collected.

3   Experiment Results

Equal Error Rate (EER) for the single-photo liveness detection system reported in Table 2 (column 1) shows that the most threatful attack is based on displaying the photo of a real user on the monitor. The lower EER for tablet attacks can be explained by the significant learning of the CNN regarding features such as black or dark borders of the tablet. We trained a first fusion system to pursue better results, using single-photo liveness scores from the two frames selected as described above from a video. The final score was obtained as a weighted sum of these scores. EER decreased significantly (Table 2 - column 2).

Experiments for interactive liveness were carried out on the same databases as for double-photo approach (Table 3). Failure To Capture (FTC) value describes the amount of trials that were discarded due to the insufficient input data (low quality or failed landmark detection in the proposed systems). This is positive when it happens on spoofed trials. However, when this happens on real trials, this may decrease the system acceptability due to user frustration. The most suitable FTC for usability was the one obtained for towards movement (Table 3). This can be explained by the low quality of the landmark detection in case of significant rotations. However, the lowest FTC was also joined to poor EER. In order to maintain the good usability though pursuing better accuracy results, we chose towards movements for the experiments on fusion of different modalities

Table 2. Single-photo, best interactive and fusion experiments results.

Attack	Single-photo	Double-photo	Interact.	Double-photo + Interact. (feature fusion)	Double-photo + Interact. (score fusion)
Paper	10.2	8.7	13.6	7	3.8
Tablet	7.4	5.3	10.4	3.5	0.6
Monitor	15.6	11.7	16	9.5	4.9

Table 3. Results of experiments with interactive liveness detection.

	Movement	Left-right	Tilt up	Tilt down	Towards
EER / FTC	Real	- / 16	- / 17	- / 53	- / 3
	Paper	1.9 / 51	3.9 / 92	3.5 / 79	13.6 / 2
	Tablet	- / 100	1.1 / 97.5	11.4 / 96	10.4 / 0
	Monitor	11.7 / 87	18.4 / 90	15.3 / 77	16 / 0

(photo liveness and interaction evaluation). We tested both feature level and score level fusion: (1) by concatenating the feature vectors of the two photos from double-photo approach with features from interactive liveness module, and retraining the final SVM; (2) by using a linear combination of the scores for the two modules as a final score. The last improvement was done by applying the logit function for single-photo scores (Table 2 - column 5). Analyzing the obtained results we concluded that feature level fusion gives a small gain in systems quality compared to each method separately. The best results for both methods were obtained on the tablet spoofing database which can be explained by the presence of borders and small face movement variation. Actually, fusion achieves acceptable results tough maintaining a low FTC for the user sake.

4   Conclusions

This research considered the specialized task of interactive liveness detection based on video recording with minimal effort for the user. A database of real trials and spoofing attacks was collected with 4 types of movements. 2 methods were presented: image quality analysis and 3D head movement analysis. The best version of the final system fuses their final scores. The proposed system achieved a less than 5% EER for paper and monitor spoofing attacks and 0.6% EER for attacks based on tablet yet maintaining the FTC lower than 3%.

Acknowledgements. This work was financially supported by the Ministry of Education and Science of the Russian Federation, Contract 14.578.21.0189 (ID RFMEFI57816X0189).

References

1. De Marsico, M., Marchionni, L., Novelli, A., Oertel, M.: FATCHA: the CAPTCHA Are You! In: 11th Biannual Conference on Italian SIGCHI Chapter, pp. 118–125 (2015)
2. Nixon, K.A., Aimale, V., Rowe, R.K.: Spoof detection schemes. In: Jain, A.K., Flynn, P., Ross, A.A. (eds.) Handbook of Biometrics, pp. 403–423. Springer, Boston (2008). https://doi.org/10.1007/978-0-387-71041-9_20
3. Tan, X., Li, Y., Liu, J., Jiang, L.: Face liveness detection from a single image with sparse low rank bilinear discriminative model. In: Daniilidis, K., Maragos, P., Paragios, N. (eds.) ECCV 2010, Part VI. LNCS, vol. 6316, pp. 504–517. Springer, Heidelberg (2010). https://doi.org/10.1007/978-3-642-15567-3_37
4. Hadid, A.: The local binary pattern approach and its applications to face analysis. In: Image Processing Theory, Tools and Application, pp. 1–9 (2008)
5. Mei, L., Yang, D., Feng, Z., Lai, J.: WLD-TOP based algorithm against face spoofing attacks. In: 10th Chinese Conference on Biometric Recognition, pp. 135–142 (2015)
6. Bao, W., Li, H., Li, N., Jiang, W.: A liveness detection method for face recognition based on optical flow field. In: International Conference on Image Analysis and Signal Processing (2009)

7. Pan, G., Sun, L., Wu, Z., Lao, S.: Eyeblink-based antispoofing in face recognition from a generic Webcamera. In: International Conference on 11th Computer Vision (2007)
8. Frischholz, R., Werner, A.: Avoiding replay-attacks in a face recognition system using head-pose estimation. In: Analysis and Modeling of Faces and Gestures, pp. 234–235 (2003)
9. Kollreider, K., Fronthaler, H., Faraj, M., Bigun, J.: Real time face detection and motion analysis with application in liveness assessment. Trans. Inf. Forensics Secur. **2**, 548–558 (2007)
10. Melnikov, A., Akhunzyanov, R., Kudashev, O., Luckyanets, E.: Audiovisual liveness detection. In: Murino, V., Puppo, E. (eds.) ICIAP 2015, Part II. LNCS, vol. 9280, pp. 643–652. Springer, Cham (2015). https://doi.org/10.1007/978-3-319-23234-8_59
11. Volkova, S.S., Matveev, Y.N.: Convolutional neural networks for face anti-spoofing. Sci. Tech. J. Inf. Technol. Mech. Opt. **18**(1), 702–710 (2018)
12. Zhang, Z., Yan, J., Liu, S., Lei, Z., Yi, D., Li, S.Z.: A face antispoofing database with diverse attacks. In: 5th IAPR International Conference on Biometrics (2012)
13. Cristinacce, D., Cootes, T.F.: Feature detection and tracking with constrained local models. In: BMVC, vol. 2, p. 6 (2006)

Indexing and Retrieval

GIF Image Retrieval in Cloud Computing Environment

Evelyn Paiz-Reyes[(✉)], Nadile Nunes-de-Lima[(✉)],
and Sule Yildirim-Yayilgan[(✉)]

Norwegian University of Science and Technology, Gjøvik, Norway
{elreyes,nadilend}@stud.ntnu.no,
sule.yildirim@ntnu.no

Abstract. GIF images have been used in the last years, especially on social media. Here it is explored a content-based image retrieval system to work specifically with GIF file format. Its implementation is extended to a cloud computing environment. Given the Tumblr GIF dataset, it is created a "search by example" image retrieval system. To describe the images, low-level features are used: (1) color, (2) texture and (3) shape. The system performs the search using just GIF images as query images. To obtain faster results on the retrieval process, a hashing indexing approach is used. The system showed a complexity of $O(n^2)$ for indexing and $O(log(n))$ for retrieval. Additionally, better results were obtained (in relation to precision and recall) for simple images, instead of images with a lot of movements.

Keywords: GIF image format · Content-based image retrieval
Hashing · Cloud computing

1 Introduction

The importance of images in people's daily life has increased along with the advances in digital technology. The emergence of imaging devices, such as smartphones, cameras, and computers, has led the world to witness the growth in quantity, availability, and value of images [1]. The need to access this type of data anytime and anywhere has increased its importance.

Content-based image retrieval (CBIR) has been widely studied [2–4]. A CBIR system retrieves the relevant images from a database to a search query based on visual characteristics, where each image in the database is mapped to a feature vector including visual, structural and conceptual characteristics [5]. On the other hand, a CBIR maintenance is considered to be a typical example of cloud computing. It offers a great opportunity for on-demand access to a wide computation and storage resources [1].

Among the many image formats that can be applied on a CBIR system, one that is interesting to mention is the GIF (Graphics Interchange Format) file format. Because of its high compression ratio and less disk space needs, this image format has been spread quickly and supported by a wide variety of applications [6]. It was designed "to allow the easy interchange and viewing of image data stored on local or remote computer systems" [7].

GIF has become well known and it is the second most common image format used on the World Wide Web after JPEG. Up until now, there have been few attempts to explore the design and development of a CBIR system for this file format. The objective of the present work is first to design and develop a CBIR system for indexing and retrieval of GIF file formats using the Tumblr GIF dataset [8]. Secondly to extend the CBIR to a cloud computing environment.

2   Related Works

2.1   Content-Based Image Retrieval System

No matter what type of CBIR system is intended to be built, the following steps are the ones needed to complete it [1,9,10]:

Image Descriptors. An image feature can be described as anything that is localized, meaningful and detectable from an image [4]. In practice, the use of multiple features is needed to be able to achieve a good description of the image. The features/signatures intended for this work are color [4], texture [4,10] and shape [4].

Dataset Indexing. Indexing can be described as the process of quantifying the dataset by utilizing an image descriptor to extract features from each image.

Definition of Similarity Metric. Images can be compared using a distance metric or similarity function. This function takes the feature vectors as inputs and its output is a number representing how "similar" the feature vectors are. The choice is highly dependent on (1) the dataset and (2) the types of features that were extracted.

Search. The search process is the following: (1) A user submits a query image to the system, (2) its features are extracted and (3) the similarity function is applied to compare the query features with the features already indexed. From there, (4) the results are sorted by relevancy and then presented to the user.

2.2   CBIR and Graphics Interchange Format (GIF)

GIF is a standard image representation and has the possibility to create animations, which made it popular on social media. There is no work related to a CBIR system specific for indexing and retrieving GIF files. The GIF format was developed in 1987 by Steve Wilhite at CompuServe Network [6]. Its purpose is to store multiple bitmap images in a single file for exchange between platforms and images. It is stream based and is made up of a series of data packets called blocks and protocol information. In GIF, lossless file compression method is applied [7].

GIF file format comprises a number of frames that are displayed in succession. Each frame is displayed with a time delay to wait until the frame is drawn [6]. Then, *why not call a GIF a video?* Because a video is a collection of both inter and intra coded frames. In a video, the inter-coded frames take advantages of the other frames, so compression is far more efficient. On the other hand, a GIF is just a collection of intra frames and each frame is coded on its own [11].

3   Methodology

The goal is a GIF-based CBIR system. A GIF is an image file and not a video file [11], but it has the characteristic of frames as video files do. Therefore, this is considered in the design of the system (Fig. 1).

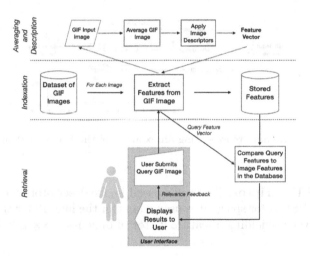

Fig. 1. Flowchart representing the architecture of the designed system.

3.1   Definition of Dataset

A collection of 2k randomly selected GIF images from the Tumblr GIF dataset (containing 100k animated GIFs in total) is used. The dataset consists of various GIFs images from Tumblr taken from random posts between May and June of 2015 [8].

Because the dataset was not previously divided into classes, the collection was manually classified into four categories where the images belonging to each category were considered similar (subjectively by the experimenter). It is important to mention that it was not possible to categorize all images. The dataset was composed of categorized plus uncategorized images. The final classes were the following:

1. Grayscale with couples.
2. Grayscale focused on faces and/or mainly just one person throughout the image.
3. Sports on a field (golf, soccer, baseball, etc.)
4. Animals.

3.2 Definition of Image Descriptor

The most basic image descriptors (color, texture, and shape) are employed. For each descriptor, a specific feature vector is created and then the three merged into a single feature vector. This means that each image in the dataset is represented and quantified using only a list of floating point numbers. Figure 2 shows this process. Additionally, the ad-hoc values selected were the ones that gave better result concerning the visual perception of the image and processing time.

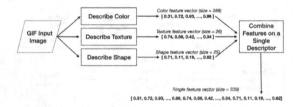

Fig. 2. Flowchart representing an example of the feature extraction.

Color-Based Descriptor. The color-based image descriptor is a 3D color histogram in the HSV color space. It is used 8 bins for the hue, 12 for the saturation, and 3 for the value, yielding a feature vector of dimension $8 \times 12 \times 3 = 288$ [10].

Texture-Based Descriptor. The method of local binary patterns (LBP) [12] is applied. First, the image is converted to grayscale and, for each pixel, a circular neighborhood of $p = 24$ points and radius $r = 8$, surrounding the center pixel is selected. An LBP value is calculated for each center pixel and stored in an output 2D array [13]. Its computed histogram is the texture-based image descriptor [12]. A total feature vector of dimension $24 + 2 = 26$ is obtained.

Shape-Based Descriptor. Zernike polynomials are orthogonal to each other and there is no redundancy of information between moments [14,15]. First, the image is converted to grayscale and segmented. Next, the Zernike moments are applied (with $r = 21$, where r is the radius of the polynomial) to characterize the shape of the object. The result is a vector with the first 25 Zernike moments from the segmented image [16].

3.3 System Architecture

The system is divided into three basic modules: (1) averaging and description of the images, (2) indexing of the data and (3) retrieval from a query. Figure 1 shows a graphical representation of the final architecture.

Averaging and Description. This module takes as an input a GIF image. A GIF image has the property of containing various images (frames) inside, and instead of working with all these data, an average image is obtained (see Algorithm 1). Next, it is computed the three feature vectors described in Sect. 3.2. The output is the combination of these vectors in a single feature vector.

Algorithm 1. Proposed averaging GIF image algorithm.

    Data: List of frames/images in the GIF file
1 **Set** sum_image to an empty image;
2 **for** *each frame in the GIF image* **do**
3 | add sum_image with the frame image pixel by pixel;
4 **end**
5 average_image = (sum_image / total number of frames);
6 **Return** average_image;

Indexing. The basic process of indexing is done as in a normal CBIR (features of each image are extracted and stored), but with the inclusion of averaging. For each image of the dataset (Sect. 3.1), the average is calculated and features are extracted. The resulting feature vectors are saved in a hash table in the form of a dictionary, where information of the image (name), a feature vector and hashed value of the feature vector are stored. The method used for indexing is the locality sensitive hashing (LSH) [17], aiming to maximize the probability of a "collision" for similar items.

Retrieval. The module works in the following way: (1) The input is a query GIF image; (2) the image is averaged and features are extracted to a single vector; (3) The query feature vector is compared with the stored feature vectors using Euclidian distance and a set of similar results is obtained; and (4) The top 5 results are retrieved and displayed to the user.

4 Experiments and Results

4.1 Indexing and Retrieval Time

In steps of 200 images, both indexing and retrieval time were tested (Fig. 3). The indexing time of each one of the image descriptors (individually) was also measured. A PC (Intel Core i5; 2.5 GHz) with macOS High Sierra and Python

2.7 was used in the experiment. The result data (from the measured time) was fitted on a curve to obtain the complexity of both indexing and retrieval. For indexing, all image descriptors (individually and combined) showed a polynomial behavior. In retrieval, the result was a logarithmic structure instead. The final outcome of the experiment revealed a complexity of $O(n^2)$ for indexing and $O(log(n^2))$ for retrieval.

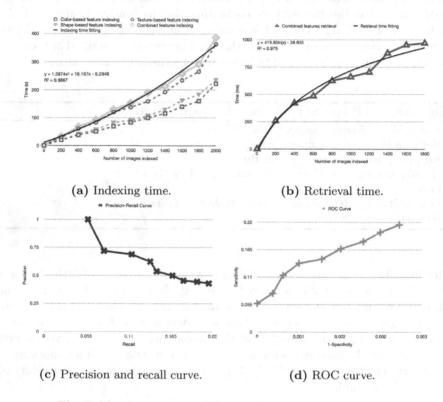

(a) Indexing time.   **(b)** Retrieval time.

(c) Precision and recall curve.   **(d)** ROC curve.

Fig. 3. Measuring curves of the system from 0 to 2000 images.

4.2   Precision and Recall of the System

On the second experiment, the precision and recall of the system were measured (Fig. 3). A total of 4 images from each category were selected randomly as query and the values of precision and recall were measured for each one of the queries (retrieving 1 to 10 images as a result). The average results were computed for each category. A final average of all the categories was the resulting precision and recall curve. Finally, a ROC curve was also computed. The same measurements of the precision-recall curve were used. Instead of estimating precision and recall, it was computed sensitivity and specificity. Figure 3 shows the resulting curves.

4.3   User Happiness

The final experiment was a user happiness evaluation. The study was performed with 6 adult volunteers from the Norwegian University of Science and Technology (NTNU). For each category (same as Sect. 3.1), a set of four images was shown. The user selected one each time and for the retrieved GIFs, the participant indicated what was considered relevant and irrelevant to him/her.

It was mentioned from their point of view that the time response for the retrieval was acceptable (83%). Also, users considered the categories 1 and 2 as similar. Finally, during the classification of what was relevant and irrelevant for the user, the semantics of the files had a strong influence. The participant tended to consider a file relevant when it contained the same actions or emotions as the query (i.e. if the query contains a person crying, the relevant results will be GIFs with people sad or crying as well).

5   Discussion and Conclusion

The complexity of the system was divided in two: indexing and retrieval. When the feature extraction is evaluated separately, it is clear that the texture description is the process that takes the majority of the time. This is because on the LBP method every single pixel in the image is computed, increasing the time needed to extract the features. Therefore, for future improvement of the system, a new method that is able to reduce the complexity of describing texture is advise.

The relevance/irrelevance of the files retrieved was judged by users and similarities between the answers were found. However, GIFs nowadays are also part of the social interaction, being used to transmit emotions and opinions towards some subject online. Therefore, only low-level features might not be enough to find the relation between the content of the file and what is the meaning the user is looking for.

The best results of the system were related to queries that did not have many motion through the images inside the file. The improvement of this condition can be a valid future work for this project. The insertion of semantics and classification would be also recommended, but first, a precise and detailed description must be done for the dataset (classifying every image). Hence, this classification would allow the use of machine learning to improve the retrieval process.

References

1. Xia, Z., Wang, X., Zhang, L., Qin, Z., Sun, X., Ren, K.: A privacy-preserving and copy-deterrence content-based image retrieval scheme in cloud computing. IEEE Trans. Inf. Forensics Secur. **11**(11), 2594–2608 (2016)
2. Zouaki, H., Abdelkhalak, B.: Indexing and content-based image retrieval. In: 2011 International Conference on Multimedia Computing and Systems, pp. 1–5, April 2011

3. Rashno, A., Sadri, S.: Content-based image retrieval with color and texture features in neutrosophic domain. In: 2017 3rd International Conference on Pattern Recognition and Image Analysis (IPRIA), pp. 50–55, April 2017

4. Kaur, M., Sohi, N.: A novel technique for content based image retrieval using color, texture and edge features. In: International Conference on Communication and Electronics Systems (ICCES), pp. 1–7, October 2016

5. Datta, R., Joshi, D., Li, J., Wang, J.Z.: Image retrieval: ideas, influences, and trends of the new age. ACM Comput. Surv. **40**(2), 5:1–5:60 (2008)

6. Zhang, Y.: The studies and implementation for conversion of image file format. In: 2015 10th International Conference on Computer Science Education (ICCSE), pp. 190–193, July 2015

7. Tiwari, N., Shandilya, D.M.: Evaluation of various LSB based methods of image steganography on gif file format. Int. J. Comput. Appl. **6**(2), 1–4 (2010)

8. Li, Y., Song, Y., Cao, L., Tetreault, J., Goldberg, L., Jaimes, A., Luo, J.: TGIF: a new dataset and benchmark on animated GIF description. In: The IEEE Conference on Computer Vision and Pattern Recognition (CVPR), June 2016

9. Yang, Z., i. Kamata, S., Ahrary, A.: Nir: content based image retrieval on cloud computing. In: 2009 IEEE International Conference on Intelligent Computing and Intelligent Systems, vol. 3, pp. 556–559, November 2009

10. Rosebrock, A.: The Complete Guide to Building an Image Search Engine with Python and OpenCV (2014). https://www.pyimagesearch.com/2014/12/01/complete-guide-building-image-search-engine-python-opencv/. Accessed 19 Sep 2017

11. Hu, W., Xie, N., Li, L., Zeng, X., Maybank, S.: A survey on visual content-based video indexing and retrieval. IEEE Trans. Syst. Man Cybern. Part C (Appl. Rev.) **41**(6), 797–819 (2011)

12. Ojala, T., Pietikainen, M., Maenpaa, T.: Multiresolution gray-scale and rotation invariant texture classification with local binary patterns. IEEE Trans. Pattern Anal. Mach. Intell. **24**(7), 971–987 (2002)

13. Rosebrock, A.: Local Binary Patterns with Python & OpenCV (2015). https://www.pyimagesearch.com/2015/12/07/local-binary-patterns-with-python-opencv/. Accessed 6 Nov 2017

14. Chaumette, F.: Image moments: a general and useful set of features for visual servoing. IEEE Trans. Rob. **20**(4), 713–723 (2004)

15. Kim, W.Y., Kim, Y.S.: A region-based shape descriptor using Zernike moments. Signal Process. Image Commun. **16**(1), 95–102 (2000)

16. Rosebrock, A.: Building a Pokedex in Python: Indexing our Sprites using Shape Descriptors (Step 3 of 6) (2014). https://www.pyimagesearch.com/2014/04/07/building-pokedex-python-indexing-sprites-using-shape-descriptors-step-3-6/. Accessed 6 Nov 2017

17. Datar, M., Immorlica, N., Indyk, P., Mirrokni, V.S.: Locality-sensitive hashing scheme based on p-stable distributions. In: Proceedings of the Twentieth Annual Symposium on Computational Geometry, pp. 253–262. ACM (2004)

Saliency-Based Image Object Indexing and Retrieval

Yat Hong Jacky Lam[✉] and Sule Yildirim Yayilgan

Norwegian University of Science and Technology, 2815 Gjøvik, Norway
yathl@ntnu.no

Abstract. We suggest a novel approach to combine visual saliency model and object recognition to provide a more semantic description of an image based on human attention priority. The idea is to index and retrieve semantically more relevant images utilizing human saliency. Based on that, we developed a content-based image indexing and retrieval system. The resultant indexing and retrieval system works, though there is room for improvement in performance. We suggest the reasons and the possibilities for further improvements to develop a practical CBIR system.

1 Introduction

Content-based image retrieval (CBIR) is a long studied topic. While there is lot of existing research on low-level features, researchers are still struggling to get a better understanding on how to represent and obtain mid-level features and high-level features. The semantic difference between low and high level features representation is commonly called as the 'semantic gap' and it is a challenge to fill this gap.

To achieve a semantically meaningful description of an image's content, one of the most important steps to do is to determine the region of interest (ROI). In this research, *we study the feasibility to combine saliency prediction model with object recognition to identify key objects in an image.* The computational image saliency model is used to predict the focus points in the image. By using the object recognition algorithm, the content of an image is generated by combining the object and the saliency information with the low-level description of the image, we obtain a high level description of it. Later, the combined description is used to index the image.

This paper includes a literature review in Sect. 2, our framework in semantic CBIR is presented in Sect. 3. Evaluation is presented in Sect. 4. Future work and conclusions are suggested in Sect. 5.

2 Literature Review

2.1 Object Recognition and Deep Learning in CBIR

Deep learning refers to a collection of machine learning techniques where information is processed in multiple layers in hierarchical architectures. Since the

© Springer International Publishing AG, part of Springer Nature 2018
A. Campilho et al. (Eds.): ICIAR 2018, LNCS 10882, pp. 269–277, 2018.
https://doi.org/10.1007/978-3-319-93000-8_31

successful use of the Deep Convolution Neural Networks in the image clas-sification task in ILSVRC1-2012 [1], deep learning became state-of-the-art in computer vision, including tasks such as image classification and object recogni-tion. There is various research based on using it, including MobileNet-SSD [2], Faster-RCNN [3] and R-FCN [4] etc. Deep learning requires a large database for training. With the development of the vast amount of multimedia source on the Internet, large amount of images annotated by users are available for the train-ing purpose. There are datasets for competitions in object recognition such as MS-COCO [5] and Kitti [6]. Those databases also cover a wide range of themes that allow to train and test the CBIR system on various images.

Object recognition provides an effective way towards higher level description of image. Image captioning is a popular application of the technique. Combining object recognition and natural language processing, it can provide a semantic description of image, including the class and characteristics of objects in the image, and also the action of animals and human beings in the image. More attention was put on instance-level image retrieval [7]. Many of them use deep learning and user-generated data on the internet.

2.2   Image Saliency in CBIR

Image saliency is the visual attention that a human observer puts on a certain position in an image. It can be used as a measure of relative importance or meaningfulness of that position in the image such that object containing that region should be given higher weighting in the indexing process. Image saliency map is introduced as a metric for CBIR by many researchers [8]. The saliency prediction can be done using a bottom-up approach using low-level features or top-down approach by including external information such as heuristics.

3   New Model to Combine Saliency Prediction and Object Recognition

3.1   Framework

In this paper, we propose a framework (Fig. 1) for combining saliency prediction and object recognition in addition to using low level features. After preprocess-ing, a vector presentation of the image is generated and stored in the database. For an image query, the procedure is similar: after generation of the feature vec-tor, the query feature vector is compared with the feature vectors stored in the database using a similarity measure. The results are sorted by similarity and top results are retrieved.

While it is similar to most of the other CBIR algorithms, the main contri-bution of this study is the introduction of a new model for representing feature vectors and defining the similarity measure.

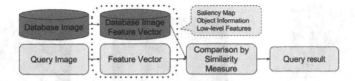

Fig. 1. The basic framework of the proposed content based image retrieval model

3.2   Object Recognition and Bounding Box

Most of the current object recognition algorithms provide bounding boxes as output. Detection is represented by a rectangular area enclosing the object. An example is shown in Fig. 2(a). Each bounding box contains three types of information:

1. Classification of object: object is represented by an integer index such as 'person' and 'toothbrush' as shown in the figure.
2. Position of the bounding box: the position is indicated by four values and also reflects the size of the object.
3. Score of detection: it is a floating point value indicating the confidence of the object recognition algorithm on the classification of the object. The classification with a low score should be rejected.

Notice that a pixel can belong to multiple bounding boxes or does not belong to any of them. Besides, due to the nature of the rectangular bounding box, some irrelevant parts of the image or the background is also included in the bounding box. In this research, object recognition is done through using a deep learning network model "Single Shot Multibox Detector (SSD) with MobileNet" [9] which is pretrained with MS-COCO data [5]. It is used due to its lightweight and speed, which is crucial for the speed performance, but the accuracy is sacrificed. The current algorithm can classify 90 different categories of objects. The number of class categories depends on the data and annotation used in the training process.

3.3   Saliency Prediction

Saliency prediction model aims to predict relative intensity of human visual attention and output as a heatmap (Fig. 2). The bright region indicates the highly salient region of the image. The Itti-Koch approach is used in our research. It is a classical model based on low level features [10]. Lower level features like colour, intensity and orientations are used to derive the saliency map. When there are alternative saliency models, especially those deep learning based approach, then they are more time consuming and hence not implemented in this study.

3.4   Feature Vector

In Fig. 3, the overall architecture for forming the feature vector is summarized:

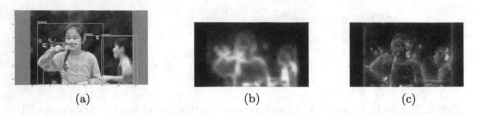

Fig. 2. (a) object recognition with bounding boxes, (b) visual attention in experiment and (c) visual attention prediction by the Koch-Itti model. Image from CAT2000 database. [11]

1. The target image is processed through the object recognition algorithm. Object bounding box (OBB) and classification of objects with high confidence ($\geq t$) are obtained.
2. The saliency map of the image is calculated based on the Itti-Koch algorithm.
3. The average saliency intensity within each bounding box is calculated.
4. The list of detected objects is sorted by the average saliency.
5. The top five objects in saliency intensity is retrieved.

To determine the value of t, there has to be a balance between the number of candidate objects and also the confidence level of the object detection result. Moreover, t value varies due to the content of the image. An iterative approach is used to determine t. By setting the initial value $t = 0.1$, the list of candidate objects is generated. If the number of OBBs in the image is less than the desired value ($N = 5$ in our model), the threshold value is reduced by half until enough number of objects are detected using the model.

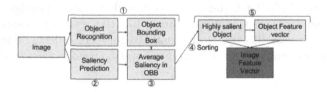

Fig. 3. Calculation of image feature vector

In our model, we have decided to choose the five most salient objects to form the primary feature vector. After the retrieval of the five highest salient objects, their category indices are used to form the primary feature vector, which provides the semantic representation of the image. The order of object in the primary feature vector is important as it shows the relative importance of the objects. However, ordering requirement can be too restrictive and it will be discussed in Sect. 5.

The object recognition algorithm provides semantic interpretation of the object. However, it misses out some important low level description of the object, including colour and size. Low level description is extracted within each bounding box to describe low level features of objects.

1. Colour: the RGB value of the pixel in the image is converted into CIELAB colour space. The average value of all pixels in the three channels gives the average L, A and B value of the object.
2. Size: the height and the width of the bounding box determine the relative size of the object in the image.

After all, there are five feature elements for each object (L,A,B, height and width). Combining with the primary feature vector (5 elements) and 5 object feature vectors, there is a 30-element image feature vector. The graphical representation is shown in Fig. 4. These feature vectors are generated both for the query and the database images.

					Object 1					Object N
Person	Car	Cat	Cat	Cat	Ave. L	Ave. A	Ave. B	Width	Height	...
1	3	4	4	4	52.0	133.6	116.5	27	18	
Primary Feature Vector					Object Feature Vector 1					...

Fig. 4. Graphical representation of the image feature vector

3.5   Similarity Measure

To retrieve similar images, we have to compare the candidate image feature vector v_c and query feature vector v_q. A distance metric $D\left(v_c, v_q\right)$ is defined and the comparison is done in our model in three steps:

1. Comparison of primary vector: check if the object category agrees between the candidate and the query. Notice the order of object matter in this case. For example, the comparison between the primary vectors $[1, 2, 3, 4, 5]$ and $[2, 3, 4, 5, 1]$ results in element-wise disagreement for all elements. For each element-wise disagreement between the primary feature vectors, a penalty P is added to D. The sum of the penalty is denoted as $P\left(v_c, v_q\right)$.
2. Comparison of object feature vector: For each element-wise matching between the primary feature vectors, the distance metric of that matching is calculated with:

$$D\left(o_c^i, o_q^i\right) = \Delta L^2 + \Delta a^2 + \Delta b^2 + \alpha\left(\Delta W^2 + \Delta H^2\right)$$

where o_c^i and o_q^i are the ith object feature vectors of the candidate and the query images respectively
ΔL is the difference in L channel
Δa is the difference in A channel
Δb is the difference in B channel
ΔW and ΔH is the difference of width and height respectively.

3. Adding step 2 and 3 then we get the distance metric:

$$D\left(v_c, v_q\right) = \sum_i D\left(o_c^i, o_q^i\right) + P\left(v_i, v_2\right)$$

As we can see from the definition, the most similar image with the query image is the query image itself as $D\left(v_q, v_q\right) = 0$. The result is sorted by the distance metric values. The value of P and α are empirically set to 10000 and 0.001.

3.6   Implementation

The implementation of the model is done in Python 3.5 with Tensorflow. Here is an example retrieval result shown in Fig. 5.

About the indexing time, we can observe that the indexing time is linearly increasing with the number of images as shown in Fig. 6 except for one outlier. The existence of outliers may be due to the threshold adjustment process. Although the image comes from the same database, there are variation of computation complexity between different catalogues.

4   Evaluation

To study the performance of the system, a subset of COREL image database [12], with 10 image categories, each containing 100 images, was used to evaluate the

(a)   (b)

Fig. 5. Example of the retrieval result in COREL database. The first image (leftmost) is the query image, which is always the first retrieval result. The others are the 2nd–5th retrieval results. Green solid bordered image represents a successful retrieval when the wrong retrieval are bounded by red dashed border.

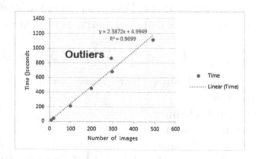

Fig. 6. Number of images vs Indexing time

system. The themes of the different categories were distinct to prevent ambiguity between categories. A retrieved image is considered as successful only if it belongs to the same category as the query. The mean average precision [13] is shown in Table 1. For comparison, we also include the average precision in 100 retrievals in our model and previous result with SIFT-LBP [14]. We also show two of the results using the ROC and precision-recall curve shown in Fig.7. Overall speaking, the results are worse than the previous result, especially the recall of the system is not very good. The precision is also quite low. This can be explained by the following reasons:

1. Limitation of object recognition algorithm: The object recognition algorithm plays an important role in the pipeline. If the class of object is not correctly determined, a heavy penalty is imposed, disregarding the similarity in low level features. For example, the category 'Horses' provides a much better result compared with other categories. In those categories, the main objects (the horses) are usually correctly determined. On the other hand, the category 'Mountains and glaciers' gives very poor result as most objects fail to be recognized. The quality of retrieval depends strongly on the object recognition algorithm, the training images and also the annotation used in the training.
2. Naive matching in primary feature vector: if an object exists in both query and candidate primary vector but in different ranking, they are still considered as mismatches. This causes high amount of mismatch in the comparison. In fact many of the images fail to match the query primary vector at all, resulting in maximum penalty (50000). These image results cannot be ranked so they are meaningless and rejected in the retrieval process. That is the reason that the maximum number of retrievals is very low in certain cases.
3. Parameters: There are three important parameters in the study: the number of bounding box, the penalty parameter P and α. These parameters are just empirically obtained and not optimized. Moreover, their optimal values are subject to various factors, including the size and context of the images.

5   Future Work and Conclusions

The first improvement is to allow for a matching of the object in different ordering. Objects in the same category in the candidate primary feature vector and the query primary feature vector should be matched by reordering. When there are multiple possible matches, the match should be chosen to minimize $D\left(v_c, v_q\right)$. Though this increases the complexity of the problem, it can improve the results. Besides, semantic segmentation [15] is a developing field in computer vision. It can be applied in our framework instead of the object recognition algorithm. The main advantage is to avoid the overlap area between bounding boxes of the objects, and it can avoid also multiple counting on the same object (for example, multiple bounding box on the same person). Thus the accuracy of the system can be improved.

Table 1. Mean average precision in COREL subset data and average precision comparison with SIFT-LBP approach

Categories	mAP (k=10)	mAP (k=100)	AP(k=100)	SIFT-LBP [14]
Africa people and villages	0.3486	0.1657	0.3540	0.57
Beach	0.3094	0.0849	0.1923	0.58
Buildings	0.2463	0.0482	0.1223	0.43
Buses	0.4970	0.2250	0.4029	0.93
Dinosaurs	0.5340	0.1885	0.2680	0.98
Elephants	0.6822	0.4926	0.5393	0.58
Flowers	0.6254	0.2782	0.3282	0.83
Horses	0.8163	0.5586	0.5979	0.68
Mountains and glaciers	0.2026	0.0391	0.1264	0.46
Food	0.6632	0.1840	0.2408	0.53
Overall	0.4925	0.2265	0.3172	0.637

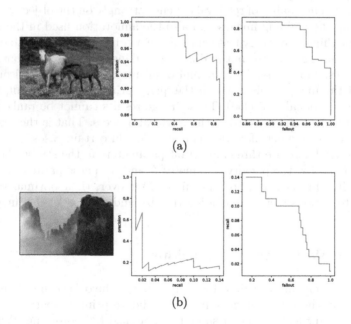

Fig. 7. (a)Retrieval example with query image from dataset 'Horses'. (b)Retrieval example with query image from dataset 'Mountains and glaciers'.

Thus, in this research, we explored the possibility to combine object recognition algorithm and image saliency prediction model with low-level features in CBIR. Although there is a significant drawback in the current technology, this framework can shed light on the direction for developing CBIR algorithms that are more semantically meaningful.

References

1. Russakovsky, O., Deng, J., Hao, S., Krause, J., Satheesh, S., Ma, S., Huang, Z., Karpathy, A., Khosla, A., Bernstein, M., et al.: Imagenet large scale visual recognition challenge. Int. J. Comput. Vis. **115**(3), 211–252 (2015)
2. Liu, W., Anguelov, D., Erhan, D., Szegedy, C., Reed, S., Fu, C.-Y., Berg, A.C.: SSD: single shot multibox detector. In: Leibe, B., Matas, J., Sebe, N., Welling, M. (eds.) ECCV 2016. LNCS, vol. 9905, pp. 21–37. Springer, Cham (2016). https://doi.org/10.1007/978-3-319-46448-0_2
3. Ren, S., He, K., Girshick, R., Sun, J.: Faster R-CNN: towards real-time object detection with region proposal networks. IEEE Trans. Pattern Anal. Mach. Intell. **39**(6), 1137–1149 (2017)
4. Dai, J., Li, Y., He, K., Sun, J.: R-FCN: Object detection via region-based fully convolutional networks. In: Advances in neural information processing systems, pp. 379–387 (2016)
5. Lin, T.-Y., Maire, M., Belongie, S., Hays, J., Perona, P., Ramanan, D., Dollár, P., Zitnick, C.L.: Microsoft COCO: common objects in context. In: Fleet, D., Pajdla, T., Schiele, B., Tuytelaars, T. (eds.) ECCV 2014. LNCS, vol. 8693, pp. 740–755. Springer, Cham (2014). https://doi.org/10.1007/978-3-319-10602-1_48
6. Geiger, A., Lenz, P., Stiller, C., Urtasun, R.: Vision meets robotics: the kitti dataset. Int. J. Robot. Res. (IJRR) **32**(11), 1231–1237 (2013)
7. Andrej, K., Li, F.-F.: Deep visual-semantic alignments for generating image descriptions. In: Proceedings of the IEEE Conference on Computer Vision and Pattern Recognition, pp. 3128–3137 (2015)
8. Papushoy, A., Bors, A.G.: Visual attention for content based image retrieval. In: 2015 IEEE International Conference on Image Processing (ICIP), pp. 971–975, September 2015
9. Howard, A.G., Zhu, M., Chen, B., Kalenichenko, D., Wang, W., Weyand, T., Andreetto, M., Adam, H.: Mobilenets: Efficient convolutional neural networks for mobile vision applications. arXiv preprint arXiv:1704.04861 (2017)
10. Itti, L., Koch, C., Niebur, E.: A model of saliency-based visual attention for rapid scene analysis. IEEE Trans. Pattern Anal. Mach. Intell. **20**(11), 1254–1259 (1998)
11. Borji, A., Itti, L.: Cat 2000: a large scale fixation dataset for boosting saliency research. In: CVPR 2015 Workshop on "Future of Datasets". arXiv preprint arXiv:1505.03581 (2015)
12. Wang, J.Z., Li, J., Wiederhold, G.: Simplicity: semantics-sensitive integrated matching for picture libraries. IEEE Trans. Pattern Anal. Mach. Intell. **23**(9), 947–963 (2001)
13. Zhou, W., Li, H., Tian, Q.: Recent advance in content-based image retrieval: A literature survey. arXiv preprint arXiv:1706.06064 (2017)
14. Yuan, X., Yu, J., Qin, Z., Wan, T.: A sift-LBP image retrieval model based on bag of features. In: IEEE International Conference on Image Processing (2011)
15. Badrinarayanan, V., Kendall, A., Cipolla, R.: Segnet: a deep convolutional encoder-decoder architecture for image segmentation. arXiv preprint arXiv:1511.00561 (2015)

Mobile-Based Painting Photo Retrieval Using Combined Features

Claudia Companioni-Brito[1], Zygred Mariano-Calibjo[1], Mohamed Elawady[2(✉)], and Sule Yildirim[1]

[1] NTNU - Norwegian University of Science and Technology, Gjøvik, Norway
sule.yildirim@ntnu.no
[2] Université de Lyon, UJM-Saint-Etienne, CNRS, IOGS, Laboratoire Hubert Curien UMR5516, 42023 Saint-Etienne, France
mohamed.elawady@univ-st-etienne.fr

Abstract. In paintings or artworks, sharing a photo of a painting using mobile phone is simple and fast. However, searching for information about specific captured photo of an unknown painting takes time and is not easy. No previous developments were introduced in the content-based indexing and retrieval (CBIR) field to ease the inconvenience of knowing the name and other information about an unknown painting through capturing photos by mobile phones. This work introduces an image retrieval framework on art paintings using shape, texture and color properties. With existing state-of-the-art developments, the proposed framework focuses on utilizing a feature combination of: generic Fourier descriptors (GFD), local binary patterns (LBP), Gray-level co-occurrence matrix (GLCM), and HSV histograms. After that, Locality Sensitive Hashing (LSH) method is used for image indexing and retrieval of paintings. The results are validated over a public database of seven different categories.

Keywords: CBIR · Image features · Similarity · Indexing · Paintings

1 Introduction

Analysis of artworks using computer vision is an interesting cross-disciplinary field that is being utilized in different industries such as architecture, advertising, design, fashion and art conservation [1,2]. Through CBIR, retrieval of similar image in the database to that of a query image through comparison of the extracted features of the images is possible [3–5]. This work focuses on art image retrieval framework respect to the museum paintings, through understanding the aesthetic and technical content of artworks. Painting photo retrieval is introduced in this paper using combined visual features based on shape, texture and color information. These features are well-detected in both global and local scale, for the purpose of efficient feature comparisons [2,4,6]. In the end, the top paintings similar to the input painting photo will be displayed together with the information about each of them. Hence, instant access to painting information about an unknown painting will become possible through mobile applications inside nowadays smart phones. The proposed framework is validated using a large-scale database of digitized painting images. The contributions of this work are (1) feature extraction using shape features in CBIR systems, and (2) combined feature representation for art paintings indexing and retrieval. The paper is organized as follows. Section 2 introduces a fully-automated image indexing and retrieval framework. In Sect. 3, the experimental results of the proposed work on paintings are shown and discussed. Finally, summary and future work were concluded in Sect. 4.

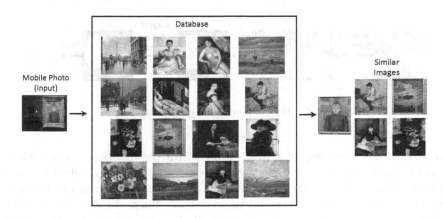

Fig. 1. Illustration of a query scheme within the corresponding retrieval results.

2 Methodology

In this work, we propose a general image retrieval system based on a combined feature representation between color, texture and shape features. As shown in Fig. 1, the proposed retrieval framework will start with an input image (i.e. real-time mobile photo). This image is known as a query image. Regardless of the resolution of the query image in RGB, it will be resized for computational efficiency and then converted to HSV color space. The dominant color of the image will be extracted as color feature vectors through a clustering-analyzing algorithm and using HSV histogram [6]. To extract the texture features, capacity, entropy and relevance of an image are calculated by the gray level co-occurrence matrix (GLCM) and local binary pattern (LBP) algorithms [7]. After extraction of texture features, shape descriptors will be used to extract the outline of the objects present in the image. As shown in Fig. 3, image signature saliency, Otsu binary thresholding and generic Fourier descriptors algorithms will be utilized because they are robust to noise and have translation, rotation and scale invariance [8–11]. After the feature extraction of a query image, these features will be matched with the same extracted ones of all images in the painting database.

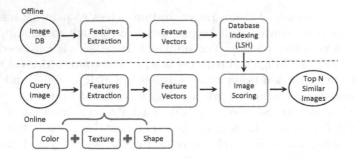

Fig. 2. The proposed framework of content-based image retrieval.

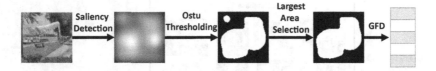

Fig. 3. Steps of shape feature extraction.

Comparison and matching of a query image with the database images will be based on low-level features previously discussed. Ranking of top similar images will be implemented by calculating $l1$ norm distance (direct comparison) between the feature vectors of the query and the database. These similar images will be ranked according to the distance from smallest to largest [6]. For the sake of computation time, similar images can be also ranked using an effective indexing algorithm called Locality Sensitive Hashing (LSH) [12]. The output of the proposed algorithm will be the top similar painting images from the large-scale database.

3   Results and Discussion

In order to evaluate the effectiveness of the proposed framework, it was applied on Kaggle Painting Database through pre-selecting 5,150 digital images representing paintings from different artists. The size of each category is as follows: abstract (993), cityscape (948), flower (334), landscape (994), marina (414), nude (513), and portrait (954). The proposed work is implemented using MATLAB (R2016b) on a Windows-based PC platform. The database images are experimentally down-sampled into 100×100 for fast computation without effecting the system performance. Figure 4 shows some sample images of selected categories. For HSV histograms, the number of quantization levels are 8:2:2 for Hue, Saturation, and Value channels respectively. The output representation of GLCM features is as follows: energy, contrast, correlation, homogeneity and entropy. The cell size for LBP feature extraction set to 3×3. The angular and radial frequencies of generic Fourier descriptors set to 12 and 5. For LSH indexing

Fig. 4. Sample images from seven categories of Kaggle database in column-wise.

method, the number of hashing tables is 3, and the length of keys is 6. The output dimensions of color, texture and shape features are: HSV (32), GLCM (5), LBP (36), and GFD (78). Afterwards, these features are normalized using $l2$ norm. The combined feature representation can be constructed by concatenating the proposed feature vectors.

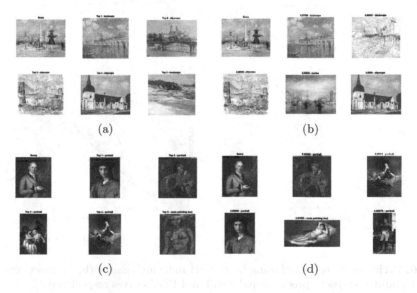

Fig. 5. Retrieval results of top 5 similar images for the Cityscape (1st row) and Portrait (2nd row) categories using: (a, c) LSH indexing and (b, d) direct comparison.

The performance of the proposed CBIR framework is presented in Fig. 5, and measured using precision-recall and ROC curves in Fig. 6. Plus statistical results present in Table 1. We compare the proposed ranking methods (LSH,

Table 1. Results of retrieval framework using LSH and Direct comparison for all queries. Time is in seconds.

	LSH			Direct comparison		
Query	Time	Recall	Precision	Time	Recall	Precision
Abstract	0.07	0.002	0.4	0.08	0.001	0.2
Cityscape	0.06	0.003	0.6	0.08	0.002	0.4
Flower	0.08	0.006	0.4	0.07	0.003	0.2
Landscape	0.06	0.005	1.0	0.08	0.005	1.0
Marina	0.06	0.007	0.6	0.08	0.004	0.4
Nude	0.07	0.008	0.8	0.07	0.008	0.8
Portrait	0.06	0.004	0.8	0.07	0.004	0.8

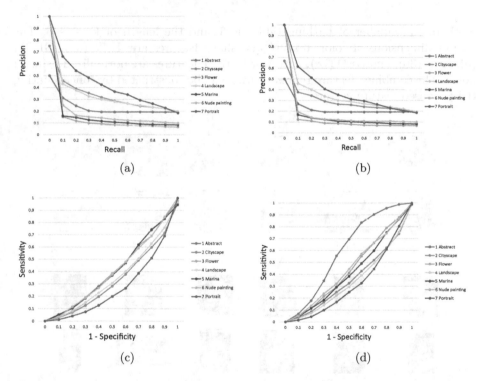

Fig. 6. Performance results of using (a, c) LSH indexing against (b, d) direct comparison. Columns represent precision and recall and ROC curves respectively.

direct comparison) to confirm the significance of indexing in reducing retrieve time. Figure 5 shows the result of two systems, with and without indexing, for a query on cityscape. Color indeed plays a significant role in image retrieval as shown by the top 5 similar images. Shapes also played a significant role, but not as dominant as color. Texture has the least effect in retrieval of similar images, with or without indexing. In the first example, cityscape was the query image and the results displayed images from marina and landscape. This kind of result will greatly affect the precision and recall of the image as well as the user satisfaction. This issue can be a topic for next researches to better understand how certain feature vectors affect the retrieval of images. In Fig. 6. Flower query has the lowest precision while portrait has the highest. As shown in Table 1, indexing indeed makes the system of retrieval faster. Though the result of recall and precision did not significantly change, as shown in Fig. 6. Having faster retrieve time will make any system efficient and effective. Hence, LSH indexing is deemed significant to the proposed framework more efficient and effective.

4   Conclusion

The proposed image retrieval framework for painting images is a significant contribution to CBIR as well as to the industries dealing with painting photographs. The qualitative and quantitative experiments showed good results using the combined feature representation, to retrieve similar painting images respect to the captured photo. This work significantly helps museums or any art institution to deliver better experience to their audience. In the future work, the shape feature extraction can be improved by segmenting the salient objects precisely from the scene background. In addition, the combined representation can be also included the deep features from pre-trained CNN models for better accuracy.

References

1. Khan, F.S., Beigpour, S., Van de Weijer, J., Felsberg, M.: Painting-91: a large scale database for computational painting categorization. Mach. Vis. Appl. **25**(6), 1385–1397 (2014)
2. Soman, S., Ghorpade, M., Sonone, V., Chavan, S.: Content based image retrieval using advanced color and texture features. In: International Conference in Computational Intelligence (ICCIA), vol. 3 (2012)
3. Kavitha, K., Sudhamani, M.: Object based image retrieval from database using combined features. In: 2014 Fifth International Conference on Signal and Image Processing (ICSIP), pp. 161–165. IEEE (2014)
4. Wang, X.Y., Chen, Z.F., Yun, J.J.: An effective method for color image retrieval based on texture. Comput. Stand. Interfaces **34**(1), 31–35 (2012)
5. Zhou, W., Li, H., Tian, Q.: Recent advance in content-based image retrieval: a literature survey. arXiv preprint arXiv:1706.06064 (2017)
6. Yue, J., Li, Z., Liu, L., Fu, Z.: Content-based image retrieval using color and texture fused features. Math. Comput. Model. **54**(3), 1121–1127 (2011)
7. Bianconi, F., Harvey, R., Southam, P., Fernández, A.: Theoretical and experimental comparison of different approaches for color texture classification. J. Electr. Imaging **20**(4), 043006–043006 (2011)
8. Amanatiadis, A., Kaburlasos, V., Gasteratos, A., Papadakis, S.: Evaluation of shape descriptors for shape-based image retrieval. IET Image Process. **5**(5), 493–499 (2011)

9. Zhang, D., Lu, G.: Content-based shape retrieval using different shape descriptors: a comparative study. In: null, p. 289. IEEE (2001)
10. Hou, X., Harel, J., Koch, C.: Image signature: highlighting sparse salient regions. IEEE Trans. Pattern Anal. Mach. Intell. **34**(1), 194–201 (2012)
11. Zhang, D., Lu, G.: Shape-based image retrieval using generic fourier descriptor. Sig. Process. Image Commun. **17**(10), 825–848 (2002)
12. Datar, M., Immorlica, N., Indyk, P., Mirrokni, V.S.: Locality-sensitive hashing scheme based on p-stable distributions. In: Proceedings of the Twentieth Annual Symposium on Computational Geometry, pp. 253–262. ACM (2004)

Lp Norm Relaxation Approach for Large Scale Data Analysis: A Review

Tien D. Bui[1]([✉]), Kha Gia Quach[2], Chi Nhan Duong[2], and Khoa Luu[2]

[1] Concordia University, Montreal, QC, Canada
bui@cse.concordia.ca
[2] Carnegie Mellon University, Pittsburgh, PA, USA
{kquach, chinhand, kluu}@andrew.cmu.edu

Abstract. In the last few years there has been a lot of attention to the techniques of sparse representation and low-rank approximation. These techniques have shown important applications in many areas in image and video processing, signal analysis, computer vision and machine learning. These techniques can also be used in unsupervised and dictionary learning to uncover high-order relations in the data and to train deep neural networks. This paper is a review to discuss the latest developments and show the effectiveness of these techniques in large scale data processing problems.

Keywords: Low-rank approximation · Sparse representation
Image and video processing · Computer vision

1 Introduction

Compressive sensing (CS) and matrix factorization (MF) have exploited sparsity and low-rankness of signals/data in various applications. Both CS and MF are originally formulated as non-convex optimization problems due to the underlying L_0-norm for sparsity and low-rankness, but it is hard to solve the problems exactly in a reasonable time. Later, the idea of using convex relaxation (i.e. using L_1-norm minimization) helps solve the non-convex problems approximately. Since using L_1-norm may produce undesired solutions, recently, a non-convex L_p-norm relaxation, a new approach being closer to optimal solutions (obtained by L_0-norm), has become more popular. This paper aims to clarify the need of using the L_p-norm to enhance sparsity over the L_1-norm, to identify problems that may need the L_p-norm enhancement, and to review some commonly used algorithms for solving the L_p-norm minimization problem.

2 Motivations

Many comparative studies have been provided for L_1-norm minimization in various problems such as compressive sensing, matrix completion, robust principal component analysis, etc. However, similar studies for L_p-functions are limited in many aspects. A full review of this new research trend is unavailable or partially mentioned in some surveys, for example, in a recent survey on CS [1], a few non-convex approaches were

© Springer International Publishing AG, part of Springer Nature 2018
A. Campilho et al. (Eds.): ICIAR 2018, LNCS 10882, pp. 285–292, 2018.
https://doi.org/10.1007/978-3-319-93000-8_33

briefly mentioned. However, there remain many questions, for example, what kinds of problems can we apply L_p-norm regularization? What types of L_p functions have been proposed? What optimization algorithms can we use to optimize a specific problem with an L_p regularization function? In theory and in practice, can those algorithms find optimal solutions? How good is the solution found by L_p-norm compared with L_1-norm? What can we say about the convergence? This review paper is an attempt to answer some of these questions with general discussions covering both theoretical and practical aspects of the state-of-the-art.

The rest of the paper is organized as follows. In Sect. 3, we summarize the properties and theoretical studies of L_p-norm and other L_p-like non-convex penalty functions. Section 4 introduces different problems that can benefit from applying L_p-norm regularization with special emphasis on the matrix decomposition problems. Our recent works in this area will also be reviewed in Sect. 4. We conclude the paper in the last section and provide potential future direction.

3 The L_p -norm $(0 < P < 1)$

3.1 Definition and Properties

Given a vector $x \in R^n$, a general definition of L_p-norm of x is given by:

$$||x||_p = (|x_1|^P + |x_2|^P + \ldots + |x_n|^P)^{1/P}.$$

We consider the unit ball in R^2 as illustrated in Fig. 1 to show the properties of the L_p-norm with the values $0 < p < 1$. When $p \geq 1$, it is a norm with the properties of a 'length function' which is convex and holds the triangle inequality. The particular cases of $p = 1$, 2 and ∞ are widely used in many optimization procedures. These norm regularizations often give a non-sparse solution, except for $p = 1$ (L_1-norm) which yields sparse results under certain conditions. When $0 < p < 1$, it is only a quasi-norm; it does not satisfy the triangle inequality but it induces a metric which is 'concave'. The resulting optimization problem involving L_p-norm is non-convex and intractable. As $p \to 0$, the solutions become sparser. Larger values of p give smooth and less sparse solutions. The curves in Fig. 1 approach the axes as $p \to 0$.

Since $\lim\limits_{p \to 0} |x_i|^p = \begin{cases} 1, & \textit{for } x_i \neq 0 \\ 0, & \textit{for } x_i = 0 \end{cases}$ hence, for $p < 1$, we consider $||x||_p^p$ rather than $||x||_p$ so that the above limit exists when $p \to 0$. This suggests that, by defining $0^0 = 0$, the zero-"norm" or L_0-"norm" (using the term norm here is an abuse of terminology, as $||x||_0$ does not satisfy all of the properties of a norm) of x is equal to the sum $|x_1|^0 + |x_2|^0 + \ldots + |x_n|^0$ which is a special case of the generalized L_p-norm. It provides a way to count the number of non-zero entries in a vector x.

Some variations appear in the naming of the norm: L_p-norm, ℓ_p-norm, or p-norm, but those terms are referring to the same thing. To be consistent we use the term L_p -norm throughout this paper to refer to the case of $0 < p < 1$. Solving L_0-norm minimization is an NP-hard problem which means that it cannot be solved by any tractable

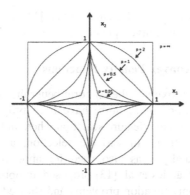

Fig. 1. Properties of the L_p norm

algorithm in polynomial time. Some works [2] showed that L_0-norm can be replaced by its nearest convex lower bound, the L_1-norm, to obtain sparse results. We consider L_p minimization as a strategy lying between two extremes, the L_0 and L_1 - minimization. One extreme is impractical to solve but gives the optimal sparse solution, the other can be solved efficiently but generates less zero coefficients. Meanwhile, L_p-minimization has some benefits, firstly, L_p-norm approximates L_0-norm better and yields more sparse results. Secondly, solving L_p-minimization is as efficient as solving its convex L_1-norm. It is noted that L_p-norm minimization has been used in different fields. However, due to space limitation we will not discuss it here.

3.2 Theoretical Analysis

In this section, we will briefly introduce recent theoretical studies on L_p-norm properties and its benefits when applied particularly in compressive sensing problems.

Chartrand [3] showed that using the L_p-norm can give exact reconstruction with substantially fewer measurements than using the L_1-norm. Later in [4], he demonstrated that with a fixed number of measurements, the non-convex case can correct the corruption of a larger number of entries. In terms of the Restricted Isometry Property (RIP), Chartrand et al. [5] generalized the result of Candes [6] to an L_p variant and determined a sufficient condition for exact recovery from perfect data via L_p -minimization. An extensive study on exact recovery condition can be found in [7]. Saab et al. [8] studied L_p-minimization in terms of its stability and robustness. They stated that L_p-minimization (with p < 1) guarantees more stable and robust than L_1-minimization does depending on the RIP constants and the noise level. Saab et al. [8] also studied the stability of L_p-minimization for the sparse and compressible signals when measurements contain some additive noise and they gave the error bounds on the reconstruction error. Ince et al. [9] proposed a sparse reconstruction method based on L_p-minimization knowing part of the signal support and they showed its stability and robustness. Gribonval and Nielsen [10] considered a family of sparseness measures L_p-norm. With such a sparseness measure, they provided conditions for getting a unique sparse representation of a signal from a dictionary and for solving all non-convex problems. In the variable selection field, Huang et al. [11] studied asymptotic property (or the oracle property) of non-convex penalized estimators.

3.3   Other Lp-like Non-convex Penalty Functions

Beside L_p-norm that can approximate the L_0-norm better than the L_1-norm, many other nonconvex surrogate functions of L_0-norm have been proposed. Most of them are proposed in the context of variable/feature selection where indeed emerged the first use of nonconvex penalty functions. In variable selection, a well-known non-convex penalty, the logarithm penalty, was also used for approximating the L_0-norm by Weston et al. [12]. While Candes et al. [13] proposed an optimization method for this penalty in sparse signal approximation problems and showed its recovering capability though experiments. In this log penalty, a small shifting quantity is added to avoid infinite value when the parameter $x_i \rightarrow 0$. This penalty has an interesting probability interpretation based on Bayesian framework with priors being a t-Student type distribution. Fan and Li [14] proposed a Smoothly Clipped Absolute Deviation (SCAD) penalty function for variable selection. They pointed out some drawbacks of the L_1 penalty such as creating noticeably large bias on large coefficients. Then, they proved that SCAD has all necessary properties i.e. sparsity, continuity and unbiasedness.

Zhang [15] proposed a Minimax Concave Penalty (MCP) that can be considered as a variant of the SCAD penalty. The MCP has a bias controlling parameter γ. With larger values of γ, it provides smoother and less computationally complex but larger bias and less accurate variable selection. The MCP path converges to the L_1 path as $\gamma \rightarrow \infty$. In the same spirit of SCAD and MCP, Gao et al. [16] proposed a non-convex penalty function which is called exponential-type penalty (ETP). The most essential point of ETP is that it bridges the L_0 and L_1 via a positive parameter γ. When this parameter approaches ∞ and 0, the limits of ETP are the L_0 and L_1 respectively. Using exponential helps to smooth the gaps between L_0 and L_1. Related to the above MCP penalty, Zhang [17] analyzed a multi-stage convex relaxation procedure with Capped-L_1 regularization. This procedure solved a non-convex problem using multiple stage refining strategy.

Geman and Yang [18] applied a new sparsity regularization, which is even and nondecreasing on $[0, \infty)$, to a derivative operator of an image. Trzasko and Manduca [19] presented a homotopic approximation of the L_0-minimization problem and applied it to recover undersampled magnetic resonance images (MRI). Their proposed method only guaranteed to find a local minimum, however, it allows accurate image reconstructions at higher undersampling rates than via L_1-minimization. Mohimani [20] introduced a continuous Gaussian-based penalty function. This function has a parameter σ (variance of Gaussian) controlling the smoothness of the L_0-norm approximation. A larger value of σ gives smoother function g_σ but far away from L_0-norm; and a smaller value of σ brings g_σ closer to L_0-norm behavior. These non-convex penalties can be used to approximate the rank function of a matrix. For examples, the Schatten p-norm [21], truncated nuclear norm [22] and log-det [23, 24].

4 L_p-norm Applicable Problems

In this section, we describe a trend of using L_p-norm in solving the matrix factorization problem. Matrix factorization may include compressive sensing, matrix completion, Robust PCA, Sparse PCA, non-negative matrix factorization, subspace clustering and dictionary learning with constraints based on rank, positivity and/or sparsity.

4.1 Compressive Sensing

Compressive sensing (CS) is a novel data acquisition theory exploiting the sparse or compressible structure of acquired signals. This theory shows that certain signals can be recovered from fewer samples than required in Nyquist theory. If the sensed signal is sparse in its original or transformed domain, i.e. low information rate, the recovery can be exact. The core of CS consists of the acquisition and reconstruction models. The CS problem can be described as follows: Given $y = \Phi x$ where $y \in R^m$ is the measurement vector, $\Phi \in R^{m \times n}$ is the measurement matrix, and $x \in R^n$ is the sparse vector to be recovered where $m \ll n$. The aim is to solve this inverse problem to find the sparsest vector x. This problem is under-determined and can be posed as the following optimization:

$$\min_x \ ||x||_0 \ \text{s.t.} \ y = \Phi x$$

where $||x||_0$ computes the number of nonzero entries in vector x. This optimization problem is combinatorial in nature and is NP-hard. To overcome this computational difficulty, Candes introduced the Basic Pursuit (BP) in which the L_0-norm is replaced by the L_1- norm. It is a convex optimization problem. However, the L_1- norm does not always give good approximation to the L_0- norm. As mentioned in the previous section, many attempts have been given to the L_p- norm solutions, i.e. to solve the non-convex optimization:

$$\arg\min_x \ ||x||_p \ \text{s.t.} \ y = \Phi x$$

In terms of the Restricted Isometry Property (RIP):

$$(1 - \delta_k)||x||_2^2 \le ||\Phi x||_2^2 \le (1 + \delta_k)||x||_2^2$$

the L_0-norm minimization (or the NP-hard problem) reconstructs a k-sparse vector x exactly if $\delta_{2k} < 1$. Candes et al. [2] showed that using L_1-norm one can recover exactly k-sparse vector x when $\delta_{3k} + 3\delta_{4k} < 2$. Later Candes [6] presented a more strict condition for exact recovery of k-sparse vector via L_1-minimization. Chartrand [3] extended this condition to L_p-minimization. He established the condition for which the RIP is satisfied. He then stated that with such sufficient condition, the exact vector x can be found for a suitable p > 0 when $\delta_{2k+1} < 1$. Foucart and Lai [7] also studied a condition on the matrix Φ which guarantees the sparest solution with the L_p-minimization.

Convergence studies on some non-convex optimization algorithms are still limited. For instances, Chartrand and Yin [25] showed that IRLS converges to a local neighborhood using ε-regularization strategy. However, it may not find the correct local neighborhood containing the global optimum.

4.2   Robust PCA Problem

The Robust PCA problem is defined as follows: Given a matrix $M \in R^{mxn}$, we want to decompose it into two components, i.e. $L, S \in R^{mxn}$, where L is the low-rank matrix and S is the sparse component. This problem can be mathematically formulated as:

$$\min_{L,S} rank(L) + \lambda||S||_0 \text{ s.t. } L + S = M$$

where $||S||_0$ computes the number of nonzero entries in matrix S and the parameter $\lambda > 0$ controls the trade-off between the sparsity level and reconstruction fidelity. Solving the above equation is difficult since it poses as a challenging NP-hard problem. Candes et al. [26] presented the Robust Principal Component Analysis (RPCA) method using a tractable and convex approximation to the objective function. In their method, the non-convex L_0 -norm and the rank functions are approximated by a convex relaxation L_1-norm and a nuclear norm respectively as shown below:

$$\min_{L,S} ||L||_* + \lambda||S||_1 \text{ s.t. } L + S = M$$

where $||L||_*$ denotes the nuclear norm, i.e. the sum of singular values of a matrix. It is also considered as the L_1-norm of the vector of singular values of that matrix.

Non-convex RPCA Formulation. In [27] we apply L_p-norm regularization on both sparse and low-rank matrices. Besides that by using the same penalty functions (and even the same p value) we can maintain the balance between low-rankness and sparsity. The parameter λ will then control this trade-off rather than penalty functions. The RPCA model is then approximated by a non-convex optimization problem:

$$\min_{L,S} ||\sigma(L)||_p^p + \lambda||S||_p^p \text{ s.t. } L + S = M$$

where $\sigma(L)$ denotes a vector of the singular values of the matrix L. In general, we denote the L_p-norm as a penalty function $g(.) = |.|^p$, thus, our proposed objective function can be redefined as follows:

$$\min_{L,S} \sum_{j=1}^{d} g(\sigma_j) + \lambda \sum_{ij=1}^{mxn} g(s_{ij}) \text{ s.t. } L + S = M$$

The above optimization problem can be solved by using the Augmented Lagrangian formulation and the ADMM in which the components are fixed alternatively while the other component is obtained iteratively.

In [27] we also presented an online/real-time version of the RPCA algorithm. This online method can decompose the matrix M into low-rank L and sparse matrix S incrementally when a new column of M is added without the need to decompose the whole matrix. An example of the application of this work is in foreground background separation in video processing.

4.3 Robust SVD Problem

In [28] a Robust SVD method was proposed to deal with the case of missing elements in the matrix M where M is decomposed into the product of two orthogonal matrices U and V and a diagonal matrix Σ. A weight matrix W is introduced to cope with missing elements, where $W_{ij} > 0$ if the data point X_{ij} exists, otherwise $W_{ij} = 0$. The notation "$\bullet$" denotes component-wise multiplications. The optimization problem is defined in terms of the L_p-norm as follows:

$$\min_{U\Sigma V} \ ||W \bullet (M - U\Sigma V^T)||_p \ \text{s.t.} \ U^T U = I, V^T V = I$$

The technique for solving the above optimization problem is given in [28]. This paper also contains many application problems including matrix completion for 3D construction from 2D images, image reconstruction from occlusions, and structure from motion.

5 Conclusion

This paper reviews the state-of-the-art of L_p-minimization techniques. These techniques contributed significantly to the efficiency of solving the matrix low-rank and sparse representations. One emerging trend is to apply low-rank approximation to deep learning in order to reduce the complexity of the learning process. In many deep networks such as CNNs there exist fully connected layers involving extremely large matrices. Low-rank approximation can help in improving the training and learning phases of deep networks.

References

1. Qaisar, S., Bilal, R.M., Iqbal, W., Naureen, M., Lee, S.: Compressive sensing: from theory to applications, a survey. J. Commun. Netw. **15**(5), 443–456 (2013)
2. Candes, E.J., Romberg, J., Tao, T.: Robust uncertainty principles: exact signal reconstruction from highly incomplete frequency information. IEEE Trans. Inf. Theory **52**(2), 489–509 (2006)
3. Chartrand, R.: Exact reconstruction of sparse signals via nonconvex minimization. IEEE Sig. Process. Lett. **14**(10), 707–710 (2007)
4. Chartrand, R.: Nonconvex compressed sensing and error correction. In: ICASSP, vol. 3, pp. 889–892 (2007)

5. Chartrand, R., Staneva, V.: Restricted isometry properties and nonconvex compressive sensing. Inverse Prob. **24**(3), 035020 (2008)
6. Candes, E.J.: The restricted isometry property and its implications for compressed sensing. C. R. Math. **346**(9), 589–592 (2008)
7. Foucart, S., Lai, M.-J.: Sparsest solutions of underdetermined linear systems via Lq-minimization for $0 < q < 1$. Appl. Comput. Harmonic Anal. **26**(3), 395–407 (2009)
8. Saab, R., Yilmaz, O.: Sparse recovery by non-convex optimization-instance opti-mality. Appl. Comput. Harmonic Anal. **29**(1), 30–48 (2010)
9. Ince, T., Nacaroglu, A., Watsuji, N.: Nonconvex compressed sensing with patialy known signal support. Sig. Process. **93**(1), 338–344 (2013)
10. Gribonval, R., Nielsen, M.: Highly sparse representations from dictionaries are unique and independent of the sparseness measure. Appl. Comput. Harmonic Anal. **3**, 335–355 (2007)
11. Huang, J., Horowitz, J.L., Ma, S.: Asymptotic properties of bridge estimators in sparse high-dimensional regression models. Ann. Stat. **36**(2), 587–613 (2008)
12. Weston, J., Elissee, A., Scholkopf, B., Tipping, M.: Use of the zero norm with linear models and kernel methods. J. Mach. Learn. Res. **3**, 1439–1461 (2003)
13. Candes, E.J., Wakin, M.B., Boyd, S.P.: Enhancing sparsity by reweighted L_1 minimization. J. Fourier Anal. Appl. **14**(5–6), 877–905 (2008)
14. Fan, J., Li, R.: Variable selection via nonconcave penalized likelihood and its oracle properties. J. Am. Stat. Assoc. **96**(456), 1348–1360 (2001)
15. Zhang, C.-H.: Nearly unbiased variable selection under minimax concave penalty. Ann. Stat. **38**(2), 894–942 (2010)
16. Gao, C., Wang, N., Yu, Q., Zhang, Z.: A feasible nonconvex relaxation approach to feature selection. In: AAAI (2011)
17. Zhang, T.: Analysis of multi-stage convex relaxation for sparse regularization. J. Mach. Learn. Res. **11**, 1081–1107 (2010)
18. Geman, D., Yang, C.: Nonlinear image recovery with half-quadratic regularization. IEEE TIP **4**(7), 932–946 (1995)
19. Trzasko, J., Manduca, A.: Highly undersampled magnetic resonance image reconstruction via homotopic-minimization. IEEE TMI **28**(1), 106–121 (2009)
20. Mohimani, H., Babaie-Zadeh, M., Jutten, C.: A fast approach for overcomplete sparse decomposition based on smoothed L_0-norm. IEEE TSP **57**(1), 289–301 (2009)
21. Mohan, K., Fazel, M.: Iterative reweighted algorithms for matrix rank minimization. J. Mach. Learn. Res. **13**(1), 3441–3473 (2012)
22. Hu, Y., Zhang, D., Ye, J., Li, X., He, X.: Fast and accurate matrix completion via truncated nuclear norm regularization. IEEE TPAMI **35**(9), 2117–2130 (2013)
23. Fazel, M., Hindi, H., Boyd, S.P.: Log-det heuristic for matrix rank minimization with applications to Hankel and Euclidean distance matrices. In: Proceedings of American Control Conference, vol. 3, pp. 2156–2162 (2003)
24. Dong, W., Shi, G., Li, X., Ma, Y., Huang, F.: Compressive sensing via nonlocal low-rank regularization. IEEE TIP **23**(8), 3618–3632 (2014)
25. Chartrand, R., Yin, W.: Iteratively reweighted algorithms for compressive sensing. In: ICASSP, pp. 3869–3872 (2008)
26. Candes, E.J., Li, X., Ma, Y., Wright, J.: Robust principal component analysis. JACM **58**(3), 11 (2011)
27. Quach, K.G., Duong, C.N., Luu, K., Bui, T.D.: Non-convex online robust PCA: enhance sparsity via L_p-norm minimization. CVIU **158**, 126–140 (2017)
28. Quach, K.G., Luu, K., Duong, C.N., Bui, T.D.: Robust L_p-norm singular value decomposition. In: NIPS Workshop on Non-convex Optimization for Machine Learning: Theory and Practice (2015)

Computer Vision

A Diffusion-Based Two-Dimensional Empirical Mode Decomposition (EMD) Algorithm for Image Analysis

Heming Wang[1], Richard Mann[2], and Edward R. Vrscay[1](✉)

[1] Department of Applied Mathematics, Faculty of Mathematics,
University of Waterloo, Waterloo, ON N2L 3G1, Canada
{h422wang,ervrscay}@uwaterloo.ca
[2] Department of Computer Science, Faculty of Mathematics,
University of Waterloo, Waterloo, ON N2L 3G1, Canada
mannr@uwaterloo.ca

Abstract. We propose a novel diffusion-based, empirical mode decomposition (EMD) algorithm for image analysis. Although EMD has been a powerful tool in signal processing, its algorithmic nature has made it difficult to analyze theoretically. For example, many EMD procedures rely on the location of local maxima and minima of a signal followed by interpolation to find upper and lower envelope curves which are then used to extract a "mean curve" of a signal. These operations are not only sensitive to noise and error but they also present difficulties for a mathematical analysis of EMD. Two-dimensional extensions of the EMD algorithm also suffer from these difficulties. Our PDEs-based approach replaces the above procedures by simply using the diffusion equation to construct the mean curve (surface) of a signal (image). This procedure also simplifies the mathematical analysis. Numerical experiments for synthetic and real images are presented. Simulation results demonstrate that our algorithm can outperform the standard two-dimensional EMD algorithms as well as requiring much less computation time.

Keywords: Empirical Mode Decomposition
Partial differential equations · Image analysis · Texture analysis
Local time-frequency analysis

1 Introduction

Empirical Mode Decomposition (EMD), introduced in [12], is a powerful tool for analyzing linear, nonlinear and nonstationary signals. Its ability to perform local time-frequency analysis for nonstationary signals has been demonstrated for real-world signals – see, for example, [1,12,13]. EMD employs a *sifting process* to extract different modes of oscillation of a signal, referred to as *Intrinsic Mode Functions* (IMF). The Hilbert transform is then applied to each IMF in order to determine its instantaneous local frequencies. A repeated application

© Springer International Publishing AG, part of Springer Nature 2018
A. Campilho et al. (Eds.): ICIAR 2018, LNCS 10882, pp. 295–305, 2018.
https://doi.org/10.1007/978-3-319-93000-8_34

of EMD produces a decomposition of a signal into components with decreasing (instantaneous) frequency. The amplitudes and instantaneous frequencies can then produce a local time-frequency analysis of the signal.

Because most of the work on EMD has focused on algorithms as opposed to theoretical analysis, there has been very little work on developing a rigorous theoretical basis for EMD as well as an understanding of why it fails for certain kinds of signals. Many EMD methods rely on rather sensitive, if not questionable, procedures of extracting upper and lower envelopes of a signal from which a mean curve is computed. The mean curve is then used to extract an IMF. In [19], we proposed a novel forward heat equation method to extract the mean envelope which is then used in the sifting process. Our approach is not only more stable but also provides a better mathematical analysis of EMD as well as identifying potential limitations.

There have been a number of efforts to extend EMD to two dimensions [2,4,6,14,16,18,20,21] – these schemes are known as bidimensional EMD (BEMD). Once again, however, these methods lack a sufficient theoretical background due to their algorithmic nature. As in the one-dimensional case, one of the major obstacles of the BEMD method is the extraction of upper and lower envelopes from which *mean surfaces* are computed. Indeed, the extraction procedures performed by many current BEMD algorithms are necessarily much more complicated.

In this paper, we propose a novel, two-dimensional PDE-based BEMD algorithm. The mean surface of a two-dimensional function, e.g., an image, is again obtained by evolving the function according to the diffusion equation, and then employed in a sifting process. Our algorithm has a solid mathematical basis and demonstrates greater effectiveness when applied to images. Moreover, its computational time is lower than that of classical BEMD methods.

2   Classical EMD and BEMD Algorithms

For a given signal $S(x)$, the classical one-dimensional EMD method may be summarized as follows:

1. Find all local maximal points and minimal points of $S(x)$.
2. Interpolate between maximal points to obtain an upper envelope function $E_{upper}(x)$ and between minimal points to obtain a lower envelope function $E_{lower}(x)$.
3. Compute the local mean function: $m(x) = \frac{1}{2} [E_{upper}(x) + E_{lower}(x)]$.
4. Define $c(x) = S(x) - m(x)$.
5. If $c(x)$ is not an IMF (see note below), iterate $m(x)$ until it is.
6. After finding the IMF, subtract it and repeat Step 2 to obtain the residual.

Note: Most EMD procedures employ the following rather a vague definition of an intrinsic mode function (IMF): (i) The number of extrema and zero-crossings of an IMF must differ at most by one and (ii) the mean of the IMF should be close to zero.

The result of the above procedure is the following decomposition of the signal $S(x)$,

$$S(x) = \sum_{k=1}^{N} c_k(x) + r(x), \tag{1}$$

where $c_k(x)$ is the kth IMF, and $r(x)$ is the residual. Two-dimensional EMD algorithms, i.e., BEMD, follow a similar procedure although the extraction of upper and lower envelopes is understandably much more complex.

As we discuss in [19], the classic EMD algorithm suffers from the following shortcomings: (i) lack of mathematical proof, (ii) errors near borders, (iii) a vague definition of the IMF and (iv) sampling effects. BEMD algorithms such as those in [2, 18, 21] are based on the classical 1D EMD algorithm which means, unfortunately, that they suffer from similar shortcomings.

One of the major problems of EMD has been the lack of a theoretical framework. There has been a number of efforts to provide a mathematical explanation and basis for EMD. Daubechies et $al.$ [5] proposed an EMD-like tool which they called a $synchrosqueezed$ $wavelet$ $transform$. Their algorithm employs wavelet analysis along with a reallocation method and provides a precise mathematical expression for a series of separable harmonic components in the signal.

El Hadji et $al.$ [7, 8] introduced a backward heat equation approach to interpret the EMD algorithm. For a prescribed $\delta > 0$, they first defined the upper and lower envelopes of a function $h(x)$ as follows,

$$U_\delta = \sup_{|y| < \delta} h(x + y), \quad L_\delta = \inf_{|y| < \delta} h(x + y), \tag{2}$$

Because of space limitations, we mention only very briefly the procedures which are then adopted. First, the Taylor expansions of the envelopes are computed from which the following mean envelope function is defined,

$$m_\delta(x) = \frac{1}{2}[U_\delta(x) + L_\delta(x)] \approx h(x) + \frac{\delta^2}{2} h''(x). \tag{3}$$

The sifting process to obtain the IMF is then defined as follows,

$$h_{n+1}(x) = h_n(x) - m_\delta(x), \quad h_0(x) = h(x). \tag{4}$$

Using the following Taylor expansion in t,

$$h_{n+1} = h(x, t + \Delta t) = h_n + \Delta t \frac{\partial h}{\partial t} + O(\Delta t^2) \tag{5}$$

the authors arrive at the following PDE,

$$\frac{\partial h}{\partial t} + \frac{1}{\delta^2} h + \frac{1}{2} \frac{\partial^2 h}{\partial x^2} = 0, \quad h(x, 0) = S(x). \tag{6}$$

Note that this PDE is a $backward$ heat equation.

Niang *et al.* [15] proposed the following fourth-order non-linear equation as the interpolator to simulate the spline interpolation of upper and lower envelope,

$$\frac{\partial s(x,t)}{\partial t} = \frac{\partial}{\partial x}\left[g(x,t)\frac{\partial^3 s(x,t)}{\partial x^3}\right], \tag{7}$$

where $g(x,t)$ is the nonlinear diffusivity function. By controlling the non-linear terms, the envelopes will pass through maximal and minimal points.

3   Proposed Diffusion-Based EMD and BEMD Algorithms

As discussed briefly in Sect. 2, most EMD algorithms obtain the mean function from upper and lower envelopes which, in turn, are obtained by interpolating local maxima and minima of a function $S(x)$. All of these procedures are time-consuming and sensitive to error and noise. Our diffusion-based EMD method, on the other hand, is based on the intuition that the mean curve $m(x)$ passes through all inflection points of $S(x)$. The idea is very simple: Instead of taking the average of two envelope functions of a signal $S(x)$ to produce a mean – Step 3 of the classical EMD algorithm in Sect. 2 – we proceed as follows. For a prescribed $\tau > 0$, we define $h_n(x) = h(x, n\tau)$ for $n = 0, 1, 2, \cdots$ and use Eqs. (3) and (4) to obtain the following equation,

$$h_{n+1} = h_n + C\frac{\partial^2 h}{\partial x^2}. \tag{8}$$

Note that from this equation, the value of h at its spatial inflection points remains the same. Now apply the following Taylor expansion to h_{n+1},

$$h_{n+1}(x) = h(x, n\tau + \tau) = h(x, n\tau) + \tau\frac{\partial h}{\partial t}(x, n\tau) + o(\tau^2). \tag{9}$$

After a few steps we arrive at the equation,

$$\tau\frac{\partial h}{\partial t} + O(\tau^2) = C\frac{\partial^2 h}{\partial x^2}. \tag{10}$$

We now assume that $C = a\tau$ and, after division by τ, arrive at the following initial value problem (IVP) for the heat/diffusion equation,

$$\frac{\partial h}{\partial t} = a\frac{\partial^2 h}{\partial x^2}, \qquad h(x,0) = S(x). \tag{11}$$

For prescribed values of the diffusivity constant $a > 0$ and time $T > 0$ (which can be adjusted) we now define the *mean function* of $S(x)$ as $m(x) = h(x, T)$, i.e., the solution of the IVP in Eq. (11) at time T. In other words, the mean function $m(x)$ is obtained from $S(x)$ by low-pass filtering.

Our method clearly differs from other EMD algorithms since it bypasses (i) the complicated procedure of extracting local maxima and minima of a signal as well as (ii) the interpolations of these points to obtain upper and lower envelopes. Instead, the mean curve $m(x)$ is obtained directly from the signal by means of smoothing. Unlike the backward heat equation in Eq. (6), the PDE employed in our EMD procedure is a *forward* heat equation. As is well known, forward diffusion is numerically more stable than backward diffusion. Niang's fourth-order PDE in Eq. (7) could be viewed as quite similar to our second-order PDE. However, as a fourth-order diffusion PDE, it will generate significantly more error when dealing with noise in image signals. As such, our second-order PDE should capture the local features of images more effectively.

We extend the above PDE-based EMD method to the two-dimensional case by simply adding another spatial variable to the PDE in (11), i.e.,

$$\frac{\partial h}{\partial t} = D(\frac{\partial^2 h}{\partial x^2} + \frac{\partial^2 h}{\partial y^2}), \qquad h(x, y, 0) = S(x, y, 0). \tag{12}$$

The *mean function* of $S(x, y)$ will be defined as $m(x, y) = h(x, y, T)$.

As in the 1D case, one of the primary motivations for this definition is that the time rate of change of $h(x, y, t)$ is zero at spatial inflection points of h. This is the basis of the following PDE-based BEMD algorithm applied to an image function $S(x, y)$:

1. Initialize: Let $n = 0$ and set $h_0(x, y, 0) = S(x, y)$.
2. Find the mean of $h_n(x, y, 0)$: Solve the PDE in (12) for $h_n(x, y, t)$ for $0 \leq t \leq T$. Then define $m_n(x, y) = h_n(x, y, T)$.
3. Extract mean: Define $c_n(x, y) = h_n(x, y, 0) - h_n(x, y, T)$.
4. If $c_n(x, y)$ is not a BIMF, let $h_{n+1}(x, y, 0) = c_n(x, y)$, $n \rightarrow n + 1$ and go to Step 2.

4   Mathematical Interpretation

As mentioned in Fladrin's paper [9], traditional EMD operates as an successive filter. In fact, we claim that traditional EMD operates as an iterative, frequency-overlapping, contrast-sensitive filter bank. This is also the case with our modified EMD and BEMD methods. In each iteration, the mean of the signal is obtained by passing it through a low-pass filter. Subsequent subtraction of the mean from the signal implies that the net procedure is equivalent to a high-pass filter. To illustrate, we consider the following special two-dimensional case,

$$S(x, y) = \sum_{i,j} [A_{ij} \sin(\omega_i x + \omega_j y + \phi_{ij})], \tag{13}$$

where each (i, j) pair represents a single sinusoidal grating basis function. Equation (12) is solved for the first mean function,

$$m_a(x, T) = \sum_{i,j} \frac{1}{\Omega_{ij}^2} [A_{ij} \sin(\omega_i x + \omega_j y + \phi_j)], \qquad \Omega_{ij} = \sqrt{\omega_i^2 + \omega_j^2}. \tag{14}$$

The magnitudes Ω_{ij} are now sorted in increasing order and denoted as Ω_k. We denote the sum of all components with the same Ω_k-value as s_k. After N iterations, our modified EMD algorithm yields the following result for $s_k(x)$,

$$h_{k,N} = (1 - e^{-a\Omega_k^2 T})h_{k,N-1} = (1 - e^{-a\Omega_k^2 T})^N s_k. \tag{15}$$

Now suppose, without loss of generality, that $\Omega_1 < \Omega_2 < \cdots < \Omega_K = \Omega_{\max}$. It is easy to show that for N sufficiently large,

$$h_N = \sum_{k=1}^N (1 - e^{-a\Omega_k^2 T})^N s_k \simeq (1 - e^{-a\Omega_K^2 T})^N s_K \simeq s_K, \tag{16}$$

where the final approximation is valid for T sufficiently large. By choosing the appropriate set of parameters, the IMF extracted after N iterations will be (at least approximately) the highest-frequency component, s_K. Our EMD algorithm, however, does not distinguish the direction of a frequency component (i.e., a particular sine grating) because the diffusion is *radial*. Instead, it will filter a group of frequency components Ω_{ij} that have the same "angular magnitude" Ω_k.

5   Experimental Results

We now show some results obtained by applying our diffusion-based EMD algorithm to some synthetic images [3], and some real images [11], A comparison of execution times between our method and classical BEMD is also presented.

Our current algorithm employs the simple explicit finite difference scheme for solving PDEs. There are two options for boundary conditions (BCs): For an image whose edges are part of the background and of the same amplitude level, we have used Dirichlet BCs. For an image with irregularly-shaped boundaries, we have used Neumann BCs.

Simple Sine Grating Image: In Fig. 1, we display results for a 512×512-pixel synthetic image which consists of a mixture of two sine gratings. It has the form,

$$S(x, y) = \sin(0.1\pi x + 0.1\pi y) + \sin(-0.4\pi x + 0.8\pi y), \tag{17}$$

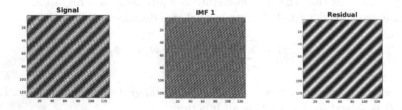

Fig. 1. Simple sine grating separation. **Left:** Sine gratings mixture. **Middle:** First BIMF. **Right:** Residual.

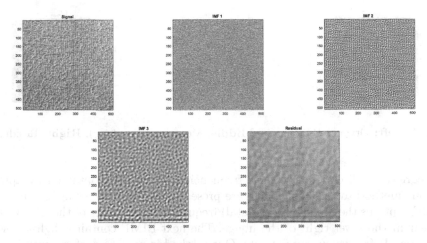

Fig. 2. Example for texture decomposition. **Top row:** Raffia texture image from Brodatz [3], first BIMF and second BIMF. **Bottom row:** Third BIMF and the residual.

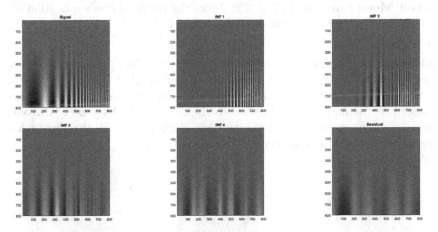

Fig. 3. Contrast sensitive function (CSF) and corresponding BIMFs. **Top row:** CSF, first and second BIMF. **Bottom row:** Third and fourth BIMFs and residual.

The second (higher frequency) component is extracted as the first BIMF and the first component comprises the residual. The two sine gratings have been separated.

Texture Image: In Fig. 2 are shown the BIMF and residual when our diffusion-based BEMD algorithm is applied to a 512 × 512-pixel texture image selected from [3]. Successive BIMFs are comprised of lower frequency components of the texture.

Contrast-Sensitive Image: The *contrast sensitivity function* (CSF) is an image which demonstrates the sensitivity of an observer to sine wave gratings of differing spatial frequencies [17]. Different frequency components are amplified

Fig. 4. Left: Original *Boat* image. **Middle:** Mean image $m_a(x,y)$. **Right:** Residual.

to degrees which depend on their frequencies. The results obtained by applying our method to the CSF image are presented in Fig. 3. Once again, the first BIMF contains the highest (horizontal) frequency components of the CSF which appear in the lower right of the image. The next BIMF contains slightly lower (horizontal) frequency components. Our method is seen to perform well in the separation of different (spatially-dependent) frequency components.

Blurred Mean Surface: In Fig. 4 is shown the result of one application of the mean surface extraction method to the 512 × 512-pixel, 8 bits-per-pixel *Boat* image, using the parameter values $a = 4/\pi^2$ and $T = 50$.

Real Image: In Fig. 5 are shown the results obtained by applying our algorithm to the 256 × 256-pixel, 8 bpp *Lena* image. Recalling that the sifting process of EMD/BEMD extracts IMFs with successively lower frequencies at each iteration, we note that the major contributions to the first two IMFs produced from the *Lena* image come, as expected, from its edges. Higher-order BIMFs contain lower-frequency features which are centered around the edges.

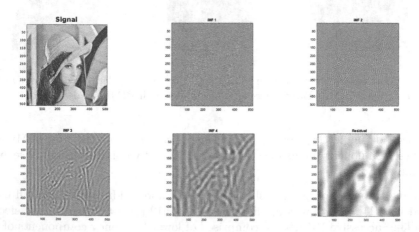

Fig. 5. *Lena* image and its BIMFs. **Top row:** *Lena* image, first and second BIMFs. **Bottom row:** Third and fourth BIMF and the residual.

5.1 Comparison of Computational Costs

Traditional EMD and BEMD methods rely on finding local maxima and minima along with interpolation to find upper and lower envelope. This is computationally expensive, especially in the case of two dimensions, i.e., images. Recall that these procedures are bypassed in our PDE-based approach and replaced by a simple diffusion procedure. As such, our method could potentially require less computational time. To test this conjecture, we have determined the computational times required for a number of iterations of the sifting process for the classical BEMD method as well as our PDE-based BEMD method. (The code based on Flandrin's toolbox [10] was implemented for the classical BEMD method.) The results that obtained by experimenting on the *Lena* image, presented in the first two columns of Table 1, show that our diffusion-based method can decompose a given image into its BIMFs much faster than traditional BEMD.

Table 1. Comparison of computational times for (i) traditional BEMD, (ii) diffusion-based BEMD and (iii) diffusion-based BEMD using Gaussian convolution (GC) in terms of total number of BIMFs computed

	Trad. BEMD	PDE-based EMD	PDE EMD with GC
1. BIMF	4.18 s	1.18 s	0.13 s
2. BIMFs	7.83 s	2.24 s	0.15 s
3. BIMFs	11.16 s	3.38 s	0.27 s
4. BIMFs	13.48 s	4.48 s	0.28 s

An even greater (on the order of tenfold) reduction in computational time is achieved if the finite difference computations involved in the determination of the mean surfaces $m_a(x, y)$ using Eq. (12) are replaced by a single Gaussian convolution, as seen in the final column of Table 1. Technically, the solution of Eqs. (11) or (12) is expressible as Gaussian convolution only in the case that the domain of definition is infinite, i.e., $\mathbb{R}$ or $\mathbb{R}^2$. By using convolution, we are essentially ignoring image boundary effects. In general, the differences between BIMFs obtained by finite differences and convolution are negligible except possibly near the image boundaries.

6 Concluding Remarks

This paper presents a diffusion-based modification of the BEMD algorithm for images. The mean surface of a signal is obtained by evolving the signal with the heat/diffusion equation, therefore avoiding any complicated methods of extracting local maxima and minima and interpolating them. Our approach provides a mathematical interpretation of the EMD algorithm as well as its limitations. The parameters in the diffusion PDE can be adjusted according to the properties of the signal or image being analyzed. Our algorithm is considerably faster than traditional BEMD. Moreover, it is possible to accelerate the algorithm by using Gaussian convolution. A number of examples have shown that our method can extract multiscale features of images effectively.

Acknowledgements. This research was supported in part by the Natural Sciences and Engineering Research Council of Canada in the form of Discovery Grants (RM and ERV). Financial support from the Faculty of Mathematics and the Department of Applied Mathematics, University of Waterloo (HW) is also gratefully acknowledged.

References

1. Bajaj, V., Pachori, R.B.: Classification of seizure and nonseizure EEG signals using empirical mode decomposition. IEEE Trans. Inf. Technol. Biomed. **16**(6), 1135–1142 (2012)
2. Bhuiyan, S.M., Adhami, R.R., Khan, J.F.: A novel approach of fast and adaptive bidimensional empirical mode decomposition. In: IEEE ICASSP 2008, pp. 1313–1316 (2008)
3. Brodatz, P.: Textures: A Photographic Album for Artists and Designers. Dover, New York (1966)
4. Chen, C.Y., Guo, S.M., Chang, W.S., Tsai, J.S.H., Cheng, K.S.: An improved bidimensional empirical mode decomposition: a mean approach for fast decomposition. Signal Process. **98**, 344–358 (2014)
5. Daubechies, I., Lu, J., Wu, H.T.: Synchrosqueezed wavelet transforms: an empirical mode decomposition-like tool. Appl. Comput. Harm. Anal. **30**(2), 243–261 (2011)
6. Diop, E., Boudraa, A., Khenchaf, A., Thibaud, R., Garlan, T.: Multiscale characterization of bathymetric images by empirical mode decomposition. MARID III, Leeds, UK, pp. 1–3 (2008)
7. El Hadji, S.D., Alexandre, R., Boudraa, A.O.: A PDE model for 2D intrinsic mode functions. In: IEEE ICIP 2009, pp. 3961–3964 (2009)
8. El Hadji, S.D., Alexandre, R., Perrier, V.: A PDE-based and interpolation-free framework for modeling the sifting process in a continuous domain. Adv. Comput. Math. **38**(4), 801–835 (2013)
9. Flandrin, P., Gonçalves, P., Rilling, G.: EMD equivalent filter banks, from interpretation to applications. In: Hilbert-Huang Transform and Its Applications, pp. 99–116. World Scientific (2014)
10. EMD Toolbox. http://perso.ens-lyon.fr/patrick.flandrin/emd.html
11. Gonzalez, R., Woods, R.E., Eddins, S.: Image Database (2010). http://www.imageprocessingplace.com
12. Huang, N.E., Shen, Z., Long, S.R., Wu, M.C., Shih, H.H., Zheng, Q., Yen, N.C., Tung, C.C., Liu, H.H.: The empirical mode decomposition and the Hilbert spectrum for nonlinear and non-stationary time series analysis. Proc. R. Soc. Lond. A **454**, 903–995 (1998)
13. Lei, Y., Lin, J., He, Z., Zuo, M.J.: A review on empirical mode decomposition in fault diagnosis of rotating machinery. Mech. Syst. Signal Process. **35**(1), 108–126 (2013)
14. Liu, G., Li, L., Gong, H., Jin, Q., Li, X., Song, R., Chen, Y., Chen, Y., He, C., Huang, Y.: Multisource remote sensing imagery fusion scheme based on bidimensional empirical mode decomposition (BEMD) and its application to the extraction of bamboo forest. Remote Sens. **9**(1), 19 (2016)

15. Niang, O., Thioune, A., El Gueirea, M.C., Deléchelle, E., Lemoine, J.: Partial differential equation-based approach for empirical mode decomposition: application to image analysis. IEEE Trans. Image Process. **21**(9), 3991–4001 (2012)
16. Nunes, J.C., Bouaoune, Y., Delechelle, E., Niang, O., Bunel, P.: Image analysis by bidimensional empirical mode decomposition. Image Vis. Comput. **21**(12), 1019–1026 (2003)
17. Robson, J.: Spatial and temporal contrast-sensitivity functions of the visual system. J. Opt. Soc. Am. **56**(8), 1141–1142 (1966)
18. Trusiak, M., Patorski, K., Wielgus, M.: Adaptive enhancement of optical fringe patterns by selective reconstruction using FABEMD algorithm and Hilbert spiral transform. Opt. Express **20**(21), 23463–23479 (2012)
19. Wang, H.M., Mann, R., Vrscay, E.R.: A novel forward-PDE approach as an alternative to empirical mode decomposition, preprint (2018)
20. Xu, Y., Liu, B., Liu, J., Riemenschneider, S.: Two-dimensional empirical mode decomposition by finite elements. Proc. R. Soc. Lond. A **462**, 3081–3096 (2006)
21. Yeh, M.H.: The complex bidimensional empirical mode decomposition. Signal Process. **92**(2), 523–541 (2012)

Extended Patch Prioritization for Depth Filling Within Constrained Exemplar-Based RGB-D Image Completion

Amir Atapour-Abarghouei[✉] and Toby P. Breckon

Computer Science and Engineering, Durham University, Durham, UK
amir.atapour-abarghouei@durham.ac.uk

Abstract. We address the problem of hole filling in depth images, obtained from either active or stereo sensing, for the purposes of depth image completion in an exemplar-based framework. Most existing exemplar-based inpainting techniques, designed for color image completion, do not perform well on depth information with object boundaries obstructed or surrounded by missing regions. In the proposed method, using both color (RGB) and depth (D) information available from a common-place RGB-D image, we explicitly modify the patch prioritization term utilized for target patch ordering to facilitate improved propagation of complex texture and linear structures within depth completion. Furthermore, the query space in the source region is constrained to increase the efficiency of the approach compared to other exemplar-driven methods. Evaluations demonstrate the efficacy of the proposed method compared to other contemporary completion techniques.

Keywords: Depth filling · Image completion
Exemplar-based inpainting · Depth map · Disparity hole filling

1   Introduction

As three dimensional scene understanding based on scene depth is becoming ever more applicable, missing or invalid depth information has resulted in the need for special case facets of subsequent processing (e.g. semantic understanding, tracking, odometry and alike), and the prevalence of low cost, yet imperfect, depth sensing has seen depth completion emerge as an important research topic.

Despite significant prior work in color image completion [1–3,6,8,11], depth filling is by contrast scantly present within the literature [4,7,9,10,13,30] emerging as a relatively new research area posing significant challenges [12]. Although there have been many attempts to use structure-based or exemplar-based color image completion approaches for depth hole filling [1–3,5], particular factors such as the absence of granular texture, clear object separation and the lack of

© Springer International Publishing AG, part of Springer Nature 2018
A. Campilho et al. (Eds.): ICIAR 2018, LNCS 10882, pp. 306–314, 2018.
https://doi.org/10.1007/978-3-319-93000-8_35

in-scene transferability of varying depth sub-regions all create notable obstacles not present in the corresponding color completion case [29].

In this paper, we propose an improved exemplar-based inpainting approach [1] for depth completion (Fig. 1) that adds additional *"boundary"* and *"texture"* terms to aid in determining the priority of the sample patches used to propagate the structure and texture into the target region (Fig. 2). High computational demands, commonly associated with such approaches, are also reduced by dynamically constraining the query space based on the location of spatially adjacent sample patch selections (Sect. 3). This is demonstrated by providing superior results within a traditional exemplar-based image completion paradigm against other leading contemporary approaches (Fig. 1).

2   Prior Work

Prior work in depth hole filling [7,9,12,14,23,24] is not as comprehensive as color image completion. In the depth filling literature, there have been attempts to fill color and depth via depth-assisted texture synthesis in stereo images [15], a myriad of approaches utilizing filters [13,16], temporal-based methods [17,18], reconstruction-based methods [19,20], and others [7,9,10,21]. We focus on some of the most relevant [4,7,10,21].

In a notable work, [7] improves upon the fast marching method-based inpainting proposed by [3] for depth filling. By assuming that the adjacent pixels with similar color values have a higher probability of having similar depth as well, they introduce an additional *"color"* term into the function to increase the contribution of the pixels with the same color.

By contrast, [21] uses a fusion-based method integrated with a non-local filtering strategy. Their framework follows [22], utilizing a scheme similar to non-local means to make accurate predictions for depth values based on image textures.

Fig. 1. Exemplar results on the KITTI dataset [25]. *RGB* denotes the color image, and *D* original (unfilled) disparity map. Results are compared with [1–3,7,9,10]. Flaws are marked in red. (Color figure online)

Herrera et al. [10] propose an approach similarly guided by the color image based on the assumption that every surface is continuous and smooth within their energy function formulation. This *"smoothness"* term encourages flat depth planes in the completion process whilst ignoring the possibility of visible texture or relief in the filled depth region and hence limiting plausible (reasonable) completion characteristics. Zhang et al. [4] improve [1] by adding a *"level set distance"* term to the priority function. A joint trilateral filter performs smoothing post process.

Overall, although such exemplar-based methods have rarely been used in depth completion, they have the tendency to preserve texture. With increased granularity in modern depth sensing and increasing detail in depth scene rendering (e.g. illumination correction), the consideration of texture detail (relief) within any depth filling process is now paramount. As such, we propose an improved exemplar-based formulation capable of efficient and plausible depth texture completion.

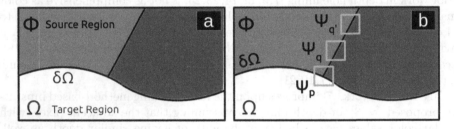

Fig. 2. Target region and target boundary (a), target/candidate patches (b).

3   Proposed Approach

In our approach, improvements are made to the framework of the exemplar-based inpainting [1] to create a more suitable and efficient depth filling approach. In the methodology of [1], the target region and its boundary are identified, a patch is selected to be inpainted and the source region is queried to find the best-matching patch via an appropriate error metric (e.g. sum of squared differences). After the candidate patch is found, all the information is updated and the process starts over. An extremely important factor in generating desirable results is the order in which these patches are selected for filling.

In [1], the priority of each patch is given by:

$$P(p) = C(p)D(p) \tag{1}$$

where $C(p)$, the *"confidence"* term, and $D(p)$, *"data"* term, are determined by:

$$C(p) = \frac{\sum_{q \in \Psi_p \cap (\mathcal{I} - \Omega)} C(q)}{|\Psi_p|} \tag{2}$$

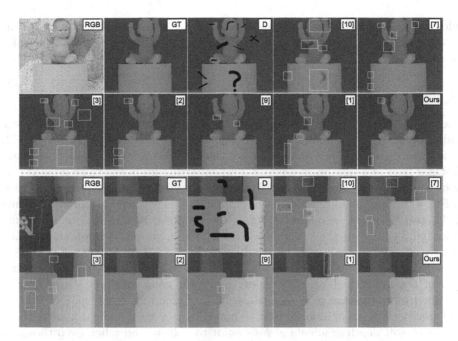

Fig. 3. Exemplar results on the Middlebury dataset [28]. *RGB* denotes the original color images, *GT* the ground truth depth, and *D* the original (unfilled) depth maps. Results are compared with [1–3,7,9,10]. All flaws are marked in red. (Color figure online)

$$D(p) = \frac{|\nabla \mathcal{I}_p^{\perp} \cdot n_p|}{\alpha} \tag{3}$$

where $|\Psi_p|$ is the area of the selected patch Ψ_p, $\mathcal{I}$ is the image, Ω is the target region, α is the normalization factor (255), n_p is a unit vector orthogonal to the target boundary, and $\perp$ is the orthogonal operator (Fig. 2). Before the inpainting begins, the *"confidence"* term is initialized as:

$$C(p) = \begin{cases} 0, & \forall p \in \Omega \\ 1, & \forall p \in \Omega - \mathcal{I} \end{cases} \tag{4}$$

The *"confidence"* term prioritizes patches constrained by more valid depth values (fewer missing neighbors) and the *"data"* term encourages the filling of patches into which isophotes (lines of equal intensity) flow. This framework creates a balance between these two terms for a more plausible inpainting [1]. However, when completing real-world depth images with large holes covering entire objects, boundaries, and isophotes, the information in the accompanying color image (within RGB-D) can be used to create a suitable depth filling approach.

In our approach, the *"confidence"* term is initialized and updated based on the depth image while the *"data"* term is calculated over the corresponding color image region (from RGB-D). To ensure a better flow of dominant linear structures into the target region, a *"boundary"* term is added based on the color image:

$$B(p) = \frac{\sum_{q \in \Psi_p \cap (\mathcal{I}-\Omega)}(|G_{x \geq \tau}(q)| + |G_{y \geq \tau}(q)|)}{|\Psi_p|} \qquad (5)$$

where $G_{x \geq \tau}$ and $G_{y \geq \tau}$ are strong intensity gradients in the color image in the x and y directions respectively, with τ being the gradient threshold (e.g. $\tau = 0.7$). This term essentially prioritizes patches that contain a larger number of pixels that are part of a significant edge or gradient structure in the color image. This ensures a better propagation of object boundaries into the target region. As seen in Fig. 4, the original exemplar-based approach [1] gives equal priority to points A, B, and C (Fig. 4, result of [1]) while the proposed method prioritizes points B and C because of the *"boundary"* term (Fig. 4, proposed approach), which greatly effects the quality of the results.

Additionally, a *"texture"* term is introduced to guarantee a better propagation of texture into the target region. Since the color and depth gradients in certain parts of an image do not always match due to factors such as lighting and perspective, color information is not always a great indicator of texture. However, soft depth gradients always point to texture and relief, even though a depth image might appear smooth to the human eye. The *"texture"* term, which is applied to the depth image, determines which parts of the image surrounding the target boundary contain texture and encourages the process to fill them earlier to propagate texture in the target region:

$$T(p) = \frac{\sum_{q \in \Psi_p \cap (\mathcal{I}-\Omega)}|G_{x < \tau}(q)| + |G_{y < \tau}(q)|}{|\Psi_p|} \qquad (6)$$

where $G_{x < \tau}$ and $G_{y < \tau}$ are slight intensity gradients in the depth image in the x and y directions respectively, with τ being the gradient threshold (e.g. $\tau = 0.3$). Smallest changes in the depth image are identified and taken into account for a better relief texture propagation. As seen in Fig. 5, in which significant edges and linear structures are hard to find, the proposed method correctly prioritizes patches with slight depth changes and functions better than the original approach [1]. After adding the two aforementioned terms, the priority evaluation function is transformed to:

$$P(p) = C(p)D(p)B(p)T(P) \qquad (7)$$

where $C(p)$, $D(p)$, $B(p)$, $T(P)$ are the *"confidence"* term (based on the depth image), *"data"* term (based on the color image), *"boundary"* (based on the color image), and the *"texture"* term (based on the depth image) respectively.

Finally, in most exemplar-based methods [1,4,6,11], the entire source region is queried for candidate patches. However, our analysis shows that most suitable candidates for any patch are located close to where the best-matching candidates

Table 1. Comparing the RMSE (root-mean-square error), PBMP (percentage of bad matching pixels), and mean run-time of the methods over the Middlebury dataset [28].

Method	Plastic (1270 × 1110) [28]			Baby (1240 × 1110) [28]			Bowling (1252 × 1110) [28]		
	RMSE	PBMP	Run-time (s)	RMSE	PBMP	Run-time (s)	RMSE	PBMP	Run-time (s)
GIF [7]	0.7947	0.0331	3.10800	0.6008	0.0095	2.58000	0.9436	0.0412	4.87500
SSI [10]	1.7573	0.0102	42.3600	2.9638	0.0180	41.2000	6.4936	0.0455	71.1200
FMM [3]	0.9580	0.0435	0.9390	0.83490	0.0120	0.79400	1.2422	0.054	1.1190
FEI [2]	**0.6952**	**0.0032**	1641.33	**0.6755**	**0.0024**	995.250	**0.4857**	**0.0035**	1937.47
FBF [9]	0.8643	**0.0023**	>20000	**0.6238**	0.0081	>20000	**0.5918**	0.0072	>20000
EBI [1]	**0.4081**	0.0066	2145.71	0.9053	**0.0025**	1196.49	0.8733	**0.0045**	2921.15
Ours	**0.3843**	**0.0051**	1538.16	**0.6688**	**0.0021**	879.730	**0.7021**	**0.0037**	1606.75

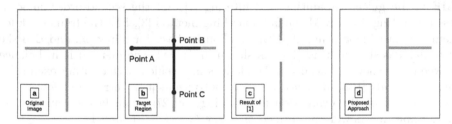

Fig. 4. A demonstration of the effect of the *"boundary"* term. (Color figure online)

were found for adjacent patches in previous patch filling iterations. As a result, a dynamic search perimeter is created when sampling candidates for a patch with previously filled neighbors (Fig. 6). The maximum and minimum of x and y indices of the selected candidates for the previously-filled adjacent patches are used to determine the perimeter. Tests run over 20 different color and depth image pairs indicate that in 91.2% of queries, the best matching patch was found inside perimeter. Although this can negatively effect the quality of the results for the remaining 8.8% of patches, the efficiency is improved by an average of 31% (with negligible standard deviation), which is significant.

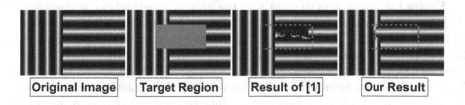

Fig. 5. A demonstration of the effect of the *"texture"* term.

4   Experimental Results

Hole filling is fraught with constant compromises between efficiency and accuracy. The proposed approach is an example of this, as it outperforms many of its predecessors qualitatively and quantitatively [1,3,7,10] while being faster than others [1,2,9]. Results were evaluated using a number of images, but in the interest of space, only a few are presented here. We utilize the Middlebury dataset [28] to provide qualitative and quantitative evaluation. Figure 3 demonstrates that the proposed method generates plausible results without significant invalid outliers, blurring, jagging or other artefacts compared to other approaches [1–3,7,9,10]. All flaws and artefacts are marked in Fig. 3. Table 1 provides quantitative evaluation of the proposed approach against the same comparator set (GIF is the guided inpainting and filtering [7], SSI the second-order smoothness inpainting [10], FMM the fast marching method [3], FEI the framework for exemplar based inpainting [2], FBF the Fourier basis for filling [9], and EBI the exemplar-based inpainting [1]). As shown in Table 1, the method is in balance between efficiency and accuracy. While it is more efficient than other exemplar-based methods [1,2], it has a smaller root-mean-square error and fewer bad pixels (based on the evaluation methodology of [27]) than faster comparators [3,7]. Experiments were performed on a 2.30 GHz CPU (Table 1).

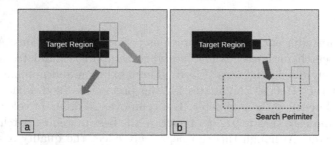

Fig. 6. Constraining the query space to improve efficiency. (Color figure online)

Figure 1 demonstrates the results of the proposed method in comparison with [1–3,7,9,10] when applied to examples from the KITTI dataset [25] (resolution, 1242×375). Depth is calculated using [26] with significant disparity speckles filtered out. The proposed method results in sharp images with fewer additional artefacts (Fig. 1). The closest performing approach, the variational framework for exemplar-based approach of [2], shows comparable quantitative performance (RMSE/PBMP, Table 1) in some aspects but our approach offers a mean computational saving of 15.2% over [2]. The faster approaches [3,7,10] have significantly worse completion performance (Table 1, Figs. 1 and 3) than our approach. We have created a video displaying the results of the work. We invite you to view the video, which can be found here: https://vimeo.com/251792601.

5   Conclusions

In this paper, the problem of depth completion is addressed in an exemplar-based framework with a focus on a balance between efficiency and attention to surface (relief) detail accuracy. While exemplar-based methods, are mostly used for color images, their ability to preserve texture in the target region makes them suitable for depth filling when texture is of importance. Here, the priority term that determines the order of patch sampling has been modified to allow for a better propagation of strong linear structures and texture into the target region. Moreover, by constraining the query space, the method performs more efficiently than other exemplar-based approaches. Our evaluation demonstrates that while the efficiency of the proposed method is better than other exemplar-based frameworks, the plausibility and statistical relevance of the depth filled results compete against the accuracy of contemporary filling approaches in the field.

References

1. Criminisi, A., Pérez, P., Toyama, K.: Region filling and object removal by exemplar-based image inpainting. IEEE Trans. Image Process. **13**(9), 1200–1212 (2004)
2. Arias, P., Facciolo, G., Caselles, V., Sapiro, G.: A variational framework for exemplar-based image inpainting. Int. J. Comput. Vis. **93**(3), 319–347 (2011)
3. Telea, A.: An image inpainting technique based on the fast marching method. Graph. Tools **9**(1), 23–24 (2004)
4. Zhang, L., Shen, P., Zhang, S., Song, J., Zhu, G.: Depth enhancement with improved exemplar-based inpainting and joint trilateral guided filtering. In: International Conference on Image Processing, pp. 4102–4106 (2016)
5. Hervieu, A., Papadakis, N., Bugeau, A., Gargallo, P., Caselles, V.: Stereoscopic image inpainting: distinct depth maps and images inpainting. In: International Conference on Pattern Recognition, pp. 4101–4104 (2010)
6. Cheng, W., Hsieh, C., Lin, S., Wang, C., Wu, J.: Robust algorithm for exemplar-based image inpainting. In: International Conference on Computer Graphics, Imaging and Visualization, pp. 64–69 (2005)
7. Liu, J., Gong, X., Liu, J.: Guided inpainting and filtering for kinect depth maps. In: International Conference on Pattern Recognition, pp. 2055–2058 (2012)
8. Goyal, P., Diwakar, S., et al.: Fast and enhanced algorithm for exemplar-based image inpainting. In: Symposium on Image and Video Technology, pp. 325–330 (2010)
9. Atapour-Abarghouei, A., de La Garanderie, G.P., Breckon, T.P.: Back to Butterworth - a Fourier basis for 3D surface relief hole filling within RGB-D Imagery. In: International Conference on Pattern Recognition, pp. 2813–2818 (2016)
10. Herrera, D., Kannala, J., Heikkilä, J.: Depth map inpainting under a second-order smoothness prior. In: Scandinavian Conference on Image Analysis, pp. 555–566 (2013)
11. Kumar, V., Mukhopadhyay, J., Kumar Das Mandal, S.: Modified exemplar-based image inpainting via primal-dual optimization. In: Kryszkiewicz, M., Bandyopadhyay, S., Rybinski, H., Pal, S.K. (eds.) PReMI 2015. LNCS, vol. 9124, pp. 116–125. Springer, Cham (2015). https://doi.org/10.1007/978-3-319-19941-2_12

12. Breckon, T.P., Fisher, R.B.: Amodal volume completion: 3D visual completion. Comput. Vis. Image Underst. **99**(3), 499–526 (2005)
13. Camplani, M., Salgado, L.: Efficient spatio-temporal hole filling strategy for kinect depth maps. In: IS&T/SPIE Electronic Imaging, p. 82900E (2012)
14. Breckon, T.P., Fisher, R.B.: A hierarchical extension to 3D non-parametric surface relief completion. Pattern Recognit. **45**, 172–185 (2012)
15. Wang, L., Jin, H., Yang, R., Gong, M.: Stereoscopic inpainting: joint color and depth completion from stereo images. In: International Conference on Computer Vision and Pattern Recognition, pp. 1–8 (2008)
16. Camplani, M., Salgado, L.: Adaptive Spatio-Temporal Filter for Low-Cost Camera Depth Maps. In: International Conference on Emerging Signal Processing Applications, pp. 33–36 (2012)
17. Matyunin, S., Vatolin, D., Berdnikov, Y., Smirnov, M.: Temporal filtering for depth maps generated by kinect depth camera. In: 3DTV Conference, pp. 1–4 (2011)
18. Berdnikov, Y., Vatolin, D.: Real-time depth map occlusion filling and scene background restoration for projected-pattern based depth cameras. In: Graphic Conference IETP (2011)
19. Chen, C., Cai, J., Zheng, J., Cham, T., Shi, G.: Kinect depth recovery using a color-guided, region-adaptive, and depth-selective framework. ACM Trans. Intell. Syst. Technol. **6**(2), 12 (2015)
20. Wang, Z., Hu, J., Wang, S., Lu, T.: Trilateral constrained sparse representation for kinect depth hole filling. Pattern Recognit. Lett. **65**, 95–102 (2015)
21. Qi, F., Han, J., Wang, P., Shi, G., Li, F.: Structure guided fusion for depth map inpainting. Pattern Recognit. Lett. **34**(1), 70–76 (2013)
22. Bugeau, A., Bertalmío, M., Caselles, V., Sapiro, G.: A comprehensive framework for image inpainting. IEEE Trans. Image Process. **19**(10), 2634–2645 (2010)
23. Bevilacqua, M., Aujol, J., Brédif, M., Bugeau, A.: Visibility estimation and joint inpainting of lidar depth maps. In: International Conference on Image Processing, pp. 3503–3507 (2016)
24. Zuo, Y., Wu, Q., An, P., Zhang, J.: Explicit measurement on depth color inconsistency for depth completion. In: International Conference on Image Processing, pp. 4037–4041 (2016)
25. Geiger A., Lenz, P., Stiller, C., Urtasun, R.: Vision meets robotics: the KITTI dataset. In: Robotics Research (2013)
26. Yamaguchi, K., McAllester, D., Urtasun, R.: Efficient joint segmentation, occlusion labeling, stereo and flow estimation. In: Fleet, D., Pajdla, T., Schiele, B., Tuytelaars, T. (eds.) ECCV 2014. LNCS, vol. 8693, pp. 756–771. Springer, Cham (2014). https://doi.org/10.1007/978-3-319-10602-1_49
27. Scharstein, D., Szeliski, R.: A taxonomy and evaluation of dense two-frame stereo correspondence algorithms. Int. J. Comput. Vis. **47**, 7–42 (2002)
28. Hirschmuller, H., Scharstein, D.: Evaluation of cost functions for stereo matching. In: Conference on Computer Vision and Pattern Recognition, pp. 1–8 (2007)
29. Atapour-Abarghouei, A., Breckon, T.P.: A comparative review of plausible hole filling strategies in the context of scene depth image completion. J. Comput. Graph. **72**, 39–58 (2018)
30. Atapour-Abarghouei, A., Breckon, T.P.: DepthComp: real-time depth image completion based on prior semantic scene segmentation. In: British Machine Vision Conference, pp. 208.1–208.13 (2017)

Real-Time Low-Cost Omni-Directional Stereo Vision via Bi-polar Spherical Cameras

Kaiwen Lin[1] and Toby P. Breckon[1,2(✉)]

[1] Department of Engineering, Durham University, Durham, UK
[2] Department of Computer Science, Durham University, Durham, UK
toby.breckon@durham.ac.uk

Abstract. With the rise of consumer-grade spherical cameras, offering full omni-directional 360° image capture, the potential for low-cost omni-directional stereo vision is ever present. Whilst this potentially offers novel low-cost omni-directional depth sensing without the need for active range sensing, it presents a number of challenges associated with the realization of contemporary dense stereo matching across this spherical imaging format. In this work, we outline an approach for omni-directional dense stereo vision, based on imagery from two consumer-grade spherical cameras mounted in a bi-polar configuration, offering 360° depth recovery at 5.5 fps. Specifically we outline the required aspects of inter-camera calibration and equirectangular image correction before detailing the required angular disparity correction that is unique to this stereo sensing formulation. Furthermore we illustrate the disparity and synchronization error achievable with the use of such consumer-grade spherical camera units, in addition to the quality of disparity (depth) available, within the context of on-road sensing for future vehicle autonomy.

1 Introduction

Recent advances in low-cost camera technology have seen the rise of widely-available consumer-grade spherical cameras, offering full omni-directional spherical panoramic video via dual-lens 180° × 180° image capture at the cost of a few hundred dollars (Ricoh Theta S; Samsung Gear 360 – 2017). The ready availability of such devices naturally facilitates the consideration of 360° depth recovery by using two within a classical stereo vision formulation. Whilst such an approach would potentially offer all-round depth recovery for a range of generalized video surveillance or vehicle autonomy sensing scenarios, a number of notable additional constraints exist for spherical-based stereo. These constraints prevent straightforward consideration of using a pair of such cameras as simply the left and right corresponding stereo views. As identified in the recent work of [10], any placement of the cameras will result in varying inter-occular distance (i.e. stereo baseline) dependent on the viewing angle as it diverges from the camera centre (illustrated by the face positions within Fig. 1A). In addition the 360° field-of-view means that

© Springer International Publishing AG, part of Springer Nature 2018
A. Campilho et al. (Eds.): ICIAR 2018, LNCS 10882, pp. 315–325, 2018.
https://doi.org/10.1007/978-3-319-93000-8_36

any side-by-side arrangement of the cameras, as per the methodology of [9,10], will indeed cause self-occlusion of a part of the field-of-view of one camera by the other (and vice-versa, Fig. 1A). Furthermore, we must address the issues of intrinsic and extrinsic camera calibration from a spherical format image in addition to that of photometric variation as we would in any stereo camera formulation. For a 360° viewpoint in an outdoor scene, photometric variation due to varying natural illumination can be considered a more significant issue than with narrow field-of-view forward facing stereo. In addition, the use of low-cost consumer-grade hardware also brings with it issues around absolute frame synchronization between the spherical stereo image pair [10].

Only a few researchers have fully considered the use of modern spherical camera hardware [8–10]. Traditional omni-directional stereo systems have involved the use of a single camera with one or more curved mirrors (e.g. Caron et al. [3]). The early seminal work of Li et al. [8] considered the use a classical equirectangular (longitude-latitude) projection model for spherical stereo vision, which was later extended to consumer-grade hardware by [9].

To consider a spherical stereo vision as a low-cost maximal depth coverage option, the fundamentals of spherical camera models must be considered. Geyer et al. [4], provide a basic practical projection model for panoramic images whilst Barreto et al. [1] described a projection model for catadioptric images [1]. These varying projection models were later unified into the spherical projection model of Mei et al. [11] that encapsulates omni-directional images by extending the work of [8] with an additional parameter, ξ, to compensate for the discrepancy between the real and spherical camera centre points during calibration.

Notably the prior work of [9] on consumer-grade hardware uses the earlier camera model of Li et al. [8], potentially explaining the poor and unstructured results obtained within that study ("look a little messy" [9]). By contrast, the recent work of [10] relies on the proprietary equirectangular projection model of the spherical camera in use (Ricoh Theta S [14]) to produce high-quality omni-directional stereo image stills using a filling arrangement to overcome the self-occlusion of their side-by-side stereo camera arrangement.

In this work, our contributions address a number of issues relating to the challenges identified within these earlier approaches [9,10]. Firstly, we adopt the camera model proposed by [11], overcoming the quality issues identified in [9] and avoiding reliance on the proprietary projection model of [10], thus illustrating the true potential of consumer-grade spherical stereo in this space. Secondly, we develop a novel bi-polar arrangement addressing the stereo self-occlusion issue identified in [10] by placing one camera directly below the other (essentially with each camera thus occupying the vertical blind-spot of the other - Fig. 1B). In addition, by adopting the calibration approach of [11], we propose a conventional target-based calibration approach akin to the seminal work of [15] but differing from natural feature point driven approach of [10]. Practically we illustrate the inter-camera synchronization achievable on unmodified consumer-grade hardware of this genre and extend the omni-directional still image stereo results of [10] to 5.5 fps (frames per second) video.

2   Approach

Our approach comprises of three main elements:- construction of a bi-polar spherical stereo rig (Sect. 2.1), calibration via an effective spherical camera model (Sect. 2.2) and final calculation of stereo disparity with additional angular correction to account for the varying stereo baseline introduced by the spherical lens configuration (Sect. 2.3).

2.1   Bi-polar Camera Configuration

As identified in the recent work of [10], the use of a conventional side-by-side stereo camera configuration with left (L) and right (R) cameras, as depicted in Fig. 1A, gives rise to the problem of inter-camera occlusion when considered for use with spherical stereo cameras (i.e. self-occlusion within the stereo rig itself). As shown in Fig. 1A any planar placement of two cameras with a 360° horizontal field-of-view in a conventional left (L) and right (R) stereo configuration will result in one camera partially occluding the field-of-view of the other. In Fig. 1A camera R occludes the field-of-view of camera L in the direction of the rightmost black arrow and conversely camera L occludes the field-of-view of camera R in the direction of the leftmost black arrow.

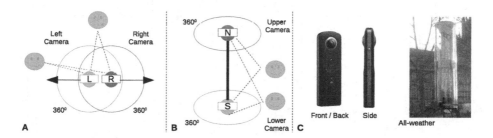

Fig. 1. Spherical stereo camera configurations—side-by-side (A), bi-polar (B) and physical construction (C).

Whilst prior work [10] has asserted this limitation is fundamental to any such configuration of omni-directional stereo cameras, by contrast we instead observe that whilst such 360° stereo coverage is highly desirable in the horizontal plane for most applications (i.e. surrounding a given sensor placement from all directions) it is significantly less attractive in the vertical plane (i.e. top to bottom). With this in mind, we can formulate an alternative bi-polar camera configuration (Fig. 1B) such that our stereo spherical cameras are now configured in a vertical offset rather than the traditional side-by-side horizontal configuration. As shown in Fig. 1B, this configuration separates the 360° horizontal field-of-view of the upper and lower (North/South bi-polar) cameras (denoted now as $\{N, S\}$) such that the opposing camera now only exists in the physical/practical bind-spot of the other. Whilst an omni-directional (360°) camera has no such blind-spot in theory, we observe that such a camera indeed has a non-zero distance between each of the 180° × 180° lenses and has physical mounting point at each pole (Fig. 1C). Furthermore, for deployment in any terrestrial environment the polar directions of the field-of-view (i.e. straight upwards/straight downwards) will be of limited practical value as ground or sky regions. Overall, this gives us a convenient methodology for bi-polar camera placement that forms a top to bottom vertical offset for the recovery of stereo depth as opposed to the conventional left-right horizontal configuration. Our vertical configuration is readily viable using a simple geometric transform of established horizontal stereo calibration and disparity estimation approaches [6].

2.2 Spherical Camera Model

To facilitate ready comparison between conventional and omni-directional stereo camera models, conventional stereo theory is initially presented to introduce terminology and notation. Subsequently, the camera model and stereo concepts within an omni-directional setup including spherical projection, epipolar geometry and final equirectangular projection are presented.

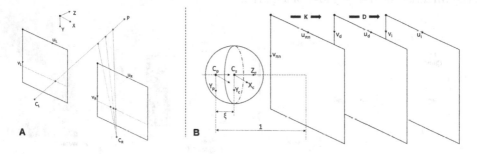

Fig. 2. Stereo camera models - conventional stereo (A) and spherical camera (B).

Conventional stereo uses two cameras, $\{L, R\}$, obeying the pin-hole camera model [6] (Fig. 2A). A pin-hole camera model projects a given scene onto a planar surface, known as the image plane (denoted by axes $U_i \leftrightarrow V_i\, i \in \{L, R\}$ in Fig. 2A). Figure 2A shows a 3D point, $P = \{X, Y, Z\}$, being projected onto the left image plane, $U_L \leftrightarrow V_L$, as a 2D point, $p_L = \{x, y\}$. Every such projection from the scene to the image plane, passes through the optical centre of a camera obeying the pin-hole camera model, denoted as C_L and C_R for the left and right camera respectively (Fig. 2A).

Within a stereo formulation, for every given point within the left image plane, the corresponding point on the right image plane needs to be identified such that triangulation can facilitate depth recovery. To reduce the search space of this stereo correspondence problem, epipolar geometry is used to limit the correspondence space of p_L to a horizontal line on the right image plane, $U_R \leftrightarrow V_R$ [6].

Figure 2 illustrates all of the corresponding points on $U_R \leftrightarrow V_R$ that may correspond to p_L. This epipolar constraint is formulated as the plane formed by the points P, C_L and C_R (denoted as epipolar planes) such that corresponding points lie on the associated horizontal lines formed on each of the left and right image planes (denoted as epipolar lines). This is expressed algebraically as:

$$p_L{}^T F p_R = 0 \tag{1}$$

where p_L and p_R are the corresponding left and right image plane projections respectively of the same scene point, P, viewed from the two different camera positions (Fig. 2A) and F is the fundamental matrix encompassing both the intrinsic (camera projection matrix, K) and extrinsic (essential matrix, E) [6] camera parameters recovered via calibration with an *a priori* target [15].

By contrast we use a spherical camera model to represent our omni-directional cameras (Fig. 2B) such that a scene point, P, is first projected to a unit sphere by:

$$P_s = \frac{P}{\|P\|} \tag{2}$$

Adoption of a spherical camera model effects our recovery of the intrinsic camera parameters, K. To recover the intrinsic parameters in this case, following the work on spherical camera models of Mei et al. [11], an additional parameter ξ is used to quantify the difference between the real camera and spherical camera centres (denoted as C_s and C_p within Fig. 2B). Given a point, $P_s = \{X, Y, Z\}$, in the spherical coordinate system of C_s, this would now be $P_s = \{X, Y, Z + \xi\}$ in the camera coordinate system of C_p. Following the outline of [11], this is then projected to the normalized plane, Π_n, with coordinates $(\frac{X}{Z+\xi}, \frac{Y}{Z+\xi}, 1)$ from which the camera projection matrix K projects from Π_n to the image plane Π_d. K is defined as follows:

$$K = \begin{bmatrix} f_u\eta & f_u\eta\alpha & u_0 \\ 0 & f_v\eta & v_0 \\ 0 & 0 & 1 \end{bmatrix} \tag{3}$$

such that f_u and f_v are the horizontal and vertical focal lengths in pixels, η is a function of lens geometry [11], α is a measure of skewness and (u_0, v_0) is the principal point of the camera image. $f_u\eta$ can be considered as an effective focal length for the u-axis, and similarly $f_v\eta$ in the orthogonal v-axis direction. A final undistortion, D, addresses remaining radial and tangential lens distortions following the outline of [11] to arrive at a rectified spherical image.

However, all modern dense stereo matching approaches operate on rectified pin-hole camera model images whereby the epipolar lines are reduced to the horizontal pixel rows of the left and right images within a conventional stereo setup [12]. By contrast, a rectified spherical camera image has a circular region of interest around the image centre (Fig. 3, left) such that pixel rows represent projections of arbitrary unknown arcs through the scene.

To facilitate the use of a conventional stereo matching approach in an unadapted form, leveraging the notable optimizations are that often present for this horizontal matching format, a final longitude-latitude (equirectangular) image projection is used to ensure that the resulting pixel rows of the rectified image are suitable for horizontal stereo correspondence. Such a projection is defined as follows:

$$u = f_s\theta$$
$$v = f_s\phi \tag{4}$$

where θ is longitude, from the X_s axis rotating clockwise around the Y_s axis, ϕ is latitude from the negative Y_s axis rotating clockwise around the X_s axis; both θ and ϕ are in radians. f_s is a scale factor converting a given angle into a linear pixel distance (effectively the radius of the spherical model that can be used to scale the image as required).

Returning to our discussion of epipolar geometry for completeness, our point $P_s = \{X, Y, Z + \xi\}$ would now be visible from both spherical cameras ($\{N, S\}$ from Fig. 1B) such that there must exist a vector from P to the principal point of the top camera (u_N, v_N) and similarly to that of the bottom camera (u_S, v_S) intersecting the spherical image plane at points (X_N, Y_N, Z_N) and (X_S, Y_S, Z_S) respectively. These two vectors along with the baseline separation, b_s, between the two cameras form an epipolar plane (see Fig. 2B) with the corresponding epipolar lines forming circles around the principal point as shown in Fig. 3 (left). Our final longitude-latitude projection (Eq. 4) projects these epipolar circles to vertical lines parallel to the v-axis for our case of vertical offset stereo (Fig. 2B).

2.3   Stereo Disparity

Following the comparative studies of [5,12], and the specific comparative findings of [10] with regard to omni-directional stereo vision, we select the seminal Semi-Global Block Matching (SGBM) dense stereo disparity estimation approach of [7] as the basis for our final stereo depth recovery. We use a post-confidence margin of 8% (i.e. selected matching cost at least 8% lower than next best matching cost) and additional speckle filter post-processing. SGBM is used with the simpler Birchfield-Tomasi sub-pixel metric [2] to overcome inter-camera photometric variation and improve overall real-time performance.

Conventionally, for a pair of pin-hole model cameras set up in a stereo configuration, depth Z can be calculated from this disparity as:

$$Z = f\frac{b}{d} \tag{5}$$

where b is the baseline (distance) between the two cameras, f is the focal length in pixels and d is the stereo disparity, $d = u_L - u_R$, where u_L and u_R are corresponding scene pixel positions in the left and right images. For spherical cameras, with reference to the equirectangular projection defined in Eq. 4, disparity is defined as:

$$d = v_N - v_S = f_s(\phi_N - \phi_S) \tag{6}$$

where v_N and v_S are the pixel coordinates in the v-axis direction for our vertical offset bipolar camera configuration. The disparity hence represents a change in

Table 1. Proof—spherical depth calculation (Eq. 7).

	Statement	Reasoning
1	$\angle C_N P C_S = \phi_N - \phi_S$	An exterior angle is the sum of the opposite interior angles (rearranged).
2	$\overline{C_N A} \perp \overline{C_S P}$	Given:
3	$\| \overline{C_N A} \| = \rho_N \sin(\phi_N - \phi_S)$	$\triangle C_N AP$ is a right angle triangle
4	$\| \overline{C_N A} \| = b_s \sin(\phi_S)$	$\triangle C_N AC_S$ is a right angle triangle
5	$\rho_N \sin(\phi_N - \phi_S) = b_S \sin(\phi_S)$	Equating statements 3 and 4
6	$\rho_N \sin\left(\dfrac{v_N}{f_s} - \dfrac{v_S}{f_s}\right)$ $= b_s \sin\left(\dfrac{v_S}{f_s}\right)$	Substituting $v = f_s\phi$ from longitude-latitude projection (Eqn. 4)
7	$\rho_N \sin\left(\dfrac{d}{f_s}\right) = b_s \sin\left(\dfrac{v_S}{f_s}\right)$	Substituting the definition of disparity (Eqn. 6)
8	$\rho_N = b_s \dfrac{\sin(v_S/f_s)}{\sin(d/f_s)}$	By re-arrangement of statement 7

arc length as opposed to the conventional linear distance. Therefore we express depth as a distance to the upper principal point (top-most, camera N) using:

$$\rho_N = b_s \frac{\sin(v_N/f_s)}{\sin(d/f_s)} \tag{7}$$

where ρ_N is the distance of a point in 3D space from the upper camera principal point and b_s is the baseline between the spherical cameras. A proof is presented in Table 1 where the left inset sub-figure shows an epipolar plane of a spherical stereo setup. The green lines represent the epipolar lines and the orange lines represent the projected rays. To prove Eq. (7), a line segment $\overline{C_N A}$ has been drawn such that it is perpendicular ($\perp$) to $\overline{C_S P}$. The following definitions shall also be used: $b_s = \overline{C_N C_S}$, $\rho_N = \overline{C_N P}$, with notation such that $\angle ijk$ represents the interior angle at point j between line segments $\overline{ij}$ and $\overline{jk}$ and $\triangle ijk$ to mean the triangle defined by vertices $\{i, j, k\}$ for $i, j, k \in \{C_N, C_S, P\}$. Hence we have retrieved the polar coordinates $\{\theta_N, \phi_N, \rho_N\}$ of our 3D point with respect to the north camera.

Equation 7, ρ_N, proven via Table 1, can be converted back into Cartesian depth, Z, as follows:

$$Z = \rho_N \sin(\phi_N) \cos(\theta_N) = \rho_N \sin\left(\frac{v_N}{f_s}\right) \cos\left(\frac{u_N}{f_s}\right) \tag{8}$$

and similarly for polar to Cartesian conversion for X and Y within $P = \{X, Y, Z\}$. This formulation (Eqs. 6–8) provides angular disparity correction for our spherical camera based stereo formulation addressing the issue of inter-occular baseline variation (shown in Fig. 1A, B).

3   Evaluation

Our stereo rig consisted of two Ricoh Theta S cameras (2017; firmware: 01.82 [14]) in a bipolar configuration (Fig. 1C) operated in live streaming mode via a USB 3.0 hub with an additional 5 V DC power injector. This delivers 1280 × 720 video at 15 fps (6 Mbps transfer) per camera which is then split into dual fish-eye images (~190° × ~190°) forming four images of resolution 640 × 640, $\{N_{front}, N_{back}, S_{front}, S_{back}\}$ as illustrated in Fig. 4.

All processing is performed on an Intel Core i7-5700HQ CPU (2.70 GHz) running Ubuntu Linux 16.04, with mild image cropping to remove the polar image regions (Fig. 4 right) and explicit parallelization of the independent front/back stereo pairs, $\{N_{front}, S_{front}\}$ and $\{N_{back}, S_{back}\}$ for SGBM based disparity calculation.

Fig. 3. Example results from original spherical camera image, longitude-latitude correction and final disparity and depth (3D point cloud) output

Calibration is performed to recover the intrinsic and extrinsic camera parameter matrices, F, K, D and baseline, b_s, using an omnidirectional specific software calibration toolbox [13], that builds on the seminal target based calibration work of [15] to facilitate recovery of the spherical camera model of [11] including ξ. A 36 × 36 mm, 9 × 6 square chessboard is used for calibration with mild relaxation of the Levenberg-Marquardt optimization termination criteria (~100 iterations) resulting in a root mean square (rms) pixel re-projection error of ~0.4 pixels [15]. Relative camera rotation is minimal over a baseline of $b_s = $ ~246 mm. Subsequent longitude-latitude projection (Sect. 2.2) is carried out, after the K

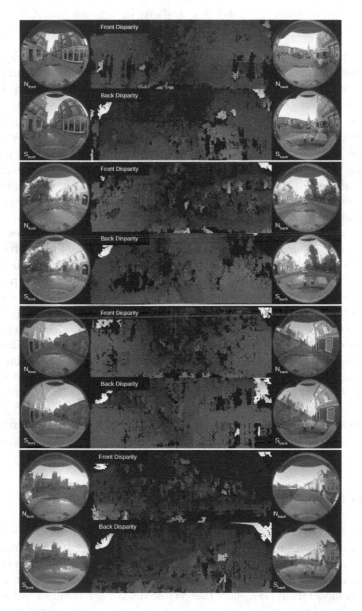

Fig. 4. Example results from vehicle mounted traverse of Durham City, UK.

and D transforms of Fig. 2B, via a specific secondary projection matrix defined as follows:

$$K' = \begin{bmatrix} \frac{|u|}{\theta_u} & 0 & 0 \\ 0 & \frac{|v|}{\phi_v} & 0 \\ 0 & 0 & 1 \end{bmatrix}, \tag{9}$$

where $|u|$ and $|v|$ are the image width and height respectively, θ_u and ϕ_v are the horizontal and vertical field-of-view in radians. For the cameras in use, $\theta_u = \phi_v = \frac{19}{18}\pi$ rad; $|u| = |v| = 640$ pixels resulting in $f_s \approx 13$ px/rad in Eq. 4 onward.

Synchronization between the camera pair is measured, by imaging metronome motion of known period, to have a mean inter-image capture delay of $t_{avg} = 860\,\mu s$ (standard deviation $\sigma = 122\,\mu s$). Assuming a Gaussian distribution for the variation of this inter-camera synchronization delay gives a maximal inter-image synchronization delay, $t_{avg} + 3\sigma = 1.23$ ms, which is negligible at only 1.8% of the maximum achievable frame rate (frames per second, fps) of the camera in use. Any reduced frame rate due to stereo processing only makes this synchronization error less significant.

Results are shown in Fig. 3 where we see the spherical images $\{N_{front}, S_{front}\}$ from the stereo rig mounted on top of a vehicle (Fig. 3 left) and the resulting longitude-latitude image projection for this pair (Fig. 3 middle) with the resulting greyscale disparity image (Fig. 3 right, upper) and 3D point cloud (depth) projection of the resulting scene (Fig. 3 right, lower). Within the disparity of Fig. 3, the structure of the building is well defined despite illumination variations. Feature-less regions and occlusion result in lesser depth coverage, as does the use of a high post-confidence margin (Sect. 2.3). Each stereo frame set took on average 125.2 ms to compute with frame rate varying between 5.5–9 fps under test. SGBM contributed 80–90% of the total computation time per frame. A stable frame rate of 5.5 fps is found over the additional sequence examples presented in Fig. 4 (video sequence available from https://youtu.be/XBjgPqwNhxo). Although flickering noise is present, this can be attributed the large-scale automatic illumination adjustment within the consumer-grade hardware in use (ISO sensitivity: 100–1600 [14]).

4   Conclusion

Overall we successfully demonstrate the recovery of spherical omni-directional stereo disparity using low-cost consumer-grade spherical camera hardware. We propose a novel bi-polar camera configuration addressing the issue of camera inter-occlusion within this domain identified by [10] and, by adopting an effective camera model from [11], show that viable disparity recovery is achievable on this genre of hardware using conventional dense stereo disparity estimation techniques. Furthermore, we outline the full end-to-end spherical camera projection model required without reliance on the proprietary equirectangular correction of prior work [10]. We investigate and report the camera synchronization and real-time spherical stereo processing frame rates that are available using contemporary hardware to achieve 360° stereo depth recovery at 5.5 fps illustrated for an on-vehicle sensing scenario.

References

1. Barreto, J.P., Araujo, H.: Issues on the geometry of central catadioptric image formation. In: Conference on Computer Vision and Pattern Recognition, vol. 2, pp. 422–427 (2001)
2. Birchfield, S., Tomasi, C.: A pixel dissimilarity measure that is insensitive to image sampling. IEEE Trans. Patt. Anal. Mach. Intell. **20**(4), 401–406 (1998)
3. Caron, G., Mouaddib, E.M., Marchand, E.: 3D model based tracking for omnidirectional vision: a new spherical approach. Robot. Auton. Syst. **60**(8), 1056–1068 (2012)
4. Geyer, C., Daniilidis, K.: A unifying theory for central panoramic systems and practical implications. In: Vernon, D. (ed.) ECCV 2000. LNCS, vol. 1843, pp. 445–461. Springer, Heidelberg (2000). https://doi.org/10.1007/3-540-45053-X_29
5. Hamilton, O.K., Breckon, T.P., Bai, X., Kamata, S.: A foreground object based quantitative assessment of dense stereo approaches for use in automotive environments. In: International Conference on Image Processing, pp. 418–422. IEEE (2013)
6. Hartley, R., Zisserman, A.: Multiple View Geometry in Computer Vision, 2nd edn. Cambridge University Press, Cambridge (2004)
7. Hirschmüller, H.: Stereo processing by semiglobal matching and mutual information. IEEE Trans. Pattern Anal. Mach. Intell. **30**(2), 328–341 (2008)
8. Li, S.: Binocular spherical stereo. IEEE Trans. Intell. Transp. Syst. **9**, 589–600 (2008)
9. Ma, C., Shi, L., Huang, H., Yan, M.: 3D Reconstruction from Full-View Fisheye Camera. Computer Vision and Pattern Recognition, abs/1506.06273, 2015
10. Matzen, K., Cohen, M.F., Evans, B., Kopf, J., Szeliski, R.: Low-cost 360 stereo photography and video capture. ACM Trans. Graph. **36**(4), 1–12 (2017)
11. Mei, C., Rives, P.: Single view point omnidirectional camera calibration from planar grids. In: IEEE International Conference on Robotics and Automation, pp. 3945–3950 (2007)
12. Mroz, F., Breckon, T.P.P.: An empirical comparison of real-time dense stereo approaches for use in the automotive environment. EURASIP J. Image Video Process. **13**, 1–9 (2012)
13. OpenCV: Omnidirectional Camara Calibration Tutorial, 3.4.1 edition, April 2018
14. Ricoh Company, Ltd.: Ricoh Theta S - User Guide (2015)
15. Zhang, Z.: A flexible new technique for camera calibration. IEEE Trans. Pattern Anal. Mach. Intell. **22**(11), 1330–1334 (2000)

The Use of Intensity-Based Measures to Produce Image Function Metrics Which Accommodate Weber's Models of Perception

Dongchang Li[1], Davide La Torre[2,3], and Edward R. Vrscay[1(✉)]

[1] Department of Applied Mathematics, Faculty of Mathematics,
University of Waterloo, Waterloo, ON N2L 3G1, Canada
d235li@edu.uwaterloo.ca, ervrscay@uwaterloo.ca

[2] Dubai Business School, University of Dubai, 14143 Dubai, UAE
dlatorre@ud.ac.ae

[3] Department of Economics, Management and Quantitative Methods,
University of Milan, 20122 Milan, Italy
davide.latorre@unimi.it

Abstract. We are concerned with the construction of "Weberized" metrics for image functions – distance functions which allow greater deviations at higher intensity values and lower deviations at lower intensity values in accordance with Weber's models of perception. In this paper, we show how the use of appropriate nonuniform measures over the image function range space can be used to produce "Weberized" metrics. In the case of Weber's standard model, the resulting metric is an L^1 distance between logarithms of the image functions. For generalized Weber's law, the metrics are L^1 distances between appropriate powers of the image functions. We then define the corresponding L^2 analogues of these metrics which are easier to work with because of their differentiability properties. Finally, we extend the definition of these "Weberized" metrics to vector-valued functions.

1 Introduction

It is well known that the commonly used mean squared error (MSE) and PSNR – both examples of L^2-based measures – perform poorly in terms of perceptual image quality [4,12]. This paper represents a continuation of earlier research [5] on methods of modifying L^2-based approximations so that they conform better to Weber's model of perception. A number of papers have incorporated Weber's model into classical image processing methods, thereby "Weberizing" them, e.g., total variation (TV) restoration [9] and Mumford-Shah segmentation [10].

One way to "Weberize" the L^2 distance between two functions u and v – or any metric involving an integration over some power of the differences $|u(x) - v(x)|$ – is to employ an *intensity-based weight function* in which regions of higher (lower) intensity values have a lower (higher) weight. A simple, seemingly *ad hoc*, yet effective method introduced in [5] is to divide the difference $|u(x) - v(x)|$ by

A. Campilho et al. (Eds.): ICIAR 2018, LNCS 10882, pp. 326–335, 2018.
https://doi.org/10.1007/978-3-319-93000-8_37

$|u(x)|$ or $|v(x)|$. If we use $|u(x)|$ and consider $v(x)$ to be an approximation to $u(x)$, we obtain the following "Weberized L^2" distance function,

$$\Delta(u,v) = \int_X \left[1 - \frac{v(x)}{u(x)} \right]^2 dx, \qquad (1)$$

where X is the support of the image functions. This distance function is convenient to employ: If $v(x)$ is a linear combination of basis functions, the minimization of $\Delta(u,v)$ yields a linear system in the expansion coefficients c_k [5].

Minimization of $\Delta(u,v)$ in Eq. (1) is also consistent with the notion that Weber's model is better accommodated when one considers *ratios* of signal/image functions u and v as we discuss in more detail below.

In this paper, we examine another method of producing Weberized distance functions, namely by employing appropriate nonuniform *measures* over the greyscale intensity space. This idea, introduced in [3], was employed in [5] to show that the logarithmic L^1 distance between two functions u and v conforms to Weber's model. In contrast to [5], however, we consider a generalized family of Weber's models of perception: Given a greyscale background intensity $I > 0$, the minimum change in intensity ΔI perceived by the human visual system (HVS) is related to I as follows,

$$\frac{\Delta I}{I^a} = C, \qquad (2)$$

where $a > 0$ and C is constant, or at least roughly constant over a significant range of intensities I [11]. In practically all applications, $a = 1$, the standard Weber model. There are, however, situations, in which other values of a, in particular, $a = 0.5$, may apply – see, for example, [7]. Equation (2) suggests that the HVS will be less/more sensitive to a given change in intensity ΔI in regions of an image at which the local image intensity $I(x)$ is high/low. As such, a Weberized distance between two functions u and v should tolerate greater/lesser differences over regions in which they assume higher/lower intensity values. The degree of toleration will be determined by the exponent a in Eq. (2).

Indeed, such a "Weberization" is built into well-known structural similarity (SSIM) measure [12,13], which demonstrates superior performance in comparison with MSE and PSNR as well as other image quality measures in terms of perceptual quality. Its luminance term, denoted as $S_1(\mathbf{x},\mathbf{y})$, characterizes the similarity between the mean values, $\bar{\mathbf{x}}$ and $\bar{\mathbf{y}}$ of two image patches $\mathbf{x}$ and $\mathbf{y}$, respectively. S_1 is a rational function $\bar{\mathbf{x}}$ and $\bar{\mathbf{y}}$ which can be rewritten as a function of the ratio $\bar{\mathbf{y}}/\bar{\mathbf{x}}$ (or $\bar{\mathbf{x}}/\bar{\mathbf{y}}$). If $\mathbf{y}$ is an approximation to $\mathbf{x}$ then greater deviations between $\bar{\mathbf{y}}$ and $\bar{\mathbf{x}}$ will be tolerated when $\bar{\mathbf{x}}$ is greater.

The primary purpose of this paper is to provide the mathematical basis for the construction of various "Weberized" image function metrics using intensity-based measures. This, in turn, is a particular case of the more general mathematical problem of what may be call "range-based function approximation." To the best of our knowledge, this is the first time that range-based measures have been employed in function approximation. We acknowledge that the rather elaborate strategy described in this paper could, in practice, be bypassed by means of standard "patch-based" methods. Indeed, earlier work on a best SSIM-based approximation method [2] may be viewed as a "patch-based" intensity-dependent approximation method. That being said, the history of signal and image processing clearly shows the numerous benefits of pursuing more general mathematical formalisms, in terms of both theory as well as applications, and we hope that this paper will inspire future efforts in both.

We summarize the basic mathematical ingredients of our formalism:

1. The **base (or pixel) space** $X \subset \mathbb{R}$ on which our signals/images are supported. In practical computations, we shall assume, unless otherwise indicated, that $X = [0, 1]$ or $[0, 1]^2$. In the case of digital images, X can be the set of pixel locations (i, j), $1 \leq i \leq n_1$, $1 \leq j \leq n_2$.
2. The **greyscale range** $\mathbb{R}_g = [A, B] \subset (0, \infty)$.
3. The **signal/image function space** $\mathcal{F} = \{u : X \to \mathbb{R}_g \mid u$ is measurable$\}$. Note that from our definition of the greyscale range $\mathbb{R}_g$, $u \in \mathcal{F}$ is positive and bounded, i.e., $0 < A \leq u(x) \leq B < \infty$ for all $x \in X$. A consequence of this boundedness is that $\mathcal{F} \subset L^p(X)$ for all $p \geq 1$, where the $L^p(X)$ function spaces are defined in the usual way. For any $p \geq 1$, the L^p norm can be used to define a metric d_p on $\mathcal{F}$: For $u, v \in \mathcal{F}$, $d_p(u, v) = \|u - v\|_p$. Our primary concern is the approximation of functions in the case $p = 2$, i.e., the Hilbert space, $L^2(X)$, with metric,

$$d_2(u, v) = \|u - v\|_2 = \left[\int_X [u(x) - v(x)]^2 \, dx \right]^{1/2}, \quad u, v \in L^2(X). \quad (3)$$

2   Distance Functions Generated by Measures on the Greyscale Range Space $\mathbb{R}_g$

With reference to the notation introduced in the previous section, we now describe a method of generating intensity-dependent metrics between functions in the space $\mathcal{F}$ by using measures that are supported on the bounded range space $\mathbb{R}_g = [A, B]$. In what follows, we let the base space be $X = [a, b]$.

Consider two functions $u, v \in \mathcal{F}$ and define the following subsets of X,

$$X_u = \{x \in X \mid u(x) \leq v(x)\} \quad X_v = \{x \in X \mid v(x) \leq u(x)\}, \quad (4)$$

so that $X = X_u \cup X_v$. A possible situation is sketched in Fig. 1 below.

The goal is to assign a distance D between u and v based on an integration over vertical strips of width dx and centered at $x \in [a, b]$. Two such strips, one lying in the set X_u and the other in X_v, are shown in Fig. 1. In most, if not all, traditional integration-based metrics, e.g., the L^p metrics for $p \geq 1$, the contribution of each strip to the integral will be an appropriate power of the height of the strip, $|u(x) - v(x)|$. This implicitly assumes a *uniform* weighting along the intensity axis since the term $|u(x) - v(x)|$ represents the Lebesgue measure of the intervals $(u(x), v(x)]$ or $(v(x), u(x)]$.

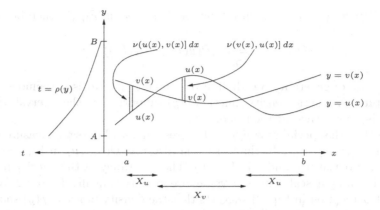

Fig. 1. Sketch of two nonnegative greyscale functions $u(x)$ and $v(x)$ with strips of width dx that will contribute to the distance $D(u, v; \nu)$.

In this study, however, the contribution of each strip will **not**, in general, be determined by the heights of the strips, i.e., the quantities $|u(x) - v(x)|$, but rather the **sizes** of the intervals $(u(x), v(x)] \subset \mathbb{R}_g$ and $(v(x), u(x)] \subset \mathbb{R}_g$ as assigned by a **measure** ν that is supported on the greyscale interval $\mathbb{R}_g = [A, B]$. The measures of the two intervals shown in the figure will be denoted as $\nu(u(x), v(x)]$ and $\nu(v(x), u(x)]$, respectively. (Note that we consider half-open intervals of the form $(y_1, y_2]$. We omit a discussion of the technical points underlying this choice.) The distance between u and v associated with the measure ν is now defined as follows,

$$D(u, v; \nu) = \int_{X_u} \nu(u(x), v(x)] \, dx \; + \; \int_{X_v} \nu(v(x), u(x)] \, dx, \qquad (5)$$

Special Case: In the case that ν is the usual (uniform) Lebesgue measure on $\mathbb{R}_g$, to be denoted as m_g, the sizes of the intervals shown in Fig. 1 become $m_g(u(x), v(x)] = v(x) - u(x)$ and $m_g(v(x), u(x)] = u(x) - v(x)$, so that

$$D(u, v, m_g) = \int_{X_u} [v(x) - u(x)] \, dx + \int_{X_v} [u(x) - v(x)] \, dx$$

$$= \int_X |u(x) - v(x)| \, dx, \qquad (6)$$

the L^1 distance between u and v.

The natural question is, "What other kind of greyscale measures ν can/should be considered on the greyscale range $\mathbb{R}_g$?" Firstly, it is convenient to consider measures which are defined by continuous, non-negative density functions $\rho(y)$. (Such measures will be *absolutely continuous* with respect to Lebesgue measure.) Given a measure ν with density function ρ, then for any interval $(y_1, y_2] \subset \mathbb{R}_g$,

$$\nu\,(y_1, y_2] = \int_{y_1}^{y_2} \rho(y) \, dy \; = P(y_2) - P(y_1), \qquad (7)$$

where $P'(y) = \rho(y)$. The distance function $D(u, v; \nu)$ in Eq. (5) then becomes

$$D(u, v; \nu) = \int_X |P(u(x)) - P(v(x))| \, dx. \tag{8}$$

Without loss of generality, we shall also assume that $\rho(y)$ is continuous on $\mathbb{R}_g$. The graph of a generic density function $\rho(y)$ supported on the interval $[A, B] \subset \mathbb{R}_g$ (y-axis) is sketched at the left of Fig. 1.

Note that the special case $\rho(y) = 1$ corresponds to Lebesgue measure on $\mathbb{R}_g$, i.e., $\nu(y_1, y_2] = y_2 - y_1$. In this case, the distance $D(u, v, \nu)$ in Eq. (8) is the L^1 distance between u and v in Eq. (6). The constancy of the density function implies that all greyscale intensity values are weighted equally. However, Weber's model of perception in Eq. (2) suggests that the density function $\rho(y)$ should be a *decreasing* function of intensity y: As the intensity value increases, the HVS will tolerate greater differences between $u(x)$ and $v(x)$ before being perceived. In [5], we presented, with a short proof, the following important result for Weber's standard model, $a = 1$:

Theorem 1: The unique measure ν on $\mathbb{R}_g$ which accommodates Weber's standard model of perception, $a = 1$ in Eq. (2), over the greyscale space $\mathbb{R}_g \subset [0, \infty)$ is, up to a normalization constant, defined by the continuous density function $\rho(y) = 1/y$. For any two greyscale intensities $I_1, I_2 \in \mathbb{R}_g$,

$$\int_{I_1}^{I_1 + \Delta I_1} \frac{1}{y} \, dy = \int_{I_2}^{I_2 + \Delta I_2} \frac{1}{y} \, dy \implies \nu(I_1, I_1 + \Delta I_1) = \nu(I_2, I_2 + \Delta I_2), \tag{9}$$

where $\Delta I_1 = CI_1$ and $\Delta I_2 = CI_2$, are the minimum changes in perceived intensity at I_1 and I_2, respectively, according to Weber's model, $a = 1$, in Eq. (2).

Equation (9) may be viewed as an invariance result with respect to perception. Its graphical interpretation in terms of equal areas enclosed by the density curve $\rho(y)$ is shown in Fig. 2 below. The measure ν defined by the density function $\rho(y) = 1/y$ is the logarithmic measure so that the distance between u and

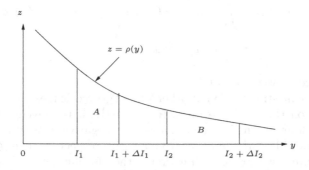

Fig. 2. Graphical interpretation of invariance result in Eq. (9). Area of A = Area of B = $\ln(1 + C)$.

v in Eq. (8) becomes

$$D(u, v; \nu) = \int_X |\ln u(x) - \ln v(x)| \, dx = \| \ln u - \ln v \|_1. \tag{10}$$

Theoretically, this is the best distance function to employ in any approximation scheme which is designed to accommodate Weber's (standard) model of perception. Unfortunately, it is difficult to work with this distance function, which leads to the consideration of more practical L^2-based analogues, as discussed in [5]. We shall discuss this further in Sect. 3 below.

We now wish to consider the generalized Weber models of perception in Eq. (2), i.e., $a \neq 1$. Once again, we expect that the density functions $\rho_a(y)$ associated with these models will be decreasing functions of y. Given that $\rho_1(y) = 1/y$, one might conjecture that the density function $\rho_a(y)$ for any $a > 0$ will be given by $\rho_a(y) = 1/y^a$. This is *asymptotically true*, as we state below.

Theorem 2: For $a > 0$, the density function $\rho_a(y)$ which accommodates Weber's model of perception in Eq. (2) is, to leading order, $\rho_a(y) \simeq 1/y^a$ as $y \to 0^+$: For any two greyscale intensities $I_1, I_2 \in \mathbb{R}_g$,

$$\int_{I_1}^{I_1 + \Delta I_1} \rho_a(y) \, dy \simeq \int_{I_2}^{I_2 + \Delta I_2} \rho_a(y) \, dy, \tag{11}$$

where $\Delta I_1 = C I_1^a$ and $\Delta I_2 = C I_2^a$ are the minimum changes in perceived intensity at I_1 and I_2, respectively, according to Weber's model in Eq. (2).

This result, which is a generalized version of the invariance result in Eq. (9), is derived in the Appendix. It may also be interpreted geometrically as shown in Fig. 2 with ΔI_1 and ΔI_2 defined in the statement of Theorem 2.

Theorem 2 may also be extended to include the case $a = 0$, essentially an absence of Weber's model. In this case $\rho_0(y) = 1$, so that $\nu = m_g$, Lebesgue measure on $\mathbb{R}_g$. Furthermore, the relation in (11) becomes an equality.

For $a \geq 0$, $a \neq 1$, substitution of (the leading-order approximations to) the density functions $\rho_a(y) = 1/y^a$ into Eq. (8) yields, up to a multiplicative constant, the following distance functions,

$$D_a(u, v) = D(u, v; \nu_a) = \int_X |u(x)^{-a+1} - v(x)^{-a+1}| \, dx. \tag{12}$$

Note that the special case $a = 0$ has already been presented in Eq. (6). And finally, the case $a = 1$ – Weber's standard model – was presented in Eq. (10).

In closing this section, we mention that as a increases, the density functions $\rho_a(y) = 1/y^a$ decrease more rapidly with respect to y. As such, regions of higher intensity values will contribute less to the distance functions $D(u, v; \nu_a)$. This effect will be demonstrated in a particular example in the next section.

3   Function Approximation Using Generalized Greyscale Measures ν_a

We now consider $u(x)$ to be a reference function and $v(x)$ to be an approximation to $u(x)$ having the standard form, $v(x) = \displaystyle\sum_{k=1}^{N} c_k \phi_k(x)$, where the set $\{\phi_k\}_{k=1}^{N}$ is assumed to be linearly independent, and perhaps orthogonal, over $X = [a, b]$. We shall denote $Y_N = \text{span}\{\phi_1, \cdots, \phi_N\}$.

Theoretically, given a $u(x) \in \mathcal{F}$ and an $a > 0$, the best Y_N-approximation of $u(x)$ in the metric space $(\mathcal{F}, D_a)$ is obtained by minimizing the distance $D(u, v; \nu_a)$ in Eq. (12). Unfortunately, these distance functions are difficult to work with, especially from a theoretical perspective, primarily because of the appearance of the absolute value in the integrand. One way to reduce such complications is to consider their L^2 analogues, defined as follows,

$$D_{2,a}(u, v; \nu_a) = \left[\int_X \left[u(x)^{-a+1} - v(x)^{-a+1} \right]^2 dx \right]^{1/2}, \quad a \neq 1, \quad (13)$$

and, for the case $a = 1$,

$$D_{2,1}(u, v; \nu_1) = \left[\int_X \left[\ln u(x) - \ln v(x) \right]^2 dx \right]^{1/2}. \quad (14)$$

We may now impose stationarity conditions on these integrals:

Case 1: $a \neq 1$. For $1 \leq p \leq N$, using Eq. (13),

$$\frac{\partial D_{2,a}}{\partial c_p} = 0 \implies \int_X \left[u(x)^{-a+1} - v(x)^{-a+1} \right] \frac{\phi_p(x)}{v(x)^a} dx = 0. \quad (15)$$

Case 2: $a = 1$. For $1 \leq p \leq N$, using Eq. (14),

$$\frac{\partial D_{2,1}}{\partial c_p} = 0 \implies \int_X \left[\ln u(x) - \ln v(x) \right] \frac{\phi_p(x)}{v(x)} dx = 0. \quad (16)$$

For a given $a > 0$, the equations for $1 \leq p \leq N$ in either (15) or (16) comprise an extremely complicated nonlinear system of equations in the unknown coefficients $c_1, c_2, \cdots, c_N$. Alternatively, one may employ some kind of gradient descent scheme to find the coefficients c_k which minimize the squared distance D_2. A convenient starting point for such schemes are the coefficients of the best L^2 approximation ($a = 0$) which are easily computed. Such an approach was employed in the following illustrative example.

Example 1: We consider the step function $u(x)$ with values 1 and 3 on half intervals of $X = [0, 1]$, as shown in Fig. 3. Also shown are plots of the best approximations for the cases $a = 0$ (best L^2), $a = 0.5$ and $a = 1$ (standard Weber) using the following orthonormal basis: $\phi_1(x) = 1$, $\phi_k(x) = \sqrt{2} \cos(k\pi x)$,

$2 \leq k \leq 5$. As expected, the approximations for $a = 0.5$ and $a = 1$ show less deviation from $u(x)$ than the best L^2 approximation over the lower intensity region $0 \leq x \leq 1/2$ and higher deviation over the higher intensity region $1/2 < x \leq 1$. Also as expected, the deviation from $u(x)$ in the lower (higher) intensity regions decreases (increases) with increasing a since the associated density functions $\rho_a(t) = 1/t^a$ decrease more rapidly with increasing a.

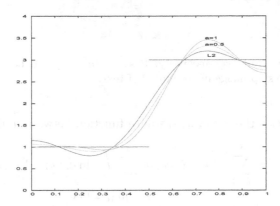

Fig. 3. Best approximations to step function $u(x)$ using $N = 5$ orthogonal cosine basis functions on $[0, 1]$ for $a = 0$ (best L^2, green), $a = 0.5$ (blue) and $a = 1$ (standard Weber, yellow). (Color figure online)

Example 2: We consider a 256×256-pixel 8 bpp image composed of four squares with greyscale values $60, 128, 128$ and 220. In Fig. 4 are shown the best approximations for $a = 0$ (best L^2) and $a = 1$ (standard Weber) obtained with the 2D basis set $\Phi_{kl}(n, m) = \phi_k(n)\phi_k(m)$, $0 \leq i, j \leq 14$, where the $\phi_i(n)$ are standard DCT basis functions. The $a = 1$ approximation exhibits greater/lesser deviation at higher/lower greyscale levels than the best L^2 approximation.

4   Weber's Model for Vector-Valued Image Functions

We now consider vector-valued image functions $\mathbf{u} : X \to \mathbb{R}^N$ having the form $\mathbf{u}(x) = (u_1(x), u_2(x), \cdots, u_N(x))$, e.g., $N = 3$ for RGB color images, $N = 224$ for AVIRIS hyperspectral images [1]. We also assume that Weber's (standard) law holds for each wavelength/channel, i.e.,

$$\Delta I_k = C_k I_k, \quad 1 \leq k \leq N. \tag{17}$$

The appropriate density function for each channel is $\rho_k(y) = 1/y$ which yields the following distance between components of $u(x)$ and $v(x)$,

$$D(u_k, v_k, \nu_k) = \int_X |\ln u_k(x) - \ln v_k(x)| \, dx. \tag{18}$$

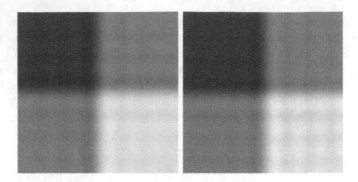

Fig. 4. Left and right, respectively: Best L^2 $(a = 0)$ and best Weber $(a = 1)$ approximations to step image in Example 2 of text.

This, in turn, yields the following distance function between u and v,

$$D(u, v, \nu) = \sum_{k=1}^{N} D(u_k, v_k, \nu_k) = \sum_{k=1}^{N} \int_X |\ln u_k(x) - \ln v_k(x)|\, dx$$
$$= \|\ln \mathbf{u} - \ln \mathbf{v}\|_1. \tag{19}$$

Once again, the L^2 analogue of this distance function is somewhat easier to work with,

$$D_{2,1}(u, v, \nu) = \left[\sum_{k=1}^{N} \int_X [\ln u_k(x) - \ln v_k(x)]^2\, dx \right]^{1/2}$$
$$= \|\ln \mathbf{u} - \ln \mathbf{v}\|_2. \tag{20}$$

Note: In the above treatment, the total distance function D in Eq. (19) could also be defined by a *weighted* sum of individual channel distances, $D(u_k, v_k, \nu_k)$. As well, associated each channel could be a measure ν_{a_k} with its own Weber exponent a_k and hence density function $\rho(y) = 1/y^{a_k}$.

Acknowledgments. We gratefully acknowledge that this research has been supported in part by the Natural Sciences and Engineering Research Council of Canada (ERV) in the form of a Discovery Grant. DLT and ERV dedicate this paper in memory of Prof. Bruno Forte (1928–2002), mentor, colleague and friend.

Appendix: Sketch of Proof of Theorem 2

We shall consider the "reverse" problem: Given the density function $\rho(y) = 1/y^a$, find the leading-order behaviour of $f(x)$ such that

$$F(x) = \int_x^{x+Cf(x)} \frac{1}{y^a}\, dy = K, \quad \text{constant.} \tag{21}$$

Differentiation with respect to x and a little manipulation yields the following differential equation (DE) for $f(x)$,

$$1 + Cf'(x) = \left[1 + \frac{Cf(x)}{x}\right]^a. \tag{22}$$

In the case $a = 1$, we easily find that $f(x) = x = x^1$. In the case $a = 0$, $f'(x) = 0$ which implies that $f(x) = x^0$. For $0 < a < 1$, we shall assume that for x sufficiently large, the RHS of Eq. (22) may be approximated using the binomial theorem, which yields the following DE for $f(x)$,

$$f'(x) = a\,\frac{f(x)}{x}. \tag{23}$$

The solution of this DE is, up to a constant, $f(x) = x^a$.

References

1. AVIRIS: Airborne Visible Infrared Imaging Spectrometer, Jet Propulsion Laboratory, California Institute of Technology. http://aviris.jpl.nasa.gov
2. Brunet, D., Vrscay, E.R., Wang, Z.: Structural similarity-based approximation of signals and images using orthogonal bases. In: Campilho, A., Kamel, M. (eds.) ICIAR 2010. LNCS, vol. 6111, pp. 11–22. Springer, Heidelberg (2010). https://doi.org/10.1007/978-3-642-13772-3_2
3. Forte, B., Vrscay, E.R.: Solving the inverse problem for function and image approximation using iterated function systems. Dyn. Contin. Discrete Impuls. Syst. **1**, 177–231 (1995)
4. Girod, B.: What's wrong with mean squared error? In: Watson, A.B. (ed.) Digital Images and Human Vision. MIT Press, Cambridge (1993)
5. Kowalik-Urbaniak, I.A., La Torre, D., Vrscay, E.R., Wang, Z.: Some "Weberized" L^2-based methods of signal/image approximation. In: Campilho, A., Kamel, M. (eds.) ICIAR 2014. LNCS, vol. 8814, pp. 20–29. Springer, Cham (2014). https://doi.org/10.1007/978-3-319-11758-4_3
6. Lee, S., Pattichis, M.S., Bovik, A.C.: Foveated video quality assessment. IEEE Trans. Multimed. **4**(1), 129–132 (2002)
7. Michon, J.A.: Note on the generalized form of Weber's Law. Percept. Psychophys. **1**, 329–330 (1966)
8. Oppenheim, A.V., Schafer, R.W., Stockham Jr., T.G.: Nonlinear filtering of multiplied and convolved signals. Proc. IEEE **56**(8), 1264–1291 (1968)
9. Shen, J.: On the foundations of vision modeling I. Weber's law and Weberized TV restoration. Physica D **175**, 241–251 (2003)
10. Shen, J., Jung, Y.-M.: Weberized Mumford-Shah model with Bose-Einstein photon noise. Appl. Math. Optim. **53**, 331–358 (2006)
11. Wandell, B.A.: Foundations of Vision. Sinauer, Sunderland (1995)
12. Wang, Z., Bovik, A.C.: Mean squared error: love it or leave it? A new look at signal fidelity measures. IEEE Signal Process. Mag. **26**, 98–117 (2009)
13. Wang, Z., Bovik, A.C., SHeikh, H.R., Simoncelli, E.P.: Image quality assessment: from error visibility to structural similarity. IEEE Trans. Image Process. **13**(4), 600–612 (2004)
14. Wang, Z., Li, Q.: Information content weighting for perceptual image quality assessment. IEEE Trans. Image Process. **20**(5), 1185–1198 (2011)

ShadowNet

Eli Kaminsky and Michael Werman[(✉)]

Computer Science, The Hebrew University of Jerusalem, Jerusalem, Israel
`michael.werman@mail.huji.ac.il`

Abstract. Finding shadows in images is useful for many applications, such as white balance, shadow removal, or obstacle detection for autonomous vehicles. Shadow segmentation has been investigated both by classical computer vision and machine learning methods. In this paper, we propose a simple Convolutional-Neural-Net (CNN) running on a PC-GPU to semantically segment shadowed regions in an image. To this end, we generated a synthetic set of shadow objects, which we projected onto hundreds of shadow-less images in order to create a labeled training set. Furthermore, we suggest a novel loss function that can be tuned to balance runtime and accuracy. We argue that the combination of a synthetic training set, a simple CNN model, and loss function designed for semantic segmentation, are sufficient for semantic segmentation of shadows, especially in outdoor scenes.

Keywords: Shadow detection · IoU - Intersection over Union
Basin-loss function

1   Introduction

This paper presents a CNN to segment shadows in an image. To that end we created a synthetic set of shadows and randomly added them to hundreds of hand picked shadow-less images. We show that training a CNN on a synthetic set of shadows with a novel loss function designed for semantic segmentation, yields satisfactory segmentation results on real images.

Past [1,6,10,12] and contemporary work [2,7–9,11] on shadow segmentation relied on manual or semi-automated labeling of shadowed pixels in an image in order to create the training, validation and test sets. Hand labeling shadows is very time consuming, and of course, not all-possible shadow shapes and intensities can be found and labeled for supervised learning. Using synthetic shadows we can simulate an unbounded range of intensities and shapes.

Resizing or reshaping an image or synthetic shadow is possible since shadows are often cast from an object not present in the image. Synthetic shadows from the test set are shown in Fig. 1. Images on the left are with cast shadows, images in the center are the ground truth shadow segmentation, and the images on the right are the CNN predicted segmentations.

This research was supported by the Israel Science Foundation and by the Israel Ministry of Science and Technology.

© Springer International Publishing AG, part of Springer Nature 2018
A. Campilho et al. (Eds.): ICIAR 2018, LNCS 10882, pp. 336–344, 2018.
https://doi.org/10.1007/978-3-319-93000-8_38

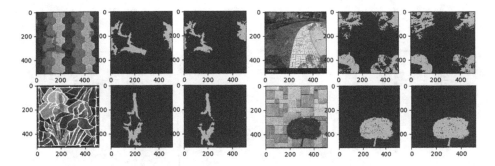

Fig. 1. In each triplet, scene with cast shadows, ground truth shadow segmentation, and the predicted segmentation

2 CNN Model Structure

In our dataset, shadows appear both in low frequencies varying slowly across the scene or as very high frequency intensity changes. Thus, we should apply different sized kernels in order to extract their features and segment them. As large kernels are computationally expensive, we can replace such kernels with cascaded smaller kernels or run them on a subsampled image. Convolving with an $n \times n$ kernel on an image resized by 0.5, has the effect of running a $2n \times 2n$ kernel on the original image. As subsampled images may lose small artifacts or high frequency features at subsampling, we ought to keep extracted features for high and low frequencies of pre-subsampling layer. The U-Net architecture [3] with multi-scaling tensors at several resolutions fulfills our requirements and we based our model on it.

As we only semantically segment shadows we did not require the full U-Net architecture. We removed the last subsampled layer and reduced the base number of convolutional kernels from 64 to 24, Fig. 2 depicts our model.

3 Loss Function

The error, or loss, between the ground truth and the predicted image is often taken to be the pixel-wise Root-Mean-Square-Error, $Loss_{RMSE}$. Using $Loss_{RMSE}$ the model converged fast. However, since shadows are often not a dominant segment of the scene this resulted in a model that ignored small shadow segments.

For semantic segmentation, it is often customary to set the loss function in terms of IoU (intersection of union).

$$IoU = \frac{\text{Area of Overlap}}{\text{Area of Union}} \tag{1}$$

With the loss function being:

$$Loss_{IoU} = 1 - IoU \tag{2}$$

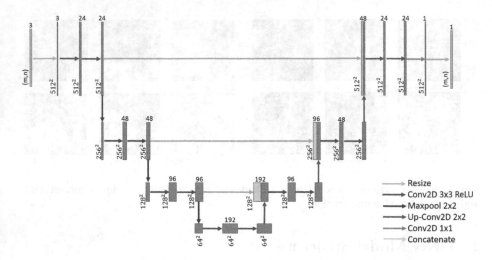

Fig. 2. A U-Net based architecture for shadow segmentation.

$Loss_{IoU}$, is indifferent to the shadow-less part of the scene. This is especially important in order not to miss small shadows segments which are often ignored by a pixel-wise loss. However, minimization of $Loss_{IoU}$ converges very slowly compared to $Loss_{RMSE}$, as it gives an equal weight to small shadow segments and to large ones in an image.

In order utilize both of their relative advantages - fast minimization, $Loss_{RMSE}$, and accuracy, $Loss_{IoU}$, we set the loss function to a combination of them. The simplest combination being linear:

$$Loss_{total} = \alpha Loss_{RMSE} + (1-\alpha)Loss_{IoU} \qquad (3)$$

In Eq. 3, $Loss_{total}$ is a plane. Gradients pointing to the most significant change in the loss function are parallel (slope of the plane), so gradients have no preference and do not converge to a single minimum at the origin. Therefore, convergence might be slow and accurate in case gradients are close to the $Loss_{IoU}$ axis, or faster and less accurate in case gradients are closer to the $Loss_{RMSE}$ axis.

For a more stable form of a loss function we used a quadratic combination of $Loss_{RMSE}$ and $Loss_{IoU}$:

$$Loss_{total} = Loss^2_{RMSE} + Loss^2_{IoU} \qquad (4)$$

Unlike Eq. 3, it is impossible to minimize only one component of the loss function without the other in training, since gradients have radial symmetry and all point to a single minimum at the origin. Figure 3 shows contours and gradients for the loss functions in Eqs. 3 and 4.

Nonetheless, while training on our sets, there was a "pull" of the gradients towards the $Loss_{RMSE}$ axis, since it was easier to minimize $Loss_{RMSE}$ than

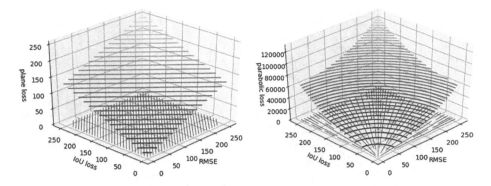

Fig. 3. 3D contours of plane loss and parabolic loss of Eqs. 3 and 4. For plane loss, projection of parallel gradients on the $Loss_{IoU}$-$Loss_{RMSE}$ plane. For parabolic loss, projection of radial gradients on the $Loss_{IoU}$-$Loss_{RMSE}$ plane.

$Loss_{IoU}$ neglecting many small shadows segments. Therefore, we chose a new loss function that forces the gradients towards the $Loss_{IoU}$ axis to increase accuracy. We required the loss function to have a basin shape with a single minimum and a basin line through which we could force the gradients to minimize the function to a preferred axis. In Eq. 4, if we divide the term $Loss_{RMSE}^2$ by $Loss_{IoU}$ and divide the term $Loss_{IoU}^2$ by $Loss_{RMSE}$, we penalize $Loss_{total}$ if one of the terms becomes dominant, as $Loss_{total}$ increases. The penalty is minimized when $Loss_{RMSE} \approx Loss_{IoU}$. The following equation achieves just that:

$$Loss_{total} = \frac{\alpha Loss_{RMSE}^2}{Loss_{IoU}} + \frac{Loss_{IoU}^2}{\alpha Loss_{RMSE}} \tag{5}$$

The hyper-parameter α, tunes the slope of the basin line of the loss function, $Loss_{total}$, which roughly represents the line $y = \alpha x$. We denote Eq. 5 as "basin-loss", illustrated in Fig. 4. Note that since $Loss_{RMSE}$ and $Loss_{IoU}$ are differentiable [4,5], Eq. 5 is also differentiable and can be used for back-propagation.

4   Training and Results

For our dataset [13], we chose 580 shadow-less images from the web, and with Photoshop created 100 shadow objects. As we used a PC-GPU, to make the most of the GPU memory we ran our model on mini-batches of size 5 for 30 iterations per epoch. We resized input images to $512 \times 512 \times 3$. For each image we randomly chose a shadow object, randomly blurred it to soften its edges, randomly set its intensity, and randomly chose an affine transformation to resize, skew, and rotate it. Finally, we added the shadow object to the image, see Fig. 1.

Our sets of images were divided $80\% - 10\% - 10\%$ for training, validation, and test, ($\alpha = 1.1$). There are two measures of accuracy; first – pixel accuracy, or percentage of pixels that are equal to 1 or 0, when comparing predicted shadow with ground truth, second – percentage of intersection over union, or

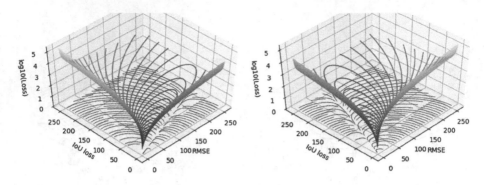

Fig. 4. Contours of basin-loss of Eq. 5, in log scale. Left: basin-loss with $\alpha = 0.3$, with a projection of the gradients on the $Loss_{IoU}$-$Loss_{RMSE}$ plane. The "pull" of the gradients is towards minimizing IoU loss. Right: basin-loss function with $\alpha = 3$, with projection of the gradients on the $Loss_{IoU}$-$Loss_{RMSE}$. The "pull" of gradients is towards minimizing RMSE loss.

IoU accuracy, of predicted shadow with ground truth. The training set converged to 96% pixel-accuracy and validation converged to 95%. For IoU accuracy, the training set converged to 82% and validation to 80%.

There is a trade-off in time-to-converge and IoU accuracy based on α. Training with $\alpha \leq 1$ caused the model to converge too slowly. If the basin-line is such that the model is forced to compensate for $Loss_{IoU}$ more than for $Loss_{RMSE}$, model convergence becomes very slow. Figure 5 shows model training results for different values of α in $Loss_{IoU}$ and $Loss_{RMSE}$.

Note in Fig. 5, that the difference in loss between the axes increased as α grows. Also setting α too large, say $\alpha = 3$, degrades IoU performance.

We used the 'Adadelta' optimization algorithm with a learning rate reduction of 90% when there is no progress. The effect of improvement in accuracy by learning rate reduction is visible in Fig. 5 (top two images), at epoch 530.

Figure 6 shows examples with real shadows we tested the shadow segmentation on and Fig. 7 shows how the CNN finds small shadows.

5   Comparison with Previous Work

We found our work to be a little better than [1] in terms of shadow segmentation. We ran our model on the test set and ground truth of test set of [1]. To improve test accuracy, we performed Otsu thresholding on our outputs and achieved 90% pixel accuracy which is 1% improvement compared to [1], and with 72% IoU accuracy - no such parameter to compare to. We could not run the code of [1] to test our samples. It is also important to note that ground truth given for these images is often incorrect both in marking non-shadows as shadows and in missing parts of the shadow. This results in a significant accuracy loss, especially in areas where our model had segmented a shadow correctly and the ground truth did not. Figure 8 shows examples.

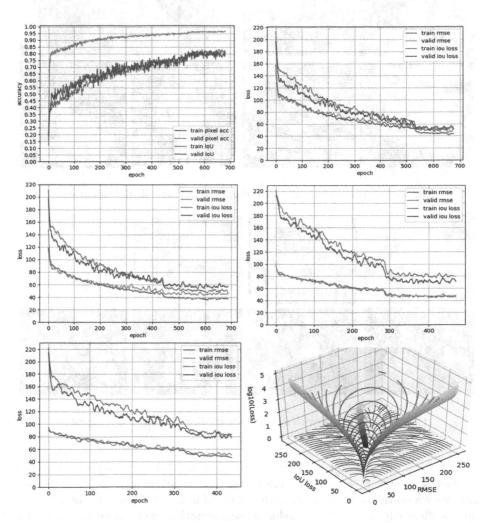

Fig. 5. Comparing training and total loss between Eqs. 4 and 5. Top left: Train/validation pixel-accuracy/IoU-accuracy for Eq. 5 with $\alpha = 1.1$. Top right: losses for basin-function with $\alpha = 1.1$. Center left: losses for basin-function with $\alpha = 2$. Center right: losses for basin-function with $\alpha = 3$. Bottom left: losses for Eq. 4, $Loss_{RMSE}$, with $Loss_{IoU}$ only measured. Bottom right: $Loss_{total}$ values illustrated on basin defined by Eq. 5 with $\alpha = 1.1$. Loss defined by Eq. 5 (basin loss) performs better for $Loss_{IoU}$.

Fig. 6. Top, outdoor images with shadows. Bottom, shadow segment.

Fig. 7. Top, images with small shadows. Bottom, shadow segment.

We were unsuccessful in applying the code of [2] due to major compilation problems. However, we present samples of our model on some of their images. Images we downloaded from [2] were mostly of indoor with lots of soft shadows and no clear edges, nevertheless, shadow segmentations were successful, as shown in Fig. 9.

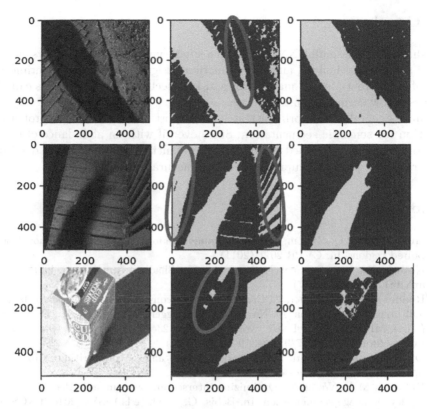

Fig. 8. Left: input images, center: our shadow segmentations and right the ground truth given in [1]. Misclassified ground truth is marked with red ellipses. Note that the given ground truth is not always reliable. (Color figure online)

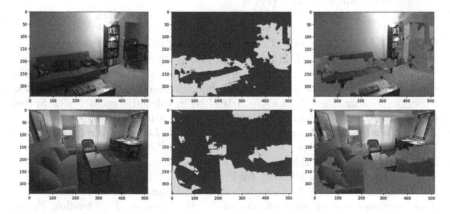

Fig. 9. Samples from [2]. Left, inputs, center our segmentation, and right are hand-marked shadows.

6 Conclusion

We showed that a small CNN trained on a small synthetic set of shadows, a small set of shadow-less images, and a loss function designed to minimize runtime and loss of both Root-Mean-Square-Error and Intersection-over-Union-Loss can give good shadow segmentations.

More generally, our work illustrates the importance of choosing a proper loss function for semantic segmentation. Since even if with an abundance of data a network can only be trained as well as its loss function allows and that designing the gradients' path can improve the overall accuracy of a network.

References

1. Guo, R., Dai, Q., Hoiem, D.: Single-image shadow detection and removal using paired regions. In: CVPR 2011 (2011)
2. Kovacs, B., Bell, S., Snavely, N., Bala, K.: Shading Annotations in the Wild. arXiv:1705.01156 (2017)
3. Ronneberger, O., Fischer, P., Brox, T.: U-Net: convolutional networks for biomedical image segmentation. In: Navab, N., Hornegger, J., Wells, W.M., Frangi, A.F. (eds.) MICCAI 2015. LNCS, vol. 9351, pp. 234–241. Springer, Cham (2015). https://doi.org/10.1007/978-3-319-24574-4_28
4. Optimizing IoU Semantic Segmentation. http://angusg.com/writing/2016/12/28/optimizing-iou-semantic-segmentation.html/
5. Rahman, M.A., Wang, Y.: Optimizing intersection-over-union in deep neural networks for image segmentation. In: Bebis, G., et al. (eds.) ISVC 2016. LNCS, vol. 10072, pp. 234–244. Springer, Cham (2016). https://doi.org/10.1007/978-3-319-50835-1_22
6. Blajovici, C., Kiss, P.J., Bonus, Z., Varga, L.: Shadow detection and removal from a single image. In: SSIP 2011 (2011)
7. Nguyen, V., Vicente, T.F.Y., Zhao, M., Hoai, M., Samaras, D.: Shadow detection with conditional generative adversarial networks. In: ICCV 2017 (2017)
8. Russell, M., Zou, J.J., Fang, G.: An evaluation of moving shadow detection techniques. Comput. Vis. Med. **2**(3), 195–217 (2016)
9. Vicente, T.F.Y., Hou, L., Yu, C.-P., Hoai, M., Samaras, D.: Large-scale training of shadow detectors with noisily-annotated shadow examples. In: Leibe, B., Matas, J., Sebe, N., Welling, M. (eds.) ECCV 2016. LNCS, vol. 9910, pp. 816–832. Springer, Cham (2016). https://doi.org/10.1007/978-3-319-46466-4_49
10. Zhu, J., Samuel, K.G., Masood, S.Z., Tappen, M.F.: Learning to recognize shadows in monochromatic natural images. In: CVPR 2010 (2010)
11. Khan, S.H., Bennamoun, M., Sohel, F., Togneri, R.: Automatic shadow detection and removal from a single image. In: PAMI 2016 (2016)
12. Lalonde, J.-F., Efros, A.A., Narasimhan, S.G.: Detecting ground shadows in outdoor consumer photographs. In: Daniilidis, K., Maragos, P., Paragios, N. (eds.) ECCV 2010. LNCS, vol. 6312, pp. 322–335. Springer, Heidelberg (2010). https://doi.org/10.1007/978-3-642-15552-9_24
13. Dataset and Source Code. http://www.cs.huji.ac.il/~werman//

Contrast Perception Across Human Cognitive Style

Anna Lewandowska[1]([✉]), Anna Samborska-Owczarek[2], and Malwina Dzisko[1]

[1] Faculty of Computer Science and Information Systems,
West Pomeranian University of Technology, Szczecin, Poland
{atomaszewska,mdzisko}@wi.zut.edu.pl
[2] FRIS®- Thinking Styles (Style Myslenia), Szczecin, Poland
anna@FRIS.pl

Abstract. In the paper we tested hypothesis that subjects' preferences to images with different contrast level is not only a function of image content but also of an individual pattern of perceptual organisation, which in terms of cognitive psychology is called a cognitive style. As reference to subjects' perceptual preferences we used FRIS® [15] that is a psychometric model and also an inventory for cognitive styles measurement. To test the hypothesis, the perceptual experiments were performed on a database included different content images. The received results confirm the given hypothesis, especially the obtained statistically significant results between idea-based thinking group and the rest of the thinking groups given for low contrast level.

1 Introduction

When analysing the images factors, that make the images a visual-pleasant, most of the researches focus on their global and local contrast. In visual perception, contrast is the difference in visual properties that makes an object (or its representation in an image) distinguishable from other objects and the background.

In visual perception of the real world, contrast is determined by the difference in the colour and brightness of the light reflected or emitted by an object and other objects within the same field of view. Therefore the contrast plays important role in image analysis and evaluation. As the Haun et al. concluded [5], contrast is a one of the functions of HVS influencing on perceived quality. In our investigations we analyse the image quality not only as a function of contrast (user preferences arising from HVS), but also from exploration of human cognitive style. We believe that such approach may deliver new interesting findings on image perception domain.

According to cognitive psychology the way an individuals perceive the world is dependent on their cognitive style that is his natural property [3]. The term 'cognitive style' refers to a psychological dimension representing consistencies in an individual's manner of cognitive functioning [1]. Therefore cognitive styles are considered stable attitudes and preferences that determine individuals' modes of

© Springer International Publishing AG, part of Springer Nature 2018
A. Campilho et al. (Eds.): ICIAR 2018, LNCS 10882, pp. 345–352, 2018.
https://doi.org/10.1007/978-3-319-93000-8_39

information perceiving and processing, thinking, decision making and problem solving habitual strategies [9]. As human cognitive styles influence the way an individual perceives information and thus make a judgement about image quality, the relation between the style and image contrast should be investigated.

In this paper, we have studied how contrast perception correlates to the observer's cognitive style. Our reference of cognitive style is metrics derived from FRIS® Thinking Styles Inventory, which is psychometrically reliable and valid [14]. The inventory offers multidimensional description of user's thinking preferences thus is suitable for variety of perceptual experiments. In our user-study, we analyse the subjects' preferences to the image contrast in confrontation to their cognitive styles. Therefore we give the Hypothesis: *There are significant differences in contrast preferences between groups of different Thinking Styles observers.*

The concept of an experiment is described in Sect. 3. Section 4 explains in detail the subjective experimental procedure that we used. The results and analysis can be found in Sect. 5. Finally, Sect. 6 concludes the paper.

2   Related Work

Contrast encoding is fundamental in development of image quality measures based on the study of the early stages of the human visual system (HVS) [5]. There were proposals that models of image quality should aim not to measure the quantity of image transmitted, but to discriminate visible differences between 'ideal'/original and degraded images, bringing image quality measurement closer to contemporary contrast psychophysics [13,20]. These newer models incorporated ideas inspired by the multi-scale spatial transform performed by the visual system, and began to acknowledge the intrinsic, efficient connection between image statistics and visual/neural encoding [2,7]. Contrast is important in a trivial sense, in that images cannot be seen without it - contrast is the carrier or medium of visual information.

However, above and beyond its importance to image detection, contrast seems to contribute qualitatively to perception. It is widely accepted that higher-contrast images look better, as shown in [12]. This could be due to higher contrast images bringing more content above threshold [11], or simply due to a psychological relation between contrast and sharpness. In a similar vein, it has been suggested repeatedly that simply adding high-frequency noise to an image improves its perceived quality (sharpness), in some cases, presumably because of a perceptual association dependence between high frequency contrast and image sharpness [4]. However, the results are based on the assumption that all of the observers perceive and process images in that same manner. But according to cognitive psychology human perceives and processes information, images included, in his/her individual way, defined as cognitive style [1,3,9].

Up to our knowledge, that point has not been taken into account in the above researches. Therefore, it is worth to verify if the way we perceive contrast depends stable on HVS only, or it is also a function of psychologically defined cognitive habits.

In order to investigate the problem, the subjective experiments should be done. Subjective image quality assessment methods originate from a wider group of psychometric scaling methods, which were developed to measure psychological attributes [19]. Given that the ultimate receivers of images are human eyes, the human subjective opinion is the most reliable value for indicating the image perceptual quality. According to [8,17,18], among procedures of perceptual experiments dedicated to image and video assessment the smallest measurement variance and thus the most accurate results can be obtained by a forced-choice method. The approach can be used to investigate the dependence between image contrast preference and types of cognitive style.

3 Conception

The aim of the paper is to examine if all of the subjects make their judgement about image quality in purely individual manner or there are some similarities in preferences among people in groups of the same cognitive styles. Therefore our research included two means for obtaining results. For the same group of observers we performed both perceptual experiment PE (described in detail in Sect. 4) and and FRIS®Thinking Styles Inventory (FRIS® TSI) [15] that is an online 76-items psychometric questionnaire (described in Subsect. 3.1). Finishing the experiment, the results derived from PE were converted to preferences of contrast level ranking PD. The questionnaire results included measures in 6 cognitive scales and individual ranking of 4 cognitive perspectives defined by FRIS® and were applied as a metrics in our research. Preprocessed PD and FRIS® measurements were composed into knowledge database KD. Then we performed analysis of contrast level preferences in subjects' groups defined by FRIS® measurements (see Fig. 1).

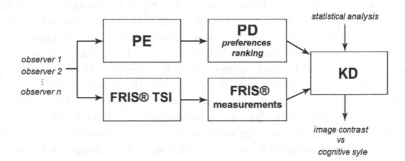

Fig. 1. The process of gathering knowledge (KD) from perceptual experiment (PE) and psychometric questionnaire (FRIS® TSI [14]) for the relation between image contrast and human cognitive style measurement retriving.

3.1   Human Cognitive Style as a Metrics

There are many approaches to human cognitive styles description and most of them define one or more bipolar scales, such as: reflectivity vs impulsivity, concrete vs abstract, relational vs analytical or field-dependence vs field-independence etc. [10] Nevertheless, even the cognitive styles are considered to be fundamental individual differences as long as temperamental types, there is no standard model or finite list of cognitive scales [16]. Some of the most widely used cognitive styles are measured by formal questionnaires or inventories. In our experiment we used as a metrics FRIS® Thinking Styles Inventory [15] that is a psychometric questionnaire measuring individual's preference ranking of 4 cognitive perspectives (cognitive styles metacategories) defined by FRIS® Model [14]:

- F: fact-based thinking (concrete, sequential, logical thinking)
- R: relation-based thinking (intuitive, field-dependent, relational thinking)
- I: idea-based thinking (abstract, lateral, global thinking)
- S: structure-based thinking (field-independent, reflective, analytical thinking)

FRIS® Thinking Styles Inventory [15] is psychometrically reliable, valid, normalised and standardised [14]. The 6 factors of the inventory are bipolar scales discriminating between pairs of cognitive perspectives: F vs I, F vs R etc. with internal consistency $0.76 - 0.82$ Cronbach's α. The 4 superfactors' internal consistency is $0, 82$ (F), $0, 88$(R) $0, 88$(I) $0, 88$(S) Cronbach's α. As a metrics in our experiment we used 1 nominal variable TS Thinking Style - the dominant (maximal) cognitive perspective of the subject (one from the set): $TS = \{F, R, I, S\}$.

4   Subjective Experiment

During experiments we investigated how contrast perception correlates with the observer cognitive style. The observers were asked to read a written instruction before the experiment. Following [6] the recommendation, the experiment started with a training session in which the observers could familiarise themselves with the task, interface, and typical images. After that session, they could ask questions or start the main experiment. To ensure that the observers fully attend the experiment, three random trials were shown at the beginning of the main session without recording the results. The images were displayed in a random order and with a different randomisation for each session. Two consecutive trials showing the same scene were avoided if possible. No session took longer than 30 min to avoid fatigue.

4.1   Experiment Design

Observers. The images were assessed by naive observers who were confirmed to have normal or corrected to normal vision. The age of the observers ranged

Fig. 2. Test images taken to the experiments.

between 20 and 70. Forty four observers completed the experiment. For additional reliability, all observers repeated each experiment three times, but no two repetitions took place on the same day in order to reduce the learning effect.

Display conditions. The experiments were run on display: NEC with, 1050×1680 pixel resolution. The display responses were measured with the Minolta CS-200 colorimeter and Specbos 1201 spectroradiometer. The measurements were used to calibrate the displays and ensure that all images were reproduced in the sRGB colour space.

Test images. The experiment was conducted on 20 images taken from Fotolia database (Fig. 2). It is subset of an image set composed for FRIS® project [15]. We used set containing different types of images contain a broad range of content type, including faces, animals, man-made objects and nature. Every image was modified by contrast level (low, reference, high). Preparing low and high contrast images we cared rather on quite equal visual difference.

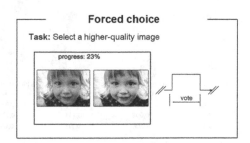

Fig. 3. Overview of the forced choice subjective quality assessment methods we investigated in this work.

Experimental procedure. We collected our data through the forced-choice experiment (Fig. 3). Forced-choice is an ordering method in which observers decide which of the two displayed images has a higher image quality. The method is popular, but is very tedious if a large number of conditions need to be compared. However, as reported in [8], it results in the smallest measurement variance and thus produces the most accurate results. Observers were shown a pair of images corresponding to different contrast level and were asked to indicate the image they prefer to put into photo album. Observers were always forced to choose one image, even if they saw no difference between them (thus, a forced-choice design). There was no time limit or minimum time in which to make the choice. The method was straightforward and was expected to be more accurate than rating methods.

5   Results and Analysis

The following sections discuss the results received from perceptual experiment and psychometrics questionary.

5.1   Screening Observers

The observers may have reported implausible impression scores because they misunderstood the experiment instruction or did not engage in the task and gave random answers. If the number of participants is low, it is easy to spot unreliable observers by inspecting the plots. However, when the number of observers is very high or it is difficult to scrutinise the plots, the [6] standard, Annex 2.3.1, provides a numerical screening procedure. We performed this procedure on our data and found no participants whose data needed to be removed.

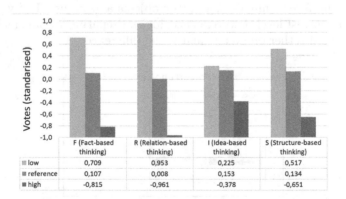

	F (Fact-based thinking)	R (Relation-based thinking)	I (Idea-based thinking)	S (Structure-based thinking)
low	0,709	0,953	0,225	0,517
reference	0,107	0,008	0,153	0,134
high	-0,815	-0,961	-0,378	-0,651

Fig. 4. Comparison of mean of observers preferences given for F, R I ans S cognitive styles. The mean votes values for different Thinking Styles are depicted below the graph.

5.2 Image Content, Contrast and Human Cognitive Style Relation

The obtained results suggest, that there are noticeable differences in preferences between groups of observers of different Thinking Styles (multicategories of cognitive styles), especially between idea-based and structure-based thinking groups (see Fig. 4). Despite the moderate number of subjects in the study, we found that the difference between the groups is statistically significant. The experiment was finished by 10 observers from F-based thinking group, 12 from R-based thinking group,10 from I-based thinking group and 16 from S-based thinking group.

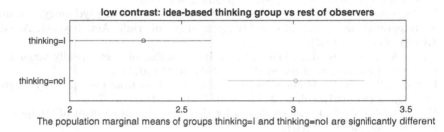

Fig. 5. ANOVA comparison of observers preferences given for low contrast, for idea-based thinking group and the rest of thinking groups.

The most significant result of the study is a difference between idea-based thinking observers and the rest of the subjects but only for low contrast level (see Fig. 5). It means, that observers from idea-based thinking group have chosen low contrast image significantly rarely than other observers. In other words, they prefer high contrast images most than the others. We assume, that probably the abstract and holistic thinking style of the idea-based thinkers includes higher than average "tolerance" for unrealistic experience. This term depicts one of the basic cognitive styles, that could be one of main traits of idea-based thinking [16]. The higher the contrast, the more unnatural the image probably is. Hence, for the idea-based thinkers with high tolerance and high expectance for unrealistic experience an image with higher contrast can be more attractive than it is for other observers.

6 Conclusions

This study is meant to provide a better understanding of image contrast perception and factors influence on human preferences. We proofed the given hypotheses that subjects' preference to images with different contrast level are a function not only of image content but also human cognitive style. The significant results were received for people characterised with abstract and holistic thinking style (idea-style) and the other cognitive styles.

The researches included in the paper are preliminary researches of a larger project concerned psychometrics tool for human cognitive styles recognition based on human perception [15]. There is also a high possibility, that after increasing the number of observers more of the differences we have noticed, would be statistically significant. Hence, we consider to intensively investigate the domain.

References

1. Ausburn, L.J., Ausburn, F.B.: Cognitive styles: Some information and implications for instructional design. Educ. Commun. Technol. **26**, 337–354 (1978)
2. Field, D.J.: What the statistics of natural images tell us about visual coding. In: Proceedings of the SPIE, vol. 1077, pp. 269–276 (1989)
3. Kozhevnikov, M.: Cognitive styles in the context of modern psychology: toward an integrated framework of cognitive style. Psychol. Bull. Am. Psychol. Assoc. **133**(3), 464–481 (2007)
4. Haun, A.M., Woods, R.L., Peli, E.: Perceived contrast of electronically magnified video. In: Proceedings of the SPIE, vol. 7865, p. 21 (2011)
5. Haun, A.M., Peli, E.: Is image quality a function of contrast perception? In: Proceedings of the SPIE, vol. 8651, id. 86510C 5 pp. (2013)
6. ITU-R.REC.BT.500-11, Methodology for the subjective assessment of the quality for television pictures (2002)
7. Klein, S.A., Carney, T.: 'Perfect' displays and 'perfect' image compression in space and time. In: Proceedings of the SPIE, vol. 1453, pp. 190–205 (1991)
8. Mantiuk, R.K., Tomaszewska, A., Mantiuk, R.: Comparison of four subjective methods for image quality assessment. Comput. Graph. Forum **31**(8), 2478–2491 (2012)
9. Messick, S.: Personality consistencies in cognition and creativity. In: Messick, S. (ed.) Individuality in Learning, pp. 4–23. Jossey-Bass, San Francisco (1976)
10. Riding, R.J., Rayner, S.G.: International Perspectives on Individual Differences: Cognitive Styles. Ablex Publishing, Stamford (1998)
11. Roufs, J.A.J.: Brightness contrast and sharpness, interactive factors in perceptual image quality. In: Proceedings of the SPIE, vol. 1077, pp. 66–72 (1989)
12. Roufs, J.A.J., Koselka, V.J., van Tongeren, A.A.: Global brightness contrast and the effect on perceptual image quality. In: Proceedings of the SPIE, vol. 2179, pp. 80–89 (1994)
13. Safranek, R.J., Johnston, J.D., Rosenholtz, R.E.: Perceptually tuned sub-band image coder. In: Proceedings of the SPIE, vol. 1249, pp. 284–293 (1990)
14. Samborska-Owczarek, A.: FRIS Thinking Styles Inventory, January 2018. https://fris.pl/FRIS-validity-data.pdf
15. Samborska-Owczarek, A.: FRIS Thinking Styles Inventory, January 2018. https://fris.pl
16. Sternberg, R.J., Zhang, L.-F.: Perspectives on Thinking, Learning, and Cognitive Styles. Lawrence Eribaum, Mahwah (New Jersey), London (2001)
17. Tomaszewska, A.L.: Time compensation in perceptual experiments. In: Chmielewski, L.J., Kozera, R., Shin, B.-S., Wojciechowski, K. (eds.) ICCVG 2014. LNCS, vol. 8671, pp. 33–40. Springer, Cham (2014). https://doi.org/10.1007/978-3-319-11331-9_5
18. Tomaszewska, A.: Scene reduction for subjective image quality assessment. J. Electron. Imaging **25**(1), 013015-1–013015-13 (2016)
19. Torgerson, W.S.: Theory and Methods of Scaling. Wiley, New York (1985)
20. Zetzsche, C., Hauske, G.: Multiple channel model for the prediction of subjective image quality. In: Proceedings of the SPIE, vol. 1077, pp. 209–216 (1989)

Vegetation Index Estimation
from Monospectral Images

Patricia L. Suárez[1]([✉]), Angel D. Sappa[1,2], and Boris X. Vintimilla[1]

[1] Facultad de Ingeniería en Electricidad y Computación, CIDIS,
Escuela Superior Politécnica del Litoral, ESPOL, Campus Gustavo Galindo,
09-01-5863, Guayaquil, Ecuador
{plsuarez,asappa,boris.vintimilla}@espol.edu.ec
[2] Computer Vision Center, Edifici O, Campus UAB, 08193
Bellaterra, Barcelona, Spain

Abstract. This paper proposes a novel approach to estimate Normalized Difference Vegetation Index (NDVI) from just the red channel of a RGB image. The NDVI index is defined as the ratio of the difference of the red and infrared radiances over their sum. In other words, information from the red channel of a RGB image and the corresponding infrared spectral band are required for its computation. In the current work the NDVI index is estimated just from the red channel by training a Conditional Generative Adversarial Network (CGAN). The architecture proposed for the generative network consists of a single level structure, which combines at the final layer results from convolutional operations together with the given red channel with Gaussian noise to enhance details, resulting in a sharp NDVI image. Then, the discriminative model estimates the probability that the NDVI generated index came from the training dataset, rather than the index automatically generated. Experimental results with a large set of real images are provided showing that a Conditional GAN single level model represents an acceptable approach to estimate NDVI index.

1   Introduction

Computer vision applications can be found in almost every domain, including topics such as medical imaging, gaming, video surveillance, multimedia, industrial applications, remote sensing, just to mention a few. In most of the cases these applications are based on images obtained from a cameras working at the visible spectrum. There are some cases, in particular in medical imaging and remote sensing, where cross-spectral and multispectral images are considered. The appealing factor of using images from different spectral bands lies on the one hand on the possibility to obtain information that cannot be seen at the visible spectrum; on the other hand, on the combined use of information that can be considered to generate some kind of high level reasoning; for instance in remote sensing the combined usage of images from different spectral bands is considered to generate vegetation indexes. These vegetation indexes are used to determine the health and strength of vegetation and their definitions involve several factors, like soil reflectance, atmosphere, vegetation density, etc.

Among the different indexes proposed in the literature, the Normalized Difference Vegetation Index (NDVI) is the most widely used [1]; in general, it is used to determine the condition, developmental stages and biomass of cultivated plants and to forecasts their yields. The values of this index go from -1 to 1, with the value zero representing the approximate where the absence of vegetation begins. Negative values represent non-vegetated surfaces. This index is calculated as the ratio between the difference and sum of the reflectance in NIR and red regions:

$$NVDI = \frac{R_{\mathrm{NIR}} - R_{\mathrm{RED}}}{R_{\mathrm{NIR}} + R_{\mathrm{RED}}}, \tag{1}$$

where R_{NIR} is the reflectance of NIR radiation and R_{RED} is the reflectance of visible red radiation.

Although interesting, cross/multi-spectral solutions need the set up of more than one camera. For instance, in the case of NDVI, an image from the visible and an image from the NIR spectra are required. In other words, we need two cameras, acquiring images at the same time of the same scene, in order to be able to compute the values of Eq. (1). It should be noticed that before computing Eq. (1) images need to be accurately registered—i.e. the information should be referred to the same reference system. Unfortunately, since images from different spectra are considered their may look different, so the problem is how to find the same set of points in both spectra [2] to be used as references. Recently, deep learning based approaches have been proposed to overcome this drawback and find correspondences in cross-spectral domains [3,4]. Once these points are obtained we can proceed by registering the images in a single reference system.

Cross/multi-spectral approaches provide unique solutions to different complex problems, however, as mentioned above, different preprocessing stages need to be performed before computing these solutions; hence, in the current work we wonder whether it is possible to obtain the same result but just using information from a single spectral band. Actually, a similar philosophy has been recently presented in [5] where vegetation index is estimated based on a learning approach from a single near infrared spectral band image. Although interesting results have been obtained, the weakness point of that approach lies on the need of having NIR images, which are not that much common like visible spectrum images. In the current work we propose to explore the possibility to estimate NDVI vegetation index using the red channel from the visible spectrum. The index is estimated from a learning based approach, where a Conditional Generative Adversarial Network (CGAN) is trained with a large data set. The CGAN architecture used in the current work is similar to the one presented in [6], but including a conditional red channel image at the final layer of the learning model to improve the details of the generated NDVI vegetation index. Additionally, a more elaborated loss function is proposed to preserve details of the given image.

The rest of the paper is organized as follows. Section 2 introduces the Generative Adversarial Network formulation. Then, Sect. 3 presents the architecture

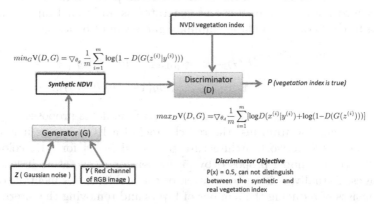

Fig. 1. Conditional Generative Adversarial process implemented on the current work to estimate NDVI vegetation index.

proposed in the current work, detailing the design, proposed loss functions and training with cross-spectral datasets. Section 4 depicts the experimental results and finally, conclusion are presented in Sect. 5.

2   Generative Adversarial Networks

Generative Adversarial Networks (GANs) are powerful and flexible tools quite useful in several computer vision problems; one of their most common applications is image generation. In the GAN framework [7], generative models are estimated via an adversarial process, in which simultaneously two models are trained: (i) a generative model G that captures the data distribution, and (ii) a discriminative model D that estimates the probability that a sample came from the training data rather than G. The training procedure for G is to maximize the probability of D making a mistake. In this architecture it is possible to apply certain conditions to improve the learning process. According to [8], to learn the generator's distribution p_g over data $\boldsymbol{x}$, the generator builds a mapping function from a prior noise distribution $p_z(z)$ to a data space $G(z; \theta_g)$ and the discriminator, $D(x; \theta_d)$, outputs a single scalar representing the probability that x came from training data rather than p_g. G and D are both trained simultaneously, the parameters for G are adjusted to minimize $log(1 - D(G(z)))$ and for D to minimize $log D(x)$ with a value function $V(G, D)$:

$$\frac{min}{G} \frac{max}{D} V(D, G) = \mathbb{E}_{x \sim p \, \text{data}_{(x)}} [log D(x)] + \tag{2}$$
$$\mathbb{E}_{z \sim p \, \text{data}_{(z)}} [log(1 - D(G(z)))].$$

Generative adversarial networks can be extended to a conditional model if both the generator and discriminator are conditioned on some extra information y. This information could be any kind of auxiliary information, such as class labels or data from other modalities. We can perform the conditioning by feeding y into both discriminator and generator as additional input layer. The objective function of a two-player minimax game would be as:

$$\frac{min}{G}\frac{max}{D}V(D,G) = \mathbb{E}_x \sim_{p\,\text{data}_{(x)}} [logD(x|y)] + \tag{3}$$
$$\mathbb{E}_z \sim_{p\,\text{data}_{(z)}} [log(1 - D(G(z|y)))].$$

In the current work a novel Conditional GAN model is proposed for vegetation index estimation from just the red channel of a RGB image; it is inspired on both the GAN network architecture presented in [9] for NIR colorization and on the triplet model proposed by [5] for learning vegetation indexes using NIR images. Actually, it is an adaptation of the architectures mentioned above, which consists of reducing the number of layers and removing the internal number of levels of learning architecture (FLAT or single). Another difference with previous approaches lies on the proposed loss function, which do not take into account only intensity level information but also it considers image structure information.

3   Proposed Approach

This section presents the approach proposed for NDVI index vegetation estimation. As mentioned above, it uses a similar architecture to the one presented in [5], where a conditional adversarial generative learning network has been proposed. A traditional scheme of layers in a deep network is considered. In the current work the usage of a Conditional GAN model is evaluated with a Flat scheme, this GAN's model has been used because it presented good performance to solve problems like colorization, dehazing, enhancement, object recognition, etc. Based on the results that have been obtained on this type of problems, where improvements in accuracy and performance have been obtained, we propose the usage of a learning model that allows the mapping of a vegetation index based on a single channel of RBG images (the red channel). The model will receive as an input a patch corresponding to red channel of a RGB image. Gaussian noise is added to each patch of the learning architecture to increase the variability in the learning process of the generation index patches, increasing the time of the convergence and generalization. A $l1$ regularization term has been added on each layer of the model in order to prevent the coefficients to overfit, which make the network learns small weights to minimize the loss, maximizes the distribution of model outputs, and improve the generalization capability of the model. Figure 1 depicts the Conditional GAN process proposed in the current work.

As mentioned above, in our case, the generator network has been implemented using a single level of layers (FLAT). Figure 2 presents an illustration of the GAN network used in this research. In all the cases, at the output of the generator network the vegetation index is obtained. This vegetation index will be validated by the discriminative network, which will evaluate the probability that the generated image (vegetation index in grayscale), is similar to the real

Conditional Generative Adversarial Architecture

(G) Generator Network

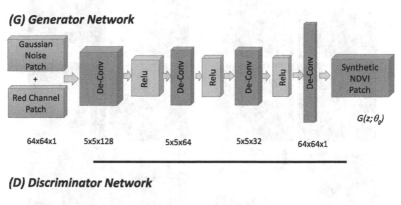

(D) Discriminator Network

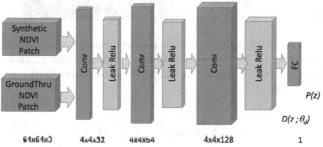

Fig. 2. GAN architecture for NDVI Vegetation Index estimation; A single level layer model (FLAT) evaluated as Generator Network; on bottom the Discriminator Network.

one used as a ground truth. Additionally, in the generator model, in order to obtain a better image representation, the CGAN framework is reformulated for a conditional generative image modeling tuple. In other words, the generative model $G(z; \theta_g)$ is trained from a red channel of a RGB image plus Gaussian noise, in order to produce a NDVI vegetation index image; additionally, a discriminative model $D(z; \theta_d)$ is trained to assign the correct label to the generated NDVI image, according to the provided real NDVI image, which is used as a ground truth. Variables (θ_g) and (θ_d) represent the weighting values for the generative and discriminative networks.

The model has been defined with a multi-term loss ($\mathcal{L}$) conformed by the combination of the Adversarial loss plus the Intensity loss (MSE) and the Structural loss (SSIM). This combined loss has been defined to avoid the usage of only a pixel-wise loss (PL) to measure the mismatch between a generated image and its corresponding ground-truth image. This multi-term loss function is better designed to human perceptual criteria of image quality, which is detailed next. The Adversarial loss is designed to minimize the cross-entropy to improve the texture loss :

Fig. 3. Pairs of patches (64×64) from *country* category (two-left columns) and *field* category (two-right columns) [10]: (*top*) RGB image; (*middle*) Red channel of the given RGB image; (*bottom*) NDVI vegetation index computed from RGB images and the corresponding NIR images.

$$\mathcal{L}_{Adversarial} = -\sum_i log D(G_w(I_{z|y}), (I_{x|y}), \tag{4}$$

where D and G_w are the discriminator and generator of the real $I_{x|y}$ and generated $I_{z|y}$ images conditioned by the red channel of the RGB of the GAN network.

The Intensity loss is defined as:

$$\mathcal{L}_{Intensity} = \frac{1}{NM} \sum_{i=1}^{N} \sum_{j=1}^{M} (NDVIe_{i,j} - NDVIg_{i,j})^2, \tag{5}$$

where $NDVIe_{i,j}$ is the vegetation index estimated by the network and $NDVIg_{i,j}$ is the ground-truth vegetation index and $N \times M$ is the size of the patches. This loss measures the difference in intensity of the pixels between the images without considering texture and content comparisons. Additionally, this loss penalizes larger errors, but is more tolerant to small errors, without considering the specific structure in the image.

To address the limitations of the simple Intensity loss function, the usage of a reference-based measure is proposed. One of the reference-based index is the Structural Similarity Index (SSIM) [11], which evaluates images accounting for the fact that the human visual perception system is sensitive to changes in local structure; the idea behind this loss function is to help the learning model to produce a visually improved image. The Structural loss for a pixel p is defined as:

$$\mathcal{L}_{SSIM} = \frac{1}{NM} \sum_{p=1}^{P} 1 - SSIM(p), \tag{6}$$

where SSIM(p) is the Structural Similarity Index (see [11] for more details) centered in pixel p of the patch P.

The Final loss ($\mathcal{L}$) used in this work is the accumulative sum of the individual Adversarial, Intensity and Structural loss functions:

$$\mathcal{L}_{Final} = \mathcal{L}_{Adversarial} + \mathcal{L}_{Intensity} + \mathcal{L}_{SSIM} \tag{7}$$

4   Experimental Results

The proposed approach has been evaluated using the red channel of RGB images and their corresponding NDVI vegetation index (ground truth), computed from Eq. (1) using NIR and red channel images; this cross-spectral data set came from [10]. The *country* and *field* categories have been considered for evaluating the performance of the proposed approach, examples of this dataset are presented in Fig. 3. This dataset consists of 477 registered images categorized in 9 groups captured in RGB (visible spectrum) and NIR (Near Infrared spectrum). The *country* category contains 52 pairs of images of (1024×680 pixels), while the *field* category contains 51 pairs of images of (1024×680 pixels). In order to train our network to generate vegetation index from each of these categories 380.000 pairs of patches of (64×64 pixels) have been cropped both, in the RGB images as well as in the corresponding NDVI images. Additionally, 3800 pairs of patches, per category, of (64×64 pixels) have been also generated for validation. It should be noted that images are correctly registered, so that a pixel-to-pixel correspondence is guaranteed.

Table 1. Root Mean Squared Errors (RMSE) and Structural Similarities (SSIM) obtained with the proposed GAN architecture by using different loss functions (SSIM the bigger the better).

Training	RMSE		SSIM	
	Country	*Field*	*Country*	*Field*
GAN with $\mathcal{L}_{Adversarial} + \mathcal{L}_{Intensity}$	3.93	4.12	0.86	0.83
GAN with $\mathcal{L}_{Adversarial} + \mathcal{L}_{SSIM}$	3.81	3.96	0.91	0.89
GAN with $\mathcal{L}_{Final}$	3.53	3.70	0.94	0.91

The Conditional Generative Adversarial network evaluated in the current work is a Flat (single level of learning layer) for NDVI vegetation index estimation. It has been trained using a 3.4 four core processor with 16GB of memory with a NVIDIA Titan XP GPU. Qualitative results are presented in Figs. 4 and 5. Figure 4 shows NDVI vegetation index images from the *country* category generated with the proposed Flat GAN network. Additionally, Fig. 5 shows NDVI vegetation index images from the *field* category generated with the proposed Flat GAN network. Quantitative evaluations for the different loss functions have been

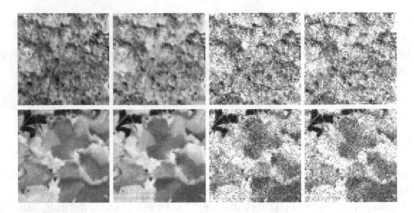

Fig. 4. (*1st.Col*) Ground truth NDVI index from the ***Country category***. (*2nd. – 4th.Col*) NDVI index obtained with the proposed GAN architecture with different loss functions: $\mathcal{L}_{Final}$, $\mathcal{L}_{Adversarial} + \mathcal{L}_{SSIM}$ and $\mathcal{L}_{Adversarial} + \mathcal{L}_{Intensity}$.

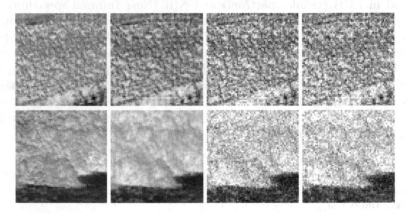

Fig. 5. (*1st.Col*) Ground truth NDVI index from the ***Field category***. (*2nd. – 4th.Col*) NDVI index obtained with the proposed GAN architecture with different loss functions: $\mathcal{L}_{final}$, $\mathcal{L}_{Adversarial} + \mathcal{L}_{SSIM}$ and $\mathcal{L}_{Adversarial} + \mathcal{L}_{Intensity}$.

obtained and provided below. Up to our humble knowledge there are not previous work on similar technique to estimate vegetation index using only the red channel of RGB images. Hence, the only way to evaluate results is by comparing the Root Mean Square Error (RMSE) of each approach. The RMSE measures the distance between the estimated NDVI with respect to the ground truth, which is the standard deviation of the residuals. Residuals are measures of how different are the images compared from each other.

The results obtained with the multi-term loss approach show that the Structural Similarity metric contributes to improve the texture of the estimated NDVI vegetation index. Furthermore, the Intensity level loss function, which measure the Mean Square Error between the estimated value and the corresponding ground truth, helps to evaluate the estimation.

Table 1 presents the average Mean Square Errors (MSE) and the Structural Similarity metric (SSMI) obtained with the the single level architecture when different loss functions ($\mathcal{L}_{Adversarial} + \mathcal{L}_{SSIM}$), ($\mathcal{L}_{Adversarial} + \mathcal{L}_{Intensity}$) and ($\mathcal{L}_{Final}$) are evaluated in the two categories used as case studies. It can be appreciated that the results obtained with the $\mathcal{L}_{Final}$ loss function reaches the best result. The results obtained show that the more elaborated the loss function is, the better results will be obtained, since the network will be more capable to learn complex scenes at a faster convergence. Having in mind that the NDVI indexes resulting from the learning process are represented as images in the range of $[0, 255]$, the results presented in Table 1 show that the average deviation of the estimated values is 1.4%. Additionally, looking at the SSIM metric, which is a perception-based model that considers image degradation as perceived change in structural information, we can observe that on average, in both categories, results are above 0.9. This value means that obtained results highly pixels inter-dependencies. These dependencies carry important information about the structure of the objects in the visual scene. This metric combined with MSE allows us to confirm that the NDVI index obtained with the proposed results is a valid approach.

5   Conclusion

This paper tackles the challenging problem of NDVI vegetation index estimation by using a novel Conditional Generative Adversarial Network model. The novelty of the proposed approach lies on the usage of just a single spectral band (the red channel of RGB images). The architecture proposed for the generative network consists of a single level structure, which combines at the final layer results from convolutional operations together with the given red channel, resulting in a sharp NVDI image. Then, the discriminative model estimates the probability that the NDVI generated index came from the training dataset, rather than the index automatically generated. Different loss functions are evaluated trying to help the learning model to produce a visually improved image. The proposed loss function takes into account both intensity level information together with image structure information. Experimental results with a large set of outdoor images shows the validity of the proposed approach to estimate NDVI index from monospectral images. As a future work the possibility to obtain the NDVI from all the channels will be considered.

Acknowledgment. This work has been partially supported by: the ESPOL project PRAIM (FIEC-09-2015); the Spanish Government under Projects TIN2014-56919-C3-2-R and TIN2017-89723-P; and the "CERCA Programme/Generalitat de Catalunya". The authors would like to thank NVIDIA for GPU donations.

References

1. Rouse Jr., J., Haas, R., Schell, J., Deering, D.: Monitoring vegetation systems in the great plains with erts (1974)
2. Ricaurte, P., Chilán, C., Aguilera-Carrasco, C.A., Vintimilla, B.X., Sappa, A.D.: Feature point descriptors: infrared and visible spectra. Sensors **14**, 3690–3701 (2014)
3. Aguilera, C.A., Aguilera, F.J., Sappa, A.D., Aguilera, C., Toledo, R.: Learning cross-spectral similarity measures with deep convolutional neural networks. In: The IEEE Conference on Computer Vision and Pattern Recognition (CVPR) Workshops, p. 9. IEEE (2016)
4. Suárez, P.L., Sappa, A.D., Vintimilla, B.X.: Cross-spectral image patch similarity using convolutional neural network. In: 2017 IEEE International Workshop of Electronics, Control, Measurement, Signals and their Application to Mechatronics (ECMSM), pp. 1–5. IEEE (2017)
5. Suárez, P.L., Sappa, A.D., Vintimilla, B.X.: Learning image vegetation index through a conditional generative adversarial network. In: 2nd Ecuador Technical Chapters Meeting (2017)
6. Suárez, P.L., Sappa, A.D., Vintimilla, B.X.: Learning to colorize infrared images. In: De la Prieta, F., Vale, Z., Antunes, L., Pinto, T., Campbell, A.T., Julián, V., Neves, A.J.R., Moreno, M.N. (eds.) PAAMS 2017. AISC, vol. 619, pp. 164–172. Springer, Cham (2018). https://doi.org/10.1007/978-3-319-61578-3_16
7. Goodfellow, I., Pouget-Abadie, J., Mirza, M., Xu, B., Warde-Farley, D., Ozair, S., Courville, A., Bengio, Y.: Generative adversarial nets. In: Advances in Neural Information Processing Systems, pp. 2672–2680 (2014)
8. Mirza, M., Osindero, S.: Conditional generative adversarial nets. arXiv preprint arXiv:1411.1784 (2014)
9. Suárez, P.L., Sappa, A.D., Vintimilla, B.X.: Infrared image colorization based on a triplet DCGAN architecture. In: Computer Vision and Pattern Recognition (2017)
10. Brown, M., Süsstrunk, S.: Multi-spectral SIFT for scene category recognition. In: 2011 IEEE Conference on Computer Vision and Pattern Recognition (CVPR), pp. 177–184. IEEE (2011)
11. Wang, Z., Bovik, A.C., Sheikh, H.R., Simoncelli, E.P.: Image quality assessment: from error visibility to structural similarity. IEEE Trans. Image Process. **13**, 600–612 (2004)

Detection of Aruco Markers Using the Quadrilateral Sum Conjuncture

José Ferrão[1], Paulo Dias[1,2], and António J. R. Neves[1,2(✉)]

[1] DETI, University of Aveiro, 3810-193 Aveiro, Portugal
{joseferrao,paulo.dias,an}@ua.pt
[2] IEETA, University of Aveiro, 3810-193 Aveiro, Portugal

Abstract. Fiducial Markers are heavily used for pose estimation in many applications from robotics to augmented reality. In this paper we present an algorithm for the detection of aruco marker at larger distance. The algorithm uses the quadrilateral sum conjecture and analyzes the sum of the cosine of the internal angles to detect squares at larger distances. Experiments conducted showed that the developed solution was able to improve the detection distance when compared to other methods that use similar marker while keeping similar pose estimation precision.

Keywords: Robotics · Digital images · Computer vision · Marker detection
Aruco

1 Introduction

Absolute pose estimation is a common problem in robotics. One possible solution to tackle this problem is the use of odometry information (coming from encoders and Inertial Units). However, this solution suffers significantly from drift error.

An alternative commonly used not only in robotics but also in areas like augmented reality is the usage of markers to estimate the position and orientation of the camera. A visual marker is something that can be easily distinguished from the rest of the ambient and have characteristics that allow it to be easily detected and identified.

The motivation for this work was the need for a marker-based solution to easily identify charging stations for robots and correcting odometry drifting using the pose estimated by the marker detector.

One of the main problems found when experimenting already existing solutions (ROS Aruco [1] and Alvar [2]) was that they are not able to identify the markers from far away or under hard perspective distortion making it difficult to discover the charging station. In this paper we propose an algorithm for the detection of aruco markers. Our approach uses the quadrilateral sum conjecture to improve the detection distance of these markers.

The remain of this paper is structured as described next. Section 2 presents base concepts related with marker encoding and detection, Sect. 3 presents the proposed algorithm and discusses pose estimation. Section 4 presents experimental results, and, finally, Sect. 5 contains result analysis and conclusion.

A. Campilho et al. (Eds.): ICIAR 2018, LNCS 10882, pp. 363–369, 2018.
https://doi.org/10.1007/978-3-319-93000-8_41

2   Aruco Markers

Aruco markers are geometrically square, they have a black border and an inner grid that is used to store a numeric identifier in binary code.

A dictionary is used to identify the marker [3]. The dictionary defines a set of rules used to calculate the marker identifier, perform validation and apply error correction.

We use the original aruco dictionary [1], that uses bits from the marker 2nd and 4th columns to store the marker identifier in natural binary code, the remaining bits are used for parity checking. Figure 1 presents the first four markers in this dictionary.

Fig. 1. Aruco markers with id's 0, 1, 2 and 3.

A signature matrix is used to validate the marker. Each row of this matrix encodes a possibility of 2 bits. An aruco marker is valid only if each of its rows are equal to one of the rows of the signature matrix, ensuring that the marker only have one valid rotation. Table 1 represents the signature matrix used in this dictionary.

Table 1.   Signature matrix, used to validate aruco markers.

Value	Data				
0	1	0	0	0	0
1	1	0	1	1	1
2	0	1	0	0	1
3	0	1	1	1	0

By analyzing the signature matrix, it is possibly to verify that it is not enough to guarantee that there is only one possible rotation for each marker, in the Fig. 2 we can see the marker 1023 that is horizontally symmetric.

Fig. 2.   Aruco marker 1023.

3 Detection Algorithm

The detection algorithm was implemented using the OpenCV library, since it provides a large set of image processing algorithms. Figure 3 shows the steps applied to detect and identify markers.

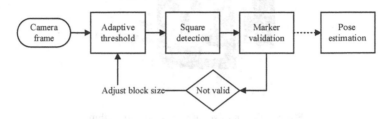

Fig. 3. Algorithm diagram

The algorithm starts by applying adaptive threshold [4] to the image, this algorithm consists in calculating for each pixel a threshold value using the histogram of its neighborhood. It is of particular interest for situations with multiple lighting conditions. Figure 4 shows the results after applying adaptive thresholding.

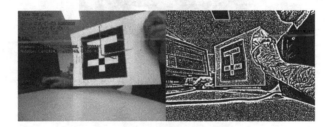

Fig. 4. Adaptive threshold result.

To determine the threshold block (neighborhood size), one block size is tested on each frame, the block size chosen is the average size from all block sizes were the maximum number of markers were found, the block size is retested when there are no markers visible.

After threshold is applied to the image, we perform square detection contours are detected using a border-following algorithm [5], followed by the Douglas-Peucker contour simplification algorithm [6].

Based on the detected contours, the Quadrilateral Sum Conjecture is used as a criterion to detect squares. Even under significant perspective distortion a square is always a convex quadrilateral. Our second criteria will be to make sure that the sum of the cosine of all inner angle is below a defined threshold.

To filter noise a third criterion was added: all contours composing a geometry with an area bellow a defined threshold will be discarded.

These three criteria allow to properly filter squares even under heavy distortion from the contour list. Figure 5 represents the obtained result for a maximum sum of cosine of 0.25 and a minimum area of 100px.

Fig. 5. Result of square detection algorithm

Perspective distortion is corrected in the detected squares, then they are resampled into a 7×7 matrix using linear interpolation, threshold is applied using the Otsu's Binarization algorithm [7], at this point we obtain a matrix with the marker data in it. Figure 6 represents the matrix obtained after the binarization process.

Fig. 6. Marker reading result

At this stage, the marker data is validated as aruco using the signature matrix. Markers might be detected in any orientation. The algorithm tests the data with different rotations (90°, 180°, 270°), if the marker is not recognized for any rotation it is then discarded.

For pose estimation the method solvePnp from OpenCV was used, in iterative mode using Levenberg-Marquardt optimization [8].

To obtain the camera position, markers need to be registered into the program, a marker is represented by its identifier and a real-world pose (position and rotation).

Corners obtained from all visible known markers are used to estimate the camera pose.

4   Algorithm Evaluation

We created a testing environment to compare the developed solution with the ones already existing in the literature. Two test markers were printed: one Aruco maker and one ARTag maker. Both markers had exactly 20 cm in size and the camera was placed on top of a box with the marker aligned with the camera. The marker was fixed with transparent tape.

A measuring tape with a millimeter scale was used to measure the distance between the camera and the markers. An image was taken for each distance tested and the markers were moved 30 cm each time until none of the algorithms was able to detect the marker. Figure 7 represents some samples of the testing images used during the experiments.

Fig. 7. Some images used to test the developed algorithm.

To measure the tolerance of the detector to perspective distortion a second testing environment was created. A marker was placed on a box and the camera was positioned 2.0 m away. The marker was rotated in steps of 10° from 0° to 80°. Table 2 presents the results obtained for marker rotation showing that the proposed method performed better than the other two algorithms used for comparison, obtaining lower error.

Table 2. Results obtained for maker rotation.

Rotation	Proposed solution		ROS Aruco		Alvar	
	Dist. (m)	Error (%)	Dist. (m)	Error (%)	Dist. (m)	Error (%)
0	1.981	0.980	2.013	0.631	1.986	0.727
10	1.983	0.872	2.032	1.583	2.017	0.858
20	1.985	0.741	2.031	1.537	2.011	0.564
30	1.989	0.528	2.029	1.415	1.974	1.308
40	2.001	0.040	2.029	1.425	1.971	1.493
50	2.002	0.121	2.03	1.468	2.028	1.357
60	2.004	0.213	2.033	1.639	1.974	1.322
70	1.993	0.341	2.029	1.421		

Camera calibration was performed using a chessboard pattern and the values obtained were stored to be used for the tests. Figure 8 presents the results obtained. It is possible to observe an improvement in the maximum detection distance when using our algorithm.

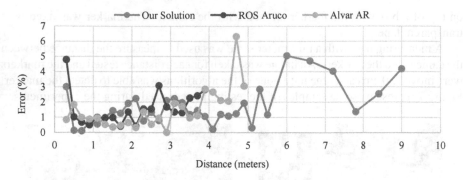

Fig. 8. Samples of the testing data

5   Conclusion

Two well known and used existing algorithms were tested (ROS Aruco and Alvar) and compared with the one proposed in this paper. All algorithms use a similar approach for marker detection: adaptive threshold, detect squares, refine corners, apply distortion correction, and decode the marker data. The proposed method uses a different approach for square detection allowed to detect markers at larger distances and more immune to rotations.

Experimental results show that algorithm detects the marker up to 9 m, when compared with 4 m and 5 m for the state of art algorithms referred before, representing a 44% increase in detection distance, with similar precision values.

The method also reveals more tolerance to perspective distortion, obtaining better precision results when detecting rotated markers.

To improve the algorithm further a corner refinement method with subpixel accuracy could be added improving the marker corner position estimation.

An implementation of the algorithm described in this document can be found at www.github.com/tentone/aruco.

Acknowledgments. This work was partially funded by FEDER (Programa Operacional Factores de Competitividade - COMPETE) and by National Funds through the FCT - Foundation for Science and Technology in the context of the project UID/CEC/00127/2013.

References

1. Garrido-Jurado, S., Muñoz-Salinas, R., Madrid-Cuevas, F.J., Marín-Jiménez, M.J.: Automatic generation and detection of highly reliable fiducial markers under occlusion. Pattern Recogn. **47**(6), 2280–2292 (2014)
2. Siltanen, S.: Theory and Applications of Marker-Based Augmented Reality. VTT Science 3
3. Garrido-Jurado, S., Muñoz-Salinas, R., Madrid-Cuevas, F.J., Medina-Carnicer, R.: Generation of fiducial marker dictionaries using mixed integer linear programming. Pattern Recogn. **51**(C), 481–491 (2016)

4. Sezgin, M., Sankur, B.: Survey over image thresholding techniques and quantitative performance evaluation. J. Electron. Imaging **13**(1), 146–165 (2004)
5. Suzuki, S., Abe, K.: Topological structural analysis of digitized binary images by border following. Comput. Vis. Graph. Image Process. **30**(1), 32–46 (1985)
6. Wu, S.-T., da Silva, A.C.G., Márquez, M.R.G.: The Douglas-peucker algorithm: sufficiency conditions for non-self-intersections. J. Braz. Comp. Soc. **9**(3), 67–84 (2004)
7. Otsu, N.: A threshold selection method from gray-level histograms. IEEE Trans. Syst. Man Cybern. **9**(1), 62–66 (1979)
8. Levenberg, K.: A method for the solution of certain non-linear problems in least squares. Q. Appl. Math. **2**(2), 164–168 (1994)

Activity Recognition

Human Action Recognition Using Fusion of Depth and Inertial Sensors

Zain Fuad and Mustafa Unel[✉]

Faculty of Engineering and Natural Sciences, Sabanci University,
Istanbul, Turkey
{zainfuad,munel}@sabanciuniv.edu

Abstract. In this paper we present a human action recognition system that utilizes the fusion of depth and inertial sensor measurements. Robust depth and inertial signal features, that are subject-invariant, are used to train independent Neural Networks, and later decision level fusion is employed using a probabilistic framework in the form of Logarithmic Opinion Pool. The system is evaluated using UTD-Multimodal Human Action Dataset, and we achieve 95% accuracy in 8-fold cross-validation, which is not only higher than using each sensor separately, but is also better than the best accuracy obtained on the mentioned dataset by 3.5%.

Keywords: Human action recognition · Sensor fusion
Depth camera · Inertial sensor · Neural Network
Logarithmic opinion pool

1 Introduction

Human action recognition consists of acquiring a person's gestures through various sensors, combining those gestures to form an action, and understanding those actions. It has found applications in domains such as surveillance, robotics, telemedicine, internet of things and human-machine interaction [1], and has extended to unorthodox areas, such as recognition of food preparation activities [2].

Recent advances such as the introduction of Microsoft Kinect and ASUS Xtion Pro Live, low-cost RGB-D cameras that acquire depth information in addition to RGB videos, have aided the capture of human motion, in contrast to the expensive detector based MoCap systems, or computationally-expensive 3-D reconstruction using stereo cameras [1]. RGB-D videos preserve discriminative information, such as shape and distance variations [3], and have reduced processing times as compared to traditional RGB cameras [4]. Thus, they have enabled researchers to use them in an action recognition structure. Han et al. [5] highlighted the utilization of Kinect for vision based algorithms, while Aggarwal et al. [6] discussed different approaches for feature extraction from 3D data and mentioned methodologies employed in the context of human activity recognition. Notable work in this area includes the proposition of a Hierarchical Recurrent

A. Campilho et al. (Eds.): ICIAR 2018, LNCS 10882, pp. 373–380, 2018.
https://doi.org/10.1007/978-3-319-93000-8_42

Neural Network framework which uses skeletal positions obtained from depth cameras, and understands the performed actions [7]. Similarly, Nie et al. [8] decomposed human actions into poses, and further decomposed these poses to mid-level spatio-temporal parts and used dynamic programming for classification purposes.

Adding to this, low-cost, small and light-weight, wearable inertial sensors have made possible the use of these sensors for human-activity recognition, as they provide very little hindrance to the person performing these actions and can be used in real life scenarios [9]. Qaiser et al. [10] studied the classification of arm action in cricket using inertial sensors, while Ermes et al. [11] analyzed the use of inertial sensors in the detection of sports activities in controlled and natural environments. In the latter, a hybrid classifier was used, which was composed of a tree structure possessing a priori knowledge and artificial Neural Networks, and 3 reference classifiers.

Each of the sensors has their own advantages and short-comings, and a fusion of these sensors results in a higher action recognition performance [1]. This fusion can occur at the data-level, feature-level or decision-level and the literature suggests different approaches in this regard. For action recognition, Ofli et al. [12] used HOG and HOF features in a Bag-of-Features framework from the depth camera, and variance of acceleration for each temporal window from the inertial sensor. Chen et al. [13] performed a decision level fusion of depth motion maps from the depth sensor and statistical features obtained based on the temporal segments from inertial sensor. On the other hand, Stein and McKenna [2] proposed the use of statistical features from both Kinect and inertial sensor to gather visual displacement components and representations of acceleration signals respectively, to recognize food preparation activities.

The notion of human action recognition using a combination of different sensors and sensor fusion is still a maturing research area. Complex algorithms although give a good accuracy of recognition, however, their slow performance or huge training times limit their uses in a lot of scenarios. On the other hand, algorithms which can be employed in a real time framework have their use limited to controlled environments.

In this paper, we propose a human action recognition system that utilizes joint locations from the depth camera and acceleration and gyro measurements from the inertial sensor. After extracting subject invariant features, we implement separate Neural Network classifiers for each sensor, and perform a decision level fusion on the outputs of these networks in a probabilistic manner. The proposed algorithm can be employed in real time and performs well under noisy measurements. Furthermore, we test our algorithm on UTD-Multimodal Human Action Dataset [14], a publicly available dataset, that mimics the real world scenario due to the variety of actions available that incorporate the movement of different joints. The fusion accuracy is higher than when using each sensor alone as well as better than highest accuracy achieved [13] on the mentioned dataset.

The organization of this paper is as follows: Sect. 2 presents the proposed algorithm which incorporates features from depth and inertial sensors. Section 3 presents the results of the proposed algorithm, and finally, Sect. 4 concludes the paper discussing the future aspects of this research.

2 Proposed Method

Intra-class variations are a common observation in a human action recognition framework, due to the variations in the body shape (size) of the person performing the action coupled with the speed variations in the performed action. A robust classification algorithm is needed in this regard, as noise due to jitters makes the classification problem more challenging.

In the proposed algorithm (Fig. 1), depth information is acquired from Microsoft Kinect and 20 joints are tracked in 3-D Cartesian coordinates. Furthermore, linear accelerations and angular velocities are obtained from a wearable inertial sensor, i.e. IMU, located on different parts of the body which consists of a 3-axis accelerometer and a 3-axis gyroscope. All the signals are made the same size with respect to the entries from a particular sensor, using bicubic interpolation, to reduce the temporal variations. After performing normalization of the skeletal joint positions to achieve user independence and extraction of mean and standard deviation of the inertial data, the data obtained from each sensor is classified separately using Neural Networks and finally, decision level fusion is performed on the output of the Neural Networks using Logarithmic Opinion pool (LOGP) [15]. In this work we assume the use of one inertial and one depth sensor, however, the implemented algorithm can be scaled up to utilize information from more sensors.

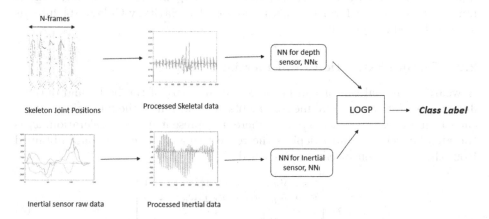

Fig. 1. Overview of the proposed method

2.1 Feature Extraction from Depth Sensor

The depth sensor outputs the 3D world coordinates of each tracked joint. Let $[x_{i,j} \; y_{i,j} \; z_{i,j}]$ be the spatial coordinates of each joint, where i is the joint number and j is the frame number. Then the output I_K of the depth sensor can be represented as

$$
I_K = \begin{bmatrix}
x_{1,1} & y_{1,1} & z_{1,1} & x_{1,2} & y_{1,2} & z_{1,2} & \cdots & x_{1,N} & y_{1,N} & z_{1,N} \\
x_{2,1} & y_{2,1} & z_{2,1} & x_{2,2} & y_{2,2} & z_{2,2} & \cdots & x_{2,N} & y_{2,N} & z_{2,N} \\
\vdots & \vdots & \vdots & \vdots & \vdots & \vdots & \vdots & \vdots & \vdots & \vdots \\
x_{M,1} & y_{M,1} & z_{M,1} & x_{M,2} & y_{M,2} & z_{M,2} & \cdots & x_{M,N} & y_{M,N} & z_{M,N}
\end{bmatrix}
\tag{1}
$$

where each row of I_k is the 3D spatial coordinates of each joint and N is the total number of frames. Since the number of joints tracked by the sensor is 20, $M = 20$.

Due to the variations in speed in performing actions, the total number of frames for each action may differ. To eliminate this, the proposed algorithm utilizes bicubic interpolation. After the interpolation operation, the number of columns in I_K reduces to

$$
\hat{N} = \lambda N_{min} \tag{2}
$$

where N_{min}, a data dependent parameter, is the least number of frames corresponding to the entry in the training dataset, and λ is a scaling constant that helps in dimensionality reduction. In our implementation, we set λ as 0.6.

Each row of I_K is divided by its norm to produce a unit vector of length one, which not only gets rid of dependence on any specific person performing the task, however, it also makes sure that the individual joint movements does not affect other joints.

The rows of the reduced matrix are stacked column-wise to produce a $20\hat{N} \times 1$ input vector to the neural network, labeled as NN_K in Fig. 1. However, there is noise present in the form of spikes and for that Savitzky-Golay [16] filter is applied to reduce the spikes.

2.2   Feature Extraction from Inertial Sensor

A wearable inertial sensor can be placed at any part of the body, and outputs 3-axis acceleration and gyro measurements. The output of the inertial sensor for each frame is $[a_x \; a_y \; a_z \; \omega_x \; \omega_y \; \omega_z]$, where a_i represent linear acceleration, ω_i is the angular velocity and i depicts the respective axis. Then the data obtained from the inertial sensor can be described as

$$
I_I = \begin{bmatrix}
a_{x,1} & a_{y,1} & a_{z,1} & \omega_{x,1} & \omega_{y,1} & \omega_{z,1} \\
a_{x,2} & a_{y,2} & a_{z,2} & \omega_{x,2} & \omega_{y,2} & \omega_{z,2} \\
\vdots & \vdots & \vdots & \vdots & \vdots & \vdots \\
a_{x,N} & a_{y,N} & a_{z,N} & \omega_{x,N} & \omega_{y,N} & \omega_{z,N}
\end{bmatrix}
\tag{3}
$$

However, if there is more than one inertial sensors utilized, the structure of I_I can be changed to incorporate them in a similar manner as skeleton joints in I_K.

As with the skeleton data, the inertial sensor data has different signal sizes. To reduce this variation, all the signals are resized using bicubic interpolation.

The size of I_I is reduced to $N_{min} \times 6$, where N_{min} is chosen from the inertial sensor training data in the same manner as in the case of the depth sensor. Furthermore, the inertial sensor measurements are partitioned into windows, the statistical features of mean and standard deviation are calculated for each window per direction and are used as features.

Finally, the features are stacked column-wise to produce a feature vector which is the input to the neural network, labeled as NN_I in Fig. 1.

2.3 Feature Classification

Data from each sensor is classified using a separate Neural Network, and each Neural network contains one hidden layer. The hidden layer of NN_K contains 86 neurons, while that of NN_I contains 90 neurons. Moreover, the networks are trained using Conjugate gradient backpropagation with Polak-Ribiére updates [17].

The implemented algorithm utilizes a probabilistic framework, which is achieved using a soft-max output layer. The output vector (4) is a $C \times 1$ vector and each entry represents the probability of the respective label being assigned to the input sample y.

$$Output = [p_q(1|y)\ p_q(2|y)\ \dots\ p_q(C|y)]^T \tag{4}$$

where C is the total number of classes, and $q \in [1,2]$ represents each sensor.

Logarithmic opinion pool (LOGP) [15] is employed to merge the individual posterior probabilities of the classifiers and estimate the global membership function given in (5). A uniform distribution is assumed when fusing the two sensors, similar to [13].

$$P(c|y) = \prod_{q=1}^{2} p_q(c|y)^{1/2} \tag{5}$$

where $c \in [1, 2, ..., C]$ represents a class label.

The final label, to any sample, is assigned to the class label that has the highest probability according to

$$Label = \underset{c=1...C}{\mathrm{argmax}}\ P(c|y) \tag{6}$$

3 Experiments

We assessed the performance of the implemented algorithm on University of Texas at Dallas Multimodal Human Action Dataset [14]. The Dataset is publicly available and comprises of data synchronized from RGB videos, skeleton joint positions and depth positions obtained from Kinect, and inertial signals obtained from a wearable inertial sensor. There are a total of 27 actions registered, performed by 8 subjects (4 male and 4 female). Each action is performed 4 times by each subject. Moreover, due to 3 corrupt sequences being removed, the size of the dataset is 861 entries. For our purpose, we use the skeletal and inertial signal information.

This dataset has been chosen because it mimics the real world scenario. The dataset comprises of actions that utilize the movement of different parts of the body. Moreover, the position for the inertial sensor is also changed for different actions (the sensor is placed on the subject's right wrist for 21 actions and placed on the subject's right thigh for 6 actions).

We perform 8-fold cross validation, as in [13], by training on 7 subjects and testing on the left out 1 subject. This procedure is repeated for every subject in turn. The results are shown and compared in Table 1.

Table 1. Recognition accuracies for subject-generic experiment

Subject-Generic Test	Skeletal Accuracy (%)	Inertial Acc. (%)	Fusion Acc. (%)
Chen et al. [13]	74.7	76.4	91.5
Proposed Algorithm	74.8	81.2	95.0

Figure 2 illustrates the performance of the algorithm for each subject. It can be seen that the fusion always results in a better accuracy than using either of the sensors alone. Moreover, the depth sensor performed better than the inertial sensor for person 1 and person 4, while during the other trials the inertial sensor was more accurate than the depth sensor. Lastly, the accuracy for person 8 (85% fusion accuracy) was fairly lower than that of the other subjects and this reduced the cross-validation accuracy.

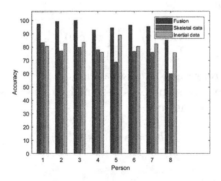

Fig. 2. Classification performance for each subject tested

Figure 3 displays the confusion matrix of the classification results when using depth sensor only, Inertial sensor only and a fusion of both. It can be seen that actions such as drawing circle clockwise (action 9) and drawing circle counterclockwise (action 10) had misclassifications amongst them, and jogging in place (action 22) was misclassified as walking in place (action 23) a number of times, which is because of these actions being of very similar nature.

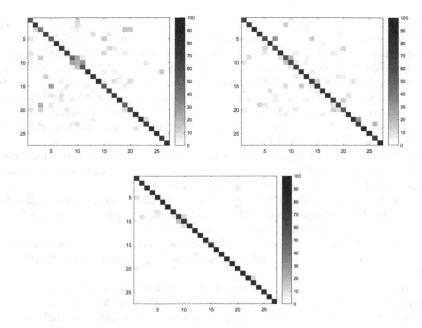

Fig. 3. Confusion Matrix of Skeletal (top left), Inertial (top right) and Fusion (bottom)

4 Conclusion

In this paper, we have presented a new approach to human action recognition that incorporates skeletal information from a depth camera, and acceleration and gyro measurements from an inertial sensor. We successfully extracted subject-invariant features that were classified using Neural Network classifiers. To improve the performance of our system we performed decision level fusion. Moreover, we performed extensive experimentation on a publicly available dataset and obtained good results. In particular, we have achieved 95% accuracy in 8-fold cross-validation, which is not only higher than using each sensor separately, but is also better than the best accuracy obtained on the mentioned dataset by 3.5%. As a future work, we plan on scaling up the system and testing it on datasets having more than one sensor of each modularity.

References

1. Chen, C., Jafari, R., Kehtarnavaz, N.: A survey of depth and inertial sensor fusion for human action recognition. Multimed. Tools Appl. **76**(3), 4405–4425 (2017)
2. Stein, S., McKenna, S.J.: Combining embedded accelerometers with computer vision for recognizing food preparation activities. In: Proceedings of the 2013 ACM International Joint Conference on Pervasive and Ubiquitous Computing. ACM (2013)

3. Ming, Y., Wang, G., Fan, C.: Uniform local binary pattern based texture-edge feature for 3D human behavior recognition. PloS one **10**(5), e0124640 (2015)
4. Ustundag, B.C., Unel, M.: Human action recognition using histograms of oriented optical flows from depth. In: Bebis, G., et al. (eds.) ISVC 2014. LNCS, vol. 8887, pp. 629–638. Springer, Cham (2014). https://doi.org/10.1007/978-3-319-14249-4_60
5. Han, J., Shao, L., Xu, D., Shotton, J.: Enhanced computer vision with microsoft kinect sensor: a review. IEEE Trans. Cybernet. **43**(5), 1318–1334 (2013)
6. Aggarwal, J.K., Xia, L.: Human activity recognition from 3d data: a review. Pattern Recogn. Lett. **48**, 70–80 (2014)
7. Du, Y., Wang, W., Wang, L.: Hierarchical recurrent neural network for skeleton based action recognition. In: Proceedings of the IEEE Conference on Computer Vision and Pattern Recognition, pp. 1110–1118 (2015)
8. Nie, B.X., Xiong, C., Zhu, S.C.: Joint action recognition and pose estimation from video. In: Proceedings of the IEEE Conference on Computer Vision and Pattern Recognition, pp. 1293–1301 (2015)
9. Altun, K., Barshan, B., Tunçel, O.: Comparative study on classifying human activities with miniature inertial and magnetic sensors. Pattern Recogn. **43**(10), 3605–3620 (2010)
10. Qaisar, S., et al.: A hidden markov model for detection & classification of arm action in cricket using wearable sensors. J. Mob. Multimed. **9**(1&2), 128–144 (2013)
11. Ermes, M., Parkka, J., Mantyjarvi, J., Korhonen, I.: Detection of daily activities and sports with wearable sensors in controlled and uncontrolled conditions. IEEE Trans. Inf. Technol. Biomed. **12**(1), 20–26 (2008)
12. Ofli, F., et al.: Berkeley MHAD: a comprehensive multimodal human action database. In: 2013 IEEE Workshop on Applications of Computer Vision (WACV), pp. 53–60. IEEE (2013)
13. Chen, C., Jafari, R., Kehtarnavaz, N.: A real-time human action recognition system using depth and inertial sensor fusion. IEEE Sens. J. **16**(3), 773–781 (2016)
14. Chen, C., Jafari, R., Kehtarnavaz, N.: UTD-MHAD: a multimodal dataset for human action recognition utilizing a depth camera and a wearable inertial sensor. In: Proceedings of IEEE International Conference on Image Processing (2015)
15. Li, W., Chen, C., Su, H., Du, Q.: Local binary patterns for spatial-spectral classification of hyperspectral imagery. IEEE Trans. Geosci. Remote Sens. **53**(7), 3681–3693 (2015)
16. Orfanidis, S.J.: Introduction to Signal Processing. Prentice-Hall, Englewood Cliffs (1996)
17. Scales, L.E.: Introduction to Non-Linear Optimization. Springer, New York (1985)

Slope Pattern Spectra for Human Action Recognition

Ignace Tchangou Toudjeu[✉] and Jules Raymond Tapamo

School of Engineering, University of KwaZulu-Natal, Durban, South Africa
itchangou@gmail.com, tapamoj@ukzn.ac.za

Abstract. Motion history image (MHI) is widely used for human action recognition (HAR) due to its simple representation of the motion information. MHI has also been used in combination with other feature extraction techniques to recognize human actions. However, there is still room for improvement. Therefore, this paper proposes a method that includes a holistic feature extraction technique not yet employed in HAR applications, named slope pattern spectra (SPS). We extract increasing slope pattern spectra from motion history images and feed them into a K-Nearest Neighbor (KNN) classifier in order to recognize various human actions. Our proposed framework has been tested on the KTH dataset, a commonly used benchmark dataset for HAR. Experimental results demonstrate that SPS are suitable feature descriptors for HAR via MHI.

Keywords: Motion history image (MHI) · Slope pattern spectra
KNN · Human action recognition · Motion templates

1 Introduction

The interpretation of human activities in video sequences remains a challenging task. Action recognition has been the center of interest for many researchers in the field of computer vision. Although there is an abundant literature on human motion understanding, propelled by the high demand in applications such as video surveillance, gesture recognition and automatic monitoring systems, computer vision based HAR still has several unresolved issues. In [1], Ahad stated that action recognition and behavior analysis are still in their infancy even though researchers have been working on these for few decades. Consequently there is still room for performance improvement, especially when action recognition relies more on the choice of suitable feature descriptors.

Motion history image (MHI) method, also referred to as a smart action representation approach by Ahad [2], has gained popularity due to its simple motion representation of a video sequence into a single grayscale image. In the MHI image, dominant motion patterns are preserved. Despite the fact that MHI method records the history of temporal changes at each pixel location, it still suffers from the problem of self-occlusion for certain actions. Many HAR based

© Springer International Publishing AG, part of Springer Nature 2018
A. Campilho et al. (Eds.): ICIAR 2018, LNCS 10882, pp. 381–389, 2018.
https://doi.org/10.1007/978-3-319-93000-8_43

applications have used MHI in combination with other techniques to extract more motion information in order to achieve better results. Common limitations of employing MHI method or its variants is the size of feature vectors produced and the fact that its use for action classification is not straightforward.

Based on the idea that if a proper feature extraction technique is applied to MHI images, then MHI can be sufficient to describe the human action in video sequences, in this paper, we propose a method that uses the extraction of slope pattern spectra (SPS) from MHI images. The use of SPS is motivated by the fact that a MHI image while describing motion occurence, a spread of temporal changes at each pixel location develops a slope progression which can be either in an increasing or decreasing order. In this work, increasing slope pattern spectra were extracted from MHI images derived from action dataset, then classified using a KNN classifier to demonstrate the importance of SPS applied to MHI for HAR.

2   Previous Work

In the literature, MHI is also referred to as a temporal template. This concept was introduced by Bobick et al. [3]. The MHI was used with the motion energy image (MEI), another temporal template, to recognize various types of aerobics exercises. The combination of MHI and MEI was motivated by the fact that when use together they described how and where the motion occurs in a image sequence. Seven Hu moments were used to recognize the aerobics movements.

Kellokumpu et al. [4] applied Local Binary Pattern (LBP) as a feature extraction technique on both MHI and MEI templates to represent action. The MHI based LBP patterns encoded the information about the direction of motion while MEI patterns described the combination of the overall pose and shape of the motion. The two types of LBP patterns were concatenated into one global histogram for each action. Hidden Markov models were used to model the sequential development of the features. Though high classification accuracy were achieved, the feature size derived from sub-volumes was up to 1920 features which could be considered large to some extent.

Ahad et al. [5] exploited the MHI, LBP and Histogram of Oriented Gradient (HOG) techniques to obtain good recognition rate. The MHI templates were generated from the input video sequence and translated into LBP codes to address the problem of self-occlusion, then HOG features were extracted from the LBP codes and classified using SVM classifier. Good recognition rate was achieved 94.3% on Pedestrian Action Dataset with just 19-dimensional feature space. This approach led to good results but at the expense of computational cost, since two feature extraction processes were involved.

Previous works highlighted some MHI limitations such as occlusion or self-occlusion of subject in the video. The development of variants of MHI were proposed. Ahad et al. [5] and Mueid et al. [6] proposed the Directional Motion History Image (DMHI) as solution to the occlusion problem. Other variants of MHI, found in the literature, are timed-motion history image (tMHI) [2], timed-DMHI [7]. However, it is worth mentioning that despite the ability of different variants of MHI to address a variety of problems as previously mentioned, they do not automatically guarantee robustness and efficiency over the MHI approach.

3   Proposed Method

This paper has for goal to improve the recognition performance of MHI-based human action recognition. The distribution of slope patterns developed in the MHI templates are extracted using the SPS algorithm. To the best of our knowledge, the application of slope pattern spectra (SPS) to HAR has not been published. We are motivated by the fact this approach, being a holistic feature extraction technique, was able to extract global motion information from MHI. The proposed method comprises two main parts: feature extraction and classification. Our proposed methodology is illustrated in Fig. 1.

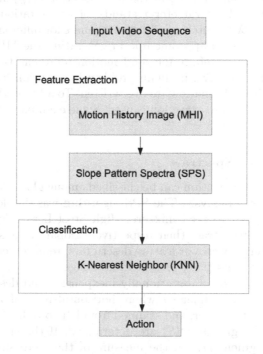

Fig. 1. Proposed methodology.

3.1   Motion History Images

The MHI templates are generated by keeping history of temporal changes at each pixel location, which then decays over time [8]. The resulting MHI is an image in which grayscale value indicates the most recent motion of the pixel in a set of video sequences. The brighter intensity values of the MHI correspond to more recent motion [9]. The concept of MHI has been used in [5] and defined as

$$H_\tau(x,y,t) = \begin{cases} \tau & \text{if } \Psi(x,y,t) = 1 \\ max(0, H_\tau(x,y,t) - \delta) & otherwise \end{cases} \tag{1}$$

where $\Psi(x,y,t)$, the update function is defined by

$$\Psi(x,y,t) = \begin{cases} 1 & \text{if } D(x,y,t) \le \epsilon \\ 0 & otherwise \end{cases} \tag{2}$$

and $D(x,y,t)$, the difference of frames is given by

$$D(x,y,t) = |I(x,y,t) - I(x,y,t \pm \lambda))| \tag{3}$$

and $I(x,y,t)$ is the intensity value at the pixel location (x,y) of tth-frame in the video sequence. Here the parameter τ stands for the duration of frames, δ for recession parameter, λ for interframe distance, and ϵ for difference threshold. All these parameters plays a important role in generating the MHI images, therefore need to be chosen carefully for good motion representation. Though MHI is computionally inexpensive, its main problem is occlusion for certain human actions where motion information are overwritten. To address this problem, SPS algorithm for global feature exraction is used. Some examples of MHI images are shown in Fig. 2.

3.2   Slope Pattern Spectra

Slope pattern spectra algorithm can be classified among global feature extraction techniques for texture analysis. The SPS algorithm was developed by Toudjeu et al. [10] and applied to seed mixture, High Steel Low Alloy (HSLA) steel, and satellite images to extract their respectively global image signatures. These signatures, as pattern spectra or feature descriptors, represented distributions of increasing slope segments (ISS) present in an image.

The algorithm is also computationally inexpensive and described as follows [10]: Consider a grayscale image I where horizontal lines of I (rows of I) are considered one after the other, and scanned from left to right. In each horizontal line, possible slope segments (SS) are determined. If the slope segment is an increasing slope segment (ISS), the measure of the increasing slope segment divided by its length, $\frac{m(ISS)}{n}$, is calculated, and the nth bin of the pattern spectra incremented with this value. If the lengths of the increasing slope segments determined at different horizontal lines are equal, the same pattern spectrum bins are respectively incremented by $\frac{m(ISS)}{n}$. These operations are repeated until the last horizontal line of I is processed.

This feature extraction technique capitalizes on the distribution of motion patterns in the MHI to extract suitable features for HAR. Examples of increasing slope pattern spectrum are shown in Fig. 2. Its derived feature size is minimum and therefore reduces computation load on the classifier.

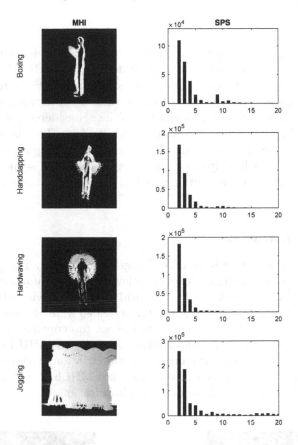

Fig. 2. Example of MHI and their SPS respectively.

3.3 K-Nearest Neighbor Classifier

The second and important part of our proposed method is classification. This plays a role in the performance of HAR. We choose the K-nearest neighbor (KNN) classifier because it is simple to implement as compared to other machine learning algorithms [11,12]. In addition, the features derived from the SPS algorithm best fit the kNN classifier since no dimension reduction technique is required to avoid the classifier to suffer the curse of dimensionality.

4   Experimental Results and Discussions

Our experiment was conducted with Matlab software as follows: Initially, MHI images were generated from all sequences without doing any partition in term of training or testing sets. Then, each MHI was translated into SPS features along with respective action label. Finally, the derived SPS feature descriptors were partitioned.

4.1 Dataset

The performance of the proposed method is evaluated using the KTH [13] dataset, one of the mostly used benchmark dataset for HAR. The KTH Action dataset consists of 25 subjects performing six human actions in four various conditions, which are outdoors, outdoors with scale variations, outdoors with clothing variation, and indoors. The human actions considered are *Boxing, Hand-waving, Handclapping, Jogging, Running*, and *Walking*. The database amounts to a total of 2391 sequences which were taken over homogeneous backgrounds with static camera with 25 fps as frame rate. In addition, sequences were also downsampled to a spatial resolution of 160×120 pixels with an average length of four seconds.

4.2 Feature Extraction

Each action video sequence is processed to generate a MHI. The parameters for MHI computation are critical to capture relevant motion information. Based on the suggestion made by Ahad in [2], we considered the following MHI parameters $(\tau, \epsilon, \delta) = (255, 40, 2)$. Fifty frames in total per video were also considered in our experiment. The generated MHI images were not too convincing as visually we could spot some kind of occlusion or noise. Specially the MHI images obtained from the video subset taken outdoors with scale variation. Example of MHI with self-occlusion and noise are shown in Fig. 3. Such MHI had costly effect on SPS extraction not leading to high accuracy in classification.

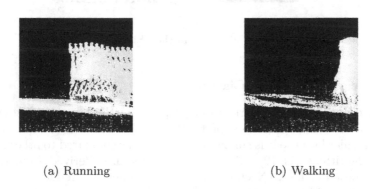

(a) Running   (b) Walking

Fig. 3. Examples of MHI for outdoor video sequence.

4.3 Classfication

The K-nearest neighbor classifier was used. The extracted SPS feature vectors were divided into two sets, training set and Testing set. The split consisted for the 600 SPS vectors was 80% and 20% for the training set and testing set respectively. Two classifications were conducted on the KTH Dataset due to

Table 1. S1 confusion matrix: mean performance of 56.67%

Actions	Box	Clap	Wave	Jog	Run	Walk
Boxing (Box)	40.0	20.0	20.0	0.00	0.0	20.0
HandClapping (Clap)	16.7	66.7	0.0	0.00	0.0	16.7
HandWaving (Wave)	0.0	0.0	75.0	12.5	0.0	12.5
Jogging (Jog)	20.0	0.0	0.0	20.0	20.0	40.0
Running (Run)	0.0	0.0	0.0	0.0	100	0.0
Walking (Walk)	0.0	25.0	25.0	0.0	0.0	50.0

Table 2. S2 confusion matrix: mean performance of 50.00%

Actions	Box	Clap	Wave	Jog	Run	Walk
Boxing (Box)	55.6	11.1	22.2	0.0	0.0	11.1
HandClapping (Clap)	33.3	66.7	0.0	0.0	0.0	0.0
HandWaving (Wave)	0.0	0.0	33.3	33.3	0.0	33.3
Jogging (Jog)	25.0	50.0	0.0	0.0	0.0	25.0
Running (Run)	0.0	0.0	20.0	0.0	80.0	0.0
Walking (W)	0.0	16.7	16.7	16.7	0.0	50.0

the complexity presented by this dataset. In the first classification, we grouped actions video with respect to their conditions (outdoor (S1), outdoor with scale variation (S2), outdoor with clothing variation (S3) and indoor(S4)). In the second classification the overall KTH Dataset was considered.

Per Scenario Classfication Results: Classification results for each scenario are summarized in a confusion matrix in Tables 1, 2, 3 and 4 Out of 150 SPS feature vectors, 120 and 30 were used for training and testing purpose respectively. A 100% classification rate per scenario is obtained for validation. The average performance for each scenario classification with respect to testing is calculated as the trace of each matrix over the total number of classified elements (e.g. From Table 1, the mean performance is 50%). Other testing average performances are indicated on respective tables. These results are quite encouraging since they demonstrate the discriminative power of SPS feature vectors and their potential to be used for recognition purpose. We can also mention that S2 classification performance is the lowest. This is justifiable by the scale variations in video sequences.

Overall Classfication Result: The overall classification result, which average is 50.83%, is illustrated in Table 5. This overall average performance is lower than the 63.50% achieved by Meng et al. [14] when using only the MHI as feature descriptors. Though the differential in accuracy rates is 13.50%, and while the length of the SPS feature vector is far less than the one of MHI making the classification computational less expensive.

Table 3. S3 confusion matrix: mean performance of 63.33%

Actions	Box	Clap	Wave	Jog	Run	Walk
Boxing (Box)	57.1	0.0	28.6	0.0	0.0	14.3
HandClapping (Clap)	25.0	25.0	25.0	0.0	0.0	25.0
HandWaving (Wave)	0.0	0.0	75.0	0.0	0.0	25.0
Jogging (Jog)	25.0	0.0	0.0	75.0	0.0	0.0
Running (Run)	0.0	0.0	0.0	28.6	71.4	0.0
Walking (Walk)	0.0	0.0	0.0	25.0	0.0	75.0

Table 4. S4 confusion matrix: mean performance of 60.00%

Actions	Box	Clap	Wave	Jog	Run	Walk
Boxing (Box)	50.0	16.7	16.7	0.0	0.0	16.7
HandClapping (Clap)	16.7	66.7	0.0	0.0	0.0	16.7
HandWaving (Wave)	20.0	0.0	80.0	0.0	0.0	0.0
Jogging (Jog)	0.0	0.0	0.0	100	0.0	0.0
Running (Run)	0.0	0.0	0.0	25.0	75.0	0.0
Walking (Walk)	20.0	0.0	0.0	60.0	0.0	20.0

Table 5. Overall confusion matrix: mean performance of 50.83%

Actions	Box	Clap	Wave	Jog	Run	Walk
Boxing (Box)	31.6	42.1	26.3	0.0	0.0	0.0
HandClapping (Clap)	16.7	50.0	27.8	0.0	0.0	5.6
HandWaving (Wave)	14.3	19.0	66.7	0.0	0.0	0.0
Jogging (Jog)	0.0	0.0	0.0	35.0	30.0	35.0
Running (Run)	0.0	5.3	5.3	15.8	64.2	10.5
Walking (Walk)	4.5	13.6	9.1	13.6	0.0	59.1

5   Conclusion

In this paper, we have proposed a HAR method based on the SPS algorithm
as a feature extraction technique. To the best of our knowledge, this is the first
time SPS is been used in HAR. The SPS features were simply computed from
the MHI images to form a low dimensional feature space that led to a robust
classification. The per scenario classification results indicated the complexity
of the KTH Action dataset. Results achieved are promising and demonstrate
the relevance of slope pattern spectra as a holistic action representation. One
direction of future work could be to tackle the issue of occlusion, self-occlusion
and background clutter which are the main causes of some poor quality of MHI
image affecting slope pattern spectra directly.

References

1. Ahad, M.A.R.: Motion History Images for Action Recognition and Understanding. Springer, London (2012). https://doi.org/10.1007/978-1-4471-4730-5
2. Ahad, M.A.R., Tan, J.K., Kim, H., Ishikawa, S.: Motion history image: its variants and applications. Mach. Vis. Appl. **23**(2), 255–281 (2012)
3. Bobick, A.F., Davis, J.W.: The recognition of human movement using temporal templates. IEEE Trans. Pattern Anal. Mach. Intell. **23**(3), 257–267 (2001)
4. Kellokumpu, V., Zhao, G., Pietikäinen, M.: Recognition of human actions using texture descriptors. Mach. Vis. Appl. **22**(5), 767–780 (2011)
5. Ahad, M.A.R., Islam, M.N., Jahan, I.: Action recognition based on binary patterns of action-history and histogram of oriented gradient. J. Multimodal User Interfaces **10**(4), 335–344 (2016)
6. Mueid, R.M., Ahmed, C., Ahad, M.A.R.: Pedestrian activity classification using patterns of motion and histogram of oriented gradient. J. Multimodal User Interfaces **10**(4), 299–305 (2016)
7. Ahad, M.A.R., Tan, J.K., Kim, H.S., Ishikawa, S.: Action recognition with various speeds and timed-DMHI feature vectors. In: 11th International Conference on Computer and Information Technology, ICCIT 2008, pp. 213–218. IEEE, December 2008
8. Xiang, T., Gong, S.: Beyond tracking: modelling activity and understanding behaviour. Int. J. Comput. Vis. **67**(1), 21–51 (2006)
9. Bilen, H., Fernando, B., Gavves, E., Vedaldi, A.: Action recognition with dynamic image networks. IEEE Trans. Pattern Anal. Mach. Intell. (2017)
10. Toudjeu, I.T., van Wyk, B.J., van Wyk, M.A., van den Bergh, F.: Global image feature extraction using slope pattern spectra. In: Campilho, A., Kamel, M. (eds.) ICIAR 2008. LNCS, vol. 5112, pp. 640–649. Springer, Heidelberg (2008). https://doi.org/10.1007/978-3-540-69812-8_63
11. Sharma, A., Kumar, S., McLachalan, N.: Representation and classification of human movement using temporal templates and statistical measure of similarity. In: WITSP 2002 Workshop on Internet Telecommunications and Signal Processing, pp. 191–196 (2002)
12. Karahoca, A. and Nurullahoglu, M.: Human motion analysis and action recognition. In: Proceedings of the WSEAS International Conference, Mathematics and Computers in Science and Engineering, No. 7. World Scientific and Engineering Academy and Society, May 2008
13. Schuldt, C., Laptev, I. and Caputo, B.: Recognizing human actions: a local SVM approach. In: Proceedings of the 17th International Conference on Pattern Recognition, ICPR 2004, vol. 3, pp. 32–36. IEEE (2004)
14. Meng, H., Pears, N., Freeman, M., Bailey, C.: Motion history histograms for human action recognition. In: Kisačanin, B., Bhattacharyya, S.S., Chai, S. (eds.) Embedded Computer Vision. Advances in Pattern Recognition, pp. 139–162. Springer, London (2009). https://doi.org/10.1007/978-1-84800-304-0_7

Recognition of Activities of Daily Living from Egocentric Videos Using Hands Detected by a Deep Convolutional Network

Thi-Hoa-Cuc Nguyen[1], Jean-Christophe Nebel[1],
and Francisco Florez-Revuelta[2]([⊠])

[1] School of Computer Science and Mathematics, Kingston University, London,
Kingston-Upon-Thames KT1 2EE, UK
{k1458932,j.nebel}@kingston.ac.uk
[2] Department of Computer Technology, University of Alicante,
P.O. Box 99, 03080 Alicante, Spain
francisco.florez@ua.es

Abstract. Ambient assisted living systems aim at supporting older and impaired people using computer technology so that they can remain autonomous while maintaining healthy living. Egocentric cameras have emerged as a powerful source of data to monitor individuals performing activities of daily living since they tend to focus on the area where the current activity takes place while showing manipulated objects and hand positions. While research has focused on activity recognition based on object recognition, this study has investigated the automatic acquisition of additional features modelling interactions between hands and objects using a deep convolutional network. Experiments conducted on a realistic dataset have demonstrated that, not only do those features improve activity recognition, but they can be accurately extracted.

Keywords: Egocentric vision · Deep convolutional network
Ambient assisted living · Activity recognition

1 Introduction

Ambient assisted living (AAL) systems aim at supporting older and impaired people using computer technology so that they can remain autonomous while maintaining healthy living. Many AAL systems are deployed in homes where they monitor individuals performing activities of daily living (ADLs), such as cooking or washing. Although those system employ different sensors, usage of cameras is becoming more popular [1] especially that automatic solutions ensuring individuals' privacy are now available [2]. While traditionally video-based AAL systems rely on fixed cameras installed in the environment, the increasing availability of wearable cameras addresses many of their shortcomings, such as

© Springer International Publishing AG, part of Springer Nature 2018
A. Campilho et al. (Eds.): ICIAR 2018, LNCS 10882, pp. 390–398, 2018.
https://doi.org/10.1007/978-3-319-93000-8_44

their limited field of view and the occlusions created by either the environment or an individual's body. Conversely, a camera attached to a person can record activities from an egocentric point of view, showing usually manipulated objects and hand positions. As a consequence, ADL recognition from data captured by egocentric cameras has become an active field of research [3], where current systems generally rely on, first, detecting and identifying the objects present in each frame and, second, using temporal information to infer the performed activities.

With the remarkable progress of deep learning and Convolutional Neural Networks (CNNs) in particular [4], significant improvement has been achieved in image recognition tasks [5]. However, even the Imagenet dataset, and its 15 million annotated images, is still far from being sufficient to train a CNN able to handle a realistic AAL video. Therefore, one can expect that recognition of ADLs relying on object identity as main information source will only progress substantially with the availability of more exhaustive object datasets. However, experiments conducted with videos, the objects of which were manually annotated, have revealed that additional information such as indication about active objects is required to perform accurate recognition of ADLs [6].

This work reports research regarding the value of automatic extraction of additional features related to hand-hand and hand-object interactions in the context of ADL recognition. First, a CNN-based method is proposed to detect the left and right hands visible on a video captured by an egocentric camera. Second, using a bag-of-visual words model, a system for recognition of activities of daily living is developed taking advantage of both object identity and interaction features. Finally, experiments are conducted on an AAL dataset captured by a wearable camera to evaluate the impact of exploiting those new features.

2 Methodology

2.1 Hand Detection Using a Region-Based CNN (R-CNN)

As Faster R-CNN is a freely available and efficient object detection framework [5], and human hands can be treated as objects, this model has been selected to detect both left and right hands in videos. Faster R-CNN operates in two steps: first, a deep fully CNN, VGG-16 [4], proposes rectangular regions of interest associated to an objectness score; second, the Fast R-CNN detector [7] takes advantage of those regions to detect and classify objects.

To detect left and right hands, the last layer of the Faster R-CNN was adapted to output left-hand and right-hand object classes using, for training, a large dataset of hands in egocentric videos. The system returns bounding boxes tagged as either left or right hand associated with a confidence score. Bounding boxes with a score above a threshold are further processed to filter out noisy results which may be produced by blurred data caused by fast hand motion: a hand detection is accepted only if it has been continuously detected for some frames.

2.2   Activity Recognition Enhanced by Hand Information

The bag-of-visual words (BoVW) model has been a popular approach applied for image classification by treating an image as a document and features as words [8]. A BoVW is a vector representing occurrences of vocabularies which are generated from local image features. BoVW is mainly composed of five steps: (i) feature extraction, (ii) feature pre-processing, (iii) codebook generation, (iv) feature encoding, and (v) pooling and normalisation [9]. Motivated by the idea that an activity can be modelled by using relevant images (key features) in a video, the BoVW model is used to generate bags of key features and then combined with the Sequences of key features approach to recognise activities [2,10].

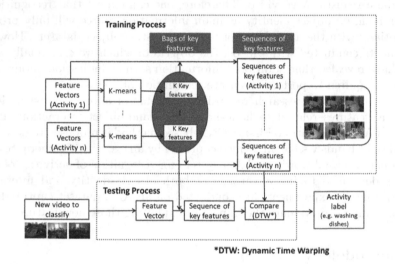

Fig. 1. Sequences of key interactions for activity recognition.

As Fig. 1 shows, during the training process, bags of key features and sequences of key features for each activity are built. First, all feature vectors extracted from all videos of each activity class are fed to a k-means clustering to obtain K representative vectors for each activity. Then, these vectors, for all the activities, are merged together into a bag of key features. Second, for each frame of a sequence, the nearest neighbour key feature in the bag is found. The successive nearest neighbour key features constitute the sequence of key features. This way, a set of sequences of key features is obtained for each activity class.

To classify an unseen video into a specific activity, three steps are followed (Fig. 1). First, a feature vector is extracted for each frame of the new video. Then, vectors are mapped to the key features generated during the training process. Second, the corresponding sequence of nearest neighbour key features is built. Third, Dynamic Time Warping (DTW) is applied to compare the new sequence with every sequence of key features created during the training. The label of the nearest neighbour sequence supplies the label of the new video.

The presence of specific objects provides rich information about performed activities. However, it is proposed to provide further information by including features exploiting spatial relationships between both, objects and hands, and left and right hands. It is expected that such data will allow modelling interactions occurring in each activity. Then, motivated by the idea that ADLs can be represented as a series of key interactions between hands and objects, the sequences of key features approach is applied to predict activities.

Egocentric videos of ADLs allow analysis of two main types of interactions. First, since hands are usually present in the images, they should provide useful information about the activity that is performed: left hand-right hand interactions are usually necessary to complete activities. Second, objects are usually manipulated by hands when activities are performed. Therefore, information interactions between hands and objects would allow not only the detection of active objects, but also discard objects which are irrelevant to the current activity. Since any object that is manipulated should eventually be in contact with a hand, the positions of both hands are used to identify active objects in a scene. Here, the active object associated to the left hand, resp. right hand, is defined as the closest object to its right, resp. left.

In this study, three features are extracted from each frame (see Fig. 2): the distance in pixel between the left and right hands ($d1$), i.e. the distance between the centres of their bounding boxes, and the distances between each hand and its active object ($d2$ and $d3$), i.e. the distances between the centre of each hand's bounding box to the centre of its active object's bounding box.

Fig. 2. Example of interaction features. $d1$: distance between left and right hands; $d2$: distance between left hand and book; $d3$: distance between right hand and book.

3   Experimental Results

3.1   Experimental Setup

Hand Detection. The Faster R-CNN model with VGG-16 network with two classes (left/right hand) was implemented using Caffe, the popular deep learning framework developed by Berkeley AI Research (BAIR) [11], its Pycaffe library supporting the Python version of Faster R-CNN [5]. A single GPU NVIDIA Titan X 12GB GDDR5X (memory speed of 10Gbps) and CUDA were used as high performance processing platform to train this very deep convolutional network.

Regarding training, the EgoHands dataset [94] which contains 48 videos of first-person interactions between two people recorded by a Google Glass was selected. Indeed, it provides 15,053 annotated (left/right) and segmented hands in a total of 4,800 images. 480,000 iterations were conducted as part of the training process: they correspond to 100 forward and backward passes of all the training examples (so called epochs) as the dataset contains 4,800 images and a batch-size of one image by batch was set. The weights of the network were tuned by Caffe during the back propagation phase. As weight pre-training is a procedure known for reducing computational time and producing improved performance, it was applied taking advantage of a VGG16 image classification model already trained using the Imagenet's Image Classification Dataset. Finally, the outputs generated by the network were post processed considering only detections with a confidence above 0.8 if they appear continuously on at least 5 frames.

The evaluation of the hand detector was conducted using 75% of Ego-Hands as training set and the remaining 25% as testing set. Performance was assessed using the standard mean Average Precision (mAP) which is algorithm-independent and specially adapted at highlighting differences between methods [12].

Activity Recognition. The most suitable dataset available to evaluate recognition of ADLs with wearable cameras is the Activities of Daily Living Dataset (ADL) [6], which comprises 1 million frames recorded by a GoPro camera. Not only does it provide annotation for 18 activities of daily living, such as *washing dishes* and *combing hair*, but objects visible in each frame are annotated within 32 distinct object categories. Even though methods for object detection have improved, performance is still relatively low: only an mAP of 0.66 was recently achieved on the large Imagenet dataset [13]. In the case of the challenging ADL dataset, where blurred and dark images are not uncommon, there is not even any suitable set for training more than a third of the objects, e.g. dental-floss, detergent and clothes. As a consequence, automatic object detection on the ADL dataset is still extremely inaccurate ($mAP < 0.2$) and, as many have done before [6], actual ground-truth object annotations are used for activity recognition.

In order to demonstrate the added value provided by the inclusion of hand-hand and hand-object interaction information, four experiments were conducted where different feature vectors were fed to the sequence of key features classifier. First, as a baseline, each frame was represented by a feature vector containing 32 binary values encoding the presence of objects belonging to the 32 categories in the ADL dataset. Second, a feature vector was created containing only the spatial distance in pixels between the left and right hands ($d1$). Third, distances in pixels between each hand and its associated active objects ($d2$) and ($d3$) were added to the previous vector (*d1*). Finally, the presence of objects belonging to the 32 categories was added to distance information, i.e. *d1*, *d2* and *d3*.

For each of those experiments, a sequence of key interactions model was trained to recognise the 18 types of activities present in the 20 videos of the ADL dataset. Evaluation was performed from pre-segmented activities using the twofold cross-validation method calculating average accuracy.

3.2   Performance

Hand Detection. The trained Faster R-CNN with VGG-16 network performs extremely well as evidenced by a mean Average Precision of 0.940. This corresponds to an improvement of over 16% when compared with the mAP of 0.807 reported at the introduction of the EgoHands dataset. Although there are rare occasions when the system produces misdetections, especially in blurry images (see Fig. 3, bottom row), such performance suggests that this classifier should be able to provide valuable information to an activity recognition system.

Fig. 3. Outputs of the hand detector: correct (top) and incorrect (bottom) detections.

Activity Recognition. Average accuracy of activity recognition using various feature vectors is reported in Table 1. Performance for the experiment conducted with the second feature vector reveals that, even without any object information, the distance between the two hands is quite informative to identify an activity among the 18 possible types (prediction with 21.0% accuracy). This is an interesting result since object detection and annotation is particularly challenging on realistic ADL datasets. If additional information about interaction with active objects is provided, accuracy increases to 23.5%. Still, comparison with baseline performance shows that object annotations are even more discriminative than knowledge about interactions (26.3%). Finally, combination of the two types of features provides richer information for ADL recognition since it allows increasing annotation-based performance by 12.5% leading to an accuracy of 29.6%.

Figure 4 shows the confusion matrix obtained for the experiment integrating all features. It reveals that relatively good results are obtained for a few activities including *drying hands* (74.2%) and *laundry* (50%). However, they are mediocre

Table 1. Average accuracy of activity recognition using various feature vectors

Feature vector	Average accuracy (%)
Object presence (baseline)	26.3
Distance between left and right hands (*d1*)	21.0
Distances between left and right hands (*d1*), and each hand and its active object (*d2* & *d3*)	23.5
Object presence and distances (*d1*, *d2* & *d3*)	29.6

for most activities, e.g. *combing hair* (12.5%), *making cold food or snack* (11.8%) and *brushing teeth* (18.1%). Moreover, the model could not detect activities involving small objects such as *dental floss*, leading to not a single recognition (0%). The main reason for these unsatisfactory performance is the lack of training data for many activities such as *make up* and *using cell-phone*. In addition, some ADLs are very difficult to discriminate since they involve similar objects and interactions, e.g. *moving dishes* and *washing dishes*. Finally, the ADL dataset includes simultaneous activities such as *drinking* and *watching TV*, the concept of which is not addressed by the proposed framework.

Usage of a more sophisticated classifier based on a spatial pyramid to approximate temporal correspondence achieved on the ADL dataset an average accuracy of 55.8% on pre-segmented activities when using the ground truth for object annotation [6]. In addition, if the ground-truth for active objects is added, the system's performance increases to 77%. This is in line with the outcome of our study which suggests that, if the proposed approach for automatic hand-hand

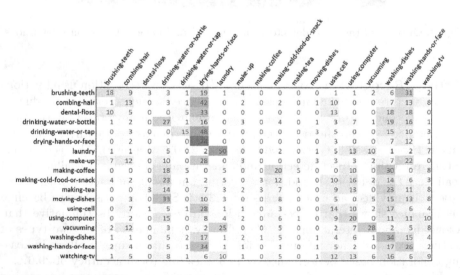

Fig. 4. Confusion matrix associated to classification of 18 activities based on both object presence and interactions.

and hand-object interactions were to be employed, performance of classifiers relying only on object identification could be substantially improved.

4   Conclusion

Usage of egocentric cameras to recognise activities of daily living has the potential to become essential to ambient assisted living. However, research so far has mainly relied on the recognition of objects visible in each video frame. Despite significant progress brought by deep learning, object recognition is still a challenge for realistic ADL datasets. This study has demonstrated that, not only does the addition of features modelling interactions between hands and objects improve activity recognition, but they can be automatically and accurately extracted using a deep network. Although the outcome of activity recognition remains unsatisfactory, exploitation of those features within state-of-the-art activity recognition systems should impact significantly on their performance.

References

1. Cardinaux, F., Bhowmik, D., Abhayaratne, C., Hawley, M.S.: Video based technology for ambient assisted living: a review of the literature. J. Ambient Intell. Smart Environ. **3**(3), 253–269 (2011)
2. Chaaraoui, A.A., Padilla-López, J.R., Ferrández-Pastor, F.J., Nieto-Hidalgo, M., Flórez-Revuelta, F.: A vision-based system for intelligent monitoring: human behaviour analysis and privacy by context. Sensors **14**(5), 8895–8925 (2014)
3. Nguyen, T.H.C., Nebel, J.C., Florez-Revuelta, F.: Recognition of activities of daily living with egocentric vision: a review. Sensors **16**(1), 72 (2016)
4. Simonyan, K., Zisserman, A.: Very deep convolutional networks for large-scale image recognition. arXiv preprint arXiv:1409.1556 (2014)
5. Ren, S., He, K., Girshick, R., Sun, J.: Faster R-CNN: towards real-time object detection with region proposal networks. IEEE Trans. Pattern Anal. Mach. Intell. **39**(6), 1137–1149 (2017)
6. Pirsiavash, H., Ramanan, D.: Detecting activities of daily living in first-person camera views. In: 2012 IEEE Conference on Computer Vision and Pattern Recognition, pp. 2847–2854, June 2012
7. Girshick, R.: Fast R-CNN. In: Proceedings of the IEEE International Conference on Computer Vision, pp. 1440–1448 (2015)
8. Csurka, G., Dance, C., Fan, L., Willamowski, J., Bray, C.: Visual categorization with bags of keypoints. In: Workshop on Statistical Learning in Computer Vision, ECCV, Prague, vol. 1, pp. 1–2 (2004)
9. Peng, X., Wang, L., Wang, X., Qiao, Y.: Bag of visual words and fusion methods for action recognition: comprehensive study and good practice. Comput. Vis. Image Underst. **150**(Supplement C), 109–125 (2016)
10. Chaaraoui, A.A., Climent-Pérez, P., Flórez-Revuelta, F.: Silhouette-based human action recognition using sequences of key poses. Pattern Recogn. Lett. **34**(15), 1799–1807 (2013). Smart Approaches for Human Action Recognition

11. Jia, Y., Shelhamer, E., Donahue, J., Karayev, S., Long, J., Girshick, R., Guadarrama, S., Darrell, T.: Caffe: convolutional architecture for fast feature embedding. In: Proceedings of the 22nd ACM International Conference on Multimedia, pp. 675–678. ACM (2014)
12. Everingham, M., Van Gool, L., Williams, C.K.I., Winn, J., Zisserman, A.: The PASCAL visual object classes (VOC) challenge. Int. J. Comput. Vis. **88**(2), 303–338 (2010)
13. Russakovsky, O., Deng, J., Su, H., Krause, J., Satheesh, S., Ma, S., Huang, Z., Karpathy, A., Khosla, A., Bernstein, M., Berg, A.C., Fei-Fei, L.: ImageNet large scale visual recognition challenge. Int. J. Comput. Vis. **115**(3), 211–252 (2015)

Sign Language Recognition Based on 3D Convolutional Neural Networks

Geovane M. Ramos Neto[✉], Geraldo Braz Junior[✉],
João Dallyson Sousa de Almeida[✉], and Anselmo Cardoso de Paiva[✉]

Computing Applied Group, Federal University of Maranhão, São Luís, Brazil
{geovane.menezes,geraldo,jdallyson,paiva}@nca.ufma.br

Abstract. The inclusion of disabled people is still a recurring problem throughout the world. For the hearing impaired, the barrier imposed by the sign language spoken by a small part of the population imposes limitations that interfere in the quality of life of these people. The popularization or even automation of sign language recognition can take their lives to a higher level. Understanding the importance of sign language recognition for the hearing impaired we propose a 3D CNN architecture for the recognition of 64 classes of gestures from Argentinian Sign Language (LSA64). We demonstrate the efficiency of the method when compared to traditional methods based on hand-crafted features and that its results outperform most deep learning-based work reaching 93.9% of accuracy.

Keywords: Sign language recognition · 3D CNN · Computer vision

1 Introduction

The inclusion of disabled people is still a recurring problem throughout the world. In the case of hearing impairment, the problem lies in the difficulty that they have in communicating using a visual language code, a Sign Language (LS). One of the major difficulties for the hearing impaired is the low number of people who are fluent in sign language, which makes learning difficult and the communication of these, especially in the early stages of the development of the individual [1,2].

Currently, solutions for the recognition of a sign language are given primarily by the use of human translators, and are therefore expensive solutions, given the necessary professional experience. Sign language recognition seeks to develop algorithms and methods that can correctly classify a sequence of signals to understand its meaning.

Given the complexity of obtain meaning for each of the elements that make up a sign language pose, many methodologies treat the recognition of sign language as a gesture recognition problem, that is, the solutions seek to identify optimal characteristics that satisfactorily represent a certain gesture and methods that can classify it correctly given a set of possible gestures.

© Springer International Publishing AG, part of Springer Nature 2018
A. Campilho et al. (Eds.): ICIAR 2018, LNCS 10882, pp. 399–407, 2018.
https://doi.org/10.1007/978-3-319-93000-8_45

The vast majority of gesture recognition studies seek to extract manually modeled features and then use them in a classifier for recognition. In this sense we find a work that uses features extracted from Kinect and Leap Motion, which based on the position and orientation of the fingers feeds a multi-class Support Vector Machine (SVM) to recognize 10 classes of American Manual Alphabet gestures present in a public dataset presented in this same paper [3].

Another work in the same direction was proposed by Ronchetti [4] through a Probabilistic SOM network (ProbSOM) [5] to recognize LSA64 [6] gestures, so that ProbSOM allows to infer statistically by grouping similar gesture classes and then determining which are the most important characteristics for the discrimination of each gesture.

Recent advances in processing capacity and the increase in the number of large databases are allowing the application of machine learning techniques that until then were almost impractical given their high computational costs and their needs for large amounts of data. Deep learning is one of the most promising techniques, being successfully used in automatic speech recognition [7–9], recommendation systems [10,11] and image recognition [12–15].

When it comes to the recognition of dynamic gestures, the work of Pigou et al. [16] employs two CNNs, whose inputs are the gray level and depth videos original from CLAP14 challenge dataset. The first network uses the original videos, while the second one cuts each frame so that the result contains only the user's hand. At the end, the characteristic vectors are combined and discriminated by the CNNs.

Also, Huang et al. [17] uses a CNN with convolutions in three dimensions (3D CNN). Each video was divided into 5, named: color-R, color-G, color-B, depth and body skeleton, each with 9 frames, the first 3 referring to the color channel of the original video. The database used in the work is private and contains 25 classes of gestures.

Although it does not deal with the recognition of Sign Language and gestures in general, it is worth mentioning the work of Molchanov et al. [18] which uses Augmentation and two 3D CNN networks in parallel. The first one has VIVA challenge's dataset [19] as input and the second uses the same images of the first but significantly reduces the dimensions of the images. The resulting probabilities of the final layer of each network are combined through conditional probability to then classify them into one of the 19 classes.

The objective of this work is to present an efficient computational methodology for the recognition of signals from the Sign Language of Argentina (LSA), through computer vision and machine learning techniques. We will present our 3D Convolutional Neural Network (3D CNN) [20] architecture and use it to represent and classify 64 LSA gestures present in the LSA64 [6] video dataset.

The main contribution of this work is to present a 3D CNN architecture specifically tuned for signal language recognition in order to produce generalist and efficient results in comparison to other works presented in the literature. We also intent to provide a method that could be applied to improve life quality, inclusion and communication over people that are no capable to use sign languages.

2   3D CNN

3D convolution [20] is a mathematical operation where each voxel present in the input volume is multiplied by voxel in the equivalent position of the convolution kernel. At the end, the sum of the results is added to the output volume. In the Fig. 1 it is possible to observe the representation of the 3D convolution operation, where the voxels highlighted in the Input are multiplied with their respective voxels in the Kernel. After these calculations, the sum of them is added to the Output, generating the value of the highlighted voxel.

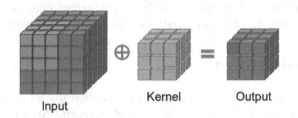

Input   Kernel   Output

Fig. 1. Representation of a 3D convolution operation.

Since the coordinates of the input volume are given by (x, y, z) and the convolution kernel has size (P, Q, R) the 3D convolution operation can be defined mathematically as:

$$O_{xyz} = \sum_{p=0}^{P-1} \sum_{q=0}^{Q-1} \sum_{r=0}^{R-1} K_{pqr} I_{(x+p)(y+q)(z+r)} \tag{1}$$

where O is a result of the convolution, I is the input volume, K is the convolution kernel and (p, q, r) are the coordinates of K.

Convolutional Neural Networks (CNNs) [21] are a specialized type of neural network for processing grid data (2D). The name of this type of neural network is closely linked to a mathematical operation called convolution, where matrix multiplications are replaced by the convolution operation 2D in at least one of its layers.

Its 3D extensions, called 3D CNN [20], differ from CNN networks because they use at least one 3D convolution. These convolutions can, in addition to extracting spatial information from matrices like 2D convolutions, extract information present between consecutive matrices. This fact allows us to map both spatial information of 3D objects and temporal information of a set of sequential images.

A layer that is not needed on a CNN 3D network however is very used is the pooling layer [16,17,22]. A typical pooling layer that calculates the maximum value of a neighborhood of a tensor is called MaxPooling. Specifically, MaxPooling 3D is the layer that calculates the maximum value of a 3D tensor [23,24].

The pooling of adjacent units can be done with the stride of more than one line, column or depth, reducing the size of the input and creating invariance to small displacements and distortions, which can increase the generalization power of the network [23].

These networks can be trained using the RMSProp (Root Mean Square Propagation) [25] optimizer. This is an adaptive step size method that scales the update of each weight through the average of its gradient norm. It is a strategy of minimizing the error, based on the robustness of the RProp [26], the efficiency of the mini-batches as well as an effective balancing of them.

Each kernel acts like filter, that is, when discriminant features are superimposed by the filter, these have a high output value (high neuron stimulus), indicating that they have found a pattern that can represent a certain feature.

3   Proposed Method

The method proposed in this work consists of configuring an architecture based on the 3D CNN concept for the recognition of Argentine Sign Language (ASL).

For all tests and model estimation, it was used the sign dataset LSA64 for Argentinian Sign Language includes 3200 videos where 10 non-expert subjects executed 5 repetitions of 64 different types of signs using one or both hands. Signs were selected among the most commonly used ones in the LSA lexicon, including both verbs and nouns [6]. Some examples of the dataset are presented in Fig. 2.

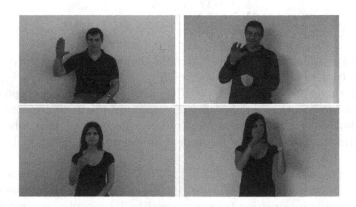

Fig. 2. Sample frames extracted from LSA64.

The dataset was collected under different luminosity conditions. Each sign was executed imposing few constraints on the subjects to increase diversity and realism in the database. The resolution of each video is 1920 by 1080, at 60 frames per second [6]. We used the LSA64 cut version, which is similar to the raw version but each video has been temporally segmented so that the frames in the beginning or end of the video with no movement in the hands were removed.

Our Method consists in a pre-processing step and subsequent model fit and evaluation using our 3D CNN architecture. The next subsections presents the details of the proposed method.

3.1 Preprocessing

Each LSA64 video has a different sizes. To normalize video sizes to 30 frames we use the Nearest Neighborhood Interpolation (NNI) [27] strategy that removes or repeats frames as needed. For example, if the original video contains 40 frames, each multiple frame of 4 is removed and if the original video contains 20 frames, each multiple frame of 2 is repeated.

In order to reduce the computational cost, the dimensions of the videos were reduced to 80 × 45 pixels. In this way we maintained the original aspect ratio so that there was no significant impact on the results.

3.2 Proposed 3D CNN Architecture

The proposed 3D CNN architecture has two stages, the first contains 3 layers of feature extraction, obtained through 3D convolutions and MaxPooling 3D. The second stage is where classification is done using the features previously extracted in 3 non-linear Fully Connected (FC) layers.

The architecture used in this work is visually represented in Fig. 3, we chose to represent the 3D convolution layers and MaxPooling 3D together in order to simplify the representation.

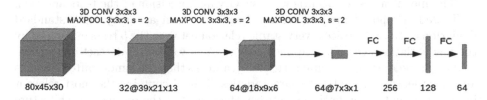

Fig. 3. Proposed 3D CNN architecture for Argentinian Sign Language recognition.

Full architecture has 3 3D convolutional layers, each followed by a 3D Max-Pooling layer. The first convolution used 32 filters (3, 3, 3) and is followed by a MaxPooling 3D layer of kernel (3, 3, 3) and strides (2, 2, 2). The second and third contains 64 filters (3, 3, 3) and both are followed by a MaxPooling 3D kernel layer (3, 3, 3) and strides (2, 2, 2). All layers are activated by ReLu function.

The network architecture was adjusted through the optimization of a parameter search space, from the number of layers, to the quantity and size of the filters. The tests performed all combinations of filters (5, 5, 3) with filters (3, 3, 3) with the amounts 32, 64, 64 filters, in that order. Each convolution layer was followed by a kernel MaxPooling layer (3, 3, 3) and strides (2, 2, 2). The motivation of the convolutions always to use kernel with size 3 in depth is that at the end of the extraction of characteristics we wanted to reduce the volume for only one image. Each setup quoted in this section has been tested 3 times and used the split ratio of the 80/20 video base, that is, 80% for training and 20% for testing.

After the last layer of MaxPooling, the architecture has 3 Fully Connected (FC) layers of 256, 128 and 64 neurons in this sequence. We did incremental tests starting with a single FC layer, until at 4 FCs the result remained practically the same as 3 layers, so we chose to leave only 3 layers.

The first two FC layers uses the ReLU activation function, while the last uses the softmax function in order to interpret the 64 outputs of the network as the probabilities of the input being one of the 64 classes present in the base.

Initially we put 300 epochs for training, but from 50 epochs the result was not increasing enough to justify the computation time, so we chose 50 epochs and batch size 32 as empirical values. As a loss function we used cross entropy, and the chosen optimizer was the RMSprop with suggested parameters [25] given its success in many studies [28,29] (learning rate of 0.001, ρ of 0.9 and decay equal to 0). To build the network we use the Keras [30] library and Theano [31] as backend.

4   Results

We evaluated the results through 5 tests, dividing the data set randomly using the proportion of 80% for training and 20% validation, resulting in 2560 videos for training and 640 videos for testing. Each set is created randomly and performing this procedure we seek to exempt the random factors present in the tests.

The mean values for accuracy, sensitivity and precision of the tests are given in Table 1. Proposed method reaches 93.9% of mean accuracy, with standard deviation of 1.4. We notice a very stable relation between the 5 tests evidenced by the low variation even when applied over random validation dataset generation.

Given the results, we compare them with works that use hand-crafted features and deep learning to extract characteristics. Table 2 contains the most relevant information in the comparisons between the results of the proposed architecture and related works.

When we compare the results with works that use hand-crafted features, we see that we have a slight advantage, reaching 2.6 percentage points more than [3]. And 2.2 percentage points over [4] that uses the same database. We can suggests

Table 1. Proposed method results.

	Accuracy (%)	Sensibility (%)	Precision (%)
Mean	93.9	93.7	94.9
σ	1.4	1.58	1.58

Table 2. Comparison with related works

Proposed	Method	Dataset	nClasses	Acc (%)
	3D CNN	**LSA64**	**64**	**93.9 ± 1.4**
[3]	Finger Position	MKLM	10	91.3
[4]	ProbSOM	LSA64	64	91.7
[16]	CNN	CLAP14	20	91.7
[17]	3D CNN	Private	25	94.2
[18]	3D CNN	VIVA challenge	19	77.5

that our approach, that capture information over spatial and temporal data using 3D CNN provide better information and outperforms these works.

The architecture was also promising when compared to other works that use deep learning. The work of [17] was the only result of related work whose result was better than the one proposed. However, we must point that the amount of information provided to the network was a great differential in this work, using 5 videos per individual while we used only one video in gray level. Finally, [16] despite using two networks for recognition, the results are pretty close and we still get 2.2 percentage points up using only a 3D CNN.

Taking into consideration the related works, there is a great indication that the proposed method is promising for the recognition of sign language, surpassing most of the comparative ones.

5   Conclusion

In this work we present a 3D CNN network architecture for the recognition of 64 classes of gesture of the Argentinian Sign Language. The results reach an accuracy rate of 93.9%, which indicates that deep learning can be adequately applied to the problem.

The great differential is the application of a 3D convolutional network to a database substantially larger than the related works, showing that its application is feasible for bases with a greater variety of classes. In view of the above, the proposed architecture has potential when compared to other architectures that also aim to recognize sign language gestures.

Some points still need to be improved such as broadening the base of gestures and diverse situations. We will also conduct studies on the use of 2D convolutions in order to provide a comparative analysis of the techniques and their real employability, in addition to testing the architecture with larger test sets.

References

1. Moeller, M.P.: Early intervention and language development in children who are deaf and hard of hearing. Pediatrics **106**(3), e43 (2000)
2. Dalton, D.S., Cruickshanks, K.J., Klein, B.E., Klein, R., Wiley, T.L., Nondahl, D.M.: The impact of hearing loss on quality of life in older adults. Gerontologist **43**(5), 661–668 (2003)
3. Marin, G., Dominio, F., Zanuttigh, P.: Hand gesture recognition with leap motion and kinect devices. In: IEEE International Conference on Image Processing (ICIP), pp. 1565–1569. IEEE (2014)
4. Ronchetti, F.: Reconocimiento de gestos dinámicos y su aplicación al lenguaje de señas. Ph.D. thesis, Facultad de Informática (2017)
5. Estrebou, C., Lanzarini, L., Hasperué, W.: Voice recognition based on probabilistic SOM. In: Proceedings of the Conference: XXXVI Conferencia Latinoamericana en Informática, At Asunción, Paraguay (2010)
6. Ronchetti, F., Quiroga, F., Estrebou, C., Lanzarini, L., Rosete, A.: LSA64: a dataset of Argentinian sign language. In: XX II Congreso Argentino de Ciencias de la Computación (CACIC) (2016)
7. Hinton, G., Deng, L., Yu, D., Dahl, G.E., Mohamed, A.r., Jaitly, N., Senior, A., Vanhoucke, V., Nguyen, P., Sainath, T.N., et al.: Deep neural networks for acoustic modeling in speech recognition: the shared views of four research groups. IEEE Signal Process. Mag. **29**(6), 82–97 (2012)
8. Graves, A., Mohamed, A.r., Hinton, G.: Speech recognition with deep recurrent neural networks. In: IEEE International Conference on Acoustics, Speech and Signal Processing (ICASSP), pp. 6645–6649. IEEE (2013)
9. Dahl, G.E., Yu, D., Deng, L., Acero, A.: Context-dependent pre-trained deep neural networks for large-vocabulary speech recognition. IEEE Trans. Audio Speech Lang. Process. **20**(1), 30–42 (2012)
10. Wang, H., Wang, N., Yeung, D.Y.: Collaborative deep learning for recommender systems. In: Proceedings of the 21th ACM SIGKDD International Conference on Knowledge Discovery and Data Mining, pp. 1235–1244. ACM (2015)
11. Wang, X., Wang, Y.: Improving content-based and hybrid music recommendation using deep learning. In: Proceedings of the 22nd ACM International Conference on Multimedia, pp. 627–636. ACM (2014)
12. He, K., Zhang, X., Ren, S., Sun, J.: Deep residual learning for image recognition. In: Proceedings of the IEEE Conference on Computer Vision and Pattern Recognition, pp. 770–778 (2016)
13. Simonyan, K., Zisserman, A.: Very deep convolutional networks for large-scale image recognition. arXiv preprint arXiv:1409.1556 (2014)
14. Cireşan, D.C., Giusti, A., Gambardella, L.M., Schmidhuber, J.: Mitosis detection in breast cancer histology images with deep neural networks. In: Mori, K., Sakuma, I., Sato, Y., Barillot, C., Navab, N. (eds.) MICCAI 2013. LNCS, vol. 8150, pp. 411–418. Springer, Heidelberg (2013). https://doi.org/10.1007/978-3-642-40763-5_51
15. Ciregan, D., Meier, U., Schmidhuber, J.: Multi-column deep neural networks for image classification. In: IEEE Conference on Computer Vision and Pattern Recognition (CVPR), pp. 3642–3649. IEEE (2012)
16. Pigou, L., Dieleman, S., Kindermans, P.-J., Schrauwen, B.: Sign language recognition using convolutional neural networks. In: Agapito, L., Bronstein, M.M., Rother, C. (eds.) ECCV 2014. LNCS, vol. 8925, pp. 572–578. Springer, Cham (2015). https://doi.org/10.1007/978-3-319-16178-5_40

17. Huang, J., Zhou, W., Li, H., Li, W.: Sign language recognition using 3D convolutional neural networks. In: IEEE International Conference on Multimedia and Expo (ICME), pp. 1–6. IEEE (2015)
18. Molchanov, P., Gupta, S., Kim, K., Kautz, J.: Hand gesture recognition with 3D convolutional neural networks. In: Proceedings of the IEEE Conference on Computer Vision and Pattern Recognition Workshops, pp. 1–7 (2015)
19. Ohn-Bar, E., Trivedi, M.M.: Hand gesture recognition in real time for automotive interfaces: a multimodal vision-based approach and evaluations. IEEE Trans. Intell. Transp. Syst. 15(6), 2368–2377 (2014)
20. Ji, S., Xu, W., Yang, M., Yu, K.: 3D convolutional neural networks for human action recognition. IEEE Trans. Pattern Anal. Mach. Intell. 35(1), 221–231 (2013)
21. LeCun, Y., Bottou, L., Bengio, Y., Haffner, P.: Gradient-based learning applied to document recognition. Proc. IEEE 86(11), 2278–2324 (1998)
22. Oyedotun, O.K., Khashman, A.: Deep learning in vision-based static hand gesture recognition. Neural Comput. Appl. 28(12), 3941–3951 (2017)
23. LeCun, Y., Bengio, Y., Hinton, G.: Deep learning. Nature 521(7553), 436 (2015)
24. Giusti, A., Ciresan, D.C., Masci, J., Gambardella, L.M., Schmidhuber, J.: Fast image scanning with deep max-pooling convolutional neural networks. In: 20th IEEE International Conference on Image Processing (ICIP), pp. 4034–4038. IEEE (2013)
25. Tieleman, T., Hinton, G.: Lecture 6.5-RmsProp: divide the gradient by a running average of its recent magnitude. COURSERA Neural Netw. Mach. Learn. 4(2), 26–31 (2012)
26. Riedmiller, M., Braun, H.: A direct adaptive method for faster backpropagation learning: the RProp algorithm. In: IEEE International Conference on Neural Networks, pp. 586–591. IEEE (1993)
27. Molchanov, P., Gupta, S., Kim, K., Pulli, K.: Multi-sensor system for driver's hand-gesture recognition. In: 11th IEEE International Conference and Workshops on Automatic Face and Gesture Recognition (FG), vol. 1, pp. 1–8. IEEE (2015)
28. Mnih, V., Badia, A.P., Mirza, M., Graves, A., Lillicrap, T., Harley, T., Silver, D., Kavukcuoglu, K.: Asynchronous methods for deep reinforcement learning. In: International Conference on Machine Learning, pp. 1928–1937 (2016)
29. Karpathy, A., Fei-Fei, L.: Deep visual-semantic alignments for generating image descriptions. In: Proceedings of the IEEE Conference on Computer Vision and Pattern Recognition, pp. 3128–3137 (2015)
30. Chollet, F., et al.: Keras (2015). https://github.com/keras-team/keras
31. Theano Development Team: Theano: a Python framework for fast computation of mathematical expressions. arXiv e-prints abs/1605.02688, May 2016

Unsupervised Human Action Categorization Using a Riemannian Averaged Fixed-Point Learning of Multivariate GGMM

Fatma Najar[1], Sami Bourouis[2,3(✉)], Atef Zaguia[3], Nizar Bouguila[4], and Safya Belghith[1]

[1] ENIT, Laboratoire RISC Robotique Informatique et Systèmes Complexes,
Université de Tunis El Manar, 1002 Tunis, Tunisie
{fatma.najjar,safya.belghith}@enit.utm.tn
[2] ENIT, Laboratoire: LR-SITI Signal Image et Technologies de l'Information,
Université de Tunis El Manar, 1002 Tunis, Tunisie
[3] Taif University, Taif, Saudi Arabia
s.bourouis@tu.edu.sa
[4] The Concordia Institute for Information Systems Engineering (CIISE),
Concordia University, Montreal, QC H3G 1T7, Canada
nizar.bouguila@concordia.ca

Abstract. We present a novel learning algorithm for Human action recognition and categorization. Our purpose here is to develop a Riemannian Averaged Fixed-Point estimation algorithm (RA-FP) for learning the multivariate generalized Gaussian mixture model's parameters (MGGMM). Experiments in a large datasets of human action images have shown the merits of our approach.

Keywords: Multivariate generalized Gaussian distribution
Mixture models · Riemannian Averaged Fixed-point estimation
Expectation-Maximization · Human action recognition

1 Introduction

Finite mixture models have been broadly applied in the last few years for several applications related to machine learning and pattern recognition [1,5,7,28]. This growing interest has led to many fascinating data modeling techniques. Human action recognition, for instance, is a well-known active research topic and has been widely used in many fields like video surveillance systems, human-to-human interaction, robotics, health care activities and video searching [11,13,24,26]. In particular, Gaussian mixture model (GMM) has been widely studied and used with success for recognizing human actions [6,9,22]. Indeed, both GMM and regression techniques have been used in [6] to build computational models of human motion learned from human examples which is used also for human action

© Springer International Publishing AG, part of Springer Nature 2018
A. Campilho et al. (Eds.): ICIAR 2018, LNCS 10882, pp. 408–415, 2018.
https://doi.org/10.1007/978-3-319-93000-8_46

classification purposes. In [22], a classification method that uses GMM, Hidden Markov Model (HMM) and skeleton features was proposed. Another adaptive GMM has been developed in [9] to classify human actions based on the background segmentation and visual information. However, the Gaussian density has several drawbacks such as its symmetry around the mean and the rigidity of its shape. Therefore, there was a growing interest in developing flexible mixture models based on the generalized Gaussian mixture models (GGMMs) [10,16,23] since they are able to provide more flexibility to fit the shape of the data better than the conventional Gaussian distribution. GGMMs have been widely used in texture image analysis [16], text independent speaker identification [23], data clustering [20] and semantic scene classification [10]. For the case of multivariate analysis, the majority of works used only the diagonal covariance matrix and ignore the richness of the full covariance matrix and this is for calculation simplicity purposes. Their justification is based also on the fact that the features of observed data are independent. However, features are not always independent and for several applications, like the case of human activities, data can be considered as correlated. Therefore, to deal with such problem, some covariance matrix estimators have been proposed in the literature such as the "Riemannian Averaged Fixed-point" estimator [4]. It is used to estimate the full covariance matrix and the shape parameter of a zero-multivariate generalized Gaussian distribution. In this work, we are mainly motivated by investigating this line of research and introducing, for the first time, a Riemannian Averaged Fixed-point estimation algorithm for learning the multivariate GGMM. Then, we derive several experiments to evaluate our proposed framework for Human activity recognition application. The remainder of this paper is organized as follows: in Sect. 2, we review the Riemannian Averaged Fixed Point estimation method for the case of multivariate generalized Gaussian distribution. Then, we present in Sect. 3 our proposed multivariate generalized Gaussian mixture model. Section 4 is dedicated for experiments and finally, we end this paper with some conclusions and future directions.

2   Mixture of Multivariate Generalized Gaussian Distributions

2.1   The Multivariate GGD

The multivariate generalized Gaussian distribution (MGGD) initially proposed in [14] is defined by its mean vector, covariance matrix and the shape parameter. The probability density function of MGGD [15] is given as:

$$p(Y|\Sigma;\beta;\mu) = \frac{\Gamma(\frac{d}{2})}{\pi^{\frac{d}{2}}\Gamma(\frac{d}{2\beta})2^{\frac{d}{2\beta}}} \frac{\beta}{m^{\frac{d}{2}}|\Sigma|^{\frac{1}{2}}} \times exp\left[-\frac{1}{2m^{\beta}}((Y-\mu)^{T}\Sigma^{-1}(Y-\mu))^{\beta}\right] \quad (1)$$

Where $Y \in R^{d}$, $\beta > 0$ is the shape parameter, m is the scale parameter and Σ is a $d \times d$ symmetric positive definite matrix (known as the covariance matrix). The MGGD can be reduced to the multivariate Gaussian distribution in the case of $\beta = 1$. The shape parameter β controls the peakedness and the spread of the distribution. The distribution is more peaky than the conventional Gaussian with heavier tails when $\beta < 1$, and it is less peaky with lighter tails when $\beta > 1$.

2.2   Learning Approach

Some of the statistical model parameter's estimation techniques have been developed in the literature. For the case of multivariate generalized Gaussian distributions, one of the robust developed algorithms is the named "Riemannian Averaged Fixed Point" method (RA-FP) [4]. The later estimator is proposed as a generalization form of the previous proposed technique called Fixed-Point (FP-estimator) [21]. The basic idea of RA-FP algorithm is to implement successive Riemannian averaged of fixed point iterates in order to estimate the covariance matrix for any positive value of the shape parameter. This process is different from the Fixed-point algorithm which estimates the covariance matrix for only the shape parameter belonging to [0, 1]. Let $(Y_1, Y_2, ..., Y_N)$ be a random sample of N observation vectors of dimension d, drawn from a zero mean MGGD with a scatter matrix $M = m\Sigma$; a scale parameter m, and a shape parameter β. The RA-FP uses the Riemannian geometry for estimating the covariance matrix. The RA-FP based estimation of m, β and Σ are determined as following:

For $t \in [0, 1]$, the Riemannian average of $\hat{\Sigma}_{k+1}$ is defined as:

$$\hat{\Sigma}_{k+1} = \Sigma_k \#_{t_k} f(\Sigma_k) \tag{2}$$
$$= \Sigma_k^{1/2} (\Sigma_k^{-1/2} f(\Sigma_k) \Sigma_k^{-1/2})^{t_k} \Sigma_k^{1/2}$$

Where $t_k = \frac{1}{k+1}, t_k \in [0, 1]$, and $f(\Sigma)$ is defined as:

$$f(\Sigma) = \sum_{i=1}^{N} \frac{d}{u_i + u_i^{1-\beta} \sum_{i \neq j} u_j^{\beta}} Y_i Y_i^T, \tag{3}$$

and

$$\hat{m} = \left[\frac{1}{N} \sum_{i=1}^{N} (u_i)^{\beta} \right]^{\frac{1}{\beta}}, \tag{4}$$

If $t_k = 1$, the RA-FP estimator is reduced to the Fixed-point estimator. Now, to compute the maximum likelihood of the shape parameter, we apply an iterative algorithm based on a Newton-Raphson technique [4] to obtain the follow:

$$\hat{\beta}_{k+1} = \hat{\beta}_k - \frac{\alpha(\hat{\beta}_k)}{\alpha'(\hat{\beta}_k)} \tag{5}$$

$$\alpha(\beta) = \frac{dN}{2\sum_{i=1}^{N} u_i^{\beta}} \sum_{i=1}^{N} \left[u_i^{\beta} ln(u_i) \right] - \frac{dN}{2\beta} \left[\psi\left(\frac{d}{2\beta}\right) + ln(2) \right]$$
$$-T - \frac{dN}{2\beta} ln\left(\frac{\beta}{dN} \sum_{i=1}^{N} u_i^{\beta}\right) \tag{6}$$

Where $u_i = Y_i^T \Sigma^{-1} Y_i$ and ψ is the digamma function.

2.3 RA-FP Multivariate Generalized Gaussian Mixture Model

We develop in this section a Riemannian Averaged Fixed-point estimation algorithm for learning a mixture of multivariate generalized Gaussian distribution. A mixture model is defined as:

$$f(Y|\Theta) = \sum_{j=1}^{M} p_j p(Y|\Sigma_j; \beta_j; \mu_j) \tag{7}$$

where $\forall j, p_j \geq 0; \sum_j p_j = 1$, each Θ_j is the set of parameters of the jth component and $\Theta = \{\Sigma_1, ..., \Sigma_M; \beta_1, ..., \beta_M; \mu_1, ..., \mu_M\}$ denotes the full parameter set. To estimate the model's parameters we maximize the Log-likelihood $log(Y|\Theta) = \sum_{i=1}^{N} log(f(Y_i|\Theta))$ through the Expectation-Maximization (EM) algorithm [2]. Later, we derive the following RA-FP steps:

1. Initialization step: We use the k-means algorithm and the method of moment [25] to initialize the model's parameters.
2. Repeat until convergence of the log-likelihood:
   - **E-step:** The responsibilities are determined over expectation step as:

$$p(j|Y_i) = \frac{p_j p(Y_i|\Sigma_j; \beta_j; \mu_j)}{\sum_{m=1}^{M} p_m p(Y_i|\Sigma_m; \beta_m; \mu_m)} \tag{8}$$

   - **M-step:** Over the maximization step, we derive the following parameters:
     - *Mean estimation*

$$\hat{\mu}_j = \frac{\sum_{i=1}^{N} p(j|Y_i)|Y_i - \mu_j|^{\beta_j-1} Y_i}{\sum_{i=1}^{N} p(j|Y_i)|Y_i - \mu_j|^{\beta_j-1}} \tag{9}$$

     - *Covariance estimation for each cluster:* After normalizing the dataset $(Y_n = Y - \mu_j)$, then we determine the covariance matrix using Eq. (2).
     - *Shape estimation:* The shape parameter is determined using Eqs. (5) and (6).
3. Finally, we apply the Bayes' rule to assign each data point to its appropriate cluster.

3 Experimental Results: Human Action Categorization

In this experiment, we propose a novel statistical approach for recognizing and categorizing human action images based on the bag of visual words representation [8,18] and the developed RA-FP multivariate generalized Gaussian mixture model.

3.1   Methodology and Data Set

The methodology that we have adopted for recognizing human actions in images can be summarized as follows. First, we have used dense SIFT descriptors [18] of 16 × 16 pixel patches computed over a grid with spacing of 8 pixels. Next, a visual vocabulary is constructed by quantizing these features into visual words [8] using K-means method. Each image is then represented as a frequency histogram over the V visual words. After that, we apply the probabilistic Latent Semantic Analysis (pLSA) [3] to the obtained histograms in order to represent each image by a D-dimensional vector where D is the number of latent aspects. Finally, we classify the overall images to their right activities using our RA-FP-MGGMM algorithm. Our experiments were conducted on UIUC Sport Event dataset [17] and Stanford dataset [27]. UIUC dataset contains 1579 diverse sport event images from 8 categories: rowing (250 images), badminton (200 images), polo (182 images), bocce (137 images), snowboarding (190 images), croquet (236 images), sailing (190 images), and rockclimbing (194 images). Stanford dataset contains 1250 diverse images from 4 categories: reading (245 images), phoning (259 images), tacking photo (197 images) and playing instrument (549 images). During training phase, we randomly select 50% images from the dataset, while the ramaining images are used for testing.

3.2   Results

We evaluate the performance of our proposed mixture model denoted by RA-FP-MGGMM and we compare obtained results w.r.t those provided by the conventional Gaussian mixture model and the generalized Gaussian mixture model. The objective of this evaluation is to emphasize the importance of considering the full covariance matrix compared to using only the diagonal covariance matrix. We propose also to compare our results with those obtained with the MGGMM learned by the Fixed-point (FP-MGGMM) algorithm [19]. We have studied the impact of the visual vocabulary sizes on the recognition accuracy for both our method (RA-FP-MGGMM) and the FP-MGGMM, as dipicted in Fig. 1. According to this result, the maximum accuracy value is obtained with visual vocabulary sizes of 50 for UIUC and 600 for Stanford dataset. Moreover, we have studied the impact of the number of aspects on the recognition accuracy as shown in Fig. 2, and we found that the optimal accuracy was obtained when the number of aspects was set to 8 for UIUC and 10 for Stanford dataset. The purpose of these studies is to have an idea about the better values for the whole recognition process.

A comparative study between different methods GMM, GGMM, FP-MGGMM and RA-FP-MGGMM is provided in Table 1. It represents the recognition accuracy for both UIUC and Stanford datasets. According to these results, it is clear that our method RA-FP-MGGMM outperforms other methods and offers the highest average accuracy rate (it is about 35% for UIUC and 43% for Stanford). It is noteworthy that the methods based on GMM and GGMM assume that the dimensions of the observed data are independent. Thus, taking

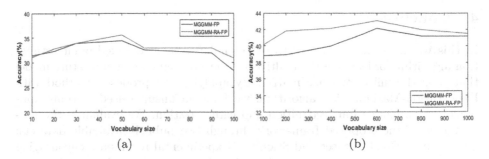

Fig. 1. Recognition accuracy w.r.t vocabulary size. (a) for UIUC dataset. (b) for Stanford dataset.

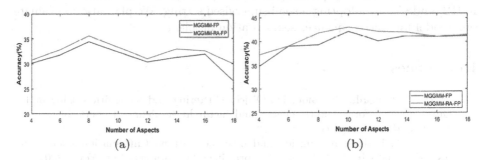

Fig. 2. Recognition accuracy w.r.t the number of aspects. (a) for UIUC dataset. (b) for Stanford dataset.

into account the full covariance matrix through the RA-FP algorithm helps in enhancing the expected performances. This means that more features are used through the covariance matrix to describe the actions, better recognition and categorization performances are obtained. In addition, it is worth mentioning that the RA-FP-MGGMM has better results compared to FP-MGGMM. This is due to the fact that RA-FP estimation algorithm uses a successive Riemannian averages of Fixed-point iterates in order to prevent them from diverging away from the true value of covariance matrix. Moreover, RA-FP technique accurately estimates Σ for any positive value of β. However, FP algorithm estimates Σ for only $\beta \in [0, 1]$.

Table 1. The average accuracy rate for different mixture models

Algorithm	UIUC dataset	Stanford dataset
GMM	30.52	34.80
GGMM	31.69	35.20
FP-MGGMM	34.41	42.13
RA-FP-MGGMM	**35.58**	**43.06**

4 Conclusion

In this work, we have developed a Riemannian Averaged Fixed-point estimation algorithm for learning the multivariate generalized Gaussian mixture model that uses the full covariance matrix. By applying the proposed method with Expectation-Maximization algorithm, we built an unsupervised learning approach for human action recognition and categorization. We evaluated the performance of the proposed framework through two publicly available datasets: UIUC Sport Event dataset and Stanford. Experimental results are encouraging and show the merits of our method compared to other methods involving only the diagonal covariance matrix. Future work could be devoted to the improvement of obtained results by taking into account more relevant visual features like in [12] and also by adopting a semi-supervised setting. We plan also to evaluate our model for video sequences segmentation problem.

References

1. Bdiri, T., Bouguila, N., Ziou, D.: Object clustering and recognition using multi-finite mixtures for semantic classes and hierarchy modeling. Expert Syst. Appl. **41**(4), 1218–1235 (2014)
2. Bishop, C.: Pattern recognition and machine learning (information science and statistics), 1st edn. (2006). corr. 2nd printing edn. Springer, New York (2007)
3. Bosch, A., Zisserman, A., Muñoz, X.: Scene classification Via pLSA. In: Leonardis, A., Bischof, H., Pinz, A. (eds.) ECCV 2006. LNCS, vol. 3954, pp. 517–530. Springer, Heidelberg (2006). https://doi.org/10.1007/11744085_40
4. Boukouvalas, Z., Said, S., Bombrun, L., Berthoumieu, Y., Adalı, T.: A new riemannian averaged fixed-point algorithm for mggd parameter estimation. IEEE Signal Process. Lett. **22**(12), 2314–2318 (2015)
5. Bourouis, S., Al Mashrgy, M., Bouguila, N.: Bayesian learning of finite generalized inverted dirichlet mixtures: application to object classification and forgery detection. Expert Syst. Appl. **41**(5), 2329–2336 (2014)
6. Bruno, B., Mastrogiovanni, F., Sgorbissa, A., Vernazza, T., Zaccaria, R.: Human motion modelling and recognition: a computational approach. In: 2012 IEEE International Conference on Automation Science and Engineering (CASE), pp. 156–161. IEEE (2012)
7. Channoufi, I., Bourouis, S., Bouguila, N., Hamrouni, K.: Image and video denoising by combining unsupervised bounded generalized gaussian mixture modeling and spatial information. Multimed. Tools Appl., February 2018. https://doi.org/10.1007/s11042-018-5808-9
8. Csurka, G., Dance, C., Fan, L., Willamowski, J., Bray, C.: Visual categorization with bags of keypoints. In: Workshop on Statistical Learning in Computer Vision, ECCV, Prague, vol. 1, pp. 1–2 (2004)
9. Dedeoglu, Y.: Human action recognition using Gaussian mixture model based background segmentation. In: Machine Learning Workshop, Bilkent University (2005)
10. Elguebaly, T., Bouguila, N.: Semantic scene classification with generalized Gaussian mixture models. In: Kamel, M., Campilho, A. (eds.) ICIAR 2015. LNCS, vol. 9164, pp. 159–166. Springer, Cham (2015). https://doi.org/10.1007/978-3-319-20801-5_17

11. Fan, W., Bouguila, N.: A variational statistical framework for clustering human action videos. In: 13th International Workshop on Image Analysis for Multimedia Interactive Services, WIAMIS 2012, Dublin, Ireland, 23–25 May, pp. 1–4 (2012)
12. Fan, W., Sallay, H., Bouguila, N., Bourouis, S.: A hierarchical Dirichlet process mixture of generalized dirichlet distributions for feature selection. Comput. Electr. Eng. **43**, 48–65 (2015)
13. Fan, W., Sallay, H., Bouguila, N., Du, J.: Human action recognition using accelerated variational learning of infinite Dirichlet mixture models. In: 14th IEEE International Conference on Machine Learning and Applications, ICMLA 2015, Miami, FL, USA, 9–11 December 2015, pp. 451–456 (2015)
14. Kelker, D.: Distribution theory of spherical distributions and a location-scale parameter generalization. Sankhyā. Indian J. Stat. Ser. A **32**, 419–430 (1970)
15. Kotz, S.: Multivariate distributions at a cross-road. Stat. Distrib. Sci. Work **1**, 247–270 (1975)
16. Kumar, K.N., Rao, K.S., Srinivas, Y., Satyanarayana, C.: Studies on texture segmentation using d-dimensional generalized gaussian distribution integrated with hierarchical clustering. Int. J. Image Graph. Sig. Process. **8**(3), 45 (2016)
17. Li, L.J., Fei-Fei, L.: What, where and who? classifying events by scene and object recognition. In: IEEE 11th International Conference on Computer Vision, ICCV 2007, pp. 1–8. IEEE (2007)
18. Lowe, D.G.: Distinctive image features from scale-invariant keypoints. Int. J. Comput. Vis. **60**(2), 91–110 (2004)
19. Najar, F., Bourouis, S., Bouguila, N., Belghith, S.: A fixed-point estimation algorithm for learning the multivariate ggmm: Application to human action recognition. Accepted, to be appear in the 31st IEEE Canadian Conference on Electrical and Computer Engineering (CCECE 2018) (2018)
20. Najar, F., Bourouis, S., Bouguila, N., Belguith, S.: A comparison between different Gaussian-based mixture models. In: 14th IEEE International Conference on. Computer Systems and Applications, Tunisia. IEEE (2017)
21. Pascal, F., Bombrun, L., Tourneret, J.Y., Berthoumieu, Y.: Parameter estimation for multivariate generalized Gaussian distributions. IEEE Trans. Signal Process. **61**(23), 5960–5971 (2013)
22. Piyathilaka, L., Kodagoda, S.: Gaussian mixture based hmm for human daily activity recognition using 3D skeleton features. In: 2013 8th IEEE Conference on Industrial Electronics and Applications (ICIEA), pp. 567–572. IEEE (2013)
23. Sailaja, V., Srinivasa Rao, K., Reddy, K.: Text independent speaker identification with finite multivariate generalized gaussian mixture model and hierarchical clustering algorithm. Int. J. Comput. Appl. **11**(11), 0975–8887 (2010)
24. Subetha, T., Chitrakala, S.: A survey on human activity recognition from videos. In: 2016 International Conference on Information Communication and Embedded Systems (ICICES), pp. 1–7. IEEE (2016)
25. Varanasi, M.K., Aazhang, B.: Parametric generalized Gaussian density estimation. J. Acoust. Soc. Am. **86**(4), 1404–1415 (1989)
26. Vrigkas, M., Nikou, C., Kakadiaris, I.A.: A review of human activity recognition methods. Front. Robot. AI **2**, 28 (2015)
27. Yao, B., Jiang, X., Khosla, A., Lin, A.L., Guibas, L., Fei-Fei, L.: Human action recognition by learning bases of action attributes and parts. In: 2011 IEEE International Conference on Computer Vision (ICCV), pp. 1331–1338. IEEE (2011)
28. Zhang, H., Huang, Y.: Finite mixture models and their applications: a review. Austin Biom. Biostat. **2**(1), 1–6 (2015)

Traffic and Surveillance

Real-Time Multispectral Pedestrian Detection with a Single-Pass Deep Neural Network

Maarten Vandersteegen$^{(\boxtimes)}$, Kristof Van Beeck, and Toon Goedemé

EAVISE, KU Leuven - Campus De Nayer,
J. De Nayerlaan 5, 2860 Sint-Katelijne-Waver, Belgium
{maarten.vandersteegen,kristof.vanbeeck,toon.goedeme}@kuleuven.be

Abstract. The need for fast and robust pedestrian detection in various applications is growing every day. The addition of a thermal camera could help solving this problem resulting in higher detection accuracy in day but especially during night and bad weather conditions. Using convolutional neural networks, the leading technology in the field of object detection and classification, we propose a network architecture and training method for an accurate real-time multispectral pedestrian detector. We select a regression based single-pass network architecture with pre-trained weights from the Pascal VOC 2007 dataset. The network is then transfer-learned without changing the architecture but taking as input three image channels composed from information of the four available image channels (RGB+T). In our experiments we compare the results of different input-channel compositions and select a top performing combination. Our results show that this simple approach easily outperforms the *improved* ACF+T+THOG detector, coming close to the accuracy of other state-of-the-art multispectral CNNs with a log-average miss-rate of 31.2% measured on the KAIST multispectral benchmark dataset. Our main contribution: it runs as fast as 80FPS, estimated 10× faster than the closest competitors.

Keywords: Real-time · Multispectral · Thermal-visible
Pedestrian detection · Deep learning · YOLOv2

1 Introduction

The task of detecting pedestrians and persons in general using optical cameras has become a wanted feature in many applications within industrial, surveillance, automotive and even consumer context. Although we still have a long way to go before we reach the detection accuracy of a human [1], we can already improve existing detectors by using additional sensors that capture useful information, such as a depth camera or a long-wave infrared (LWIR) camera (also known as a thermal camera). In this work, we consider the LWIR camera as additional sensor. In contrast to a classic camera or a near infrared (NIR) surveillance camera, which use reflected light waves to trigger their pixels, a thermal camera

© Springer International Publishing AG, part of Springer Nature 2018
A. Campilho et al. (Eds.): ICIAR 2018, LNCS 10882, pp. 419–426, 2018.
https://doi.org/10.1007/978-3-319-93000-8_47

measures the radiated heat of objects within its field-of-view causing the body warmth of a human to be spotted easily. Hwang *et al.* [2] and De Smedt *et al.* [3] already proved that a thermal-visible camera combination outperforms a regular person detector at day time but especially at night or under low light and bad weather conditions (e.g. dust and fog).

Besides a high detection accuracy, speed and resources are the next big thing to worry about when it comes to the tinyfication of products. Many vehicles like cars and UAVs or small traffic monitoring systems require small computation units that demand these kind of requirements. Combining the complementary strength of a thermal-visible sensor system and a fast and real-time detector architecture is therefore a very interesting topic of research.

The main contribution of this paper is to bring a new speed record to the latest deep-learning-based thermal-visible object detection techniques while achieving a similar detection accuracy. We do this by transfer learning a fast RGB single-pass network architecture to a multispectral object detector. We selected the darknet YOLOv2 [4] object detector to start from because of its well balanced trade-off between accuracy and speed [5]. In contrast to other state-of-the-art multispectral detectors we compare to [3,6–8], we use three image input channels composed from information of four image channels (RGB+T) instead of using all four channels at once. By doing so, we can use the fast transfer learning procedure from a regular RGB detector to train our network and since we don't introduce any new layers or input channels, the original time performance of the YOLOv2 architecture is preserved.

The remainder of this paper is structured as follows. The related work is discussed in Sect. 2. In Sect. 3 we motivate our choices about the selection of different input compositions. In Sect. 4 we train a model for each selected input composition by means of transfer learning on the KAIST multispectral benchmark dataset [2]. Section 5 discusses the test results where we compare our top performing compositions against the *improved* ACF+T+THOG [3] thermal-visible object detector and the current state-of-the-art, where we assess the added value of a thermal-visible pair against a standalone visible or thermal YOLOv2 and where we asses the real-time capabilities of our proposed detector.

2   Related Work

Traditional object detection techniques mostly use a trained classifier on top of hand crafted features to classify an object. Localization is done using exhaustive search algorithms such as the sliding window approach. Among the most popular methods for classification are the Histogram of Oriented Gradients (HOG) [9], Integral Channel Features (ICF) [10] and Aggregated Channel Features (ACF) [11]. The HOG-feature based detectors have proven to be very good at the detection of pedestrians and persons in general, dominating the object detection market for many years. The channel based approaches easily allowed the addition of channels from other sensors like a thermal camera. Hwang *et al.* [2] extended the ACF detector in this way by adding a thermal channel plus a set of thermal-HOG channels resulting in the ACF+T+THOG detector.

De Smedt *et al.* [3] improved its accuracy by improving the classifier resulting in the *improved* ACF+T+THOG detector, which we use as a benchmark baseline in our experiments.

Nowadays, deep convolutional neural networks are the cutting edge technology when it comes to object detection and classification. Since object detection requires localization, one of the first CNN-based detectors are of the (Fast(er)) R-CNN [12] family which consist of a two-stage approach: a region proposal stage and a classification network. Wagner *et al.* [8] created one of the first thermal-visible detectors based on R-CNN using ACF+T+THOG as a region proposal generator combined with a thermal-visible halfway fusion classifier. Liu *et al.* [7] did similar experiments with Faster R-CNN and Choi *et al.* [13] tried using individual RPNs for the visible and thermal channels in combination with a Support Vector Regression (SVR) for the final classification. Nowadays, state-of-the-art accuracy on the KAIST benchmark dataset is achieved by König *et al.* [6] which uses a halfway-fused thermal-visible RPN with a BDT classifier.

Single-stage or single-pass detection networks see object detection as a regression optimization problem and are faster by nature [5]. Among the most popular state-of-the-art single-pass networks are SSD [14] and YOLOv2 [4], the successor of YOLO. SSD however is surpassed in most of its configurations by YOLOv2 both in speed and accuracy. For our research, we will be using YOLOv2 because it gives the best trade-off between accuracy and speed compared to two-stage object detectors.

3   Composing Three Image Channels from RGB+T

In this section we discuss a number of channel compositions to be able to fit the three input channels of YOLOv2.

In the first experiment we trade one of the RGB channels with the thermal channel in the assumption that the thermal channel contains more valuable information than one colour channel on its own. We train three different models using this type of composition where we replace the *red*, *green*, and *blue* image channel with the thermal channel T, leaving the other two colour channels in their original input position. We name the models respectively *YOLO_TGB*, *YOLO_RTB* and *YOLO_RGT*.

In a second experiment we first colour-convert the RGB channels to a representation where the amount of image information in the individual resulting channels is less balanced. If we then trade one of the channels containing less important information with the thermal channel, we throw away less information. Inspired by the ICF [10] and ACF [11] channel based object detectors, a colour conversion to LUV (CIELUV) is chosen since those detectors use the L or luminance channel to calculate their HOG feature maps which is their major source of information. For this experiment we combine the luminance channel and the thermal channel with one of the U or V colour difference channels. We train two models coined *YOLO_TLV* and *YOLO_TLU*.

In the last experiment we minimize the image information loss as much as possible. By summing the pixel values of the thermal channel with each of the

Fig. 1. Day/night examples of the three different channel composition experiments on the KAIST test set. From left to right *YOLO_TGB*, *YOLO_TLV* and *YOLO_RGB+T*. Detection bounding boxes are shown from the associated models. (Color figure online)

three RGB colour channels, we obtain a thermal-overlayed colour image without the need for throwing away an image channel. To avoid clipping, we use a weighted combination as shown in Eq. 1:

$$X = \frac{R+T}{2} \quad Y = \frac{G+T}{2} \quad Z = \frac{B+T}{2} \tag{1}$$

We train a last model called *YOLO_RGB+T* based on this composition. Figure 1 shows channel composition examples of three models for a day and a night image from the KAIST dataset with corresponding detections overlay.

4 Training

Training a deep neural network requires a huge amount of data. Many large and challenging datasets are created to help solving the problems of image classification and object detection (ImageNet, Microsoft COCO, VOT, Pascal VOC, Caltech). Unfortunately only a few small thermal-visible datasets are available due to the cost and complexity of the camera combination [2,15]. Training a few million weights only from a limited amount of data is unfortunately not feasible.

König *et al.* [6] solves this problem by initializing the first layers of its RPN with weights pretrained on the ImageNet dataset [16] followed by fine-tuning its visible input stage on a visible-only dataset and fine-tuning its thermal input stage on a thermal-only dataset. The final RPN is then transfer-learned on the KAIST dataset.

In contrast to this long and complex training procedure, our proposed training scheme consists of a simpler single-stage procedure. We initialize the YOLOv2 architecture with pretrained weights from the PASCAL VOC 2007 dataset [17] which is already optimized for object detection. We then use the KAIST thermal-visible benchmark dataset directly to transfer-learn our network to a thermal-visible object detector.

We sample the videos from the KAIST training sets, analogous to [18] with a 2-frame skip. Next to that all frames containing instances labelled *people, cyclist* or *person?* and frames containing pedestrians smaller than 50 pixels are removed. This leaves us with 19022 frames of training data with 5013 frames containing annotated pedestrians. All other frames are just scenery without objects of interest. We discovered that by not removing all scenery images, the model converges better resulting in surprisingly better test results.

We prepare the YOLOv2 architecture according to the procedure described in [19] for a single class object detector. We resize the input resolution of the network to fit the KAIST image resolution (640 × 512) so we can better cope with smaller objects. Resizing is possible thanks to the fact that YOLOv2 is fully convolutional.

During training we allow the weights of all network layers to be updated instead of only the weights of the last layers. This leads to longer training but gives the network a chance to adapt to the new view of a thermal-visible channel composition, resulting in a better model. To stabilize, the first 100 iterations (mini batches) use a learning rate of 0.0001. After that we continue with a learning rate of 0.001 to speed up the training process. We stop after about 15000 iterations with an average training loss of 0.7. For most models, this appears to be the optimal point before we start to over-fit. Training time for each model takes less than 12 h on an NVIDIA GTX1080TI graphics card.

5   Experiments

Evaluation is done on the *reasonable* test set of the KAIST benchmark dataset [2]. We follow the evaluation protocol defined in [20] and compare against the *improved* ACF+T+THOG thermal-visible pedestrian detector [3] in three different cases: *day, night* and *all*, respectively representing the *reasonable day, reasonable night*

Table 1. Log-average miss rates for each detector model on *reasonable all, reasonable day* and *reasonable night* KAIST test sets. Note that all YOLO_* models and the *improved* ACT+T+THOG are compared here with an IoU of 0.4. All detectors we compare to use four input image channels.

Detector	All	Day	Night
YOLO_TGB	**31.2%**	34.7%	23.1%
YOLO_RTB	38.9%	40.2%	34.8%
YOLO_RGT	52.7%	56.1%	44.6%
YOLO_TLU	32.5%	36.7%	23.8%
YOLO_TLV	**31.2%**	35.1%	22.7%
YOLO_RGB+T	42.6%	45.5%	36.9%
YOLO_RGB	40.8%	39.1%	45.9%
YOLO_TTT	40.5%	46.8%	24.4%
improved ACF+T+THOG [3]	37.8%	39.1%	34.1%
R-CNN based Wagner *et al.* [8]	43.80%	46.15%	37.00%
Faster R-CNN based Liu *et al.* [7]	36.99%	36.84%	35.49%
RPN + BDT König *et al.* [6]	**29.83%**	N.A	N.A

and *reasonable all* subsets. The test set is sampled with a 20-frame skip resulting in 2252 images. Following the *reasonable* test set criteria, annotations are ignored if their label is different from *person*, if the bounding box height is smaller than 50 pixels and if they are marked as *heavily occluded*. This leaves us with 1627 annotated pedestrians. We experimentally discovered that due to the nature of YOLOv2's course grid cells, less accurate location predictions are made for small objects compared to the *improved* ACF+T+THOG. For this reason, we use an IoU threshold of 0.4 instead of 0.5 as proposed by the standard.

Table 1 summarizes the log-average miss rates of all models we trained on the *reasonable all, reasonable day* and *reasonable night* test sets. *YOLO_TGB* and *YOLO_TLV* both surpass all our other models with a log-average miss rate of 31.2% which is better than the proposed model from Liu *et al.* [7] and closely approaches the state-of-the-art 29.83% from König *et al.* [6]. Figure 2 shows the miss rate vs. FPPI curves on the *all, day* and *night* test sets for our top performing models (*YOLO_TGB, YOLO_TLV*), the *improved* ACF+T+THOG detector, YOLOv2 learned on RGB images only (*YOLO_RGB*) and a YOLOv2

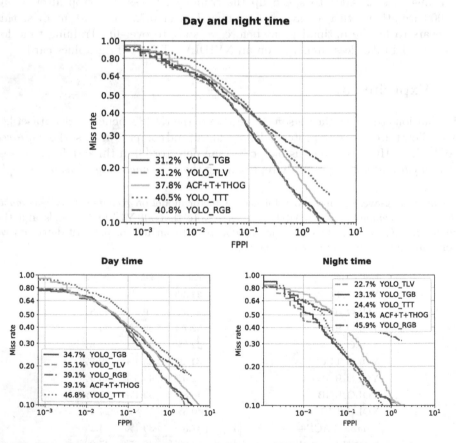

Fig. 2. Detection curves respectively on the *reasonable all, reasonable day* and *reasonable night* subsets. (Color figure online)

learned on thermal images only (*YOLO_TTT*). *YOLO_TLV* outperforms the *improved* ACF+T+THOG baseline detector by 6.6% and at night, the difference is even 11.4%. Since the *YOLO_TLV* and *YOLO_TGB* models perform equally well, we propose to use the *YOLO_TGB* model since it doesn't need a colour conversion stage which benefits the speed for use in real-time applications.

Apart from achieving top accuracy results, our models are capable of running at speeds of 80FPS on an NVIDIA GTX1080TI graphical card because of the efficient C - CUDA implementation of darknet [4]. The detectors from Liu *et al.* and König *et al.* are respectively based on and derived from a MATLAB implementation of Faster R-CNN which is, according to [4,5] 10× slower, making it safe to state that our proposed detector currently is probably the fastest neural network for thermal-visible pedestrian detection, achieving overall state-of-the-art accuracy.

6   Conclusion

In this paper, we investigated the possibility to create a real-time multispectral pedestrian detector using the latest technology of deep convolutional neural networks. Inspired by the speed of single-pass CNNs, we proposed to use the YOLOv2 architecture to train a thermal-visible pedestrian detector. We accomplished overall state-of-the-art performance by the simple approach of composing three input channels based on the information of four image channels (RGB+T), thereby avoiding the introduction of new layers or channels resulting in the preservation of YOLOv2's speed. Our results demonstrate that our proposed model *YOLO_TGB*, which uses only the thermal, green and blue image channels, achieves a log-average miss rate of 31.2%, closely approaching the current state-of-the-art benchmark on the KAIST multispectral dataset. Thanks to the fast single-pass architecture of YOLOv2, the detector is benchmarked on an NVIDIA GTX1080TI graphical card at 80FPS which gives it sufficient head room for real-time applications.

In future work, we will port this detector to an embedded platform, using it to detect pedestrians from a UAV.

References

1. Zhang, S., Benenson, R., Omran, M., Hosang, J., Schiele, B.: How far are we from solving pedestrian detection? In: Proceedings of the IEEE Conference on Computer Vision and Pattern Recognition, pp. 1259–1267 (2016)
2. Hwang, S., Park, J., Kim, N., Choi, Y., So Kweon, I.: Multispectral pedestrian detection: benchmark dataset and baseline. In: Proceedings of the IEEE Conference on Computer Vision and Pattern Recognition, pp. 1037–1045 (2015)
3. De Smedt, F., Puttemans, S., Goedemé, T.: How to reach top accuracy for a visual pedestrian warning system from a car? In: 2016 6th IEEE International Conference on Image Processing Theory Tools and Applications (IPTA), pp. 1–6 (2016)

4. Redmon, J., Farhadi, A.: Yolo9000: better, faster, stronger. In: Proceedings of the IEEE Conference on Computer Vision and Pattern Recognition, pp. 6517–6525 (2017)
5. Tijtgat, N., Van Ranst, W., Volckaert, B., Goedemé, T., De Turck, F.: Embedded real-time object detection for a UAV warning system. In: The International Conference on Computer Vision, ICCV 2017, pp. 2110–2118 (2017)
6. König, D., Adam, M., Jarvers, C., Layher, G., Neumann, H., Teutsch, M.: Fully convolutional region proposal networks for multispectral person detection. In: 2017 IEEE Conference on Computer Vision and Pattern Recognition Workshops (CVPRW), pp. 243–250. IEEE (2017)
7. Liu, J., Zhang, S., Wang, S., Metaxas, D.: Multispectral deep neural networks for pedestrian detection. In: Proceedings of BMVC, pp. 73.1–73.13, September 2016
8. Wagner, J., Fischer, V., Herman, M., Behnke, S.: Multispectral pedestrian detection using deep fusion convolutional neural networks. In: 24th European Symposium on Artificial Neural Networks, Computational Intelligence and Machine Learning (ESANN), pp. 509–514 (2016)
9. Dalal, N., Triggs, B.: Histograms of oriented gradients for human detection. In: 2005 IEEE Computer Society Conference on Computer Vision and Pattern Recognition, CVPR 2005, vol. 1, pp. 886–893. IEEE (2005)
10. Dollár, P., Tu, Z., Perona, P., Belongie, S.: Integral channel features (2009)
11. Dollár, P., Appel, R., Belongie, S., Perona, P.: Fast feature pyramids for object detection. IEEE Trans. Pattern Anal. Mach. Intell. **36**(8), 1532–1545 (2014)
12. Ren, S., He, K., Girshick, R., Sun, J.: Faster R-CNN: Towards real-time object detection with region proposal networks. In: Advances in neural information processing systems, pp. 91–99 (2015)
13. Choi, H., Kim, S., Park, K., Sohn, K.: Multi-spectral pedestrian detection based on accumulated object proposal with fully convolutional networks. In: 2016 23rd International Conference on Pattern Recognition (ICPR), pp. 621–626. IEEE (2016)
14. Liu, W., Anguelov, D., Erhan, D., Szegedy, C., Reed, S., Fu, C.-Y., Berg, A.C.: SSD: single shot multibox detector. In: Leibe, B., Matas, J., Sebe, N., Welling, M. (eds.) ECCV 2016. LNCS, vol. 9905, pp. 21–37. Springer, Cham (2016). https://doi.org/10.1007/978-3-319-46448-0_2
15. González, A., Fang, Z., Socarras, Y., Serrat, J., Vázquez, D., Xu, J., López, A.M.: Pedestrian detection at day/night time with visible and FIR cameras: a comparison. Sensors **16**(6), 820 (2016)
16. Krizhevsky, A., Sutskever, I., Hinton, G.E.: Imagenet classification with deep convolutional neural networks. In: Advances in neural information processing systems, pp. 1097–1105 (2012)
17. Everingham, M., Van Gool, L., Williams, C.K., Winn, J., Zisserman, A.: The pascal visual object classes (VOC) challenge. Int. J. Comput. Vis. **88**(2), 303–338 (2010)
18. Hosang, J., Omran, M., Benenson, R., Schiele, B.: Taking a deeper look at pedestrians. In: Proceedings of the IEEE Conference on Computer Vision and Pattern Recognition, pp. 4073–4082 (2015)
19. Puttemans, S., Callemein, T., Goedemé, T.: Building robust industrial applicable object detection models using transfer learning and single pass deep learning architectures. In: Proceedings of the International Conference on Computer Vision Theory and Applications (2018, to appear)
20. Dollar, P., Wojek, C., Schiele, B., Perona, P.: Pedestrian detection: An evaluation of the state of the art. IEEE Trans. Pattern Anal. Mach. Intell. **34**(4), 743–761 (2012)

Encoding Stereoscopic Depth Features for Scene Understanding in off-Road Environments

Christopher J. Holder$^{(\boxtimes)}$ and Toby P. Breckon

Durham University, Durham, UK
c.j.holder@durham.ac.uk

Abstract. Scene understanding for autonomous vehicles is a challenging computer vision task, with recent advances in convolutional neural networks (CNNs) achieving results that notably surpass prior traditional feature driven approaches. However, limited work investigates the application of such methods either within the highly unstructured off-road environment or to RGBD input data. In this work, we take an existing CNN architecture designed to perform semantic segmentation of RGB images of urban road scenes, then adapt and retrain it to perform the same task with multi-channel RGBD images obtained under a range of challenging off-road conditions. We compare two different stereo matching algorithms and five different methods of encoding depth information, including disparity, local normal orientation and HHA (horizontal disparity, height above ground plane, angle with gravity), to create a total of ten experimental variations of our dataset, each of which is used to train and test a CNN so that classification performance can be evaluated against a CNN trained using standard RGB input.

Keywords: Deep learning · RGBD · Scene understanding

1 Introduction

Scene understanding is a widely researched topic, and although the majority of scene understanding work only considers conventional 2D colour images (RGB), it has been demonstrated that the addition of 3D depth information (D) can improve classification performance in semantic scene understanding tasks, whether a laser scanner [1], stereoscopic camera [2] or structured light sensor [3] is utilised to provide a combined colour-depth (RGB-D) input.

More recently, deep-learning based methods have come to dominate scene understanding research, with convolutional neural networks (CNNs) achieving state of the art results on many image recognition tasks [4, 5]. The approaches of Fully Convolutional Network (FCN) [6] and SegNet [7] demonstrate leading performance for full pixelwise labelling of RGB images in a wide variety of contexts, particularly with SegNet in road scene understanding.

Prior attempts to utilise depth information in CNN classification tasks have shown that such features can bring about an improvement over results obtained from standard colour images: Gupta et al. [8] encode each pixel height, orientation and disparity into a 3 channel depth image to achieve state-of-the-art RGB-D object detection results,

© Springer International Publishing AG, part of Springer Nature 2018
A. Campilho et al. (Eds.): ICIAR 2018, LNCS 10882, pp. 427–434, 2018.
https://doi.org/10.1007/978-3-319-93000-8_48

while Pavel et al. [9] utilise Histogram of Oriented Gradients and Histogram of Oriented Depth, computed from the output of a consumer depth camera (Microsoft Kinect), to obtain competitive results in an object segmentation task.

There is, however, relatively little scene understanding work focused on the off-road environment, where distinct but visually similar classes and a lack of regular structure can pose particular problems for computer vision. The approach of Jansen et al. [10] classifies pixels using colour based features and Gaussian Mixture Models, while Manduchi et al. [1] uses a combination of features from colour imagery and 3D geometry from a laser range-finder. In [11] a CNN is used to classify off-road imagery, with promising results achieved using only scene colour.

In this work, we examine the relevance of depth information within this context. Following the work of [11], we adapt the SegNet CNN architecture [7] to take multi-channel images comprising three RGB channels plus some combination of depth features $(D_{f1} D_{f2} \dots D_{fn})$ as input. Using our own stereoscopic off-road data set, we create ten different encodings and train a network to perform pixelwise classification on each.

2   Methodology

Our method comprises a CNN architecture that takes multiple-channel input images and outputs a single class label for every pixel. Input images consist of 3-channel RGB information combined with one or more additional channels containing some 3D information derived from stereo disparity.

2.1   Network Architecture

The convolutional neural network architecture we use is nearly identical to that of SegNet, as described in [7]. We carry out minor alterations so that it can take multiple-channel images as input, and adapt the final layer to output the six classes found in our off-road scene data set.

The SegNet architecture is comprised of a symmetrical network of thirteen 'encoder' layers followed by thirteen 'decoder' layers. The encoder layers correspond to the convolution and pooling layers of the VGG16 [12] object classification network, while the decoder layers up-sample their input so that the final output from the network has the same dimensions as the input. During the encoding phase, each pooling layer down-samples its input by a factor of two and stores the location of the maximum value from each 2×2 pooling window. During the decoding phase, these locations are used by the corresponding up-sampling layer to populate a sparse feature map, with the convolution layers on the decoder side trained to fill the gaps. This technique facilitates full pixel-wise classification in real-time, making SegNet an ideal architecture for use in autonomous vehicle applications.

For each of our input configurations, we initialise a network with randomised weights and train for 20,000 iterations, an amount empirically found to give the network ample time to achieve optimum performance. We use stochastic gradient descent (backpropagation) with a fixed learning rate of 0.001 and a momentum of 0.9, the values originally used to benchmark the SegNet architecture.

2.2 Data

We train the network using our own off-road data set, using images captured by stereo camera at an off-road driving centre in England. Our images have a resolution of 480×360 with a stereo baseline of 400 mm giving us good depth resolution for a considerable distance in front of the vehicle. We manually label our ground truth images, with each pixel being assigned one of six class labels: {*sky, water, dirt, grass, tree, man-made obstacle*}. Ten variants of the data set are created, each with one of five combinations of RGB-D features and one of two stereo algorithms, and each set is split into 80% training and 20% testing data sets.

2.3 Stereo Disparity

We compute two sets of stereo disparities, D, using Semi Global Block Matching (SGBM) [13] and Adaptive Support Weights (ASW) [14] methods, from which we also compute height above ground plane (H), normal orientation (N) and angle with gravity (A) of each point.

Stereo disparity measures the distance, in pixels, between the horizontal position of a feature in the left and right images of a rectified stereo image pair. Our data set contains disparities of between 1 and 64 pixels, which translates to a theoretical range of between 3 m and 200 m in front of the camera.

SGBM is widely used in real-time applications due to its combination of accuracy and speed. The algorithm first calculates the cost for every potential disparity match, in our case using the method from [15], and then attempts to minimise a global smoothness constraint while aggregating these costs along a one-dimensional path across the image.

In the ASW method, a local support weight window is computed for each pixel taking account of colour as well as spatial proximity, so that when matching is performed, neighbouring pixels that are part of the same surface, and therefore likely to be similar in colour to the pixel being matched, are given precedence. Despite being a more computationally complex algorithm, ASW has been shown to be easily parallelizable [16], allowing for real-time performance when run on a GPU. Furthermore, ASW has been empirically shown to provide a greater level of depth texture granularity than SGBM due to its ability to account for surface edges and the absence of a global smoothness prior.

For the disparity channel included in the CNN input, we normalise each stereo depth output to 0–255 to create an 8-bit image.

From this disparity information, we derive three further four-channel encodings: RGBD, RGBH and RGBA; and two six-channel encodings: RGBN, with N_x, N_y, and N_z each comprising one channel, and RGBDHA, combining disparity, height above ground plane and angle with gravity in the same manner as HHA encoding in [8]. These five encoding types combined with two stereo algorithms give us a total of ten data sets, in addition to our original RGB data set, for evaluation. Figure 1 visualises four of our depth encoding methods.

Fig. 1. Four of the methods we use to encode depth data (clockwise from top left): disparity computed using the ASW method; Height above an assumed ground plane; Surface Normal (R, G and B values represent X, Y and Z respectively); Angle with gravity.

2.4   Height Above Ground Plane

From each disparity map we create height map H, encoding each pixel height above an assumed ground plane. Due to the rough nature of off-road environments, fitting a ground plane, as in [8] is not reliable, so we assume a ground plane fixed relative to the camera based on the known vehicle dimensions.

Each pixel height above this plane can be calculated using the pixel disparity value and known camera parameters. We clamp this value between 0 and 2 h, where h is the height of the camera above the ground, then normalise to 0–255 to create an 8-bit image.

2.5   Normal Orientation

A normal map N encodes local orientation information at each point in an image. By calculating the 3D positions of three points surrounding each pixel, we can describe an imagined plane encompassing them, the orientation of which gives us a local normal vector. We multiply each component of this vector by 255 to create an image of three 8-bit channels encoding the normal vector X, Y and Z values at each pixel.

2.6 Angle with Gravity

In [8], angle with gravity was found to be a useful feature when performing RGB-D object classification with a CNN. We compute each pixel angle with gravity, A, by comparing its normal vector with a gravity vector as in Eq. 1. As our data does not include vehicle orientation information and plane fitting is unreliable in the off-road environment, we assume gravity to always be $(0, -1, 0)$ relative to the camera. Each pixel value is then multiplied by 255 to create an 8-bit image.

$$A_{x,y} = N_{x,y} \cdot (0, -1, 0) \tag{1}$$

3 Evaluation

We assess our trained CNNs using the testing portion of our data set. Our primary metric for assessing classification performance is overall accuracy, defined as the number of correctly labelled pixels divided by the total number of labelled pixels in the test data. We also observe mean average precision and recall over our six classes (Table 1).

Table 1. Shows the performance of each variant of input. The best performing configuration was RGBH (height above ground plane) generated from SGBM stereo disparity, achieving an overall accuracy of 0.88. This shows that height is a particularly useful feature when considering the problem of off-road classification, where several classes can be delineated fairly consistently by their vertical positions.

Input format	Overall accuracy	Mean average precision	Mean average recall
RGB	0.87	0.82	0.85
RGBD (SGBM)	0.86	0.76	0.85
RGBA (SGBM)	0.84	0.81	0.78
RGBH (SGBM)	**0.88**	0.84	**0.87**
RGBN (SGBM)	0.83	0.8	0.77
RGBDHA (SGBM)	0.87	0.86	0.84
RGBD (ASW)	0.87	0.81	0.85
RGBA (ASW)	0.87	**0.88**	0.83
RGBH (ASW)	0.84	0.82	0.83
RGBN (ASW)	0.82	0.8	0.8
RGBDHA (ASW)	0.84	0.84	0.79

Overall results obtained from ASW stereo were not as good as those from SGBM, which would seem to suggest that the additional encoded detail is of limited utility and cannot counter the adverse effects of the extra noise introduced by the lack of any smoothness constraint. The worst performing encoding with both stereo algorithms was RGBN, which re-encodes a single disparity channel as three normal orientation channels. This may indicate that the addition of extra data channels can impact the ability of the CNN to converge on an optimal configuration, as a channel containing information that is redundant or otherwise not useful effectively decreases the signal to noise ratio of the input data. Despite this, the six channel RGBDHA configuration derived from SGBM stereo, performed fairly well, with a mean average precision higher than that of the RGB benchmark, suggesting that by careful selection of the data contained within additional channels, they can prove useful, even when they contain different encodings of identical information.

Figure 2 demonstrates our CNN output, with results obtained from RGB images compared to those from SGBM RGBH images. A slightly greater amount of detail can be seen in the RGBH images, with edges appearing slightly better defined than in their RGB counterparts, however the noise present in the image containing a large body of water illustrates the inability of stereo techniques to cope with transparent or reflective surfaces, representing a key area for future work.

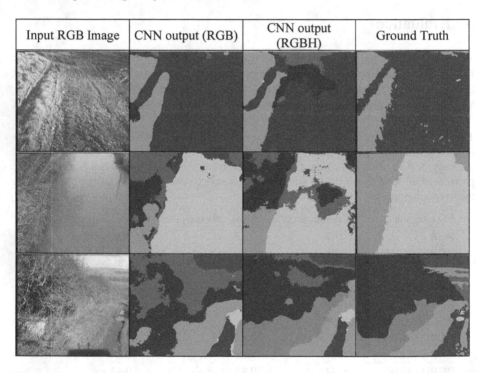

Fig. 2. CNN output labels generated from RGB input, compared to those generated with the addition of a channel encoding pixel height above ground plane (RGBH), computed using semi global block matching disparities.

4   Conclusions

Our results show that the additional information contained in stereo disparity can provide marginal improvement to CNN classification performance compared to standard RGB images in this particularly challenging problem of off-road scene understanding. However, careful consideration of how this information is encoded is necessary, and in our case the combination of RGB data with each pixel's height above ground plane was shown to give the best results.

The performance gains demonstrated are small, however this is mostly due to the efficacy of the existing CNN architecture at classification from conventional colour images (RGB), with results so good to begin with that it becomes ever harder to gain extra performance.

This is counter to results such as those from Gupta et al. [8] and Pavel et al. [9], who claim that RGBD data provides significant improvements in CNN classification performance over RGB imagery. This demonstrates that while depth information may improve CNN performance in an indoor object detection task, it is of limited utility in the more challenging off-road environment, where poorly defined class boundaries and inconsistent object shape can hamper classification accuracy.

References

1. Manduchi, R., Castano, A., Talukder, A., Matthies, L.: Obstacle detection and terrain classification for autonomous off-road navigation. Auton. Robots **18**(1), 81–102 (2005)
2. Ess, A., Mueller, T., Grabner, H., Van Gool, L.J.: Segmentation-based urban traffic scene understanding. In: British Machine Vision Conference (2009)
3. Gupta, S., Arbelaez, P., Girshick, R., Malik, J.: Indoor scene understanding with RGB-D images: bottom-up segmentation, object detection and semantic segmentation. Int. J. Comput. Vis. **112**(2), 133–149 (2014)
4. Krizhevsky, A., Sutskever, I., Hinton, G.E.: ImageNet classification with deep convolutional neural networks. In: Advances in Neural Information Processing Systems (2012)
5. He, K., Zhang, X., Ren, S., Sun, J.: Deep residual learning for image recognition. arXiv: 1512.03385 (2015)
6. Long, J., Shelhamer, E., Darrell, T.: Fully convolutional networks for semantic segmentation. In: IEEE Conference on Computer Vision and Pattern Recognition (2015)
7. Badrinarayanan, V., Handa, A., Cipolla, R.: SegNet: a deep convolutional encoder-decoder architecture for robust semantic pixel-wise labelling. arXiv:1505.07293 (2015)
8. Gupta, S., Girshick, R., Arbeláez, P., Malik, J.: Learning rich features from RGB-D images for object detection and segmentation. In: Fleet, D., Pajdla, T., Schiele, Bernt, Tuytelaars, Tinne (eds.) ECCV 2014. LNCS, vol. 8695, pp. 345–360. Springer, Cham (2014). https://doi.org/10.1007/978-3-319-10584-0_23
9. Pavel, M.S., Schulz, H., Behnke, S.: Recurrent convolutional neural networks for object-class segmentation of RGB-D video. In: International Joint Conference on Neural Networks (2015)
10. Jansen, P., van der Mark, W., van den Heuvel, J.C., Groen, F.C.: Colour based off-road environment and terrain type classification. In: IEEE Intelligent Transportation Systems (2005)
11. Holder, C.J., Breckon, T.P., Wei, X.: From on-road to off: transfer learning within a deep convolutional neural network for segmentation and classification of off-road scenes. In: Hua, G., Jégou, H. (eds.) ECCV 2016. LNCS, vol. 9913, pp. 149–162. Springer, Cham (2016). https://doi.org/10.1007/978-3-319-46604-0_11
12. Simonyan, K., Zisserman, A.: Very deep convolutional networks for large-scale image recognition. arXiv:1409.1556 (2014)

13. Hirschmuller, H.: Accurate and efficient stereo processing by semi-global matching and mutual information. In: IEEE Computer Society Conference on Computer Vision and Pattern Recognition (2005)
14. Yoon, K.-J., Kweon, I.-S.: Adaptive support-weight approach for correspondence search. IEEE Trans. Pattern Anal. Mach. Intell. **28**(4), 650–656 (2006)
15. Birchfield, S., Tomasi, C.: A pixel dissimilarity measure that is insensitive to image sampling. IEEE Trans. Pattern Anal. Mach. Intell. **20**(4), 401–406 (1998)
16. Kowalczuk, J., Psota, E.T., Perez, L.C.: Real-time stereo matching on CUDA using an iterative refinement method for adaptive support-weight correspondences. IEEE Trans. Circuits Syst. Video Technol. **23**(1), 94–104 (2013)

Sleep Deprivation Detection for Real-Time Driver Monitoring Using Deep Learning

Miguel García-García[1,2](✉) [ORCID], Alice Caplier[2], and Michele Rombaut[2]

[1] Innov+, Batiment 503, Centre Universitaire d'Orsay, 91400 Orsay, France
miguel.garcia@innov-plus.com
[2] Univ. Grenoble Alpes, CNRS,
Grenoble INP, GIPSA-lab, 38000 Grenoble, France
{alice.caplier,michele.rombaut}@gipsa-lab.fr

Abstract. We propose a non-invasive method to detect sleep deprivation by evaluating a short video sequence of a subject. Computer Vision techniques are used to crop the face from every frame and classify it (within a Deep Learning framework) into two classes: "rested" or "sleep deprived". The system has been trained on a database of subjects recorded under severe sleep deprivation conditions. A prototype has been implemented in a low-cost Android device proving its viability for real-time driver monitoring applications. Tests on real world data have been carried out and show encouraging performances but also reveal the need of larger datasets for training.

Keywords: Mobilenet · Road safety · Driver drowsiness
Sleep deprivation

1 Introduction

Sleep deprivation is the condition of not having enough sleep. Its physical impact have been studied [1], as well as its effects on cognitive [2] and driving performance [3]. It is estimated that having less than 8 h of sleep is analogue to drinking a certain amount of alcohol [4].

Drowsy driving is a major threat to road safety. In 2014, 846 fatalities related to drowsy drivers were recorded in the United States [5], but it is believed that this number is systematically underestimated and the real cipher may be near 6,000 fatal crashes each year [6]. Therefore, drowsiness detection is an important challenge for the automotive industry, which proposes several options either for alerting the driver in real time, for offering coaching sessions to correct risky behaviors, or for handing over the control to an autonomous vehicle.

There are two main categories of real-time drowsiness detectors: vehicle-focused or driver-focused. Vehicle-focused detectors try to infer drowsiness from a deterioration on driving performance by monitoring the behavior of vehicle.

© Springer International Publishing AG, part of Springer Nature 2018
A. Campilho et al. (Eds.): ICIAR 2018, LNCS 10882, pp. 435–442, 2018.
https://doi.org/10.1007/978-3-319-93000-8_49

They are limited to certain specific conditions, such as highway driving. Driver-focused detectors may infer drowsiness from psychophysiological parameters of the subject (electroencephalogram, electrooculogram, electromyogram, skin conductivity) but need the usage of invasive captors, which can be uncomfortable. Computer Vision based methods are getting popular within the industry as they can evaluate in real-time certain driver parameters without invasive instruments.

Sleep deprivation is not the only cause for drowsy driving, but it leads almost inevitably to it. Hence, being able to detect if a driver has not had enough sleep may be a good way to improve the performance of Advanced Driver Assistance Systems (ADAS) and therefore to prevent road accidents. We propose here a method to estimate sleep deprivation based on Computer Vision and Deep Learning techniques. We prove its feasibility by building a prototype on a low cost device which evaluates driver status in real time.

2   Related Work

Recent studies have detailed the effects of sleep deprivation on facial appearance [7], specifically particular patterns on eyes, mouth and skin after a prolonged wake of 31 h. Classical approaches for drowsiness detection use one or several of these features, such as blinking frequency, eye closure or yawning frequency [8]. Other studies use the Facial Action Coding System [9] to perform the classification, obtaining very subject-dependent results [10]. These methods do not work with all the possible information facial features can offer.

Another approaches have tried to use the information of the whole facial area to infer fatigue. Several studies have been carried out over NTHU Driver Drowsiness Detection dataset [11], which provides data from 8 subjects performing a set of facial expressions simulating different scenarios [12,13]. Best results are achieved by Lyu et al. [14], who use a Long-term Multi-granularity Deep Framework for a performance of 90.05%. However, the use of simulated data does not seem appropriated for sleep deprivation detection, as some of the effects revealed by [7] are impossible to imitate consciously (skin tone, circles around eyes, etc.).

Dwivedi et al. [15] used a private dataset of 30 male subjects playing a video game after midnight at different fatigue levels and analyzed the whole face with a shallow convolutional neural network, obtaining an accuracy score of 78%. Drowsiness was induced by increasing fatigue, not by sleep deprivation.

Our goal will be the detection of sleep deprivation using information of the whole face and non-simulated data with objective ground truth.

3   Proposed System

3.1   Face Classification

The goal of the system is to classify images within two classes: "rested" and "sleep deprived". Faces are extracted from the videos using OpenCV Haar Cascades [16], cropping the central 80% area to avoid border effects and normalizing.

Although we considered using FaceNet [17] (a state of the art face recognition model) for face classification, we ultimately chose MobileNets [18] as we intended to embed it on a smartphone-based system. MobileNets are a class of highly efficient non-linear models created specifically for mobile and embedded vision applications. They are based on 3×3 depthwise separable convolutions, which need 8 to 9 times less computation than standard convolutions with only a small loss in performance. Standard convolutions perform a filtering and then combine the outputs in one step in order to produce a new representation. Depthwise separable convolutions split the operation into two steps: depthwise convolutions apply a single filter per each input channel and their outputs are linearly combined by 1×1 pointwise convolutions. The entire architecture has 28 layers.

Two hyper-parameters may be tuned in order to construct smaller and less computationally expensive networks. The width multiplier ($\alpha \in (0, 1]$) thins the network uniformly at each layer, scaling the computational cost and the number of parameters by α^2. The resolution multiplier ($\rho \in (0, 1]$) changes the resolution of the input image scaling the computational cost by ρ^2. A 1.0 MobileNet-224 model ($\alpha = 1, \rho = 1$) was chosen, as it is the one that offers the best performance in ImageNet classification [18].

The output of MobileNet for a frame n is $P_{sd}(n)$, which represents an estimation of the probability of the frame to belong to "sleep deprived" class. If $P_{sd}(n) > 0.5$, the subject in the frame n is classified as "sleep deprived".

3.2 Video Classification

The proposed system is conceived to perform image classification. However, sleep deprivation is a behavior with a certain persistence over time. Thus, in a short video sequence, every frame should belong to the same class. This consistence allows for an improvement of the performance if the decision is made over the entire sequence by reducing the impact of outliers in the classification results.

In order to maximize the weight of the frames classified with higher confidence we applied a logistic function [19] with empirical parameters $L = 1, k = 20, x_0 = 0, 5$, and averaged the result over the entire sequence. Let n be a frame from a sequence of N frames, and $P_{sd}(n)$ the probability that the MobileNet step assigns to a facial image to be drowsy; the subject in the video sequence is classified as "sleep deprived" if $\overline{P_{SD}} > 0.5$ in Eq. 1.

$$\overline{P_{SD}} = \frac{1}{N} \sum_{n=0}^{N-1} \frac{1}{1 + e^{-20[P_{sd}(n)-0.5]}} \tag{1}$$

4   Experimental Settings

4.1   Datasets

The ULg Multi-modality Drowsiness Database (DROZY). Drozy [20] provides multi-modal data of 14 healthy people (3 males and 11 females aged

22.7 ± 2.3, without any alcohol dependency, drug addition or sleep disorder) who were asked to perform three 10-min psycho-motor vigilance tests (PVT) under conditions of increasing sleep deprivation induced by prolonged wake: first day at 10:00 AM (normal sleep patterns), second day at 3:30 AM (20 h of sleep deprivation) and second day at 11:00 AM (28 h of sleep deprivation). Subjects were instructed to monitor a red rectangular box over a black background on a computer screen, and to press a response button as soon as they noticed the appearance of a yellow stimulus counter within the box. Videos are recorded with an artificial near-infrared illumination using a Microsoft Kinect v2 sensor which provides frames of size 512×424 pixels at 30 frames per second for a duration of 10 min. Figure 1 shows examples of NIR frames.

Fig. 1. Examples of NIR frames from DROZY database.

Toucango Dataset. As part of the Toucango project [21], we conducted a naturalistic data acquisition campaign between March 2015 and February 2017 with the participation of professional drivers [22]. We equipped operational medium size vans and buses with portable devices carrying a near-infrared camera mounted in the dashboard. Videos were recorded at 30 frames per second and with a size of 640×480 pixels under artificial near-infrared illumination. Trips were filmed at day and night, with natural changing lightning conditions. As per the agreement between the companies involved, videos and images must remain confidential and thus samples cannot be shown here.

For the particular purpose of sleep deprivation detection, we selected video sequences from 5 drivers at two separate times: at daytime at the beginning of a work shift ("rested") and just before dawn at the end of a work shift ("sleep deprived"). Subjects are professional drivers in operation, so sleep deprivation conditions are not as extreme as in the DROZY dataset.

4.2   Implementation for Real-Time Classification on Android

Training and offline tests were performed on a laptop equipped with an Intel Core i7-6500U CPU (3.1 GHz), 8 GB RAM and a GPU Nvidia GeForce 920M.

In order to evaluate is feasibility for an usage in real time we implemented the system in Android. It was embedded in a smartphone Lenovo K6 Note, equipped with a Qualcomm Snapdragon 430 MSM8937 chipset (Octa-core 1.4 GHz Cortex-A53 CPU, Adreno 505 GPU, 3 GB RAM) running a standard version of Android 7.0. In order to replicate the conditions of the training dataset, we used a ELP-USB100W04H-RL35 1.0 Megapixel camera illuminated by 8 near-infrared LEDs, connected and powered via an On-The-Go USB cable.

We used the Android Face API to crop and normalize faces, and a Tensorflow Lite framework to compile the MobileNet model previously trained on a laptop. The prototype records the subject's face during 10 s and make the decision over all the frames processed in the time window. In our experimental set-up, we achieved a frame rate of around 5–10 frames per second. Improvements of this performance would be possible with optimized code and the usage of reduced MobileNet networks (with a consequent decrease in accuracy).

5   Experimental Results

DROZY was selected for training purposes as it provides objective ground truth on sleep deprivation. We trained the model using data from the first and second PVT only (respectively labeled as "rested" and "sleep deprived") of 11 subjects randomly selected (every subject but numbers 3, 8 and 14). We applied knowledge transfer [23] to a 1.0 MobileNet-224 pre-trained on Inception network. (by freezing all but the last layer, for a total of 2004 free parameters).

5.1   Intraindividual Model

First we evaluated the intraindividual performance by training a model on each subject. Data was split into training (80%), validation (10%) and test (10%) subsets. Accuracy scores are very high (more than 99% both for image and video classification) but the models are fit to one subject and are not translatable.

5.2   Interindividual Model

For evaluating interindividual performance, we randomly selected 1000 frames per subject and class for a total of 22,000 images, which were divided into two subsets: 85% for training and 15% for validation. The remaining frames, which were not included in the training were reserved for test purposes. On 236,981 frames, image classification got an accuracy score of 90.48%. Video classification improved this result, with an accuracy score of 93.48% over 966 sequences.

Evaluating Videos from the Third PVT. The samples of the class "sleep deprived" used for training were all from the second PVT, the subjects being awake for 20 h. Data from the third PVT (more than 28 h of sleep deprivation) was not seen by the model during the training phase, and should be classified as "sleep deprived". The model trained on the first two PVTs was tested on the videos from the third PVT (for the same 11 subjects). The videos were cropped in the same way as we did for the other two classes, obtaining 100,561 images and 485 video sequences. When applying classification, accuracy score was 77.82% on images and 91.13% on video sequences.

Extending to Subjects Not Previously Seen by the Model. The next test consisted in classifying images and videos from the three subjects who were not included in the training phase (subjects 3, 8 and 14) and who had not been seen by the model yet. Videos from the first PVT are labeled as "rested", and videos from the second and third PVTs are labeled as "sleep deprived". The resulting dataset had 124,289 images and 486 video sequences. Accuracy score reached 82.9% on images and improved to 86.21% on videos.

The final accuracy score over the entire DROZY dataset is 85.68% on 461,831 images and 91.07% on 1,937 videos. Confusion matrices in Fig. 2 show that the system is really good in avoiding false positives and gets to identify most of the sleep deprived sequences.

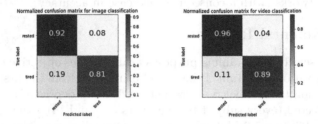

Fig. 2. Confusion matrices for image (left) and video classification (right) on DROZY

Applying the Model to Real World Data. Finally, we evaluated the application of the system to the classification of sequences from real drivers, recorded under naturalistic conditions with Toucango devices. We used the model previously trained on the DROZY dataset. applying the system to this data, the system got an accuracy score of 68.7% for image classification on 9473 frames, and an accuracy score of 72.73% for video classification on 44 sequences.

Confusion matrices in Fig. 3 show that the system performs well when classifying sequences of rested drivers but struggles with tired drivers. This is coherent with the limitations of this new dataset, described in Sect. 4.1; as the conditions of sleep deprivations are less severe, the system only classifies a portion of them as "sleep deprived".

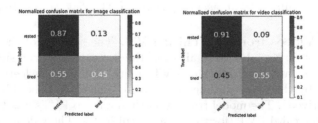

Fig. 3. Confusion matrices for image (left) and video classification (right) on Toucango

Facial features for sleep deprivation differ to those for fatigue. Therefore, in order to improve results on the Toucango dataset, we should look toward the retraining of the system using more videos from drowsy drivers specifically.

6 Discussion, Applications and Future Work

We propose a new way to evaluate fitness-to-drive by detecting sleep deprivation. The decision is made by classifying every frame from a video into two classes ("rested" and "sleep deprived") and averaging the results over the length of the sequence. Intraindividual accuracy is very good, and interindividual performance observed on several experiments over a controlled dataset are satisfactory. Early applications to real world data are also encouraging.

We imagine two separate applications for its usage in Advanced Driver Assistance Systems (ADAS) in order to evaluate subject's fitness to drive (FTD). First one is implementing a FTD test that needs to be passed by the driver as a condition to start the trip. The subject would have to record himself with the ADAS (or with a smartphone). The system would estimate then if he is well rested or if he is too tired to drive. Another possible application is real-time drowsiness detection. In this case, this estimation should be combined among other well-known parameters (eye closure, blinking frequency, yawning, etc.). The feasibility of the system have been demonstrated with our Android prototype. A system like this can be easily implemented in a low cost device and work in real-time, which makes possible its deployment in a commercial ADAS.

However, the system has relevant limitations. The database used for training is too small and sleep deprivation conditions are too extreme (more than 20 h). In addition, the dataset lacks of subject diversity regarding ethnicity, age, facial hair, physical characteristics or glasses usage.

Future work should try to assess these limitations by retraining the system on a much larger dataset including a wider variety of sleep deprivation conditions but also more subject diversity. It should also evaluate the usage of 3D Convolutional Neural Networks in order to include spatio-temporal features.

References

1. Taheri, S., et al.: Short sleep duration is associated with reduced leptin, elevated ghrelin, and increased body mass index. PLoS Med. **1**(3), e62 (2004). Ed. Philippe Froguel. PMC
2. Durmer, J.S., Dinges, D.F.: Neurocognitive consequences of sleep deprivation. Semin. Neurol. **25**(1), 117–129 (2005). Copyright 2005 by Thieme Medical Publishers Inc, 333 Seventh Avenue, New York, NY 10001, USA
3. Peters, R.D.: Effects of partial and total sleep deprivation on driving performance. US Department of Transportation, February 1999
4. Metzgar, C.: Moderate sleep deprivation produces impairments in cognitive and motor performance equivalent to legally prescribed levels of alcohol intoxication. Prof. Saf. **46**(1), 17 (2001)

5. Drowsy Driving NHTSA reports. https://www.nhtsa.gov/risky-driving/drowsy-driving. Accessed 02 June 2017
6. Masten, S.V., Stutts, J.C., Martell, C.A.: Predicting daytime and nighttime drowsy driving crashes based on crash characteristic models. In: 50th Annual Proceedings, Association for the Advancement of Automotive Medicine, Chicago, October 2006
7. Sundelin, T., et al.: Cues of fatigue: effects of sleep deprivation on facial appearance. Sleep **36**(9), 1355–1360 (2013)
8. Sahayadhas, A., Sundaraj, K., Murugappan, M.: Detecting driver drowsiness based on sensors: a review. Sensors **12**(12), 16937–16953 (2012)
9. Ekman, P.: Facial action coding system (FACS). A human face (2002)
10. Vural, E., Cetin, M., Ercil, A., Littlewort, G., Bartlett, M., Movellan, J.: Drowsy driver detection through facial movement analysis. In: Lew, M., Sebe, N., Huang, T.S., Bakker, E.M. (eds.) HCI 2007. LNCS, vol. 4796, pp. 6–18. Springer, Heidelberg (2007). https://doi.org/10.1007/978-3-540-75773-3_2
11. Weng, C.-H., Lai, Y.-H., Lai, S.-H.: Driver drowsiness detection via a hierarchical temporal deep belief network. In: Chen, C.-S., Lu, J., Ma, K.-K. (eds.) ACCV 2016. LNCS, vol. 10118, pp. 117–133. Springer, Cham (2017). https://doi.org/10.1007/978-3-319-54526-4_9
12. Shih, T.-H., Hsu, C.-T.: MSTN: multistage spatial-temporal network for driver drowsiness detection. In: Chen, C.-S., Lu, J., Ma, K.-K. (eds.) ACCV 2016. LNCS, vol. 10118, pp. 146–153. Springer, Cham (2017). https://doi.org/10.1007/978-3-319-54526-4_11
13. Huynh, X.-P., Park, S.-M., Kim, Y.-G.: Detection of driver drowsiness using 3D deep neural network and semi-supervised gradient boosting machine. In: Chen, C.-S., Lu, J., Ma, K.-K. (eds.) ACCV 2016. LNCS, vol. 10118, pp. 134–145. Springer, Cham (2017). https://doi.org/10.1007/978-3-319-54526-4_10
14. Lyu, J., Zejian Y., Dapeng C.: Long-term multi-granularity deep framework for driver drowsiness detection. arXiv:1801.02325 (2018)
15. Dwivedi, K., Biswaranjan, K., Sethi, A.: Drowsy driver detection using representation learning. In: 2014 IEEE International Advance Computing Conference (IACC) , 21–22 February 2014
16. Bradski, G., Adrian, K.: OpenCV. Dr. Dobb's journal of software tools 3 (2000)
17. Schroff, F., Dmitry, K., James, P.: Facenet: a unified embedding for face recognition and clustering. In: Proceedings of the IEEE Conference on Computer Vision and Pattern Recognition (2015)
18. Howard, A.G., Zhu, M., Chen, B., Kalenichenko, D., Wang, W., Weyand, T., Andreetto, M., Adam, H.: Efficient convolutional neural networks for mobile vision applications. CoRR, Mobilenets (2017)
19. Reed, L.J., Berkson, J.: The application of the logistic function to experimental data. J. Phys. Chem. **33**(5), 760–779 (1929)
20. Massoz, Q., Langohr, T., Francois, C., Verly, J.G.: The ULG Multimodality Drowsiness Database (called DROZY) and Examples of Use, WACV (2016)
21. http://www.innov-plus.com/en/toucango/
22. García-García, M., Caplier, A., Rombaut, M.: Driver head movements while using a smartphone in a naturalistic context. In: 6th International Symposium on Naturalistic Driving Research, The Hague, Netherlands, vol. 8, Jun 2017
23. Pan, S.J., Yang, Q.: A survey on transfer learning. IEEE Trans. Knowl. Data Eng. **22**(10), 1345–1359 (2010)

Transfer Learning Based Strategy for Improving Driver Distraction Recognition

Chaojie Ou$^{(\boxtimes)}$, Chahid Ouali, and Fakhri Karray

Center for Pattern Analysis and Machine Intelligence, Department of Electrical
and Computer Engineering, University of Waterloo, Waterloo, ON, Canada
{c9ou,couali,karray}@uwaterloo.ca

Abstract. This paper describes a deep learning-based approach for
driver distraction recognition. The proposed strategy consists of applying
transfer learning to overcome the scarcity of training images. More specifically, ResNet-50 model pre-trained on ImageNet is used as the basis
for a more specific training aimed at classifying three driving behaviors: normal driving, texting while driving, and talking on the phone
while driving. We propose different training strategies using two different datasets composed of images collected from the Internet and from
real world simulations. The experimental results show that the best performance is achieved when the model is fine-tuned using a combination
of images from both datasets. Specifically, the proposed system achieves
accuracies of 98% and 95% when tested separately on the simulation and
the Internet datasets, respectively. In addition, we evaluate the proposed
system under different light conditions and show its robustness to light
variations. In the worst case, the proposed system loses only 5.09% in
accuracy when compared to its performance without light variations.

Keywords: Driver distraction · Deep learning · Transfer learning

1 Introduction

While there have been significant advances in designing next generation
autonomous vehicles, human in the loop remains an important aspect of large
portion of semi-drivereless cars. As such, we can still anticipate a high percentage
of roadway accidents mainly caused by humans. A substantial portion of these
crashes are mainly caused by distracted or drowsy drivers. In fact, according to
a 2015 study by the National Highway Traffic Safety Administration (NHTSA),
there were 3,477 people killed and more than 391,000 injured in the United
States alone due to vehicle crashes caused by distracted drivers [1]. Distracted
driving includes activities such as talking on the phone, texting, and operating
the radio while driving, among a number of other activities. In this perspective,
driver distraction detection and recognition have gained great interests in both
academia and industry due to the severity of the problem.

© Springer International Publishing AG, part of Springer Nature 2018
A. Campilho et al. (Eds.): ICIAR 2018, LNCS 10882, pp. 443–452, 2018.
https://doi.org/10.1007/978-3-319-93000-8_50

The impact of driver distraction on road traffic accidents has been frequently studied, resulting in numerous strategies and recommendations to minimize the risk of road accidents [2]. These strategies include organizing education campaigns, introducing legislation to combat the use of electronic devices while driving and developing safety performance standards for technologies that limit driver distraction. However, these solutions did not seem to have a major impact, and the problem continues to be even more prevalent. In fact, the NHTSA stated that fatal distracted-driving crashes involving cell-phone have increased from 12% in 2011 to 14% in 2015 [1].

On the other hand, significant research efforts have been made to develop preventive technologies that detect distracted driving and alert the driver when distracted behavior is recognized [3]. A good review of previous approaches used to detect driving distraction can be found in [4]. The main approaches used in driver distraction detection rely on computer vision, and involve placing a camera in front of the driver to analyze physiological changes such as percentage of eye closure [5], eyelid activity [6], head movements [7,8], and the fusion of multiple visual cues [9–13]. However, these methods are more suitable for driver fatigue detection than distraction [1].

Traditional computer vision techniques have been widely used for driver distraction detection including Scale Invariant Feature Transform (SIFT) [14], Speeded-Up Robust Features (SURF) [15], and Histogram of Oriented Gradients (HOG) [16]. These visual features are employed with diverse machine learning classification algorithms such as Support Vector Machine (SVM) and Artificial Neural Networks (ANNs). Like on many other computer vision applications, deep Convolutional Neural Networks (CNNs) [17] have shown superior performance compared to traditional machine learning techniques in detecting driver distraction as demonstrated in [18]. However, one of the main issues in building good, deep CNN models is the limited amount of data available for training. To solve this problem, transfer learning [19,20] has been used as an effective solution.

The idea behind transfer learning is to use a model pre-trained on a large dataset and fine-tune it using a relatively small dataset to perform classification on a related domain [19]. In [18], three deep CNN models, namely AlexNet [17], VGG-16 [21] and ResNet-152 [22], pre-trained on ImageNet [23] are used as baselines for the driver distraction detection task. To fine-tune ResNet-152, the authors replaced the fully connected layer by 10 outputs (i.e. the number of classes) initialized with random weights, while maintaining the pre-trained weights for the rest of the layers. A similar strategy is used with AlexNet and VGG-16 by initializing the last two fully connected layers with random weights. These models are then trained using a dataset containing about twenty thousand dashboard camera images for multiple drivers. The results ranked ResNet-152 first compared to the other models with a detection performance of 85%. A similar strategy was used in [24] to fine-tune the InceptionV3 network [25], pre-trained on ImageNet, for distracted driver posture classification. Evaluation results of this method showed that the fine-tuned InceptionV3 model outperforms AlexNet model trained from the scratch (i.e. without transfer learning).

In this paper, we extend our work on driver distraction recognition introduced in [26]. The proposed strategy consists of adapting the well-known ResNet-50 model to the task of driver distraction recognition. To overcome the limited diversity of images collected from simulation experiments, we propose to combine images of driving from the Internet with images from simulations. We explore and compare several strategies of training using these two kinds of images. In addition, we enhance the robustness of the proposed system against luminosity changes by randomly adding luminosity adjustments to training images.

2 Proposed Approach

In this study, we propose to recognize distracted driving activities from images captured using a side view dash camera by employing an end-to-end deep learning system. We study two types of distraction activities: talking on the phone and texting.

The driver distraction recognition problem is treated as a multi-class classification problem to map input observations into one of three classes (two distracted driving classes and a normal driving class). The recognition system receives an image I_i at every time point i then, by a CNN, classifies it according to the distraction activity shown in it, and results in a probability distribution

$$Act_i = [Act_{i1}, \ Act_{i2}, \ \ldots, \ Act_{iK}], \tag{1}$$

where Act_{iK} represents the probability that at time point i the driver is performing a distraction activity K. Moreover, $\sum_{j=1}^{K} Act_{ij} = 1$ since Act_i is a probability distribution. In other words, the classifier models the conditional probability

$$Act_{ij} = P(Act_j | I_i) = \frac{P(I_i, Act_j)P(Act_j)}{p(I_i)}, \ j \in \{1, \ldots, K\}. \tag{2}$$

As illustrated in Fig. 1, our system is an adaptation structure of ResNet-50 network [22], which is a state-of-the-art CNN that achieved excellent performance on the ImageNet Large Scale Visual Recognition Challenge [23]. The architecture of ResNet-50 is a stack of several blocks composed of convolutional layers, pooling layers, and fully connected layers. In a convolutional layer, an input image (or feature maps) is convolved with a set of convolutional kernels $\mathbf{W} = \{w_1, w_2, \ldots, w_N\}$. After adding biases $\mathbf{B} = \{b_1, b_2, \ldots, b_N\}$, these results pass an element-wise non-linear transform $\sigma(\cdot)$. Each kernel w_n, with a b_n, produces a feature map f_n. Thus, for a convolutional layer l, the feature map is expressed as

$$f_n^l = \sigma(W_n^l * f^{l-1} + b_n^l). \tag{3}$$

For every pixel in a pooling operation, values of the neighboring feature map patch are aggregated using a permutation invariant function, typically the Max operation. Thus, for a pooling layer $l+1$, the value of resulting nth feature map at position $[i, j]$ is

$$f_n^{l+1}[i, j] = \max f_n^l[i - s : i + s, j - s : j + s], \tag{4}$$

where s is the stride of pooling operations. A pooling operation reduces dimensions of feature maps, induces a certain amount of translation invariance, and increases the receptive field of subsequent layers. For classification or regression tasks, it is common to insert fully connected layers at the end of the network, where the number of outputs in the last layer is equal to the number of classes or regression outputs. For a classification task, activations in the final layer are fed into a softmax function to generate probability distribution over classes. Thus,

$$Act_{ij} = \frac{e^{f_j}}{\sum_{j=1}^{K} e^{f_j}}, \tag{5}$$

where f_j is the jth output in the last layer given the input image I_i.

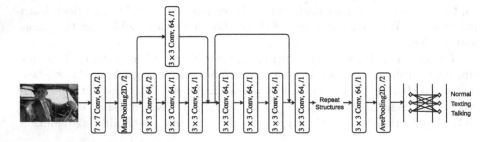

Fig. 1. A schematic representation of our system with ResNet-50.

The main difficulty for developing this deep learning classification system is on collecting a comprehensive dataset of drivers who are performing distraction activities. Constructing such dataset is time-consuming if not impossible since extracting images of distracted drivers from large naturalistic driving study datasets requires huge manual and human effort[1]. A possible solution for the limited training data is to generate images by simulation. However, in simulation experiments, images are usually extracted from video clips, in which there is a large similarity in terms of backgrounds, drivers' body positions, etc. The generalization ability of deep neural networks trained on these datasets would be limited. On the other hand, a huge number of images of various driving scenarios are publicly available on the Internet. Camera positions, image backgrounds, and luminosity conditions are diverse in these images, which makes them suitable to train a deep neural network with high generalization ability. In this work, we explore and compare four different strategies of using images from the Internet and from simulation experiments to train the classification system.

3   Experiment and Analysis

In this section, we describe the experimental results of the proposed driver distraction recognition system. First, we present the two datasets used to train and

---

[1] Distracted driver detection dataset from Kaggle competition is not available for academic use.

test the system. Then, we evaluate the classification performance of the proposed system on these two datasets by training the CNN model with several strategies. Finally, we evaluate the classification capability of the system under different simulated light conditions.

3.1 Datasets Collection

Activities in Car Dataset: the dataset Activities in Car, represented as S_v, is collected from the Internet. Figure 2 shows few examples of images from this dataset. We have defined several selection criteria when constructing this dataset. First, a phone should be visible in images of distracted driving. Second, the images are taken from both inside and outside the vehicle with short camera distances. The resulting dataset contains images with different backgrounds, different camera distances, and different camera angles. The numbers of images belonging to the three different classes are shown in the second column of Table 1.

Simulation Dataset: Images of the Simulation dataset, represented by S_d, are obtained using a driving simulator. The difference between these images and those in S_v is that all the images in S_d have a fixed camera position.

The camera is located such that the steering wheel of the car and the driver's upper-body as well as his hands are captured. A set of 640 × 480 RGB videos with a frame rate of 5 frames per second are obtained. In this experiment, the simulations are performed under the same lighting conditions. These situations are illustrated in Fig. 3. The experiment was carried out using participants of different ages, genders, and ethnicities. 23 drivers were involved in the experiments. Each driver was instructed to perform the following driving activities: normal/safe driving, text messaging using the right hand, phone calling using the right hand. The numbers of images for each class is shown in the third column of Table 1.

Fig. 2. Sample pictures from the Activities in Car Dataset.

Fig. 3. Sample pictures from the Simulation Dataset.

Table 1. Number of samples in Car Datasets.

Class	Number of samples	
	Activities in Car	Simulation
Normal driving	666	4600
Talking	326	9200
Texting	222	9000

3.2   Experimental Settings

Before we train the CNN, we perform a preprocessing step similar to [22]. First, we reshape each image to 224 × 224 pixels so that it can be fed into the neural network (ResNet-50 takes as input 224 × 224 RGB image). Then, we subtract the means of the RGB values from these images, as proposed in the original ResNet-50 model. Fully connected layers in the original ResNet-50 model were replaced with two fully connected layers and a softmax layer. These two new fully connected layers have 256 and 128 neurons respectively, rectified linear unit activation functions, and randomly-initialized parameters. Moreover, to improve the generalization ability of our neural networks, the dropout method introduced in [27] is used. The deep neural network is trained on a desktop PC with an Intel Core i5 Quad Core 3.5 Ghz, 16 GB of RAM, and a GTX1070 8 GB GPU card. To make the proposed system robust under different lighting conditions, we change the pixel intensities by adding all three image channels with a random value from this set: $[-100, -80, \cdots, 80, 100]$. These numbers are chosen to represent a large range, the system should also work other values in this range.

3.3   Results and Analysis

We analyze the recognition performance by exploring 4 different training strategies. For each strategy, we randomly choose 5 drivers and used their images (971 images from S_v) for training then test the system on images of the remaining 18 drivers. We repeat this procedure for 10 different training driver combinations, and the results shown in the following sections are averaged over testing results of these 10 combinations. Figure 4 shows the changing process of accuracies for these strategies while training with different numbers of epochs. We also give in Table 2 the best performances corresponding to the optimal numbers of epochs.

The first strategy consists of training the neural network using only S_v. It can be seen from the 4th row of Table 2 that this strategy gives the lowest accuracy (78.69%) compared to the other strategies when tested on S_d. The accuracy on S_v is much better and reaches 89.58%, which is an expected result since the model is trained and tested on the same dataset. This is similar to the results obtained with the second strategy where the neural network is trained on only S_d. The accuracy results of this latter strategy (5th row of Table 2) show that although the system achieves a high testing accuracy on S_d, it only gives a low

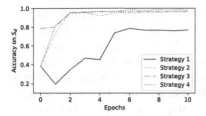

Fig. 4. Accuracy results on S_d for the 4 training strategies for 10 epochs.

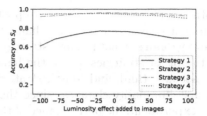

Fig. 5. Accuracy results on S_d for the 4 strategies under different simulated luminosity conditions (2 epochs).

testing accuracy of 44.19% on S_v. This difference shows that the classification task of S_v is more difficult than the one of S_d since the images are more diverse as to their background, camera positions, and luminosity conditions. This also justifies the usage of S_v as an additional training dataset.

The third strategy consists of training the neural network on S_v then fine-tuning it on S_d. The testing results in the 6th row of Table 2 show that this strategy performs much better than the first two strategies. In fact, fine-tuning the model trained on S_v improves the performances by 17% and 6% when tested on S_d and S_v, respectively.

In the fourth strategy, the system is trained using a mixture of S_v and S_d. This strategy provides the best performance on S_d as shown in the last row of Table 2. In fact, training the system on a mixture of the two datasets provides the system with a better discriminative ability on S_d, without losing this ability on the other, more difficult dataset.

Table 2. Testing performance of 4 different training strategies.

Training		Testing			
		S_d		S_v	
		Accuracy(%)	Cross-entropy	Accuracy(%)	Cross-entropy
S_v		78.69 ± 1.30	0.51 ± 0.03	89.58 ± 0	0.44 ± 0
	S_d	96.16 ± 2.49	0.11 ± 0.06	44.19 ± 6.95	1.45 ± 0.25
S_v	S_d	96.58 ± 0.80	0.11 ± 0.02	95.60 ± 1.28	0.18 ± 0.04
S_v & S_d		98.30 ± 1.17	0.06 ± 0.03	95.50 ± 3.08	0.20 ± 0.15

A major difficulty in computer vision-based methods for driver distraction is training a CNN model that can maintain good performance under different lighting conditions [28–30]. Our solution to this problem consists of simulating various lighting conditions by adding different luminosity values to all channels of the training images (more details can be found in Sect. 3.2). Figure 5 shows testing results on S_d after two epochs of training. The x-axis represents the luminosity values added to all channels of images in S_d during testing. From this figure we can see that the first strategy still achieves lower performance compared to the other strategies for all the luminosity levels. The classification results of the second, third, and fourth strategies are similar and show good robustness against luminosity changes (since the system is trained on only two epochs in this experiment, the performance of the second strategy is slightly better in some luminosity conditions). In addition, the performance of the fourth strategy goes from 95.41% with no luminosity adjustment to 90.32% with the most severe luminosity change of +100, which is a drop of 5.09% in performance. For the second strategy, the worst case (i.e. +100) results in an accuracy of 94.47% with a slight loss of performance of 1.65%.

4   Conclusion

In this paper, we proposed a driver distraction recognition system based on transfer learning. The proposed approach is to adapt and fine-tune a pre-trained ResNet-50 model with a relatively small dataset of images obtained using a driving simulator. Besides, we exploit images of driving collected from the Internet to overcome the lack of diversity of the images collected from the simulation experiments. We investigated several training strategies using these two different datasets, and we showed that the distraction classification system gains the best generalization ability by combining the images of the two datasets. The proposed system achieved an accuracy of 98% when tested on the simulation dataset. On images collected from the Internet, the system gave an accuracy of 95%. In addition, we demonstrated the robustness of the system by testing it in different lighting conditions. The experimental results showed that the proposed system is able to maintain a good classification accuracy even with a relatively large change in luminosity.

References

1. National Center for Statistics and Analysis: Distracted driving 2015. Technical report, The National Highway Traffic Safety Administration (2017)
2. Young, K., Regan, M., Hammer, M.: Driver distraction: a review of the literature. In: Distracted Driving, pp. 379–405 (2007)
3. Koesdwiady, A., Soua, R., Karray, F., Kamel, M.S.: Recent trends in driver safety monitoring systems: State of the art and challenges. IEEE Trans. Veh. Technol. (2016)
4. Fernández, A., Usamentiaga, R., Carús, J.L., Casado, R.: Driver distraction using visual-based sensors and algorithms. Sensors 16(11), 1805 (2016)
5. Dinges, D.F., Grace, R.: Perclos: a valid psychophysiological measure of alertness as assessed by psychomotor vigilance. US Department of Transportation, Federal Highway Administration, Publication Number FHWA-MCRT-98-006 (1998)
6. Ioannis, G., Damousis, I.G., Tzovaras, D.: Fuzzy fusion of eyelid activity indicators for hypovigilance-related accident prediction. IEEE Trans. Intell. Transp. Syst. 9(3), 491–500 (2008)

7. Smith, P., Shah, M., de Vitoria Lobo, N.: Determining driver visual attention with one camera. IEEE Trans. Intell. Transp. Syst. **4**(4), 205–218 (2003)
8. Bergasa, L.M., Buenaposada, J.M., Nuevo, J., Jimenez, P., Baumela, L.: Analysing driver's attention level using computer vision. In: International IEEE Conference on Intelligent Transportation Systems, pp. 1149–1154 (2008)
9. Senaratne, R., Hardy, D., Vanderaa, B., Halgamuge, S.: Driver fatigue detection by fusing multiple cues. In: Advances in Neural Networks, pp. 801–809 (2007)
10. Craye, C., Rashwan, A., Kamel, M.S., Karray, F.: A multi-modal driver fatigue and distraction assessment system. Int. J. Intell. Transp. Syst. Res. **14**(3), 173–194 (2016)
11. Ji, Q., Zhu, Z., Lan, P.: Real-time nonintrusive monitoring and prediction of driver fatigue. IEEE Trans. Veh. Technol. **53**(4), 1052–1068 (2004)
12. Bergasa, L.M., Nuevo, J., Sotelo, M.A., Barea, R., Lopez, M.E.: Real-time system for monitoring driver vigilance. IEEE Trans. Intell. Transp. Syst. **7**(1), 63–77 (2006)
13. Li, L., Werber, K., Calvillo, C.F., Dinh, K.D., Guarde, A., König, A.: Multi-sensor soft-computing system for driver drowsiness detection. In: Snášel, V., Krömer, P., Köppen, M., Schaefer, G. (eds.) Soft Computing in Industrial Applications. AISC, vol. 223, pp. 129–140. Springer, Cham (2014). https://doi.org/10.1007/978-3-319-00930-8_12
14. Lowe, D.G.: Distinctive image features from scale-invariant keypoints. Int. J. Comput. Vis. **60**(2), 91–110 (2004)
15. Bay, H., Ess, A., Tuytelaars, T., Van Gool, L.: Speeded-up robust features (SURF). Comput. Vis. Image Underst. **110**(3), 346–359 (2008)
16. Dalal, N., Triggs, B.: Histograms of oriented gradients for human detection. In: IEEE Conference on Computer Vision and Pattern Recognition, vol. 1, pp. 886–893 (2005)
17. Krizhevsky, A., Sutskever, I., Hinton, G.E.: Imagenet classification with deep convolutional neural networks. In: Advances in Neural Information Processing Systems, pp. 1097–1105 (2012)
18. Hssayeni, M.D., Saxena, S., Ptucha, R., Savakis, A.: Distracted driver detection: deep learning vs handcrafted features. Electr. Imaging **2017**(10), 20–26 (2017)
19. Pan, S.J., Yang, Q.: A survey on transfer learning. IEEE Trans. Knowl. Data Eng. **22**(10), 1345–1359 (2010)
20. Shin, H.-C., Roth, H.R., Gao, M., Lu, L., Xu, Z., Nogues, I., Yao, J., Mollura, D., Summers, R.M.: Deep convolutional neural networks for computer-aided detection: Cnn architectures, dataset characteristics and transfer learning. IEEE Trans. Med. Imaging **35**(5), 1285–1298 (2016)
21. Simonyan, K., Zisserman, A.: Very deep convolutional networks for large-scale image recognition. arXiv preprint arXiv:1409.1556 (2014)
22. He, K., Zhang, X., Ren, S., Sun, J.: Deep residual learning for image recognition. In: IEEE Conference on Computer Vision and Pattern Recognition, pp. 770–778 (2016)
23. Russakovsky, O., Deng, J., Hao, S., Krause, J., Satheesh, S., Ma, S., Huang, Z., Karpathy, A., Khosla, A., Bernstein, M., et al.: Imagenet large scale visual recognition challenge. Int. J. Comput. Vis. **115**(3), 211–252 (2015)
24. Abouelnaga, Y., Eraqi, H.M., Moustafa, M.N.: Real-time distracted driver posture classification. arXiv preprint arXiv:1706.09498 (2017)
25. Szegedy, C., Vanhoucke, V., Ioffe, S., Shlens, J., Wojna, Z: Rethinking the inception architecture for computer vision. In: IEEE Conference on Computer Vision and Pattern Recognition, pp. 2818–2826 (2016)

26. Koesdwiady, A., Bedawi, S.M., Ou, C., Karray, F.: End-to-end deep learning for driver distraction recognition. In: International Conference on Image Analysis and Recognition, pp. 11–18. Springer (2017)
27. Hinton, G.E., Srivastava, N., Krizhevsky, A., Sutskever, I., Salakhutdinov, R.R.: Improving neural networks by preventing co-adaptation of feature detectors. arXiv preprint arXiv:1207.0580 (2012)
28. Li, N., Jain, J.J., Busso, C.: Modeling of driver behavior in real world scenarios using multiple noninvasive sensors. IEEE Trans. Multimed. **15**(5), 1213–1225 (2013)
29. Li, N., Busso, C.: Predicting perceived visual and cognitive distractions of drivers with multimodal features. IEEE Trans. Intell. Transp. Syst. **16**(1), 51–65 (2015)
30. Ragab, A., Craye, C., Kamel, M.S., Karray, F.: A visual-based driver distraction recognition and detection using random forest. In: Campilho, A., Kamel, M. (eds.) ICIAR 2014. LNCS, vol. 8814, pp. 256–265. Springer, Cham (2014). https://doi. org/10.1007/978-3-319-11758-4_28

Vehicle Detection in Infrared Imagery Using Neural Networks with Synthetic Training Data

Chris P. Moate, Stephen D. Hayward$^{(\boxtimes)}$, Jonathan S. Ellis,
Lee Russell, Ralph O. Timmerman, Richard O. Lane,
and Thomas J. Strain

QinetiQ Ltd, Malvern Technology Centre, St Andrews Road, Malvern, UK
{cpmoate, sdhayward}@qinetiq.com

Abstract. We present a new approach to the detection, localization, and recognition of vehicles in infrared imagery using a deep Convolutional Neural Network that completely avoids the need for manually-labelled training data by using synthetic imagery and a transfer learning strategy. Synthetic imagery is generated from CAD models using a rendering tool, allowing the network to be trained against a complete set of vehicle aspects and with automatically generated meta-data encoding the position of the vehicle in the image. The proposed approach is fast since a single network is used to compute class probabilities for individual pixels in the image. Results are presented illustrating the robust recognition and localization performance achievable with the novel approach for vehicle detection in real high-resolution infrared imagery.

Keywords: Vehicle detection · Neural networks · Infrared imagery

1 Introduction

Real-time automatic detection, localization and recognition of vehicles and other objects in imagery is of significant continuing interest in many defence, security and commercial applications. Requirements for persistent situational awareness will be met in the future by intelligent computer vision systems which will reduce the burden on human operators, improving accuracy and response times and increasing safety. The performance of commercially available infrared (IR) cameras continues to increase as costs decrease, making IR the wave-band of choice where day/night operation is required.

The principle contributions of this paper are: (1) deep learning networks developed for visible-band colour imagery can be adapted for object detection in IR imagery through transfer learning; (2) synthetically rendered IR images of target objects can be used to train deep learning networks to successfully detect these objects in real IR imagery without the need for training on real images; (3) object location meta-data can be automatically generated for synthetically rendered images completely avoiding the need for manual annotation.

We review a selection of related work in Sect. 2. In Sect. 3 we describe our proposed approach to vehicle detection, with examples and results presented in Sect. 4.

© Springer International Publishing AG, part of Springer Nature 2018
A. Campilho et al. (Eds.): ICIAR 2018, LNCS 10882, pp. 453–461, 2018.
https://doi.org/10.1007/978-3-319-93000-8_51

2 Related Work

Previous work on vehicle identification was reported in [1] where template matching was employed using fast correlator hardware, and a template library was generated from computer-aided design (CAD) vehicle models. More recently neural networks have been proposed [2–4] as solutions to the problem of vehicle recognition in visible band imagery, but typically these approaches are restricted to classifying vehicles imaged from specific viewpoints, and are limited by the difficulty in obtaining large training datasets of labelled images.

Object classification in IR imagery using deep neural networks had little attention in the literature previously, with one exception being the work described in [5], where the performance of two state-of-the-art Convolutional Neural Network (CNN) approaches to object detection and localization is compared. In [6] an approach combining Histogram of Oriented Gradients (HOG) features and a Bag of Words model is described for Automatic Target Recognition (ATR) in IR imagery.

The use of synthetic imagery for training CNNs is described in [7] for the detection of food objects through object segmentation, where the use of layers from a pre-trained Inception network is described. Unlike the current work, object classification is not considered, but because the approach in [7] is fully convolutional it has the advantage that it can be applied to an image of any size. The connection between the use of synthetic training data and Model-Based Reasoning is formalised in [8].

Other work on automatic segmentation is reported in [9], where a discriminative convolutional network is trained jointly with two objectives for a given image patch, producing a class-agnostic segmentation mask and the likelihood of the patch being centred on a full object. Transfer learning to different wavelengths, simulated training data or classification is not considered.

3 The Proposed Approach

3.1 The Model

Our approach to the vehicle detection, localization and recognition problem is to take a pre-trained deep CNN and replace the final fully-connected layers with two new layers which are trained using our own IR image dataset to segment an image into regions containing targets. The advantage of CNNs is that they have shown good performance in image analysis problems and enable an easy-to-implement transfer learning approach. By using the Inception V3 network [10] as implemented within Keras [11], with weights that have been learnt on the ImageNet challenge problem [12], we avoid the time-consuming process of training the lower convolutional layers.

The Inception convolutional layers are pre-trained to transform an image to a set of features. The new fully-connected layers in our network consist of a hidden layer with 1024 neurons, and a second layer which learns to predict the position, shape and class of a vehicle in the image, by estimating a set of segmentation masks, with pixels set to 1 if the vehicle is present, and 0 if it is not. The final layer is reshaped to:

$$\left(n_b, n_x, n_y, n_c\right) \tag{1}$$

where n_b is the number of images in a batch, n_x and n_y are the size of the mask and n_c is the number of classes.

Our work so far has considered two different vehicle types: van and land rover. The vehicles were chosen for ease of access to CAD models and real measurements. Because the network needs to learn how to reject non-target objects we set $n_c= 3$ and include a third class which is "background". Inclusion of a third mask for the background allows us to apply a softmax activation across the classes for each pixel which we find to improve overall performance. The network is trained to output numbers between 0 and 1, and target detections are formed as an additional output by applying a fixed threshold to the output of the softmax activation function. Training was performed using mini-batch gradient descent with RMSprop adaptive learning rate control using a rho (squared gradient decay) parameter value of 0.9 and an initial learning rate of 10^{-5}, a batch size of 16, and 30 epochs. No other regularisation was used.

We find that detection and localization performance can be greatly improved by adding random Gaussian noise to the features generated by the Inception network. Four different cases are considered with noise added during either training or testing, during both, or not at all. Adding noise at training time should improve the robustness of the model and help prevent overfitting as it is similar to the dropout technique [13]. In contrast test time noise is observed to change the detections reported by the model, and is applied to each image many times, Monte Carlo fashion, with the resulting pixel detections combined before being reported.

To control false alarm rates we use a novel constraint procedure involving the use of two models, trained simultaneously in the same manner, ready for use with or without additive test-time noise. Detections from the noisy classifier are declared only where they are adjacent to or overlap detections from the noise-free classifier.

We note that test-time noise may simply have the effect of perturbing the network outputs, allowing a lower output (without noise) to sometimes exceed the detection threshold. In this case, test-time noise may just be equivalent to lowering the detection threshold. We therefore also try lowering the detection threshold of the model. We do this while still using the above constraint procedure based on two models. In this case, the first model uses a high threshold and the second model uses a lower threshold to detect further adjacent pixels.

3.2 Image Data

IR imagery has been collected for algorithm testing and characterisation of background scenes, without targets, using a Zenmuse XT system with a FLIR IR camera and a DJI gimbal. The camera had a field-of-view of 47 deg × 36 deg and a focal length of 13 mm. The total number of images of each class used in the test set is 285 (van), 394 (land rover) and 185 (background). Example imagery of the three classes is shown in Fig. 1.

Van	Land rover	Background

Fig. 1. Example real data used for testing the model.

The weather was sunny with scattered cloud and air temperatures of around 20 °C during the data collection.

Synthetic images of the two vehicles were generated from 3D models using CameoSim, a renderer capable of generating physically accurate images at wavelengths between 0.36 and 14 microns [14]. The vehicle CAD models were modified slightly to better match the target vehicles by making broad changes to the proportions of the models and removing superfluous details, without changing the underlying mesh topology.

In CameoSim, the thermal and optical properties of objects are controlled by defining the properties of the materials. In this work we mostly used the standard materials defined in CameoSim, although some of these were modified to create customised materials. Another source of variability in IR imagery is the environment. In CameoSim the location, time of day, and atmospheric properties can all be adjusted. Most of the synthetic images used in this paper were generated for a day-time scene under a clear, sunny sky.

Images were generated for wavelengths in the range 8 to 12 microns (covering the spectral range of the real long-wave IR camera). Each image was rendered at a resolution of 720 × 480 pixels, and the field of view was adjusted to match the actual camera as closely as possible.

3.3 Training and Test Databases

To train the model we need to present simulated images of the vehicles in such a way that the model does not learn false features separating them from the background. For example if the simulated images are shown against an empty background the presence of either vehicle could be inferred trivially from the background pixels. To avoid this problem we combine simulated vehicle image chips with real IR backgrounds, but with no attempt to realistically scale or position the vehicle. Therefore, the superimposed vehicle is just as likely to appear in the sky of the background image as it is on the ground. Methods for inserting synthetic image chips into real backgrounds accounting for context are a topic for future work.

The synthetic image chips are not expected to be a perfect match for the real vehicle images, so data augmentation in the form of random spatial transformations (e.g. rotation, shear, stretch and zoom) as well as brightness and contrast modulation is applied before the image chips are inserted into the background images.

For each input image used to train our model a set of segmentation masks is required. These are easily produced by the simulation software. A total of 10000 images were used for training, split equally across the three classes. For the test database comprising real imagery, the masks are needed as ground-truth to enable computation of the Intersection over Union (IoU) metric, the ratio between the areas of intersection and union of estimated and ground-truth segmentation masks. In this case there was no alternative but to generate masks by hand for each of the test images. Example masks are shown in Fig. 2.

Fig. 2. Example manual segmentation of the test data.

In summary, our approach to training and testing of the model is to use only simulated images of the vehicles for training and only real images of the vehicles for testing. For the background images, we use real IR images in both cases but the training and test sets have no images in common and were captured as separate data collections.

4   Results

4.1   Metrics

We have used a variety of metrics to quantify the detection, segmentation and clas sification performance of our algorithms.

For each vehicle class a detection is declared if there is at least one pixel in the corresponding segmentation ground-truth (as defined by the mask) with model output above the detection threshold. We do not insist that the pixels are correctly classified at this stage, so if the model detects either the van or land rover, a detection will be recorded irrespective of whether it is actually the correct vehicle. The Probability of Detection (PD) for each class is then just the ratio of the number of detected images to the total number of images of that class.

For background images a false alarm is declared if any pixels in the output vehicle segmentation masks pass the detection threshold. For images containing a van or land rover a false alarm is declared if there are any detections more than 3 pixels beyond the boundary of the ground-truth segmentation. Dilating the ground-truth segmentation masks prevents segmentation errors contributing to the Probability of False Alarm (PFA).

Since detection metrics are counted at the image rather than pixel level, we do not distinguish between an image with many false alarm pixels and an image with only one – both contribute the same to the PFA and the same is true for PD.

To measure segmentation accuracy we compute IoU between the ground-truth segmentation and the model output for the correct class. To measure classification performance we have computed confusion matrices between the van and land rover classes. These confusion matrices are normalised so that rows (corresponding to inputs) sum to 100%. Only images in which the vehicles are detected contribute to the confusion matrices.

4.2 Results for Single Models

Results are shown in Table 1 for models trained and tested using different levels of additive random noise. Key conclusions from these results are that the van is generally significantly under-segmented without including test-time noise, giving a low IoU value. Including test-time noise improves this at the expense of increased PFA, particularly in images of the land rover and background images. Classification performance is good.

Table 1. Results for single models with and without noise. Detection threshold is 0.5. Results order for PD, IoU, Confusion matrix: van, land rover; for PFA: van, land rover, background.

Metric\Model	1. No noise	2. Train noise	3. Test noise	4. Train & test noise
PD	0.92, 1.00	0.99, 1.00	1.00, 1.00	1.00, 1.00
PFA	0.00, 0.06, 0.03	0.00, 0.12, 0.04	0.07, 0.80, 0.77	0.02, 0.79, 0.6
IoU	0.19, 0.65	0.29, 0.71	0.65, 0.63	0.57, 0.61
Confusion matrix	$\begin{pmatrix} 91.2 & 8.8 \\ 0.0 & 100.0 \end{pmatrix}$	$\begin{pmatrix} 84.3 & 15.7 \\ 0.0 & 100.0 \end{pmatrix}$	$\begin{pmatrix} 92.3 & 7.7 \\ 0.0 & 100.0 \end{pmatrix}$	$\begin{pmatrix} 84.6 & 15.4 \\ 0.0 & 100.0 \end{pmatrix}$

We next investigate the impact of lowering the detection threshold from 0.5 to 0.1. Results are shown in Table 2.

Table 2. Results for single models with and without noise. Detection threshold is 0.1.

Metric\Model	1. No noise	2. Train noise	3. Test noise	4. Train & test noise
PD	0.99, 1.00	1.00, 1.00	1.00, 1.00	1.00, 1.00
PFA	0.00, 0.43, 0.10	0.01, 0.99, 0.43	0.58, 1.00, 1.00	0.39, 1.00, 0.97
IoU	0.46, 0.71	0.57, 0.60	0.67, 0.41	0.62, 0.33
Confusion matrix	$\begin{pmatrix} 89.8 & 10.2 \\ 0.0 & 100.0 \end{pmatrix}$	$\begin{pmatrix} 85.3 & 14.7 \\ 0.0 & 100.0 \end{pmatrix}$	$\begin{pmatrix} 92.3 & 7.7 \\ 0.0 & 100.0 \end{pmatrix}$	$\begin{pmatrix} 83.5 & 16.5 \\ 0.0 & 100.0 \end{pmatrix}$

Lowering the detection threshold improves PD and IoU for the van, at the expense of PFA. Classification performance is largely unchanged.

4.3   Results for Two Simultaneous Models

The aim of combining two models is to reduce PFA while maintaining good segmentation performance. Table 3 gives results for combining the outputs of models 3 or 4, which have test-time noise, with the output of model 1, which has no noise, used as a constraint.

Table 3. Results for two models, combining with and without noise. Detection threshold is 0.5.

Metric\Model	3. Test noise	4. Train & test noise
PD	0.93, 1.00	0.99, 1.00
PFA	0.00, 0.11, 0.03	0.00, 0.14, 0.04
IoU	0.62, 0.66	0.57, 0.63
Confusion matrix	$\begin{pmatrix} 91.7 & 8.3 \\ 0.0 & 100.0 \end{pmatrix}$	$\begin{pmatrix} 85.8 & 14.2 \\ 0.0 & 100.0 \end{pmatrix}$

Compared to Table 2 these results show the higher values for IoU of ~ 0.6, and the lower values for PFA of ~ 0.1, achieving our aim of good segmentation with a low PFA. Further results were generated using two models with different detection thresholds, but these did not improve on the results shown in Table 3.

In our view the best overall result is achieved with the test-time noise model combined with the noise-free model, both using a detection threshold of 0.5. Example image segmentation results from this approach are shown in Fig. 3. We note that the vehicles are detected reliably and classified robustly. However, the outlines are not pixel-wise accurate which may result from the use of simulated training data and transfer learning from a base model learnt on optical rather than IR imagery.

In the last row, we show a weak result for each class. In column 1 the van is shown misclassified as the land rover which typically happens from rear aspects. In column 2 a second vehicle is misclassified as a land rover. In the background image in column 3 an off-road type vehicle is wrongly declared to be a land rover. This latter result can also be seen in an encouraging light, as the vehicle is similar to the land rover and is likely not in the background training images the model was trained to reject.

Fig. 3. Results for the best performing model. Columns show van, land rover and background images. Typical results in the first 2 rows with pixels declared to be the van coloured red, and those declared to be the land rover coloured green. The last row shows some problem cases. (Color figure online)

5 Conclusions

To the authors' knowledge our results show for the first time that complicated objects, such as vehicles, can be detected and localised in imagery using CNNs which are trained without the need for any measured target imagery at all. This is important because the provision of large quantities of manually labelled and annotated training data can be both time-consuming and expensive. In addition we have shown that deep learning networks developed for visible-band colour imagery can be adapted for object detection in IR imagery through transfer learning.

Further work is planned to extend the number of object classes recognised by the system, to include frame-to-frame tracking of the objects detected, and to test algorithms in a wider variety of environmental conditions. It is expected that fine-tuning the whole network by enabling training for all layers will improve performance.

Acknowledgements. The authors are grateful to Dr. Jeremy Ward, CTO QinetiQ, for sponsoring this work under QinetiQ's Internal Research and Development programme.

References

1. McDonald, G.J., Ellis, J.S., Penney, R.W., Price, R.W.: Real-time vehicle identification performance using FPGA correlator hardware. IEEE Trans. Intell. Transp. Syst. **13**(4), 1891–1895 (2012)
2. Xie, S., Yang, T., Wang, X., Lin, Y.: Hyper-class augmented and regularized deep learning for fine-grained image classification. In: IEEE Conference on Computer Vision and Pattern Recognition, pp. 2645–2654 (2015)
3. Tang, T., Zhou, S., Deng, Z., Zou, H., Lei, L.: Vehicle detection in aerial images based on region convolutional neural networks and hard negative example mining. Sensors **17**(2), 336 (2017)
4. Gao, Y., Lee, H.J.: Vehicle make recognition based on convolutional neural network. In: 2nd International Conference on Information Science and Security (ICISS), pp. 1–4 (2015)
5. Abbott, R., Del Rincon, J.M., Connor, B., Robertson, N.: Deep object classification in low resolution LWIR imagery via transfer learning. Mathematics in Defence (2017)
6. Khan, M.N.A., Fan, G., Heisterkamp, D.R., Yu, L.: Automatic target recognition in infrared imagery using dense HOG features and relevance grouping of vocabulary. In: IEEE Conference on Computer Vision and Pattern Recognition Workshop, pp. 293–298 (2014)
7. Pinheiro, P., Collobert, R., Dollar, P.: Learning to Segment Object Candidates, arXiv:1506. 06204v2 [cs.CV] (2015)
8. Le, T.A., Baydin, A.G., Zinkov, R., Wood, F.: Using Synthetic Data to Train Neural Networks is Model-Based Reasoning. arXiv preprint arXiv:1703.00868 (2017)
9. Rajpura, P.S., Bojinov, H., Hegde, R.S.: Object Detection Using Deep CNNs Trained on Synthetic Images, arXiv:1706.06782v2 [cs.CV] (2017)
10. Szegedy, C., Vanhoucke, V., Ioffe, S., Shlens, J.: Rethinking the Inception Architecture for Computer Vision. arXiv:1512.00567v3 [cs.CV] (2015)
11. Chollet, F.: Keras, GitHub repository (2016). https://github.com/fchollet/keras
12. Russakovsky, O., Deng, J., Su, H., Krause, J., Satheesh, S., Ma, S., Huang, Z., Karpathy, A., Khosla, A., et al.: ImageNet large scale visual recognition challenge (2014)
13. Srivastava, N., Hinton, G., Krizhevsky, A., Sutskever, I., Salakhutdinov, R.: Dropout: a simple way to prevent neural networks from overfitting. J. Mach. Learn. Res. **15**, 1929–1958 (2014)
14. Brady, A., Kharabash, S.: Further Studies into Synthetic Image Generation using CameoSim (No. DSTO-TR-2589). Defence Science and Technology Organisation, Edinburgh, Australia (2011)

Applications

A Preliminary Study of Image Analysis for Parasite Detection on Honey Bees

Stefan Schurischuster[1], Beatriz Remeseiro[2(✉)], Petia Radeva[3], and Martin Kampel[1]

[1] Computer Vision Lab, Vienna University of Technology, Vienna, Austria
schurischuster@caa.tuwien.ac.at, martin.kampel@tuwien.ac.at
[2] Department of Computer Science, Universidad de Oviedo, Gijón, Spain
bremeseiro@uniovi.es
[3] Departament de Matemàtiques i Informàtica,
Universitat de Barcelona, Barcelona, Spain
petia.ivanova@ub.edu

Abstract. Varroa destructor is a parasite harming bee colonies. As the worldwide bee population is in danger, beekeepers as well as researchers are looking for methods to monitor the health of bee hives. In this context, we present a preliminary study to detect parasites on bee videos by means of image analysis and machine learning techniques. For this purpose, each video frame is analyzed individually to extract bee image patches, which are then processed to compute image descriptors and finally classified into mite and no mite bees. The experimental results demonstrated the adequacy of the proposed method, which will be a perfect stepping stone for a further bee monitoring system.

Keywords: Honey bees · Varroa destructor · Bee localization
Mite characterization · Parasite detection

1 Introduction

For almost a decade now, it is a well-known fact that honey bee (*apis mellifera*) population is reducing in a global scale. Beekeepers and those in favor of honey bees are at the mercy of this phenomenon. At the time of this work, there are no known solutions to stopping this paradox. This is mainly due to the fact that the reasons are manifold and ambiguous [4].

Beekeepers and researchers are facing the problem by extending the health surveillance of their bee hives. This includes time consuming manual tests to control the great amount of parasites that bees are coping with [6]. These manual processes can be performed in different ways, such as sampling living bees using alcohol or powder sugar or opening brood cells to check for mites, and have a number of drawbacks. First, they rely completely on statistical projections to estimate the parasite load of a bee hive. To get statistically accurate results for each inspection, a minimum of 300 bees have to be tested per hive. Second, most

© Springer International Publishing AG, part of Springer Nature 2018
A. Campilho et al. (Eds.): ICIAR 2018, LNCS 10882, pp. 465–473, 2018.
https://doi.org/10.1007/978-3-319-93000-8_52

accurate procedures are invasive in the sense that bees die during the monitoring procedures which adds additional strain to the colonies.

The idea of automatically monitoring the entrance of apiaries for flight estimations dates back over several decades [7]. This was long before computer enhanced monitoring became part of a beekeeper's life. First micro-processor monitoring was presented by Struye et al. [12], who used small tunnels equipped with infrared sensors to successfully count the number of bees flying in and out.

Chiron et al. [3] stated the need for observation of bees to monitor abnormal behavior, which can be used to diagnose the health state of a hive. In particular, they are interested in the number of bees and trajectories, and used a stereo camera system to capture video footage. The company Keltronixinc is marketing bee monitoring as a service [1], by using a system that consists of a camera and a computer, both setup at the bee hive. The camera is looking at the bee hive and monitors the bee activity with a tracking algorithm, allowing to distinguish between healthy and not healthy hives. A recent sensor study for visual observation of honey bees was presented in [10], in which the camera system proposed can be mounted at the entrance of a standard honey bee hive.

With the ultimate goal of automating the parasite monitoring, this paper presents a novelty approach for varroa mite detection on honey bees (see Fig. 1). The proposed framework makes three important contributions: (1) it includes a foreground detection approach to localize bees on video frames, (2) it provides a pipeline system susceptible to be applied to other types of bee parasites, and (3) it allows to reliably detect varroa mites with maximum accuracy over 80%.

The remainder of this manuscript is organized as follows: Sect. 2 presents the bee dataset and the proposed methods for parasite detection, Sect. 3 includes the experimentation carried out and the validation results, and Sect. 4 closes with the conclusions and future lines of research.

2   Materials and Methods

2.1   Data Collection

Videos of honey bees, when they are entering or leaving the hive, are used as input data in this research. The acquisition of the videos was carried out by a camera system that can be mounted at the entrance of standard bee hives [10]. Figure 1 (right) illustrates a representative frame of these videos.

The main properties of these videos are: (1) the camera position and focus are fixed creating a static environment, (2) the background is also static due to the tunnel setup that includes artificial lightning to ensure constant filming conditions, (3) the tunnel is covered with a dark adhesive foil to minimize reflections and create a homogeneous background.

2.2   Video Frame Processing

Once the videos are recorded, the next step entails processing them frame by frame. The target here is to detect the foreground first, and then to extract

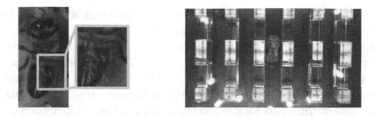

Fig. 1. Representative honey bee in which a varroa mite appears highlighted (left), and video frame of bees entering or leaving the hive (right).

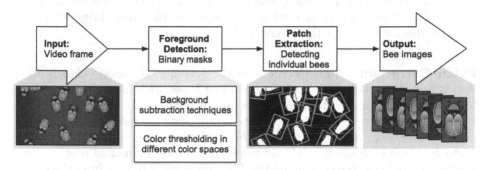

Fig. 2. Workflow for video frame processing with the different proposed methods.

image patches containing individual bees. Figure 2 shows the different steps for video frame processing, which are following explained in depth.

Foreground Detection. This task consists in separating the foreground from the background in each single video frame, getting a trade-off between noise and honey bee details. The foreground is defined as all non-static *regions of interest* (ROIs) in the image, being the rest of the regions part of the background. In the problem at hand, the ROIs are the honey bees passing through the tunnels. From a technical point of view, the result of this step is a binary image serving as a mask. This mask assigns to each pixel in the original image (video frame) one of the binary values depending if the pixel belongs to a ROI or not.

Taking into account the properties of the input data, especially the static camera setup, the following methods were considered:

– **Background subtraction** [11]. The idea is to subtract the intensity values of the image with the intensities of the background, and then classify each pixel as foreground if it is greater than a proposed threshold, t. Therefore, the binary image, M_i of the i-th frame, F_i is computed as: $M_i = |F_i - B| > t$, where B is the background image. Two different approaches were considered to calculate the background image, B. The first one uses the median image over the complete video as a model for the background. The second one calculates the background using Gaussian Mixture Models (GMMs), being the idea to model each pixel intensity value as a linear combination of Gaussian distributions calculated over the histogram of the image.

– **Color thresholding.** This approach uses a simple thresholding in different color spaces, both individually and combined. The threshold defines a region in a given color space, in such a way that all the pixels that fall into this region are treated as foreground, whereas the rest is background. Raw image data is organized in the RGB format, which addresses the color of each pixel as a mix of the three base colors: red, green, and blue. When looking at color as a potential feature, the RGB format is not always optimal, mainly because the brightness information of each pixel is directly linked to the color information. For this reason, two color models that separate color from brightness have been also considered: CIELab and HSV.

Patch Extraction. Since the input of the subsequently image classification step is one single foreground object, bounding boxes with individual bees need to be extracted from the foreground previously detected. To this end, the foreground image is processed using connected component analysis to determine the biggest component and its direction, whilst all other components are removed. The procedure is as follows: (1) find the boundaries of segmented bees, (2) calculate the bounding boxes of individual bees and extract images from them, and (3) post-process the patch images to remove other bees and rotate if needed.

2.3   Image Classification

In this stage, image patches previously extracted from video frames are used as input data. A set of features is extracted from each single patch to create an image descriptor that finally feeds a classifier in order to categorize it into *mite* or *no mite*. Figure 3 shows the different steps, which are subsequently described.

Data Pre-processing. In order to improve the contrast of input images, Contrast Limited Adaptive Equalization (CLAHE) [14] has been considered. This method operates on small regions of the image, by applying the contrast transform function to each region individually, rather than to the entire image.

Taking into account the distinctive color of varroa mites, other color spaces apart from RGB have been analyzed. So, the pre-processing step also includes the transformation of input images from RGB to CIELab and HSV.

Feature Extraction. Varroa mites are parasites with a button shape and a reddish-brown color (see Fig. 1). In order to detect them in bee images, different feature extraction methods have been considered:

– **Color histograms.** Binned color histograms of the input images in the different color spaces have been computed. Note that histograms for each color component have up to 256 bins.

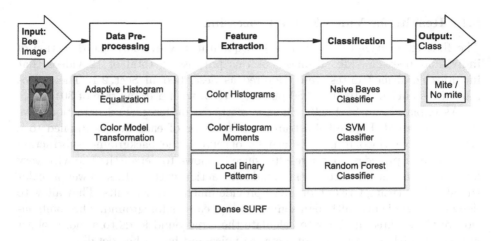

Fig. 3. Workflow for image classification with the different proposed methods.

- **Color histogram moments.** In addition to using color histograms as feature vectors, a few statistical measures have been computed from them and used as features: mean, standard deviation, skewness, and kurtosis.
- **Local binary patterns** [8]. This technique allows to compute a local representation of texture. It partitions input images into non-overlapping regions, and then it calculates the LBP value for the center pixel of each region.
- **Dense SURF** [2]. Inspired in the popular scale-invariant feature transform (SIFT) descriptor, it also allows to compute local features but being faster and more robust against image transformations.

Classification. The last step consists in classifying the input image, by means of its feature vector, into one of the two classes considered: *mite* or *no mite*. Three popular classifiers were selected aiming to provide different approaches of the learning process [5]: naive Bayes, based on the Bayesian theorem; support vector machine (SVM), based on the statistical learning theory; and random forest, a combination of decision trees.

3   Experimental Results

This section presents the evaluation of the proposed method for parasite detection on honey bees, including the results for video processing and image classification. Note that the source code was implemented in Python, making use of the OpenCV[1] library for image analysis and Scikit-learn[2] for machine learning.

---

[1] https://opencv.org/.
[2] http://scikit-learn.org/.

3.1   Results for Video Frame Processing

The first experiments were designed to qualitatively evaluate the detection of individual bees on video frames. For this purpose, a total of 12 videos that includes confirmed mites were acquired as described in Sect. 2.1. The videos have a resolution of 1920 × 1080 pixels in RGB, with a frame rate of 30 fps.

As explained in Sect. 2.2, different methods for foreground detection have been considered. Figure 4 illustrates the behavior of each one as applied to a representative video frame. As can be observed, the background subtraction with median provides poorer results, since it allows to detect the bee with very low precision. As opposite, background subtraction with GMMs as well as color thresholding (using CIELab or HSV) provide much better results. They allow to detect the whole bee, although some noise appears as foreground. The combination of these three methods to calculate the foreground leads to a more robust approach, with a good trade-off between noise and honey bee details.

Fig. 4. Comparing different foreground detection methods applied to the video frame of Fig. 1. From left to right: background subtraction with median, background subtraction with GMMs, color thresholding with HSV, color thresholding with CIELab, and HSV-CIELab color thresholding combined with GMM background subtraction.

3.2   Results for Image Classification

After processing the 12 videos acquired from bee hives, a total of 1300 patches were obtained, each one containing a single bee. These images were manually labeled with one of the two classes considered: *mite* vs. *no mite*. Only 103 of these images correspond to bees with mites, resulting in a high imbalanced dataset. For this reason, a balanced dataset was created by randomly selecting 103 negative samples to match the available positive ones. Based on a 80–20% split, two distinct subsets were selected: a 163-sample train set and a 43-sample test set.

The experimental results were analyzed in terms of the two following metrics: *accuracy*, the percentage of correctly classified instances; and *F1-measure*, the harmonic mean of precision and recall. Due to the size of the train set, a 3-fold cross-validation [9] was used to evaluate the hyper-parameters of each feature extraction method, such as the number of bins used for color histograms (30–256 bins), or the grid-size of SURF features (30–80 px).

The goal of this second experiment was to find the feature vector that best describes the underlaying data. For this purpose, the three different color models considered, as well as their individual color components, were combined with the four feature extraction methods. Given the great number of combinations obtained, only the most relevant ones are included in Table 1.

As can be observed, R from RGB, L from Lab, and H from HSV are the individual components that provide better results, similar to the three components of each one. Regarding feature extraction, the color histogram moments and SURF are the most competitive ones when combined with other methods. With respect to the classifiers, random forest provides the highest values for the two performance measures considered, followed closely by SVM. And finally, the use of CLAHE as a pre-processing step seems not to be necessary, in general, since the best results for most of the combinations are obtained when no image equalization is applied. However, the best results for both accuracy and F1-score, 0.81 and 0.83 respectively, are obtained when using the following configuration: (1) CLAHE and HSV color space as pre-processing, (2) LBP (radius: 1 px, 8-neighborhood) and SURF (grid-size: 80 px) feature extraction on all three color channels, and (3) random forest classifier for final classification.

Table 1. Image classification results obtained with different combinations of colors models and feature extraction methods, with no equalization (top) and after applying CLAHE (bottom). Results are shown in terms of accuracy and F1-measure using three different classifiers. The best result per column, top and bottom, appears in bold.

Color model	Features applied	Naive Bayes		SVM		Random forest	
		Acc	F1	Acc	F1	Acc	F1
RGB	Moments, SURF	0.72	0.74	**0.79**	**0.82**	0.67	0.67
Lab	Moments, SURF	0.61	0.71	0.65	0.65	0.72	**0.79**
HSV	Histog., Moments, SURF	0.56	0.58	0.51	0.53	**0.81**	**0.79**
R	Hist., Momen., LBP, SURF	0.70	0.70	**0.79**	**0.82**	0.70	0.67
L	Hist., Momen., LBP, SURF	0.72	0.74	0.65	0.69	**0.81**	**0.79**
H	Histog., Moments, SURF	**0.77**	**0.78**	0.56	0.56	0.65	0.61
RGB	Histog., moments, SURF	0.56	0.63	0.61	0.64	0.77	0.77
Lab	Moments, SURF	0.67	**0.76**	0.51	0.68	0.77	0.81
HSV	LBP, SURF	**0.70**	0.74	**0.67**	0.68	**0.81**	**0.83**
R	Histog., moments, SURF	0.51	0.59	0.58	0.59	0.77	0.78
L	Moments, SURF	0.56	0.64	0.63	**0.70**	0.77	0.79
H	Histograms, moments	0.49	0.56	0.56	0.58	0.72	0.74

Note that, in addition to the pipeline illustrated in Fig. 3, an object detection pipeline similar to the Viola/Jones face detector [13] was applied to the problem at hand. The main performance advantage of this approach comes from efficient computation of Haar-like features, using integral images in combination with a cascading classifier. Nonetheless, this alternative pipeline provides a maximum accuracy of 0.65 and F1-score of 0.71, mainly because an object detection approach of this type needs a greater amount of data samples for training.

4   Conclusion

Varroa mites are harmful parasites that affect bee colonies, causing the destruction of hives. Automatic monitoring systems play an important role to help beekeepers that traditionally perform a time consuming manual sampling.

This manuscript presents a first, novel approach to detect parasites in honey bees recorded when entering and leaving their hive. Video frames are individually processed in order to extract single images of each bee, which are further analyzed to classify them as *mite* or *no mite*. Experimentation results demonstrated the adequacy of the proposed pipeline, which includes both image analysis and machine learning techniques. The proposed methods are able to classify bee images with maximum accuracy and F1-measure over 80%.

Our future research is focused on the use of deep learning approaches for image classification and techniques to handle the class imbalance problem.

Acknowledgments. This work was partly supported by Vienna Business Agency under grant Innovation 2016 - 1583681, Ministerio de Ciencia e Innovación of the Gobierno de España (project TIN2015-66951-C2), SGR 1219, CERCA, *ICREA Academia 2014* and Marató TV3 (grant 20141510).

References

1. EYESONHIVES. http://www.keltronixinc.com/. Accessed April 2018
2. Bay, H., Ess, A., Tuytelaars, T., Van Gool, L.: Speeded-up robust features (SURF). Comput. Vis. Image Underst. **110**(3), 346–359 (2008)
3. Chiron, G., Gomez-Krämer, P., Ménard, M.: Detecting and tracking honeybees in 3D at the beehive entrance using stereo vision. EURASIP J. Image Video Process. **2013**(1), 1–17 (2013)
4. Evans, H.: ARNIA: Using Remote Hive Monitoring Data. http://www.beeculture. com/arnia-using-remote-hive-monitoring-data/. Accessed April 2018
5. Kantardzic, M.: Data Mining: Concepts, Models, Methods, and Algorithms. Wiley, Chichester (2011)
6. Lee, K.V., Moon, R.D., Burkness, E.C., Hutchison, W.D., Spivak, M.: Practical sampling plans for Varroa destructor in Apis mellifera colonies and apiaries. J. Econ. Entomol. **103**(4), 1039–1050 (2010)
7. Lundie, A.E.: Flight Activities of the Honey Be. US Department of Agriculture Bulletin 1328 (1925)
8. Pietikäinen, M.: Local binary patterns. Scholarpedia **5**(3), 9775 (2010)
9. Refaeilzadeh, P., Tang, L., Liu, H.: Cross-validation. In: Encyclopedia of Database Systems, pp. 532–538 (2009)
10. Schurischuster, S., Zambanini, S., Kampel, M., Lamp, B.: Sensor Study for Monitoring Varroa Mites on Honey bees (Apis Mellifera). In: Visual Observation and Analysis of Vertebrate and Insect Behavior Workshop (2016)
11. Sobral, A., Vacavant, A.: A comprehensive review of background subtraction algorithms evaluated with synthetic and real videos. Comput. Vis. Image Underst. **122**, 4–21 (2014)
12. Struye, M., Mortier, H., Arnold, G., Miniggio, C., Borneck, R.: Microprocessor-controlled monitoring of honeybee flight activity at the hive entrance. Apidologie **25**(4), 384–395 (1994)

13. Viola, P., Jones, M.J.: Robust real-time face detection. Int. J. Comput. Vis. **57**(2), 137–154 (2004)
14. Zuiderveld, K.: Contrast limited adaptive histogram equalization. In: Graphics gems IV, pp. 474–485 (1994)

Plant Bounding Box Detection from Desirable Residues of the Ultimate Levelings

Wonder A. L. Alves[1,2(✉)], Charles F. Gobber[1], and Ronaldo F. Hashimoto[2]

[1] Informatics and Knowledge Management Graduate Program,
Universidade Nove de Julho, São Paulo, Brazil
wonder@uni9.pro.br
[2] Department of Computer Science, Institute of Mathematics and Statistics,
Universidade de São Paulo, São Paulo, Brazil

Abstract. Ultimate levelings are operators that extract important image contrast information from a scale space based on levelings. During the residual extraction process, it is very common that some residues are extracted from undesirable regions, but they should be filtered out. In order to attend this problem it can be used some strategies to filter residues extracted by ultimate levelings. In this paper, we selected desirable regions from the residual extraction process through a binary classifier. The selected regions are used later in a solution to the bounding box detection problem applied in a plant images dataset.

1 Introduction

An operator in Mathematical Morphology (MM) can be seen as a mapping between complete lattices [1]. In particular, mappings on the set of all gray level images are called morphological operators. Furthermore, when a morphological operator satisfies the properties of being increasing and idempotent, it is called *morphological filter* [1]. By using these properties, information content reductions are expected after applying morphological filters [2]. Relying on these characteristics, morphological filters remove selectively undesirable contents from images such as noise, background irregularities, etc.; while preserving desired contents [3–5]. However, this is not always an easy task. A complementary strategy is to effectively erase the desirable portion of an image, and then restore it through a difference with the original image. This gives rise to the idea of *residual operators*. Simply put, residual operators are transformations that involve combinations of morphological operators with differences. Morphological gradient, top-hat transforms, skeleton by maximal balls and ultimate levelings are some examples of residual operators widely used in image processing applications.

There is a class of important residual operators called *ultimate levelings* [6]. Those residual operators analyze the evolution of the residual values between

© Springer International Publishing AG, part of Springer Nature 2018
A. Campilho et al. (Eds.): ICIAR 2018, LNCS 10882, pp. 474–481, 2018.
https://doi.org/10.1007/978-3-319-93000-8_53

two consecutive operators on a scale-space of levelings and keep the maximum residues for each pixel. During the residual extraction process, it is very common that undesirable regions of the input image contain residual information that should be filtered out. These undesirable residual regions often include desirable residual regions (which should be preserved) due to the design of the ultimate levelings which consider maximum residues. In this sense, several researches have been proposed in recent years, introducing strategies to filter undesirable residues during the residual extraction process [6–10].

In this paper, we selected desirable regions from the residual extraction process using a binary classifier. We explore several approach to select regions from a morphological tree, since we know that the ultimate levelings can be computed from these trees. Then, the regions that would be used from the morphological tree to produced the result of the ultimate levelings, are used later in a solution to the bounding box detection problem applied in a plant images dataset.

2 Theoretical Background

Image representations through trees have been proposed in recent years to carry out tasks of image processing and analysis such as filtering, segmentation, pattern recognition, contrast extraction, registration, compression and others. In this scenario, as illustrated in Fig. 1, the first step consists of constructing a representation of the input image by means of a tree; then the task of image processing or analysis is performed through information extraction from or modifications in the tree itself, and finally an image is reconstructed from the modified tree.

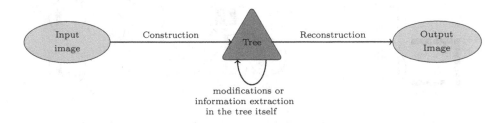

Fig. 1. Image representation through a tree.

In order to build the trees considered in this paper, we need the following definitions. First, we consider images as mappings from a Cartesian grid $\mathcal{D} \subset \mathbb{Z}^2$ to a discrete set of $k \geq 1$ integers $\mathbb{K} = \{0, 1, \ldots, k-1\}$. These mappings can be decomposed into *lower (strict)* and *upper (large)* level sets, i.e., for any $\lambda \in \mathbb{K}$, $\mathcal{X}_{\downarrow}^{\lambda}(f) = \{p \in \mathcal{D} : f(p) < \lambda\}$ and $\mathcal{X}_{\lambda}^{\uparrow}(f) = \{p \in \mathcal{D} : f(p) \geq \lambda\}$. From these sets, we define two other sets $\mathcal{L}(f)$ and $\mathcal{U}(f)$ composed by the connected components (CCs) of the lower and upper level sets of f, i.e., $\mathcal{L}(f) = \{\tau \in CC(\mathcal{X}_{\downarrow}^{\lambda}(f)) : \lambda \in \mathbb{K}\}$ and $\mathcal{U}(f) = \{\tau \in CC(\mathcal{X}_{\lambda}^{\uparrow}(f)) : \lambda \in \mathbb{K}\}$, where $CC(\mathcal{X})$ denotes the sets of either 4 or 8-CCs of $\mathcal{X}$, respectively.

The ordered pairs consisting of the CCs of the lower and upper level sets and the usual inclusion set relation, i.e., $(\mathcal{L}(f), \subseteq)$ and $(\mathcal{U}(f), \subseteq)$, induce two dual trees [11,12] called *component trees*. It is possible to combine them into a single tree in order to obtain the so-called *tree of shapes*. Then, let $\mathcal{P}(\mathcal{D})$ denote the *powerset* of $\mathcal{D}$ and let $sat : \mathcal{P}(\mathcal{D}) \to \mathcal{P}(\mathcal{D})$ be the operator of saturation [12] (or filling holes). Then, $\mathcal{SAT}(f) = \{sat(\tau) : \tau \in \mathcal{L}(f) \cup \mathcal{U}(f)\}$ be the family of CCs of the upper and lower level sets with holes filled. The elements of $\mathcal{SAT}(f)$, called *shapes*, are nested by the inclusion relation and thus the pair $(\mathcal{SAT}(f), \subseteq)$ induces a tree which is called *tree of shapes* [12].

In tree of shapes, and also component trees (max-tree and min-tree), each pixel $p \in \mathcal{D}$ is associated only to the smallest Connected Component (CC) of the tree containing it; and through parenthood relationship, it is also associated to all its ancestor nodes. Then, we denote by $SC(\mathcal{T}, p)$ the smallest CC containing p in tree $\mathcal{T}$. Similarly, we say $p \in \mathcal{D}$ is a *compact node pixel* (CNP) of a given CC $\tau \in \mathcal{T}$ if and only if τ is the smallest CC containing p, i.e., $\tau = SC(\mathcal{T}, p)$. Moreover, we denote by $\hat{\tau}$ the set composed by only CNPs of τ, i.e., $\hat{\tau} = \{p \in \mathcal{D} : \tau = SC(\mathcal{T}, p)\}$. Figure 2 shows examples of min-tree, max-tree, and tree of shapes, where CNPs are highlighted in red.

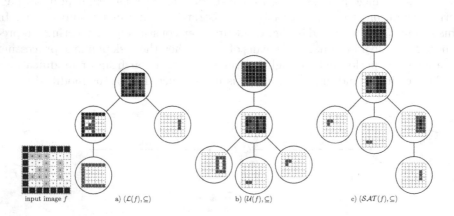

input image f a) $(\mathcal{L}(f), \subseteq)$ b) $(\mathcal{U}(f), \subseteq)$ c) $(\mathcal{SAT}(f), \subseteq)$

Fig. 2. Min-tree (a), max-tree (b) and tree of shapes (c) as compact representations of $(\mathcal{L}(f), \subseteq)$ and $(\mathcal{U}(f), \subseteq)$, and $(\mathcal{SAT}(f), \subseteq)$, respectively, of the input image f. Only Component Node Pixels (CNPs) are stored and they are highlighted in red. (Color figure online)

3   Ultimate Levelings

Ultimate levelings constitute a wider class of residual operators defined from a scale-space of levelings $\{\psi_i : i \in \mathcal{I}\}$ [6,8,9]. An ultimate leveling analyzes the evolution of residual values from a family of consecutive primitives, i.e. $r_i^+(f) = [\psi_i(f) - \psi_{i+1}(f) \vee 0]$ and $r_i^-(f) = [\psi_i(f) - \psi_{i+1}(f) \vee 0]$, keeping the maximum positive and negative residues for each pixel. Thus, contrasted objects can be detected if a relevant residue is generated when they are filtered out by one of these levelings. More precisely, the ultimate leveling $\mathcal{R}$ is defined for any image f as follows:

$$\mathcal{R}(f) = \mathcal{R}^+(f) \vee \mathcal{R}^-(f), \tag{1}$$

where $\mathcal{R}^+(f) = \sup_{i \in \mathcal{I}} \{r_i^+(f)\}$ and $\mathcal{R}^-(f) = \sup_{i \in \mathcal{I}} \{r_i^-(f)\}$.

Residual values of these operators can reveal important contrasted structures in the image. In addition to these residues, other associated information can be obtained such as properties of the operators that produced the maximum residual value. For example, Beucher [13] introduced a function $q_{\mathcal{I}_{max}} : \mathcal{D} \to \mathcal{I}$ that associates to each pixel the major index that produces the maximum non-null residue, i.e.,

$$p \in \mathcal{D}, q_{\mathcal{I}_{max}}(p) = \begin{cases} q_{\mathcal{I}_{max}}^+(p), & \text{if } [\mathcal{R}_\theta(f)](p) > [\mathcal{R}_\theta^+(f)](p), \\ q_{\mathcal{I}_{max}}^-(p), & \text{otherwise.} \end{cases} \tag{2}$$

where $q_{\mathcal{I}_{max}}^+(p) = \max\{i + 1 : [r_i^+(f)](p) = [\mathcal{R}_\theta^+(f)](p) > 0\}$ and $q_{\mathcal{I}_{max}}^-(p) = \max\{i + 1 : [r_i^-(f)](p) = [\mathcal{R}_\theta^-(f)](p) > 0\}$.

The ultimate levelings can be efficiently implemented thanks to the theorem proposed in Alves et al. [11], which shows that an increasing family of levelings $\{\psi_i : i \in \mathcal{I}\}$ can be obtained through a sequence of pruned trees $(\mathcal{T}_f^0, \mathcal{T}_f^1, \ldots, \mathcal{T}_f^{\mathcal{I}MAX})$ from the structure of the max-tree, min-tree or tree of shapes $\mathcal{T}_f$ constructed from the image f. Then, the i-th positive (resp. negative) residue $r_i^+(f)$ can be obtained from the nodes $\mathcal{N}r(i) = \mathcal{T}_f^i \setminus \mathcal{T}_f^{i+1}$, i.e., $\forall \tau \in \mathcal{N}r(i)$,

$$r_{\mathcal{T}_f^i}^+(\tau) = \begin{cases} \texttt{level}(\tau) - \texttt{level}(\texttt{Parent}(\tau)), & \text{if } \texttt{Parent}(\tau) \notin \mathcal{N}r(i), \\ \texttt{level}(\tau) - \texttt{level}(\texttt{Parent}(\tau)) \\ \quad + r_{\mathcal{T}_f^i}^+(\texttt{Parent}(\tau)), & \text{otherwise,} \end{cases} \tag{3}$$

where $\texttt{level}$ and $\texttt{Parent}$ are functions that represent the gray level and the parent node of τ in $\mathcal{T}_f$, respectively. Thus, the i-th positive (resp. negative) residue $r_i^+(f)$ is given as follows:

$$\forall p \in \mathcal{D}, [r_i^+(f)](p) = \begin{cases} r_{\mathcal{T}_f^i}^+(SC(\mathcal{T}_f^i, p)), & \text{if } SC(\mathcal{T}_f^i, p) \in \mathcal{N}r(i), \\ 0, & \text{otherwise.} \end{cases} \tag{4}$$

Those facts lead to efficient algorithms for computing ultimate levelings and its variations [8, 14].

Ultimate levelings are operators that extract residual information from primitive families. During the residual extraction process, it is very common that undesirable regions of the input image contain residual information that should be filtered out. These undesirable residual regions often include desirable residual regions due to the design of the ultimate levelings which consider maximum residues. Thus, residual information can be improve by filtration of residues extracted from undesirable regions [6–9]. To decide whether a residue $r_i^+(f)$ (resp., $r_i^-(f)$) is filtered out or not, just checking nodes $\tau \in \mathcal{N}r(i)$ that satisfy a given filtering criterion $\Omega : \mathcal{P}(\mathcal{D}) \to \{\text{desirable}, \text{undesirable}\}$. Thus, just calculate the ultimate leveling $\mathcal{R}$ for residues r_i^+ (resp., r_i^-) such that satisfy the criterion Ω. So, positive (resp. negative) residues are redefined as follows:

$$\forall \tau \in \mathcal{N}r(i), r_{T_f^i}^{\Omega+}(\tau) = \begin{cases} r_{T_f^i}^+(\tau), & \text{if } \exists C \in \mathcal{N}r(i) \\ & \text{such that } \Omega(C) \text{ is desirable}; \\ 0, & \text{otherwise}, \end{cases} \qquad (5)$$

and thus redefined the ultimate levelings with strategy for filtering from undesirable residues as follows: $\mathcal{R}_\Omega(f) = \mathcal{R}_\Omega^+(f) \vee \mathcal{R}_\Omega^-(f)$, where, $\mathcal{R}_\Omega^+(f) = \sup\{r_i^{\Omega+}(f) : i \in \mathcal{I}\}$ and $\mathcal{R}_\Omega^-(f) = \sup\{r_i^{\Omega-}(f) : i \in \mathcal{I}\}$.

Given the above considerations, in this paper we are interested in the maximum desirable residues provided by Ultimate Levelings. In this sense, is presented in the Sect. 4 three approaches to construct the classifier Ω.

4   Plant Bounding Box Detection Based on Desirable Residues of the Ultimate Levelings

In this section, we present the construction of a classifier Ω to filter undesirable residues from the ultimate levelings based on an attribute $\kappa : \mathcal{P}(\mathcal{D}) \to \mathbb{R}^+$ inspired in three robust theories. This means that some desirable residual regions are selected according to the attribute κ and a parameter threshold $\varepsilon \in \mathbb{R}^+$. Thus, to decide whether a residue $r_i^+(f)$ (resp., $r_i^-(f)$) is desirable, simply check if there exists at least one node $\tau \in \mathcal{N}r(i)$ that satisfies the filtering criterion:

$$\Omega_\kappa(\tau) = \begin{cases} \text{desirable}, & \text{if } \kappa(\tau) \geq \varepsilon, \\ \text{undesirable}, & \text{otherwise}. \end{cases} \qquad (6)$$

Then, following the Eq. 6 we design three classifiers $\Omega_{\kappa_{ms}}$, $\Omega_{\kappa_{mser}}$ and $\Omega_{\kappa_{tbmr}}$ using three attributes κ_{ms}, κ_{mser} and κ_{tbmr} describe as follows:

1. *Mumford-Shah energy functional* introduced in [15] and is widely applied in the segmentation problem where objective is minimize an energy function on the image partition. In this direction, in [16] was proposed an attribute (denoted by κ_{ms}) based on Mumford-Shah energy functional subordinated to a morphological tree and this attribute and a parameter ϵ_{ms} is used in this paper.
2. *Maximally Stable Extremal Regions (MSER)* originally introduced in [17] have been widely used in a variety of applications in computer vision as region detector. The regions detected by this method are the regions of level sets with maximum stability and are invariant to affine transformations. Then, the regions that correspond to the local maximum of stability function (denoted by κ_{mser}) are called MSERs.
3. *Tree-Based Morse Regions (TBMR)* introduced in [18] and is a topological approach to local invariant feature detection motivated by Morse theory. The idea is to select regions (that is, critical points) of a component tree according to its topology. Thus, we defined the function $\kappa_{tbmr}(\tau) = 1$ if and only if the region τ were selected, otherwise $\kappa_{tbmr}(\tau) = 0$.

It is worth mentioning that the parameters $\varepsilon_m s$ and ε_{mser} were obtained using the cross-validation tuning technique.

Finally, the representation of our approach is showed in Fig. 3. First, the max-tree of the green channel of the input image is constructed. After, the ultimate leveling based on either (i) Mumford-Shah energy functional or (ii) MSER or (iii) TBMR is applied. As some images present incomplete regions, then a post-processing to merge those regions is computed, and, finally, we can obtain the bounding box coordinates.

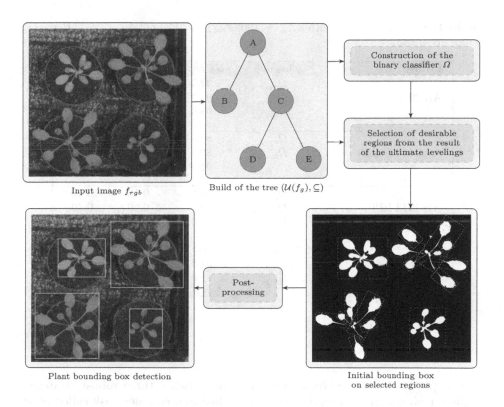

Input image f_{rgb} · Build of the tree $(\mathcal{U}(f_g), \subseteq)$ · Construction of the binary classifier Ω · Selection of desirable regions from the result of the ultimate levelings · Post-processing · Plant bounding box detection · Initial bounding box on selected regions

Fig. 3. Overview of our approach to plant bounding box detection.

5 Results and Experiments

One of the most significant current discussions in vision task problem is the plant bounding box detection. The plant morphology is very complex, so the plant bounding box detection is a difficult task. In addition, we choose an important plant dataset provided by [19]. In respect of plant bounding box detection task, the dataset is composed by three subsets: Ara2012, Ara2013-Canon and Ara2013-Rpi, totalizing 70 images with size of 3108 × 2324 and 2592 × 1944 pixels.

In order to compare the $\Omega_{\kappa_{ms}}$, $\Omega_{\kappa_{mser}}$ and $\Omega_{\kappa_{tbmr}}$ strategies, we chose the measurements presented by Minervine et al. [19]. Those measurements are: SBD that provides a measure about accuracy; DIC that is the difference between the plant detection using the bounding box annotated and the bounding box predicted and $|DIC|$ is the absolute value of DIC. The results obtained using our approach are shown in Table 1 and they reveal its robustness. Those values reveal in a general way that $\Omega_{\kappa_{tbmr}}$ showed better results in comparison of $\Omega_{\kappa_{ms}}$ and $\Omega_{\kappa_{mser}}$.

Table 1. Results obtained with $\varepsilon_{\kappa_{ms}} = 190$, $\varepsilon_{\kappa_{mser}} = 11$ and $\varepsilon_{\kappa_{tbmr}} = 1$. Reported values are mean.

Dataset	Classifier	$SBD[\%]$	DiC	$|DiC|$
Ara2012	$\Omega_{\kappa_{ms}}$	92.0	0.20	0.20
	$\Omega_{\kappa_{mser}}$	91.9	0.20	0.20
	$\Omega_{\kappa_{tbmr}}$	93.6	0.00	0.00
Ara2013-Canon	$\Omega_{\kappa_{ms}}$	87.5	0.10	0.30
	$\Omega_{\kappa_{mser}}$	89.4	0.10	0.10
	$\Omega_{\kappa_{tbmr}}$	92.0	0.20	0.20
Ara2013-RPi	$\Omega_{\kappa_{ms}}$	80.3	0.10	0.40
	$\Omega_{\kappa_{mser}}$	83.2	0.20	0.40
	$\Omega_{\kappa_{tbmr}}$	84.0	0.30	0.30
All	$\Omega_{\kappa_{ms}}$	85.8	0.00	0.30
	$\Omega_{\kappa_{mser}}$	87.6	0.10	0.20
	$\Omega_{\kappa_{tbmr}}$	89.3	0.10	0.10

6   Conclusion

This paper presented results of a comparison between three robust strategies to filter residues from ultimate levelings applied to a complex task called plant bounding box detection. In addition, the results shows that the strategy $\Omega_{\kappa_{tbmr}}$ presented better results in comparison of $\Omega_{\kappa_{ms}}$ and $\Omega_{\kappa_{mser}}$ collaborating with the conclusions published in [18]. It is recommended that further research be undertaken in intent of extends the ultimate levelings to colored images.

Acknowledgments. The authors would like to thank UNINOVE and FAPESP - São Paulo Research Foundation (Process 2016/02547-5) by financial support.

References

1. Serra, J.: Image Analysis and Mathematical Morphology. Volume 2: Theoretical Advances. Academic Press, London (1988)
2. Serra, J., Vincent, L.: An overview of morphological filtering. Circ. Syst. Sign. Process. **11**, 47–108 (1992)
3. Najman, L., Talbot, H.: Mathematical Morphology. Wiley, London (2013)
4. Bangham, J.A., Chardaire, P., Pye, C.J., Ling, P.D.: Multiscale nonlinear decomposition: the sieve decomposition theorem. IEEE Trans. Pattern Anal. Mach. Intell. **18**, 529–539 (1996)
5. Bangham, J.A., Ling, P.D., Harvey, R.: Scale-space from nonlinear filters. IEEE Trans. Pattern Anal. Mach. Intell. **18**, 520–528 (1996)
6. Alves, W.A., Hashimoto, R.F., Marcotegui, B.: Ultimate levelings. Comput. Vis. Image Underst. **165**, 60–74 (2017)
7. Hernández, J., Marcotegui, B.: Shape ultimate attribute opening. Image Vis. Comput. **29**, 533–545 (2011)
8. Alves, W.A.L., Hashimoto, R.F.: Ultimate grain filter. In: IEEE International Conference on Image Processing, Paris, France, pp. 2953–2957 (2014)
9. Alves, W., Morimitsu, A., Castro, J., Hashimoto, R.: Extraction of numerical residues in families of levelings. In: 2013 26th SIBGRAPI - Conference on Graphics, Patterns and Images (SIBGRAPI), pp. 349–356 (2013)
10. Gobber, C., Alves, W.A.L., Hashimoto, R.F.: Ultimate leveling based on Mumford-Shah energy functional applied to plant detection. In: Mendoza, M., Velastín, S. (eds.) CIARP 2017. LNCS, vol. 10657, pp. 220–228. Springer, Cham (2018). https://doi.org/10.1007/978-3-319-75193-1_27
11. Alves, W.A.L., Morimitsu, A., Hashimoto, R.F.: Scale-space representation based on levelings through hierarchies of level sets. In: Benediktsson, J.A., Chanussot, J., Najman, L., Talbot, H. (eds.) ISMM 2015. LNCS, vol. 9082, pp. 265–276. Springer, Cham (2015). https://doi.org/10.1007/978-3-319-18720-4_23
12. Caselles, V., Monasse, P.: Geometric Description of Images as Topographic Maps. Springer, Heidelberg (2010). https://doi.org/10.1007/978-3-642-04611-7
13. Beucher, S.: Numerical residues. Image Vis. Comput. **25**, 405–415 (2007)
14. Fabrizio, J., Marcotegui, B.: Fast implementation of the ultimate opening. In: Proceedings of the 9th International Symposium on Mathematical Morphology, pp. 272–281 (2009)
15. Mumford, D., Shah, J.: Optimal approximations by piecewise smooth functions and associated variational problems. Commun. Pure Appl. Math. **42**, 577–685 (1989)
16. Xu, Y., Géraud, T., Najman, L.: Hierarchical image simplification and segmentation based on Mumford-Shah-salient level line selection. Pattern Recogn. Lett. **83**(Part 3), 278–286 (2016)
17. Matas, J., Chum, O., Urban, M., Pajdla, T.: Robust wide-baseline stereo from maximally stable extremal regions. Image Vis. Comput. **22**, 761–767 (2004). British Machine Vision Computing 2002
18. Xu, Y., Monasse, P., Géraud, T., Najman, L.: Tree-based Morse regions: a topological approach to local feature detection. IEEE Trans. Image Process. **23**, 5612–5625 (2014)
19. Minervini, M., Fischbach, A., Scharr, H., Tsaftaris, S.A.: Finely-grained annotated datasets for image-based plant phenotyping. Pattern Recogn. Lett. **81**, 80–89 (2016)

A Fast and Robust Approach for Touching Grains Segmentation

Peterson A. Belan, Robson A. G. de Macedo, Marihá M. A. Pereira,
Wonder A. L. Alves, and Sidnei A. de Araújo$^{(\boxtimes)}$

Informatics and Knowledge Management Graduate Program,
Nove de Julho University (UNINOVE), São Paulo, Brazil
`saraujo@uni9.pro.br`

Abstract. The visual properties of agricultural grains are important factors for determining their market prices and assisting their choices by consumers. Despite the importance of visual inspection processes for agricultural grains quality, such tasks are usually handled manually and therefore subject to many failures. Thus, a computer vision approach that is able to segment correctly the grains contained in an image for further classification and detection of defects consists of an important practical application, which can be employed by visual quality inspection systems. In this work we propose an approach based on mathematical morphology and correlation-based granulometry techniques, guided by a set of heuristics, for grains segmentation. Experimental results showed that the proposed approach is able to segment the grains contained in an image, with high accuracy and very low computational time, even in cases where there are many grains glued together (touching grains).

Keywords: Touching grains · Segmentation
Mathematical morphology · Correlation-based granulometry
Heuristics

1 Introduction

The world production of grains in the last decade has been over 2 billion tons per year. A matter of extreme importance in the commercialization of agricultural grains, both with respect to the act of buying and selling, is knowing exactly what is being marketed. In many cases, visual properties of agricultural products such as color, shape and size are the main characteristics evaluated by consumers and constitute important factors for determining their market price [1].

Despite the importance of visual inspection tasks on the quality of agricultural products (including grains), they have historically been carried out manually by a human operator. However, this form of quality assessment usually takes a lot of time, is tedious, generates high operating costs, is liable to human failures, and presents difficulties in standardizing the results [2]. In this context, the use of computational systems aiming at the automation of such tasks can bring a competitive differential for the companies.

© Springer International Publishing AG, part of Springer Nature 2018
A. Campilho et al. (Eds.): ICIAR 2018, LNCS 10882, pp. 482–489, 2018.
https://doi.org/10.1007/978-3-319-93000-8_54

In the last decade several works have been presented in the literature proposing the development of computational systems to solve tasks of visual inspection of agricultural grains and seeds, such as [2–6].

Patil et al. [2] and Rodríguez-Pulido et al. [3] presented proposals for inspecting grains, but they do not address the task of segmentation. On the other hand, the approaches for segmentation proposed in [6] fail in images were the grains are glued to each other (touching grains). For this reason, in the experiments conducted in these works, the grains are placed spaced from each other purposely before acquiring the image to facilitate the segmentation, or only previously manual segmented grains are processed. This is a severe limitation that hinders the applicability of such approaches in industrial processes of food quality control. It is imperative that touching grains in an image should be segmented rightly before their appearance features are extracted and evaluated by a inspection system.

Recently, Araújo et al. [4] proposed a robust correlation-based granulometry module for beans segmentation that is able to segment touching grains, overcoming the aforementioned limitation. This approach segmented correctly $29,993$ grains out of $30,000$ (hit rate of 99.98%) in experiments with touching bean grains images. Another similar approach was proposed to segment touching rice grains by Dubosclard et al. [5], who claim that their algorithm achieved good results, although they do not present any measure of accuracy. In addition, the drawback of these two approaches is the time consumption. While the Araújo's approach spends 11 s for segmenting an image of 800×600 pixels, the Dubosclard's approach spends 90 s in the same task.

Clearly, other approaches have been proposed to segment touching grains such as Yao et al. [7]. However, as far as we know, the best hit rate from the literature was obtained by Araújo et al. [4]. In this context, a remaining challenge is to propose an approach that allow to inspect (segment and classify), in real time, the grains put on a conveyor belt, similar to the scenario found in a food industry, with high rates such as those achieved by Araújo et al. [4]. Trying to solve the most critical task of this challenge (segmentation), using an approach fast and robust at the same time, is the main objective of this work. Moreover, differently from other works dealing with food grains segmentation, which only provide the hit rate of grains detected, we present a more robust evaluation that includes the measures of Accuracy, Specificity, Sensitivity and the Area Under the ROC Curve (AUC).

2   Theoretical Background

Consider an image as a function I from a set of pixels $\mathcal{D} \subseteq \mathbb{Z}^2$ to set of values $\mathbb{K} = \{0, 1, ..., 2^{bits} - 1\}$, i.e., $I : \mathcal{D} \rightarrow \mathbb{K}$. It can be interpreted as a weighted graph $G_I = (\mathcal{D}, \mathcal{A}, \omega)$ consisting of a set $\mathcal{D}$ of vertices that represent image pixels, a set $\mathcal{A}$ of arcs weighted by ω, a function from $\mathcal{A}$ to some nonnegative scalar domain. The arcs $\mathcal{A}$ can be defined by a binary relation on $\mathcal{D}$, for example, 4-neighborhood or 8-neighborhood in case of 2D images. We use $t \in \mathcal{A}(s)$ and

$(s,t) \in \mathcal{A}$ to indicate that t is adjacent to s. Each arc $(s,t) \in \mathcal{A}$ has a fixed weight $\omega(s,t) \geq 0$ that is represented by gradient of image I. For a given image graph $(\mathcal{D}, \mathcal{A}, \omega)$, a path $\pi_t = \langle t_1, t_2, ..., t \rangle$ is a sequence of adjacent pixels with terminus at a pixel t. A path is trivial when $\pi_t = \langle t \rangle$. A path $\pi_t = \pi_s \cdot \langle s, t \rangle$ indicates the extension of a path π_s by an arc $\langle s, t \rangle$. A image graph $(\mathcal{D}', \mathcal{A}', \omega)$ is subgraph of $(\mathcal{D}, \mathcal{A}, \omega)$ if $\mathcal{D}' \subseteq \mathcal{D}$, $\mathcal{A}' \subseteq \mathcal{A}$ and $\mathcal{A}' \subseteq \mathcal{D}' \times \mathcal{D}'$. A forest $\mathcal{F}$ of G_I is an acyclic subgraph $\mathcal{F}$ of G_I. Trees are connected components of the forest, i.e., any two vertices of a tree are connected by a path.

Let $S \subseteq \mathcal{D}$ be a set of particular vertices s_i called seeds. For a given image graph $(\mathcal{D}, \mathcal{A}, \omega)$ and a set S of seeds, the Image Foresting Transform (IFT) returns a forest $\mathcal{F}$ of $(\mathcal{D}, \mathcal{A}, \omega)$ such that (i) there exists for each vertice $v \in \mathcal{D}$ a unique and simple path $\pi(s_i, v)$ in $\mathcal{F}$ from a seed vertice $s_i \in S$ to v and (ii) each such path is optimum, i.e., has a minimum cost for linking v to some seed of S, according to the specified path-cost function f [8]. This forest $\mathcal{F}$ can be simply represented by a predecessor map optPathForest and path-cost map pathCost. Thus, we say that optPathForest(v) is predecessor of vertice v in the minimum path and pathCost(v) is the minimum cost for linking v to some seed of S. Then, the Algorithm 1 computes a path-cost map pathCost, which converges to optimum-path forest optPathForest, if f is a smooth function [8].

Algorithm 1. IFT Computation

Input: Image graph $G_I = (\mathcal{D}, \mathcal{A}, \omega)$ and function f.
Output: Optimum-path forest optPathForest and the path-cost map pathCost
1 **begin**
2   Initialize priority queue $\mathcal{Q}$
3   **foreach** $t \in \mathcal{D}$ **do**
4   optPathForest$(t) \leftarrow$ NIL
5   wasProcessed$(t) \leftarrow$ False
6   pathCost$(t) \leftarrow f(\langle t \rangle)$
7   **if** pathCost$(t) \neq +\infty$ **then**
8   add $(\mathcal{Q}, t, $pathCost$(t))$

9   **while** $\mathcal{Q}$ *is not empty* **do**
10          $s \leftarrow$ removeMinPriority$(\mathcal{Q})$
11   wasProcessed$(s) \leftarrow$ True
12   **foreach** *pixel* $t \in \mathcal{D}$ *such that* $\langle s,t \rangle \in \mathcal{A}$ *and* wasProcessed$(t) = $ False **do**
13   costTMP $\leftarrow f(\pi_s^{\text{optPathForest}} \cdot \langle s,t \rangle)$
14   **if** costTMP $<$ pathCost(t) **then**
15   **if** pathCost$(t) \neq +\infty$ **then** remove t from $\mathcal{Q}$
16   optPathForest$(t) \leftarrow s$
17   pathCost$(t) \leftarrow$ costTMP
18   add $(\mathcal{Q}, t, $pathCost$(t))$

Depending on the path-cost function f utilized and other input parameters (adjacency relation $\mathcal{A}$ and arc weights ω), the IFT can compute different image processing operations, for example: distance transforms, connected filters, segmentation by watershed and others [8,9]. More specifically, the watershed transform by IFT assumes that (i) the seeds correspond to regional minima of the image (or to imposed minima, i.e. markers); (ii) the path-cost function $f_{\max}$ defined by the maximum arcs as follows:

$$f_{\max} = (\langle v \rangle) = \begin{cases} 0, & \text{if } v \in S \\ +\infty & \text{otherwise}, \end{cases} \qquad (1)$$
$$f_{\max} = (\pi_u \cdot \langle v \rangle) = \max\{f_{\max}(\pi_u), \omega(u, v)\}.$$

3   Proposed Approach

Based on the considerations presented in Sect. 2, we were inspired in function $f_{\max}$ to design a path-cost function f_{beans} that takes in consideration the shapes of grains through heuristics. It is worth noting that segmentation based on watershed normally suffers from the problem of over segmentation [10,11], especially if the image is corrupted with different kinds of noise during its acquisition. To overcome this problem a sequence of pre-processing and post-processing is performed, as follows:

1. In the first step of the proposed approach the color space of original image is converted from RGB to CIELab. This conversion showed an interest strategy to improve the next pre-processing step, that is the binarization of the image.
2. In the second step the CIELab input image I_{lab} is mapped to a grayscale image I_{gray} as follows: each pixel $p \in \mathcal{D}$ is mapped to black if the color of $I_{\text{lab}}(p)$ is a typical color of beans (foreground), and to white if the color of $I_{\text{lab}}(p)$ is a typical background color, as described in [4]. Formally, let B and F be two sets of colors constructed from training images containing colors of beans and their backgrounds, respectively, this pre-processing filtering is given by:

$$\forall p \in \mathcal{D}, I_{\text{gray}}(p) = \frac{dist(\text{ColorF}, I_{\text{lab}}(p))}{dist(\text{ColorF}, I_{\text{lab}}(p)) + dist(\text{ColorB}, I_{\text{lab}}(p))}, \qquad (2)$$

   where $dist(\text{ColorA}, \text{ColorB})$ is the Euclidean distance between ColorA and ColorB,

$$\text{ColorF} = \arg\min\{dist(\text{Color}, I_{\text{lab}}(p)) : \text{Color} \in F\} \qquad (3)$$

   and

$$\text{ColorB} = \arg\min\{dist(\text{Color}, I_{\text{lab}}(p)) : \text{Color} \in B\}. \qquad (4)$$

   Differently from [4], in this work we used a look-up table to compute this filter very efficiently. So, instead to conduct a training for each image, the filtering is done directly based on the look-up table previously created. The modifications in this step allowed a significant reduction in processing time. To finish this step, a binary image I_{bin} is obtained from I_{gray} by applying a simple binarization procedure.
3. In the third step, we compute an Euclidean Distance Transform (EDT) [10] in binary image I_{bin} using IFT constrained to propagate inwards from the connected grains boundaries. In this case, the following path-cost function f_{euc} is used:

$$f_{\text{euc}}(\langle v \rangle) = \begin{cases} 0, & \text{if } v \in I_{\text{bin}} \\ +\infty & \text{otherwise,} \end{cases} \tag{5}$$
$$f_{\text{euc}}(\pi_u \cdot \langle v \rangle) = (x_v - x_r)^2 + (y_v - y_r)^2$$

where r is the initial pixel of π_u. The EDT I_{EDT} is obtained by computing the IFT and the squared root of its resulting path-cost map `pathCost`. Thus, we can extract a set of seeds $S \subset \mathcal{D}$ from local maximum to start the flooding process of IFT.

4. In the fourth step, we execute more one IFT to compute the segmentation of beans using the path-cost function f_{beans} which fills one or more basins, selected by a seed $s \in S$, up to levels specified by center of beans, given by: I_{EDT}, as follows:

$$f_{\text{beans}}(\langle v \rangle) = \begin{cases} I_{\text{gray}}(v), & \text{if } v \in S \text{ and } I_{\text{EDT}}(v) > \text{DistMin} \\ +\infty & \text{otherwise,} \end{cases}$$
$$f_{\text{beans}}(\pi_u \cdot \langle v \rangle) = \begin{cases} f_{\text{beans}}(\pi_u), & \text{if } f_{\text{beans}}(\pi_u) > I_{\text{gray}}(v) \text{ and } v \in I_{\text{bin}} \\ +\infty & \text{otherwise.} \end{cases} \tag{6}$$

Thus, for improving the segmentation, we employed additional post-processing operations of merging in trees of optimum-path forest `optPathForest` using heuristic information (i.e., average size of grain, distance between the centers of grains and orientation of grains). The merger of two trees is made when the distance between the centers of grains (tree roots) is smaller than the average size of a grain.

5. Finally, for grains greater than or equal to twice the average size of a typical grain (errors of the segmentation process described in the previous step) we applied the correlation-based granulometry approach described in [4], using the same kernels indicated by authors. Since the cross-correlation is usually time-consuming, in this work it is applied only in a few areas represented by the trees, without compromising the processing time of proposed approach. Figure 1 shows the output images obtained in the five processing steps previously described.

4   Experimental Results

The employed image database is composed by 50 RGB color images of most consumed Brazilian beans (i.e. Carioca, Mulatto and Black), as shown in Fig. 2. Each image contains 100 mixed grains, distributed according to Table 1, and was manually segmented to generate its binary version, which is used to evaluate the proposed segmentation approach. It is valid to emphasize that: (i) in all images there are many cases of touching grains and (ii) the images considered in the computation of the lookup table mentioned in Sect. 3, to extract the background of original color image, did not belong to the dataset used in the evaluation step.

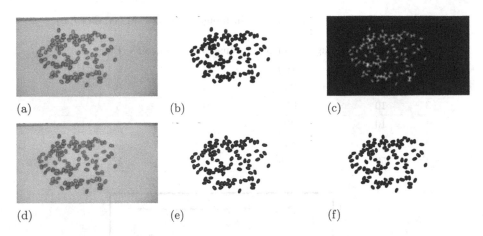

Fig. 1. Processing steps of proposed approach: (a) input image; (b) binary image I_{bin}; (c) EDT image I_{EDT}; (d) overlap of grayscale image and the set of seeds S obtained in step 3; (e) overlap of segmentation f_{beans} and the set of seeds; (f) final result of segmentation.

Fig. 2. Types of Brazilian beans contained in images considered in the experiments. (a) Carioca; (b) Mulatto; (c) Black. (Color figure online)

The conditions for image acquisition were based on the specifications presented by Anami and Savakar [12]. The images were acquired by a Microsoft LifeCam HD5000 webcam with resolution of 1280 × 720 pixels, using the RGB (24-bit) color system. The adopted focal length was 30 cm, and the measured illuminance was 930 Lux (in average) throughout the acquisition region. Such light intensity is generated by a LED strip which covers an area of 40 × 40 cm and is positioned inside the image acquisition chamber, above the webcam.

For each image of employed database, the following performance measures were calculated: sensitivity (evaluates the rate of true positives), specificity (evaluates the rate of true negatives) and accuracy (evaluates the rate of pixels correctly classified). From conducted experiments, the following results are obtained: Accuracy = 0.862, Specificity = 0.692, Sensitivity = 0.996. These measures allow to compute the ROC curve [13] presented in Fig. 3.

Table 1. Brazilian beans varieties in images from considered database

Subset	Total of images	Carioca grains	Mulatto grains	Black grains
1	10	100	0	0
2	10	95	5	0
3	10	95	0	5
4	10	90	5	5
5	10	85	10	5
Total	50	465	20	15

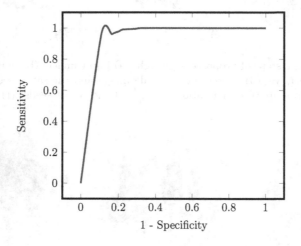

Fig. 3. ROC curve.

The AUC (0.9394) calculated from ROC curve showed in Fig. 3 demonstrates good performance of the proposed approach, which was able to detect correctly 4,978 grains out of 5,000 (hit rate of 99.56%), even in images containing many touching grains. Regarding computational cost, our approach takes, in average, 0.7 s to segment an image with resolution of 1280×720 pixels, without using multithreading or special optimization techniques. These results make it clear that the objective of this work was reached since the proposed approach allows to segment beans with a hit rate very close to that reported in Araujo et al. [4], with much less processing time.

5   Conclusion

The overall results of the proposed segmentation approach (AUC: 0.9394, accuracy: 86.2%, specificity: 69.2%, sensitivity: 99.6%) indicate that it could be used as part of an online visual quality inspection of beans, especially if we consider its robustness and speed. Planned future work includes: (*i*) an investigation for improving the heuristics used in order to maintain the accuracy of proposed approach avoiding the use of cross correlation operation, which will lead to a reduction of processing time and (ii) conducting experiments by coupling the proposed approach in a real-time system for beans inspection.

Acknowledgements. The authors would like to thank UNINOVE, CNPq–Brazilian National Research Council for the research scholarship granted to S. A. Araújo (Proc. 311971/2015-6) and FAPESP–São Paulo Research Foundation (Proc. 2017/05188-9).

References

1. Fernandez, L., Castillero, C., Aguilera, J.: An application of image analysis to dehydration of apple discs. J. Food Eng. **67**(1), 185–193 (2005)
2. Patil, N.K., Yadahalli, R.M., Pujari, J.: Comparison between HSV and YCbCr color model color-texture based classification of the food grains. Int. J. Comput. Appl. **34**(4), 51–57 (2011)
3. Rodríguez-Pulido, F.J., Gordillo, B., González-Miret, M.L., Heredia, F.J.: Analysis of food appearance properties by computer vision applying ellipsoids to colour data. Comput. Electron. Agric. **99**, 108–115 (2013)
4. De Araújo, S.A., Pessota, J.H., Kim, H.Y.: Beans quality inspection using correlation-based granulometry. Eng. Appl. Artif. Intell. **40**, 84–94 (2015)
5. Dubosclard, P., Larnier, S., Konik, H., Herbulot, A., Devy, M.: Deterministic method for automatic visual grading of seed food products. In: 4th International Conference on Pattern Recognition Applications and Methods (2015)
6. Zareiforoush, H., Minaei, S., Alizadeh, M.R., Banakar, A., Samani, B.H.: Design, development and performance evaluation of an automatic control system for rice whitening machine based on computer vision and fuzzy logic. Comput. Electron. Agric. **124**, 14–22 (2016)
7. Yao, Q., Zhou, Y., Wang, J.: An automatic segmentation algorithm for touching rice grains images. In: 2010 International Conference on Audio Language and Image Processing (ICALIP), pp. 802–805. IEEE (2010)
8. Falcão, A.X., Stolfi, J., de Alencar Lotufo, R.: The image foresting transform: theory, algorithms, and applications. IEEE Trans. Pattern Anal. Mach. Intell. **26**(1), 19–29 (2004)
9. Audigier, R., de Alencar Lotufo, R.: Watershed by image foresting transform, tiezone, and theoretical relationships with other watershed definitions. In: Mathematical Morphology and its Applications to Signal and Image Processing (ISMM), pp. 277–288 (2007)
10. Soille, P.: Morphological Image Analysis: Principles and Applications. Springer, Heidelberg (2013). https://doi.org/10.1007/978-3-662-05088-0
11. Najman, L., Talbot, H.: Mathematical Morphology: From Theory to Applications, ISTE-Wiley, Hoboken (2010). 520 pp., ISBN 9781848212152
12. Anami, B.S., Savakar, D.G.: Influence of light, distance and size on recognition and classification of food grains' images. Int. J. Food Eng. **6**(2), 1–21 (2010)
13. Fawcett, T.: An introduction to ROC analysis. Pattern Recogn. Lett. **27**(8), 861–874 (2006)

Quantification and Prediction of Damage in SAM Images of Semiconductor Devices

Dženana Alagić[1,2]([✉]), Olivia Bluder[1], and Jürgen Pilz[2]

[1] KAI - Kompetenzzentrum Automobil- und Industrieelektronik GmbH,
Europastraße 8, 9524 Villach, Austria
`Dzenana.Alagic@k-ai.at`
[2] Institut für Statistik, Alpen-Adria-Universität, Universitätsstraße 65-67,
9020 Klagenfurt, Austria

Abstract. The importance of statistical lifetime models for the reliability assessment of semiconductors is increasing steadily, because resources and time are limited. The devices are tested under accelerated electrical and thermal conditions which causes degradation in metal layers. To visualize the damage, Scanning Acoustic Microscopy (SAM) is used. In this work, an approach combining image processing and statistical modeling is presented in order to quantify and predict the damage intensity in SAM images. The image processing algorithm automatically locates and quantifies the maximum damaged areas in SAM images. The damage intensity is coded as an ordered categorical variable and a cumulative link model for damage prediction is defined. Both the algorithm and the proposed statistical model show good results.

Keywords: SAM · Image processing · Cumulative link model
Semiconductor reliability · Lifetime model

1 Introduction

To get information about the functionality and robustness of the semiconductor devices in a reasonable amount of time, accelerated lifetime tests are performed. The applied stress causes signs of damage in metal layers, which can be visualized by means of 8-bit SAM images. To describe and model the damage propagation, an image processing algorithm to automatically locate and quantify the maximum damaged areas in a series of SAM images is needed.

Figure 1 illustrates the structure of the investigated SAM images. This image represents a Device under Test (DUT) with two channels out of which only one is stressed. The black circles surround the area of the so-called nailheads of the bondwires. The main goal of the algorithm is to mark and quantify the maximum damage in the Double diffused Metal Oxide Semiconductor (DMOS) area (illustrated with black rectangles) excluding the nailheads. It can be seen that the applied stress caused metal degradation in the DMOS area of the stressed channel, which is visible as change to dark gray. The "darkest" areas in the

© Springer International Publishing AG, part of Springer Nature 2018
A. Campilho et al. (Eds.): ICIAR 2018, LNCS 10882, pp. 490–496, 2018.
https://doi.org/10.1007/978-3-319-93000-8_55

stressed channel are the areas of maximum degradation. To enable statistical reliability analysis, they need to be located and quantified automatically by an image processing algorithm.

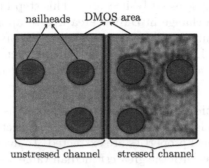

nailheads   DMOS area

unstressed channel   stressed channel

Fig. 1. SAM image of the metal layer of interest

Quantitative analysis of SAM images (see Sect. 2) enables the objective comparison of damage in metal layers. However, to determine the factors which influence the degradation process and describe the damage propagation, a statistical model is necessary (see Sect. 3).

2   Algorithm for Damage Quantification in SAM Images

The algorithm for the damage quantification in SAM images is implemented in ImageJ [1,2]. The main steps and the output of the algorithm are explained below.

Input Images. All images are put into a stack (array of images sharing the same window) to perform image processing operations on all images at once.

Image Transformation. Since the images differ in size, contrast and rotation, they need to be aligned first. Let $\mathbf{x} = (x_1, x_2)$ denote the coordinate of the pixel in the input image. To align the images in a stack, the following transformation is performed

$$f(\mathbf{x}) = \lambda \begin{pmatrix} \cos\theta & -\sin\theta \\ \sin\theta & \cos\theta \end{pmatrix} \cdot \mathbf{x} + \Delta\mathbf{x}, \tag{1}$$

where $f(\mathbf{x})$ represents the output coordinate, λ is a scalar resizing factor and $\Delta\mathbf{x}$ is a constant vector determining the amount of translation. This type of transformation is called **scaled rotation** [3]. Every image is transformed in such a way that it matches with the previous image in the stack.

Feature Extraction. The number, position and size of the nailheads that cover one part of the DMOS area (see Fig. 1) differ for different device types. Since they have similar gray values as damaged area, a mask is created to exclude them from the consideration. Next, the unstressed and stressed channels are cropped and separated in 2 stacks. To reduce the noise in the images, Gaussian Blur filter with a radius $\sigma = 2$ is applied on both stacks. The median gray value of the unstressed DMOS area of each image in the stack is computed and subtracted from the corresponding stressed DMOS area. This step highlights the damaged areas. The greater the change in DMOS area due to applied stress, the higher the gray value in the subtracted stack. To separate the pixels indicating damage from the background, local thresholding of the subtracted stack is performed. For each pixel in the image, the threshold is calculated according to the grayscale information of the neighboring pixels.

Damage Quantification. Image binarization enables easy selection of damaged areas that have irregular shapes. These areas are selected on the subtracted stack and their statistical properties are extracted. To avoid bias due to a single outlying pixel, the areas with the greatest median value are marked as maximum damaged areas.

Output. The algorithm saves the images of the original stressed channel with marked maximum damaged areas (see Fig. 2a). To reduce complexity, only the five areas with the highest median values are marked. The boundaries of the damaged areas are denoted with yellow lines, while the red numbers indicate the damage intensities. Higher values imply higher damage intensities.

To see how the degradation process develops over time, eight devices of two different device types were tested under the same electro-thermal conditions, but with increasing number of test cycles. The SAM images of these devices are analyzed with the developed image processing algorithm. The change of the maximum damage intensity with respect to the number of cycles expressed in arbitrary units (a.u.) is illustrated in Fig. 2b. For both device types, the damage intensity increases with increasing number of test cycles. Further, the analysis of more SAM images shows that saturation in damage intensity occurs around 120. Physical failure inspection shows that at that point another type of failure mechanism starts. The relation visible in Fig. 2b indicates that the results provided by the algorithm are reliable and deserve further investigation and statistical analysis.

3   Statistical Model to Predict the Maximum Damage

The SAM images investigated in this work represent DUTs tested under different electrical and thermal stress conditions. In the reliability test system [4], the following parameters can be adjusted: pulse shape (triangular or rectangular), voltage (V), current (I), pulse length (t_p), time between two pulses (t_{rep}), pulse energy (E) and device temperature at the beginning of a test (T_{case}). The maximum temperature rise is denoted with ΔT and testing time is measured in number of test cycles (N). Expert knowledge suggests that the geometry of the devices can also influence the degradation process. Therefore, the size of the channel area $(chArea)$ is considered as an additional parameter.

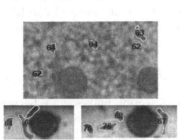

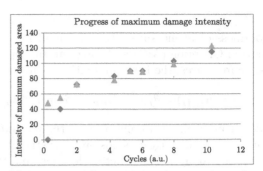

(a) Marked maximum damaged areas

(b) Progress of maximum damage intensity over time

Fig. 2. Output results of the developed image processing algorithm

The aim of the statistical model is to predict the maximum damage of the metal layer based on the applied stress conditions. To enable objective comparison of the parameters with different units and scales, all parameters are standardized by subtracting the corresponding mean value and dividing the difference with the standard deviation. A dataset with 607 observations is split into a training set (80%), used to build the model and determine its coefficients and a test set (20%), used to evaluate the model performance. According to the intensity of the maximum damaged area (d_{max}), three damage categories are built: $1 = small\ damage\ (0 \leq d_{max} \leq 40)$, $2 = medium\ damage\ (40 < d_{max} \leq 60)$ and $3 = large\ damage\ (d_{max} > 60)$. Hence, the response variable is categorical with ordered categories. Therefore, the class of ordinal logistic models is used to train the model and make predictions. More precisely, cumulative link models are investigated [5].

Our response variable Y_i (=damage category) follows a multinomial distribution with parameter π. The cumulative probabilities are defined as

$$\gamma_{ij} = P(Y_i \leq j) = \pi_{i1} + \pi_{i2} + \pi_{i3}, \quad j = 1, 2, 3 \tag{2}$$

where π_{ij} represents the probability that the ith observation is in the category j. To select the most important parameters describing the damage data, the logit link defined as $\text{logit}(\pi) = \log[\pi/(1 - \pi)]$, is used. Hence, cumulative logits are defined as

$$\text{logit}(\gamma_{ij}) = \log \frac{P(Y_i \leq j)}{1 - P(Y_i \leq j)} \quad j = 1, 2. \tag{3}$$

For category 3, the denominator in (3) would be equal 0, so the cumulative logit for the 3rd category is not defined [5,6]. A cumulative logit model is then given by $\text{logit}(\gamma_{ij}) = \theta_j + x_i^T\beta$, where β denotes the set of regression coefficients and $\{\theta_j\}$ provide cumulative logits and act as intercepts. Note that the regression part $x_i^T\beta$ does not depend on the category, i.e. β has the same effect for each of the 2 cumulative logits.

The model with optimal set of parameters is selected based on the statistical goodness-of-fit measures, like likelihood ratio statistic, Wald test, Akaike Information Criterion (AIC) and Bayesian Information Criterion (BIC) [5]. Based on these measures, the best cumulative logit model is defined by

$$\text{logit}(\gamma_{ij}) = \theta_j + \beta_1 T_{case} + \beta_2 N + \beta_3 t_p + \beta_4 I + \beta_5 chArea + \beta_6 \Delta T. \quad (4)$$

Also from a physical point a view, the parameter selection makes sense because the observed damage depends on the distribution of the thermo-mechanical stress in the metal layer. The selected electrical and thermal parameters have an impact on this distribution and hence will lead to different damage intensities.

The choice of an appropriate link function may have a significant influence on the model performance. Therefore, the model (4) is refitted with other link functions. The obtained models are compared by means of goodness-of-fit measures (see Table 1). A closer look at the table reveals that the log-log link outperforms the other functions. Therefore, it is used in the remainder of this paper.

Table 1. Comparison of goodness-of-fit for different link functions for model (4)

Link function	Formula	AIC	BIC	Log-likelihood
logit	$\log \frac{\gamma}{1-\gamma}$	675.26	708.74	-329.63
probit	$\Phi^{-1}(\gamma)$	676.76	710.23	-330.38
log-log	$-\log(-\log(\gamma))$	**670.38**	**703.86**	**-327.19**
complementary log-log	$\log(-\log(1-\gamma))$	703.97	737.45	-343.99
cauchit	$\tan(\pi(\gamma - 0.5))$	689.52	722.99	-336.76

4   Results

To measure the accuracy of the defined model, a test dataset is used. The easiest way to validate the model with categorical response is via confusion matrix (see Table 2). The rows represent observations in the actual class, while the columns represent the observations in the predicted class. The observations on the main diagonal are classified correctly. Thus, the model accuracy is 66%.

Table 2. Confusion matrix of the test dataset

		Predicted class		
		Small damage	Medium damage	Large damage
Actual class	Small damage	47	2	1
	Medium damage	18	3	16
	Large damage	4	0	31

But a closer look at the probabilities according to which the observations are assigned to a certain class reveals that the model accuracy is way better. To be more precise, the majority of observations from category 2 that are misclassified to category 1, have damage intensities around 40, i.e. close to the boundary between the two classes. In such a case, the difference between the probabilities of belonging to one or the other class predicted by the model is very small. The same holds for medium/large damage relations.

Additional investigation of the observations in the upper right and bottom left corner, which are more of a concern, indicates two important points. First, the observation in the upper right corner is correctly classified by the model, but the algorithm did not locate the damaged areas precisely enough. Hence, there is place for algorithm improvement. One could try to apply e.g. machine learning algorithms, since the number of available SAM images is large. Second, the 4 observations in the lower bottom corner are misclassified by the model. This inaccuracy can be explained by the fact that the metal layer of interest of these devices has different properties with respect to the other investigated devices. Hence, to improve the model, additional parameters of the metal layer must be considered.

5   Conclusion

In this work the SAM images of semiconductor devices after thermo-mechanical stress are investigated. An image processing algorithm for detection and quantification of maximum damaged areas in a series of SAM images is presented. Additionally, a statistical model that predicts the damage intensity of the device dependent on the applied stress conditions and testing time is developed. Both the algorithm and the model provide reliable and valuable results. However, there is still place for improvement. With larger number of SAM images it is possible to use machine learning algorithms for certain image processing tasks. To improve the model quality, additional physical properties of the devices can be included into the model.

Acknowledgments. This work was jointly funded by the Austrian Research Promotion Agency (FFG, Project No. 854247) and the Carinthian Economic Promotion Fund (KWF, contract KWF-1521/28101/40388).

References

1. Rasband, W.S.: ImageJ. U.S. National Institutes of Health, Bethesda, Maryland, USA (1997–2016). http://imagej.nih.gov/ij/
2. Alagić, D.: A statistical measure for fatigue induced degradation in metal layers. Master thesis, Alpen-Adria University of Klagenfurt (2017)
3. Thévenaz, P., Ruttimann, U.E., Unser, M.: A pyramid approach to subpixel registration based on intensity. IEEE Trans. Image Process. **7**(1), 27–41 (1998). http://bigwww.epfl.ch/publications/thevenaz9801.html

4. Glavanovics, M., Köck, H., Kosel, V., Smorodin, T.: A new cycle test system emulating inductive switching waveforms. In: Proceedings of the 12th European Conference on Power Electronics and Applications, pp. 1–9 (2007)
5. Agresti, A.: An Introduction to Categorical Data Analysis. Wiley, Hoboken (2007)
6. Christensen, R.H.B.: Analysis of ordinal data with cumulative link models estimation with the R-package ordinal (2015). https://cran.r-project.org/web/packages/ordinal/vignettes/clm_intro.pdf

Automatic Cartoon Face Composition Using Caricature Traits

Tanasai Sucontphunt[✉] and Jaturong Mahaisavariya

Graduate School of Applied Statistics, National Institute of Development
Administration, Bangkok, Thailand
tanasai@as.nida.ac.th

Abstract. We develop a system that can automatically generate a cartoon avatar from a single photograph. This system aims to mimic how artists create a cartoon face with a specific style using a cartoon-face composite application. The cartoon style used in this work was intentionally designed to be very plain and simple in order to bring cuteness to the avatar as well as to add the signature design. This simplicity removes higher details of the face except the prominent features, thus, it causes difficulty in making the cartoon face unique for a human identity. In practice, to make the identity unique for the avatar, artists must match human shapes to their correspondence cartoon shapes from their experience. To mimic this experience, in this work, the mapping operation from human shapes and their cartoon shapes is constructed first. To begin, the training dataset of pairs of a photograph and its artist-created cartoon face is analyzed to capture their patterns. To emphasize more on the facial uniqueness, our "caricature traits" are designed to capture the cartoon style further. Finally, to maintain the cartoon style, our shape search engine will search for the proper cartoon shapes in our pre-fab cartoon libraries. Our evaluation demonstrates that our system can generate a cartoon face for any individual with reasonable similarity comparing to the real artist creation. Cartoon faces from our system are in the form of a 3D model by default. Thus, they can be employed in a variety of applications such as avatars using in games, social network, and virtual reality applications. However, in this work, the main purpose of this application is to 3D-print the model figure of the person.

Keywords: 3D face modeling · Cartoon faces · Avatar creation

1 Introduction

Creating a cartoon face resembling to an individual person requires artistic skills. Many face Creating a cartoon face resembling to an individual person requires a great deal of artistic skills. Many face composite applications such as FACES software [2] allow typical users to create a face by selecting facial components from a shape collection. These applications provide users a list of facial components such as eyes, eyebrows, nose, mouth and face shape to be selected. Thus, it

© Springer International Publishing AG, part of Springer Nature 2018
A. Campilho et al. (Eds.): ICIAR 2018, LNCS 10882, pp. 497–504, 2018.
https://doi.org/10.1007/978-3-319-93000-8_56

is easier for users to just select the target shapes and assembly them by just a few clicks rather than crafting it from scratch. However, selecting the right shapes from the shape collection, provided enough shapes, still requires artistic skills. Normally, users will ask skillful artists to use these applications to compose a face for them. For a cartoon-face composition, artists also require to be familiar with the cartoon style in order to properly choose the right combination of the shapes. Thus, in this work, we make cartoon face composition fully automatic from a single photograph.

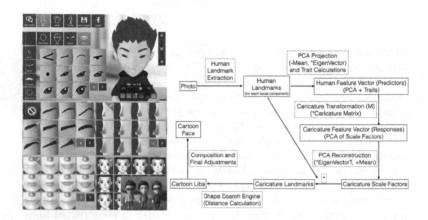

Fig. 1. The cartoon face composition application and its work flow. A user can select proper face component shapes from a variation of 31 eyes, 14 eyebrows, 18 noses, 26 mouths, and 17 faceshapes in the cartoon shape library. Some of the shapes are shown in the picture.

Conceptually, this system should only have a job to search for resembled cartoon shapes from input human shapes. However, cartoon and human shape matching is not a straightforward procedure. Mostly, cartoon shapes contain only some level of abstraction of human shapes. Therefore, input human shapes are required to be transformed to the similar abstraction level as the cartoon shapes. Thus, the abstraction level of the cartoon style need to be defined first. This can be achieved by analyzing the relationship between examples of created cartoon faces and their correspondence human faces. In this work, around 600 pairs of cartoon-human examples are used as a training set. These examples are collected from created cartoon face orders from the MiNOCKIO website [8]. Although this website provides an online cartoon face composite application (Fig. 1) for everyone who wants to order a 3D printed avatar (as shown in the bottom right corner in Fig. 1), however, customers always send a photograph to artists to create a face for them. Thus, all cartoon face examples are created by artists and are carefully picked from orders of which cartoon faces matched the photographs the most. To increase variation, a face is partitioned into five face components (i.e. eyes, eyebrows, nose, mouth, and face shape). Since not all cartoon shapes have real human shape examples, only 10 popular cartoon shapes for each face component are analyzed first. From our observation, a human face shape is transformed to its cartoon face shape by a particular deformation. To simplify this deformation, each human shape is firstly translated, rotated, and scaled so that they are similar to its cartoon shape as much as possible. Finally, only scaling factor for each dimension (x, y, and z separately) is the main factor in the deformation. Hence, scaling factors are extracted from the examples. Furthermore, to add more uniqueness to the cartoon, a caricature technique is employed to exaggerate the scaling factor. The input human face is then first transformed to its cartoon abstraction using these scaling factors. Then, this cartoon abstraction shape is used to search through the cartoon shape library to for resembled cartoon shapes. Finally, refine adjustments e.g. position and rotation of some facial components are made to convey the overall uniqueness of the person.

2   Related Work

This section covers only most recent research works on cartoon and caricature face modeling that are most related to our work. For a survey on caricature modeling before 2010, please refer to Sadimon et al. [9]. Here, we briefly grouped the works to geometric-based and collection-based modeling approaches.

Geometric-Based Modeling: This approach mainly deforms a face with specific rules to create a specific cartoon style with or without a small set of examples. Meng et al. [7] generate a paper-cut style portrait from a photograph using templates created by artists. Clarke et al. [4] use a 2D image example to synthesize a 3D caricature deformation. Sucontphunt [11] combines a human and a cartoon face to generate a cartoon with human identity using PCA-based facial recognition. Xie et al. [5] provide a smart sketching interface that can reshape any drawing to a better face sketch. Selim et al. [10] transfer any painting style to any portrait photograph by using convolutional neural network.

Collection-Based Modeling: This approach analyzes the relationship between human faces and artistic faces from a collection of examples. Normally, this approach requires medium to large set of examples to be analyzed properly. Wang and Tang [12] synthesize a face sketch from photograph and vice versa using Markov Network. Li et al. [6] generates a cartoon face image from a photograph using guidance from a pool of examples. Berger et al. [3] generate portrait sketches with different abstractions by analyzing artist stroke examples. Recently, Zhou et al. [13] generate 3D cartoon face from 3D human face using regression for multiple facial regions.

Our work follows the collection-based modeling approach in order to capture cartoon abstraction. However, none of the previous works in both approaches can generate a cartoon face with exact cartoon shapes in the shape library while maintaining its likeness level to artist creation as in our work.

3 System Overview

Figures 1 and 2 shows work flow and output flow of our system. Considering the choices of facial data for analyzing, we prefer feature-based (e.g. using facial landmarks) over holistic (e.g. using face image) approach because our cartoon-style is created mainly on salient shape rather than overall appearance. From our empirical experiment, analyzing shapes using feature landmarks yields higher precision than using image pixels. Thus, the 59 landmarks designed to capture prominent facial feature points are used in this work. The landmarks are 8 for eye, 8 for eyebrow, 8 for nose, 18 for mouth, and 17 for faceshape as shown in Fig. 2. In this work, we use faceplusplus [1] to extract the landmarks from an input image. After the facial landmarks are extracted from the input image, the landmarks are transformed to create its cartoon abstraction using Cartoon Abstraction Transformation (Sect. 4). Then, the cartoon abstraction landmarks are searched for its proper cartoon shape in the cartoon library collection and composed to the complete cartoon face (Sect. 5). Section 6 shows our results and evaluation.

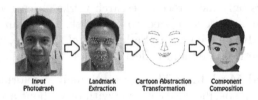

Input Photograph   Landmark Extraction   Cartoon Abstraction Transformation   Component Composition

Fig. 2. Output flow starts from an input photograph; the landmarks are extracted, the cartoon abstraction is created; and the final cartoon face is composed. Noting that the hair style and skin color are pre-selected by a user.

4 Cartoon Abstraction Transformation

Cartoon Abstraction: To capture cartoon abstraction from input human landmarks, the semantic mapping between human landmarks and cartoon landmarks needs to be constructed first. With a medium number of examples as in our work, multivariate regression analysis is used to create this map. Also, since many cartoon shapes still lack of their human shape examples, using regression to predict possible values is ideal. The mapping equation (M) or Caricature Transformation in Fig. 1 is the multivariate linear regression of $M * Predictors = Responeses$. To calculate for M, we need to construct predictors and their responses properly. To prepare predictors, the human landmarks are projected to their orthogonal space using Principle Component Analysis (PCA) calculated from the example set (Human Feature Vector in Fig. 1). This will make all predictors independent to each other. However, constructing the proper responses is not straightforward because there is no direct relationship from human landmarks to cartoon landmarks in term of their positions. In fact, creating a cartoon from a human face requires proper deformations which are scaling factors.

Scaling Factors: From our experiment on classification by using human landmarks as predictors and cartoon library ID as responses, it gave about 2–5% in accuracy. If we grouped the similar libraries together, for example: small-eye and medium-eye and large-eye group, it gave about 10–20% in accuracy. This is because there is no direct relationship between human landmarks and cartoon library or groups of them. In fact, even artists sometimes have difficulty in selecting proper cartoon library. However, each human landmark contains relationship to each cartoon landmark in fine scaling factors. From our observation, the main difference between human landmarks and cartoon landmarks is how they are distributed. The cartoon landmarks, though visually similar to its human counterpart, have significantly different range of distribution. This relationship can be defined as the scaling factor from human landmarks to cartoon landmarks. Thus, the responses are calculated directly from scaling factors of each human landmark and cartoon landmark in each dimension separately (Caricature Feature Vector in Fig. 1). Also, to make the responses independent to each other, they are also projected to their PCA space first. We can then calculate for M with these predictors and responses. Then, we will use M to calculate the customized scaling factors specially for any input human landmarks. However, some facial uniquenesses such as smaller eye or bigger eye could not be captured well with just separated human landmarks. Thus, some semantic informations are added to the predictors in order to create such relationships.

Caricature Traits: In caricature technique, the human face is exaggerated to emphasize its uniqueness toward a specific trait. The uniqueness is mostly defined by artistic aspects rather than landmark positions especially its size (small or big). The size of a component can be defined by area covered by a specific group of landmarks divided by total area of the whole face. It can be also defined by aspect ratio i.e. width/height of the component. These values can be added to the existing predictors to emphasize these traits in the relationship. In this work, artists who designed the cartoon library defined the traits to be area ratio, aspect ratio, and tip area ratio (e.g. tip of the nose area/nose area). Different facial component has some or all of the traits depending on its characteristic.

5 Component Composition

Shape Search Engine: From cartoon abstraction landmarks, our shape search engine will rank the best matched shapes according to their similarity. In this work, we use PCA-based to capture the landmark patterns. Thus, all cartoon landmarks are first projected to their PCA space. Then, the similarity of each cartoon shape is then measured using cosine similarity from the projected cartoon abstraction landmarks. The cosine similarity is used because the difference between cartoon shapes mainly comes from deformation direction rather than distance. After we rank the matched cartoon shapes for each facial component, the best candidates from each face component are then selected and composited into a complete cartoon face.

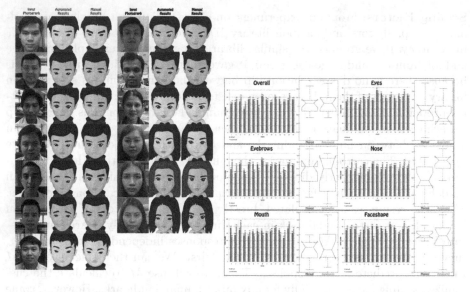

Fig. 3. Total scores of manual (from real artists) and automated creation of 15 faces are shown in bar-chart. The total scores are the summation of rating scores from all participants for each face. The ANOVA results are calculated from an average of rating scores of all the faces for each participant. Example results comparing input photographs, automated cartoon creation from our system, and manual cartoon creation from real artists. Noting that the hair style and skin color are pre-selected by real artists.

Inter-Face-Component Adjustment: After the cartoon shape libraries are selected, they will be placed to their proper positions and orientations. In our cartoon style, the only components that can be adjusted for positions and orientations are eyes and eyebrows. Thus, the example set of eye positions and orientations are trained similar to the Cartoon Abstraction Transformation (Sect. 4). The predictors in this case are PCA of human landmarks plus the traits of distance to chin (for eyes) or distance to eyes (for eyebrows) and their inclined degrees from vertical line. Responses are more straightforward in this case because there are position in height and orientation in degree directly from the example set.

6   Results and Evaluation

Figure 3 shows some of the results generated by our automated system comparing to the results created by real artists. All photographs used in this test set are not used in the training process but they have their cartoon faces created by real artists available to compare. To evaluate our generated results, a user study was conducted by a survey. The survey asks participants (mostly computer science students) to rate the similarity of the photograph to its cartoon face. The rating is starting from 1 (least similar) to 5 (most similar). In each question, participants are asked to rate for similarities of 6 components which are (1) overall face, (2) eyes, (3) eyebrows, (4) nose, (5) mouth, and (6) face-shape separately. There are 15 photograph-cartoon faces to rate in each survey. There are two separate surveys: one is for the results created from our automated system, and, another one is for the results created from real artists. Participants do not know which survey they are rating since the surveys are randomly distributed. Since our work focuses only on creating facial components, other components such as hair style, glasses, facial hair, and cloth are created from real artists and used on both surveys. There are 30 participants (15 for our results and 15 for real artist's results) in our user study. Figure 3 shows the total scores and ANOVA results from the surveys. The results imply that our automated results have similar and, in some cases, even better quality comparing to the results created from real artists.

7 Conclusion

This work imitates a cartoon face creation from artists using face composition. The pre-collected examples created from artists are analyzed in order to capture the relationship between human facial shapes and their cartoon shapes. Our system is initially designed to assist artists in using cartoon face composite application to create a cartoon face for an individual. However, our evaluation indicates that our system can be used to replace tedious manual cartoon creation by artists with similar quality. With regression analysis together with the search engine scheme, even the cartoon shapes those are not in the training set can also be selected if the predicted cartoon shape abstraction going in the same direction. The system developed in this work is now used on a commercial website [8]. On the website, we experimented on new 50 faces and found only 3 cases those required artist intervention. The cartoon-and-human likeness can be significantly improved by (1) having more cartoon shape libraries that covers more variation of shapes and (2) having more human-cartoon example set to be analyzed. With limited cartoon shape variations, several face shapes can only be mapped to the same cartoon shape in many-to-one mapping scheme. Having more examples can also give more option in using other major non-linear algorithms such as multi-layer neural network or deep learning. In order to keep improving our results, we also develop a data collection system to collect input photographs and their adjusted cartoon faces those approved by artists. Also, this work intends to use for Asian faces only but we are now expanding our dataset to cover all ethnicities. This will create a better example training set for constructing a better system. Furthermore, enhanced details can also be added to this automated system such as skin color, hair styles, glasses detection by using similar approach to this work.

References

1. faceplusplus.com
2. Faces. http://www.iqbiometrix.com/
3. Berger, I., Shamir, A., Mahler, M., Carter, E., Hodgins, J.: Style and abstraction in portrait sketching. ACM Trans. Graph. **32**(4), 55:1–55:12 (2013)
4. Clarke, L., Chen, M., Mora, B.: Automatic generation of 3d caricatures based on artistic deformation styles. IEEE Trans. Visual Comput. Graph. **17**(6), 808–821 (2011)
5. Jun, X., Aaron, H., Wilmot, L., Holger, W.: Portraitsketch: face sketching assistance for novices. In: Proceedings of the 27th Annual ACM Symposium on User Interface Software and Technology. ACM (2014)
6. Li, H., Liu, G., Ngan, K.N.: Guided face cartoon synthesis. IEEE Trans. Multimed. **13**(6), 1230–1239 (2011)
7. Meng, M., Zhao, M., Zhu, S.-S.: Artistic paper-cut of human portraits. In: Proceedings of the 18th ACM International Conference on Multimedia, MM 2010, pp. 931–934. ACM, New York (2010)
8. MiNOCKIO. Minockio.com
9. Sadimon, S.B., Sunar, M.S., Mohamad, D., Haron, H.: Computer generated caricature: a survey. In: 2010 International Conference on Cyberworlds, pp. 383–390, October 2010
10. Selim, A., Elgharib, M., Doyle, L.: Painting style transfer for head portraits using convolutional neural networks. ACM Trans. Graph. **35**(4), 129:1–129:18 (2016)
11. Sucontphunt, T.: 3D artistic face transformation with identity preservation. In: Christie, M., Li, T.-Y. (eds.) SG 2014. LNCS, vol. 8698, pp. 154–165. Springer, Cham (2014). https://doi.org/10.1007/978-3-319-11650-1_14
12. Wang, X., Tang, X.: Face photo-sketch synthesis and recognition. IEEE Trans. Pattern Anal. Mach. Intell. **31**(11), 1955–1967 (2009)
13. Zhou, J., Tong, X., Liu, Z., Guo, B.: 3d cartoon face generation by local deformation mapping. Visual Comput. **32**(6), 717–727 (2016)

Automatic Text Extraction from Arabic Newspapers

Nikos Vasilopoulos[1(✉)], Yazan Wasfi[2], and Ergina Kavallieratou[1]

[1] University of the Aegean, Karlovasi, 83200 Samos, Greece
nvasilopoulos@aegean.gr
[2] Media Observer, Caracas Complex, Yajouz St 8, Amman, Jordan

Abstract. A system for extracting the textual information from document images with complex layouts is presented. It is based on both layout analysis and text localization techniques. Layout analysis is first applied to segment the page in text and non-text blocks and then text localization is used to detect text that may be embedded inside images, charts, diagrams, tables etc. Detailed experiments on scanned Arabic newspapers showed that combining layout analysis and text localization methods can lead to improved page segmentation and text extraction results.

Keywords: Layout analysis · Page segmentation · Text localization
Text extraction

1 Introduction

Although layout analysis methods achieve to extract the main text blocks of a document image, they often fail to detect text that may be contained in non-text components like photos, graphs, banners etc. This information is sometimes useful and should rather be extracted as well. Layout analysis can thus be followed by a text localization technique to detect text included inside non-text regions.

A combination of a layout analysis [1] and a text localization [2] method for extracting all the textual information from document images is presented. It is inspired by the background analysis methods of Baird et al. [3] and Breuel [4]. They both use geometric models and data structures to computationally find all the white rectangular covers, while in this paper the morphological opening transform is applied to the binary image considering only tall and long rectangles. This way, the major line and column blank spaces are correctly detected even in pages with very small or very large inter-block gaps. To overcome the limitation to Manhattan layouts, a foreground analysis task is added. This is inspired by the multiresolution morphology methods of Bloomberg [5] and Bukhari et al. [6]. Instead of sub-sampling the input image however, structuring elements of different sizes are automatically adjusted to the font size of the main text of the document. The exact size is calculated before segmentation, therefore no a priori knowledge is needed. The text localization algorithm that is presented in this work is based on edge detection. It differentiates from previous methods [7] particularly for combining contour tracing, mathematical morphology and a set of criteria based on spatial and geometrical features of the connected components in order to filter out non-text regions. The algorithm is evaluated on a dataset that contains Arabic newspapers. A sample page is shown in Fig. 1.

A. Campilho et al. (Eds.): ICIAR 2018, LNCS 10882, pp. 505–510, 2018.
https://doi.org/10.1007/978-3-319-93000-8_57

Fig. 1. An Arabic newspaper frontpage with a complex layout (left). Layout analysis and text localization results (right).

2   The Proposed System

2.1   Layout Analysis

Background Analysis. The image is first transformed to grayscale and then binarized. Otsu's algorithm is used for thresholding. The background is processed in order to localize long white columns and rows. The binarized image is morphologically opened with two structuring elements: a horizontal line and a vertical line. The length of the first one is equal to half the image width while the length of the second one is equal to

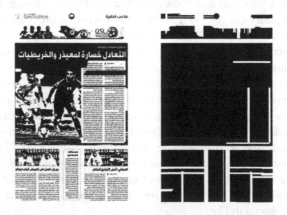

Fig. 2. The binarized image of Fig. 1 (left), morphologically opened with long lines (right).

a quarter of the image height. A separators mask is created, containing all the column and row separators of the document (Fig. 2).

Foreground Analysis. The foreground analysis (Fig. 3) is applied to the inverted image, so that foreground pixels are white while the background is now black. The border-following algorithm [8] is applied to the image and the external contours of all the connected components are detected. The contours are used to determine the size of the main body of small text characters (x-height). That is the distance between the baseline and the mean-line of the lower-case letters. The contours of the connected components are filled before proceeding to the next step, to better distinguish between the small text and the large text regions. The minimum size of the bounding box will be the value of the filling color. The result is a grayscale image, showing small text in dark gray and bigger text and images in lighter color. The grayscale image containing the filled contours is dilated by a square structuring element. The size of the structuring element is equal to one third of the main body height, selected by experimental trial. This way the small letters are connected and form text blocks, while the larger letters are not fully connected yet. One more dilation is required, to cover the remaining space between the larger letters and image parts. The size of the square structuring element is now equal to half the main body height. This way large letters and image parts are also connected and form blocks. To split merged regions and improve segmentation results the logical AND is applied to the dilated image and the invert separator mask of Fig. 2. Long horizontal blocks are considered as titles while the rest of the bright blocks are considered as images. Very large blocks, classified as images, are further being processed by the text localization algorithm so that embedded text can also be extracted.

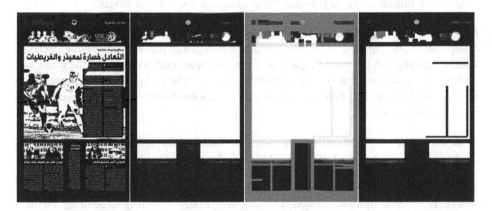

Fig. 3. Result of the first and the second dilation of the foreground. The separators mask is used to split merged regions after the second dilation. (Color figure online)

2.2 Text Localization

Edge Detection. The Canny operator is performed and the edges are detected (Fig. 4). To preserve the sharp and clean strokes of the characters, neither histogram equalization nor Gaussian smoothing are applied to the image. Both thresholds of the operator are set to the maximum value, so that only the stronger edges are selected.

Fig. 4. The results of Canny edge detection of the large frame in Fig. 1 (left) and morphological closing with dashes (right).

Contour Tracing. The border-following algorithm [8] is used to extract the contours of all the connected components. For each contour, the following spatial and geometrical values are calculated: (i) the position of the four vertices of the contour's bounding rectangle, (ii) the orientation of the minimum area rectangle enclosing the component, (iii) the gaps between the contour and its closest left and right neighbors and (iv) the x-height (the minimum value between the component's width and height).

Size and Position Filtering. Before proceeding further, the very small and very large components are removed. Next, the spatial information of the remaining components is used to distinguish between aligned (at least one more component is at the same line and has the same orientation) and non-aligned ones. The components are supposed to be aligned if either their bottom or their top vertices are collinear. Non-aligned components are removed.

Contour Filling. The aligned components are filled according to their x-height values, so that small ones have a dark gray color while large ones are brighter.

Morphological Closing. In order to group adjacent characters into text strings, the image is morphologically closed. Closing is a dilation with a structuring element followed by an erosion with the same element. The element that is used is a short dash of width equal to the mean gap between neighboring connected components. The result is an image that contains merged components that can be either text or non-text (Fig. 4).

Non-text Regions Filtering. The candidate regions can be classified as either text or non-text assuming that adjacent characters belonging to the same word have similar sizes, similar stroke widths and regular distances between each other. Removing the non-text regions leaves the uniform and robust regions in the image that are supposed to include only text. The outlines of the minimum area rectangles of the text regions are drawn over the grayscale input image (Fig. 1).

3   Experimental Results

A dataset of 74 scanned pages from different newspapers in Arabic, provided by Media Observer (www.mediaobserver-me.com), has been used for the experiments. To train the system, 4 images of the dataset have been selected. All the predefined parameters (e.g. the sizes of the structuring elements and the classification criteria), described in the previous sections, have been fine-tuned according to the training data.

The algorithm has been coded in C# language. The morphological operations, the contour tracing function, the Otsu thresholding and the Canny method implementations of the OpenCV library have been applied. To improve speed, both training and evaluation input images were linearly resized to 50% of their initial dimensions.

Table 1 shows precision and recall results for the proposed layout analysis (LA) algorithm as well as the unified layout analysis and text localization (LA & TL) system. The ground truth of a text block (title, paragraph etc.) is the bounding polygon of the block, while the ground truth of embedded text (in photos, graphs, diagrams etc.) is the bounding rectangle of the corresponding word or text line. A result region is considered as correct if it completely overlaps only one ground truth region. Errors that do not violate the reading order (like merging text columns of the same article) are allowed. The area of either a ground truth or a result region is the total number of the included foreground pixels. Precision is then calculated as the area of the correct result regions divided by the area of all the result regions, while recall is calculated as the area of the correct result regions divided by the area of all the ground truth regions.

Table 1. Results.

System setup	Precision	Recall
LA only	90.4%	51.8%
LA & TL	88.1%	76.3%

The results have shown that text localization significantly improves recall. The layout analysis algorithm seems to produce very few false positive results compared to the text localization method, therefore precision is higher when only the layout analysis step is performed.

Although the experiments proved that the algorithm performs well even with low quality document images, a few limitations have been identified. The proposed layout analysis method assumes there is always a gap between components of different classes. In case there are either overlapping or collided regions it usually fails. It can also hardly discriminate between large characters and small photos. Since the criteria are the size and shape of the components, quite large letters and numbers can sometimes be classified as graphics. As for the text localization method, it will fail to extract partially occluded words or characters. It should also be noted that the proposed method can process linear text but not curved text.

4 Conclusion

In this paper, a mixed layout analysis and text localization method has been presented. Evaluated on images of Arabic newspapers, the system achieved promising results. The text localization part of the algorithm performs very well in regions where the layout analysis fails. On the other hand, the layout analysis part can extract the major text and non-text blocks of the image much faster, keeping the mean processing time low.

References

1. Vasilopoulos, N., Kavallieratou, E.: Complex layout analysis based on contour classification and morphological operations. Eng. Appl. Artif. Intell. **65**, 220–229 (2017)
2. Vasilopoulos, N., Kavallieratou, E.: Unified layout analysis and text localization framework. J. Electron. Imaging **26**(1), 013009 (2017)
3. Baird, H.S., Jones, S.E., Fortune, S.J.: Image segmentation by shape-directed covers. In: Proceedings of the 10th International Conference on Pattern Recognition, 1990, vol. 1, pp. 820–825. IEEE (1990)
4. Breuel, T.M.: Two geometric algorithms for layout analysis. In: Lopresti, D., Hu, J., Kashi, R. (eds.) DAS 2002. LNCS, vol. 2423, pp. 188–199. Springer, Heidelberg (2002). https://doi.org/10.1007/3-540-45869-7_23
5. Bloomberg, D.S.: Multiresolution morphological approach to document image analysis. In: Proceedings of the International Conference on Document Analysis and Recognition, Saint-Malo, France (1991)
6. Bukhari, S.S., Shafait, F., Breuel, T.M.: Improved document image segmentation algorithm using multiresolution morphology. In: IS&T/SPIE Electronic Imaging, pp. 78740D–78740D–8. International Society for Optics and Photonics (2011)
7. Karatzas, D., Gomez-Bigorda, L., Nicolaou, A., et al.: ICDAR 2015 competition on robust reading. In: 2015 13th International Conference on Document Analysis and Recognition (ICDAR), pp. 1156–1160. IEEE (2015)
8. Suzuki, S., et al.: Topological structural analysis of digitized binary images by border following. Comput. Vis. Graph. Image Process. **30**(1), 32–46 (1985)

Biomedical Image Analysis

Multi-scale Fully Convolutional DenseNets for Automated Skin Lesion Segmentation in Dermoscopy Images

Guodong Zeng and Guoyan Zheng[(✉)]

Institute for Surgical Technology and Biomechanics,
University of Bern, Bern, Switzerland
guoyan.zheng@istb.unibe.ch

Abstract. This paper addresses the problem of automated skin lesion segmentation in dermoscopy images. We propose a novel Multi-Scale Fully Convolutional DenseNets (MSFCDN) for skin lesion segmentation. The MSFCDN adopts fully convolutional architecture, which after training, can perform semantic segmentation of an image with arbitrary size. We conduct extensive experiments on ISBI 2017 "Skin Lesion Analysis Towards Melanoma Detection" Challenge dataset. Our method achieves an average Dice coefficient of 86.9% and an average accuracy of 95.3% for skin lesion segmentation.

Keywords: Deep learning · Skin lesion segmentation
Dense convolutional networks

1 Introduction

The importance of early diagnosis of melanoma should not be under-estimated as melanoma can be cured with a simple excision if detected early. Significant efforts have been dedicated to the development of computerized image analysis techniques for automated recognition of melanomas from dermoscopy images, which is usually solved with a two-stage approach consisting of a segmentation stage and a classification stage [1]. These two stages can be done jointly or separately. More specifically, the segmentation aims to partition an image into skin lesion regions and background, and is often the first step in an automated recognition of melanoma from dermoscopy images, while the classification handles the problem distinguishing melanomas from non-melanoma skin lesions.

For skin lesion segmentation, there exist both semi-automatic methods and fully automatic methods [2]. These methods can be roughly classified as low-level image processing-based methods [3,4], active contour-based methods [5] and supervised learning-based methods [6]. With the advance of deep learning techniques [7–10], many researchers have proposed deep learning based methods for automated melanoma recognition in dermoscopy images that can learn the features that optimally represent the data. For example, Codella et al. [11]

© Springer International Publishing AG, part of Springer Nature 2018
A. Campilho et al. (Eds.): ICIAR 2018, LNCS 10882, pp. 513–521, 2018.
https://doi.org/10.1007/978-3-319-93000-8_58

proposed to integrate transfer feature learning from the domain of natural photographs, sparse coding-based unsupervised feature learning and Support Vector Machine (SVM) for melanoma recognition. Kawahara et al. [12] proposed a multi-resolution-tract convolutional neural network (CNN) architecture for skin lesion classification, which was designed to learn based on information from multiple image resolutions while leveraging pretrained CNNs. More recently, two different studies [13,14] emphasized the importance of the network depth as a major factor of model expressiveness. Though dermatologist-level classification results were reported [14], the problem with very deep networks lies in that these networks usually generate a large number of feature maps in each layer and they have plenty of parameters to be tuned.

In this paper, we propose a deep learning based method to automatically segment skin lesion in dermoscopy images. In order to overcome the challenge in training very deep neural networks (more than 50 layers), we employ DenseNets that was originally introduced in [15] for effective and accurate skin lesion segmentation. More specifically, we propose a novel Multi-Scale Fully Convolutional DenseNets (MSFCDN). The MSFCDN adopts fully convolutional architecture, which after training, can perform semantic segmentation of an image with arbitrary size. To further improve the gradient flow within the network and to further stabilize the learning process, we incorporate multi-scale branch paths. Experimental results demonstrate the performance improvement of the proposed method.

2   Method

In this section, the proposed method for automatic skin lesion segmentation will be described. We will first briefly review the background and the basics of DenseNets, followed by the detailed description of the proposed multi-scale deeply supervised fully convolutional DenseNets.

2.1   Background of DenseNets

Suppose a neural network consisting L layers, and x_l is the output of each layer l. H_l is a non-linear transformation on layer l, and usually composites of several functional operations such as batch normalization [17], rectified linear unit (ReLU) [18], pooling [19], and convolution.

In a standard convolutional neural network, each layer x_l only connects with its previous layer x_{l-1}.

$$x_l = H_l(x_{l-1}) \tag{1}$$

To facilitate the training of deep neural networks, ResNets [10] employs a skip-connection between the identity mapping of the input x_{l-1} and the output $H_l(x_{l-1})$.

$$x_l = H_l(x_{l-1}) + x_{l-1} \tag{2}$$

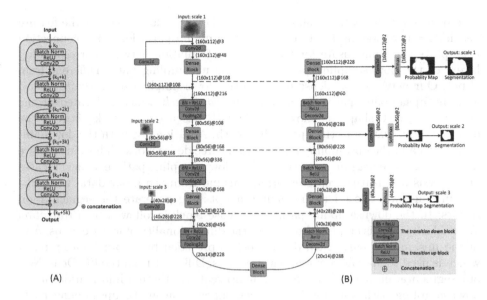

Fig. 1. (A) A schematic view of the design of one dense block; and (B) A schematic view of the proposed Multi-scale Fully Convolutional DenseNets (MSFCDN). The network consists of a downsampling path, a *bottleneck*, and an upsampling path. Dense blocks are used in the downsampling path, the *bottleneck*, and the upsampling path. The digits in the figure take a format as "feature width × feature height@the number of feature maps". See text for detailed description.

where skip-connection in residual blocks help to back-propagate gradients to previous layer in the phase of training. To further improve the gradient flow, DenseNets [15] adopt a more complicated connectivity in each dense block.

$$x_l = H_l(x_{l-1}, x_{l-2}, ...x_0) \tag{3}$$

where the current layer receives feature maps of all preceding layers $x_{l-1}, ..., x_0$ as input. During training, the dense connection improve the direct information flow to all proceeding layers. Figure 1-(A) illustrates the architecture of a dense block. In a dense block, the output of each layer is concatenated with all preceding layers. The output dimension of each layer in a dense block has k feature maps where k is regarded as the growth rate parameter of the dense block. As it can be seen in Fig. 1-(A), the number of feature maps grows lineally with the depth l of the dense block. Specifically, the number of feature maps after l layers is $k_0 + l \times k$, where k_0 is the number of input feature maps.

2.2   Skin Lesion Segmentation

Network Design. Our segmentation network is inspired by the Fully Convolutional DenseNets (FC-DenseNet) as introduced in [16], which takes advantage of both the U-net like architecture [9] and the dense convolutional network [15]. Similar to U-net [9], our network consists of a downsamping path, a *bottleneck* and an upsampling path, as shown in Fig. 1-(B). In order to recover the feature lost induced by pooling layers in the downsampling path, long skip connection is employed to compensate for fine-grained information between corresponding layers of the downsampling path and of the upsampling path. Different from U-net, Our network uses dense blocks in the downsampling path, the *bottlenek*, and the upsampling path. Specifically, the *bottleneck*, which is located at the bottom of the U-shape as shown in Fig. 1-(B), is a dense block between the downsampling path and the upsampling path. Additionally, both the downsampling path and the upsampling path contain three dense blocks. Thus, in total we use seven dense blocks in our network. The downsampling path (encoder) focuses on analysis and feature representation learning from the input data, while the upsampling path (decoder) are mainly adopted to generate the segmentation results. In the downsampling path, each dense block is followed by a *transition down* block which is employed to reduce the dimensionality of feature maps. And in the upsampling path, each dense block is preceded by a *transition up* block which is used to upscale previous feature maps. Different from the FC-DenseNet, our segmentation network introduces multi-scale contextual information in the downsampling path and multi-scale deep supervision in the upsampling path, respectively. By doing this, we enjoy two advantages in network training: the incorporation of multi-scale contextual information in the downsampling path is designed to enhance the feature representation learning in the forward process while the multi-scale deep supervision in the upsampling path can enable more efficient information flow in back propagation process during training.

For each dense block, it consists five convolutional layers with a growth rate of 12. Each *transition down* block consists of a batch normalization layer, a ReLU layer, a convolutional layer and a pooling layer while each *transition up* block contains a batch normalization layer, a ReLU layer and a deconvolutional layer.

It has been shown that small convolutional kernels are more beneficial for training and performance [20]. In our deeply supervised network, all convolutional layers in the dense block use kernel size of 3×3 and strides of 1 and all max pooling layers use kernel size of 2×2 and strides of 2. The convolutional layers in the *transition down* block use kernel size of 1×1 while the deconvolutional layers in the *transition up* block use kernel size of 3×3. In the dense blocks, the *transition down* blocks and the *transition up* blocks, batch normalization and rectified linear unit are adopted to speed up the training and to enhance the gradient back propagation.

Integration of Multi-Scale Contextual Information. In order to further improve feature learning in the downsampling path, multi-scale contextual information is incorporated. Specifically, whenever the output of a dense block is fed into the *transition down* block in the downsampling path, it will be concatenated with the contextual information of the same size, which was obtained by applying convolutional operations to the corresponding down-scaled input image. In Fig. 1-(B), we incorporate context information of three different scales (i.e., Input:scale1, Input:scale2 and Input:scale3 in Fig. 1-(B)). The lower the resolution of the context information is, the bigger the number of the feature maps used as the context information.

Multi-scale Deep Supervision. Training deep neural networks is challenging. As the matter of gradient vanishing, final loss cannot be efficiently back propagated to shallow layers, which is more difficult for DenseNets with more layers than normal neural networks. To address this issue, in addition to the main classifier (i.e., Output:scale 1 in Fig. 1-(B), we inject two down-scaled branch classifiers into our segmentation network (i.e., Output:scale 2 and Output:scale 3 in Fig. 1-(B)). By doing this, segmentation is performed at multiple output layers in different scales. For the classifier at the coarse scale (Output:scale 3) which is closer to the downsampling path, it generates segmentation results with the coarsest resolution, while the classifiers at the middle (Output:scale 2) and the fine (Output:scale 1) scales generate segmentation results with the intermediate and the finest resolutions, respectively. As a result, classifiers in different scales can take advantage of multi-scale context. Furthermore, with the loss calculated by the prediction from classifiers at different scales, more effective gradient back propagation can be achieved by direct supervision on the hidden layers.

Let W be the weights of main network and $w = \{w^0, w^1, \dots w^{M-1}\}$ be the weights of classifiers at different scales, where M is the number of classifier branches. For the training samples $S = (X, Y)$, where X represents training images and Y represents the class labels while $Y \in \{0, 1\}$.

$$L_{cls}(X, Y; W, w) = \sum_{m=0}^{M-1} \sum_{(x_i, y_i) \in S^m} \alpha_m l^m (x_i, y_i | W, w^m) \qquad (4)$$

where $S = \{S^0, S^1, \dots S^{M-1}\}$; S^0 is a training image while S^m contains the examples (x_i, y_i) at scale of $m > 0$, which is obtained by downsampling S^0 by a factor of 2^m along each dimension; w^m is the weights of the classifier at scale of m; α_m is the weight of l^m, which is the loss calculated by a training sample x_i, y_i at scale of m.

$$l^m(x_i, y_i | W, w^m) = -\log p(y_i = t(x_i) | x_i; W, w^m)) \qquad (5)$$

where $p(y_i = t(x_i) | x_i; W, w^m)$ is the probability of predicted class label $t(x_i)$ corresponding to sample $x_i \in S^m$.

The total loss of our multi-scaled deeply supervised model will be:

$$L(X, Y; W, w) = L_{cls}(X, Y; W, w) + \lambda(\psi(W) + \sum_m \psi(w^m)) \qquad (6)$$

where $\psi()$ is the regularization term (L_2 norm in our experiment) with hyper parameter λ.

Training and Testing. In the phase of training, images and ground truth are resized into 160×112. Data augmentation is used to enlarge the training samples by clockwise rotation of $(90, 180)$ degrees and flipped horizontally for each image. Before training, all weights were initialized from Gaussian distribution

($\mu = 0, \sigma = 0.01$). Each time, the model was trained for 10,000 iterations and the weights were updated by the stochastic gradient descent (SGD) algorithm (momentum = 0.9, weight decay = 0.005). The initial learning rate was 1×10^{-3} and halved by 3000 every training iterations. The hyper parameters were chosen as follows: $\lambda = 0.005$, $\alpha_0 = 1.0$, $\alpha_1 = 0.67$, and $\alpha_2 = 0.33$.

In the phase of testing, we first downscale the input test image into 160×112 and feed it to the trained network to get prediction probability maps. After that, we get initial segmentation result and upscale it to the original size of the input test image. Finally, we conduct morphological operations to remove isolated small regions and internal holes.

3 Experimental Results

We evaluated our method on ISBI 2017 "Skin Lesion Analysis Towards Melanoma Detection" Challenge dataset [21][1]. As the submission of test dataset results is not possible at this moment and the ground truth of test dataset is not released, we only evaluate the proposed method on the training dataset, which consists of 2000 images. In this paper, we conducted a 4-fold cross-validation study to evaluate the performance of the present method. More specifically, the 2000 images were randomly partitioned into 4 equal size subsamples (each subsample has 500 images). Of the 4 subsamples, each time a single subsample (500 images) was used as the test data while the remaining 3 subsamples (the rest 1500 images) were used as training data. This process was repeated 4 folds, with each one of the 4 subsamples used exactly once as the test data. Sensitivity (SE), specificity (SP), accuracy (AC), Jaccard index (JA) and Dice coefficient (DI) are adopted as evaluation criteria for the skin lesion segmentation.

Quantitative Results. To demonstrate the capability of the proposed MSFCDN, we conduct a comparison experiment between U-Net [9], FC-DenseNets [16] and the proposed MSFCDN. Table 1 shows segmentation results obtained by these three neural networks. From the results, it is clear that FC-DenseNets performs better than U-Net in four metrics (AC, DI, JA, SE) except SP, while the proposed MSFCDN achieves better performance than FC-DenseNets in four metrics (AC, DI, JA, SP) except SE. The quantitative comparison results demonstrate the efficacy of the proposed MSFCDN for skin lesion segmentation task. When implemented with Python using TensorFlow framework, our network took about 1.2 s on average to process one test image.

Qualitative Results. Figure 2 shows qualitative comparison of these three networks (U-Net, FC-DenseNets, MSFCDN). From left to right, the difficulty of skin lesion segmentation task increases. For the easy case shown in Fig. 2(a), all methods achieve good results. For the case with medium difficulty as shown in Fig. 2(b), U-Net achieves the poorest result while FC-DenseNets and MSFCDN achieve relatively good results. For the cases with hard difficulty and very hard difficulty as shown in Fig. 2(c) and (d), respectively, the performance of all three

---

[1] https://challenge.kitware.com/#challenge/583f126bcad3a51cc66c8d9a.

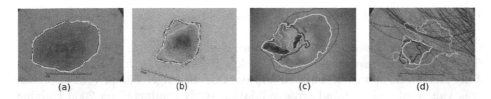

(a)   (b)   (c)   (d)

Fig. 2. Qualitative Comparison of U-Net, FC-DenseNets and MSFCDN. Red contours indicate ground truth of the skin lesion borders, while green, blue and yellow contours represent segmentation generated by U-Net, FC-DenseNets and MSFCDN, respectively. (Color fig online)

Table 1. Comparison of the performance of three different networks for skin lesion segmentaiton task. In each column, the best performance is highlighted with bold font.

	AC	DI	JA	SE	SP
U-Net	0.947	0.853	0.767	0.888	**0.967**
FC-DenseNets	0.948	0.857	0.770	**0.903**	0.960
MSFCDN	**0.953**	**0.869**	**0.785**	0.901	**0.967**

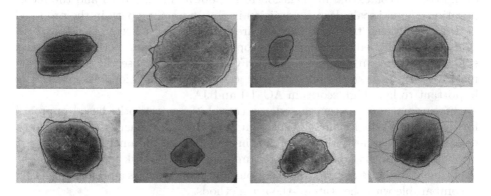

Fig. 3. Randomly selected examples of skin lesion segmentation results. The first and second rows list cases with non-melanoma and melanoma lesions, respectively. The red and blue contours represent the ground truth and the results generated by MSFCDN, respectively. (Color figure online)

methods gets worse but it still can be observed that the proposed MSFCDN achieves much better segmentation than the other two networks.

Figure 3 shows several randomly selected segmentation examples on images containing non-melanoma lesions (the top row) and melanoma lesions (the bottom row). For all the cases, the proposed MSFCDN achieves satisfactory results which are accurate enough to be used to crop the skin lesions out from the input images for further classification task.

4   Discussions and Conclusions

Automated skin lesion segmentation in dermoscopy images is a challenging task. The goal of the present study is to develop and validate a deep learning based, fully automatic approach that can address this challenge. The present approach was validated with a 4-fold cross validation study conducted on 2000 training images of the ISBI 2017 "Skin Lesion Analysis Towards Melanoma Detection" Challenge. The experimental results demonstrated that the present approach was able to accurately segment the skin lesions in dermoscopy images.

The performance of the proposed skin lesion segmentation method is compared with other methods with a similar network architecture [9,16]. The comparison results are presented in Table 1. In comparison with U-net [9], which is one of the most popular fully convolutional networks (FCN) used in medical image analysis [22], both FC-DenseNets [16] and the proposed segmentation method achieved better results in terms of AC, DI, JA and SE. We attribute the better performance to the incorporation of dense blocks. When compared with FC-DenseNets [16], the proposed method achieved better performance in terms of AC, DI, JA and SP. This probably can be explained by the integration of multi-scale contextual information in the downsampling path and the incorporation of multi-scale deep supervision in the upsampling path in the proposed network. By doing this, a better feature learning and a better back propagation can be achieved. Although the proposed segmentation method achieved a slightly worse SE in comparison with FC-DenseNets, to use the segmentation mask to crop the skin lesion region for the later classification task, it is more important to have high scores in AC, DI and JA.

In summary, we presented a dense convolutional networks based approach for automated skin lesion segmentation in dermoscopy images. The proposed dense convolution networks have following advantages: parameter efficiency and implicit deep supervision, which are important for the task at our hand. The experimental results demonstrate that our approach achieves a performance that is comparable with the state-of-the-art methods.

References

1. Mishra, N.K., Celebi, M.E.: An overview of melanoma detection in dermoscopy images using image processing and machine learning. arXiv:1601.07843, 15 p. (2016)
2. Celebi, E.M., et al.: A state-of-the-art survey on lesion border detection in dermoscopy images. In: Dermoscopy Image Analysis, pp. 97–129 (2015)
3. Peruch, F., et al.: Simpler, faster, more accurate melanocytic lesion segmentation through MEDS. IEEE Trans. Biomed. Eng. **61**(2), 557–565 (2014)
4. Abbas, Q., et al.: Unified approach for lesion border detection based on mixture modeling and local entropy thresholding. Skin Res. Technol. **19**(3), 314–319 (2013)
5. Mete, M., Sirakov, N.M.: Lesion detection in dermoscopy images with novel density-based and active contour approaches. BMC Bioinform. **11**(Suppl. 6), s23 (2010)

6. Sadri, A.R., et al.: Segmentation of dermoscopy images using wavelet networks. IEEE Trans. Biomed. Eng. **60**(4), 1134–1141 (2013)
7. Simonyan, K., Zisserman, A.: Very deep convolutional networks for large-scale image recognition. arXiv:1409.1556 (2014)
8. Long, J., Shelhamer, E., Darrell, T.: Fully convolutional networks for semantic segmentation. In: CVPR 2015, pp. 3431–3440 (2015)
9. Ronneberger, O., Fischer, P., Brox, T.: U-Net: convolutional networks for biomedical image segmentation. In: Navab, N., Hornegger, J., Wells, W.M., Frangi, A.F. (eds.) MICCAI 2015. LNCS, vol. 9351, pp. 234–241. Springer, Cham (2015). https://doi.org/10.1007/978-3-319-24574-4_28
10. He, K., et al.: Deep residual learning for image recognition. In: CVPR 2016, pp. 770–778 (2016)
11. Codella, N., Cai, J., Abedini, M., Garnavi, R., Halpern, A., Smith, J.R.: Deep learning, sparse coding, and SVM for melanoma recognition in dermoscopy images. In: Zhou, L., Wang, L., Wang, Q., Shi, Y. (eds.) MLMI 2015. LNCS, vol. 9352, pp. 118–126. Springer, Cham (2015). https://doi.org/10.1007/978-3-319-24888-2_15
12. Kawahara, J., Hamarneh, G.: Multi-resolution-tract CNN with hybrid pretrained and skin-lesion trained layers. In: Wang, L., Adeli, E., Wang, Q., Shi, Y., Suk, H.-I. (eds.) MLMI 2016. LNCS, vol. 10019, pp. 164–171. Springer, Cham (2016). https://doi.org/10.1007/978-3-319-47157-0_20
13. Yu, L., et al.: Automated melanoma recognition in dermoscopy images via very deep residual networks. IEEE Trans. Med. Imaging **36**(4), 994–1004 (2017)
14. Esteva, A., et al.: Dermatologist-level classification of skin cancer with deep neural network. Nature **542**(7639), 115–118 (2017)
15. Huang, G., et al.: Densely connected convolutional networks. In: CVPR 2017, pp. 4700–4708 (2017)
16. Jegou, S., et al.: The One Hundred Layers Tiramisu: Fully Convolutional DenseNets for Semantic Segmentation. arXiv:1611.09326 (2016)
17. Ioffe, S., Szegedy, C.: Batch normalization: accelerating deep network training by reducing internal covariate shift. In: ICML 2015, pp. 448–456 (2015)
18. Glorot, X., Bordes, A., Bengio, Y.: Deep sparse rectifier neural networks. In: Proceedings of the Fourteenth International Conference on Artificial Intelligence and Statistics, PMLR 15, pp. 315–323 (2011)
19. LeCun, Y., et al.: Gradient-based learning applied to document recognition. Proc. IEEE **86**(11), 2278–2324 (1998)
20. Szegedy, G., et al.: Going deeper with convolutions, arXiv:1409.4842 (2014)
21. Codella, N., Gutman, D., Celebi, M.E., et al.: Skin Lesion Analysis Toward Melanoma Detection: A Challenge at the 2017 International Symposium on Biomedical Imaging (ISBI), Hosted by the International Skin Imaging Collaboration (ISIC), arXiv:1710.05006 (2017)
22. Litjens, G., et al.: A survey on deep learning in medical image analysis. Med. Image Anal. **42**, 60–88 (2017)

Transfer Learning of Spectrogram Image for Automatic Sleep Stage Classification

Ali Abdollahi Gharbali[1,2(✉)], Shirin Najdi[1,2], and José Manuel Fonseca[1,2]

[1] CTS, Uninova, 2829-516 Caparica, Portugal
[2] Faculdade de Ciências e Tecnologia, Universidade Nova de Lisboa Campus da Caparica,
Quinta da Torre, 2829-516 Monte de Caparica, Portugal
{a.gharbali,s.najdi}@campus.fct.unl.pt, jmrf@fct.unl.pt

Abstract. Most of the existing methods for automatic sleep stage classification are relying on hand-crafted features. In this paper, the goal is to develop a deep learning-based method that automatically exploits time-frequency spectrum of Electroencephalogram (EEG) signal, removing the need for manual feature extraction. Using Continuous Wavelet Transform (CWT), we extracted the time-frequency spectrogram for EEG signal of 10 healthy subjects and converted to RGB images. The images were classified using transfer learning of a pre-trained Convolutional Neural Network (CNN), AlexNet. The proposed method was evaluated using a publicly available dataset. Evaluation results show that our method can achieve state of the art accuracy, while having higher overall sensitivity.

Keywords: Sleep stage classification · Spectrogram · Deep learning
Transfer learning · Convolutional Neural Network
Discrete Wavelet Transform

1   Introduction

Sleep studies support doctors in diagnosing sleep disorders such as insomnia, narcolepsy or sleep apnea and set the starting point for proper follow up. sleep stages are commonly assessed using the physiological criteria based on Electroencephalogram (EEG), Electro-oculogram (EOG), Electromyogram (EMG), heart rate, snoring, and respiration. Holland, Dement, and Raynal in 1974, proposed the term Polysomnography (PSG) for describing the recording, analysis and interpretation of multiple, simultaneous physiologic parameters recorded during sleep. According to American Academy of Sleep Medicine (AASM) [1], sleep is divided in two main stages, Non-Rapid Eye Movement stage (NREM) which by itself includes three stages: N1, N2, and N3 and Rapid-Eye Movement stage (REM). Wakefulness is also included in analysis as the fifth stage. In the manual process of sleep scoring each 30 s of PSG signals, called an epoch, is associated with one of five sleep stages. This process is tedious, subjective and costly. Therefore, over the last years, extensive research efforts have been taken to purse for an automatic sleep stage classification based on machine learning techniques. Most of the existing work rely on the hand-crafted features that require prior knowledge of the domain expert [2, 3]. Additionally, these systems are strongly dependent to available labeled data. Recently, deep learning method have been used in sleep stage classification

© Springer International Publishing AG, part of Springer Nature 2018
A. Campilho et al. (Eds.): ICIAR 2018, LNCS 10882, pp. 522–528, 2018.
https://doi.org/10.1007/978-3-319-93000-8_59

systems, trying to enhance the performance of feature extraction and classification steps. Inspired by the ability of deep networks, this work proposes a method for classification of spectrogram images, extracted from each epoch of sleep EEG, using a pre-trained Convolutional Neural Network, called AlexNet.

This paper is organized as follows. Section 2 gives a brief overview of how sleep stage classification using deep learning methods is treated in the literature. Section 3 provides detailed description of the proposed algorithm. In Sect. 4, the process of performance evaluation is described. In Sect. 5, the evaluation results are presented and discussed. Section 6 finalizes the paper with conclusions and future directions.

2 Related Works

One of the first deep learning-based sleep scoring systems was proposed by Längkvist et al. [5]. In this paper, the focus was to extract meaningful feature representations from unlabeled PSG recordings. Three different setups for sleep stage classification were implemented. Comparison results showed that the best accuracy was achieved by Deep Belief Network (DBN)-based feature extraction followed by Gaussian Mixture Model (GMM). DBNs once again were used in [4], in which, sparse DBN extracted the features from raw EEG, filtered EEG, EOG and EMG data. Different classifiers were applied on features of different signals: SVM for EEG, KNN for EOG and HMM for EMG. The accuracies for wake, N1, N2, N3 and REM were 98.49%, 80.05%, 91.2%, 98.22% and 95.31%, respectively, and the total accuracy of sleep stage classification was 91.31%. The results demonstrated that the sparse DBN is an efficient feature extraction method for sleep data.

In [6], an end-to-end deep learning method was proposed to perform temporal sleep stage classification using multivariate sleep signals, i.e. EEG, EOG, and EMG. This algorithm basically had three key steps. First, linear spatial filtering was applied on the input signals with the aim of enhancing the information contained in the data. Second, feature extraction architecture, where temporal convolution, rectified linear operator, and max pooling were applied to signals serially. The outputs of the second step were concatenated to form the feature space. Finally, the features were fed to nonlinear SoftMax classifier. Comparison with three state of the art methods yielded comparable performance with the state of the art methods.

With rapid development of wearable devices and increased accessibility of EEG signal, single channel deep learning models are getting more attention. For instance, Supratak et al. [7] proposed DeepSleepNet, this model is based on raw sleep EEG signal and contains two different CNNs to extract time-invariant features and one bidirectional Long Short-Term Memory (LSTM) for sequence residual learning [8]. The performance evaluation with two different datasets demonstrated that this method was able to learn features from raw EEG signal and classify them efficiently compared to the methods that use hand-crafted features.

In another work, the idea of single channel system is combined with transfer learning. Vilamala et al. [9] tested the hypothesis that sleep stage classification can be supported by transfer learning on the data obtained from Physionet Sleep-EDF database [10]. They created spectral images from each window of EEG signal using a method called multi-taper spectral estimation [11]. These images then were fed to a pre-trained Convolutional Neural Network (CNN), VGGNet [12], to be classified into one of five sleep stages. Empirical evaluation results showed that this method reaches the performance of the state of art methods.

3   Proposed Method

3.1   Database

In this paper, we benchmarked our work with EEG recordings of a publicly available database. We used an open-access comprehensive ISRUC-Sleep dataset [13]. This dataset includes data from healthy subjects as well as subjects with sleep disorders and subjects under the effect of sleep medication. Sampling frequency was 200 Hz for all EEG, EOG, chin EMG and ECG signals. Sleep annotations, including wake, REM, N1, N2, and N3, were obtained from the hypnograms at every 30 s according to AASM. In this dataset a pre-processing was done by the providers of the database, as follows:

- A notch filter was applied on EEG, EOG, chin EMG and ECG to remove 50 Hz electrical noise,
- EEG and EOG recordings were filtered in the interval of 0.3 to 35 Hz with the aid of a bandpass Butterworth filter,
- EMG channels were filtered in the interval of 10 to 70 Hz using a bandpass Butter-worth filter.

We used EEG recordings from healthy subjects. Nine males and one female subjects aged between 30 and 58 participated in the recordings. Since C3-A2 channel is the commonly used EEG channel in sleep stage classification [3, 14–16] and also it is among the recommended channels by AASM, we selected C3-A2 EEG channel.

3.2   Time-Frequency Spectrogram Image

EEG is a nonstationary signal and temporal or spectral representation by itself cannot reflect the information hidden in EEG. The Continues Wavelet Transform (CWT) [17] is a proper method to analyze the non-stationary signals such as EEG. As the window of CWT gets shrunk and dilated, it maps the variations of signal into a time-frequency spectrogram. In this paper, each epoch of EEG data is presented by time-frequency spectrogram image. Epochs are concatenated in a way that there is no overlap between them. There are a set of parameters that affect the CWT spectrogram, including the mother wavelet and number of frequency bins. After extracting the spectrogram for each epoch, we converted it to an RGB image by using a color map (or color table) to map pixel values into the actual color values.

3.3   Deep Network Architecture

Our approach is based on transfer learning, which is developed based on the fact that human brain is able to discover the underlying structure in previously learned knowledge and transfer this knowledge to new tasks [18]. Transfer learning is a machine learning method where the learning of new task is improved through using the previous task as a starting point [19]. The main advantage of transfer learning is the reduction in the number of training samples necessary for achieve a desired performance on correlated problems.

We chose AlexNet [20] which is a CNN trained on a subset of ImageNet database [21]. CNNs are deep feed-forward neural networks with trainable weights. These networks are mainly used for visual tasks since 1980s [22], minimizing the need for pre-processing related to feature extraction. AlexNet is trained 1.2 high resolution images and can classify images into 1000 categories. This network comprises of 25 layers. Eight of these layers have learnable weight including 5 convolutional layers and 3 fully connected layers. The input size is 227 in 227 pixels RGB image.

4   Performance Evaluation

Images were created for C3-A2 sensor EEG signal for healthy subjects as explained in Sect. 3.1. To reduce the computational complexity while preserving the information in the EEG, a decimation with factor 2 was applied to signals. Then, using Discrete Wavelet Transform (DWT) [17], the signals were filtered with lower cut-off frequency of 0.1 and higher cut-off frequency of 40. CWT mother wavelet was set to cmor15-1. For the time-frequency representation of each epoch, the number of frequency bins was chosen to be 2048 with the aim of capturing properly the sleep dynamics. The time-frequency spectrograms were created in the range of 0.3 Hz and 35 Hz, according to the guidelines of AASM. The spectrograms were converted to RGB images using Jet color map with 256 colors. The mapping of spectrogram to image was done through linear mapping. Although the dynamic range of sleep spectrograms was relatively high, using logarithmic/exponential mapping would either highlight the unwanted noise in the signals or fade out the desired high activity areas. While the generated image resolution was 3000 (points in time) in 2048 (points in frequency), the final image resolution was set to AlexNet input size (227 in 227) through the image resizing. The last three layers of AlexNet are by default configured for 1000 classes. We transferred these layers to fit five-stage sleep classification problem by replacing these layers with a fully connected Softmax layer. Simulations were done using a PC with 3.40 GHz Intel® Core™ i7-3770 CPU, 8 GB of RAM, Windows 10 (64 bits), and MATLAB R2015b. Several sets of training parameters were tested to determine the optimal set of parameters. AlexNet was trained using Stochastic Gradient Descent (SGD) with learning rate of 10-4 on mini-batches of 64 samples. To assess the generalization ability, the proposed model was validated by 10-fold cross validation.

5   Results and Discussion

Figure 1 shows sample RGB images of each sleep stage, as typical inputs to the pretrained CNN. Each individual image depicts the signal energy distribution during an epoch, i.e. 30 s of EEG signal (horizontal axis) and frequency interval of 0.3 to 35 Hz (vertical axis). These images can be easily interpreted using AASM guidelines. The spectrogram for wake stage (Fig. 1.a) shows high Alpha band activity in the frequency interval of 8 to 13 Hz. Figure 1.b, corresponding to N1, shows activity in the range of 4-7 Hz with slow background activity (in frequencies less than 2 Hz).

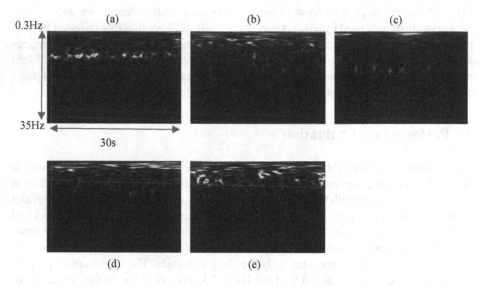

Fig. 1. Sample RGB image for five sleep stages created from time-frequency spectrogram (a) Wake, (b) N1, (c) N2, (d) N3, and (e) REM.

As the subject moves to N2, low amplitude activity in the range of 12-14 Hz, together with low frequency K complexes, are noticeable. During N3, slow wave activity in frequencies less than is typical. Mixed frequency, low amplitude activity, resembling N1 stage is present in REM spectrogram.

The proposed method performance was evaluated using per stage and overall performance scores, including per stage sensitivity, specificity, accuracy and overall accuracy as shown in Table 1. The most correctly classified stage is wake (96.3%) followed by N3 (89.2%), N2 (84.1%) and REM (82.4%). As typical for automatic sleep stage classification systems, the least classification accuracy is for N1. The main reason is that EEG signals have similar patterns in N1, REM and even N2. On the other hand, the distribution of the stages in sleep data is not balanced. Usually N1 stage is rare compared to other stages and the classification system cannot learn enough and predict it correctly. The sensitivity results confirm the above-mentioned similarity of EEG patterns in N1, N2, and REM. The specificity or true negative results for all stages are higher than 90%. Our results can be compared to the state of the art works presented in [9], although our system was trained with lower number of samples. In contrast to our work, they achieved the highest per stage accuracy in N3 (94%). The accuracy for wake stage was 87% compared to 96.3% in our work. The system in [9] outperformed our system in classifying N1 stage (75% vs. 64%). On the other hand, overall sensitivity of our system is higher. Both systems reached state of the art overall accuracy [23, 24].

Table 1. Sensitivity, specificity, accuracy per stage, and overall accuracy for proposed method All numbers are in percentage.

	Sensitivity	Specificity	Accuracy (per stage)
Wake	92	97	96.3
N1	64	94	67.6
N2	79	91	84.1
N3	85	95	89.2
REM	78	96	82.4
Overall Accuracy			**84**

6 Conclusion and Future Work

In this paper, a new sleep scoring algorithm based on image classification was proposed. The idea of using 2D images instead of conventional hand-crafted feature is an emerging trend in sleep stage classification. The main advantage of this method is eliminating the need for manual feature extraction and selection, while taking advantage of the advancements in deep image classification domain. High resolution time-frequency spectrograms of sleep epochs were extracted using CWT and converted to RGB images. The extracted images were intuitive and interpretable according to AASM guidelines. These images were fed to pre-trained CNN, AlexNet. Classification results showed that although our system was trained with lower number of samples compared to similar studies, it was able to achieve state of the art accuracy and higher overall sensitivity. Future work can include testing the proposed system with other datasets, further optimization of parameters and utilizing different pre-trained CNNs.

Acknowledgment. Authors would like to thank professor André Damas Mora for the useful comments and suggestions on sleep image processing. This work was partially funded by FCT Strategic Program UID/EEA/00066/203 of UNINOVA, CTS.

References

1. Berry, R.B., et al.: AASM - Manual for the Scoring of Sleep and Associated Events version 2.1 (2014)
2. Najdi, S., Gharbali, A.A., Fonseca, J.M.: A comparison of feature ranking and rank aggregation techniques in automatic sleep stage classification based on polysomnographic signals. In: 4th International Conference, IWBBIO, pp. 230–241 (2016)

3. Şen, B., Peker, M., Çavuşoğlu, A., Çelebi, F.V.: A comparative study on classification of sleep stage based on EEG signals using feature selection and classification algorithms. J. Med. Syst. **38**(3), 18 (2014)
4. Zhang, J., Wu, Y., Bai, J., Chen, F.: Automatic sleep stage classification based on sparse deep belief net and combination of multiple classifiers. Trans. Inst. Meas. Control **38**(4), 435–451 (2016)
5. Längkvist, M., Karlsson, L., Loutfi, A.: Sleep stage classification using unsupervised feature learning. Adv. Artif. Neural Syst. **2012**, 1–9 (2012)
6. Chambon, S., Galtier, M., Arnal, P., Wainrib, G., Gramfort, A.: A deep learning architecture for temporal sleep stage classification using multivariate and multimodal time series, July 2017
7. Supratak, A., Dong, H., Wu, C., Guo, Y.: DeepSleepNet: a model for automatic sleep stage scoring based on raw single-channel EEG. IEEE Trans. Neural Syst. Rehabil. Eng. **25**(11), 1998–2008 (2017)
8. He, K., Zhang, X., Ren, S., Sun, J.: Deep residual learning for image recognition. In: 2016 IEEE Conference on Computer Vision and Pattern Recognition (CVPR), pp. 770–778 (2016)
9. Vilamala, A., Madsen, K.H., Hansen, L.K.: Deep convolutional neural networks for interpretable analysis of EEG sleep stage scoring, October 2017
10. PhysioNet, The Sleep-EDF Database (Expanded) (2015). https://physionet.org/physiobank/database/sleep-edfx/. Accessed 01 Feb 2017
11. Thomson, D.J.: Spectrum estimation and harmonic analysis. Proc. IEEE **70**(9), 1055–1096 (1982)
12. Simonyan, K., Zisserman, A.: Very deep convolutional networks for large-scale image recognition, September 2014
13. Khalighi, S., Sousa, T., Santos, J.M., Nunes, U.: ISRUC-Sleep: a comprehensive public dataset for sleep researchers. Comput. Methods Programs Biomed. **124**, 180–192 (2016)
14. Kim, J.: A comparative study on classification methods of sleep stages by using EEG. J. Korea Multimed. Soc. **17**(2), 113–123 (2014)
15. Obayya, M., Abou-Chadi, F.E.Z.: Automatic classification of sleep stages using EEG records based on Fuzzy c-means (FCM) algorithm. In: 2014 31st National Radio Science Conference (NRSC), pp. 265–272 (2014)
16. Liang, S.-F., Kuo, C.-E., Hu, Y.-H., Pan, Y.-H., Wang, Y.-H.: Automatic stage scoring of single-channel sleep EEG by using multiscale entropy and autoregressive models. IEEE Trans. Instrum. Meas. **61**(6), 1649–1657 (2012)
17. Mallat, S.: A wavelet tour of signal processing (2009)
18. Raina, R., Ng, A.Y., Koller, D.: Constructing informative priors using transfer learning. In: Proceedings of the 23rd International Conference on Machine Learning, pp. 713–720 (2006)
19. Torrey, L., Shavlik, J.: Transfer learning. In: Handbook of Research on Machine Learning Applications and Trends, pp. 242–264. IGI Global (2009)
20. Krizhevsky, A., Sutskever, I., Hinton, G.E.: ImageNet classification with deep convolutional neural networks. In: Advances in Neural Information Processing Systems, vol. 25, pp. 1–9 (2012)
21. ImageNet. http://www.image-net.org/. Accessed 23 Jan 2018
22. LeCun, Y., et al.: Backpropagation applied to handwritten zip code recognition. Neural Comput. **1**(4), 541–551 (1989)
23. Tsinalis, O., Matthews, P.M., Guo, Y.: Automatic sleep stage scoring using time-frequency analysis and stacked sparse autoencoders. Ann. Biomed. Eng. **44**(5), 1587–1597 (2016)
24. Tsinalis, O., Matthews, P.M., Guo, Y., Zafeiriou, S.: Automatic sleep stage scoring with single-channel EEG using convolutional neural networks, October 2016

A Kernelized Morphable Model
for 3D Brain Tumor Analysis

David A. Jimenez$^{(\boxtimes)}$, Hernán F. García, Andres M. Álvarez,
Álvaro A. Orozco, and G. Holguín

Grupo de Investigación en Automática, Universidad Tecnológica de Pereira,
Pereira, Colombia
{david.jimenez,hernan.garcia,andres.alvarez1,aaog,gahol}@utp.edu.co

Abstract. Abnormal tissue analysis in brain volumes is a difficult task, due to the shape variability that the brain tumors exhibit between patients. The main problem in these processes is that the common techniques use linear representations of the input data which makes unsuitable to model complex shapes as brain tumors. In this paper, we present a kernelized morphable model (3D-KMM) for brain tumor analysis in which the model variations are captured through nonlinear mappings by using kernel principal component analysis. We learn complex shape variations through a high-dimensional representation of the input data. Then from the trained model, we recover the pre-images from the features vectors and perform a non-rigid matching procedure to fit the modeled tumor to a given brain volume. The results show that by using a kernelized morphable model, the non-rigid properties (i.e., nonlinearities and shape variations) of the abnormal tissues can be learned. Finally, our approach proves to be more accurate than the classic morphable model for shape analysis.

Keywords: Brain tumor analysis · Kernelized morphable model
3D Shape fitting

1 Introduction

Brain tumor analysis has a significant impact on applications derived from a medical diagnostic, cerebral disorders, structure representation, visualization and patient-specific surgery planning [1,2]. Since brain tumors are non-rigid structures, the main challenge in this field is to model the high variability such as size, shape, and volumetry that they present between patients [3]. Therefore, is hard to follow a specific pattern to detect this kind of abnormalities, which makes this task unsuitable and reproducible for patient-independent analysis [4]. Besides, due to the nature of brain tumors a nonlinear relation is needed, because it generates high and complex variations that a linear relation cannot do, allowing to model properly this kind of tissues (Brain Tumors) [5].

In the medical imaging modeling field, the most common techniques make use of low-dimensional representation retaining as much information as possible

© Springer International Publishing AG, part of Springer Nature 2018
A. Campilho et al. (Eds.): ICIAR 2018, LNCS 10882, pp. 529–537, 2018.
https://doi.org/10.1007/978-3-319-93000-8_60

(i.e. capturing relevant information of the brain volumetry) [6]. To this end, several state-of-the-art methods employs principal component analysis (PCA) such as active shape models [7] and 3D morphable models (3D-MM) [8]. These methods, make use of linear projections in a given latent space to represent the observed data [9]. However, the latent representation of complex shapes (i.e., brain tumors) through linear methods, leads to inaccurate modeling of the observed data (i.e., mainly when the size of the training set is lower than the dimension of the model itself) [10]. Wang et. al. in [11], made a further research to improve the core of the morphable models and deal with missing data (i.e., low samples of the training set), by including a covariance matrix that represents synthetic deformations. However, these assumption requires handling the full matrix through linear projections, which is unsuitable for large data nonlinear modeling as in the medical imaging context [12].

Kernel PCA (KPCA) extends the linear latent variable model framework of principal component analysis by using nonlinear mappings (i.e., the kernel trick) to project in a feature space the input data (possibly infinite dimensional) [13]. This variation allows computing the eigenvalue decomposition in the feature space induced by the kernel [13]. Hence, we can deal with nonlinearities and missing data (i.e., low samples of the training set). In this paper, we present a kernelized morphable model (3D-KMM) for brain tumor analysis in which we captured the model variations through nonlinear mappings of the observed data. Our approach is an extension of the classic point distribution model (PDM), that learns the shape variations related to those structures that present abnormal tissues (brain tumors). From the trained kernelized model, we perform a fitting process based on non-rigid iterative closest point (ICP) [14], to match the modeled shape of the tumor to the brain volume (MRI). Our contribution is based on the extension of the classical morphable model to handle nonlinear mappings, with the aim of relaxing the projected data in a more representative latent space. In other words, we pretend to extend the model to be able to deal with missing data (i.e., low samples of the training set), complex shapes and nonlinearity properties related to large deformations over different patients (i.e., different brain tumors). The rest of the paper proceeds as follows. Section 2 provides a detailed discussion of materials and methods. Section 3 presents the experimental results and some discussions about the proposed method. The paper concludes in Sect. 4, with a summary and some ideas for future research.

2   Materials and Methods

2.1   Database

In this work we used the Brain Tumor Image Segmentation Challenge (Brats[1]) 2015 [15]. This Database contains high-grade tumors, Low-grade tumors and labels maps made by experts based on landmarks. The tumors of this database are located in different brain regions. The label have four different labels 1- for Necrosis,

---

[1] https://www.smir.ch/BRATS/Start2015.

2- for the Edema, 3- for Non-enhancing tumor and 4- for Enhancing tumor. We make us of the label of the enhancing tumor (4).

2.2 Kernelized 3D Morphable Model

In order to build our model, we use the volume label information for each patient. From these volumes, we extract the cloud of points that represent the 3D shape of the tumor area. Then, we use marching cubes algorithm[2] to extract the real world coordinates $(g(h) \rightarrow \Omega)$ as in [16].

Definition: Let us define a given $3D$ shape as $\Gamma_i = [\mathbf{x_i, y_i, z_i}] \in \mathbb{R}^{M x 3}$ where $\mathbf{x_i,\ y_i,\ z_i} \in \mathbb{R}^{M x 1}$ contain the $\mathbf{x, y}$ and $\mathbf{z}$ locations of M vertex of the point cloud data related to the tumor volume. Hence, the training set is built from N- $3D$ tumor shapes as $\mathcal{S} = \{\mathbf{s_i}\}_{i=1}^{N} \in \mathcal{I}$, where $\mathbf{s_i} = [\mathbf{x_i}^\top, \mathbf{y_i}^\top, \mathbf{z_i}^\top]^\top$ is the vectorized form of Γ_i.

We define the high-dimensional feature space $\mathcal{F}$, containing the features vectors of the training data obtained after a non-linear mapping Φ from the input space $\Phi : \mathcal{I} \rightarrow \mathbb{R}$. Assuming that the data in $\mathcal{F}$ is centered, $\sum_{k=1}^{l} \Phi(\mathbf{s_k}) = 0$ (zero mean), the covariance matrix of the feature vectors can be calculated as

$$\mathbf{C} = \frac{1}{N} \sum_{k=1}^{N} \Phi(\mathbf{s_k})\Phi(\mathbf{s_k})^T. \tag{1}$$

From this covariance matrix a singular value decomposition is computed to find the eigenvalues $\beta \geq 0$ and eigenvectors $\mathbf{B} \in \mathcal{F}$, satisfying $\beta\mathbf{B} = \mathbf{CB}$. Since all solutions of $\mathbf{B}$ lie in span$\{\Phi(\mathbf{s_1}), \ldots, \Phi(\mathbf{s_l})\}$, we can consider the equivalent system as follows

$$\beta(\Phi(\mathbf{s_k}) \cdot \mathbf{B}) = (\Phi(\mathbf{s_k})) \cdot \mathbf{CB}) \text{ for } k = 1, ..., l, \tag{2}$$

$$\mathbf{B} = \sum_{k=1}^{l} \alpha_i \Phi(\mathbf{s_k}), \quad \text{where } l \leq N. \tag{3}$$

Consequently, we can define a kernel matrix $\mathbf{K} \in \mathbb{R}^{N \times N}$, consisting of inner products of the feature vectors $\Phi(\mathbf{s_1}), \ldots, \Phi(\mathbf{s_N})$, whose entries are given by $\mathbf{K}_{kj} := < \Phi(\mathbf{s_k}), \Phi(\mathbf{s_j}) >$ in the feature space $\mathcal{F}$. By substituting (1) and (3) in (2), and α as a column vector with entries $\alpha_1, \ldots, \alpha_l$, we obtain that $l\beta\mathbf{K}\alpha = \mathbf{K}^2\alpha$. Therefore, to solve this equation we perform an eigenvalue decomposition as in [17]. Finally, the principal components can be extracted by projecting a test point $\Phi(\mathbf{s})$ onto a eigenvector $\mathbf{B}_{:k}$ (which is a column vector of the matrix $\mathbf{B}$), according to $(\mathbf{B}_{:k} \cdot \Phi(\mathbf{s})) = \sum_{j=1}^{l} \alpha_j^k (\Phi(\mathbf{s_j}) \cdot \Phi(\mathbf{s}))$.

---

[2] We use the implementation available at http://iso2mesh.sourceforge.net/cgi-bin/index.cgi.

Simplifying the derivation above, it has been previously assumed that the data has zero mean in both input and feature space. Besides, by using a centered version of the features vectors as $\bar{\Phi}(\mathbf{s_i}) := \Phi(\mathbf{s_i}) - \frac{1}{N} \sum_{k=1}^{N} \Phi(\mathbf{s_k})$, the centered kernel matrix can be computed as

$$\bar{\mathbf{K}} = \mathbf{K} - \mathbf{1}_N \mathbf{K} - \mathbf{K} \mathbf{1}_N + \mathbf{1}_N \mathbf{K} \mathbf{1}_N, \tag{4}$$

where $\mathbf{1}_N$ is a N-dimensional column vector with all entries equal to $\frac{1}{N}$.

As in [17], we use a Gaussian Kernel $\mathbf{K} = \exp\left(-\frac{\|s - s'\|^2}{2\sigma^2}\right)$, to compute new instances of features vector as follows

$$\phi(\mathbf{s_i})_{\mathcal{H}} = \bar{\phi}(\mathbf{s}) + \beta \mathbf{B}. \tag{5}$$

Pre-Image: We solved the pre-image problem to create new brain tumors from the trained kernelized model [17]. To this end, the pre-image of Gaussian Kernel is computed by minimizing $\hat{\mathbf{s}}_i = \arg \min_{\hat{\mathbf{s}}_i \in \mathcal{X}} -\sum_{k=1}^{N} \gamma_i \mathbf{K}(\hat{\mathbf{s}}_i, \mathbf{s_k})$. After applying an iterative fixed point algorithm, the pre-image is obtained as

$$\hat{\mathbf{s}}_{i\,k+1} = \frac{\sum_{k=1}^{N} \gamma_i \exp\left(-\frac{\|\hat{\mathbf{s}}_i - \mathbf{s_k}\|^2}{2\sigma^2}\right) \mathbf{s_k}}{\sum_{k=1}^{N} \gamma_i \exp\left(\frac{-\|\hat{\mathbf{s}}_i - \mathbf{s_k}\|^2}{2\sigma^2}\right)}, \tag{6}$$

where $\gamma_i = \sum_{k=1}^{l} \beta_k \alpha_k$. Finally, Fig. 1 shows the scheme of the proposed method. First we train two morphable models as: (1) the kernelized morphable model (3D-KMM), and (2) the classic morphable model (3D-MM) based on linea PCA. Besides, we compute the pre-images of the brain tumors in the 3D-KMM. Then, we perform non-rigid iterative closest point to match the trained models to a given brain volume.

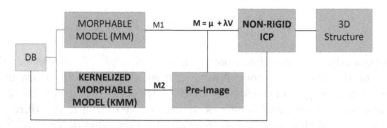

Fig. 1. Scheme of the proposed method. DB stands for Database. We compare our approach by building the classic morphable model based on PCA framework. Both models are matched to a given shape using non-rigid ICP approach. Where M represent the model, λ eigenvalues and V eigenvectors.

3   Results and Discussions

In this section we report the experimental results for our 3D Kernelized Morphable Model for brain tumor analysis. On Sect. 3.1, we show the results of the 3D shape model for the brain tumor modeling. Then, Sect. 3.2 shows the results for the fitting process of our morphable model using non-rigid ICP. The results are compared against the classic morphable model.

3.1   Training Results for 3D-KMM

Figure 2, shows the mean shape computed from the training set with different sizes of training data. The figure reveals that by using feature vectors as latent representations of the tumor data, the model exhibits more shape variability than using the linear approach.

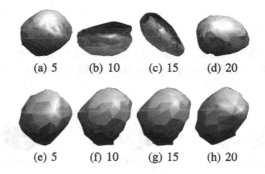

(a) 5   (b) 10   (c) 15   (d) 20

(e) 5   (f) 10   (g) 15   (h) 20

Fig. 2. Mean shape for the brain tumor modeling using our approach (top row) vs the classical MM (bottom row), with different size of training data (5, 10, 15 and 20 patients respectively).

Figure 3 shows the model variations of the kernelized morphable model and the classical morphable model. The figure shows that by using nonlinear latent representations, our approach can model more complex shapes. This can be noticed in the top row of Fig. 3 in which the most relevant components of the eigen-decomposition retained in the feature space are used to compute pre-images of modeled brain tumors. Here, our approach holds more variability in the modeled tumors than using the classic approach. These results suggest that modeling shape variations in the feature space, lie in a more spanned latent space. Besides, we can see in Fig. 3(c) and (d) even with twenty training data, the model cannot be compared to the proposed 3D-KMM with only five training data.[3]

---

[3] We set the shape of the training tumors Γ_i to have the same size, that means all vertices were adjusted to the smallest one.

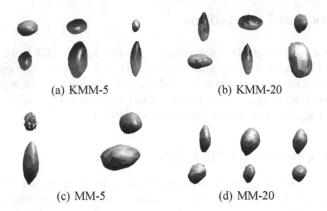

(a) KMM-5   (b) KMM-20

(c) MM-5   (d) MM-20

Fig. 3. Variation modes from $-3\sqrt{\beta}$ (top row) to $3\sqrt{\beta}$ (bottom row) of the KMM and classical MM, with different size of training data.

3.2 Fitting Results

In order to match the kernelized morphable model to the brain volume a fitting strategy is needed. In this sense, we use non-rigid ICP (Iterative Close Point).

(a) Real   (b) **KMM**.   (c) MM.

Fig. 4. Fitting results for a given 3D brain tumor with the our approach and the classic morphable model using twenty training data.

Figure 4 shows the experimental results of the model deformation using the classic morphable model based on PCA and our proposed kernelized method. Here, Fig. 4(c) shows that the modeled tumor is inaccurate due to the lack of variability that can be captured through the linear model. This result leads to sharped corners and the inability to fit the model to the real tumor properly. Therefore, Fig. 4(b) shows that by using the kernelized approach, the modeled tumor trained from the KPCA method, exhibits a better representation of the shape structure deriving in a smoother and well-defined 3D tumor model. In addition, to evaluate the shape curvedness of the modeled tumors, we compute the Laplacian curvature of the modeled shapes using both approaches, the classic 3D-MM, and the 3D-KMM. Figure 5, shows the experimental results for the curvature computed for a given brain tumor and the tumor modeled for the two approaches. In Figs. 5(b) and (c), we can show how the proposed model captures better the curvature of the brain tumor with respect to the linear approach. The results also show that the Laplacian curvature exhibited for the fitted model through the linear approach present less curvedness (see Fig. 5(c)), which leads to an inaccurate representation of the brain tumor.

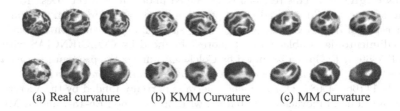

(a) Real curvature   (b) KMM Curvature   (c) MM Curvature

Fig. 5. Curvature of the KMM and MM for vs the real curvature of a given brain tumor.

Finally, Table 1 shows a quantitative evaluation of the fitting process for two approaches. The results show that our approach is more accurate than the classic morphable model based on PCA. For instance, the Volume Ratio shows better results for our approach in comparison with the linear morphable model. However the classical morphable model shows a lower structural similarity index (0.72 for 3D-MM and 0.92 for our approach) which means that some parts of the surface match properly the brain tumor. In addition, the results also show that the root-mean-square error (RMSE) of the Laplacian curvature for the fitted models proves that our approach models more accurately a given brain tumor.

Table 1. Model Performance of the fitting strategy in terms of structural similarity index (SSIM), Volume Ratio, and RMSE-Curvature.

Model	SSIM	Volume ratio	RMSE-Curvature
Classic 3D-MM	0.72 ± 0.15	0.86 ± 0.25	0.15 ± 0.25
Kernelized 3D-MM	0.92 ± 0.2	0.95 ± 0.22	0.05 ± 0.12

4 Conclusions and Future Works

In this paper, we present a kernelized morphable model (3D-KMM) for brain tumor analysis in which we captured the model variations through nonlinear mappings of the observed data. Our approach is an extension of the classic point distribution model (PDM), that learns the shape variations related to those structures that present abnormal tissues (brain tumors). From the trained kernelized model, we perform a fitting process based on non-rigid iterative closest point (ICP), to match the modeled shape of the tumor to the brain volume (MRI). The results show that by using a nonlinear mapping induced by a Gaussian kernel the model can learn a given brain tumor with less data and become more representative than the classical model. Leading to a more accurate structure in the fitting processes.

As future works, we plan to analyze a Gaussian processes latent variable model in to relax in a probabilist framework the classic morphable model.

Acknowledgments. This research is developed under the project "Desarrollo de un sistema de soporte clínico basado en el procesamiento estócasitco para mejorar la resolución espacial de la resonancia magnética estructural y de difusión con aplicación al procedimiento de la ablación de tumores" financed by COLCIENCIAS with code 111074455860. H.F. García is funded by Colciencias under the program: *Formación de alto nivel para la ciencia, la tecnología y la innovación - Convocatoria 617 de 2013* with code 111065740687. D. A. Jimenez Sierra is partially funded by the Vicerrectoria de Investigaciones, Innovación y Extensión with project code *E*6-18-7 and by Maestría en Ingeniería Eléctrica both from the Universidad Tecnológica de Pereira.

References

1. Sen, M., Rudra, A.K., Chowdhury, A.S., Elnakib, A., El-Baz, A.: Cerebral white matter segmentation using probabilistic graph cut algorithm. Multi Modality State-of-the-Art Medical Image Segmentation and Registration Methodologies, pp. 41–67. Springer, New York (2011)
2. Singh, K.K., Singh, A.: A study of image segmentation algorithms for different types of images different types of images. Int. J. Comput. Sci. Issues **7**(5), 414–417 (2010)
3. Li, Y., Jia, F., Qin, J.: Brain tumor segmentation from multimodal magnetic resonance images via sparse representation. Artif. Intell. Med. **73**, 1–13 (2016)
4. Zhan, T., Gu, S., Feng, C., Zhan, Y., Wang, J.: Brain tumor segmentation from multispectral mris using sparse representation classification and markov random field regularization. Int. J. Sign. Process. Image Process. Pattern Recogn. **8**(9), 229–238 (2015)
5. Singh, A., et al.: Review of brain tumor detection from MRI images. In: 3rd International Conference on Computing for Sustainable Global Development (INDIA-Com), IEEE, pp. 3997–4000 (2016)
6. Bishop, C.: Neural networks for pattern recognition. Oxford University Press, oxford (1995). Google Scholar
7. Cootes, T.F., Taylor, C.J., Cooper, D.H., Graham, J.: Active shape models-their training and application. Comput. Vis. image Underst. **61**(1), 38–59 (1995)
8. Blanz, V., Vetter, T.: A morphable model for the synthesis of 3D faces. In: Proceedings of the 26th Annual Conference on Computer Graphics and Interactive Techniques, pp. 187–194. ACM Press/Addison-Wesley Publishing Co. (1999)
9. Bishop, C.: Pattern recognition and machine learning (Information Science and Statistics), 1st Edn. 2006. corr. 2nd printing Edn. Springer, New York (2007)
10. Le, Y.H., Kurkure, U., Kakadiaris, I.A.: PDM-ENLOR: Learning ensemble of local PDM-based regressions. In: Proceedings of the IEEE Conference on Computer Vision and Pattern Recognition, pp. 1878–1885 (2013)
11. Wang, Y., Staib, L.H.: Boundary finding with prior shape and smoothness models. IEEE Trans. Pattern Anal. Mach. Intell. **22**(7), 738–743 (2000)
12. Joshi, S.C., Banerjee, A., Christensen, G.E., Csernansky, J.G., Haller, J.W., Miller, M.I., Wang, L.: Gaussian random fields on sub-manifolds for characterizing brain surfaces. In: Duncan, J., Gindi, G. (eds.) IPMI 1997. LNCS, vol. 1230, pp. 381–386. Springer, Heidelberg (1997). https://doi.org/10.1007/3-540-63046-5_30

13. Schölkopf, B., Smola, A., Müller, K.-R.: Kernel principal component analysis. In: Gerstner, W., Germond, A., Hasler, M., Nicoud, J.-D. (eds.) ICANN 1997. LNCS, vol. 1327, pp. 583–588. Springer, Heidelberg (1997). https://doi.org/10.1007/BFb0020217

14. Amberg, B., Romdhani, S., Vetter, T.: Optimal step nonrigid ICP algorithms for surface registration. In: CVPR, IEEE Computer Society (2007)

15. Kistler, M., Bonaretti, S., Pfahrer, M., Niklaus, R., Büchler, P.: The virtual skeleton database: an open access repository for biomedical research and collaboration. J. Med. Internet Res. **15**(11), e245 (2013)

16. Nair, P., Cavallaro, A.: 3-D face detection, landmark localization, and registration using a point distribution model. IEEE Trans. Multimed. **11**(4), 611–623 (2009)

17. Kwok, J.Y., Tsang, I.H.: The pre-image problem in kernel methods. IEEE Trans. Neural Netw. **15**(6), 1517–1525 (2004)

Normal Brain Aging: Prediction of Age, Sex and White Matter Hyperintensities Using a MR Image-Based Machine Learning Technique

Mariana Bento[1,2(✉)] ⓘ, Roberto Souza[1,3] ⓘ, Marina Salluzzi[1,3] ⓘ,
and Richard Frayne[1,2,3] ⓘ

[1] Radiology and Clinical Neuroscience, Hotchkiss Brain Institute,
University of Calgary, Calgary, AB, Canada
mariana.pinheirobent@ucalgary.ca
[2] Calgary Image Processing and Analysis Centre, Foothills Medical Centre,
Calgary, AB, Canada
[3] Seaman Family MR Research Centre, Foothills Medical Centre,
Calgary, AB, Canada

Abstract. A better understanding of normal human brain aging is
required to better study age-related neurodegeneration including cognitive impairment. We propose an automatic deep-learning method to
analyze the predictive ability of magnetic resonance images with respect
to age, sex and the presence of an age-related pathology (white matter hyperintensity, WMH). Experiments performed in a large dataset,
containing 200 normal subjects, resulted in average accuracy rates to
predict subject age (82.0%), sex (79.5%), and WMH occurrence (72.5%)
when combining handcrafted texture and convolutional features. Positive
and negative correlations between other extracted features and the subject characteristics (age, sex and WMH occurrence) were also observed.
Even though human brain variability due to age, sex and WMH occurrence in structural magnetic resonance imaging may be subtle (and often
not observable by human specialists), our results demonstrate that MR
images alone contain relevant information that can better characterize
the aging process and some demographic information of the population.

Keywords: Medical imaging · Normal aging
Magnetic resonance imaging · Classification

1 Introduction

Cerebral aging presents a high degree of inter-individual variability, representing a complex process to be analyzed [1]. The study of normal brain aging with
magnetic resonance (MR) imaging may assist in the diagnosis and monitoring of age-related neurodegenerative diseases [2]. These conditions can include

© Springer International Publishing AG, part of Springer Nature 2018
A. Campilho et al. (Eds.): ICIAR 2018, LNCS 10882, pp. 538–545, 2018.
https://doi.org/10.1007/978-3-319-93000-8_61

Alzheimer's disease, vascular dementia and other forms of cognitive decline, that impose economic and other social burdens to society [3]. Thus, the identification of modifiable risk factors that can reduce the rate of brain tissue degeneration and decrease the burden of these diseases is required [4].

MR imaging allows the quantitative evaluation of changes in the brain tissue and its structure that are commonly seen in normal aging and age-related diseases [5–7]. Age-related analysis on MR imaging have been performed to describe the brain variability related with the aging process [8]. Specially, machine learning techniques were developed to non-invasively study neurological conditions on MR images, providing biomarkers and suggestions for further analysis about the human brain tissue [9,10]. In a recent challenge including patients with brain tumor[1], for example, the possibility of predicting overall survival by using MR imaging was assessed. The best results (classification accuracy of around 65%) included age as one of the most discriminant features, suggesting that age related studies are required and relevant.

While MR image changes are often evident in the presence of a disease, the image variability of brain tissue in healthy control groups requires further evaluation. We propose a MR image-based machine learning technique to better understand normal brain aging by evaluating MR images changes with respect to: (1) age, (2) sex, and (3) the presence of age-related pathology (white matter hyperintensity, WMH). WMH are common pathologies that are associated with cognitive decline [3]. Our goal is to distinguish and identify subtle changes during the healthy adult lifespan from only structural MR imaging in a homogeneous dataset.

Contributions: Our main contribution is the development and demonstration of a technique to yield quantitative information about the normal aging process that uses only structural MR brain imaging. Our findings may be used to better understand cognitive impairment in healthy elderly and/or to aid the diagnosis of age related neurodegenerative diseases.

2   Methods

2.1   MR Dataset

Two hundred (200) oblique axial T2-weighted fluid attenuated inversion recovery (FLAIR) images from healthy controls were acquired on a 3-T scanner (Discovery 750, GE Healthcare, Waukesha, WI) with slice thickness = 3 mm, repetition time (TR) = 9000 ms, echo time (TE) = 141.4 ms and inversion time (TI) = 2250 ms as part of the Calgary Normative Study (CNS) [2]. MR image bias field correction was performed using the N4 non-uniformity correction method, compensating for possible non-uniformity in the MR receptive field [11]. The images were then skull stripped using an automated brain extraction tool [12] and their intensity normalized to the range [0, 255].

---

[1] http://braintumorsegmentation.org/.

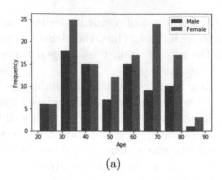 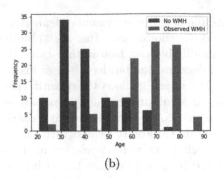

(a)   (b)

Fig. 1. Age distribution of dataset by (a) sex and (b) WMH occurrence.

Participants with significant incidental findings on their MR images or that obtained scores < 26 (out of 30) on the Montreal Cognitive Assessment (MoCA) test [13] were excluded from the study. Both sexes and a large range of ages were included in the study (Fig. 1a). A visual assessment of the FLAIR images was performed to detect possible WMH occurrences. As expected, most of the subjects with observed WMH were elderly (Fig. 1b).

For each subject, three labels were given related to: (1) age considering 65 years as the threshold (adult or elderly) [14,15], (2) sex (male or female), and (3) WMH occurrence (yes or no; see Table 1 and Fig. 2). The final classes may present high intra-class variability (*i.e.*, elderly class contains MR images acquired from subjects ranging from 65 to 90 years), and in some cases low observable inter-class variability (*i.e.*, sex differences are subtle).

Table 1. Dataset label distribution: age (adult: 18 to 65 years, or elderly: >65 years), sex (female or male) and WMH occurrence (no WMH or observed WMH).

Age	Adult: 141 (70.5%)/elderly: 59 (29.5%)
Sex	Female: 119 (59.5%)/male: 81 (40.5%)
WMH occurrence	No WMH: 96 (48.0%)/observed WMH: 104 (52.0%)

2.2 Classification by Age, Sex and WMH Occurrence

We developed a support vector machine (SVM) classifier [16] that combines handcrafted and convolutional features to analyze the MR variability due to: age, sex and WMH presence in healthy subjects (Fig. 3). Handcrafted features comprise statistics (such as mean, standard deviation, among others) computed from different texture analysis approaches, such as histogram [17], gray level and morphological gradients [18], local binary pattern [18], and frequency domain methods, such as Haar features [19]. The convolutional features were computed with a VGG16 network using imagenet weights [20], computed in the central 2D

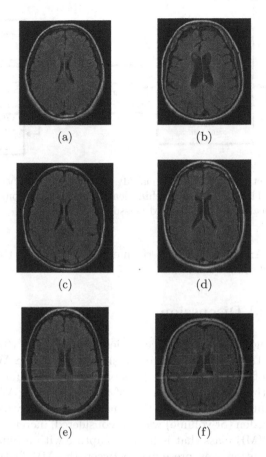

Fig. 2. Representative samples drawn from the experimental dataset with (a, b) varying age (matching sex and WMH occurrence); (c, d) sex (matching age and WMH occurrence); and (e, f) WMH occurrence (matching age and sex): (a) adult (age < 65), (b) elderly (age > 65), (c) female, (d) male, (e) no WMH and (f) observed WMH data.

axial, sagittal and coronal slices. VGG16 was used to perform feature extraction by removing the last layer (fully connected layer).

Three SVM classifiers were developed to perform different prediction tasks: distinguish MR images based on subjects age (adult vs elderly, using a 65-year threshold), sex (female vs male) and WMH burden (no WMH vs observed WMH). The SVM classifiers were evaluated by using five-fold cross validation [21].

Aside from estimating the classifier accuracy rates, we also evaluated the correlation between the analyzed characteristics (age, sex, WMH occurrence) and features extracted from the FLAIR images. For visualization purposes, a principal component analysis (PCA) was applied [22] and the top-two components (PCA1, PCA2) were used in the correlation analysis to represent the MR

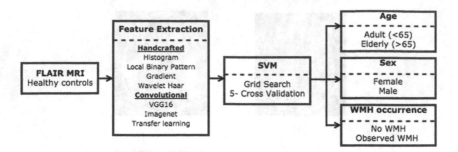

Fig. 3. Proposed method flow chart to classify healthy controls based on age, sex and WMH occurrence. The MR-based machine learning technique combines handcrafted and convolutional features to train SVM classifiers.

imaging findings. An analysis was performed that compared the correlation (ρ) between pairs of characteristics [23].

3   Results and Discussion

Classification by age and sex had accuracies of 82.0% and 79.5%, respectively (Figs. 4a and b). The most challenging task was predicting WMH occurrence (overall accuracy of 72.5%) (Fig. 4c). Possible explanations for the lower WMH accuracy include the inherent challenges of manual labeling WMH occurrences (as some subtle white matter changes that may not be visually detected). In addition, the WMH burden (or volume) was not considered, increasing the variability within observed WMH class that is hard to capture with a binary variable.

A strong correlation was presented between the MR features (PCA1 and PCA2) and age: age/PCA1 ($\rho = -0.75$) and age/PCA2 ($\rho = +0.60$). Mild correlations were found between age/WMH occurrence ($\rho = +0.25$), sex/WMH occurrence ($\rho = -0.35$) and sex/PCA2 ($\rho = +0.25$). The other pairs examined low correlation ($|\rho| \leq 0.10$) (Fig. 5).

Classifications based on age, sex and WMH occurrence presented good results (*i.e.*, >50%, or better than chance), therefore, our study suggests that machine learning-based techniques may be used to characterize normal aging, improving the understanding of the normal aging process within a variable population. In addition, the observed positive and negative correlation between the MR findings and other subject characteristics provide a proof-of-concept that structural MR images may be used to evaluate and classify normal aging, working as biomarkers to the normal aging process. Further investigation on the selected features and other complementary MR modalities is needed.

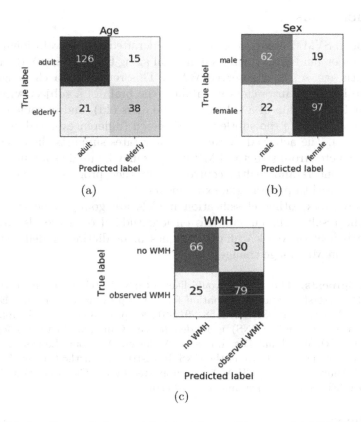

Fig. 4. SVM classifier confusion matrices by (a) age, (b) sex, and (c) WMH occurrence.

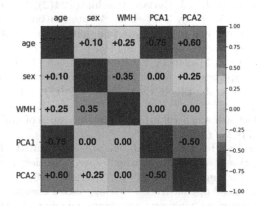

Fig. 5. Symmetric correlation matrix between normal aging characteristics (age, sex, WMH occurrence) and PCA-derived features from the corresponding FLAIR images. Positive correlations represent variables that change in the same direction. Negative values represent changes in the opposite direction.

4   Conclusions

We developed SVM classifiers combining handcrafted and convolutional features to better understand brain changes in normal aging by analyzing MR variability related with age, sex and observed WMH. This represents a challenging task since there is a large intra-class variability (the brain of a subject with 65 year is different from a brain of a subject with 90 years old), and in some cases, the MR characteristics are too subtle to be detected (differences based on sex with matching age). The achieved average accuracy rates supports the concept that features extracted from structural MR imaging may be used as an initial screening to better understand healthy controls, verify their progression in comparison to the group used to perform the experiments.

In future work, other classification models are going to be evaluated to improve the results. Similar analyses on longitudinal data are also needed to assess the benefit of ML learning techniques in predicting or defining normal aging based on MR image changes.

Acknowledgments. The authors would like to thank Hotchkiss Brain Institute, the Hopewell Professorship, and Coordination for the Improvement of Higher Education Personnel (CAPES, PVE 88881.062158/2014-01) for providing financial support. The Calgary Normative Study (CNS) is funded by the Canadian Institutes for Health Research (CIHR). We thank Drs. Linda B. Andersen, M. Louis Lauzon and Cheryl R. McCreary for their assistance in the CNS. Infrastructure at the Calgary Image Processing and Analysis Centre (CIPAC) was supported by the Canadian Foundation for Innovation (CFI) and the Government of Alberta.

References

1. Gunning-Dixon, F.M., Brickman, A.M., et al.: Aging of cerebral white matter: a review of MRI findings. Int. J. Geriatr. Psychiatr. **24**(2), 109–117 (2009)
2. Tsang, A., Lebel, C.A., Bray, S.L., et al.: White matter structural connectivity is not correlated to cortical resting-state functional connectivity over the healthy adult lifespan. Front. Aging Neurosci. **9**(144), 1–13 (2017)
3. Lampe, L., Kharabian-Masouleh, S., Kynast, J., et al.: Lesion location matters: the relationships between white matter hyperintensities on cognition in the healthy elderly. J. Cereb. Blood Flow Metab. (2017). https://doi.org/10.1177/0271678X17740501
4. Lockhart, S.N., DeCarli, C.: Structural imaging measures of brain aging. Neuropsychology **24**(3), 271–289 (2014)
5. Spilt, A., Geeraedts, T., Craen, A.J., et al.: Age-related changes in normal-appearing brain tissue and white matter hyperintensities: more of the same or something else? New Engl. J. Med. **26**(4), 725–729 (2005)
6. Leite, M., Rittner, L., Appenzeller, S.: Etiology-based classification of brain white matter hyperintensity on magnetic resonance imaging. J. Med. Imaging **2**(1), 014002-1–014002-10 (2015)
7. Dichgans, M., Wardlaw, J., Smith, E., et al.: Metacohorts for the study of vascular disease and its contribution to cognitive decline and neurodegeneration: an initiative of the joint programme for neurodegenerative disease research. Alzheimer's Dement. **12**(12), 1235–1249 (2016)

8. Fillmore, P.T., Phillips, M.C., Richards, J.E.: Age-specific MRI brain and head templates for healthy adults from 20 through 89 years of age. Front. Aging Neurosci. **7**, 44 (2015)
9. Griffanti, L., Zamboni, G., Khan, A., et al.: BIANCA (Brain Intensity Abnormality Classification Algorithm): a new tool for automated segmentation of white matter hyperintensities. NeuroImage **141**, 191–205 (2016)
10. Despotovic, I., Goossens, B., Philips, W.: MRI segmentation of the human brain: challenges, methods, and applications. Comput. Math. Methods Med. **2015**(1), 1–23 (2015)
11. Tustison, N.J., Avants, B.B., Cook, P.A., et al.: N4ITK: improved N3 bias correction. IEEE Trans. Med. Imaging **29**(6), 1310–1320 (2010)
12. Jenkinson, M., Beckmann, C.F., Behrens, T.E., et al.: FSL. Neuroimage **62**, 782–790 (2012)
13. Nasreddine, Z.S., Phillips, N.A., Bédirian, V., et al.: The montreal cognitive assessment, MoCA: a brief screening tool for mild cognitive impairment. J. Am. Geriatr. Soc. **53**(4), 695–699 (2005)
14. Bates, A.T., Divino, C.: Laparoscopic surgery in the elderly: a review of the literature. Aging Dis. **2**(6), 149–155 (2015)
15. Chen, S.C., Shoemaker, S.: Age and cohort effects: the American senior tourism market. Ann. Tour. Res. **48**, 58–75 (2014)
16. Yichuan, T.: Deep learning using linear support vector machines. In: Proceedings of International Conference on Machine Learning (2013)
17. Woods, R., Gonzalez, R.C.: Digital Image Processing (2000)
18. Pedregosa, F., Varoquaux, G., Gramfort, A., et al.: Scikit-learn: machine learning in Python. J. Mach. Learn. Res. **12**(1), 2825–2830 (2011)
19. Schwartz, W.R., Siqueira, F.R., Pedrini, H.: Evaluation of feature descriptors for texture classification. J. Eletron. Imaging **21**(2), 1–17 (2012)
20. Shin, H., Roth, H., Gao, M., et al.: Deep convolutional neural networks for computer-aided detection: CNN architectures, dataset characteristics and transfer learning. IEEE Trans. Med. Imaging **35**(5), 1285–1298 (2016)
21. Kohavi, R.: A study of cross-validation and bootstrap for accuracy estimation and model selection. In: Proceedings of the 14th International Joint Conference on Artificial Intelligence, San Francisco, vol. 2, pp. 1137–1143 (1995)
22. Minka, T.: Automatic choice of dimensionality for PCA. NIPS **13**, 514 (2000)
23. McKinney, W.: Data structures for statistical computing in Python. In: Proceedings of the 9th Python in Science Conference (2010)

Boosted Cascaded Convnets for Multilabel Classification of Thoracic Diseases in Chest Radiographs

Pulkit Kumar, Monika Grewal, and Muktabh Mayank Srivastava[✉]

Paralleldots, Inc., Gurgaon, India
{pulkit,monika,muktabh}@paralleldots.com

Abstract. Chest X-ray is one of the most accessible medical imaging technique for diagnosis of multiple diseases. With the availability of ChestX-ray14, which is a massive dataset of chest X-ray images and provides annotations for 14 thoracic diseases; it is possible to train Deep Convolutional Neural Networks (DCNN) to build Computer Aided Diagnosis (CAD) systems. In this work, we experiment a set of deep learning models and present a cascaded deep neural network that can diagnose all 14 pathologies better than the baseline and is competitive with other published methods. Our work provides the quantitative results to answer following research questions for the dataset: (1) What loss functions to use for training DCNN from scratch on ChestX-ray14 dataset that demonstrates high class imbalance and label co occurrence? (2) How to use cascading to model label dependency and to improve accuracy of the deep learning model?

1 Introduction

Computer Aided Diagnosis (CAD) has been a well sought research field ever since the inception of medical imaging techniques and the interest is increasing with the advent of sophisticated medical imaging techniques. Among the existing medical imaging techniques, X-ray imaging is most commonly used technique for screening and diagnosis of lung related diseases e.g. pneumonia, cardiomegaly, lung nodules etc. The cost effectiveness of X-rays makes it most accessible diagnostic method for chest diseases in third world countries. The diagnosis of disease from a radiograph is, however, a time-consuming and challenging task. Thus, development of a CAD system for evaluation would increase the productivity of physicians and accessibility of better healthcare services in remote areas.

Recent years have observed significant rise in use of deep learning methods for analysis of medical imaging datasets. Deep learning methods have been rigorously applied for disease classification and image segmentation tasks. The gradual rise of interest in deep learning based diagnostic solutions can be attributed to their tremendous potential in modeling complex relationships between input

---

P. Kumar and M. Grewal contributed equally.

© Springer International Publishing AG, part of Springer Nature 2018
A. Campilho et al. (Eds.): ICIAR 2018, LNCS 10882, pp. 546–552, 2018.
https://doi.org/10.1007/978-3-319-93000-8_62

and output variables and faster inference. However, training highly accurate deep learning systems in any domain requires a large annotated dataset. Recently, Wang et al. [1] developed a large dataset of chest X-ray images along with annotations for chest diseases through Natural Language Processing (NLP). The dataset is the largest open dataset for chest X-ray images, and therefore paves a path for development of better algorithms for automated diagnosis of chest diseases.

ChestX-ray14 dataset provides labels for 14 lung related diseases for 112,120 radiograph images of 1024 by 1024 resolution with above 90% label accuracy. Most of the radiographs are labelled with more than one disease making it a typical multi-label classification problem. Apart from the inherent challenges posed by multi-label classification, the dataset has heavy imbalance in number of instances of individual classes. Moreover, the co-occurrence instances of each class with every other class are very high. For instance, the disease 'Cardiomegaly' co-occurs with disease 'Effusion' in 1060 images, whereas the total images of the diseases are 2772 and 13307, respectively. These challenges make the multi label classification task quite difficult and necessitate the incorporation of label dependencies along with employing robust learning approaches.

The standard approach to multi-label classification is Binary Relevance (BR), wherein the problem of multilabel classification for n classes is transformed into n binary classification problems [2]. However, BR approach does not account for the interdependence of different class labels. The prevalent approaches to account for label dependencies include chain classification [3], label power set of k-labels [4], and modeling with recurrent neural network [5]. The label power set approaches improve upon performance, but the modeling becomes intractable as the number of classes increase. Moreover, the use of recurrent neural network might not be able to model complex dependencies between class labels.

Another approach for multi label classification includes Pairwise Error (PWE) loss that inherently models label dependencies in the sense that it tries to maximize the margin between positive and negative labels within an example [6,7]. Different variants of PWE loss are widely used for multi label classification in natural image classification and natural language processing tasks. However, the popular PWE losses such as hinge loss, margin loss are non-smooth and as such pose difficulty in optimization. Further, there exist empirical evidences that the ensemble approaches e.g. cascading, boosting, etc., demonstrate increased performance as compared to single classifiers. Although, the exact mechanism of how ensembling helps increase generalizability is still debatable.

In the present work, we experiment with a series of deep learning methods for the diagnosis of chest diseases from the ChestX-ray14 dataset while systematically addressing the challenges mentioned in above paragraphs. To begin with, we train the popular DenseNet architecture [8] with basic BR approach. We also train the baseline architecture with PWE and compare the performance with cross entropy loss in BR method. Further, we propose a novel cascading architecture that takes benefits from both ensemble and hard example mining techniques.

We design the architecture such that it models the labels dependencies between classes inherently. The contributions of this paper can be summarized as:-

1. We train deep learning architecture from scratch for multi label classification of ChestX-ray14 dataset and achieve better results from baseline which used transfer learning.
2. We experiment two standard loss functions for multi label classification: BR and PWE loss, and present comparison results.
3. We design a boosted cascade architecture that is specifically tailored for multi label classification task of type of ChestX-ray14 dataset. The proposed approach models complex dependencies between class labels and benefits from the training strategy of boosting methods to provide improved performance as compared to single classifiers trained using cross-entropy and PWE loss.

2 Related Work

Multi label classification problem has been extensively explored for the tasks outside the domain of medical imaging e.g. object detection, text categorization. Last year Wang et al. published a large dataset of chest X-ray images [1] that is a typical example of multi label classification problem in medical imaging domain.

We have developed our method using DenseNet161 [8] architecture and used the smoother version of pairwise error loss as described in [9]. Our approach is inspired from boosted cascade of classifiers method [10] and basic Adaboost [11] method that weighs individual examples while training different classifiers. The approach of forwarding output of preceding cascade level to next level bears similarity with the approach by Zeng et al. [12] used for object detection. Different from their work, we forward the outputs of all preceding cascade levels to next cascade level in the architecture.

3 Methods

We methodically experimented a series of approaches and evaluated their performance. We used DensNet161 [8] as baseline neural network architecture, due to its well known performance for a variety of datasets. The selection of the DenseNet architecture was additionally motivated by its efficiency in modeling with lesser number of parameters, which reduced the risk of over-fitting while still benefiting from deep architecture. Below, we briefly explain the approaches that we experimented:-

3.1 Binary Relevance

For starter, we transformed the task as independent binary classification task for each class. Since the positive instances of any class are very less as compared to negative instances, we used weighted cross entropy loss by penalizing the errors on positive class instances by n/p, where n and p correspond to frequencies of negative and positive instances, respectively. Moreover, we undersampled majority classes and oversampled minority classes to avoid bias due to imbalance in class occurrence and co-occurrence frequencies.

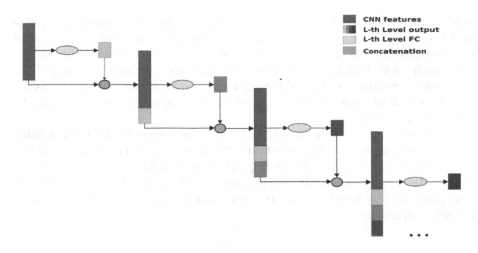

Fig. 1. Architecture for 4 levels of cascade

3.2 PairWise Error (PWE) Loss

The major disadvantage of the BR approach is that it does not model the inter-class relations within an example. As an alternative, PWE loss maximizes the margin between the scores of each positive class to each negative class, and is based on simple logical reasoning that learning relations between pairs of each positive to negative class is sufficient to learn inter-class relations between all classes. We used smooth PWE loss [7] to separate probability scores of each positive class from each negative class within an example. The probability scores were computed as sigmoid output from the classifier layer. We used the sampling technique mentioned for BR approach to avoid adverse effects of class imbalance.

3.3 Boosted Cascade

There exist empirical evidences that cascading multiple predictions using binary relevance improves performance of multi-label classification. Following this hypothesis, we trained a cascaded network to improve upon initial predictions from baseline networks using BR approach with cross-entropy loss, and PWE loss. We refer to these experiments as C-BR and C-PWE, respectively. Different from conventional cascading approaches, we designed our cascade network such that each succeeding level in the cascade network received predictions from all the preceding levels as input, as shown in Fig. 1. This allowed the different levels in the cascade network model non-linear dependencies between each class along with learning from mistakes of all preceding levels.

Conventionally, the different levels in the cascade are trained from differ-ent splits of the original training set. This is motivated by standard ensemble methods, wherein an ensemble of many weak classifiers is trained, each of which are independently tuned for smaller datasets. The said approach, thus consider-ably reduces the amount of training data for individual classifiers. Therefore its applicability is limited to ensembles of simpler models e.g. decision trees, support vector machines etc., as neural networks are prone to over-fitting if trained with smaller dataset. Therefore we trained different levels of the cascade network with entire training set. Further, we employed weighted sampling of the data points according to their difficulty level such that each successive cascade level was trained more for the data points which were difficult to classify by previous cascade level.

After each cascade level was trained, loss was computed for each training example, which gave an estimate of difficulty level of each data point according to the classifier at l-th level. The data points were sorted according to decreasing loss and then sampled according to probability p for training next cascade level. The probability of selection for i-th data point p_i was computed according to following equation:-

$$p_i = \frac{e^{\frac{-iR}{N}}}{\sum\limits_{n=1}^{n=N} e^{\frac{-nR}{N}}} \tag{1}$$

Where, N is total number of training data points; n belongs to [1, N]; R is rate of probability decay (higher the R, higher is the selection probability of difficult data points over easier data points). In this way, every succeeding classifier in the cascade focuses on more and more difficult examples.

4   Implementation

We used ChestX-ray14 dataset published by Wang et al. [1], which contained 112,110 frontal X-ray images of 30,805 unique patients. The dataset contained labeling for fourteen different thoracic diseases. Following the method used in original paper, we randomly separated 20% dataset for testing and utilized the rest for training.

We used DenseNet161 architecture and modified the last fully connected (fc) layer to contain twice the number of classes as output units. The output was reshaped to compute independent softmax activation for each class against background. Finally, weighted cross-entropy loss was computed.

We used 6-levels of cascading for both cross entropy and PWE loss. Each level in cascading composed of two fc layers. We used RELU non-linearity and a dropout of 0.5 between fc layers. The inference from cascading was made by taking average of the predictions from each level.

The training for each approach was done using Stochastic Gradient Descent (SGD) with learning rate 0.1 and momentum 0.9. The learning rate was reduced to $1/10^{th}$ of the original value after $1/3^{rd}$ and $2/3^{rd}$ of the training finished. The network weights were initialized using He norm initialization [13].

5   Results and Discussion

Table 1 represents the Area Under the Curve (AUC) of the Receiver Operating Characteristic (ROC) curve of the binary classification for all the classes from all the experiments. Both PWE loss and BR with cross entropy loss performed comparable. Whereas, the combination of boosted cascade approach gave increased performance as compared to single classifier for both the losses. Wang et al. [1] have provided baseline classification results for the dataset. Our baseline models: BR with cross-entropy, and PWE loss outperformed the baseline in 9 and 10 classes, respectively. Further, the addition of boosted cascade approach with both the losses outperforms the baseline in all the classes by a large margin.

Table 1. Comparison of AUCs of ROC curve for classification of diseases in ChestX-ray14 dataset. The experiments of this paper are marked with asterisk (*).

	Wang et al. [1]	Yao et al. [14]	Rajpurkar et al. [15]	BR*	PWE*	C-BR*	C-PWE*
Atelectasis	0.7158	0.772	**0.8209**	0.7453	0.7158	0.7618	0.7433
Cardiomegaly	0.8065	0.904	0.9048	0.8947	0.8777	**0.9133**	0.8930
Effusion	0.7843	0.859	**0.8831**	0.8396	0.8507	0.8635	0.8615
Infiltration	0.6089	0.695	**0.7204**	0.67	0.666	0.6923	0.6746
Mass	0.7057	0.792	**0.8618**	0.6964	0.7137	0.7502	0.7894
Nodule	0.6706	0.717	**0.7766**	0.6134	0.6023	0.6662	0.7035
Pneumonia	0.6326	0.713	**0.7632**	0.55108	0.6073	0.7145	0.6378
Pneumothorax	0.8055	0.841	**0.8932**	0.8198	0.8408	0.8594	0.8531
Consolidation	0.7078	0.788	**0.7939**	0.7606	0.7324	0.7838	0.7604
Edema	0.8345	0.882	**0.8932**	0.8669	0.8563	0.8880	0.8824
Emphysema	0.8149	0.829	**0.926**	0.8474	0.8993	0.8982	0.9164
Fibrosis	0.7688	0.767	**0.8044**	0.7236	0.7171	0.7559	0.7520
PT	0.7082	0.765	**0.8138**	0.7405	0.7388	0.7739	0.7566
Hernia	0.7667	0.914	**0.9387**	0.7122	0.898	0.8024	0.8636

Two other groups have reported their results on the ChestX-ray14 dataset. Yao et al. [14] proposed an LSTM based approach to model the label dependencies. Our proposed boosted cascade approach achieves comparable performance to [14]. Further, Rajpurkar et al. [15] trained 121-layer DenseNet architecture by initializing network weights from a model pretrained on ImageNet dataset. Our approach yielded comparable AUCs in all the classes as compared to [15], although not better. The better performance of their model may be attributed to the beneficial effects of pretraining, which are ubiquitously known to the deep learning community. We would like to highlight that the key objective of our study was to explore the stand-alone effects of different loss functions and boosted cascade approach on the performance of the model. We believe that our proposed approach of boosted cascading with pretraining would yield further improved results.

6   Conclusion

We experiment a set of deep learning methods for the multi label classification of ChestX-ray14 dataset and provide results comparable to the state-of-the-art.

We provide comparison results for cross entropy and pairwise error loss for the task of multi label classification of the dataset. Further, we implement a cascade network that improves upon the performance of deep learning models along with modeling label dependencies. In summary, the present work provides optimistic results for the automatic diagnosis of thoracic diseases. However, future work related to disease localization and improvement of classification performance is suggested.

References

1. Wang, X., Peng, Y., Lu, L., Lu, Z., Bagheri, M., Summers, R.M.: ChestX-ray8: hospital-scale chest X-ray database and benchmarks on weakly-supervised classification and localization of common thorax diseases (2017)
2. Nam, J., Kim, J., Gurevych, I., Fürnkranz, J.: Large-scale multi-label text classification - revisiting neural networks. CoRR abs/1312.5419 (2013)
3. Cheng, W., Hüllermeier, E., Dembczynski, K.J.: Bayes optimal multilabel classification via probabilistic classifier chains. In: Fürnkranz, J., Joachims, T. (eds.) Proceedings of the 27th International Conference on Machine Learning (ICML 2010), pp. 279–286. Omnipress (2010)
4. Read, J., Pfahringer, B., Holmes, G., Frank, E.: Classifier chains for multi-label classification. Mach. Learn. **85**(3), 333–359 (2011)
5. Yao, L., Poblenz, E., Dagunts, D., Covington, B., Bernard, D., Lyman, K.: Learning to diagnose from scratch by exploiting dependencies among labels (2017)
6. Gong, Y., Jia, Y., Leung, T., Toshev, A., Ioffe, S.: Deep convolutional ranking for multilabel image annotation. CoRR abs/1312.4894 (2013)
7. Li, Y., Song, Y., Luo, J.: Improving pairwise ranking for multi-label image classification (2017)
8. Huang, G., Liu, Z., Weinberger, K.Q., Van Der Maaten, L.: Densely Connected Convolutional Networks (2016)
9. Yeh, C.K., Wu, W.C., Ko, W.J., Wang, Y.C.F.: Learning deep latent spaces for multi-label classification (2017)
10. Viola, P., Jones, M.: Rapid object detection using a boosted cascade of simple features. In: Proceedings of the 2001 IEEE Computer Society Conference on Computer Vision and Pattern Recognition, CVPR 2001, vol. 1, p. I. IEEE (2001)
11. Schapire, R.E.: A brief introduction to boosting. In: Proceedings of the 16th International Joint Conference on Artificial Intelligence, IJCAI 1999, San Francisco, vol. 2, pp. 1401–1406. Morgan Kaufmann Publishers Inc. (1999)
12. Zeng, X., Ouyang, W., Wang, X.: Multi-stage contextual deep learning for pedestrian detection. In: Proceedings of the IEEE International Conference on Computer Vision (2013)
13. He, K., Zhang, X., Ren, S., Sun, J.: Delving deep into rectifiers: surpassing human-level performance on imagenet classification. In: Proceedings of the IEEE International Conference on Computer Vision, pp. 1026–1034 (2015)
14. Yao, L., Poblenz, E., Dagunts, D., Covington, B., Bernard, D., Lyman, K.: Learning to diagnose from scratch by exploiting dependencies among labels. arXiv preprint arXiv:1710.10501 (2017)
15. Rajpurkar, P., Irvin, J., Zhu, K., Yang, B., Mehta, H., Duan, T., Ding, D., Bagul, A., Langlotz, C., Shpanskaya, K., Lungren, M.P., Ng, A.Y.: CheXNet: radiologist-level pneumonia detection on chest X-rays with deep learning, November 2017

A Deep Learning Approach for Red Lesions Detection in Video Capsule Endoscopies

Paulo Coelho[1(✉)], Ana Pereira[2], Argentina Leite[3], Marta Salgado[4], and António Cunha[3]

[1] Polytechnic Institute of Leiria, Leiria, Portugal
[2] University of Trás-os-Montes e Alto Douro, 5000-801 Vila Real, Portugal
paulo.coelho@ipleiria.pt
[3] INESC TEC (Formerly INESC Porto) and UTAD – University of Trás-os-Montes e Alto Douro, 5000-801 Vila Real, Portugal
[4] Centro Hospitalar Porto, Porto, Portugal

Abstract. The wireless capsule endoscopy has revolutionized early diagnosis of small bowel diseases. However, a single examination has up to 10 h of video and requires between 30–120 min to read. Computational methods are needed to increase both efficiency and accuracy of the diagnosis. In this paper, an evaluation of deep learning U-Net architecture is presented, to detect and segment red lesions in the small bowel. Its results were compared with those obtained from the literature review. To make the evaluation closer to those used in clinical environments, the U-Net was also evaluated in an annotated sequence by using the Suspected Blood Indicator tool (SBI). Results found that detection and segmentation using U-Net outperformed both the algorithms used in the literature review and the SBI tool.

Keywords: Lesion detection · Gastrointestinal bleeding
Machine learning · Capsule endoscopy · Deep learning · U-Net

1 Introduction

Approximately 300,000 hospitalizations per year in the United States of America are associated with gastrointestinal bleeding and in 5% of those cases it is not possible to immediately identify the bleeding's source [14]. The small bowel is one of the major organs where bleeding from unknown sources occurs (also named as Obscure Gastrointestinal Bleeding - OGIB). Full and direct visualization of the small bowel is not possible through high endoscopy or colonoscopy, due to the organ's length and its morphological diversity [8]. To overcome this issue, direct visualization of the small bowel through endoscopic methods with emphasis to the Wireless Capsule Endoscopy (WCE), have greatly evolved in the last decades, revolutionizing the knowledge and clinical approach of several pathologies [10].

© Springer International Publishing AG, part of Springer Nature 2018
A. Campilho et al. (Eds.): ICIAR 2018, LNCS 10882, pp. 553–561, 2018.
https://doi.org/10.1007/978-3-319-93000-8_63

Recently, several Computer Aided Diagnostic (CAD) designs have been developed allowing for an automatic or semi-automatic lesion detection (e.g. polyps, ulcers, tumors and bleeding). Extensive reviews of these CAD systems can be found in [3,4,9]. Rapid Reader commercial software has been one of the most used diagnostic support tool since it provides, amongst other tools, the Suspected Blood Indicator (SBI), which identifies frames with possible red lesions in the gastrointestinal (GI) tract, based on color. However, several studies have shown that the results obtained using this tool are not completely satisfactory [1,4,6,16].

Computational methods for automatic image processing and analysis, such as smoothing filters, noise removal, contour detection or segmentation, can be used to facilitate the detection of anomalies/pathologies and to homogenize the response between different clinicians. Since 2012, Convolutional Neural Network (CNN), commonly known as "deep learning", started to present significantly better results than previous methods, automatically extracting characteristics from data and thus supporting new developments in CAD systems [9]. In this paper, an evaluation of deep learning U-Net architecture is presented for detecting and segmenting red lesions in the small bowel. Moreover, the comparison between its results and those found in the literature review is also presented.

2   Deep Learning Approach

CNN is a technology for learning generic resources in computational tasks that uses a hierarchy of computational layers and begins by mapping an input (image) to obtain an output (class). The lower layers are composed by convolution, normalization and pooling layers, alternating between each other, while the upper layers are fully connected and correspond to traditional neural networks [9].

The model used in this study is the U-Net architecture, proposed by Ronneberger et al. to segment images [7]. It is a CNN modification and presents a U shape due to symmetrical form presented by the contracting path (the left branch) and the expansive path (the right branch), as illustrated in Fig. 1.

Summarily, a repetitive pattern of convolution operation, followed by a Rectified Linear Unit (ReLU) and a down-sampling process – with a step of 2 – is performed in the contraction path. Regarding the expansive path, it includes an up-sampling operation of the previously obtained feature map, followed by a convolution (has the effect of halving the feature channels) and the concatenation with the characteristics map obtained in the contracting path. A final convolutional layer is added to map feature vectors to the desired number of classes [7]. The contraction path intents to capture context and the expanding path allows an accurate feature location.

3   Datasets and Experiments

3.1   Datasets

For this study it was necessary to compile 2 custom datasets with frames from the small bowel since, in the best of our knowledge, there is no publicly available

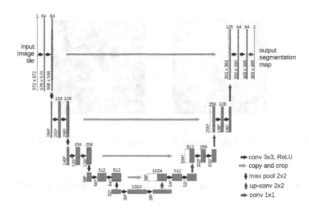

Fig. 1. The architecture of U-Net, reproduced from [7]. Each blue box in this figure represents a multi-channel feature map. The data pass through the horizontal lines simultaneously. The deep blue arrows represent activation functions. (Color figure online)

Table 1. Datasets characterization.

	Set 1	Set 2	Total
Lesion	1,131	439	1,570
No lesion	2,164	161	2,325
Total	3,295	600	

dataset with annotated red lesions in Video Capsule Endoscopy (VCE) images and with adequate size to train the U-Net architecture. The datasets characterization are presented in Table 1.

As criteria for compilation of Set 1, it was decided to have a dataset with images as diverse as possible - from different cameras, such as MiroCam, PillCam SB1, SB2 and SB3 - and with different red lesions, such as angioectasias, angiodysplasias, bleeding and others. It has 3,295 frames from which 1,131 have lesions. This set has a similar size to other aforementioned works [5]. All lesions were annotated manually. The images have 320×320 or 512×512 resolutions, although they were all resampled to 512×512 when applied to the U-Net.

Figure 2 presents a frame and the respective annotation mask example. The annotation process is subjective and very time consuming. For example, it is difficult for a human being to rigorously annotate the smooth border of blood diluted in small bowel fluids, which result in annotations with wide variability and impacts the segmentation results.

For Set 2, it was decided to have a dataset with a sequence of 600 images from a PillCam SB3 video to get an evaluation of the model closer to the clinical reality. The set contains 73% of frames with red lesions, each one labelled manually as Blood/Non-blood based on the human judgment for Ground Truth

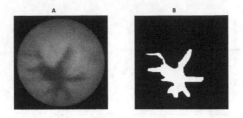

Fig. 2. a. Bleeding example; b. Manually annotated mask.

(GT) and on the result of the Given SBI to get an evaluation of the SBI tool in the set[1].

3.2 Evaluation Criteria

The metrics used to evaluate the U-Net performance in the detection process are derived from the basic cardinalities of the confusion matrix, namely the true positives (TP), the false positives (FP), the true negatives (TN) and the false negatives (FN) [11]. These measures assume that there is an overlap between two partitions, in this particular case the actual existence of red lesions in a given image and the possibility of this being predicted through the proposed method. From the aforementioned measures, one can obtain test validity indicators such as Accuracy - ACC (1), True Positive Rate (Sensitivity) - TPR (2), True Negative Rate (Specificity) - TNR (3):

$$ACC = \frac{TP + TN}{TP + FP + TN + FN} \tag{1}$$

$$TPR = \frac{TP}{TP + FN} \tag{2}$$

$$TNR = \frac{TN}{TN + FP} \tag{3}$$

The ACC is defined as the portion of correctly classified elements to the total number of elements. TPR is a quantification of the algorithm capacity to correctly classify an image truly containing red lesions, i.e., it is the portion of frames with lesion that had a positive classifier result. Analogously, the TNR is a quantification of the algorithm capability in correctly classifying images truly without red lesions, i.e., it is the portion that non-lesion frames will be classified as normal by the classifier.

As segmentation metric the Dice Coefficient – DICE (4) was used [11]:

$$DICE = \frac{2 \cdot tp}{2 \cdot tp + fp + fn} \tag{4}$$

---

[1] At the time of submission these datasets were waiting for publication approval from the Ethical Council. In case of approval it will be available at https://rdm.inesctec.pt/dataset/nis-2018-003.

The Dice coefficient is a relative metric that provides a similarity index between predicted and ground truth segmentations. The tp are the total number of pixels belonging to the lesion in both masks: predicted and ground truth. The fp are the total number of pixels predicted as lesion but are not in the ground truth mask. The fn are the total number of pixels predicted as not belonging to lesion but are present in the ground truth mask.

3.3   Implementation Details

The U-Net network was trained from scratch with Set 1, which was split randomly in 80% for training and 20% for validation, to detect and segment red lesions. The training was made using Dice coefficient as cost function, in 3 cycles of 120 epochs with the Adam optimizer. The learning rate was 1E-4, 1E-5 and 1E-6 in each cycle, respectively. The model evaluation was performed by comparing its predictions with the annotated masks, used as ground truth, based on Sect. 3.2 evaluation metrics. The network was implemented in Python 2.7 and all experiments were performed on a machine with an Intel Xeon CPU E5-2650 and 64 GB RAM. The U-Net was implemented using Keras with TensorFlow as backend and was accelerated on an NVIDIA GTX-1080Ti GPU (11 GB on-board memory).

4   Results and Discussion

The SBI tool and most of state of the art methods are used as blood detectors. So, it was decided to evaluate the U-Net model - trained on Set 1 for segmentation - as a detector and the results compared with state of the art bleeding detection with datasets greater than 1,000 images, as showed in Table 2. The authors point out that the relative comparison with other works is carried out under different experimental conditions, since the datasets are different.

Table 2. Comparison between U-Net trained on Set 1 and state of the art bleeding detection.

Author(s)	Images/Patients	ACC(%)	TPR(%)	TNR(%)
Sainju et al. [8]	1,500/3	93.00	96.00	90.00
Figueiredo et al. [2]	4,000/10	92.70	92.90	>90.00
Usman et al. [13]	8,500	92.00	94.00	91.00
Xiong et al. [15]	3,596/5	94.10	91.69	94.59
U-Net	3,295/>5	95.88	99.56	93.93

The U-Net model learned very well to detect red lesions, with only 1 FN frame and 26 FP. Indeed, it has a very good accuracy (ACC = 95.88%), sensitivity (TPR = 99.56%) and specificity (TNR = 93.93%), outperforming Xiong et al.

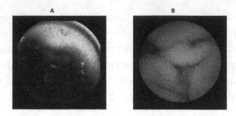

Fig. 3. a. FN frame; b. FP frame example. (Color figure online)

work (the overall most precise present in the literature review) by 1.78% in accuracy and in 7.87% in sensitivity. The specificity is lower 0.66% from the Xiong et al work, but is still higher than other state of the art works. From the analysis of the FN frames it was verified that these occur in lesions in which the background presents similar colors as the one shown in Fig. 3a.

In the case of the 26 FP, in 15 of them the system predicted very small areas that could be ignored, 12 of them appearing in between intestinal folds. Of the remaining 11 cases, 7 are dubious, even after the system's prediction result, since they were manually annotated as not containing red lesions. However, the U-Net considers them as having lesions and, in fact, it can be considered as correct. Finally, the last 4 cases present one or several considerable areas, also located in intestinal folds as can be seen in Fig. 3b.

The segmentation metric for red lesions was obtained from the evaluation of the Set 1 TP frames by averaging the Dice coefficient (DICE = 87.08%). This rate value is biased by the human manual ground truth segmentation in the smooth border of diluted blood in small bowel fluids. In the literature, this result can be compared with the study presented by Tuba et al. [12], that presents an average value for DICE of 84%. In this case, the U-Net outperforms it in 3.08%.

According to Yung et al. [16], SBI showed high sensitivity (TPR = 98.8%) but with low specificity (TNR = 64.0%) even for clinical scenarios for active bleeding. For small bowel pathology with bleeding potential, it shows moderate sensitivity (TPR = 55.3%) and specificity (TNR = 57.8%). To get a fair comparison, the model was evaluated with 600 consecutive new frames belonging to the small bowel and compared with SBI, Set 2, as can be seen in Table 3.

With 4 FN frames and 15 FP, the U-Net obtained a very good accuracy (ACC = 96.83%) and an excellent sensitivity (TPR = 99.09%), much better than SBI, with 185 FN frames. U-Net outperforms SBI by 27.66% in accuracy and 41.23% in sensitivity, but in specificity, it underperforms SBI (without FP frames), by 9.32%. The 15 FP that have been wrongly marked contain small areas in intestinal folds.

Figure 4 presents an interesting view of U-Net's performance for clinical application. The chart shows the Set 2 sequence with the area (total of pixels) of the segmented bleeding lesions plotted in black and in background the frames with bleeding are represented in red - for the ground truth - and in blue for the SBI tool.

Table 3. Comparison between U-Net (trained on Set 1) and SBI, when applied to Set 2.

	ACC (%)	TPR (%)	TNR (%)
SBI	69.17	57.86	100.00
U-Net	96.83	99.09	90.68

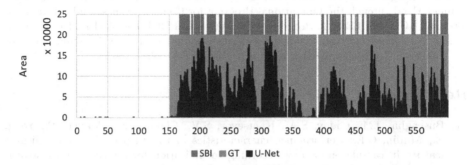

Fig. 4. Set 2: chart of U-Net segmented area versus blood detection in ground truth and SBI. (Color figure online)

In the first 150 sequence frames there are no red lesions. It can be seen that there are some frames with very small areas (black dots) that are detected by the U-Net but unrecognized as blood by the human. The SBI does not detect any red lesion until approximately frame 160, were U-Net are about 1E4 pixels.

After frame 150, the human marked almost all the frames with red lesion, as it can be seen by the continuous red color. The U-Net area has a very good match with GT, as expected (ACC = 96.83%) and also translates the amount of blood in each frame. It can be seen a coherent continuity of blood amount along the sequence and that in the few frames without blood in the interval, around frames 340 and frames 390. The SBI show lots of false negative red lesions, noticed in the frequent discontinuation of blue color, in accordance with SBI ACC = 69.17%. From the chart it seems like the SBI is tuned to identify red lesions without false positives, as the TNR = 100% indicates.

Thus, it can be stated that the U-Net model did very well in the detection and segmentation of bleeding in videos of endoscopy and presents high potential to be useful in clinical environment.

5 Conclusion

In this paper, the U-Net model was evaluated in detecting and segmenting red lesions in endoscopy videos. The U-Net model learned very well to detect red lesions, outperforming the works that showed the best results in the state of the art by 1.78% in accuracy and in 7.87% in sensitivity and having a specificity lower by 0.66%. It was evaluated in a sequence of images and compared with SBI achieving much better accuracy and excellent sensibility, much better than SBI (more 27.66% and 41.23%, respectively). The SBI got a specificity of 100%, 9.32% better than the U-Net model. Thus, the U-Net model had an excellent performance in the detection and segmentation of red lesions in endoscopy videos, presenting an high potential to be useful in clinical environments.

Acknowledgments. This work is financed by the ERDF – European Regional Development Fund through the Operational Program for Competitiveness and Internationalization - COMPETE 2020 Program within project «POCI-01-0145-FEDER-006961», and by National Funds through the Portuguese funding agency, FCT - Fundação para a Ciência e a Tecnologia as part of project «UID/EEA/50014/2013».

References

1. Buscaglia, J.M., Giday, S.A., Kantsevoy, S.V., Clarke, J.O., Magno, P., Yong, E., Mullin, G.E.: Performance characteristics of the suspected blood indicator feature in capsule endoscopy according to indication for study. Clin. Gastroenterol. Hepatol. **6**(3), 298–301 (2008). http://linkinghub.elsevier.com/retrieve/pii/S1542356507012062
2. Figueiredo, I.N., Kumar, S., Leal, C., Figueiredo, P.N.: Computer-assisted bleeding detection in wireless capsule endoscopy images. Comput. Methods Biomech. Biomed. Eng. Imaging Vis. **1**(4), 198–210 (2013). http://www.tandfonline.com/doi/abs/10.1080/21681163.2013.796164
3. Iakovidis, D.K., Koulaouzidis, A.: Software for enhanced video capsule endoscopy: challenges for essential progress. Nat. Rev. Gastroenterol. Hepatol. **12**(3), 172–186 (2015). http://dx.doi.org/10.1038/nrgastro.2015.13%5Cn10.1038/nrgastro.2015.13
4. Koulaouzidis, A., Iakovidis, D.K., Karargyris, A., Plevris, J.N.: Optimizing lesion detection in small-bowel capsule endoscopy: from present problems to future solutions. Expert Rev. Gastroenterol. Hepatol. **9**(2), 217–235 (2015)
5. Koulaouzidis, A., Iakovidis, D.K., Yung, D.E., Rondonotti, E., Kopylov, U., Plevris, J.N., Toth, E., Eliakim, A., Wurm Johansson, G., Marlicz, W., Mavrogenis, G., Nemeth, A., Thorlacius, H., Tontini, G.E.: KID Project: an internet-based digital video atlas of capsule endoscopy for research purposes. Endosc. Int. Open **5**(6), E477–E483 (2017). http://www.thieme-connect.de/DOI/DOI?10.1055/s-0043-105488
6. Park, S.C., Chun, H.J., Kim, E.S., Keum, B., Seo, Y.S., Kim, Y.S., Jeen, Y.T., Lee, H.S., Um, S.H., Kim, C.D., Ryu, H.S.: Sensitivity of the suspected blood indicator: an experimental study. World J. Gastroenterol (WJG) **18**(31), 4169–4174 (2012)
7. Ronneberger, O., Fischer, P., Brox, T.: U-Net: convolutional networks for biomedical image segmentation. Med. Image Comput. Comput. Assisted Interv. (MICCAI) **15**(1), 348–356 (2015). https://doi.org/10.1007/978-3-319-24574-4_28
8. Sainju, S., Bui, F.M., Wahid, K.A.: Automated bleeding detection in capsule endoscopy videos using statistical features and region growing. J. Med. Syst. **38**(4), 25 (2014). http://link.springer.com/10.1007/s10916-014-0025-1
9. Seguí, S., Drozdzal, M., Pascual, G., Radeva, P., Malagelada, C., Azpiroz, F., Vitrià, J.: Generic feature learning for wireless capsule endoscopy analysis. Comput. Biol. Med. **79**, 163–172 (2016). http://linkinghub.elsevier.com/retrieve/pii/S0010482516302712

10. Spada, C., Hassan, C., Munoz-Navas, M., Neuhaus, H., Deviere, J., Fockens, P., Coron, E., Gay, G., Toth, E., Riccioni, M.E., Carretero, C., Charton, J.P., Van Gossum, A., Wientjes, C.A., Sacher-Huvelin, S., Delvaux, M., Nemeth, A., Petruzziello, L., de Frias, C.P., Mayershofer, R., Aminejab, L., Dekker, E., Galmiche, J.P., Frederic, M., Johansson, G.W., Cesaro, P., Costamagna, G.: Second-generation colon capsule endoscopy compared with colonoscopy. Gastrointest. Endosc. **74**(3), 581–589 (2011). http://dx.doi.org/10.1016/j.gie.2011.03.1125
11. Taha, A.A., Hanbury, A.: Metrics for evaluating 3D medical image segmentation: analysis, selection, and tool. BMC Med. Imaging **15**(1) (2015). https://doi.org/10.1186/s12880-015-0068-x
12. Tuba, E., Tuba, M., Jovanovic, R.: An algorithm for automated segmentation for bleeding detection in endoscopic images. In: International Joint Conference on Neural Networks (IJCNN), pp. 4579–4586. IEEE, May 2017. http://ieeexplore.ieee.org/document/7966437/
13. Usman, M.A., Satrya, G., Usman, M.R., Shin, S.Y.: Detection of small colon bleeding in wireless capsule endoscopy videos. Comput. Med. Imaging Graph. **54**, 16–26 (2016). https://doi.org/10.1016/j.compmedimag.2016.09.005
14. Wilcox, C.M., Cryer, B.L., Henk, H.J., Zarotsky, V., Zlateva, G.: Mortality associated with gastrointestinal bleeding events: comparing short-term clinical outcomes of patients hospitalized for upper GI bleeding and acute myocardial infarction in a US managed care setting. Clin. Exp. Gastroenterol. **2**, 21–30 (2009). http://www.ncbi.nlm.nih.gov/pmc/articles/PMC3108636/
15. Xiong, Y., Zhu, Y., Pang, Z., Ma, Y., Chen, D., Wang, X.: Bleeding detection in wireless capsule endoscopy based on MST clustering and SVM. In: IEEE Workshop on Signal Processing Systems (SiPS), vol. 35, pp. 1–4. IEEE, October 2015. http://ieeexplore.ieee.org/lpdocs/epic03/wrapper.htm?arnumber=7345001
16. Yung, D.E., Sykes, C., Koulaouzidis, A.: The validity of suspected blood indicator software in capsule endoscopy: a systematic review and meta-analysis. Expert Rev. Gastroenterol. Hepatol. **11**(1), 43–51 (2017). https://www.tandfonline.com/doi/full/10.1080/17474124.2017.1257384

Hierarchical Framework for Automatic Pancreas Segmentation in MRI Using Continuous Max-Flow and Min-Cuts Approach

Hykoush Asaturyan[(✉)] and Barbara Villarini

Computer Science Department, University of Westminster, London, UK
h.asaturyan@my.westminster.ac.uk, b.villarini@westminster.ac.uk

Abstract. Accurate, automatic and robust segmentation of the pancreas in medical image scans remains a challenging but important prerequisite for computer-aided diagnosis (CADx). This paper presents a tool for automatic pancreas segmentation in magnetic resonance imaging (MRI) scans. Proposed is a framework that employs a hierarchical pooling of information as follows: identify major pancreas region and apply contrast enhancement to differentiate between pancreatic and surrounding tissue; perform 3D segmentation by employing continuous max-flow and min-cuts approach, structured forest edge detection, and a training dataset of annotated pancreata; eliminate non-pancreatic contours from resultant segmentation via morphological operations on area, curvature and position between distinct contours. The proposed method is evaluated on a dataset of 20 MRI volumes, achieving a mean Dice Similarity coefficient of $75.5 \pm 7.0\%$ and a mean Jaccard Index coefficient of $61.2 \pm 9.2\%$.

Keywords: Automatic pancreas segmentation
Computer aided diagnosis (CADx)
Continuous max-flow and min-cuts · Contrast enhancement · MRI
Structured forests

1 Introduction

The accurate segmentation and classification of the pancreas plays a key role in computer-aided diagnosis (CADx) systems [7,18], providing image analysis for disorders such as Type 2 diabetes mellitus [1] and detection of pancreatic neoplasms [13]. Studies have reported variations in the pancreas contour can be linked to ductal adenocarcinoma [3], and enhanced contour analysis can help stratify normal variations against pancreatic tumours [11]. However, the pancreas has very high structural variability and a full inspection from a scan is problematic due to location and surrounding abdominal fat, and vessels. Differing from CT imaging, the low resolution and slower imaging speed of MRI presents additional edge based artefacts, especially for the pancreas [2].

© Springer International Publishing AG, part of Springer Nature 2018
A. Campilho et al. (Eds.): ICIAR 2018, LNCS 10882, pp. 562–570, 2018.
https://doi.org/10.1007/978-3-319-93000-8_64

In recent research literature, various approaches to pancreas segmentation have relied upon training databases of manually annotated pancreata in MRI and CT volumes. A number of methods have been employed including region growing [16], atlas guided approach and discriminative dictionary learning [17], deformable image registration [14] and patch-based label propagation using relative geodesic distances [19]. Furthermore, most recently, deep learning based networks such as convolutional neural networks (CNNs) have been widely reported in pancreas segmentation tasks [2,13].

The proposed approach performs automatic pancreas segmentation in MRI volumes using a training dataset of annotated image volumes. The identification of the major pancreas region, coupled with effective contrast enhancement, reveals rich pancreatic features which are extracted using continuous max-flow and min-cuts, and structured forest edge detection.

In Sect. 2, the methodology for 3D pancreas segmentation and refinement is covered. Section 3 presents and discusses the segmentation results' outcome with comparison to those reported in recent literature, and strategies for further optimisation. Section 4 provides a conclusion for the proposed framework.

2   Methodology

The methodology of the proposed framework, as illustrated in Fig. 1, progresses through three main stages, each one of which is discussed below.

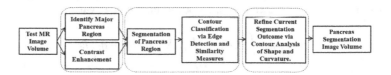

Fig. 1. Overview of framework for the automatic segmentation of the pancreas from an MRI volume.

2.1   Analysis of Image Structure and Intensities

An effective application of contrast enhancement in an MRI volume can differentiate pancreatic tissue and boundaries against background classes of blood vessels, stomach fundus and the first section of the small intestine. In this approach, a sigmoid function is applied to a given test image volume by incorporating a gain, g, which controls the actual contrast, and a cut-off value, c, which represents the (normalised) grey value about which contrast level is changed. Every i-th slice, s_i, in the image volume undergoes contrast enhancement, $C(s_i)$, as described in Eq. 1:

$$C(s_i) = \frac{1}{1 + \exp\left[g(c-s_i)\right]} \tag{1}$$

Figure 2(a) and (b) depicts a slice from an image volume before and after contrast enhancement, respectively. By assigning optimum gain values to images in the training dataset, a non-linear regression model is developed to predict the gain from a test image volume. Overall, the value of the gain changes in proportion to the mean of pixel intensities in the image volume. Similarly, a linear regression model is developed for predicting the cut-off value.

Next, the major pancreas region is identified using the method reported in [7]. A random forest is trained on a selection of extracted features in image patches of 25×25 pixels. These features describe texture and the probability of a patch being "pancreas" based on voxel intensity analysis in the training data. Figure 2(c) displays a red outline over a sample slice that embodies the area predicting "pancreas" at a probability of 0.85. This represents the major pancreas region for that particular slice in a test image volume.

2.2 Segmentation of Pancreas Tissue and Surroundings

The image volume is further processed through a 3D segmentation algorithm described in [20], which uses maximal-flow and minimum graph-cuts approach in a continuous domain. Allow Ω to serve as a closed and continuous 3D domain representing the major pancreas region volume as a graph. At every position, $x \in \Omega$, the spatial flow passing x can be written as $q(x)$. Additionally, the directed source flow from terminal s to x can be denoted by $q_s(x)$, and the directed sink flow from x to terminal t by $q_t(x)$. The continuous max-flow and min-cuts model can be described through the introduction of a multiplier known as the "dual variable", denoted by μ to some flow conservation:

$$\max_{q_s,q_t,q} \min_{\mu} \int_{\Omega} q_s dx + \int_{\Omega} \mu(\nabla \cdot q - q_s + q_t)dx \qquad (2)$$

such that $q_s(x) \leq C_s(x)$, $q_t(x) \leq C_t(x)$ and $|q(x)| \leq |C(x)|$, where $C(x)$, $C_s(x)$ and $C_t(x)$ describe given capacity functions, and $\nabla \cdot q$ calculates the total spatial flow nearby x. From here, the "Multiplier-Based Maximal-Flow Algorithm" described in [20] is employed to perform unsupervised image segmentation on the entire image volume within the major pancreas region. Figure 2(d) displays the resulting segmentation of a single slice from a given test image volume.

Edge Detection and Boundary Matching. The segmented image volume undergoes a transformation via structured forest learning [4] where the boundaries or edges of pancreatic issue and surroundings are detected. The edges of segments in each slice are measured against the boundaries of equally sized pancreas segments provided in the training dataset. The measure of similarity between these edges are performed via modified Hausdorff distance (MHD) [6] and structural similarity (SSIM) index [5]. Whenever the error between a region in the training data and its corresponding region in the segmentation slice falls below 15% for MHD and below 30% for SSIM, a boundary match is assigned to a compilation of pancreas contour similarities, otherwise the segment is disregarded. Figure 2(e) depicts the boundaries of different tissue in a segmented slice after max-flow and min-cuts segmentation. Notice the variation in contour intensity against the background.

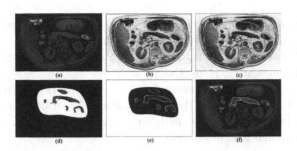

Fig. 2. Visualisation of results for a slice from image volume. (a) Original MRI slice, (b) MRI slice after contrast enhancement, (c) Red bounding box depicts major pancreas region, (d) Segmentation following max-flow and min-cuts approach, (e) Boundary detection using structured forest learning, (f) Final contour segmentation after refinement. (Color figure online)

2.3   Fine Extraction of Pancreas

Once an image volume of rough segmentation has been extracted, a stage of post-processing eliminates surrounding contours identified as "non-pancreas". Figure 2(f) displays the final segmentation outcome for a single slice in a test image volume following stages of refinement.

Morphological Operations on Pancreatic Contours. Analysing a given set of annotated training image volumes, the following is deduced: the mean range of slices for a theoretical image, with careful consideration to heavy outliners; the mean slice number where the pancreas features become visible for the first time, s_{start}, reach maximum area, s_{max}, and the last slice after which pancreas features are not visible any longer, s_{end}. By considering the total number of slices in each image volume, t_s (which is constant), a discrete set of four slice ranges are established: $r_1 : [1, s_{start}-1]$, $r_2 : [s_{start}, s_{max}-1]$, $r_3 : [s_{max}, s_{end}-1]$ and $r_4 : [s_{end}, t_s]$, where r_1, r_2, r_3 and $r_4 \in \mathbb{Z}$. A k-medoids cluster approach is employed in order to generate N_{r_1}, N_{r_2}, N_{r_3} and N_{r_4} groups of constraints for every slice range. Every group of constraints includes a measure of area, triangularity and ratio of width-to-height. For each slice range, individual contours in the segmentation image volume are simultaneously measured against corresponding groups of constraints; if the error for each observation is larger than 15%, then this contour is regarded as "non-pancreas" and removed from the overall segmentation result, otherwise it is retained. Let $N_{r_i}(\alpha)$, $N_{r_i}(\beta)$ and $N_{r_i}(\gamma)$ represent individual constraints of area, triangularity and ratio of spatial dimensions. Thus, for every N_{r_i}, this operation can be defined as:

$$p_c = \begin{cases} 1 & \text{if } 0 \leq E_{r_i}^{\alpha}, \, E_{r_i}^{\beta}, \, E_{r_i}^{\gamma} \leq 0.15 \\ 0 & \text{otherwise} \end{cases} \tag{3}$$

where p_c represents a segmented contour whose value of 1 corresponds to "pancreas" and a value of 0 corresponds to "non-pancreas". $E_{r_i}^{\alpha}$, $E_{r_i}^{\beta}$ and $E_{r_i}^{\gamma}$ represent the error between $N_{r_i}(\alpha)$, $N_{r_i}(\beta)$ and $N_{r_i}(\gamma)$ and an observed segmentation contour's similar measures, respectively.

Another morphological operation involves computation of mean curvature [9] for each distinct contour in the segmentation. If an observed contour falls below a threshold computed from analysing curvatures of unique contours in the training dataset, then it is discarded.

Position of Contours. The slice-by-slice inspection of pancreatic regions in the training dataset reveals that whole or distinct pancreatic contours are embodied in a shape resembling a horseshoe, an inverted-V, transverse, sigmoidal [8] but more commonly, oblique or L-shaped [3]. By considering a bounding box, F_s, to contain all the contours in each segmentation slice, it is possible to generate an L-shaped template that behaves like a "trail-map" for identifying contours deemed as "pancreas" or otherwise. This trail-map can be viewed as a collection of neighbouring paths that begin from a set of points, $B_{XY} = \{(x_1, y_{max}), ..., (x_n, y_{max})\}$, on the bottom horizontal of the bounding box and rise by corresponding angles, $\theta = \{\theta_1, ..., \theta_n\}$, to respective points on the top horizontal of the bounding box. From here, the trail descends by angles, $\phi = \{\phi_1, ..., \phi_n\}$, to respective terminating points (on the bounding box). It is noted that $B_X = \{x_1, ..., x_n\}$ are values that refer to a set of n distances measured from the bottom right-hand vertex, i.e. (x_{max}, y_{max}), hence, $B_X \in \mathbb{R} \mid x_{min} \leq B_X \leq x_{max}$. Values of θ and ϕ are co-dependent on the width and height of the bounding box.

3   Results and Discussion

The proposed approach employs a dataset of T2-weighted (fat-suppressed) abdominal MRI scans obtained from 130 volunteers using a Siemens Trio 3T scanner. The training and test evaluation dataset is split into 110 and 20 MRI volumes respectively. For each image volume, the pancreas has been manually annotated by an expert-operator using a commercially available image analysis software. Every image volume in the dataset consists of 80 slices with 1.6 mm spacing, with each slice of spatial size 320×260 and 1.1875 mm pixel interval in the axial and sagittal direction.

For each experiment, the values described in Sect. 2.3 are such that the curvature threshold is 0.27 and $n = 4$, respectively.

The segmentation program ran via a workstation with i7-59-30k-CPU at 3.50 GHz, and the mean time for segmentation of one case (MRI volume) is 25 min.

This run-time can be potentially reduced by a factor of 10 by using a GeForce Titan X GPU.

The performance of the proposed approach is evaluated using the Dice Similarity Coefficient (DSC) and Jaccard Index (JI) method. Table 1 displays the DSC and JI for the evaluation dataset as mean ± standard deviation [lowest, highest], in comparison to other automatic approaches reported in research literature.

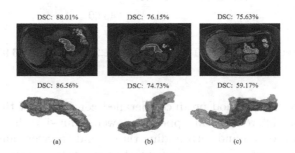

Fig. 3. Segmentation results for three different volunteers. From left, first column displays sample MRI axial slices with segmentation outcome (green) against ground-truth (red), and computed DSC; second column displays 3D reconstruction of entire pancreas (green) segmentation against its ground-truth (red), with computed overall DSC. (Color figure online)

However, direct comparison with other methods in literature is difficult due to differences in imaging modalities, the scanner imaging protocols, spatial resolution and dimensions, as well as the number of image volumes used in the experiments. That said, the approach presented in this paper does report better quantitative pancreas segmentation results in comparison to other state-of-the-art techniques. Although the accuracy results reported in [2] are relatively higher in comparison, this proposed approach reveals a tighter standard deviation. Moreover, employing this method produces detailed contouring of the pancreas for every protrusion and indentation as opposed to an approximate or mean tracing of the organ.

A methodology reported in [15] employs probabilistic atlas-based graph cut and achieves a mean JI coefficient of 77.0 ± 10.2% for 15 CT volumes. Since the technique is interactive based, a medical expert identifies a "seed" (or location) from where the segmentation is performed. The proposed method for this paper is fully automatic and does not require user intervention. Also, the modality of choice is MRI, as opposed to CT, and therefore tackles greater problems relating to image artefacts. Also, the max-flow and min-cuts based approach, described in this paper, employs rich statistical information about wide variations and irregularities in pancreas shape and size.

Figure 3 displays the final pancreas segmentation from three different MRI scans. Notice the variation between image contrast and intensity in the axial MRI

Table 1. Overall DSC and JI shown as mean ± standard deviation [lowest, highest] for automatic segmentation methods

Method	DSC (%)	JI (%)	Data (size)
Wang et al. [19]	65.5 ± 18.6 [2.4, 90.2]	–	CT (100)
Tong et al. [17]	71.1 ± 14.7	56.90 ± 15.2	CT (150)
Roth et al. [13]	71.8 ± 10.7 [25.0, 86.9]	–	CT (82)
Cai et al. [2]	76.1 ± 8.7 [47.4, 87.1]	–	MRI (78)
Okada et al. [10]	–	46.60	CT (28)
Shimizu et al. [14]	–	57.90	CT (20)
Proposed Method	75.5 ± 7.0 [65.0, 86.9]	61.2 ± 9.2 [48.1, 76.9]	MRI (20)

slices. Although this method produces detailed contouring of the organ, there are also evident differences can appear less-well defined with blurred boundaries between the organ and surrounding tissue, and therefore affect the overall segmentation accuracy. The main source of segmentation error, currently preventing a relatively higher accuracy score, can be attributed to accumulation of surrounding pancreas tissue such as the superior mesenteric vein, the splenic vein, the duodenum and nearby vessels. The potential for optimisation involves removal of surrounding tissue such as splenic arteries prior to max-flow and min-cuts segmentation. Incorporating a deep learning based model for automatically learning to identify pancreatic features can enhance the segmentation outcome [2,12]. Moreover, the proposed approach can be further developed by improving computation of optimum parameters, such as threshold and contrast level for pancreatic tissue enhancement prior to segmentation.

4   Conclusion

This paper presents a framework for automatic pancreas segmentation in MRI volumes. Although direct comparison with other methods is difficult due to differences in datasets, the proposed approach performs close to performs better than state-of-the-art techniques.

Acknowledgments. The authors would like to thank the University of Westminster for providing a large medical imaging database that fosters research for health and wellbeing.

References

1. Burute, N., Nisenbaum, R., Jenkins, D.J., Mirrahimi, A., Anthwal, S., Colak, E., Kirpalani, A.: Pancreas volume measurement in patients with type 2 diabetes using magnetic resonance imaging-based planimetry. Pancreatology **14**, 268–274 (2014)
2. Cai, J., Lu, L., Xie, Y., Xing, F., Yang, L.: Pancreas segmentation in MRI using graph-based decision fusion on convolutional neural networks. In: Descoteaux, M., Maier-Hein, L., Franz, A., Jannin, P., Collins, D.L., Duchesne, S. (eds.) MICCAI 2017. LNCS, vol. 10435, pp. 674–682. Springer, Cham (2017). https://doi.org/10.1007/978-3-319-66179-7_77
3. Cruickshank, A.H., Benbow, E.W.: Pathology of the Pancreas, pp. 10–15. Springer, London (1995). https://doi.org/10.1007/978-1-4471-3005-5
4. Dollár, P., Zitnick, C.L.: Structured forests for fast edge detection. In: Proceedings of the 2013 IEEE International Conference on Computer Vision, ICCV 2013, pp. 1841–1848. IEEE CS (2013)
5. Dosselmann, R., Yang, X.D.: A comprehensive assessment of the structural similarity index. SIViP **5**(1), 81–91 (2011)
6. Dubuisson, M., Jain, A.: A modified Hausdorff distance for object matching. In: Proceedings of the 12th IAPR International Conference, vol. 1, pp. 566–568 (1994)
7. Farag, A., Lu, L., Roth, H.R., Liu, J., Turkbey, E., Summers, R.M.: A bottom-up approach for pancreas segmentation using cascaded superpixels and (deep) image patch labeling. IEEE Trans. Image Process. **26**(1), 386–399 (2017)
8. Hagen-Ansert, S.: Textbook of Diagnostic Sonography, pp. 305–308. Mosby, St. Louis (2017)
9. Williams, D.J., Shah, M.: A fast algorithm for active contours and curvature estimation. CVGIP **55**, 14–26 (1992)
10. Okada, T., et al.: Abdominal multi-organ segmentation of CT images based on hierarchical spatial modeling of organ interrelations. In: Yoshida, H., Sakas, G., Linguraru, M.G. (eds.) ABD-MICCAI 2011. LNCS, vol. 7029, pp. 173–180. Springer, Heidelberg (2012). https://doi.org/10.1007/978-3-642-28557-8_22
11. Omeri, A.K., Matsumoto, S., Kiyonaga, M., Takaji, R., Yamada, Y., Kosen, K., Mori, H., Miyake, H.: Contour variations of the body and tail of the pancreas: evaluation with MDCT. Jpn. J. Radiol. **35**(6), 310–318 (2017)
12. Ronneberger, O., Fischer, P., Brox, T.: U-Net: convolutional networks for biomedical image segmentation. In: Navab, N., Hornegger, J., Wells, W.M., Frangi, A.F. (eds.) MICCAI 2015. LNCS, vol. 9351, pp. 234–241. Springer, Cham (2015). https://doi.org/10.1007/978-3-319-24574-4_28
13. Roth, H.R., Lu, L., Farag, A., Shin, H.-C., Liu, J., Turkbey, E.B., Summers, R.M.: DeepOrgan: multi-level deep convolutional networks for automated pancreas segmentation. In: Navab, N., Hornegger, J., Wells, W.M., Frangi, A.F. (eds.) MICCAI 2015. LNCS, vol. 9349, pp. 556–564. Springer, Cham (2015). https://doi.org/10.1007/978-3-319-24553-9_68
14. Shimizu, A., Kimoto, T., Kobatake, H., Nawano, S., Shinozaki, K.: Automated pancreas segmentation from three-dimensional contrast-enhanced computed tomography. Int. J. Comput. Assist. Radiol. Surg. **5**(1), 85–98 (2010)
15. Suzuki, T., Takizawa, H., Kudo, H., Okada, T.: Interactive segmentation of pancreases from abdominal CT images by use of the graph cut technique with probabilistic atlases. BioMed Res. Int. **45**, 575–584 (2016)

16. Tam, T.D., Binh, N.T.: Efficient pancreas segmentation in computed tomography based on region-growing. In: Vinh, P.C., Vassev, E., Hinchey, M. (eds.) ICTCC 2014. LNICST, vol. 144, pp. 332–340. Springer, Cham (2015). https://doi.org/10.1007/978-3-319-15392-6_31
17. Tong, T., Wolz, R., Wang, Z., Gao, Q., Misawa, K., Fujiwara, M., Mori, K., Hajnal, J.V., Rueckert, D.: Discriminative dictionary learning for abdominal multi-organ segmentation. Med. Image Anal. **23**(1), 92–104 (2015)
18. Villarini, B., Asaturyan, H., Thomas, E., Mould, R., Bell, J.: A framework for morphological feature extraction of organs from MR images for detection and classification of abnormalities. IEEE (2017)
19. Wang, Z., et al.: Geodesic patch-based segmentation. In: Golland, P., Hata, N., Barillot, C., Hornegger, J., Howe, R. (eds.) MICCAI 2014. LNCS, vol. 8673, pp. 666–673. Springer, Cham (2014). https://doi.org/10.1007/978-3-319-10404-1_83
20. Yuan, J., Bae, E., Tai, X.C.: A study on continuous max-flow and min-cut approaches. In: Proceedings of the IEEE Computer Society Conference on Computer Vision and Pattern Recognition, pp. 2217–2224 (2010)

Nerve Structure Segmentation from Ultrasound Images Using Random Under-Sampling and an SVM Classifier

C. Jimenez[1]([✉]), D. Diaz[2], D. Salazar[2], A. M. Alvarez[1], A. Orozco[1],
and O. Henao[1]

[1] Automatics Research Group, Universidad Tecnologica de Pereira, Pereira, Colombia
craljimenez@utp.edu.co
[2] VitalCare, Pereira, Colombia

Abstract. The identification of nerve structures is a crucial issue in the field of anesthesiology. Recently, ultrasound images have become relevant for performing Peripheral Nerve Blocking (PNB) procedures since it offers a non-invasive visualization of the nerve and the anatomical structures around it. However, the location of nerve structures from ultrasound images is a difficult task for the specialist due to the artifacts, i.e., speckle noise, which affect the intelligibility of a given image. Here, we proposed an automatic nerve structure segmentation approach from ultrasound images based on random under-sampling (RUS) and a support vector machine (SVM) classifier. In particular, we use a Graph Cuts-based technique to define a region of interest (ROI). Then, such an ROI is split into several correlated areas (superpixels) using the well-known Simple Linear Iterative Clustering algorithm. Further, a nonlinear Wavelet transform is applied to extract relevant features. Afterward, we use a classification scheme based on RUS and SVM to predict the label of each parametrized superpixel. Thus, our approach can deal with the imbalance issues when classifying a superpixel as nerve or non-nerve. Attained results on a real-world dataset demonstrate that our method outperforms similar works regarding both the dice segmentation coefficient and the geometric mean-based classification assessment.

Keywords: Nerve segmentation · SVM · Ultrasound images
Under-sampling

1 Introduction

Regional anesthesia has become an attractive alternative for general anesthesia in the context of medical surgeries because it increases post-operative mobility and reduces morbidity and mortality [1]. Regarding this, the Peripheral Nerve Blocking (PNB) is a well-known regional anesthesia technique that consists in the administration of an anesthetic nearby the nerve structure. However, the success of the PNB procedure depends on a precise localization of the nerve

© Springer International Publishing AG, part of Springer Nature 2018
A. Campilho et al. (Eds.): ICIAR 2018, LNCS 10882, pp. 571–578, 2018.
https://doi.org/10.1007/978-3-319-93000-8_65

structure. So, four methods are recognized to find the right place to perform PNB: Anatomical surface landmarks, Elicitation of paresthesia, Nerve stimulation, and Ultrasound imaging. The first one is not useful in clinical processes because of the anatomical differences among each patient. The second one is rarely used due to the inconveniences imposed upon the patient. On the other hand, nerve simulation is recommended for performing PNB, but it causes a contraction in the area innervated by the nerve [2]. Lastly, the ultrasound image permits non-invasive visualization of the nerve, the structures around it, the needle used, and the injected anesthesia to ensure adequate distribution.

Nevertheless, ultrasound images-based nerve structure segmentation is a difficult task due to these images are affected by several artifacts, namely: attenuation, acoustic shadows, and speckle noise; moreover, nerves are not static structures. Therefore, their location and shape depend on body position, gravity, and external forces. Some methods have been proposed for the segmentation of anatomical structures in ultrasound images. Recently, two methodologies have been introduced for dealing with the problem of nerve structure segmentation as a binary classification task [3,4]. Notwithstanding, they ignore the imbalance between the classes nerve and non-nerve region, obtaining biased results [5].

In this work, we propose a nerve structure segmentation approach from ultrasound images based on random under-sampling (RUS) and support vector machines (SVM) to counteract the effect of imbalanced data [6]. Thereby, we use a Graph Cuts-based technique to find a region of interest (ROI) that allows ensuring stable results on real-world images. Then, the ROI is divided into several superpixels using a Simple Linear Iterative Clustering algorithm. Afterward, a feature extraction space is computed based on a nonlinear Wavelet transform. Finally, RUS and an SVM-based classifier are trained to predict the label of each parametrized superpixel. As benchmarks we test a Gaussian Process classifier (GPC) [4], a weighted lagrangian twin support vector machine (WLTSVM) [5], and a standard SVM. Results obtained on a real-world dataset show that our approach outperforms the baseline methods concerning both the dice segmentation coefficient and the geometric mean-based classification assessment.

The remainder of this paper is organized as follows: Sect. 2 describes the materials and methods of the approach proposed for nerve structure segmentation. Section 3 and 4 describe the experimental set-up and the results obtained, respectively. Finally, the concluding remarks are outlined in Sect. 5.

2   Nerve Structure Segmentation from Ultrasound Images

Preprocessing and Feature Estimation. Let $\{Z^n \in \mathbb{R}^{W_n \times H_n}, L^n \in \{-1,$ $+1\}^{W_n \times H_n}\}_{n=1}^{N_I}$ be an input set holding N_I ultrasound images labeled by an specialist; namely, the pair of matrices Z^n and L^n contain the n-th image pixel intensities and labels (nerve/non-nerve), respectively. First, to highlight a relevant region within the n-th image, we extract a *Region of Interest*–(ROI) from each Z^n matrix towards a Graph-cut approach [2]. In turn, the ROI is filtered based on a median function aiming to attenuate speckle noise artifacts, and then, opening and closing morphological operators are used to refine the preprocessing results [4]. Further, each ROI is divided into K superpixels to impose pairwise constraints regarding the pixel location and intensity while enhancing the nerve structure representation. In particular, we employ the well-known *Simple Linear Iterative Clustering*–(SLIC) technique, which combines five-dimensional color and image plane spaces to efficiently generate compact and nearly uniform K superpixels [7]. So, a superpixel can be written as the set $\Omega_k^n = \{z_r^n \in Z^n, l_r^n \in L^n : r \in \chi_k^n\}$, where $r = [w, h]$ is an index vector, $w \in \{1, 2, \ldots, W_n\}$, $h \in \{1, 2, \ldots, H_n\}$, and the set χ_k^n comprises the pixel coordinates belonging to the k-th superpixel in the n-th ROI. Besides, the superpixels are represented towards a non-linear wavelet-based transform aiming to highlight discriminant patterns to segment nerve and nonnerve structures. In particular, a dual-lifting scheme is performed. Thereby, B representation bands are deemed to compute their mean, standard deviation, and entropy. In this sense, we obtain the feature matrix $X \in \mathbb{R}^{N_S \times P}$ and the label vector $y \in \{-1, +1\}^{N_S}$ after row-based vector concatenation of the wavelet-based feature vectors $x_i \in \mathbb{R}^P$ ($i \in \{1, 2, \ldots, N_S\}$), where $N_S = N_I \times K$, $P = B \times 3$, and $y_i = \mathrm{mode}_r(l_r^n)$ for the i-th superpixel in the n-th ROI. In turn, the segmentation of nerve structure configures a binary classification problem.

Random Under-Sampling and Classification. Since the number of super-pixels belonging to the non-nerve is higher than the nerve class, we apply a *random under-sampling*–(RUS) over superpixels belonging to the non-nerve class, $\{x_i : y_i = -1\}$, to balance the dataset through random elimination of samples belonging to non-nerve group. By that, we obtain a re-sampling feature matrix $X' \in \mathbb{R}^{N_S' \times P}$ and a label vector $y' \in \{-1, +1\}^{N_S'}$ with $N_S' < N_S$. Next, we define a non-linear mapping function from $\mathbb{R}^P$ to a Reproducing Kernel Hilbert Space–(RKHS), $\phi : \mathbb{R}^P \to \mathcal{H}$, for embedding any $x_i \in X'$ into $\phi(x_i) \in \mathcal{H}$. Then, a *support vector machine*–(SVM) classifier is trained as a separating functional $f(x) = w^\top \phi(x) + b = 0$, where $w \in \mathcal{H}$ and $b \in \mathbb{R}$. The optimal values of w and b are obtained by solving the following optimization problem:

$$\min_{w,b,\xi} \ \frac{1}{2}\|w\|_2^2 + C \sum_{j=1}^{N_S'} \xi_j \quad \text{s.t} \quad y_j\left(w^\top \phi(x_j) + b\right) \geq 1 - \xi_j; \quad \xi_j \geq 0 \quad (1)$$

where $\xi_j = |y_j - f(x_j)|$ is the j-th slack variable and $C \in \mathbb{R}^+$ is a regularization parameter. According to the Wolfe dual form, the above minimization problem can be written as [8]:

$$\min_{\alpha} \frac{1}{2} \sum_{i=1}^{N_S'} \sum_{j=1}^{N_S'} y_i y_j \alpha_i \alpha_j k\left(x_i, x_j\right) - \sum_{i=1}^{M} \alpha_i \quad \text{s.t} \quad \sum_{j=1}^{M} y_j \alpha_j = 0; \quad 0 \leq \alpha_j \leq C, \quad (2)$$

where $\alpha_j \in \mathbb{R}$ is a Lagrange multiplier, and $k(\cdot, \cdot) : \mathbb{R}^P \times \mathbb{R}^P \to \mathbb{R}$ is a kernel function. In this sense, a new feature vector x belonging to a given superpixel can be labeled as: $y = \sum_{j=1}^{N_S'} \alpha_j k(x, x_j) + b$. Lastly, a post-processing step is required to recover the full nerve region after RUS and SVM-based nerve structure estimation. This stage is carried out using the morphological-based filtering described in [9]. Figure 1 shows the block diagram of the proposed RUS-SVM-based nerve structure segmentation from ultrasound images.

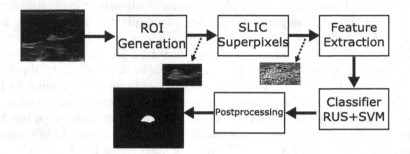

Fig. 1. RUS-SVM-based nerve structure segmentation pipeline.

3   Experimental Set-Up

To test the introduced RUS-SVM-based nerve structure segmentation, we use a dataset of the Universidad Tecnológica de Pereira and the Hospital de Santa Mónica, termed UI-UTP, which comprises several ultrasound images (UI) from patients prosecuted to regional anesthesia for PNB. Namely, UI-UTP contains 38 UI: 22 from the median nerve and 16 from the ulnar nerve. Each UI was collected using a Sonosite Nano-Maxx device with a resolution of 640×480 pixels. Besides, each image was labeled by one specialist in anesthesiology to indicate the location of nerve structures. As baseline, four classification approaches are tested: a Gaussian Process-based classifier (GPC) [4], an SVM without RUS, and a weighted lagrangian twin support vector machine (WLTSVM) [5]. We measure the segmentation performance regarding the Dice coefficient (DC) and the geometric mean (GM). The DC is used in medical imaging to assess the overlap between the target and the estimated segmentation and can be computed as follows: $DC = 2TP/(2TP + FN + FP)$, where TP is the number of pixels belonging to a nerve and classified as nerve, FN codes the number of pixels belonging to a nerve and classified as non-nerve, TF the number of pixels belonging to non-nerve and classified as non-nerve, and FP the number of pixels belonging to non-nerve and classified as nerve. Now, the GM is commonly used to test imbalanced tasks as follows: $GM = \sqrt{\nu \times \zeta}$, where $\nu = TP/(TP + FN)$ and $\zeta = TF/(TN + FP)$. For all the experiments, we perform a leave-one-out cross-validation scheme due to the small number of images.

Concerning the RUS-SVM free parameters, we experimentally fix the ROI size to $K = 600$ superpixels. Besides, we deem $B = 4$ bands, yielding to $P = 12$ features. We select the classifiers free parameters using a 10-fold cross-validation scheme over 20 images chosen randomly. Furthermore, the SVM kernel is fixed as a Gaussian function with bandwidth value fixed from the set $\sigma \in \{0.1\sigma_0, \ldots, \sigma_0\}$, being $\sigma_0 = \text{median} \left(\|x_i - x_j\|_2 \right)$ and median $(\cdot)$ stands for the median operator. Moreover, the regularization parameter value C is computed from the set $C \in \{2^{-5}, 2^{-3}, \ldots, 2^{15}\}$.

4   Results and Discussion

First, a Principal Component Analysis–(PCA) algorithm is applied to the entire data and the RUS-based subset aiming to visualize the main sample relationships. As seen in Fig. 2, the RUS approach can code the main data dependencies for both nerve and non-nerve classes, while balancing the number of samples from one to six to one to one imbalance ratio, aiming to favor further classification stages. Though RUS eliminates some samples belonging to the non-nerve class, the achieved subset preserves the original data structures, avoiding information loss concerning the nerve structure discrimination.

Now, Fig. 3 presents an illustrative example for the RUS-SVM-based nerve structure identification form UI. In fact, Fig. 3(a) and (b), show the original and the labeled UI, respectively. Then, Fig. 3(c) reveals the ROI extracted, which contains mainly pixels belonging to the nerve class. In particular, removing the ROIs allows reducing the imbalance issue between regions (nerve/non-nerve), which is enormous if analyzed from the original UIs, and favors the computational burden of further feature estimation and discrimination stages. In addition, Fig. 3(d) displays the obtained SLIC-based superpixels to estimate relevant features regarding the studied structures. In turn, in Figs. 3(e) to (h) the attained segmentations are presented for SVM, WLTSVM, GPC, and the RUS-SVM proposed. As seen, GPC and RUS-SVM algorithms obtain the best segmentations

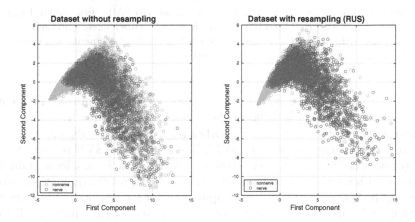

Fig. 2. Left: PCA-based projection of the original (complete) dataset. Right: PCA-based projection of the subset identified by RUS. The red points are samples belonging to the non-nerve class meanwhile the blue ones are related to the nerve class. (Color figure online)

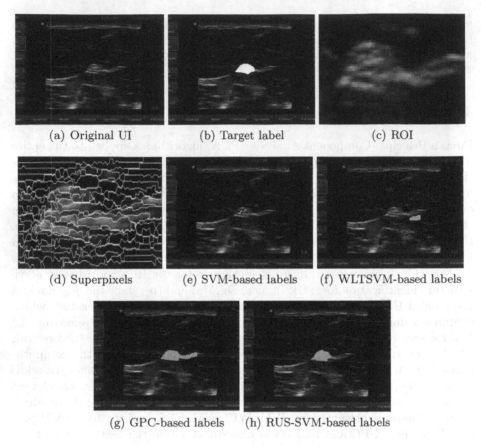

(a) Original UI   (b) Target label   (c) ROI

(d) Superpixels   (e) SVM-based labels   (f) WLTSVM-based labels

(g) GPC-based labels   (h) RUS-SVM-based labels

Fig. 3. An illustrative example of the proposed RUS-SVM-based nerve structure segmentation. (a) shows the ultrasound image original. (b) is the first image tagged by a specialist. (c) is the ROI extracted. (d) shows the superpixels obtained by SLIC Superpixel algorithm. (e), (f), (g) and (h) show the result of segmentation using SVM, WLTSVM, GPC and SVM with RUS respectivity

concerning to the specialist labels. Indeed, the GPC-based approach also includes a RUS-based resampling to balance the classes. However, our RUS-SVM-based segmentation is able to achieve a smoother result than the GPC one because of the generalization capability of the SVM. Remarkably, the SVM segmentation in Fig. 3(e) does not reveal the nerve structure due to such a classifier is trained on a dataset with a six to one imbalance ratio, reducing its discrimination virtues. Likewise, the WLTSVM algorithm computes a poor segmentation due to its optimization problem aims to separate the classes based on the minimum distance to two different hyperplanes, without considering the overlapping between them.

Finally, Table 1 summarizes the segmentation results in terms of the DC and the GM-based assessment. Outstandingly, our RUS-SVM approach achieves the best results regarding the average and the standard deviation. So, our proposal

Table 1. DC and GM results for nerve structure segmentation from UI. The average ± the standard deviation are presented.

Approach	Dice coefficient	Geometric mean
SVM	0.3459 ± 0.2920	0.4031 ± 0.3256
GPC [4]	0.6524 ± 0.0085	**Not provided**
WLTSVM [5]	0.0837 ± 0.1832	0.1036 ± 0.2216
RUS-SVM (proposal)	**0.6706 ± 0.1554**	**0.9360 ± 0.0502**

is able to identify the main data structures based on RUS and then it builds a reliable classifier towards a SVM-based strategy.

5 Conclusions

In this study, we propose a new nerve structure segmentation methodology from UI based on RUS and SVM approaches to counteract the inherent imbalanced issue behind the classification between nerve and non-nerve. Accordingly, we employ a Graph Cuts-based algorithm to highlight an ROI from each UI, and such an ROI is divided into several superpixels. Then, a Wavelet-based feature strategy is carried out. Lastly, RUS and an SVM are applied to predict the label (nerve or non-nerve) of each parametrized superpixel. The approach proposed is tested in a real-world dataset that consists of UI from patients were prosecuted regional anesthesia for PNB. The nerve structure segmentation performance is tested concerning the well-known DC coefficient and the GM. Obtained results show that our RUS-SVM-based algorithm outperforms state-of-the-art methods and allows highlighting smooth regions to support PNB tasks. As future work, authors plan to develop more elaborated undersampling approaches to favor further classification stages.

Acknowledgments. Under grants provided by COLCIENCIAS project 1110-744-55958: "Desarrollo de un sistema de identificación de estructuras nerviosas en imágenes de ultrasonido para la asistencia de bloqueo de nervios periféricos". C. Jimenez is partially funded by the project E6-18-09: "Clasificador de máquinas de vectores de soporte para problemas desbalanceados con selección automática de parámetros" (Vicerrectoria de Investigaciones, Innovación y Extensión) and by Maestría en Ingeniería Eléctrica, both from Universidad Tecnológica de Pereira.

References

1. González, J.G., Álvarez, M.A., Orozco, Á.A.: Peripheral nerves segmentation in ultrasound images using non-linear wavelets and Gaussian processes. In: Paredes, R., Cardoso, J.S., Pardo, X.M. (eds.) IbPRIA 2015. LNCS, vol. 9117, pp. 603–611. Springer, Cham (2015). https://doi.org/10.1007/978-3-319-19390-8_68
2. González, J.G., Álvarez, M.A., Orozco, Á.A.: Automatic segmentation of nerve structures in ultrasound images using graph cuts and Gaussian processes. In: 37th Annual International Conference on Engineering in Medicine and Biology Society (EMBC), pp. 3089–3092. IEEE (2015)

3. Gil-González, J., Álvarez-Meza, A., Echeverry-Correa, J., Orozco-Gutiérrez, A., Álvarez-López, M.: Enhancement of nerve structure segmentation by a correntropy-based pre-image approach. Tecno Lógicas **20**(39), 199–210 (2017)
4. González, J.G., Álvarez, M.A., Orozco, Á.A.: A probabilistic framework based on SLIC-superpixel and Gaussian processes for segmenting nerves in ultrasound images. In: IEEE 38th Annual International Conference on Engineering in Medicine and Biology Society (EMBC), pp. 4133–4136. IEEE (2016)
5. Shao, Y.H., Chen, W.J., Zhang, J.J., Wang, Z., Deng, N.Y.: An efficient weighted Lagrangian twin support vector machine for imbalanced data classification. Pattern Recognit. **47**(9), 3158–3167 (2014)
6. Branco, P., Torgo, L., Ribeiro, R.P.: A survey of predictive modeling on imbalanced domains. ACM Comput. Surv. (CSUR) **49**(2), 31 (2016)
7. Han, C.Y.: Improved SLIC imagine segmentation algorithm based on k-means. Clust. Comput. **20**(2), 1017–1023 (2017)
8. Duda, R.O., Hart, P.E., Stork, D.G.: Pattern Classification. Wiley, New York (2012)
9. Chang, C.Y., Lei, Y.F., Tseng, C.H., Shih, S.R.: Thyroid segmentation and volume estimation in ultrasound images. IEEE Trans. Biomed. Eng. **57**(6), 1348–1357 (2010)

Assessment of Anti-tumor Immune Response in Colorectal Carcinomas from Whole Slide Images

Tiédé Armand Djiro, Camille Kurtz, and Nicolas Loménie[(✉)]

LIPADE, University Paris Descartes, Paris, France
{tiedearmand.djiro,camille.kurtz,nicolas.lomenie}@parisdescartes.fr

Abstract. Digital pathology is considered as one of the most promising techniques for diagnostic medicine, enabling to automate different steps in the visual interpretation process of biological tissues. In order to assess treatment efficiency in colorectal carcinomas, we developed a methodology to characterize the anti-tumor immune response based on the analysis of Whole Slide Images. This method relies both on marker separation and lymphocyte detection image processing modules, coupled to a novel strategy to locally quantify the lymphocyte infiltration relative to the tumor boundary, according to a specific clinical protocol. The quantitative assessments obtained are already used in a pre-clinical analysis of tumor evolution and improve repeatability of clinical studies.

1 Introduction

Cancer is a major public health problem in many parts of the world [1] and several medical studies in the field of histopathology have concluded that evaluating the antitumor immune response of the tumor is a key factor to characterize the progression of the latter [2,3], particularly by the evaluation of lymphocyte infiltration through the tumor border. The evaluation of the anti-tumor immune response is generally done downstream of a treatment by a pathologist to determine the treatment effectiveness as a "companion test".

Digital pathology consists of converting tissue biopsies into Whole Slide Images (WSI), which are very high-resolution and large-scale digital images. It is currently considered as one of the most promising techniques for diagnostic medicine, enabling to automate different steps in the visual interpretation process of biological tissues. In our context, the evaluation or quantification of the antitumor immune response from digital images require multiple steps. The methods related to these steps can be grouped into three groups: the stain separation, the detection of the biological objects of interest, and then the extraction of these biological objects.

Staining of tissue samples is usually done using a biomarker staining a few cells of a light color together with a counter stain staining the rest of the cells of a different color [4]. The stain separation is then a pre-treatment to guide object

© Springer International Publishing AG, part of Springer Nature 2018
A. Campilho et al. (Eds.): ICIAR 2018, LNCS 10882, pp. 579–588, 2018.
https://doi.org/10.1007/978-3-319-93000-8_66

detection and segmentation [5] and although more recent methods of stain separation are presented in the literature [6,7], color deconvolution remains mainly used in practice. For instance, a classical method is based on Beer Lambert's law of absorption [8]. A simple and fast method for stain separation based on the observation of the different RGB channels was also proposed in [5].

In the specific context of the assessment of anti-tumor immune response in colorectal carcinomas, the method proposed by [9] relies on a quantification of CD3+ and CD45R0+ sub-populations of lymphocytes within the tumor borders; more technically, the extraction of the lymphocytes is based on a color thresholding followed by a watershed transformation and finally an area filtering. One of the main limit of the method is to perform the quantification of the lymphocyte infiltration only from different patches superimposed over the lesion border in localized areas, resulting in a partial analysis of the lymphocyte infiltration. Furthermore, such patches are manually drawn by a pathologist, potentially leading to subjective and non-reproducible results.

In this work, we propose a novel method improving the workflow originally presented in [9]. Our method relies both on marker separation and lymphocyte detection image processing modules. The principal contribution is then a novel strategy to spatially quantify the lymphocyte infiltration, relative to the global tumor boundary, according to a specific clinical protocol. The main strength is the use of a distance map for the quantification of lymphocyte infiltration from a representation of the whole tumor boundary, avoiding the consideration of specific patches from the images, and leading to a full analysis of the lymphocyte infiltration in tumor areas.

The paper is organized as follows. Section 2 describes our image analysis method for the assessment of the anti-tumor immune response in colorectal carcinomas from Whole Slide Images. Section 3 describes the experiments carried out with this methodology. Finally we conclude and present some perspectives of our work in Sect. 4.

2   Methodology

The proposed method aims to quantify the infiltration of lymphocytes in colorectal carcinomas relative to the global tumor boundary out of Whole Slide Images. The method takes as input a color image and provides as output a curve of lymphocyte infiltration profile. Figure 1 summarizes the whole pipeline from tumor boundary annotation to the quantification of lymphocyte infiltration. The different steps of this method are presented in the next sections.

The first step consists in annotating the regions of interest in the input WSI image to delineate the tumor borders, avoiding the processing of the entire image. In this preliminary work, this step is done manually without a phase of automatic segmentation of the tumor. The lesions are delineated by a pathologist using an interactive web-based image annotation tool[1] leading to polygonal regions of interest where the analysis of lymphocyte infiltration will be carried out.

---

[1] http://www.cytomine.be/.

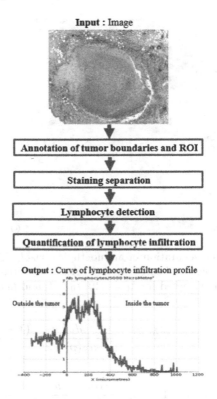

Fig. 1. Pipeline of the proposed method from the tumor boundary annotation on the input WSI to the generation of a curve modeling the lymphocyte infiltration profile.

2.1 Staining Separation

Our images are stained with aminoethylcarbazole (AEC) and hematoxylin (H), which are respectively immunohistochemical and histological stainings.

Staining separation with color deconvolution is a very sensitive step for estimating the optical density matrix associated with each image acquisition device. The optical density vectors of the RGB channels of each single staining should be defined from the stained sample by that staining alone, as described by [8]. This process of defining the matrix is not straightforward.

Thus, inspired by the work of [5], we propose for color separation a function that takes as input a WSI color image and a specific reference stain color and that returns a novel gray level image (enabling to better differentiate the lymphocytes from the other biological objects) where the value of each pixel represents the distance (value) relative to the hue, saturation and reference luminance of the stain. Such a function is defined as follows.

Let an image I defined from a two-dimensional pixel space $\mathbb{N}^2$ with a color space function associated $I(p)$ assigning the gray level intensities to each pixel $p \in \mathbb{N}^2$, in terms of d_H, d_S and d_L that are respectively the distances of hue (h), saturation (s) and luminance (l) of the pixel considered relative to the reference values (h_0, s_0, and l_0):

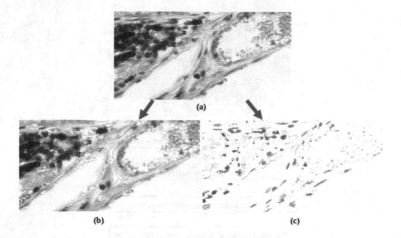

Fig. 2. Illustration of the separation of aminoethylcarbazole (AEC) and hematoxylin (H). (a) RGB image of colorectal carcinoma; (b) AEC extracted for $h_0 = 0$, $s_0 = 1$ and $l_0 = 0$. (c) Hematoxylin extracted for $h_0 = 240$; $s_0 = 1$; and $l_0 = 0$.

$$I(p) = 1 - \left[\frac{(1 - d_H(p)) \times (1 - d_S(p)) \times (1 - d_L(p))}{1 - d_S(p) + \varepsilon'}\right], \tag{1}$$

where:

$$d_H(p) = 1 - \exp\left[\frac{\cos(h - h_0) - 1}{\cos(h - h_0) + 1 + \varepsilon}\right], \tag{2}$$

$$d_S(p) = |s - s_0| \quad \& \quad d_L(p) = |l - l_0| \tag{3}$$

with $h \in [0, 360]$; $s, l, I(p), d_H, d_S, d_L \in [0, 1]$ and control parameters $c, \varepsilon' \in]0, 1[$. The ideal value of ε' is $\frac{1}{255}$ and $I(p)$ can be normalized between $[0, 255]$.

To make easier for the user the selection of the reference values of hue, saturation and luminance (h_0, s_0, and l_0), we developed an interactive software tool. These reference values can be selected in two ways:

1. by interactively selecting and considering the HSL values of a pixel of the WSI image formally identified as stained. To this end our tool enables the user to click on a (stained) pixel of interest in the image content;
2. by considering pre-defined HSL values of the color used to mark the biological objects.

An illustrative example of this step is presented in Fig. 2.

2.2 Lymphocyte Detection

This part gathers the steps of segmentation, separation and extraction of the objects of interest (mentioned in Sect. 1), in our case the lymphocytes, generally applied to stain marked by histological dye material.

As our approach relies on a quantification of the density of the lymphocytes in a particular ROI, we do not need a precise extraction of each individual biological object of interest but rather an estimation of the density of pixels labeled as lymphocytes (applicable to histological and immunohistochemical staining).

In this work, we used the Otsu binarization algorithm on the image resulting from Sect. 2.1 to separate the pixels belonging to lymphocytes from the rest of the image content. However, this often leads to many false positive pixels that are incorrectly considered as lymphocytes due to the imbalance in the pixels of interest distribution. To deal with this issue, we apply the K-Means algorithm on the pixels extracted by Otsu thresholding to split them into two clusters: one for the pixels belonging to lymphocytes and the other for the remainder pixels (that can be considered here as "noise"). Their respective centers are *a priori* determined as follows:

- Cluster 1 (lymphocytes): we set the center value as the average of the gray level values (obtained from the image resulting from Sect. 2.1) of the darkest pixels detected by Otsu;
- Cluster 2 ("noise"): we set the center value as the average of the gray level values (obtained from the image resulting from Sect. 2.1) of the pixels detected by Otsu.

A focus is thus made on the pixels corresponding to lymphocytes and the initialization of the centers is always adapted to the content of the input image.

Some illustrative results are shown in Fig. 3. With the reference luminance and saturation always set at 0 and 1 respectively, this method proved to be less sensitive to the different variations of a marker.

2.3 Quantification of Lymphocyte Infiltration

The last step consists in quantifying the infiltration of the lymphocyte through the whole tumor boundary. To this end, we use a distance map in order to build iso-curves that are parallel to the tumor boundary annotated by an expert. To do that, we implemented an efficient algorithm (involving a parallelization procedure) to compute distance map for closed polygons over large images. This results in two distance maps, encoding the euclidean distance values from the inner (resp. outer) pixels of the lesion to its border.

We then opted for quantification of lymphocytes by local pixel density. The detected pixels of lymphocytes belonging to the ROI are clustered together according to their distance from the tumor boundary (they are all included in the area between two consecutive iso-curves) and are quantified with respect to the surface unit according to the density as detailed below.

Let α and β respectively be the set of stained pixels and the set of unstained pixels of a group of pixels of the ROI at a distance x from the tumor boundary, δ and θ respectively the number of pixels per surface unit and the number of pixels per lymphocyte defined with respect to the resolution of the image. At a distance α from the tumor boundary will be associated a density f defined

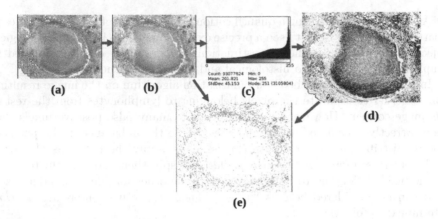

Fig. 3. Illustration of lymphocyte detection. (a) RGB image of colorectal carcinoma. (b) Staining separation step. (c) Histogram of the image. (d) Result of Otsu binarization. (e) Result of K-means clustering of pixels detected by Otsu (only the cluster corresponding to lymphocyte pixels is depicted).

by: $f(\alpha) = [\frac{\alpha \times \delta}{\theta \times (\alpha + \beta)}]$. From the set of $f(\alpha)$ (for all $\alpha \in$ ROI), we automatically compute a *lymphocyte infiltration curve* of the ROI (see Fig. 5(e)). The horizontal axis represents distances to the tumor front (including negative values attributed to objects outside the tumor, positive values to objects inside the tumor). The vertical axis on the center of the graph represents the density of infiltrated lymphocytes per unit of surface ($5000 \mu m^2$) inside (resp. outside) the tumor.

3   Experimental Study

We used the proposed approach to evaluate the infiltration of lymphocytes in colorectal carcinomas, assessing treatment efficiency in the context both of a preclinical and a clinical study in collaboration with biologists and pathologists.

3.1   Material

For our experimental study we built up a database of 25 WSI images including 5 clinical images and 20 preclinical images (3 images from untreated mice, 9 images from mice treated with radiofrequency alone and 8 images from mice treated with radiofrequency + GMCSF-BCG gel). Four types of reference groups were defined from previous studies on the quantification of lymphocyte infiltration [9,10] depending on the shape of the lymphocyte infiltration curve (Fig. 4):

– Level 1: No lymphocyte infiltration (Fig. 6(G, H));
– Level 2: Low lymphocyte infiltration of the tumor front (Fig. 6(E, F));
– Level 3: Lymphocyte infiltration centered on the tumor front (Fig. 6(C, D));
– Level 4: Good lymphocyte infiltration of the tumor front and the interior of the tumor (Fig. 6(A, B)).

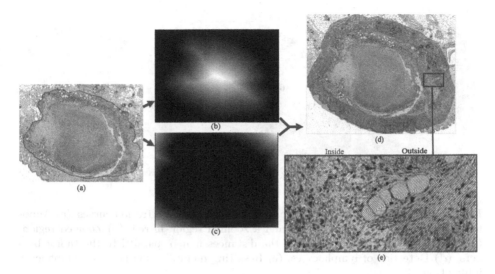

Fig. 4. Illustration of creating iso-curves, parallel to the tumor borders. (a) Annotation of a tumor boundary (ROI). (b) and (c) Normalised outside (inside) distance map. (d) and (e) parallel iso-curves (successive borders) with a resolution of 5 μm.

The objective of this experimental study was twofold: (1) to reproduce the basic assessment done in clinical studies with a more flexible and automatic method than the one originally used [9] and (2) to quantify the infiltration on preclinical studies to assess the efficiency of a new pharmaceutical treatment. The section below summarizes our preliminary results.

3.2 Experimental Results

Clinical Validation. We processed the clinical WSI images, leading to 5 lymphocyte infiltration curves. These curves were then interpreted by a pathologist who classified each lymphocyte infiltration profile in a particular reference group (Level 1 to Level 4).

For comparison purposes, we compared our results with initial results obtained in the study in [9] with the method "VISILOG". Based on a qualitative evaluation of the results by two experts pathologists involved in the previous studies, the results are more precise with our method. Table 1(b) shows a good concordance with the previous results and a possible confusion between type 3 and type 4 profiles. This can be due to the fact that our method analyzes more space and respects better the tumor border. However, type 3 and 4 are both considered by experts as a strong response without much distinction.

In addition, the analysis conducted with regions of interest (ROI) and tumor boundaries in the same locations as the analysis that produced the reference results, revealed a perfect match of the typing for the confusing images in Table 1(b) of our experimental study in the context of the clinical study.

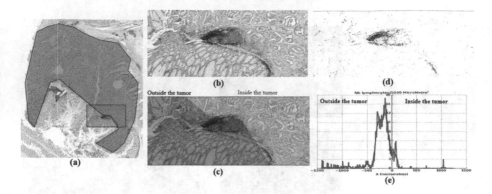

Fig. 5. Illustration of the process of creating lymphocyte infiltration curves. (a) Annotation of the tumor border in blue and a zoomed region in red. (b) Zoomed region. (c) Creation of the iso-curves (from the distances maps), parallel to the tumor borders. (d) Detection of lymphocytes. (e) Resulting quantification curve of lymphocyte infiltration.

Table 1. (a) Results of typing 20 preclinical images. (b) Comparison of typing results of clinical images

Treatment vs. Infiltration Level	1	2	3	4
Untreated	2	1		
RFA only			3	6
RFA and Gel			8	

Reference Level	Updated Level
3	4
4	3
1	1
3	3
4	4

Preclinical Use. We also used our approach to assess the efficiency of a new treatment with mice models. We processed the 20 preclinical WSI images (3 images from untreated mice, 9 images from mice treated with radiofrequency alone and 8 images from mice treated with radiofrequency + GMCSF-BCG gel), leading to novel lymphocyte infiltration curves.

In agreement with the biologists, we observed a difference of interpretation (typing) of the lymphocyte quantification curves between a preclinical study and a clinical study. This difference in interpretation is due to the difference in size of the tumors and the effectiveness of the treatment applied to the tumor. Indeed, tumors in mice are smaller compared to that in humans and for effective treatment, they are quickly destroyed. However, for untreated mice, we observed a low lymphocyte density in the tumor environment. This phenomenon corresponds to type 1 and 2, due to the small recognition of tumor cells. For treated mice by radiofrequency (RFA) only, a good lymphocyte density at the border and inside the tumor is observed. This is due to partial recognition of tumor cells and this corresponds to type 4. Last, for the mice treated by RFA + gel, a high

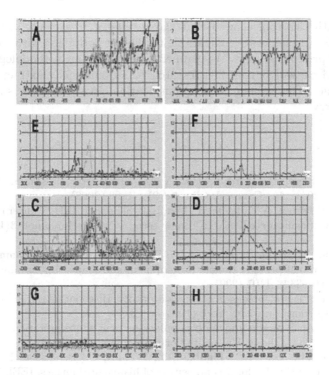

Fig. 6. Illustration of the four types of lymphocyte infiltration profiles (image from [9]). **A, E, C, G**: Curves derive from different measures performed on 4 tumors. **B, F, D, H**: Different pattern of lymphocytic infiltration defined according to the mean curve derived from the different measures in A, E, C and G respectively, From High density of positive lymphocytes within the tumors (**B**) to a Uniform low lymphocyte density pattern (**H**).

lymphocyte density only at the border is observed due to the strong recognition of the tumor cells. This corresponds to type 3.

Table 1(a) summarizes the type of infiltration depending on the type of treatments. The quantitative assessments obtained are already used in a preclinical analysis of tumor evolution and, according to the involved biologists, they improve repeatability of clinical studies.

4   Conclusion

The proposed method provides a reproducible and fine quantification of lymphocyte infiltration through tumors, in the context of the treatment of colorectal carcinomas. This method relies both on marker separation and lymphocyte detection image processing modules. Our principal contribution is the definition of an efficient color distance to extract stained pixels and a novel strategy to locally quantify the lymphocyte infiltration, relative to the global tumor boundary, using a strategy of iso-curves parallel to the tumor borders. The results obtained with this tool showed that the results of treatments are those predicted by biologists and are comparable to the ones obtained with the reference tool used in previous studies. We planned to validate our methodology on larger datasets and we will pursue this research to automatically extract the tumor boundary and ROIs, as well as the quantification of colored objects in immunohistochemistry.

References

1. Jemal, A., Siegel, R., Ward, E., Hao, Y., Xu, J., Murray, T., Thun, M.J.: Cancer statistics, 2008. CA: Cancer J. Clin. **58**(2), 71–96 (2008)
2. Dunn, G.P., Bruce, A.T., Ikeda, H., Old, L.J., Schreiber, R.D.: Cancer immunoediting: from immunosurveillance to tumor escape. Nature Immunol. **3**(11), 991–998 (2002)
3. Shankaran, V., Ikeda, H., Bruce, A.T., White, J.M., et al.: IFN gamma and lymphocytes prevent primary tumour development and shape tumour immunogenicity. Nature **410**(6832), 1107 (2001)
4. Winsor, L.: Tissue processing. In: Laboratory Histopathology, p. 4.2-1–4.2-39. Churchill Livingstone, New York (1994)
5. Ali, M.A.: Analyse statistique de populations pour l'interprétation d'images histologiques. Ph.D. thesis, Université Sorbonne Paris Cité (2015)
6. Gavrilovic, M., Azar, J.C., Lindblad, J., Wählby, C., Bengtsson, E., Busch, C., Carlbom, I.B.: Blind color decomposition of histological images. IEEE Trans. Med. Imaging **32**(6), 983–994 (2013)
7. Tadrous, P.: Digital stain separation for histological images. J. Microsc. **240**(2), 164–172 (2010)
8. Ruifrok, A.C., Johnston, D.A., et al.: Quantification of histochemical staining by color deconvolution. Anal. Quant. Cytol. Histol. **23**(4), 291–299 (2001)
9. Allard, M.A., Bachet, J.B., Beauchet, A., Julie, C., Malafosse, R., Penna, C., Nordlinger, B., Emile, J.F.: Linear quantification of lymphoid infiltration of the tumor margin: a reproducible method, developed with colorectal cancer tissues, for assessing a highly variable prognostic factor. Diagn. Pathol. **7**(1), 156 (2012)
10. Emile, J.F., Charlotte, F., Chassagne-Clement, C., Copin, M.C., Fraitag, S., Mokhtari, K., Moreau, A.: Classification histologique et altérations moléculaires des histiocytoses. La Presse Médicale **46**(1), 46–54 (2017)

Vessel Preserving CNN-Based Image Resampling of Retinal Images

Andrey Krylov[1(✉)], Andrey Nasonov[1], Konstantin Chesnakov[1],
Alexandra Nasonova[1], Seung Oh Jin[2], Uk Kang[3], and Sang Min Park[4]

[1] Laboratory of Mathematical Methods of Image Processing,
Faculty of Computational Mathematics and Cybernetics,
Lomonosov Moscow State University, Moscow, Russia
kryl@cs.msu.ru
[2] Korea Electrotechnology Research Institute, Busan, Korea
[3] Biomedical Research Institute, Seoul National University Hospital,
Seoul, Korea
[4] Department of Biomedical Science and Family Medicine,
Seoul National University College of Medicine,
Seoul, Korea

Abstract. High quality resolution enhancement of eye fundus images is an important problem in medical image processing. Retinal images are usually noisy and contain low-contrast details that have to be preserved during upscaling. This makes the development of retinal image resampling algorithm a challenging problem.

The most promising results are achieved with the use of convolutional neural networks (CNN). We choose the popular algorithm SRCNN for general image resampling and investigate the possibility of using this algorithm for retinal image upscaling.

In this paper, we propose a new training scenario for SRCNN with specific preparation of training data and a transfer learning. We demonstrate an improvement of image quality in terms of general purpose image metrics (PSNR, SSIM) and basic edges metrics—the metrics that represent the image quality for strong isolated edges.

1 Introduction

Image resampling is a process of generating a high-resolution (HR) image from a low-resolution (LR) image. It is used in a wide range of practical applications, especially in medical image processing and surveillance systems [1]. Some important practical examples of this problem for retinal fundus images are:

- upscaling to a predefined size to work with images of different size from different databases or captured by different cameras [2–4]. Downsampling of all images to a minimal size is not the best solution in many cases;
- processing of low-resolution stereo pair of retinal images [5,6];
- processing of low-resolution retinal images that are captured using smartphone fundoscopy [7,8].

© Springer International Publishing AG, part of Springer Nature 2018
A. Campilho et al. (Eds.): ICIAR 2018, LNCS 10882, pp. 589–597, 2018.
https://doi.org/10.1007/978-3-319-93000-8_67

There is no unique way to construct a high-resolution image from a low-resolution image. Thus, different data-dependent constraints are used.

One of such constraints for medical image enhancement is the preservation of image details. The algorithms should keep non-smooth regions and should not add artifacts like blur or ringing effect. When image details are corrupted, the results of further image analysis become unreliable and may lead to a wrong diagnosis.

One of the most important parts of retinal images is blood vessels. Thin blood vessels usually have low contrast. Also retinal images suffer from camera shot noise due to low light capturing conditions, which prevent general purpose image resampling algorithms like bilinear, bicubic, Lanczos interpolation from producing satisfactory results. Retinal images resampling algorithms should preserve as many details as possible and reduce noise during resampling.

Edge-directional image upscaling algorithms use the information about image edges to produce an adaptive image interpolation kernel at each pixel. Algorithms EGII [9], ICBI [10] and DCCI [11] use a combination of two directional kernels for pixel interpolation depending on the directions of edges at this pixel. They work well for straight and diagonal edges, but fail at image corners, textured regions with multiple directions and noisy areas.

A group of state-of-the-art image resampling methods use a mapping transform between low-resolution (LR) image patches and high-resolution (HR) patches. Algorithm NEDI [12] obtains this mapping individually for each pixel from a self-similarity property of natural images at different scales. Learning-based methods obtain this transform from a training dataset containing LR and corresponding HR images. The method SI [13] classifies the LR patch into one of 625 classes and uses individual interpolation kernel for each class. Sparse representation is also used to construct the mapping transform between LR and HR patches [14,15].

Convolutional neural networks (CNN) is another class of methods for constructing an LR-to-HR mapping function for example-based image upscaling. In practice it provides the most promising results. The mapping function consists of a number of convolutional layers with non-linear transformation. CNN based upscaling algorithms mostly differs in the number of convolutional layers and their spatial sizes, however, the quality of the resulting HR images mostly depends on sufficiency of the training dataset and adequate matching of input image class with image classes from the training data.

At the same time, the results of CNN-based algorithms greatly depend on the training data. The training data should be sufficient and match the input images, otherwise the results may become unpredictable. For example, if the training data consists only of high-quality images but the real input images are noisy, the image resampling algorithm will try to restore false details from noise. This may result in incorrect diagnosis in medical image analysis.

In this paper, we propose a retinal image resampling algorithm that is based on SRCNN algorithm [16]. It uses the same CNN model but differs from SRCNN in training procedure.

2   Network Model

We use the same model for CNN as described in SRCNN algorithm [16,17]. This model takes a low-resolution input image, then upscales it using bicubic interpolation with a certain factor, and finally maps it to a high-resolution image by applying three convolutional filters with bias and rectified linear unit (ReLU) activation function applied at each layer. Table 1 describes the CNN model.

Table 1. SRCNN model for image upscaling

Layer	Layer type	Filter size	Number of filters
Layer 1	conv + bias	9×9	64
Layer 2	conv + bias	$5 \times 5 \times 64$	32
Layer 3	conv + bias	$5 \times 5 \times 32$	1

3   Training Procedure

Training procedure consists of finding the coefficients of the convolution filters that minimize the loss between the reconstructed images and the ground truth high-resolution images from the training set. We use Mean Squared Error (MSE) as the loss function.

This leads to higher PSNR values as an objective image quality metric. Though it has weak correlation with human perception, the minimization of the MSE-based loss function produces satisfactory upscaling results, even if they are assessed using other objective metrics, e.g., SSIM, MSSIM.

The loss is minimized using stochastic gradient descent with standard back-propagation. We have used Caffe package for training procedure [18].

3.1   Training Dataset

The most obvious idea is to take real retinal images and build the training dataset of high-resolution retinal images and their downsampled versions. But this idea has led to poor results. Retinal images have many flat and noisy areas and few vessels. This makes the training dataset imbalanced.

Another idea is to exclude flat regions from training dataset and to train CNN only on patches containing blood vessels and other structures. But experiments have shown that this dataset is also inconsistent and the resampling quality is still not good enough.

After a series of experiments, we have come to the following algorithm:

1. We take a set of photographic images and perform normal training procedure. We have used a collection of 124 photographic images of nature, buildings and humans (WebShots Premium Collections, October 2007) with average resolution 1600×1200.

2. Then we freeze the coefficients in the first and the second layers, take a set of retinal images and optimize the coefficients of the third layer only. We have used the images from DRIVE [19] database. This database consists of 20 retinal images with blood vessel masks. We use these masks to keep only patches containing vessels.

3.2   Handling Noise and Blur

Compared to photographic images, retinal images are more noisy and slightly more blurry. In order to improve the results of retinal image resampling, the training images should be preprocessed.

We apply Zero Component Analysis (ZCA) transformation to the reference images [17,20]. ZCA enhances important details such as edges and textures and also helps to remove unwanted high-frequency noise by normalizing the variance of the data in the direction of each eigenvector of its covariance matrix. We apply ZCA transformation globally to the whole image, and the output of this transformation is of the same size as input. ZCA preprocessing step is widely used for image classification problems, and we adopt this technique for CNN-based image resampling.

The idea of adding noise to HR images only without affecting LR images has proven effective for noisy image upscaling [21]. To take into account both blur and noise effects, we apply Gaussian blur with $\sigma = 0.5$ to HR images and then add Gaussian noise with $\sigma = 6$.

4   Evaluation

We have tested our algorithm on DiaretDB database [22]. We take 100 images, downsample them with a factor of 2 using bicubic interpolation and then upsample them using the proposed method. The results are compared with reference images using objective metrics PSNR and SSIM [23]. Also we measure the sharpness value.

4.1   Blur Estimation

One of the properties that correlates to subjective image quality is sharpness. We use the edge width estimation algorithm [24] that measures the sharpness of the basic edges [25]—strong edges that are the most suitable for image quality analysis.

Figure 1 shows an example of basic edge detection for a retinal image.

4.2   Results

The results of the application of the SRCNN algorithm with different training strategies to retinal images are shown in Figs. 2, 3 and 4. Table 2 shows the average metric values calculated over DiaretDB retinal database [22].

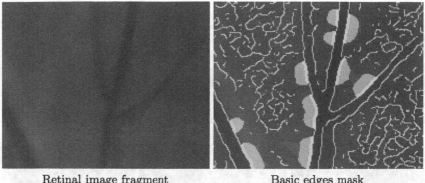

Retinal image fragment   Basic edges mask

Fig. 1. The basic edges for a retinal image. The basic edges are marked with yellow color and its neighborhood is marked with green color. (Color figure online)

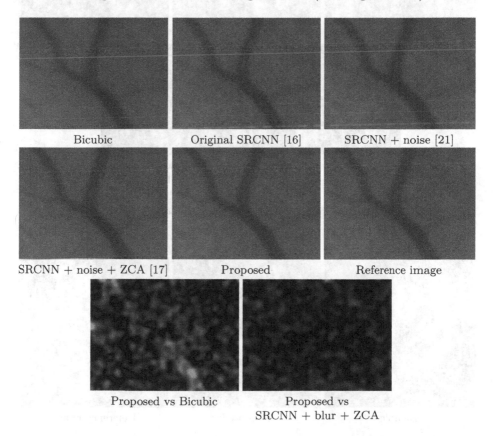

Bicubic   Original SRCNN [16]   SRCNN + noise [21]

SRCNN + noise + ZCA [17]   Proposed   Reference image

Proposed vs Bicubic   Proposed vs
                                    SRCNN + blur + ZCA

Fig. 2. The results of retinal image upscaling (blood vessels fragment). The bottom row is a visualization of the difference between error images of image upscaling methods. Positive values corresponding to quality improvement are green while negative values are red. (Color figure online)

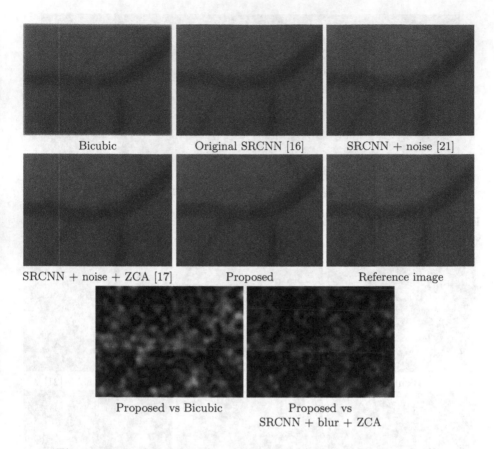

Bicubic   Original SRCNN [16]   SRCNN + noise [21]

SRCNN + noise + ZCA [17]   Proposed   Reference image

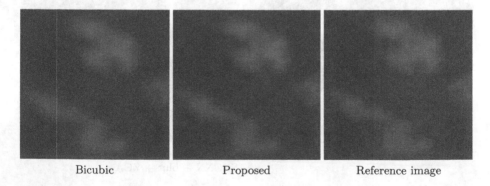

Proposed vs Bicubic   Proposed vs
                             SRCNN + blur + ZCA

Fig. 3. The results of retinal image upscaling (blood vessels fragment).

Bicubic   Proposed   Reference image

Fig. 4. The results of retinal image upscaling (lesions fragment). Compared to blood vessels, there is no visible difference between different SRCNN implementations. At the same time, sharpness is improved compared to bicubic interpolation.

Table 2. Average metric values for the DiaretDB images for different SRCNN training procedures.

Method	PSNR	SSIM	Blur level
Reference	—	—	1.19
Original SRCNN [16]	45.73	0.972	1.24
SRCNN + noise [21]	47.58	0.987	1.22
SRCNN + noise + ZCA [17]	48.42	0.988	1.20
SRCNN + blur + noise + ZCA	48.65	0.988	1.20
Proposed (ZCA, noise, blur, transfer learning)	48.74	0.990	1.19

It can be seen that the original SRCNN trained by its authors amplifies the noise and reveals its pattern structure. Adding noise to the HR images from the training set results in lower noise level. Applying the ZCA transform and Gaussian blur to the HR images results in increased sharpness. Transfer learning further improves the image quality—its effect appears as slightly better vessel contrast.

5 Conclusion

A novel training procedure for CNN-based upscaling algorithm for retinal images has been proposed. The best results have been achieved using a combination of the special training dataset preparation and the transfer learning. The proposed ideas have been applied to SRCNN algorithm and demonstrated its effectiveness with the retinal images from standard database. It can be added that the proposed data preparation procedure can be used for retinal image enhancement with other CNN models.

References

1. Kim, W.H., Lee, J.S.: Blind single image super resolution with low computational complexity. Multimed. Tools Appl. **76**(5), 7235–7249 (2017)
2. Li, Z., Huang, F., Zhang, J., Dashtbozorg, B., Abbasi-Sureshjani, S., Sun, Y., Long, X., Yu, Q., ter Haar Romeny, B., Tan, T.: Multi-modal and multi-vendor retina image registration. Biomed. Opt. Express **9**(2), 410–422 (2018)
3. Deng, K., Tian, J., Zheng, J., Zhang, X., Dai, X., Xu, M.: Retinal fundus image registration via vascular structure graph matching. J. Biomed. Imaging **2010**, 14 (2010)
4. Abdel-Hamid, L., El-Rafei, A., El-Ramly, S., Michelson, G.: Performance dependency of retinal image quality assessment algorithms on image resolution: analyses and solutions. Signal Image Video Process. **12**(1), 9–16 (2018)
5. Xu, J., Chutatape, O.: Auto-adjusted 3-d optic disk viewing from low-resolution stereo fundus image. Comput. Biol. Med. **36**(9), 921–940 (2006)

6. Nakagawa, T., Suzuki, T., Hayashi, Y., Mizukusa, Y., Hatanaka, Y., Ishida, K., Hara, T., Fujita, H., Yamamoto, T.: Quantitative depth analysis of optic nerve head using stereo retinal fundus image pair. J. Biomed. Opt. **13**(6), 064026 (2008)

7. Jebadurai, J., Peter, J.D.: Super-resolution of retinal images using multi-kernel SVR for IoT healthcare applications. Future Gener. Comput. Syst. **83**, 338–346 (2018)

8. Xu, X., Ding, W., Wang, X., Cao, R., Zhang, M., Lv, P., Xu, F.: Smartphone-based accurate analysis of retinal vasculature towards point-of-care diagnostics. Sci. Rep. **6**, 34603 (2016)

9. Zhang, L., Wu, X.: An edge-guide image interpolation via directional filtering and data fusion. IEEE Trans. Image Process. **15**, 2226–2235 (2006)

10. Giachetti, A., Asuni, N.: Real time artifact-free image interpolation. IEEE Trans. Image Process. **20**(10), 2760–2768 (2011)

11. Zhou, D., Shen, X., Dong, W.: Image zooming using directional cubic convolution interpolation. IET Image Process. **6**(6), 627–634 (2012)

12. Li, X., Orchard, M.: New edge-directed interpolation. IEEE Trans. Image Process. **10**, 1521–1527 (2001)

13. Choi, J.S., Kim, M.: Super-interpolation with edge-orientation based mapping kernels for low complex 2x upscaling. IEEE Trans. Image Process. **25**(1), 469–483 (2015)

14. Yang, J., Wright, J., Huang, T.S., Ma, Y.: Image super-resolution via sparse representation. IEEE Trans. Image Process. **19**(11), 2861–2873 (2010)

15. Dong, W., Zhang, L., Lukac, R., Shi, G.: Sparse representation based image interpolation with nonlocal autoregressive modeling. IEEE Trans. Image Process. **22**(4), 1382–1394 (2013)

16. Dong, C., Loy, C.C., He, K., Tang, X.: Learning a deep convolutional network for image super-resolution. In: Fleet, D., Pajdla, T., Schiele, B., Tuytelaars, T. (eds.) ECCV 2014, Part IV. LNCS, vol. 8692, pp. 184–199. Springer, Cham (2014). https://doi.org/10.1007/978-3-319-10593-2_13

17. Nasonov, A., Chesnakov, K., Krylov, A.: CNN Based Retinal Image Upscaling Using Zero Component Analysis, pp. 27–31. ISPRS-International Archives of the Photogrammetry, Remote Sensing and Spatial Information Sciences (2017)

18. Jia, Y., Shelhamer, E., Donahue, J., Karayev, S., Long, J., Girshick, R., Guadarrama, S., Darrell, T.: Caffe: convolutional architecture for fast feature embedding (2014). arXiv preprint: arXiv:1408.5093

19. Staal, J., Abramoff, M., Niemeijer, M., Viergever, M., van Ginneken, B.: Ridge based vessel segmentation in color images of the retina. IEEE Trans. Med. Imaging **23**, 501–509 (2004)

20. Krizhevsky, A.: Masters Thesis "Learning multiple layers of features from tiny images" (2009). www.cs.utoronto.ca/~kriz/learning-features-2009-TR.pdf

21. Nasonov, A., Chesnakov, K., Krylov, A.: Convolutional neural networks based image resampling with noisy training set. In: International Conference on Signal Processing (ICSP2016), Chengdu, China, pp. 62–66 (2016)

22. Kälviäinen, R., Uusitalo, H.: DIARETDB1 diabetic retinopathy database and evaluation protocol. In: Medical Image Understanding and Analysis (2007)

23. Wang, Z., Bovik, A.C., Sheikh, H.R., Simoncelli, E.P.: Image quality assessment: from error visibility to structural similarity. IEEE Trans. Image Process. **13**(4), 600–612 (2004)

24. Nasonov, A., Nasonova, A., Krylov, A.: Edge width estimation for defocus map from a single image. In: Battiato, S., Blanc-Talon, J., Gallo, G., Philips, W., Popescu, D., Scheunders, P. (eds.) ACIVS 2015. LNCS, vol. 9386, pp. 15–22. Springer, Cham (2015). https://doi.org/10.1007/978-3-319-25903-1_2
25. Nasonov, A.V., Krylov, A.S.: Edge quality metrics for image enhancement. Pattern Recogn. Image Anal. **22**(1), 346–353 (2012)

Diagnosis of Non-Small Cell Lung Cancer Using Phylogenetic Diversity in Radiomics Context

Antonino C. dos S. Neto$^{(\boxtimes)}$, Pedro H. B. Diniz, João O. B. Diniz,
André B. Cavalcante, Aristófanes C. Silva, Anselmo C. de Paiva,
and João D. S. de Almeida

Applied Computing Group - NCA, Federal University of Maranhao - UFMA,
Av. dos Portugueses, SN, Campus do Bacanga, Bacanga,
Sao Luis, MA 65085-580, Brazil
{antoninocalisto,jdallyson}@nca.ufma.br, ari@dee.ufma.br,
phb.diniz@gmail.com, joao.obd@gmail.com, abcborges@gmail.com,
anselmo.c.paiva@gmail.com
http://nca.ufma.br/

Abstract. Lung cancer is the most common type of cancer and has
the highest mortality rate in the world. The automatic process for the
diagnosis by computer vision systems, through medical images, provides
an interpretation regarding the pathology. The idea of this work is to use
the texture features using phylogenetic diversity indexes, to classify Non-
Small Cell Lung Cancer. This work presents the development of texture
descriptors based on phylogenetic diversity indices for characterization
of the nodule. The tests showed promising results of 98.47% accuracy, a
Kappa index of 0.979 and an ROC of 0.999.

Keywords: Lung cancer · NSCLC · Phylogenetic diversity
Radiomics · Extract features

1 Introduction

Cancer is the denomination for a set of more than 100 pathologies characterized
by the disordered growth of cells that invade tissues or organs. There are several
causes, both internal (linked to the capacity of the body to defend itself) or
external (relating to the environment and habits or customs). Currently, lung
cancer is the type of carcinoma with the highest mortality rate among men. In
women, lung cancer loses only to the breast [1].

One of the most effective methods for diagnosis is imaging. Computed tomography (CT) has emerged as an effective way to aid in detection and diagnosis of
pulmonary nodules and is of great use in the treatment of cancer.

Thus, with the great help of technology, it became easier to extract high-
performance quantitative features that resulted in the conversion of images into
data, and in the use of these data for decision support. This practice is called

Radiomics [2,3]. Radiomics database is one that, through laboratory analysis of tissues of the patient's nodules, provided predictions about those tissues, and it has been shown that images of these same tissues force features that can predict in the same way (or better) a decision according to laboratory tests.

However, the analysis of an examination can cause some problems in the diagnosis, because it is performed subjectively, causing errors in its analysis, caused by visual fatigue, distraction, among others. Because of this, techniques for processing, analyzing and recognizing patterns in images associated with Computer-Aided Diagnosis (CADx) systems have emerged in order to improve diagnostic accuracy, serving as a "second opinion" for decision-making.

In this context, as contribution of the work can be highlighted: (a) the use of phylogenetic diversity indexes that a priori was used in the context of biology and was brought to the problem of medical images; (b) the generalization capacity of these indices, which are only used as five features and presented very promising results; and (c) the application in a large database, showing that the present methodology is effective in the classification task of in CT scans of patients with Non-Small Cell Lung Cancer (NSCLC).

2 Related Works

In the literature, many studies are related to the development of automatic systems for the classification of pulmonary nodules. The following is a summary of the most recent work related to the proposed method.

In [4] Radiomics features were extracted based on conebeam CT (CBCT) for patients with NSCLC being a part of the base used for training (132 patients) and another for testing (62 and 94 patients), and this test base has NSCLC patients with stage of I-IV. A total of 1119 features were extracted and 149 were used after a selection of features. The Harrell's concordance index was used as a validation metric, with a value of 0.69 for CT images.

In [5] evaluates that the Radiomics features are capable of predicting the pathological response in locally established NSCLC patients. CT scans of 127 patients were used, extracting 15 selected Radiomics features regarding the relevance and stability of the power to predict the pathological response. The validation metric used was the area under the Receiver Operating Characteristic (ROC) curve. The features had a value of 0.63 for the area under the ROC curve.

Work proposed by [6] demonstrates that features on a Radiomics basis in early-stage NSCLC CT scans being treated with stereotactic body radiation therapy have predictive power. 12 Radiomics features were selected according to their relevance and stability. The validation metrics for its prognostic value were using the index of agreement *Kappa*. The index of *Kappa* had a predictive value of 0.67.

These are examples of systems that have been developed for feature extraction on NSCLC CT scans in the context of the Radiomics approach. Two important common points in these works: the validation indexes obtained low values and the small number of cases. In our method, we will try to exploit these deficiencies in order to improve the metrics that evaluate the performance, such as accuracy, area under the ROC curve and *Kappa* index, in a greater number of cases and with a quantity smaller of features.

3   Proposed Method

The methodology developed to classify NSCLC (large cell carcinoma, squamous cell carcinoma, adenocarcinoma, adenocarcinoma of mutation negative and unspecified) followed a few steps: initially the acquisition of the images; the pulmonary nodules were then extracted (VOI) according to the base markings; then, the features were extracted from phylogenetic diversity indexes (developed by [7]); finally, we used the WEKA tool [8] for classification. Figure 1 illustrates the flow of the methodology.

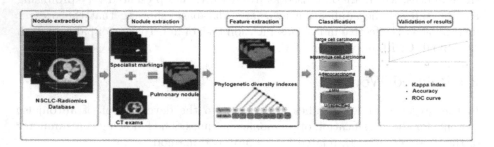

Fig. 1. Flow of the methodology.

3.1   Image Acquisition

For the application of the developed algorithms, the NSCLC-Radiomics public image database provided by Cancer Imaging Archive was used. This image database contains images of 422 patients with NSCLC, and each patient may belong to one of the 5 classes: large cell carcinoma, squamous cell carcinoma, adenocarcinoma, adenocarcinoma of mutation negative and unspecified [9].

The creation of NSCLC-Radiomics resulted in a database consisting of 51,513 slices, each exam containing a RT-STRUCT (Radiotherapy Structure Set) file with base markings (nodule location, patient's class, age, among others) [9].

3.2   Descriptors of Phylogenetic Diversity Features

The feature extraction of the CADx model was developed from the texture analysis with application of phylogenetic diversity indexes adapted to the context of Radiomics of NSCLC, which will be detailed in the course of the work.

The extraction of phylogenetic diversity indexes through phylogenetic trees are used in biology to compare behavior samples among species belonging to different regions, in the area of computation will be used to classify which pattern of NSCLC. Therefore, a correlation between the biology and the proposed methodology should be made, where the community represents the nodules of the CT image; The species is each Hounsfield unit of the nodule; The individual is each voxels of the nodule; And the species richness represents the number of voxels of each node.

The intensive quadratic entropy index J [10] will represent the number of species and their taxonomic relationships when they are the same values of abundance of species. This index is defined by Eq. 1.

$$J = [\frac{\sum dij}{s^2}] \tag{1}$$

where d_{ij} represents the distance between the species i and j; s represents the number of species.

An extension of index J was created the extensive quadratic entropy F [10], representing the sum of species differences. Equations 2 and 3 represents this index.

$$d_{ij} = [Q_j - Q_i, i < j] \tag{2}$$

$$F = \sum_{i<j} d_i j \tag{3}$$

where d_{ij} represents the distance between the species i and j, Q_j and Q_i the values of the species (HU) j and i, respectively.

The indexes of average taxonomic distinction($AvTD$) [11] and total taxonomic distinction(TTD) [12] were originally developed taking into account the taxonomic relations, being possible to adapt them to be used in phylogeny [13]. Equation 3 represents the taxonomic distinction between any pairs of species randomly chosen [11]. Equations 4 and 5 represents the $AvTD$ e TTD, respectively.

$$AvTD = \frac{[\sum \sum_{i<j} d_i j]}{\frac{s(s-1)}{2}} \tag{4}$$

$$TDD = \sum_i [\frac{\sum_{i<j} d_i j}{(s-1)}] \tag{5}$$

where for Eqs. 3 and 4, d_{ij} indicates the distance between species i e j.

The last index belonging to this group is denominated pure diversity index(Dd), responsible for checking the distance value of a species for its nearest neighbor [14]. These indexes are represented by Eqs. 6 and 7.

$$d_{imin} = MIN[d_i For All_j], i < j \tag{6}$$

$$D_d = \sum d_{imin} \tag{7}$$

where d_{imin} represents the shortest distance (MIN) of specie i for all other species j.

4   Results and Discussion

It is not possible to make a reliable comparison with the related works, since they do not use a public or available database for NSCLC analysis and also because the set of cases is different.

To validate the methodology developed, efficiency test with the NSCLC-Radiomics database was performed using 319 of the 422 exams due to the fact that 103 of the available public-base exams were unmarked. The validation metrics used were the accuracy [15]; *Kappa* index [15]; and area under the curve ROC [15] in classifiers *Random Forest* [8], *Logistic* [8] and *Suport Virtual Machine* (SVM) [8].

Analyzing the results in Table 1 it can be observed that Random Forest classifier obtained a better result with an accuracy of 98.47%, where the SVM had the lowest result of the classifiers with an accuracy of 98.35%. However, it can be observed that the results are similar, which shows, once again, the generalization capacity of the features used in the proposed method.

Table 1. Results for diagnosis using phylogenetic diversity indexes based on pairs of species.

Classifier	Accuracy	ROC	Kappa
Random Forest	**98.47%**	**0.999**	**0.979**
SVM	97.35%	0.983	0.962
Logistic	97.78%	0.991	0.962

In Table 2 some of the works with results considered promising in the context of the Radiomics approach are shown.

Table 2. Comparison of papers in the context of the Radiomics approach.

Works	Kappa	ROC	No. of features	Database	Samples
[4]	-	0.690	1119	Private base	288
[5]	-	0.630	15	Private base	127
[6]	0.670	-	12	Private base	-
Method	**0.979**	**0.999**	**5**	**NSCLC-Radiomics**	**319**

In Table 2, it is observed that the results are promising. It is emphasized that the phylogenetic indexes used in the images made more evident intrinsic properties making it possible to distinguish well the classes of the test bases. As can be seen in Fig. 2, two images of nodules from different classes are classified as a class in common, because their textures are similar.

Fig. 2. Corrects classification: A and B; Incorrect classification: C.

5   Conclusion

This work presented an automatic method to classify NSCLC in: large cell carcinoma; squamous cell carcinoma; adenocarcinoma; negative mutation adenocarcinoma; and unspecified, serving as a diagnostic aid tool for specialists.

The results confirm a promising result of texture extraction techniques in the Radiomics context, with an accuracy rate of 98.47% and a ROC of 0.999, in addition to being more significant compared to the published literature, confirming that the images can provide effective features for the prediction of NSCLC cancer by providing early treatment and with a greater chance of a more favorable prognosis to the patient.

For future work, we intend to use classification methods using Deep Learning approaches, in order to compare with the classifiers used in the proposed method. In addition, we can combine the proposed indexes with other indexes of texture or indexes of shape, to observe better results.

References

1. Setio, A.A.A., Ciompi, F., Litjens, G., Gerke, P., Jacobs, C., van Riel, S.J., Wille, M.M.W., Naqibullah, M., Sánchez, C.I., van Ginneken, B.: Pulmonary nodule detection in CT images: false positive reduction using multi-view convolutional networks. IEEE Trans. Med. Imaging **35**(5), 1160–1169 (2016)
2. Gillies, R.J., Kinahan, P.E., Hricak, H.: Radiomics: images are more than pictures, they are data. Radiology **278**(2), 563–577 (2015)
3. Kumar, D., Chung, A.G., Shaifee, M.J., Khalvati, F., Haider, M.A., Wong, A.: Discovery radiomics for pathologically-proven computed tomography lung cancer prediction. In: Karray, F., Campilho, A., Cheriet, F. (eds.) ICIAR 2017. LNCS, vol. 10317, pp. 54–62. Springer, Cham (2017). https://doi.org/10.1007/978-3-319-59876-5_7
4. van Timmeren, J.E., Leijenaar, R.T., van Elmpt, W., Reymen, B., Oberije, C., Monshouwer, R., Bussink, J., Brink, C., Hansen, O., Lambin, P.: Survival prediction of non-small cell lung cancer patients using radiomics analyses of cone-beam CT images. Radiother. Oncol. **123**(3), 363–369 (2017)
5. Coroller, T.P., Agrawal, V., Narayan, V., Hou, Y., Grossmann, P., Lee, S.W., Mak, R.H., Aerts, H.J.: Radiomic phenotype features predict pathological response in non-small cell lung cancer. Radiother. Oncol. **119**(3), 480–486 (2016)
6. Huynh, E., Coroller, T.P., Narayan, V., Agrawal, V., Hou, Y., Romano, J., Franco, I., Mak, R.H., Aerts, H.J.: CT-based radiomic analysis of stereotactic body radiation therapy patients with lung cancer. Radiother. Oncol. **120**(2), 258–266 (2016)

7. de Carvalho Filho, A.O., Silva, A.C., de Paiva, A.C., Nunes, R.A., Gattass, M.: Computer-aided diagnosis of lung nodules in computed tomography by using phylogenetic diversity, genetic algorithm, and SVM. J. Digit. Imaging **30**(6), 812–822 (2017)

8. Dean, J.: Big Data, Data Mining, and Machine Learning: Value Creation for Business Leaders and Practitioners. John Wiley & Sons, Hoboken (2014)

9. Aerts, H., Rios Velazquez, E., Leijenaar, R.T., Parmar, C., Grossmann, P., Carvalho, S., Lambin, P.: Data from NSCLC-radiomics. The cancer imaging archive (2015)

10. Izsák, J., Papp, L.: A link between ecological diversity indices and measures of biodiversity. Ecol. Model. **130**(1–3), 151–156 (2000)

11. Clarke, K., Warwick, R.: Change in Marine Communities: An Approach to Statistical Analysis and Interpretation, 2nd edn. (1994)

12. Pienkowski, M., Watkinson, A., Kerby, G., Clarke, K., Warwick, R.: A taxonomic distinctness index and its statistical properties. J. Appl. Ecol. **35**(4), 523–531 (1998)

13. Schweiger, O., Klotz, S., Durka, W., Kühn, I.: A comparative test of phylogenetic diversity indices. Oecologia **157**(3), 485–495 (2008)

14. Faith, D.P.: Phylogenetic pattern and the quantification of organismal biodiversity. Phil. Trans. R. Soc. Lond. B **345**(1311), 45–58 (1994)

15. Hanley, J.A., McNeil, B.J.: The meaning and use of the area under a receiver operating characteristic (ROC) curve. Radiology **143**(1), 29–36 (1982)

Analyzing Social Network Images with Deep Learning Models to Fight Zika Virus

Pedro H. Barros[1], Bruno G. C. Lima[1], Felipe C. Crispim[1], Tiago Vieira[1(✉)], Paolo Missier[2], and Baldoino Fonseca[1]

[1] Federal University of Alagoas, Maceió, Brazil
{pedro_h_nr,bgcl,fcc,tvieira,baldoino}@ic.ufal.br
[2] Newcastle University, Newcastle, UK
paolo.missier@newcastle.ac.uk
http://www.ic.ufal.br/
http://www.ncl.ac.uk/

Abstract. Zika and Dengue are viral diseases transmitted by infected mosquitoes (Aedes aegypti) found in warm, humid environments. Mining data from social networks helps to find locations with highest density of reported cases. Differently from approaches that process text from social networks, we present a new strategy that analyzes Instagram images. We use two customized Deep Neural Networks. The first detects objects commonly used for mosquito reproduction with 85% precision. The second differentiates mosquitoes as Culex or Aedes aegypti with 82.5% accuracy. Results indicate that both networks can improve the effectiveness of current social network mining strategies such as the VazaZika project.

Keywords: Deep Neural Networks · Zika · Aedes aegypti
Social networks

1 Introduction

Zika has become a big problem for health organizations. Among worst disease implications, we highlight microcephaly [12] in newborns of contaminated mothers. Transmitted by the Aedes aegypti mosquito, reported contaminations of Zika are mainly present in countries with warm and humid weather. To pinpoint Aedes aegypti breeding sites, one mines data from social networks. Based on user's posts, authorities may retrieve information such as the number of reported cases and their location. VazaZika[1] [11] is a platform where users may report cases, resulting in a geographical map containing inferred mosquitoes concentration.

We use pictures from Instagram and two Deep Neural Networks. One detects objects commonly used by mosquitoes for egg deposition (tires, bottles and jars).

---

[1] http://vazadengue.inf.puc-rio.br/.

© Springer International Publishing AG, part of Springer Nature 2018
A. Campilho et al. (Eds.): ICIAR 2018, LNCS 10882, pp. 605–610, 2018.
https://doi.org/10.1007/978-3-319-93000-8_69

The other classifies whether a mosquito is a Culex (common) or Aedes aegypti (vector of Zika and other diseases). We argue that our solution, attached to the VazaZika platform, improves the effectiveness of health agencies actions by pinpointing relevant loci. To the extent of our knowledge, no work with this purpose has been presented so far.

We aim at answering the following Research Questions: (**RQ1**): How effective is our deep learning model for detecting objects associated with mosquito proliferation? (**RQ2**): How accurate is our mosquito classification model? (**RQ3**): What is the classification performance when applied to pictures from Instagram?

Our contribution is twofold. First, we collected and annotated an image database comprising: (1) Culex and Aedes aegypti mosquitoes and; (2) tires, empty bottles and plant pots – common mosquito breeding sites. Second, we trained deep models which performed well when tested on pictures from Instagram.

2   Related Work

Hay et al. [7] used sophisticated airborne and satellite-sensor technology, often unavailable alternatives to poor nations due to high costs. Wang et al. [16] used feature extraction and classification of high resolution close-up images, differently from our approach which deals with uncontrolled images. Jahangir et al. [1] studied insect's characteristics for species classification. Fuchida et al., classified insects as whether mosquito or another bug [5]. Their approach differs from ours since we classify a mosquito between two genera: Aedes and Culex. SVM was also used in [4] to classify species and genus of fruit flies and mosquitoes using only images of their wings. In [8] authors generate a Wavelet representation of mosquitoe's sounds, passing it as input to a Convolutional Neural Network (CNN) classifier. Authors in [14] propose a novel method based on CNN for mosquito larva classification, using Alexnet architecture for the deep model. Dong et al. [2] evaluated Deep Convolutional Neural Network to identify cells infected with malaria. Mehra et al. [10] collected data from multiples sources, combining RGB and thermal images in order to detect the presence of water puddles through an ensemble of Bayesian classifiers. Neural networks have also been used for object detection tasks, for example, detecting vehicle [9], pedestrians [6] and faces [15].

We emphasize that, to the extent of our knowledge, no work has been presented so far with the specific goal of using Deep Learning to analyze images from social networks to fight proliferation of mosquito transmitted diseases. Therefore, we present no quantitative comparison with previous works.

3   Methodology

From ImageNet[2] and Google Images, we firstly gathered pictures using the following keywords: (i) `aedes aegypti`; (ii) `culex`; (iii) `soda bottle`;

---

[2] www.image-net.org.

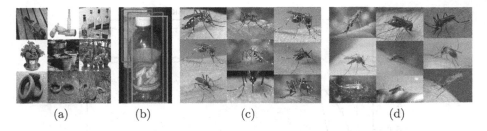

(a)   (b)   (c)   (d)

Fig. 1. Dataset samples. (a) Bottles, recipient and tires. (b) True-positive (green), false-positive (red) and ground-truth (blue). (c) Aedes. (d) Culex. (Color figure online)

(iv) `car tire`[3]; (v) `flowerpot`. Secondly, we collected mosquito pictures from Instagram in order to test the classification model and obtain real performance metrics.

For the object detection dataset (Fig. 1(a)), we used 170 images with tires, 167 with bottles and 182 with flower pots (85% of them for training and 15% for testing) with the Faster RCNN Resnet [13] model and following augmentation options: (i) `random horizontal flip`; (ii) `random vertical flip`; (iii) `random 90 deg rotation`.

The accuracy metric is the Intersection Over Union (IOU) (PASCAL Visual Object Classes Challenge 2007 [3]). For each training step, we evaluated: Average Precision per class AP and Mean Average Precision mAP for all classes. IOU ratio for each bounding box (BB) must exceed a threshold of 0.5 to be considered a "true positive", meaning a "false positive" otherwise. Figure 1(b) shows an example of a true and a false positive.

We also gathered 226 images of Aedes and 322 Culex (Fig. 1(c) and (d), respectively). All images were thoroughly verified by experts from local authority in Zoonoses Control Center (ZCC). We also used data augmentation: Random scaling, Rotation in 3 directions (90°, 180° and 270°) and random flip (horizontal and vertical). The final dataset is based on 80 original images for testing (15% of total) and was increased to 3804 by data augmentation. Finally, we collected 60 pictures of mosquitoes from Instagram to test the trained model, as presented in Fig. 2.

(a)   (b)

Fig. 2. Example images belonging to (a) Aedes class, and (b) Culex category posted on Instagram.

---

[3] Particularly suited to mosquitoes for providing black camouflage.

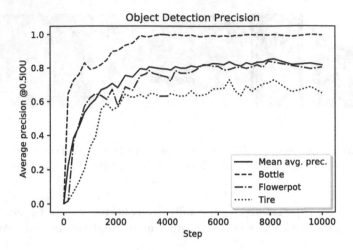

Fig. 3. Average Precision per step index.

4 Results

RQ1. Average detection Precision (AP) is presented in Fig. 3. On the best check-point, APs achieved 99%, 84% and 73%, for bottle, flowerpot and tire, respectively (Mean Average Precision, mAP = 85%).

RQ2. We proposed the following model: (i) Input image is resized to 225 × 225. (ii) Rectifier Linear Units is used as activation function. (iii) Training batch with a size of 32. (iv) 6-fold cross-validation. (v) Random drop-out was used as an attempt to reduce overfitting and improve the network robustness to unseen data. This topology provided a training accuracy of 82.5%.

RQ3. Finally, the model trained over the mosquito dataset was tested on pictures collected from Instagram. Since users do not often post mosquito photographs, it was difficult to gather many images (we found 78 images, but 18 of them were present in our training dataset and were excluded). Hence, we applied the classification model onto 60 images and the results are shown in Fig. 4 (Receiver Operating Characteristic curve and Confusion Matrix).

5 Discussion

Results are shown in Fig. 3. Class "bottle" performs best (99%) since pictures were reasonably well behaved, with few or no occlusions at all. The "flowerpot" class, presenting many images with partial occlusion caused by leaves, flowers and garden utilities, followed with 84% precision. "Tires" presented worst precision (73%) likely due to the large variety of positions (often with big stocks of tires) and occlusion. Model performed satisfactorily overall, achieving a mAP of 85%.

For the classification problem, a Deep Convolutional Neural Network is capable of achieving good training results (82.5%) on a challenging dataset using

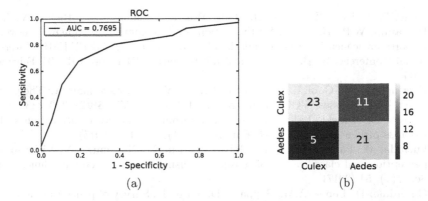

Fig. 4. Results from applying the mosquito classification model to real images collected from Instagram. (a) Receiver Operating Characteristic curve showing an Area Under Curve of 0.77. (b) Confusion matrix.

only supervised learning. Testing the model on very few images (60) collected from Instagram provided 73.33% classification accuracy. This reduction might be expected due to the small amount of training and test image (low generalization capabilities of the network) and due to the variety (scale and rotation) of images in the test set (*cf.* Fig. 2). In some images the mosquito is very small and sometimes squashed dead. A more comprehensive analysis is to be pursued by using more pictures. Testing different network topologies (auto-encoders) might improve results.

6   Conclusion

We presented two Deep Learning Models aimed at processing images and extracting information associated with mosquito activity. To train the models we collected many images from Google Images and Image-Net. Even tough no direct comparison is possible with previous works, training performances were high for both models (85% for detection and 82.5% for classification) and we tested the classification model on real pictures posted on Instagram (73% accuracy). More comprehensive experiments are being executed using the VazaZika platform and results will be eventually reported.

Acknowledgments. The authors would like to thank: (1) National Council for Scientific and Technological Development (CNPq, grant 447336/2014-2). (2) Deep Learning program provided by the Nervana Academy (Intel®). (3) FAPEAL grant 60030 1201/2016.

References

1. Jahangir Alam, S.M., Guoqing, H., Chen, C.: Characteristics analysis and detection algorithm of mosquitoes. TELKOMNIKA Indones. J. Electr. Eng. **17**, 5368–5378 (2013)

2. Dong, Y., Jiang, Z., Shen, H., Pan, W.D., Williams, L.A., Reddy, V.V.B., Benjamin, W.H., Bryan, A.W.: Evaluations of deep convolutional neural networks for automatic identification of malaria infected cells. In: 2017 IEEE EMBS International Conference on Biomedical Health Informatics (BHI), pp. 101–104, February 2017

3. Everingham, M., Gool, L.V., Williams, C.K.I., Winn, J., Zisserman, A.: The pascal visual object classes (VOC) challenge. Int. J. Comput. Vis. **88**(2), 303–338 (2009)

4. Favret, C., Sieracki, J.M.: Machine vision automated species identification scaled towards production levels. Syst. Entomol. **41**(1), 133–143 (2015)

5. Fuchida, M., Pathmakumar, T., Mohan, R., Tan, N., Nakamura, A.: Vision-based perception and classification of mosquitoes using support vector machine. Appl. Sci. **7**(1), 51 (2017)

6. Geronimo, D., Lopez, A.M., Sappa, A.D., Graf, T.: Survey of pedestrian detection for advanced driver assistance systems. IEEE Trans. Pattern Anal. Mach. Intell. **32**(7), 1239–1258 (2010)

7. Hay, S., Snow, R., Rogers, D.: From predicting mosquito habitat to malaria seasons using remotely sensed data: practice, problems and perspectives. Parasitol. Today **14**(8), 306–313 (1998)

8. Kiskin, I., Orozco, B.P., Windebank, T., Zilli, D., Sinka, M., Willis, K., Roberts, S.: Mosquito detection with neural networks: the buzz of deep learning (2017)

9. Manana, M., Tu, C., Owolawi, P.A.: A survey on vehicle detection based on convolution neural networks. In: 2017 3rd IEEE International Conference on Computer and Communications (ICCC), pp. 1751–1755, December 2017

10. Mehra, M., Bagri, A., Jiang, X., Ortiz, J.: Image analysis for identifying mosquito breeding grounds. 2016 IEEE International Conference on Sensing, Communication and Networking (SECON Workshops) (2016)

11. Missier, P., McClean, C., Carlton, J., Cedrim, D., Sousa, L., Garcia, A., Plastino, A., Romanovsky, A.: Recruiting from the network: discovering Twitter users who can help combat Zika epidemics (2017)

12. Rasmussen, S., Jamieson, D.J., Honein, M., Petersen, L.: Zika Virus and birth defects - reviewing the evidence for causality. New Engl. J. Med. **374**, 1981–1987 (2016)

13. Ren, S., He, K., Girshick, R., Sun, J.: Faster R-CNN: towards real-time object detection with region proposal networks. IEEE Trans. Pattern Anal. Mach. Intell. **39**(6), 1137–1149 (2017)

14. Sanchez-Ortiz, A., Fierro-Radilla, A., Arista-Jalife, A., Cedillo-Hernandez, M., Nakano-Miyatake, M., Robles-Camarillo, D., Cuatepotzo-Jimenez, V.: Mosquito larva classification method based on convolutional neural networks. Univ Americas Puebla, Dept Comp Elect & Mechatron; IEEE (2017). 27th International Conference on Electronics, Communications and Computers (CONIELECOMP)

15. Srivastava, A., Mane, S., Shah, A., Shrivastava, N., Thakare, B.: A survey of face detection algorithms. In: 2017 International Conference on Inventive Systems and Control (ICISC), pp. 1–4, January 2017

16. Wang, J., Lin, C., Ji, L., Liang, A.: A new automatic identification system of insect images at the order level. Know. Based Syst. **33**, 102–110 (2012)

Diagnosis and Screening of Ophthalmic Diseases

Retinal Image Synthesis for CAD Development

Pujitha Appan K.[(✉)] and Jayanthi Sivaswamy

Center for Visual Information Technology, IIIT, Hyderabad, India
pujitha.ak@research.iiit.ac.in, jsivaswamy@iiit.ac.in

Abstract. Automatic disease detection and classification have been attracting much interest. High performance is critical in adoption of such systems, which generally rely on training with a wide variety of annotated data. Availability of such varied annotated data in medical imaging is very scarce. Synthetic data generation is a promising solution to address this problem. We propose a novel method, based on generative adversarial networks (GAN), to generate images with lesions such that the overall severity level can be controlled. We demonstrate the reliability of the generated synthetic images independently as well as by training a computer aided diagnosis (CAD) system with the generated data. We showcase this approach for heamorrhage detection in retinal images with 4 levels of severity. Quantitative assessment results show that the generated synthetic images are very close to the real data. Haemorrhage detection was found to improve with inclusion of synthetic data in the training set with improvements in sensitivity ranging from 20% to 27% over training with just expert marked data.

Keywords: Synthetic images · Generative adversarial networks
Deep neural net

1 Introduction

Generation of synthetic medical data is aimed at addressing a range of needs. Early examples are generating digital brain phantoms [1] and synthesizing a whole retinal image [11] using complex modeling. These were aimed at aiding the development of algorithms for denoising, reconstruction and segmentation. Recently simulation of brain tumors in MR images [13] has also been explored to aid CAD algorithm development. With the advent of deep learning, modeling of complex structures and synthesizing images has become easier with a class of neural networks called generative adversarial networks or GAN [4].

GAN is an architecture composed of two networks, namely, a generator and a discriminator. Functionally, the generator synthesizes images from noise while

---

This work was supported by the Dept. of Electronics and Information Technology, Govt. of India under Grant: DeitY/R&D/TDC/13(8)/2013.

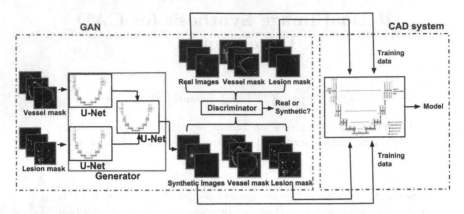

Fig. 1. Proposed end-to-end pipeline for generation of abnormal retinal images and its use in a CAD system for detection of haemorrhages.

the discriminator differentiates between real and synthetic images. GAN have recently been explored for a variety of applications: detection of brain lesions [15], predicting CT from MRI images [12], synthesizing normal retinal images from vessel mask [2], segmenting anatomical structures such as vessels [6] and optic disc/cup [17].

We propose a GAN for generating images with pathologies in a *controlled manner* and illustrate how the generated synthetic images can be used to address the data sparsity problem which hampers the development of robust CAD solutions for abnormality detection. We choose *staging* of diabetic retinopathy (DR) from given color retinal images as a case study. The ETDRS standard for staging of DR is based on the number and location of haemorrhages [19]. However, very few images are publicly available with local markings of haemorrhages. Recent deep learning-based methods [5,20] overcome this problem by sampling a large public dataset (with only image-level annotations) to get local annotations for a much smaller subset of images which are abnormal. These annotations are privately held and hence such measures are not beneficial to a wide community for building a robust CAD solution.

2   Method

The proposed method consists of three modules: (i) pre-processing, (ii) synthetic image generation and (iii) CAD for haemorrhage detection. As a part of the pre-processing step, given retinal images are corrected for non-uniform illumination using luminosity and contrast normalization [7].

2.1   GAN for Synthesis of Retinal Images with Pathologies

Generating *normal* retinal images from vessel mask has been attempted earlier [2] with a single U-net for the generator and a 5-layer convolutional neural network for the discriminator. Our interest is in generating images with haemorrhage (HE) towards synthesis of exemplars for different stages of DR. HE are often indistinguishable from vessel fragments and therefore the input to the generator has to enable distinguishing between these both structures. Further, exemplar generation requires gaining control of the locations, size and density of HE. Hence, we propose a GAN architecture (shown in Fig. 1) with a generator consisting of two parallel networks: one with a vessel mask as input and another with a lesion mask as input. The output of the networks, based on the U-net architectures, are merged and fed to a third U-net architecture which generates the whole retinal image with lesions. The generator thus maps from vessel (v_i) and lesion (l_i) masks to a retinal image (r_i). A 5-layer convolutional neural network as in [2] is used for the discriminator to distinguish between the real and synthetic sets of images, with each set consisting of vessel and lesion masks along with retinal images.

The GAN learns a model as follows: the discriminator iteratively reduces its misclassification error by more accurately classifying the real and synthetic images while the generator aims to deceive the discriminator by producing more realistic images. The overall loss function that is to be optimized is chosen as a weighted combination of 3 loss functions: L_{adv}, L_{SSIM} and L_1 as defined below in Eqs. 1−4 to produce sharp and realistic images (here, G and D, represent generator and discriminator respectively).

(i) The adversarial loss function L_{adv} is defined as

$$L_{adv}(G, D) = \mathbb{E}_{(v,l),r \sim p_{data}((v,l),r)}[log(D((v,l),r))] \\ + \mathbb{E}_{v,l \sim p_{data}(v,l)}[log(1 - D((v,l), G(v,l)))] \tag{1}$$

where $\mathbb{E}_{(v,l),r \sim p_{data}}$ represents the expectation of the log-likelihood of the pair $((v,l),r)$ being sampled from the underlying probability distribution of real pairs $p_{data}((v,l),r)$, while $p_{data}(v,l)$ is the distribution of real vessel and lesion masks.

(ii) The Structure Similarity (SSIM) [18] index is useful in quantitatively measuring the structural similarity between two images $(r, G(v,l))$. It also has been shown to perform well for reconstruction and generation of visually pleasing images.

$$SSIM(p) = \frac{2\mu_r\mu_{G(v,l)} + C_1}{\mu_r^2 + \mu_{G(v,l)}^2 + C_1} \cdot \frac{2\sigma_{rG(v,l)} + C_2}{\sigma_r^2 + \sigma_{G(v,l)}^2 + C_2} \tag{2}$$

where $(\mu_r, \mu_{G(v,l)})$ and $(\sigma_r, \sigma_{G(v,l)})$ are the means and standard deviation computed over patch centered on pixel p, C_1 and C_2 are constants. The loss L_{SSIM} can be computed as:

$$L_{SSIM} = 1 - \frac{1}{N}\sum_{p \in P} SSIM(\tilde{p}) \tag{3}$$

where $\tilde{p}$ is the center pixel of a patch P in the image I.

(iii) The loss function L_1 is used mainly to reduce artifacts and blurring and is defined as

$$L_1 = \mathbb{E}_{(v,l),r \sim p_{data}((v,l),r)}(\|r - G(v,l)\|_1) \tag{4}$$

The overall loss function to be minimized is taken to be

$$L(G,D) = L_{adv} + \lambda_1 L_1 + \lambda_2 L_{SSIM} \tag{5}$$

where λ_1 and λ_2 control the contribution of the L_1 and L_{SSIM} loss functions respectively.

2.2   CAD for Haemorrhage Detection

We chose the U-Net [16] to build a CAD solution for detection of HE (referred to as CADH). This is used to demonstrate that the synthetic images (generated by our proposed GAN) are a reliable resource in training the U-net. The U-net architecture consists of a contracting and an expansive path. The contracting path is similar to a typical CNN architecture, whereas in the expanding path, max-pooling is replaced by up-sampling. There are skip connections between contracting and expanding paths to ensure localization. The U-net is modified in terms of the number of filters at each convolutional layer and the loss function. The number of filters at each stage is reduced to half to simplify computations. The loss is modified to account for the misclassification of lesions.

The U-net architecture provides the segmentation of HE. The segmented HE are counted and the image is classified into the respective grade accordingly (as given in Sect. 3.1: training data for CADH).

3   Implementation

3.1   Datasets

Both GAN and CADH were trained on *pathological* images. These are drawn from DRiDB [14] (31 images) and a locally sourced dataset denoted as *LoD* (58 images). Testing of CADH was done at (i) lesion level on 40 pathological images from DIARETDB1 [8] and (ii) at a stage-level on 308 abnormal images + 892 normal images (without HE) from MESSIDOR [3].

Lesion markings are available for DIARETDB1 from four experts, while for DRIDB and *LoD* it is from one expert. The consensus of 3 experts was considered to derive a binary mask for DIARETDB1. The ground truth of all the three datasets were overlapped with the respective images and thresholded to get a pixel-level lesion mask. The vessel masks, whenever unavailable were derived using method described in [10]. Images from all datasets was cropped and resized 512 × 512 before feeding them to GAN or CADH.

Training Data for GAN. Training of the GAN requires both lesion and vessel masks. the lesion masks for the training data are available, but vessels masks are available only for DRiDB. It is tedious and time consuming to mark the vessels in each of the retinal images. Hence, vessel masks were derived using a method [10] which has proved to perform relatively well for vessel segmentation even in the presence of pathologies.

Training Data for CADH. For training the CADH, a heterogeneous mixture of data were combined, namely, expert annotated data and synthetic data and augmented data. The DRiDB and *LoD* datasets were sources of expert annotated data. Augmented data was derived by applying random transformations to the images. This included random rotation between -25^0 to 25^0, random translation in vertical/horizontal directions in the range of 50 pixels, and random horizontal/vertical flips.

Finally, the synthetic retinal images were generated using GAN as follows. The vessel and lesion masks were taken randomly from *LoD* and DRiDB. The lesion masks were modified using the same random transformations such as flipping the lesions sector wise, flipping horizontally and vertically, rotations and translations. Retinal images containing HE are graded with severity levels as in [3]: grade 0/1 (no HE), grade 2 (1–5 HE) and grade 3 (more than 5 HE). The lesions masks were derived to provide exemplars for each level using these rules. The number of lesions in each category were maintained by masking out few lesions or adding new lesions from another lesion mask randomly. Figure 2 shows a sample of the vessel, lesion masks and generated synthetic images at grade 2 and 3 severity levels.

3.2 Computing Details

The models were implemented in Python using Keras with Theano as backend and trained on a NVIDIA GTX 970 GPU, 4 GB RAM. Training was done with random initialized weights for 2000 epochs by minimizing the loss functions described in Sect. 2.1 using Adam optimizer. For model parameters, learning rate was initialized to 2×10^{-4} for GAN and 1×10^{-5} for CADH. A batch size of 4 was considered for both cases and other parameters were left at default values. Class weights were outlined as the inverse ratio of the number of positive samples to negative samples and modified empirically.

3.3 Evaluation Metrics

The synthetically generated images were evaluated quantitatively and qualitatively. The mean and standard deviation of the Q_v score described in [9] was computed over all images (40 abnormal) in DIARETDB1.

The performance of CADH was evaluated using Sensitivity (SN) and Positive Predictive Value (PPV) which are defined as follows: $SN = \frac{TP}{TP+FN}$ and $PPV = \frac{TP}{TP+FP}$. To evaluate against the given local annotations by experts, the pixel

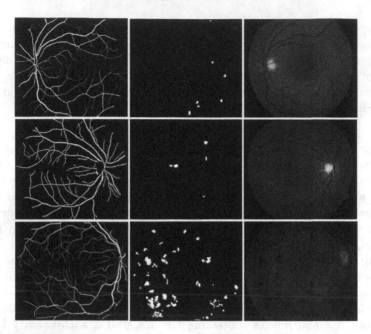

Fig. 2. Vessel, lesion masks and synthetic images generated at grade 2 (first two rows) and grade 3 (last row) levels.

wise classification was converted to region wise detection by applying connected component analysis and requiring at least 50% (but not exceeding more than 150%) overlap with manually marked regions to identify true positive detections (TP); else it is false positive (FP). If a region is marked by the expert but was not detected by the model then it is a False negative (FN). The area under the SN vs PPV curve (AUC) is also taken as a measure of performance.

4   Experiments and Results

4.1   Synthetic Image Generation (GAN)

Figure 3 shows two sample synthetic retinal images (containing HE) generated by the proposed GAN model. The first two columns show the vessel and lesion masks given as input to the GAN. Third and fourth columns show the synthetic and the corresponding real images, respectively. The synthetic images appear realistic yet differ from the real images in terms of background color, texture and illumination. Lesion locations are roughly similar but sizes are different as lesion masks are not results of exact segmentations of lesions.

The mean/standard deviation of Q_v computed over all images with pathologies in DIARETDB1 is 0.0516/ 0.0144 and over all the synthetic images generated from vessel and lesion mask from DIARETDB1 is 0.0675/0.0239. The Q_v score is higher for images of greater quality, this indicates synthetic images are considered better as they contain less noise.

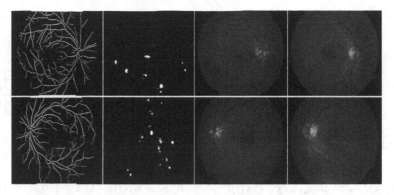

Fig. 3. Results of GAN-based image synthesis. From left to right: vessel mask, lesion mask, synthetic image and corresponding real image.

4.2 CAD for Haemorrhage Detection (CADH)

The utility of the synthetic data for CAD development was tested by training 4 different CADH models by varying the training set content. Denoting the set of real images with expert annotations as E and the set of synthetic images generated by GAN with the corresponding lesion masks as S, the variants of the training set considered are: (i) only E, (ii) E with data augmentation (E+A), (iii) E and S, (iv) E, S with data augmentation (E+S+A). The computed SN at a fixed PPV and AUC values for these variants are reported in Table 1. The SN vs PPV curve is shown in Fig. 4.

The tabulated results indicate that addition of synthetic data (E+S) boosts SN by 20.4% and 10% over E and E+A, respectively. The full set of E+S+A yields the best performance with an improvement (over E) in SN by 27.4% and AUC by 19%. This establishes the effectiveness of synthetic data in general and in CAD development. Increasing the number of synthetic images serves to improve the performance (row 5). In order to assess if synthetically derived data has artifacts, the E+S+A variant was tested on an exclusive set of separately generated synthetic images using vessel and lesion masks of DIARETDB1. The obtained results (row 6) shows a minor degradation over that for real images (row 4), implying the generated data is free of artifacts. A recent fast CNN method [5] for binary (HE/no HE) classification used local markings by experts and report a SN/SP on the MESSIDOR dataset of 91.9/91.4% which is lower than 94/ 91.7% achieved by CADH trained on E+S(141)+A. Since this dataset provides severity grades for each image, testing of CADH model was done at grade level and the obtained values for SN/ SP are 92/94.4% for grade 2 and 89.4/90.1% for grade 3. This indicates that the model trained with synthetic data (can be generated in abundance) is better than that trained with expert annotated data (which is difficult to obtain).

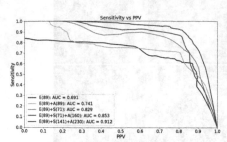

Fig. 4. SN vs PPV curve for CADH.

Table 1. CADH performance on DIARETDB1.

Training data (# images)	SN (%)	PPV (%)	AUC
1. E (89)	63.1	79.4	0.691
2. E (89) + A (89)	70.6	79.6	0.741
3. E (89) + S (71)	79.3	79.6	0.829
4. E (89) + S (71)+ A (160)	86.9	79.8	0.853
5. E (89) + S (141)+ A (230)	92.7	79.4	0.912
6. E (89)+ S (71)+ A (160)^a	84.2	80	0.834

^{a} detection performance on only synthetic images.

5   Concluding Remarks

We proposed a novel solution to develop retinal images with HE using generative adversarial networks. The network is trained to generate the retinal image using vessel and lesion masks. Hence, we can develop retinal image with any type of severity, by providing the corresponding lesion mask. The synthetic abnormal images generated are shown to be realistic in the type of lesions produced and also the color, texture using the Q_v metric. These generated images are valuable in developing a CAD system which detects and localizes haemorrhages as addition of synthetic data led to improvement in both SN and AUC by 17%. Our proposed approach can be extended to other lesions (such as hard exudates) and image modalities and thus has a wide potential.

References

1. Collins, D.L., et al.: Design and construction of a realistic digital brain phantom. IEEE Trans. Med. Imaging **17**(3), 463–468 (1998)
2. Costa, P., et al.: End-to-end adversarial retinal image synthesis. IEEE Trans. Med. Imaging **37**(3), 781–791 (2017)
3. Decenciere, E., et al.: Feedback on a publicly distributed database: the messidor database. Image Anal. Stereol. **33**, 231–234 (2014)
4. Goodfellow, I., et al.: Generative adversarial nets. In: Advances in Neural Information Processing Systems 27, pp. 2672–2680 (2014)
5. van Grinsven, M.J.J.P., et al.: Fast convolutional neural network training using selective data sampling: application to hemorrhage detection in color fundus images. IEEE Trans. Med. Imaging **35**, 1273–1284 (2016)
6. Guibas, J.T., et al.: Synthetic Medical Images from Dual Generative Adversarial Networks. ArXiv e-prints, September 2017
7. Joshi, G.D., et al.: Colour retinal image enhancement based on domain knowledge. In: Computer Vision, Graphics Image Processing, ICVGIP, pp. 591–598, December 2008

8. Kalesnykiene, V., et al.: DIARETDB1 diabetic retinopathy database and evaluation protocol, June 2007
9. Kohler, T., et al.: Automatic no-reference quality assessment for retinal fundus images using vessel segmentation. In: International Symposium on Computer-Based Medical Systems, CBMS 2013, pp. 95–100 (2013)
10. Maninis, K.-K., Pont-Tuset, J., Arbeláez, P., Van Gool, L.: Deep retinal image understanding. In: Ourselin, S., Joskowicz, L., Sabuncu, M.R., Unal, G., Wells, W. (eds.) MICCAI 2016. LNCS, vol. 9901, pp. 140–148. Springer, Cham (2016). https://doi.org/10.1007/978-3-319-46723-8_17
11. Menti, E., Bonaldi, L., Ballerini, L., Ruggeri, A., Trucco, E.: Automatic generation of synthetic retinal fundus images: vascular network. In: Tsaftaris, S.A., Gooya, A., Frangi, A.F., Prince, J.L. (eds.) SASHIMI 2016. LNCS, vol. 9968, pp. 167–176. Springer, Cham (2016). https://doi.org/10.1007/978-3-319-46630-9_17
12. Nie, D., Trullo, R., Lian, J., Petitjean, C., Ruan, S., Wang, Q., Shen, D.: Medical image synthesis with context-aware generative adversarial networks. In: Descoteaux, M., Maier-Hein, L., Franz, A., Jannin, P., Collins, D.L., Duchesne, S. (eds.) MICCAI 2017. LNCS, vol. 10435, pp. 417–425. Springer, Cham (2017). https://doi.org/10.1007/978-3-319-66179-7_48
13. Prastawa, M., et al.: Simulation of brain tumors in MR images for evaluation of segmentation efficacy. Med. Image Anal. 13, 297–311 (2009)
14. Prentasic, P., et al.: Diabetic retinopathy image database (DRiDB): a new database for diabetic retinopathy screening programs research. In: Image and Signal Processing and Analysis, ISPA, pp. 704–709 (2013)
15. Rezaei, M., et al.: Conditional adversarial network for semantic segmentation of brain tumor. CoRR abs/1708.05227, August 2017
16. Ronneberger, O., et al.: U-net: convolutional networks for biomedical image segmentation. In: Medical Image Computing and Computer-Assisted Intervention, MICCAI, pp. 234–241 (2015)
17. Shankaranarayana, S.M., Ram, K., Mitra, K., Sivaprakasam, M.: Joint optic disc and cup segmentation using fully convolutional and adversarial networks. In: Cardoso, M.J., et al. (eds.) FIFI/OMIA -2017. LNCS, vol. 10554, pp. 168–176. Springer, Cham (2017). https://doi.org/10.1007/978-3-319-67561-9_19
18. Wang, Z., et al.: Image quality assessment: from error visibility to structural similarity. IEEE Trans. Image Process. 13(4), 600–612 (2004)
19. Wilkinson, C.P., et al.: Proposed international clinical diabetic retinopathy and diabetic macular edema disease severity scales. Ophthalmology 110(9), 1677–1682 (2003)
20. Yang, Y., et al.: Lesion detection and grading of diabetic retinopathy via two-stages deep convolutional neural networks. CoRR abs/1705.00771 (2017)

Deep Convolutional Artery/Vein Classification of Retinal Vessels

Maria Ines Meyer[1(✉)], Adrian Galdran[1], Pedro Costa[1],
Ana Maria Mendonça[1,2], and Aurélio Campilho[1,2]

[1] INESC-TEC - Institute for Systems and Computer Engineering,
Technology and Science, Porto, Portugal
{maria.i.meyer,adrian.galdran}@inesctec.pt
[2] Faculdade de Engenharia da Universidade do Porto, Porto, Portugal
{amendon,campilho}@fe.up.pt

Abstract. The classification of retinal vessels into arteries and veins in eye fundus images is a relevant task for the automatic assessment of vascular changes. This paper presents a new approach to solve this problem by means of a Fully-Connected Convolutional Neural Network that is specifically adapted for artery/vein classification. For this, a loss function that focuses only on pixels belonging to the retinal vessel tree is built. The relevance of providing the model with different chromatic components of the source images is also analyzed. The performance of the proposed method is evaluated on the RITE dataset of retinal images, achieving promising results, with an accuracy of 96% on large caliber vessels, and an overall accuracy of 84%.

1 Introduction

The retina is routinely examined in medical settings as a means of diagnosis for several different pathologies. In particular, several types of alterations in the vasculature are known to be indicative of disease. For instance, decreased arteriolar caliber may indicate coronary artery disease, while increased venular caliber is associated with diabetic retinopathy and risk of stroke [11]. To assess these alterations, a commonly employed biomarker is the ratio between arteriolar and venular diameters (AVR) [2]. Abnormal AVR has been correlated with high cholesterol levels or high blood pressure [7]. In addition, a decreased AVR is an early sign of Diabetic Retinopathy. This is caused by a pathological widening of the veins produced by retinal hypoxia, arising after retinal microvascular degradation due to high blood sugar levels [5]. The early detection of such symptoms can increase the chance of disease detection and enable early adoption of preventive treatments to avoid vision loss.

To examine the retinal vessels, ophthalmologists often rely on images of the retina acquired by fundus cameras. However, objective visual analysis of the retinal vasculature on these images is a time consuming task that requires expert knowledge. For this reason, in recent years a large number of techniques have

© Springer International Publishing AG, part of Springer Nature 2018
A. Campilho et al. (Eds.): ICIAR 2018, LNCS 10882, pp. 622–630, 2018.
https://doi.org/10.1007/978-3-319-93000-8_71

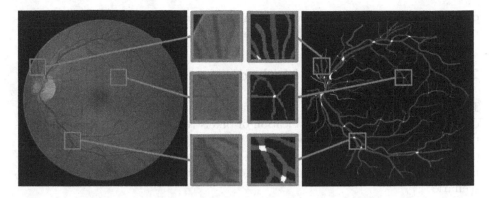

Fig. 1. Left: Retinal image. Right: Expert A/V annotations, encoded as: blue: veins; red: arteries, white: crossings; yellow: uncertain labels. Center: Zoomed regions illustrating the main visual features and challenges related to the A/V problem. Top Row: Arteries show brighter intensities. Center Row: Fine veins and arteries are hardly distinguishable. Bottom Row: Central reflex effect. Reflex size is slightly larger for arteries. (Color figure online)

been proposed to automate several retinal image analysis tasks, *e.g.*, vessel segmentation [10], optic disk localization [3], or detection of markers for disease [1]. The classification of retinal vessels into arteries or veins is another relevant challenge, since this differentiation is necessary for measuring AVR. An automated approach to artery/vein (A/V) classification could lead to a systematic approach for AVR estimation, which would be a very useful tool for ophthalmologists (Fig. 1).

Existing techniques can be grouped into graph-based and dense methods. Graph-based methods reduce the segmented vasculature to a linear skeleton, further divided into separate edges, considering junction and ending points as nodes, and building an undirected graph on which geometry and connectivity can be more easily analyzed [4,5,14]. Dense methods assign an artery or vein label to each pixel in a pre-existing segmentation of the retinal vessel tree. This classification is achieved by supplying to a machine learning model representations of artery and vein pixels in terms of visual descriptors that model differences between both classes. These descriptors attempt to capture relevant color, size, or geometrical information [9,12,17,18]. A notable exception are recent deep-learning based approaches, which automatically learn the most useful representation [16].

In this work, we propose to solve the A/V classification task by means of a Deep Convolutional Neural Network. This allows us to avoid generating an initial skeletonized vessel map representation, and directly classify every pixel in a vessel. We bypass the implementation of cumbersome tracking mechanisms to propagate predictions along vessels, and other type of post-processing. We also provide an experimental analysis of the influence of each particular color component on the resulting model, which allows us to discard non-relevant information and leads to a more efficient training.

2   A/V Classification Method

The proposed method builds on a Convolutional Neural Network specifically designed to deal with the classification of pixels lying on one-dimensional structures (vessels), which are embedded in a two-dimensional space (the background of the retinal image). Below we detail the selected architecture and a suitable modification of a standard pixel-wise loss function to take into account this scenario.

2.1   Adapting CNNs for A/V Classification

Over the past few years Convolutional Neural Networks (CNNs) have achieved remarkable success in medical image analysis tasks. When applied for the task of image segmentation, we are interested in assigning a prediction to each pixel on the image. CNNs can be reformulated to perform image segmentation based on the notions of *Fully-Convolutional Neural Networks* (F-CNN) and *skip connections*, which allow to link coarse and fine layers of a CNN.

A popular F-CNN architecture is U-net, introduced in [13] for the task of segmenting biological tissue images. In this architecture, the upsampling of the feature map is done symmetrically to the regular contracting CNN section. Specifically, the output feature map of the last layer of the contracting path is upsampled so that it has the same dimension as the second last layer. The resulting feature map is fused with the feature map from the corresponding layer in the contracting section. This procedure is repeated until the output of the upsampling operation has the same dimension as the input of the network. This results in a U-shaped network, where the output feature maps of the layers in the contracting section are fused with the output from the upsampling operations.

The problem of classifying retinal vessels can also be formulated as a pixel-wise classification problem, suitable for the application of a U-net-like network. Nevertheless, solving a three-class segmentation in the context of retinal images is a complex challenge that remains unsolved [5]. As such, in this work we focus on the simpler problem of classifying pixels belonging to retinal vessels, while ignoring the task of separating the vasculature from the background.

In its common formulation the convolution operation is not suitable for the task of vessel pixel classification, since the input of a CNN must be a rectangular image region and all of its pixels must classified. Accordingly, a U-net-like model returns a prediction for each pixel, and a third class accounting for background pixels needs to be considered. The solution adopted in this paper for solving the two class A/V problem consists on weighting the penalization of pixels belonging to different classes. For that, we propose to modify the cross-entropy loss function, typically used for classification problems, as follows:

$$L_i = \frac{1}{N} \sum_{i=1}^{N} \sum_{j=1}^{3} w_j \ y_{ij} \log(\hat{y}_{ij}), \quad w_j = \begin{cases} 0, \ j = 1 \\ 1, \ j = 2,3 \end{cases} \tag{1}$$

where $\hat{y}_{ij}$ is the prediction associated to a pixel i with ground-truth label given by y_{ij}. In this case, $j \in \{1, 2, 3\}$ models each of the possible classes occurring in a retinal image, *i.e.* background ($j = 1$), artery ($j = 2$), and vein ($j = 3$), and w_n is the weight attributed to each class. In order to obtain classifications only for the vessel tree, the background class is assigned a weight $w = 0$ at training time. With this formulation, Eq. (1) returns a score penalizing only incorrect classification of vessel pixels, and the error is backpropagated through the network (Fig. 2).

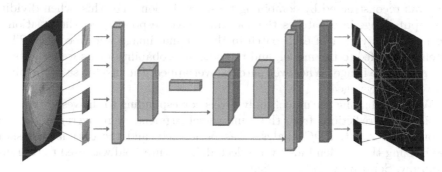

Fig. 2. Proposed U-Net-like architecture adapted for A/V classification

Implementation and Training. In our implementation of the U-net architecture, each convolution layer uses a stride of two, and is followed by Rectified Linear Unit activations, batch normalization and Dropout. The feature maps between the shallow contracting layers and the deep expanding layers are fused by a concatenation operation. The final layer is a convolution followed by a softmax activation in order to map each feature vector onto the classes of interest.

The model is optimized by minimizing the pixel mis-classification error, according to the cross-entropy function given by Eq. (1). The minimization follows stochastic mini-batch gradient descent, with the gradients computed by standard backpropagation. The Adam algorithm [8] is used for optimization, with learning rate 1×10^{-2}. The loss was monitored on the validation set, and training was stopped when it did not decrease anymore. Training took approximately 20 h on a NVIDIA GeForce GTX 1080 GPU. After training, the model can generate a prediction for 90 64 × 64 pixels patches (the minimum number of patches needed to create a reconstruction of the original image) in approximately 10.4 s.

3   Experimental Evaluation

3.1   Data and Evaluation

The method was trained and evaluated on the RITE dataset [6], which contains A/V ground-truth of the retinal images from the publicly available DRIVE dataset [15]. DRIVE contains 40 images of size 565 × 584, divided into 20 training and 20 test images. Before training, 4 images were randomly selected for validation.

Images in RITE contain labels for artery, vein, crossing and uncertain. Pixels labeled as crossing or uncertain were ignored during training. The images were divided into patches of 64 × 64 pixels centered on randomly selected pixels of both classes. At test time predictions were performed patch-wise, and the vessel tree was reconstructed by combining these predictions. For this, when dividing the input image into patches the coordinates corresponding to the position of the upper left corner of each patch in the original image were recorded. These patches were fed to the model, and the output probability maps were combined into a full-size image. Whenever patches overlapped, the pixel-wise probabilities were simply averaged.

When evaluating the models only pixels corresponding to the vessel tree were considered. Predictions from the same vessel segments were averaged to reach a consistent result. ROC analysis was performed, and the optimal threshold maximizing the Youden Index was selected. This threshold was used to compute Accuracy, Sensitivity and Specificity.

3.2   Chromatic Component Analysis for the A/V Problem

When dealing with color images, RGB is the typical choice for most computer-aided diagnosis tasks. However, it is well-known that, in the case of retinal images, the blue channel contains large quantities of noise, whereas the green channel is the component of choice for vessel segmentation methods due to its good contrast between background and vessels. On the other hand, the red component seems to be visually relevant for the discrimination of vessel types.

In order to analyze the contribution of each color channel for classifying vessels, we take advantage of CNNs being agnostic feature extractors: the most relevant information is extracted by the model driven only by the misclassification loss, thus bypassing manual feature engineering. We conduct a simple experiment: we train seven equal models, considering different inputs for each of them. We provide to each model different combinations of chromatic components, spanning from single channels to every possible pair, and finally to the three color channels. All models are trained for 150 epochs with the same hyperparameter configuration. The results of these experiments are shown in Table 1.

As expected, when considering individual channels, the performance of the model trained on the Red component only was higher than when trained on

Table 1. Classification performance when considering different chromatic components.

	R	G	B	RG	RB	BG	RGB
Accuracy	0.82	0.79	0.74	0.83	**0.84**	0.82	**0.84**
AUC	0.89	0.87	0.81	0.91	**0.92**	0.89	0.91

Green, and training with the Blue channel obtained the worst performance. However, when considering combinations of two different channels, we observed that the Red channel was slightly better complemented by the Blue component than by the Green channel, although the difference was marginal. The combination of chromatic components that ignored the Red channel obtained the worst result, indicating that Red is an essential component to consider when solving the A/V classification problem. In addition, the combination of the three components did not lead to any improvement in performance when compared to employing either the Red and Green components or Red and Blue. Since considering less input channels leads to removing redundant information and a more efficient memory usage, we discarded the option of training on the entire RGB information for the next section.

3.3   Quantitative Comparison with Previous Approaches

Since the difference in performance between using RG and RB chromatic component combinations was not significant, we decided to select both input types and train two models until full convergence. In order to test our approach against other A/V classification techniques, we present in Table 2 a comparison of our method and the methods introduced in [4,12] for the same dataset. Both methods originally reported performance when classifying only major vessels with a caliber greater than 3 pixels. For a fair comparison, we also computed the performance of the technique introduced in this paper on these vessels.

4   Discussion and Future Work

The proposed model achieves a competitive performance in terms of accuracy when compared with other approaches. It is also interesting to note that the model trained on Red-Blue components achieved similar AUC, but greater specificity than the one trained on Red-Green channels, indicating that the information in each channel may be complementary. It must be stressed that this performance was computed only for predictions on thick vessels. This is a useful

Table 2. Performance of the proposed models on thick vessels.

	Sensitivity	Specificity	Accuracy	AUC
Dashtbozorg et al. [4]	0.90	0.84	0.874	–
Niemejer et al. [12]	0.80	0.80	–	0.88
Proposed approach – **RG**	**0.96**	0.93	0.95	**0.99**
Proposed approach – **RB**	0.95	**0.96**	**0.96**	**0.99**

scenario, since for AVR measurements only large arcades are typically considered. However, when predictions are computed on the entire vessel tree, the performance drops significantly, as shown in Table 1. In Fig. 3 we show the predictions for all vessel pixels. The displayed predictions correspond to the best, the average, and the worst results. We can observe how, while the classification of the main arcades is mostly correct, thin vessels are wrongly predicted in a substantial amount. The performance of other recent methods, when predicting the entire vessel tree, is greater than the proposed model [5,16], indicating that there is a wide margin for improvement. Accordingly, the next steps will consist of designing domain-related regularizing mechanisms for the presented deep CNN, mainly taking into account geometrical constraints on the distribution of arteries and veins within the retina.

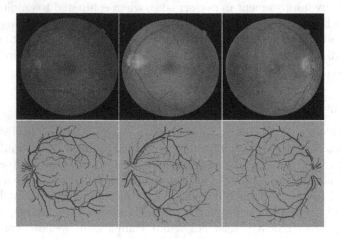

Fig. 3. Left: Best classification result (RB); Middle: Average classification result; Right: Worse classification result. Color code: Red, correctly predicted arteries. Blue, correctly predicted veins. Green, wrongly predicted veins. Yellow, wrongly predicted arteries. (Color figure online)

5   Conclusions

We have introduced a novel approach for classification of retinal vessels into arteries and veins. The method builds on a Deep Neural Network, and the loss function that drives the model learning is suitably modified to account for vessel pixels only, while ignoring the background. The method achieves promising results in the task of artery/vein classification, with high performance on thick vessels.

Acknowledgments. This work is funded by the North Portugal Regional Operational Programme (NORTE 2020), under the PORTUGAL 2020 Partnership Agreement, and the European Regional Development Fund (ERDF), within the project "NanoSTIMA:

Macro-to-Nano Human Sensing: Towards Integrated Multimodal Health Monitoring and Analytics/NORTE-01-0145-FEDER-000016".

References

1. Costa, P., Campilho, A.: Convolutional bag of words for diabetic retinopathy detection from eye fundus images. IPSJ Trans. Comput. Vis. Appl. **9**(1), 10 (2017)
2. Dashtbozorg, B., Mendonça, A.M., Campilho, A.: An automatic method for the estimation of arteriolar-to-venular ratio in retinal images. In: IEEE International Symposium on Computer-Based Medical Systems, pp. 512–513, June 2013
3. Dashtbozorg, B., Mendonça, A.M., Campilho, A.: Optic disc segmentation using the sliding band filter. Comput. Biol. Med. **56**, 1–12 (2015)
4. Dashtbozorg, B., Mendonca, A.M., Campilho, A.: An automatic graph-based approach for artery/vein classification in retinal images. IEEE Trans. Image Process. **23**(3), 1073–1083 (2014)
5. Estrada, R., Allingham, M.J., Mettu, P.S., Cousins, S.W., Tomasi, C., Farsiu, S.: Retinal artery-vein classification via topology estimation. IEEE Trans. Med. Imaging **34**(12), 2518–2534 (2015)
6. Hu, Q., Abràmoff, M.D., Garvin, M.K.: Automated separation of binary overlapping trees in low-contrast color retinal images. In: Mori, K., Sakuma, I., Sato, Y., Barillot, C., Navab, N. (eds.) MICCAI 2013. LNCS, vol. 8150, pp. 436–443. Springer, Heidelberg (2013). https://doi.org/10.1007/978-3-642-40763-5_54
7. Ikram, M.K., de Jong, F.J., Vingerling, J.R., Witteman, J.C.M., Hofman, A., Breteler, M.M.B., de Jong, P.T.V.M.: Are retinal arteriolar or venular diameters associated with markers for cardiovascular disorders? The rotterdam study. Invest. Ophthalmol. Vis. Sci. **45**(7), 2129–2134 (2004)
8. Kingma, D., Ba, J.: Adam: a method for stochastic optimization. In: International Conference on Learning Representations, pp. 1–13 (2014)
9. Kondermann, C., Kondermann, D., Yan, M.: Blood vessel classification into arteries and veins in retinal images. In: Image Processing, p. 651247 (2007)
10. Meyer, M.I., Costa, P., Galdran, A., Mendonça, A.M., Campilho, A.: A deep neural network for vessel segmentation of scanning laser ophthalmoscopy images. In: Karray, F., Campilho, A., Cheriet, F. (eds.) ICIAR 2017. LNCS, vol. 10317, pp. 507–515. Springer, Cham (2017). https://doi.org/10.1007/978-3-319-59876-5_56
11. Nguyen, T.T., Wong, T.Y.: Retinal vascular changes and diabetic retinopathy. Curr. Diabetes Rep. **9**(4), 277–283 (2009)
12. Niemeijer, M., van Ginneken, B., Abramoff, M.D.: Automatic classification of retinal vessels into arteries and veins. In: SPIE medical imaging. International Society for Optics and Photonics, November 2016, vol. 7260, pp. 1–8 (2009)
13. Ronneberger, O., Fischer, P., Brox, T.: U-Net: convolutional networks for biomedical image segmentation. In: Navab, N., Hornegger, J., Wells, W.M., Frangi, A.F. (eds.) MICCAI 2015. LNCS, vol. 9351, pp. 234–241. Springer, Cham (2015). https://doi.org/10.1007/978-3-319-24574-4_28
14. Rothaus, K., Jiang, X., Rhiem, P.: Separation of the retinal vascular graph in arteries and veins based upon structural knowledge. Image Vis. Comput. **27**(7), 864–875 (2009)
15. Staal, J.J., Abramoff, M.D., Niemeijer, M., Viergever, M.A., Ginneken, B.V.: Ridge based vessel segmentation in color images of the retina. IEEE Trans. Med. Imaging **23**(4), 501–509 (2004)

16. Welikala, R., Foster, P., Whincup, P., Rudnicka, A., Owen, C., Strachan, D., Barman, S.: Automated arteriole and venule classification using deep learning for retinal images from the UK biobank cohort. Comput. Biol. Med. **90**, 23–32 (2017)
17. Yu, H., Barriga, S., Agurto, C., Nemeth, S., Bauman, W., Soliz, P.: Automated Retinal Vessel Type Classification in Color Fundus Images, vol. 8670 (2013)
18. Zamperini, A., Giachetti, A., Trucco, E., Chin, K.S.: Effective features for artery-vein classification in digital fundus images. In: Proceedings - IEEE Symposium on Computer-Based Medical Systems (2012)

Improved Accuracy and Robustness of a Corneal Endothelial Cell Segmentation Method Based on Merging Superpixels

Juan P. Vigueras-Guillén[1,3](✉) iD, Angela Engel[1] iD, Hans G. Lemij[2] iD,
Jeroen van Rooij[2] iD, Koenraad A. Vermeer[1] iD, and Lucas J. van Vliet[3] iD

[1] Rotterdam Ophthalmic Institute, Rotterdam, The Netherlands
[2] The Rotterdam Eye Hospital, Rotterdam, The Netherlands
[3] Department of Imaging Physics, Delft University of Technology,
Delft, The Netherlands
J.P.ViguerasGuillen@tudelft.nl

Abstract. Clinical parameters related to the corneal endothelium can only be estimated by segmenting endothelial cell images. Specular microscopy is the current standard technique to image the endothelium, but its low SNR make the segmentation a complicated task. Recently, we proposed a method to segment such images by starting with an oversegmented image and merging the superpixels that constitute a cell. Here, we show how our merging method provides better results than optimizing the segmentation itself. Furthermore, our method can provide accurate results despite the degree of the initial oversegmentation, resulting into a precision and recall of 0.91 for the optimal oversegmentation.

Keywords: Specular microscopy · Oversegmentation · Watershed

1 Introduction

The endothelium of the cornea, a monolayer of hexagonal shaped cells on the posterior corneal surface, plays a key role in keeping an optimal state of corneal hydration [2]. Human endothelial cell density decreases naturally with increasing age, and regeneration of endothelial cells has not been observed under normal circumstances. Instead, endothelial cells grow and migrate to occupy the space that is freed by the dying cells. Intraocular surgery, trauma, and certain diseases may accelerate cell loss. If cell density drops below 700 cells/mm^2, the resulting corneal edema may disrupt vision [3]. Accurate quantification of the endothelial cell morphology is crucial for the assessment of the health status of the cornea.

Non-contact specular microscopy and contact confocal microscopy are commonly used in clinical practice to image the endothelium *in vivo*. Characterized by its non-invasive nature and fast acquisition time, non-contact specular

This work was supported by ZonMw under Grants 842005004 and 842005007.

microscopy provides reliable and reproducible measurements [8]. In comparison, contact confocal microscopy requires corneal contact and has longer acquisition time, but it provides higher quality endothelial images in diseased and edematous corneas [5]. Furthermore, ocular microsaccades, respiration, and pulse are important, limiting factors in the acquisition of good quality images *in vivo*.

Endothelial cell density (ECD), cell size variation (CV), and hexagonality (HEX) are the three main parameters to assess the endothelium. Microscope manufacturers provide built-in software to automatically segment endothelium images and estimate these parameters. However, many studies have indicated that current microscope software may provide unreliable estimations, specifically in the cases with low or high cell density or a high degree of CV [6–8].

In recent years, several cell segmentation techniques for *in vivo* corneal endothelium images were proposed. More studies were focused on segmenting confocal images [10,11] rather than specular [9], probably because of its better image quality and signal-to-noise ratio (SNR). Hence, there is a need to develop algorithms that can accurately segment specular microscopy endothelial images.

1.1   Our Aim

We have recently developed an automatic algorithm to segment *in vivo* specular microscopy images [12]. Briefly summarized, our method aims to generate an accurate segmentation by starting with an oversegmented endothelial cell image and merging those superpixels that together comprise a whole cell (Fig. 1). We showed how a machine learning approach (based on Support Vector Machines) can use features related to shape, intensity, size, etc., to identify the superpixels that constitute a complete cell. During the merging process, all combinations of two and three neighboring superpixels are evaluated simultaneously, using a dedicated classifier for the merger of two or three superpixels. The binary classification is then transformed into a probabilistic output, which allows to sort the combinations. In a iterative process, the combination with the highest probability is merged until no more acceptable combinations ($p > 0.5$) remain.

Although any method that can generate oversegmented endothelial cell images could be used as a starting point, we chose to adapt Selig *et al.*'s approach [10] because of its simplicity to generate and adjust oversegmentation. Selig *et al.* designed a seeded watershed algorithm in a stochastic manner to segment *in vivo* confocal microscopy images, which requires fine-tuning of several parameters in order to achieve a satisfactory result. In our approach [12], parameter tuning was not necessary as we aimed for oversegmentation.

In this paper, we show how our method can improve the accuracy of Selig *et al.*'s [10] optimal segmentation when applied to *in vivo* specular microscopy images. By using precision and recall to evaluate the segmentation, we obtained the best parameter values for Selig *et al.*'s method and computed the corresponding segmentation (named *"watershed optimized result"*). After applying our merging method [12] to the watershed optimized result, we evaluated the segmentation results. Furthermore, we generated several oversegmented images with different degrees of oversegmentation, applied our merging method to all of

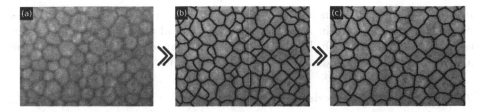

Fig. 1. (a) Input image. (b) Initial oversegmentation. (c) Output of merging process.

them, and evaluated the resulting segmentation, thereby showing the robustness of our method against various degrees of oversegmentation.

2 Method

2.1 Materials

The dataset contains 30 corneal endothelium images from the central cornea of 30 glaucomatous eyes, acquired in The Rotterdam Eye Hospital with a non-contact specular microscope (SP-1P, Topcon, Japan) for an ongoing study regarding the implantation of a Baerveldt glaucoma drainage device. Each image covers an area of $0.25\,\mathrm{mm} \times 0.55\,\mathrm{mm}$ and they were saved as 8-bits grayscale images of 241×529 pixels. The dataset shows a large variability in cell morphology, with a range of 1400–2700 cells/mm^2 in ECD, 19%–35% in CV, and 44%–73% in HEX. The acquisition occurred with informed consent and followed the tenets of the Declaration of Helsinki. One expert created the gold standard by performing manual segmentation of the edges using an image manipulation program, GIMP.

2.2 Description of Selig *et al.*'s Method

Selig *et al.*'s method [10] employs a seeded stochastic watershed algorithm to segment endothelial cell images. The seeds are arranged in a hexagonal grid to mimic the endothelial cells pattern. The grid size is derived by estimating the most common cell size, which can be computed from the Fourier spectrum of the image (see Sect. 2.3). The seeded watershed algorithm is repeatedly applied, $m = 100$ times (value derived in [1]), to a randomly rotated and translated grid. Uniformly distributed noise in the range of $[0, u]$ is added to the image at each iteration, which avoids the occurrence of spurious segmentation lines [1]. The result of all seeded watershed segmentations are summed together, providing an image named *likelihood map* (or PDF), which indicates how often each pixel was selected as edge. To smooth the result, a Gaussian smoothing filter is applied to the PDF, whose optimal σ_{PDF} is related to the cell size. To adapt σ_{PDF} to the cell size of each image, Selig *et al.* defined a parameter $k_\sigma = \sigma_{PDF} f^*$, where f^* is the characteristic frequency estimated from the Fourier spectrum of the image. An H-minima transform is then applied to the PDF, $h = k_h m / \sigma_{PDF}$, to discard small minima. Finally, the classical watershed is applied to the PDF, resulting in the final segmentation. Selig *et al.* observed that the smoothing was very sensitive to errors in the estimation of f^*, and so they suggested to re-estimate f^* from the PDF. In summary, three parameters are to be tuned in the algorithm: noise amplitude u, smoothing size k_σ, and local minima depth k_h.

2.3   Frequency Analysis

The 2D Fourier transform (2D FT) of an endothelial image shows a distinctive concentric ring due to the fairly regular size and pattern of the cells [4]. The ring's radius, called *characteristic frequency* (f^*), is related to the most common cell size in the image, $l = 1/f^*$ [10]. To determine the radius, we compute the 1D radial magnitude by angular averaging of the magnitude of the 2D FT,

$$\mathcal{F}_{RM}(f) = \frac{1}{2\pi} \int_0^{2\pi} |\mathcal{F}(f,\theta)| d\theta, \tag{1}$$

where $\mathcal{F}(f,\theta)$ is the Fourier transform of the intensity image in polar coordinates. Thus, the ring radius in the 2D FT appears as a peak in the 1D radial magnitude. Since specular microscopy images have lower SNR, lower contrast, and lower resolution than confocal images, the ring appears almost imperceptible in the radial magnitude (Fig. 2a, arrow). Selig *et al.* [10] proposed a method, named reconstruction by dilation, to enhance the peak (Fig. 2b) and find its value by fitting a parabola. While the enhancement method works well in specular microscopy images, the parabola fitting must be applied with caution because it is prone to generate wrong estimations. Instead, we propose to fit a function that is comprised of a decaying exponential and a Gaussian,

$$g(f; a, b, c, \mu, \sigma) = a \exp(-bf) + \frac{1}{\sqrt{2\pi\sigma^2}} \exp\left(\frac{-(f-\mu)^2}{2\sigma^2}\right) + c, \tag{2}$$

where g is the model, f is the spatial frequency, a and b are the scale parameters of the exponential, μ and σ are the mean and standard deviation of the Gaussian respectively, and c is the offset. A non-linear least-squares solver was used to find the parameters. The characteristic frequency is then estimated as the position of the Gaussian (μ). As suggested by Selig *et al.* [10], the estimation of f^* can be improved if the model is fitted to the Fourier transform of the PDF (Fig. 2c).

2.4   Generating Oversegmentation

Oversegmentation can easily be induced by creating a denser grid of seeds in Selig *et al.*'s method [10]. Given the total image area A_I, the expected number of cells in the image is $n_{seeds} = NA_I f^{*2}$, with $N = 1$ for the watershed optimized segmentation. In our merging method, we used a value $N = 3$, which is equivalent to a three times higher cell density. In this paper, we generate nine oversegmented images by taking the integer values $N = 1, 2, ..., 9$.

Two scenarios to create oversegmentation were considered. If f^* is reestimated in the PDF after oversegmentation was applied, the frequency spectrum will show the components of the smaller superpixels in the PDF (Fig. 2d). Then,

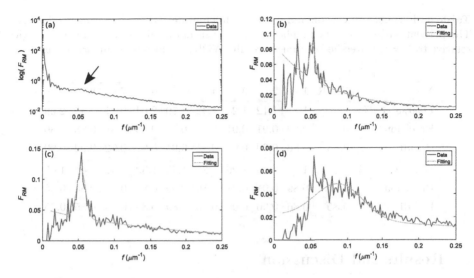

Fig. 2. The radial magnitude of the FT after angular averaging at different stages of preprocessing in order to estimate f^*. (a) No preprocessing; f^* is almost indiscernible (arrow). (b) After reconstruction by dilation in the FT of the image (fitting gives a $f^* = 0.0527$). (c) After reconstruction by dilation in the FT of the PDF (fitting indicates a $f^* = 0.0541$). (d) After reconstruction by dilation in the FT of the PDF where an oversegmentation with $N = 8$ was applied (fitting provides a $f^* = 0.0880$).

the fitting function will provide an f^* balanced between the average cell size and the smaller superpixels in the PDF. This simply creates a higher degree of oversegmentation with more irregular sizes of superpixels. Alternatively, we can avoid re-estimation (or to re-estimate it using $N = 1$). Nonetheless, both cases were evaluated here, named *oversg. 1* for the former (re-estimation of f^* in the PDF) and *oversg. 2* for the latter. The degree of oversegmentation in both cases is indicated in Table 1.

2.5 Evaluating the Segmentation

In order to evaluate the segmentation, we computed two values from the segmented images, the total number of superpixels (n_{total}) and the number of cells correctly segmented (n_{corr}), as well as one value from the gold standard, the number of real cells (n_{real}). We considered a cell is correctly segmented based on the following rule: given the area of a cell in the segmentation A_S, the area of a cell in the gold standard A_G, and the intersection of those two areas $A_I = A_S \cap A_G$, the cell in the segmentation is correctly segmented if $A_I > 0.75 \times max(A_S, A_G)$. That margin was added to allow small deviations in the cell boundary locations and was selected after visual analysis.

The precision $p = n_{corr}/n_{total}$ and the recall $r = n_{corr}/n_{real}$ were computed and combined into the F-measure, $F = 2pr/(p + r)$. Although both, over- and under-segmented cells affect both metrics, precision decreases more acutely with oversegmentation and recall decreases more strongly with undersegmentation.

Table 1. Estimated precision and recall for different degrees of oversegmentation (N). The percentage indicates the number of superpixels in the initial oversegmented images relative to N = 1. Watershed optimized result (WOR) is added for comparison purposes.

N	WOR	1	2	3	4	5	6	7	8	9
Oversg. 1 (%)	-	1	1.12	1.24	1.42	1.70	2.04	2.21	2.45	2.68
Precision	0.83	0.89	0.91	0.91	0.91	0.90	0.89	0.88	0.88	0.86
Recall	0.85	0.86	0.90	0.91	0.91	0.91	0.92	0.92	0.92	0.90
Oversg. 2 (%)	-	1	1.10	1.20	1.28	1.35	1.39	1.42	1.44	1.47
Precision	0.83	0.89	0.91	0.91	0.89	0.89	0.88	0.86	0.85	0.85
Recall	0.85	0.86	0.90	0.90	0.89	0.89	0.88	0.86	0.85	0.85

3   Results and Discussion

3.1   Watershed Optimized Result

Selig *et al.*'s algorithm was applied to all images in the dataset for all values of u between 0 and 50 in steps of 10, values of k_σ between 0.10 and 0.25 in steps of 0.01, and values of k_h between 0.000 and 0.010 in steps of 0.001. The F-measure was computed for each image. In a leave-one-out approach, the parameters for image i were estimated as the ones that yielded the largest average F when computed for all images in the dataset excluding i. For all images, the optimal parameters were the same: $u_i = 20$, $k_{\sigma,i} = 0.20$, and $k_{h,i} = 0$.

When evaluated the segmentation without merging, the mean and standard deviation of the precision and recall with the optimal parameters were $p = 0.83 \pm 0.07$ and $r = 0.85 \pm 0.06$, yielding $F = 0.84 \pm 0.07$. This suggested that over- as well as under-segmentation were present.

3.2   Solving the Oversegmentation

Based on the optimal parameters obtained in Sect. 3.1, nine oversegmented images (per image in the dataset) were generated for each type of oversegmentation (as described in Sect. 2.4) after which the merging method [12] was applied to all of them without retraining. The evaluation of the resulting segmentations shows that the watershed optimized result can be directly improved by just applying our merging method (WOR vs. $N = 1$, in Table 1). In a visual evaluation (Fig. 3b, f), it is clear that the watershed optimized result generates under- (red arrows) and over-segmentation (magenta edges). Whereas the latter is mostly solved by the merging method (large increase in precision from WOR to $N = 1$ in Table 1), the former cannot be easily fixed as the number of possible splits grows exponentially with the number of edge pixels per undersegmented superpixel. It is then crucial for our merging method to start with an oversegmented image where no undersegmentation occurs.

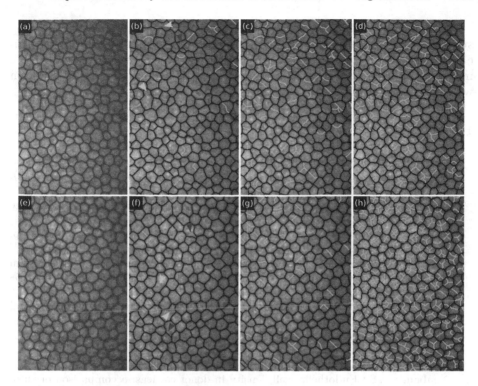

Fig. 3. Two representative examples: *oversg. 2* in (a–d), and *oversg. 1* in (e–h). (a, e) Gold standard segmentation in blue, superimposed over the intensity image. (b, c, d, f, g, h) Resulting segmentation in black, and edges removed during merging process in magenta, for an oversegmentation of $N = 1$ in (b, f), $N = 3$ in (c, g), and $N = 9$ in (d, h). Note that watershed optimized result is (b, f) with all edges (black and magenta). Red arrows indicate undersegmentation. Blue arrows indicate inaccurate segmentation. (Color figure online)

The optimal degree of oversegmentation occurs at $N = 3$ for both types of oversegmentation ($F_{oversg.1} = 0.910$, and $F_{oversg.2} = 0.906$). All true edges seem to be detected at that point, and the degree of oversegmentation is not excessive. For higher values of N, it would be expected that more (presumably unnecessary) initial oversegmentation would only increase the chances of more errors. Interestingly, this hardly happens for the cases in *oversg. 1*. The reason lies in the inaccurate segmentation of some edges due to a limitation of the stochastic watershed: when a strong false edge is detected close to a real edge (blue arrows in Fig. 3f), the latter cannot be detected unless we force a large amount of oversegmentation (Fig. 3h). Whereas such a degree of oversegmentation would suggest a higher error probability, the merging method can satisfactorily overcome this problem. Nonetheless, this evaluation suggests that the best setup is using *oversg. 1* with $N = 3$, as it is more robust.

In summary, we have shown how a segmentation method based on merging superpixels can improve the accuracy of another segmentation method specifically designed to solve confocal images. Furthermore, we have proven how such a merging method is strongly robust against the degree of initial oversegmentation without requiring any retraining.

References

1. Bernander, K.B., Gustavsson, K., Selig, B., Sintorn, I.M., Luengo Hendriks, C.L.: Improving the stochastic watershed. Pattern Recogn. Lett. **34**(9), 993–1000 (2013). https://doi.org/10.1016/j.patrec.2013.02.012
2. Bourne, W.M.: Biology of the corneal endothelium in health and disease. Eye (Lond.) **17**(8), 912–918 (2003). https://doi.org/10.1038/sj.eye.6700559
3. Bourne, W.M., McLaren, J.W.: Clinical responses of the corneal endothelium. Exp. Eye Res. **78**(3), 561–572 (2004). https://doi.org/10.1016/j.exer.2003.08.002
4. Foracchia, M., Ruggeri, A.: Automatic estimation of endothelium cell density in donor corneas by means of fourier analysis. Med. Biol. Eng. Comput. **42**(5), 725–731 (2004). https://doi.org/10.1007/BF02347557
5. Hara, M., Morishige, N., Chikama, T., Nishida, T.: Comparison of confocal biomicroscopy and noncontact specular microscopy for evaluation of the corneal endothelium. Cornea **22**(6), 512–515 (2003). https://doi.org/10.1097/00003226-200308000-00005
6. Hirneiss, C., Schumann, R.G., Gruterich, M., Welge-Luessen, U.C., Kampik, A., Neubauer, A.S.: Endothelial cell density in donor corneas: a comparison of automatic software programs with manual counting. Cornea **26**(1), 80–83 (2007). https://doi.org/10.1097/ICO.0b013e31802be629
7. Huang, J., Maram, J., Tepelus, T.C., Sadda, S.R., Chopra, V., Lee, O.L.: Comparison of noncontact specular and confocal microscopy for evaluation of corneal endothelium. Eye Contact Lens (2017). https://doi.org/10.1097/ICL.0000000000000362
8. Salvetat, M.L., Zeppieri, M., Miani, F., Parisi, L., Felletti, M., Brusini, P.: Comparison between laser scanning in vivo confocal microscopy and noncontact specular microscopy in assessing corneal endothelial cell density and central corneal thicknes. Cornea **30**(7), 754–759 (2011). https://doi.org/10.1097/ICO.0b013e3182000c5d
9. Scarpa, F., Ruggeri, A.: Development of a reliable automated algorithm for the morphometric analysis of human corneal endothelium. Cornea **35**(9), 1222–1228 (2016). https://doi.org/10.1097/ICO.0000000000000908
10. Selig, B., Vermeer, K.A., Rieger, B., Hillenaar, T., Luengo Hendriks, C.L.: Fully automatic evaluation of the corneal endothelium from in vivo confocal microscopy. BMC Med. Imaging **15**, 1–13 (2015). https://doi.org/10.1186/s12880-015-0054-3
11. Sharif, M.S., Qahwaji, R., Shahamatnia, E., Alzubaidi, R., Ipson, S., Brahma, A.: An efficient intelligent analysis system for confocal corneal endothelium images. Comput. Methods Programs. Biomed. **122**(3), 421–436 (2015). https://doi.org/10.1016/j.cmpb.2015.09.003
12. Vigueras-Guillén, J.P., Andrinopoulou, E.R., Engel, A., Lemij, H.G., van Rooij, J., Vermeer, K.A., van Vliet, L.J.: Corneal endothelial cell segmentation by classifier-based merging of oversegmented images (2018, submitted)

Hard Exudate Detection Using Local Texture Analysis and Gaussian Processes

Adrián Colomer[1]([✉]), Pablo Ruiz[2], Valery Naranjo[1], Rafael Molina[3],
and Aggelos K. Katsaggelos[2]

[1] Instituto de Investigación e Innovación en Bioingeniería (I3B), Universitat
Politècnica de València, Camino de Vera s/n, 46022 Valencia, Spain
adcogra@upv.es
[2] Department of Electrical Engineering and Computer Science,
Northwestern University, Evanston, USA
[3] Dpto. de Ciencias de la Computación e I.A.,
Universidad de Granada, Granada, Spain

Abstract. Exudates are the most noticeable sign in the first stage of
diabetic retinopathy. This disease causes about five percent of world
blindness. Making use of retinal fundus images, exudates can be detected,
which helps the early diagnosis of the pathology. In this work, a novel
method for automatic hard exudate detection is presented. After an
exhaustive pre-processing step, Local Binary Patterns Variance (LBPV)
histograms are used to locally extract texture information. We then use
Gaussian Processes to distinguish between healthy and pathological retinal patches. The proposed methodology is validated using the *E-OPHTA
exudates* database. The experimental results demonstrate that Gaussian
Process classifiers outperform the current state of the art classifiers for
this problem.

Keywords: Hard exudate · Local Binary Patterns
Gaussian Processes · Bayesian modeling · Variational inference

1 Introduction

Diabetic Retinopathy (DR) causes about five percent of world blindness and
signs of this eye disease are found in around 33% of the diabetes population
[1]. There exist two types of DR: Non-Proliferative and Proliferative Diabetic
Retinopathy [2]. Non-Proliferative DR is the earliest stage of the pathology and
it is characterized by deposits of extra fluid and small amounts of blood, from

This work has been supported in part by the Ministerio de Economía y Competitividad under contracts DPI2016-77869-C2-{1,2}-R, and the Department of Energy
grant DE-NA0002520. The work of Adrián Colomer has been supported by the Spanish FPI Grant BES-2014-067889. We gratefully acknowledge the support of NVIDIA
Corporation with the donation of the Titan Xp GPU used for this research.

© Springer International Publishing AG, part of Springer Nature 2018
A. Campilho et al. (Eds.): ICIAR 2018, LNCS 10882, pp. 639–649, 2018.
https://doi.org/10.1007/978-3-319-93000-8_73

the vessels into the retina, called exudates and microaneurysms/hemorrhages (Fig. 1a).

RGB fundus images are acquired by a retinal camera using non-invasive protocols. This kind of images is commonly used by ophthalmologists to diagnose diabetic retinopathy. Exudates are revealed as yellow whitish areas of random size and shape generated by the accumulation of fats and lipids. As these lesions are the most noticeable sign of non-proliferative diabetic retinopathy, indicating the first stage of the disease, the exudate detection is a key step in the early diagnosis of the pathology. Due to the large population at risk of DR, there exists the need of developing automatic algorithms able to discriminate regions where exudates are present.

Fundus databases contain images with different resolutions, non-uniform illumination, reflects and noise or artefacts (Figs. 1b and c), due to the uncalibrated conditions in the acquisition process. Besides these problems, the physiological properties of the retina produce other image variabilities such as highlights near the vessels, characteristic of young retinas (Fig. 1d), and different fundus colour depending on age, ethnicity, retina pigmentation and other anatomical human factors (Fig. 1e). In most of the state-of-the-art works, conflictive images are removed from the original dataset when proposed algorithms are evaluated [3]. However, a computer-aided diagnose system must deal with the high variability among fundus images, so we will not eliminate problematic images.

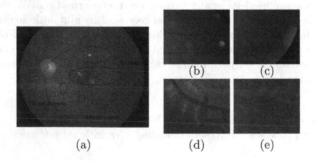

Fig. 1. (a) Noisy image, (b) Image with reflects, (c) Highlighted retina, (d) Tessellated image due to ethnicity. (Color figure online)

In the literature, the most common procedure to detect exudates exploits their shape information. In [4–6], exudates are segmented by applying mathematical morphology and thresholding techniques. Another common way to detect these lesions is to extract global information from the fundus images and identify the unhealthy regions through supervised or unsupervised classification techniques [3,7,8].

The main contribution of this work is the validation of a new methodology to distinguish between healthy and pathological retinal tissues. Our methodology is based on local texture analysis and makes use of Gaussian Processes for

Classification (GPC). To the best of our knowledge, in the literature to detect exudates, features have only been extracted from the whole image and local features and GPs have not been used before for exudate detection. A comparison with the most commonly used classification methods for solving this problem is also carried out.

The rest of the paper is organized as follows: in Sect. 2 the fundus image pre-processing is detailed. Then, in Sect. 3 the local texture analysis method is described. Section 4 details the Variational Gaussian Process for classification approach. Finally, Sect. 5 provides the experimental validation and in Sect. 6 conclusions and some future work directions are reported.

2   Fundus Image Pre-processing

As mentioned in Sect. 1, databases usually contain images with different resolutions propitiating that some structures and lesions are not comparable. The first preprocessing step aims to normalize the image dimensions following the method described in [9].

Blood vessels are considered as noise or artefacts that hamper the classification of pathologies based on background textures. The contribution of these structures to the texture descriptor must be removed. In this work, diffusion-based inpainting techniques [10] are applied to eliminate the vascular tree.

Another factor that contributes to the heterogeneity of fundus databases is the difference among background colours. This fact is due to the particular physiological properties of each human's retina. With the aim of developing a system invariant to high-lighted retinas and tesselated images, a colour normalization is carried out. Geometric transformations to the chromatic histogram (plane r-g) are performed taking into account a reference image with the ideal background colour [11].

After these steps, the green channel of the RGB fundus images is selected (Fig. 2b) because this component maximizes the contrast between lesions and background [6].

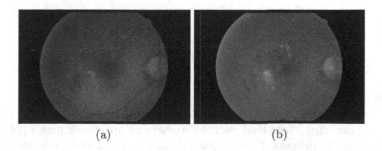
(a)   (b)

Fig. 2. (a) Original image and (b) Green component of the pre-processed image. (Color figure online)

3   Local Texture Analysis

Local Binary Patterns (LBP) is a grey-scale texture descriptor. The basic LBP version assigns a label to each pixel (i, j) taking into account its neighbourhood as follows:

$$LBP_{P,R}(i,j) = \sum_{p=0}^{P-1} s(g_p - g_c) \cdot 2^p, \quad s(x) = \begin{cases} 1 \text{ if } x \geq 0 \\ 0 \text{ if } x < 0 \end{cases} \tag{1}$$

where P represents the number of samples on the symmetric circular neighbourhood of radious R, g_c is the gray value of pixel (i, j) and g_p the gray value of each neighbour.

Although many variants of LBP exist in the literature, due to the properties of the rotation-invariant uniform (riu2) LBP presented in [12], we use it in this work to encode a selected subset of patterns. When LBP is used for texture description it is common to additionally include a contrast measure by defining the Rotational Invariant Local Variance (VAR) as:

$$VAR_{P,R}(i,j) = \frac{1}{P} \sum_{p=0}^{P-1} (g_p - \mu)^2, \quad \mu = \frac{1}{P} \sum_{p=0}^{P-1} g_p \tag{2}$$

Lesions due to diabetic retinopathy vary in size depending on the stage of the disease. In most cases, lesions represent less than one percent of the total number of pixels in the retinal fundus image. For this reason, the texture descriptor is applied locally to obtain relevant features for a large variety of images.

The LBP and VAR images, both of dimensions $M_1 \times M_2$, are extracted from the green channel of the preprocessed original image. These resulting images are divided into patches using a sliding window and normalized histograms are computed for each patch taking into account the information provided by both images (Fig. 3). LBP variance (LBPV) histogram [13] accumulates the VAR value for each LBP label inside the window according to the following equation:

$$LBPV_{P,R}(k) = \sum_{i=1}^{M_1} \sum_{j=1}^{M_2} w(LBP_{P,R}(i,j), k), \quad k \in [0, K] \tag{3}$$

$$w(LBP_{P,R}(i,j), k) = \begin{cases} VAR_{P,R}(i,j), & LBP_{P,R}(i,j) = k \\ 0, & otherwise. \end{cases} \tag{4}$$

where K is the maximal LBP label.

The window used to compute the local histograms is a $b \times b$ square with overlap of $(\Delta x, \Delta y)$. Note that patches containing optic disk pixels [14] are not considered in the process. Patches should also be completely contained within the field of view of the retinal image.

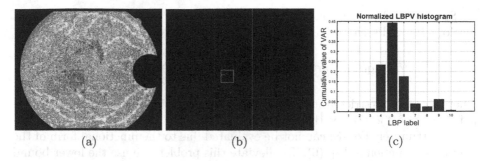

Fig. 3. Local texture analysis. (a) LBP and (b) VAR image with different highlighted patches and (c) the LBPV normalized histogram computed for the yellow patch. (Color figure online)

4 Variational Gaussian Process for Classification

Let $\mathbf{X} = [\mathbf{x}_1, \ldots, \mathbf{x}_N]^{\mathrm{t}}$ be the matrix containing the samples, where each $\mathbf{x}_i \in \mathbb{R}^K$ is the descriptor for the i-th patch, calculated as described in Sect. 3, N is the number of patches used for training, and K is the number LBPV features. Let $\mathbf{y} \in \{0,1\}^N$ be the vector of labels, where 1 refers to "pathologic patches" and 0 refers to "healthy patches".

To model the relationship between samples and labels, the GPC formulation [15] introduces a latent variable $\mathbf{f} \in \mathbb{R}^N$, which is in fact a prior on the functions over the feature space. This latent variable has the following Gaussian prior distribution

$$p(\mathbf{f}|\varOmega) = \mathcal{N}(\mathbf{f}|\mathbf{0}, \mathbf{K}), \tag{5}$$

where $\mathbf{K}$ is the covariance matrix, which depends on a set of parameters $\varOmega$ to be estimated and has the form $\mathbf{K}_{ij} = \mathbf{k}(\mathbf{x}_i, \mathbf{x}_j)$ where $\mathbf{k}(\cdot, \cdot)$ is a kernel function (see [15]) . $\mathbf{K}$ is the way in which GPs exploit the correlation between samples, since each $\mathbf{K}_{ij}$ is calculated by evaluating a kernel function (an inner product in a transformed vector space) on the samples $\mathbf{x}_i$ and $\mathbf{x}_j$. Although $\mathbf{K}$ depends on $\mathbf{X}$, we have removed it from dependencies in $p(\mathbf{f}|\varOmega)$ for simplicity.

The relationship between $\mathbf{f}$ and the labels $\mathbf{y}$ is modeled by the so-called logistic likelihood function

$$p(\mathbf{y}|\mathbf{f}) = \prod_{i=1}^{N} p(y_i|f_i) = \prod_{i=1}^{N} \left(\frac{1}{1 + e^{-f_i}}\right)^{y_i} \left(\frac{1}{1 + e^{f_i}}\right)^{1-y_i}. \tag{6}$$

Notice that for large positive values of f_i, $p(y_i = 1|f_i) \approx 1$, and for negative values of f_i with large absolute value $p(y_i = 1|f_i) \approx 0$.

The joint distribution of $\mathbf{y}$, $\mathbf{f}$, and $\varOmega$ is

$$p(\mathbf{y}, \mathbf{f}, \varOmega) = p(\mathbf{y}|\mathbf{f})p(\mathbf{f}|\varOmega)p(\varOmega). \tag{7}$$

where we have used a flat improper prior for $\varOmega$.

Since $p(\mathbf{f}, \Omega|\mathbf{y})$ can not be calculated, we resort to the mean field approximation [16] and solve the problem

$$\hat{q}(\mathbf{f}), \hat{q}(\Omega) = \arg \min_{q(\mathbf{f}), q(\Omega)} \int q(\mathbf{f})q(\Omega) \ln \frac{q(\mathbf{f})q(\Omega)}{p(\mathbf{y}, \mathbf{f}, \Omega)} d\mathbf{f}d\Omega, \quad (8)$$

where $\hat{q}(\Omega)$ is restricted to be a degenerate distribution, to finally obtain $p(\mathbf{f}, \Omega|\mathbf{y}) \approx \hat{q}(\mathbf{f})\hat{q}(\Omega)$, see [17] for details.

Unfortunately Eq. (8) can not be evaluated due to the functional form of the likelihood function in Eq. (6). To alleviate this problem we use the lower bound provided in [17],

$$\log p(\mathbf{y}|\mathbf{f}) \geq \log \mathbf{H}(\mathbf{y}, \mathbf{f}, \boldsymbol{\xi}) = \quad (9)$$

$$\mathbf{f}^t(\mathbf{y} - \frac{1}{2}\mathbf{1}) - \mathbf{f}^t \boldsymbol{\Lambda}\mathbf{f} + \boldsymbol{\xi}^t \boldsymbol{\Lambda}\boldsymbol{\xi} + \frac{1}{2}\boldsymbol{\xi}^t\mathbf{1} - \sum_{i=1}^{N} \log(1 + e^{\xi_i}),$$

where $\boldsymbol{\xi} = (\xi_1, \ldots, \xi_N)^t$ is a set of nonnegative parameters to be estimated, $\boldsymbol{\Lambda} = \mathrm{diag}(\lambda(\xi_1), \ldots, \lambda(\xi_N))$, with $\lambda(\xi) = \frac{1}{2\xi}(\frac{1}{1+e^{-\xi}} - \frac{1}{2})$, and $\mathbf{1}$ is a column vector with all components equal to 1.

The joint distribution in Eq. (7) can then be lower bounded as $p(\mathbf{y}, \mathbf{f}, \Omega) \geq \mathbf{M}(\mathbf{y}, \mathbf{f}, \Omega, \boldsymbol{\xi}) = \mathbf{H}(\mathbf{y}, \mathbf{f}, \boldsymbol{\xi})p(\mathbf{f}|\Omega)p(\Omega)$, which produces

$$\int q(\mathbf{f})q(\Omega) \ln \frac{q(\mathbf{f})q(\Omega)}{p(\mathbf{y}, \mathbf{f}, \Omega)} d\mathbf{f}d\Omega$$

$$\leq \min_{\xi \geq 0} \int q(\mathbf{f})q(\Omega) \log \frac{q(\mathbf{f})q(\Omega)}{\mathbf{M}(\mathbf{y}, \mathbf{f}, \Omega, \boldsymbol{\xi})} d\mathbf{f}. \quad (10)$$

Let $\boldsymbol{\xi}^k$ be the current value of $\boldsymbol{\xi}$, then

$$\min_{q(\mathbf{f})} \int q(\mathbf{f}) \log \frac{q(\mathbf{f})}{\mathbf{M}(\mathbf{y}, \mathbf{f}, \Omega, \boldsymbol{\xi}^k)} d\mathbf{f} = \mathrm{const}$$

$$- \ln \mathcal{N}\left(\frac{1}{2}(\mathbf{y} - \frac{1}{2})|\mathbf{0}, \frac{1}{2}\boldsymbol{\Lambda}^k + \boldsymbol{\Lambda}^k \mathbf{K}_\Omega \boldsymbol{\Lambda}^k\right) \quad (11)$$

which produces Ω^k, the current estimate of the vector where $\hat{q}(\Omega)$ is degenerate,

$$\Omega^k = \arg \max_{\Omega} \mathcal{N}\left(\frac{1}{2}(\mathbf{y} - \frac{1}{2})|\mathbf{0}, \frac{1}{2}\boldsymbol{\Lambda}^k + \boldsymbol{\Lambda}^k \mathbf{K}_\Omega \boldsymbol{\Lambda}^k\right). \quad (12)$$

Fixing $\boldsymbol{\xi}$ to $\boldsymbol{\xi}^k$ and Ω to Ω^k we obtain

$$q^k(\mathbf{f}) = \mathcal{N}(<\mathbf{f}>_k, \boldsymbol{\Sigma}_k) \quad (13)$$

where $<\mathbf{f}>_k = \boldsymbol{\Sigma}_k(\mathbf{y} - \frac{1}{2}\mathbf{1})$ and $\boldsymbol{\Sigma}_k = (\mathbf{K}_{\Omega^k}^{-1} + 2\boldsymbol{\Lambda}^k)^{-1}$. Finally, solving

$$\boldsymbol{\xi}^{k+1} = \max_{\boldsymbol{\xi}} < \ln \mathbf{M}(\mathbf{y}, \mathbf{f}, \Omega^k, \boldsymbol{\xi}) >_{q^k(\mathbf{f})} \quad (14)$$

we obtain

$$\xi_i^{k+1} = \sqrt{<f_i>^2 + \Sigma_k(i,i)}. \tag{15}$$

In Algorithm 1 we summarize the estimation procedure.

Algorithm 1. Learning Algorithm

Require: Initial $\boldsymbol{\xi}^1 = \mathbf{1}$ and $k = 1$.
1: **repeat**
2:     Calculate Ω^k using $\boldsymbol{\xi}^k$ in Eq. (12).
3:     Calculate $q^k(\mathbf{f})$ using Ω^k and $\boldsymbol{\xi}^k$ in Eq. (13).
4:     Calculate $\boldsymbol{\xi}^{k+1}$ using $q^k(\mathbf{f})$ and Ω^k in Eq. (15).
5:     $k = k + 1$
6: **until** convergence

Given a new patch $\mathbf{x}_*$ we would like to calculate

$$p(y_*|\mathbf{y}) = \int_{f_*} p(y_*|f_*) \left(\int_{\mathbf{f}} p(f_*|\mathbf{f})p(\mathbf{f}|\mathbf{y})d\mathbf{f} \right) df_*$$
$$\approx \int_{f_*} p(y_*|f_*) \left(\int_{\mathbf{f}} p(f_*|\mathbf{f})\hat{q}(\mathbf{f})d\mathbf{f} \right) df_*, \tag{16}$$

where the approximated posterior $\hat{q}(\mathbf{f})$ has been calculated, at convergence, in Algorithm 1, and $p(y_*|f_*)$ is given by Eq. (6). The conditional distribution $p(f_*|\mathbf{f})$ can be calculated from Eq. (5) as

$$p(f_*|\mathbf{f}) = \mathcal{N}(f_*|\mathbf{h}^t\mathbf{K}^{-1}\mathbf{f}, c - \mathbf{h}^t\mathbf{K}^{-1}\mathbf{h}), \tag{17}$$

with $\mathbf{h} = (k(\mathbf{x}_*, \mathbf{x}_1), \ldots, k(\mathbf{x}_*, \mathbf{x}_N))^t$, $c = k(\mathbf{x}_*, \mathbf{x}_*)$. The probability that patch $\mathbf{x}_*$ belongs to class "pathological" can be written then as

$$p(y_* = 1|\mathbf{y}) \approx \int \frac{1}{1 + e^{-f_*}} \mathcal{N}(f_*|m(f_*), v^2(f_*))df_*, \tag{18}$$

with $m(f_*) = \mathbf{h}^t\mathbf{K}^{-1}<\mathbf{f}>$ and $v^2(f_*) = c - \mathbf{h}^t(\mathbf{K} + (2\Lambda)^{-1})^{-1}\mathbf{h}$. The integral in Eq. (18) is approximated as in [17], to obtain

$$p(y_* = 1|\mathbf{y}) \approx \left(1 + \exp\left\{ -m(f_*)(1 + \frac{1}{8}\pi v^2(f_*))^{-1/2} \right\} \right)^{-1}. \tag{19}$$

As can be observed in Fig. 2a, pathological areas represent only a small region of the whole image, which results in a very unbalanced dataset. Training a classifier with an unbalanced dataset can produce overfitting to the majority class "healthy" [18]. To avoid this problem we proceed as follows. Let us assume that the number of healthy samples is T times the number of pathological ones, then the set of all healthy samples is partitioned into T subsets with the same cardinality as the number of pathological samples. A committee of T GPCs is then learned with training sets formed by joining all pathological training samples and each partition of healthy training samples. Soft majority voting is used as the final criterion. If the obtained probability is higher than a given threshold δ, the patch is assigned to the class "pathological". Notice that this is not a bagging procedure [19], since sampling is not uniform and with replacement.

5   Experimental Results

To validate the proposed methodology, the *E-OPHTHA exudates* public database [20] was selected. This database is composed by a large variety of images with different resolutions containing tesselations, round spots, brights near the blood vessels, reflects. The performance of our algorithm was tested using the forty seven pathological images and their corresponding ground truth manually annotated by experts. From these forty seven pre-processed images, healthy and pathological patches are extracted as explained in Sect. 3 using $b = 64$ and $(\Delta x, \Delta y) = (32, 32)$. Afterwards, LBPV normalized histograms are computed for $LBP_{8,1}^{riu2}$ obtaining $K = 10$ features from each patch.

In addition to validating the proposed methodology, we also compared it to both, baseline and the state-of-the-art algorithms, for the hard exudate detection problem. The baseline method is Linear Support Vector Machine (LIN-SVM) with a Linear kernel [21], while the state-of-the-art methods are SVM with Radial Basis Function (RBF) kernel [21] and Random Forest (RF) [22].

RBF kernel is also used for GPC . Unlike GPC, SVM and RF do not provide estimation methods for their respective parameters. To perform a fair comparison, cross-validation is used to set the "cost" and "length-scale" parameters in SVM, and "number of trees" in RF.

To avoid biased results produced by training and testing sets selection, in this work we use a leave-one-out cross-validation procedure. The whole dataset with 47 images is divided into 5 partitions, (3 with 9 images, and 2 with 10 images). Then patches in 4 partitions are used for training a classifier as described in Sect. 4, and the remaining patches are used for testing. The procedure is carried out 5 times, leaving out a different partition in each repetition. Since the testing set is also unbalanced, for each classifier we select the decision threshold δ obtaining the best trade-off between sensitivity and specificity.

The mean numeric results for GPC are reported in Table 1, where 0.7840, 0.7840, 0.7833, and 0.6044 of accuracy (Acc.), sensitivity (Sens.), specificity (Spec.) and Matthews correlation coefficient (MCC) [23] are obtained, respectively. The mean numerical results for LIN-SVM, RBF-SVM and RF methods are also reported in Table 1. We can observe that GPC obtains the best result with respect to all metrics of performance. For AUC, GPC is almost 2% better than RF and RBF-SVM, and 4% than the baseline method LIN-SVM. For accuracy, sensitivity, and specificity, GPC is approximately 1%, 2%, and 4% better than RF, RBF-SVM, and LIN-SVM, respectively.

The mean ROC curve for GPC is plotted in red in Fig. 4a, which obtains a 0.8645 of Area Under ROC Curve. Based on [24], the proposed methodology can be considered a "good diagnostic test" for the hard exudate detection.

Table 1. Figures of merit for the compared methods.

	Acc.	Sens.	Spec.	AUC	MCC
LIN-SVM	0.7481	0.7475	0.7471	0.8299	0.4292
RBF-SVM	0.7642	0.7625	0.7635	0.8447	0.4718
RF	0.7701	0.7741	0.7687	0.8473	0.5275
GPCs	**0.7840**	**0.7840**	**0.7833**	**0.8645**	**0.6044**

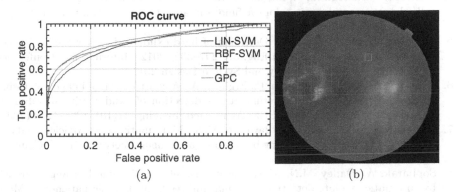

(a)   (b)

Fig. 4. (a) ROC curves for the compared methods and (b) exudate detection using GPCs in a representative image (TP in red, FP in green and TN in blue). (Color figure online)

Mean ROC curves for LIN-SVM, RBF-SVM and RF methods are also plotted in Fig. 4a. We can observe that GPC obtains a better performance than all of them for both, high and low false positive rates. RF works better than RBF-SVM for low false positive rates, however RBF-SVM obtains better results than RF for high false positives rates. Figure 4b shows the exudate detection results in a representative image of *E-OPHTHA* database.

6   Conclusions

In this paper, we presented a system, based on local texture analysis and Gaussian Processes, to detect exudates for DR diagnosis. Local texture description allows to identify pathological tissue providing robustness against the high fundus image variability and spatial information of the lesions. The obtained ROC curves provide evidence that GPCs result in the best classification solution independently of the decision threshold. The proposed methodology outperforms the current state of the art algorithms, namely RBF-SVM and RF. Future work will deal with the detection of dark lesions in order to develop a computer-aided diagnosis system for automatic DR detection. In addition, other texture descriptors will be explored to improve the classification results.

References

1. World Health Organization (WHO): Universal eye health: a global action plan 2014–2019. Technical report (2015)
2. American Academy of Ophtalmology (AAO) Retina/Vitreous Panel: Preferred Practice Pattern ® Guidelines. Diabetic Retinopathy, San Francisco (2016)
3. Morales, S., Engan, K., Naranjo, V., Colomer, A.: Retinal disease screening through local binary patterns. IEEE J. Biomed. Health Inform. **21**(1), 184–192 (2017)
4. Welfer, D., Scharcanski, J., Marinho, D.R.: A coarse-to-fine strategy for automatically detecting exudates in color eye fundus images. Comput. Med. Imaging Graph. **34**(3), 228–235 (2010)
5. JayaKumari, C., Maruthi, R.: Detection of hard exudates in color fundus images of the human retina. Procedia Eng. **30**, 297–302 (2012). International Conference on Communication Technology and System Design 2011
6. Walter, T., Klein, J.C., Massin, P., Erginay, A.: A contribution of image processing to the diagnosis of diabetic retinopathy - detection of exudates in color fundus images of the human retina. IEEE Trans. Med. Imaging **21**(10), 1236–1243 (2002)
7. Karegowda, A.G., Nasiha, A., Jayaram, M.A., Manjunath, A.S.: Article: exudates detection in retinal images using back propagation neural network. Int. J. Comput. Appl. **25**(3), 25–31 (2011)
8. Sopharak, A., Dailey, M.N., Uyyanonvara, B., et al.: Machine learning approach to automatic exudate detection in retinal images from diabetic patients. J. Mod. Opt. **57**(2), 124–135 (2010)
9. Zhang, X., Thibault, G., et al.: Spatial normalization of eye fundus images. In: ISBI 2012 : 9th IEEE International Symposium on Biomedical Imaging, IEEE (2012)
10. Guillemot, C., Le Meur, O.: Image inpainting: overview and recent advances. IEEE Sig. Process. Mag. **31**(1), 127–144 (2014)
11. Colomer, A., Naranjo, V., Angulo, J.: Colour normalization of fundus images based on geometric transformations applied to their chromatic histogram. In: 2017 IEEE International Conference on Image Processing (ICIP), pp. 3135–3139, September 2017
12. Ojala, T., Pietikainen, M., Maenpaa, T.: Multiresolution gray-scale and rotation invariant texture classification with local binary patterns. IEEE Trans. Pattern Anal. Mach. Intell. **24**(7), 971–987 (2002)
13. Guo, Z., Zhang, L., Zhang, D.: Rotation invariant texture classification using LBP variance (LBPV) with global matching. Pattern Recognit. **43**(3), 706–719 (2010)
14. Morales, S., Naranjo, V., Angulo, J., Alcaniz, M.: Automatic detection of optic disc based on pca and mathematical morphology. IEEE Trans. Med. Imaging **32**(4), 786–796 (2013)
15. Rasmussen, C.E., Williams, C.K.I.: Gaussian processes for machine learning. Adaptive computation and machine learning. MIT Press, Cambridge (2006)
16. Parisi, G.: Statistical Field Theory. New edn. Perseus Books, Reading (1998)
17. Bishop, C.: Pattern Recognition and Machine Learning. 1st edn. Springer, New York (2006). Corr. 2nd printing 2011 edn., February 2010
18. Tapia, S.L., Molina, R., de la Blanca, N.P.: Detection and localization of objects in passive millimeter wave Images. In: 2016 24th European Signal Processing Conference (EUSIPCO), pp. 2101–2105, August 2016
19. Breiman, L.: Bagging predictors. Mach. Learn. **24**(2), 123–140 (1996)
20. Decencière, E., Cazuguel, G., Zhang, X., et al.: Teleophta: machine learning and image processing methods for teleophthalmology. IRBM **34**(2), 196–203 (2013)

21. Cristianini, N., Shawe-Taylor, J.: An Introduction to Support Vector Machines and Other Kernel-based Learning Methods. Cambridge University Press, Cambridge (2000)
22. Breiman, L.: Random Forests. Mach. Learn. **45**(1), 5–32 (2001)
23. Matthews, B.: Comparison of the predicted and observed secondary structure of t4 phage lysozyme. Biochim. Biophys. Acta (BBA) Protein Struct. **405**(2), 442–451 (1975)
24. Swets, J.A.: Measuring the accuracy of diagnostic systems. Science **240**(4857), 1285–1293 (1988)

Construction of a Retinal Atlas for Macular OCT Volumes

Arunava Chakravarty[✉], Divya Jyothi Gaddipati, and Jayanthi Sivaswamy

Center for Visual Information Technology, KCIS, IIIT Hyderabad, Hyderabad, India
{arunava.chakravarty,divyajyothi.gaddipati}@research.iiit.ac.in,
jsivaswamy@iiit.ac.in

Abstract. Optical Coherence Tomography (OCT) plays an important role in the analysis of retinal diseases such as Age-Related Macular Degeneration (AMD). In this paper, we present a method to construct a normative atlas for macula centric OCT volumes with a mean intensity template (MT) and probabilistic maps for the seven intra-retinal tissue layers. We also propose an AMD classification scheme where the deviation of the local similarity of a test volume with respect to the MT is used to characterize AMD. The probabilistic atlas was used for layer segmentation where we achieved an average dice score of 0.82 across the eight layer boundaries. On the AMD detection task, the classification accuracy and Area under the Receiver Operating Characteristic curve were 98% and 0.996 respectively, on 170 OCT test volumes.

1 Introduction

Atlas plays an important role in medical image analysis by providing a standard coordinate frame to represent the anatomy. It is often in the form of a mean intensity template (MT) obtained by the average of a set of co-registered images along with a probability template (PT) which gives the probability of observing a particular structure at a given location. Normalization of images to a single coordinate frame via registration to the MT is useful in applications such as the segmentation of anatomical structures, disease detection and therapy planning.

Optical Coherence Tomography (OCT) has emerged as an important modality in retinal imaging by providing a high resolution 3D cross-sectional view of the intra-retinal tissue in a non-invasive manner. The intra-retinal tissue can be anatomically categorized into seven adjacent layers separated by eight boundaries [2] as depicted in Fig. 1a. Quantitative measurements of the thickness and morphology of various layers are directly correlated to the health of the eye. For eg., in Age Related Macular Degenration (AMD), the drusen deposits occur in the Retinal Pigment Epithelium (RPE) layer leading to undulations in the Bruch's membrane (see Fig. 1b.) around the macular region. The region between the ILM and Bruch's membrane is known as the Total Retina (TR) [3].

This work is partially supported by Tata Consultancy Services (TCS) under their doctoral Research Scholarshp Program.

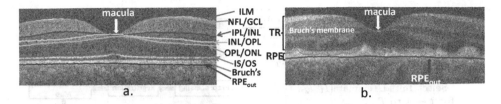

Fig. 1. a. A healthy OCT B-scan with eight layer boundaries. b. OCT B-scan of an AMD case with three relevant layer boundaries.

Though a Normative OCT atlas can have a wide range of applications in retinal image analysis including tissue layer segmentation, ocular disease detection and localization of abnormalities, its construction has received little attention. In [1], the similarity between pairs of A-scans was explored for the inter-subject registration of OCT volumes. The main challenges in the construction of an OCT atlas include the presence of speckle noise, vessel shadows and the inter or intra-scanner intensity variations across the A-scans. The curvature of the retinal surface also leads to large shifts in the retinal tissue across the B-scans.

The contribution of this paper is two-fold. (i) A Normative Atlas is constructed for the macular OCT volumes comprising a MT and the corresponding PT maps for seven retinal tissue layers. The OCT atlas is publicly available for research use at: https://researchweb.iiit.ac.in/~arunava.chakravarty/Atlas_mat_files.zip. (ii) The utility of the atlas is demonstrated through two applications, namely, the segmentation of intra-retinal tissue layers using label transfer and the detection of AMD in OCT volumes by leveraging the deviations in the local similarity between the MT and the registered test OCT Volumes.

2   Method

An overview of the atlas construction method is depicted in Algorithm 1 and discussed in Sect. 2.1. The application of the atlas to layer segmentation and AMD detection (see Fig. 2) is detailed in Sect. 2.2. The preprocessing step comprises resizing, denoising, intensity standardization and retinal curvature flattening of the OCT volumes. Each B-scan in the OCT volume is resized to normalize the pixel dimensions to $3.6\ \mu m$ by $8.6\ \mu m$. Denoising is done via speckle reducing anisotropic diffusion [15] (30 iterations, timestep=0.1) and intensity standardization is achieved with a method reported in [9].

Algorithm 1. Atlas Construction

Input : Set of Normal OCT volumes
$\{I_1, I_2 ... I_N\}$
Output: Atlas Mean Template $\mathcal{M}_T$

1 $\mathcal{M}_0 \leftarrow$
Select_Initial_Template$(I_1, I_2 ... I_N)$

2 **for** $t \leftarrow 1$ **to** T **do**

3 | $\hat{I}_i \leftarrow$ Pairwise_Register $(I_i, \mathcal{M}_{t-1})$,
| $\forall 1 \leq i \leq N$
| $\mathcal{M}_t \leftarrow$ Weighted_Average$(\hat{I}_1, ... \hat{I}_N)$

4 **end**

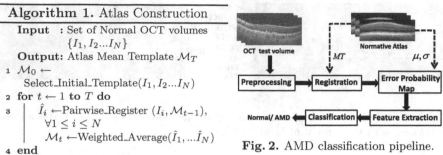

Fig. 2. AMD classification pipeline.

Retinal flattening is performed in two steps. First, each B-scan is individually flatenned using the method in [2] as follows. An approximate estimate of the outer RPE boundary is obtained by finding the brightest pixel in each A-scan, removing the outlier pixels and fitting a quadratic polynomial which is then mapped onto a straight line by shifting each column. In the second step, the B-scans are aligned across the volume. Each B-scan is sequentially aligned to its previous slice by an exhaustive search of the axial pixel translations that maximizes the normalized cross correlation (NCC) between them.

2.1 Atlas Construction

The construction of the atlas involves a groupwise registration of a set of pre-processed OCT volumes followed by computing their average to obtain the MT. A Sharp Means [14] based iterative method was adapted for this task. In each iteration (see algorithm 1), all OCT volumes are registered to the current mean intensity template $\mathcal{M}_{t-1}$ and their weighted average is used to update $\mathcal{M}_t$. The main challenge in the atlas construction is the large inter-subject variation which can result in a blurred $\mathcal{M}_t$, particularly in the initial iterations. To prevent blurring, the weights are adapted patchwise at each spatial location across each volume based on the local similarity between the registered volume $\hat{I}_i$ and $\mathcal{M}_{t-1}$ [14]. The final MT was obtained after $T = 10$ iterations and the patch size was decreased from $19 \times 19 \times 19$ to $1 \times 1 \times 1$ in steps of 2 at each iteration.

Our implementation differs from [14] in two ways: (a) The initial template $\mathcal{M}_0$ is selected as the volume that lies closest to the geometric mean of the set using geodesic distance; (b) Since size of the OCT volumes ($216 \times 770 \times 100$) is much larger than the typical size encountered in neuroimaging, we replace the Demon's registration approach in [14] with the discrete registration framework in [5] for the pairwise registrations to improve the computational efficiency.

The Pairwise Registration Algorithm: The pairwise registration between a fixed (I_f) and moving (I_m) volume is performed in two steps. Since, registration along the axial direction is critical for the alignment of the anatomical layers, an initial rigid translation is performed along the axial direction by maximizing the global NCC of the entire volume using an exhaustive search of pixel translations. Next, a *symmetric* deformable registration is performed using a discrete optimization based method [5] which estimates the deformation field $\boldsymbol{u}$ as

$$\underset{u}{\text{argmin}}\, E(u; I_f, I_m) = \sum_{p \in \Omega} S(I_f, I_m, u_p) + \alpha.|\nabla u|^2, \tag{1}$$

where p denotes each voxel location in the entire image domain Ω. NCC is chosen as the similarity function $S(I_f, I_m, u_p)$ and computed between local patches centered around p. The deformable registration is performed at 3 scales. The maximum displacement was restricted to ± 7, ± 4 and ± 2 voxels from the coarse to fine scale respectively, along all the 3 axis. The regularization parameter σ which indirectly controls the regularization weight α was set to 1 and the radius of local cost aggregation r was set to 2. (see [5] for more details).

Initial Template Selection: A method similar to [10], is used to select $\mathcal{M}_0$. Each OCT volume is represented as a node in a graph by constructing an adjacency matrix using the geodesic distance between each pair of volumes.

We define the geodesic distance between (I_i, I_j) as the registration error $E(u^*; I_i, I_j)$ where u^* represents the displacement field obtained after registering I_j to I_i. In contrast, the bending energy of u^* alone was used in [10] to define the distance neglecting the similarity between the two image.

An adjacency matrix for the set of OCT volumes is constructed using the geodesic distance and Multidimensional Scaling (MDS) is applied to obtain a feature representation for each I_i such that the Euclidean distances in the feature space best approximates the corresponding geodesic distances in terms of the mean squared error [10]. Finally, the volume with the MDS feature closest to the mean feature of the entire set is selected as $\mathcal{M}_0$.

2.2 Applications

Our OCT atlas has the potential to become a useful resource in the field of retinal image analysis with various applications in layer segmentation, abnormality localization and ocular disease detection. In this work, we demonstrate its utility with two preliminary applications, the segmentation of intra-retinal tissue layers and the detection of AMD in OCT volumes.

OCT Layer Segmentation
In order to use the atlas for intra-retinal tissue layer segmentation, the PT maps for the corresponding layers must be pre-computed during training. To compute the PT maps, a set of OCT volumes with manually segmented layers are employed. These OCT volumes are registered to the reference MT and its displacement field is applied to deform the corresponding groundtruth segmentation label maps. Finally, for each voxel in the atlas space, a probability value is computed for each label as the fraction of the registered volumes that have the label at that location.

During testing, a probabilistic segmentation is obtained by registering the atlas MT to a test OCT volume and applying the corresponding deformation field to the atlas PT maps for each layer. Further details on the datasets used in the PT map construction and it's performance are provided in Sect. 3.

AMD Classification

The OCT atlas can aid in the detection of ocular diseases by enabling the extraction of a clinically relevant Region of Interest (ROI). Moreover, the higher registration errors for the abnormal images when registered to a Normative atlas can be leveraged to extract relevant features for disease classification.

We demonstrate this on the task of AMD detection. An atlas based approach has not been explored for AMD detection so far. Existing methods extract the RPE layer to define the (ROI) and employ handcrafted features such as Local Binary Patterns (LBP) [6], Histogram of Oriented Gradients (HoG) [11] or Bag of visual words (BoW) [13] to detect AMD. The local features are aggregated using histogram [13] and employ multi-scale [11] or spatial pyramid [6] approaches to encode the spatial context. The details of the proposed atlas based method are outlined in Fig. 2 and described below.

ROI Extraction: A test OCT volume is first preprocessed and registered to the MT to obtain I_{tst}. Since the morphological changes in AMD are found in the area surrounding the macula in the RPE layer, a ROI is extracted in the atlas space for computational efficiency. The ROI is defined to span 31 B-scans and 180 A-scans centered at the macula. In the axial direction, the ROI is restricted to a small region around the *RPE* layer (rows 124-210 in the atlas space).

Error Probability Map Extraction: A local similarity measure for I_{tst} is evaluated at each voxel p within the ROI by extracting a $3 \times 3 \times 3$ patch $I_{tst}(p)$ around p and computing the NCC similarity $S(I_{tst}(p))$ with respect to the corresponding patch in the MT. The AMD cases (volumes) are expected to have smaller values for $S(I_{tst}(p))$ within the ROI.

However, the absolute value of the $S(I_{tst}(p))$ may not be meaningful. Depending on the complexity of the anatomical structure at a voxel location, the distribution of the local similarity of the Normal OCT volumes also varies across p. Hence the $S(I_{tst}(p))$ values are used to derive an error probability map $P_{err}(I_{tst})$. The $P_{err}(I_{tst})$ at location p measures the probability that $S(I_{tst}(p))$ is sampled from the distribution of similarity values at p that is encountered in the Normal OCT volumes. Assuming a Gaussian distribution for the similarity at each p independently, a mean $(\mu(p))$ and standard deviation $\sigma(p)$ map is generated for the ROI from the Normal OCT volumes used in the atlas construction. During testing, $P_{err}(I_{tst})$ is computed as $\frac{1}{\sqrt{2\pi\sigma(p)^2}} exp\{\frac{(S(I_{tst}(p))-\mu(p)).^2}{2\sigma(p)^2}\}$.

Feature Extraction and Classification: To obtain a global feature representation from the P_{err}, it is scaled to $[0,1]$ across the samples. Thereafter, a 10 bin (uniform bins of width 0.1, centered at 0.05 to 0.95) histogram is computed. Though the abnormality can occur at any column position in the ROI, it should lie close to the bruch's membrane. Hence, the spatial location of the error probabilities along the rows may be important for classification. To incorporate this information, the ROI was further sub-divided into 6 equal row-wise sections and a separate histogram of the P_{err} was also computed for each sub-region. Finally, all histogram features were concatenated resulting in a $(10 + 10 \times 6 =)70$-D feature. A binary linear SVM classifier was employed for AMD classifcation.

3   Results

Dataset: The proposed method was evaluated using 290 (102 Normal, 188 AMD cases) 3D macular OCT volumes from a public dataset released in [3], henceforth referred to as the DUKE-3D dataset. The volumes were acquired from 4 clinics at a size of $512 \times 1000 \times 100$ with a voxel resolution of $(3.25, 6.7, 67)$ $\mu m/voxel$ along the axial, lateral and azimuthal directions. However, the ground truth(GT) segmentation for only the RPE and TR tissue regions are provided in DUKE-3D. Therefore, two additional public datasets, OCTRIMA [12] and the dataset released in [2] (henceforth referred to as the DUKE-2D dataset) were employed to compute and evaluate the PT maps for the inner layers within the TR region (See Fig. 1). Both OCTRIMA and DUKE-2D contain 10 OCT volumes each, acquired using different OCT scanners at varying resolutions (See [2,12] for details). The two datasets provide the GT markings of seven retinal layers for only a few non-consecutive linearly spaced B-scans per volume (10 B-scans per volume in DUKE-2D and 11 B-scans per volume in OCTRIMA).

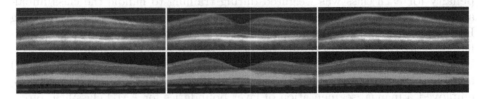

Fig. 3. (left to right) the mean intensity atlas ($1^{s}t$ row) and the corresponding probability maps for the seven tissue layers for the 30th, 50th and 60th B-scans.

Intra-retinal Layer Segmentation: The MT and PT maps for the TR and RPE regions were computed using 40 Normal OCT volumes and evaluated on the remaining (102-40) 62 Normal volumes in the DUKE-3D dataset. After thresholding the probabilities at 0.5, a mean dice score of 0.91 ± 0.02 and $\pm 0.78/0.06$ was achieved for the TR and RPE regions respectively.

To evaluate the localization of the inner layers, the PT maps were computed using the DUKE-2D dataset. Since, GT for only a few B-scans are available, the PT maps for each B-scan in the atlas was computed individually by registering to it, the nearest B-scan (with respect to the distance from macula) from each volume in DUKE-2D. The PT maps for the seven tissue layers are depicted in Fig. 3. The localization of all the seven layers were evaluated on the OCTRIMA dataset and benchmarked against three open source OCT segmentation softwares, the Iowa Reference Algorithm (IRA) version 3.8.0 based on [4], CASEREL based on [2] and OCTSEG based on [7]. CASEREL provides segmentation of seven boundaries (except the bruch's membrane) and OCTSEG segments six boundaries (except the bruch's membrane and INL/OPL). The quantitative results in Table 1 show our performance to be comparable to the existing methods. The probabilistic segmentation can also be used to provide a good initialization to deformable models such as [8] to further fine-tune the layer segmentation.

Table 1. Dice coefficients (mean ± standard deviation) for the segmentation of 7 retinal tissue layers on the OCTRIMA dataset.

	NFL	GCL-IPL	INL	OPL	ONL-IS	OS	RPE
Dice							
CASEREL	0.81±0.13	0.78±0.11	0.50±0.14	0.62±0.12	0.90±0.06	—	—
OCTSEG	0.77±0.18	0.76±0.22	—	—	0.91±0.06	—	—
IRA	0.60±0.15	0.61±0.12	0.45±0.11	0.64±0.10	0.92±0.03	0.88±0.05	0.91±0.04
Proposed	0.79±0.08	0.89±0.07	0.81±0.07	0.75±0.08	0.93±0.03	0.74±0.11	0.83±0.06

AMD Classification: The μ and σ used to compute the P_{err} was computed from the 40 volumes from DUKE-3D used in the atlas construction. These volumes were excluded and the remaining OCT volumes in DUKE-3D were randomly divided into a separate training and test set consisting of 80 (22 Normal and 58 AMD cases) and 170 (40 Normal and 130 AMD cases) respectively. The cost paramter of the linear SVM classifier set to 100 and the mis-classification penalty for each class was weighted during training to handle the class imbalance. The classification performance is depicted in Table 2 and the corresponding ROC plot in Fig. 4. The good performance of our method with a linear classifier demonstrates the discriminative power of the proposed feature. Our atlas based feature outperforms the existing Bag of Words, multiscale HoG (MS-HoG) and the pyramid based SP-LBP features explored in [6,11,13] respectively. [3] employed a manual segmentation of layer boundaries for AMD classification.

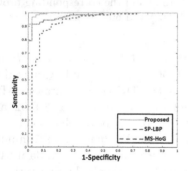

Fig. 4. ROC for AMD detection.

Table 2. AMD classification performance.

	Sens.	Spes.	Acc.	AUC
MS-HoG [11]	0.90	0.85	0.90	0.930
SP-LBP [6]	0.93	0.92	0.92	0.978
BoW [13]	0.96	0.92	0.94	0.984
Manual Seg. [3]	–	–	–	0.992
Proposed	0.97	0.98	0.98	0.996

4   Conclusion

In this paper, we have constructed an atlas for normal OCT volumes which can be used in many applications such as extraction a clinically relevant ROI for analysis, characterize abnormalities as deviations from the Normative atlas or to provide intra-retinal tissue layer segmentations. The probabilistic segmentation maps of seven retinal tissue regions have been obtained which can be transferred onto the test images by registering them to the atlas MT. It achieved an average dice of 0.82 across the seven layers. Better registration algorithms specifically adapted for OCT volumes can be investigated in the future to further improve on the segmentation performance. We have also proposed a novel classification scheme for AMD which demonstrates state of the art performance with an accuracy of 98% and area under the ROC curve of 0.996 on a test set of 170 OCT volumes. Future work would investigate the characterization of additional pathologies such as cysts in the atlas space that appears in the TR region.

References

1. Chen, M., Lang, A., Sotirchos, E., Ying, H.S., Calabresi, P.A., Prince, J.L., Carass, A.: Deformable registration of macular OCT using a-mode scan similarity. In: IEEE International Symposium on Biomedical Imaging, pp. 476–479 (2013)
2. Chiu, S.J., Li, X.T., Nicholas, P., Toth, C.A., Izatt, J.A., Farsiu, S.: Automatic segmentation of seven retinal layers in sdoct images congruent with expert manual segmentation. Opt. Express **18**(18), 19413–19428 (2010)
3. Farsiu, S., Chiu, S.J., O'Connell, R.V., Folgar, F.A., Yuan, E., Izatt, J.A., Toth, C.A., et al.: Quantitative classification of eyes with and without intermediate age-related macular degeneration using optical coherence tomography. Ophthalmology **121**(1), 162–172 (2014)
4. Garvin, M.K., Abràmoff, M.D., Wu, X., Russell, S.R., Burns, T.L., Sonka, M.: Automated 3-D intraretinal layer segmentation of macular spectral-domain optical coherence tomography images. IEEE Trans. Med. Imaging **28**(9), 1436–1447 (2009)
5. Heinrich, M.P., Papież, B.W., Schnabel, J.A., Handels, H.: Non-parametric discrete registration with convex optimisation. In: Ourselin, S., Modat, M. (eds.) WBIR 2014. LNCS, vol. 8545, pp. 51–61. Springer, Cham (2014). https://doi.org/10.1007/978-3-319-08554-8_6
6. Liu, Y.Y., Chen, M., Ishikawa, H., Wollstein, G., Schuman, J.S., Rehg, J.M.: Automated macular pathology diagnosis in retinal OCT images using multi-scale spatial pyramid and local binary patterns in texture and shape encoding. Med. Image Anal. **15**(5), 748–759 (2011)
7. Mayer, M.A., Hornegger, J., Mardin, C.Y., Tornow, R.P.: Retinal nerve fiber layer segmentation on FD-OCT scans of normal subjects and glaucoma patients. Biomed. Opt. Express **1**(5), 1358–1383 (2010)
8. Novosel, J., Thepass, G., Lemij, H.G., de Boer, J.F., Vermeer, K.A., van Vliet, L.J.: Loosely coupled level sets for simultaneous 3D retinal layer segmentation in optical coherence tomography. Med. Image Anal. **26**(1), 146–158 (2015)
9. Nyúl, L.G., Udupa, J.K., Zhang, X.: New variants of a method of MRI scale standardization. IEEE Trans. Med. Imaging **19**(2), 143–150 (2000)
10. Park, H., Bland, P.H., Hero, A.O., Meyer, C.R.: Least biased target selection in probabilistic atlas construction. In: Duncan, J.S., Gerig, G. (eds.) MICCAI 2005. LNCS, vol. 3750, pp. 419–426. Springer, Heidelberg (2005). https://doi.org/10.1007/11566489_52
11. Srinivasan, P.P., Kim, L.A., Mettu, P.S., Cousins, S.W., Comer, G.M., Izatt, J.A., Farsiu, S.: Fully automated detection of diabetic macular edema and dry age-related macular degeneration from optical coherence tomography images. Biomed. Opt. Express **5**(10), 3568–3577 (2014)

12. Tian, J., Varga, B., Somfai, G.M., Lee, W.H., Smiddy, W.E., DeBuc, D.C.: Real-time automatic segmentation of optical coherence tomography volume data of the macular region. PloS One **10**(8), e0133908 (2015)
13. Venhuizen, F.G., van Ginneken, B., Bloemen, B., van Grinsven, M.J., Philipsen, R., Hoyng, C., Theelen, T., Sánchez, C.I.: Automated age-related macular degeneration classification in OCT using unsupervised feature learning. In: SPIE Medical Imaging, p. 94141I (2015)
14. Wu, G., Jia, H., Wang, Q., Shen, D.: Sharpmean: groupwise registration guided by sharp mean image and tree-based registration. NeuroImage **56**(4), 1968–1981 (2011)
15. Yu, Y., Acton, S.T.: Speckle reducing anisotropic diffusion. IEEE Trans. Image Process. **11**(11), 1260–1270 (2002)

Arterioles and Venules Classification in Retinal Images Using Fully Convolutional Deep Neural Network

Sufian AlBadawi[✉] and M. M. Fraz[✉]

School of Electrical Engineering and Computer Science,
National University of Science and Technology, Islamabad, Pakistan
{sufian.badawi,moazam.fraz}@seecs.edu.pk

Abstract. The abnormalities in size, shape and other morphological attributes of retinal vasculature have been prospectively associated as a physio-marker and predictor of many microvascular, systemic and ophthalmic diseases. The progression of retinopathy has a very different evolution in venules and arterioles with some biomarkers associated with only one type of vessel. The robust classification of retinal vasculature into arteriole/venule (AV) is the first step in the development of automated system for analyzing the vasculature biomarker association with disease prognosis.

This paper presents an encoder-decoder based fully convolutional deep neural network for pixel level classification of retinal vasculature into arterioles and venules. The feature learning and inference will be done directly from the image without the requiring the segmented vasculature as a preliminary step. The complex patterns are automatically learned from the retinal image without requiring the handcrafted features. The methodology is trained and evaluated on a subset of the images collection obtained from a population-based study in the UK (EPIC Norfolk), producing 93.5% detection rate. This proposed technique will be optimized further and may replace the AV classification module in the QUARTZ software which is developed earlier by our research group.

Keywords: Computer aided diagnosis · Deep learning
Arteriole/venule classification · Fully convolutional neural networks
Semantic segmentation

1 Introduction

The analysis of shape, appearance, tortuosity and other morphological attributes of human retinal blood vessels can be the important diagnostic indicator of various ophthalmic and system disease which includes diabetic retinopathy, hypertensive retinopathy, arteriolar narrowing, arteriosclerosis and age related macular degeneration [1]. The association of abnormalities in retinal vasculature with cardiovascular disease has been reported in the studies [2]. The effect of onset of systemic and ophthalmic disease on arterioles and venules is very much different. For instance, generalized arteriolar narrowing is one among the early signatures of hypertensive retinopathy. The decrease

© Springer International Publishing AG, part of Springer Nature 2018
A. Campilho et al. (Eds.): ICIAR 2018, LNCS 10882, pp. 659–668, 2018.
https://doi.org/10.1007/978-3-319-93000-8_75

in Arteriole to Venule Ratio (AVR) is a well-known predictor of stroke and other cardiovascular disease in later life. Moreover, Arterio-Venous (AV) nicking is associated with long term risk of hypertension [2].

The advancement in retinal image acquisition and the availability of retinal fundus images make it possible to run the large population based screening programs to examine the early biomarkers of these diseases. Besides improving the diagnostic efficiency, the computerized retinal image analysis can help in reducing the workload of ophthalmologists. Therefore an efficient algorithm for classification of retinal vasculature into the constituent venules and arterioles is an essential part of automated diagnostic retinal image analysis system.

The arterioles/venules in the retinal images look like much similar to each other with only very few known discriminating features [3]. The venules appear to be a little bit wider than the arterioles particularly at the place closer to the optic disc. The arterioles exhibit clearer and wider center light reflex as compared to the venules. The venules appear to be a bit darker in color than arterioles. Moreover, generally the arterioles do not cross other arterioles and venules do not cross other venules within the retinal vasculature tree. The intra/inter image variability in color, contrast and illumination are further added challenges in developing automated AV classification system. The width as well as the color of retinal vessels change across their length as they originated from optic disc and spread in the retinal. The color change is due to the variability in oxygenation level.

Deep learning [4] is gaining importance in the last few years due to the ability to efficiently solve complex nonlinear classification problems. The main advantage of deep learning is the automated feature learning from the raw data. The convolutional neural network (CNN) [5] architectures have been used for variety of image classification and detection tasks with the human level performance. The CNNs have been used to detect diabetic retinopathy in retinal images in recent Kaggle competition with very encouraging results. The promising results of CNN based architectures in retinal image analysis motivates us to investigate the application of deep learning for pixel level classification and labeling.

In this paper, we have modeled the vessel classification task as semantic segmentation. Semantic segmentation [6] refers to the pixel level understanding of an image, and each pixel in the image will be assigned to a particular object class. For vessel classification, the aim is to assign every pixel in the retinal image to either of the three classes i.e. the arteriole, the venule or the background. We have presented a CNN based architecture for pixel level classification of retinal blood vessels into arterioles and venules. The proposed methodology can perform end-to-end vessel classification directly on the retinal image without the need of separately segmenting the blood vessels, or delineating the vessel centerlines as proposed in other algorithms. To the limit of our knowledge, the deep learning-based pixel level semantic segmentation has been utilized for the first time for classifying retinal blood vessels into arterioles/venules. The proposed AV classification algorithm will replace the current AV classification module in the QUARTZ retinal image analysis software tool [7], which is developed by our research group for quantification of retinal vessel morphology, with the aim to help epidemiologists analyze the association of retinal vessel morphometric properties with the prognosis of various systemic/ophthalmic disease biomarkers.

The rest of this paper is arranged as follows: a review of the related techniques is reported in Sect. 2. The following section provides the detailed description of proposed methodology. In Sect. 4, the experimental results are presented. The discussions and conclusion are illustrated in Sect. 5.

2   Related Work

A number of techniques are reported in the literature for arteriole/venule classification in retinal images [8]. These approached may be categorized into two major groups; the graph based approaches and the feature based approaches.

The feature based approaches prepare set of features for each pixel that eventually used as input to a classification algorithm. The first step in the majority of the approaches is segmenting the vasculature tree, followed by vessel skeletonization. The next step is the identification of bifurcations and crossovers. The complete vasculature is divided into vessel segments by removing the pixels at the crossover/bifurcation point in the vessel centerline images. The features are computed from these vessel segments which are further classified by a suitable classifier to be arteriole or venule. The graph based approaches usually represent the vasculature tree into a graph planner. The contextual information in the graph is utilized in making local decisions for a pixel whether it belongs to the arteriole or the venule.

Li [9] introduced a Gaussian filter model designed to detect vessel's center light reflex and used Minimum Mahalanobis distance classifier. However, the classification accuracy is mentioned at artery/vein level, and not at pixel level. Grisan [10] proposed the dividing the retinal image into four quadrants assuming that each of the divided regions has at least one arteriole/venule and afterwards applied fuzzy clustering. Saez [11] and Vazquez [12] improved the quadrant based approach, computed the pixel level features from RGB and HSL color spaces and utilized K-Mean clustering for AV classification. Kondarmann [13] proposed background normalization followed by computing the features of vessel centerline pixels in the 40-pixel square neighborhood and use Neural Network classifier for AV classification. Niemijar et al. [14] have computed a 27 dimensional feature vector for each pixel and classify the vasculature segments using linear discriminate classifier. Fraz [15] introduced features at different levels (pixel, segment, profile based) and use ensemble classifier for pixel level classification. Relan [16] computed the features set from the circular neighborhood around the current pixel within a specific radius and used the least square SVM classifier. Xu [17] built an innovative feature set from first and second order texture based and pass it to KNN classified for pixel classification.

Rothaus et al. [18] and Dashtbuzorg et al. [19] have built the planner graph from the vessel centerlines such that the branches and crossovers in the vascular network represent the nodes in the graph and the vessel segments represent the link between the graph nodes. The contextual information i.e. the link orientation across nodes, and the count of links associated with each graph node is used to identify the node type. After identification of all the nodes on the graph, the links corresponding to the vessel segment can be identified as arteriole or venule. Rothaus et al. [18] also created vessel graph, initialize few vessel segments manually and employ a rule based algorithm to propagate the vessel labels across the graph. Dashtbozorg et al. [19] combine the supervised pixel classification approach with graph based methodology to obtain pixel level classification. A color information based 30-D feature vector is computed for every centerline pixel followed by linear discriminant analysis classifier. The classification results are combined with graph labeling to attain excellent results. Estrada [20] applied global likelihood model to assign the a/v label to the links.

The feature based and graph based approaches can struggle in case the vascular tree is not correctly segmented. Moreover, these approaches are heavily relying on the hand crafted features. Welikala et al. [21] have employed the deep learning for the first time in the context of AV classification, and used a six layers convolutional neural network for feature learning from the retinal vasculature. The methodology achieves significant results in terms of accuracy, but it also relies on the accurate segmentation of vessels in the retinal image. We have proposed an end-to-end pixel-level AV classification techniques based on encoder-decoder based fully convolutional neural network. The proposed technique does not rely on the segmented vasculature, rather it learns and classify the pixels directly from the image.

3   The Methodology

In this work, we have presented a fully convolutional encoder-decoder based deep neural network architecture for pixel-wise segmentation of retinal vasculature and classification of arterioles and venules simultaneously. The proposed network architecture takes inspiration from SegNet [22] and perform the semantic segmentation of retinal images by associating each pixel of an image with a class label, i.e. background, arteriole or venule, without performing retinal vasculature segmentation separately, which usually had been a preliminary step in the traditional computer vision based AV classification approaches.

The network is composed of convolutional layers without any fully-connected layers which are usually found at the end of the traditional CNN. The encoder-decoder based fully convolutional neural networks take the input of arbitrary size and produce correspondingly-sized output. The feature learning and inferencing is performed as a whole-image-at-a-time basis by dense feedforward computation and backpropagation.

The encoder part of the network takes an input image and generates a high-dimensional by learning the features at multiple abstractions and aggregating the features at multiple levels. The decoder part of the network takes a high dimensional feature vector and generates a semantic segmentation mask. The building blocks of the network are convolutional layers, down-sampling and up-sampling. The learning is performed within subsampled layers using stride convolutions and max pooling. The up sampling layers in the network enable pixel wise prediction by applying unpooling and deconvolutions.

3.1 The Deep Network Architecture

The architecture consists of a sequence of encoder-decoder pairs which are used to create feature maps followed by pixel wise classification. The encoder-decoder architecture is illustrated in Fig. 1. The complete network consists of three layers of encodes-decoder blocks as shown Fig. 1(b). The input encoder block and output decoder block is presented in Fig. 1(a) and Fig. 1(c) respectively.

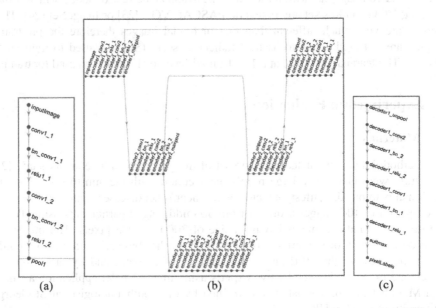

(a)   (b)   (c)

Fig. 1. The network architecture; (a) The input block of encoder part; (b) The complete network diagram; (c) The output block of decoder part.

The encoder part of the network closely resembles the VGG16 [5] architecture with the difference that only convolution layers are retained while the fully connected layers are excluded which makes it smaller and easier to train. A set of feature maps is produced by performing convolutions with filter bank. The feature map is batch normalized and element wise Rectified Linear Unit (RELU) activation is performed. Afterwards, a 2×2 max pooling with a non-overlapping stride of 2 units is applied. We have modified the architecture by reducing the number of layers to seven; hence the number of trainable parameters is also reduced.

The decoder part is comprised of nonlinear up sampling and convolution layers. The feature map is up sampled by the decoder network by utilizing the maxpooling indices which have been computed from the corresponding encoder phase. The pooling indices of encoder and decoder parts are connected with each other hence incorporating the capability to retain high frequency details in the neural network. As a result of up sampling, sparse feature maps are produced. Afterwards, dense feature-maps are generated by convolving previously generated sparse feature maps with a trainable filter bank. Softmax classifier is applied after the restoration of feature maps to the original resolution. The softmax performs independent classification of each pixel as arteriole, venule or background and produces the final multiclass segmentation.

3.2 Learning Details

The methodology is evaluated on a dataset of 100 images, such that 90 images are used for training and 10 images are used for testing. The available pertained models which include AlexNet, VGG and ResNet are trained on PASCAL VOC [23] or ImageNet [24]. These datasets are very much different than that of retinal images therefore the pre-trained weights are not used. The Stochastic Gradient Descent (SGD) is used to train all the network. The learning rate fixed at 0.1 and a mini-batch of 12 images is used for training.

4   Experimental Evaluation

4.1   Materials

The methodology is evaluated on a sub set of images from EPIC Norfolk study [25]. The study was started as a large multi-center cohort with the aim to investigate the relationship among diet, lifestyle factors and cancer/other disease prognosis. The subset is comprised of 100 images acquired from 50 middle aged participants using Topcon non-mydratic fundus cameras having a size of 3000×2002 pixels. The images are captured from both of the left and right eyes. The other biomarkers are also recorded which includes weight, BMI and family history of diabetes and hypertension. The vessels are manually labeled by two experts using image labeler application available with Matlab R2017b. The labels are verified by the ophthalmologists at St Georges University of London UK.

4.2   Performance Measures

The performance measures used to quantitatively evaluate the algorithm performance are summarized in Table 1.

Table 1. Performance metrics for vessel classification

Metric	Description
Global accuracy	It measures the percentage of pixels correctly classified in the dataset. $Global\,Accuracy = \dfrac{(TP + TN)}{(TP + FP + FN + TN)}$
Mean accuracy	The fraction of correctly classified pixels averaged over the classes
Mean Intersection over Union (mIoU)	Mean IoU is used to compare the similarity between the predicted class and the actual ground truth class
Weighted Intersection over Union (wIoU)	Performs IoU average weighted by the count of pixels in each class
Mean BF score	The measure depicts that how well predicted objects boundaries match ground truth boundaries

TP, FP, and TN and FN refers to true positive, false positive, true negative, false negative respectively

4.3 Experimental Results

The attained performance measures by the proposed methodology are summarized in Table 2.

Table 2. Performance measures of AV Classification

Global accuracy	Mean accuracy	Mean IoU	Weighted IoU	Mean BF score
0.9352	0.8228	0.7905	0.9457	0.8201

The comparison of the algorithm accuracy with previously published algorithms is shown in Table 3.

Table 3. Performance comparison with different vessel classification methods

S. No	Algorithm	Accuracy
1	Grisan [14]	87.58%
2	Kondarmann [13]	95.32%
3	Niemijar [14]	93.5%
4	Vazquez [12]	87.68%
5	Fraz [15]	83.27%
6	Relan [16]	89.4%
7	Xu [17]	92.3%
8	Dashtbuzorg [19]	87.4%
9	Estrada [20]	93.5%
10	Welikala [21]	91.97%
11	Proposed Methodology	93.5%

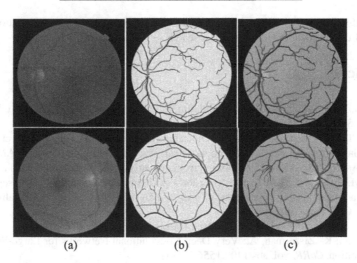

Fig. 2. Vessel Classification Results: (a) Original images (b) labels (c) segmentation results (Color figure online)

Figure 2 shows the classification results of the proposed methodology. The first column is the retinal image, the ground truth and the classification results are shown in 2nd the 3rd column respectively. The background is marked with yellow color and the arterioles and venules are marked with red and blue color respectively.

5   Discussion and Conclusion

In this paper a novel deep learning based methodology for AV classification of retinal blood vessels is presented. An encoder-decoder based deep convolutional neural network is proposed for pixel level classification of retinal vessels into the arterioles and venules. The methodology does not rely on prior segmentation of retinal blood vessels, which have been the preliminary step for approximately all of the AV classification techniques available in the literature. The proposed network architecture has taken inspiration from SegNet, which is used in semantic segmentation paradigm but to the best of our knowledge, has been utilized for the first time in the context of automated AV classification.

The major contribution of this paper is the application of novel encoder-decoder based fully convolutional deep network for robust AV classification. In future we aim to extend this methodology such that it will be used in place of current AV classification module in the QUARTZ software [7], which is developed by our research group for automated quantification the retinal vessel morphometry, with the aim study associations between vessel change and systemic/ophthalmic disease prognosis. Furthermore, we aim to use the proposed methodology as a preliminary step in the development the modules in QUARTZ for identification of venous beading and measurement of arteriovenous nicking.

Acknowledgements. We thankfully appreciate the support of NVIDIA Corporation with the donation of the TitanX GPU used for this research.

References

1. Kanski, J.J., Bowling, B.: Clinical Ophthalmology: A Systematic Approach, 8th edn. Elsevier Health Sciences (UK), London (2015)
2. Wong, T.Y., Klein, R., Sharrett, A.R., Duncan, B.B., Couper, D.J., Tielsch, J.M., et al.: Retinal arteriolar narrowing and risk of coronary heart disease in men and women. JAMA, J. Am. Med. Assoc. **287**, 1153–1159 (2002). http://jama.ama-assn.org/content/287/9/1153.abstract
3. Fraz, M.M., Barman, S.A.: Computer vision algorithms applied to retinal vessel segmentation and quantification of vessel caliber. In: Image Analysis and Modeling in Ophthalmology, pp. 49–84. CRC Press (2014)
4. LeCun, Y., Bengio, Y., Hinton, G.: Deep learning. Nature **521**, 436 (2015)
5. Simonyan, K., Zisserman, A.: Very Deep Convolutional Networks for Large-Scale Image Recognition. *CoRR,* vol. abs/1409.1556 (2014)
6. Garcia-Garcia, A., Orts, S., Oprea, S., Villena-Martinez, V., Rodríguez, J.G.: A Review on Deep Learning Techniques Applied to Semantic Segmentation. *CoRR,* vol. abs/1704.06857 (2017)

7. Fraz, M.M., Welikala, R.A., Rudnicka, A.R., Owen, C.G., Strachan, D.P., Barman, S.A.: QUARTZ: quantitative analysis of retinal vessel topology and size – an automated system for quantification of retinal vessels morphology. Expert Syst. Appl. **42**, 7221–7234 (2015)

8. Miri, M., Amini, Z., Rabbani, H., Kafieh, R.: A comprehensive study of retinal vessel classification methods in fundus images. J. Med. Sig. Sens. **7**, 59–70 (2017)

9. Li, H., Hsu, W., Lee, M.L., Wang, H.: A piecewise gaussian model for profiling and differentiating retinal vessels. In: Proceedings 2003 International Conference on Image Processing (Cat. No.03CH37429), vol. 1, pp. I-1069-72 (2003)

10. Grisan, E., Ruggeri, A.: A divide et impera strategy for automatic classification of retinal vessels into arteries and veins. In: Engineering in Medicine and Biology Society (2003) Proceedings of the 25th Annual International Conference of the IEEE, vol. 1, pp. 890–893 (2003)

11. Saez, M., González-Vázquez, S., González-Penedo, M., Barceló, M.A., Pena-Seijo, M., Coll de Tuero, G., et al.: Development of an automated system to classify retinal vessels into arteries and veins. Comput. Methods Programs Biomed. **108**, 367–376 (2012)

12. Vázquez, S.G., Cancela, B., Barreira, N., Penedo, M.G., Rodríguez-Blanco, M., Seijo, M.P., et al.: Improving retinal artery and vein classification by means of a minimal path approach. Mach. Vis. Appl. **24**, 919–930 (2013)

13. Kondermann, D., Kondermann, C., Yan, M.: Blood vessel classification into arteries and veins in retinal images. In: Medical Imaging, p. 651247 (2007)

14. Niemeijer, M., Xu, X., Dumitrescu, A.V., Gupta, P., Ginneken, B.V., Folk, J.C., et al.: Automated measurement of the arteriolar-to-venular width ratio in digital color fundus photographs. IEEE Trans. Med. Imaging **30**, 1941–1950 (2011)

15. Fraz, M.M., Rudnicka, A.R., Owen, C.G., Strachan, D.P., Barman, S.A.: Automated arteriole and venule recognition in retinal images using Ensemble classification. In: 2014 International Conference on Computer Vision Theory and Applications (VISAPP), pp. 194–202 (2014)

16. Relan, D., MacGillivray, T., Ballerini, L., Trucco, E.: Automatic retinal vessel classification using a least square-support vector machine in VAMPIRE. In: 2014 36th Annual International Conference of the IEEE Engineering in Medicine and Biology Society, pp. 142–145 (2014)

17. Xu, X., Ding, W., Abràmoff, M.D., Cao, R.: An improved arteriovenous classification method for the early diagnostics of various diseases in retinal image. Comput. Methods Programs Biomed. **141**, 3–9 (2017)

18. Rothaus, K., Jiang, X., Rhiem, P.: Separation of the retinal vascular graph in arteries and veins based upon structural knowledge. Image Vis. Comput. **27**, 864–875 (2009)

19. Dashtbozorg, B., Mendonça, A.M., Campilho, A.: An automatic graph-based approach for artery/vein classification in retinal images. IEEE Trans. Image Process. **23**, 1073–1083 (2014)

20. Estrada, R., Allingham, M.J., Mettu, P.S., Cousins, S.W., Tomasi, C., Farsiu, S.: Retinal artery-vein classification via topology estimation. IEEE Trans. Med. Imaging **34**, 2518–2534 (2015)

21. Welikala, R.A., Foster, P.J., Whincup, P.H., Rudnicka, A.R., Owen, C.G., Strachan, D.P., et al.: Automated arteriole and venule classification using deep learning for retinal images from the UK Biobank cohort. Comput. Biol. Med. **90**, 23–32 (2017)

22. Badrinarayanan, V., Kendall, A., Cipolla, R.: SegNet: a deep convolutional encoder-decoder architecture for image segmentation. IEEE Trans. Pattern Anal. Mach. Intell. **39**, 2481–2495 (2017)

23. Everingham, M., Van Gool, L., Williams, C.K.I., Winn, J., Zisserman, A.: The pascal visual object classes (VOC) challenge. Int. J. Comput. Vis. **88**, 303–338 (2010)

24. Shuhan, C., Ben, W., Jindong, L., Xuelong, H.: Semantic image segmentation using region-based object detector. In: 2017 13th IEEE International Conference on Electronic Measurement & Instruments (ICEMI), pp. 505–510 (2017)

25. EPIC-Norfolk.: European Prospective Investigation of Cancer (EPIC), February 2013. http://www.srl.cam.ac.uk/epic/

Creation of Retinal Mosaics
for Diabetic Retinopathy Screening:
A Comparative Study

Tânia Melo[1]($\boxtimes$) (iD), Ana Maria Mendonça[1,2] (iD), and Aurélio Campilho[1,2] (iD)

[1] INESC TEC - Institute for Systems and Computer Engineering,
Technology and Science, Porto, Portugal
`tania.f.melo@inesctec.pt`
[2] Faculty of Engineering of the University of Porto, Porto, Portugal
`{amendon,campilho}@fe.up.pt`

Abstract. The creation of retinal mosaics from sets of fundus photographs can significantly reduce the time spent on the diabetic retinopathy (DR) screening, because through mosaic analysis the ophthalmologists can examine several portions of the eye at a single glance and, consequently, detect and grade DR more easily. Like most of the methods described in the literature, this methodology includes two main steps: image registration and image blending. In the registration step, relevant keypoints are detected on all images, the transformation matrices are estimated based on the correspondences between those keypoints and the images are reprojected into the same coordinate system. However, the main contributions of this work are in the blending step. In order to combine the overlapping images, a color compensation is applied to those images and a distance-based map of weights is computed for each one. The methodology is applied to two different datasets and the mosaics obtained for one of them are visually compared with the results of two state-of-the-art methods. The mosaics obtained with our method present good quality and they can be used for DR grading.

Keywords: Diabetic retinopathy screening · Retinal mosaicking
Image registration · Image blending · Qualitative evaluation

1 Introduction

Diabetic retinopathy (DR) is an eye disease that affects the vision of a high number of diabetic people worldwide. It is characterized by the presence of several retinal lesions, being a leading cause of blindness [7]. In order to prevent the development of DR, regular eye examinations need to be done in the diabetic patients.

However, in a screening program, there is a large number of retinal images to be manually examined by the medical doctors, which is labor intensive, time consuming and expensive [6]. Furthermore, in these screening programs, there

© Springer International Publishing AG, part of Springer Nature 2018
A. Campilho et al. (Eds.): ICIAR 2018, LNCS 10882, pp. 669–678, 2018.
https://doi.org/10.1007/978-3-319-93000-8_76

is usually more than one image per eye, since the analysis of a single image may not be enough to make a good eye evaluation. Thus, the creation of retinal mosaics from images of the same eye can reduce substantially the time spent by the medical doctors on DR screening. Through the analysis of mosaics, the ophthalmologists can do a complete eye examination at a single glance instead of examining each portion of the eye in a different image [2].

Therefore, a methodology for retinal mosaic creation is herein proposed. The main novelty of this methodology is related to the sequence of operations performed for combining the overlapping images.

Section 2 presents a brief introduction about image mosaicking and a summary of the most relevant state-of-the-art methods in this research area. A description of the proposed methodology is presented in Sect. 3. The results obtained are shown and discussed in Sect. 4 and the main conclusions are stated in Sect. 5.

2   Image Mosaicking Methods

Image mosaicking is the process of obtaining a wider field-of-view of a 3D scene through the alignment of a set of overlapping images which represent part of that scene [4]. Due to its wide range of applications, this process has become an attractive research area and, thus, a high number of image mosaicking algorithms have been developed over the last years. A large number of those methods are focused on the creation of retinal mosaics.

The image mosaicking methods comprise two main steps: image registration and image blending. The first step consists in the identification of common regions in the images and their alignment into the same coordinate system based on the estimated geometric transformations; the second step aims to minimize the discontinuities in the transition regions. As mentioned in [4], the image mosaicking methods can be classified according to the algorithms used in these two steps.

Regarding to the registration step, the methods can be classified as global, local or hybrid methods. While global methods align the images based on the similarity of the pixel intensities, local methods detect relevant keypoints in the images, find the correspondences between those points and use them in order to estimate the geometric transformation that registers the images. Hybrid methods combine both strategies [5]. Legg et al. [8] developed a global method which computes the mutual information between "windows" of the images to be registered. Since the mutual information is obtained by computing the entropy from the probability distribution of the data, the authors also propose the use of an adaptive probability distribution estimation in order to increase the accuracy of the registration procedure. In a different way, Hernandez-Matas et al. [5] apply the Scale Invariant Feature Transform (SIFT) [9] to detect and describe some relevant keypoints in the images and then estimate the geometric transformation based on the correspondences established between the points detected. In order to discard the incorrect correspondences (outliers) and obtain more accurate estimations of the transformation matrix, the authors employ the Random

Sample Consensus (RANSAC) method [3]. Stewart et al. [11] also developed a local method, but instead of applying a feature detector to obtain the salient points, the authors use vascular landmarks (branching and cross-over points) for registering the images. Adal et al. [1] proposed a hybrid model that aligns the images based on a vasculature-weighted mean squared difference similarity metric. With this metric the authors combine both global and local cues. In general, local or feature-based methods present best performance in the registration of image pairs with a small overlap in comparison to global or area-based methods.

Regarding to the transformation models used for warping the images, some of the state-of-the-art methods apply 2D linear transformations. For instance, Matsopoulos et al. [10] detect the vessel centerlines, extract the vessel bifurcation points and use a novel implementation of self organizing maps for establishing the correspondences between those points. Then, the parameters of the affine transform are estimated based on those correspondences. However, since linear transformations do not take into account the curvature of the eye, several authors apply non-linear transformations to obtain more accurate results. For instance, Adal et al. [1] use a deformation model with increasing complexity in order to estimate the 12 parameters of a global quadratic model. Since the non-linear transformations do not take necessarily into account the shape and size of the eye, Hernandez-Matas et al. [5] apply a 3D model of the eye to estimate the transformation that relates the views from which the images to be registered were acquired.

Although the methods used for registering retinal images are slightly different from those used for aligning other types of images (because the scenes which are captured have different shapes and different landmarks), the methods applied for blending images of different 3D scenes can be similar. As mentioned in [4], these methods can be divided into three main groups: feathering-based, pyramid-based and gradient-based methods [4]. Feathering-based methods blend the images through a weighted combination of the overlapping images, pyramid-based methods convert the input images into band-pass pyramids to obtain the final mosaics and the gradient-based methods set the gradients across seams to zero for smoothing out the color differences [4].

3   Methodology

Like most of the state-of-the-art methods, the methodology herein proposed for retinal mosaicking comprises two main steps: retinal image registration and blending.

Although the methods applied for registering the retinal images have already been used by other authors for this purpose, the operations performed in the blending step in order to smooth the transitions between the overlapping images are novel in this application field.

In the following subsections a detailed description of these methods is done.

3.1   Registration of Retinal Images

In order to accurately align two retinal images, a sequence of operations is performed (Fig. 1).

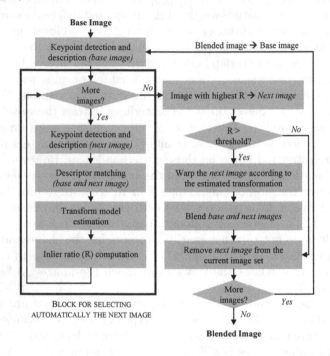

Fig. 1. General scheme of the methodology implemented

First, several keypoints are detected in both images and described based on the Scale Invariant Feature Transform (SIFT) [9]. The advantage of using SIFT is that the detected keypoints are invariant to image scaling and rotation, they are distributed over the entire image and the descriptor is distinctive, which allows a keypoint to find its correct match with high probability [5,9].

Then, for each keypoint detected in the next image (image which is being registered), the corresponding keypoint (closest neighbor) in the base image is found through the computation of the Euclidean distance between the keypoint descriptors. Since the keypoints which are located outside the overlapping region have not a corresponding keypoint in the base image, a large number of incorrect matches are expected. In order to exclude these matches, a threshold is applied to the ratio between the distances to the closest and the second closest neighbors of each keypoint [9].

Since some incorrect matches still remain after this filtering, the RANSAC method is used for finding the consistent matches and estimating the parameters of the geometric transformation. Taking into account the curvature of the eye, a non-linear quadratic transformation is applied. Then, the inlier ratio is computed by dividing the number of matches used by the RANSAC method for estimating the twelve parameters of the polynomial transformation by the total number of matches.

Knowing that the main goal of this work is to create retinal mosaics from sets of two or more images, it is necessary to define the order by which the images are registered. In order to do that automatically, the steps described above are repeated for all pairs that can be formed by the base image and the images which have not yet been attached. The next image to be registered is associated with the image pair with the highest inlier ratio (see Fig. 1).

In order to avoid the incorrect alignment of images that do not overlap, the next image is only reprojected into the same coordinate system of the base image if the inlier ratio is greater than 0.1. Otherwise, that image is discarded and it does not appear in the final mosaic.

3.2   Blending of the Overlapping Images

After reprojecting the overlapping images into the same coordinate system, the pixels of the overlapping regions have to be combined in order to smooth the transitions between the images and obtain mosaics with high quality.

Considering that the overlapping images can present different illumination patterns and corresponding points can have different intensities in the two images, an illumination correction is performed (Fig. 2).

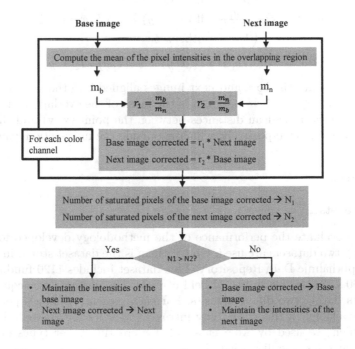

Fig. 2. Overall scheme of the illumination correction process

For that, the mean of the pixel intensities in the overlapping region is computed for each image separately. Then, two parameters (r_1 and r_2) are computed based on those mean values (see Fig. 2) and multiplied by the registered images in order to obtain the intensity compensated images. The image which is definitively corrected after this process is the one which presents the lowest number of saturated pixels. The pixel intensities of the other image remain constant.

After the illumination correction process, the two overlapping images are combined for obtaining the final mosaic (Fig. 3).

In order to identify the region where the two images intersect, their masks have to be obtained. For that, thresholding and morphological operations are applied. The mask of the overlapping region results from the intersection of the masks of the registered images.

A map of weights is also computed for each image (Fig. 3E and F) based on the Euclidean distances between the pixels of the overlapping region and the closest point of that image which is outside the intersection zone (see Eqs. 1 and 2). In the end, the pixel intensities of the composite image are a weighted sum of the pixel intensities of the base and next images (Eq. 3).

$$
w_1(x,y) = \begin{cases} 0 & \text{if } m_1(x,y) = 0 \\ \frac{d_2}{d_1+d_2} & \text{if } m_1(x,y) = 1 \wedge R(x,y) = 1 \\ 1 & \text{otherwise} \end{cases} \tag{1}
$$

$$
w_2(x,y) = \begin{cases} 0 & \text{if } m_2(x,y) = 0 \\ \frac{d_1}{d_1+d_2} & \text{if } m_2(x,y) = 1 \wedge R(x,y) = 1 \\ 1 & \text{otherwise} \end{cases} \tag{2}
$$

$$
I(x,y) = w_1(x,y) * I_1(x,y) + w_2(x,y) * I_2(x,y) \tag{3}
$$

where I_1 and I_2 are the base and next images aligned into the same coordinate system, m_1 and m_2 are their masks, R is the mask of the overlapping region and d_1 and d_2 are the Euclidean distances between the point (x, y) and the closest point in m_1 and m_2, respectively, which is outside the intersection zone.

4   Results

4.1   Datasets

In order to evaluate the performance of the methodology developed for retinal mosaicking, two datasets are used. One of them is the dataset stored in the Rotterdam Ophthalmic Data Repository. This dataset includes 1120 fundus images of size 2000×1312 pixels and a 45° field-of-view. The images were acquired from 70 patients during two different visits. For each patient, 4 images per eye and visit are available. In this work, only intravisit mosaics are created. Therefore, images which are used by Adal et al. [2] for creating other types of mosaics (intervisit mosaics) are discarded.

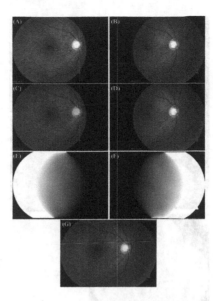

Fig. 3. Image blending: (A-B) Input images reprojected into the same coordinate system; (C-D) Images A and B, respectively, after color compensation (only the intensities of the image A were changed during the process); (E-F) Weight maps associated with C and D, respectively; (G) Blended image

Since the final intravisit mosaics obtained from these images through the methods proposed in [2,11] are also publicly available, they are used in this work for comparison purposes. However, these mosaics were obtained from the images of this dataset after performing the normalization referred in [2]. In order to obtain similar mosaics and be possible the comparison with the other methods, the normalized images provided with the dataset are used as input images in our method.

The performance of the methodology herein presented is also evaluated for a private dataset provided by Hospital S. João (Porto). In this dataset, there are images from the two eyes of 21 patients. For each eye, 3 images with a 45° field-of-view and 7 images with a 30° field-of-view are available. However, for this dataset there are not other mosaics to compare with the results of our method.

4.2 Discussion of the Results

In this work, the quality of the final mosaics obtained from the images captured in the Rotterdam Eye Hospital is visually evaluated by comparison with the mosaics obtained by the methods proposed in [2,11].

Although most image sets give rise to high quality mosaics, there is a small number of mosaics which are not composed by the four images or have at least one image misplaced. Figures 4 and 5 show an example of a good and a bad result, respectively.

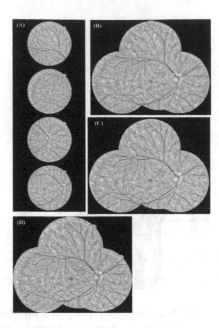

Fig. 4. Retinal mosaicking - example 1: (A) Original images; (B-C) Mosaics obtained with the methods described in [11] and [2], respectively; (D) Mosaic obtained with the method herein proposed

Through the analysis of Fig. 4, it is possible to observe that the mosaic obtained with our method from the images shown in Fig. 4A is very similar to the results obtained with the other state-of-the-art methods. Taking into account that the other two mosaics were classified as "acceptable" by an experienced grader [2], we can also infer that the mosaic created with our method also has an "acceptable" quality and it can be used for DR grading.

In the other hand, the low quality of the original images presented in Fig. 5A, as well as the low degree of overlap between them, interferes with the number of keypoints detected in the overlapping regions. Because of this, the RANSAC method is not able to detect a sufficient number of consistent matches and the method considers that the images do not overlap. In this way, the images are not registered and an incomplete mosaic is obtained. However, the mosaics obtained by the other methods (Fig. 5B and C) for the same set of images also have at least one image misplaced.

Although the registration step fails in special cases, the transitions between overlapping images are imperceptible in all mosaics. This allows to conclude that the operations proposed in this work for image blending produces very good results.

In order to show that this method can be applied to different datasets, the methodology herein proposed is also applied to the dataset provided by Hospital S. João (see an example in Fig. 3). For this set of images, the final mosaics also present a good quality, which proves the robustness of our method.

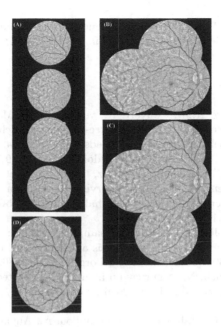

Fig. 5. Retinal mosaicking - example 2: (A) Original images; (B-C) Mosaics obtained with the methods described in [11] and [2], respectively; (D) Mosaic obtained with the method herein proposed

5   Conclusions

In this work, it is possible to conclude that the mosaics obtained with our method are very similar to the mosaics obtained using the methods proposed in [2, 11]. Although most mosaics present high quality and can be used for DR grading, there is a small number of mosaics that appear incomplete or have at least one image misplaced. This happens mainly when the original images present low quality or the overlapping degree between them is too small that few keypoints are detected in the overlapping region. In this way, the use of a more robust keypoint detector can improve the performance of the method herein proposed, specially in the cases where the overlapping degree between the images is small.

Although the registration step fails in these special cases, all mosaics present imperceptible transitions between the overlapping images, which demonstrates the good performance of the operations introduced in the blending step.

Although the scores given by two experienced graders to the mosaics obtained using the methods described in [2, 11] have been used as reference for evaluating the performance of the methodology herein proposed, as future work we propose the use of a quantitative measure for evaluating more accurately the quality of the final mosaics.

Acknowledgments. This work is financed by the ERDF - European Regional Development Fund through the Operational Programme for Competitiveness and Internationalisation - COMPETE 2020 Programme, and by National Funds through the FCT - Fundação para a Ciência e a Tecnologia within project CMUP-ERI/TIC/0028/2014.

References

1. Adal, K.M., Ensing, R.M., Couvert, R., van Etten, P., Martinez, J.P., Vermeer, K.A., van Vliet, L.J.: A hierarchical coarse-to-fine approach for fundus image registration. In: Ourselin, S., Modat, M. (eds.) WBIR 2014. LNCS, vol. 8545, pp. 93–102. Springer, Cham (2014). https://doi.org/10.1007/978-3-319-08554-8_10
2. Adal, K.M., van Etten, P.G., Martinez, J.P., van Vliet, L.J., Vermeer, K.A.: Accuracy assessment of intra- and intervisit fundus image registration for diabetic retinopathy screening. Invest. Ophthalmol. Vis. Sci. 56(3), 1805–1812 (2015). https://doi.org/10.1167/iovs.14-15949
3. Fischler, M.A., Bolles, R.C.: Random sample consensus: a paradigm for model fitting with applications to image analysis and automated cartography. Commun. ACM 24(6), 381–395 (1981). https://doi.org/10.1145/358669.358692
4. Ghosh, D., Kaabouch, N.: A survey on image mosaicing techniques. J. Vis. Commun. Image Represent. 34, 1–11 (2016). https://doi.org/10.1016/j.jvcir.2015.10.014
5. Hernandez-Matas, C., Zabulis, X., Triantafyllou, A., Anyfanti, P., Argyros, A.A.: Retinal image registration under the assumption of a spherical eye. Comput. Med. Imaging Graph. 55, 95–105 (2017). https://doi.org/10.1016/j.compmedimag.2016.06.006
6. Jelinek, H., Cree, M.: Automated Image Detection of Retinal Pathology. CRC Press, Boca Raton (2009)
7. Lee, R., Wong, T.Y., Sabanayagam, C.: Epidemiology of diabetic retinopathy, diabetic macular edema and related vision loss. Eye Vis. 2(1), 17 (2015). https://doi.org/10.1186/s40662-015-0026-2
8. Legg, P.A., Rosin, P.L., Marshall, D., Morgan, J.E.: Improving accuracy and efficiency of mutual information for multi-modal retinal image registration using adaptive probability density estimation. Comput. Med. Imaging Graph. 37(7), 597–606 (2013). https://doi.org/10.1016/j.compmedimag.2013.08.004
9. Lowe, D.G.: Distinctive image features from scale-invariant keypoints. Int. J. Comput. Vis. 60(2), 91–110 (2004). https://doi.org/10.1023/B:VISI.0000029664.99615.94
10. Matsopoulos, G.K., Asvestas, P.A., Mouravliansky, N.A., Delibasis, K.K.: Multimodal registration of retinal images using self organizing maps. IEEE Trans. Med. Imaging 23(12), 1557–1563 (2004). https://doi.org/10.1109/TMI.2004.836547
11. Stewart, C.V., Tsai, C.L., Roysam, B.: The dual-bootstrap iterative closest point algorithm with application to retinal image registration. IEEE Trans. Med. Imaging 22(11), 1379–1394 (2003). https://doi.org/10.1109/TMI.2003.819276

Segmentation of the Retinal Reflex in Brückner Test Images Using U-Net Convolutional Network

Italo Francyles Santos da Silva$^{(\boxtimes)}$, João Dallyson Sousa de Almeida,
Jorge Antonio Meireles Teixeira, Geraldo Braz Junior,
and Anselmo Cardoso de Paiva

Applied Computing Group (NCA), Federal University of Maranhão (UFMA),
Av. dos Portugueses, 1966, Bacanga, São Luís, Maranhão, Brazil
jorgemeireles1@gmail.com
{francyles,jdallyson,geraldo,paiva}@nca.ufma.br
http://nca.ufma.br/

Abstract. Brückner test is an eye exam characterized by the evaluation of brightness of red retinal reflex in pupillary area. The reflex region segmentation is important for a computational method that automatizes that examination and detects eye pathologies by the image analysis. This work presents an automatic method for retinal reflex segmentation in images of Brückner test using the fully convolutional network U-Net. The method reaches 87.73% of Dice coefficient, 78.95% of Jaccard index, 90.63% recall and 88.03% precision.

Keywords: Brückner test · Retinal reflex · Image segmentation
Fully Convolutional Network · U-Net

1 Introduction

Brückner Test, also known as red reflex examination, is an important eye exam which is useful for early detection of eye diseases. The use of this test as part of the routine of exams in newborns helps for early identification of ocular problems, including congenital cataract, refractive error and retinoblastoma [10].

During the examination, a coaxial light source is used to illuminate both eyes of the subject from a distance of about one meter. The examiner compares the brightness of the reflexes for an evidence of asymmetry [8]. When the light contacts the blood vessels inside the eye, they reflect the red color. It means that the main internal structures of the eye are transparent, allowing the contact between the light and the retina. But, there are cases in which the reflex does not have a good quality, that is, the reflected light has another color or is totally absorbed. That kind of reflex is often observed in flash photography.

This work presents a method to segment the retinal reflex in Brückner Test images using the network U-Net [9], a fully convolutional network architecture.

© Springer International Publishing AG, part of Springer Nature 2018
A. Campilho et al. (Eds.): ICIAR 2018, LNCS 10882, pp. 679–686, 2018.
https://doi.org/10.1007/978-3-319-93000-8_77

Given an input image containing the eye, U-Net must be able to yield a segmentation mask for the region of reflex even if it does not have the red color. The segmentation of the reflex is important for a computational method that automatizes examination and detects eye pathologies by the image analysis.

Fully Convolutional Networks (FCN) [7] are an architecture of convolutional network proposed for segmentation of images. They are constituted by two stages: contracting and expansion. In the first one, the feature maps are generated in the same way that in CNN, using convolution and pooling layers. But, the fully connected layer is removed and the yielded maps in the last layer are the input for the next stage. During the expansion stage, new feature maps are yielded by upsampling the ones previously obtained. This process can predict the object location. U-Net has already presented promising results in segmentation of biomedical images [9]. In this work, the effectiveness of U-Net is verified in the proposed task of segmentation.

There are in the literature several approaches for the retinal reflex detection (red reflex detection). Some works try to detect the red reflex in these images using thresholding [1,6,12]. But, there are works proposing the red reflex detection locating first the eye spots [5]. These approaches are linked to the task of image correction to remove the red reflex because that phenomenon is considered a problem in image acquisition. The work presented here address the segmentation of the retinal reflex using a Deep Learning-based approach.

This work is organized as follows: the Sect. 2 shows the proposed methodology and explains in more detail both the database and U-Net architecture. The Sect. 3 shows the results and discuss that. Finally, the conclusion and future works are presented in Sect. 4.

2   Materials and Methods

This section explains the procedures executed in the development of the proposed method and presents informations about the dataset used to validate our proposal.

2.1   Image Dataset

Brückner Test uses a light source to illuminate both eyes of the subject. The examiner took photographs of the patients during the exam. In these cases, the light source is the camera flash. The region of the reflex was manually annotated in each image by the authors and validated by the specialist. A segmentation mask was generated for each sample based on its respective annotation.

In this work, the proposed method aims to segment the region of the reflex. The region of each eye was obtained manually based on the segmentation map of its reflex. First, the center of each annotation is located. After this, values for width and height are defined in order to crop that part of the image. Therefore, the dataset is composed of images of eyes and its masks (Fig. 1). The image dataset used is composed of 118 samples for both eyes and masks. The images

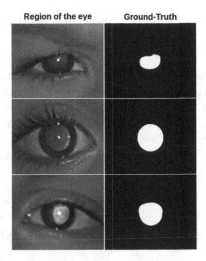

Fig. 1. Samples images of eyes resulting from the Bruckner test and segmentation map (ground-truth).

used in the present study were taken of patients from an ophthalmology clinic in the city of São Luís-MA, Brazil. Patients who volunteered to participate in the study signed a consent form, and approval from the ethics committee was obtained for the use of human images in this study.

2.2 Segmentation of the Region of the Reflex

The proposed approach uses the U-Net fully convolutional network for the segmentation of the retinal reflex in Brückner test images. This network is trained to yield the segmentation mask of the region of interest for each input sample. Figure 2 summarizes the steps of the proposed method.

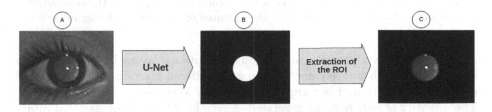

Fig. 2. Proposed method: (A) Image of the eye region, (B) segmentation map generated, (C) region of interest.

As seen in Fig. 2, the input is an image of an eye (Fig. 2(A)). So, U-Net yields the segmentation mask (Fig. 2(B)) for that reflex and the final image containing the ROI (Fig. 2(C)) is obtained using the generated mask. The following section explains in more detail the U-Net convolutional network and the structure implemented in this work.

U-Net: Convolutional Network for Segmentation. The leading strategy that differentiates U-Net from the others FCN architectures is the combination among the contraction stage feature maps and its corresponding symmetric in the expansion stage, allowing the propagation of context information to the high-resolution feature maps [9]. Thus, U-Net architecture can be represented by the shape of the letter "U". Figure 3 presents the architecture used in this work based on Ronneberger et al. [9].

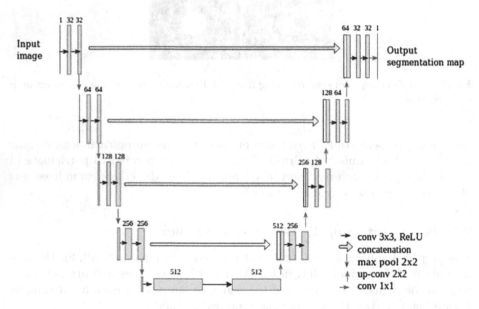

Fig. 3. U-Net architecture. Blue boxes correspond to a feature map. The number of channels is indicated on the top of each box. White boxes represent the concatenated feature maps. Colored arrows indicate the executed operations. (Color figure online)

Proposed network architecture has 19 convolutional layers. In the contraction stage, each level has a sequence of two convolutional layers using kernels 3×3 and ReLU activation. They are followed by the Max Pooling operator (2×2). The quantity of feature maps generated in each level is the double of that established for the previous one. In this work, this quantity starts with 32 maps. And each convolutional layer yields 512 feature maps in the last level of the contraction path. U-Net does not have a fully connected layer as well as others FCN architectures. Hence, the output of the last convolutional layer in the contraction path is the input to the first layer in the expansion path.

The inputs for each level of the expansion stage are subjected to the upconvolution operation which is responsible for enlarge the resolution of the feature maps. In each level there are also two convolutional layers followed by a Max Pooling operator. Furthermore, each input map is concatenated with its corresponding symmetric in the contraction stage. This allows the network to use original features together with the new ones obtained by upconvolution. Finally, in the last level, there are three convolutional layers: the first two generate maps using a kernel 3×3 and ReLU activation, whereas the last one generates the segmentation map using a kernel 1×1 and Sigmoid activation whose output tends to be 0 if a pixel is not part of the region of interest or 1, otherwise.

2.3 Evaluation Metrics

In order to evaluate the similarity between the segmentation maps generated by U-Net compared with the dataset, the following metrics are used: Dice Coefficient, Jaccard Index, Recall and Precision.

The Dice coefficient is the most used to validate segmentations of medical images [11]. It is defined as showed in Eq. 1 where X and Y represent the compared masks for each input image, in this case, the ground-truth and the U-Net generated mask. On the other hand, the Jaccard Index is the ratio between the intersection of the sets X and Y and the result of the union of them (Eq. 2). This index is also known as Intersection over Union (IoU).

$$DICE = \frac{2 * |X \cap Y|}{|X| + |Y|} \tag{1}$$

$$IoU = \frac{|X \cap Y|}{|X \cup Y|} \tag{2}$$

Recall and Precision measure the rate of correct predictions. They are defined by Eqs. 3 and 4 respectively. In the context of segmentation, the true positives (Tp) are those pixels that make part of the ROI in both ground-truth and generated mask. The false negatives (Fn) are pixels that make part of the ROI and the false positives do not. But they were predicted wrong by the method.

$$Recall = \frac{Tp}{Tp + Fn} \tag{3}$$

$$Precision = \frac{Tp}{Tp + Fp} \tag{4}$$

2.4 Experiment Details

In the experiment performed, U-Net is implemented using the Keras Framework [2]. The dataset contains RGB images with fixed-size 309×400 pixels. However, for reasons of memory limitation, that images are resized to 160×160 and are passed to the network input. The U-Net is trained for 100 epochs using the Adam optimizer [4]. Others image processing procedures are implemented using OpenCV 3.3 [3]. Training and evaluation was performed on a single GPU NVIDIA GeForce GTX 1060ti.

3   Experiment Results

This section presents the experiment results for the proposed method for segmentation of the retinal reflex in Brückner Test images.

The dataset contains 118 images and was divided into training, validation and test sets as follows: 70% training, 30% test and 20% of training set is used for validation. Each set contains randomly chosen samples. Training and test procedures was performed 5 times in order to evaluate the method's performance using that metrics mentioned in the Sect. 2.3. No data augmentation was used.

Experiments using two others image segmentation approaches was also performed in our dataset in order to compare the proposed method with them. One approach is based on Kumar et al. [5] and the other is a graph-based method using Spectral Clustering and superpixels. This one was configured with number of clusters k = 12. The results are shown in Table 1.

Table 1. Results of the proposed method in comparison with different methods on the same dataset

Evaluation metrics	Proposed method	Kumar et al. (2009)	Spectral clustering
Dice coeff	**87.73**% ± **0.63**	62.46% ± 0.35	69.00% ± 0.13
Jaccard index	**78.95**% ± **0.97**	53.45% ± 0.31	54.08% ± 0.15
Recall	**90.63**% ± **0.81**	68.47% ± 0.38	96.72% ± 0.07
Precision	**88.03**% ± **0.88**	59.09% ± 0.34	55.47% ± 0.17

Similarity measures were obtained from the comparison between the generated masks and the ground-truth. For all of them, the best is the nearest 100%. Standard deviation is also calculated for all metrics. As seen in Table 1, the proposed method that uses U-Net surpass the others in great part of the metrics. It means the trained network generates a mask whose shape and size are quite similar to the ground-truth in many samples. Thus, the generated segmentation maps have many pixels in common with the ground-truth. It can be confirmed by Dice and Jaccard values and is also verified in Fig. 4.

Notice that Spectral Clustering and the method based on Kumar et al. [5] show a great difference between Recall and Precision. It indicates a high occurrence of false positives, when some masks generated by these approaches are bigger than the ground-truth.

Figure 5 demonstrates some occurrences of wrong segmentations. They occur because of the annotated mask set has many cases in which the patients' eyes are fully opened, so the pupil's mask has a uniform circular shape. So, the lack of shape variations in that mask set, mainly caused when the eyelid covers the pupil, does the network to learn the shape features of the most cases and yield some wrong predictions. Despite that, analyzing all value results and the generated images, it is noticed that our method performs well in segmentation both for the red reflection and for the other tones (white or golden).

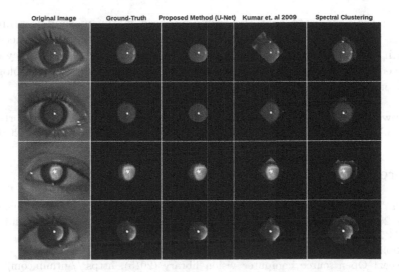

Fig. 4. Images segmentations results. First column is the original image followed by the ground-truth. Next columns compare the obtained performance of our method using the U-Net convolutional network with other two approaches.

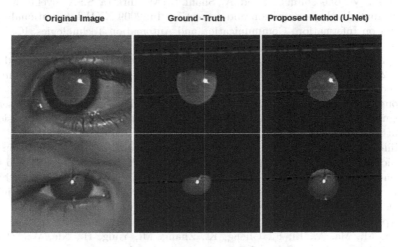

Fig. 5. Some wrong segmentations produced by the proposed method. (Color figure online)

4   Conclusion

This paper presented a method for segmentation of the retinal reflex in Brückner Test images using the U-Net convolutional network. The proposed method performed a segmentation more accurate according the evaluation metrics as discussed in Sect. 3. The obtained results are satisfactory and corroborate to using fully convolutional networks for segmentation task.

The results indicate that the technique used in the method is promising because it achieved matching rate superior to 88%. However, it is necessary perform tests on a larger image dataset, in order to confirm the efficiency of the proposed method. As a future work, is proposed to develop a methodology for detection of eye diseases using the segmented image of the reflex.

Acknowledgments. Our research group acknowledges financial support from FAPEMA (Grant Number:001082/16) and CNPQ (Grand Number: 423493/2016-7).

References

1. Ali, T., Khan, A., Kim, I.: Automatic detection and correction of red-eye effect. In: 2009 2nd International Conference on Computer, Control and Communication, IC4 2009, pp. 1–4. IEEE (2009)
2. Chollet, F., et al.: Keras (2015). https://github.com/keras-team/keras
3. Itseez: Open source computer vision library (2015). https://github.com/itseez/opencv
4. Kingma, D.P., Ba, J.: Adam: A method for stochastic optimization. arXiv preprint arXiv:1412.6980 (2014)
5. Kumar, V., Bhooshan, S., Sood, A., Shahi, R., Mendiratta, S.: A novel technique for automated red eye detection and correction. In: 2009 XXII International Symposium on Information, Communication and Automation Technologies, ICAT 2009, pp. 1–5. IEEE (2009)
6. Lepisto, L., Launiainen, A., Kunttu, I.: Red eye detection using color and shape. In: 2009 International Workshop on Local and Non-Local Approximation in Image Processing, LNLA 2009, pp. 153–157. IEEE (2009)
7. Long, J., Shelhamer, E., Darrell, T.: Fully convolutional networks for semantic segmentation. In: Proceedings of the IEEE Conference on Computer Vision and Pattern Recognition, pp. 3431–3440 (2015)
8. Miller, J.M., Hall, H.L., Greivenkamp, J.E., Guyton, D.L.: Quantification of the brückner test for strabismus. Invest. Ophthalmol. Vis. Sci. **36**(5), 897–905 (1995)
9. Ronneberger, O., Fischer, P., Brox, T.: U-Net: convolutional networks for biomedical image segmentation. In: Navab, N., Hornegger, J., Wells, W.M., Frangi, A.F. (eds.) MICCAI 2015. LNCS, vol. 9351, pp. 234–241. Springer, Cham (2015). https://doi.org/10.1007/978-3-319-24574-4_28
10. Sun, M., Ma, A., Li, F., Cheng, K., Zhang, M., Yang, H., Nie, W., Zhao, B.: Sensitivity and specificity of red reflex test in newborn eye screening. J. Pediatr. **179**, 192–196 (2016)
11. Taha, A.A., Hanbury, A.: Metrics for evaluating 3D medical image segmentation: analysis, selection, and tool. BMC Med. Imaging **15**(1), 29 (2015)
12. Yoo, S., Park, R.H.: Red-eye detection and correction using inpainting in digital photographs. IEEE Trans. Consum. Electron. **55**(3), 1006–1014 (2009)

Hybrid Statistical Framework for Diabetic Retinopathy Detection

Sami Bourouis[1,2]($\boxtimes$), Atef Zaguia[2], and Nizar Bouguila[3]

[1] Université de Tunis El Manar, ENIT, Laboratoire: LR-SITI Signal Image
et Technologies de l'Information, 1002 Tunis, Tunisie
s.bourouis@tu.edu.sa
[2] College of Computers and Information Technology, Taif University,
Taif, Kingdom of Saudi Arabia
zaguia.atef@tu.edu.sa
[3] The Concordia Institute for Information Systems Engineering (CIISE),
Concordia University, Montreal, QC H3G 1T7, Canada
nizar.bouguila@concordia.ca

Abstract. We present in this paper a novel hybrid statistical framework for retinal image classification and diabetic retinopathy detection. Our purpose here is to develop a probabilistic SVM-based kernel combined with a finite mixture of Scaled Dirichlet distributions. The developed method offers more flexibility in data modeling and classification since it takes advantage of both generative and discriminative models. Quantitative results obtained from a large dataset of real retinal images confirm the effectiveness of the proposed framework.

Keywords: Retinal images · Diabetic retinopathy · SVM
Scaled Dirichlet mixture · Fisher score kernel

1 Introduction and Related Research Work

Diabetic retinopathy (DR) is an eye disease which causes blindness in both developing and developed countries. According to several studies such as the one in [18], it is possible to avoid and prevent visual loss if the we detect and analyse at early stage the DR. Nevertheless, this kind of disease often shows few symptoms that makes its detection too difficult. The most common signs of DR are: exudates, microaneurysms (MA), cotton wool spots (CWS), and hemorrhages (HA) [2]. It should be noted that the protocol followed by specialist for DR screening takes always a lot of time. Even several approaches have been proposed to solve the problem of diabetic retinopathy detection, however, the major problems facing researchers in developing accurate methods are related to the inter- and intra- variability in appearance that causes a lot of false positives. Thus, there is a need for developing more efficient DR screening tools allowing early revealing of diseases and timely treatment. This emerging topic has gained a lot of importance and several computer-aided screening methods

© Springer International Publishing AG, part of Springer Nature 2018
A. Campilho et al. (Eds.): ICIAR 2018, LNCS 10882, pp. 687–694, 2018.
https://doi.org/10.1007/978-3-319-93000-8_78

have been developed in the literature in which several image processing techniques are developed to analyse retinal images and detect diabetic retinopathy [1,24,25,27–29]. For example in [3] DR is identified based on the extraction of a set of features of higher-order spectra and SVM classifier. Another interesting work is developed in [4] in which a hierarchical clustering algorithm is combined with a relevant features extraction (AM-FM) tool to achieve better DR lesions detection. Some signs of DR like the "exudates" pathologies have been analysed with different algorithms like the computational intelligence technique developed in [24]and the fuzzy FCM algorithm combined with some morphological operators as proposed in [30]. Other type of lesions which are "microaneurysms (MA)" are also detected with other methods such as dynamic thresholding and multi-scale correlation filtering [31]; ensemble-based framework detector [6]; wavelet transform-based template matching [26]; local rotating cross-section profile [20], etc. Comparing existing methods is a quite hard problem since a lot of works are based a variety of hypothesis (for example, the nature of the input data to model and classify). However, it is possible to distinguish two main approaches: discriminative approaches and generative approaches. Discriminative approaches have received a lot of attention in several applications (i.e text classification, speech recognition) and are usually used in the construction of decision boundaries and recognition problems [9]. Generative approaches have the advantage of offering a principled effective way for handling uncertainty and they are practical especially when dealing with missing and incomplete data [16,21,22]. In many settings, traditional discriminative approaches such as SVMs fail to perform precise classification performances because they are often relying on classic kernels which are not significant for all applications like the case of DR classification. Thus, finding a suitable kernel is usually a challenging task. To deal with such limitation, we propose in this paper to develop a hybrid framework that takes advantages from both generative and discriminative approaches [10]. In this study, we tackle the problem of retinal image classification by developing a new hybrid framework driven by SVM-based kernel from finite mixture of scaled Dirichlet [23] in order to distinguish between normal and abnormal retina with possible DR lesions. The consideration of scaled Dirichlet mixture is motivated by its flexibility and the excellent results recently obtained in several real-life applications [23]. In fact, SDD has been proposed as a powerful alternative to the well-known Dirichlet mixture model [12–15,17]. The proposed method involves mixture models based on the scaled Dirichlet family of distributions (SDMM) as the generative part and support vector machines as the discriminative counterpart. To the best of our knowledge there is no prior work that has considered both probabilistic generative-discriminative approaches, based on SDMM mixtures with SVM, for DR detection and classification. The remainder of this paper is organized as follows. Section 2 outlines the proposed probabilistic framework for retinal images classification based on SVM and a scaled Dirichlet mixture model. Then, in Sect. 3, obtained results for this model and a comparative study are presented. Finally, we end with conclusions of this work in Sect. 4.

2   Probabilistic Framework for DR Classification

Our focus here is to derive a probabilistic SVM kernel [11] based on Fisher score from mixture of scaled Dirichlet distributions (SDMM) to tackle the problem of retinal images classification. SVM is one of the most successful learning algorithms for binary classification and SDMM is able to take into account the intrinsic structure of the data. In this manner, the constructed kernel function is generated directly from data and then it can provide more better results than standard kernels [8, 19]. In the following we provide a detailed description of the proposed framework.

2.1   The Scaled Dirichlet Mixture Model (SDMM)

Let $\mathcal{X} = \{\boldsymbol{X}_1, \boldsymbol{X}_2, \dots, \boldsymbol{X}_N\}$, a set of proportional vectors, be a realization from a K-component mixture distribution. Each sample vector $\boldsymbol{X}_n = (X_{n1}, \dots, X_{nD})$ is D-dimensional. The corresponding likelihood is:

$$p(\mathcal{X}|\Theta) = \prod_{n=1}^{N} \sum_{k=1}^{K} p_k p(\boldsymbol{X}_n|\theta_k) \tag{1}$$

where $\Theta = (\boldsymbol{p}, \theta)$, the $\{p_k\}$'s are the mixing parameters that are positive and sum to one, $\boldsymbol{p} = (p_1, \dots, p_K)$, and the $\theta = \{\theta_k\}$'s are component-specific parameter vectors. Each $\boldsymbol{X}_n$ is supposed to arise from one of the K components. In our mixture model, $p(\boldsymbol{X}_n|\theta_k)$ is a scaled Dirichlet distribution denoted by

$$p(\boldsymbol{X}_n|\theta_k) = \frac{\Gamma(\alpha_{k+})}{\prod_{d=1}^{D} \Gamma(\alpha_{kd})} \frac{\prod_{d=1}^{D} \beta_{kd}^{\alpha_{kd}} X_{nd}^{\alpha_{kd}-1}}{(\sum_{d=1}^{D} \beta_{kd} X_{nd})^{\alpha_{k+}}} \tag{2}$$

where Γ denotes the Gamma function, $\alpha_{k+} = \sum_{d=1}^{D} \alpha_{kd}$ and $\theta_k = (\boldsymbol{\alpha}_k, \boldsymbol{\beta}_k)$ is our model parameter. $\boldsymbol{\alpha}_k = (\alpha_{k1}, \dots, \alpha_{kD})$ is the shape parameter and $\boldsymbol{\beta}_k = (\beta_{k1}, \dots, \beta_{kD})$ is the scale parameter of the scaled Dirichlet distribution. The scale parameter controls how the density plot is spread out and the shape parameter describes the shape of the scaled Dirichlet distribution. The flexibility of this parameter is very important in finding patterns and shapes inherent in a dataset. To estimate the model's parameters, we process here with one of the most interesting estimator methods which is called the "Maximum Likelihood (ML)". In practice, the parameters are estimated through the well known EM algorithm that takes into account the latent variables. In this case, latent vectors are defined with $\boldsymbol{Z}_i = (Z_{n1}, \dots, Z_{nK}), n = 1, \dots, N$, Where $Z_{nk} = 1$ if $\boldsymbol{X}_n$ belongs to class j and 0, otherwise. $\mathcal{Z} = \{\boldsymbol{Z}_1, \boldsymbol{Z}_2, \dots, \boldsymbol{Z}_N\}$. Once the data $\mathcal{X}$ combined with the latent variables $\mathcal{Z}$, we can find the $\Theta_{MLE} = \arg\max_\Theta log(p(\mathcal{X}, \mathcal{Z}|\Theta))$. We call $(\mathcal{X}, \mathcal{Z})$ the complete data and its complete log-likelihood is given by:

$$\mathcal{L}(\mathcal{X}, \mathcal{Z}|\Theta) = \sum_{n=1}^{N} \sum_{k=1}^{K} \hat{Z}_{nk} \, log[p_k p(\boldsymbol{X}_n|\theta_k)]. \tag{3}$$

In the expectation step of the EM algorithm, the goal is to replace the latent variables by the expectation values of class assignment which is the posterior probability of each data vector assigned to a particular cluster j:

$$\hat{Z}_{nk} = p(\theta_k | \boldsymbol{X}_n) = \frac{p_k p(\boldsymbol{Y}_n | \theta_k)}{\sum_{j=1}^{K} p_j p(\boldsymbol{Y}_n | \theta_j)}. \tag{4}$$

In the maximization step, we update the model parameters to refine the learned model which result in maximizing the expectation of the complete log-likelihood. The maximization of $\mathcal{L}(\mathcal{X}, \mathcal{Z} | \Theta)$ under the constraint $\sum_{k=1}^{K} p_k = 1$ gives:

$$p_k = \frac{1}{N} \sum_{n=1}^{N} \hat{Z}_{nk}. \tag{5}$$

By setting the first derivatives of $\mathcal{L}(\mathcal{X}, \mathcal{Z} | \Theta)$ equal to zero with respect to the mixture components parameters we obtain the optimal parameters for (α_k, β_k) via the MLE framework:

$$\frac{\partial \mathcal{L}(\mathcal{X}, \mathcal{Z} | \Theta)}{\partial \alpha_{kd}} = (\Psi(\alpha_+) - \Psi(\alpha_d)) \sum_{n=1}^{N} \hat{Z}_{nk} + log\beta_d + logx_{nd} - log(\sum_{d=1}^{D} \beta_d x_{nd}) \tag{6}$$

$$\frac{\partial \mathcal{L}(\mathcal{X}, \mathcal{Z} | \Theta)}{\partial \beta_{kd}} = \sum_{n=1}^{N} \hat{Z}_{nk} \left(\frac{\alpha_d}{\beta_d} \frac{\alpha_+ x_{nd}}{\sum_{d=1}^{D} \beta_d x_{nd}} \right) \tag{7}$$

where $\Psi(\alpha) = \frac{\partial log \Gamma(\alpha)}{\partial \alpha} = \frac{\frac{\partial \Gamma(\alpha)}{\partial \alpha}}{\Gamma(\alpha)}$ is the digamma function.

According to these previous equations, it is clear that a closed-form solution is intractable and does not exist for the model parameters Θ_k. Thus, we use an iterative multivariate optimization method called Newton-Raphson method to estimate these parameters. It is expressed as:

$$\theta_k^{(t+1)} = \theta_k^{(t)} - H(\theta_k^{(t)})^{-1} \frac{\partial \mathcal{L}(\mathcal{X}, \mathcal{Z} | \Theta^{(t)})}{\partial \theta_k^{(t)}} \tag{8}$$

where $H(\theta_k^{(t)})^{-1}$ is called the inverse of the Hessian matrix. To calculate this Hessian matrix, we must compute the second and mixed derivatives of our log-likelihood function.

2.2   Fisher-Based SVM Kernel

Fisher-based SVM Kernel, initially introduced by [19], is calculated at the estimated statistical manifold parameter Θ as follows:

$$\mathcal{K}(\boldsymbol{X}, \boldsymbol{X}_n) = U_X^{tr}(\Theta) F(\Theta)^{-1} U_{X_n}(\Theta) = U_X^{tr}(\Theta) I(\Theta)^{-1} U_{X_n}(\Theta) \tag{9}$$

where $F(\Theta)$ the Fisher information matrix. Each component of $U_X(\Theta) = \nabla \log(p(\mathcal{X} | \Theta))$ denotes the Fisher score. In our case, the Fisher kernel for the

Table 1. Results using DRIVE data set.

	AUC	Accuracy
Finite scaled Dirichlet mixture	0.79	83.35
Fisher Kernel+ finite scaled Dirichlet mixture	0.87	90.87
Finite Dirichlet mixture	0.78	81.88
Fisher Kernel+ finite Dirichlet mixture	0.84	88.54
Finite Gaussian mixture	0.74	78.91
Fisher Kernel + finite Gaussian mixture	0.79	85.08

scaled Dirichlet mixture model is calculated with respect to the parameters $\Theta = (p_k, \alpha_k, \beta_k)$ where k represents each component in the model:

$$\frac{\partial \log(\mathcal{X}|\Theta)}{\partial \alpha_{kd}} = \sum_{n=1}^{N} \hat{Z}_{nk} \left\{ \Psi(\alpha_+) - \Psi(\alpha_d) + \log \beta_d + \log x_{nd} - \log(\sum_{d=1}^{D} \beta_d x_{nd}) \right\} \tag{10}$$

$$\frac{\partial \log(\mathcal{X}|\Theta)}{\partial \beta_{kd}} = \sum_{n=1}^{N} \hat{Z}_{nk} (\frac{\alpha_d}{\beta_d} \frac{\alpha_+ x_{nd}}{\sum_{d=1}^{D} \beta_d x_{nd}}) \tag{11}$$

$$\frac{\partial \log(\mathcal{X}|\Theta)}{\partial p_n} = \sum_{n=1}^{N} \frac{\hat{Z}_{nk}}{p_k} \tag{12}$$

where $\Psi(\alpha) = \frac{\partial \log \Gamma(\alpha)}{\partial \alpha}$ is the digamma function.

3 Experiments and Results

In this section, we apply our framework to the important problem of DR detection using local features. We have tested and evaluated our methods on three well-known publicly available datasets: DRIVE, HRF, and VDIS [5]. A crucial step for diabetic Retinopathy classification, after pre-processing for which we applied the steps describes in [5], is the extraction of features. In our work we have considered SURF features [7]. Each image was then represented as a set of SURF features which we modeled using our finite scaled Dirichlet mixture model. The main goal here is to compare the results obtained when using directly finite scaled Dirichlet mixture model and the results when this model is integrated within SVM as a kernel. Concerning the multi-class SVM using the 1-vs-1 MaxVotes. The SVM was trained with the proposed probabilistic kernels. The used data sets were split into two groups: one for training and the other for testing. Then, the kernel parameters were selected by cross-validation using 70% of the training group for training and the rest for validation. After finding the best parameters, the SVM was trained using all the training data. Tables 1, 2, and 3 display the results when applying different approaches to the DRIVE, HRF, and VDIS data sets, respectively.

Table 2. Results using HRF data set.

	AUC	Accuracy
Finite scaled Dirichlet mixture	0.81	83.31
Fisher Kernel+ finite scaled Dirichlet mixture	0.87	90.87
Finite Dirichlet mixture	0.77	81.94
Fisher Kernel+ finite Dirichlet mixture	0.85	89.22
Finite Gaussian mixture	0.73	80.18
Fisher Kernel + finite Gaussian mixture	0.84	89.02

Table 3. Results using VDIS data set.

	AUC	Accuracy
Finite scaled Dirichlet mixture	0.76	80.48
Fisher Kernel+ finite scaled Dirichlet mixture	0.87	90.87
Finite Dirichlet mixture	0.75	80.03
Fisher Kernel+ finite Dirichlet mixture	0.84	88.55
Finite Gaussian mixture	0.73	79.80
Fisher Kernel + finite Gaussian mixture	0.80	86.13

According to the results, it is clear that the SVM based on the Fisher Kernel extracted from the scaled Dirichlet finite mixture outperforms the other approaches. It is clear also that the hybrid generative discriminative approaches outperforms the purely generative finite mixture approaches. We can notice also that the finite scaled Dirichlet mixture outperforms the finite Dirichlet and the finite Gaussian mixtures.

4 Conclusion

In this paper, we propose a diabetic Retinopathy detection approach based on a hybrid generative discriminative framework. The generative part is a finite scaled Dirichlet mixture model from which a Fisher kernel is generated to be deployed within SVM. According to the obtained results, the proposed approach is promising and takes simultaneously the advantages of both generative and discriminative families. Future works could be devoted to the generation of other kernels. Another future work could be the handling of larger databases of images and their description with different features to produce a comprehensive analysis and detection system.

References

1. Abràmoff, M.D., Niemeijer, M., Suttorp-Schulten, M.S., Viergever, M.A., Russell, S.R., Van Ginneken, B.: Evaluation of a system for automatic detection of diabetic retinopathy from color fundus photographs in a large population of patients with diabetes. Diabetes care **31**(2), 193–198 (2008)
2. Abràmoff, M.D., Reinhardt, J.M., Russell, S.R., Folk, J.C., Mahajan, V.B., Niemeijer, M., Quellec, G.: Automated early detection of diabetic retinopathy. Ophthalmology **117**(6), 1147–1154 (2010)
3. Acharya, R., Chua, C.K., Ng, E., Yu, W., Chee, C.: Application of higher order spectra for the identification of diabetes retinopathy stages. J. Med. Syst. **32**(6), 481–488 (2008)
4. Agurto, C., Murray, V., Barriga, E., Murillo, S., Pattichis, M., Davis, H., Russell, S., Abràmoff, M., Soliz, P.: Multiscale am-fm methods for diabetic retinopathy lesion detection. IEEE Trans. Med. Imaging **29**(2), 502–512 (2010)
5. Amin, J., Sharif, M., Yasmin, M., Ali, H., Fernandes, S.L.: A method for the detection and classification of diabetic retinopathy using structural predictors of bright lesions. J. Comput. Sci. **19**, 153–164 (2017)
6. Antal, B., Hajdu, A.: An ensemble-based system for microaneurysm detection and diabetic retinopathy grading. IEEE Trans. Biomed. Eng. **59**(6), 1720–1726 (2012)
7. Bay, H., Ess, A., Tuytelaars, T., Gool, L.V.: Speeded-up robust features (surf). Comput. Vis. Image Underst. **110**(3), 346–359 (2008)
8. Bdiri, T., Bouguila, N.: Bayesian learning of inverted dirichlet mixtures for SVM kernels generation. Neural Comput. Appl. **23**(5), 1443–1458 (2013)
9. Boser, B.E., Guyon, I.M., Vapnik, V.N.: A training algorithm for optimal margin classifiers. In: Proceedings of the Fifth Annual Workshop on Computational Learning Theory, pp. 144–152. ACM (1992)
10. Bouguila, N.: Bayesian hybrid generative discriminative learning based on finite liouville mixture models. Pattern Recogn. **44**(6), 1183–1200 (2011)
11. Bouguila, N., Amayri, O.: A discrete mixture-based kernel for svms: application to spam and image categorization. Inf. Process. Manage. **45**(6), 631–642 (2009)
12. Bouguila, N., Ziou, D.: On fitting finite dirichlet mixture using ECM and MML. In: Singh, S., Singh, M., Apte, C., Perner, P. (eds.) ICAPR 2005. LNCS, vol. 3686, pp. 172–182. Springer, Heidelberg (2005). https://doi.org/10.1007/11551188_19
13. Bouguila, N., Ziou, D., Vaillancourt, J.: Unsupervised learning of a finite mixture model based on the dirichlet distribution and its application. IEEE Trans. Image Process. **13**(11), 1533–1543 (2004)
14. Bourouis, S., Al Mashrgy, M., Bouguila, N.: Bayesian learning of finite generalized inverted dirichlet mixtures: application to object classification and forgery detection. Expert Syst. Appl. **41**(5), 2329–2336 (2014)
15. Bourouis, S., Al-Osaimi, F., Bouguila, N., Sallay, H., Aldosari, F., Al Mashrgy, M.: Video forgery detection using a Bayesian RJMCMC-based approach. In: IEEE/ACS 14th International Conference on Computer Systems and Applications (AICCSA), pp. 71–75 (2017)
16. Channoufi, I., Bourouis, S., Bouguila, N., Hamrouni, K.: Image and video denoising by combining unsupervised bounded generalized Gaussian mixture modeling and spatial information. Multimedia Tools and Applications, pp. 1–16 (2018)
17. Fan, W., Sallay, H., Bouguila, N., Bourouis, S.: A hierarchical dirichlet process mixture of generalized dirichlet distributions for feature selection. Comput. Electr. Eng. **43**, 48–65 (2015)

18. Garg, S., Davis, R.M.: Diabetic retinopathy screening update. Clin. Diabetes **27**(4), 140–145 (2009)
19. Jaakkola, T., Haussler, D.: Exploiting generative models in discriminative classifiers. In: Advances in neural information processing systems, pp. 487–493 (1999)
20. Lazar, I., Hajdu, A.: Retinal microaneurysm detection through local rotating cross-section profile analysis. IEEE Trans. Med. Imaging **32**(2), 400–407 (2013)
21. McLachlan, G., Peel, D.: Finite mixture models. Wiley, New York (2004)
22. Najar, F., Bourouis, S., Bouguila, N., Belghith, S.: A comparison between different Gaussian-based mixture models. In: 14th IEEE/ACS International Conference on Computer Systems and Applications, AICCSA, Tunisia, pp. 704–708 (2017)
23. Oboh, B.S., Bouguila, N.: Unsupervised learning of finite mixtures using scaled Dirichlet distribution and its application to software modules categorization. In: IEEE International Conference on Industrial Technology (ICIT), 2017, pp. 1085–1090. IEEE (2017)
24. Osareh, A., Shadgar, B., Markham, R.: A computational-intelligence-based approach for detection of exudates in diabetic retinopathy images. IEEE Trans. Inf. Technol. Biomed. **13**(4), 535–545 (2009)
25. Philip, S., Fleming, A.D., Goatman, K.A., Fonseca, S., Mcnamee, P., Scotland, G.S., Prescott, G.J., Sharp, P.F., Olson, J.A.: The efficacy of automated "disease/no disease" grading for diabetic retinopathy in a systematic screening programme. Br. J. Ophthalmol. **91**(11), 1512–1517 (2007)
26. Quellec, G., Lamard, M., Josselin, P.M., Cazuguel, G., Cochener, B., Roux, C.: Optimal wavelet transform for the detection of microaneurysms in retina photographs. IEEE Trans. Med. Imaging **27**(9), 1230–1241 (2008)
27. Sánchez, C.I., Niemeijer, M., Išgum, I., Dumitrescu, A., Suttorp-Schulten, M.S., Abràmoff, M.D., van Ginneken, B.: Contextual computer-aided detection: improving bright lesion detection in retinal images and coronary calcification identification in CT scans. Med. Image Anal. **16**(1), 50–62 (2012)
28. Sopharak, A., Dailey, M.N., Uyyanonvara, B., Barman, S., Williamson, T., Nwe, K.T., Moe, Y.A.: Machine learning approach to automatic exudate detection in retinal images from diabetic patients. J. Mod. Opt. **57**(2), 124–135 (2010)
29. Sopharak, A., Uyyanonvara, B., Barman, S.: Simple hybrid method for fine microaneurysm detection from non-dilated diabetic retinopathy retinal images. Comput. Med. Imaging Graph. **37**(5), 394–402 (2013)
30. Sopharak, A., Uyyanonvara, B., Barman, S., Williamson, T.H.: Automatic detection of diabetic retinopathy exudates from non-dilated retinal images using mathematical morphology methods. Comput. Med. imaging Graph. **32**(8), 720–727 (2008)
31. Zhang, B., Wu, X., You, J., Li, Q., Karray, F.: Detection of microaneurysms using multi-scale correlation coefficients. Pattern Recogn. **43**(6), 2237–2248 (2010)

BIOMISA Retinal Image Database
for Macular and Ocular Syndromes

Taimur Hassan[1](✉) (iD), M. Usman Akram[1] (iD), M. Furqan Masood[2], and Ubaidullah Yasin[3]

[1] Department of Computer and Software Engineering,
National University of Sciences and Technology (NUST), Islamabad, Pakistan
engr.taimoorhassan@gmail.com, usmakram@gmail.com
[2] Center for Advanced Studies in Engineering (CASE), Islamabad, Pakistan
mfurqanmasood@gmail.com
[3] Armed Forces Institute of Ophthalmology (AFIO), Rawalpindi, Pakistan
talhaubaid@gmail.com

Abstract. Retinopathy is a collective group of macular and ocular syndromes that damages the human retina due to increased fluid pressure or hyperglycemia. The major forms of retinopathy include macular edema (ME), exudative or non-exudative age related macular degeneration (AMD) and glaucoma. Various eye testing techniques are being used by ophthalmologists to grade retinopathy. Furthermore, different researchers are developing fully autonomous systems to mass screen eye patients across the globe. However, to validate the performance of these systems, they must be tested on publicly available standardized datasets. Therefore, this paper presents a retinal image database containing high quality 64 fundus and 2497 OCT brightness scans (B-scans). The proposed dataset is first of its kind in providing detailed annotations of retinal hemorrhages, hard exudates, intra-retinal and sub-retinal fluids, drusen, retinal pigment epithelium (RPE) atrophy and cup to disc (CDR) ratios from both retinal fundus and OCT imagery. The proposed dataset is also compared with the publicly available databases where it outmatched them by providing high quality fundus and OCT scans along with detailed markings through which different researchers can automatically diagnose different pathological conditions of human retina.

Keywords: Optical coherence tomography (OCT) · Fundus photography
Retinopathy

1 Introduction

A human eye is the sense organ which allows vision by reacting to the light and pressure and it has the capability to distinguish between approximately 10 million colors [1]. A human eyeball is structured into three layers i.e. sclera, choroid and retina [2]. Retina is the innermost layer of an eye ball where the vision is formed. Human retina is subdivided into two regions i.e. the macular region and the ocular region. The human vision is formed scaled and inverted on the central portion of a macular region known as fovea and afterwards the vision information is passed to the brain through optic nerve for interpretation [2]. Retinopathy consists of multiple retinal syndromes that often leads to

© Springer International Publishing AG, part of Springer Nature 2018
A. Campilho et al. (Eds.): ICIAR 2018, LNCS 10882, pp. 695–705, 2018.
https://doi.org/10.1007/978-3-319-93000-8_79

blindness if there are not timely treated. Some of the commonly occurring retinal diseases are ME, exudative or non-exudative AMD and glaucoma. There are various imaging techniques that can be used to diagnose retinopathy. However, the most commonly used and non-invasive techniques are fundus photography and OCT imaging. Many researchers have worked on developing retinal clinical decision support systems (CDSS) [3–8] on publicly available datasets such as duke datasets, structured analysis of the retina (STARE) and digital retinal images for vessel extraction (DRIVE) etc. However, all of these datasets are based on single imagery source and to the best of our knowledge, there is no publicly available dataset that contains detailed markings for different complications of human retina from both retinal fundus and OCT scans. So, this paper presents a high quality retinal database that contains detailed retinal fundus and OCT volumetric scans for the diagnosis of various retinal diseases such as ME, exudative and non-exudative AMD and glaucoma. The proposed dataset is unique as it contains markings of different abnormalities such as retinal hemorrhages, hard exudates, drusen, intra-retinal and sub-retinal fluid segments, RPE atrophy, CDR ratios from both retinal fundus and OCT scans. Furthermore, the proposed system also contains the detailed annotations of intra-retinal layers from both healthy and diseased pathology and they have been marked by expert doctors. The proposed dataset has been acquired from Armed Forces Institute of Ophthalmology (AFIO), Pakistan. Figure 1 shows a randomly selected retinal fundus and OCT scans from the proposed dataset that depicts different retinal anomalies.

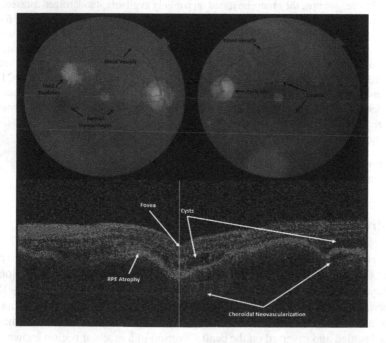

Fig. 1. Abnormal retinal fundus and OCT scans reflecting different retinal abnormalities

2   Related Publicly Available Datasets

Different research groups across the globe have published their detailed and high quality retinal image databases such as DUKE VIP DATASETS, AVRDB, STARE, VICAVR, DRIVE, HRF and MESSIDOR. All of these datasets contain detailed markings of macular and ocular syndromes from multiple experts. The detailed description of these datasets is given below:

2.1   DUKE VIP Datasets

The Vision and Image Processing (VIP) lab at Duke University have published datasets [9–11] containing spectral domain optical coherence tomography (SD-OCT) scans of healthy, diabetic macular edema (DME) and AMD affected subjects. Farsiu et al. [9] published their SD-OCT dataset containing 38,400 B-scans from 269 AMD patients and 115 normal subjects. Srinivasan et al. [10] published SD-OCT scans of 15 DME, 15 AMD and 15 healthy subjects. Chiu et al. [11] published SD-OCT dataset of 10 DME affected subjects. All of these datasets have been acquired using Spectralis SD-OCT (Heidelberg Engineering Inc.) OCT machine.

2.2   AVRDB

AVRDB [12] is the dataset that is publicly available that contains 100 retinal fundus scans for the automated grading of hypertensive retinopathy (HR) [12]. Apart from this, AVRDB contains detailed markings of optic nerve head (ONH), cotton wool spots, hard exudates and arteriovenous ratios (AVR). The dataset has been acquired using TOPCON TRC-NW8 machine in AFIO, Rawalpindi Pakistan.

2.3   STARE

STARE is one of the most commonly used database which covers different retinal complications within macular and ocular region. STARE contains around 400 annotated fundus scans covering various complications of human retina [13].

2.4   HRF

High resolution fundus (HRF) dataset [14] was developed by the research community in order to validate CDSS in automatically analyzing and diagnosing retinal anomalies. The dataset contains 45 high resolution fundus scans depicting glaucomatous and DR pathologies. The dataset has been acquired using CANON CF-60 UVi camera has the spatial resolution of 3504×2336 pixels with 24-bits RGB color space. Apart from this, the dataset contains detailed markings which are performed by the group of expert ophthalmologists.

2.5 DIARETDB0

DIARETDB0 stands for standard diabetic retinopathy database calibration level 0 and it is an online dataset that consists of 130 colored retinal fundus scans in which 20 scans are of healthy subjects and 110 shows pathological symptoms of DR such as soft and hard exudates, neovascularization, hemorrhages and microaneurysms [15].

2.6 DIARETDB1

DIARETDB1 stands for standard diabetic retinopathy database calibration level 1 and it is another online dataset [16] which contains 89 fundus images from which 5 scans are of healthy subjects and remaining 84 scans shows symptoms of DR. DIARETDB1 has been marked against exudates and bright lesions by four experts.

2.7 DRIONS

Digital retinal images for optic nerve segmentation (DRIONS) is a freely available dataset online [17] and it is designed for ONH segmentation. The dataset contains 110 optic disc (OD) fundus scans which are acquired using an analog camera. The scans are later on digitized using HP-PhotoSmart-S20 scanner. The scanned images have the spatial resolution of 600×400 with the 8 bits per pixel (BPP) and ONH region has been marked by 2 experts.

2.8 MESSIDOR

MESSIDOR stands for methods to evaluate segmentation and indexing techniques in the field of retinal ophthalmology and it is a publicly available dataset [18] containing approximately 1200 fundus scans acquired from 654 diabetes and 546 healthy patients [19] and all of these scans are divided into 3 sets. Each set has been annotated against various complications of DR and ME.

2.9 DRIVE

DRIVE stands for digital retinal images for vessel extraction is also retinal fundus dataset and it is a publicly available dataset [20] to study different pathological symptoms of DR. The 44 fundus images within the dataset has been captured through Cannon CR5 3CCD camera with the spatial resolution of 768×584, 8-BPP. Out of these 40 images, 33 are of healthy subjects while 7 contains mild symptoms of DR.

Table 1 shows the comparison of proposed dataset against state of the art publicly available dataset. It can be observed from Table 1 that the proposed dataset provides the dataset that contains detailed markings of different retinal complications for both fundus and OCT scans. Furthermore, the proposed dataset not only provides the markings of fundus and OCT imagery but it also relates them together for the objective diagnosis of underlying pathology. Therefore, the proposed dataset can be utilized efficiently by the research community to test and validate the fully automated self-diagnosis system.

Table 1. Dataset comparison

Dataset	D*	CDR*	AVR*	Fluids*	R*	VA*	RL*	GA*	HE*	OA*	NI*
DUKE			✓	✓		✓					38,000+
AVRDB		✓			✓			✓	✓	✓	100
STARE					✓					✓	400
DIARETDB0									✓		130
DIARETDB1									✓		89
HRF						✓		✓		✓	45
DRIONS										✓	110
BIOMISA	✓	✓	✓	✓	✓	✓	✓	✓	✓	✓	**2561**

D: Drusen, CDR: Cup to Disc Annotations on OCT, AVR: Arteriovenous Ratio, Fluids: Intra-retinal and Sub-Retinal Fluids, R: RPE Atrophic Profiles, VA: Vascular Annotations, RL: Retinal Layers Annotations, GA: Glaucoma Annotations, HE: Hard Exudates, OA: Optic Nerve Annotations, NI: Number of images in dataset

3 Proposed Dataset Description

We present a complete dataset suite that incorporates both retinal fundus and optical coherence tomography (OCT) imagery. The dataset is primarily designed for researchers to validate their CDSS to diagnose and mass screen various complications of retinal pathology. The dataset contains detailed annotations for both fundus and OCT analysis where each annotation is characterized according to the respective underlying retinal morphology. Apart from this, the dataset is unique in its way that it includes both retinal fundus as well as OCT B-scans and C-scans, giving the capabilities of correlating cross-sectional retinal pathology with prominent fundus anomalies for accurate and objective diagnosis. The dataset has been made available to research community on request through our website: http://biomisa.org/contact.html.

3.1 Image Acquisition

The proposed dataset has been acquired from AFIO, Pakistan. The data acquisition phase was carried out under the strict observation of multiple expert ophthalmologists. Apart from this, the annotations were carried out individually by each ophthalmologist based on their knowledge and expertise, in an isolated zone. All the images are acquired using TOPCON 3D OCT 2000 machine. Fundus scans are centered on both macular and ocular region, with the dimensions of 2032×1934 pixels. OCT images are characterized as B-scans and C-scans where B-scans are acquired with the resolution 951×456 pixels and C-scans contains 128 frames where each frame has a resolution of 760×576 pixels. Fundus and OCT B-scans are stored in JPEG uncompressed images while OCT C-scans are stored in WMV format with 15 frames per second. Table 2 presents the detailed summary of the dataset.

The dataset contains 64 fundus scans (20 maculae centered and 44 OD centered) and 2497 OCT B-scans (2453 are of macular region and 44 are of OD region). Out of these 2497 B-scans, 2432 B-scans are embedded into 19 C-scans of 128 frames. The total patient count for macular region is 59 (14 AMD subjects, 13 ME subjects and 32 healthy

Table 2. Dataset summary

Dataset	Fundus Scans		OCT B-scans		OCT C-scans	
	Healthy	Diseased	Healthy	Diseased	Healthy	Diseased
Resolution	2032 x 1934 pixels	2032 x 1934 pixels	951 x 456 pixels	951 x 456 pixels	128 frames of 760x 576 pixels	128 frames of 760x 576 pixels
Maculae Centered	9	11	9	12	8	11
Optic Disc (OD) Centered	19	25	19	25		
Presence of Exudates and Retinal Fluids		7		8		7
Presence of Hemorrhages		2				
Presence of Drusen and RPE Atrophy		4		4		4
Cup to Disc Ratio	12	14	12	14		

subjects) and for ocular region, it is 44 (26 glaucomic and 18 healthy subjects). Furthermore, all the scans are arranged patient wise in the dataset and for each patient, the scans are distinguished w.r.t left and right eye.

Apart from this, 29 out of 64 fundus images contains healthy pathology while 35 images contain retinal anomalies, which are further characterized into exudates, hemorrhages and drusen etc. Similarly, 1181 OCT B-scans contains no abnormal symptoms while remaining 1316 contains retinal fluids, RPE atrophic profile and glaucoma etc. To the best of our knowledge, the proposed dataset is first of its kind in providing detailed annotations for different pathological conditions that appears in various retinal diseases on both fundus and OCT imagery. In OCT images, the dataset contains detailed annotations for up to nine retinal layers in both healthy and diseased pathology as shown in Fig. 2. This is apart from all the other disease specific annotations which are also present within the proposed dataset. Similarly, the dataset contains detailed annotations for drusen, hemorrhages and hard exudates from fundus scans. For OD centered fundus scans, we have provided the mean cup to disc ratio (CDR) calculated by expert graders for both healthy and glaucomic pathology.

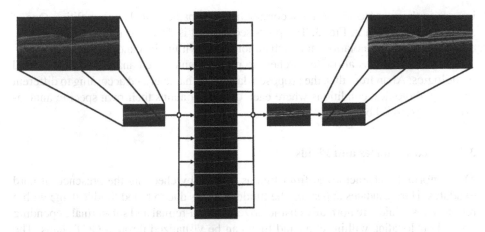

Fig. 2. Marked annotations of up to nine retinal layers from healthy OCT B-scan.

3.2 Data Annotations

The dataset contains detailed annotation carried out by multiple expert ophthalmologists. All the annotations were performed through BIOMISA Retinal Image Illustrator software. These annotations are used for the characterization of different retinal diseases like ME, exudative or non-exudative AMD and glaucoma. Moreover, there are many

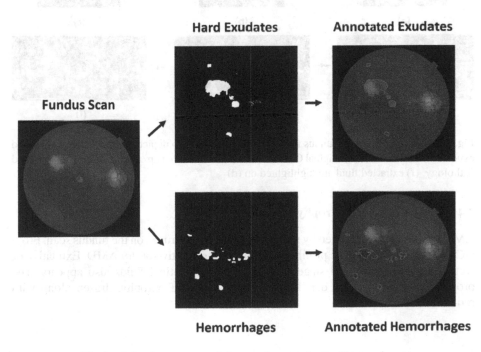

Fig. 3. A fundus scan containing exudates and retinal hemorrhages

images in the proposed dataset that contain multiple pathological abnormalities. One of such cases is shown in Fig. 3. The proposed dataset is designed in such a way that it contains separate annotations for each abnormality within the candidate images.

These annotations allow researchers to perform automated analysis on the desired pathologies. Apart from this, the proposed dataset is characterized according to different retinal pathological conditions where each disease contains their own specific annotations, as discussed below.

3.3 Hard Exudates and Fluids

ME is normally characterized from fundus images by checking the presence of hard exudates. Hard exudates appear on the fundus images due to blood fluid leakage within retina. These fluids are normally characterized as intra-retinal and sub-retinal depending upon their location within retina and they can be visualized through OCT scans. The proposed dataset contains the annotations of hard exudates from fundus photographs and intra-retinal and sub-retinal fluids from OCT B-scans. A randomly selected fundus and OCT scan containing ME pathological symptoms is shown in Fig. 4.

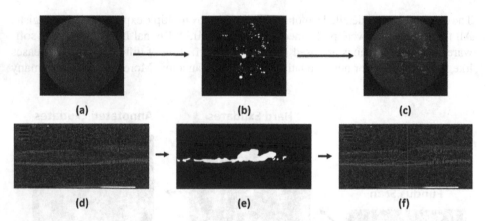

Fig. 4. Retinal imagery (a) fundus image, (b) annotation map depicting exudates, (c) extracted exudates marked on (a), (d) original OCT B-scan, (e) annotation map containing intra-retinal fluid pathology, (f) extracted fluid are highlighted on (d)

3.4 Drusen and RPE Atrophy

AMD is mainly characterized by seeing the presence of drusen on the fundus scan. From OCT B-scan, RPE atrophic profile highlights non-exudative or dry AMD. Exudative or wet AMD is an advanced stage of AMD in which retinal fluids also appears. The proposed dataset contains detailed annotations for RPE atrophy, drusen along with retinal fluids.

3.5 Cup to Disc Annotations

Glaucomic patients are often identified by measuring CDR from both OD centered fundus and OCT imagery. The proposed dataset contains 44 OD centered fundus scans and 44 ocular OCT B-scans, where 19 scans in each category shows healthy pathology and 25 scans contains pathological symptoms of glaucoma. Furthermore, the proposed dataset contains detailed CDR as shown in Fig. 5 and they are calculated by multiple expert ophthalmologists for both healthy and glaucomic scans. These CDR help researchers in analyzing the performance of the automated CDSS.

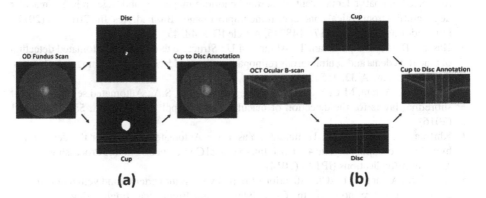

Fig. 5. CDR markings (a) from fundus scan, (b) from OCT scans

4   Conclusion

A high-quality dataset has been proposed here that contains retinal fundus and OCT scans for the diagnosis and grading of retinopathy. The proposed dataset is first of its kind in providing highly objective markings of different pathological symptoms of human retina from both retinal fundus and OCT imagery. The dataset has been obtained from AFIO, Rawalpindi Pakistan and it contains detailed annotations of retinal hemorrhages, hard exudates, drusen, retinal fluids, RPE atrophic profiles and CDR ratios from 64 fundus and 2497 OCT scans. The dataset has been designed in such a way that it does not focus only on one disease or on one imagery source, rather it can be utilized to study different complications of macular and ocular pathology from both fundus and OCT scans. Furthermore, the dataset proposed in this paper has been compared with other publicly available databases where it outmatched others in providing detailed markings of different retinal pathological conditions.

Acknowledgement. This work is sponsored by Ignite National Technology Fund and we would like to thank AFIO, Rawalpindi for providing the dataset.

References

1. Judd, D.B., Wyszecki, G.: Color in Business, Science and Industry. Wiley Series in Pure and Applied Optics, 3rd edn., p. 388. Wiley-Interscience, New York (1975)
2. Human Eye, Encyclopedia Britannica Ultimate Reference Suite 2009 (2009)
3. Syed, A.M., Hassan, T., Akram, M.U., Naz, S., Khalid, S.: Automated diagnosis of macular edema and central serous retinopathy through robust reconstruction of 3D retinal surfaces. Comput. Methods Programs Biomed. **137**, 1–10 (2016). ISSN 0169-2607
4. Khalid, S., Akram, M.U., Hassan, T., Nasim, A., Jameel, A.: Fully automated robust system to detect retinal edema, central serous chorioretinopathy, and age related macular degeneration from optical coherence tomography images. Biomed. Res. Int. 2017, 15 (2017). https://doi.org/10.1155/2017/7148245, Article ID 7148245
5. Hassan, B., Raja, G., Hassan, T., Akram, M.U.: Structure tensor based automated detection of macular edema and central serous retinopathy using optical coherence tomography images. J. Opt. Soc. Am. A **33**, 455 (2016)
6. Hassan, T., Akram, M.U, Hassan, B., Syed, A.M., Bazaz, S.A.: Automated segmentation of subretinal layers for the detection of macular edema. Appl. Optics, OSA. **55**(3), 454–461 (2016)
7. Khitran, S., Akram, M.U., Usman, A., Yasin, U.: Automated System for the detection of hypertensive retinopathy. In: 4th IEEE International Conference on Image Processing Theory, Tools and Applications (IPTA) (2014)
8. Irshad, S., Akram, M.U.: Classification of retinal vessels into arteries and veins for detection of hypertensive retinopathy. In: Cairo International Biomedical Engineering Conference (CIBEC) (2014)
9. Farsiu, S., Chiu, S.J., O'Connell, R.V., Folgar, F.A., Yuan, E., Izatt, J.A., Toth, C.A.: Quantitative classification of eyes with and without intermediate age-related macular degeneration using optical coherence tomography. Ophthalmology **121**(1), 162–172 (2014)
10. Srinivasan, P.P., Kim, L.A., Mettu, P.S., Cousins, S.W., Comer, G.M., Izatt, J.A., Farsiu, S.: Fully automated detection of diabetic macular edema and dry age-related macular degeneration from optical coherence tomography images. Biomed. Optics Express **5**(10), 3568–3577 (2014)
11. Chiu, S.J., Allingham, M.J., Mettu, P.S., Cousins, S.W., Izatt, J.A., Farsiu, S.: Kernel regression based segmentation of optical coherence tomography images with diabetic macular edema. Biomed. Optics Express **6**(4), 1172–1194 (2015)
12. Akbar, S., Hassan, T., Akram, M.U., Yasin, U.U., Basit, I.: AVRDB: annotated dataset for vessel segmentation and calculation of arteriovenous ratio. In: 21st International Conference on Image Processing, Computer Vision and Pattern Recognition (IPCV), Las Vegas, Nevada, USA, pp. 129–134, July 2017
13. Structured analysis of the retina dataset. http://www.ces.clemson.edu/~ahoover/stare/. Accessed 28 Jan 2018
14. High resolution fundus (HRF) image database. https://www5.cs.fau.de/research/data/fundus-images/. Accessed 28 Jan 2018
15. Standard diabetic retinopathy database calibration level 0 (DIARETDB0). http://www.it.lut.fi/project/imageret/diaretdb0/. Accessed 28 Jan 2018
16. Standard diabetic retinopathy database calibration level 1 (DIARETDB1). http://www.it.lut.fi/project/imageret/diaretdb1/. Accessed 28 Jan 2018
17. Digital retinal images for optic nerve segmentation (DRIONS) database. http://www.ia.uned.es/~ejcarmona/DRIONS-DB.html. Accessed 28 Jan 2018

18. Methods to evaluate segmentation and indexing techniques in the field of retinal ophthalmology (MESSIDOR). http://messidor.crihan.fr/index-en.php. Accessed 28 Jan 2018
19. Methods to evaluate segmentation and indexing techniques in the field of retinal ophthalmology. MiProblems at http://www.miproblems.org/datasets/messidor/. Accessed 28 Jan 2018
20. Digital retinal images for vessel extraction (DRIVE). http://www.isi.uu.nl/Research/Databases/DRIVE/. Accessed 28 Jan 2018

Automatic Detection and Characterization of Biomarkers in OCT Images

Melinda Katona[1], Attila Kovács[4], László Varga[1], Tamás Grósz[2],
József Dombi[3], Rózsa Dégi[4], and László G. Nyúl[1(✉)]

[1] Department of Image Processing and Computer Graphics,
University of Szeged, Szeged, Hungary
{mkatona,vargalg,nyul}@inf.u-szeged.hu
[2] MTA-SZTE Research Group on Artificial Intelligence,
University of Szeged, Szeged, Hungary
groszt@inf.u-szeged.hu
[3] Department of Computer Algorithms and Artificial Intelligence,
University of Szeged, Árpád tér 2, Szeged 6720, Hungary
dombi@inf.u-szeged.hu
[4] Department of Ophthalmology, University of Szeged,
Korányi fasor 10-11, Szeged 6720, Hungary
{kovacs.attila,degi.rozsa}@med.u-szeged.hu

Abstract. Optical Coherence Tomography (OCT) is one of the most
advanced, non-invasive method of eye examination. Age-related macular degeneration (AMD) is one of the most frequent reasons of acquired
blindness. Our aim is to develop automatic methods that can accurately
identify and characterize biomarkers in OCT images, related to AMD.
We present methods for quantizing hyperreflective foci (HRF) with deep
learning. We also describe an algorithm for determining pigmentepithelial detachment (PED) and localizing outer retinal tubulation (ORT)
that appears between the layers of the retina.

Keywords: Age-related macular degeneration · Biomarker
Pigmentepithelial detachment · Hyperreflective foci
Outer retinal tubulation · Optical coherence tomography

1 Introduction

Age-related Macular Degeneration (AMD) is a health problem worldwide, that
is the leading cause of vision loss in the Western World. While symptoms are
rare in patients below 50 years of age, an increasing prevalence of AMD can be
detected in the elderly population. AMD means degeneration of the macula, the
region of the retina responsible for central vision. Since only this specific part
of the retina is affected by AMD, untreated patients lose their fine shape- and
face recognition, reading ability, and central vision [4]. AMD can be divided

© Springer International Publishing AG, part of Springer Nature 2018
A. Campilho et al. (Eds.): ICIAR 2018, LNCS 10882, pp. 706–714, 2018.
https://doi.org/10.1007/978-3-319-93000-8_80

into two subtypes; the dry (non-exudative) and the wet (exudative, neovascular) form. The latter one causes rapid and serious visual impairment and accounts for 10% of the cases. In this more acute, neovascular type of the disease, abnormal angiogenesis causes fluid and blood leakage into the retinal layers thus resulting in photoreceptor lesion. Albeit the exact pathomechanism of the disease is still unclear, it is known that the vascular endothelial growth factor (VEGF) plays crucial role in the pathogenesis [10]. The first choice of treatment in neovascular AMD is anti-VEGF intravitreal injection, a periodic injection into the eye.

During the last decade, optical coherence tomography (OCT) has become a basic tool in diagnosing and monitoring neovascular AMD and its response to anti-VEGF treatment. With the help of OCT, we are capable of detecting the layers of the retina, and also the effects of the disease, the so-called OCT biomarkers, such as subretinal/intraretinal fluid accumulation, pigmentepithelial detachment (PED), outer retinal tubulation (ORT) or hyperreflective foci (HRF) (Fig. 1). These markers help the clinical decision-making process for observing/treating/re-treating a patient. To improve the treatment procedure, there is a need for more precise measurements, hence our aim was to create algorithms which can automatically identify and quantify some of the above mentioned biomarkers, namely PED, ORT and HRF.

A large number of publications in the scientific literature deal with cysts, subretinal fluid detection and retinal layer segmentation, however only a small number of papers are available on PED. Haq et al. [3] defined 12 retinal layer with a multi resolution graph-search method and the PED was calculated from the relative position of the lower two layers. The algorithm of Shi et al. [9] applied machine learning for PED detection. We have not come across any papers about automatic segmentation of ORT. In case of the HRFs there are some simple techniques for the detection (see, e.g., [8]), but we have not found any methods in use related to AMD.

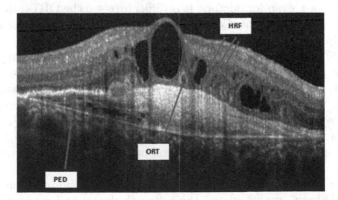

Fig. 1. Optical Coherence Tomography (SD-OCT) image of the retina with biomarkers

2   Materials and Methods

In this section, we present several algorithms to detect HRF, PED and ORT. The OCT images were acquired using Heidelberg Spectralis (Spectralis, Heidelberg Engineering, Heidelberg, Germany) OCT scans on wet age-related macular degeneration. Patients were either treated naively or with anti-VEGF intravitreal injections. The annotated images contained many biomarkers, such as subretinal fluid, PED, subretinal and hyperreflective material. The currently used data consist of images of different patients taken at different times. All image sequences consisted of 49 slices taken with a 6 × 6 mm pattern size and 122 μm slice distance. The slices were generated by averaging 30 frames on each B-scan. Slices had a resolution of 512 × 496 pixels with pixel sizes 11.45 and 3.87 μm and a quality score above 16 dB.

We evaluated our PED and ORT segmentation method by comparing the results to manual segmentations of ophthalmologists for 2 image sequences. The database of HRF consisted of 11 image sequences taken from 7 clinical patients. The annotation was performed by two clinical doctors, independently marking the hyperreflective foci.

2.1   PED Detection and ORT Localization

Pigment epithelium detachment (PED) can be an important medical feature of the disease. PED estimation can be made relatively easily after the retinal pigment epithelium (RPE) layer is detected. Determining the outer boundaries, such as the internal limiting membrane (ILM) and RPE layers are defined in our previous work [5]. We calculated a possible normal layer boundary using the known RPE boundaries to characterize the detachment. We took 1% of the points from both sides of the image and we fitted a smoothed cubic spline to these points, giving the possible boundary.

In many cases, even for doctors, it is difficult to see the ORTs, they can only guess their place and extent. Consequently, an approximate segmentation result can also help.

The ORT has hyperreflective contour and contains hyper- hyporeflective points. The procedure is based on finding hyperreflective points. As we can see in Fig. 1, the input image is noisy, so we used a Wiener filter with a 3 × 5 pixel kernel. Our input image size was 509 × 496, so a smaller kernel was sufficient. Reflective points were localized using a Hessian detector [1]. Then, we performed a non-maximum suppression and considered the 100 highest points. The result image may also contain a several points that are not relevant for ORT localization.

For filtering the false points, we used some prior information about the biomarkers. Firstly, we calculated the retina thickness and we kept only those points which are located in the lower third of the retina. Since we know that ORT is close to the RPE layer and in the distorted retina region or nearby surroundings, by estimating the beginning and end of the distortion on the slices additional points can be removed. We used our published algorithm [5] to detect the extent and location of the distortion of the retina and the detection of cyst and liquid areas. Limiting the specific extent of the ORT in many cases is very difficult, because there is no clear distinction between the hyperreflective wall and its surroundings. We performed adaptive histogram equalization in the image so that at least a part of the possible contours became separable by hysteresis thresholding. The two threshold values are given as the lower and upper third of the maximum intensity value in the image. At the end of the last filtering, we kept only those points which were part of an object in the binary image. Then, we calculated distance map for the points, thresholded and finally computed the convex hull of the objects. The key stages of the procedure are summarized in Fig. 2.

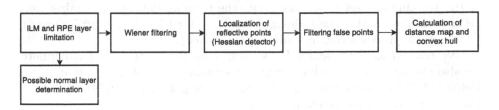

Fig. 2. Flowchart of the proposed PED detection and ORT localization algorithm.

2.2   Quantifying Change in HRFs Using Deep Neural Networks

One of the aims of this work was to quantify the number of HRF pixels in the OCT slices. Although this included the segmentation of HRF pixels, our goal was not a detection, but rather the tracking slight changes in the amount of HRFs. This can help the doctors to objectively track the progress of the disease and aid the treatment planning. For this task, we used Deep Neural Networks (DNNs), which were trained using annotated images by ophthalmologists.

We applied several types of networks, namely the standard Artificial Neural Networks with one hidden layer, Deep Rectifier Neural Networks (DRNs) [2] and Convolution Neural Networks (CNNs) [7], which were successfully used in many previous medical studies [6]. The goal of these networks was to classify one single pixel from a given feature vector. The full image classification was performed by classifying each pixel of the image, separately. We gave the networks two types of input data. The first one was the raw pixel data, which consisted of raw pixel intensities in 25×25 pixel vicinity of the pixel to classify. The other type of input consisted of feature vectors extracted from the OCT images. These features were:

– Weighted sum of pixel intensities in the neighborhood weighted with a Laplacian of Gaussian (LoG) kernels of different σ values. LoG filter σ value ranged from 1 to 2 with a step of 0.1;
– Distance of the pixel from the ILM and RPE layers;
– Distance from subretinal fluid;

– To help the networks recognize shadows of veins we added 25 average intensity values of 40 pixel long vertical strips under the pixel in question, i.e., $\left\{ \sum_{j=1}^{40} I(x-i, y-j), \quad i \in \{-12, -11, \ldots, 11, 12\} \right\}$, where $I(x,y)$ is the pixel of question with x and y coordinates.

The marked targets by ophthalmologist were the bright spots of the images having equal or higher reflectivity than the RPE band, and a diameter of approximately $20 - 40$ μm (2–4 pixels). The annotation consisted of the delineation the HRF pixels of the slices. Before the training phase, we separated the dataset into two partitions, 7 out of 11 sequences were used for training the networks. The other 4 sequences were kept for testing. The images in the test set were taken from 4 different patients. The data of these patients were not included in the training dataset in any way (i.e., the training data set was taken from other patients). Within the training dataset, we used 1 out of every 7 slices for development purposes (i.e. hyperparameter tuning).

We trained an ANN and a DRN using only the pixel data. Furthermore, we also changed the network structure by splitting the first hidden layer of the DRN; half the neurons were connected to the raw pixel input and the other half was connected only to the extracted features.

The structure of the networks were determined empirically by seeking the structures giving the best results. The ANNs had only one hidden layer and 7000 hidden neurons, the DRNs had 5 hidden layers each having 1000 rectifier neurons. To train the ANNs and the DRNs we applied stochastic gradient descent (i.e. backpropagation) training with a mini-batch size of 100. The initial learn rate was set to 0.001, which was halved after each iteration if the performance on the validation set did not improve. During the preliminary experiments we found that the optimal value of the sampling parameter (λ) was 0.8.

The CNN had 3 convolutional layers having a kernel size of 5×5 and output size of 32, 32 and 64, respectively, followed by a fully connected layer of 2 neurons, and a softmax layer. The CNN was trained with backpropagation method with a fixed learning rate of 0.001, momentum of 0.9, and weight decay of 0.004. The batch size was 128. Before training and evaluation we normalized the data to the interval $[-1, 1]$. The net was initialized with random values of uniform distribution, and we did not use any pre-training.

3   Evaluation and Results

3.1   PED and ORT Detection

For calculating accuracy, we used the Jaccard coefficient of similarity, which measures the overlap of the annotated segment and the detected biomarker region. The result of the pigmentepithel detachment localization depends on the location of the pre-determined RPE layer. It may also appear as subretinal hyperreflective material, which is not distinguished from the detachment, so this appears as a false detected region in evaluation. Figure 3 represent the Jaccard values for

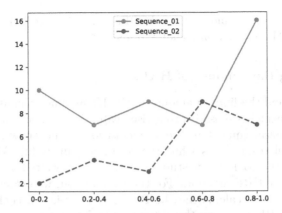

Fig. 3. Jaccard histogram of 2 image sequences. Horizontal axis represents Jaccard values and vertical axis is the number of slices with Jaccard index falling into the given ranges.

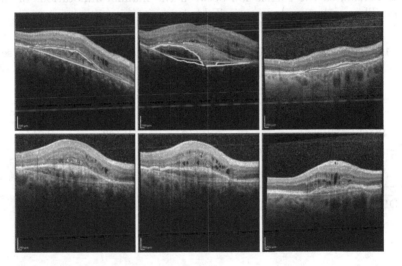

Fig. 4. Illustration of detected and annotated PED and ORT. Upper images show PED regions (magenta - detected, yellow - annotated) and lower pictures represent ORT (red - detected, blue - annotated). (Color figure online)

the two annotated sequences. It can be concluded that the procedure in most cases closely approximates the PED area designated by the ophthalmologist.

In the case of ORT, we analyse the result in two different ways, because not only the localization is important for the ophthalmologist, but sometimes it is also appropriate to determine, if ORT appears on images or not. We achieved a Jaccard value of 0.530 for the two sequences, but we filtered images which do not contain ORT with 97.6% success. Figure 4 illustrates the results of the proposed methods.

Running time of the method was 0.401 ms, PED detection was 0.006 ms on average and ORT localization took 0.091 ms per slice.

3.2 Tracking the Amount of HRFs

The small size and the limited amount of the HRFs made the use of simple (F1 score, or Dice coefficient-based) pixel-wise evaluation metrics meaningless, since only a 1 pixel misalignment in the segmentation would show significant error on the 2–4 pixel sized HRFs while the result is still useful. Also, segmenting HRF-s was not the goal of this study as the doctors wanted a method to track the changes in the HRF amounts. For the comparison, we evaluated the performance of the nets by calculating the Pearson's correlation coefficient between the number of HRF pixels on the automatic and manual segmentations. Using 196 slices, we pairwise compared the pixel counts got by the automatic segmentations to those of the gold standard annotation. As a baseline for the study, we also calculated the correlation between the manual annotations of the two doctors. The results can be seen in Table 1.

Table 1. Pearsons correlation coefficient between the automatic and manual segmentations. In columns one can see the comparison of segmentations sources (NN - Neural network; MD.# - physician).

Data (optimizer goal)	NN ⇔ MD.1	NN ⇔ MD.2	MD.1 ⇔ MD.2
ANN - pixel (accuracy)	0.778	0.789	0.812
ANN - pixel & feature (accuracy)	0.698	0.775	
DRN - pixel (accuracy)	0.812	0.783	
DRN - pixel & feature (accuracy)	0.796	0.782	
split DRN - pixel & feature (accuracy)	0.812	0.790	
DRN - pixel & feature (dice)	0.802	0.788	
CNN - pixel (accuracy)	0.845	0.862	

We argue, that if a neural network can reach a higher correlation than the one between the annotations of the doctors (0.812), then its outputs are useful, since they reflect the number of HRFs on a slice as well as the annotation of a medical expert would. In most of the cases, the networks were able to provide good results as almost all of them achieved a correlation value above 0.78. Interestingly, using the extracted features did not improve the quality of the segmentation, suggesting that the nets learned to extract those informations from the raw data. Furthermore, switching the loss function to the Dice loss was neither beneficial.

The best results were achieved by the CNN, with correlation coefficients over 0.845. This indicates that it can produce an acceptable, and reliable quantization. We should also note that the hand made full delineation of HRFs in an OCT sequence leading to an accurate quantization is time consuming, and our method can give a quick automatic estimation of the amount of HRFs.

Based on the above results, we can say that our methods are capable of tracking the number of HRFs in OCT images, and they could aid the doctors during the planning of the treatment, by speeding up the decision making process.

4   Conclusions

We have described procedures for analysing some OCT features of AMD patients. The methods include detection of PED, localization of ORT between retinal layers, and the quantization of HRF. We determined the possible normal layer boundary for the characterization of PED and we introduced a method to localize ORT. We compared our results with the annotated data by medical colleagues. Furthermore, automatic detection of these specified biomarkers can be used not only in AMD patients, so it can help the doctor during patient examination.

Our HRF quantization method achieved a correlation coefficient as good as the one between the annotations by the ophthalmologists. Hence, we argue that they are suitable for aiding the diagnosis and treatment planning process.

Acknowledgements. We would like to thank the NVIDIA Corporation for the donation of the Tesla K40 GPU used for this research. Tamás Grósz was supported by the ÚNKP-17-3 New National Excellence Programme of the Ministry of Human Capacities.

References

1. Beaudet, P.: Rotationally invariant image operators. In: International Joint Conference on Pattern Recognition, Kyoto, Japan, pp. 579–583 (1978)
2. Glorot, X., Bordes, A., Bengio, Y.: Deep sparse rectifier neural networks. In: Proceedings of the Fourteenth International Conference on Artificial Intelligence and Statistics, vol. 15, pp. 315–323. PMLR (2011)
3. Haq, A., Wilk, S.: Detection of wet age-related macular degeneration in OCT images: a case study. Innovations in Biomedical Engineering. AISC, vol. 623, pp. 43–51. Springer, Cham (2018). https://doi.org/10.1007/978-3-319-70063-2_5
4. Hee, M.R., et al.: Optical coherence tomography of age-related macular degeneration and choroidal neovascularization. Ophthalmology **103**(8), 1260–1270 (1996)
5. Katona, M., Kovács, A., Dégi, R., Nyúl, L.G.: Automatic detection of subretinal fluid and cyst in retinal images. In: Battiato, S., Gallo, G., Schettini, R., Stanco, F. (eds.) ICIAP 2017. LNCS, vol. 10484, pp. 606–616. Springer, Cham (2017). https://doi.org/10.1007/978-3-319-68560-1_54
6. Kayalibay, B., Jensen, G., van der Smagt, P.: CNN-based Segmentation of Medical Imaging Data. CoRR abs/1701.03056 (2017)
7. Krizhevsky, A., Sutskever, I., Hinton, G.E.: Imagenet classification with deep convolutional neural networks. Adv. Neural Inf. Process. Syst. **25**, 1097–1105 (2012)
8. Mokhtari, M., Kamasi, Z.G., Rabbani, H.: Automatic detection of Hyperreflective foci in optical coherence tomography b-scans using morphological component analysis. In: 2017 39th Annual International Conference of the IEEE Engineering in Medicine and Biology Society (EMBC), pp. 1497–1500 (July 2017)

9. Shi, F., et al.: Automated 3-D retinal layer segmentation of macular optical coherence tomography images with serous pigment epithelial detachments. IEEE Trans. Med. Imaging **34**(2), 441–452 (2015)
10. Velez-Montoya, R., et al.: Current knowledge and trends in age-related macular degeneration: today's and future treatments. Retina **334**, 1487–1502 (2013)

Challenge on Breast Cancer Histology Images

Two-Stage Convolutional Neural Network for Breast Cancer Histology Image Classification

Kamyar Nazeri, Azad Aminpour, and Mehran Ebrahimi^(✉)

Faculty of Science, University of Ontario Institute of Technology,
2000 Simcoe Street North, Ontario, Oshawa L1H 7K4, Canada
{kamyar.nazeri,azad.aminpour,mehran.ebrahimi}@uoit.ca
http://www.ImagingLab.ca/

Abstract. This paper explores the problem of breast tissue classification of microscopy images. Based on the predominant cancer type the goal is to classify images into four categories of normal, benign, in situ carcinoma, and invasive carcinoma. Given a suitable training dataset, we utilize deep learning techniques to address the classification problem. Due to the large size of each image in the training dataset, we propose a patch-based technique which consists of two consecutive convolutional neural networks. The first "patch-wise" network acts as an auto-encoder that extracts the most salient features of image patches while the second "image-wise" network performs classification of the whole image. The first network is pre-trained and aimed at extracting local information while the second network obtains global information of an input image. We trained the networks using the ICIAR 2018 grand challenge on BreAst Cancer Histology (BACH) dataset. The proposed method yields 95% accuracy on the validation set compared to previously reported 77% accuracy rates in the literature. Our code is publicly available at https://github.com/ImagingLab/ICIAR2018.

Keywords: Breast cancer · Whole slide images
Convolutional neural networks · Patch-wise learning
Microscopy image classification

1 Introduction

Breast cancer is one of the leading causes of cancer-related death in women around the world [1]. According to Canadian Cancer Society, over 26,000 women were diagnosed with breast cancer in Canada in 2017 which represents 25% of all new cancer cases in women. In the same year, more than 5,000 women in Canada lost their lives due to breast cancer which represents 13% of all cancer deaths in women.

It is evident that early diagnosis can significantly increase treatment success. Breast cancer symptoms and signs are varied and diagnosis includes physical

© Springer International Publishing AG, part of Springer Nature 2018
A. Campilho et al. (Eds.): ICIAR 2018, LNCS 10882, pp. 717–726, 2018.
https://doi.org/10.1007/978-3-319-93000-8_81

exam, mammography, ultrasound testing, and biopsy. Biopsy is generally performed after detection of some abnormality using mammography and ultrasound.

In biopsy, a sample of tissue is surgically removed to be analyzed. This can indicate which cells are cancerous, and if so which type of cancer these are associated to. Microscopy imaging data of biopsy samples are large in size and complex in nature. Therefore, pathologists face a substantial workload increase for histopathological cancer diagnosis. In recent years, the development of computer aid diagnosis (CAD) systems have helped reducing this workload. Digital pathology continues to gain momentum worldwide for diagnostic purposes [2].

Recently, deep learning techniques have emerged to address many problems in the field of medical image processing. We propose a classification scheme for breast cancer tissue image classification based on deep convolutional neural networks (CNN). Convolutional networks are considered state of the art technique for classification problems when the input is high-dimensional data such as images. These networks "learn" to extract local features from images and classify the input according to the extracted features. Size of microscopy images are very large and due to hardware barriers, several patch-based CNN methods have been proposed in the literature [3–5] to process the input image as a set of smaller patches. In these models, each image is divided into smaller patches and each patch is classified with a "patch-wise" classifier network and assigned to a label. To classify at the whole image level, the patch-wise network is followed by another classifier that receives output labels from the first network as input and generates label scores. These techniques achieve high accuracy with high confidence on image patches, however, they fail to capture global attributes of the image: Once all image patches are labeled, the spatial information is ignored and any possible feature that is shared between patches is lost.

We propose a novel two-stage convolutional neural network pipeline in a patch-wise fashion that is designed to utilize both local and global information of the input. The proposed method does not require a large memory footprint of the end-to-end training. In this scheme, the sole purpose of the patch-wise network is to extract spatially smaller feature maps from each patch. Once trained, this network is then used to extract the most salient feature maps from all patches in an image based on their local information. These feature maps are stacked together to form a spatially smaller 3D input for the "image-wise" network. This network is trained to classify images based on local features extracted from image and global information shared between different patches. We trained our network using the ICIAR 2018 grand challenge on BreAst Cancer Histology (BACH) dataset [6] containing 400 Hematoxylin and Eosin (H&E) stained breast histology microscopy images. Our model has achieved 95% accuracy on the validation set, outperforming [3] in terms of classification accuracy.[1]

---

[1] Our code and pre-trained weights are available at https://github.com/ImagingLab/ICIAR2018.

2 Related Works

Due to the importance of detection and classification of breast cancer in microscopic tissue images, many new methods have emerged in recent years [3–5]. Computer aided diagnosis (CAD) systems appear to become fast and inexpensive alternatives to second opinion methods. Recently, deep learning techniques have made a huge impact in various problems including medical image processing.

In the past few years, several works aimed at breast cancer detection and classification using CNNs have been published [5,7–12]. Although the aim of all of these works are very similar, each work considers a specific type of problem. For example, [7–9] are proposing a two class (malignant and benign) classifier. Other works in [10,11] consider more complex 3-class classification (normal, in situ carcinoma, and invasive carcinoma). Finally, [5,12] develop a segmentation scheme for breast cancer.

Our work is similar to the work of Araújo et al. [3] in nature. To the best of our knowledge they were the first team to consider a four class classifier for breast tissue images. They developed a CNN followed by a support vector machines (SVM) classifier. In their technique, first the original image is divided into twelve contiguous non-overlapping patches. The patch class probability is computed using the patch-wise trained CNN and CNN+SVM classifiers. Finally, the image-wise classification is obtained using three different patch probability fusion methods. These three methods namely include "majority voting", "maximum probability", and "sum of probabilities" [3].

3 Methods

Given a high resolution (2048 × 1536) histology image, our goal is to classify the image into four classes: *normal tissue, benign tissue, in situ carcinoma* and *invasive carcinoma*.

3.1 Patch-Based Method with CNN

The high resolution nature of the images in our dataset and the need to extract relevant discriminatory features from them impose extra limitations in implementing a regular feed forward convolutional network. Training a CNN on high resolution image requires either a very large memory footprint, which is not available in most cases, or to progressively reduce the spatial size of the image such that the downsampled version could be stored in the memory. However, downsampling an image increases the risk of losing discriminative features such as nuclei information and their densities to correctly classify carcinoma versus non-carcinoma cells. Also, if trained on the large microscopy image, the network might learn to rely only on the most distinctive features and totally discard everything else.

We follow the patch-wise CNN method proposed by [3–5] followed by an image-wise CNN that classifies histology images into four classes. Given a microscopy image, we extract fixed size patches by sliding a patch (window) of size $k \times k$ with stride of s over an image. This makes a total number of $[1 + \frac{I_W - k}{s}] \times [1 + \frac{I_H - k}{s}]$ patches where I_W and I_H are image width and height respectively. In our experiments, we follow [3] and choose patch size of $k = 512$ considering the amount of GPU memory available. We also choose a stride of $s = 256$, which results in $7 \times 5 = 35$ overlapping image patches. We argue that allowing the overlap is essential for the patch-wise network to learn features shared between patches. The proper stride s is chosen by considering the receptive field of both networks when they "work" together, as explained later. An overview of our two-stage CNN is presented in Fig. 1. Note that the labels in the training set are provided only for the whole image and individual patch labels are unknown, yet we train the patch-wise network using categorical cross-entropy loss based on the label of the corresponding microscopy image. This network works like an auto-encoder that learns to extract the most salient features of image patches. Once trained, we discard the classifier layer of this network and use the last convolutional layer to extract feature maps of size $(C \times 64 \times 64)$ from any number of patches in an image, where C is another hyper-parameter in our proposed system that controls the depth of output feature maps as explained later.

To train the image-wise network, we no longer extract overlapping patches from the image: with stride of $s = 512$ patches do not overlap and the total patches extracted from an image becomes 12. We found non-overlapping patches work slightly better in our validation set. We argue that it is because overlapping patches introduce redundant features for a single concept and as a result accuracy of the image-wise network will suffer. The extracted feature-maps from all 12 patches are concatenated together to form a spatially smaller 3D input of size $(12 \times C, 64, 64)$ for the image-wise network. This network is trained against image-level labels using categorical cross-entropy loss and learns to classify images based on local features extracted from image patches and global information shared between different patches.

Once both networks are trained, we use them jointly to infer image-level class predictions.

3.2   Network Architecture

Inspired by [13], we design our patch-wise CNN using a series of 3×3 convolutional layers followed by a pooling layer with the number of channels being doubled after each downsampling. All convolutional layers are followed by *batch normalization* [14] and *ReLU non-linearity* [15]. We followed the guideline in [16] to implement a homogeneous fully convolutional network with occasional dimensionality reduction by using a stride of 2. In our tests, we found that 2×2 kernel with stride of 2 worked better than conventional max-pooling layers in terms of performance. Instead of fully connected layers for the classification task, we use a 1×1 convolutional layer to obtain the spatial average of feature maps from the convolutional layer below it, as the confidence categories and the resulting vector is fed into the *softmax layer* [17]. We use this feature map later as

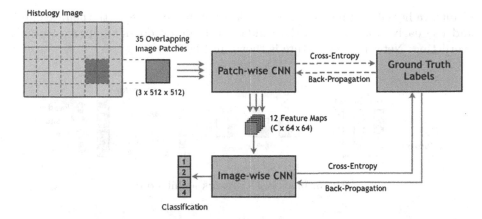

Fig. 1. An overview of the proposed workflow. A CNN is trained on image patches. Feature maps extracted from all image patches are stacked together and passed to a second CNN that learns to predict image-level labels.

an input to the image-wise CNN. To further control and experiment the effect of using spatial averaging layer, we introduce another hyper-parameter C that controls the depth of the output feature maps. Both batch normalization and global average pooling are *structural regularizers* [14,17] which natively prevent overfitting. As a result, we did not introduce any dropout or weight decay in our model. Overall, there are 16 convolutional layers in the network with the input being downsampled 3 times at layers 3, 6, and 9. Figure 2 illustrates the overall structure of the proposed patch-wise network.

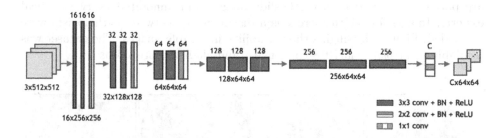

Fig. 2. Patch-wise network architecture

For the proposed image-wise network we follow a similar pattern. Series of 3×3 convolutional layers are followed by a 2×2 convolution with stride of 2 for downsampling. Each layer is followed by batch normalization and ReLU activation function. We use the same 1×1 convolutional layer as before to obtain the spatial average of activation maps before the classifier. The convolutional layers are followed by 3 fully connected layers with a softmax classifier at the end. Unlike the patch-wise network, overfitting is a major problem for this network, as a result, we heavily regularize this network using dropout [18] with the rate of 0.5 and use early stopping once the validation accuracy doesn't improve to limit overfitting. Network architecture is shown in Fig. 3.

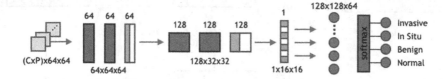

Fig. 3. Image-wise network architecture

The receptive field of the last convolutional layer with respect to the patch-wise network is 252 [19]. In principle, this number has to be the maximum stride value s we can choose in extracting patches, in order to cover the whole surface of the input image. In our experiments we found $s = 256$ has almost the same accuracy. We argue that having large patch size (512×512) makes our network invariant to small changes in s. Note that small values of s makes training time slower and the network prone to overfitting.

4 Experiments and Results

Our dataset is composed of 400 high resolution Hematoxylin and Eosin (H&E) stained breast histology microscopy images labelled as *normal, benign, in situ carcinoma,* and *invasive carcinoma* (100 images for each category). These images are patches extracted from whole-slide images and annotated by two medical experts. Images for which there was a disagreement between pathologists were discarded. Figure 4 highlights the variability in sample images. The dataset was available at https://iciar2018-challenge.grand-challenge.org/dataset/.

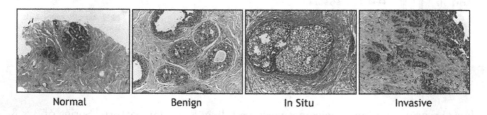

Fig. 4. Samples of ICIAR 2018 challenge on BreAst Cancer Histology (BACH) dataset

The size of dataset is relatively small for our convolutional network. To prevent patch-wise network from overfitting, we apply several data augmentations on patches extracted from the microscopy image. Pathology images do not have

Table 1. Accuracy of the proposed method for one-channel output compared to [3]

	Patch-wise			Image-wise	
	Sum	Max	Maj	CNN	Ensemble
Proposed	91.25	92.50	90.00	93.75	**95.00**
Araújo et al. [3]	77.8	72.2	77.8	-	-

canonical orientation and the classification problem is rotation invariant [3, 12]. To augment the dataset we rotate each patch by 4 multiples of 90°, with and without mirroring, which results in 8 valid variations for each patch. We further apply random color perturbations to these variations as suggested by [20] and produce 8 more patches. The color augmentation process would help our model to learn color-invariant features and make pre-processing color normalization [21] step unnecessary. The total size of our patch-wise dataset becomes $16 \times 35 \times 400$.

We train both networks on a single NVIDIA Titan XP GPU using Adam [22] optimizer, mini-batch size of 64 and initial learning rate of 0.001, with a decay of 0.1 every 20 epochs. We train the patch-wise model on 80% of our dataset for 30 epochs and used the remaining 20% for cross-validation. We use the same train/validation sets for image-wise network.

The accuracy of the proposed method is measured as the ratio between correct samples and the total number of evaluated images. For our validation set of 80 images, our best model achieved 93.75% accuracy (Table 1) and mean Area Under Curve (AUC) of 98.3 corresponding to (98.9, 97.7, 98.5, 98.1) for the four classes (Table 2) based on Receiver Operating Characteristic (ROC) analysis. In addition, we experimented with an ensemble model, averaging across 8 variations of rotation/flip in the input image as suggested by [20] and further improved the accuracy to 95.00%.

To compare our results with those of Araújo et al. [3], the image-wise labels through a decision making scheme on outputs of the patch-wise network is also presented in (Table 1). The image label is obtained using one of the three different patch probability fusion methods. These methods include, *majority voting*, where the image label is selected as the most common patch label, *maximum probability*, where the patch with higher class probability decides the image label, and *sum of probabilities*, where the patch class probabilities are summed up and the class with the largest value is assigned. As shown in (Table 1), our proposed patch-wise network is outperforming previous methods by a large margin. To further experiment the effect of using spatial average layer at the end of the patch-wise network, we use the hyper-parameter C that controls the depth of the output feature maps. We examined different values of C and measured the accuracy using our validation set (Table 2). In our tests, the network with only one output channel outperforms the others corroborating the idea that having many filters for a single concept impose extra burden on the next network, which needs to adjust with all variations from the previous network [17]. The ROC curves for $C = 1$ and $C = 4$ are illustrated in Fig. 5.

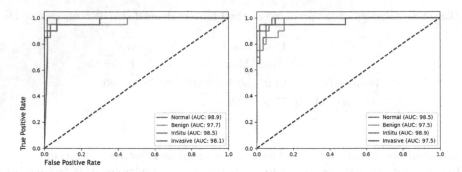

Fig. 5. Receiver Operating Characteristic (ROC) curves for two output sizes of the patch-wise network. Left: 1-Channel feature map, Right: 4-Channel feature map

Table 2. Detailed results of both networks over different classes

Feature maps	Class	Patch-wise			Class	Image-wise			
		Precision	Recall	Accuracy		Precision	Recall	AUC	Accuracy
64 × 64 × 1	Normal	0.80	0.81	0.82	Normal	0.95	1.00	0.99	**0.94**
	Benign	0.81	0.77		Benign	0.95	0.95	0.98	
	InSitu	0.76	0.85		InSitu	0.86	0.95	0.99	
	Invasive	0.93	0.86		Invasive	1.00	0.85	0.98	
64 × 64 × 3	Normal	0.81	0.86	0.86	Normal	0.94	0.85	0.97	0.90
	Benign	0.85	0.79		Benign	0.86	0.90	0.96	
	InSitu	0.86	0.88		InSitu	0.83	0.95	0.98	
	Invasive	0.93	0.90		Invasive	1.00	0.90	0.98	
64 × 64 × 4	Normal	0.81	0.90	0.86	Normal	0.79	0.95	0.98	0.88
	Benign	0.85	0.79		Benign	1.00	0.70	0.97	
	InSitu	0.90	0.84		InSitu	0.86	0.90	0.99	
	Invasive	0.90	0.93		Invasive	0.90	0.95	0.97	
64 × 64 × 16	Normal	0.77	0.86	0.82	Normal	0.78	0.90	0.98	0.85
	Benign	0.85	0.68		Benign	0.83	0.75	0.96	
	InSitu	0.80	0.87		InSitu	0.94	0.80	0.96	
	Invasive	0.86	0.85		Invasive	0.86	0.95	0.99	

5   Conclusions and Future Work

In this manuscript, we considered the problem of breast cancer classification using microscopy tissue images. We utilized deep learning techniques and proposed a novel two-stage CNN pipeline to overcome the hardware limitations imposed by processing of very large images. The first so called *patch-wise* network acts on the smaller patches of the whole image and outputs spatially smaller feature maps. The second network is performing on top of the patch-wise network. It receives stack of feature maps from the patch-wise network as input and generates image-level label scores. In this framework, patch-wise network is responsible for capturing the local features of the input while the image-wise network is learning to combine those features and find the relationship between neighbouring patches to globally infer characteristics of the image and generate class confident scores. The main contribution of this work is presenting a pipeline which is able to process large scale images using minimal hardware.

We trained the networks using the ICIAR 2018 grand challenge on BreAst Cancer Histology (BACH) dataset. The proposed method yields 95% accuracy on the four-class validation set compared to previously reported 77% accuracy rates in [3]. It is worth noting that inference time of our scheme is in the order of milliseconds. The pre-trained weights of our networks are relatively small in size (7.9MB patch-wise, 1.6MB image-wise) compared to other state-of-the-art networks (hundreds of MB) which makes them suitable for practical settings.

We trained two networks separately on the same labels with the same loss function. One might fairly argue that training the patch-wise network with the same labels as the image-wise network is a disadvantage to the performance of our model. Clearly, not every patch in an image represents the same category.

One alternative would be to train both networks end-to-end using only one loss function that back-propagates through both networks. In this scheme, both networks are interconnected to let the flow of gradient and therefore cost is minimized by updating both networks' parameters together. In our experiments, we found that such model requires a very large memory footprint that makes it impractical to apply in practice. We plan to further investigate this framework in the future and focus on its improvements.

Acknowledgments. This research was supported in part by a Natural Sciences and Engineering Research Council of Canada (NSERC) Discovery Grant (DG) for ME. AA would like to acknowledge UOIT for a doctoral graduate international tuition scholarship (GITS). The authors gratefully acknowledge the support of NVIDIA Corporation for their donation of Titan XP GPU used in this research through its Academic Grant Program.

References

1. Siegel, R.L., Miller, K.D., Jemal, A.: Cancer statistics, 2016. CA: Cancer J. Clin. **66**(1), 7–30 (2016)
2. Ghaznavi, F., Evans, A., Madabhushi, A., Feldman, M.: Digital imaging in pathology: whole-slide imaging and beyond. Annu. Rev. Pathol. Mech. Dis. **8**, 331–359 (2013)
3. Araújo, T., Aresta, G., Castro, E., Rouco, J., Aguiar, P., Eloy, C., Polónia, A., Campilho, A.: Classification of breast cancer histology images using convolutional neural networks. PloS one **12**(6), e0177544 (2017)
4. Hou, L., Samaras, D., Kurc, T.M., Gao, Y., Davis, J.E., Saltz, J.H.: Patch-based convolutional neural network for whole slide tissue image classification. In: Proceedings of the IEEE Conference on Computer Vision and Pattern Recognition, pp. 2424–2433 (2016)
5. Cruz-Roa, A., Basavanhally, A., González, F., Gilmore, H., Feldman, M., Ganesan, S., Shih, N., Tomaszewski, J., Madabhushi, A.: Automatic detection of invasive Ductal carcinoma in whole slide images with convolutional neural networks. In: SPIE medical imaging, International Society for Optics and Photonics, vol. 9041, pp. 904103–904103 (2014)

6. ICIAR 2018 grand challenge: In: 15th International Conference on Image Analysis, Recognition. https://iciar2018-challenge.grand-challenge.org/
7. Kowal, M., Filipczuk, P., Obuchowicz, A., Korbicz, J., Monczak, R.: Computer-aided diagnosis of breast cancer based on fine needle biopsy microscopic images. Comput. Biol. Med. **43**(10), 1563–1572 (2013)
8. George, Y.M., Zayed, H.H., Roushdy, M.I., Elbagoury, B.M.: Remote computer-aided breast cancer detection and diagnosis system based on cytological images. IEEE Syst. J. **8**(3), 949–964 (2014)
9. Filipczuk, P., Fevens, T., Krzyzak, A., Monczak, R.: Computer-aided breast cancer diagnosis based on the analysis of cytological images of fine needle biopsies. IEEE Trans. Med. Imaging **32**(12), 2169–2178 (2013)
10. Brook, A., El-Yaniv, R., Isler, E., Kimmel, R., Meir, R., Peleg, D.: Breast cancer diagnosis from biopsy images using generic features and SVMs. IEEE Transactions on Information Technology in Biomedicine (2006)
11. Zhang, B.: Breast cancer diagnosis from biopsy images by serial fusion of random subspace ensembles. In: 4th International Conference on Biomedical Engineering and Informatics (BMEI), vol. 1, pp. 180–186 IEEE (2011)
12. Cireşan, D.C., Giusti, A., Gambardella, L.M., Schmidhuber, J.: Mitosis detection in breast cancer histology images with deep neural networks. In: Mori, K., Sakuma, I., Sato, Y., Barillot, C., Navab, N. (eds.) MICCAI 2013. LNCS, vol. 8150, pp. 411–418. Springer, Heidelberg (2013). https://doi.org/10.1007/978-3-642-40763-5_51
13. Simonyan, K., Zisserman, A.: Very deep convolutional networks for large-scale image recognition (2014). arXiv preprint arXiv:1409.1556
14. Ioffe, S., Szegedy, C.: Batch normalization: Accelerating deep network training by reducing internal covariate shift. In: International Conference on Machine Learning, pp. 448–456 (2015)
15. Maas, A.L., Hannun, A.Y., Ng, A.Y.: Rectifier nonlinearities improve neural network acoustic models. In: Proceedings of the ICML, vol. 30 (2013)
16. Springenberg, J.T., Dosovitskiy, A., Brox, T., Riedmiller, M.: Striving for simplicity: the all convolutional net (2014). arXiv preprint arXiv:1412.6806
17. Lin, M., Chen, Q., Yan, S.: Network in network (2013). arXiv preprint:1312.4400
18. Srivastava, N., Hinton, G.E., Krizhevsky, A., Sutskever, I., Salakhutdinov, R.: Dropout: a simple way to prevent neural networks from overfitting. J. Mach. Learn. Res. **15**(1), 1929–1958 (2014)
19. Luo, W., Li, Y., Urtasun, R., Zemel, R.: Understanding the effective receptive field in deep convolutional neural networks. In: Advances in Neural Information Processing Systems, pp. 4898–4906 (2016)
20. Liu, Y., Gadepalli, K., Norouzi, M., Dahl, G.E., Kohlberger, T., Boyko, A., Venugopalan, S., Timofeev, A., Nelson, P.Q., Corrado, G.S., et al.: Detecting cancer metastases on Gigapixel pathology images (2017). arXiv preprint arXiv:1703.02442
21. Macenko, M., Niethammer, M., Marron, J., Borland, D., Woosley, J.T., Guan, X., Schmitt, C., Thomas, N.E.: A method for normalizing histology slides for quantitative analysis. In: IEEE International Symposium on Biomedical Imaging: From Nano to Macro, 2009, ISBI'09., pp. 1107–1110, IEEE (2009)
22. Kingma, D., Ba, J.: Adam: A method for stochastic optimization (2014). arXiv preprint arXiv:1412.6980

Towards Interactive Breast Tumor Classification Using Transfer Learning

Nick Weiss[1]([⊠]), Henning Kost[2], and André Homeyer[2]

[1] Fraunhofer MEVIS, Maria-Goeppert-Straße 3, 23562 Lübeck, Germany
nick.weiss@mevis.fraunhofer.de
[2] Fraunhofer MEVIS, Am Fallturm 1, 28359 Bremen, Germany

Abstract. The diagnosis of breast cancer relies on the accurate classification of morphological subtypes in histological sections. Recent advances in image analysis using convolutional neural networks have yielded promising automated methods for this classification task. These networks are usually trained from scratch and depend on hours-long training with thousands of labeled examples to produce good results. Once trained these methods can not easily be adapted in cases of misclassification or to novel tasks. We aim to develop methods that can quickly be adapted in an interactive way. As a first step in this direction we present a classification method that enables fast training with a limited number of samples and achieves state-of-the-art results.

Keywords: Histology · Breast cancer · Automated image analysis
Transfer learning · Neural networks

1 Introduction

Background. Breast cancer is the second most common cancer in the world and the most frequent cancer among women [9]. In case of suspected breast cancer, it is strictly required to take a biopsy and classify the obtained tissue [20]. Whether the tissue is cancerous or not is determined by a pathologist looking at sections of histological tissue. These two categories, cancerous and non-cancerous, are further divided into morphological subtypes that are indispensable for an accurate diagnosis, prognosis and treatment. Although an ever-growing number of subtypes exists, the most commonly used categories for breast cancer are ductal carcinoma in situ and invasive ductal carcinoma [18].

The histological assessment is usually carried out manually by a pathologist using a standard bright-field microscope. The growing number of breast cancer incidences results in an increasing workload for pathologists who have to accurately process each tissue slide [9,25]. Furthermore, it has been shown that there is limited inter-observer consensus in interpreting breast biopsy specimens [8]. Both, high workload and inter-observer variability, have motivated the development of several automatic analysis methods based on digitized histological slides [15,25]. Among these are methods using convolutional neural networks (CNNs)

A. Campilho et al. (Eds.): ICIAR 2018, LNCS 10882, pp. 727–736, 2018.
https://doi.org/10.1007/978-3-319-93000-8_82

that have recently shown very promising results [15]. These methods could help to objectively assess most of the standard cases with minimal interaction giving the pathologists more time for the complex cases.

In this paper, we consider the classification of suspected breast cancer histology images into one of the following categories: *normal, benign, in situ* or *invasive*.

Related Work. The interest in developing algorithms for breast cancer related image analysis tasks has been very high [10,15,17,25]. This is especially visible in challenges and open data repositories on breast cancer that have appeared since 2012 [15]. One dataset to mention in the context of breast cancer classification is the BreakHis dataset [23] from 2016. It contains thousands of H&E stained images with labels of four distinct benign and four malignant subtypes. Another dataset is made available as part of the BACH challenge [1] and contains 100 H&E stained images of each of the subtypes *normal, benign, in situ* or *invasive*. It is used for evaluating our automatic classification approach in this paper. Additionally, a publicly available subset of this dataset of 285 images presented by Araújo et al. [2] is used for comparison.

Araújo et al. [2] use a CNN to classify breast cancer histology images into the stated categories. After normalization [16], they divide the microscopic images of 2048×1536 pixels into overlapping image patches of 512×512 pixels to train a CNN from scratch. The training dataset is further extended using data augmentation, involving rotation and reflection. To obtain image-wise classification they use different methods but find majority voting to work best. They report an average accuracy on two test sets of 0.78.

Cruz-Roa et al. [5] try to identify regions of invasive ductal carcinoma (IDC) in 162 whole slide images of different patients. The reference segmentations are available for all images. The whole slide images are preprocessed to non-overlapping image patches of 100×100 pixels. These are used to train a simple 3-layer CNN architecture to classify the image patches correctly to IDC or non-IDC. They achieve an overall f1-measure of 0.72. They also test methods with handcrafted features and a random forest classifier achieving an inferior overall f1-measure of 0.68 compared to their CNN approach.

Janowczyk el al. [12] use a slightly adapted AlexNet [13] as their CNN to tackle various breast cancer related histological segmentation tasks such as nuclei, epithelium, lymphocyte, mitosis, tubule or invasive ductal carcinoma segmentation. The latter problem is the same as the described in the previous approach by Cruz-Roa et al. [5]. They are using the same data and could improve the overall f1-measure to 0.77.

Spanhol et al. [24] try different CNN architectures for their classification into benign and malignant breast tumor tissue. They also use the BreakHis dataset consisting of 7909 microscopic images from 82 patients. They train their CNN with randomly selected image patches with 64×64 pixels from downsampled microscopic images of 350×230 pixels. After fusing the image patch predictions to a final image-wise prediction an average accuracy of 0.90 is achieved using an adapted AlexNet. Compared to their best handcrafted features method this is an improvement of about 0.05.

Another recent approach by Spanhol et al. [22] utilizes the idea of transfer learning to solve the previously described classification task. They use an adapted AlexNet model trained on the ImageNet dataset [6] as a feature extractor for a logistic regression classifier. Features from all three top layers of the model are considered. The method reaches an image-wise average accuracy of 0.84. Although they mention this method offers a faster and more robust training with less data, no experiments are provided confirming these statements.

A similar framework is considered by Xu et al. [26] and applied to histological brain tumor and colon cancer images. They also use a pretrained AlexNet model but only use the final layer as feature extractor for a linear SVM classifier. Li et al. [14] use a closely related method for gland segmentation in colon images but finetune their AlexNet model with the training data. They find that the CNN features outperform the handcrafted features and that fusing both, CNN and handcrafted features, does not necessarily contribute to a superior classifier.

Overall, there is a clear tendency in using CNN architectures for the classification of breast cancer histology images. Using a CNN in these cases usually results in a more accurate classification than using handcrafted features with a standard classifier. Moreover, a CNN learns the most meaningful features for a given task itself. However, this does not come for free. Instead of spending the time with the clever design of discriminative features it is nowadays spent with the collection of enough labeled data, the artificial generation of more data and the training process itself. Although training neural networks has become much easier in recent years, it still takes up a lot of time and data when trained from scratch. Transfer learning holds promise to tackle this problem by using powerful generic CNN features from one task and apply them to another. In general, these features are evaluated with a standard classifier like SVM and then applied to a new dataset. In many cases, the performance of these approaches is close to the performance of a normally trained CNN. However, they offer a clear advantage regarding the time and data needed for training.

Contributions. Transfer learning approaches as described above are the starting point for our approach. We are interested in fast interactive classification methods for histological breast tissue images. *Interactive* should imply that once the features are extracted for a new unlabeled dataset, a few image labels should be sufficient to train a standard classifier within a few seconds and present the results on the screen. The solution can be further refined by adding more labels and rapidly train the classifier again.

In our work, we therefore quantify both, the amount of time and data needed in a transfer learning approach with CNN features. This has not been evaluated in any of the approaches presented above. Furthermore, we do not limit ourselves to the top layers of CNN networks but also test features extracted from lower layers. Instead of the AlexNet we use the more recent CNN models VGG [21],

ResNet [11] and Xception [4]. Finally we evaluate our approach as part of the BACH challenge and compare it to a CNN based approach by Araújo et al. [2].

2   Methods

In this section we describe all parts of our supposed approach for training and predicting breast cancer subtypes in histological breast cancer images. Some parts of the approach are optional or interchangeable, especially the preprocessing steps and the feature extractor. That way several methods can be deduced from the approach. A selection of these methods is presented in Sect. 3.

Normalization. Histological images show a great range of color even when exhibiting the same kind of tissue and using the same staining procedure. This variation is hardly captured by any limited set of training images, so reducing it beforehand often increases the performance of image analysis methods on unseen data [7, 16]. To reduce the variation in color we therefore apply the normalization method introduced by Macenko et al. [16].

Data Augmentation. It is not guaranteed that features extracted from pre-trained CNNs are invariant to the position or orientation of the tissue within an image or an image patch. To address this we apply vertical and horizontal flipping of the images. That increases the chances of a subsequent classifier to rely on mostly invariant features or at least to adjust to the variation within one feature.

Feature Extraction. Three architectures are considered as a feature extractor: VGG16 [21], ResNet50 [11] and Xception [4]. They have shown promising results on various image classification tasks and can be found as pretrained models in deep learning frameworks such as Keras [3]. They have been trained using the ImageNet data [6], which consists of millions of images showing animals, plants, vehicles and other objects. Although the task of classifying these images is not closely related to our task of classifying breast cancer images, these architectures have been found suitable for transfer learning in various approaches [14, 22, 26]. As mentioned in the related work section these approaches limit themselves to use features extracted from the top layers, whereas Yosinski et al. [27] suggest that higher layers provide less generic features with decreased performance on the target task. The clear hierarchical structure found in most CNN architectures network offers us the possibility to extract features at several prominent positions and further explore their transferability. These prominent positions are specific layers of each building block found in different network architecture, namely we selected the pooling layers in VGG16 and the addition layers found in ResNet50 and Xception. To limit the number of total features, each extraction layer is followed by a global average pooling. This way the response of each filter in a convolutional layer is reduced to just one feature. This results in a total of 1472 features for VGG16, 7960 features for Xception and 15104 features for ResNet50.

Classification. The training data is processed by the previously described steps and the final features are then, along with their corresponding label, used to train a linear classifier. Given the high number of features, the limited number of samples and the need for a fast training, we decided to use a simple logistic regression. We found the multinomial logistic regression with the limited-memory BFGS optimizer to train fast enough for our interactive approach [19].

3   Experiments

Datasets. The **BACH challenge** [1] is held as part of the ICIAR 2018. For part A it provides a training set that is used for evaluation in this paper. An additional test set has not yet been released. The training set consists of 400 labeled microscopic H&E stained breast tissue images with 2048×1536 pixels and a pixel size of $0.42\,\mu\mathrm{m}$ x $0.42\,\mu\mathrm{m}$. Each of the four subtypes *normal, benign, in situ* and *invasive* are equally represented in the training set. The patient IDs are only partly available for the training set, so that it is not possible to automatically create independent folds of different patients for cross-validation. Hence, mixing the images for cross-validation might present an overly optimistic accuracy. We therefore decided to construct one independent test set based on patients 13, 18, 19, 20, 21, 23, 31, 32, 37, 38. This results in 50 nearly balanced images from all 4 subtypes. We call this test set *independent*. From the other 350 images we randomly select another 50 images to build a test set called *dependent*.

Araújo et al. also made the dataset available that they used for their evaluation in [2]. It has a training set of 249 images which is just a subset of the challenge training set. Additionally they provide two separate balanced test sets, which are not part of the challenge training set. An *initial* test set of 20 images and an *extended* test set of 16 images of increased ambiguity. These datasets are used for direct comparison of our methods with the CNN based approach in [2].

Selection of Methods. All methods considered for evaluation use the described image normalization, data augmentation and logistic regression. Before feature extraction we additionally downsample all images from 2048×1536 to 1024×768 to slightly decrease the processing time without losing too much information. Besides the image size we also keep the regularization factor in the logistic regression fixed to 0.01. Following this, we focus on evaluating methods with different feature extractors and name the methods accordingly: **VGG Features, ResNet Features** and **Xception Features**.

4   Results

Araújo et al. Dataset. The selected methods produced the image-wise accuracies shown in Table 1. The features extracted by the deeper architectures ResNet and Xception outperformed the features of the VGG network. Furthermore, the results of the ResNet and Xception features are at par with the results achieved by a CNN trained from scratch in [2]. The training itself was performed on 249 labeled images and completed in about 2 s. The feature extraction was run beforehand and took about 0.4 s per image. Compared to the proposed methods the training from scratch took at least several minutes if not hours and is therefore not suited for an interactive training.

In another experiment we reduced the number of images used for training the proposed methods. The results are presented in Table 2. We found the Xception features to be most robust. This method was able to achieve a combined accuracy of 0.70 with 100 randomly selected sample images. With 50 randomly selected samples it still obtained a combined accuracy of 0.67.

Table 1. Accuracy depending on used method and test set (initial, extended and both combined). Additionally the time for feature extraction and training is shown.

Method	Accuracy			Time* (s)	
	initial	*extended*	combined	extract	train
VGG features	0.65	0.62	0.64	89.5	0.2
ResNet features	**0.85**	0.69	**0.78**	88.2	2.5
Xception features	0.75	**0.75**	0.75	91.6	1.5
Reference CNN [2]	0.80	**0.75**	**0.78**	-	-

* Intel Core i7-7700 CPU @ 3.60GHz, 32 GB, Nvidia GeForce GTX 1080.

Table 2. Accuracy depending on method, test set and number of training images used.

Method	50 images		100 images		200 images	
	initial	*extended*	*initial*	*extended*	*initial*	*extended*
VGG features	0.60	0.62	0.60	0.56	0.70	0.50
ResNet features	**0.70**	0.62	0.65	0.62	**0.85**	0.69
Xception features	0.65	**0.69**	**0.70**	**0.69**	0.75	**0.75**

BACH Challenge Dataset. The results found using the extended BACH challenge dataset in Table 3 confirm the results presented above and, in particular, the superiority of the Xception features. The design of the dependent and especially the independent test set helped to see how the extracted features generalize to unseen patients. There is a significant accuracy drop from unseen images of the same patients to images of unseen patients for all methods. Still, the overall accuracy reached by the Xception features is 0.75, matching the results from Table 1. Finally, the method we submit to the challenge is trained using all 400 images of the BACH dataset and evaluated with the *initial* and *extended* test sets, showing a combined accuracy of 0.83.

Table 3. Accuracy depending on used method and test set. For the last entry no accuracy values are given for the BACH test sets, as they were both included in the training set.

Method	Accuracy			
	initial	*extended*	*dependent*	*independent*
VGG features	0.60	**0.69**	0.72	0.50
ResNet features	**0.75**	0.62	0.80	0.64
Xception features	**0.75**	**0.69**	**0.82**	**0.70**
Xception features*	0.90	0.75	-	-

* Challenge method, trained using all images except *initial* and *extended*.

Finally we present accuracy results limiting the Xception features to one block at a time in Fig. 1. The accuracy serves as an indicator for the transferability of the features found in each building block. Again, we use all 400 provided images for training and the *initial* and *extended* test sets for evaluation. The accuracy increases monotonically from 0.56 in the first block up to 0.76 in the 11th block. Using the features extracted from the 12th block decreases the accuracy compared to the previous block. It can also be seen that combining features from all building blocks yields the best result with an overall accuracy of 0.83.

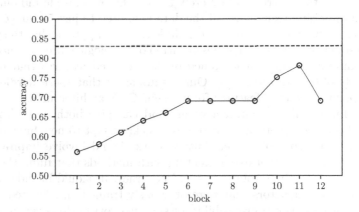

Fig. 1. Overall accuracies on *initial* and *extended* test set obtained by only using extracted features from one specific building block of the Xception network. The dotted line shows the overall accuracy achieved by combining all features.

5   Discussion and Conclusions

The results show the general transferability of features from CNN networks trained on ImageNet to histological image data. That confirms the results recently achieved by similar methods in [22,26].

Unlike these methods our approach also considered features from layers at various positions within the network and not only the top. As we further investigated the transferability of these features in our last experiment, we also found features from layers of the top building blocks to work best in our setup. The higher level features trained for the ImageNet classification still have a high transferability for histological image data. The performance drop at block 12 in Fig. 1 suggests that this transferability has its limits as the features become too specific to the original classification problem, the CNNs were trained for. A further decrease is expected in the layers following block 12 up to the ImageNet category classification. These final layers are fully connected dense layers that are very task specific and are generally cut off beforehand.

For our proposed challenge method we combined features from all 12 blocks found in the Xception network. Using these features in combination with the suggested averaging of the response of each filter outperforms all individually evaluated feature layers. The averaging reduces the number of features and further helps to make the features more generic, especially the ones found in the first layers, which otherwise would provide nearly pixel-wise information.

The combined Xception features used with the logistic regression classifier deliver state-of-the-art results when compared to the CNN method suggested in [2]. Using exactly the same datasets, our proposed method achieves an overall accuracy of 0.75 compared to 0.78 reported in [2].

This level of accuracy is achieved without using task specific features and with a classifier that is trained in merely 2 s. Furthermore, we found our method to provide promising results even if the data is limited to just 50 image samples. Fulfilling these two requirements we conclude that our approach has the potential to set the stage for an interactive classification of histological breast cancer tissue. Previous interactive approaches relied on handcrafted features that could not deliver state-of-the-art results [5]. Our results show that these hurdles can be overcome using extracted features from recent CNN architectures.

In the future such an interactive method can give both, pathologists and image analysis researchers, a great tool to quickly adapt to new histological use cases or rare subtypes of cancer. Future work should involve improving such interactive tools by further experimenting with methods that fulfill the requirements of processing time, robustness and accuracy. It should include the use of CNNs as feature extractors that were previously trained on a related histological task to increase the transferability of such networks. Moreover, it would be interesting to train CNNs for feature extraction without the need for labeled data using autoencoder architectures.

Acknowledgements. This work was conducted under the QuantMed project funded by the Fraunhofer Society, Munich, Germany.

References

1. Araújo, T., Aresta, G., Aguiar, P., Eloy, C., Polónia, A.: Bach challenge (2018). https://iciar2018-challenge.grand-challenge.org
2. Araújo, T., Aresta, G., Castro, E., et al.: Classification of breast cancer histology images using Convolutional Neural Networks. PLOS ONE **12**(6), e0177544 (2017)
3. Chollet, F., et al.: Keras (2015). https://github.com/fchollet/keras
4. Chollet, F.: Xception - deep learning with depthwise separable convolutions. In: CVPR, pp. 1800–1807 (2017)
5. Cruz-Roa, A., Basavanhally, A., González, F., et al.: Automatic detection of invasive ductal carcinoma in whole slide images with convolutional neural networks. In: SPIE, pp. 904103–904115 (2014)
6. Deng, J., Dong, W., Socher, R., et al.: ImageNet: a large-scale hierarchical image database. In: CVPR, pp. 248–255 (2009)
7. Ehteshami Bejnordi, B., Litjens, G., Timofeeva, N., et al.: Stain specific standardization of whole-slide histopathological images. IEEE Trans. Med. Imaging **35**(2), 404–415 (2016)
8. Elmore, J.G., Longton, G.M., Carney, P.A., et al.: Diagnostic concordance among pathologists interpreting breast biopsy specimens. JAMA **313**(11), 1122–1132 (2015)
9. Ferlay, J., Soerjomataram, I., Dikshit, R., et al.: Cancer incidence and mortality worldwide: sources, methods and major patterns in GLOBOCAN 2012. Int. J. Cancer **136**(5), E359–86 (2015)
10. Ghaznavi, F., Evans, A., Madabhushi, A., Feldman, M.: Digital imaging in pathology: whole-slide imaging and beyond. Ann. Rev. Pathol. **8**, 331–359 (2013)
11. He, K., Zhang, X., Ren, S., Sun, J.: Deep residual learning for image recognition. In: CVPR, pp. 770–778 (2016)
12. Janowczyk, A., Madabhushi, A.: Deep learning for digital pathology image analysis: a comprehensive tutorial with selected use cases. J. Pathol. Inf. **7**(1), 29–18 (2016)
13. Krizhevsky, A., Sutskever, I., Hinton, G.E.: ImageNet classification with deep convolutional neural networks. In: Advances in Neural Information Processing Systems 25, pp. 1097–1105 (2012)
14. Li, W., Manivannan, S., Akbar, S., et al.: Gland segmentation in colon histology images using hand-crafted features and convolutional neural networks. In: ISBI, pp. 1405–1408 (2017)
15. Litjens, G., Kooi, T., Bejnordi, B.E., et al.: A survey on deep learning in medical image analysis. Med. Image Anal. **42**, 1–29 (2017)
16. Macenko, M., Niethammer, M., Marron, J.S., et al.: A method for normalizing histology slides for quantitative analysis. In: ISBI, pp. 1107–1110 (2009)
17. Madabhushi, A., Lee, G.: Image analysis and machine learning in digital pathology: challenges and opportunities, pp. 1–6 (2016)
18. Makki, J.: Diversity of breast carcinoma: histological subtypes and clinical relevance. Clin. Med. Insights Pathol. **8**, 23–31 (2015). CPath.S31563–9
19. Pedregosa, F., Varoquaux, G., Gramfort, A., et al.: Scikit-learn - machine learning in python. J. Mach. Learn. Res. **12**, 2825–2830 (2011)
20. Senkus, E., Kyriakides, S., Penault-Llorca, F., et al.: Primary breast cancer: ESMO Clinical Practice Guidelines for diagnosis, treatment and follow-up. Ann. Oncol. **24**(Suppl. 6), vi7–vi23 (2013)
21. Simonyan, K., Zisserman, A.: Very deep convolutional networks for large-scale image recognition. In: Computing Research Repository (2014)

22. Spanhol, F.A., Oliveira, L.S., Cavalin, P.R., Petitjean, C., Heutte, L.: Deep features for breast cancer histopathological image classification. In: SMC, pp. 1868–1873 (2017)

23. Spanhol, F.A., Oliveira, L.S., Petitjean, C., Heutte, L.: A dataset for breast cancer histopathological image classification. IEEE Trans. Biomed. Eng. **63**(7), 1455–1462 (2016)

24. Spanhol, F.A., Oliveira, L.S., Petitjean, C., Heutte, L.: Breast cancer histopathological image classification using Convolutional Neural Networks. In: IJCNN (2016)

25. Veta, M., Pluim, J.P.W., Van Diest, P.J., Viergever, M.A.: Breast cancer histopathology image analysis: a review. IEEE Trans. Biomed. Eng. **61**(5), 1400–1411 (2014)

26. Xu, Y.: Large scale tissue histopathology image classification, segmentation, and visualization via deep convolutional activation features. BMC Bioinform. **18**(1), 1–17 (2017)

27. Yosinski, J., Clune, J., Bengio, Y., Lipson, H.: How transferable are features in deep neural networks? In: Proceedings of the 27th International Conference on Neural Information Processing Systems, vol. 2, pp. 3320–3328 (2014)

Deep Convolutional Neural Networks for Breast Cancer Histology Image Analysis

Alexander Rakhlin[1](✉), Alexey Shvets[2], Vladimir Iglovikov[3], and Alexandr A. Kalinin[4]

[1] Neuromation OU, 10111 Tallinn, Estonia
rakhlin@neuromation.io
[2] Massachusetts Institute of Technology, Cambridge, MA 02142, USA
shvets@mit.edu
[3] Lyft Inc., San Francisco, CA 94107, USA
iglovikov@gmail.com
[4] University of Michigan, Ann Arbor, MI 48109, USA
akalinin@umich.edu

Abstract. Breast cancer is one of the main causes of cancer death worldwide. Early diagnostics significantly increases the chances of correct treatment and survival, but this process is tedious and often leads to disagreement between pathologists. Computer-aided diagnosis systems show potential for improving the diagnostic accuracy. In this work, we develop the computational approach based on deep convolution neural networks for breast cancer histology image classification. Hematoxylin and eosin stained breast histology microscopy image dataset is provided as a part of the ICIAR 2018 Grand Challenge on Breast Cancer Histology Images. Our approach utilizes several deep neural network architectures and gradient boosted trees classifier. For 4-class classification task, we report 87.2% accuracy. For 2-class classification task to detect carcinomas we report 93.8% accuracy, AUC 97.3%, and sensitivity/specificity 96.5/88.0% at the high-sensitivity operating point. To our knowledge, this approach outperforms other common methods in automated histopathological image classification. The source code for our approach is made publicly available at https://github.com/alexander-rakhlin/ICIAR2018.

Keywords: Medical imaging · Computer-aided diagnosis (CAD)
Computer vision · Image recognition · Deep learning

1 Introduction

Breast cancer is the most common cancer diagnosed among women in the United States (excluding skin cancers) [23]. Breast tissue biopsies allow the pathologists to histologically assess the microscopic structure the tissue. Histopathology aims

© Springer International Publishing AG, part of Springer Nature 2018
A. Campilho et al. (Eds.): ICIAR 2018, LNCS 10882, pp. 737–744, 2018.
https://doi.org/10.1007/978-3-319-93000-8_83

to distinguish between normal tissue, non-malignant (benign) and malignant lesions (carcinomas), and to perform a prognostic evaluation [7]. A combination of hematoxylin and eosin (H&E) is the principal stain of tissue specimens for histopathological diagnostics. There are multiple types of breast carcinomas that embody characteristic tissue morphology, see Fig. 1. Breast carcinomas arise from the mammary epithelium and cause a pre-malignant epithelial proliferation within the ducts, called ductal carcinoma *in situ*. Invasive carcinoma is characterized by the cancer cells gaining the capacity to break through the basal membrane of the duct walls and infiltrate into surrounding tissues [20].

Morphology of tissue and cells is regulated by complex biological mechanisms related to cell development and pathology [13]. Traditionally, morphological assessment were visually performed by a pathologist. This process is tedious and subjective, causing inter-observer variations even among senior pathologists [6,16]. The subjectivity of morphological criteria in visual classification motivates the use of computer-aided diagnosis (CAD) to improve the diagnosis accuracy, reduce human error, increase inter-observer agreement and reproducibility [20].

There are many methods developed for the digital pathology image analysis, from rule-based to applications of machine learning [20]. Recently, deep learning based approaches were shown to outperform conventional machine learning methods in many image analysis tasks, automating end-to-end processing [4,10,12]. In the domain of medical imaging, convolutional neural networks (CNN) have been successfully used for diabetic retinopathy screening [19], bone disease prediction [26] and age assessment [11], and other problems [4,22]. Previous deep learning based applications in histological microscopic image analysis have demonstrated their potential to provide utility in diagnosing breast cancer [1,2,20,24].

In this paper, we present an approach for histology microscopy image analysis for breast cancer type classification. Our approach utilizes deep CNNs for feature extraction and gradient boosted trees for classification and, to our knowledge, outperforms other similar solutions.

2   Methods

2.1   Dataset

The dataset is an extension of the dataset from [1] and consists of 400 H&E stain images (2048 × 1536 pixels) of 4 classes. All the images are digitized with the same acquisition conditions: a magnification of 200× and a 0.42 μm × 0.42 μm pixel size. Each image is labeled with one of the four balanced classes: normal, benign, *in situ* carcinoma, and invasive carcinoma, where class is defined as a predominant cancer type in the image, see Fig. 1. The image-wise annotation was performed by two medical experts [9]. The goal of the challenge is to provide an automatic classification of each input image.

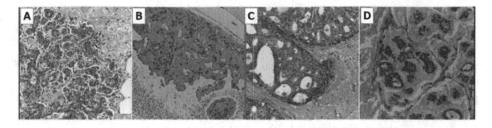

Fig. 1. Examples of microscopic biopsy images in the dataset: (A) normal; (B) benign; (C) *in situ* carcinoma; and (D) invasive carcinoma

2.2 Approach Overview

The limited size of the dataset poses a significant challenge for the training of a deep CNN [4]. Very deep architectures (ResNet, Inception) that contain millions of parameters have achieved state-of-the-art results in many computer vision tasks [25]. However, training these models from scratch requires a large number of images, as training on a small dataset leads to overfitting. A typical remedy in these circumstances is fine-tuning, when only a part of the pre-trained neural network is being fitted to a new dataset. Since fine-tuning did not demonstrate good performance on this task, we employed a different approach known as deep convolutional feature representation [8]. It uses deep CNNs, trained on large datasets like ImageNet (10M images, 20K classes) [5] for unsupervised feature representation extraction. In this study, images are encoded with state-of-the-art general-purpose networks to obtain sparse descriptors of low dimensionality (1408 or 2048). This unsupervised dimensionality reduction step significantly reduces the risk of overfitting on the next stage of supervised learning.

We use LightGBM, the fast, distributed, high performance implementation of gradient boosted trees, for supervised classification [14]. Gradient boosting models are widely used in machine learning due to their speed, accuracy, and robustness against overfitting [17].

2.3 Data Pre-processing and Augmentation

To bring the microscopy images into a common space to enable improved quantitative analysis, we normalize the amount of H&E stained on the tissue as described in [15]. For each image, we perform 50 random color augmentations. Following [21] the amount of H&E is adjusted by decomposing the RGB color of the tissue into H&E color space, followed by multiplying the magnitude of H&E of every pixel by two random uniform variables from the range $[0.7, 1.3]$. Furthermore, we downscale images in half to 1024×768 pixels. From the downscaled images we extract crops of 400×400 pixels and 650×650 pixels. Thereby, each image was represented by 20 crops that are encoded into 20 descriptors. Then, the set of 20 descriptors is combined through 3-norm pooling [3] into a single descriptor:

$$\mathbf{d}_{pool} = \left(\frac{1}{N} \sum_{i=1}^{N} (\mathbf{d}_i)^p \right)^{\frac{1}{p}},$$ (1)

where the hyperparameter $p = 3$ as suggested in [3,27], N is the number of crops, $\mathbf{d}_i$ is descriptor of a crop and $\mathbf{d}_{pool}$ is pooled descriptor of the image. The p-norm of a vector gives the average for $p = 1$ and the max for $p \to \infty$. As a result, for each original image, we obtain 50 (number of color augmentations) ×2 (crop sizes) ×3 (CNN encoders) = 300 descriptors.

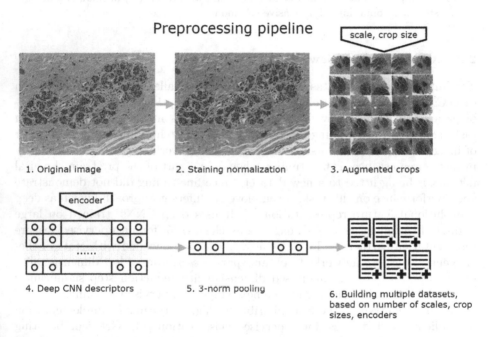

Fig. 2. An overview of the pre-processing pipeline.

2.4   Feature Extraction

Overall pre-processing pipeline is depicted in Fig. 2. For features extraction, we use pre-trained ResNet-50, InceptionV3 and VGG-16 networks. We remove fully connected layers from each model to allow the networks to consume images of an arbitrary size. In ResNet-50 and InceptionV3, we convert the last convolutional layer consisting of 2048 channels via `GlobalAveragePooling` into a one-dimensional feature vector with a length of 2048. With VGG-16 we apply the `GlobalAveragePooling` operation to the four internal convolutional layers: `block2`, `block3`, `block4`, `block5` with 128, 256, 512, 512 channels respectively. We concatenate them into one vector with a length of 1408, see Fig. 3.

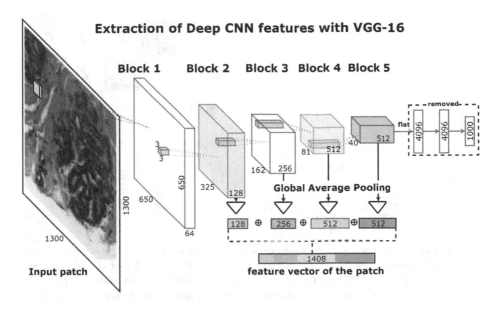

Fig. 3. Schematic overview of the network architecture for deep feature extraction.

2.5 Training

We split the data into 10 stratified folds to preserve class distribution, while all descriptors of the same image are contained in the same fold to prevent information leakage. Augmentations increase the size of the dataset ×300 (2 patch sizes x 3 encoders x 50 color/affine augmentations). For each combination of the encoder, crop size and scale we train 10 gradient boosting models per fold. This allows us to increase the diversity of the models with limited data (bagging). Furthermore, we recycle each dataset 5 times with different random seeds in LightGBM adding augmentation on the model level. As a result, we train 10 (number of folds) ×5 (seeds) ×4 (scale and crop) ×3 (CNN encoders) = 600 gradient boosting models. At the cross-validation stage, we predict every fold only with the models not trained on this fold. For the test data, we similarly extract 300 descriptors for each image and use them with all models trained for particular patch size and encoder. The predictions are averaged over all augmentations and models. Finally, the predicted class is defined by the maximum probability score.

3 Results

To validate the approach we use 10-fold stratified cross-validation.

For 2-class non-carcinomas (normal and benign) vs. carcinomas (*in situ* and invasive) classification accuracy was $93.8 \pm 2.3\%$, the area under the ROC curve was 0.973, see Fig. 4a. At high sensitivity setpoint 0.33 the sensitivity of the

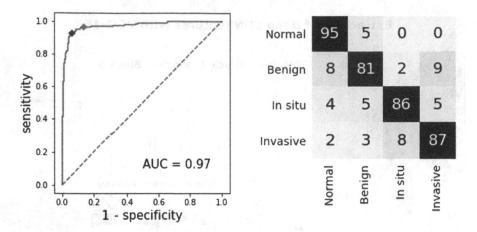

Fig. 4. (a) Non-carcinoma vs. carcinoma classification, ROC. High sensitivity set-point $= 0.33$ (green): 96.5% sensitivity and 88.0% specificity to detect carcinomas. Set-point $= 0.50$ (blue): 93.0% sensitivity and 94.5% specificity (b) Confusion matrix, without normalization. Vertical axis - ground truth, horizontal - predictions. (Color figure online)

Table 1. Accuracy (%) and standard deviation for 4-class classification evaluated over 10 folds via cross-validation. Results for the blended model is in the bottom. Model name represented as ⟨CNN⟩-⟨crop size⟩, thereby VGG-650 denotes LightGBM trained on deep features extracted from 650×650 crops with VGG-16 encoder. Each column in the table corresponds to the fold number.

	f1	f2	f3	f4	f5	f6	f7	f8	f9	f10	**mean**	**std**
ResNet-400	92.0	77.5	86.5	87.5	79.5	84.0	85.0	83.0	84.0	82.5	84.2	4.2
ResNet-650	91.0	77.5	86.0	89.5	81.0	74.0	85.5	83.0	84.5	82.5	83.5	5.2
VGG-400	87.5	83.0	81.5	84.0	84.0	82.5	80.5	82.0	87.5	83.0	83.6	2.9
VGG-650	89.5	85.5	78.5	85.0	81.0	78.0	81.5	85.5	89.0	80.5	83.4	4.4
Inception-400	93.0	86.0	71.5	92.0	85.0	84.5	82.5	79.0	79.5	76.5	83.0	6.5
Inception-650	91.0	84.5	73.5	90.0	84.0	81.0	82.0	84.5	78.0	77.0	82.5	5.5
std	1.8	3.5	5.7	2.8	2.0	3.7	1.8	2.1	3.9	2.7	3.0	-
Model fusion	92.5	82.5	**87.5**	87.5	**87.5**	**90.0**	85.0	**87.5**	87.5	**85.0**	**87.2**	**2.6**

model to detect carcinomas was 96.5% and specificity 88.0%. At the setpoint 0.50 the sensitivity of the model was 93.0% and specificity 94.5%, Fig. 4a. Out of 200 carcinomas cases only 9 *in situ* and 5 invasive were missed, Fig. 4b.

Table 1 shows classification accuracy for 4-class classification. Accuracy averaged across all folds is $87.2 \pm 2.6\%$. Data augmentation and model fusion are particularly evident. The fused model accuracy is by 4–5% higher than any of its individual constituents. The standard deviation of the ensemble across 10 folds is as twice as low than the average standard deviation of individual models. Moreover, all results are slightly improved by averaging across 5 seeded models.

4   Conclusions

In this paper, we propose a simple and effective method for the classification of H&E stained histological breast cancer images in the situation of very small training data (few hundred samples). To increase the robustness of the classifier we use strong data augmentation and deep convolutional features extracted at different scales with publicly available CNNs pretrained on ImageNet. On top of it, we apply accurate and prone to overfitting implementation of the gradient boosting algorithm. Unlike some previous works, we purposely avoid training neural networks on this amount of data to prevent suboptimal generalization.

To our knowledge, the reported results are superior to the automated analysis of breast cancer images reported in literature.

Acknowledgments. The authors thank the Open Data Science community [18] for useful suggestions and other help aiding the development of this work.

References

1. Araújo, T., Aresta, G., Castro, E., Rouco, J., Aguiar, P., Eloy, C., Polónia, A., Campilho, A.: Classification of breast cancer histology images using convolutional neural networks. PloS One **12**(6), e0177544 (2017)
2. Bejnordi, B.E., Veta, M., van Diest, P.J., van Ginneken, B., Karssemeijer, N., Litjens, G., van der Laak, J.A., Hermsen, M., Manson, Q.F., Balkenhol, M., et al.: Diagnostic assessment of deep learning algorithms for detection of lymph node metastases in women with breast cancer. JAMA **318**(22), 2199–2210 (2017)
3. Boureau, Y.L., Ponce, J., LeCun, Y.: A theoretical analysis of feature pooling in visual recognition. In: Proceedings of the 27th International Conference on Machine Learning (ICML-10), pp. 111–118 (2010)
4. Ching, T., Himmelstein, D.S., Beaulieu-Jones, B.K., Kalinin, A.A., Do, B.T., Way, G.P., Ferrero, E., Agapow, P.M., Zietz, M., Hoffman, M.M., Xie, W., Rosen, G.L., Lengerich, B.J., Israeli, J., Lanchantin, J., Woloszynek, S., Carpenter, A.E., Shrikumar, A., Xu, J., Cofer, E.M., Lavender, C.A., Turaga, S.C., Alexandari, A.M., Lu, Z., Harris, D.J., DeCaprio, D., Qi, Y., Kundaje, A., Peng, Y., Wiley, L.K., Segler, M.H.S., Boca, S.M., Swamidass, S.J., Huang, A., Gitter, A., Greene, C.S.: Opportunities and obstacles for deep learning in biology and medicine. J. R. Soc. Interface **15**(141), 20170387 (2018)
5. Deng, J., Dong, W., Socher, R., Li, L.J., Li, K., Fei-Fei, L.: Imagenet: a large-scale hierarchical image database. In: IEEE Conference on Computer Vision and Pattern Recognition, CVPR 2009, pp. 248–255. IEEE (2009)
6. Elmore, J.G., Longton, G.M., Carney, P.A., Geller, B.M., Onega, T., Tosteson, A.N., Nelson, H.D., Pepe, M.S., Allison, K.H., Schnitt, S.J., et al.: Diagnostic concordance among pathologists interpreting breast biopsy specimens. JAMA **313**(11), 1122–1132 (2015)
7. Elston, C.W., Ellis, I.O.: Pathological prognostic factors in breast cancer. i. the value of histological grade in breast cancer: experience from a large study with long-term follow-up. Histopathology **19**(5), 403–410 (1991)
8. Guo, Y., Liu, Y., Oerlemans, A., Lao, S., Wu, S., Lew, M.S.: Deep learning for visual understanding: a review. Neurocomputing **187**, 27–48 (2016)

9. ICIAR 2018 Grand Challenge on Breast Cancer Histology Images. https://iciar2018-challenge.grand-challenge.org/. Accessed 31 Jan 2018
10. Iglovikov, V., Mushinskiy, S., Osin, V.: Satellite imagery feature detection using deep convolutional neural network: a kaggle competition. arXiv preprint arXiv:1706.06169 (2017)
11. Iglovikov, V., Rakhlin, A., Kalinin, A., Shvets, A.: Pediatric bone age assessment using deep convolutional neural networks (2017). arXiv preprint arXiv:1712.05053
12. Iglovikov, V., Shvets, A.: Ternausnet: U-net with vgg11 encoder pre-trained on imagenet for image segmentation (2018). arXiv preprint arXiv:1801.05746
13. Kalinin, A.A., Allyn-Feuer, A., Ade, A., Fon, G.V., Meixner, W., Dilworth, D., Jeffrey, R., Higgins, G.A., Zheng, G., Creekmore, A., et al.: 3d cell nuclear morphology: microscopy imaging dataset and voxel-based morphometry classification results. bioRxiv, 208207 (2017)
14. Ke, G., Meng, Q., Finley, T., Wang, T., Chen, W., Ma, W., Ye, Q., Liu, T.Y.: Lightgbm: a highly efficient gradient boosting decision tree. In: Advances in Neural Information Processing Systems, pp. 3149–3157 (2017)
15. Macenko, M., Niethammer, M., Marron, J., Borland, D., Woosley, J.T., Guan, X., Schmitt, C., Thomas, N.E.: A method for normalizing histology slides for quantitative analysis. In: IEEE International Symposium on Biomedical Imaging: From Nano to Macro, ISBI 2009, pp. 1107–1110. IEEE (2009)
16. Meyer, J.S., Alvarez, C., Milikowski, C., Olson, N., Russo, I., Russo, J., Glass, A., Zehnbauer, B.A., Lister, K., Parwaresch, R.: Breast carcinoma malignancy grading by bloom-richardson system vs proliferation index: reproducibility of grade and advantages of proliferation index. Mod. Pathol. **18**(8), 1067 (2005)
17. Natekin, A., Knoll, A.: Gradient boosting machines, a tutorial. Front. Neurorobot. **7**, 21 (2013)
18. Open Data Science (ODS). https://ods.ai. Accessed 31 Jan 2018
19. Rakhlin, A.: Diabetic retinopathy detection through integration of deep learning classification framework. bioRxiv, 225508 (2017)
20. Robertson, S., Azizpour, H., Smith, K., Hartman, J.: Digital image analysis in breast pathology-from image processing techniques to artificial intelligence. Transl. Res. **194**, 19–35 (2017)
21. Ruifrok, A.C., Johnston, D.A., et al.: Quantification of histochemical staining by color deconvolution. Anal. Quant. Cytol. Histol. **23**(4), 291–299 (2001)
22. Shvets, A., Rakhlin, A., Kalinin, A.A., Iglovikov, V.: Automatic instrument segmentation in robot-assisted surgery using deep learning. arXiv preprint arXiv:1803.01207 (2018)
23. Siegel, R.L., Miller, K.D., Jemal, A.: Cancer statistics, 2018. CA Cancer J. Clin. **68**(1), 7–30 (2018). https://doi.org/10.3322/caac.21442
24. Spanhol, F.A., Oliveira, L.S., Petitjean, C., Heutte, L.: Breast cancer histopathological image classification using convolutional neural networks. In: 2016 International Joint Conference on Neural Networks (IJCNN), pp. 2560–2567. IEEE (2016)
25. Szegedy, C., Ioffe, S., Vanhoucke, V., Alemi, A.A.: Inception-v4, inception-resnet and the impact of residual connections on learning. In: AAAI, vol. 4, p. 12 (2017)
26. Tiulpin, A., Thevenot, J., Rahtu, E., Lehenkari, P., Saarakkala, S.: Automatic knee osteoarthritis diagnosis from plain radiographs: a deep learning-based approach. Sci. Rep. **8**, 1727 (2018)
27. Xu, Y., Jia, Z., Ai, Y., Zhang, F., Lai, M., Eric, I., Chang, C.: Deep convolutional activation features for large scale brain tumor histopathology image classification and segmentation. In: 2015 IEEE International Conference on Acoustics, Speech and Signal Processing (ICASSP), pp. 947–951. IEEE (2015)

Classification of Breast Cancer Histopathological Images using Convolutional Neural Networks with Hierarchical Loss and Global Pooling

Zeya Wang[1,2(✉)] ⓘ, Nanqing Dong[1,3] ⓘ, Wei Dai[1], Sean D. Rosario[1], and Eric P. Xing[1]

[1] Petuum Inc., Pittsburgh, PA 15222, USA
{zeya.wang,nanqing.dong,wei.dai,sean.drosario,eric.xing}@petuum.com
[2] Rice University, Houston, TX 77005, USA
[3] Cornell University, Ithaca, NY 14850, USA

Abstract. Deep learning-based computer-aided diagnosis (CAD) has been gaining popularity for analyzing histopathological images. However, there has been limited work that addresses the problem of accurately classifying breast biopsy tissue with hematoxylin and eosin stained images into different histological grades. We propose a system which can automatically classify breast cancer histology images into four classes, namely normal tissues, benign lesion, *in situ* carcinoma and invasive carcinoma. Our framework uses a Convolutional Neural Network (CNN) with a hierarchical loss, where failing to distinguish between carcinoma and non-carcinoma is penalized more than failing to distinguish between normal and benign or between *in situ* and invasive carcinoma. The network also includes a patch-wise design with global pooling directly on input images. By incorporating the hierarchical and global information of the input images, our framework can outperform the previous system by a large margin.

Keywords: Convolutional Neural Networks · Image classification
Histopathology · Breast cancer · Hierarchical loss

1 Introduction

Breast cancer is one of the leading causes of death by cancer in women, and early detection can give patients more treatment options. Breast cancer can be detected by microscopic analysis [1,2]. During a screening examination, breast tissue biopsies can be obtained from suspected patients, which pathologists analyze for tumor progression and type [2,3]. The tumor type is evaluated in terms of the extent of variation of structure from normal tissues, and how cancer spreads during detection. Benign lesion, *in situ* carcinoma, and invasive carcinoma are three types of tumors that can be determined from biopsy through histological analysis. Benign lesions lack the ability to invade neighbors, so they are non-malignant. *In situ* and invasive carcinoma are malignant, hence spread to other areas. Invasive tissues, unlike *in situ*, invade the surrounding normal tissues beyond the mammary ductal-lobular system [2]. After the microscopic examination of biopsies at specific magnification levels, pathologists generate stained images by applying Hematoxylin-Eosin (H&E) staining to enhance the nuclei (purple) and cytoplasm (pinkish) for the purpose of diagnosis [3]. Stained images are labeled using manual methods based on the experience of pathologists, which is costly in terms of workload. Since the majority of biopsies are normal and benign, most of the work is redundant. CAD approaches for automatic diagnosis improve efficiency by allowing pathologists to focus on more difficult diagnosis cases [3,4]. CAD can reduce the workload of classifying histopathological images, using machine learning methods. Several existing machine learning approaches perform classification for two-class (malignant/benign) and three-class (normal, *in situ*, invasive) through extraction of nuclei-related information [3]. With the rise in computing power, deep learning algorithms are widely adopted for analysis of medical images [5]. In the Camelyon Grand Challenge 2016, several works demonstrated high accuracy for a similar four-class classification task on TNM breast cancer staging system [6]. These works follow a two-stage pipeline. In the first stage, patches that constitute the whole slide image are classified as tumor or normal. In the second stage, the tumor region features extracted from these classified patches are input into a random forest classifier in order to classify the cancer type [7]. That challenge provided pixel-wise annotation of tumors, which is expensive to collect, and not frequently available. In [3], the authors propose a CNN framework to solve the four-class classification problem (normal, benign, *in situ*, invasive) on H&E stained microscopic images by retrieving nuclei and tissue structure information. We believe there is scope for improving classification performance by using better network design. In this paper, we design a loss function that leverages hierarchical information of the histopathological classes. We also incorporate embedded feature maps with information from the input image to maximize grasp on the global context.

2   Data and Methods

2.1   Dataset

The dataset used in this paper is provided by Universidade do Porto, Instituto de Engenharia de Sistemas e Computadores, Tecnologia e Ciência (INESC TEC) and Instituto de Investigação and Inovação em Saúde (i3S), in TIF format. The dataset consists of 400 high resolution (2048 × 1536) H&E stained breast histology microscopic images with 200× magnification. Each pixel of an image corresponds to $0.42\,\mu m \times 0.42\,\mu m$ of the biopsy. These images are labeled with four classes: normal, benign, *in situ*, and *invasive*, and each class consists of 100 images.

Prior to the quantitative analysis, inconsistencies brought by the way of staining the histology slides should be minimized. We perform normalization on all images using the method proposed in [8]. This method first converts RGB values to their corresponding optical density (OD) values through a logarithmic transformation. Then singular value decomposition (SVD) is applied to find the two directions with higher variances of the OD tuples. All the OD transformed pixels are projected onto the plane created from the two SVD directions to find the robust extremes. These extremes are converted to the OD space and then used for deconvolving the original images to the H&E components. Concentrations for each stain are scaled to have the same pseudo-maximum. Finally, all images are recreated using normalized stain concentrations and the reference mixing matrix [9].

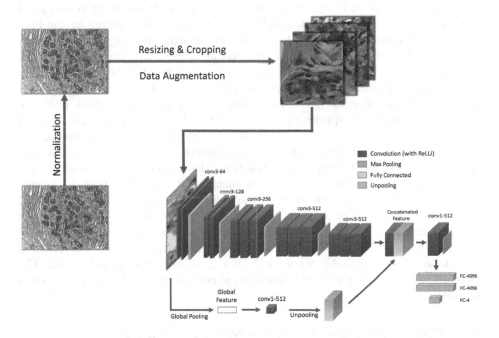

Fig. 1. Illustration of our classification pipeline.

2.2   Image-Wise Classification Framework

Our cancer-type classification framework consists of a data augmentation stage, a patch-wise classification stage, and an image-wise classification stage. After normalizing for staining inconsistencies, we rescale and crop each image to small patches with a size that can be fed as input to the CNN for patch-wise classification (See Fig. 1). The label of each patch is consistent with the label of the image which the patch is cropped from. During the training phase, the cropped patches are augmented to increase the robustness of the model as a method of regularization. A VGG-16 network with a hierarchical loss and global image pooling is trained for classifying these patches into four classes [10–12]. In the inference phase, we generate patches from each test image and combine patch classification results to classify the image [3]. We implement three patch probability score fusion methods for assigning the class label, namely, majority voting, maximum probability, and sum of probabilities [3]. In addition to these fusion techniques, we also adopt dense evaluation over the test image to get a class score map and select the class with the highest score [13]. This is detailed in Sect. 3.

2.3 Data Augmentation

We obtain 280 normalized images in the training set of size 2048×1536. The original images are too large to be fed into the network, so we crop images of size 224×224. Cropping small patches from a 2048×1536 image at the high magnification level of $200\times$ can break the overall structural organization of the image, and therefore leave out important tissue architecture information. While training a CNN model, images are conventionally resized. However, for microscopic images, resizing could decrease magnification level. There is no consensus on the best magnification level, so we isotropically resize the whole image to a relatively small size, specifically, 1024×768 and 512×384 [14]. Each scaled image is then cropped to 224×224 patches with 50% overlap. In our experiments, the final choice for isotropic image resizing is 512×384, which generates a total of 3360 different patches from the original 280 training images. Contrast-limited adaptive histogram equalization (CLAHE) is then performed on the Lightness component after converting the RGB image to LAB format, and then the image is converted back to RGB, for enhancing the local contrast of cropped images [15]. Mean subtraction is performed by subtracting the average value from the R, G and B channels separately. The training set is augmented by image rotation with $\frac{k\pi}{2}$, where $k \in \{0, 1, 2, 3\}$, and vertical reflections. The patches after cropping and augmentation share the same label as the original stained image.

2.4 CNN Architecture for Patch-Wise Classification

The VGG-16 network is chosen to classify the 224×224 histology image patches, in order to explore the scale and organization features of nuclei and the scale features of the overall structure, which do not have complicated semantic information [10]. A 16-layer structure suffices for exploring these features. The VGG-19 network is also used for the sake of comparison in our experiments. To leverage the whole contextual information from the cropped images, we add global context to the last convolutional layer of the VGG network. Similar to ParseNet [12], the input images are passed to two independent branches, our VGG network and a global average pooling layer [12]. With a $B \times H \times W \times C$ input (B is batch size; W and H is the width and height; C is the number of channels), the output of the global pooling layer is $B \times 1 \times 1 \times C$. One 1×1 convolutional layer will transform the last dimension of output to the desired number, which in our case is 512. The transformed output is unpooled to the same shape as that of the feature maps after the last convolutional layer of VGG network and is then concatenated with it. These two feature maps are fused by another 1×1 convolutional layer and then passed through three fully-connected (FC) layers for classification (See Fig. 1).

2.5   Hierarchical Loss

Hierarchical loss is a novel addition to this classification work. As mentioned before, we can further group normal/benign into non-carcinoma, and *in situ*/invasive into carcinoma. The classes have a tree organization, where normal/benign can be considered as leaves from the node non-carcinoma, and *in situ*/invasive as leaves from the node carcinoma. From the root, we have two nodes for carcinoma and non-carcinoma, respectively connected to two leaves normal/benign and *in situ*/invasive. This structure motivates us to apply a hierarchical loss for classification instead of the vanilla cross entropy loss. The hierarchical loss uses an ultrametric tree to calculate the amount of metric "winnings" [11]. Hence, failing to distinguish between carcinoma and non-carcinoma is penalized more than failing to distinguish between normal and benign or between *in situ* and invasive, which follows intuition. The amount of the "winnings" is calculated from the weighted sum of the estimated probability score of each node along the path from the first non-root node to the correct leaf. The probability score of each node is obtained by summing up the scores from its child nodes. The weights are given in Fig. 2. Finally, the loss (the negative of "winnings") uses the negative logarithm as in computing cross entropy loss.

$$L(\hat{\boldsymbol{y}}, \boldsymbol{y}) = -\sum_{i=1}^{N}\sum_{c=1}^{C} y_i^c \log \{\frac{1}{2}\hat{y}_i^c + \frac{1}{2}(\hat{y}_i^c + \sum_{c' \in siblings(c)} \hat{y}_i^{c'})\} \qquad (1)$$

For class hierarchy with a height equal 2, the loss function is defined as shown in Eq. 1, where y_i^c is the binary label of sample i belonging to class c, $\hat{y}_i^c$ is softmax output for the labeled class channel c, C the number of channels, N the number of samples, and $siblings(\cdot)$ denotes the sibling set of classes for a specified class node.

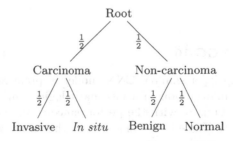

Fig. 2. Tree representation of "winnings" in the hierarchical loss.

3   Experiments

In this section, we present our evaluation results in terms of accuracy for patch-wise and image-wise classification as per [3]. We demonstrate the performance of our proposed framework through a series of ablation studies.

3.1   Experimental Setup

We first randomly split all images to 280 images for training, 60 images for validation and 60 images for testing. All four classes are distributed equally between splits. The objective of the model is to minimize the hierarchical loss using a momentum optimizer with momentum 0.9 and batch size 32 [16]. The weights of the network are initialized with the pre-trained weights of the VGG-16 model on ImageNet [17]. The learning rate is initialized to 0.0002 and decreases exponentially every 1000 mini-batch iterations with a decay factor of 0.9. The weights are regularized with weight decay with L2 penalty multiplier of 0.003. Dropout with ratio 0.5 is applied to the first two fully-connected layers. Training usually converges very quickly (after around 5 epochs). At test time, we first pre-process and resize test images, and then classify each test image using the aforementioned fusion methods. In the dense evaluation, we convert the last three FC layers in VGG networks to convolutional layers, and then densely apply the converted networks over the rescaled test image to get a class score map. The class with the highest score is selected [13]. Our final results are shown below in Table 1. For each performance reported, the patch-wise classification accuracy is calculated with the same model used in image-wise classification.

Table 1. Image-wise classification accuracy (%) of best model setting with different post-processing methods (patch-wise accuracy (%) given in the bracket).

	Majority vote	Sum probability	Maximum probability	Dense evaluation
Validation set	0.92 (0.87)	0.92 (0.87)	0.92 (0.87)	0.92 (0.87)
Test set	0.93 (0.85)	0.90 (0.85)	0.92 (0.85)	0.92 (0.85)
Average	0.93	0.91	0.92	0.92

3.2   VGG-19 vs. VGG-16

As described previously, a shallow CNN model is preferred by virtue of the content of semantic information in a histopathological image. To support this heuristic choice, we compare with the performance of the deeper VGG-19 (See Table 2 compared with Table 1) to demonstrate that a network with an appropriate depth is able to perform better.

Table 2. Image-wise classification accuracy (%) of using VGG-19 with different post-processing methods (patch-wise accuracy (%) given in the bracket).

	Majority vote	Sum probability	Maximum probability	Dense evaluation
Validation set	0.85 (0.76)	0.83 (0.76)	0.80 (0.74)	0.82 (0.76)
Test set	0.80 (0.72)	0.80 (0.73)	0.80 (0.71)	0.80 (0.74)
Average	0.83	0.82	0.80	0.81

Table 3. Image-wise classification accuracy (%) of removing hierarchical loss with different post-processing methods (patch-wise accuracy (%) given in the bracket).

	Majority vote	Sum probability	Maximum probability	Dense evaluation
Validation set	0.88 (0.82)	0.87 (0.82)	0.88 (0.82)	0.87 (0.81)
Test set	0.88 (0.83)	0.87 (0.81)	0.85 (0.81)	0.87 (0.83)
Average	0.88	0.87	0.87	0.87

3.3 Hierarchical Loss vs. No Hierarchical Loss

To emphasize the importance of using hierarchical loss, we include a comparison experiment that just uses the vanilla cross entropy loss. The results of the experiment are shown below in Table 3 (compared with Table 1).

3.4 Global Image Pooling vs. No Global Image Pooling

Global image pooling is another important feature we integrate into our network architecture. This structure, which is often used for global information extraction from high resolution feature maps, can pass global context from the input image to the last convolution layer in deep networks, thus improving the final performance. We also include an experiment without image pooling layers with its results (see Table 4 compared with Table 1), to demonstrate its improvement of model performance.

Table 4. Image-wise classification accuracy (%) of removing global average pooling with different post-processing methods (patch-wise accuracy (%) given in the bracket).

	Majority vote	Sum probability	Maximum probability	Dense evaluation
Validation set	0.93 (0.90)	0.93 (0.90)	0.93 (0.90)	0.93 (0.90)
Test set	0.87 (0.84)	0.87 (0.84)	0.90 (0.84)	0.87 (0.84)
Average	0.90	0.90	0.92	0.90

3.5 Different Scales

The microscopic images are obtained with a high magnification level of 200×, for capturing the nuclei-scale feature. We pre-process the large image into different

224 × 224 patches that can be fed into the VGG networks. However, this crop-ping could result in a loss of most of the structural information. Thus, we first isotropically resize the 2048 × 1536 image into a smaller scale before cropping. In our presented performance, the width and height are both down-scaled 4× to 512 × 384 respectively. This scale is used because it can maintain most of the nuclei structural information from the original whole image, while keeping most information of tissue structural organization for the cropped patches. We include a larger scale 1024 × 768 for comparison with results shown in Table 5 (compared with Table 1).

Table 5. Image-wise classification accuracy (%) of resizing images to 1024 × 768 with different post-processing methods (patch-wise accuracy (%) given in the bracket).

	Majority vote	Sum probability	Maximum probability	Dense evaluation
Validation set	0.82 (0.72)	0.82 (0.72)	0.83 (0.72)	0.83 (0.72)
Test set	0.75 (0.68)	0.75 (0.68)	0.78 (0.68)	0.78 (0.68)
Average	0.79	0.79	0.81	0.81

4   Discussion

In this work, we present a CNN-based approach with preprocessing and post-processing methods to classify of H&E stained histopathological images for breast cancer tissue classification. We propose to resize and crop images after considering the trade-off between capturing nuclei associated scale information and the overall structural organization. We utilize the VGG-16 network, which has been successful in general image recognition tasks [10,17]. Additionally, we apply a hierarchical loss based on the biological nature of the problem, and use global average pooling to incorporate the global information in an image. Our approach succeeds in classification of cancer types and shows competitive performance on the given dataset.

Magnification is an important factor for analyzing microscopic images for diag-nosis. The most informative magnification is still debatable, so we compare two possible scales in our work. In future work, we will study the influence of other scales on the performance.

References

1. Siegel, R.L., Miller, K.D., Jemal, A.: Cancer statistics, 2016. CA Cancer J. Clin. **66**(1), 7–30 (2016)
2. American Cancer Society: Breast Cancer Facts & Figures 2017–2018. American Cancer Society, Inc., Atlanta (2017)
3. Araújo, T., Aresta, G., Castro, E., Rouco, J., Aguiar, P., Eloy, C., Polónia, A., Campilho, A.: Classification of breast cancer histology images using convolutional neural networks. PloS One **12**(6), e0177544 (2017)

4. Gurcan, M.N., Boucheron, L.E., Can, A., Madabhushi, A., Rajpoot, N.M., Yener, B.: Histopathological image analysis: a review. IEEE Rev. Biomed. Eng. **2**, 147–171 (2009)
5. Litjens, G., Kooi, T., Bejnordi, B.E., Setio, A.A.A., Ciompi, F., Ghafoorian, M., van der Laak, J.A.W.M., van Ginneken, B., Sánchez, C.I.: A survey on deep learning in medical image analysis. Med. Image Anal. **42**, 60–88 (2017)
6. Ehteshami Bejnordi, B., Veta, M., van Diest, P.J., et al.: Diagnostic assessment of deep learning algorithms for detection of lymph node metastases in women with breast cancer. JAMA **318**(22), 2199–2210 (2017)
7. Wang, D., Khosla, A., Gargeya, R., Irshad, H., Beck, A.H.: Deep learning for identifying metastatic breast cancer. arXiv preprint arXiv:1606.05718 (2016)
8. Macenko, M., Niethammer, M., Marron, J.S., Borland, D., Woosley, J.T., Guan, X., Schmitt, C., Thomas, N.E.: A method for normalizing histology slides for quantitative analysis. In: IEEE International Symposium on Biomedical Imaging: From Nano to Macro, ISBI 2009, pp. 1107–1110. IEEE (2009)
9. Veta, M., van Diest, P.J., Willems, S.M., Wang, H., Madabhushi, A., Cruz-Roa, A., Gonzalez, F., Larsen, A.B., Vestergaard, J.S., Dahl, A.B., et al.: Assessment of algorithms for mitosis detection in breast cancer histopathology images. Med. Image Anal. **20**(1), 237 (2015)
10. Simonyan, K., Zisserman, A.: Very deep convolutional networks for large-scale image recognition. arXiv preprint arXiv:1409.1556 (2014)
11. Wu, C., Tygert, M., LeCun, Y.: Hierarchical loss for classification. arXiv preprint arXiv:1709.01062 (2017)
12. Liu, W., Rabinovich, A., Berg, A.C.: Parsenet: Looking wider to see better. In: CoRR. Citeseer (2015)
13. Sermanet, P., Eigen, D., Zhang, X., Mathieu, M., Fergus, R., Lecun, Y.: Overfeat: integrated recognition, localization and detection using convolutional networks. In: International Conference on Learning Representations (ICLR2014), CBLS, April 2014
14. Komura, D., Ishikawa, S.: Machine learning methods for histopathological image analysis. arXiv preprint arXiv:1709.00786 (2017)
15. Pizer, S.M., Amburn, E.P., Austin, J.D., Cromartie, R., Geselowitz, A., Greer, T., ter Haar Romeny, B., Zimmerman, J.B., Zuiderveld, K.: Adaptive histogram equalization and its variations. Comput. Vis. Graph. Image Process. **39**(3), 355–368 (1987)
16. Sutskever, I., Martens, J., Dahl, G., Hinton, G.: On the importance of initialization and momentum in deep learning. In: International Conference on Machine Learning, pp. 1139–1147 (2013)
17. Deng, J., Dong, W., Socher, R., Li, L.-J., Li, K., Fei-Fei, L.: Imagenet: a large-scale hierarchical image database. In: IEEE Conference on Computer Vision and Pattern Recognition, CVPR 2009, pp. 248–255. IEEE (2009)

Breast Cancer Histological Image Classification Using Fine-Tuned Deep Network Fusion

Amirreza Mahbod[1,2(✉)], Isabella Ellinger[1], Rupert Ecker[2], Örjan Smedby[3], and Chunliang Wang[3]

[1] Institute of Pathophysiology and Allergy Research, Medical University of Vienna, Vienna, Austria
[2] Department of Research and Development, TissueGnostics GmbH, Vienna, Austria
amirreza.mahbod@tissuegnostics.com
[3] Department of Biomedical Engineering and Health Systems, Division of Biomedical Imaging, KTH Royal Institute of Technology, Stockholm, Sweden

Abstract. Breast cancer is the most common cancer type in women worldwide. Histological evaluation of the breast biopsies is a challenging task even for experienced pathologists. In this paper, we propose a fully automatic method to classify breast cancer histological images to four classes, namely normal, benign, *in situ* carcinoma and invasive carcinoma. The proposed method takes normalized hematoxylin and eosin stained images as input and gives the final prediction by fusing the output of two residual neural networks (ResNet) of different depth. These ResNets were first pre-trained on ImageNet images, and then fine-tuned on breast histological images. We found that our approach outperformed a previous published method by a large margin when applied on the BioImaging 2015 challenge dataset yielding an accuracy of 97.22%. Moreover, the same approach provided an excellent classification performance with an accuracy of 88.50% when applied on the ICIAR 2018 grand challenge dataset using 5-fold cross validation.

Keywords: Breast cancer · Histological images · Classification
Deep learning

1 Introduction

Breast cancer is the most frequent cancer among women. Moreover, it ranks at place one as cause of death from cancer in women [1]. Early detection of breast cancer is crucial, since more than 90% of women diagnosed with breast cancer at the earliest stage survive their disease for at least 5 years. Distant organ tumor metastases, in contrast, are essentially incurable and cause over 90% of cancer deaths. Thus, in many countries screening methods such as mammography have been implemented as important tools for early cancer detection in order to reduce breast cancer mortality [2,3].

© Springer International Publishing AG, part of Springer Nature 2018
A. Campilho et al. (Eds.): ICIAR 2018, LNCS 10882, pp. 754–762, 2018.
https://doi.org/10.1007/978-3-319-93000-8_85

Suspicious breast lesions detected by screening require the histological evaluation of the biopsies by pathologists. Examination of hematoxylin and eosin (H&E) stained samples remains the most important and fundamental method for breast cancer diagnosis and should discriminate normal or healthy breast tissue from benign lesions, *in situ* and invasive breast cancer (see Fig. 1 for examples). The vast majority of breast lesions are benign [4]. Among breast malignancies, more than 95% arise from epithelial cells. *In situ* carcinoma are neoplastic lesions still confined to the breast ducts and lobules, while in invasive carcinomas, tumor cells start to infiltrate the surrounding tissue. Overall, benign lesions as well as breast carcinomas are heterogenous groups of lesions that differ in microscopic appearance and biologic behavior [5,6].

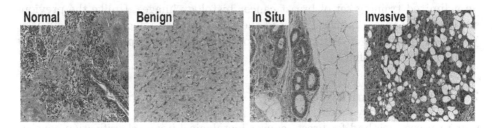

Fig. 1. Examples of different forms of breast tissue biopsies, H&E stained and acquired with 200x magnification. (Images are adapted from ICIAR 2018 grand challenge on breast cancer histology classification).

Even for experienced pathologists, manual analysis always causes intra- or inter-observer variation [7], which can result in an inaccurate evaluation. At the same time, the demand for accuracy in histopathologic breast cancer diagnosis is increasing. In addition, there is a lack of pathologists in many parts of the world. In this context, digital pathology and automated image analysis tools offer the possibility for pathologists to make faster and more accurate assessments. Diverse image processing techniques to assist histopathologic breast cancer diagnosis have evolved over the past years [8].

In some studies, nuclei level information (fine details) were analyzed for tissue classification. In classical approaches, hand-crafted nuclei features such as texture and morphological features were extracted in order to train a classical classifier such as artificial neural networks or support vector machine [9–11]. In some other studies, beside nuclei information, hand-crafted tissue features (context information) were also utilized for algorithm training [12].

With the advent of convolutional neural networks (CNNs) and their excellent performance for natural image classification [13,14], there is a growing trend to adapt them for medical images. In contrast to conventional machine learning approaches for image classification, they do not rely on hand-crafted features, but utilize large amount of images to derive task-specific image features that can be represented by convolution kernels through their special contracting architectures [13,14]. Several studies on using CNNs for breast cancer histological image analysis have been reported in the literature. In most of the early studies, patch-wise classification using CNNs were investigated, while image-wise classification is based on the combination of patch probabilities. The patch size varied in different studies (e.g. from 32×32 to 512×512) and in most cases a novel CNN architecture was trained on a limited dataset from scratch [15–18].

In this study, we propose a fully automatic computerized method based on fusion of fine-tuned deep neural networks for classifying breast histological image to four classes, including normal tissue, benign lesion, *in situ* carcinoma and invasive carcinoma. In our approach, instead of training relative small CNNs from scratch, we utilize very deep neural networks that are pre-trained on Ima-geNet [19]. This work is based on our previous work on ensemble multiple CNNs for skin lesion classification [20], with the extension of fine-tuning the networks on a limited training set of breast cancer histology images. Unlike the previous studies using image patches, we feed the whole resized images to the networks. We also experiment several normalization techniques to improve the robustness of the trained classifier.

2   Materials and Methods

Our proposed method for breast cancer histological image classification consists of two major steps: image pre-processing and normalization, and deep learning based image classification. In the following subsections, we describe in details all steps of our approach.

2.1   Dataset

We used two datasets in this work which were the BioImaging 2015 chal-lenge (BI) dataset[1] and the ICIAR 2018 grand challenge (ICIAR) dataset[2]. The second dataset was an extended version of the first dataset and both con-tained 24 bits RGB H&E stained breast histological images with pixel size of $0.42\,\mu m \times 0.42\,\mu m$, acquired with 200x magnification and extracted from whole slide image biopsies. Both datasets contained four different classes of breast can-cer histological images, namely normal tissues, benign lesions, *in situ* cracinomas and invasive carcinomas. The first dataset contained 249 training images that were equally distributed among the four classes. It also contained 36 test images that were divided in two groups, namely initial group (20 images that were less challenging for classification) and extended group (16 images that were more challenging for classification). The second dataset contained 100 images in each class, i.e., in total 400 training images, which included the training and testing images from the BI dataset. The testing images of the second dataset were kept away from challenge participants at the time of the submission of this report and will be used for evaluation of different approaches by the challenge organiz-ers. The size of each image in all datasets was 2048×1536 pixels. Labeling of

---

[1] https://rdm.inesctec.pt/dataset/nis-2017-003.

[2] https://iciar2018-challenge.grand-challenge.org/dataset/.

the images was performed by two medical experts and images where there was disagreement between pathologists were discarded.

2.2 Pre-processing

In our proposed pipeline, we used two major pre-processing steps before feeding the images to the deep networks:

Normalization. Staining variation is very common in histology images. This is due to many factors such as variations in chemical agent manufactures, storage condition prior to use and staining protocols [21]. Some examples of this staining variability is shown in Fig. 1. In order to deal with this problem, we tried two different normalization techniques to reduce the color scheme variation and improve the robustness of the following classification method. These two methods were:

- **RGB histogram matching**: We chose a random reference image from the dataset and calculated its cumulative histogram for all intensity levels for each individual RGB channels and then, we matched the RGB histogram of all other training and test images accordingly [22]. Although the background pixels of the both reference and target images were used during the histogram computations, the background pixels were ignored in the transformation. For background detection, Otsu's thresholding method was utilized [23].
- **Macenko et al. method** [21]: The RGB values were converted to optimal density (OD) for both reference and target images. Next, part of data which had an intensity value less than a threshold, β, were removed. Then, the singular value decomposition (SVD) was applied on OD tuples. In the next step, a plane was created using the two largest values from SVD directions and afterwards the data were projected to the created plane to form the stain separation vectors. The stain separation vectors which represented H&E staining of the reference image were used to change H&E intensity values of the target image. More detailed information about this approach can be found in [21]. Similar to RGB histogram matching, background pixels remained unchanged during this pre-processing step.

After applying the aforementioned normalization techniques, we subtracted the mean RGB value of the ImageNet dataset from all training and test images as the utilized networks in our approach were initially trained on this dataset [13].

Resizing. The utilized deep pre-trained networks with fully connected (FC) layers expect the input images to have a certain size. Thus, we resized all images to have appropriate size (224×224) using bicubic interpolation. The aspect ratio of the original images was changed during this resizing step.

2.3 CNN Fine-Tuning and Fusion

We utilized two well-established pre-trained deep CNNs, ResNet-50 and ResNet-101 [14] which have shown excellent performance for natural image classification. Deep residual networks have a specialized layer architecture referred as residual blocks with shortcut connections which is followed by a FC layer at the top of the network. ResNet-50 has 17 residual blocks while ResNet-101 is much deeper and consists of 33 residual blocks. More details about the architecture of these networks can be found in [14]. Since these networks were initially trained on several hundred thousands of natural images, it was not possible to use them directly for breast cancer histological image classification. Hence, we used the transfer learning method by taking the ResNet networks pre-trained on natural images and fine-tuning them on breast histological slides, to be able to exploit them in our classification problem.

For fine-tuning, we removed the last FC layers of the networks and replaced them by two new FC layers with 64 and 4 nodes to perform classification for 4 classes. The weights of these newly added layers were randomly chosen from a Gaussian distribution with zero mean and standard deviation of 0.01. Then, we retrained all layers including FC and convolution layers, but kept the learning rate (LR) of the new FC layers 10 times bigger compared to all other learnable layers. We used stochastic gradient descent with momentum and L2 regularization term for fine-tuning of the networks. We chose an initial LR of 0.001 which dropped by a factor of 10 after each 5 epochs. We chose weight decay of 0.0001 and momentum of 0.9 for performing optimization and retrained the network for 25 epochs.

In order to prevent the network from overfitting to our limited datasets, we artificially increased our training data size through data augmentation. We used rotation (0, 90, 180 and 270°) and horizontal flipping as the main augmentation techniques. During the inference stage on the test data, we applied similar data augmentation techniques. This means that 8 images (rotated and horizontally flipped images) were created from a single test image and were fed to the fine-tuned network. The average output probabilities of the network applied on these images was chosen as the final classification result for a specific test image.

Moreover, we tested the network fusion scheme to see its effect on method's performance. For fusing the results on a test image, we took the average over the network's prediction vectors.

2.4 Evaluation

Evaluation of the proposed method was performed by calculating the overall accuracy of all four classes which is also the main evaluation metric in both the BI and ICIAR challenge. In order to obtain overall accuracy, we chose the maximum value in each 4 elemental prediction vector for each test image and then set its corresponding label as the method's chosen class.

3   Results

The reported results in this section are derived from the BI and the ICIAR datasets. For the BI dataset, 36 provided test images were used for evaluation which consisted of 20 easy samples (initial group) and 16 challenging cases (extended group) for classification. For the ICIAR dataset since the test data are not available at the time of submitting this paper, we used 5-fold cross validation on the training set and averaged the accuracy over all test folds. Since one of the dataset is an extended version of the other dataset, we isolated the networks for reporting the results (i.e. the trained networks for the second dataset were not used for evaluation of the test data of the first dataset).

We started our experiments by investigating the normalization effect on general performance. The summarized results of this part for the BI dataset are shown in Tables 1 and 2. The results reported in these tables are obtained by running the whole algorithm for 5 times and taking the average over network outputs to obtain the final classification prediction. As we observed better overall performance using the RGB histogram matching normalization technique, we did not use the other normalization techniques in further experiments.

Table 1. Effects of various normalization techniques on accuracy (acc) using fine-tuned ResNet-50 applied on the BI dataset.

Normalization	Initial acc (%)	Extended acc (%)	Overall acc (%)
RGB histogram matching	95.00	87.50	91.67
Macenko et al. [21]	90.00	81.25	86.11
No normalization	90.00	75.00	83.33

Table 2. Effects of various normalization techniques on accuracy (acc) using fine-tuned ResNet-101 applied on the BI dataset.

Normalization	Initial acc (%)	Extended acc (%)	Overall acc (%)
RGB histogram matching	95.00	75.00	86.11
Macenko et al. [21]	85.00	81.25	83.33
No normalization	80.00	75.00	77.78

Results in Table 3 show the network fusion effect on accuracy performance. The last row of Table 3 also shows the results from a previous study on the BI dataset which was based on patch wise classification, training a novel and rather small CNN from scratch and using Macenko et al. normalization method [15].

Table 3. Network fusion comparison based on accuracy (acc).

Network	Overall acc on the BI dataset (%)	Overall acc on the ICIAR dataset (%)
ResNet-50	91.67	87.75
ResNet-101	86.11	88.00
ResNet-50 + ResNet-101	97.22	88.50
Araujo et al. method [15]	77.8	N/A

4   Discussion and Conclusion

In this study, we present a new approach for breast cancer histological image classification based on fusion of fine-tuned deep networks.

As results in Tables 1 and 2 suggest, using a proper normalization technique could improve the classification accuracy. However, how to choose the best reference image remains a difficult question, which should be addressed in future studies. Moreover, the accuracy obtained from the extended images were inferior compared to the initial images due to increased complexity of the extended dataset which was also reported in [15].

It can be inferred from Table 3 that even using a single fine-tuned ResNet instead of training a new CNN from scratch which was suggested in [15], delivers better accuracy by high margin. The effect of network output fusion is also shown in Table 3. As the results suggest, network output combination can deliver better performance compared to each individual network. Our best results were obtained by fusing ResNet-50 and ResNet-101 networks' output for both BI and ICIAR datasets. However, as the test data size in both cases are relative small (i.e. 36 images for the BI and 80 images for the ICIAR using 5-fold cross validation), investigating the real effect of fusion scheme is not trivial.

In conclusion, in this paper a fully automatic method is proposed for breast cancer histological image classification based on fusion of fine-tuned deep networks applied on RGB histogram matched images which delivers excellent performance for two datasets used in this work. Improving the performance could be potentially achieved by utilizing better normalization techniques, using more extensive training data and fusing more fine-tuned deep models. These suggestions are open for investigation in further studies.

Acknowledgments. This project is supported by Horizon 2020 Framework of the European Union in the CaSR Biomedicine project, No. 675228.

References

1. Torre, L.A., Bray, F., Siegel, R.L., Ferlay, J., Lortet Tieulent, J., Jemal, A.: Global cancer statistics, 2012. CA Cancer J. Clin. **65**(2), 87–108 (2015)
2. Saadatmand, S., Bretveld, R., Siesling, S., Tilanus-Linthorst, M.M.A.: Influence of tumour stage at breast cancer detection on survival in modern times: population based study in 173 797 patients. BMJ **351**, h4901 (2015)
3. Myers, E.R., Moorman, P., Gierisch, J.M., Havrilesky, L.J., Grimm, L.J., Ghate, S., Davidson, B., Mongtomery, R.C., Crowley, M.J., McCrory, D.C.: Benefits and harms of breast cancer screening: a systematic review. JAMA **314**(15), 1615–1634 (2015)
4. Guray, M., Sahin, A.A.: Benign breast diseases: classification, diagnosis, and management. Oncol. **11**(5), 435–449 (2006)
5. Malhotra, G.K., Zhao, X., Band, H., Band, V.: Histological, molecular and functional subtypes of breast cancers. Cancer Biol. Ther. **10**(10), 955–960 (2010)
6. Makki, J.: Diversity of breast carcinoma: histological subtypes and clinical relevance. Clin. Med. Insights Pathol. **8**, 23 (2015)
7. Elmore, J.G., Longton, G.M., Carney, P.A., Geller, B.M., Onega, T., Tosteson, A.N.A., Nelson, H.D., Pepe, M.S., Allison, K.H., Schnitt, S.J.: Diagnostic concordance among pathologists interpreting breast biopsy specimens. JAMA **313**(11), 1122–1132 (2015)
8. Robertson, S., Azizpour, H., Smith, K., Hartman, J.: Digital image analysis in breast pathology-from image processing techniques to artificial intelligence. Translational Research **194**, 19–35 (2018)
9. Kowal, M., Filipczuk, P., Obuchowicz, A., Korbicz, J., Monczak, R.: Computer-aided diagnosis of breast cancer based on fine needle biopsy microscopic images. Comput. Biol. Med. **43**(10), 1563–1572 (2013)
10. Filipczuk, P., Fevens, T., Krzyzak, A., Monczak, R.: Computer-aided breast cancer diagnosis based on the analysis of cytological images of fine needle biopsies. IEEE Trans. Med. Imaging **32**(12), 2169–2178 (2013)
11. Brook, A., El-Yaniv, R., Isler, E., Kimmel, R., Meir, R., Peleg, D.: Breast cancer diagnosis from biopsy images using generic features and SVMs. Technical report, Technion - Israel Institute of Technology (2006)
12. Belsare, A.D., Mushrif, M.M., Pangarkar, M.A., Meshram, N.: Classification of breast cancer histopathology images using texture feature analysis. In: TENCON 2015–2015 IEEE Region 10 Conference, pp. 1–5. IEEE (2015)
13. Krizhevsky, A., Sutskever, I., Hinton, G.E.: Imagenet classification with deep convolutional neural networks. Adv. Neural Inf. Process. Syst. **25**, 1097–1105 (2012)
14. He, K., Zhang, X., Ren, S., Sun, J.: Deep residual learning for image recognition. In: Proceedings of the IEEE Conference on Computer Vision and Pattern Recognition, pp. 770–778 (2016)
15. Araújo, T., Aresta, G., Castro, E., Rouco, J., Aguiar, P., Eloy, C., Polónia, A., Campilho, A.: Classification of breast cancer histology images using convolutional neural networks. PloS One **12**(6), e0177544 (2017)
16. Spanhol, F.A., Oliveira, L.S., Petitjean, C., Heutte, L.: Breast cancer histopathological image classification using convolutional neural networks. In: 2016 International Joint Conference on Neural Networks (IJCNN), pp. 2560–2567. IEEE (2016)
17. Cireşan, D.C., Giusti, A., Gambardella, L.M., Schmidhuber, J.: Mitosis detection in breast cancer histology images with deep neural networks. In: Mori, K., Sakuma, I., Sato, Y., Barillot, C., Navab, N. (eds.) MICCAI 2013. LNCS, vol. 8150, pp. 411–418. Springer, Heidelberg (2013). https://doi.org/10.1007/978-3-642-40763-5_51

18. Cruz-Roa, A., Basavanhally, A., González, F., Gilmore, H., Feldman, M., Ganesan, S., Shih, N., Tomaszewski, J., Madabhushi, A.: Automatic detection of invasive ductal carcinoma in whole slide images with convolutional neural networks. In: SPIE Medical Imaging. International Society for Optics and Photonics, vol. 9041, pp. 904103 (2014)
19. Deng, J., Dong, W., Socher, R., Li, L.J., Li, K., Fei-Fei, L.: Imagenet: a large-scale hierarchical image database. In: IEEE Conference on Computer Vision and Pattern Recognition, CVPR 2009, pp. 248–255. IEEE (2009)
20. Mahbod, A., Ecker, R., Ellinger, I.: Skin lesion classification using hybrid deep neural networks. arXiv preprint arXiv:1702.08434 (2017)
21. Macenko, M., Niethammer, M., Marron, J.S., Borland, D., Woosley, J.T., Guan, X., Schmitt, C., Thomas, N.E.: A method for normalizing histology slides for quantitative analysis. In: IEEE International Symposium on Biomedical Imaging: From Nano to Macro, ISBI 2009, pp. 1107–1110. IEEE (2009)
22. Jain, A.K.: Fundamentals of Digital Image Processing. Prentice-Hall, Inc., Englewood Cliffs (1989)
23. Otsu, N.: A threshold selection method from gray-level histograms. IEEE Trans. Syst. Man Cybern. 9(1), 62–66 (1979)

Classification of Breast Cancer Histology Images Through Transfer Learning Using a Pre-trained Inception Resnet V2

Carlos A. Ferreira[1]([✉]) [iD], Tânia Melo[1] [iD], Patrick Sousa[1] [iD],
Maria Inês Meyer[1] [iD], Elham Shakibapour[1] [iD], Pedro Costa[1] [iD],
and Aurélio Campilho[1,2] [iD]

[1] INESC-TEC - Institute for Systems and Computer Engineering,
Technology and Science, Porto, Portugal
{carlos.a.ferreira,tania.f.melo,patrick.sousa,maria.i.meyer,
elham.shakibapour,pvcosta}@inesctec.pt
[2] Faculty of Engineering, University of Porto, Porto, Portugal
campilho@fe.up.pt

Abstract. Breast cancer is one of the leading causes of female death worldwide. The histological analysis of breast tissue allows for the differentiation of the tissue suspected to be abnormal into four classes: normal tissue, benign tumor, *in situ* carcinoma and invasive carcinoma. Automatic diagnostic systems can help in that task. In this sense, this work propose a deep neural network approach using transfer learning to classify breast cancer histology images. First, the added top layers are trained and a second fine-tunning is done on some feature extraction layers that are frozen previously. The used network is an Inception Resnet V2. In order to overcome the lack of data, data augmentation is performed too. This work is a suggested solution for the ICIAR 2018 BACH-Challenge and the accuracy is 0.76 in the blind test set.

Keywords: Breast cancer diagnosis
Breast histology images classification · Convolutional neural network
Inception resnet v2 · Transfer learning · Data augmentation
Fine-tuning

1 Introduction

Breast cancer consists in a malignant proliferation of the epithelial cells present in the ducts or lobes of the breast [1]. It is the most diagnosed cancer in women worldwide and the second leading cause of death among them. Fortunately, in the last years, the morbidity and mortality rates have decreased due to better screening procedures, which allow to do an early detection of the disease, and the improvement of treatment options [2].

Breast cancer is commonly detected by clinical examination of the breast via palpation or mammograms. Most masses detected in the screening examinations are benign. Unlike the malignant tissue, the benign lesions do not grow uncontrollably and are not life-threatening [3]. When the detected mass is suspicious, a pathologist performs a histological examination of the tissue obtained from a needle biopsy. This examination allows to distinguish between normal, benign and malignant tissues based on the analysis of tissue architecture and nuclei organization [4]. However, this analysis is not trivial and different pathologists can classify the same sample in a different way, which leads to overinterpreted and underinterpreted diagnoses [5]. Furthermore, it is a time-consuming task.

In order to reduce the cost and increase the efficiency of the classification, in this work, we present a methodology for automatic classification of hematoxylin and eosin (H & E) stained breast microscopy images into four classes: normal tissue, benign abnormality, malignant *in situ* carcinoma and malignant invasive carcinoma (Fig. 1). A benign tumor is characterized by the accumulation of a significant number of cells in the ducts and lobes. Unlike the malignant tissues, the variation of cells' size and shape in this type of lesions is minimal. In turn, the classification of a malignant tissue as invasive carcinoma or *in situ* carcinoma depends on the presence of abnormal cells in other breast regions beyond the ducts and lobes. The staining enhances nuclei (purple) and cytoplasm (pinkish). The lumen appears white.

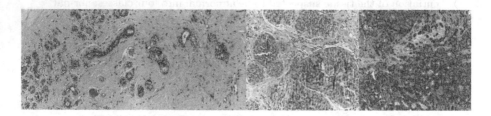

Fig. 1. Hematoxylin and eosin stained breast histology microscopy images (from left to right): normal tissue, benign lesion, *in situ* and invasive carcinoma (Color figure online)

2 Related Work

Taking into account that a benign tissue can be distinguished from a malignant tissue based on the analysis of nuclei morphology, several authors extract nuclei-based features from stained microscopy images and use them for classifying the tissues into benign and malignant (binary classification) [6–8]. Filipczuk et al. [7] use the circular Hough transform for an initial detection of the nuclei candidates and a support vector machine (SVM) to discriminate "correct candidates" from "incorrect candidates". Morphological and texture features are then extracted from the candidates that were classified as "correct" in the previous step. In [8] the authors refine the nuclei contour using a watershed and in [6] four clustering algorithms for nuclei segmentation are tested. Belsare et al. [9] segment the epithelial cells surrounding the lumen using a spatio-color-texture graph segmentation method, extract texture features and then compare the performance of a linear discriminant analyzer classifier with k-Nearest Neighbors classifier and SVM.

Although all works mentioned above present methodologies to classify the breast histology images into benign or malignant, other authors considered the classification of these images as a multiclass problem. For instance, in [10] the author used a fusion of two Random Subspace classifier ensembles in order to classify the images into 3 classes: normal, *in situ* carcinoma and invasive carcinoma. In this approach, one of the ensembles consists of SVM classifiers and the other is based on multiple layer perceptrons. Regarding to the feature extraction step, Zhang [10] combines a local binary pattern texture analysis with Curvelet Transform.

In the last years, the deep learning models have become more and more popular. Therefore, several authors also extended the use of Convolutional Neural Networks (CNNs) for classifying breast histology images. Cruz-Roa et al. [11] presented a deep learning approach for the detection of invasive ductal carcinoma in whole slide images. In this approach, a CNN is trained over a large amount of tissue regions (patches) with size 100×100 pixels. Since the features extracted contain information about not only the nuclei but also the tissue organization, this approach outperforms the other state-of-the-art methods. Recently, Araújo et al. [4] also proposed a deep learning approach for classifying breast histology images into four classes: normal tissue, benign lesion, *in situ* carcinoma and invasive carcinoma. Similarly to [11], the architecture of the CNN used in [4] also retrieves information at different scales. In this work, a data augmentation method was also applied to increase the amount of training data. For comparative purposes, Araújo et al. [4] trained a SVM with the features detected by the CNN. The accuracy of the approach presented in [4] is 77.8% and the sensitivity for cancer cases is 95.6%.

2.1 Deep Convolutional Neural Networks

Deep convolutional neural networks (DCNN) have achieved unprecedented performance in the field of image classification and recognition. A DCNN recognizes an object by looking for low level features such as edges, lines and curves, and then building up more abstract features. The use of these methods becomes particularly interesting and useful in approaches where feature extraction is required. The input image passes through a series of filters before entering into a neural network. Instead of having fixed numbers in kernels, they are trained on the data. While the convolutional network is trained, the kernel will get better and better at filtering a given image for relevant information. Therefore, the model parameters are optimized in order to minimize the loss function.

There is often a direct relationship between the amount of data needed and the performance of the model. The larger the training dataset, the greater the diversity of data, and the better the generalization achieved. However, most of the times, the amount of data needed to build models is impossible to find, especially in the medical field. One usual solution to overcome this issue is the transfer learning. Models trained on one task capture relations in the data type and can easily be reused for different problems in the same domain. Output reusable features of a pre-trained model in a large dataset are used to allow the learning process to be closer to the optimal solution parameters for the problem. The data augmentation is another methodology that allows to overcome the limitation of data. Often rotations, flips, zooms, shears do not change the classes of the images and allow to have a high amount of data and obtain models with a greater generalization.

Regarding the architecture, VGG networks, ResNets or Inception Networks are usually used for classification with transfer learning. The VGG networks follow the traditional layout of basic convolutional neuronal networks: a series of convolutional, max-pooling, and activation layers before some fully-connected classification layers which are in the end. On the other hand, the ResNet has the essential structure of a shortcut connection which is flexible and dependent on the tasks. Shortcut connections can skip one or more layers. Finally, an inception network uses convolution kernels of multiple sizes as well as pooling within one layer.

3   Methods

3.1   Material

This paper describes an approach to solve the part I of the challenge held of ICIAR 2018 conference: the classification of breast histology images. The dataset is composed by high-resolution (2048×1536 pixels) RGB images. All images were digitized in the same acquisition conditions, with magnification of 200x and pixel size of $0.42\,\mu m \times 0.42\,\mu m$. The training dataset contains a total of 400 images (100 per each class). Of the 100 images per class, 70, 20 and 10 were sub-selected for training, testing and validation before the release of the evaluation dataset by the challenge organizers. The division was random. The images that are part of the validation and test set are indicated in the appendix. The blind test set contains 100 images.

The processor used was Intel (R) Core TM i7-5829K CPU @ 3.30 GHz, the RAM was 32 GB and the GPU was 8 GB.

3.2   DCNN Model

Given the reduced dataset size, the use of transfer learning and data augmentation methods is indispensable. In this case a pre-trained Inception-Resnet-v2 network [12] for the ImageNet without the fully-connected layers is used. The ImageNet database is often used for pre-trained models of transfer learning as it contains a great diversity of intra and inter classes and it is publicly available. The pre-trained top layers are removed previously because they are very specific to the training occurrence. This architecture uses the tricks and decisions of an inception network with residual connection variants. This was used since it is one of the architectures that obtained better results for the ImageNet dataset. It was expected that most of the filters used in the extraction of features were already adjusted to features suitable for this classification problem. No pre-processing is done. The images are first reshaped to 244 × 244 pixels, a very common input size for DCNN and rescaled to [0-1]. DCNN usually work better with square images. The reshape of the images does not greatly affect the accuracy and the shape of the cellular structures and it allows to reduce the computational cost.

The top layers consist of a global average pooling layer, a fully connected layer of 256 neurons (with activation of rectified linear unit) and finally the neurons that allow classification in each of the four classes (with softmax activation). The global average pooling and dropout of 0.5 after the fully connected layer help to reduce overfitting.

In a first phase, only the fully-connected layers are trained. In a second phase, the DCNN is retrained on top layer but also there is fine-tuning of the weights of some pretrained network layers. It is common to keep the weights of some bottom layers (due to overfitting issues) and only perform fine-tunning of high-level features. The most generic features (e.g. edges and blobs) are maintained. In this case the weights are frozen until the layer 678. Figure 2 represents a schematic of the proposed architecture.

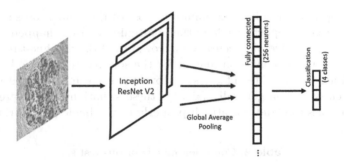

Fig. 2. Implemented CNN architecture

Data augmentation increases the amount and generality of the data. In this case it is built through the application in the training set of 18 rotations, vertical and horizontal flips, zooms of 10% and vertical and horizontal shifts of 10%. The shifts and the zoom range is not too large, otherwise the anatomical structures could be lost in the transformation.

Early stopping is used in both phases, i. e., no more epochs are ran when the validation loss does not reach a minimum over 20 consecutive epochs. The weights used for the evaluation are from the epoch in which the loss of the validation set is minimum. The loss is categorical cross-entropy. The optimizer used is the SGD. SGD tends to converge to better solutions but in return takes longer time. In the training of the top layers, a high learning rate of 0.2 is used, while with fine-tuning of the bottom layer, a low learning rate of 0.0001 is used. The value is smaller since the solution was already close to the intended one.

4   Results

The performance of the method was evaluated based on accuracy. Besides that, a confusion matrix was computed to understand which classes are more misclassified and the log loss was considered since it takes into account the uncertainty of prediction. Table 1 presents the obtained results.

Table 1. Accuracy and loss of the datasets

	Accuracy	Loss
Training	0.99	0.23
Validation	0.93	0.23
Test	0.90	0.59
Evaluation	0.76	Not available

In the top layer training, the minimum loss of the evaluation set is reached at approximately 65 epochs while in the fine-tuning phase it happens at approximately 35 epochs. Overall, accuracy improved by 0.15 with fine-tuning.

Table 2 shows the confusion matrix for the selected test set. False negatives are spread across the different classes. However, some images have very white areas and classification generally fails for these situations. These are damaged tissues or tissues that did not attach properly to the blade preparation.

Table 2. Confusion matrix of this test set

		Real			
		Normal	Benign	*In situ*	Invasive
Predict	Normal	19	0	1	0
	Benign	0	18	1	2
	In situ	1	2	17	0
	Invasive	0	0	1	18

Throughout the training, there is a little overfitting. The existence of overfitting leads to a large decrease in accuracy for the blind test set over previously known and evaluated datasets. For future work, some strategies can be adopted in order to avoid overfitting: use the lower unfreeze layers, apply few neurons in the top layers, increase the number of images for validation and testing, promote greater similarity between datasets and/or introduce cross-validation and regularization techniques. Figure 3 shows an example in which the proposed algorithm works well and another one in which the result does not correspond to the entire image. Both are invasive carcinoma situations. In the first one (Fig. 3 (a)), it is possible to verify a spreading of cells along all the image. In the second example (Fig. 3 (c)), lumen structures (white) with a small amount of cells are distinguishable. This has the appearance of a benign tumor and the algorithm is not robust enough to perceive the particulars of the invasive carcinoma. This conclusion can be achieved through saliency maps (the hottest colors represent the most relevant locations for classification).

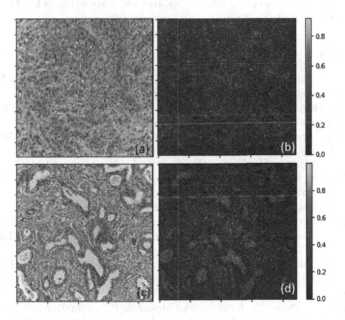

Fig. 3. Classification results for two invasive carcinomas: (a and c) original images; (b and d) saliency maps

5   Conclusion

This work proposes a Inception ResNet V2 which through transfer learning, finetunning and data augmentation allows to classify histological images of breast cancer stained with H & E. The network learns the relevant features for classification which becomes particularly important since it is not always easy to understand which features should be extracted using traditional methods. The classification of each individual class produce reliable results that overcomes some state-of-art works. In order to improve the results, an approach with image patches, some pre and post-processing methods will be tested. Other strategies will also be applied to reduce the overfitting.

Acknowledgments. This work is financed by the North Portugal Regional Operational Programme (NORTE 2020), under the PORTUGAL 2020 Partnership Agreement, and the European Regional Development Fund (ERDF), within the project "NanoSTIMA: Macro-to-Nano Human Sensing: Towards Integrated Multimodal Health Monitoring and Analytics/NORTE-01-0145-FEDER-000016".

A   Appendix

Each class has images numbered from 1 to 100. In each class, the following images were used to construct the datasets: Test set - 2, 3, 4, 15, 20, 27, 38, 39, 42, 44, 47, 54, 60, 61, 67, 69, 75, 80, 93 and 96; Validation set - 11, 18, 21, 23, 45, 49, 55, 87, 89 and 99; Training set - remaining images.

References

1. Kasper, D., Fauci, A., Hauser, S., Longo, D., Jameson, J.: Harrison's Principles of Internal Medicine. McGraw-Hill Education, New York (2015)
2. National Breast Cancer Foundation Inc: Breast Cancer Facts. http://www.nationalbreastcancer.org/breast-cancer-facts
3. American Cancer Society: Breast Cancer Facts&Figures 2017–2018. American Cancer Society, Inc., Atlanta (2017)
4. Araújo, T., Aresta, G., Castro, E., Rouco, J., Aguiar, P., Eloy, C., Polónia, A., Campilho, A.: Classification of breast cancer histology images using Convolutional Neural Networks. PLOS ONE **12**(6), 1–14 (2017)
5. Elmore, J., Longton, G., Carney, P., Geller, B., Onega, T., Tosteson, A., Nelson, H., Pepe, M., Allison, K., Schnitt, S., O'Malley, F., Weaver, D.: Diagnostic concordance among pathologists interpreting breast biopsy specimens. JAMA **313**(11), 1122–1132 (2015)
6. Kowal, M., Filipczuk, P., Obuchowicz, A., Korbicz, J., Monczak, R.: Computer-aided diagnosis of breast cancer based on fine needle biopsy microscopic images. Comput. Biol. Med. **43**(10), 1563–1572 (2013)
7. Filipczuk, P., Fevens, T., Krzyzak, A., Monczak, R.: Computer-aided breast cancer diagnosis based on the analysis of cytological images of fine needle biopsies. IEEE Trans. Med. Imaging **32**(12), 2169–2178 (2013)
8. George, Y., Zayed, H., Roushdy, M., Elbagoury, B.: Remote computer-aided breast cancer detection and diagnosis system based on cytological images. IEEE Syst. J. **8**(3), 949–2178 (2013)
9. Belsare, A., Mushrif, M., Pangarkar, M., Meshram, M.: Classification of breast cancer histopathology images using texture feature analysis. In: TENCON 2015–2015 IEEE Region 10 Conference, Macau (2015)
10. Zhang, B.: Breast cancer diagnosis from biopsy images by serial fusion of Random Subspace ensembles. In: 4th International Conference on Biomedical Engineering and Informatics, Shanghai (2011)
11. Cruz-Roa, A., Basavanhally, A., González, F., Gilmore, H., Feldman, M., Ganesan, S., Shih, N., Tomaszewk, J., Madabhushi, A.: Automatic detection of invasive ductal carcinoma in whole slide images with convolutional neural networks. In: Proceedings of the Medical Imaging 2014: Digital Pathology, San Diego, vol. 9041 (2014)
12. Szegedy, C., Ioffe, S., Vanhoucke, V.: Inception-v4, inception-resnet and the impact of residual connections on learning (2016). arXiv:1602.07261

Multi-classification of Breast Cancer Histology Images by Using a Fine-Tuning Strategy

Nadia Brancati[1]([✉]), Maria Frucci[1], and Daniel Riccio[1,2]

[1] Institute for High Performance Computing and Networking,
National Research Council of Italy (ICAR-CNR), Naples, Italy
{nadia.brancati,maria.frucci}@cnr.it
[2] University of Naples "Federico II", Naples, Italy
daniel.riccio@unina.it

Abstract. The adoption of automatic systems to support the diagnosis of breast cancer from histology images analysis is rapidly becoming more widespread. Most of the works in literature focus principally on a two-class problem, namely benign and malignant tumors. However, the development of multi-classification approaches would also be greatly appreciated in order to support the determination of an ideal therapeutic schedule for the treatment of breast cancer. The multi-classification of histology images is particularly challenging due to the broad variability of appearance of the image, the great differences in the spatial arrangement of the histological structures, and the heterogeneity in the color distribution. In this work, a fine-tuning strategy of ResNet, a residual convolutional neural network, is presented to address the problem of multi-classification for breast cancer histology images in normal tissue, benign lesions, in situ carcinomas and invasive carcinomas. We have combined three configurations of ResNet, differing from each other in terms of the number of layers, by using a maximum probability rule to balance out their individual weaknesses during the testing. The proposed approach achieved a remarkable performance on the images provided for the Grand Challenge on Breast Cancer Histology Images (BACH), within the context of the International Conference ICIAR 2018.

Keywords: Breast cancer multi-classification · Histology images
Deep convolutional network · Fine-tuning

1 Introduction and Background

According to the World Cancer Report [21], breast cancer is the most common cancer with the highest rate of mortality among women worldwide, with nearly 1.7 million new cases arise per year. A correct diagnosis and an optimal personalized therapy for the specific cancer could help to decrease the incidence of this disease. An erroneous diagnosis could be made by pathologists due to the high

© Springer International Publishing AG, part of Springer Nature 2018
A. Campilho et al. (Eds.): ICIAR 2018, LNCS 10882, pp. 771–778, 2018.
https://doi.org/10.1007/978-3-319-93000-8_87

variability in the appearances of the high-resolution images, the great differences in the spatial arrangement of the histological structures and the heterogeneity in the color distribution. On the other hand, it is very difficult to transfer the knowledge deriving from the professional experience of expert pathologists to primary-level clinicians. Moreover, manual multi-classification is a very expensive and time-consuming task, due to the huge number of histology images that are produced every day. Thus, an automatic system for the multi-classification of breast cancer histology images is extremely important in order both to reduce the number of erroneous diagnoses and to lighten the workload of pathologists.

Most of the approaches in literature address the classification of breast cancer histology images as a two-class problem, namely benign and malignant tumors, a broad survey being available in [6,7,23]. These methods can be divided into two groups. The former adopts unsupervised methods for the feature extraction and K-Nearest Neighbor (KNN) or Support Vector Machine (SVM) to classify the images. The latter relies on neural networks for both the feature extraction and image classification. As regards the methods in the first group, graph-based algorithms have been proposed to quantitatively characterize the spatial arrangement and distribution of histological structures such as cancer nuclei, lymphocytes and glands [11]. In [14], an image segmentation is obtained by using a k-means clustering based algorithm, following which a wide range of features are merged by means of a KNN classifier. In [16], an algorithm for the automated classification of the breast cancer, based on local descriptors [15,17] and an SVM classifier, is presented. All the above-mentioned methods extract hand-crafted features, which might not be very effective on heterogeneous sets of images. To overcome these limitations, the methods belonging to the second group are generally based on a Deep Neural Network. A Convolutional Neural Network (CNN) was used in [20] for the classification of the breast cancer histology images of different magnification factors. The highest accuracy was obtained for the minimum magnification factor. A transfer learning architecture of a CNN was used in [9] and fusion rules of the results at different magnification factors were applied. In [8] a CNN magnification-independent method was proposed, where all the available data were used for the training, independently of their magnification factors. In [24] also, a magnification-independent strategy was used to train the proposed CNN network. The test dataset was randomly obtained and a high accuracy was achieved.

Recently, several attempts have been made to perform a multi-classification of breast cancer histology images. In particular, in [12], a CNN Class Structure-based approach was used on the Breast Cancer Histopathological (BreakHis) dataset [19], in order to leverage the hierarchical feature representation. At the image level, an accuracy of about 92% for all magnification factors was achieved in respect of a multi-classification in eight classes, and an approximate accuracy of 96% was achieved for the binary classification. Another approach was presented in [5], where the performance was evaluated on the dataset provided by the Bioimaging 2015 challenge [2,3]. A CNN and a combination of a CNN and an SVM were proposed, achieving accuracies of 77.8% for the four class test and 83.3% for the carcinoma/non-carcinoma test.

In this paper a supervised method for the multi-classification of breast cancer histology images based on the fine-tuning strategy of a ResNet model [13] is presented. The classification of a breast cancer histology image is obtained by combining three configurations of the ResNet with a different number of layers according to the maximum probability rule. The method has been tested on the Grand Challenge on Breast Cancer Histology Images (BACH) dataset [4], within the context of the 15th International Conference on Image Analysis and Recognition (ICIAR 2018) and on the dataset provided by the Bioimaging 2015 challenge. In these datasets the histology images are classified into four classes, normal tissue, benign lesions, in situ carcinomas, and invasive carcinomas. Different experiments have been performed, using different training modalities of ResNet. The best accuracy was obtained by applying the fine-tuning strategy, training all the layers of the networks. The accuracy achieved was 97.3% for the multi-classification in four classes and 98.7% for carcinoma/non-carcinoma test on the BACH training set. The performance of our approach has also been evaluated by using the testing set provided by the Bioimaging 2015 challenge, achieving an accuracy of 97.2% for both the four classes and two classes tests. Finally, the approach has also been tested on the dataset provided by the Bioimaging 2015 challenge and the accuracy achieved was 88.9% for both the four classes and two classes tests. Following the release of the BACH testing set, according to the preliminary results of the BACH competition, the accuracy achieved was 86% for the four classes.

2   Our Approach

The training of a CNN from scratch proves to be a very challenging task, since the training dataset often consists of a reduced number of images, as is the case in respect of many medical applications. For this reason, a fine-tuning strategy of a pre-trained deep neural network is an effective way of borrowing parameters from other large datasets [22]. Models, such as VGG-Net [18], Google-Net [10] or ResNet [13] were pre-trained on a very large natural image dataset, namely ImageNet [1]. In this work, we have performed a fine-tuning on a pre-trained ResNet model.

ResNet won the first place in the ImageNet and COCO 2015 competitions, which covered image classification, object detection, and semantic segmentation. It is a residual neural network deeper but having lower complexity than VGG-Net or Google-Net. The main idea of residual networks is based on the degradation problem: as the number of layers increases, the accuracy rapidly degrades. To address this issue, the original mapping in the network is replaced with a residual mapping, which is easier to optimize. This kind of network is realized by introducing "shortcut connections", which can skip one or more layers. In particular, in ResNet, the residual mapping is the identity mapping and the connections are realized in such a way that the output of the identity is added to the output of the stacked layer. Such a connection allows you to obtain a smaller number of parameters and a lower complexity than other deep neural networks.

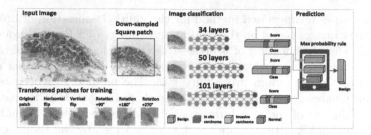

Fig. 1. Workflow of our approach.

Deep neural networks encounter problems with very high resolution images, as the training time and the computational cost grow proportionately until they become intractable. Most methods address this problem by splitting the image into patches, so that the network training and image classification is performed on single patches. In this way, a very large number of images is generated to train a deep network. Since, in this work, we are adopting a pre-trained network which means that we do not need a very large number of images to train it from scratch, a different strategy has been adopted to tackle the problem of image resolution. The input image is down-sampled by a factor k and only the central square patch of size $m \times m$ is extracted and submitted as input to the network. The value m is set to the value equal to the minimum size between the width and height of the re-sized image. This strategy shows the further advantage of having a single response by the network for the whole test image. Indeed, when the image is partitioned into multiple patches, which are separately classified by the network, a merging strategy is mandatory to achieve a final decision for the whole image. In so doing, a wrong decision on a malignant image could be made if the number of patches affected by the carcinoma is very small.

Usually the fine-tuning strategy is applied updating only the last layer of a pre-trained model, by using a specific training dataset. In this work, we have adopted a fine-tuning strategy for all the layers of ResNet. A ResNet model can be configured with a different number of layers. We have chosen three different configurations, 34, 50 and 101 layers. Each configuration is trained on the training dataset and the classification of a test image is obtained by computing the highest class probability provided by the three configurations. In Fig. 1, the main steps of our approach are shown.

3   Experiments

The proposed approach was validated on the Grand Challenge on Breast Cancer Histology (BACH) images, which is a follow-up of the dataset provided by the Bioimaging 2015 breast histology classification challenge. All images have a resolution of 2040×1536 pixels, with a magnification factor of $200\times$ and a pixel size of $0.42\,\mu m \times 0.42\,\mu m$. The annotated $H\&E$ stain images are uncompressed and associated with a label with four possible values: normal tissue, benign lesion, in situ carcinoma and, invasive carcinoma. The dataset includes 400 images and was released to the participants at the challenge. To increase the training set, we have also considered a set of 5 transformations for each image (i.e. horizontal flip, vertical flip, and three clock-wise rotations of 90°).

The input image is reduced by a factor k and the central square patch of size $m \times m$ is extracted, where m is the minimum size between the width and height of the reduced image. Our experiments were performed considering two different values for k, 80% and 60%, so providing two corresponding values for m, i.e. 308 pixels and 615 pixels. The extracted patch is provided as input to the network to train L layers (34, 50 and 101). All the networks have been trained by using stochastic gradient descent, a learning rate equal to 0.001 and a batch size equal to 8. Since the testing set of the BACH images was released after the submission of the proposed algorithms to the challenge, the original training set was divided into two parts. In particular, 75 images (the first 15 of benign class, the first 22 of normal class, the first 18 of in situ class and the first 20 of invasive class) of the BACH dataset (about 20%) were selected as the testing set, namely D1, while the remaining images were used to train the network. A further testing set, namely D2, was also considered. The dataset D2 includes 36 test images provided by the Bioimaging 2015 challenge.

In Table 1, we report the classification accuracy of two experiments for different values of k and m, showing also the classification accuracy obtained by single networks ($L = 34$, $L = 50$, and $L = 101$) and that obtained with the maximum probability rule. It is worth noting that, unlike the images in D2, the images in D1 are quite similar to those in the training set. This entails two important implications: (i) the accuracies obtained on D1 are slightly better than those achieved on D2 and (ii) an improvement is provided by the maximum probability rule, when D2 is used as the testing set. Independently of the considered testing set, the best accuracy is obtained for $m = 308$ pixels and when the maximum probability rule is applied. For this reason, all the following experiments were performed by only considering such a configuration.

The results in Table 1 were obtained by considering the training of all layers of the pre-trained ResNet configurations. For the sake of completeness, we have also considered two further strategies to train the proposed ResNet configurations: (i) only the last fully connected layer is trained on the BACH images and (ii) all the layers are trained from scratch on the BACH images. The accuracies obtained are reported in Table 2. By comparing the accuracies in Tables 1 and 2, it emerges that the proposed fine tuning strategy significantly outperforms the commonly used training approaches.

In Table 3, we report the confusion matrices of the proposed approach on D1 and D2. The obtained accuracies for the two-class problem (benign and malignant tumors) are 98.7% and 97.2% on D1 and D2, respectively.

Thus, for the sake of comparison with the state of the art, we also tested our approach on the whole dataset provided by the Bioimaging 2015 challenge. This has allowed us to compare the obtained classification accuracy with that provided by the approach proposed in [5]. The training dataset is constituted

Table 1. The classification accuracy on the (a) D1 and (b) D2 testing sets.

	k=80% m=308px	k=60% m=615px
L=34	93.3%	93.3%
L=50	97.3%	89.3%
L=101	97.3%	81.3%
Max.Prob.Rule	97.3%	89.3%

(a)

	k=80% m=308px	k=60% m=615px
L=34	88.9%	83.3%
L=50	88.9%	80.5%
L=101	88.9%	86.1%
Max.Prob.Rule	97.2%	88.9%

(b)

Table 2. The classification accuracy for the different training strategies.

Test set	Train. last FC layer	Train. from scratch
D1	92%	77.3%
D2	69.4%	52.8%

Table 3. The confusion matrices of the proposed approach on the (a) D1 and (b) D2 testing sets.

	N	B	IS	IV
N	22	0	0	0
B	1	14	0	0
IS	0	1	17	0
IV	0	0	0	20

(a)

	N	B	IS	IV
N	9	0	0	0
B	0	8	1	0
IS	0	0	9	0
IV	0	0	0	9

(b)

Table 4. The classification accuracy on the whole dataset of the Bioimaging 2015 challenge.

Method	Four classes	Two classes
Proposed approach	88.9%	88.9%
Arujo et al. [5]	77.8%	83.3%

by 249 images, of which 20% we have been used for the validation phase. Our approach outperforms the method proposed in [5] (see Table 4). Moreover, our approach was tested by the organizers of the BACH challenge on a testing set of 100 images, achieving an accuracy of 86% for the four classes, so resulting in the top-three rank of the competition. Finally, no results can be provided for the two classes problem, since the images, but not the corresponding labels, were released for the BACH testing set.

4   Conclusions

In this work, we have presented a multi-classification approach for breast cancer histology images, which combines fine-tuned ResNet-34/50/101 configurations, using a maximum probability rule on the results provided by the single configurations. Different experiments have been performed to evaluate the performance of the proposed approach. In particular, before the release of the BACH testing set, two different testing sets have been adopted for the evaluation on the BACH dataset: a testing set, which consisted of about 20% of the training dataset of the BACH images, and a second testing set provided by the Bioimaging 2015 challenge. Considering the first testing set, the achieved accuracy was 97.3% for the multi-classification in the four classes and 98.7% for the binary classification. The images of the second testing set are slightly different from those of the training set, so the classification accuracy was 97.2% for both the four classes and two classes tests. A further experiment has been performed on the whole dataset provided by the Bioimaging 2015 challenge, obtaining an increment in terms of accuracy of about 11.1% for the multi-classification and of 5.6% for the binary classification with respect to a recent state of the art multi-classification method. After the release of the BACH testing set, according to the preliminary results of the BACH challenge, the classification accuracy achieved was 86% for the four classes. The results suggest that the proposed approach provides a high performance in terms of classification accuracy.

References

1. Imagenet. http://www.image-net.org/
2. Bioimaging 2015 (2015). http://www.bioimaging2015.ineb.up.pt/dataset.html
3. Breast (2017). https://rdm.inesctec.pt/dataset/nis-2017-003
4. ICIAR 2018 Grand Challenge on Breast Cancer Histology images (BACH) (2018). https://iciar2018-challenge.grand-challenge.org/dataset/
5. Araújo, T., Aresta, G., Castro, E., Rouco, J., Aguiar, P., Eloy, C., Polónia, A., Campilho, A.: Classification of breast cancer histology images using convolutional neural networks. PloS One 12(6), e0177544 (2017)
6. Arevalo, J., Cruz-Roa, A., et al.: Histopathology image representation for automatic analysis: A state-of-the-art review. Revista Med. 22(2), 79–91 (2014)
7. Aswathy, M., Jagannath, M.: Detection of breast cancer on digital histopathology images: present status and future possibilities. Inform. Med. Unlocked 8, 74–79 (2016)
8. Bayramoglu, N., Kannala, J., Heikkilä, J.: Deep learning for magnification independent breast cancer histopathology image classification. In: 2016 23rd International Conference on Pattern Recognition (ICPR), pp. 2440–2445. IEEE (2016)
9. Das, K., Karri, S.P.K., Roy, A.G., Chatterjee, J., Sheet, D.: Classifying histopathology whole-slides using fusion of decisions from deep convolutional network on a collection of random multi-views at multi-magnification. In: 2017 IEEE 14th International Symposium on Biomedical Imaging (ISBI 2017), pp. 1024–1027. IEEE (2017)

10. Donahue, J., Jia, Y., Vinyals, O., Hoffman, J., Zhang, N., Tzeng, E., Darrell, T.: Decaf: a deep convolutional activation feature for generic visual recognition. In: International Conference on Machine Learning, pp. 647–655 (2014)

11. Doyle, S., Agner, S., Madabhushi, A., Feldman, M., Tomaszewski, J.: Automated grading of breast cancer histopathology using spectral clustering with textural and architectural image features. In: 5th IEEE International Symposium on Biomedical Imaging: From Nano to Macro, 2008, pp. 496–499. IEEE (2008)

12. Han, Z., Wei, B., Zheng, Y., Yin, Y., Li, K., Li, S.: Breast cancer multi-classification from histopathological images with structured deep learning model. Sci. Rep. **7**(1), 4172 (2017)

13. He, K., Zhang, X., Ren, S., Sun, J.: Deep residual learning for image recognition. In: Proceedings of the IEEE Conference on Computer Vision and Pattern Recognition, pp. 770–778 (2016)

14. Kumar, R., Srivastava, R., Srivastava, S.: Detection and classification of cancer from microscopic biopsy images using clinically significant and biologically interpretable features. J. Med. Eng. **2015**, 1–14 (2015)

15. Ojala, T., Pietikainen, M., Maenpaa, T.: Multiresolution gray-scale and rotation invariant texture classification with local binary patterns. IEEE Trans. Pattern Anal. Mach. Intell. **24**(7), 971–987 (2002)

16. Ojansivu, V., Linder, N., Rahtu, E., Pietikäinen, M., Lundin, M., Joensuu, H., Lundin, J.: Automated classification of breast cancer morphology in histopathological images. Diagn. Pathol. **8**(1), S29 (2013)

17. Rahtu, E., Heikkilä, J., Ojansivu, V., Ahonen, T.: Local phase quantization for blur-insensitive image analysis. Image Vis. Comput. **30**(8), 501–512 (2012)

18. Simonyan, K., Zisserman, A.: Very deep convolutional networks for large-scale image recognition. arXiv preprint arXiv:1409.1556 (2014)

19. Spanhol, F.A., Oliveira, L.S., Petitjean, C., Heutte, L.: A dataset for breast cancer histopathological image classification. IEEE Trans Biomed. Eng. **63**(7), 1455–1462 (2016)

20. Spanhol, F.A., Oliveira, L.S., Petitjean, C., Heutte, L.: Breast cancer histopathological image classification using convolutional neural networks. In: 2016 International Joint Conference on Neural Networks (IJCNN), pp. 2560–2567. IEEE (2016)

21. Stewart, B.W., Wild, C.: World Cancer Report 2014, World Health Organization, International Agency for Research on Cancer, vol. 505 (2014)

22. Tajbakhsh, N., Shin, J.Y., Gurudu, S.R., Hurst, R.T., Kendall, C.B., Gotway, M.B., Liang, J.: Convolutional neural networks for medical image analysis: full training or fine tuning? IEEE Trans. Med. Imaging **35**(5), 1299–1312 (2016)

23. Veta, M., Pluim, J.P., Van Diest, P.J., Viergever, M.A.: Breast cancer histopathology image analysis: a review. IEEE Trans. Biomed. Eng. **61**(5), 1400–1411 (2014)

24. Wei, B., Han, Z., He, X., Yin, Y.: Deep learning model based breast cancer histopathological image classification. In: 2017 IEEE 2nd International Conference on Cloud Computing and Big Data Analysis (ICCCBDA), pp. 348–353. IEEE (2017)

Improve the Performance of Transfer Learning Without Fine-Tuning Using Dissimilarity-Based Multi-view Learning for Breast Cancer Histology Images

Hongliu Cao[1,2(✉)], Simon Bernard[2], Laurent Heutte[2], and Robert Sabourin[1]

[1] Laboratoire d'Imagerie, de Vision et d'Intelligence Artificielle,
École de Technologie Supérieure, Université du Québec, Montreal, Canada
[2] Université de Rouen Normandie, LITIS (EA 4108),
BP 12, 76801 Saint-Étienne du Rouvray, France
caohongliu@gmail.com

Abstract. Breast cancer is one of the most common types of cancer and leading cancer-related death causes for women. In the context of ICIAR 2018 Grand Challenge on Breast Cancer Histology Images, we compare one handcrafted feature extractor and five transfer learning feature extractors based on deep learning. We find out that the deep learning networks pretrained on ImageNet have better performance than the popular handcrafted features used for breast cancer histology images. The best feature extractor achieves an average accuracy of 79.30%. To improve the classification performance, a random forest dissimilarity based integration method is used to combine different feature groups together. When the five deep learning feature groups are combined, the average accuracy is improved to 82.90% (best accuracy 85.00%). When handcrafted features are combined with the five deep learning feature groups, the average accuracy is improved to 87.10% (best accuracy 93.00%).

Keywords: Breast cancer · Dissimilarity · Random forest
Deep learning · Multi-view · Transfer learning
High dimensional low sample size

1 Introduction

The detection and treatment of cancer are still very challenging. The normal process of cancer detection is from certain signs and symptoms to the further investigation by medical imaging and at last confirmed by biopsy [1,2]. The diagnosis of breast cancer usually uses the biopsy tissue. The pathologists can histologically assess the microscopic structure and elements of the tissue from breast tissue biopsies [3].

One of the most important method for tumor histological examination in pathology is Hematoxylin and eosin (H&E) staining [4]. However, manual analysis is experience based, qualitative and always causes intra- or inter-observers

© Springer International Publishing AG, part of Springer Nature 2018
A. Campilho et al. (Eds.): ICIAR 2018, LNCS 10882, pp. 779–787, 2018.
https://doi.org/10.1007/978-3-319-93000-8_88

variation even for experienced pathologists [5]. Hence developing a more efficient, accurate, quantitative and automated system is necessary and urgent. Due to the high performance of deep learning networks, more and more studies used deep learning for the classification of breast cancer images [6]. However, the number of images available has always been an obstacle for the use of deep learning. Many studies divide images into patches for data augmentation, but the new problem is that there are no label information for patches.

In this paper, transfer learning without fine-tuning is proposed to solve the above problems. Six different feature extractors are compared, including five deep learning architectures and a traditional feature extractor combining PFTAS (Parameter-Free Threshold Adjacency Statistics) and GLCM (Gray Level Co-Occurrence Matrices) features. When all features are combined, there are mainly three challenges from the machine learning point of view: (i) small sample size: size: like most other medical applications, the number of breast cancer histology images is very small (400 images); (ii) high dimensional feature space: as six groups of features may be combined, the size of the feature space may be up to 31855, which is over 80 times bigger than the sample size; (iii) multiple feature groups: it may be hard to improve the learning performance by exploiting the complementary information that different groups contain [7]. To deal with these three challenges, we propose to treat breast cancer histology image classification as a multi-view learning problem. A multi-view RFSVM method proposed in our previous work [7] is then used as a solution.

The remainder of this paper is organized as follows: the six feature extractors are detailed in Sect. 2; in Sect. 3, the dissimilarity based multi-view learning solution is introduced; we describe in Sect. 4 the data sets chosen in this study and provide the protocol of our experimental method; we analyze in Sect. 5 the results of our experiments; the final conclusion and future works are drawn in Sect. 6.

2   Feature Extractors

In total six different feature extractors are used in this work: handcrafted features, ResNet-18, ResNeXt, NASNet-A, ResNet-152 and VGG16. In this section, a brief introduction of each feature extractor is given. The handcrafted features include PFTAS and GLCM and have been chosen due to their good performance on breast cancer histology image classification [8]. The five deep learning networks have been chosen for their performance and because they are built on different structures with different depths, and the pre-trained models are available online[1,2].

Handcrafted Features: Two kinds of feature extractors are combined together to form the handcrafted feature group: PFTAS and GLCM. TAS (Threshold

---

[1] https://github.com/Cadene/pretrained-models.pytorch.
[2] https://github.com/pytorch/vision/tree/master/torchvision.

Adjacency Statistics) is a simple and fast morphological measure for cell phenotype image classification presented by Hamilton et al. in [9]. Similar to the work of [8], we use the Parameter-Free Threshold Adjacency Statistics (PFTAS) from the python library Mahotas [10] to build a 162-dimensional PFTAS-feature vector. GLCM features are widely used to describe the texture of tumor in cancer applications. Same as PFTAS, the library Mahotas is used to calculate the GLCM features leading to a 175-dimensional GLCM-feature vector.

ResNet-18 and ResNet-152: ResNet is one of the deepest deep learning architectures proposed by Microsoft researchers. The deep residual nets based methods have won the first places on the tasks of ImageNet detection, ImageNet localization, COCO detection, and COCO segmentation as well as the first place on the ILSVRC 2015 classification task [11]. We use two ResNet in this work: ResNet-18 and ResNet-152. Both networks take as input a $\{3, 224, 224\}$ RGB image and are pretrained on ImageNet with 1000 classes[3,4]. Features are extracted from the average pool layer (i.e. before the last classification layer), which results in 512 features for ResNet-18 and 2048 features for ResNet-152.

ResNeXt: ResNeXt is one of the state-of-the-art techniques for object recognition. It builds upon the concepts of repeating layers while exploiting the split-transform-merge strategy to bring about a new and improved architecture [12]. The input space of ResNeXt is a $\{3, 224, 224\}$ RGB image and we use the network pretrained on ImageNet with 1000 classes[5]. 2048 features are extracted from the average pool layer (i.e. before the last classification layer).

NASNet-A: In the work of [13], the authors proposed to search for an architectural building block on a small dataset and then transfer the block to a larger dataset to reduce the computation cost and improve the efficiency. They used NAS (Neural Architecture Search) framework from [14] as the main search method for their NASNets. The three networks constructed from the best three searches are named NASNet-A, NASNet-B and NASNet-C respectively. In this work, a NASNet-A pretrained on ImageNet is used. The input space of NASNet-A is a $\{3, 331, 331\}$ RGB image and we use the network pretrained on ImageNet with 1001 classes (ImageNet+background)[6]. 4032 features are extracted from the last layer before the classification layer.

VGG16: The VGG Network was introduced by the researchers at Visual Graphics Group at Oxford [15]. This network is specially characterized by its pyramidal shape. VGG16 takes as input a $\{3, 224, 224\}$ RGB image and we use the network

---

[3] https://download.pytorch.org/models/resnet18-5c106cde.pth.

[4] http://data.lip6.fr/cadene/pretrainedmodels/fbresnet152-2e20f6b4.pth.

[5] http://data.lip6.fr/cadene/pretrainedmodels/resnext101-64x4d-e77a0586.pth.

[6] https://data.lip6.fr/cadene/pretrainedmodels/nasnetalarge-a1897284.pth.

pretrained on ImageNet with 1000 classes[7]. Features are extracted from the last max pooling layer, which results in $512 \times 7 \times 7$ features.

3 Dissimilarity-Based Learning

In our previous work [7], we proposed to use RFSVM to integrate information from different views together (each feature group is a view in multi-view learning framework). We have shown that RFSVM offers a good performance on Radiomics data. The RFSVM method can deal well with high dimensional low sample size multi-view data because: (i) RFSVM uses random forest dissimilarity measure to transfer each view of the data to a dissimilarity matrix so that the data dimension is reduced without feature selection, and at the same time the data in each view become directly comparable; (ii) RFSVM can take advantage of the complementary information contained in each view by combining the dissimilarity matrices together. We now recall the RFSVM method.

Random Forest: Given a training set $\mathbf{T}$, a Random Forest classifier $\mathbf{H}$ is a classifier made up of M trees denoted as in Eq. (1):

$$\mathbf{H}(\mathbf{X}) = \{h_k(\mathbf{X}), k = 1, \dots, M\} \tag{1}$$

where $h_k(\mathbf{X})$ is a random tree grown using the Bagging and the Random Feature Selection techniques as in [16]. For predicting the class of a given query point $\mathbf{X}$ with such a tree, $\mathbf{X}$ goes down the tree structure, from its root till its terminal node. The prediction is given by the terminal node (or leaf node) in which $\mathbf{X}$ has landed. We refer the reader to [16] for more information about this process. Hence if two query points land in the same terminal node, they are likely to belong to the same class and they are also likely to share similarities in their feature vectors, since they have followed the same descending path.

Random Forest Dissimilarity (RFD): the RFD measure is inferred from a RF classifier $\mathbf{H}$, learned from $\mathbf{T}$. Let us firstly define a dissimilarity measure inferred by a decision tree $d^{(k)}$: let L_k denote the set of leaves of the kth tree, and let $l_k(\mathbf{X})$ denote a function from $\mathbb{X}$ to L_k that returns the leaf node of the kth tree where a given instance $\mathbf{X}$ lands when one wants to predict its class. The dissimilarity measure $d^{(k)}$, inferred by the kth tree in the forest is defined as in Eq. (2): if two training instances $\mathbf{X}_i$ and $\mathbf{X}_j$ land in the same leaf of the kth tree, then the dissimilarity between both instances is set to 0, else set to 1.

$$d^{(k)}(\mathbf{X}_i, \mathbf{X}_j) = \begin{cases} 0, & \text{if } l_k(\mathbf{X}_i) = l_k(\mathbf{X}_j) \\ 1, & \text{otherwise} \end{cases} \tag{2}$$

---

[7] https://download.pytorch.org/models/vgg16-397923af.pth.

The RFD measure $d^{(\mathbf{H})}$ consists in calculating the $d^{(k)}$ value for each tree in the forest, and to average the resulting dissimilarity values over the M trees, as in Eq. (3):

$$d^{(\mathbf{H})}(\mathbf{X}_i, \mathbf{X}_j) = \frac{1}{M} \sum_{k=1}^{M} d^{(k)}(\mathbf{X}_i, \mathbf{X}_j) \tag{3}$$

Multi-view Learning Dissimilarities: For multi-view learning tasks, the training set $\mathbf{T}$ is composed of K views: $\mathbf{T}^{(k)} = \{(\mathbf{X}_1^{(k)}, y_1), \ldots, (\mathbf{X}_N^{(k)}, y_N)\}$, $k = 1..K$. Firstly, for each view $\mathbf{T}^{(k)}$, the RFD matrix is computed and noted as $\{\mathbf{D}_{\mathbf{H}}^k, k = 1..K\}$. In multi-view learning, the joint dissimilarity matrix can typically be computed by averaging over the K matrices as in Eq. (4):

$$\mathbf{D_H} = \frac{1}{K} \sum_{i=1}^{K} \mathbf{D_H}^i \tag{4}$$

Multi Random Forest kernel SVM (RFSVM): From the joint RFD matrix $\mathbf{D_H}$ of Eq. (4), one can calculate the joint similarity matrix $\mathbf{S_H}$ as in Eq. (5):

$$\mathbf{S_H} = \mathbf{1} - \mathbf{D_H} \tag{5}$$

where $\mathbf{1}$ is a matrix of ones. SVM is one of the most successful classifier. Apart from the most used gaussian kernel, a lot of custom kernels can also be used: we use the joint similarity matrix $\mathbf{S_H}$ inferred from the RF classifier $\mathbf{H}$ as a kernel in a SVM classifier.

4 Experiments

The dataset used in this work is from ICIAR 2018 Grande Challenge on BreAst Cancer Histology images[8]. It is composed of Hematoxylin and eosin stained breast histology microscopy images. Microscopy images are labeled as normal, benign, in situ carcinoma or invasive carcinoma according to the predominant cancer type in each image. It is a balanced dataset with in total 400 images.

The protocol of the experiments is as follows:

- First, the 6 feature extractors described in Sect. 2 are used to extract features from histology image data. As there is no patch label provided, to simplify the feature extracting process, all images are rescaled to the network input size.
- Second, for each group of features, a random forest with 500 trees is built. The performance of each feature group is measured by the classification accuracy of the random forest. The random forest dissimilarity matrix is calculated for each group too.

---

[8] https://iciar2018-challenge.grand-challenge.org/dataset/.

– Finally, the RFSVM method described in Sect. 3 is used to combine all the groups together. Two RFSVMs are used: *RFSVM (DL only)* combines the five deep learning based feature groups; *RFSVM-All* combines all the six feature groups. For RFSVM, the search range of parameter C for SVM is {0.01, 0.1, 1, 10, 100, 1000}.

Note that in [17], the authors found that when dealing with high dimensional low sample size data, stratification of the sampling is central for obtaining minimal misclassification. In this work, the stratified random splitting procedure is repeated 10 times, with 75% as training data and 25% as testing data. In order to compare the methods, the mean and standard deviations of accuracy were evaluated over the 10 runs. However, for the contest, only one model can be submitted. Hence the best performance among the 10 runs is also presented and chosen as the model for the contest.

5   Results

The results of the experiments are shown in Table 1. We can tell that the best feature extractor is ResNet-152 with an average accuracy of 79.30% and best accuracy of 83.00%. Followed by ResNeXt with an average accuracy of 78.60% and the best accuracy of 81.00%. Surprisingly, the worst feature extractor is handcrafted features with PFTAS and GLCM with an average accuracy of 67.00%. In the work of [8], PFTAS and GLCM are the best features for breast cancer histology image classification. By comparing the performance of the six feature extractors, we can see that even though the deep learning networks are pretrained on ImageNet dataset, which is very different from histology images, they still have a better performance as a feature extractor for breast cancer data than the best handcrafted feature extractor used in the field of breast cancer histology image classification.

Table 1. The image wise classification results with 75% training data and 25% test data. *Average* is the average accuracy over 10 runs, *Best* is the best accuracy among the 10 runs.

	Average	Best
Handcrafted	67.00% ± 5.46	76.0%
ResNet-18	75.10% ± 5.46	78.0%
ResNeXt	78.60% ± 1.74	81.0%
NASNet-A	74.70% ± 2.33	78.0%
ResNet-152	79.30% ± 3.20	83.0%
VGG16	68.00% ± 5.04	78.0%
RFSVM(DL only)	82.90% ± 1.37	85.0%
RFSVM-All	**87.10% ± 2.17**	**93.0%**

Table 2. The confusion matrix, sensitivity and specificity of our best model.

	Benign	InSitu	Invasive	Normal
Benign	23	1	0	1
InSitu	0	23	0	2
Invasive	1	0	24	0
Normal	2	0	0	23
Sensitivity	92%	92%	96%	92%
Specificity	85%	96%	100%	85%

With *RFSVM (DL only)* integrating all the five deep learning based feature groups together, the average accuracy is improved to 82.90% and the best performance is improved to 85.00%. However, when all feature groups are combined with *RFSVM-All*, the average accuracy is improved to 87.10% and the best performance is improved to 93.00%. It shows that even though the handcrafted features do not have a very good performance individually, they can still provide useful complementary information for breast cancer classification when combined with deep learning based feature groups.

The confusion matrix, sensitivity and specificity of our best model are shown in Table 1. From the results we can see that our model has very high sensitivity on all four classes, and very high specificity too for two classes, i.e. *InSitu* and *Invasive*.

Note that the state of the art performance on this dataset is considered to be from [3]. In this work, the authors used CNN patch-wise training on a previous version of the dataset with 249 images for training and 20 images for testing (7.4% of the whole dataset as test data). They obtained as best performance an accuracy of 85.00%. In our work, 300 images are used for training and 100 images are used as test data. Hence, even if the results are not directly comparable with [3], the accuracy of our best model is 8% higher than the accuracy reported in [3] while using 25% of the whole dataset as test data, which is much more than 7.4% in [3] (Table 2).

6 Conclusion

In this work, we firstly compared the popular handcrafted features used in breast cancer histology image classification with five deep learning based feature extractors pretrained on ImageNet. Not surprisingly, the experimental results show that the deep learning based features are better than the handcrafted. To improve the performance of transfer learning, we tackled the problem of breast cancer histology image classification as an HDLSS multi-view learning task and applied an RFSVM method previously proposed for the classification of Radiomics data. The results obtained with *RFSVM (DL only)* show that the performance of transfer learning can be improved by combining multiple feature extractors together. The results obtained with *RFSVM-All* show that even though deep learning based features have better performance than hand-crafted features for breast cancer histology image classification, the accuracy can be improved significantly when they are combined together and surpass the state of the art performance on the dataset used.

Acknowledgment. This work is part of the DAISI project, co-financed by the European Union with the European Regional Development Fund (ERDF) and by the Normandy Region.

References

1. Coroller, T.P., Grossmann, P., Hou, Y., Velazquez, E.R., Leijenaar, R.T., Hermann, G., Lambin, P., Haibe-Kains, B., Mak, R.H., Aerts, H.J.: CT-based radiomic signature predicts distant metastasis in lung adenocarcinoma. Radiother. Oncol. **114**(3), 345–350 (2015)
2. Aerts, H., Velazquez, E.R., Leijenaar, R., Parmar, C., Grossmann, P., Cavalho, S., Bussink, J., Monshouwer, R., Haibe-Kains, B., Rietveld, D., et al.: Decoding tumour phenotype by noninvasive imaging using a quantitative radiomics approach. Nat. Commun. **5**, 1–8 (2014)
3. Araújo, T., Aresta, G., Castro, E., Rouco, J., Aguiar, P., Eloy, C., Polónia, A., Campilho, A.: Classification of breast cancer histology images using convolutional neural networks. PLoS ONE **12**(6), e0177544 (2017)
4. Chan, J.K.: The wonderful colors of the hematoxylin-eosin stain in diagnostic surgical pathology. Int. J. Surg. Pathol. **22**(1), 12–32 (2014)
5. Meyer, J.S., Alvarez, C., Milikowski, C., Olson, N., Russo, I., Russo, J., Glass, A., Zehnbauer, B.A., Lister, K., Parwaresch, R.: Breast carcinoma malignancy grading by Bloom-Richardson system vs proliferation index: reproducibility of grade and advantages of proliferation index. Modern Pathol. **18**(8), 1067 (2005)
6. Spanhol, F.A., Oliveira, L.S., Petitjean, C., Heutte, L.: Breast cancer histopathological image classification using convolutional neural networks. In: International Joint Conference on Neural Networks (IJCNN), pp. 2560–2567. IEEE (2016)
7. Cao, H., Bernard, S., Heutte, L., Sabourin, R.: Dissimilarity-based representation for radiomics applications. arXiv preprint arXiv:1803.04460 (2018)
8. Spanhol, F.A., Oliveira, L.S., Petitjean, C., Heutte, L.: A dataset for breast cancer histopathological image classification. IEEE Trans. Biomed. Eng. **63**(7), 1455–1462 (2016)
9. Hamilton, N.A., Pantelic, R.S., Hanson, K., Teasdale, R.D.: Fast automated cell phenotype image classification. BMC Bioinform. **8**(1), 110 (2007)
10. Coelho, L.P.: Mahotas: open source software for scriptable computer vision. J. Open Res. Softw. **1** (2013)
11. He, K., Zhang, X., Ren, S., Sun, J.: Deep residual learning for image recognition. In: Proceedings of the IEEE Conference on Computer Vision and Pattern Recognition, pp. 770–778 (2016)
12. Xie, S., Girshick, R., Dollár, P., Tu, Z., He, K.: Aggregated residual transformations for deep neural networks. In: IEEE Conference on Computer Vision and Pattern Recognition (CVPR), pp. 5987–5995. IEEE (2017)
13. Zoph, B., Vasudevan, V., Shlens, J., Le, Q.V.: Learning transferable architectures for scalable image recognition. arXiv preprint arXiv:1707.07012 (2017)

14. Zoph, B., Le, Q.V.: Neural architecture search with reinforcement learning. arXiv preprint arXiv:1611.01578 (2016)
15. Simonyan, K., Zisserman, A.: Very deep convolutional networks for large-scale image recognition. arXiv preprint arXiv:1409.1556 (2014)
16. Biau, G., Scornet, E.: A random forest guided tour. Test **25**(2), 197–227 (2016)
17. Bill, J., Fokoué, E.: A comparative analysis of predictive learning algorithms on high-dimensional microarray cancer data. Serdica J. Comput. **8**(2), 137–168 (2014)

Context-Aware Learning Using Transferable Features for Classification of Breast Cancer Histology Images

Ruqayya Awan[1], Navid Alemi Koohbanani[1,2], Muhammad Shaban[1], Anna Lisowska[1], and Nasir Rajpoot[1,2,3(✉)]

[1] Department of Computer Science, University of Warwick, Coventry, UK
n.m.rajpoot@warwick.ac.uk
[2] The Alan Turing Institute, London, UK
[3] Department of Pathology, University Hospitals Coventry & Warwickshire, Coventry, UK

Abstract. Convolutional neural networks (CNNs) have been recently used for a variety of histology image analysis. However, availability of a large dataset is a major prerequisite for training a CNN which limits its use by the computational pathology community. In previous studies, CNNs have demonstrated their potential in terms of feature generalizability and transferability accompanied with better performance. Considering these traits of CNN, we propose a simple yet effective method which leverages the strengths of CNN combined with the advantages of including contextual information, particularly designed for a small dataset. Our method consists of two main steps: first it uses the activation features of CNN trained for a patch-based classification and then it trains a separate classifier using features of overlapping patches to perform image-based classification using the contextual information. The proposed framework outperformed the state-of-the-art method for breast cancer classification.

Keywords: Digital pathology · Convolutional neural network
Context-aware learning · Transferable features · Breast cancer

1 Introduction

Breast cancer is the most common type of cancer diagnosed and is the second most common type of cancer with high mortality rate after lung cancer in women [1]. Due to the increased incidence of breast cancer and subjectivity in diagnosis, there is an increasing demand for automated systems. To this end, deep neural networks (DNNs) have been widely used to produce the state-of-the-art results for a variety of histology image analysis tasks such as nuclei detection and classification [2], tissue classification [3,4] and segmentation [5,6].

The CAMELYON16 challenge [6] is the best demonstration of using deep learning for automatic tissue analysis, outperforming the pathologists in terms

---

R. Awan and N. A. Koohbanani—Joint first authors.

© Springer International Publishing AG, part of Springer Nature 2018
A. Campilho et al. (Eds.): ICIAR 2018, LNCS 10882, pp. 788–795, 2018.
https://doi.org/10.1007/978-3-319-93000-8_89

of detection of tumors within the whole slide images (WSIs). The objective of this challenge was to automatically detect the metastasis in haematoxylin and eosin (H&E) stained WSIs of lymph node sections. Cruz-Roa *et al.* [3] presented a deep learning architecture for automated basal carcinoma detection. This method first learns image representation via autoencoder and then a CNN is applied on this representation to capture both translation invariant features and a compact image representation. Spanhol *et al.* [7] applied a simple CNN for classifying the BreaKHis database [8] consisting of microscopic images of benign and malignant breast tumor biopsies. Small patches were extracted at different magnification levels to train the network and during inference, final output was produced by combining the predictions of the small patches.

The generalizability property of DNN makes their features transferable to other applications which encouraged the researchers to employ transfer learning for histology images as in [5,9,10]. These features have also been used to train separate classifiers for predictions [11–14], which are particularly useful when there is not enough dataset for training the CNN from scratch. In some recent studies [15,16], context-aware based learning architecture has been introduced, in which first CNN is trained using high pixel resolution patches to extract features at a cellular level that are then fed to a second CNN, stacked on top of the first for expanding the context from a single patch to a large tissue region. The experimental results of these studies suggest that the contextual information plays a crucial role in identifying abnormalities in heterogeneous tissue structures.

Our contribution in this work is twofold. First, we propose to use CNN features as a generic descriptor for a small dataset, provided as a part of a challenge dataset. We extract transferable features from a number of networks, each trained on a different dataset for the purpose of classification by a separate classifier trained on these features. As our second contribution, we combine these features to learn context of a large patch to improve our classification performance. To this end, we use transferable features for a block of consecutive patches to train a SVM model to classify the H&E stained breast images into normal, benign, carcinoma *insitu* (CIS) and breast invasive carcinoma (BIC).

2   Dataset and Experimental Setup

We used the dataset provided as a part of the ICIAR 2018 challenge for the classification of breast cancer histology images. This dataset comprises of 400 high resolution images of size 2048×1536 pixels at $20\times$ magnification, stained with H&E stain. The pixel resolution for these images is $0.42\,\mu m$. Each image belongs to one of the four classes: normal, benign, *insitu* carcinoma or invasive carcinoma. The ground truth was provided by the two pathologists. To study the feature transferability of CNN, we experimented with other part of the challenge dataset provided for segmentation task. Ten WSIs with coarse annotations were provided for this task. We extracted patches from these WSIs after manually refining the original annotations.

The challenge dataset for a classification task consists of training images used in [14] along with 151 additional images. To evaluate the effectiveness of our proposed approach, we splitted the challenge dataset for two settings. In the first setting, we use the same images for training and testing which were used in [14] for a fair comparison. We included the additional images in our validation set while training the network. The test dataset contains two sets of images, with equal number of images in each class. The testing data is not provided with the challenge data but is made publicly available by the authors in two sets. The first test set contains 20 images while the second set contains 16 images and is referred as 'test extended' dataset in this paper. In the second setting which is used for submission to the challenge, we combined the whole challenge dataset from task-1 and the test dataset and randomly split them into 75% training and 25% validation set.

Regarding the implementation, we used residual neural network with 50 layers for patch-based classification in Tensorflow. For context-aware image-based classification, support vector machine (SVM) classifier with radial basis function (RBF) was used and implemented in MATLAB. SVM parameters are determined using cross-validation and grid search. Further details on both these steps are given in the *Methods* section.

3   Methods

In this paper, we introduce an effective model for the purpose of image-based classification using more context information, particularly for a small dataset. To this end, we design our model in two main steps: patch-based classification and context-aware image-based classification. The overall system architecture is shown in Fig. 1.

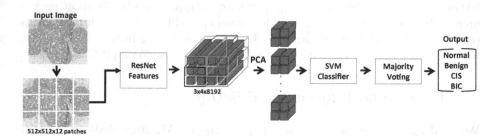

Fig. 1. Flow Diagram of our classification framework. Twelve non-overlapping patches are extracted from the input image. A 8192-dimensional feature vector is then obtained for each patch using a trained ResNet. PCA is applied to reduce the dimensionality of these features. For context-based classification, 2×2 overlapping block of features are extracted for the input image and are fed to SVM classifier, to predict label for each block. The predicted label for each block of features are then used to predict the label for the input image using majority voting.

3.1 Preprocessing

Stain inconsistency of digitized WSIs is a significant issue affecting the performance of machine learning (ML) systems. The dataset provided for this challenge contains images with large stain variation. To this end, we performed stain normalization using the Reinhard method [17], available in our group's *Stain Normalization Toolbox* [18]. This method transforms the color distribution of an image to the color distribution of a target image by matching the mean and standard deviation of the source image to that of target image. This transformation is carried out for each channel separately, in the Lab colorspace. Fig. 2 shows the output of stain normalization.

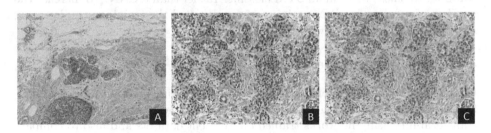

Fig. 2. Output of stain normalization: A, B and C show the target image, the original image and the stain normalized version of B respectively.

3.2 Patch-Based Classification

ResNet [19] introduced in 2015 by Microsoft has been shown to outperform several architectures including VGG [20], GoogleNet [21], PReLU-net [22] and BN-inception [23]. This network also outperformed best performing networks with a significant margin for the classification of histopathology colorectal images [24]. The state-of-the-art results of ResNet on different datasets motivated us to use it for our patch-based classification. For our experiments, we used ResNet with 50 layers, with trainable parameters initialized to random values. For network training, overlapping patches of size 512×512 pixels were extracted from the images. The network was trained for 16 epochs with batch size of 12. The best trained network was selected, based on the validation accuracy, for further processing. The training was done using stochastic gradient descent with momentum set to 0.95. The learning rate was initially set to 0.001 and was decremented after each update. Due to the very small dataset and also to make our network robust to feature transformation, we performed data augmentation involving random rotation (90 to 360° with step of 90°) and flipping during the training stage.

3.3 Context-Aware Image-Wise Classification

The above patch-based classification network learns a limited contextual representation for each class by using small patches of size 512×512 pixels. To train a classifier with larger context, we divided each image into twelve non-overlapping patches and for each patch, we then extracted 8192 dimensional feature vector from the last layer of our patch-based network. Principal component analysis (PCA) was performed to reduce the dimensionality of these features while preserving 99% of the variance. We then trained an SVM classifier with the flattened features of 2×2 overlapping blocks of patches which is equivalent to training the classifier with the features of patch 1024×1024 pixels in size. During testing, image-level label was decided by applying majority voting on the SVM predicted labels for the overlapping feature blocks of an image. This approach has been shown to improve the results in previous studies by training a CNN using the features of bigger blocks of patches. Due to the limited availability of dataset for training, we chose to train an SVM classifier rather than a CNN. To increase the number of samples for SVM training, we augmented the training samples using rotation and flipping.

4   Experimental Results

For the evaluation of our proposed method, we experimented with different configurations to show the significance of contextual information, effect of feature transferability using networks trained on different datasets and also to compare our method with the results of [14].

Firstly, we experimented with contextual information captured from the varying size of block of patches. We trained SVM with the context of 1×1 block (512×512 pixels), 2×2 block (1024×1024 pixels) and 3×3 block (1536×1536 pixels) of patches. As shown in Fig. 3(a), we obtained better accuracy with 2×2 block as compared to the 1×1 block but we observed a decline in accuracy for 3×3 block of context. It is due to the fact that the increase in context using the large block of patches reduces the amount of data for training SVM. Otherwise, incorporating a larger context could have improved our results if we had enough dataset. For our further experiments, we used 2×2 block of context for classification.

To study the feature transferability, we used activation features from three networks, each trained on a different dataset: training images used in [14], challenge dataset (WSIs) for segmentation task and the Camelyon dataset [6]. To enrich the SVM training, we added half of the additional challenge dataset to our training set. Our results demonstrate that the features learned by the first network tend to provide the most appropriate representation for training the SVM. The network trained on the WSIs has been shown to be the second best feature descriptor as the dataset used to train this network is similar to the evaluation data. While our third network, since it is trained on a completely different dataset did not perform well as compared to the other networks.

For comparative analysis of our proposed method, we compared our results with the results of previously published work of the organizers of BACH challenge [14]. For a fair comparison, we used the same dataset as in [14] for training and testing. Along with 4-class classification, we also present comparison using 2-class classification, for which we grouped normal and benign images in one class while CIS and BIC were grouped in the other class. The 2-class and 4-class comparative results are shown in Fig. 3(c) and (d) respectively. Our method achieved higher accuracy compared to [14] which demonstrates the capability of the contextual information for discriminating different classes.

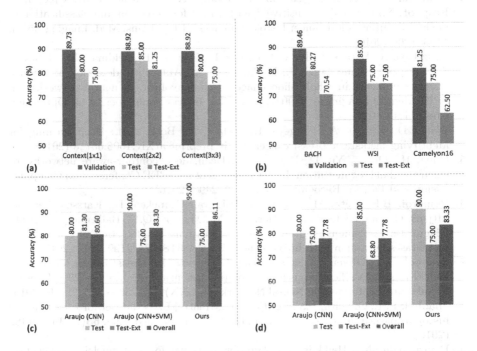

Fig. 3. Summary of our experimental results. (a) Accuracy obtained using the context of various size of blocks where Context (1×1), Context (2×2) and Context (3×3) represent contextual block of size 512×512, 1024×1024 and 1536×1537 pixels. (b) Analysis of transferable features using three networks, each trained with a different dataset where BACH, WSI and Camelyon16 represent challenge dataset for classification, challenge dataset for segmentation and Camelyon16 challenge dataset respectively. (c) and (d) show comparative analysis of our approach with the previous study [14] using both 2-class and 4-class classification respectively.

5   Conclusion

In this paper, we proposed a context-aware network for automated classification of breast cancer histology images. The proposed method leverages the power of CNNs to encode the representation of a patch into high dimensional space and uses traditional machine method (SVM) to aggregate the contextual information from the high dimensional features while having a limited dataset. Our proposed approach outperformed the existing methods proposed for the same task. The proposed method is not limited to breast cancer classification task. It could be applied to other problems where both high resolution and contextual information are required to make an optimal prediction.

References

1. Siegel, R.L., Miller, K.D., Jemal, A.: Cancer statistics, 2016. CA Cancer J. Clin. **66**(1), 7–30 (2016)
2. Sirinukunwattana, K., Raza, S.E.A., Tsang, Y.-W., Snead, D.R., Cree, I.A., Rajpoot, N.M.: Locality sensitive deep learning for detection and classification of nuclei in routine colon cancer histology images. IEEE Trans. Med. Imaging **35**(5), 1196–1206 (2016)
3. Cruz-Roa, A., Basavanhally, A., González, F., Gilmore, H., Feldman, M., Ganesan, S., Shih, N., Tomaszewski, J., Madabhushi, A.: Automatic detection of invasive ductal carcinoma in whole slide images with convolutional neural networks. In: SPIE Medical Imaging, vol. 9041, p. 904103. International Society for Optics and Photonics (2014)
4. Wang, D., Khosla, A., Gargeya, R., Irshad, H., Beck, A.H.: Deep learning for identifying metastatic breast cancer, arXiv preprint arXiv:1606.05718 (2016)
5. Chen, H., Qi, X., Yu, L., Heng, P.-A.: Dcan: deep contour-aware networks for accurate gland segmentation. In: Proceedings of the IEEE Conference on Computer Vision and Pattern Recognition, pp. 2487–2496 (2016)
6. Bejnordi, B.E., Veta, M., van Diest, P.J., van Ginneken, B., Karssemeijer, N., Litjens, G., van der Laak, J.A., Hermsen, M., Manson, Q.F., Balkenhol, M., et al.: Diagnostic assessment of deep learning algorithms for detection of lymph node metastases in women with breast cancer. JAMA **318**(22), 2199–2210 (2017)
7. Spanhol, F.A., Oliveira, L.S., Petitjean, C., Heutte, L.: Breast cancer histopathological image classification using convolutional neural networks. In: 2016 International Joint Conference on Neural Networks (IJCNN), pp. 2560–2567. IEEE (2016)
8. Spanhol, F.A., Oliveira, L.S., Petitjean, C., Heutte, L.: A dataset for breast cancer histopathological image classification. IEEE Trans. Biomed. Eng. **63**(7), 1455–1462 (2016)
9. Bayramoglu, N., Heikkilä, J.: Transfer learning for cell nuclei classification in histopathology images. In: Hua, G., Jégou, H. (eds.) ECCV 2016. LNCS, vol. 9915, pp. 532–539. Springer, Cham (2016). https://doi.org/10.1007/978-3-319-49409-8_46
10. Han, Z., Wei, B., Zheng, Y., Yin, Y., Li, K., Li, S.: Breast cancer multi-classification from histopathological images with structured deep learning model. Sci. Rep. **7**(1), 4172 (2017)
11. Xu, Y., Jia, Z., Wang, L.-B., Ai, Y., Zhang, F., Lai, M., Eric, I., Chang, C.: Large scale tissue histopathology image classification, segmentation, and visualization via deep convolutional activation features. BMC Bioinform. **18**(1), 281 (2017)
12. Valkonen, M., Kartasalo, K., Liimatainen, K., Nykter, M., Latonen, L., Ruusuvuori, P.: Dual structured convolutional neural network with feature augmentation for quantitative characterization of tissue histology. In: Proceedings of the IEEE Conference on Computer Vision and Pattern Recognition, pp. 27–35 (2017)
13. Xu, Y., Jia, Z., Ai, Y., Zhang, F., Lai, M., Eric, I., Chang, C.: Deep convolutional activation features for large scale brain tumor histopathology image classification and segmentation. In: 2015 IEEE International Conference on Acoustics, Speech and Signal Processing (ICASSP), pp. 947–951. IEEE (2015)
14. Araújo, T., Aresta, G., Castro, E., Rouco, J., Aguiar, P., Eloy, C., Polónia, A., Campilho, A.: Classification of breast cancer histology images using convolutional neural networks. PloS One **12**(6), e0177544 (2017)

15. Agarwalla, A., Shaban, M., Rajpoot, N.M.: Representation-aggregation networks for segmentation of multi-gigapixel histology images, arXiv preprint arXiv:1707.08814 (2017)
16. Bejnordi, B.E., Zuidhof, G., Balkenhol, M., Hermsen, M., Bult, P., van Ginneken, B., Karssemeijer, N., Litjens, G., van der Laak, J.: Context-aware stacked convolutional neural networks for classification of breast carcinomas in whole-slide histopathology images. J. Med. Imaging 4(4), 044504 (2017)
17. Reinhard, E., Adhikhmin, M., Gooch, B., Shirley, P.: Color transfer between images. IEEE Comput. Graph. Appl. 21(5), 34–41 (2001)
18. Khan, A.M., Rajpoot, N., Treanor, D., Magee, D.: A nonlinear mapping approach to stain normalization in digital histopathology images using image-specific color deconvolution. IEEE Trans. Biomed. Eng. 61(6), 1729–1738 (2014)
19. He, K., Zhang, X., Ren, S., Sun, J.: Deep residual learning for image recognition. In: Proceedings of the IEEE Conference on Computer Vision and Pattern Recognition, pp. 770–778 (2016)
20. Simonyan, K., Zisserman, A.: Very deep convolutional networks for large-scale image recognition, arXiv preprint arXiv:1409.1556 (2014)
21. Szegedy, C., Liu, W., Jia, Y., Sermanet, P., Reed, S., Anguelov, D., Erhan, D., Vanhoucke, V., Rabinovich, A.: Going deeper with convolutions. In: Proceedings of the IEEE Conference on Computer Vision and Pattern Recognition, pp. 1–9 (2015)
22. He, K., Zhang, X., Ren, S., Sun, J.: Delving deep into rectifiers: surpassing human-level performance on imagenet classification. In: Proceedings of the IEEE International Conference on Computer Vision, pp. 1026–1034 (2015)
23. Ioffe, S., Szegedy, C.: Batch normalization: accelerating deep network training by reducing internal covariate shift. In: International Conference on Machine Learning, pp. 448–456 (2015)
24. Korbar, B., Olofson, A.M., Miraflor, A.P., Nicka, C.M., Suriawinata, M.A., Torresani, L., Suriawinata, A.A., Hassanpour, S.: Deep learning for classification of colorectal polyps on whole-slide images. J. Pathol. Inf. 8, 30 (2017)

Hierarchical ResNeXt Models for Breast Cancer Histology Image Classification

Ismaël Koné[✉][iD] and Lahsen Boulmane[iD]

2MIA Research Group, LEM2A Lab, Faculté des Sciences, Université Moulay Ismail,
Meknes, Morocco
i.kone@edu.umi.ac.ma, l.boulmane@umi.ac.ma

Abstract. Microscopic histology image analysis is a cornerstone in early detection of breast cancer. However these images are very large and manual analysis is error prone and very time consuming. Thus automating this process is in high demand. We proposed a hierarchical system of convolutional neural networks (CNN) that classifies automatically patches of these images into four pathologies: normal, benign, in situ carcinoma and invasive carcinoma. We evaluated our system on the BACH challenge dataset of image-wise classification and a small dataset that we used to extend it. Using a train/test split of 75%/25%, we achieved an accuracy rate of 0.99 on the test split for the BACH dataset and 0.96 on that of the extension.

Keywords: CNN · ResNeXt · Learning rate · Histology images

1 Introduction

Every year, breast cancer kills more than 500,000 women around the world [19]. Early detection can help take proper actions before the spread of cancerous tissues. This has been proved to reduce death rate in US [2]. Histology image analysis is necessary to perform early diagnosis [17]. However these images are too large so manually analyzing them is very time consuming and error prone. Thus an automated system is more than welcome to reduce the burden of manual analysis.

In this scope, the BreAst Cancer Histology (BACH) Challenge[1] has been organized to stimulate scientific interest in solving this problem and finding a solution that will be a step closer to the equipment of clinical centers with such system. Specifically, it is about classifying histology images in four pathological groups: *Normal, Benign, In situ carcinoma* and *Invasive carcinoma*.

Our main contribution is a hierarchy of Convolutional Neural Network (CNN) models that gradually classify images from general pathological groups namely carcinoma and non-carcinoma and then into the four groups cited above. We trained our system on 75% of the challenge dataset (Sect. 2.2) and evaluated it on the remaining 25% (Sect. 3.3). We also extended this dataset with another one and performed the same training and evaluation.

---

[1] https://iciar2018-challenge.grand-challenge.org/dataset/.

© Springer International Publishing AG, part of Springer Nature 2018
A. Campilho et al. (Eds.): ICIAR 2018, LNCS 10882, pp. 796–803, 2018.
https://doi.org/10.1007/978-3-319-93000-8_90

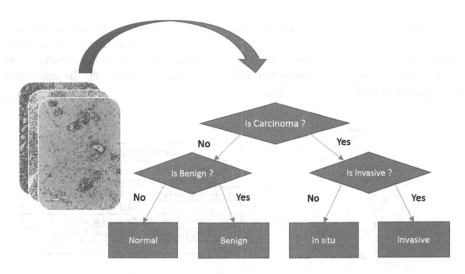

Fig. 1. Binary tree structure of the hierarchy of models for classifying images into the four pathological groups. Each question is answered by a specific model. The model in charge of classifying images into Carcinoma and Non Carcinoma deals with the top question. For the remaining questions, their models classify images into their respective children in the tree structure.

2   Method

Instead of classifying images directly into the four pathological groups that may be difficult to differentiate, our approach is about starting by a simplified version of the problem that is classifying images into two categories:

- Carcinoma: which includes In Situ and Invasive pathologies.
- Non Carcinoma: which includes Normal and Benign pathologies.

Then we classify images from each category into the two pathologies that composed them. We use a CNN model for each classification. So a CNN model that we call the general model is in charge of this simplified version of the problem. Then we have two specialized CNN models that classify respectively the Carcinoma category into In Situ and Invasive and the Non Carcinoma category into Normal and Benign. Thus we have a hierarchy of three CNN models in a binary tree structure where each model/node classifies incoming images into two types. Figure 1 synthesizes visually the structure of the hierarchy of models where each one answers a question. We describe below the underlying CNN model used and how we train them.

2.1   Model

Architecture: For all three models, we used the ResNeXt50 architecture [16] which is structured in repetitive blocks composed of convolution and non-linear operations as general CNNs. However, in a ResNeXt block, operations are performed across many branches and results are aggregated together with the block input (see Fig. 2(a)). As ResNeXt is a 1000-categories ImageNet classifier, we substituted its last fully connected layer by some custom layers to make it a 2-categories classifier (see Fig. 2(b)).

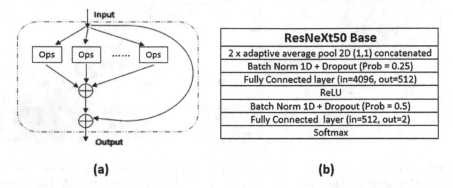

(a)   **(b)**

Fig. 2. (a) ResNeXt block. Ops stands for convolution and non-linear operations. (b) ResNeXt50 adapted to our task. ResNeXt50 Base is the original ResNeXt50 without its last layer. Below are custom last layers we added for our classification.

Baseline: instead of learning from scratch, we started from a pretrained ResNeXt50 for each model of our hierarchical system. This is one way of doing transfer learning [11] which is using a model trained for one task and re-targeting it for another related task. This is suggested in [14] as a baseline for any recognition task.

Then we fine tuned each model to its corresponding two classes. For the general model, we used the ImageNet [15] pretrained weights. For the two specialized models, we have chosen the best of: one fine tuned from ImageNet and the other from the general model. The idea of fine tuning from the general model is that it has already seen these images and learned to extract meaningful features from them.

2.2 Training

We trained each CNN model of our system following these steps:

- choosing an optimal learning rate η.
- training for 3 epochs the last layers randomly initialized using [5] while keeping pretrained ones fixed.
- training middle and last layers with different learning rates:
  - $\eta/5$ for middle layers
  - η for last layers

Additionally, during each training, we vary the optimal learning rate with a specific scheduling method. We will go over it and each step stated above with their explanations.

Optimal Learning Rate Choice: the learning rate η is one of the most important hyperparameter when training any CNN [9]. In general it is set based on trial and error. We used a method in [9] for setting an optimum value for η. The idea is to make one training run for few epochs while increasing η from a very small value after each iteration. Then we plot the accuracy against the learning rate η and note the value η_{max} where the accuracy starts diverging or decreasing after increasing. The optimal η is $1/3$ or $1/4$ of η_{max}. However we utilized an implementation of this method that uses the loss plot instead. We have found that in this case it works better when using $1/10$ of η_{max}.

Learning Rate Scheduling via Stochastic Gradient Descent with Warm Restarts (SGDR): It is a method to schedule the learning rate variation during training so as to converge rapidly. It has been proposed in [10] and achieved new state-of-the-art results on CIFAR-10 and CIFAR-100 datasets. In this approach, we decrease the optimal learning rate η following the cosine annealing scheme until nearly zero. Then we suddenly set η to its initial value and repeat again. This sudden jump of η allows to look for another local minima around that may be better. That is the idea of "Warm Restarts".

Training with Different Learning Rates: This idea has been introduced by Jeremy Howard in [6]. It is based on [20] where authors show that first layers of CNNs learn to extract generic features like edges, corners, blobs and latter ones are more specialized on the task in hand. So we avoid to alter first layers as these features are useful for any task. In the same way, we slightly alter middle layers because there are getting specialized on the task in hand and finally alter last layers with the optimal learning rate η found. That is why we choose to use $\eta/5$ and η respectively for middle layers and last layers. The number is arbitrary and chosen based on trial and error but the idea of having decreasing learning rates from last to first layers remains. Here we set the learning rate of first layers to zero.

3   Experiments and Results

3.1   Dataset

The dataset is a set of images of hematoxylin and eosin (H&E) stained breast histology microscopy. It is one of the two tracks of the ICIAR 2018 Grand Challenge on BreAst Cancer Histology (BACH) Challenge. It has 400 images equally distributed among four pathologies: *Normal, Benign, In situ carcinoma* and *Invasive carcinoma*. Images are conventional color images and are high resolution 2048×1536 pixels with a pixel scale of 0.42μm $\times 0.42\mu$m. This dataset is an extension of the BioImaging 2015 challenge [13].

We also used an additional public dataset from Bio-Image Semantic Query User Environment (BISQUE)[2] [3]. It is a very small dataset containing 58 histology images as the challenge but with less resolution: 896 × 768 pixels. But the idea is to get a system that generalizes well so heterogeneous source of data is welcome. Images are distributed among two pathological groups: *Benign* (32) and *Malignant* (26). These pathologies are excellent candidates for the two general pathological groups of the top model of our hierarchical system: *Benign* belongs to Non carcinoma and *Malignant* to Carcinoma. But for the specialized CNN models, we used only images labeled as Benign for the one that classifies between Normal and Benign.

3.2 Setup

We trained our system on a Nvidia Tesla K80 equipped environment and used the following settings for training all three compounding CNNs:

- splitting the dataset into 75% for training and 25% for validation.
- resizing all images to 299 × 299.
- augmenting the dataset by random rotations, reflections and cropping.
- setting batch size to 10.

Concerning the resize operation, we first resized the image to $(299 \times ratio) \times 299$ which preserves the ratio equals to 4/3. So the resolution became 399 × 299. Then we cropped a 299 × 299 square at the center of the resized image. This reduces of the risk of missing important parts of the image which are likely to be around its center. We did so to accelerate the training.

We implemented our system with a new library namely, fastai [7] which is based on Pytorch [12], a framework for deep learning and GPU computations.

3.3 Results Based on the Training Set

We evaluated our method on 25% of the dataset unused during training. Table 1 presents results. We performed better on the initial dataset than the extended one. Figure 3 shows the confusion matrix of results on the BACH dataset. Only one out of 100 images was misclassified. We obtained these results in less than 60 epochs of training for each model which is very fast thanks to the training approach.

3.4 Final System for the Competition and Result

For the competition we assemble four different versions of the general or *Carci* model and three versions of the specialized ones: *NorBe* and *InvIs* as named in Table 1.

---

[2] http://bioimage.ucsb.edu/research/bio-segmentation.

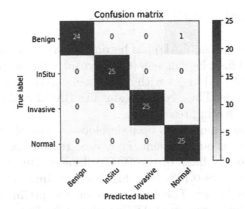

Fig. 3. Confusion matrix of the results on the BACH validation dataset.

Table 1. Performance of the method based on the validation set. Init. and Ext. are respectively BACH and BISQUE datasets. Carci is the top model of the system. NorBe and InvIs are specialized models that classify respectively into Normal and Benign and into In situ and Invasive. Last column is the preliminary competition test set result.

Models	Init.	Init. + Ext.	Competition
Carci	1.00	0.98	–
NorBe	0.98	0.965	–
InvIs	1.00	–	–
Whole system	**0.99**	0.963	**0.81**

1. **Carci:** two versions are in Table 1. They correspond to 'Init.' and 'Init. + Ext.' columns. We have built the third version by training on the whole dataset (BACH and BISQUE combined). The last one is a snapshot of 'Init' column when accuracy was 0.99.
2. **NorBe:** similar to the first three versions of *Carci* model.
3. **InvIs:** Table 1 contains one version which we obtained by using *Carci* as a pretrained model. The second version used the ImageNet pretrained model. Finally, we trained the model on the whole BACH dataset to build the last version.

When training on the whole dataset, there is no way to check overfitting in contrast to having separate train and validation sets where losses of both help check it. Thus we trusted more these latter than those trained on the whole dataset. As reported in Table 1, this system reached an accuracy of 0.81 on the preliminary competition test set and rank us the 8th place out of 50.

4   Related Work and Discussions

Computer-Aided Diagnosis (CAD) has become a major area of research in medical imaging included histology images [8]. There are many works on breast cancer detection from histology images with different datasets. It makes it difficult to fairly compare methods. Thus, competitions like BACH challenge are well suited for that and help advancing researches.

In [1], a CNN based model has been developed to classify histology images in the same four classes as our problem. They used the BioImaging 2015 challenge [13] dataset which is the basis of the BACH dataset. Our reported accuracy is better than them: 0.81 vs 0.778. But this does not imply our method is better since this dataset is larger. The best result on the preliminary results of the BACH challenge is an accuracy of 0.87 which not far from us. Besides, looking at Table 1, we may suspect our system to overfit as there is a gap of 0.19 between validation and competition test set accuracies. To combat overfitting, we used dropout [18] twice respectively with probabilities 0.25 and 0.5 (see Fig. 2(b)). Thus, we inclined towards our validation choice which may be similar to the training set. Additionally, mainly using 75% of the data could have prevented our system to discover new patterns in validation data to perform better. Likewise, not only the resize operation induces lost of image parts but may also hamper the system to capture helpful details.

5   Conclusion and Perspectives

We proposed a hierarchical system of three CNN models to solve the image-wise classification of the BACH challenge. This system classifies gradually images into two categories carcinoma and non-carcinoma and then into the four classes of the challenge. When training CNN models, we followed a scheme that accelerate convergence. We got an accuracy of 0.81 on the competition test set and rank 8th out of 51 teams. The first way to improve our system is training on the whole dataset using a strategy described in [4]. It consists in training the whole dataset until the loss reaches that of the best accuracy obtained during validation. Regarding the resize operation, we can use a left and right crop with the center crop during training. Not only this will avoid losing part of images but serve as a data augmentation strategy as well. Finally, we could increase images' size but not exceeding the original size.

References

1. Araújo, T., Aresta, G., Castro, E., Rouco, J., Aguiar, P., Eloy, V., et al.: Classification of breast cancer histology images using convolutional neural networks. PLOS ONE **12**(6), 1–14 (2017). https://doi.org/10.1371/journal.pone.0177544
2. Berry, D., Cronin, K., Plevritis, S., Fryback, D., Clarke, L., Zelen, M., et al.: Effect of screening and adjuvant therapy on mortality from breast cancer. New England J. Med. **353**(17), 1784–1792 (2005). https://doi.org/10.1056/NEJMoa050518

3. Gelasca, E., Byun, J., Obara, B., Manjunath, B.: Evaluation and benchmark for biological image segmentation. In: 15th IEEE International Conference on Image Processing, pp. 1816–1819 (2008). https://doi.org/10.1109/ICIP.2008.4712130
4. Goodfellow, I., Warde-Farley, D., Mirza, M., Courville, A., Bengio, Y.: Maxout networks. In: Proceedings of the 30th International Conference on Machine Learning. Proceedings of Machine Learning Research, vol. 28, pp. 1319–1327 (2013)
5. He, K., Zhang, X., Ren, S., Sun, J.: Delving deep into rectifiers: surpassing human-level performance on imagenet classification. In: 2015 IEEE International Conference on Computer Vision (ICCV), pp. 1026–1034 (2015). https://doi.org/10.1109/ICCV.2015.123
6. Howard, J.: Lesson 2: Deep learning v2. practical deep learning for coders (2018)
7. Howard, J., et al.: The fast.ai deep learning library, github (2018)
8. Kunio, D.: Computer-aided diagnosis in medical imaging: Historical review, current status and future potential. Comput. Med. Imaging Graph. 31(4), 198–211 (2007). https://doi.org/10.1016/j.compmedimag.2007.02.002
9. Leslie, N.: Cyclical learning rates for training neural networks. In: 2017 IEEE Winter Conference on Applications of Computer Vision (WACV), pp. 464–472 (2017). https://doi.org/10.1109/WACV.2017.58
10. Loshchilov, I., Hutter, F.: SGDR: Stochastic gradient descent with restarts. In: 6th International Conference on Learning Representations (ICLR) (2017)
11. Pan, S., Yang, Q.: A survey on transfer learning. IEEE Trans. Knowl. Data Eng. 22(10), 1345–1359 (2010). https://doi.org/10.1109/TKDE.2009.191
12. Paszke, A., Gross, S., Chintala, S., Chanan, G., Yang, E., De Vito, Z., et al.: Automatic differentiation in pytorch. In: 31st Conference on NIPS 2017 Workshop Autodiff (2017)
13. Pêgo, A., Aguiar, P.: Bioimaging 2015. In: 4th International Symposium in Applied Bioimaging the Pre-Clinical Challenge in 3D (2015)
14. Razavian, A., Azizpour, H., Sullivan, J., Carlsson, S.: CNN features off-the-shelf: an astounding baseline for recognition. In: 2014 IEEE Conference on Computer Vision and Pattern Recognition Workshops, pp. 512–519 (2014). https://doi.org/10.1109/CVPRW.2014.131
15. Russakovsky, O., Deng, J., Su, H., Krause, J., Satheesh, S., Ma, S., et al.: Imagenet large scale visual recognition challenge. Int. J. Comput. Vis. 115, 211–252 (2015). https://doi.org/10.1007/s11263-015-0816-y
16. Saining, X., Ross, G., Piotr, D., Zhuowen, T., Kaiming, H.: Aggregated residual transformations for deep neural networks. In: The IEEE Conference on Computer Vision and Pattern Recognition (CVPR), pp. 1492–1500 (2017)
17. Society, A.C.: Breast cancer facts & figures 2017–2018 (2017)
18. Srivastava, N., Hinton, G., Krizhevsky, A., Sutskever, I., Salakhutdinov, R.: Dropout: a simple way to prevent neural networks from overfitting. J. Mach. Learn. Res. 15, 1929–1958 (2014)
19. WHO: WHO position paper on mammography screening. WHO Press, 20 Avenue Appia, 1211 Geneva 27, Switzerland (2014)
20. Zeiler, M.D., Fergus, R.: Visualizing and understanding convolutional networks. In: Fleet, D., Pajdla, T., Schiele, B., Tuytelaars, T. (eds.) ECCV 2014. LNCS, vol. 8689, pp. 818–833. Springer, Cham (2014). https://doi.org/10.1007/978-3-319-10590-1_53

Classification of Breast Cancer Histology Image using Ensemble of Pre-trained Neural Networks

Sai Saketh Chennamsetty[1], Mohammed Safwan[2], and Varghese Alex[3(✉)]

[1] Bangalore, India
sakari1994@gmail.com
[2] Gurgaon, India
kp.mohd.safwan@gmail.com
[3] Chennai, India
varghesealex90@gmail.com

Abstract. Breast cancer is one of the most commonly occurring types of cancer and the treatment administered to a subject is dependent on the grade or type of the lesion. In this manuscript, we make use of an ensemble of convolutional neural networks (CNN) to classify histology images as Normal, In-situ, Benign or Invasive. The performance of CNN is dependent on the network architecture, number of training instances and also on the data normalization scheme. However, there exists neither a single architecture nor a pre-processing regime that promises best performance. For the reason stated above, we use 3 CNNs trained on different pre-processing regimes to form an ensemble. On the held out test data (n = 40), the proposed scheme achieved an accuracy of 97.5%. On the challenge data (n = 100) provided by the organizers, the proposed technique achieved an accuracy of 87% and was jointly adjudged as the top performing algorithm for the task of classification of breast cancer from histology images.

Keywords: Breast cancer · Histology · CNN · Ensemble

1 Introduction

Breast cancer is one of the major causes of death among women, thus early detection and diagnosis of the breast cancer is of utmost importance so as to reduce the risk of progression and thereby improve the life span of the subject. In a clinical setup the presence of lesion is found by mammography, while the grade of lesion is found by performing histology studies on the biopsy tissues.

For various classification and pattern recognition based tasks, convolutional neural networks (CNN) is currently the technique that produces state of the art performance [1–3]. The improved performance of CNNs comes at the cost

---

All authors have contributed equally.

© Springer International Publishing AG, part of Springer Nature 2018
A. Campilho et al. (Eds.): ICIAR 2018, LNCS 10882, pp. 804–811, 2018.
https://doi.org/10.1007/978-3-319-93000-8_91

of requiring a large amount of annotated data. However, in the field of medical image analysis, presence of such high quality labeled dataset is rare and sparse. Such conditions are circumvented by first training (pre-training) the CNNs on datasets such as natural images where the amount of labeled data is large. Further, the networks are then trained on limited labeled medical images or volumes. This process is called as fine-tuning of pre-trained networks. This app-roach has been widely used for numerous medical image analysis applications such as detection of thoraco-abdominal lymph node & interstitial lung disease (ILD) from medical volumes [4], polyp detection from colonoscopy video frames [5], classification of mammograms [6], etc.

For classification related tasks, an ensemble of classifiers typically outperform single classifier as an ensemble reduces variance in the final prediction [7]. In the context of CNNs, an ensemble of classifiers can be built by either changing the architecture of the network or by training a network on data pre-processed using different variants of data normalization schemes.

The tasks presented to the participants of ICIAR-2018 breast histology chal-lenge [8] were two folds; namely, "microscopy images" classification and "whole-slide image" pixel-wise classification. This manuscript reports our submission to the microscopy image classification using an ensemble of classifiers (CNNs). Given a test data, each CNN in the ensemble predicts the image as one of the four classes (normal, in-situ, benign or invasive). The final prediction associated with the test data was done by performing maximum voting scheme.

2   Materials and Methods

2.1   Data

The data was made available as part of the ICIAR-2018 grand challenge. The dataset consists of 400 images which were equally distributed across the four classes: normal, benign, in situ carcinoma and invasive carcinoma. Figure 1(a d) illustrates the aforementioned 4 classes when the tissue is viewed under a micro-scope after appropriate staining.

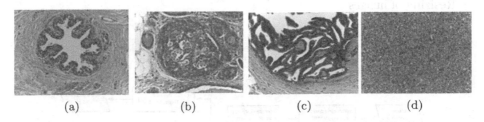

(a)   (b)   (c)   (d)

Fig. 1. Histology images. (a) Normal tissue (b) Benign lesion (c) in situ carcinoma (d) Invasive carcinoma

2.2 Convolutional Neural Networks

Traditional CNNs such as AlexNet, VGG-16, VGG-19, etc. comprises of convolutional layers, pooling layers and fully connected layer. Max pooling is one of the oft used pooling technique so as to reduce the spatial dimension of the feature maps as the depth of the network increases. Furthermore, it also aids in learning translation invariant features from the data. As the depth of the network increases, the features learned by the network becomes more abstract and thus the features learned by a layer are typically considered to be a higher level representation of the data than the features learned in the preceding layers in the network. The features of the highest abstraction are then vectorized to form the fully connected layers. In traditional CNNs, the class associated to an incoming data is predicted based on the activation produced by the penultimate layer in the network. The downside of using traditional CNNs are: (1) the presence of multiple fully connected layers which lead to a drastic increase in the number of trainable parameters, and (2) making decision or the classification based solely on the highest level of abstraction of the data.

The introduction of skip and residual connections between different layers of the network aid in building deeper and newer variants of CNNs such as deep Residual Networks (ResNets) [9] and Densely connected Networks (DenseNets) [10]. When compared to traditional networks, both DenseNets and ResNets comprises fewer number of fully connected layers, resulting in fewer number of trainable parameters. Despite having fewer parameters, the presence of the skip and residual connections in the Densely connected Networks and Residual Networks achieve better classification performance as the decision making is based on both high and low level features extracted by the network.

In this manuscript, we make use of a Densely connected CNN and a deep Residual CNN pre-trained on natural images [11] for classifying the histology slides. The pre-trained networks were made available by PyTorch [12].

2.3 Preprocessing of Data

In this work, the preprocessing pipeline comprises of:

- Resizing of images
- Z-score Normalization

The pre-processing pipeline is illustrated in Fig. 2.

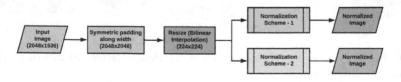

Fig. 2. Pre-processing pipeline.

Both the networks were pre-trained on images with same dimensions along the height and width of the data, however, the histology data provided by the organizers had a dimension of 2048 × 1536. The images were symmetrically padded along the width to produce an image with same dimension along height and width. The resultant images were resized to 224 × 224 using bilinear interpolation. The resized images were then normalized using z-score normalization.

Z-score normalization, an often used normalization scheme in machine learning helps in achieving zero mean and unit variance data, Eq. 1.

$$x_{norm} = \frac{x - \mu}{\sigma} \tag{1}$$

In Eq. 1, x_{norm} is the normalized data, x is the data, μ is the mean of the entire training data while σ is the standard deviation of the pixel intensities of all images that constitute the training database. Two variants of the dataset were made by using:

1. Normalizing the histology data using the statistics (mean and standard deviation) computed from the data that used to pre-train the network [ImageNet data]. We refer this as *Normalization Scheme* − 1 in the pre-processing pipeline.
2. Normalizing the histology data using the statistics computed from the entire training histology data. This is referred as *Normalization Scheme* − 2 in the pipeline.

Normalizing the entire dataset with the aforementioned normalization schemes gave rise to 2 distinct datasets. These datasets were then used to train classifiers in the ensemble.

2.4 Training of CNNs

Training of ResNet-101. The pre-trained network made available by the PyTorch community was fine-tuned with 70 images from each class. The network was validated and tested on 20 and 10 images from each class respectively. The hindmost layer in ResNet-101 was modified from 1000 neurons to 4 neurons (Normal, In-situ, Benign, Invasive) & the parameters of the network were learned by minimizing the cross entropy loss with the learning rate set to 0.0001 and ADAM [13] as the optimizer. The data normalized by statistics attained from the ImageNet dataset (Normalization scheme-1) was used to train the network.

Training of DenseNet-161. The network pre-trained on ImageNet database was fine-tuned with both variants of the histology data. The parameters of the network were learned by minimizing the cross entropy between the predictions made by the network and the true label/class associated with the data. The network was trained for 30 number of epochs with the learning rate set to 0.0001 and ADAM as the optimizer. Two variants of the same network were achieved by training the model on two distinct normalization schemes explored in this work.

2.5   Testing

The image to be tested is first passed through the pre-processing pipeline to get two images normalized using different statistics. These images are then passed through appropriate models in the classifier to get multiple predictions. A majority voting criterion was used on the list of predictions by the ensemble of classifiers to assign the final prediction to the test data. The testing regime is shown in Fig. 3.

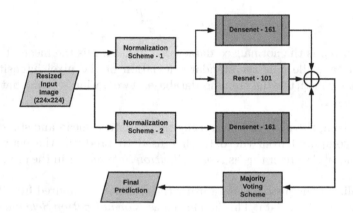

Fig. 3. Proposed testing pipeline.

3   Results

The trained models were tested on a held out test dataset (n = 40) and on the challenge data (n = 100). The held out test data comprises of equal number of images from each class.

3.1   Effect of Using Pre-trained Models

Since the models were trained on a large cohort of natural images (ImageNet), kernels in the networks would respond to edges, patterns and textures in the images. Thus initializing the network with pre-trained weights is analogous to providing a good weight initialization scheme to the network. Three models namely AlexNet, ResNet-18 and DenseNet-121 were trained from scratch and the weights of the network were initialized using Xavier initialization. Furthermore, ResNet-18 and DenseNet-121 model have fewer number of parameters when compared to the models such as Densnet-161 and ResNet-101. The accuracy attained by each classifier on the validation and held out test data is given in Table 1. It was observed that the model initialized with pre-trained weights (DenseNet-161) and performing a transfer learning approach aided in achieving better validation and testing accuracy when compared to models trained from scratch.

Table 1. Performance of different networks. Except for DenseNet-161, weights and biases in other networks were initialized using Xavier initialization.

Model	Validation accuracy	Testing accuracy	No. of Parameters
AlexNet	0.68	0.53	57020228
ResNet-18	0.71	0.63	11178564
DenseNet-121	0.79	0.65	6957956
DenseNet-161	0.98	0.83	26480836

3.2 Effect of Using Ensemble of Models

The performance of each model in the ensemble is given in Table 2(a–c). It was observed that each model had an associated bias and variance. Ensembling the models and using majority voting scheme for final prediction aids in producing performance better than individual models, (Table 2(d)). On the limited dataset (n = 40), the technique achieved an accuracy of 97.5%.

It was observed that the sensitivity of scheme utilized in the manuscript for classes namely Normal, In-Situ & Benign were 100%, while the sensitivity for Invasive class was 91%. The specificity of the ensemble of classifiers associated to classes Normal, In-Situ and Invasive were 100%, while the specificity for Benign was 97%.

Table 2. Confusion matrix showing result achieved by different models

(a) DenseNet-161-NS-2

		Prediction		
		Benign	Insitu	Invasive	Normal
	Benign	8	0	2	0
Truth	Insitu	1	9	0	0
	Invasive	3	0	7	0
	Normal	1	0	0	9

(b) ResNet-101-NS-1

		Prediction		
		Benign	Insitu	Invasive	Normal
	Benign	9	0	1	0
Truth	Insitu	0	9	0	1
	Invasive	1	0	9	0
	Normal	0	0	0	10

(c) DenseNet-161-NS-1

		Prediction		
		Benign	Insitu	Invasive	Normal
	Benign	8	0	1	1
Truth	Insitu	0	10	0	0
	Invasive	0	0	10	0
	Normal	0	0	0	10

(d) Ensemble

		Prediction		
		Benign	Insitu	Invasive	Normal
	Benign	9	0	1	0
Truth	Insitu	0	10	0	0
	Invasive	0	0	10	0
	Normal	0	0	0	10

The ability of the classifier to demarcate between more aggressive stages of the disease from less malignant stages of the disease is studied by clubbing various classes. For example, classes such as In-Situ and Invasive were clubbed to form a new class "Carcinoma", while images labeled as Normal and Benign were jointly called as "Non-Carcinoma", Table 3. For the 2-class problem, we observed that the proposed scheme achieved a sensitivity and specificity of 95% and 100% respectively.

Table 3. Performance of the ensemble of classifier in distinguishing more aggressive class (Invasive and In-Situ) from less malignant class (Normal and Benign).

		Prediction	
		Carcinoma	Non-Carcinoma
Truth	Carcinoma	20	0
	Non-Carcinoma	1	19

3.3   Performance on the Challenge Data

The efficacy of the proposed technique was determined by computing the performance of the technique on the test data provided by the challenge organizers. A total of 100 images without their associated ground truths were provided to all the participating teams in the challenge and performance of each team was computed by the challenge organizers. On the leader-board generated by the organizers [14], our technique shared the spot of the top performing algorithm, Table 4.

Table 4. Performance of the proposed technique on the challenge data (n = 100)

Position	Team number	Accuracy (%)
1	216 (Ours)	87
1	248	87
3	1	86

4   Conclusion

In this paper, we present an ensemble of models trained for the classification of breast cancer histology images into four classes namely Benign, Insitu, Invasive and Normal. The absence of large number training instances were circumvented by fine-tuning pre-trained models. Networks with different architectures were trained on different variants of data obtained by adopting two different normalization schemes. A total of 3 CNNs were used to form an ensemble of classifier and during the testing phase, each entity in the ensemble produced a prediction. From the 3 predictions, the final classification was done based on majority voting.

On the held out test data (n = 40), it was observed that the ensemble of classifiers produced better results than the individual entities in the ensemble. The proposed scheme achieved an accuracy of 97.5% and achieved a sensitivity of 100% for the classes "Normal", "In-Situ" and "Benign". For the task of differentiating carcinoma input images from non-carcinoma images, the technique achieved a sensitivity and specificity of 95% and 100% respectively.

On the challenge data (n = 100), the proposed technique was adjudged jointly as the top performing submission, thus indicating good generalization capabilities of the trained networks.

References

1. Krizhevsky, A., Sutskever, I., Hinton, G.E.: Imagenet classification with deep convolutional neural networks. In: Advances in Neural Information Processing Systems 2012, pp. 1097–1105 (2012)
2. Simonyan, K., Zisserman, A.: Very deep convolutional networks for large-scale image recognition. arXiv preprint arXiv:1409.1556, 4 September 2014
3. Szegedy, C., Liu, W., Jia, Y., Sermanet, P., Reed, S., Anguelov, D., Erhan, D., Vanhoucke, V., Rabinovich, A.: Going deeper with convolutions. In: Proceedings of the IEEE Conference on Computer Vision and Pattern Recognition, pp. 1–9 (2015)
4. Shin, H.C., Roth, H.R., Gao, M., Lu, L., Xu, Z., Nogues, I., Yao, J., Mollura, D., Summers, R.M.: Deep convolutional neural networks for computer-aided detection: CNN architectures, dataset characteristics and transfer learning. IEEE Trans. Med. Imaging 35(5), 1285–98 (2016)
5. Tajbakhsh, N., Shin, J.Y., Gurudu, S.R., Hurst, R.T., Kendall, C.B., Gotway, M.B., Liang, J.: Convolutional neural networks for medical image analysis: full training or fine tuning? IEEE Trans. Med. imaging 35(5), 1299–312 (2016)
6. Carneiro, G., Nascimento, J., Bradley, A.P.: Unregistered multiview mammogram analysis with pre-trained deep learning models. In: Navab, N., Hornegger, J., Wells, W.M., Frangi, A.F. (eds.) MICCAI 2015. LNCS, vol. 9351, pp. 652–660. Springer, Cham (2015). https://doi.org/10.1007/978-3-319-24574-4_78
7. Konstantinos, K., Wenjia, B., Enzo, F., Steven, M., Matthew, S., Nick, P., Martin, R., Matthew, L., Bernhard, K., Daniel, R., Ben, G.: Ensembles of Multiple Models and Architectures for Robust Brain Tumour Segmentation. arXiv preprint arXiv:1711.01468, 04 Nov 2017
8. https://iciar2018-challenge.grand-challenge.org/
9. He, K., Zhang, X., Ren, S., Sun, J.: Identity mappings in deep residual networks. In: Leibe, B., Matas, J., Sebe, N., Welling, M. (eds.) ECCV 2016. LNCS, vol. 9908, pp. 630–645. Springer, Cham (2016). https://doi.org/10.1007/978-3-319-46493-0_38
10. Huang, G., Liu, Z., Weinberger, K.Q., van der Maaten, L.: Densely connected convolutional networks. arXiv preprint arXiv:1608.06993, 25 August 2016
11. Deng, J., Dong, W., Socher, R., Li, L.J., Li, K., Fei-Fei, L.: Imagenet: a large-scale hierarchical image database. In: IEEE Conference on Computer Vision and Pattern Recognition, CVPR 2009, pp. 248–255. IEEE, 20 June 2009
12. Paszke, A., Gross, S., Chintala, S., Chanan, G., Yang, E., DeVito, Z., Lin, Z., Desmaison, A., Antiga, L., Lerer, A.: Automatic differentiation in PyTorch (2017)
13. Kingma, D.P., Ba, J.: Adam: a method for stochastic optimization. arXiv preprint arXiv:1412.6980v9, 30 January 2017
14. https://iciar2018-challenge.grand-challenge.org/results/

Classification of Breast Cancer Histology Images Using Transfer Learning

Sulaiman Vesal[1], Nishant Ravikumar[1(✉)], AmirAbbas Davari[1],
Stephan Ellmann[2], and Andreas Maier[1]

[1] Pattern Recognition Lab, Friedrich-Alexander-Universität Erlangen-Nürnberg,
Erlangen, Germany
sulaiman.vesal@fau.de, mta08nr@gmail.com
[2] Radiologisches Institut, Universitätsklinikum Erlangen, Erlangen, Germany

Abstract. Breast cancer is one of the leading causes of mortality in
women. Early detection and treatment are imperative for improving survival rates, which have steadily increased in recent years as a result of
more sophisticated computer-aided-diagnosis (CAD) systems. CAD systems are essential to reduce subjectivity and supplement the analyses
conducted by specialists. We propose a transfer learning based approach,
for the task of breast histology image classification into four tissue subtypes, namely, normal, benign, *in situ* carcinoma and invasive carcinoma.
The histology images, provided as part of the BACH 2018 grand challenge, were first normalized to correct for color variations induced during
slide preparation. Subsequently, image patches were extracted and used
to fine-tune Google's Inception-V3 and ResNet50 convolutional neural
networks (CNNs), both pre-trained on the ImageNet database, enabling
them to learn domain-specific features, necessary to classify the histology images. Classification accuracy was evaluated using 3-fold cross validation. The Inception-V3 network achieved an average test accuracy of
97.08% for four classes, marginally outperforming the ResNet50 network,
which achieved an average accuracy of 96.66%.

1 Introduction

According to a recent report published by the American Cancer Society, breast
cancer is the most prevalent form of cancer in women, in the USA. In 2017 alone,
studies indicate that approximately 252,000 new cases of invasive breast cancer
and 63,000 cases of *in situ* breast cancer are expected to be diagnosed, with
40,000 breast cancer-related deaths expected to occur [1]. Consequently, there
is a real need for early diagnosis and treatment, in order to reduce morbidity
rates and improve patients' quality of life. Histopathology remains crucial to the
diagnostic process and the gold standard for differentiating between benign and
malignant tissue, and distinguishing between patients suffering from *in situ* and
invasive carcinoma [2]. Diagnosis and identification of breast cancer sub-types
typically involve collection of tissue biopsies from masses identified using mammography or ultrasound imaging, followed by histological analysis. Tissue samples are usually stained with Hematoxylin and Eosin (H&E) and subsequently,

visually assessed by pathologists using light microscopy. Visual assessment of tissue microstructure and the overall organization of nuclei in histology images is time-consuming and can be highly subjective, due to the complex nature of the visible structures. Consequently, automatic computer-aided-diagnosis systems are essential to reduce the workload of specialists by improving diagnostic efficiency, and to reduce subjectivity in disease classification.

Classification of histology images into cancer sub-types and metastases detection in whole-slide images are challenging tasks. Numerous studies have proposed automated approaches to address the same in recent years. Kothari et al. [3] examined the utility of biologically interpretable shape-based features for classification of histological renal tumor images. They extracted shape-based features that captured the distribution of tissue structures in each image and employed these features within a multi-class classification model. Doyle et al. [4] proposed an automated framework for distinguishing between low and high grades of breast cancer, from H&E-stained histology images. They employed a large number of image-derived features together with spectral clustering to reduce the dimensionality of the feature space. The reduced feature set was subsequently used to train a support vector machine classifier to distinguish between cancerous and non-cancerous images, and low and high grades of breast cancer. Wang et al. [5] proposed an award-winning (at the International Symposium on Biomedical Imaging) deep learning framework for whole-slide classification and cancer metastases detection in breast sentinel lymph node images. In a recent study [6], the authors proposed a convolutional neural network (CNN) based approach to classifying H&E-stained breast histology images into four tissue classes, namely, healthy, benign, in situ carcinoma and invasive carcinoma, with a limited number of training samples. The features extracted by the CNN were used for training a Support Vector Machine classifier. Accuracies of 77.8% for four class classification and 83.3% for carcinoma/non-carcinoma classification were achieved. In this study, we investigate the efficacy of transfer-learning for the task of image-wise classification of H&E-stained breast cancer histology images and examine the classification performance of the pre-trained Inception-V3 [7] and ResNet50 [8] networks, on the BACH 2018 challenge data set.

2 Methods

The data set used in this study was provided as part of BACH 2018 grand challenge[1], comprising H&E-stained breast histology microscopy images. The images are high-resolution (2040 × 1536 pixels), uncompressed, and annotated as normal, benign, in situ carcinoma or invasive carcinoma, as per the predominant tissue type visible in each image. The annotation was performed by two medical experts and images with disagreements were discarded. All images were digitized using the same acquisition conditions, with a magnification of 200×. The data set comprises 400 images (100 samples per class), with a pixel scale of 0.42 μm × 0.42 μm. It was partitioned into training, validation (80 samples) and test

---

[1] https://iciar2018-challenge.grand-challenge.org/home/.

(20 samples) sets, by selecting images at random for each class independently (Fig. 1).

2.1 Stain Normalization

A common problem with histological image analysis is substantial variation in color between images due to differences in color responses of slide scanners, raw materials and manufacturing techniques of stain vendors, and staining protocols. Consequently, stain normalization is essential as a pre-processing step, prior to conducting any analyses using histology images. Various strategies have been proposed for stain normalization in histological images. In this paper, we used the approach proposed by Reinhard et al. [9] which matches the statistics of color histograms of a source and target image, following transformation of the RGB images to the de-correlated LAB color space. Here, the mean and standard deviation of each channel in the source image is matched to that of the target by means of a set of linear transforms in the LAB color space. Histogram matching techniques assume that the proportions of stained tissue components for each staining agent are similar across the images being normalized. Figure 2 illustrates the effect of stain normalization on a few samples from the breast cancer histology image data set using the method proposed in [9].

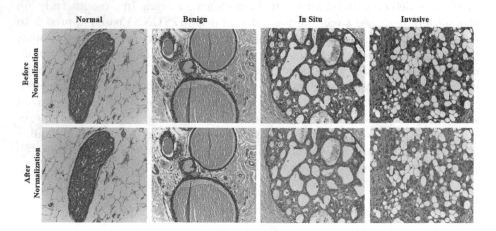

Fig. 1. Examples of histology images from each class before (top row) and after (bottom row) stain normalization.

2.2 Pre-processing

Deep learning approaches are heavily dependent on the volume of training data available, with models of higher complexity requiring more data to generalize well and avoid over-fitting to the training samples. A common challenge in the medical domain is a lack of sufficient data, as was the case with the BACH

2018 challenge. Additionally, the breast histology images provided in the challenge data set are very large in size, spanning 2040×1536 pixels. In order to address the issues of limited data and large image sizes, we extracted patches from each image and augmented the data set using a variety of rigid transformations, thereby increasing the number of training samples. Image-wise classification into tissue/cancer sub-types requires learning features describing overall tissue architecture and localized organization of nuclei. Consequently, we chose to extract patches of size 512×512 pixels from each image, while ensuring 50% overlap between patches (similar to [6]), as there was no guarantee that smaller patches would contain information relevant to the class assigned to the whole image. This resulted in the extraction of 35 patches from each image and a final data set comprising 11,200 patches.

Additionally, to enrich the training set we augmented the data by applying varying degrees of rotation and flipping the extracted patches. This mode of data augmentation emulates a real-world scenario as there is no fixed orientation adopted by pathologists when analyzing histology slides/images. Such a patch extraction and dataset augmentation approach have been used previously for an identical classification problem [6]. The training data was augmented by flipping the extracted patches along their horizontal and vertical edges. Thus, each patch was transformed to create 2 additional, unique patches resulting in a total of 33,600 training and validation patches from the original 320 training images. During the training, we also applied real-time augmentation to rotate the patches randomly by $90, 180, 270°$. The label for each patch was inherited from the class assigned to the original image. The remaining 'unseen' 80 images were used as test data, to evaluate the classification accuracy of the methods investigated.

2.3   Pre-trained CNN Architectures

The application of CNNs pre-trained on large annotated image databases, such as ImageNet for example, to images from different modalities/domains, for various classification tasks, is referred to as transfer learning. Pre-trained CNNs can be fine-tuned on medical image data sets, enabling large networks to converge quicker and learn domain-/task-specific features. Fine-tuning pre-trained CNNs is crucial for their re-usability [10]. With such an approach, the original network architecture is maintained and the pre-trained weights are used to initialize the network. The initialized weights are subsequently updated during the fine-tuning process, enabling the network to learn features specific to the task of interest. Recently, numerous studies have demonstrated that fine-tuning is effective and efficient for a variety of classification tasks in the medical domain [11]. In this study, we investigate two well known pre-trained CNN architectures, namely, Google's Inception-V3 [7] and deep residual convolutional (ResNet50) network [8], which are fine-tuned to learn domain and modality specific features for classifying breast histology images. ResNet50 is based on a residual learning framework where, layers within a network are reformulated to learn a residual mapping rather than the desired unknown mapping between the inputs and outputs. Such a network is easier to optimize and consequently, enables training of deeper networks, which correspondingly leads to an overall improvement in network capacity and performance. A recent study showed that Google's Inception-V3 network, pre-trained on ImageNet and fine-tuned using images of skin lesions, achieved very high accuracy for skin cancer classification, comparable to that of numerous dermatologists [12]. The Inception-V3 network employs factorized inception modules, allowing the network to choose suitable kernel sizes for the convolution layers. This enables the network to learn both low-level features with small convolutions and high-level features with larger ones.

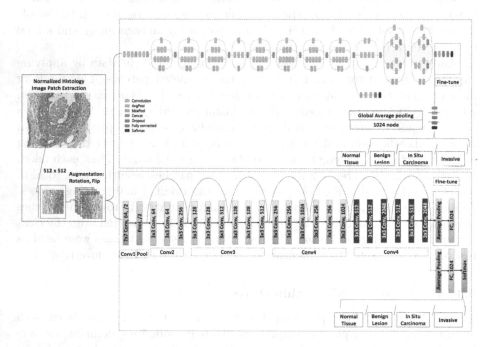

Fig. 2. Breast histology image classification workflow by fine-tuning Google's Inception-V3 and ResNet50 network architectures. The block on the left represents the pre-processing steps and the blocks on the right depict the Inception-V3 (top) and ResNet50 (bottom) network architectures.

The dataset was pre-processed as described in the previous section and used to fine-tune Google's Inception-V3 and ResNet50 networks. While such a transfer learning approach has been adopted for a variety of classification and detection tasks in medical images, few studies have employed the same for breast cancer histology image classification. Figure 2 describes our proposed workflow for the Inception-V3 and ResNet50 network architectures. The original Inception network is modified by replacing the last 5 layers with an average global pooling layer, 1 fully connected layer, and a softmax classifier. The latter outputs probabilities for each of the four classes of interest, for each patch, fed as input to the network during the fine-tuning process. The stochastic gradient descent optimizer with momentum was employed to train the Inception-V3 network, with a batch size of 32 for both training and validation. A learning rate and Nesterov momentum of 0.0001 and 0.9, respectively, were found to be suitable. The network stopped learning after 100 epochs. The same fine-tuning approach was applied to the ResNet50 network with identical optimization parameters. Model performance was measured by first classifying several patches extracted from each unseen test image, and then combining the classification results of all patches through a majority voting process, to obtain the final class label for each image. We trained and evaluated classification accuracy of both networks with the same configuration using 3-fold cross-validation to ensure consistency.

3   Results

We conducted several experiments on the challenge data set to evaluate the classification performance of the networks investigated. First, the overall prediction accuracy of the networks was assessed as the ratio between the number of images classified correctly and the total number of images evaluated in the cross validation experiments. Average patch-wise and image-wise classification accuracy are presented in Table 1 for Inception-V3 and ResNet50. We also implemented the CNN model proposed in [6] to compare the performance of these transfer learning approaches with a CNN trained from scratch (refer to Table 1). Patch-wise classification accuracy of Inception-V3 for the validation and test sets were 93.40% and 92.95%, respectively. The ResNet50 network on the other hand achieved patch-wise classification accuracies of 93.02% and 92.95% for the validation and test sets, respectively. Additionally, the results presented in Table 1 indicate that transfer learning approaches achieve significant improvements in classification accuracy compared to a state-of-the-art CNN model trained from scratch [6]. As discussed previously, whole image classification was achieved using a majority voting process, based on the patch-wise class labels estimated using each network. Inception-V3 achieved image-wise classification accuracies of 96.66% and 97.08%, for the validation and test sets, respectively. Meanwhile, the ResNet50 network achieved classification accuracies of 95.41% and 96.66% for the validation and test sets, respectively. Overall, Inception-V3 and ResNet50 consistently outperformed the [6] network, achieving higher patch-wise and image-wise classification accuracy, for both the validation and test data.

We also computed the average receiver operating characteristic (ROC) curves (evaluated across the cross validation experiments) for each network, depicted in Fig. 3. ROC curves plot the true positive rate (TPR) versus the false positive rate (FPR) at different threshold settings. TPR also known as sensitivity, represents the proportion of correctly classified samples and FPR, also known as fall-out, represents the proportion of incorrectly classified samples. Thus classification accuracy was measured as the area under the ROC curve (AUC), with an area of 1 representing perfect classification on the test set. We assessed network performance for each class individually by computing their average ROCs and calculated their corresponding AUCs (presented in Fig. 3). The overall specificity and sensitivity of both Inception-V3 and ResNet50 is approximately 99.0%.

Table 1. Average patch-wise and image-wise classification accuracy (%) for all three networks.

Model	Patch-Wise		Image-Wise	
	Validation Set(%)	Test Set(%)	Validation Set(%)	Test Set(%)
Inception-V3	93.40	92.95	96.66	97.08
ResNet50	93.02	92.95	95.41	96.66
Araujo et al. [6]	88.95	88.15	82.91	93.33

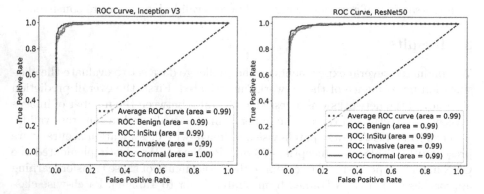

Fig. 3. ROC curves for unseen test set using Google's Inception-V3 and ResNet50 fine-tuned architectures.

4   Conclusions

A transfer learning-based approach for the classification of breast cancer histology images is presented in this study. The network learns features using Google's Inception-V3 and residual network (ResNet50) architectures, which have been pre-trained on ImageNet. The data set of images provided for the BACH 2018 grand challenge are classified into four tissue classes, namely, normal, benign, *in situ* carcinoma and invasive carcinoma. We trained all the networks using 80% of the data set for training and validation, in all 3-fold cross validation experiments, and tested their performance on the remaining 20% of images. The proposed transfer-learning approach is simple, effective and efficient for automatic classification of breast cancer histology images. The investigated networks successfully transferred ImageNet knowledge encoded as convolutional features to the problem of histology image classification, in the presence of limited training data. The residual network (ResNet50) and Google's Inception-V3 outperformed a CNN network trained from scratch consistently, in terms of classification accuracy. The presented work demonstrates the applicability and powerful classification capacity of transfer learning approaches, for the automatic analysis of breast cancer histology images. However, majority voting is a limitation of this study as there is a possibility that cancerous cells are present in only a small part of the image, while the rest of the image depicts healthy or benign tissue. Such cases lead to high false negative rates. Future work will look to address this limitation of majority voting by devising a suitable alternative approach.

References

1. DeSantis, C.E., Ma, J., Goding Sauer, A., Newman, L.A., Jemal, A.: Breast cancer statistics, 2017, racial disparity in mortality by state. CA Canc. J. Clin. **67**(6), 439–448 (2017)
2. Xu, Y., Jia, Z., Wang, L.B., Ai, Y., Zhang, F., Lai, M., Chang, E.I.C.: Large scale tissue histopathology image classification, segmentation, and visualization via deep convolutional activation features. BMC Bioinform. **18**(1), 281 (2017)
3. Kothari, S., Phan, J.H., Young, A.N., Wang, M.D.: Histological image classification using biologically interpretable shape-based features. BMC Med. Imaging **13**(1), 9 (2013)
4. Doyle, S., Agner, S., Madabhushi, A., Feldman, M., Tomaszewski, J.: Automated grading of breast cancer histopathology using spectral clustering with textural and architectural image features. In: 5th IEEE International Symposium on Biomedical Imaging: From Nano to Macro, ISBI 2008, pp. 496–499. IEEE (2008)
5. Wang, D., Khosla, A., Gargeya, R., Irshad, H., Beck, A.H.: Deep learning for identifying metastatic breast cancer. arXiv preprint arXiv:1606.05718 (2016)
6. Araújo, T., Aresta, G., Castro, E., Rouco, J., Aguiar, P., Eloy, C., Polónia, A., Campilho, A.: Classification of breast cancer histology images using convolutional neural networks. PLOS ONE **12**(6), 1–14 (2017)
7. Szegedy, C., Vanhoucke, V., Ioffe, S., Shlens, J., Wojna, Z.: Rethinking the inception architecture for computer vision. In: Proceedings of the IEEE Conference on Computer Vision and Pattern Recognition, pp. 2818–2826 (2016)
8. He, K., Zhang, X., Ren, S., Sun, J.: Deep residual learning for image recognition. In: Proceedings of the IEEE Conference on Computer Vision and Pattern Recognition, pp. 770–778 (2016)
9. Reinhard, E., Adhikhmin, M., Gooch, B., Shirley, P.: Color transfer between images. IEEE Comput. Graph. Appl. **21**(5), 34–41 (2001)
10. Yosinski, J., Clune, J., Bengio, Y., Lipson, H.: How transferable are features in deep neural networks? In: Proceedings of the 27th International Conference on Neural Information Processing Systems, NIPS 2014, vol. 2, pp. 3320–3328. MIT Press, Cambridge (2014)
11. Shin, H.C., Roth, H.R., Gao, M., Lu, L., Xu, Z., Nogues, I., Yao, J., Mollura, D., Summers, R.M.: Deep convolutional neural networks for computer-aided detection: CNN architectures, dataset characteristics and transfer learning. IEEE Trans. Med. Imaging **35**(5), 1285–1298 (2016)
12. Esteva, A., Kuprel, B., Novoa, R.A., Ko, J., Swetter, S.M., Blau, H.M., Thrun, S.: Dermatologist-level classification of skin cancer with deep neural networks. Nature **542**(7639), 115 (2017)

Candy Cane: Breast Cancer Pixel-Wise Labeling with Fully Convolutional Densenets

Sameh Galal$^{(\boxtimes)}$ and Veronica Sanchez-Freire

Chicago, IL, USA
sameh.galal@alumni.stanford.edu, sanchez.freire@gmail.com

Abstract. Breast cancer is one of the leading cancer-related death causes worldwide. Analysis of histology whole-slide and microscopy images is essential for early diagnosis. However this task is time consuming and has to be performed by specialists. Computer-aided Diagnosis can accelerate the process and reduce cost. Candy Cane, a system for performing pixel-wise labelling of whole-slide images in four classes: normal tissue, benign lesion, in situ carcinoma and invasive carcinoma is introduced. It uses fully convolutional Densenet architecture which performs successive convolutions and downsampling on input image followed by successive upsampling and transpose convolution to predict the label image. This allows the system to examine both microscopic low level details as well as high level features and organization of the tissue to make its pixel labeling decision. Accuracy s score of 0.501 are achieved in four-class pixelwise labeling of images on test set.

Keywords: Breast cancer · Deep learning · Semantic segmentation
Fully convolutional networks

1 Introduction

Breast cancer is the leading cause of death by cancer for women. Early detection and diagnosis of the tumor is essential in treatment and lowering its mortality rate. Screening is done through regular check ups and if abnormal tissue growth is suspected a breast tissue biopsy is performed. The tissue histology and microscopic features are studied by pathologists to determine if the tissue is normal or containing benign abnormality or carcinoma. Furthermore carcinoma progression can be classified as in situ or invasive. In situ carcinoma cells are restrained inside the mammary ductal-lobular system, whereas invasive carcinoma cells spread beyond that structure.

Computer aided diagnosis (CAD) systems are used to improve the diagnosis efficiency and assist specialists in classifying the tissues. Systems based on convolutional neural networks have been used to classify the type of tissue based on an image of a region of interest [1]. This paper takes a step further by introducing a framework for learning pixel-wise labeling for whole-slide images using fully convolutional networks.

© Springer International Publishing AG, part of Springer Nature 2018
A. Campilho et al. (Eds.): ICIAR 2018, LNCS 10882, pp. 820–826, 2018.
https://doi.org/10.1007/978-3-319-93000-8_93

2   Candy Cane

2.1   Dataset

The dataset is composed of hematoxylin and eosin (H&E) stained breast histology whole-slide images provided by the grand challenge on breast cancer histology images [2]. The whole-slide images are high resolution images containing the entire sampled tissue (e.g. resolution of 62000 × 42000 pixels) with pixel scaling of 0.467 μ/pixel. The images were pixel-wise annotated into one of four categories: normal tissue, benign, in situ carcinoma and invasive carcinoma as shown in Fig. 1. The annotation was performed by two medical experts and images where there was disagreement were discarded. 10 such labeled whole-slide images were provided from 10 different patients.

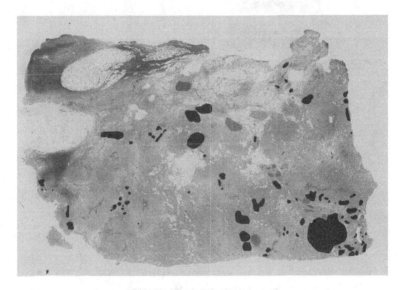

Fig. 1. An example labeled breast histology whole-slide image (red: benign, green: in situ, blue: invasive) (Color figure online)

2.2   Architecture

Convolutional neural networks (CNNs) have been very successful at image classification tasks and the state of the art is advancing rapidly. It involves training sets of convolutions on an image to learn low level features in the lower layers of the network. In subsequent layers of the network, the resolution of these low level features are successively reduced and used to train others sets of convolutions to learn hierarchically higher level features of an image. As such it is able to perform high level classification tasks such as detecting a cat in a picture.

Semantic segmentation is the task of pixel-wise classification of an image instead of classifying the whole image. Fully Convolutional Networks (FCNs)

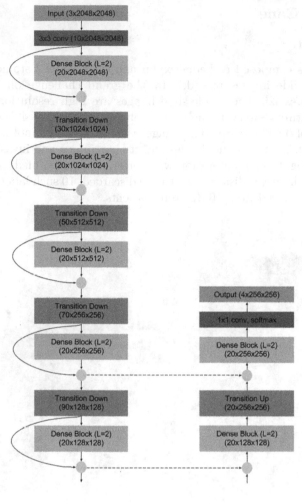

Intermediate layers removed for space limitation...

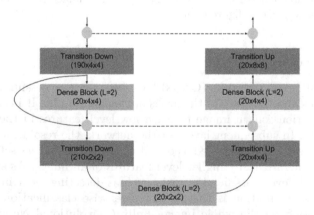

Fig. 2. Candy cane architecture

were introduced to handle such a task [4]. It extends CNNs by introducing an upsampling path to transmit high level features information back to high resolution pixel labeling. To preserve low level feature information skip connections are introduced between feature maps of the same size in the downsampling and upsampling paths. This allow the network to combine both high level and low level features in its pixel labeling allowing high accuracy of the network.

Fully Convolutional Densenet (FC-Densenet)is a particular flavor of FCNs where Densenets architecture is used as a main building block [5]. Densenet is a recent architectural innovation which allows training deeper networks easier and with better results [3]. In a densenet, for each layer, the feature-maps of all preceding layers are used as inputs and the outputs are used as inputs to all subsequent layers. This improves gradient descent and encourages feature reuse.

To achieve high accuracy, pixel-labeling of breast cancer slide images, a few insights were discovered through training and trying different configurations. First, to perform classification properly, both microscopic low level features as well as high level features of the tissue has to be taken into account. Looking at high level context for example can help determine the cancer is in situ or invasive. Additionally, the granularity of the labels are much lower resolution than the microscopic images of the slide. As an analogy the algorithm is mimicking an expert looking at a microscope in few adjacent regions to examine the tissue but then the labeling is done on large parts of the tissue.

These insights inspired the architecture of the network we chose for breast cancer labeling. The architecture uses as input relatively large 2048 × 2048 images which are sampled from the whole slide images. It uses a fully convo-

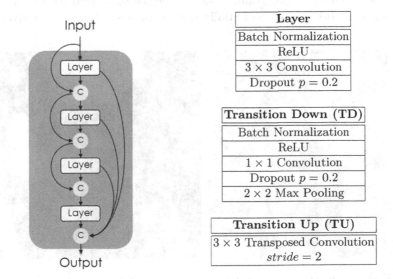

Fig. 3. Building blocks of fully convolutional DenseNets: dense block, layer used in dense block, Transition Down (TD) and Transition Up (TU). Reproduced from [5].

lutional Densenet with a deep downsampling path going all the way to 2×2 resolution, while the upsampling path is shallow going up to 256×256 output pixel label. The architecture is illustrated in Fig. 2. The reduced resolution of the output label doesn't affect performance as the labeled region are very big compared to the high resolution images. This shortening of the upsampling path allows for a deeper downsampling path to fit in GPU memory and is key to achieve high performance and give the labeling algorithm "microscopic" vision capability. The long downsampling path of the network compared to the short upsampling path results in the architecture shape resembling a candy cane and hence the name of the architecture.

For the parameters of the architecture, drop out of 0.2 was used, the dense blocks were 2 layers deep $(L = 2)$ and the number of feature maps per layer is 10. Figure 3 illustrates all the building blocks used in the network.

2.3 Training

For training, input images with resolution of 2048×2048 were sampled randomly on the fly from different whole slide-images at pixel scaling of 1.87 μ/pixel. Corresponding label images were downsampled 8× to the resolution of 256×256 at pixel scaling of 14.93 μ/pixel. Sampling improves training and reduce overfitting by making sure that the data the training observes are different for different epochs especially that we have only 10 whole-slide images. Sampling was biased towards the non-normal labeled regions and the probabilities of sampling were skewed to make sure every label type is sampled as frequently as other labels. Random rotations and flipping were performed on the sampled images to increase data augmentation. Training was performed using Pytorch [6] and fast.ai [7] packages. Learning rate was initialized at 0.001 and adjusted adaptively.

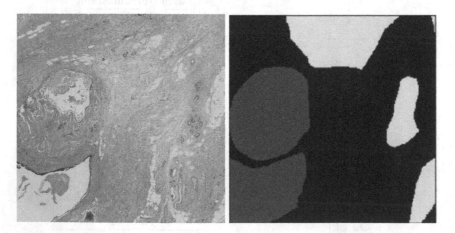

Fig. 4. A 2048×2048 image sampled from the whole slide image with its corresponding 256×256 label

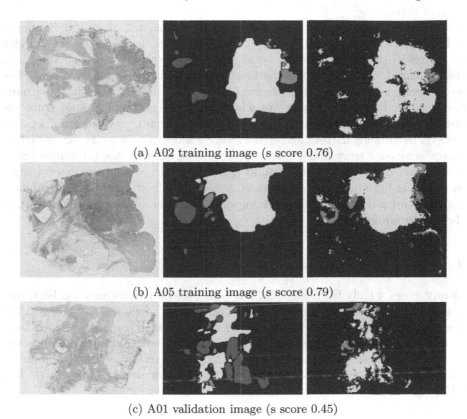

(a) A02 training image (s score 0.76)

(b) A05 training image (s score 0.79)

(c) A01 validation image (s score 0.45)

Fig. 5. Candy Cane pixel labeling results. Each row from left to right: original whole-slide image, ground truth and the model prediction

2.4 Whole-Slide Label Reconstruction

For pixel-labeling of a whole-slide image, a sliding window of size 2048 × 2048 and stride of 512 pixels is used to generate overlapping label images which are combined and stitched together to produce final label. Output label probabilities from overlapping images are averaged and the label with highest probability is used to produce final pixel label.

3 Results

For training dataset, 9 whole-slide images were sampled to generate training images. One last whole-slide image was used for validation. For evaluation of the accuracy of the prediction, the following s score is used:

$$s = 1 - \frac{\sum_i^N |pred_i - gt_i|}{\sum_i^N max(|gt_i - 0|, |gt_i - 3|) \times [1 - (1 - pred_{i,bin})(1 - gt_{i,bin})]} \quad (1)$$

where "pred" is the predicted class (0: normal, 1: benign, 2: in situ carcinoma or 3: invasive carcinoma), and "gt" is the ground truth class, i is the linear index of a pixel in the image, N is the total number of pixels in the image and bin is the binarized value, i.e., is 0 if the label is 0 and 1 if the label is 1, 2 or 3. The score aims at penalizing more the predictions that are farther from the ground truth value. However, the cases in which the prediction and ground truth are both 0 (normal class) are not counted, since these can be seen as true negative cases. The training dataset achieves average s score of 0.78 while the validation image achieves s score of 0.45. Test set achieves s score of 0.501. Figure 5 shows whole-slide image along with ground truth label images and predicted images from model both from training dataset as well as validation dataset. The model does a good job of fitting the training data and generalizes well for predicting the validation image.

4   Conclusion

Candy cane, a Fully Convolutional Network based on Densenets has been proposed as a viable architecture for pixel-wise labeling of whole-slide breast tissue images. Big high resolution images of the tissues used in conjunction with lower resolution labels are proposed as a trade-off to achieve good performance and accuracy. The network achieves good fitting with relatively small amount of data and generalizes well to the validation set. Increasing the amount of data will probably result in further accuracy and better performance.

References

1. Araújo, T., Aresta, G., Castro, E., Rouco, J., Aguiar, P., Eloy, C., et al.: Classification of breast cancer histology images using Convolutional Neural Networks. PLoS One 12: e0177544. pmid: 28570557 (2017)
2. ICIAR 2018 Grand Challenge on Cancer Breast Histology Images. https://iciar2018-challenge.grand-challenge.org/
3. Huang, G., Liu, Z., Weinberger, K.Q., van der Maaten, L.: Densely connected convolutional networks. In: IEEE Conference on Computer Vision and Pattern Recognition (CVPR) (2017)
4. Long, J., Shelhamer, E., Darrell, T.: Fully convolutional networks for semantic segmentation. In: IEEE Conference on Computer Vision and Pattern Recognition (CVPR) (2015)
5. Jégou, S., Drozdzal, M., Vázquez, D., Romero, A., Bengio, Y.: The one hundred layers Tiramisu: fully convolutional DenseNets for semantic segmentation. In: IEEE Conference on Computer Vision and Pattern Recognition Workshops (CVPRW) (2017)
6. Paszke, A., et al.: Automatic differentiation in PyTorch NIPS-W (2017)
7. fast.ai deep learning library. https://github.com/fastai/fastai

Breast Cancer Histology Image Classification Based on Deep Neural Networks

Yao Guo, Huihui Dong, Fangzhou Song, Chuang Zhu$^{(\boxtimes)}$, and Jun Liu

Center for Data Science, School of Information and Communication Engineering,
Beijing Laboratory of Advanced Information Networks,
Beijing Key Laboratory of Network System Architecture and Convergence,
BUPT, Beijing 100876, China
{2013211938,donghuihui,czhu,liujun}@bupt.edu.cn

Abstract. Automatic histopathology image recognition system plays a key role in speeding up diagnosis and reducing the error rate. In this work, we propose a new histopathology image recognition scheme. First, hybrid Convolutional Neural Network (CNN) architecture is designed based on GoogLeNet to merge more key information in decision. Second, bagging technique and hierarchy voting tactic are executed to reduce generalization error and improve performance. At last, transfer learning and data augment strategies are employed to address the limitations of the small amount of data. The classification accuracy of our adopted method is 87.5% for four class, which far outperforms the existing state-of-the-art.

Keywords: Breast cancer · Image classification · CNN
Hybrid CNN units · Hierarchy voting

1 Introduction

Breast cancer is the most prevalent disease among women, and this type of cancer causes hundreds of thousands of deaths each year worldwide [1]. The early stage diagnosis and treatment will significantly reduce the mortality rate [2]. In general, to conduct breast cancer diagnosis, the materials obtained in the operating room are first processed by formalin and then embedded in paraffin [3]. After that, the tissue is cut by a high precision instrument and mounted on glass slides. To make the nuclei and cytoplasm visible, the slides are dyed with hematoxylin and eosin (H & E). Finally, the pathologists finish diagnosis through visual inspection of histological slides under the microscope. However, the traditional manual diagnosis needs intense workload, and diagnostic errors are prone to happen with the prolonged work of pathologists. Thus, automatic histopathology image recognition system plays a key role in speeding up diagnosis and reducing the error rate.

© Springer International Publishing AG, part of Springer Nature 2018
A. Campilho et al. (Eds.): ICIAR 2018, LNCS 10882, pp. 827–836, 2018.
https://doi.org/10.1007/978-3-319-93000-8_94

Extensive pieces of literature [4–9] are reported on trying to design automatic histo-pathology image recognition schemes. Typically, the algorithms of the literature can be classified into two categories. In the first category, nuclei segmentation is performed first and then hand-crafted features, such as morphological and texture features, are extracted from the segmented nuclei. Finally, the generated features are put into classifiers for automatic image type decision [4–6]. Generally, great efforts and effective expert domain knowledge are required to design appropriate features for this type of method. In the second category, different Convolutional Neural Networks (CNN) are adopted to recognize histopathology image [7–9]. Deep feature DeCAF is used to perform breast cancer recognition in work [7], and some previously existing CNN architectures are evaluated in work [8]. A set of comprehensive experiments demonstrates that the CNN achieves better results than the other traditional machine learning models [8]. Recently, Teresa et al. [9] present a new breast cancer image dataset and design a CNN to retrieve information at different scales in image recognition. The proposed method achieves state-of-the-art performance. However, the adoption of a patch-level CNN will inevitably cause the loss of the global information.

In this work, we propose a new histopathology image recognition scheme which will take more global information into account. The main contributions of this paper are summarized in the following:

(1) To merge more key information in decision, hybrid CNN architecture is designed based on GoogLeNet. One patch-level CNN is responsible for local information extraction and another image-level CNN is used to produce global features. Both local classification score and global classification score are weighted together to select the best matching type for each image.
(2) To reduce generalization error and improve performance, bagging technique and hierarchy voting tactic are executed. Several models are trained first by using different data splitting and sampling manners, and then hierarchy (patch-level and image-level) voting is applied for image classification.
(3) To reduce training time and prevent overfitting, transfer learning and data augmentation strategies are employed. Large-scale knowledge, such as the low-level features, in ImageNet are transferred to breast cancer classification by initializing the pre-trained network into our model. Besides, various transformations are adopted to enhance the training dataset.

The rest of the paper is organized as follows: In Sect. 2, we review the related works on breast cancer histology image classification. Then, the proposed method is introduced in Sect. 3. At last, the experiments and the conclusion of our paper will be elaborated in Sects. 4 and 5, respectively.

2   Related Work

The automatic cancer diagnosis has been considered as a research topic for more than 40 years [10] and great efforts have been made in designing automatic histopathology image recognition system. Traditionally, in order to perform recognition, hand-crafted features are extracted for the segmented nuclei and put into the properly designed classifiers [4–6]. The recent research shows that the CNN-based algorithms achieve promising results, which outperform the best traditional machine learning method [6]. In the following, we will review the automatic histopathology image recognition based on deep learning.

Geert et al. [11] introduce deep learning to improve the analysis of histopathologic slide and conclude that it holds great promise in increasing diagnosis efficacy. Dan et al. [12] use deep max-pooling CNN to detect mitosis, which is an important indicator for breast cancer. The proposed method won the ICPR 2012 mitosis detection competition. To recognize the subtype of breast cancer, Sungmin et al. [13] propose to adopt the hybrid model, which contains a graph CNN and a relation network. The authors in work [8] train the existing CNN based on the extraction of patches from the high-resolution images, and achieve some accuracy improvement when compared to the traditional machine learning methods. Both single task CNN and multi-task CNN architectures are proposed to classify breast cancer histopathology images [14]. In order to save the training time of works [8] and [14], Fabio et al. extract DeCAF features by using a pre-trained CNN and then learn a classifier for the new classification task. In recent work [9], the authors introduce a new breast cancer image dataset and propose an image-level classification method. In the presented public dataset, the breast histology images are classified into four types: normal tissue, benign lesion, *in situ* carcinoma and invasive carcinoma. The reported classification accuracy is 77.8% for the four classes.

3   Approach

3.1   Architecture Introduction

The whole architecture in this paper is shown in the Fig. 1. As the figure shows, we divide the architecture into training process and inference process.

In training process, given sets of stained histopathology images, we eliminate the color difference among them in the preprocessing stage at first. Then, different data augmentation strategies are applied to generate more training images. To reduce generalization error, bagging strategies are used. Through random sampling with replacement, we can extend the original datasets to several and train different classifiers using these extended datasets. The sampling process will be detailed in Sect. 4. In training process, two types of CNNs are trained, which are called patch model and global model, respectively.

Analogously, in the inference process, a preprocessing stage is also needed to eliminate the color difference at first. To merge more key information when in decision, a hybrid CNN unit is proposed, which contains the patch model and global model trained before. Besides, a patch-level voting module and a merging module are also introduced inside the unit. From the Fig. 1, we can see that several hybrid CNN units participate in the classification process. After passing through these hybrid units, we get several prediction results.

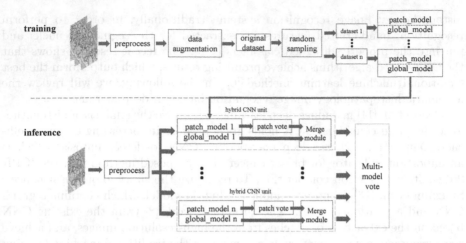

Fig. 1. The whole architecture of the approach

At last, using bagging strategies, a multi-model voting module is placed to give a final decision at the end of the architecture.

3.2   Preprocessing

The breast histology microscopy we used in this paper is stained by H & E. This universal staining method can help medical workers better observe the internal morphology of the tissue cells. However, it is extremely difficult to ensure the same dye concentration and amount used in each image in the staining process, which results in differences in the color of the stained histology microscopy. Other factors such as the brightness of the ambient light in image acquisition process also have an impact on the color of the histology images. These color differences of the histology images can adversely affect the training and inference process in CNNs. In this case, we need to uniform the data to eliminate the differences in the color of the histology images.

In this paper, we adopt the image processing methods in [15], which give an approach for a more general form of color correction that borrows one image's color characteristics from another. This method uses a simple statistical analysis to impose one image's color characteristics on another, and can achieve color correction by choosing an appropriate source image and apply its characteristic to another image. We give the sample preprocessed result shown in Fig. 2(b).

3.3   Dataset Augmentation

To avoid overfitting, there is a need of larger datasets for the training process. The strategies we used in this paper include random rotation, flipping transformation and shearing transformation.

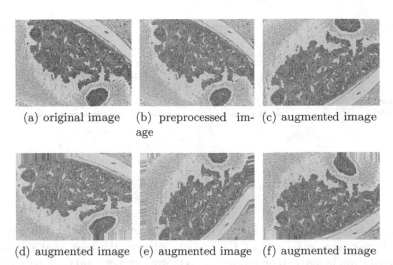

(a) original image   (b) preprocessed image   (c) augmented image

(d) augmented image   (e) augmented image   (f) augmented image

Fig. 2. Preprocessing and augmentation of the datasets. (c–f) represent different augmentation results produced by different augmentation methods. Through flipping transformation, we can get the result shown as (c). Through shearing transformation on image (b), we get the image with blank areas. Filling the blank area, image (d) is acquired. The filling method we used is introduced in [18]. Similarly, (e) and (f) are also the results of shearing transformation.

Unlike the augmentation methods in [9], we rotate the images in the experiment randomly. Besides, shearing transformation method is also used, which can zoom in or zoom out images in different directions. The augmentation sample results are shown in the Fig. 2(c–f).

3.4   Proposed Hybrid CNN Unit Structure in Inference

To extract and merge more key information in the decision, a hybrid CNN unit is proposed shown in Fig. 3, which contains two different types of CNN models, one patch-level voting module, and one merging module.

We use two methods to deal with the high-resolution image sized at 2048 × 1536. One of the methods is to crop the image in patches of 512 × 512 with 50% overlap and resize the patches to the target size 224 × 224 when finishing the cropping work. We note that the patches of the images after cropping retain the local features of the original image. The other method is to resize the original image to the target size 224 × 224 directly. This operation preserves the global features of the original image, however, part of the local features are lost during the resizing process. In this case, we designed the hybrid CNN unit to extract the features as much as possible when in decision and merge these local and global features to help make the prediction.

The two different types of CNN models are trained based on GoogLeNet using transfer learning strategies. The patch model, which is trained using patches of

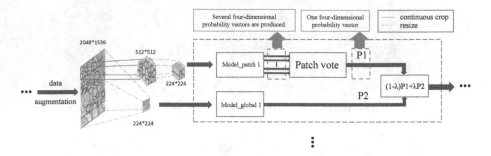

Fig. 3. The architecture of the classifier

images, is responsible for local information extraction. Analogously, the global model is responsible to extract the global features. We note that one original high-resolution image can be cropped into many patches, and each patch passing through the patch model could have a four-dimensional probability vector, and each element in the vector represents the probability of each category images. To take full advantage of these local prediction information and improve accuracy, we place a patch-level voting module after the patch model.

In the training process, we find that the sensitivity of Invasive generally far outweighs the sensitivity of Benign on the validation dataset, and this phenomenon is partly the reflection of different classification difficulties of different data. If the maximum of the predicted probabilities for all classes is less than a specific threshold, we think contradiction happens with the above phenomenon. In this paper, we proposed a forced class decision strategy (shown in Algorithm 1) in patch vote to solve the contradiction. The symbols P_0, P_1, P_2, P_3 represent the probability of categories **Benign, Insitu, Invasive, Normal** respectively

The steps of patch-level voting are shown as follows: (a) For each probability vector, we get the prediction label using Algorithm 1 and set the possibility of the label in the vector to 1, others to 0.; (b) Add up the processed vectors and normalize them. After the voting process, we acquire the patch-level prediction probability vector distribution P_1. Through the global model, the resized original image produces an image-level prediction probability vector distribution P_2. Then, we merge the local features and global features using the merging module. The parameter λ is set as the weight. Finally, the unit makes the decision and predicts the histology image label.

3.5 Voting

To reduce generalization error and improve performance, bagging strategies and hierarchy voting tactic are executed.

Bagging is proposed by Leo Breiman in 1994 to improve classification by combining classifications of randomly generated training sets. In this work, we use a random sampling with replacement method to generate different datasets. Using these datasets, we can train different classification models. Then, in the

Algorithm 1. A forced class decision strategy

Input: the patch's probability of each type: P_i, $i = 0, 1, 2, 3$
Output: the label of the patch: $label$
1: **if** $maxP_i < 0.5$ **then**
2:     **if** $P_0 + P_3 > P_1 + P_2$ **then** $label = 0$
3:     **else** $label = \underset{1,2}{argmax}(P_1, P_2)$
4:     **end if**
5: **else**
6:     $label = \underset{i}{argmax}(P_i)$
7: **end if**

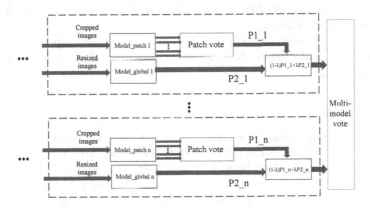

Fig. 4. The architecture of the classifier

inference process, each unit could make a decision and predicts the histology image label. Using a multi-model voting module, the classifier makes the final prediction.

In the process of bagging, we form the hierarchy voting tactic. As Fig. 4 shows, the patch-level voting in the hybrid CNN unit and the multi-model voting represent different hierarchies of voting. All these voting tactics help improve the performance of the classifiers.

4   Experiments

4.1   Dataset

The dataset is provided by The Grand Challenge on Breast Cancer Histology Images 2018, which consists of four categories of histology images for a total of 400 pieces, and each category has 100 pieces. We randomly choose 10 images in each category as the test dataset, totally sized at 40 pieces. The remaining 90 images in each category, totally sized at 360 pieces, are divided into five folds, so each fold has 72 images. When conducting an experiment, we choose one fold as the validation datasets, the remaining four folds as training datasets.

To get a bigger and stronger dataset, we extend the 72 images in each fold to 1440 by data augmentation, expanded by 20 times. We conduct five experiments by choosing one fold from the five folds as validation datasets by turns. The remaining 4 folds, which has 5760 images, as original training datasets. By bagging, we can extend the original training set to a size of 7200.

4.2 Baseline Experiments

In order to give a clearer comparison, we conduct several experiments as the baselines:

(1) Fine-tune the GoogLeNet model trained by ImageNet to classify four types of pathological images.
(2) Reproduce the schemes in [17] using GoogLeNet. We crop the pictures and train them, and classify them by majority voting. And we call this method patch voting.

4.3 Training

We use our own Centos 7.0 server to conduct the experiments. The training process uses 1 NVIDIA GTX 1080Ti 12 GB GPU (NVIDIA Corporation, Santa Clara, CA) and the NVIDIA Deep Learning GPU Training System (DIGITS 4.0) using the Caffe deep learning framework by the Berkeley Learning and Vision Center (BLVC). Through experiment many times, the λ is set as 0.4 in Figs. 3 and 4.

4.4 Comparison with the State-of-the-art

The experiment results are shown in Table 1. From the table, we can see that our proposed hybrid CNN unit have the highest overall accuracy. Our classifier has an excellent performance in detecting *in situ* carcinoma and invasive carcinoma, and it can well identify normal category images. Though it has a relatively low sensitivity in detecting the benign tumor, its accuracy has reached 80%. The overall accuracy achieves 77% when predicting the test dataset provided by the ICIAR 2018 challenge later.

Table 1. Experiment results

Network	Overall accuracy	Sensitivity			
		Benign	*in situ*	Invasive	Normal
GoogLeNet	0.8	0.6	0.9	0.8	0.9
Patch voting	0.825	0.6	0.9	0.9	0.9
Hybrid CNN unit	0.875	0.8	0.9	0.9	0.9

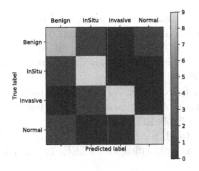

Fig. 5. The confusion matrix of the experiment results

The confusion matrix of the experiment results is shown in Fig. 5. We use different colors to represent the classification results. The color *yellow* represents the most pieces of images, while the color *dark blue* represents the least. From Fig. 5 we can see that the classification results of category benign has been most scattered, which reflects a relatively low accuracy. And other categories such as *in situ* carcinoma, invasive carcinoma and normal have the high accuracy.

5   Conclusions

In this paper, we propose a high-performance, scalable architecture to address the four-category problem of breast cancer based on deep CNN networks. Our proposed hybrid CNN unit could make full use of the local and global features of an image and make a more accurate prediction. The bagging strategies and hierarchy voting tactic are also introduced to help improve the classifier. Through experiments, our approach has a better performance than the state of art in overall accuracy and sensitivity in classification of each category of the images. In future work, we plan to modify and crop the GoogLeNet model structure to reduce the complexity of the model.

Acknowledgments. This work is supported in part by the Beijing Natural Science Foundation (4182044), the National Natural Science Foundation of China (61671078, 61701031, 61602011), Director Funds of Beijing Key Laboratory of Network System Architecture and Convergence (2017BKL-NSAC-ZJ-06), Basic scientific research project of Beijing University of Posts and Telecommunications (2018RC11), and 111 Project of China (B08004, B17007). This work is conducted on the platform of Center for Data Science of Beijing University of Posts and Telecommunications.

References

1. Network, C.G.A.: Comprehensive molecular portraits of human breast tumours. Nature **490**(7418), 61–70 (2012)
2. Smith, R.A., Cokkinides, V., Eyre, H.J.: American cancer society guidelines for the early detection of cancer. CA Cancer J. Clin. **54**(1), 41–52 (2004)

3. Veta, M., Pluim, J.P.W., Van Diest, P.J., et al.: Breast cancer histopathology image analysis: a review. IEEE Trans. Biomed. Eng. **61**(5), 1400–1411 (2014)
4. Kowal, M., Filipczuk, P., Obuchowicz, A., et al.: Computer-aided diagnosis of breast cancer based on fine needle biopsy microscopic images. Comput. Biol. Medi. **43**(10), 1563–1572 (2013)
5. Filipczuk, P., Fevens, T., Krzyzak, A., et al.: Computer-aided breast cancer diagnosis based on the analysis of cytological images of fine needle biopsies. IEEE Trans. Med. Imaging **32**(12), 2169–2178 (2013)
6. Spanhol, F.A., Oliveira, L.S., Petitjean, C., et al.: A dataset for breast cancer histopatho-logical image classification. IEEE Trans. Biomed. Eng. **63**(7), 1455–1462 (2016)
7. Spanhol, F.A., Cavalin, P.R., Oliveira, L .S., et al.: Deep features for breast cancer Histopathological image classification. In: IEEE International Conference on Systems, Man, and Cybernetics (SMC), IEEE (2017)
8. Spanhol, F.A., Oliveira, L.S., Petitjean, C., et al.: Breast cancer Histopathological image classification using convolutional neural networks. In: International Joint Conference on Neural Networks (IJCNN), IEEE, pp. 2560–2567 (2016)
9. Arajo, T., Aresta, G., Castro, E., et al.: Classification of breast cancer histology images using Convolutional Neural Networks. PloS one **12**(6), e0177544 (2017)
10. Stenkvist, B., Westman-Naeser, S., Holmquist, J., Nordin, B., Bengts-son, E., Vegelius, J., Eriksson, O., Fox, C.H.: Computerized nuclearmorphometry as an objective method for characterizing human cancercell populations. Cancer Res. **38**(12), 4688–4697 (1978)
11. Litjens, G., Snchez, C.I., Timofeeva, N., et al.: Deep learning as a tool for increased accuracy and efficiency of histopathological diagnosis. Sci. Rep. **6**, 26286 (2016)
12. Cireşan, D.C., Giusti, A., Gambardella, L.M., Schmidhuber, J.: Mitosis detection in breast cancer histology images with deep neural networks. In: Mori, K., Sakuma, I., Sato, Y., Barillot, C., Navab, N. (eds.) MICCAI 2013. LNCS, vol. 8150, pp. 411–418. Springer, Heidelberg (2013). https://doi.org/10.1007/978-3-642-40763-5_51
13. Rhee, S., Seo, S., Kim, S.: Hybrid approach of relation network and localized graph convolutional filtering for breast cancer subtype classification (2017). arXiv preprint arXiv:1711.05859
14. Bayramoglu, N., Kannala, J., Heikkilä, J.: Deep learning for magnification independent breast cancer histopathology image classification. In 23rd International Conference on Pattern Recognition (ICPR), IEEE, pp. 2440–2445 (2016)
15. Reinhard, E., Adhikhmin, M., Gooch, B., Shirley, P.: Color transfer between images. IEEE Comput. Graph. Appl. **21**(5), 34–41 (2001)
16. Szegedy, C., Liu, W., Jia, Y., Sermanet, P., Reed, S., Anguelov, D., Erhan, D., Vanhoucke, V., Rabinovich, A.: Going deeper with convolutions. In: IEEE Conference on Computer Vision and Pattern Recognition, pp. 1–9 (2015)
17. Arajo, T., Aresta, G., Castro, E., Rouco, J., Aguiar, P., Eloy, C., Polnia, A., Campilho, A.: Classification of breast cancer histology images using convolutional neural networks. Plos One **12**(6), e0177544 (2017)
18. Keras Documentation: Image Preprocessing in Keras Documentation (2017). https://keras.io/preprocessing/image/
19. Zintgraf, L.M, Cohen, T.S., Adel, T., Welling, M.: Visualizing deep neural network decisions: Prediction Difference Analysis (2017)

Classification of Breast Cancer Histology Using Deep Learning

Aditya Golatkar[✉], Deepak Anand, and Amit Sethi

Indian Institute of Technology Bombay, Mumbai, India
chelsea.aditya@gmail.com, deepakanandece@gmail.com, amitsethi@gmail.com

Abstract. Breast cancer is a major cause of death among women worldwide. Hematoxylin and eosin (H&E) stained breast tissue samples from biopsies are observed under microscopes for primary diagnosis of breast cancer. In this paper, we propose a deep learning-based method for classification of H&E stained breast tissue images released for BACH challenge [1] by fine-tuning Inception-v3 convolutional neural network (CNN) [9]. These images are to be classified into four classes – (i) normal tissue, (ii) benign lesion, (iii) *in situ* carcinoma and (iv) invasive carcinoma. Our strategy is to extract patches based on nuclear density and rejecting patches that are not rich in nuclei, e.g. from non-epithelial regions. This allowed us to discard uninformative regions of the images as compared to random or grid sampling, because visual signs of tumors are most evident in the epithelium. Every patch with high nuclear density in an image is classified in one of the four above mentioned categories. The class of the entire image is determined using majority voting over the nuclear classes. We obtained an average accuracy of 85% over the four classes and 93% for non-cancer (i.e. normal or benign) vs. malignant (*in situ* or invasive carcinoma), which significantly improves upon a previous benchmark [2].

Keywords: Deep learning · Histopathology · Breast cancer · CNN
Transfer learning

1 Introduction

In 2012, breast cancer caused 522,000 deaths worldwide along with 1.68 million new cases [7]. Early diagnosis of the disease and proper treatment is essential to improve the survival rates. Examination of breast tissue biopsy using hematoxylin and eosin (H&E) stain plays a crucial role in determining the type of lesion for primary diagnosis. Hematoxylin stains the nuclei purple and eosin stains the cytoplasm pinkish. This staining helps the pathologist identify the grade of carcinoma, which in turn determines the type of treatment to be provided to the patient. In this work we designed a deep learning based method to classify breast cancer slides. This work is part of our entry in the BACH challenge [1]. Solutions to this problem can potentially be used to reduce diagnoses

© Springer International Publishing AG, part of Springer Nature 2018
A. Campilho et al. (Eds.): ICIAR 2018, LNCS 10882, pp. 837–844, 2018.
https://doi.org/10.1007/978-3-319-93000-8_95

errors, increase the throughput of pathologists, or be used in second opinion or teaching tools.

Tumors are believed to progress in phases. Normal breast tissues have large regions of cytoplasm (pinkish regions) with a dense cluster of nuclei forming glands in H&E stained slides (Fig. 1-A). Benign lesion consists of multiple adjacent clusters of small-sized nuclei (Fig. 1-B). Unchecked benign lesions can progress to *in situ* carcinoma in which the size of nuclei in the clusters increases and nucleoli within the nucleus become prominent, but the tumor seems to be circumscribed in round clusters while losing some of their glandular appearance (Fig. 1-C). In invasive carcinoma the enlarged nuclei break their clustered structure and spread to the nearby regions in fragments (Fig. 1-D). Carcinoma images have a high nuclear density with an absence of structure in inter-nuclear arrangement as compared to *in situ* carcinoma images, which still have a preserved inter-nuclear structure.

The recent success of CNNs for natural image classification has inspired others and us to use them on medical images, e.g. for histopathology image classification. Spanhol *et al.* [8] used an ImageNet [5] based CNN architecture for classifying benign and malignant tumors. They extracted patches of sizes 32×32 and 64×64 from the images to train their CNN. In their results they showed that the accuracy of their CNN decreases with increase in magnification. Ciresan *et al.* [3], who won the ICPR 2012 mitosis detection contest, trained a CNN on 101×101 size patches extracted from images. This enabled them to analyze nuclei of different sizes. Cruz-Roa *et al.* [4] trained a CNN on 100×100 size patches extracted out of whole slide images. They addressed the problem of detecting invasive carcinoma regions in whole slide images. Their CNN was able to extract structural as well as nucleus-based features. Their method established the-state-of-the-art by achieving an F1-score of 0.78. A recently proposed method by Araújo *et al.* [2] addressed the problem of classifying H&E stained images as normal, benign, *in situ*, or invasive carcinoma. In their approach they normalized the images using the method proposed in [6]. They extracted 512×512 patches from the normalized images to train their proposed CNN architecture. They also trained a CNN+SVM classifier for patch classification. Dataset augmentation was also performed by mirroring and rotating the patches. Images were classified by combining the patch probabilities using (i) majority voting, (ii) maximum probability and (iii) sum of probabilities.

Challenges in the BACH dataset include vast areas in images without any epithelium (where the cancer starts) and areas of seemingly intermediate visual patterns between two neighboring classes.

2   Dataset

The Breast Cancer Histology Challenge (BACH) 2018 dataset consists of high resolution H&E stained breast histology microscopy images from [1]. These images are RGB color images of size 2048×1536 pixels. Each pixel covers $0.42\,\mu m \times 0.42\,\mu m$ of tissue area. The images in this dataset are annotated

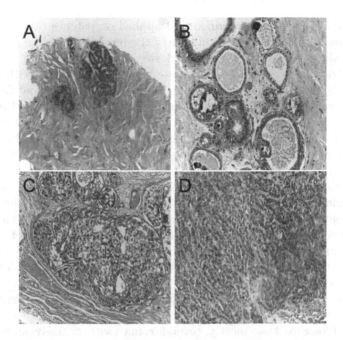

Fig. 1. Examples of H&E stained images from the BACH challenge: (A) normal tissue, (B) benign lesion, (C) *in situ* carcinoma and (D) invasive carcinoma. Hematoxylin stains the nuclei purple while eosin stains the stroma pink.

by two medical experts and cases of disagreement among the experts were discarded. The images are to be classified into four categories: (i) normal tissue, (ii) benign lesion, (iii) *in situ* carcinoma, and (iv) invasive carcinoma as per the agreed upon diagnosis of the two experts. The dataset contains 100 images in each category amounting to a total of 400 images. For our experiments we have used 75 random images from each category for training and the remaining 25 images for validation. Thus in total, we used 300 images for training and 100 images for validating our method.

3 Methods

In this section we describe the details of our methods. First we will discuss about the novelty of our pre-processing method. Then we will discuss the details of patch-level classifier using transfer learning [11]. Finally we will explain the aggregation policy for generating the image-level classification, from patch-level classifier.

3.1 Nuclei-Based Patch Extraction

CNNs trained on only a few hundred whole H&E stained images of size 2048×1536 pixels are prone to poor generalization due to overfitting. So, it is clear that CNNs have to be trained and applied on patches rather than whole images. This opens up the question of how the patches should be sampled from the whole slide images. The shape and size of a nucleus along with its surrounding structure is essential for accurate tissue classification. With this line of thinking in mind, it has previously been proposed to extracted patches centered at nuclei from the given H&E stained images [10]. These extracted patches are also flipped horizontally and vertically, shifted horizontally and vertically and also rotated randomly within 180 degree for data augmentation. These methods not only help in increasing the dataset size by at least 8 folds but also makes our model more robust.

For patch extraction we divided the image into 299 × 299 pixels patches with a 50% overlap. We chose this patch size for two reasons. First, because fine-tuning Inception-v3 – our base architecture – requires images of that size, and we wanted to avoid inaccuracies that can come due to rescaling of images due to bilinear or cubic interpolations used in image resizing. Secondly, this patch size ensures that the CNN extracts nuclei based features along with features of inter-nuclear arrangements.

However, we do not use all the patches which are extracted from the image. Instead we only choose to keep those patches which have high nuclear density and discard patches that mostly cover stroma (with sparsely located nuclei) in majority of their area. To extract epithelial patches dense in nuclei we first compute a mask that identifies bluish pixels for each H&E stained image by comparing the ratio of blue and red channel intensities with to an appropriate threshold. By trial and error on the training images, we arrived at a threshold of 1.587. For each patch we define a blue density metric as the proportion of bluish pixels in the patch. All patches with more than 2% bluish pixels were kept, and the rest were discarded. One challenge that we faced was that a few H&E stained images in the given dataset have a large part of their area filled with stroma. In such cases very few pixels will be bluish and the image may not yield any patches for analysis. To overcome this problem, we first sort the extracted patches (>2% bluish pixels) in decreasing order of the proportion of bluish pixels. Then we define a blue density metric as the proportion of bluish pixels in the whole image. For images with metric more than 1% we keep all the patches for scoring with CNN. For images with metric in range 0.5% − 1%, 0.1% − 0.5% and <0.1% we extract 10, 5 and 1 patch respectively for scoring with CNN. The reason for choosing less patches from such images is that stroma does not provide the model with any significant information regarding the type of tumor present in the image. Images with large regions of stroma are inconclusive and can even cause medical experts to have divided opinions. Figure 2 shows a benign image taken from the dataset along with its mask image. It can be seen that our model only extracts patches from regions dense with nuclei. Each of the patch has the same class label as the original image.

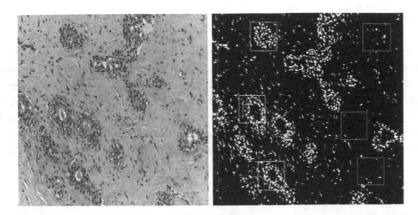

Fig. 2. A sample image with H&E stained benign lesion (left), and its map of bluish pixels (right), with bounding boxes of accepted (green) and rejected patches (red). (Color figure online)

3.2 Transfer Learning for Patch-Wise Classification

As mentioned earlier, the paucity of training images prevents us from training Inception-v3 from scratch with random initialization [9]. Therefore, we employed transfer learning [11] and only fine-tuned Inception-v3 pre-trained on the ImageNet dataset [5]. However, we have made some modifications to the Inception-v3 architecture. We removed the fully connected layer at the top of the network and added a global average pooling layer, followed by a fully connected layer with 1,024 neurons, and finally a softmax classifier with 4 neurons. Our training process had two stages. In the first stage we froze the convolutional layers and only trained the top (newly added) layers. In the second stage we fine-tuned the last two inception blocks along with the top layers. We used a Keras-based implementation of Inception-v3 [9]. We used RMSProp optimizer for 25 epochs for the first stage and SGD optimizer for the second stage with a learning rate of 0.0001 and momentum of 0.9 for 50 epochs. Disease label of an image was given to all its patches. And, although this can lead to erroneous labels, because of the strategy to sample only nucleus-rich patches and the curation of the BACH dataset by its organizers, we expect that the patch-level labels are largely correct.

3.3 Decision Aggregation from Patches to Patients

We combined the patch-based predictions using majority voting to determine the class of the entire image. In majority voting, the class of the entire image is the class to which maximum number of patches extracted from that image belong. In case of a tie we use the following precedence order to classify the image: (i) invasive, (ii) *in situ*, (iii) benign and (iv) normal. The reason behind using this order was to avoid false negatives for a more dangerous disease class.

4 Results

We employed two fold validation to evaluate our method by using patient-level accuracy on a held-out set of patients, with 25 such patients in each of the four classes. Accuracy for each class is defined as the ratio of correctly classified images to the total number images for that class in the validation set. Along with the four class classification we have also evaluated the accuracy of our method for identifying carcinoma images against non-carcinoma images. The non-carcinoma class consists of benign and normal images while the carcinoma class consists of *in situ* and invasive carcinoma images. Along with the image-wise classification we have also computed the patch-wise accuracy for the bluish patches.

4.1 Patch-Level Accuracy

After performing the above-mentioned experiment we got an average patch-wise accuracy of 79% across all the four classes. This metric compares favorably to a previous benchmark of 66.7% [2]. We attribute our success to nuclei-based patch extraction, which takes away lots of variability in patch appearance on which the CNN has to learn to be invariant.

4.2 Image-Level Accuracy

We used majority voting to fuse the results obtained from the patch classification to predict the class of the entire image. The confusion matrices are shown in Tables 1 and 2.

We can see in Table 1 that the our model confuses the normal class with benign. This can be attributed partly to the high similarity between benign and normal images in the dataset. Similarly, images of *in situ* images carcinoma are confused with normal images due to a similar reason. The overall image-level accuracy was 85%, which was higher than the patch-level accuracy due to the voting strategy.

Table 1. Four class confusion matrix

	Actual			
	Normal	Benign	*In situ*	Invasive
Normal	20	1	3	0
Benign	4	23	1	1
In situ	1	1	20	2
Invasive	0	0	1	22

Table 2. Two class confusion matrix

	Actual	
	Non-Carcinoma	Carcinoma
Non-Carcinoma	48	5
Carcinoma	2	45

Table 2 shows the image-level accuracy for non-carcinoma vs. carcinoma. The non-carcinoma super-class consisted of normal tissue as well as benign lesions. The carcinoma super-class was based on *in situ* and invasive carcinomas. Accuracy on this task was 93%.

A comparison of our proposed method with a previous benchmark is shown in in Table 3.

Table 3. Comparison of our results with a previous benchmark [2] using same dataset.

Method	Proposed method	Araújo *et al.* [2]
Pre-processing	Nuclei based patch extraction	Grid Sampling
Patch Classifier	Modified Inception-v3	Custom CNN
Patch-wise accuracy (4 class)	79%	67%
Image-wise accuracy (4 class)	85%	78%
Image-wise accuracy (2 class)	93%	83%

5   Conclusion and Discussion

We developed a two-stage approach for classification of the H&E tissue images in four classes normal, benign, *in situ*, and invasive. One of our key contributions was a pre-processing technique to consider only *relevant* regions from tissue images for training and testing. We also used transfer learning for training the patch-level classifier with a large neural network architecture (Inception-v3) by using weights pre-trained on ImageNet dataset. We have achieved a classification accuracy of 79% at patch-level. The image-level classification was done by majority-voting over patch-level classification results, resulting in an average accuracy of 85% over the four classes and carcinoma versus non-carcinoma classification accuracy of 93%. These figures were significantly higher than those achieved by a previous state-of-the-art [2].

As far medical imaging is concerned, the application of deep learning has two major challenges namely *the size of the image* and *lack of region-of-interest annotations* for a large number of images. Several approaches can be used to further tackle these challenges apart from our static algorithm for patch selection. Multi-column CNNs that examine the tissue at multiple resolutions can be tried. Additionally, graph-based approaches to explicitly model inter-nuclear arrangements can also be tried. To account for staining variation in H&E stained images following approach can be used. First color-normalize the images using [10], extract nuclei based patches, estimate the patient class of each patch, and then aggregate the estimated class decision for each tissue-image. The idea behind using nuclear-based patches as opposed to randomly or densely located patches is to give primacy to identifying nuclear structure and inter-nuclear arrangements based on our preliminary understanding of pathology in [10]. Additionally, multiple instance learning-based approaches that work with weakly supervised data can also be tried.

Acknowledgments. Authors thank Nvidia Corporation for donation of GPUs used for this research.

References

1. BACH, ICIAR 2018, Grand Challenges on BreAst Cancer Histology images (2018). https://iciar2018-challenge.grand-challenge.org/
2. Araújo, T., Aresta, G., Castro, E., Rouco, J., Aguiar, P., Eloy, C., Polónia, A., Campilho, A.: Classification of breast cancer histology images using convolutional neural networks. PloS one **12**(6), e0177544 (2017)
3. Cireşan, D.C., Giusti, A., Gambardella, L.M., Schmidhuber, J.: Mitosis detection in breast cancer histology images with deep neural networks. In: Mori, K., Sakuma, I., Sato, Y., Barillot, C., Navab, N. (eds.) MICCAI 2013. LNCS, vol. 8150, pp. 411–418. Springer, Heidelberg (2013). https://doi.org/10.1007/978-3-642-40763-5_51
4. Cruz-Roa, A., Basavanhally, A., González, F., Gilmore, H., Feldman, M., Ganesan, S., Shih, N., Tomaszewski, J., Madabhushi, A.: Automatic detection of invasive ductal carcinoma in whole slide images with convolutional neural networks. In: Medical Imaging 2014: Digital Pathology. vol. 9041, p. 904103. International Society for Optics and Photonics (2014)
5. Deng, J., Dong, W., Socher, R., Li, L.J., Li, K., Fei-Fei, L.: Imagenet: A large-scale hierarchical image database. In: IEEE Conference on Computer Vision and Pattern Recognition, 2009. CVPR 2009, IEEE, pp. 248–255 (2009)
6. Macenko, M., Niethammer, M., Marron, J., Borland, D., Woosley, J.T., Guan, X., Schmitt, C., Thomas, N.E.: A method for normalizing histology slides for quantitative analysis. In: International Symposium on Biomedical Imaging: From Nano to Macro, 2009. ISBI '09, IEEE, pp. 1107–1110 (2009)
7. McGuire, S.: World cancer report 2014. Geneva, Switzerland: World Health Organization, International agency for research on cancer, WHO press, 2015. Advances in Nutrition. An International Review Journal **7**(2), 418–419 (2016)
8. Spanhol, F.A., Oliveira, L.S., Petitjean, C., Heutte, L.: Breast cancer histopathological image classification using convolutional neural networks. In: International Joint Conference on Neural Networks (IJCNN), pp. 2560–2567. IEEE (2016)
9. Szegedy, C., Vanhoucke, V., Ioffe, S., Shlens, J., Wojna, Z.: Rethinking the inception architecture for computer vision. In: Proceedings of the IEEE Conference on Computer Vision and Pattern Recognition. pp. 2818–2826 (2016)
10. Vahadane, A., Peng, T., Sethi, A., Albarqouni, S., Wang, L., Baust, M., Steiger, K., Schlitter, A.M., Esposito, I., Navab, N.: Structure-preserving color normalization and sparse stain separation for histological images. IEEE Trans. Med. Imaging **35**(8), 1962–1971 (2016)
11. Yosinski, J., Clune, J., Bengio, Y., Lipson, H.: How transferable are features in deep neural networks? In: Advances in neural information processing systems, pp. 3320–3328 (2014)

Breast Cancer Microscope Image Classification Based on CNN with Image Deformation

Yaqi Wang[1], Lingling Sun[1,2(✉)], Kaiqiang Ma[1], and Jiannan Fang[1]

[1] Key Laboratory of RF Circuits and Systems, Ministry of Education,
Hangzhou Dianzi University, Hangzhou 310018, China
sun11@hdu.edu.cn
[2] Zhejiang Provincial Laboratory of Integrated Circuits Design, Hangzhou Dianzi University,
Hangzhou 310018, China

Abstract. In recent years, digital pathology, computational storage and computing capabilities have been evolved rapidly. Computer software provides a possibility to automatically identify tissue types of high-resolution microscopic images, thus greatly improving the accuracy of physician diagnosis and reducing the workload of physicians. In this paper, the convolution neural network (CNN) and hybrid CNN model such as CNN + SVM are adopted to classify the breast cancer microscope images on ICIAR2018 dataset. Part A of the challenge is to automatically classify H&E-stained breast histological microscopy into four categories: normal, benign, carcinoma in situ and invasive carcinoma. In case that the data set is too small, VGG16 network and transfer learning are used, together with a variety of data augmentation methods. In addition to the traditional method of natural image augmentation, this study introduces a deformation to the microscope image and then uses a multi-model vote to achieve a 92.5% accuracy on 80 validation sets, an ACC of 91.7% on the test set of [7]. This approach yielded test set ACC's of 0.83 on the first task of the Grand Challenge on Breast Cancer Histology Images.

Keywords: Breast cancer histopathology images · Transfer learning ·
Image analysis · Deformation

1 Introduction

Breast cancer is the second most common cancer in women after skin cancer. Though it occurs in both men and women, men account lower proportion. Among 100,000 females, the number of new cases of breast cancer was 124.9 per year, and the number of deaths was 21.2 per year in the US [1]. These rates were age-adjusted and based on 2010–2014 cases and deaths.

Cancer stage at diagnosis, which refers to the extent of a cancer in the body, determines treatment options and has a strong influence on the length of survival. The earlier breast cancer is caught, the better chance a person has of surviving five years after being diagnosed. For female breast cancer, 61.8% are diagnosed at the local stage. The 5-year survival for localized female breast cancer is 98.9%.

© Springer International Publishing AG, part of Springer Nature 2018
A. Campilho et al. (Eds.): ICIAR 2018, LNCS 10882, pp. 845–852, 2018.
https://doi.org/10.1007/978-3-319-93000-8_96

Pathology Artificial intelligence has been applied in a variety of tumors, including gastric cancer [2] and intestinal cancer [3], with a focus on benign and malignant diagnoses, grading of disease, staining and early tumor Screening and so on. Artificial intelligence has scored remarkable successes in breast cancer screening, diagnosis of sentinel lymph nodes for cancer cells, and human epidermal growth factor receptor staining scores. The winner of the Camelyon 16 challenge [4] achieved 92.5% AUC and 75% sensitivity in 100 pathological sections of benign and malignant disease [5].

Based on breast cancer patients' breast shape, margins, density, age and breast imaging data system scoring, with deep learning method, Shirazi et al. [6] analyzed and validated 822 cases of breast cancer patients, so as to verify the stage of disease detection up to 95%.

Araújo [7] used convolutional neural networks to classify the histological images of breast cancer, with an accuracy of 77.8% for the four categories (normal tissue, benign disease, carcinoma in situ and invasiveness), 83.3% for the two categories (cancer and non-cancer Tissue), with 95.6% of the sensitivity of tumor detection.

Here, an in-depth learning-based approach is put forward to classify breast cancer images from microscopic images. 400 microscopic images are used to train a deep convolutional neural network, and a variety of data enhancement methods are added to distinguish patch-level predictions from normal, benign, carcinoma in situ, and invasive carcinoma. Then, the effects of various preprocessing methods are compared, such as introducing image warping and Sample Pairing to improve the classification accuracy. In the meantime, the classification results of CNN and CNN + SVM are also compared under this data set. The system is based on Section A of the ICIAR2018 Grand Prix and outperforms the Bioimaging 2015 accuracy. In this paper, the method of multi-network convergence and a variety of pre-processing methods for augmentation are used to better depict the rich intrinsic information of data and improve the accuracy of classification.

2   Dataset and Evaluation Metrics

2.1   Dataset

The dataset was composed of Hematoxylin and eosin (H&E) stained breast histology microscopy and whole-slide images. Microscopy images were labeled as normal, benign, in situ carcinoma or invasive carcinoma according to the predominant cancer type in each image. The annotation was performed by two medical experts and im-ages where there was disagreement were discarded.

The image dataset was composed of high-resolution (2048 × 1536 pixels), uncompressed, and annotated H&E stain images from the ICIAR 2018 Grand Challenge on breast cancer histology images [8]. This challenge was a follow-up of the one of Bioimaging 2015. All the images were digitized with the same acquisition conditions, with magnification of 200 × and pixel size of 0.42 μm × 0.42 μm.

The labeling was performed by two pathologists, who only provided a diagnostic from the image contents, without specifying the area of interest for the classification. Cases of disagreement between specialists were discarded. The goal of the challenge was to provide an automatic classification of each input image.

The dataset contained a total of 400 microscopy images, each of which was labeled with one of four classes: normal tissue, benign lesion, in situ carcinoma and invasive carcinoma. Each category had 100 images. 20 pictures, a total of 80, were randomly selected from each category as a test set. The remaining 320 images were used as the training set, with each class including 80 pictures.

2.2 Evaluation Metrics

Submissions to the competition were evaluated on the following metric:

The performance of our method was evaluated in terms of sensitivity and accuracy. The model was also assessed with values for sensitivity and specificity, as well as AUC values.

3 Method

3.1 Image Pre-processing

In this section, our classification of breast cancer microscopy images is described.

Before training, we selected 80% (320) as the training, 20% (80) as a validation set. Since the data set was small, a variety of data augmentation methods were used.

The biggest challenge was the small dataset with only 400 training images; hence the image enhancement and dataset augmentation were necessary.

Random Crop. First, random cropping method was adopted, which could effectively increase the diversity of data. The microscope image was scaled to 256 * 256 and randomly cropped by using a 224 * 224 sliding window. A small angle rotation (5 degrees) was then performed to amplify the image.

Z-score Standardization. Third, the Z-score standardization method was adopted, which standardized the data by giving the mean of the raw data.

Random Rotation. Followed by several attempts and comparison, the random rotation 90/180/270°, horizontal flip, vertical flip and other methods were added. Better experimental results were obtained.

Deformation. This study applied the deformation method [9] to the microscopic image, and transformed the deformation data by changing three parameters, including the probability of deformation, the size of the mesh and the range. An image deformation method was used based on Moving Least Squares by using various classes of linear functions including affine, similarity and rigid transformations. There was method being provided to create smooth deformations of images which used either points or lines as handles to control the deformation.

Two kinds of setting deformation parameters were chosen: 1. size = 15, range = 50 (range a little larger) 2. size = 30, range = 30, (size bigger).

Others. In addition, Gaussian filters, sharpening, contrast enhancement and other augmentation methods were also involved. However, the experimental results showed that the effect was not good and the accuracy rate was declined. After a number of comparative experiments, it's found that the color change was not obvious for this experimental effect, hence these methods were not recommended in this dataset (Fig. 1).

Fig. 1. Several primary data preprocessing method employed, such as random crop, random rotation, horizontal flip deformation.

3.2 Image Classification Based on Hybrid Convolution Neural Network

In addition to the selection of CNN network structure, there are many factors that affect image classification, such as the size of the input data, the depth of the network selected, training parameters and other issues.

Performance was evaluated with four well-known deep learning network architectures during this training session by using 224×224 pixel inputs. In our framework, VGG [10] was used because of its more stable feature. After several experiments, ResNet and Inception v3 performed worse than VGG. The too deep and complex network model did not have good generalization ability for small data sets.

Add Sample Pairing. The VGG16 structure with input size 224×224 (default) was adopted to evaluate the initialization value of the pre-trained existing model. And Sample Pairing [11] was added to amplify and then train with the VGG16 network, saving that weight when loss was not significantly reduced.

As shown in Fig. 2, two images were randomly selected from the augmented data, and then they were superimposed together to generate a new image.

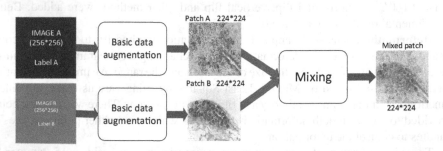

Fig. 2. Several primary data preprocessing method employed, such as random crop, random rotation, horizontal flip deformation. During the model training, the patch-based classification stage was to input all microscopic images and image annotations entered, predicting the label of the test set output microscope image.

Basic data augmentation includes: random cropping, random 90 °, 181 °, 270 ° rotation, random horizontal inversion, and random vertical rotation. Mixing operation in the figure was to add patch A after patch A and patch B were averaged to obtain a mixed patch. Our breast cancer classification framework is shown in Fig. 3.

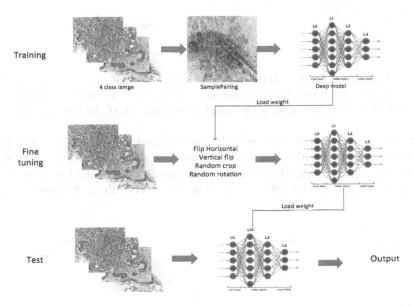

Fig. 3. This is to add sample pairing and transfer learning classification network framework.

4   Experimental Results

4.1   Evaluation Results on the Validation Dataset

In addition, the classification results of VGG and VGG + SVM were compared on this microscope image dataset.

After the fine-tuning, the network was trained with our SamplePairing. This study used the same training data during the fine-tuning phase, but only the most basic data augmentation (random cropping, random 90 °, 180 °, 270 ° rotation, random horizontal inversion, and random vertical rotation). Also it used the VGG16 model and loaded previously trained weights for fine-tuning. The forecasting stage loaded the trained weights to predict the test set (Fig. 4).

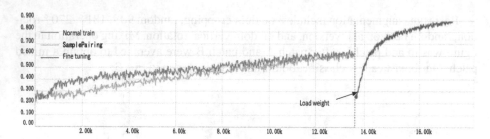

Fig. 4. The yellow in the figure is the ACC curve added to the Sample Pairing training; the red is the ACC curve of the Sample Pairing training without joining; and the blue is the ACC curve of the fine adjustment phase added to the Sample Pairing training. (Color figure online)

It can be clearly seen that in the beginning the yellow curve rises more slowly than the red one, but eventually it reaches the same ACC as the yellow one, and the fine-tuning gives higher results. This shows that this augmentation method to a certain extent has the same regularization effect, so as to prevent over-fitting and improve accuracy (Fig. 5).

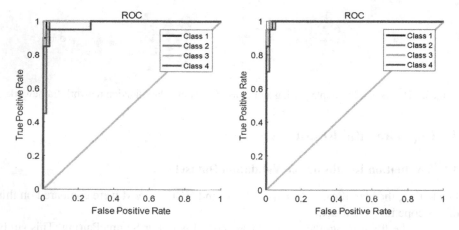

Fig. 5. Receiver Operating Characteristic (ROC) curve of Slide-based Classification. The graph on the left is the model without the deformation method, and the model on the right is the deformation model.

The model was trained with 80% of the training set and the remaining images were validated. The validation set was randomly chosen for each epoch. The selected loss function was classified cross-entropy using a momentum optimization algorithm with a learning rate set at 0.0001, decaying at 0.97 times per 200 steps. The best model is to add a de-averaging preprocessing, which means to calculate the mean for each channel separately and then subtract the mean. That is, color standardization, by the average of the red, green and blue channels, respectively subtracted. After adding the deformation augmentation method, the CNN verification set accuracy rate is 92. 5; that of CNN + SVM is 81.25.

Deformation was better in the third sample, invasive carcinoma, than non-deforming, and it could also be seen from the ROC that its AUC was larger and the model had better generalization (Tables 1 and 2).

Table 1. Test results on 80 validation set data.

Classifier	Classes	Accuracy
CNN	4	92. 5%
CNN + SVM	4	81.25%

Table 2. Table captions should be placed above the tables.

	Precision	Sensitivity	Specificity	Support	AUC
normal	1.00	0.85	1.00	20	0.9920
benign	0.86	0.95	0.95	20	0.9933
insitu	0.79	0.95	0.92	20	0.9992
invsive	1.00	0.95	1.00	20	0.9967

4.2 Evaluation Results on the Test Dataset

This challenge was a follow-up of the one of Bioimaging2015 Challenge. Since Teresa Araujo et al. have done a lot of great researches, we tried to partially benchmark their method by comparing with their articles. In addition, we are pleased to receive the test set data sent by them.

The test set data contains 36 microscope images, including 20 for Initial and 16 for Extended.

As can be seen from Table 3, the classification accuracy of the proposed method is better than the accuracy of the paper [7], and the method of multi-network fusion and multiple pre-processing methods can better depict the richness of data information, thereby improving the classification accuracy. This approach yielded test set ACC's of 0.83 on the first task of the Grand Challenge on Breast Cancer Histology Images. In terms of the single-net performance, our architecture achieves the result (83% test accuracy).

Table 3. Comparison of the results of the microscopic images in the model and article [7].

Classifier	No classes	Accuracy
CNN in [7]	4	72.5
CNN + SVM in [7]	4	72.9
CNN in this work	4	91.7
CNN + SVM in this work	4	80.6

5   Conclusion

In this paper, we have considered the problem of multi-classification of breast tissue HE staining pathological image, and proposed a classification model. We have combined the image deformation with the CNN network, analyzed the impact of each preprocessing on the classification results and selected the best combination of preprocessing methods; then extracted the features and classified them by using SVM, compared CNN with CNN + SVM. Finally, two different image sets were checked. The application of image deformation to the enhancement of the microscope image has obviously improved performance compared with the traditional affine transformation. The results demonstrated that the proposed method can greatly improve the accuracy and has a better sensitivity.

Acknowledgments. We are grateful to all the ICIAR 2018 conference organizers for the Challenge, with special thanks to Teresa Araújo and the INESC TEC Organizer Test Set. We are grateful to mentor Sun Lingling. Acknowledgments We thank all the Organizers of the 2018 ICIAR Grand Challenge.

References

1. DeSantis, C.E., Ma, J., Goding, S.A., Newman, L.A., Jemal, A.: Breast cancer statistics, 2017, racial disparity in mortality by state. CA Cancer J. Clin. **67**(6), 439 (2017)
2. Chougrad. H., Zouaki, H., Alheyane, O.: Convolutional Neural Networks for Breast Cancer Screening: Transfer Learning with Exponential Decay (2017). arXiv preprint arXiv: 1711.10752
3. Roth, H., Oda, M., Shimizu N, et al.: Towards dense volumetric pancreas segmentation in CT using 3D fully convolutional networks (2017). arXiv preprint arXiv:1711.06439
4. Camelyon (2016). Accessed 17 Jan 2018. https://camelyon16.grand-challenge.org/
5. Wang, D., et al.: Deep learning for identifying metastatic breast cancer (2016). arXiv preprint arXiv:1606.05718
6. Shirazi, A.Z, Chabok, S.J.S. M., Mohammadi, Z.: A novel and reliable computational intelligence system for breast cancer detection. Med. Biol. Eng. Comput., 1–12 (2017)
7. Araújo, T., Aresta, G., Castro, E., et al.: Classification of breast cancer histology images using Convolutional Neural Networks. PloS one **12**(6), e0177544 (2017)
8. ICIAR 2018 Grand Challenge. Accessed 29 Jan 2018. https://iciar2018-challenge.grand-challenge.org/
9. Schaefer, S., McPhail, T., Warren, J.: Image deformation using moving least squares. ACM Trans. Graph. (TOG) **25**(3), 533–540 (2006)
10. Simonyan, K., Zisserman, A.: Very deep convolutional networks for large-scale image recognition (2014). arXiv preprint arXiv:1409.1556
11. Inoue, H.: Data Augmentation by Pairing Samples for Images Classification (2018). arXiv preprint arXiv:1801.02929

Convolutional Capsule Network for Classification of Breast Cancer Histology Images

Tomas Iesmantas[(✉)] and Robertas Alzbutas

Kaunas University of Technology, K. Donelaičio g. 73, 44249 Kaunas, Lithuania
tomas.iesmantas@ktu.lt

Abstract. Automatization of the diagnosis of any kind of disease is of great importance and its gaining speed as more and more deep learning solutions are applied to different problems. One of such computer-aided systems could be a decision support tool able to accurately differentiate between different types of breast cancer histological images – normal tissue or carcinoma (benign, in situ or invasive). In this paper authors present a deep learning solution, based on convolutional capsule network, for classification of four types of images of breast tissue biopsy when hematoxylin and eosin staining is applied. The cross-validation accuracy, averaged over four classes, was achieved to be 87% with equally high sensitivity.

Keywords: Capsule network · Breast cancer · Classification

1 Introduction

Breast cancer is one of the most frequent types diagnosed for women – it accounts for 30% of all new cancer diagnoses in women [1]. However, it is a multifaceted disease with varying biological as well as clinical behaviors [2]. This heterogeneity resulted to an endeavor to classify this cancer into meaningful classes [3]. One may consider histological types, which refers to the growth patterns of the tumors, or molecular subtypes.

Histological grading is particularly important, because if the initial check-up for breast cancer (e.g. by palpation, mammography, ultrasound) is positive the breast tissue biopsies enables histological assessment of the severity of the cancer. However, histological analysis requires experience and extensive knowledge of the cytologist. Therefore, computer-aided decision systems would be of great help in detecting abnormalities and assessing their severity.

2 Related Work

Advances of past decade in the deep learning techniques as well as computing power enabled systems for automatic classification of images: whether it is classification of many images found on internet of thousands general categories (see ImageNet competitions), to dermatologist-level skin cancer classification [4], to animal recognition in their habitats [5].

© Springer International Publishing AG, part of Springer Nature 2018
A. Campilho et al. (Eds.): ICIAR 2018, LNCS 10882, pp. 853–860, 2018.
https://doi.org/10.1007/978-3-319-93000-8_97

An attempt to apply deep learning techniques for breast cancer histological images has already been made – convolutional neural networks proved to be of great use in this task [6] allowing to achieve accuracies of 77.8% for four class (normal, benign, *in situ* and invasive) and 83.3% for carcinoma vs. non-carcinoma classification task. The accuracies achieved by convolutional neural network are truly high, considering that it requires no elaborate feature extraction methods before training the classifier – an advantage for which deep learning algorithms are often prized.

There are several other important examples of breast histological image analysis. Kowal et al. [10] used K-means, fuzzy C-means, competitive learning neural networks and Gaussian mixture models for nuclei segmentation and the results of this analysis were used in a medical decision support system for breast cancer diagnosis, where the cases were classified as benign or malignant (similar works were done by Filipczuk et al. [11] and George et al. [12]). Brooks et al. [13] considered a problem of classifying 361 images as normal, in situ and benign by support vector machines and achieved ~93% accuracies for all classes. Zhang et al. [14] ensembles of SVM and neural networks to achieve 97% classification accuracy for a 3-class (normal, benign and in situ) problem.

Above references are great examples of what machine learning/deep learning can achieve. In this paper a 4-class problem is considered: normal, benign, in situ and invasive types of histological images. In Materials and methods section, we briefly discuss the data and preprocessing steps together with more extensive presentation of Convolutional capsule networks (CapsNet) – a new type of networks [7].

3   Dataset and Preprocessing

The dataset[1] is composed of hematoxylin and eosin (H&E) stained breast histology microscopy images. In total 400 images (in equal class proportions) was used. All images were of equal dimensions (2048×1536), with $0.42\,\mu m \times 0.42\,\mu m$ pixel size. Each image is labelled with one of four classes: (i) normal tissue, (ii) benign lesion, (iii) in situ carcinoma and (iv) invasive carcinoma.

The images differed in the shading of the coloring probably due to slightly varying conditions and protocols of staining (see Fig. 1). Therefore, color transfer by Reinhard's method [9] was performed. In addition, to increase the number of trainable samples, three rotations of images were used: by 0 degrees (i.e. no rotation), by 90 and by 180°. After an image rotation, 100 random patches of size 256×256 were cut. Hence, 300 patches were extracted from one image (3 rotations × 100 random patches).

Because patches were generated randomly, no knowledge about the degree of overlap is retained. It is not clear whether such random cutting results to better performance. This aspect was not investigated any further.

---

[1] Additional test dataset was provided latter after the paper submission deadline.

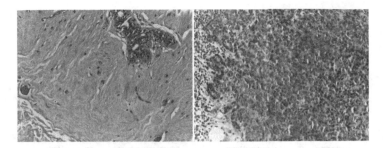

Fig. 1. Examples of different stain shades.

4 Capsule Networks

Convolutional neural networks (CNN) suffer from several conceptual drawbacks: (1) max-pooling operation throws away information about the position of some entity that the network tries to recognize and (2) convolutional neural networks do not take into account many spatial relations between simpler objects. On the other hand, CNNs with max-pooling layers resulted to the rapid development of deep learning field. So, it was probably a matter of time till the method with CNN capabilities and without its disadvantages was developed - capsule network with dynamic routing [7]. The concept of capsules is not anything new, because Hinton, major figure in deep learning field, has been thinking about it for a while (see for example [8], although the idea goes back several decades ago, according to Hinton himself). It just never worked before, up until dynamic routing algorithm was proposed [7]. In what follows, the concept of Convolutional capsule network (CapsNet) will be presented in more details.

First of all, a capsule is a group of neurons whose outputs are interpreted as various properties of the same object. Each capsule has two ingredients: a pose matrix, and an activation probability. These are like activities of a standard neural network. The length of the output vector of a capsule can be interpreted as the probability that the entity represented by the capsule is present in the current input. There can be several layers of capsules. In our architecture, we used a layer of primary capsules (reshaped and squashed output of the last convolutional layer) and a layer of CancerCaps (i.e. capsules representing 4 types of images: normal/noncancerous, benign, in-situ and invasive).

Before the layer of primary capsules, one can have as many convolutional layers as it fits. Only, the max-pool layers are missing; instead, to reduce the dimensionality, one used convolution with strides larger than 1 (if the stride is 2, then dimension are reduced by the factor of 2, etc.). The output of CancerCaps are used to make the decision about the class of the input image. An entire architecture of the network used in this work is presented in Fig. 2 and Table 1 contains information about the dimensions. The total number of trainable parameters was 9850816.

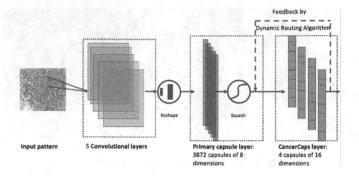

Fig. 2. Architecture of the convolutional capsule network used to classify breast cancer histological images.

Table 1. Considered convolutional capsule network architecture.

	Layer type	Maps and neurons/ capsules	Filter size/Strides or Capsule dimensions
0	Input	3 M × 512 N × 512 N	1 × 1
1	Convolutional	64 M × 255 N × 255 N	4 × 4/2
2	Convolutional	128 M × 126 N × 126 N	4 × 4/2
3	Convolutional	256 M × 61 N × 61 N	6 × 6/2
4	Convolutional	256 M × 28 N × 28 N	6 × 6/2
5	Convolutional	256 M × 11 N × 11 N	8 × 8/2
6	Primary capsule layer	3872 C	8
7	CancerCaps layer	4 C	16

Each capsule in primary capsule layer is connected to every other capsule in Cancer-Caps layer. However, an algorithm, called routing-by-agreement, enables better learning as compared to the max-pooling routing. Routing-by-agreement is sort of a feedback algorithm which increases the contribution of those capsules which agree most with the parent output. Thus, even more strengthening its contribution.

The above-mentioned squashing function is a multidimensional alternative to the one-dimensional activation functions in regular neural networks (e.g. hyperbolic tangent, etc.) and is calculated as follows:

$$v_j = \frac{\left\|s_j\right\|^2}{1 + \left\|s_j\right\|^2} \frac{s_j}{\left\|s_j\right\|},$$

where v_j is the vector output of capsule j and s_j is its total input.

Another novelty introduced together with capsule networks was the use of margin-loss. For each cancer capsule, k the incurred loss is as follows:

$$L_k = T_k \max\left(0, m^+ - \|v_k\|\right)^2 + \lambda\left(1 - T_k\right)\max\left(0, \|v_k\| - m^-\right)^2,$$

where $T_k = 1$ if and only if an image of class k is present and $m^+ = 0.9$ and $m^- = 0.1$. We use $\lambda = 0.5$.

5   Results

5-fold cross-validation was used with 25% on whole images leaving for testing and the rest 75% were used for network training. Adam optimizer [16] was used with parameter 0.0001 to train the entire network.

5.1   Image-Wise Classification

Image patches, due to the significantly smaller sizes than original images, were not all equally informative. Consider example in Fig. 3. The small patch in Fig. 3 (inside the black box) contains no information whether the entire image is taken from invasive carcinoma tissue or not. In other words, information contained in one large image is dispersed over the larger number of patches, some of which may not be of any value at all.

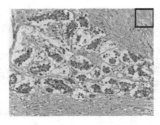

Fig. 3. Original image of invasive carcinoma and its patch (bounded by a black box)

Such information dispersion results to the noisy learning (i.e. loss function is noisy) and it is possible to quickly over-train the network with those uninformative patches. To avoid this the training was stopped when loss-function (computed on training samples) was less than 0.1. Only image-wise prediction was considered, i.e. accuracies were analyzed only for entire images and not for separate patches. The majority voting was used to decide on the label of the image.

Table 2. The confusion matrix for the cross-validation (mean values, %).

True vs. Predicted	Benign	In situ	Invasive	Normal
Benign	87	6	4	6
In situ	6	84	5	3
Invasive	5	5	88	1
Normal	2	5	4	90

Cross-validation procedure results were as in Table 2. The overall accuracy, as obtained from cross validation is 87%.

The results on the test set of the competition was 72%. However, some errors were made during the network training phase and therefore the results on the test set does not correspond to the properly trained network. At the time of submission of the paper competition organizers did not released the labels of the test set and the true results are not known (cross validation above corresponds to the correctly trained network).

Even though the cross-validation accuracies are high, it is clear that the network has difficulty to differentiate between Benign and Normal tissues. In addition, invasive type can be mixed up with benign and this type of mistakes can have severe consequences, as the invasive type of breast cancer requires immediate treatment.

5.2   Feature Visualization

It is difficult to give any meaning to the different layers of the network and therefore it is not possible to understand clearly what gives the network the ability to discriminate between different classes. However, as exemplified in the Fig. 4, at least first convolutional layers try to recognize different parts of the histological image – nuclei, cytoplasm, and other objects. Going deeper into a network, the interpretability is lost due to the complexity of the network and calculations that it performs.

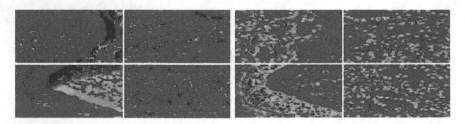

Fig. 4. Example on the left of first convolutional layer features where other than nuclei and cytoplasm areas are enhanced. Example on the right of first convolutional layer features, where nuclei are enhanced

It is also interesting to look at the visualization of the output of CancerCaps layer (i.e. layer consisting of 4 cancer capsules of 16 dimensions). For this purpose, t-SNE method [15], a parametric embedding technique for dimensionality reduction, was applied.

In Fig. 5 a visualization of how different four classes are. All image classes overlap significantly. But this is expected because, as was noted previously, an entire histology image was divided into much smaller patches, many of which carried no information about the specific class or that information was misleading.

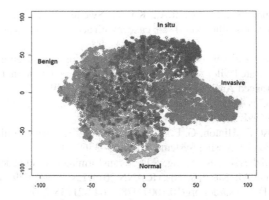

Fig. 5. t-SNE visualization of CancerCaps layer features.

6 Conclusions and Further Discussion

A convolutional capsule network was presented to solve the classification task of breast cancer histological images. The cross-validation accuracy was 87% for the benign carcinoma tissue images, 84% for the *in situ* carcinoma, 88% for invasive type and 89% for normal tissue images. As of now, testing phase results remain unknown and will be added shortly.

It is unknown whether different variations of network architecture would've resulted to similar or better results. In the future, more in depth analysis will be performed to optimize the architecture: number of convolutional layers, dimensions of capsules in primary and CancerCaps layers. Also, no regularization was considered, although decoding part of autoencoder after capsule layers was suggested to have a positive impact on the learning and generalization. However, cross-validation results are very promising, hinting that capsule networks are of equal or even better capabilities as compared to the classical convolutional neural networks.

It is probably safe to speculate, that a computer-aided decision system, which would help to diagnose breast cancer faster and more accurately, can be envisaged in a near future.

Acknowledgement. Tomas Iesmantas was supported by the Postdoctoral fellowship (supervisor Robertas Alzbutas) grant kindly provided by the Kaunas University of Technology and the Faculty of Mathematics and Natural Sciences.

References

1. Siegel, R.L., Miller, K.D., Jemal, A.: Cancer statistics. CA Cancer J. Clin. **68**, 7–30 (2018)
2. Vargo-Gogola, T., Rosen, J.M.: Modelling breast cancer: one size does not fit all. Nat. Rev. Cancer **7**, 659–672 (2007)
3. Weigelt, B., Reis-Filho, J.S.: Histological and molecular types of breast cancer: is there a unifying taxonomy? Nat. Rev. Clin. Oncol. **6**, 718–730 (2009)

4. Esteva, A., Kuprel, B., Novoa, R.A., Ko, J., Swetter, S.M., Blau, H.M., Thrun, S.: Dermatologist-level classification of skin cancer with deep neural networks. Nature **542**, 115–118 (2017)
5. Nguyen, H., et al.: Animal recognition and identification with deep convolutional neural networks for automated wildlife monitoring. In: 2017 IEEE International Conference on Data Science and Advanced Analytics (DSAA), Tokyo, Japan (2017)
6. Arajo, T., et al.: Classification of breast cancer histology images using Convolutional Neural Networks. PLoS ONE **12**(6), e0177544 (2017)
7. Sabour, S., Frosst, F., Hinton, G. E.: Dynamic routing between capsules. In: Advances in Neural Information Processing Systems, pp. 3859–3869 (2017)
8. Hinton, G.E., Krizhevsky, A., Wang, S.D.: Transforming auto-encoders. In: Honkela, T., Duch, W., Girolami, M., Kaski, S. (eds.) ICANN 2011. LNCS, vol. 6791, pp. 44–51. Springer, Heidelberg (2011). https://doi.org/10.1007/978-3-642-21735-7_6
9. Reinhard, E., Ashikigmin, M., Gooch, B., Shirley, P.: Color transfer between Images. IEEE Comput. Graph. Appl. **21**, 34–41 (2001)
10. Kowal, M., Filipczuk, P., Obuchowicz, A., Korbicz, J., Monczak, R.: Computer-aided diagnosis of breast cancer based on fine needle biopsy microscopic images. Comput. Biol. Med. **43**(10), 1563–1572 (2013)
11. Filipczuk, P., Fevens, T., Krzyzak, A., Monczak, R.: Computer-aided breast cancer diagnosis based on the analysis of cytological images of fine needle biopsies. IEEE Trans. Medical. Imag. **32**(12), 2169–2178 (2013)
12. George, Y.M., Zayed, H.H., Roushdy, M.I., Elbagoury, B.M.: Remote computer-aided breast cancer detection and diagnosis system based on cytological images. IEEE Syst. J. **8**(3), 949–964 (2014)
13. Brook, A., El-Yaniv, R., Issler, E., Kimmel, R., Meir, R., Peleg, D.: Breast cancer diagnosis from biopsy images using generic features and SVMs, p. 1–16 (2007)
14. Zhang, B.: Breast cancer diagnosis from biopsy images by serial fusion of Random Subspace ensembles. In: 2011 4th International Conference on Biomedical Engineering and Informatics (BMEI), Shanghai, vol. 1, pp. 180–186. IEEE (2011)
15. Van Der Maaten, L.J.P., Hinton, G.E.: Visualizing high-dimensional data using t-sne. J. Mach. Learning. Res. **9**, 2579–2605 (2008)
16. Kingma, D.P., Ba, J.: Adam: A method for stochastic optimization. In: ICLR (2015)

Ensemble Network for Region Identification in Breast Histopathology Slides

Bahram Marami$^{(\boxtimes)}$, Marcel Prastawa, Monica Chan, Michael Donovan,
Gerardo Fernandez, and Jack Zeineh

The Center for Computational and Systems Pathology,
Department of Pathology, Icahn School of Medicine at Mount Sinai
and The Mount Sinai Hospital, New York, USA
bahram.marami@mssm.edu

Abstract. Accurate analysis of tissue structures in breast cancer histopathology slides is crucial for staging treatments and predicting outcome. Such analysis depends on identification of tissue architecture in different regions, and determining the different types of cancer morphology which includes in-situ carcinoma, invasive tumor, and benign tumor. We propose an automated classification method for identifying these micro-architectures using an ensemble of convolutional neural networks. This ensemble is constructed by combining multiple networks, trained using different data subset sampling and image perturbation models. Our proposed approach results in a high performing detector with robustness to data variations.

1 Introduction

Breast cancer diagnosis and prognosis are critical for addressing mortality rates among females. Accurate analysis of tissue structures in breast cancer histopathology is an essential step for staging treatments and predicting outcome. This analysis is conducted by pathologists based on the tissue architecture in slides stained with hematoxylin and eosin (H&E) [1]. Due to the size and amount of whole slide images, this analysis can benefit greatly from automation by reducing clinician workload. Automated algorithms would also perform with higher reproducibility and reliability for large volume tasks.

Identifying different types of tumor regions in whole slide images using machine learning has been proposed using pre-defined morphological or intensity features. Rexhepaj et al. [2] used texture image features for isolating melanoma cells. Filipczuk et al. [3] used cellular structures obtained through nuclei segmentation for performing diagnosis. Recent developments in deep learning have enabled new approaches that automate the creation of features present in a large collection of labeled image datasets.

Deep learning, particularly convolutional neural networks, have been applied to a variety of clinical tasks in breast histopathology analysis. Ciresan et al. used

© Springer International Publishing AG, part of Springer Nature 2018
A. Campilho et al. (Eds.): ICIAR 2018, LNCS 10882, pp. 861–868, 2018.
https://doi.org/10.1007/978-3-319-93000-8_98

convolutional neural network combined with data augmentation techniques to detect mitotic figures in breast pathology images [4]. Spanhol et al. [5] uses the AlexNet architecture [6] for classifying breast tissue image regions into benign and malignant. Cruz-Roa et al. proposed a detector for invasive tumor in whole slide images using convolutional neural network applied to image patches [7]. Araújo et al. [8] proposed a classifier for different tumor region types using a combination of convolutional neural network features and a support vector machine.

A major issue hindering practical adoption of machine learning techniques in histopathology analysis is the lack of consensus among pathologists and the variability due to different staining techniques, tissue processing, and patient demographics. We propose an ensemble network combining recent developments in deep learning for image classification. Our approach combines variations of the inception network [9] architectures trained on different subsets of the data. We also incorporate image perturbation models specifically designed for digital pathology images when we train our classifiers, resulting in a robust classifier with increased generalizability for real world image data.

2   Method

Tissue areas in breast cancer histopathology slide images can be divided into four general region types: normal tissue, benign tumor, invasive cancer, and in-situ carcinoma [8]. Construction of a classifier is performed using labeled image patches within the slides, where each patch is associated with a label belonging to the four classes. We train multiple variations of a supervised classifier using these labels, each trained on different subsets and with different image perturbations.

2.1   Data Composition and Augmentation

We use the image datasets provided as part of the public BACH challenge[1], composed of 400 field images (2048×1536) labeled with four classes (normal, benign, invasive, and in-situ) as well as 10 whole slide images labeled with three classes (benign, invasive, and in-situ). A pathologist adds annotation of normal tissue regions to the 10 whole slide images, expanding the whole slide annotation labels to the same four classes as provided for the field images with 3480 fields labeled as normal. We also utilize data from another public challenge called BreakHis[2], which contains 7909 images labeled as benign or malignant. We extract 623 field images labeled as benign to expand the training data. In this paper, we construct and train our neural network models using the following sets of data:

(A) BACH field images (4 classes).
(B) BACH whole slide images (3 classes, no normal class).

---

[1] https://iciar2018-challenge.grand-challenge.org.
[2] https://web.inf.ufpr.br/vri/databases/breast-cancer-histopathological-database-breakhis.

(C) BACH field images (4 classes) and whole slide images (3 classes, no normal class).

(D) BACH field images (4 classes) and whole slide images with expanded annotation for normal tissue (4 classes).

(E) BACH field images (4 classes), whole slide images with expanded annotation for normal tissue (4 classes), and BreakHis images for the benign tissue class.

Table 1 shows the number of fields for each tissue category in the training data. Training is performed by oversampling data from different classes to equal amounts per class, in order to reduce the effect of unbalanced amount of labeled data for different classes.

Table 1. Training data compositions used for building different ensemble networks, with number of fields per tissue class.

Training data	Resolution	Classes			
		Normal	Benign	In-situ	Invasive
A	2048 × 1536	100	100	100	100
B	2048 × 1536	0	490	152	5240
C	2048 × 1536	100	590	252	5340
D	2048 × 1536	3580	590	252	5340
E	2048 × 1536	3580	590	252	5340
	700 × 460	0	623	0	0

We augment the training data by randomly manipulating the images, in order to reduce bias to certain color or geometric features. We apply random flips to the images, following Ciresan et al. [4], to reduce directional bias in our network. We also apply random color perturbation to our training images to reduce dependency on absolute color values and improve the generalizability of our classifier. We use the stain-specific color model proposed by Bejnordi et al. [10] instead of standard hue-saturation color model used by Liu et al. [11] for deep learning. Random augmentation is applied to different subsets of the training data to generate richer sets of data that reduces risk of convergence to local optima during training.

2.2 Ensemble Network for Classification

We use the deep neural network architecture called the inception network proposed by Szegedy et al. [9], with modifications as shown in Fig. 1. This architecture utilizes complex structure with parallel convolutional networks being combined in the basic inception block. The added complexity in each inception block can capture image properties at multiple scales and generate a richer set of features. Variations of the Inception-v3 network are trained separately on different subsets of the labeled image data in the training set. During inference, we

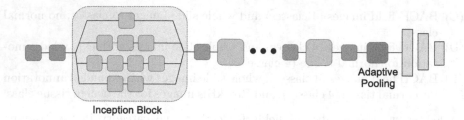

Inception Block

Adaptive
Pooling

Fig. 1. Conceptual view of the proposed tissue classifier based on the inception network architecture. We modify the inception network by using adaptive pooling before applying fully connected layers to obtain class probabilities. Adaptive pooling increases the practical utility of our trained network, as it can be applied to images with minor scale changes from the input training images.

classify the image regions by averaging the outputs of these networks to create an ensemble network. This approach yields a combined network that is more robust to potential inconsistencies and corruption in the labeled data.

When processing whole slide images, we apply a secondary classifier after the ensemble that separates tissue regions from background areas. The secondary classifier is constructed using the residual network (ResNet34) architecture [12] and trained using data derived from manually outlined tissue regions (with both tumor and non-tumor areas). We extract two classes of field images from the whole slide: tissue areas from inside the outlines and background areas outside the outlines. The background class includes ink marker regions, which tend to be misclassified by the ensemble network as they are not trained on ink regions. This secondary classifier reduces potential misclassification of marker ink regions, which were not explicitly annotated in the original training data and have different characteristics to the four classes of tissue sub-types.

3   Results

We construct and train the ensemble network models on annotated field images of size 512×512 pixels. For each 2048×1536 fields, we combine the output for the different subfields by either majority voting on subfield labels or by taking the maximum of the sum of subfield class probabilities. We utilize the test dataset from the 2015 Bioimaging and 2018 BACH challenges, with descriptions and performance measures shown in Table 2.

Detailed performance of our ensemble networks trained on different data collections measured on the field annotation ground truth from the 2015 Bioimaging challenge are shown in Table 3. We show example field images from this test dataset with discordant classification in Table 2. We used the Bioimaging 2015 test dataset for detailed performance measures, as annotated test data for the 2018 challenge are currently not available for use by participants. In the first part of the 2018 BACH challenge, we perform classification on selected field

Table 2. Description of test datasets used for evaluating performance in field classification and whole slide classification tasks. Performance of our classifier trained on augmented dataset E are shown in the last two columns. We use the modified accuracy measure for whole slide images, detailed in Eq. 1.

Test data	Resolution	Number	Accuracy	Modified Accuracy
Bioimaging 2015	2048 × 1536	36 fields	94.4	
BACH 2018 Part A	2048 × 1536	100 fields	84.0	
BACH 2018 Part B	varies (˜20K × 20K)	10 whole slides		0.5526

Table 3. Detailed performance of ensemble networks trained on a variety of data compositions, as listed in Sect. 2.1, measured on the field image data annotated with four classes of region types. We measure performance on the annotated test datasets provided from the 2015 Bioimaging challenge, which is improved with data expansion.

Training Data	Sub-field Fusion	Non-carcinoma Normal	Benign	Carcinoma In-situ	Invasive	Accuracy
A	Majority	100		100		91.7
		78	100	100	89	100
	Sum	100		94		88.9
		78	100	89	89	97.2
C	Majority	100		100		100
		89	100	100	100	97.2
	Sum	100		100		100
		89	100	100	100	97.2
D	Majority	94		100		97.2
		89	89	100	100	94.4
	Sum	100		100		100
		89	100	100	100	97.2
E	Majority	100		100		100
		78	100	100	100	94.4
	Sum	100		100		100
		78	100	100	100	94.4

images with four classes. Performance on the BACH 2018 test data were evaluated by the challenge organizers, and our network trained on dataset E obtained an accuracy measure of 84.0 (https://iciar2018-challenge.grand-challenge.org/results/).

In the second part of the 2018 BACH challenge, we perform classification on whole slide images and compare the generated regions against manually generated outlines. We use the score defined for the 2018 BACH challenge for measuring whole slide classification performance:

	02	21	28	35
Ground Truth	Normal	Normal	In-situ	Invasive
Network-A	Benign	Benign	Normal	In-situ
Network-C	Normal	Benign	In-situ	Invasive
Network-D	Normal	Benign	In-situ	Invasive
Network-E	Normal	Benign	In-situ	Invasive

Fig. 2. Example fields with discrepancies from the ground truth annotation. Benign and normal class have subtle changes which tend to overlap. In-situ and invasive carcinomas are another pair of categories with potential misclassification.

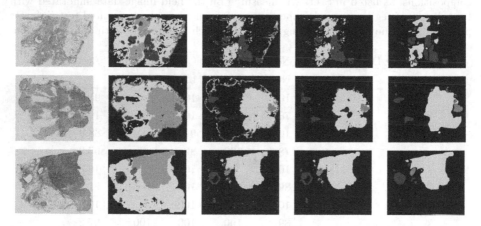

Fig. 3. Example prediction on whole slide images generated using network-E. Exclusion of normal areas (column 3) and further exclusion of background regions using a secondary ResNet classifier (column 4) generates maps that matches the ground truth outlines (last column).

$$s = 1 - \frac{\sum_{i=1}^{N} |\mathtt{pred}_i - \mathtt{gt}_i|}{\sum_{i=1}^{N} max(|\mathtt{gt}_i - 0|, |\mathtt{gt}_i - 3|) \times [1 - (1 - \mathtt{pred}_{i,bin})(1 - \mathtt{gt}_{i,bin})]} \quad (1)$$

where $\mathtt{pred}$ is the predicted class $(0, 1, 2, 3)$, and $\mathtt{gt}$ is the ground truth class, i is the index of a pixel in the image, N is the total number of pixels in the image and bin is the binarized value (i.e., it is 0 if the label is 0 and 1 if the label is 1, 2, or 3). This score is based on the accuracy metric, which aims at giving higher penalty to predictions that are farther from the ground truth value. Note that, in the denominator, the cases in which prediction and ground truth are both 0 (normal class) are not counted since these can be seen as true negative cases.

We applied our classifier that was trained on expanded dataset E to 10 whole slide test images, and we obtained a score of 0.5526 as evaluated by the challenge organizers.

4   Conclusions

We have proposed a robust classifier for identifying regions in breast histopathology slides, constructed as an ensemble of deep convolutional neural networks. The use of an ensemble with variations on data sampling and perturbation yields in improvements on classifier performance and generalizability when applied to whole slide image region classification (Fig. 3). We have not observed substantial improvement in classification of individual field images with the expanded datasets (Table 3), which we believe are due to the limited focus on field images with definitive classification to one of the four tissue classes.

In the future, we plan to further increase the practical utility of the network by using a richer set of networks in the ensemble, along with more advanced data sampling and perturbation models in the training process.

References

1. Elston, C.W., Ellis, I.O.: Pathological prognostic factors in breast cancer. I. The value of histological grade in breast cancer: experience from a large study with long-term follow-up. Histopathology **19**(5), 403–410 (1991)
2. Rexhepaj, E., Agnarsdottir, M., Bergman, J., Edqvist, P.H., Bergqvist, M., Uhlen, M., Gallagher, W.M., Lundberg, E., Ponten, F.: A texture based pattern recognition approach to distinguish melanoma from non-melanoma cells in histopathological tissue microarray sections. PLoS ONE **8**(5), e62070 (2013)
3. Filipczuk, P., Fevens, T., Krzyzak, A., Monczak, R.: Computer-aided breast cancer diagnosis based on the analysis of cytological images of fine needle biopsies. IEEE Trans. Med. Imag. **32**(12), 2169–2178 (2013)
4. Cireşan, D.C., Giusti, A., Gambardella, L.M., Schmidhuber, J.: Mitosis detection in breast cancer histology images with deep neural networks. In: Mori, K., Sakuma, I., Sato, Y., Barillot, C., Navab, N. (eds.) MICCAI 2013. LNCS, vol. 8150, pp. 411–418. Springer, Heidelberg (2013). https://doi.org/10.1007/978-3-642-40763-5_51
5. Spanhol, F., Soares de Oliveira, L., Petitjean, C., Heutte, L.: Breast cancer histopathological image classification using convolutional neural networks. In: International Joint Conference on Neural Networks (IJCNN), June 2016
6. Krizhevsky, A., Sutskever, I., Hinton, G.E.: Imagenet classification with deep convolutional neural networks. In: Advances in Neural Information Processing Systems (2012)
7. Cruz-Roa, A., Gilmore, H., Basavanhally, A., Feldman, M., Ganesan, S., Shih, N.N.C., Tomaszewski, J., González, F., Madabhushi, A.: Accurate and reproducible invasive breast cancer detection in whole-slide images: A deep learning approach for quantifying tumor extent. Sci. Rep. **7**, 46450 (2017)
8. Araújo, T., Aresta, G., Castro, E., Rouco, J., Aguiar, P., Eloy, C., Polónia, A., Campilho, A.: Classification of breast cancer histology images using convolutional neural networks. PLoS ONE **12**(6), 1–14 (2017)

9. Szegedy, C., Vanhoucke, V., Ioffe, S., Shlens, J., Wojna, Z.: Rethinking the inception architecture for computer vision. In: 2016 IEEE Conference on Computer Vision and Pattern Recognition (CVPR), pp. 2818–2826 (2016)
10. Bejnordi, B.E., Litjens, G., Timofeeva, N., Otte-Holler, I., Homeyer, A., Karssemeijer, N., van der Laak, J.A.: Stain specific standardization of whole-slide histopathological images. IEEE Trans. Med. Imag. **35**(2), 404–415 (2016)
11. Liu, Y., Gadepalli, K., Norouzi, M., Dahl, G.E., Kohlberger, T., Boyko, A., Venugopalan, S., Timofeev, A., Nelson, P.Q., Corrado, G.S., Hipp, J.D., Peng, L., Stumpe, M.C.: Detecting cancer metastases on gigapixel pathology images. CoRR abs/1703.02442 (2017)
12. He, K., Zhang, X., Ren, S., Sun, J.: Deep residual learning for image recognition. arXiv preprint arXiv:1512.03385 (2015)

Classification Of Breast Cancer Histology Images Using ALEXNET

Wajahat Nawaz$^{(\boxtimes)}$, Sagheer Ahmed, Ali Tahir, and Hassan Aqeel Khan

National University of Sciences and Technology, Islamabad, Pakistan
{Wnawaz.msee16seecs,sahmed.msee16seecs,ali.tahir,
hassan.aqeel}@seecs.edu.pk

Abstract. Training a deep convolutional neural network from scratch requires massive amount of data and significant computational power. However, to collect a large amount of data in medical field is costly and difficult, but this can be solved by some clever tricks such as mirroring, rotating and fine tuning pre-trained neural networks. In this paper, we fine tune a deep convolutional neural network (ALEXNET) by changing and inserting input layer convolutional layers and fully connected layer. Experimental results show that our method achieves a patch and image-wise accuracy of 75.73% and 81.25% respectively on the validation set and image-wise accuracy of 57% on the *ICIAR*-2018 breast cancer challenge hidden test set.

Keywords: Deep learning · Convolution neural network
Transfer learning · Pathologists · Carcinoma cancer

1 Introduction

Breast cancer is the most frequent type of diagnosed cancer and cause of death in women aged between 20 and 59 years [1]. Generally, breast cancer is considered as one disease, but it has many different types. There are non-carcinoma and carcinoma type cancers. Figure 1 shows the microscopic images of breast tissues of non-carcinoma (normal and benign) and carcinoma (*InSitu* and invasive).

Non-carcinoma class is divided into normal and benign. Benign represents minor changes in the structure of normal breast tissue that cannot be termed as advancement in cancer. Carcinoma class is further divided into two classes *InSitu* and invasive. *InSitu* also termed as non-invasive carcinoma or Ductal carcinoma *InSitu* (DCIS). In *InSitu* type, abnormal tissue contained in milk ducts has not further spread to nearby breast tissues. If not treated, it develops into invasive type; in which carcinoma cancer cells from original site have advanced to other nodes like lymph nodes or to other body parts. That is why the invasive carcinoma is very difficult to treat.

Initial breast cancer detection is performed by palpation, mammography or ultrasound imaging. If these processes indicate the growth of malignant tissue then further diagnosis is performed by breast tissue biopsy [2]. Breast tissues

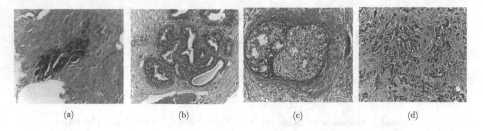

Fig. 1. Microscopy images of Breast tissues. Where (a) & (b) represent non- carcinoma (Normal & Benign) and (c) & (d) carcinoma (In situ & Invasive) tissues respectively.

biopsies allow the pathologists to examine the microscopic structure and elements of tissues histologically; which in turn allows them to distinguish between non-carcinoma, *InSitu* carcinoma or invasive carcinoma [3] types. Hematoxylin and Eosin (H&E) staining prior to inspection is performed on these breast tissues during a biopsy. In the next step, pathologists manually inspect the (H&E) stained breast tissues; this makes it a soporific, fallible and time-taking process. Moreover, pathologists often disagree on the final diagnosis. The reason is that normal and benign as well as *InSitu* and invasive share same type of features.

The aforementioned drawbacks are overcome by automating the diagnostics system. Automatic diagnostics systems are robust and time efficient, and thus quite helpful where disagreement occurs between pathologists.

2 Related Work

Conventionally, pathologists visually examine the breast tissues which is a time-taking and non-trivial process. This problem is addressed by automating the process of classifying histology images.

In previous studies, handcrafted features are used to train a classifier for automating the aforementioned problem, achieving accuracy between 84 to 93%. Filipczuk [4] and George [5] both used circular Hough Transform for detection of nucleic regions in features extracted from fine needle biopsy images. They augmented it with false-positive reduction using different types of thresholding. Their proposed methodology [4] achieved 98.5% accuracy using 11 images from each patient while [5] achieved an accuracy of 71.9–97.15% in 92 images from each individual.

Belsare [6] also considered tissue organization besides nucleic information for binary classification of more complex images. They used 70 images from a private dataset containing 40× magnification breast histology H&E stained biopsy images. Features such as spatio-color textures were used to represent segmented epithelial layer surrounding the cells' lumen graphically while final classifiers were trained using statistical features achieving an accuracy of 70–100%. Brook [7] and Zhang [8] have used breast cancer histology images from the Israel Institute of Technology dataset [9] to classify tissue images in normal, *InSitu* carcinoma and invasive carcinoma type cases. Brook [7] used multiple thresholding levels to binarize and train a support vector machine (SVM) classifier using connected components, achieving an accuracy of 93.4–96.4%. On the other hand, Zhang [8] applied cascaded classification to train SVM classifier using multiple techniques achieving an accuracy of 97%.

Recently, Deep CNN models have outperformed other techniques in image classification challenges related to different domains [10,12]; among them biomedical image analysis [13] and histopathology images [14]. Inspired by Imagenet Network [10], Spanhol [15] train deep CNN using 32×32 and 64×64 pixel patches extracted from an initial set of images to classify H&E stained breast cancer histology images into bengin and malignant classes. Final image prediction is based on sum, product or maximum rules for patch probability. They have also reported that higher magnification causes degradation in accuracy.

Researchers have modified the CNN architecture successfully for breast histology problems. Ciresan [12] trained a CNN model for mitosis detection in breast histology images and won the ICPR 2012 Mitosis Detection challenge with F1-score of 0.782. They used patches of size 101×101 extracted from initial images for training and sliding window method for mitosis detection. Cruz-Roa [16] trained a CNN using whole-slide patch size of 100×100 pixels, for invasive carcinoma region detection. Their network outperformed the state-of-the-art by achieving F1-score of 0.780%. Araújo [17], trained a CNN model on a dataset provided by Bioimaging 2015 breast histology classification challenge [17]. They opted for a bigger patch size of (512×512) for training the CNN model and and achieving an accuracy of 77.80% outperforming other approaches. They also trained a Support Vector Machine classifier using CNN based learned features.

3   Transfer Learning

One of the problems associated with convolution neural network parameter learning is that it requires massive amounts of data and significant computing power. The computational problem can be overcome by employing GPU computing. However, collecting very large sized medical imaging datasets can be difficult

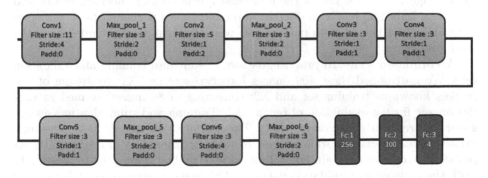

Fig. 2. TK-ALEXNET architecture after changing in ALEXNET.

and time-consuming. This problem, however, can be solved to some extent by some clever tricks such as mirroring, rotating images, extracting overlapping patches [12] and fine tuning [18] (Transfer learning). Transfer learning basically takes an existing pre-trained deep neural network such as ALEXNET [10] or GOOGLE-NET [11] and fine tunes its parameters by changing the last three layers based on the application specific dataset (as in our case, the medical images data set).

4   Proposed Solution

Unlike previous approaches, we propose a transfer learning based approach for the classification breast cancer H&E stained histology images inspired by [18]. For this purpose, we fine tune ALEXNET for breast cancer images. ALEXNET is composed of stacks of multiple layers of neuron-like units on top of each other. It consists of multiple sets of convolutional layers, pooling layers and fully-connected layers stacked on top of each other. The job of the convolutional layers is to extract local features in the input images. A convolutional layer is typically followed by a pooling layer that reduces computational complexity by performing non-linear down-sampling. Pooling layers also introduce translation invariance into the network.

In the upper and final layers, all the units are generally connected to each other and thus are termed fully-connected layers. Initially, it is trained on "Imagenet" dataset which contains 1000 distinct classes consisting of 1.2 million labelled images.

5   Dataset Description

The provided breast cancer dataset consists of high quality (2048×1536 pixels) non-compressed and labeled H&E stained images. Image digitization is done under similar acquisition settings (magnification = $200\times$ and pixel size of $0.42\,\mu m \times 0.42\,\mu m$. This data consists of 400 images (100 for each class) and each image is assigned one of the four class labels (benign, normal, *InSitu* and invasive). Labelling has been done by two experienced pathologists. The images for which the labels of both pathologists were different were excluded from the final dataset.

According to standard practice, dataset is split into training and validation sets. We partitioned these 400 images into two sets i.e., X1: consisting of 320 images known as training set and X2: consisting of 80 images termed as validation set for the evaluation of our model. Training and validation images are separated randomly into disjoint sets. The aim of this challenge is to automate breast histology classification process to make it faster and more accurate. As per standard practice; stain normalization was applied during pre-processing to both the training and validation datasets. This is equivalent to the staining used for the preparation of slides.

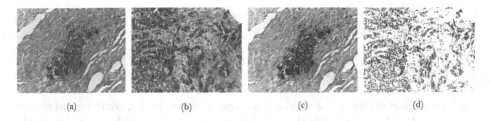

(a)   (b)   (c)   (d)

Fig. 3. Microscopy images before and after stain normalization. Where the original images are shown in (a) & (b) and their corresponding stain normalized images are shown in (c) & (d).

During the first step, the logarithmic transformation is applied to color image. This is followed by singular value decomposition for identification of high variance projections. Finally, the original image is transformed via the resultant color space transform, and histogram stretching is applied to ensure that the dynamic range spans the lower 90% data. Figure 3 demonstrates the impact of normalization on two sample histology images. It is highlighted that stain normalization tends to give an improvement in quantitative analysis, as report in [19]. During our preliminary analysis we also observed that stain normalization did result in performance gain; when compared to training on original (non-normalized) images.

6   Model Training

We fine-tuned ALEXNET for breast cancer histology images dataset by changing the layer structure with respect to the provided dataset. To fine-tune a deep CNN, a large amount of training data is required. For this purpose, we extended the training set X1 by making mirrored and rotated versions of images in X1, inspired by [12]. Furthermore, we extracted overlapping patches of size 512×512 from the training images. Now we have roughly 38,400 images having 9600 images per class.

In our experimental setup, we changed the input layers of ALEXNET to size 512×512 instead of using 227×227. We also removed all the fully connected (FC) layers and added convolution (256 filter of size 3×3), activation (ReLU) and max pooling layer of same size. We also reduced the size of fully connected layer as (FC-1:256) followed by ReLU (but no dropout layer), which was again followed by a fully connected layer of size (FC-2:100) in order to avoid overfitting. At the end, we added a 4 class Fully connected layer for respective classes. We named our extended ALEXNET version as *TK-ALEXNET*. Figure 2 shows the architecture of our new model.

We trained the above mentioned model with an intial learning rate 10^{-4} for 5 epochs. Then we tested performance on X2, the validation data set. For the classification of a whole image, non-overlapping patches are extracted from the image and passed through the classifier. The final decision regarding the class of the whole image is made by applying majority voting to the results of individual patches contained within the image.

7   Performance Evaluation

Performance evaluation was conducted using accuracy and sensitivity and results are presented here for both the validation set and the hidden test set of the *ICIAR*-2018 Grand Challenge on Breast Cancer histology images. The ground truth for the hidden test set was not visible to us at the time of paper submission. Our model had to predict one out of four classes (normal, benign, InSitu and invasive).

7.1   Patch-Wise Classification

Patch-wise accuracy and sensitivity for four classes in shown in Table 1. Patch-wise dataset is generated by extracting non-overlapping patches (e.g. for 20 images 240 patches are extracted for each class as shown in Table 1.). Accuracy of our model is 75.73% for four classes.

Table 1. Patch-wise accuracy (%) & sensitivity (%) of four classes.

Dataset	Normal	Benign	*InSitu*	Invasive
Validation set	20(240)	20(240)	20(240)	20(240)
Patch-wise sensitivity (%)	82.08	68.75	80.83	71.25
Overall accuracy (%)	75.73			

7.2   Image-Wise Classification

For classification of the whole image, first the image is converted into twelve non-overlapping patches and then passed through the model. Labels of images are predicted based on one of three different techniques explained in [17]. Image wise accuracy of our model for four classes is 81.25% on validation dataset. Performance metrics for different classes, on the validation set, are shown in Table 2. The accuracy of our model on the hidden set of the challenge was 57.00%.

Table 2. Image-wise accuracy (%) & sensitivity (%) of four classes

Dataset	Normal	Benign	*InSitu*	Invasive
Validation set	20	20	20	20
Image-wise sensitivity (%)	85.00	85.00	80.00	75.00
Overall accuracy (%)	81.25			

This decrease in accuracy might have resulted due to the complexity of the hidden test set. We have access to only the accuracy on the hidden test set and therefore, cannot present performance metrics for the individual classes (as we have done for the validation set).

8 Conclusion

This work presents the details of a modified version of ALEXNET for classification of Breast Cancer slide images which was part of our entry to the *ICIAR*-2018 challenge on this topic. In this work, instead of designing our own CNN model, we fine tuned a good pre-trained model (ALEXNET) on breast cancer H & E Stained Dataset. Our approach includes convolutional, activation & max-pooling layers; while reducing the size of fully connected layer in order to avoid overfitting. Experimental evidence shows that our method gives an overall accuracy of 57% on the hidden test set. As part of our future work we intend to expand on this research and improve our performance using custom built deep architectures for cancer classification.

References

1. Siegel, R.L., Miller, K.D., Jemal, A.: Cancer statistics, 2015. CA Cancer J. Clin. **65**(1), 5–29 (2015)
2. National Breast Cancer Foundation. Breast Cancer Diagnosis (2015). http://www.nationalbreastcancer.org/breast-cancer-diagnosis
3. Elston, C.W., Ellis, I.O.: Pathological prognostic factors in breast cancer. I. The value of histological grade in breast cancer: experience from a large study with long-term follow-up. Histopathology. **19**(5), 403–10 (1991)
4. Filipczuk, P., Fevens, T., Krzyzak, A., Monczak, R.: Computer-aided breast cancer diagnosis based on the analysis of cytological images of fine needle biopsies. IEEE Trans. Med. Imag. **32**(12), 2169–2178 (2013)
5. George, Y.M., Zayed, H.H., Roushdy, M.I., Elbagoury, B.M.: Remote computer-aided breast cancer detection and diagnosis system based on cytological images. IEEE Syst. J. **8**(3), 949–64 (2014)
6. Belsare, A.D., Mushrif, M.M., Pangarkar, M.A., Meshram, N.: Classification of breast cancer histopathology images using texture feature analysis. In: 2015 IEEE Region 10 Conference, TENCON 2015, Macau, p. 1–5. IEEE (2015)
7. Brook, A., El-Yaniv, R., Issler, E., Kimmel, R., Meir, R., Peleg, D.: Breast cancer diagnosis from biopsy images using generic features and SVMs, pp. 1–16 (2007)
8. Zhang, B.: Breast cancer diagnosis from biopsy images by serial fusion of Random Subspace ensembles. In: 2011 4th International Conference on Biomedical Engineering and Informatics (BMEI), vol. 1. IEEE (2011)
9. Israel Institute of Technology dataset. ftp.cs.technion.ac.il/pub/projects/medic-image
10. Krizhevsky, A., Ilya S., Hinton, G.E.: Imagenet classification with deep convolutional neural networks. In: Advances in Neural Information Processing Systems (2012)

11. Szegedy, C.: Going deeper with convolutions. In: Proceedings of the IEEE conference on computer vision and pattern recognition (2015)
12. Cireşan, D.C., Giusti, A., Gambardella, L.M., Schmidhuber, J.: Mitosis detection in breast cancer histology images with deep neural networks. In: Mori, K., Sakuma, I., Sato, Y., Barillot, C., Navab, N. (eds.) MICCAI 2013. LNCS, vol. 8150, pp. 411–418. Springer, Heidelberg (2013). https://doi.org/10.1007/978-3-642-40763-5_51
13. Litjens, G.: Deep learning as a tool for increased accuracy and efficiency of histopathological diagnosis. Sci. Rep. **6**, 26286 (2016)
14. Sirinukunwattana, K.: Locality sensitive deep learning for detection and classification of nuclei in routine colon cancer histology images. IEEE Trans. Med. Imag. **35**(5), 1196–1206 (2016)
15. Chi, J.: Thyroid nodule classification in ultrasound images by fine-tuning deep convolutional neural network. J. Digit. Imag. **30**(4), 477–486 (2017)
16. Cruz-Roa, A.: Automatic detection of invasive ductal carcinoma in whole slide images with convolutional neural networks. In: International Society for Optics and Photonics, SPIE Medical Imaging, vol. 9041 (2014)
17. Araújo, T.: Classification of breast cancer histology images using Convolutional Neural Networks. PloS one **12**(6), e0177544 (2017)
18. Bayramoglu, N., Heikkilä, J.: Transfer learning for cell nuclei classification in histopathology images. In: Hua, G., Jégou, H. (eds.) ECCV 2016. LNCS, vol. 9915, pp. 532–539. Springer, Cham (2016). https://doi.org/10.1007/978-3-319-49409-8_46
19. Macenko, M.: A method for normalizing histology slides for quantitative analysis. In: 2009 IEEE International Symposium on Biomedical Imaging, ISBI2009, From Nano to Macro. IEEE (2009)

Ensembling Neural Networks for Digital Pathology Images Classification and Segmentation

Artem Pimkin[1,2,3], Gleb Makarchuk[1,2,3], Vladimir Kondratenko[1,2,3],
Maxim Pisov[2,3(✉)], Egor Krivov[1,2,3], and Mikhail Belyaev[1,2]

[1] Skolkovo Institute of Science and Technology, Moscow, Russia
gleb.makarchuk@gmail.com, e.a.krivov@gmail.com, m.belyaev@skoltech.ru
[2] Kharkevich Institute for Information Transmission Problems, Moscow, Russia
[3] Moscow Institute of Physics and Technology, Moscow, Russia
{artem.pimkin,vladimir.kondratenko,maksim.pisov}@phystech.edu

Abstract. In the last years, neural networks have proven to be a powerful framework for various image analysis problems. However, some application domains have specific limitations. Notably, digital pathology is an example of such fields due to tremendous image sizes and quite limited number of training examples available. In this paper, we adopt state-of-the-art convolutional neural networks (CNN) architectures for digital pathology images analysis. We propose to classify image patches to increase effective sample size and then to apply an ensembling technique to build prediction for the original images. To validate the developed approaches, we conducted experiments with *Breast Cancer Histology Challenge* dataset and obtained 90% accuracy for the 4-class tissue classification task.

Keywords: Convolutional networks · Ensembles · Digital pathology

1 Introduction

Histology is a key discipline in cancer diagnosis thanks to its ability to evaluate tissues anatomy. The classical approach involves glass slide microscopy and requires thoughtful analysis by a pathologist. Digital pathology imaging provides a statistically equivalent way to analyze tissues [13], so it's a natural application area for machine learning methods [10]. Recent advances in deep learning suggest that these methods can be useful for a set of digital pathology image analysis problems including cell detection and counting and segmentation [7]. One of the most important and challenging tasks is tissue classification, and recent studies (e.g., [1]) demonstrate promising results. However, these image analysis problems differ from standard one in different ways. A crucial limiting factor

---

A. Pimkin, G. Makarchuk, V. Kondratenko, M. Pisov—Equal contribution.

© Springer International Publishing AG, part of Springer Nature 2018
A. Campilho et al. (Eds.): ICIAR 2018, LNCS 10882, pp. 877–886, 2018.
https://doi.org/10.1007/978-3-319-93000-8_100

is a combination of relatively small sample sizes (usually hundreds of examples) and extremely high resolution (the typical image size is 50000 × 50000). For comparison, the ImageNet dataset contains millions of 256 × 256 images [3]. This combination leads to high variance of deep learning models predictions and requires careful design of data processing pipelines. In this work, we propose two methods for digital pathology images segmentation and classification. Both methods include data preprocessing, intensive usage of modern deep learning architectures and an aggregation procedure for decreasing model variability.

2   Problem

Generally, our task was to recognize benign and malignant formations on breast histology images. We were solving this problem in two formulations: image classification and segmentation.

2.1   Data

In this paper we use the *Breast Cancer Histology Challenge* (BACH-18) dataset which consists of *hematoxylin and eosin* stained microscopy images as well as whole-slide images.

Microscopy Images. The first subset consists of 400 microscopy images of shape 2048 × 1536 × 3, where 3 stands for the number of channels, the color space is RGB.

The images were obtained as patches from much larger microscopy images, similar to those described further in current subsection.

Every dataset entry is labeled as belonging to one of the four classes: Normal (n, 0), Benign (b, 1), Carcinoma in situ (is, 2) or Invasive Carcinoma (iv, 3). The labels are evenly distributed between the 400 images (Fig. 1).

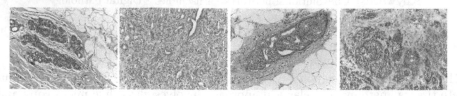

Fig. 1. Samples from the first subset (from left to right): Normal, Benign, Carcinoma in situ and Invasive Carcinoma

Whole-Slide Images. The second subset consist of 20 whole-slide images of shape (approx.) 40000 × 60000 × 3, where, similarly, 3 stands for the number of channels, and the color space is RGB.

For half of the images segmentation masks of corresponding spatial shape are provided. Each pixel of the mask is labeled from 0 to 3 (from Normal to Invasive Carcinoma). During the model training only this half of the dataset was used (Fig. 2).

Fig. 2. A sample from the second subset: whole-slide image (left) and the corresponding mask overlayed on the image (right). The black color stands for Invasive Carcinoma, gray - Benign, the rest - Normal. Note the roughness of the ground truth segmentation.

3   Microscopy Images Classification

3.1   Preprocessing

One of the common problems in work with histology slides is preprocessing. As it turned out, network pays attention to areas of inhomogeneity. For this reason, our image preparation was aimed at normalization and contrast enhancement of the slide. We tried a couple of well-known methods of digital pathology images preprocessing (e.g., [9]), but it didn't increase the performance. Also, we tested simple data transformations like inversion, channel-wise mean subtraction, conversion to different color spaces, etc. A simple channel-wise mean subtraction provided the largest performance boost (about 10% of accuracy score), so we ended up using only this preprocessing approach.

3.2   Training

We used two popular architectures for image classification: ResNet [5] and DenseNet [6]:

ResNet is a convolutional neural network which won the 1st place on ILSVRC 2015 classification task. We used ResNet34 implemented in *torchvision*[1] with slight architectural changes: we replaced the pooling layer before the fully-connected layer by an *average spatial pyramid pooling layer* [4]. We tried several levels of pyramid pooling depth from 1 (global average pooling) to 3.

DenseNet is a convolutional neural network which has a slightly smaller error rate on the ImageNet dataset than ResNet. We used DenseNet169 and DenseNet201 from *torchvision*'s implementation with similar architectural changes as for ResNet.

In our experiments we used Adam optimizer [8] with an exponential-like learning rate policy: each 20 epochs the learning rate decreased by a factor of 2. Initially the learning rate was taken equal to 0.01.

---

[1] http://pytorch.org/docs/0.3.0/torchvision/models.html

Experiments have shown that feeding the images directly into the network yields poor results due to quite large images shape. In order to overcome this difficulty we chose to train out models on patches extracted from the original images: during training each patch was randomly (with a 2D uniform distribution) extracted from an image, also picked at random, with the label being the same as for the original image. This approach led to a performance increase of about 15%.

Also, we observed that preprocessing each individual patch instead of preprocessing the whole image yields slightly better results.

Each network was trained on patches of shape 500×500 pixels, with batches of size ≈ 10 (this value differs between models). The training process lasted for 120 epochs, and every epoch 300 batches were fed into the network.

We also tried pretraining our models on similar datasets: BreakHis[2] and *Breast carcinoma histological images from the Department of Pathology*, "Agios Pavlos" General Hospital of Thessaloniki, Greece [14]. See Table 1 for performance comparison.

3.3   Model Selection and Stacking

While building models, we experimented with different architectures, learning rate policies and pretraining. Thus, we ended up with 29 different models built and evaluated using 3-fold cross-validation (CV). We had a goal of combining these models in order to make more accurate predictions.

During inference we deterministically extracted patches according to a grid with a stride of 100 pixels. Thus, every multiclass network would generate a matrix of shape 176×4 containing 4 class probabilities for 176 patches extracted from the image. Similarly, every one-vs-all network would generate a matrix of shape 176×1.

We extracted various features from these class probabilities predictions:

- min, max and mean values of the probabilities of each class
- (for multiclass networks only) on how many patches each class has the highest probability
- 10, 25, 75 and 90 percentile probability values of each class
- on how many patches probabilities go above 15% and 25% threshold values for each class.

After building the features, the problem was reduced to tabular data classification. So, for our final classifier, we have chosen XGBoost [2] as one of the state-of-the-art approaches for such tasks. Our pipeline was the following:

- Choose reasonable XGBoost hyperparameters (based on cross-validation score) for the classifier built on top of all (29) models we have.
- Use greedy search for model selection: keep removing models while the accuracy on CV keeps increasing.
- Fine-tune the XGBoost hyperparameters on the remaining models set.

---

[2] https://omictools.com/breast-cancer-histopathological-database-tool.

By following this procedure we reduced the number of models from 29 to 12. It is also worth mentioning that we compared accuracies for different sets of models and hyperparameters by averaging accuracy score from 10-fold CV across 20 different shuffles of the data to get statistically significant results (for such a small dataset) and thus optimize based on merit rather than on randomness.

3.4   Inference

Given the relatively small dataset, we decided that we might take advantage from retraining the networks on the whole dataset. However, this approach leaves no possibility to assess the stacking quality.

As a trade-off, we decided to use 6-fold CV (instead of 3-fold CV), so that the network would see 83% (vs 66%) of data: a substantial increase in performance (compared to the 3-fold CV models) would mean that retraining on the whole dataset might be beneficial.

In the 6-fold CV setting, the performance of every individual network increased significantly. We also have fine-tuned the composition for 6-split networks that resulted in two more models being held out and slightly changed hyperparameters (see Table 1 for a comparison of networks' performances). However, the resulting ensemble classifier could not surpass the one build on top of 3-fold CV.

Nevertheless, for our final classifier we chose to average the patch predictions across all 6 networks and use the XGBoost classifier built on top of 6-fold CV. This approach is computationally inefficient, but allows us to reduce variance of the predictions.

4   Whole-Slide Images Segmentation

4.1   Preprocessing

Similarly to the first problem, we use channel-wise mean subtraction as a preprocessing strategy. Also, given the unusually big images, we tried to downsample it by various factors: the downsampling by a factor of 40 along each spatial dimension proved to be very effective. Thereby, downsampled input is used in some ensemble models.

4.2   Training

In our segmentation experiments we also used the same optimizer and learning rate policy as in Sect. 3.2.

In case when downsampling was included in the preprocessing pipeline the images were fed directly into the network, and the network was trained for 1500 epochs. Otherwise, the network was trained for 150 epochs with patches of shape 300×300 (40 patches per batch), similarly to the procedure described in Sect. 3.2.

4.3 Models

For the segmentation task, we introduce T-Net, a novel architecture based on U-Net [11]. It can be regarded as a generalization, which applies additional convolutions to the connections between the downsampling and upsampling branches (Fig. 3).

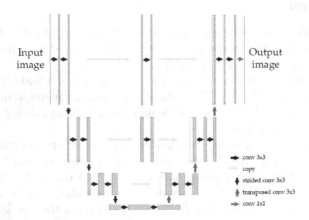

Fig. 3. A schematic example of the T-Net architecture.

We used 3 different models:

- T-Net for binary segmentation Normal-vs-all trained on patches (T-Net 1).
- T-Net for a similar task but trained on images downsampled by a factor of 40 along each dimension (T-Net 2). We also used a weighted-boundary log loss, which adds linearly decreasing weights to the pixels near the ground-truth regions' boundaries. Basically, it can be reduced to multiplying the ground truth mask by the corresponding weights and calculating the log loss for the resulting "ground truth".
- T-Net for multiclass segmentation trained on images downsampled by a factor of 40 along each dimension (T-Net 3).

4.4 Postprocessing

While working with output of network trained on patches of the non-downsampled whole-slide images we faced the fact that output probability maps were too heterogeneous, which resulted in holes in segmented areas after thresholding, although ground truth consists of 1-connected domains. So, for primary processing we use Gaussian blur with square kernel of fixed size (processing hyperparameter) to reduce the hole sizes on the next steps. Then we threshold the probability map and get several clusters of areas with holes, many of which we merge with the morphological closing operation [12]. Finally, we discard the connected components with areas less than $\sqrt[a]{\overline{S^a}}$, where $\overline{S^a}$ is the mean of component areas in the power of a (a is a hyperparameter). The postprocessing steps are shown in Fig. 4.

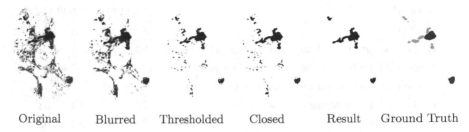

Original   Blurred   Thresholded   Closed   Result   Ground Truth

Fig. 4. Example of postprocessing. (Original) and (blurred) is the probability maps. Black on (Ground truth) is 'iv', gray is 'is'. Black on the other images means abnormal.

4.5 Ensembling

Due to strong class imbalance ($75\% - n : 1\% - b : 1\% - is : 23\% - iv$) we focused our research on the Normal-vs-All task to adjust the output more precisely. Experiments have shown that the network trained on whole-slide images (T-Net 1) predicts quite "ragged" regions while the network trained on downsampled images (T-Net 2) predicts a lot of false-positive pixels.

Our approach is T-Net ensemble that consists of blending these two models, letting them to compensate each other's mistakes, and transforming output binary mask into a multiclass one using (T-Net 3)'s prediction:

$$Result = 3 \cdot BinaryMask + (TNet3) \cdot (1 - BinaryMask) \tag{1}$$

However, given the fact that the metric proposed by the organizers of the BACH-18 challenge is biased towards the abnormal classes (1, 2, 3), we decided to use a much simpler approach - shifted blending, by setting the binary positive class to Invasive Carcinoma and the negative class to Benign:

$$Result = 1 + 2 \cdot BinaryMask \tag{2}$$

It significantly increased the proposed metric. Also, since it is shifted we provide more common metrics for both approaches. See Sect. 5.2 for details.

Each model was trained and evaluated with 3-fold CV. To evaluate performance of the ensemble we used 5-fold CV (on top of the test predictions from 3-fold CV).

5 Results

5.1 Microscopy Images Classification

Table 1 shows the models' accuracies. Note the significant performance boost gained from stacking.

Table 1. Models' accuracy for the microscopy images classification task: multiclass (first block), one-vs-all (second block), final ensemble built on top of 3- and 6-fold CV (third block)

Network	3-fold CV	6-fold CV
ResNet 34	.83 ± .01	.86 ± .03
ResNet 34, pretrained on patches from whole slides	.83 ± .05	.85 ± .04
ResNet 34, pretrained on BreakHis Dataset	.81 ± .04	.87 ± .06
ResNet 34, pretrained on Agios Pavlos dataset	.83 ± .03	.86 ± .03
ResNet 34, patch mean subtraction	.79 ± .04	.83 ± .03
DenseNet 169	.78 ± .06	.85 ± .02
DenseNet 201	.80 ± .03	.82 ± .06
ResNet 34, Benign vs all	.90 ± .01	.91 ± .02
ResNet 34, InSitu vs all	.90 ± .05	.93 ± .02
ResNet 34, Invasive vs all	.90 ± .03	.91 ± .03
Ensemble (stacking)	**.90 ± .05**	**.90 ± .05**

Table 2. Segmentation results

Network	BachScore	Dice(b)	Dice(is)	Dice(iv)	Dice(abnormal)
T-Net 1	.54 ± .16			.61 ± .19	.69 ± .16
T-Net 2	.59 ± .20			.68 ± .21	.71 ± .19
T-Net 3	.56 ± .19	.01 ± .01	.03 ± .04	.59 ± .21	.66 ± .21
T-Net ensemble	.64 ± .20	.01 ± .02	.01 ± .02	.71 ± .23	.72 ± .20
T-Net shifted blending	**.70 ± .06**	**.04 ± .06**	**.03 ± .04**	**.73 ± .21**	**.74 ± .18**

5.2   Whole-Slide Images Segmentation

In the BACH-18 challenge the following metric is used:

$$BachScore = 1 - \frac{\sum_i |pred_i - gt_i|}{\sum_i max\{gt_i, 3 - gt_i\} \cdot \mathbb{I}[gt_i > 0 \& pred_i > 0]}, \quad (3)$$

where the summation is performed across all the pixels and $gt_i, pred_i$ are the i-th pixel values of the ground truth and prediction respectively.

Table 2 shows the models' performances according to BachScore, as well as the Dice score - a more common segmentation quality measure (it is computed for each channel separately and also from the point of "normal/abnormal" task).

6   Conclusion

We proposed a two-stage procedure for **digital pathology images classification** problem. To increase effective sample size, we used random patches for training. The developed ensembling technique allowed us not only to increase the prediction quality due to averaging but also combine results for individual patches into the whole image prediction. In overall, a promising classification accuracy was obtained.

As for the **whole-slide images segmentation** task, we obtained controversial results: on the one hand we obtained promising Bach and Dice scores, but on the other hand most of our work was aimed at roughening the obtained predictions in accordance with the given labeling. Moreover, the results of our top performing ensemble were heavily improved by hard biasing which doesn't allow us to say how well this result depicts our method's performance.

References

1. Araújo, T., Aresta, G., Castro, E., Rouco, J., Aguiar, P., Eloy, C., Polónia, A., Campilho, A.: Classification of breast cancer histology images using convolutional neural networks. PLoS ONE **12**(6), e0177544 (2017)
2. Chen, T., Guestrin, C.: Xgboost: A scalable tree boosting system. In: Proceedings of the 22nd ACM SIGKDD International Conference on Knowledge Discovery and Data Mining, KDD 2016, pp. 785–794 (2016)
3. Deng, J., Dong, W., Socher, R., Li, L.J., Li, K., Fei-Fei, L.: Imagenet: a large-scale hierarchical image database. In: 2009 IEEE Conference on Computer Vision and Pattern Recognition, CVPR 2009, pp. 248–255. IEEE (2009)
4. He, K., Zhang, X., Ren, S., Sun, J.: Spatial pyramid pooling in deep convolutional networks for visual recognition. In: Fleet, D., Pajdla, T., Schiele, B., Tuytelaars, T. (eds.) ECCV 2014. LNCS, vol. 8691, pp. 346–361. Springer, Cham (2014). https://doi.org/10.1007/978-3-319-10578-9_23
5. He, K., Zhang, X., Ren, S., Sun, J.: Deep residual learning for image recognition, pp. 770–778 (2016)
6. Huang, G., Liu, Z., Weinberger, K.Q., van der Maaten, L.: Densely connected convolutional networks. IEEE Trans. Neural Netw. Learn. Syst. **1**(2), 3 (2017)
7. Janowczyk, A., Madabhushi, A.: Deep learning for digital pathology image analysis: a comprehensive tutorial with selected use cases. J. Pathol. Inform. **7**, 29 (2016)
8. Kingma, D.P., Ba, J.: Adam: A method for stochastic optimization. arXiv preprint arXiv:1412.6980 (2014)
9. Macenko, M., Niethammer, M., Marron, J.S., et al.: A method for normalizing histology slides for quantitative analysis. J. Magn. Reson. Imag. **9**, 1107–1110 (2009)
10. Madabhushi, A., Lee, G.: Image analysis and machine learning in digital pathology: challenges and opportunities. Med. Image Anal. **33**, 170–175 (2016)
11. Ronneberger, O., Fischer, P., Brox, T.: U-Net: convolutional networks for biomedical image segmentation. In: Navab, N., Hornegger, J., Wells, W.M., Frangi, A.F. (eds.) MICCAI 2015. LNCS, vol. 9351, pp. 234–241. Springer, Cham (2015). https://doi.org/10.1007/978-3-319-24574-4_28
12. Serra, J.: Image Analysis and Mathematical Morphology. Academic Press Inc, Orlando, FL, USA (1983)

13. Snead, D.R., Tsang, Y.W., Meskiri, A., Kimani, P.K., Crossman, R., Rajpoot, N.M., Blessing, E., Chen, K., Gopalakrishnan, K., Matthews, P., et al.: Validation of digital pathology imaging for primary histopathological diagnosis. Histopathology **68**(7), 1063–1072 (2016)
14. Zioga, C., Kamas, A., Patsiaoura, K., Dimitropoulos, K., Barmpoutis, P., Grammalidis, N.: Breast carcinoma histological images from the department of pathology, "agios pavlos" general hospital of thessaloniki, Greece, July 2017

Automatic Breast Cancer Grading of Histological Images Based on Colour and Texture Descriptors

Auxiliadora Sarmiento$^{(\boxtimes)}$ (iD) and Irene Fondón (iD)

Departamento de Teoría de la Señal y Comunicaciones,
Universidad de Sevilla, C/ Descubrimientos s/n, 41092 Sevilla, Spain
sarmiento@us.es

Abstract. The early diagnosis of breast cancer is extremely important to save lives, but breast cancer diagnosis and prediction is very complex and time consuming. In this article we propose a CAD tool for automated malignancy assessment of breast tissue histological images into four classes: normal, benign, in situ and invasive. The problem is very complex, since histological images exhibit a highly variable appearance, even within the same malignancy level. We compute a features vector related to nuclei, colour regions and textures for each image that serves as an input to a Support Vector Machine (SVM) classifier with a quadratic kernel. System performance has been measure as its classification accuracy using 10-fold cross-validation within an initial set of 400 images. Our approach yields good results with an overall accuracy of 79.2%, and outperforms several other state of the art algorithms.

Keywords: Breast cancer · Computer-aided diagnosis
Digital pathology · Pattern recognition and classification
Tissue malignancy

1 Introduction

Breast cancer is the second most common cancer in worldwide representing about 25% of all cancers in women [1]. It starts when cells in the breast begin to divide and grow out of control in an abnormal way. Pathologists play an essential role in the diagnosis of the disease evaluating breast biopsy samples stained with hematoxylin and eosin (H&E). Most breast lesions detected by pathologists are benign: that is, they are not cancerous. Common benign lesions are developmental abnormalities, epithelial and stromal proliferations, inflammatory lesions, and neoplasms. The majority of these benign lesions are not related with an increased risk for subsequent breast cancer.

Breast cancers can be grouped into two categories: carcinomas and sarcomas. Carcinomas are cancers that begin in the lining layer (epithelial cells) of the breast, whereas sarcomas, which represent less than 1% of primary breast

© Springer International Publishing AG, part of Springer Nature 2018
A. Campilho et al. (Eds.): ICIAR 2018, LNCS 10882, pp. 887–894, 2018.
https://doi.org/10.1007/978-3-319-93000-8_101

cancers, begin in the connective tissue (stromal). Carcinomas in turn are divided into two broad categories: in situ and invasive. In situ carcinoma means that cancer cells remain confined inside the pre-existing normal lobules or ducts. Is there is any evidence of cancer cell invasion into the surrounding stroma, however limited, the lesion is classified as invasive carcinoma. An example of each image type is depicted in Fig. 1.

In this paper, we present a CAD tool for automatic classification of tissue malignancy based on some colour and texture features of histological images. Our method is capable of distinguishing among four malignancy levels, as is performed in clinical practice, with high accuracy, and outperforms various other proposed methods. MATLAB implementations of the proposed algorithm are freely available from [2].

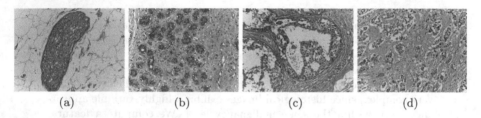

| (a) | (b) | (c) | (d) |

Fig. 1. Representative histological H&E stained images of normal (a), benign (b), in situ (c), and invasive (d) cases.

2 Previous Work

Currently, there are two families of methods that address this problem. The first family is composed of methods that use machine learning algorithms based on feature descriptors. The majority of these approaches consider only two possible output classes: malignant or benign. For example, in [3], the authors computed some features based on nuclei detection and Gabor decomposition coefficients. The accuracy obtained with $k = 10$ cross-validation on a set of 58 images was 80.2% using the H&E colour space. The approach presented in [4] relies on the accurate segmentation of nuclei, performed with random walker technique in the H plane of the H&E colour space. The accuracy levels claimed were between 84.86% and 87.14% with a 10-splits Monte Carlo cross-validation. Up to our knowledge, [5] is the only feature-based method that considers four levels of severity. It extracts some features based on nuclei detection, color region and texture. A Quadratic SVM classifier was trained with 120 images, obtaining an overall accuracy of 75.8% with a 5-fold cross validation and 75% with an external validation set of 20 images.

The other family of methods is based on deep learning techniques, in which the relevant features are learned directly by the network. In particular, convolutional neural networks (CNNs) have been used to handle two-class breast cancer classification in [6–8] and the classification into four classes in [9]. However, histopathological datasets are often small, and in this scenario, CNN-based methods might result in overfitting and poor generalization. To overcome this serious problem, CNN-based methods for cancer classification usually expand their dataset by taking image patches and by artificially generating samples via affine transformations. The augmented dataset is then used to train the network. Finally, they perform a patch-wise classification and decide the label of the whole image by simple decision fusion methods, such as max-pooling and voting. For example, the method presented in [9] divides the image into twelve non-overlapping patches, and composes an augmented dataset rotating and mirroring these patches. Then, it computes the patch class probability with a trained CNN or a CNN+SVM, and finally, it decides the image class using a majority voting approach. The network was trained with 120 images and the method obtained a mean accuracy of 77.8% with an external validation.

3   Method

H&E images are full of information at many levels, from the lowest level structures, nuclei, to the highest levels of complexity structures, milk ducts. The automatic study of all possible structures is probably unapproachable, but we can study the overall architecture in a more abstract way using not only nuclei based features, but also region colour and texture features.

Our method is conceptually simple: after an initial contrast enhancement step, we compute for each image two types of characteristics: colour based and texture based, which are concatenated to build a vector with a final size of 126 features. This feature vector serves as the input for the classifier. As presented in results section, we have tested a total number of 10 classifiers, obtaining the best model using the SVM classifier with a Quadratic kernel.

In order to obtain a successful processing of the histological image it is necessary to choose the best colour model tailored to the microscopic stain and tissue type under consideration. In our experiments we have found that BACH dataset images have better classification result if CMYK colour space is used to extract the features. In fact, the CMYK colour model allows both distinguishing different textures and retrieving their proper colour for further analysis. As pre-processing step, we have employed a simple but effective histogram equalization method with a gamma correction (gamma $= 1.5$) on all the CMYK colour planes.

3.1   Colour Features

Our algorithm studies structures through the detection of nuclei in the images, as well as overall architecture characteristics based on colour regions.

In our approach, we initially identify the presence or absence of violet areas as nuclei using the well-known K-means clustering algorithm on the C, M and Y colour planes. If the image presents some quantity of violet, then the processing will be continued. Otherwise, all the features corresponding to colour are set to zero. To evaluate the presence of violet in the images we have used the well-known K-means clustering algorithm on the C, M and Y colour planes. We automatically select the number of clusters K and the initial centroids by studying the colour histogram of the images with a hill-climbing technique [10]. When the K-means algorithm ends, the resulting centroids are compared to an empirical reference violet. If the Euclidean distance of at least one of them is less than 0.3, we assume that there are violet regions and the algorithm continues. Then, we isolate nuclei by processing the complete image in blocks of fixed size of 200 × 200 pixels. First, we compute a mask of violet regions using the results of the K-means algorithm and Otsu threshold. Then, a Cha-Vese active contour is used to accurately delineate the boundaries of nucleus. The next step consists of separating adjacent nuclei by computing the distance image, imposing the minima, and applying the traditional watershed method. We show in Fig. 2 the nuclei segmentation results for two different images.

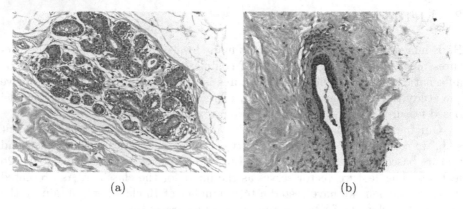

(a)   (b)

Fig. 2. The ultimately obtained nuclei marked in green overlaid on two of the original images.

We extract from the resulting nuclei the following features: the number of nuclei in the image, mean and variance of the area, mean and variance of the Euler number, mean and variance of nuclei extent, mean and variance of eccentricity, mean and variance of perimeter, mean and variance of solidity and mean and variance of saturation.

We have also study the degree of dispersion of the nuclei in the images by calculating the Euclidean distance between all the nuclei. We have fitted the Euclidean distances between nuclei to a Rayleigh distribution. We show in Fig. 3 a representative normalized histogram of the Euclidean distance on each grade of cancer. On average, the nuclei seem to be more clustered in the non-cancerous images, that is, normal and benign cases, than in the cancerous images. We have computed also the number of nuclei with another nuclei close to it, where the term close refers to a Euclidean distance lower than 60. The b parameter of the distribution and the proportion of nuclei that are close to at least one other nucleus with respect to the total number of nuclei have been also included in the feature vector.

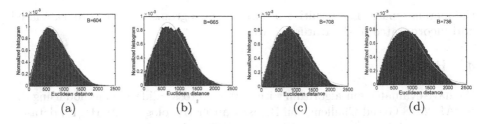

Fig. 3. Representative histograms of Euclidean distances between nuclei, fitted Rayleigh distribution models (in red) and parameter b of the distribution in the cases normal (a), benign (b), in situ (c) and invasive (d).

In Fig. 1, one can see that the pattern of colour changes as the tissue transforms from non-cancerous to cancerous. This is mainly due to the fact that the nuclei of the cells, which stain violet, invade stroma and lumen regions, which are pink and white respectively. This change may be captured by computing some area proportions: pink/violet, pink/white and white/violet. On average, the proportion pink/violet and white/violet seems to be higher in normal and benign images than in situ and invasive images. We also computed the mean area of white regions to account for the small amount of white in invasive images, where the white areas are small and sparse.

3.2   Texture Features

H&E images feature high variability in their appearance due to the presence or absence of certain structures or the arrangement of nuclei in determined shapes. From the perspective of texture, all of these distributions are different textures occurring on the images. In the proposed algorithm, we have computed two sets of texture descriptors: fractal dimension [11,12] and local binary patterns [13].

There is a significant association between fractal measurements and breast tumour characteristics [14]. Our method computes two fractal descriptors. The first one is the Segmentation-based Fractal Texture Analysis (SFTA) feature vector [11]. This method decompose the input image into a set of binary images and then it computes the fractal dimensions of the region's borders. We think that this feature allows us to capture detailed duct structures. The second one is the Image Landscape's Fractal Dimension (ILF), which is based on the analysis of two 1-D sequences, called the horizontal and vertical landscapes, through the computation of Higuchi's fractal dimension [12]. For calculation of the Higuchi's fractal dimension we used a moving window length of 100 points, moved each time 1 point, with $k_{max} = 8$ on the C plane.

LPB technique allows to represent the underlying textural characteristics of the images in small-scale neighbourhoods with low computational effort. Among all the variants of LBP codes, we have employed a multi-resolution uniform rotational invariant pattern $LBP_{P,R}^{riu2}$ [13] in the C and M planes, with (P, R) values of $(8, 1)$ and $(16, 2)$. The radius R determines the spatial resolution of the operator and the number of neighbourhood pixels P controls the quantization of the angular space. The resulting occurrence histograms have been concatenated and incorporated to the feature vector.

4   Results

We have evaluated our algorithm with a 10-fold cross validation method using the ICIAR 2018 Grand Challenge on Breast Cancer Histology (BACH) [15] dataset. The image database consists of a total of 400 high-resolution anonymous annotated H&E straining images from breast tumour biopsies, digitized with the same acquisition conditions and with a magnification of 200×. The images have a fixed size of 2048 × 1536 and are stored in tagged image file format (TIF). The image database was annotated/classified by two pathologists as normal, benign, in situ carcinoma or invasive carcinoma according to the predominant cancer type in each image. The sensitivity or true positive rate (TPR), precision or positive predictive value (PPV) and overall accuracy for all the classifiers under test is presented in Table 1.

Table 1. Obtained sensitivity (TPR), precision (PPV) and overall accuracy (ACC) with the classifiers under test

Classifier	Sensitivity (TPR) (%)				Precision (PPV) (%)				Accuracy (ACC) (%)
	Class				Class				
	1	2	3	4	1	2	3	4	
Simple tree	43.0	43.0	74.0	50.0	60.6	36.1	48.4	87.7	52.5
Medium tree	65.0	55.0	58.0	67.0	67.0	48.2	55.2	79.8	61.3
Complex tree	74.0	53.0	56.0	71.0	67.9	50.0	59.6	78.0	63.5
Bagged tree	72.0	64.0	64.0	77.0	69.9	57.7	70.3	81.1	69.2
AdaBoost tree	72.0	61.0	67.0	72.0	75.0	60.4	58.3	81.8	68.0
KNN cosine	79.0	48.0	59.0	72.0	65.3	60.8	60.8	69.9	64.5
KNN cubic	80.0	57.0	60.0	61.0	64.0	57.0	59.4	82.4	64.5
Lineal SVM	79.0	65.0	70.0	75.0	75.2	65.7	74.1	76.5	72.2
Quadratic SVM	**86.0**	**71.0**	77.0	**83.0**	**78.2**	**74.0**	**76.2**	**89.2**	**79.2**
Cubic SVM	79.0	67.0	**80.0**	79.0	75.2	69.8	74.1	86.8	76.2

The best classifier, Quadratic SVM, obtains an overall accuracy of 79.2%, while the worst, simple tree, obtains an accuracy of 52.5%. All the classifiers show variability in performance across grade types. With the best classifier normal and invasive images are consistently and accurately ($TPR \geq 83\%$) assigned to the correct type. While the most difficult case is benign type with $TPR = 71\%$. The performance of the Cubic SVM classifier appears to be close to that of the Quadratic SVM classifier.

In order to compare our method with other approaches, we have also classified the images in two classes, non carcinoma (normal and benign cases) and carcinoma (in situ and invasive cases). Results are showed in Table 2. In comparison, our method outperforms the state-of-the-art significantly in both the classification in two and four classes. In particular our feature-based method's performance is slightly superior than the CNN-based approach of [9], even though we use a bigger and more challenging dataset. In fact, BACH dataset contains a large variety of images, very different from each other in each of the classes considered.

Table 2. Comparison of the overall accuracy (ACC) with other feature-based (FB) and CNN-based methods for two and four classes. The number of images in the dataset (training/validation) and the type of validation employed is also showed.

Classifier	Number of images in the dataset	Accuracy (%) two classes	Accuracy (%) four classes
Proposed with Quadratic SVM	400 (10-cross val.)	**87.5**	**79.2**
Proposed with Cubic SVM	400 (10-cross val.)	85.0	76.2
CNN+SVM of *Araújo et al.* [9]	120/36 (external val.)	83.3	77.8
FB of *Li et al.* [3]	58 (10-cross val.)	80.2	-
FB of *Chekkoury et al.* [4]	30/70 (Monte-Carlo val.)	84.86–87.14	-
FB of *Fondón et al.* [5]	120/20 (external val.)	-	75

5   Conclusion

In this paper we have addressed the problem of breast carcinoma malignancy assessment from the point of view of histopathological image processing. This is a key point in early cancer detection that remains unsolved, mainly due to the intrinsic complexity of breast cancer images.

Our main contribution is a new and efficient system that provides promising results in histopathological image classification and that completely and automatically gives four labels of malignancy: normal, benign, in situ and invasive cancer. For label assignment, our tool automatically computes several features from the images that are used by an Quadratic SVM classifier. These features are colour and texture based according to local characteristics and global image properties. We have validated the algorithm with 10-fold cross validation performed on BACH dataset that provides four grades for the cancer diagnosis. The proposed technique has achieved high levels of accuracy, 79.2%, and outperforms other state-of the art algorithms for both four and two classes classification.

Acknowledgements. This work was supported by the Government of Spain [grant number TEC2014-53103-P and TEC2017-82807-P].

References

1. World Cancer Research Fund International. http://www.wcrf.org/int/cancer-facts-figures/data-specific-cancers/breast-cancer-statistics

2. Sarmiento, A., Fondón, I.: Breast Cancer Diagnosis CAD (2018). http://personal. us.es/sarmiento/downloads/
3. Li, X., Plataniotis, K.N.: Color model comparative analysis for breast cancer diagnosis using H and E stained images. In: SPIE 9420, Medical Imaging 2015: Digital Pathology, vol. 9420 (2015). https://doi.org/10.1117/12.2079935
4. Chekkoury, A., Khurd, P., Ni, J., Bahlmann, C., Kamen, A., Patel, A., Grady, L., Singh, M., Groher, M., Navab, N., Krupinski, E., Johnson, J., Graham, A., Weinstein, R.: Automated malignancy detection in breast histopathological images. In: SPIE 8315, Medical Imaging 2012: Computer-Aided Diagnosis, vol. 8315, pp. 831515-1–831515-13 (2012). https://doi.org/10.1117/12.911643
5. Fondón, I., Sarmiento, A., Garca, A.I., Silvestre, M., Eloy, C., Polónia, A., Aguiar, P.: Automatic classification of tissue malignancy for breast carcinoma diagnosis. Comput. Biol. Med. **96**, 41–51 (2018). https://doi.org/10.1016/j.compbiomed. 2018.03.003
6. Spanhol, F.A., Oliveira, L.S., Petitjean, C., Heutte, L.: Breast cancer histopathological image classification using convolutional neural networks. In: Proceedings of International Joint Conference on Neural Networks, pp. 2560–2567 (2016). https:// doi.org/10.1109/IJCNN.2016.7727519
7. Wang, D., Khosla, A., Gargeya, R., Irshad, H., Becktitle, A.H.: Deep learning for identifying metastatic breast cancer. arXiv:1606.05718 (2016)
8. Weil, B., Han, Z., He, X., Yin, Y.: Deep learning model based breast cancer histopathological image classification. In: Proceedings of 2nd IEEE International Conference on Cloud Computing and Big Data Analysis, pp. 348–353 (2017). https://doi.org/10.1109/ICCCBDA.2017.7951937
9. Araújo, T., Aresta, G., Castro, E., Rouco, E., Aguiar, P., Eloy, C., Polónia, A., Campilho, A.: Classification of breast cancer histology images using convolutional neural networks. PLoS One **12**, 1–14 (2017). https://doi.org/10.1371/journal.pone. 0177544
10. Ohashi, T., Al Aghbari, Z., Makinouchi, Z.: Fast segmentation of texture image regions based on hill-climbing. In: Proceedings of IEEE Pacific Rim Conference on Communications, Computers and Signal Processing, (PACRIM), vol. 2, pp. 848–851 (2003)
11. Costa, A.F., Humpire-Mamani, G., Traina, A.J.M.: An efficient algorithm for fractal analysis of textures. In: 25th SIBGRAPI Conference on Graphics, Patterns and Images, Ouro Preto, pp. 39–46 (2012). https://doi.org/10.1109/SIBGRAPI. 2012.15
12. Klonowski, W., Pierzchalski, M., Stepien, P., Stepien, R.A.: New fractal methods for diagnosis of cancer. In: Proceedings of 38th International Symposium on Biomedical Engineering and Medical Physics, pp. 70–73 (2013). https://doi.org/ 10.1007/978-3-642-34197-7_18
13. Ojala, T., Pietikainen, M., Maenpaa, T.: Multiresolution gray-scale and rotation invariant texture classification with local binary pattern. IEEE Trans. Pattern Anal. Mach. Intell. **24**(7), 971–987 (2002)
14. Di Giovanni, P., Ahearn, T.S., Semple, S.I.K., Lovell, L.M., Miller, I., Gilbert, F.J., Redpath, T.W., Heys, S.D., Staff, R.T.: The biological correlates of macroscopic breast tumour structure measured using fractal analysis in patients undergoing neoadjuvant chemotherapy. Breast Cancer Res. Treat. **133**(3), 1199–1206 (2001). https://doi.org/10.1007/s10549-012-2014-8
15. ICIAR 2018 Grand Challenge on Breast Cancer Histology (BACH). https:// iciar2018-challenge.grand-challenge.org/home/

Micro and Macro Breast Histology Image Analysis by Partial Network Re-use

Quoc Dang Vu, Minh Nguyen Nhat To, Eal Kim,
and Jin Tae Kwak[(⊠)]

Department of Computer Science and Engineering,
Sejong University, Seoul 05006, Korea
dangvuquoc1993@gmail.com, tnnhatminh@gmail.com,
laoavae@naver.com, jkwak@sejong.ac.kr

Abstract. Convolutional neural networks (CNN) have shown to be effective in medical image processing and analysis. Herein, we propose a CNN approach to perform patch- and pixel-wise histology labeling on breast microscopy and whole slide images (WSI), respectively. We devise a processing block that is capable of extracting compact features in an efficient manner. Based upon the processing block, classification and segmentation networks are built. Two networks share an encoder via partial transformation and transfer learning to maximally utilize the trained network and available dataset. 400 microscopy images and 10 WSI were employed to evaluate the proposed approach. For patch classification, an accuracy of 71% and 65% were obtained on the training and testing dataset, respectively. As for segmentation, we achieved an overall score of 0.7343 and 0.4945 on the training and testing dataset, respectively.

Keywords: Breast cancer · Tissue segmentation · Histology analysis
CNN

1 Introduction

Breast cancer is one of the most prevalent causes of cancer-related death in women [1] and early diagnosis significantly increases the patient survival rate. In breast pathology, manual histologic assessment of tissue specimens forms the gold standard for cancer diagnosis, prognosis, and treatment. The manual process, however, not only limits speed and throughput but also places a huge demand on clinical services. It also suffers from substantial intra- and inter-observer variability [2]. Automated, robust, and precise tools for analyzing tissues will, therefore, aid in improving breast pathology.

With the advent of high-resolution and cost-effective digital scanners, numerous machine learning approaches have been applied to improve the analysis of digitized tissue specimen images [3]. Recently, deep learning, in particular convolutional neural networks (CNN), has been increasingly applied for pathology images [4, 5]. Its great learning capability has been recognized and confirmed by multiple applications such as detection of mitosis [6], invasive ductal carcinoma [7], and metastases [8] in breast and gland segmentation [5]. CNN approaches often fall into two categories: (1) region or patch classification and (2) segmentation (or pixel-wise classification). Although the

© Springer International Publishing AG, part of Springer Nature 2018
A. Campilho et al. (Eds.): ICIAR 2018, LNCS 10882, pp. 895–902, 2018.
https://doi.org/10.1007/978-3-319-93000-8_102

ultimate goal and overall structure (slightly) differ, both networks try to extract and utilize high-level feature representation of tissues. The networks, therefore, could be shared or transferred from one to the other. This may aid in overcoming the limited availability of dataset and ground truth in image analysis of breast pathology.

In earlier CNN architectures, convolution and pooling layers are, in general, (repeatedly) stacked on top of each other, forming a processing block of the network such as in VGG [12] and Unet [7], and shown to be effective in various tasks [13]. Later, a more efficient layout like residual blocks [14] further improves upon the performance of CNN [15]. A processing block, however, often generates high-dimensional features, i.e., the number of convolution kernels becomes much larger than the spatial dimension of the input and convolution kernels. It is likely that the resultant feature maps are redundant [9]. This redundancy not only decreases the learning capability of the network but also wastes memory storage. Therefore, a processing block that is able to learn a set of compact and efficient features will lead to a more efficient and powerful network.

In this manuscript, we present a deep learning approach for analyzing breast histology images at both micro-level (patch-based image classification) and macro-level (whole slide image (WSI) segmentation). Both breast image classification and segmentation networks are built based upon identical processing blocks, which attempt at producing high-level, compact feature representation of the breast images. Moreover, the architecture and weights of the two networks are shared to maximally utilize the networks and available dataset. The proposed networks have been evaluated using tissue specimen imaging dataset provided by the ICIAR 2018 BACH Challenge.

2 Methodology

The proposed approach contains two networks: (1) a classification network to conduct patch-based image classification and (2) a segmentation network to provide segmentation maps for WSI (Fig. 1).

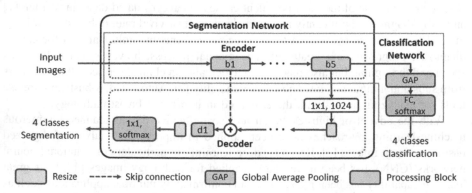

Fig. 1. Overview of the proposed approach. A classification network consists of an encoder and two processing layers. A segmentation network contains an encoder and decoder.

2.1   Processing Block

A processing block (Fig. 2) is composed of three units: the top and the bottom units are standard convolutions for spatial/feature dimensionality reduction; the unit in the middle follows the design principle of DenseNet [10] where a series of convolutions (designated as a sub-unit) are performed, each of which takes all the preceding inputs via concatenation (called as feature re-use). Feature re-use is known to reduce the number of parameters without losing the learning capability of the network. Each sub-unit is designed to find a more compact and structured feature representation by conducting two convolutions with a dilation rate of 1 (standard) and 2 (dilated) [11]; the first convolution is followed by a squeeze excitation (or self-gating) mechanism [12] to facilitate dynamic feature selection; the second convolution adopts a split-transform-merge strategy (or grouped convolution) [13] to improve feature correlation, leading to a more structured feature representation as well as a dilation rate of 2 to incorporate contextual information. In addition, the pre-activation [14] layout of Batch Normalization – ReLU – Convolution is adopted for all the convolutions in the proposed networks to ease the gradient flow during the optimization procedure. The top unit of each processing block lacks ReLU [15].

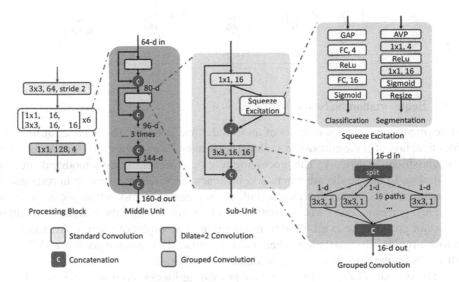

Fig. 2. Layout of the processing block *b2* in the encoder. GAP and AVP denote global average pooling and average pooling, respectively.

2.2   Classification Network

A classification network is comprised of five processing blocks (called as "encoder"), global average pooling (GAP) layer and fully-connected (FC) softmax layer (Table 1). The middle unit in the first processing block does not use the squeeze excitation.

Table 1. Architecture of the proposed approach. [AVP, 17 x 17, 8] denotes the region-wise squeeze excitation using average pooling (AVP) with kernel size of 17 x 17 and stride 8.

		b1	b2	b3	b4	b5
Encoder						
Classification		3x3, 64	3x3, 64, stride 2	3x3, 128, stride 2	3x3, 256, stride 2	3x3, 512, stride 2
		3x3, 64, 16	[1x1, 16, / 3x3, 16, 16] x6	[1x1, 16, / 3x3, 16, 16] x12	[1x1, 16, / 3x3, 16, 16] x24	[1x1, 16, / 3x3, 16, 16] x32	Global AVP, FC, softmax
		3x3, 64	1x1, 128, 4	1x1, 256, 8	1x1, 512, 16	1x1, 512, 32
Segmentation		3x3, 64	3x3, 64, stride 2	3x3, 128, stride 2	3x3, 256, stride 2	3x3, 512, stride 2
		3x3, 64, 16	[1x1, 16, / AVP, 17x17, 8 / 3x3, 16, 16] x6	[1x1, 16, / AVP, 9x9, 4 / 3x3, 16, 16] x12	[1x1, 16, / AVP, 5x5, 2 / 3x3, 16, 16] x24	[1x1, 16, / AVP, 3x3, 1 / 3x3, 16, 16] x32
		3x3, 64	1x1, 128, 4	1x1, 256, 8	1x1, 512, 16	1x1, 512, 32

		d4	d3	d2	d1	
Decoder						
Segmentation		5x5, 256	5x5, 128	5x5, 64	5x5, 32	
		[5x5, 128, / 5x5, 128, 32] x2	[5x5, 64, / 5x5, 64, 16] x2	[5x5, 32, / 5x5, 32, 8] x2	[5x5, 16, / 5x5, 16, 4] x2	1x1, Softmax
		1x1, 256	1x1, 128	1x1, 64	1x1, 32	

2.3 Segmentation Network

A segmentation network consists of an encoder and decoder. The encoder utilizes the identical layout of the encoder from the classification. Weights are also transferred from the classification network. The processing blocks, however, utilize a modified squeeze excitation. In the classification network, it excites the whole feature map in response to a pertinent class, which contradicts with the segmentation task where a class label is assigned per pixel. Pixel-wise excitation is not applicable since the intermediate output does not preserve the exact location information of an object of interest. Alternatively, a local, region-wise excitation, where GAP is replaced by average pooling (AVP) with stride, is applied per feature map as illustrated in Fig. 2.

The decoder (Table 1) includes four processing blocks, each of which is followed by a nearest neighbor resizing layer (up-sampling), instead of other popular techniques such as deconvolution [4] or un-pooling [16]. Each processing block obtains two inputs, one from the preceding layer in the decoder and the other from the encoder via a skip connection [4, 16–18]. No squeeze excitation is employed. All the convolutions use no padding and a stride 1.

3 Dataset and Training Details

3.1 ICIAR2018 BACH Challenge Dataset

Hematoxylin and eosin (H&E) stained breast histology images are provided by ICIAR2018 Grand Challenge on Breast Cancer Histology images (BACH).

Training Dataset. For classification, 400 microscopy image patches that are labeled as one of four classes (normal, benign, in situ carcinoma or invasive carcinoma; 100 images per class) are employed. Each patch is of size 2048 x 1536 pixels with the pixel scale of 0.42 um x 0.42 um. For segmentation, 10 WSI images are used that was acquired through Leica SCN400 with a pixel resolution of 0.467 um/pixel. Three distinct regions are marked as benign (red), in situ carcinoma (green) and invasive carcinoma (blue). The rest of tissues are considered to be normal (black). For both tasks, the ground truth annotation was performed by two medical experts and those image patches or WSI regions on which they disagree were not included.

Testing Dataset. A total of 100 image patches are used for classification task. Each path is of size 2048 x 1536. For segmentation, a total of 10 WSI images are utilized. The ground truth annotation is blinded to the challenge participants.

3.2 Training Details

Classification. The classification network (encoder) is trained and evaluated via a 5-fold cross validation. The original image patches are down-sampled by a factor of 4 (scale x0.25) and then directly used to train the network without any additional pre-processing steps. During training, a random cropping, resizing [19], horizontal and vertical flipping are applied for data augmentation. The network is initialized with He method [20] and trained via Stochastic Gradient Descent for 120 epochs. The learning rate is initially set to 3.5e−3 and decreases by a factor of 10 at every 60 epochs.

Segmentation. WSI dataset is massive and highly imbalanced. By resizing WSI at x0.25 scale and manually sampling sub-regions, we sought to efficiently obtain the segmentation network that is less biased. 6,129 sub-regions of size 1000 x 1000, maintaining roughly the same number of regions per class and accounting for 17% the total volume of the WSI dataset, are utilized for training. For each sub-region, the center region of 630 x 630 is fed into the network to avoid the zero-padding during augmentation, and the segmentation map is generated for the inner most central region of size 204 x 204. Moreover, we re-use the weight of the encoder from the classification network. He method [20] is used to initialize the decoder and the extended layers. During training, random affine transformations (shifting, scaling, rotation and minor shearing) are applied to ensure the robustness of the network. Alongside the (main) loss for the targeted four classes, an auxiliary loss is jointly computed, at the same level as the main loss, to emphasize the closeness among the four classes; it is computed via categorical cross-entropy for normal and benign group versus in situ and invasive carcinoma group. The network is trained for 30 epochs using Adam optimizer with default parameter values. The learning rate is initially set to 3.5e−5 and reduced by a factor of 10 at each subsequent 15th epoch.

4 Experimental Results and Discussion

4.1 Evaluation Metric

For classification task, the overall prediction accuracy, which is the ratio of correctly predicted patches to the total number of patches, is measured. As for segmentation task, the performance is assessed using the following formula $s = 1 -$

$$\frac{\sum_{i=1}^{N} |\text{pred}_i - \text{gt}_i|}{\sum_{i=1}^{N} \max(|\text{gt}_i - 0|, |\text{gt}_i - 3|) \times [1 - (1 - \text{pred}_{i,\text{bin}})(1 - \text{gt}_{i,\text{bin}})]}$$ where "*pred*" is the predicted class (0, 1, 2 or 3), and "*gt*" is the ground truth class, i is the linear index of a pixel in an image, N is the total number of pixels in an image and bin is the binarized value, i.e., is 0 if the label is 0 and 1 if the label is 1, 2 or 3. This score aims at penalizing more the predictions that are farther from the ground truth label (or value).

4.2 Classification and Segmentation Performance

To evaluate the performance of the proposed networks, we conducted two separate experiments per network. Each network was evaluated based upon the training dataset and then tested on the testing dataset. The performance on the testing dataset was evaluated by the challenge organizer. The testing results are available online at https://iciar2018-challenge.grand-challenge.org/results/.

Classification. In a 5-fold cross-validation on the training dataset, an average accuracy of 71% with 6.4% standard deviation was obtained. By using the best model from the 5-fold cross validation, an accuracy of 65% was obtained on the testing dataset.

Segmentation. Trained on the manually selected sub-regions and tested on the remaining regions, the network achieved an overall score of 0.7343 at x0.25 scale. Tested on the testing dataset, we obtained a score of 0.4945 at x0.5 scale.

5 Conclusion

In this manuscript, we propose a CNN approach for micro-level and macro-level analysis of breast tissue images. The two networks share the architecture and weights, in particular the encoder in the network, to improve the utility of the trained network and available dataset. Both networks are built based upon a processing block that is designed for compact and efficient feature learning. The future work will entail the investigation of an optimal design of a processing block and CNN that can maximize its memory capacity and learning capability and the extended study on other types of tissues and disease.

Acknowledgments. This study is supported by the National Research Foundation of Korea (NRF) grant funded by the Korea government (MSIP) (No. 2016R1C1B2012433).

References

1. Siegel, R.L., Miller, K.D., Jemal, A.: Cancer statistics, 2016. CA Cancer J. Clin. **66**, 7–30 (2016)
2. Elmore, J.G., Longton, G.M., Carney, P.A., et al.: Diagnostic concordance among pathologists interpreting breast biopsy specimens. JAMA **313**, 1122–1132 (2015)
3. Madabhushi, A., Lee, G.: Image analysis and machine learning in digital pathology: challenges and opportunities. Med. Image Anal. **33**, 170–175 (2016)
4. Ronneberger, O., Fischer, P., Brox, T.: U-Net: convolutional networks for biomedical image segmentation. In: Navab, N., Hornegger, J., Wells, W.M., Frangi, A.F. (eds.) MICCAI 2015. LNCS, vol. 9351, pp. 234–241. Springer, Cham (2015). https://doi.org/10.1007/978-3-319-24574-4_28
5. Chen, H., Qi, X., Yu, L., Dou, Q., Qin, J., Heng, P.A.: DCAN: deep contour-aware networks for object instance segmentation from histology images. Med. Image Anal. **36**, 135–146 (2017)
6. Ciresan, D.C., Giusti, A., Gambardella, L.M., Schmidhuber, J.: Mitosis detection in breast cancer histology images with deep neural networks. Med. Image Comput. Comput. Assist. Interv. **16**, 411–418 (2013)
7. Cruz-Roa, A.A., Arevalo Ovalle, J.E., Madabhushi, A., Gonzalez Osorio, F.A.: A deep learning architecture for image representation, visual interpretability and automated basal-cell carcinoma cancer detection. Med. Image Comput. Comput. Assist. Interv. **16**, 403–410 (2013)
8. Litjens, G., Sanchez, C.I., Timofeeva, N., Hermsen, M., Nagtegaal, I., Kovacs, I., Hulsbergen-van de Kaa, C., Bult, P., van Ginneken, B., van der Laak, J.: Deep learning as a tool for increased accuracy and efficiency of histopathological diagnosis. Sci. Rep. **6**, 26286 (2016)
9. Chen, W., Wilson, J.T., Tyree, S., Weinberger, K.Q., Chen, Y.: Compressing neural networks with the hashing trick. ArXiv e-prints, vol. 1504 (2015)
10. Huang, G., Liu, Z., Weinberger, K.Q., van der Maaten, L.: Densely connected convolutional networks. ArXiv e-prints, vol. 1608 (2016)
11. Yu, F., Koltun, V.: Multi-scale context aggregation by dilated convolutions. ArXiv e-prints, vol. 1511 (2015)
12. Hu, J., Shen, L., Sun, G.: Squeeze-and-excitation networks. ArXiv e-prints, vol. 1709 (2017)
13. Xie, S., Girshick, R., Dollár, P., Tu, Z., He, K.: Aggregated residual transformations for deep neural networks. ArXiv e-prints, vol. 1611 (2016)
14. He, K., Zhang, X., Ren, S., Sun, J.: Identity mappings in deep residual networks. ArXiv e-prints, vol. 1603 (2016)
15. Dong, X., Kang, G., Zhan, K., Yang, Y.: EraseReLU: a simple way to ease the training of deep convolution neural networks. ArXiv e-prints, vol. 1709 (2017)
16. Badrinarayanan, V., Kendall, A., Cipolla, R.: SegNet: a deep convolutional encoder-decoder architecture for image segmentation. ArXiv e-prints, vol. 1511 (2015)
17. Lin, G., Milan, A., Shen, C., Reid, I.: RefineNet: multi-path refinement networks for high-resolution semantic segmentation. ArXiv e-prints, vol. 1611 (2016)
18. Peng, C., Zhang, X., Yu, G., Luo, G., Sun, J.: Large Kernel matters – improve semantic segmentation by global convolutional network. ArXiv e-prints, vol. 1703 (2017)

19. Szegedy, C., Liu, W., Jia, Y., Sermanet, P., Reed, S., Anguelov, D., Erhan, D., Vanhoucke, V., Rabinovich, A.: Going deeper with convolutions. ArXiv e-prints, vol. 1409 (2014)
20. He, K., Zhang, X., Ren, S., Sun, J.: Delving deep into rectifiers: surpassing human-level performance on ImageNet classification. ArXiv e-prints, vol. 1502 (2015)

Assessment of Breast Cancer Histology Using Densely Connected Convolutional Networks

Matthias Kohl[1], Christoph Walz[2], Florian Ludwig[1], Stefan Braunewell[1], and Maximilian Baust[1(✉)]

[1] Konica Minolta Laboratory Europe, Munich, Germany
maximilian.baust@konicaminolta.eu
[2] Institute of Pathology, Faculty of Medicine, LMU Munich, Munich, Germany
http://research.konicaminolta.eu/

Abstract. Breast cancer is the most frequently diagnosed cancer and leading cause of cancer-related death among females worldwide. In this article, we investigate the applicability of densely connected convolutional neural networks to the problems of histology image classification and whole slide image segmentation in the area of computer-aided diagnoses for breast cancer. To this end, we study various approaches for transfer learning and apply them to the data set from the 2018 grand challenge on breast cancer histology images (BACH).

Keywords: Digital pathology · Breast cancer · Deep learning

1 Introduction

This work presents approaches for the classification of microscopy images as well as the segmentation of whole slide images (WSIs) in the area of computer-aided diagnosis for breast cancer. In particular, it describes how the recently invented densely connected convolutional neural networks [13] can be applied to the aforementioned tasks on data from the 2018 grand challenge in Breast Cancer Histology Images (BACH).

Clinical Background. According to the global cancer statistics 2012 [24], breast cancer is the most frequently diagnosed cancer and the leading cause of cancer-related death among females worldwide, with an estimated 1.6 million new cases and over 0.5 million deaths per year. With tumor stage remaining the most important determinant of the outcome [27], an early detection of breast cancer is crucial for reducing mortality rates. Among other factors, such as patient age, axillary lymph node status, tumor size, hormone receptor status, and HER2 status, histological features play an important role for categorizing patients with invasive breast cancer in order to assess prognosis and determine the appropriate therapy [20]. While the importance of histomorphological grading for breast cancer has been acknowledged almost 30 years ago [10], the computerized assessment of histological features has become increasingly popular during the last decade. Tumor grading in breast cancer is typically based on the following three criteria suggested by Elston and Ellis [10]:

1. *mitotic activity* as a measure of cellular proliferation,
2. *nuclear pleomorphism*, i.e. how different the tumor cells are in comparison to normal cells, and
3. *glandular and tubular differentiation*, i.e. how well the tumor resembles normal structures.

Current developments in the area of digital pathology are driven by the observation that genetic and phenotypic intra-tumor heterogeneity have a direct impact on both diagnosis and disease management [18] as well as the availability of effective machine learning techniques, such as deep convolutional neural networks. Particularly the segmentation of WSIs, i.e. the second part of the BACH challenge, plays an increasingly important role as it facilitates not only a standardized assessment of resection margins, but also novel scoring approaches, such as the ImmunoScore [11], and a better understanding of tumor heterogeneity and micro-environment, e.g. via phenotype-guided genetic readouts.

Related Work in digital pathology can be categorized with respect to approaches which focus on the three aforementioned criteria for breast cancer grading as well as approaches for WSI segmentation. In the following discussion we focus on the most recent approaches for beast cancer and breast cancer metastases that are based on deep learning. For a more exhaustive overview, we refer the interested reader to recent overview articles, such as [19] or [15].

Possibly the largest class of methods focuses on the computational assessment of mitotic activity. This field has been extensively promoted by the recent success of deep-learning-based approaches starting with the seminal work of [6]. Referring the interested reader to the review paper of [25] for an overview of all methods for mitosis detection until 2015, we specifically want to mention the more recent works on leveraging the potential of crowdsourcing for training deep networks [1], on deep regression networks [5] and on using deep residual Hough voting [28]. The next category, comprises methods aiming at cellular or nuclear features. Recent examples include works on stacked sparse auto encoders for nuclei detection [29] and on hierarchical learning [14]. Regarding the assessment of glandular and tubular structures, there are only a few works in the field of breast cancer, such as [9] or [2]. However, for a general overview on the computational assessment of relevant pathological structures and primitives, we refer the interested reader to [15].

In contrast to the approaches for particular histopathological tasks, there is the group of methods that are aiming at classification of whole tissue regions or at WSI-segmentation, which requires learning of features on both cellular and structural level. A good example is the recent work of the BACH challenge organizers presenting a classification method for Hematoxylin- and Eosin-stained (HE-stained) histological images from breast cancer patients, cf. Araujo *et al.* [3].

Regarding WSI-segmentation, there exists a series of methods is related to the recent challenges on cancer metastasis detection in lymph node (CAMELYON16 & CAMELYON17). Examples for notable works using the associated data sets are the ones of the organizers [4,16], as well as the works of Wang *et al.* [26] or Liu *et al.* [17]. Conceptually, these approaches are also comparable to the recent works of Su *et al.* [22] and Cruz-Roa *et al.* [7].

Contributions and Organization. We participated in the BACH challenge due to our interest in the learning and integration of features from multiple levels and their application to WSI-segmentation, particularly in case of small data sets. As several contributions for the CAMELYON challenges were based on the popular Inception-v3 architecture proposed by [23], we wanted to assess the performance of another recently published and very promising architecture, i.e. the densely connected convolutional networks proposed by Huang *et al.* [13]. As the data set of the challenge is too small for training such large architectures from scratch, we investigated two approaches for transfer learning: One based on weights obtained from training on ImageNet [8] and one based one weights obtained from training the network on data from the CAMELYON challenges, which is described in Sect. 2. The evaluation of these two approaches for both sub-challenges is described in Sect. 3 and discussed in Sect. 4, before we conclude this paper with Sect. 5.

2 Methodology

The BACH challenge comprises two sub-challenges, i.e. classification of histology images (part A) and segmentation of WSIs (part B). In order to achieve these goals, we train classifiers $C : p \mapsto \ell$ to predict the correct label ℓ for a given microscopic image (in case of part A) or a patch extracted from a WSI (in case of part B) p. Thereby $\ell \in \{0, 1, 2, 3\}$, where the numeric values encodes one of the four class labels: normal (0), benign (1), carcinoma *in situ* (2), invasive carcinoma (3). As explained later in Sects. 2.2 and 2.3, these classifiers are implemented via densely connected convolutional neural networks (DenseNets).

2.1 Pre-training on CAMELYON Data

As the size of both data sets for part A and part B is too small for training deep networks from scratch, we decided to employ transfer learning with pre-trained networks. Besides using a network which has been pre-trained on ImageNet data [8], we also investigated the possibility of using a network pre-trained on data from the two CAMELYON challenges [4]. As of now, the data from these challenges consists of approximately 691 WSIs, of which 210 are tumor cases. The tumor cases contain metastases of breast cancer in lymph nodes, ranging from large metastatic areas to small to individual cancerous cells in lymph node tissue. All non-tumor WSIs are control cases exhibiting no pathological findings.

Preparatory to patch extraction, we subtracted the background as described in [16] to ensure that only patches from foreground regions are sampled. To speed up this process for the large CAMELYON dataset, background subtraction is done at a level where each extracted patch is represented by a single pixel with a value obtained through interpolation. Then we covered the entire WSI with a regular grid of patch center points and extracted a patch along with its label according to the grid center point. Thereby, we ensure that the extracted patches exhibit a random portion of overlap of classes, which should help to reduce over-fitting on large homogeneous regions. After downscaling all extracted patches to match the physical resolution of the BACH data set, we obtained in total 274,272 image patches of physical size $132\,\mu m \times 132\,\mu m$ at 157×157 pixels from both CAMELYON data sets. For pre-training the network, we randomly split the data with a ratio of 80% and 20% for training and validation, respectively, making sure that data from all sub-groups of the two challenges is equally represented in training and validation. This way, we obtained 119,705 normal and 101,347 invasive patches for training and 30,240 normal and 22,980 invasive patches for validation.

For pre-training the network, we used a uniform Xavier initialization and trained the network for 90 epochs starting with a learning rate of 1×10^{-3}, which is decreased by a factor of 0.5 every 20 epochs. The employed data augmentation strategy is identical to the one used for fine tuning, which is described in Sect. 2.3.

2.2   Classification of Histological Images (A)

Data Preparation, Scale Selection and Augmentation. The data of part A consists of 400 images of size 2048×1536 pixels with a pixel resolution of $0.42\,\mu m \times 0.42\,\mu m$. The images have been assigned one of the four aforementioned classes, if two medical experts agreed to the predominant type of cancer in each image. For classification, we rescaled all images by a factor of 10 resulting in images of size 205×154 pixels.

It is important to note that this data set contains multiple subsets of images acquired from the same patient. In order to evaluate a classification method in a clinically correct way, it is essential to prevent images from the same patient being present in both training and validation set. Due to the limited amount of data, however, we decided to explicitly drop this constraint and performed a 5-fold cross-validation with a data distribution of 80% and 20% for training and validation, respectively. This way, we wanted to ensure that the network has seen the maximum variability of the data during training.

As pathological images do not have a canonical orientation, we used arbitrary rotations as well as horizontal and vertical flips for data augmentation. In order to achieve slight scale-invariance we also used random scale changes in the range $[0.5, 2.0]$. To achieve robustness against spatial recognition of features, we employed random shifting of up to 50% of the width and height for each image. Pixels outside of the range of the original image are replaced by their nearest neighbors inside the image. Finally, we normalized each image by the mean and the standard deviation of all images in the data set.

Network Architecture and Training. We used a DenseNet-161 architecture as proposed by Huang *et al.* [13] which generalizes the concept of residual learning introduced by He *et al.* [12]. The architecture consists of seven stages, six spatial reduction stages and one classifier stage. Each spatial reduction uses a stride of 2×2. The first two stages consist of a single convolution (kernel size 7×7) and a single max pooling (kernel size 3×3), respectively. The next four stages consist of densely connected convolutions (kernel sizes 3×3 and 1×1) followed by a full 2×2 max pooling. The head of the classifier consists of a global average pooling of the spatial feature map and a single fully-connected layer. We employ a categorical cross-entropy loss and retain the weights with highest classification accuracy on the validation set. Neither dropout nor weight-decay were used.

For transfer learning, we first trained only the fully connected layer for 25 epochs with a learning rate of 1×10^{-3} in order to avoid over-fitting. Next, we trained the whole network for 250 epochs with a learning rate of 2×10^{-3}. One epoch consists of all possible batches of size 32 of the training data. The training data was randomly shuffled between each epoch.

2.3   Segmentation of Whole Slide Images (B)

Data Preparation, Scale Selection and Augmentation. The data of part B consists of 30 whole slide images of which only 10 are annotated with regard to the aforementioned tissue classes. All WSIs have a spatial resolution of $0.467\,\mu m \times 0.467\,\mu m$ per pixel.

From the ten annotated WSIs, we extracted patches of physical size $330\,\mu m \times 330\,\mu m$ into 157×157 pixels, corresponding to a down-sampling factor of 4.5. We followed a similar procedure as described in Sect. 2.1. The only difference is that the background subtraction is done at the patch-level, with a patch being considered background if at least 80% of its pixels are considered background. We obtained a total of 24,406 patches, with 13,280 being labeled normal, 903 benign, 354 in situ, and 9,869 invasive. Due to the very limited amount of data in the benign and the carcinoma in situ classes, we refrained from splitting training and validation data according to the individual WSIs and performed a random splitting, as done for part A of the challenge, and refrained from performing a cross-validation. Again, our motivation was to expose the maximum variability to the network during training.

We employed a similar strategy for data augmentation as described in Sect. 2.2: The main difference is that missing pixels are replaced by the actual pixels from the larger image, except on the borders of the WSI where they are replaced by their nearest neighbors. Finally, in order to achieve robustness with respect to color perturbations introduced by varying staining conditions for example, we employed the color augmentation procedure suggested by [17]. All other augmentation parameters are kept as in Sect. 2.2

Additional Data. To further reduce data shortage, we added additional data by partially annotating 16 of the 20 originally non-annotated WSIs.

This was done with the help of a trained pathologist. In particular, we aimed at reducing the problem of imbalanced classes and specifically annotated regions containing benign malformations and carcinoma in situ.

After performing the data extraction again as described above, we extracted a total of 41,506 image patches, with 25,230 normal, 1,723 benign, 1,759 in situ and 12,794 invasive tissue regions.

Network Architecture and Training. We used the same DenseNet-161 architecture as in part A, as described in Sect. 2.2. For transfer learning, we first trained only the fully connected layers for 6 epochs with a learning rate of 5×10^{-3} in order to avoid over-fitting. Next, we trained the whole network for 60 epochs with a learning rate of 1×10^{-3} and 40 epochs with a learning rate of 5×10^{-4}. In order to compensate for the highly imbalanced classes, we employed log-balanced class weights, i.e. the weight for class c is defined as $\log(N/N_c)$, where N denotes the number of all training patches and N_c the number of training patches belonging to class c.

Patch-Based Segmentation and Post-processing. In order to produce a segmentation of a full WSI, we first down-scale the WSI to obtain the expected resolution of the classifier. We then classify every grid center point of a grid with cell size 32×32 pixels. In total, the down-sampling factor is approximately 144.

The resulting label image is then post-processed by applying a median filter to smooth the segmentation and a small dilation of all non-normal classes (overlapping classes are resolved in the order benign < in-situ < invasive) to slightly decrease the false-negative rate and slightly increase the size of tumor regions after decreasing them with the median filter.

3   Evaluation

We conducted several experiments for both parts of the challenge on a dedicated workstation with Intel i7-6850K processor, 64 GB RAM and two NVIDIA Geforce GTX 1080 Ti graphics cards. As an operating system we used Ubuntu 16.04 LTS, endowed with docker and NVIDIA-docker. For implementing the network architecture and conducting the training we used python 2.7.12, keras 2.1.3 and tensorflow 1.4.0 backend (official tensorflow docker). Training time on this machine (using one GPU) was around 10 h for pre-training on the CAMELYON data set and between 7 and 9 h for transfer learning. The inference time per image or patch is around 37 ms and for a full WSI is around 30 min.

3.1   Classification of Histological Images (A)

The results of our experiments for part A of the BACH challenge are summarized in Table 1. In lines one and two, we report the achieved accuracies for baseline approaches based on the VGG-19 and Inception-v3 architectures [21,23].

Table 1. Classification Accuracy of Various Trainings (part A): Baseline approaches (in the first two rows) are compared with less aggressive data augmentation but same hyper-parameters (DA-) and the DenseNet-161 architecture tested with different pre-trainings (last two rows).

Architecture	Pre-training on	Splitting	Accuracy
VGG-19	ImageNet	5-fold cross-validation	92.5%
Inception-v3	ImageNet	5-fold cross-validation	91.25%
DenseNet-161	ImageNet	5-fold cross-validation	**94%**
DenseNet-161	CAMELYON	5-fold cross-validation	76.75%

The DenseNet-161 architectures, which were trained using the same hyper-parameter settings as described in Sect. 2.2, but less aggressive data augmentation. The performed experiments show that the baseline architectures exhibit worse performance in our setting. Although we did not perform a grid search for hyper-parameter tuning, we believe that the discrepancy between these architectures is not solely caused by a discrepancy in quality of the hyper-parameters, such that the reported results give a fair qualitative impression of the performance of these architectures. In line three and four of Table 1, we report the results of the proposed approach using ImageNet-data and CAMELYON data for pre-training, respectively. These two experiments suggest that pre-training using ImageNet-data seems to outperform pre-training on CAMELYON data. For composing the challenge submission, we selected the best performing network pre-trained on ImageNet from the cross-validation experiment, cf. line three of Table 1.

3.2 Segmentation of Whole Slide Images (B)

For the second part of the challenge we conducted two main experiments: At first, we limited ourselves to the 10 annotated WSIs, using a random stratified split into 80% training and 20% validation data. We tested this approach using networks pre-trained on CAMELYON as well as pre-trained on ImageNet. Secondly, we added additional data from selected WSIs as described in Sect. 2.3 and repeated the training, comparing the obtained results with VGG-19 and Inception-v3 architectures as a baseline approaches, cf. Table 2.

Similar to part A, the DenseNet architecture outperforms the Inception architecture and pre-training on ImageNet outperforms pre-training on CAMELYON. We chose the model trained on the extended data set for submission as it achieves highest accuracy. Since the remaining four unlabeled WSIs do not exhibit sufficient variability in order to assess the network performance based on the score suggested by the challenge, we based our decision solely on patch-accuracy.

Table 2. Patch-Based Classification Accuracy of Various Trainings (part B): Comparison of different architectures, pre-trainings and datasets w.r.t. patch-accuracy on WSIs.

Architecture	Pre-training on	Data	Patch-based acc.
DenseNet-161	ImageNet	Annotated 80/20 split	95.75%
DenseNet-161	CAMELYON	Annotated 80/20 split	95.33%
VGG-19	ImageNet	Ext. annotated 80/20 split	96.04%
Inception-v3	ImageNet	Ext. annotated 80/20 split	95.51%
DenseNet-161	ImageNet	Ext. annotated 80/20 split	**96.24%**

4 Discussion

Regarding the results for part A of the challenge, it becomes apparent that the DenseNet architecture outperforms the other baseline methods. More interesting than this first qualitative comparison, however, is the fact that pre-training on ImageNet is considerably better than pre-training on CAMELYON data. We hypothesize that this discrepancy arises from the fact that features learned from the CAMELYON data base do not generalize well enough to the specific appearance of the images from part A.

Comparing the achieved results to the ones reported by Araujo *et al.* [3] is not straightforward: In [3] a classification accuracy of 78% for the same task is reported, however, the used dataset is even smaller (285 images) and we do not have any information regarding the splitting of the data.

Regarding the results for part B, we observe again that the DenseNet architecture outperforms the baseline approaches, i.e. the VGG-19 and Inception-v3 architectures. Furthermore, we observed comparable results for the DenseNet trained on the original ten WSIs and the extended data base of 26 WSIs. As we observed a better generalization performance in preliminary experiments, where we gradually added additional training data, we decided to submit the network which has seen the largest data variability during training to the challenge phase.

In both parts, we observed a better performance for networks pre-trained on ImageNet data in comparison to the ones pre-trained on CAMELYON data. By training networks on the CAMELYON data base we were hoping to learn features, particularly in the first layer, which are better suited to digital pathology images. On the other hand, networks pre-trained on ImageNet are known to learn very robust and general features due to the high variability of the ImageNet data base and it might be that the features learnt from the CAMELYON data base generalize less well to the data of this challenge.

5 Conclusion

The conducted experiments demonstrate that densely connected convolutional networks are well-suited for transfer learning, even in case the considered data set is small. In order to develop classification algorithms which can be used in clinical practice, a significantly larger amount of data is necessary. We want to emphasize that the chosen splittings for training and validation (in both part A and B) are not suited for a clinical evaluation. In addition to this, a data base for training such a network possibly requires more precise and also different annotations. This cannot only be observed by inspecting the rather coarse annotations of the WSIs, but also by the fact that part A only contains images where two pathologists agreed. In fact, computer-assisted diagnoses would be particularly helpful in those excluded cases. However, future work should not be limited to the creation of larger and carefully annotated data bases. The development of sophisticated feature visualization techniques will be crucial to not only understand performance differences of differently trained networks, but also to make the computed decision more understandable to the medical expert.

References

1. Albarqouni, S., Baur, C., Achilles, F., Belagiannis, V., Demirci, S., Navab, N.: AggNet: deep learning from crowds for mitosis detection in breast cancer histology images. IEEE Trans. Med. Imaging 35(5), 1313–1321 (2016)
2. Apou, G., Schaadt, N.S., Naegel, B., Forestier, G., Schönmeyer, R., Feuerhake, F., Wemmert, C., Grote, A.: Detection of lobular structures in normal breast tissue. Comput. Biol. Med. 74, 91–102 (2016)
3. Araújo, T., Aresta, G., Castro, E., Rouco, J., Aguiar, P., Eloy, C., Polónia, A., Campilho, A.: Classification of breast cancer histology images using convolutional neural networks. PloS One 12(6), e0177544 (2017)
4. Bejnordi, B.E., Veta, M., van Diest, P.J., van Ginneken, B., Karssemeijer, N., Litjens, G., van der Laak, J.A., Hermsen, M., Manson, Q., Balkenhol, M., et al.: Diagnostic assessment of deep learning algorithms for detection of lymph node metastases in women with breast cancer. JAMA 318(22), 2199–2210 (2017)
5. Chen, H., Wang, X., Heng, P.A.: Automated mitosis detection with deep regression networks. In: 2016 IEEE 13th International Symposium on Biomedical Imaging (ISBI), pp. 1204–1207. IEEE (2016)
6. Cireşan, D.C., Giusti, A., Gambardella, L.M., Schmidhuber, J.: Mitosis detection in breast cancer histology images with deep neural networks. In: Mori, K., Sakuma, I., Sato, Y., Barillot, C., Navab, N. (eds.) MICCAI 2013. LNCS, vol. 8150, pp. 411–418. Springer, Heidelberg (2013). https://doi.org/10.1007/978-3-642-40763-5_51
7. Cruz-Roa, A., Gilmore, H., Basavanhally, A., Feldman, M., Ganesan, S., Shih, N., Tomaszewski, J., González, F., Madabhushi, A.: Accurate and reproducible invasive breast cancer detection in whole-slide images: a deep learning approach for quantifying tumor extent. Sci. Rep. 7, 46450 (2017)
8. Deng, J., Dong, W., Socher, R., Li, L.J., Li, K., Fei-Fei, L.: ImageNet: a large-scale hierarchical image database. In: IEEE Conference on Computer Vision and Pattern Recognition, pp. 248–255 (2009)
9. Dong, F., Irshad, H., Oh, E.Y., Lerwill, M.F., Brachtel, E.F., Jones, N.C., Knoblauch, N.W., Montaser-Kouhsari, L., Johnson, N.B., Rao, L.K., et al.: Computational pathology to discriminate benign from malignant intraductal proliferations of the breast. PloS One 9(12), e114885 (2014)

10. Elston, C., Ellis, I.: Pathological prognostic factors in breast cancer. I. The value of histological grade in breast cancer: experience from a large study with long-term follow-up. Histopathology 19(5), 403–410 (1991)
11. Fridman, W.H., Pagès, F., Sautès-Fridman, C., Galon, J.: The immune contexture in human tumours: impact on clinical outcome. Nat. Rev. Cancer 12(4), 298–306 (2012)
12. He, K., Zhang, X., Ren, S., Sun, J.: Deep residual learning for image recognition. In: IEEE Conference on Computer Vision and Pattern Recognition, pp. 770–778 (2016)
13. Huang, G., Liu, Z., van der Maaten, L., Weinberger, K.: Densely connected convolutional networks. In: IEEE Conference on Computer Vision and Pattern Recognition, pp. 4700–4708 (2017)
14. Janowczyk, A., Doyle, S., Gilmore, H., Madabhushi, A.: A resolution adaptive deep hierarchical (radhical) learning scheme applied to nuclear segmentation of digital pathology images. Comput. Methods Biomech. Biomed. Eng. Imaging Vis. 6(3), 270–276 (2016)
15. Janowczyk, A., Madabhushi, A.: Deep learning for digital pathology image analysis: a comprehensive tutorial with selected use cases. J. Pathol. Inform. 7(1), 29 (2016)
16. Litjens, G., Sánchez, C., Timofeeva, N., Hermsen, M., Nagtegaal, I., Kovacs, I., Hulsbergen-Van De Kaa, C., Bult, P., Van Ginneken, B., Van Der Laak, J.: Deep learning as a tool for increased accuracy and efficiency of histopathological diagnosis. Sci. Rep. 6, 26286 (2016)
17. Liu, Y., Gadepalli, K., Norouzi, M., Dahl, G.E., Kohlberger, T., Boyko, A., Venugopalan, S., Timofeev, A., Nelson, P.Q., Corrado, G.S., et al.: Detecting cancer metastases on gigapixel pathology images. arXiv preprint arXiv:1703.02442 (2017)
18. Martelotto, L., Ng, C., Piscuoglio, S., Weigelt, B., Reis-Filho, J.: Breast cancer intra-tumor heterogeneity. Breast Cancer Res. 16(3), 210 (2014)
19. Robertson, S., Azizpour, H., Smith, K., Hartman, J.: Digital image analysis in breast pathology-from image processing techniques to artificial intelligence. Transl. Res. 194, 19–35 (2017)
20. Schnitt, S.: Classification and prognosis of invasive breast cancer: from morphology to molecular taxonomy. Mod. Pathol. 23, S60–S64 (2010)
21. Simonyan, K., Zisserman, A.: Very deep convolutional networks for large-scale image recognition. arXiv preprint arXiv:1409.1556 (2014)
22. Su, H., Liu, F., Xie, Y., Xing, F., Meyyappan, S., Yang, L.: Region segmentation in histopathological breast cancer images using deep convolutional neural network. In: IEEE International Symposium on Biomedical Imaging, pp. 55–58. IEEE (2015)
23. Szegedy, C., Vanhoucke, V., Ioffe, S., Shlens, J., Wojna, Z.: Rethinking the inception architecture for computer vision. In: IEEE Conference on Computer Vision and Pattern Recognition, pp. 2818–2826 (2016)
24. Torre, L., Bray, F., Siegel, R., Ferlay, J., Lortet-Tieulent, J., Jemal, A.: Global cancer statistics, 2012. CA Cancer J. Clin. 65(2), 87–108 (2015). https://doi.org/10.3322/caac.21262D
25. Veta, M., Van Diest, P., Willems, S., Wang, H., Madabhushi, A., Cruz-Roa, A., Gonzalez, F., Larsen, A., Vestergaard, J., Dahl, A., et al.: Assessment of algorithms for mitosis detection in breast cancer histopathology images. Med. Image Anal. 20(1), 237–248 (2015)
26. Wang, D., Khosla, A., Gargeya, R., Irshad, H., Beck, A.: Deep learning for identifying metastatic breast cancer. arXiv preprint arXiv:1606.05718 (2016)

27. Warner, E.: Breast-cancer screening. N. Engl. J. Med. **365**(11), 1025–1032 (2011)
28. Wollmann, T., Rohr, K.: Deep residual Hough voting for mitotic cell detection in histopathology images. In: International Symposium on Biomedical Imaging, pp. 341–344. IEEE (2017)
29. Xu, J., Xiang, L., Liu, Q., Gilmore, H., Wu, J., Tang, J., Madabhushi, A.: Stacked sparse autoencoder (SSAE) for nuclei detection on breast cancer histopathology images. IEEE Trans. Med. Imaging **35**(1), 119–130 (2016)

Deep Learning Framework for Multi-class Breast Cancer Histology Image Classification

Yeeleng S. Vang$^{(\boxtimes)}$, Zhen Chen, and Xiaohui Xie

University of California Irvine, Irvine, CA 92697, USA
{ysvang,zhenc4}@uci.edu, xhx@ics.uci.edu

Abstract. In this work, we present a deep learning framework for multi-class breast cancer image classification as our submission to the International Conference on Image Analysis and Recognition (ICIAR) 2018 Grand Challenge on BreAst Cancer Histology images (BACH). As these histology images are too large to fit into GPU memory, we first propose using Inception V3 to perform patch level classification. The patch level predictions are then passed through an ensemble fusion framework involving majority voting, gradient boosting machine (GBM), and logistic regression to obtain the image level prediction. We improve the sensitivity of the Normal and Benign predicted classes by designing a Dual Path Network (DPN) to be used as a feature extractor where these extracted features are further sent to a second layer of ensemble prediction fusion using GBM, logistic regression, and support vector machine (SVM) to refine predictions. Experimental results demonstrate our framework shows a 12.5% improvement over the state-of-the-art model.

1 Introduction

In the United States, breast cancer continues to be the leading cause of cancer death among women of all races [1]. Studies have shown that improvement to survival rate over the last decade can be attributed to early diagnosis and awareness of better treatment options [2–4]. Common non-invasive screening test includes clinical breast exam which involves a visual check of the skin and tissue and a manual check for unusual texture or lump, mammography which requires taking an x-ray image of the breast to look for changes, and breast MRI which uses radio waves to obtain a detailed image inside the breast. Of the latter two diagnostic modals, many computer-aided diagnosis (CAD) systems have been developed to assist radiologists in their effort to identify breast cancer in its early stages [5]. On the other end of the screening toolbox are biopsies which are minimally invasive procedures whereby tissue samples are physically removed to be stained with hematoxylin and eosin (H&E) and visualized under a microscope. These histopathology slides allow pathologists to distinguish between normal, non-malignant, and malignant lesions [11] to assist in their diagnosis. However, even among trained pathologists the concordance between their

A. Campilho et al. (Eds.): ICIAR 2018, LNCS 10882, pp. 914–922, 2018.
https://doi.org/10.1007/978-3-319-93000-8_104

unanimous agreement is a mere 75% [6]. This high degree of discord motivates the development of automatic CAD systems using machine learning to assist these professionals in their diagnosis.

From November 2017 to January 2018, the International Conference on Image Analysis and Recognition (ICIAR) held the 2018 Grand Challenge on BreAst Cancer Histology images (BACH) to solicit submissions of automatic image analysis systems for the task of four-class classification of breast cancer histology images. Here we present a deep learning framework for the task of multi-class breast cancer histology image classification. Our approach uses the Inception (GoogLeNet) V3 [18] architecture to discriminate between invasive carcinoma, in situ carcinoma, benign lesion, and normal tissue patches. We then fuse these patch level predictions to obtain image level prediction using an ensemble framework. Our system improves the sensitivity over the benign and normal classes by using a Dual Path Network (DPN) [23] to extract features as input into a second level ensemble framework involving GBM, SVM, and logistic regression. Experimental results on a held out set demonstrate our framework shows a 12.5% improvement over the state-of-the-art model.

2   Relate Work

Several works have been published in the area of applying machine learning algorithms for biomedical image detection and classification [12–14, 20, 24–26]. In the specific area of breast cancer histopathology classification, the Camelyon 16 competition led to numerous new approaches utilizing techniques from deep learning to obtain results comparable to highly trained medical doctors [9,10,17]. The winning team used Inception V3 to create a tumor probability heatmap and perform geometrical and morphological feature selection over these heatmaps as input into a random forest classifier to achieve near 100% area under the receiver operating characteristic curve (AUC) score [9]. However, this competition involved only binary class prediction of tumor and normal whole slide images. For 4-class breast cancer classification, Araujo et al. [11] published a bespoke convolutional neural network architecture that achieved state-of-the-art accuracy results and high sensitivity for carcinoma detection.

3   ICIAR2018 Grand Challenge Datasets and Evaluation Metric

In this section, we describe the ICIAR2018 dataset provided by the organizers for the subchallenge of multi-class breast cancer histology image classification and the evaluation metric used. The interested reader is encouraged to refer to the competition page for details regarding the other subchallenge.

3.1   ICIAR2018 Dataset

The ICIAR2018 breast cancer histology image classification subchallenge consist of hematoxylin and eosin (H&E) stained microscopy images as shown in Table 1. The dataset is an extended version of the one used by Araujo et al. [11]. All images were digitized with the same acquisition conditions, with resolution of 2040×1536 pixels and pixel size of $0.42 \,\mu m \times 0.42 \,\mu m$. Each image is labeled with one of four classes: (i) normal tissue, (ii) benign lesion, (iii) in situ carcinoma and (iv) invasive carcinoma according to the predominant cancer type in each image. The images were labeled by two pathologists who only provided a diagnostic from the image contents without specifying the area of interest. There are a total of 400 microscopy images with an even distribution over the four classes. We randomly perform a 70%−20%−10% training-validation-test split. The training and validation sets are used for model development while the test set is held out and only used for evaluation.

Table 1. ICIAR2018 H&E histopathology dataset

Type		Training	Validation	Test	Total
Microscopy	Normal	70	20	10	400
	Benign	70	20	10	
	In situ	70	20	10	
	Invasive	70	20	10	

3.2   Evaluation Metric

This challenge consists of classifying H&E-stained breast cancer histology images into four classes: normal, benign, in situ carcinoma and invasive carcinoma. Performance on this challenge is evaluated based on the overall prediction accuracy, i.e. the ratio of correct predictions over total number of images.

4   Method

In this section, we describe our framework and approach to this problem of multi-class breast cancer histology image classification.

4.1   Image-Wise Classification of Microscopy Images

Stain Normalization Pre-processing. Stain normalization is a critically important step in the pre-processing of H&E stain images. It is known that cell nucleus are stained with a large amount of pure hematoxylin and a small amount of Eosin whereas cytoplasm is stained with a large amount of pure eosin and small amount of hematoxylin [8]. Variations in H&E images can be attributed to such factors as differences in lab protocols, concentration, source manufacturer, scanners, and even staining time [21]. These variations makes it difficult for software trained on a particular stain appearance [22] and therefore necessitates careful preprocessing to reduce such variances.

Many methods have been proposed for stain normalization including [7,8,22] that are based on color devolution where RGB pixel values are decomposed into their stain-specific basis vectors. In addition to color information, Bejnordi et el. takes advantage of spatial information to perform this deconvolution step [21], however their approach currently only works for whole slide images.

In our framework, we utilized both Macenko [7], which used singular value decomposition (SVD), and Vahadane [8] normalizations, which used sparse non-negative matrix factorization (SNMF), as part of our ensemble framework. This was due to the fact that initial empirical results showed Macenko-normalized images obtained high sensitivity for invasive and in situ classes whereas Vahadane-normalized images showed high sensitivity for benign and normal classes. Both set of normalized datasets were normalized using "iv001.tif" as the target image. An example of both normalization schemes are shown in Fig. 1.

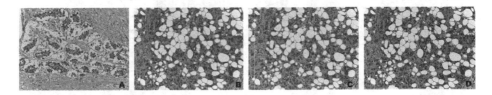

Fig. 1. *A* target image, *B* original image, *C* image after Macenko normalization, *D* image after Vahadane normalization.

Image-Wise Classification Framework. The microscopy classification framework consists of a patch level classification stage, an image level heatmap post-processing stage, and possibly a refinement stage, as depicted in Fig. 2. During model training of the patch-based classifier, each patch input is of size 512×512. We extracted 500 patches from each microscopy slide in the training and validation sets for both Macenko-normalized and Vahadane-normalized datasets. 35 of those patches comes from sliding over the normalized microscopy image with strides of 256 while the remaining patches were randomly sub-sampled. As with the assumption used in [11], these patches are given the same label as the original slide image with which they where obtained from.

A pretrained Inception V3 model [18], is modified to accept image patch of this size and trained to discriminate between the four classes. At training time, images data are dynamically augmented before being fed through the model. Similar to the color perturbation scheme used in [10], brightness is perturbed with a delta of 5/255, contrast with a delta of .05, saturation with a delta of .05, and hue with a delta of 0.02. In addition to color perturbation, images were randomly flipped vertically and/or horizontally, and randomly rotated by 90 degrees to obtain all eight valid orientations.

The Inception V3 model was fine-tuned on 4 GPUs (2 Nvidia Titan X and 2 Nvidia GTX 1080Ti) where each GPUs receive a batch of 8 images. The model is trained for 30 epochs with learning rates set as: 5e−5 for the bottom 5 convolution layers, 5e−4 for the eleven inception modules, and 5e-2 for the top fully connected layer. Learning rate was decreased by 0.95 every 2 epochs. The RMSprop optimizer with 0.9 momentum is used and the best performing model on the validation set is saved.

At inference time for a single microscopy image, a heatmap tensor of size [8 × 4 × 3 × 4] is obtained. The first dimension corresponds to the 8 valid orientations of the image, the second dimension to the 4 classes, and the third and fourth dimension corresponds to the spatial dimensions of the image using non-overlapping patching.

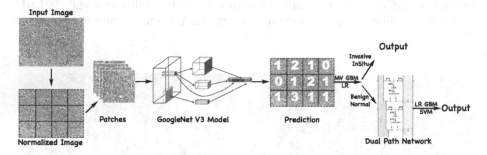

Fig. 2. The framework of image-wise classification. The normalized input image is patched into twelve non-overlapping patches. 8 sets of these patches are generated corresponding to the 8 valid orientations. These 8 sets of patches are passed through the Inception (GoogLeNet) V3 model to generate a patch level heatmap probability tensor. The heatmap tensor is then fused using majority voting (MV), gradient boosting machine (GBM), and logistic regression (LR) across both macenko-normalized and vahadane-normalized version of the input image. If the model predicts invasive or in situ carcinoma, the model outputs this prediction. Otherwise the normalized images are pass through the DPN network to extract features for a second fusing step involving LR, GBM, and support vector machine (SVM) to output prediction for benign and normal class.

Heatmap-Based Post-processing. Three data fusion strategies were investigated for this competition. The first strategy involved finding the average probabilities along the first dimension of the heatmap and then assigning labels to each 3 × 4 patches corresponding to the most probable class, which we will call the class map. From this 3 × 4 class map, a final label for the microscopy is obtained by majority voting. The second and third strategies involved finding the class map for each of the 8 orientation separately first, and then obtaining a histogram of the classes across all 8 orientations. The histogram data is then used to train two separate models: a logistic regression with $L1$ regularization and a gradient boosting machine (GBM) classifier (num. of estimator = 280, max depth = 4, learning rate = .9) to ultimately classify the image similar to [16]. If the model predicts benign or normal, the vahadane-normalized image was further passed through a refinement stage as will be describe in the next section.

Refinement Model for Benign and Normal Classes. Since the Inception model yielded low sensitivity for both normal and benign classes with many interclass misclassification between these two classes, we proposed training a slimed-down version of the dual path network (DPN) [23] to serve as a feature extractor for use with Vahadane-normalized images. DPN was chosen due to its compact size and having beneficial characteristics of both residual-like and densenet-like architectures to utilize feature reuse and new feature exploration respectively. Using the architecture notation of [23], we build a 26 layers DPN (DPN-26) by replicating the bottleneck blocks in conv2, conv3, conv4, and conv5 layers 2 times each. The input and output channels of these 4 bottleneck blocks are (6, 12, 24, 48) and (16, 32, 64 ,128) respectively. The dense layers in each of these blocks are (2, 4, 8, 16). Using the features extracted by the DPN-26, we train three additional models: GBM, Support Vector Machine (SVM), and Logistic regression with $L1$ for binary classification. The results for our entire pipeline is presented below in Table 2.

5   Experimental Results

The performance of our framework on image-wise classification is shown below in Table 2. As a baseline, we compare against Araujo et al. [11] which, although using a smaller subset of this dataset, tested on a held-out set of roughly the same size. Their best accuracy performance on this 4-class classification problem was 77.8%. Our framework achieves an accuracy score of 87.5%, a 12.5% improvement over the baseline score. Even without the refinement model, our model offers a 6% improvement over the baseline.

Table 2. Image-wise classification results

		Accuracy	
		Validation set	Test set
Macenko normalization	MV	0.800	0.775
	LR	0.750	0.775
	GBM	0.775	0.775
Vahadane normalization	MV	0.788	0.775
	LR	0.763	0.775
	GBM	0.750	0.800
Ensemble		0.825	0.825
Ensemble with refinement		0.838	0.875

Comparing the sensitivity to baseline, we see they achieved sensitivities of 77.8%, 66.7%, 88.9%, and 88.9% for normal, benign, in situ, and invasive classes respectively. From Table 3, we showed higher sensitivity across all four classes using our framework. Of noticeable improvement is the benign class which we saw an almost 20% improvement. This validates our decision to incorporate a binary class refinement phase specifically for the benign and normal classes.

Table 3. Image-wise test set contingency table

Ground truth	Prediction				
	Invasive	In situ	Benign	Normal	Sensitivity
Invasive	9	0	1	0	0.90
In situ	0	10	0	0	1.00
Benign	1	1	8	0	0.80
Normal	0	0	2	8	0.80

6 Discussion

In this work we proposed a deep learning framework for the problem of multi-class breast cancer histology image classification. To leverage recent advances from computer vision, we propose using the successful Inception V3 model for initial four-class classification. We propose a new ensemble scheme to fuse patch probabilities for image-wise classification. To improve the sensitivity of the benign and normal class, we propose a two-class refinement stage using a dual path network to first extract features from the vahadane-normalized images and then using gradient boosting machine, support vector machine, and logistic regression to fuse all our predictions into a final result. Experimental results on the ICIAR2018 Grand Challenge dataset demonstrates an improvement of 12.5% over the state-of-the-art system.

References

1. U.S. Cancer Statistics Working Group: United States Cancer Statistics: 1999–2014 Incidence and Mortality Web-based Report. U.S. Department of Health and Human Services, Centers for Disease Control and Prevention and National Cancer Institute, Atlanta (2017). www.cdc.gov/uscs
2. Saadatmand, S., et al.: Influence of tumour stage at breast cancer detection on survival in modern times: population based study in 173 797 patients. Bmj **351**, h4901 (2015)
3. Berry, D.A., et al.: Effect of screening and adjuvant therapy on mortality from breast cancer. New Engl. J. Med. **353**(17), 1784–1792 (2005)
4. de Gelder, R., et al.: The effects of population-based mammography screening starting between age 40 and 50 in the presence of adjuvant systemic therapy. Int. J. Cancer **137**(1), 165–172 (2015)

5. Hadjiiski, L., et al.: Advances in CAD for diagnosis of breast cancer. Curr. Opin. Obstet. Gynecol. **18**(1), 64 (2006)
6. Elmore, J.G., et al.: Diagnostic concordance among pathologists interpreting breast biopsy specimens. Jama **313**(11), 1122–1132 (2015)
7. Macenko, M.: A method for normalizing histology slides for quantitative analysis. In: IEEE International Symposium on Biomedical Imaging: From Nano to Macro, ISBI 2009. IEEE (2009)
8. Vahadane, A., et al.: Structure-preserved color normalization for histological images. In: 2015 IEEE 12th International Symposium on Biomedical Imaging (ISBI). IEEE (2015)
9. Wang, D., et al.: Deep learning for identifying metastatic breast cancer. arXiv preprint arXiv:1606.05718 (2016)
10. Liu, Y., et al.: Detecting cancer metastases on gigapixel pathology images. arXiv preprint arXiv:1703.02442 (2017)
11. Araújo, T., et al.: Classification of breast cancer histology images using convolutional neural networks. PloS one **12**(6), e0177544 (2017)
12. Nayak, N., et al.: Classification of tumor histopathology via sparse feature learning. In: 2013 IEEE 10th International Symposium on Biomedical Imaging (ISBI). IEEE (2013)
13. Gorelick, L., et al.: Prostate histopathology: learning tissue component histograms for cancer detection and classification. IEEE Trans. Med. Imaging **32**(10), 1804–1818 (2013)
14. Xu, Y., et al.: Weakly supervised histopathology cancer image segmentation and classification. Med. Image Anal. **18**(3), 591–604 (2014)
15. Ciompi, F., et al.: The importance of stain normalization in colorectal tissue classification with convolutional networks. arXiv preprint arXiv:1702.05931 (2017)
16. Hou, L., et al.: Patch-based convolutional neural network for whole slide tissue image classification. In: Proceedings of the IEEE Conference on Computer Vision and Pattern Recognition (2016)
17. Bejnordi, B.E., et al.: Diagnostic assessment of deep learning algorithms for detection of lymph node metastases in women with breast cancer. Jama **318**(22), 2199–2210 (2017)
18. Szegedy, C., et al.: Going deeper with convolutions. In: CVPR (2015)
19. Otsu, N.: A threshold selection method from gray-level histograms. IEEE Trans. Syst. Man Cybern. **9**(1), 62–66 (1979)
20. Wang, W., et al.: Detection and classification of thyroid follicular lesions based on nuclear structure from histopathology images. Cytom. Part A **77**(5), 485–494 (2010)
21. Bejnordi, B.E., et al.: Stain specific standardization of whole-slide histopathological images. IEEE Trans. Med. Imaging **35**(2), 404–415 (2016)
22. Khan, A.M., et al.: A nonlinear mapping approach to stain normalization in digital histopathology images using image-specific color deconvolution. IEEE Trans. Biomed. Eng. **61**(6), 1729–1738 (2014)
23. Chen, Y., et al.: Dual path networks. In: Advances in Neural Information Processing Systems (2017)
24. Zhu, W., et al.: DeepLung: deep 3D dual path nets for automated pulmonary nodule detection and classification. In: IEEE WACV (2018)

25. Zhu, W., Lou, Q., Vang, Y.S., Xie, X.: Deep multi-instance networks with sparse label assignment for whole mammogram classification. In: Descoteaux, M., Maier-Hein, L., Franz, A., Jannin, P., Collins, D.L., Duchesne, S. (eds.) MICCAI 2017. LNCS, vol. 10435, pp. 603–611. Springer, Cham (2017). https://doi.org/10. 1007/978-3-319-66179-7_69
26. Zhu, W., et al.: Adversarial deep structured nets for mass segmentation from mammograms. In: IEEE ISBI (2018)

Automated Breast Cancer Image Classification Based on Integration of Noisy-And Model and Fully Connected Network

Chao-Hui Huang[1(✉)], Jens Brodbeck[2], Nena M. Dimaano[3], John Kang[3], Belma Dogdas[3], Douglas Rollins[4], and Eric M. Gifford[1]

[1] MSD, Singapore, Singapore
chao.hui.huang@merck.com
[2] Merck, Palo Alto, CA, USA
[3] Merck, Rahway, NJ, USA
[4] West Point, PA, USA

Abstract. In this paper, we proposed an automated pathological image classification approach for supporting breast cancer (BC) diagnosis, *e.g.*, BC image classification for categories of normal, benign, *in-situ* and invasive. The proposed model is consist of two components: first, a dual path network (DPN), which is a deep convolutional neural network used to convert R.G.B. features of the given input image into a probability map of each possible category; and second, a integration of a noisy-and model and a fully connected neural network is used as a classifier, which takes both global and local features into account in order to achieve a better performance. Based on 10-fold cross validation using the given training set, the accuracy of the proposed approach was ~91.75%. The accuracy on the test set provided by the contest, the accuracy was ~64.00%.

Keywords: Digital pathology · Histopathology · Dual path networks
Noisy-and · Multiple instance learning

1 Introduction

Breast cancer (BC) is the top leading cause of cancer death of women in some countries. In United States, the average risk of a woman developing breast cancer sometime in her life is about 12% [1]. Studies suggested that early diagnosis can significantly increase treatment success and survival rate [1]. Analysis of pathology images is a critical task during cancer diagnosis. During the clinical diagnosis procedure, pathologists evaluate tissue organization by using conventional microscopy or digital pathology platform. However, the massive size of image data and the complexity of this professional task make this process time-consuming and labor-intensive. Thus, the development of automated pathological image analyzing platform becomes an interesting topic, which is challenging, but also valuable for both the fields of medical and health-care business.

© Springer International Publishing AG, part of Springer Nature 2018
A. Campilho et al. (Eds.): ICIAR 2018, LNCS 10882, pp. 923–930, 2018.
https://doi.org/10.1007/978-3-319-93000-8_105

Studies and investigations on digital pathology have been benefited from the recent surge in activity around machine intelligence technologies. Advances in deep learning is also driving dramatic progress on improving the automated cancer detection using haematoxylin & eosin (H&E) stained whole slide images (WSIs) [2].

In 2018, a grant challenge has been held together with the 15th International Conference on Image Analysis and Recognition (ICIAR2018). The organizers proposed two tasks and looked for participants for tackling these problems. The first task was automated classifying microscopic breast cancer images, including normal, benign, *in situ* and invasive; the second task was to detect the category pixel-wisely on BC whole-slide images.

In this paper, we proposed an efficient deep learning model for dealing with the automated BC pathological image categorization tasks: an integration of noisy-and model and fully connected network combining with a dual path network (DPN) [3]. In the approach, we used the DPN as a preprocessing step so that the color signal on the given was converted to the probability map. Then, a combination of noisy-and model and fully connected network (FCN) was used as the classifier: the noisy-and model was included in order to manage the MIL (multiple instance learning, see below) problems [4] and the FCN was used to evaluate the global picture of the given image. In the follows, we will introduce the further details of the proposed approach, followed by our results; performance metrics and our conclusions.

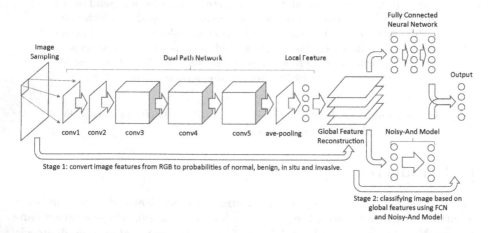

Fig. 1. The architecture of the proposed method.

2   Method

The proposed approach included two parts: a dual path network (DPN) [3] and a combination of a noisy-and model [4] and a fully connected network, as shown in Fig. 1. These two components will be introduced as follows:

2.1   Dual Path Networks

DPN is a high efficient modularized deep convolutional neural network, proposed by Chen *et al.*, combining residual network (ResNet) and densely convolutional network (DenseNet) within the a higher order recurrent neural network (HORNN) framework. According to Chen *et al.*, ResNet enables feature re-usage and DenseNet explores new features. Both capabilities are important for learning representative image features. DPN was chosen due to the fact that DPN is able to provide similar or better accuracy for image classification while requires relatively lower costs of memory and processing time [3,5].

Table 1. The structure of DPN used in the experiment.

Stage	Output	Structure	Repeat
conv1	112×112	$7 \times 7, 96$, stride 2	N/A
conv2	56×56	$1 \times 1, 160$ $3 \times 3, 160, G = 40$ $1 \times 1, 256 \ (+16)$	3
conv3	28×28	$1 \times 1, 320$ $3 \times 3, 320, G = 40$ $1 \times 1, 512 \ (+32)$	6
conv4	14×14	$1 \times 1, 640$ $3 \times 3, 640, G = 40$ $1 \times 1, 1024 \ (+32)$	20
conv5	7×7	$1 \times 1, 1280$ $3 \times 3, 1280, G = 40$ $1 \times 1, 2048 \ (+128)$	3
Final	1×1	global average pooling 4-d fully-connected softmax (for optimization)	N/A

The architecture of the DPN used in the experiment is shown in Table 1. The implementation was based on the original DPN proposed by Chen *et al.* [3]. The number of classes was modified in order to fit our requirements.

2.2   Noisy-And Model

Our implementation involved segmenting a given image into multiple image samples. For example, cropped a 256×256 image in every 128-stride along the x- and y- directions. This mechanism is common solution of data augmentation for biomedical image classification and segmentation. However, not every image sample contains the needed features. For example, Fig. 2 shows one of

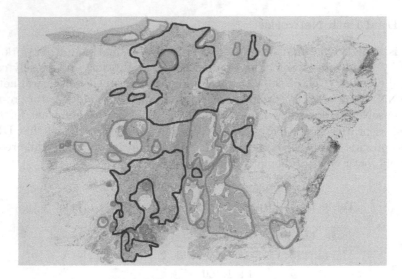

Fig. 2. An annotated pathology image example provided by the ICIAR2018BACH challenge, where red regions represent benign, greens are *in situ* and blues are invasive. Note that the other regions are considered as normal tissue (obtained from the contest website: https://iciar2018-challenge.grand-challenge.org/). (Color figure online)

the images provided by the contest. The image was annotated accordingly. The labels included benign (red), *in situ* (green) and invasive (blue). Note that the regions not annotated were either considered as normal or was not relevant. Once a image has been divided into multiple parts, there will be no guarantee that which training instance contains which label.

Biomedical microscopy image classification and segmentation problems can be considered as a multiple instance learning (MIL) problem [4]. In a MIL problem, the data instances are arranged in a set of data bags. The label of each instance is ambiguous, only the label of each bag is given. A bag is defined positive if at the least one instance in the bag is positive. On the other hand, a bag is labeled as negative if all instances in the bag are negative.

The problems of breast cancer image classification can be considered as a MIL problem. That is, assume a whole slide image is segmented into N image samples, if any portion is labeled as positive (*e.g.*, invasive), the whole image will be determined as an invasive case. In some scenario, an image may or may not contain multiple labels. This is called a multiple label multiple instance learning problem, which is also an interesting, although it will not be discussed in this paper. As Kraus *et al.* suggested, noisy-and model (NAM) can enable the capabilities of MIL for a convolutional neural network [4]. Based on this concept, we integrated the noisy-and model so that a more efficient deep learning model can be used in this problem.

A noisy-and model can be described as: [4]:

$$P_i = \frac{\sigma\left(q_i - \beta_i\right) - \sigma\left(-\alpha\beta_i\right)}{\sigma\left(\alpha\left(1 - \beta_i\right)\right) - \sigma\left(-\alpha\beta_i\right)}, i = 1\cdots, N, \tag{1}$$

where

$$q_i = \frac{1}{M} \sum_j \frac{e^{p_{ij}}}{\sum_{k=1}^N e^{p_{kj}}}, j = 1,\cdots, M, \tag{2}$$

$N = 4$ as we were dealing with 4 categories; M is the number of samples cropped from an image, and $\sigma(\cdot)$ is a sigmoid function; $\alpha \in \mathbb{R}$ and $\beta_i \in \mathbb{R}\forall i$ are parameters obtained during the training phase. Equation (2) represents the mean value of the sigmoid outputs along 4 classes for all of the inputs: p_{ij}, where each $p_{ij} \in [0, 1]$. In text, p_{ij} represents the probability that the jth local region of the given image belongs the ith category. P_i represents the probability that the given image is classified as the ith category based on the concept of MIL.

Then, a fully connected layer were defined as:

$$y_{\mathrm{NAM},i} = ReLU\left(\mathbf{W}_{\mathrm{NAM}}P_i + \mathbf{b}_{\mathrm{NAM}}\right), \tag{3}$$

where $\mathbf{W} \in \mathbb{R}^{N \times N}$ and $\mathbf{b} \in \mathbb{R}^N$ are the corresponding parameters; $N = 4$ for the given 4 categories; and $ReLU(\cdot)$ is the chosen activation function.

For optimizing the model, a joint cross-entropy cost function was defined as:

$$J_{\mathrm{NAM}} = -\sum_{i=1}^N \left(\log p\left(t_i|P_i\right) + \log p\left(t_i|y_{\mathrm{NAM},i}\right)\right), \tag{4}$$

where $t_i \in [0, 1]$ indicates the corresponding ground-truth; $P_i \in \{p|0 \le p \le 1\}$ and $y_{\mathrm{NAM},i} \in \mathbb{R}$, $i = 0,\cdots, N$, are obtained from the Eqs. (1) and (3).

2.3 Fully Connected Network

The noisy-and model was used to evaluate the local feature of each region on the given image. However, relying ONLY on the noisy-and model will result losing the grip on the global picture of the given image. Thus, in our model, we integrated a FCN parallelly with the noise-and model so that both local- and global features were taking into account. As the used FCN is a conventional neural network, to save space, here we only define the notations for parameter set of the FCN, γ_{FCN}, and its output: $y_{\mathrm{FCN},i} \in \mathbb{R}, i = 0,\cdots, N$, for the ith classification output.

2.4 Integration

Finally, the outputs of NAM y_{NAM} and FCN, y_{FCN}, were concatenated and integrated using an additional fully connected layer:

$$y_i = ReLU\left(\mathbf{W}[y_{\mathrm{NAM},0},\cdots, y_{\mathrm{NAM},N}, y_{\mathrm{FCN},0},\cdots, y_{\mathrm{FCN},N}]^T + \mathbf{b}\right), \tag{5}$$

2.5   Four Phase Training Strategy

The training process of the proposed approach consisted of 4 steps as follows:

Local Feature Sampling: In this phase, we performed image sampling on the given image set, *e.g.*, sampling multiple $256 \times 256 \times 3$ over the whole of each image evenly. Each sample may or may not be flipped, rotated or shifted, depending on the need of data augmentation. Then, we performed Mechenko's staining normalization so that the dynamic ranges of color space of all images are synchronized, as Wang *et al.* has highlighted, proper staining normalization can improve automated pathology image classification [2].

Local Feature Training: Then, we trained the DPN model by using the normalized image samples (see Fig. 1).

Global Feature Sampling: Once the DPN model was trained, we used it to classify each sampled region of a whole image. Assume $I \in \mathbb{R}^{H \times W \times C}$ represents a given input image, where $H \in \mathbb{Z}_{\leq 0}$, $W \in \mathbb{Z}_{\leq 0}$ are the size of the image and $C = 3$ is the number of channels (in our case, $H = 1536$, $W = 2048$ and $C = 3$ for the RGB channels), we had the trained DPN model, θ, to perform

$$f_\theta : I \to j, \tag{6}$$

where $j \in \mathbb{R}^{h \times w \times d}$. $0 < w \leq W$, $0 < h \leq H$ and $d = 4$ represents the probability map of a set of sites on the given image.

Global Feature Training: Finally, the combination of noisy-and model showing in Eq. (1) and the FCN were trained and the obtained parameter set γ_{NAM} and γ_{FCN} was used to classify an input image as:

$$g_{\gamma_{\text{NAM}}, \gamma_{\text{FCN}}} : j \to \mathbf{y}, \tag{7}$$

$\mathbf{y} = [y_i | y_i \in \mathbb{R}, i = 0, \cdots, N]$. Finally, we defined the image predictor as:

$$i^* = \operatorname*{argmax}_i y_i, i = 0, \cdots, N. \tag{8}$$

where

$$i^* = \begin{cases} 0, \text{Benign} \\ 1, \textit{In Situ} \\ 2, \text{Invasive} \\ 3, \text{Normal} \end{cases}. \tag{9}$$

3   Results

3.1   Setup

The given dataset was consists of 4 categories: (1) normal, (2) benign, (3) *in situ*, and (4) invasive. Each category included 100 images. In which, 10% (40 images) were selected for validation and the rests 90% (360 images) were for training.

Table 2. The confusion matrix.

Results	Ground Truth			
	normal	benign	*in situ*	invasive
normal	3312	360	0	0
benign	288	2628	0	0
in situ	0	180	3600	36
invasive	0	432	0	3564

Table 3. The accuracy comparison of different configurations.

	DPN only	DPN+NoisyAnd	DPN+NoisyAnd+FCN
accuracy	71.5%	89%	91.75%

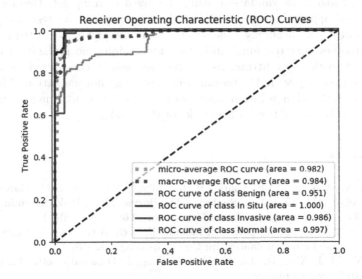

Fig. 3. The multi-label receiver operating characteristic (ROC) curves of the proposed approach.

In order to expand the size of the dataset, we performed data augmentation on each of the j's in Eq. (6). The strategies of data augmentation included shifting, flipping along w and h dimensions in Eq. (6). As we were conducting 10-cross validation, we obtained 129,600 instances for training and 14,400 instances for validation.

The obtained accuracy was ∼91.75%. The corresponding confusion matrix is shown in Table 2. Note that the worst was on the category of benign, in which , the majority of misclassified category was invasive. The plot of receiver operating characteristic (ROC) curves is shown in Fig. 3.

We also investigated the contributions of each components, including DPN, NAM and FCN, by evaluating the performance when different components were absent. The comparison is shown in Table 3.

4   Conclusions

In this paper, we introduced a combination of dual path network (DPN) with an integration of a noisy-and model (NAM) and a fully connected network (FCN) for addressing the problem of breast cancer Hematoxylin & Eosin (H&E) image classification. The categories included normal, benign, *in situ* and invasive.

The proposed approach first cropped samples from the given image evenly. Then, used DPN to evaluate the cropped image patches. Finally, used NAM and FCN to obtain the predicted result for the given image. In our experiments, based on 10-fold cross validation using the given training set, the accuracy of the proposed approach was ~91.75%. The accuracy on the test set provided by the contest, the accuracy was ~64.00%. There was a over fitting problem as the outcomes were too much different. The staining normalization might be contributed to the over fitting, as the test set wasn't considered as a part of the inputs when adjusting the parameters of staining normalization. The chosen staining normalization solution may sensitive to the input images. Improving this part can be one of the future works of this study.

References

1. Howell, A., Anderson, A.S., Clarke, R.B., Duffy, S.W., Evans, D.G., Garcia-Closas, M., Gescher, A.J., Key, T.J., Saxton, J.M., Harvie, M.N.: Risk determination and prevention of breast cancer. Breast Cancer Res. **16**(5), 446 (2014)
2. Wang, D., Khosla, A., Gargeya, R., Irshad, H., Beck, A.H.: Deep learning for identifying metastatic breast cancer. In: CoRR, q-bio.QM (2016)
3. Chen, Y., Li, J., Xiao, H., Jin, X., Yan, S., Feng, J.: Dual path networks, pp. 4470–4478 (2017). papers.nips.cc
4. Kraus, O.Z., Ba, J.L., Frey, B.J.: Classifying and segmenting microscopy images with deep multiple instance learning. Bioinformatics **32**(12), 52–59 (2016)
5. Ning, G., He, Z.: Dual path networks for multi-person human pose estimation. In: CoRR, cs.CV (2017)

Multiclass Classification of Breast Cancer in Whole-Slide Images

Scotty Kwok[(✉)]

Seek AI Limited, Hong Kong, China
scottykwok@gmail.com

Abstract. Breast cancer is one of the leading cause of cancer-related death worldwide. During the diagnosis of breast cancer, the histopathological assessment of Haemotoxylin and Eosin(H&E) stained slides provides important clinical values. By applying computer-aid diagnosis on whole-slide image(WSI), the efficiency and consistency of such assessment could be improved. In this paper, we propose a deep learning-based framework that classifies H&E stained WSIs into regions of normal tissue, benign lesion, in-situ carcinoma and invasive carcinoma. The framework utilizes both microscopy images and WSIs to train a patch classifier in two stages. The underlying classifier is based on Inception-Resnet-v2. This framework won both parts of the *ICIAR2018 Grand Challenge on Breast Cancer Histology Images* [4] competition, achieved a part A multiclass accuracy of 87% and part B score of 0.6929.

Keywords: Breast cancer · Deep learning · Whole-Slide Images
Multiclass classification

1 Introduction

Breast cancer is one of the leading cause of cancer-related death worldwide. According to the estimation of American Cancer Society, among US women in 2017, there will be an estimated 252,710 new cases of invasive breast cancer, 63,410 new cases of breast carcinoma in situ, and 40,610 breast cancer deaths [3]. The diagnosis of breast cancer involves the histopathological assessment of Haemotoxylin and Eosin (H&E) stained sections under microscope. The assessment result provides the basis for clinical treatment and management decisions, which significantly impact the mortality and quality of life of patients. Nevertheless, this manual assessment task is challenging due to the following reasons: (1) this task required experienced pathologists, (2) this task is tedious and time consuming, and (3) the result is subjected to variability in inter-rater and/or intra-rater concordance [6, 8, 11]. Computer-aided diagnosis (CAD) is therefore an appealing option for tackling these problems.

© Springer International Publishing AG, part of Springer Nature 2018
A. Campilho et al. (Eds.): ICIAR 2018, LNCS 10882, pp. 931–940, 2018.
https://doi.org/10.1007/978-3-319-93000-8_106

2   Related Work

Among the many CAD techniques, studies have shown that CNN-based analysis outperformed other methods in various pathological classification tasks. Specifically for studies related to breast cancer histopathology, researchers have published related works based on: BreakHis [13], Camelyon16 [1], Camelyon17 [2] and the enriched Bioimaging 2015 dataset [5]. For BreakHis, a recent study by Habibzadeh et al. [7] reported a binary classification accuracy of 98.7% using ResNet-152. For Camelyon16, the winning team, Wang et al. [16], achieved an area under the receiver operating curve (AUC) of 0.925 by using GoogleLeNet to detect metastases in lymph nodes. Later in Camelyon17, the winning team, Zhong et al. [16], achieved a Kappa score of 0.8958 in classifying the pN-stage of patients by using Resnet-101 and spatial pyramid pooling.

Despite most of studies focused on binary classification (normal vs tumor), multiclass classification actually offer more clinical values for an informed decision. The study of Araújo et al. [5] addressed this issue by enriching the Bioimaging 2015 dataset and using a CNN-based approach to classify histology images into four classes: normal, benign, in-situ carcinoma and invasive carcinoma. The authors achieved a state-of-the-art multiclass accuracy of 77.8% and binary accuracy of 83.3%.

Built on top of the enriched Bioimaging 2015 dataset, the ICIAR 2018 Grand Challenge on Breast Cancer Histology Images (BACH2018) dataset further enriched the data with more microscopy images and added WSI into the collection. In this paper, we will present the framework that we used to participate in BACH2018, which has achieved promising results in the challenge. The schematic overview of the framework is in Fig. 1.

3   Materials

3.1   Part a - Microscopy Images

The train set consists of 400 microscopy images of size 2048×1536 pixels, with pixel scale $0.42\,\mu m$. The images were evenly sampled from each classes: Normal (100), Benign (100), In-situ carcinoma (100) and Invasive carcinoma (100). This dataset is an extension of the one used by Araújo et al. [5], the data collection methodology was explained in details in their article. The patient-wise origin of each microscopy image is only partially available due to the anonymization process. The test set consists of another 100 microscopy images of the same scale. The ground truth is hidden.

3.2   Part B - Whole-Slide Images

The train set consists of 10 WSIs in various sizes (e.g. 42113×62625 pixels), with pixel scale $0.467\,\mu m$. These whole-slide images are high resolution images containing the entire sampled tissue. The annotation was prepared by two medical

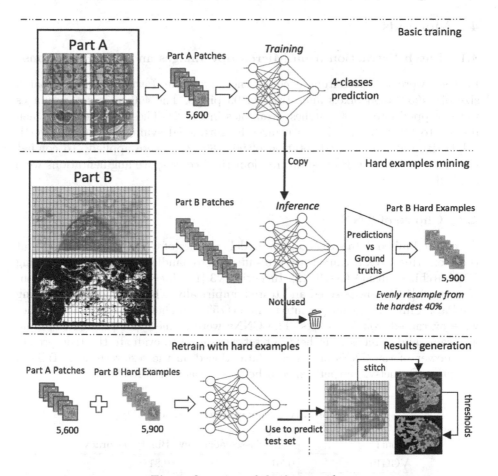

Fig. 1. Overview of the framework

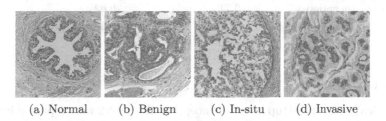

(a) Normal   (b) Benign   (c) In-situ   (d) Invasive

Fig. 2. Sample Part A Patches

experts and images where there was disagreement were discarded. The ground truth annotations are multiple regions that were labelled as: Benign, In-situ carcinoma or Invasive carcinoma. The patient-wise origin of the whole-slide images are fully available. (Note the train set also contains another 20 whole-slide images without ground truth, these 20 slides were not used in our approach). The test set consists another 10 WSIs of the same scale. The ground truth is hidden.

4   Methods

4.1   Patch Extraction from Microscopy Images and Augmentations

Patches were cropped from each of the images in Part A, using a patch size of 1495×1495 pixels and stride of 99 pixels. The 400 microscopy images were cropped into 5,600 patches (examples in Fig. 2). These patches were then resized to 299×299 pixels. To utilize the rotational symmetry, random vertical/horizontal flipping and rotation of 90, 180, 270° were applied. To combat the color variation of H&E stain, random HSV color space augmentations were applied.

4.2   Choice of CNN

Given the limited data size and high model capacity of CNN, we postulated that those existing CNN architectures are sufficient to handle this task. Four existing CNN architectures (VGG19 [12], Inception-v3 [15], Inception-v4 and Inception-Resnet-v2 [14]) were selected and tested empirically. The test involved splitting the Part A microscopy images into train set(75%) and held-out set(25%). Patches were extracted from each sets. The CNNs were trained and tuned to optimal accuracy, and patches from held-out set were used to evaluate the true predictive power of the CNNs on unseen data. Based on the test results in Table 1, Inception-Resnet-v2 outperformed others and was therefore chosen.

Table 1. Accuracy of different models

Model	Four-classes accuracy	Binary accuracy
VGG19	0.70	0.81
Inception-v3	0.74	0.85
Inception-v4	0.71	0.82
Inception-Resnet-v2	0.79	0.91

4.3   Basic Training

In technical details: the top layers of Inception-Resnet-v2 were replaced by a fully connected layer with 2048 units, followed by a dropout layer with 50% dropout rate, and a fully connected output layer with Sigmoid as activation function. The output probabilities need to be normalized to sum to unity due to the use of Sigmoid. The network were initialized using ImageNet pre-trained weights. The back propagation was performed by Stochastic Gradient Descent with a constant learning rate(0.001), Nesterov momentum (0.9), batch size(64) and categorical cross-entropy as the objective function. Note only Part A patches were used in this training. Using a machine with two GPUs (GeForce GTX 1080 Ti), the model converged to its optimal accuracy within 25 epochs, in <35 mins.

4.4   Patch Extraction from WSIs

The Part B WSIs need to be converted to patches before they can be used. The conversion began with our customized foreground extraction. Unlike many prior works, where Otsu thresholding [10] or gray value thresholding [9] were used, our extraction method made use of the color characteristics of H&E stain to threshold tissue regions. In our method, WSI was down-sampled and converted from RGB to CIE L*a*b* color space. The mean intensity of the a* channel were then computed. And by applying a binary threshold on the a* channel, all the pixels that were above mean by 10% became the foreground. A sample result was shown in Fig. 3. The rationale of this method is based on the fact that H&E stained tissues are predominantly red/magenta in color, whereas the a* channel is a good approximation of how red/magenta a pixel is.

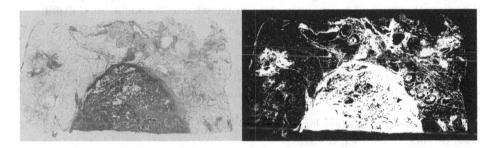

Fig. 3. The original WSI and the computed foreground mask (Color figure online)

Next, the WSIs were then cropped into patches of the same scale as that was done in Part A. Patches with less than 5% foreground pixels were considered as empty and discarded. The coordinates of the patches were stored in file for the later use during heatmap stitching.

Lastly, the WSIs ground truth annotations were converted into patch-wise class labels by the following method: each class were mapped to a pixel value based on its invasiveness, that is Normal = 0, Benign = 1, In-Situ Carcinoma = 2 and Invasive Carcinoma = 3. The patch-wise invasiveness was then be computed by taking the mean overall all the pixels in the patch. The mean invasiveness was then rounded to the nearest class and became the patch-wise class label.

4.5   Hard Examples Mining

The patch classifier (we trained earlier using Part A patches) was then used to predict Part B patches. By comparing the prediction verse the ground truth, the difficulty of each patch can be quantified. The patch difficulty was computed by: the absolute class distance between the ground truth class and the predicted class, multiplied by the predicted probability. For example: if given an invasive carcinoma patch, the classifier predicted 90% chance benign, then the difficulty of this patch is: abs(3 − 1) * 0.9 = 1.8. This value enabled us to sort the patches according to difficulties.

To further narrow down the selection, patches with less than 70% foreground pixels were excluded. Finally, patches were sorted by difficulty and the top 40 percentile were sampled as candidates. The resultant number of patches were imbalanced: Normal (28,000), Benign (4,500), In-Situ Carcinoma (1,500) and Invasive Carcinoma (19,700). In order to re-balance the classes, a total of 5,900 patches were evenly sampled from each classes to become our final hard examples collection.

4.6 Retrain with Hard Examples

The patch classifier was retrained by combing Part A patches (5,600) and Part B hard examples (5,900), using the same CNN architecture and hyper-parameters. The model converged to its optimal accuracy within 15 epochs, in <40 min.

4.7 Results Generation

The test set was converted to patches in the same way and fed through the patch classifier to obtain predictions, except that image augmentation was disabled during inference.

Part A results are class labels. They were generated by averaging the patch-wise predictions in each images.

Part B results are color-coded class maps. They were generated by two steps: (1) First a heatmap was computed by stitching all the patch-wise predictions into one single image buffer, the pixel intensity were then normalized to a value between 0 and 1. The higher the value, the more likely that the pixel was invasive carcinoma. (2) Then in order to quantize the pixel intensity into four classes, the optimal thresholds were probed empirically. In our implementation, the thresholds for Normal, Benign, In-situ Carcinoma and Invasive Carcinoma were: 0, 0.35, 0.7, 0.75 respectively. Note when compared to the default thresholds (0, 0.25, 0.5, 0.75), our thresholds were biased towards predicting more Normal/Benign and less In-situ Carcinoma (Fig. 4).

5 Results and Analysis

5.1 Part a Results

The primary evaluation metric for Part A is multiclass accuracy. Our approach achieved a multi-classes accuracy of **87%** when presented with the test set. This is a **9%** improvement comparing to the previous best result reported by Araújo et al. [5], where their CNN+SVM approach achieved a multiclass accuracy of 77.8%.

Together with another team (Chennamsetty et. al.) that also achieved 87% accuracy in the challenge, we won the first place in Part A of the competition.

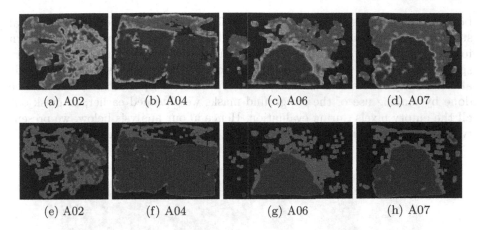

(a) A02   (b) A04   (c) A06   (d) A07

(e) A02   (f) A04   (g) A06   (h) A07

Fig. 4. (a)–(d) are the heatmaps generated by stitching patch-wise predictions into single image. (e)–(h) are the color-coded class map generated by applying thresholds to the heatmaps

The other evaluation metrics were not available because the test set ground truth were not disclosed at the time of this writing. The binary accuracy and the root-mean-square error should provide further insight to differentiate the model performances.

5.2 Part B Results

The primary evaluation metric for Part B is based on the following score, s:

$$s = 1 - \frac{\sum_{i=1}^{N} |\text{pred}_i - \text{gt}_i|}{\sum N_{i=1} max(|\text{gt}_i - 0|, |\text{gt}_i - 3|) \times [1 - (1 - \text{pred}_{i,bin})(1 - \text{gt}_{i,bin})]}$$

where "pred" is the predicted class (0, 1, 2 or 3), and "gt" is the ground truth class, i is the linear index of a pixel in the image, N is the total number of pixels in the image and bin is the binary value.

Our approach achieved a score of **0.6929** when presented with the test set. Again, it won the first place in Part B of the competition. To our knowledge, there were no prior studies for comparison, but our score outperformed the second (**0.5527**) and the third (**0.5230**) team by a large margin.

5.3 Part B Analysis

The evaluation methods and results of Part B deserved a more detailed analysis. Unfortunately, the test set ground truth were not disclosed at the time of this writing, so here we present the analysis using the train set WSIs (A01 to A10).

Firstly, inspection of the ground truth revealed that some annotated regions enclosed considerable amount of empty spaces (Fig. 5). This was inevitable because (1) human annotations were high level, and (2) some of the histological structure enclosed empty spaces by itself. These empty spaces were not a concern for human interpretation, but for the evaluation of model performance, empty spaces could distort the true score. A simple and effective remedy was to exclude all the empty spaces in both the ground truth and the predictions. This can be done by making use of the foreground masks we obtained earlier, to mask out all the empty pixels during evaluation. Hence in our analysis below, we present two sets of scores: the basic scores and the scores that excluded empty spaces.

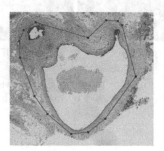

Fig. 5. Some annotated region enclosed considerable amount of empty pixels

Secondly, we established a baseline prediction by blindly predicting all pixels as Benign. This baseline strategy was based on the fact that the evaluation score does not weight the four classes equally. According to the organizers, the evaluation score was designed to penalize predictions that are farther from the ground truth value. And in the denominator, cases in which the prediction and ground truth are both 0 (normal class) are not counted, this was to avoid over-evaluating the correct predictions of normal cases. We tested this metric statistically and found that if the four classes are equally likely, then the expected score of predicting Normal, Benign, In-situ Carcinoma and Invasive Carcinoma are 0.14, 0.60, 0.60 and 0.40 respectively. In other words, the dominant strategy was to at least predict a pixel as Benign. Hence in our analysis below, we enriched the analysis by comparing our scores with this baseline.

Finally, listed in Table 2a are the scores of individual WSI predicted using the baseline verse our framework. Listed in Table 2b are the same set of scores but with empty spaces excluded in the evaluation. The bottom rows are the average scores.

In Table 2a, the average score of the baseline is 0.60. This suggests that any model that scores below 0.60 is no better than a blind prediction. Our approach achieved an average score of 0.75.

The individual scores of each WSIs in Table 2a reveal that our approach underperformed the baseline in some conditions, such as in slide A03 (0.66 > 0.63) and A08 (0.66 > 0.57). By inspection, we found that our classifier was weak at detecting the in-situ carcinoma regions in A03, and the small invasive carcinoma regions of A08.

Table 2. Part B analysis

WSI	Baseline	Our framework	WSI	Baseline	Our framework
A01	0.65	0.68	A01	0.61	0.70
A02	0.60	0.71	A02	0.52	0.75
A03	0.66	0.63	A03	0.64	0.65
A04	0.44	0.92	A04	0.37	0.67
A05	0.61	0.82	A05	0.53	0.86
A06	0.61	0.85	A06	0.51	0.90
A07	0.54	0.87	A07	0.45	0.91
A08	0.66	0.57	A08	0.65	0.56
A09	0.62	0.73	A09	0.52	0.78
A10	0.62	0.74	A10	0.53	0.79
Avg. Score	0.60	0.75	Avg. Score	0.53	0.79
(a) Scores			(b) Scores excl. empty spaces		

The differences in average scores of Table 2b (0.53 vs 0.79) are more prominent than those in Table 2a (0.60 vs 0.75). This suggests that the exclusion of empty spaces helps to further differentiate models performance.

6   Conclusion

We presented a framework that classifies H&E stained breast cancer WSIs into regions of: normal tissue, benign lesion, in-situ carcinoma and invasive carcinoma. The framework made use of Inception-Resnet-v2 as the underlying patch classifier. The training employed a two-stage approach to utilize both the microscopy images and WSIs. In the first stage, patch classifier was trained using microscopy images. In the second stage, hard examples were extracted from WSIs and the patch classifier was retrained. Prediction results were aggregated from patch-wise predictions back onto image-wise prediction and WSI annotations. Analysis shown that the bias in the evaluation metric deserves much attention. The prediction outcomes are satisfactory but has room for improvement, especially in the detection of in-situ carcinoma and small regions of invasive carcinoma.

This framework won the first place in both Part A and Part B of ICIAR 2018 Grand Challenge on Breast Cancer Histology Images. It achieved a Part A accuracy of 87% which is a 9% improvement over the state-of-the-art. And a Part B score of 0.6929 which outperformed the second place (0.5527) by a large margin.

Acknowledgements. We would like to thank the organizers of ICIAR2018 and BACH2018 who supported and organized this challenge.

References

1. Camelyon16 (2016). https://camelyon16.grand-challenge.org/results/
2. Camelyon17 (2017). https://camelyon17.grand-challenge.org/results/
3. Breast Cancer Facts and Figures 2017–2018 (2018). https://www.cancer.org/research/cancer-facts-statistics/breast-cancer-facts-figures.html
4. ICIAR 2018 Grand Challenge on Breast Cancer Histology Images (2018). https://iciar2018-challenge.grand-challenge.org/
5. Araújo, T., Aresta, G., Castro, E., Rouco, J., Aguiar, P., Eloy, C., Polónia, A., Campilho, A.: Classification of breast cancer histology images using convolutional neural networks. PLOS ONE **12**(6), 1–14 (2017). https://doi.org/10.1371/journal.pone.0177544
6. Elmore, J.G., Longton, G.M., Carney, P.A., Geller, B.M., Onega, T., Tosteson, A.N.A., et al.: Diagnostic concordance among pathologists interpreting breast biopsy specimens. JAMA **313**(11), 1122–1132 (2015). https://doi.org/10.1001/jama.2015.1405
7. Habibzadeh, M.N., Jannesary, M., Aboulkheyr, H., Khosravi, P., Elemento, O., Totonchi, M., Hajirasouliha, I.: Breast cancer histopathological image classification: a deep learning approach. bioRxiv (2018). https://www.biorxiv.org/content/early/2018/01/04/242818
8. Jain, R.K., Mehta, R., Dimitrov, R., Larsson, L.G., Musto, P.M., Hodges, K.B., Ulbright, T.M., Hattab, E.M., Agaram, N., Idrees, M.T., Badve, S.: Atypical ductal hyperplasia: interobserver and intraobserver variability. Mod. Pathol. **24**, 917–923 (2011)
9. Janowczyk, A., Madabhushi, A.: Deep learning for digital pathology image analysis: a comprehensive tutorial with selected use cases. J. Pathol. Inform. 7(1), 29 (2016). http://www.jpathinformatics.org/article.asp?issn=2153-3539;year=2016;volume=7;issue=1;spage=29;epage=29;aulast=Janowczyk;t=6
10. Otsu, N.: A threshold selection method from gray-level histograms. IEEE Trans. Syst. Man Cybern. **9**(1), 62–66 (1979)
11. Schnitt, S., Connolly, J., Tavassoli, F.A., Fechner, R., Kempson, R.L., Gelman, R., Page, D.: Interobserver reproducibility in the diagnosis of ductal proliferative breast lesions using standardized criteria. Am. J. Surg. Pathol. **16**(12), 1133–1143 (1992)
12. Simonyan, K., Zisserman, A.: Very Deep Convolutional Networks for Large-Scale Image Recognition. ArXiv e-prints, September 2014
13. Spanhol, F.A., Oliveira, L.S., Petitjean, C., Heutte, L.: A dataset for breast cancer histopathological image classification. IEEE Trans. Biomed. Eng. **63**(7), 1455–1462 (2016)
14. Szegedy, C., Ioffe, S., Vanhoucke, V., Alemi, A.: Inception-v4, Inception-ResNet and the Impact of Residual Connections on Learning, ArXiv e-prints, February 2016
15. Szegedy, C., Liu, W., Jia, Y., Sermanet, P., Reed, S., Anguelov, D., Erhan, D., Vanhoucke, V., Rabinovich, A.: Going Deeper with Convolutions. ArXiv e-prints, September 2014
16. Zhong, A., Li, Q.: HMS-MGH-CCDS Camelyon17 presentation (2017). https://camelyon17.grand-challenge.org/serve/public_html/presentations/HMS-MGH-CCDS_Camelyon17_presentation.pptx

Author Index